FOUNDATIONS SERIES

Prentice Hall

Algebra 2

Randall I. Charles
Basia Hall
Dan Kennedy
Allan E. Bellman
Sadie Chavis Bragg
William G. Handlin
Siegfried Haenisch
Stuart Murphy
Grant Wiggins

PEARSON

Boston, Massachusetts • Chandler, Arizona • Glenview, Illinois • Upper Saddle River, New Jersey

Acknowledgments appear on page 1015, which constitutes an extension of this copyright page.

ISBN-13: 978-0-7854-6929-2
ISBN-10: 0-7854-6929-X
5 6 7 8 9 10 V057 13 12 11 10

Contents *in Brief*

Welcome to Pearson's *Prentice Hall Algebra 2* student book. Throughout this textbook, you will find content that has been developed to cover all of the American Diploma Project's (ADP) math benchmarks. The End-of-Course Assessment is modeled after the ADP Algebra 2 test and can serve as practice before taking the actual ADP test.

Percents and Percent Application, 865; Operations With Fractions, 866; Ratios and Proportions, 867; Simplifying Expressions With Integers, 868; Area and Volume, 869; The Coordinate Plane, Slope, and Midpoint, 870; Operations With Exponents, 871; Factoring and Operations With Polynomials, 872; Scientific Notation and Significant Digits, 873; The Pythagorean Theorem and the Distance Formula, 874; Bar and Circle Graphs, 675; Descriptive Statistics and Histograms, 876; Operations With Rational Expressions, 877

Measures, 878; Symbols, 879; Properties and Formulas, 880; Formulas From Geometry, 886

Series *Authors*

Randall I. Charles, Ph.D., is Professor Emeritus in the Department of Mathematics and Computer Science at San Jose State University, San Jose, California. He began his career as a high school mathematics teacher, and he was a mathematics supervisor for five years. Dr. Charles has been a member of several NCTM committees and is the former Vice President of the National Council of Supervisors of Mathematics (NCSM). Much of his writing and research has been in the area of problem solving. He has authored more than 75 mathematics textbooks for kindergarten through college.

Dan Kennedy, Ph.D., is a classroom teacher and the Lupton Distinguished Professor of Mathematics at the Baylor School in Chattanooga, Tennessee. A frequent speaker at professional meetings on mathematics education reform, Dr. Kennedy has conducted numerous workshops and institutes for high school teachers. He is coauthor of calculus and precalculus textbooks, and, from 1990 to 1994, he chaired the College Board's AP Calculus Development Committee. He is a 1992 Tandy Technology Scholar and a 1995 Presidential Award winner.

Basia Hall is currently Manager of Instructional Programs for the Houston Independent School District. Ms. Hall has been a department chair, instructional supervisor, school improvement facilitator, and professional development trainer. She has developed curricula for high school mathematics and co-developed the Texas state mathematics standards. A 1992 Presidential Awardee, Ms. Hall is past president of the Texas Association of Supervisors of Mathematics and is a state representative for NCSM.

Consulting *Authors*

Stuart Murphy is a visual learning author and consultant. He is the author of *MathStart*, a series of children's books that presents mathematical concepts in the story contexts. A graduate of the Rhode Island School of Design, Mr. Murphy has worked extensively in educational publishing and has been on the authorship teams of a number of mathematics programs. He is a frequent presenter at meetings of the National Council of Teachers of Mathematics and the International Reading Association.

Grant Wiggins, Ed.D., is the President of Authentic Education in Hopewell, New Jersey. Dr. Wiggins consults with schools, districts, and state education departments on reform matters; organizes conferences and workshops; and develops materials on curricular change. With Jay McTighe, he is co-author of *Understanding by Design* and *The Understanding by Design Handbook*, published by ASCD. His work has been supported by the Pew Charitable Trusts, the Geraldine R. Dodge Foundation, and the National Science Foundation.

Siegfried Haenisch, Ed.D, has taught mathematics from elementary to graduate school, most recently as Professor in the Department of Mathematics and Statistics at the College of New Jersey. Dr. Haenisch was the site director for the training of teachers in the New Jersey Algebra Project. Dr. Haenisch currently serves as a mathematics curriculum consultant to school districts. The Mathematical Association of America granted him the 1995 Award for Distinguished Teaching of Mathematics.

Program *Authors*
Algebra 1 and Algebra 2

Allan E. Bellman, Ph.D., is a Lecturer/Supervisor in the School of Education at the University of California, Davis. Before coming to Davis, he was a mathematics teacher for 31 years in Montgomery County, Maryland. He has been an instructor for both the Woodrow Wilson National Fellowship Foundation and the T^3 program. He has been involved in the development of many products from Texas Instruments. Dr. Bellman has a particular expertise in the use of technology in education and speaks frequently on this topic. He was a 1992 Tandy Technology Scholar and has twice been listed in Who's Who Among America's Teachers.

Sadie Chavis Bragg, Ed.D., is Senior Vice President of Academic Affairs at the Borough of Manhattan Community College of the City University of New York. A former professor of mathematics, she is a past president of the American Mathematical Association of Two-Year Colleges (AMATYC), co-director of the AMATYC project to revise the standards for introductory college mathematics before calculus, and an active member of the Benjamin Banneker Association. Dr. Bragg has coauthored more than 50 mathematics textbooks for kindergarten through college.

William G. Handlin, Sr., is a classroom teacher and Department Chairman of Technology Applications at Spring Woods High School in Houston, Texas. Awarded Life Membership in the Texas Congress of Parents and Teachers for his contributions to the well-being of children, Mr. Handlin is also a frequent workshop and seminar leader in professional meetings throughout the world.

Geometry

Laurie E. Bass is a classroom teacher at the 9–12 division of the Ethical Culture Fieldston School in Riverdale, New York. A classroom teacher for more than 30 years, Ms. Bass has a wide base of teaching experience, ranging from Grade 6 through Advanced Placement Calculus. She was the recipient of a 2000 Honorable Mention for the Radio Shack National Teacher Awards. She has been a contributing writer for a number of publications, including software-based activities for the Algebra 1 classroom. Among her areas of special interest are cooperative learning for high school students and geometry exploration on the computer. Ms. Bass is a frequent presenter at local, regional, and national conferences.

Art Johnson, Ed.D., is a professor of mathematics education at Boston University. He is a mathematics educator with 32 years of public school teaching experience, a frequent speaker and workshop leader, and the recipient of a number of awards: the Tandy Prize for Teaching Excellence, the Presidential Award for Excellence in Mathematics Teaching, and New Hampshire Teacher of the Year. He was also profiled by the Disney Corporation in the American Teacher of the Year Program. Dr. Johnson has contributed 18 articles to NCTM journals and has authored over 50 books on various aspects of mathematics.

Reviewers *National*

Tammy Baumann
K-12 Mathematics Coordinator
School District of the City
  of Erie
Erie, Pennsylvania

Sandy Cowgill
Mathematics Department Chair
Muncie Central High School
Muncie, Indiana

Kari Egnot
Mathematics Teacher
Newport News High School
Newport News, Virginia

Sheryl Ezze
Mathematics Chairperson
DeWitt High School
Lansing, Michigan

Dennis Griebel
Mathematics Coordinator
Cherry Creek School District
Aurora, Colorado

Bill Harrington
Secondary Mathematics
  Coordinator
State College School District
State College, Pennsylvania

Michael Herzog
Mathematics Teacher
Tucson Small School Project
Tucson, Arizona

Camilla Horton
Secondary Instruction Support
Memphis School District
Memphis, Tennessee

Gary Kubina
Mathematics Consultant
Mobile County School System
Mobile, Alabama

Sharon Liston
Mathematics Department Chair
Moore Public Schools
Oklahoma City, Oklahoma

Ann Marie Palmeri Monahan
Mathematics Supervisor
Bayonne Public Schools
Bayonne, New Jersey

Indika Morris
Mathematics Department Chair
Queen Creek School District
Queen Creek, Arizona

Jennifer Petersen
K-12 Mathematics Curriculum
  Facilitator
Springfield Public Schools
Springfield, Missouri

Tammy Popp
Mathematics Teacher
Mehlville School District
St. Louis, Missouri

Mickey Porter
Mathematics Teacher
Dayton Public Schools
Dayton, Ohio

Steven Sachs
Mathematics Department Chair
Lawrence North High School
Indianapolis, Indiana

John Staley
Secondary Mathematics
  Coordinator
Office of Mathematics, PK-12
Baltimore, Maryland

Robert Thomas, Ph.D.
Mathematics Teacher
Yuma Union High School
  District #70
Yuma, Arizona

Linda Ussery
Mathematics Consultant
Alabama Department of
  Education
Tuscumbia, Alabama

Denise Vizzini
Mathematics Teacher
Clarksburg High School
Montgomery County,
  Maryland

Marcia White
Mathematics Specialist
Academic Operations,
  Technology and Innovations
Memphis City Schools
Memphis, Tennessee

Merrie Wolf
Mathematics Department Chair
Tulsa Public Schools
Tulsa, Oklahoma

From the *Authors*

Welcome

Math is a powerful tool with far-reaching applications throughout your life. We have designed a unique and engaging program that will enable you to tap into the power of mathematics and mathematical reasoning.

Developing mathematical skills and problem-solving strategies is an ongoing process—a journey both inside and outside the classroom. This course is designed to help make sense of the mathematics you encounter in and out of class each day.

You will learn important mathematical principles. You will also learn how the principles are connected to one another and to what you already know. You will learn to solve problems and learn the reasoning that lies behind your solutions.

Each chapter begins with the "big ideas" of the chapter and some essential questions that you will learn to answer. Through this question-and-answer process you will develop your ability to analyze problems independently and solve them in different applications.

Your skills and confidence will increase through practice and review. Work the examples so you understand the concepts and methods presented and the thinking behind them. Then do your homework. Ask yourself how new concepts relate to old ones. Make the connections!

Everyone needs help sometimes. You will find that this program has built-in opportunities, both in this text and online, to get help whenever you need it.

This course will also help you succeed on the tests you take in class and on other tests like the SAT, ACT, and state exams. The practice problems in each lesson will prepare you for the format and content of such tests. No surprises!

The reasoning habits and problem-solving skills you develop in this program will serve you in all your studies and in your daily life. They will prepare you for future success not only as a student, but also as a member of a changing technological society.

Best wishes,

PowerAlgebra.com

Welcome to Algebra 2. *Prentice Hall Algebra 2* is part of an integrated digital and print environment for the study of high school mathematics. Take some time to look through the features of our mathematics program, starting with **PowerAlgebra.com,** the site of the digital features of the program.

Hi, I'm Darius. My friends and I will be showing you the great features of the Prentice Hall Algebra 2 program.

In each chapter opener, you will be invited to visit the **PowerAlgebra.com** site to access these online features. Look for these buttons throughout the lessons.

Big *Ideas*

We start with **Big Ideas.** Each chapter is organized around Big Ideas that convey the key mathematics concepts you will be studying in the program. Take a look at the Big Ideas on pages xx and xxi.

BIG ideas

1 Models
Essential Question How do you model a quantity that changes regularly over time by the same percentage?

2 Equivalence
Essential Question How are exponents and logarithms related?

3 Functions
Essential Question How are exponential functions and logarithmic functions related?

The **Big Ideas** are organizing ideas for all of the lessons in the program. At the beginning of each chapter, we'll tell you which Big Ideas you'll be studying. We'll also present an **Essential Question** for each Big Idea.

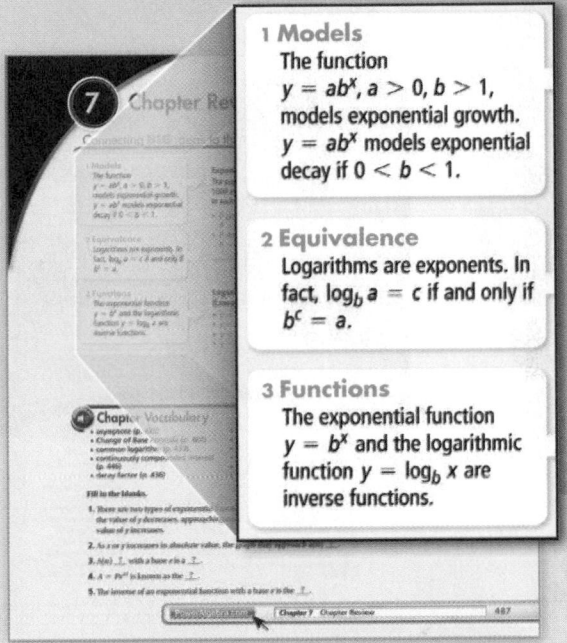

1 Models
The function
$y = ab^x$, $a > 0$, $b > 1$,
models exponential growth.
$y = ab^x$ models exponential decay if $0 < b < 1$.

2 Equivalence
Logarithms are exponents. In fact, $\log_b a = c$ if and only if $b^c = a$.

3 Functions
The exponential function $y = b^x$ and the logarithmic function $y = \log_b x$ are inverse functions.

In the **Chapter Review** at the end of the chapter, you'll find the answers to the Essential Question for each Big Idea. We'll also remind you of the lesson(s) where you studied the concepts that support the Big Ideas.

Exploring *Concepts*

The lessons offer many opportunities to explore concepts in different contexts and through different media.

Hi, I'm Serena. I never have to power down when I am in math class now.

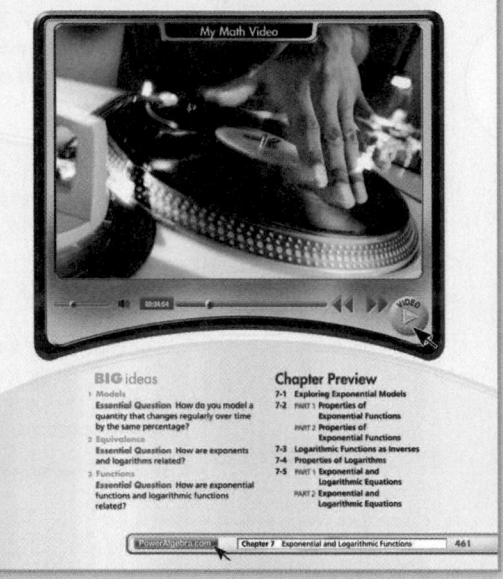

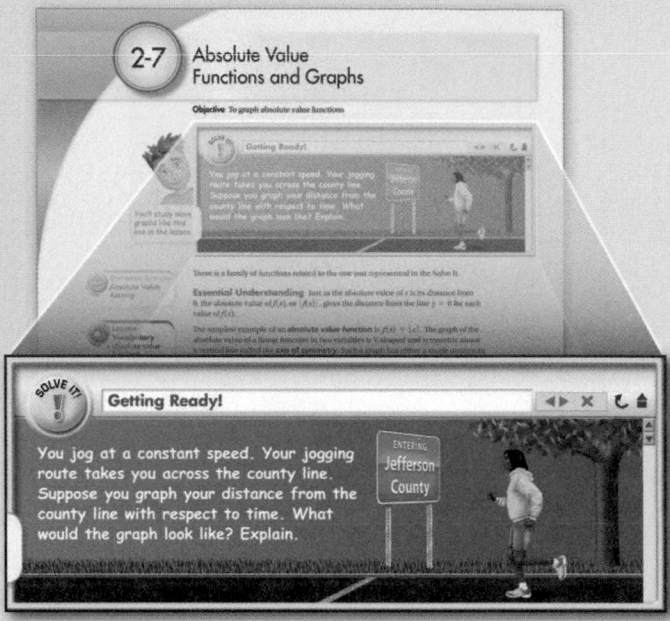

For each chapter, there is a video that you can access at **PowerAlgebra.com.** The video presents concepts in a real-life context. And you can contribute your own math video.

Here's another cool feature. Each lesson opens with a **Solve It,** a problem that helps you connect what you know to an important concept in the lesson. Do you notice how the Solve It frame looks like it comes from a computer? That's because all of the Solve Its can be found at **PowerAlgebra.com.**

Exploring concepts in print and digitally helps you develop important **21st Century Skills,** such as technological literacy.

21st Century Skills

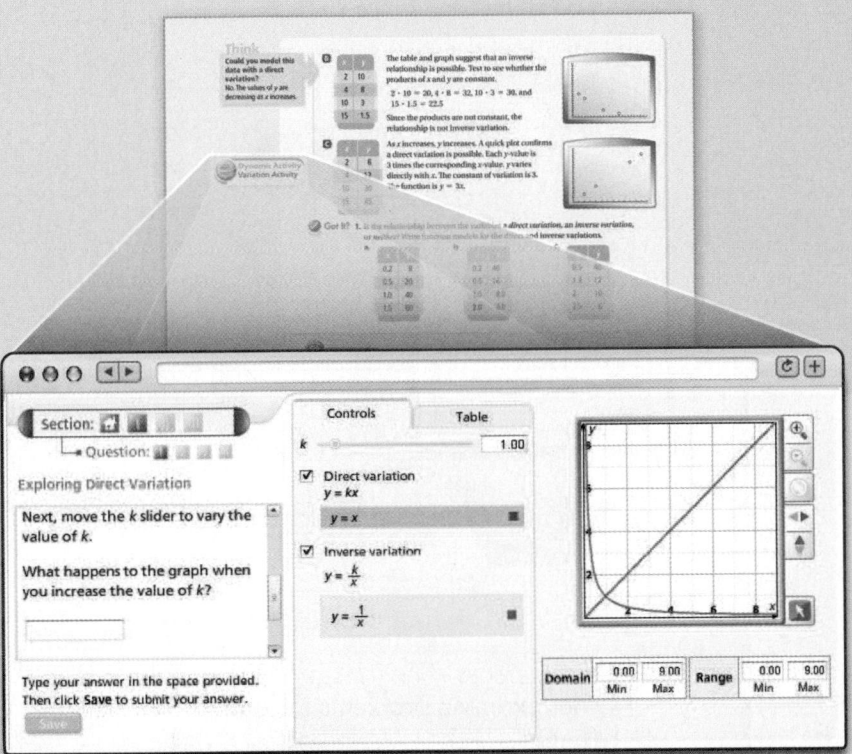

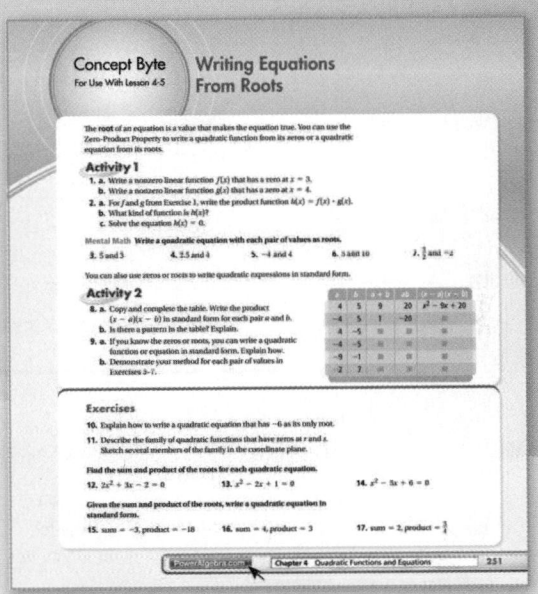

Try a **Concept Byte!** In a Concept Byte, you might explore technology, do a hands-on activity, or try a challenging extension.

Want to do some more exploring? Look for this icon in your book. It lets you know that there is a **Dynamic Activity** at **PowerAlgebra.com.** With the Dynamic Activity, you can continue to explore the concept that is presented in the lesson.

Thinking *Mathematically*

Mathematical reasoning is the key to solving problems and making sense of math. Throughout the program you'll learn strategies to develop mathematical reasoning habits.

Hello, I'm Tyler. These Think-Write boxes help me plan my work.

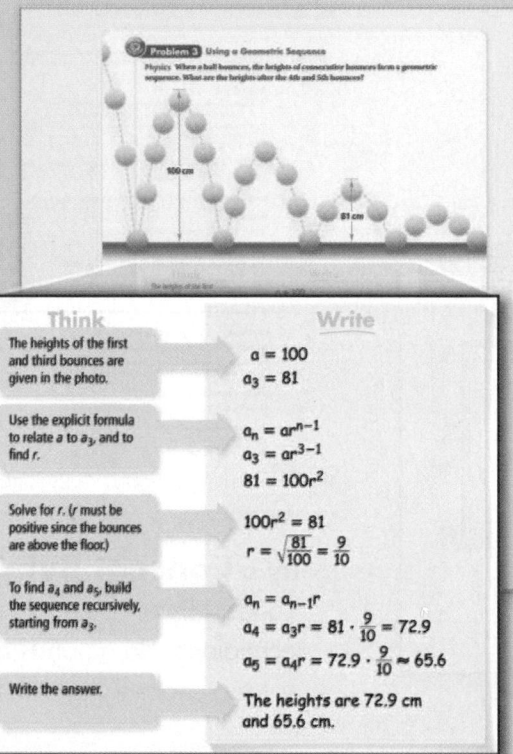

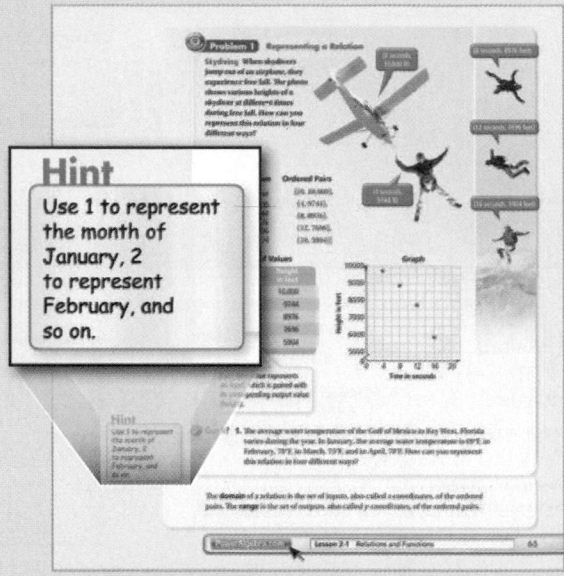

Hint

Use 1 to represent the month of January, 2 to represent February, and so on.

The worked-out problems include call-outs that reveal the strategies and reasoning behind the solution. The **Think-Write** problems model the thinking behind each step of a solution.

Also, look for the boxes labeled **Plan** and **Think.**

Other example problems include **Hints**, to help you remember a skill you already know or to point you to a different strategy.

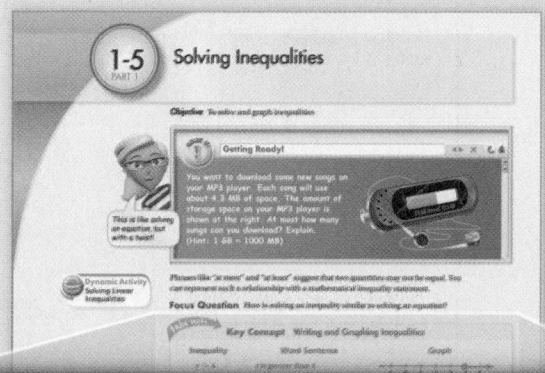

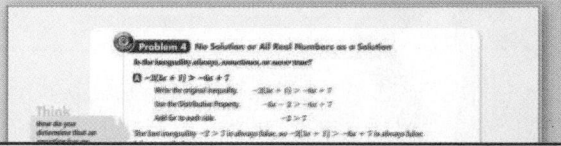

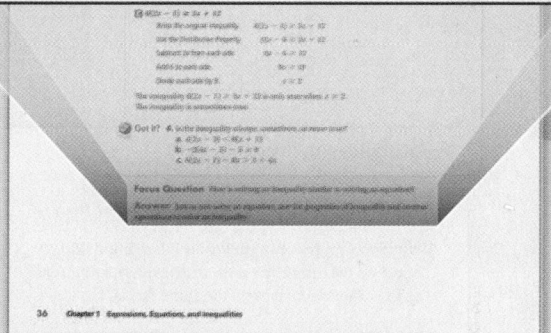

Focus Question How is solving an inequality similar to solving an equation?

Answer Just as you solve an equation, use the properties of inequality and inverse operations to solve an inequality.

A **Take Note** box highlights key concepts in a lesson. You can use these boxes to review concepts throughout the year.

Part of Thinking Mathematically is figuring out the main reason behind learning a new concept. The **Focus Questions** and **Answers** help you get there.

Active *Learning*

Through active learning, you become a successful, independent problem solver. The **Student Companion** has graphic organizers and other tools to help you master skills and problem solving.

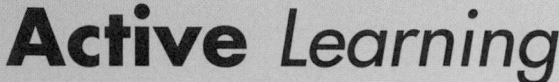

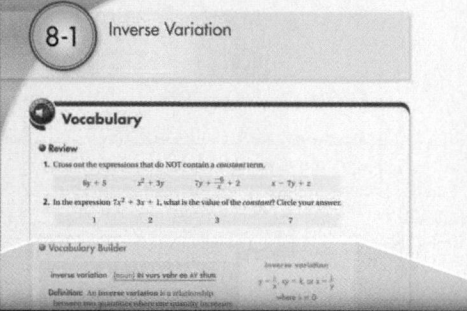

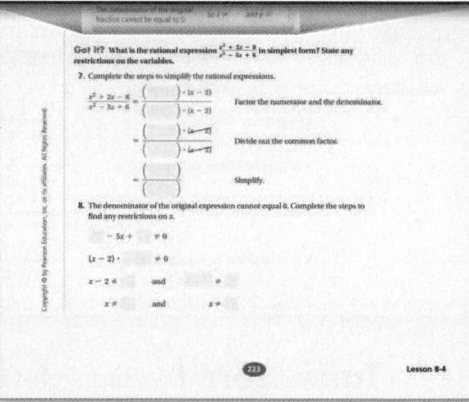

The **Think-Write** format allows you to organize your thinking in order to solve a problem.

The Companion has a **Vocabulary Builder** for each lesson. After reading the definitions, examples and nonexamples in the Vocabulary Builder, you use the vocabulary in realistic contexts.

Efficient and effective problem solvers are likely to score well on state and national assessments and be better prepared for college studies.

SAT® and ACT®

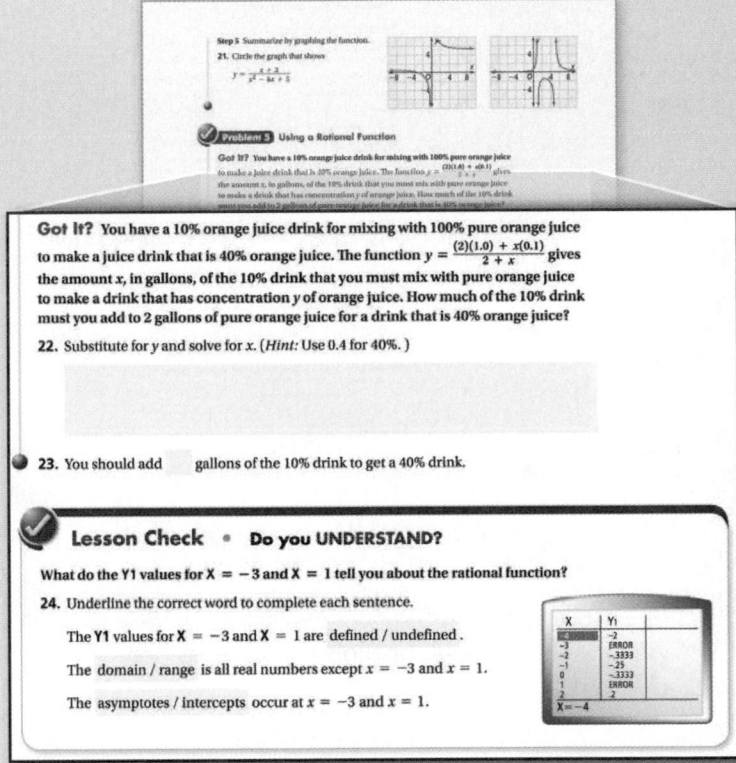

Got It? You have a 10% orange juice drink for mixing with 100% pure orange juice to make a juice drink that is 40% orange juice. The function $y = \frac{(2)(1.0) + x(0.1)}{2 + x}$ gives the amount x, in gallons, of the 10% drink that you must mix with pure orange juice to make a drink that has concentration y of orange juice. How much of the 10% drink must you add to 2 gallons of pure orange juice for a drink that is 40% orange juice?

22. Substitute for y and solve for x. (*Hint:* Use 0.4 for 40%.)

23. You should add ____ gallons of the 10% drink to get a 40% drink.

Lesson Check • Do you UNDERSTAND?

What do the Y1 values for $X = -3$ and $X = 1$ tell you about the rational function?

24. Underline the correct word to complete each sentence.

The **Y1** values for $X = -3$ and $X = 1$ are defined / undefined .

The domain / range is all real numbers except $x = -3$ and $x = 1$.

The asymptotes / intercepts occur at $x = -3$ and $x = 1$.

Use the **Got Its** and **Lesson Checks** to actively participate in the presentation of a lesson. These will help you make sure you understand a lesson before you do your homework.

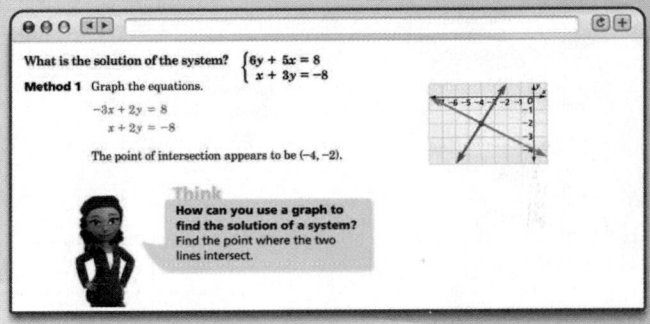

Not sure you "got it" yet? Try out the **Online Problems** at **PowerAlgebra.com.** You will find some problems with stepped-out solutions as well as some helpful math tools, such as the graphing utility.

Practice *Makes Perfect*

Ask any professional and you'll be told that the one requirement for becoming an expert is practice, practice, practice.

Hello, I'm Anya. I can leave my book at school and still get my homework done. All of the lessons are at PowerAlgebra.com

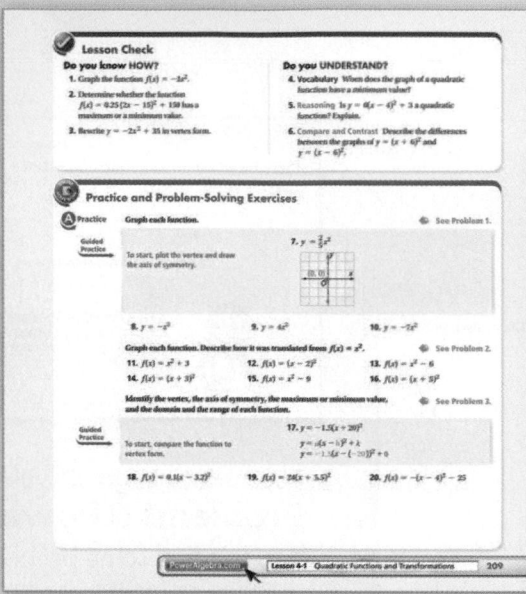

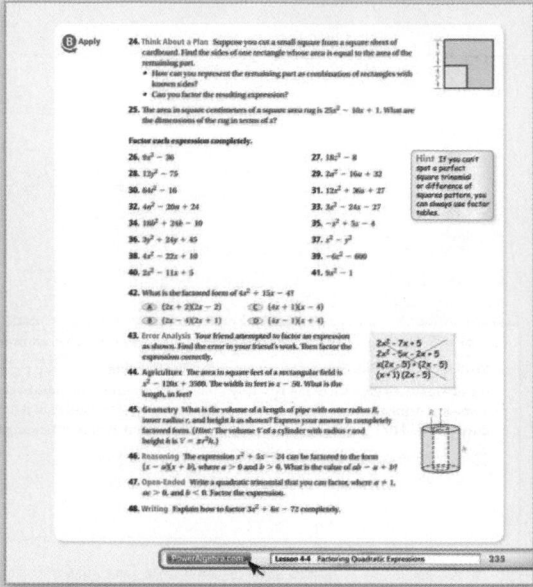

We give you lots of practice! There are **Practice** exercises for each concept or skill. Having difficulty with any of them? The green arrow tells you what problem with a worked-out solution to revisit in the lesson. The blue arrow of the guided practice points to information to help you get started on an exercise.

In the **Apply** section, you apply the concepts or skills to different situations or contexts. Be on the lookout for hints to exercises here.

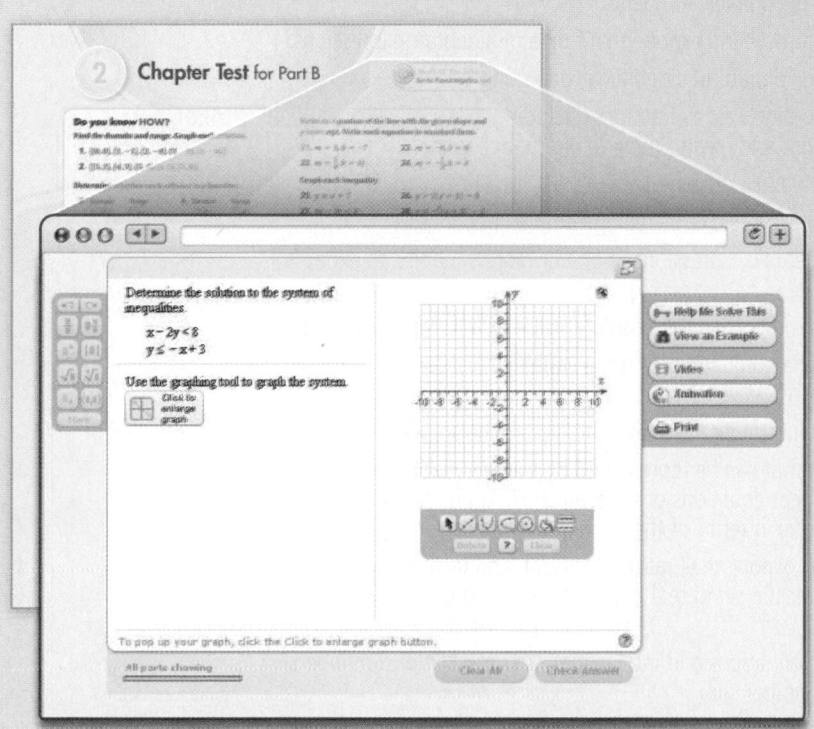

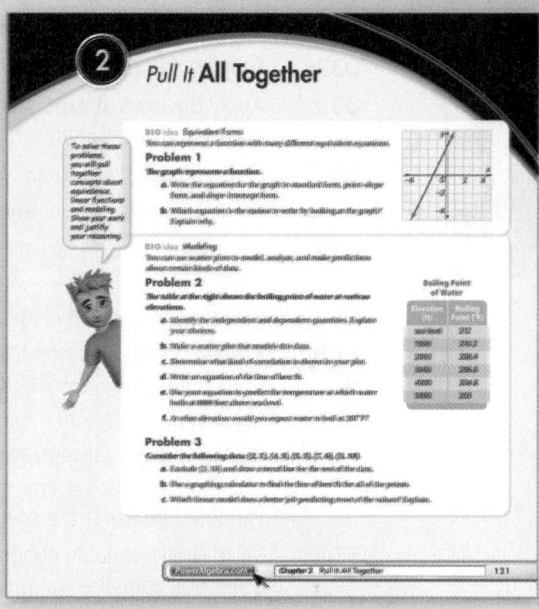

Want more practice? Look for this icon 🔵 in your book. Check out all of the opportunities in **MathXL® for School.** Your teacher can assign you some practice exercises or you can choose some on your own. And you'll know right away if you got the right answer!

But the best practice occurs when you **Pull It All Together** — understanding of concepts, mathematical thinking, and problem solving — to solve interesting problems. And look: there are those Big Ideas again.

ADP *End-of-Course Exam Content*

Hi! I'm Max. Here is a list of important topics you will learn this year. These topics are on the national ADP test.

O1.a Convert between and among radical and exponential forms of numerical expressions.

O1.b Simplify and perform operations on numerical expressions containing radicals.

O1.c Apply the laws of exponents to numerical expressions with rational and negative exponents to order and rewrite them in alternative forms.

O2.a Represent complex numbers in the form $a + bi$, where a and b are real; simplify powers of pure imaginary numbers.

O2.b Perform operations on the set of complex numbers.

O3.a Convert between and among radical and exponential forms of algebraic expressions.

O3.b Simplify and perform operations on radical algebraic expressions.

O3.c Apply the laws of exponents to algebraic expressions, including those involving rational and negative exponents, to order and rewrite them in alternative forms.

O3.d Perform operations on polynomial expressions.

O3.e Perform operations on rational expressions, including complex fractions.

O3.f Identify or write equivalent algebraic expressions in one or more variables to extract information.

E1.a Solve equations and inequalities involving the absolute value of a linear expression.

E1.b Express and solve systems of linear equations in three variables with and without the use of technology.

E1.c Solve systems of linear inequalities in two variables and graph the solution set.

E1.d Recognize and solve problems that can be represented by single variable linear equations or inequalities or systems of linear equations or inequalities involving two or more variables. Interpret the solution(s) in terms of the context of the problem.

E2.a Solve single-variable quadratic, exponential, rational, radical, and factorable higher-order polynomial equations over the set of real numbers, including quadratic equations involving absolute value.

E2.b Solve single variable quadratic equations and inequalities over the complex numbers; graph real solution sets on a number line.

E2.c Use the discriminant, $D = b^2 - 4ac$, to determine the nature of the solutions of the equation $ax^2 + bx + c = 0$.

E2.d Graph the solution set of a two-variable quadratic inequality in the coordinate plane.

E2.e Rewrite nonlinear equations and inequalities to express them in multiple forms in order to facilitate finding a solution set or to extract information about the relationships or graphs indicated.

P1.a Determine key characteristics of quadratic functions and their graphs.

P1.b Describe and represent the effect that changes in the parameters of a quadratic function have on the shape and position of its graph.

P1.c Describe the effect that changes in the parameters of a quadratic function have on the shape and position of its graph.

P1.d Recognize, express, and solve problems that can be modeled using quadratic functions. Interpret their solutions in terms of the context.

P2.a   Determine key characteristics of power functions in the form $f(x) = ax^n$, $a \neq 0$, for positive integral values of n and their graphs.

P2.b   Determine key characteristics of polynomial functions and their graphs.

P2.c   Represent polynomial functions using tables, graphs, verbal statements, and equations. Translate among these representations.

P2.d   Determine key characteristics of simple rational functions and their graphs.

P2.e   Represent simple rational functions using tables, graphs, verbal statements, and equations. Translate among these representations.

P2.f   Recognize, express, and solve problems that can be modeled using polynomial and simple rational functions. Interpret their solutions in terms of the context.

X1.a   Determine key characteristics of exponential functions and their graphs.

X1.b   Represent exponential functions using tables, graphs, verbal statements, and equations. Represent exponential expressions in multiple forms. Translate among these representations.

X1.c   Describe and represent the effect that changes in the parameters of an exponential function have on the shape and position of its graph.

X1.d   Recognize, express, and solve problems that can be modeled using exponential functions, including those where logarithms provide an efficient method of solution. Interpret their solutions in terms of the context.

F1.a   Combine functions by addition, subtraction, multiplication, and division.

F1.b   Determine the composition of two functions, including any necessary restrictions on the domain.

F2.a   Describe the conditions under which an inverse relation is a function.

F2.b   Determine and graph the inverse relation of a function.

F3.a   Determine key characteristics of absolute value, step, and other piecewise-defined functions.

F3.b   Represent piecewise-defined functions using tables, graphs, verbal statements, and equations. Translate among these representations.

F3.c   Recognize, express, and solve problems that can be modeled using absolute value, step, and other piecewise-defined functions. Interpret their solutions in terms of the context.

S1.a   Summarize and compare data sets using statistical methods.

S1.b   Determine, use, and identify potential misuses of weighted averages.

S1.c   Use a computer or calculator to find a linear regression equation (least squares line) as a model for data that suggest a linear trend, and determine the correlation coefficient.

S2.a   Analyze the strength of the linear relationship indicated by the regression line.

S2.b   Interpret data and communicate conclusions effectively.

S2.c   Make judgments regarding accuracy, reasonableness, and bias in the use of data.

S2.d   Critique and justify various methods of sampling and data collection used in real-world problems.

R1.a   Determine the number of ways events can occur using permutations, combinations, and other systematic counting methods.

R1.b   Relate the expansion of $(x + y)^n$ (i.e., the binomial theorem) with the possible outcomes of a binomial experiment and/or the nth row of Pascal's triangle.

R1.c   Apply probability concepts to calculate the probability of events and to make informed decisions in practical situations.

R1.d   Analyze and interpret actual data to estimate probabilities and predict outcomes, including those involving relative frequency.

R1.e   Compare theoretical probabilities with the results of simple experiments (e.g., tossing number cubes, flipping coins, spinning spinners).

R1.f   Compute and graph cumulative frequencies.

R2.a   Identify and distinguish between discrete and continuous probability distributions.

R2.b   Identify the principal characteristics of the normal distribution and use them to estimate probabilities.

R2.c   Identify and describe the key characteristics of and create frequency distributions of both discrete and continuous data.

L1.a   Apply the properties of logarithms and use them to manipulate logarithmic expressions.

L1.b   Solve logarithmic equations, paying attention to the possibility of extraneous roots.

L2.a   Determine key characteristics of logarithmic functions.

L2.b   Represent logarithmic functions using tables, graphs, verbal statements, and equations. Translate among these representations.

L2.c   Describe the effect that changes in the parameters of a logarithmic function have on the shape and position of its graph.

L2.d   Recognize, express, and solve problems that can be modeled using logarithmic functions. Interpret their solutions in terms of the context of the problem.

T1.a   Recognize periodic phenomena and determine key characteristics of such phenomena.

T1.b   Use the relationship of the sine and cosine functions to a central angle of the unit circle to determine the exact trigonometric ratio of angles on the unit circle. (0° to 360°, 0 to 2pi)

T1.c   Explain and use both degree and radian measure for angles.

T1.d   Represent trigonometric functions using tables, graphs, verbal statements, and equations. Translate among these representations.

T1.e   Determine key characteristics of trigonometric functions and their graphs.

T1.f   Describe the effect that changes in the parameters of an equation of a trigonometric function in the form, $f(x) = A \sin B(x - C) + D$ (or the similar cosine function) have on the shape and position of its graph.

T1.g   Recognize, express, and solve problems that can be modeled using trigonometric or other periodic functions.

M1.a   Perform addition, subtraction, and scalar multiplication of matrices.

M1.b   Perform matrix multiplication.

M2.a   Find the determinant of a 2×2 or 3×3 matrix.

M2.b   Determine the inverse of a 2×2 or 3×3 matrix or indicate that no inverse exists.

M2.c   Represent 2-variable and 3-variable systems of linear equations using matrices and use them to solve the system.

M2.d   Solve a matrix equation.

M3.a   Use matrix tools to represent and transform geometric objects in the coordinate plane.

M4.b   Add, subtract, and compute the dot product of two-dimensional vectors; multiply a two-dimensional vector by a scalar.

C1.a   Identify a parabola, circle, ellipse, or hyperbola from its equation, description, or key characteristics.

C1.b   Represent conic sections whose axes are parallel to the x- and y-axes using graphs, verbal statements, and equations. Translate among these representations. Represent the equations of conic sections in multiple forms to extract information about the parabola, circle, ellipse, or hyperbola.

C1.c   Describe the effect that changes in the parameters of a particular conic section have on its shape and position.

C1.d   Recognize, express, and solve problems that can be modeled using conic sections. Interpret their solutions in terms of the context of the problem.

I1.a   Represent the general term of an arithmetic or geometric sequence and use it to generate the sequence or determine the value of any particular term.

I1.b   Represent partial sums of an arithmetic or geometric sequence and determine the value of a particular partial sum or sum of a finite sequence.

I1.c   Recognize when an infinite geometric sum can be determined and determine the sum when possible.

I1.d   Convert the recursive model for linear growth ($a_1 = a$, $a_{n+1} = a_n + d$, where a is the first term and d is the constant difference) to a closed linear form ($a_n = a + (n - 1)d$).

I1.e   Convert the recursive model of geometric growth ($p_1 = a$, $p_{n+1} = rp_n$ where a is the first term and r is the constant growth rate) to a closed exponential form ($p_n = ar^{n-1}$).

I1.f   Recognize, express, and solve problems that can be modeled using a finite geometric series. Interpret their solutions in terms of the context of the problem.

I2.a   Use recursion to generate and describe, analyze, and interpret patterned relationships other than arithmetic or geometric sequences.

I2.b   Use iterative methods to solve problems.

BIGideas

These Big Ideas are the organizing ideas for the study of important areas of mathematics: algebra, geometry, and statistics.

Stay connected! These Big Ideas will help you understand how the math you study in high school fits together.

Algebra

Properties

- In the transition from arithmetic to algebra, attention shifts from arithmetic operations (addition, subtraction, multiplication, and division) to use of the *properties* of these operations.
- All of the facts of arithmetic and algebra follow from certain properties.

Variable

- Quantities are used to form expressions, equations, and inequalities.
- An expression refers to a quantity but does not make a statement about it. An equation (or an inequality) is a statement about the quantities it mentions.
- Using variables in place of numbers in equations (or inequalities) allows the statement of relationships among numbers that are unknown or unspecified.

Equivalence

- A single quantity may be represented by many different expressions.
- The facts about a quantity may be expressed by many different equations (or inequalities).

Solving Equations & Inequalities

- Solving an equation is the process of rewriting the equation to make what it says about its variable(s) as simple as possible.
- Properties of numbers and equality can be used to transform an equation (or inequality) into equivalent, simpler equations (or inequalities) in order to find solutions.
- Useful information about equations and inequalities (including solutions) can be found by analyzing graphs or tables.
- The numbers and types of solutions vary predictably, based on the type of equation.

Proportionality

- Two quantities are *proportional* if they have the same ratio in each instance where they are measured together.
- Two quantities are *inversely proportional* if they have the same product in each instance where they are measured together.

Function

- A function is a relationship between variables in which each value of the input variable is associated with a unique value of the output variable.
- Functions can be represented in a variety of ways, such as graphs, tables, equations, or words. Each representation is particularly useful in certain situations.
- Some important families of functions are developed through transformations of the simplest form of the function.
- New functions can be made from other functions by applying arithmetic operations or by applying one function to the output of another.

Modeling

- Many real-world mathematical problems can be represented algebraically. These representations can lead to algebraic solutions.
- A function that models a real-world situation can be used to make estimates or predictions about future occurrences.

Statistics and Probability

Data Collection and Analysis

- Sampling techniques are used to gather data from real world situations. If the data are representative of the larger population, inferences can be made about that population.
- Biased sampling techniques yield data unlikely to be representative of the larger population.
- Sets of numerical data are described using measures of central tendency and dispersion.

Data Representation

- The most appropriate data representations depend on the type of data—quantitative or qualitative, and univariate or bivariate.
- Line plots, box plots, and histograms are different ways to show distribution of data over a possible range of values.

Probability

- Probability expresses the likelihood that a particular event will occur.
- Data can be used to calculate an experimental probability, and mathematical properties can be used to determine a theoretical probability.
- Either experimental or theoretical probability can be used to make predictions or decisions about future events.
- Various counting methods can be used to develop theoretical probabilities.

Geometry

Visualization

- Visualization can help you connect properties of real objects with two-dimensional drawings of these objects.

Transformations

- Transformations are mathematical functions that model relationships with figures.
- Transformations may be described geometrically or by coordinates.
- Symmetries of figures may be defined and classified by transformations.

Measurement

- Some attributes of geometric figures, such as length, area, volume, and angle measure, are measurable. Units are used to describe these attributes.

Reasoning & Proof

- Definitions establish meanings and remove possible misunderstanding.
- Other truths are more complex and difficult to see. It is often possible to verify complex truths by reasoning from simpler ones using deductive reasoning.

Similarity

- Two geometric figures are similar when corresponding lengths are proportional and corresponding angles are congruent.
- Areas of similar figures are proportional to the squares of their corresponding lengths.
- Volumes of similar figures are proportional to the cubes of their corresponding lengths.

Coordinate Geometry

- A coordinate system on a line is a number line on which points are labeled, corresponding to the real numbers.
- A coordinate system in a plane is formed by two perpendicular number lines, called the x- and y-axes, and the quadrants they form. The coordinate plane can be used to graph many functions.
- It is possible to verify some complex truths using deductive reasoning in combination with the distance, midpoint, and slope formulas.

1

Expressions, Equations, and Inequalities

3

Linear Systems

2 Functions, Equations, and Graphs

Visual See It!

Reasoning Try It!

Practice Do It!

4 Quadratic Functions and Equations

Visual See It!

Reasoning Try It!

Practice Do It!

5

Polynomials and Polynomial Functions

6 Radical Functions and Rational Exponents

Visual See It!

Reasoning Try It!

Practice Do It!

7

Exponential and Logarithmic Functions

8 Rational Functions

Visual See It!

Reasoning Try It!

Practice Do It!

Sequences and Series

10 Quadratic Relations and Conic Sections

Visual See It!

Reasoning Try It!

Practice Do It!

Probability and Statistics

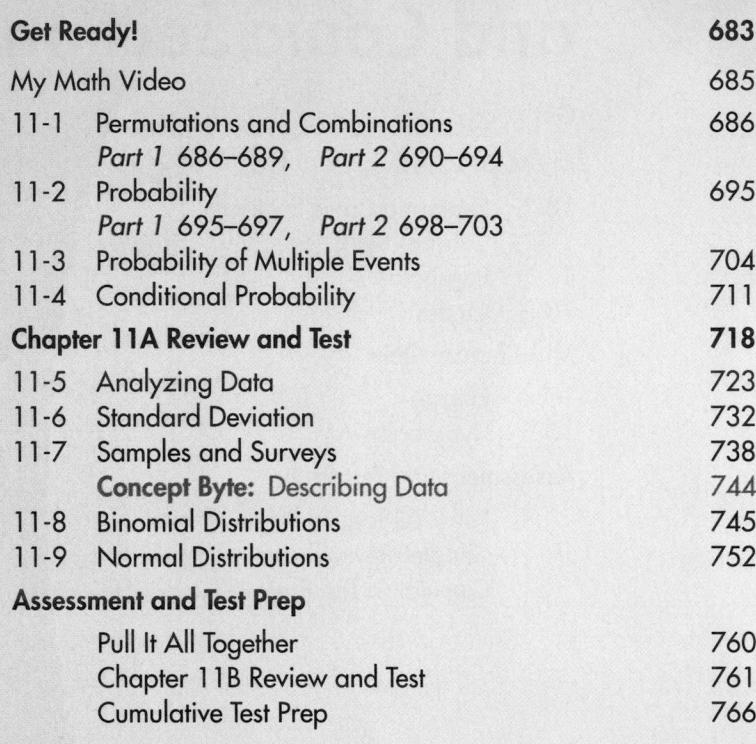

12 Matrices

Trigonometry Concepts

Visual See It!

Reasoning Try It!

Practice Do It!

Entry-Level Assessment

Multiple Choice

Read each question. Then write the letter of the correct answer on your paper.

1. Let $A = \{1, 2, 3, 4\}$ be a set in the universe $U = \{1, 2, 3, 4, 5, 6, 7, 8\}$. What is the complement of A?

   Ⓐ $\{2, 3\}$ Ⓒ $\{1, 2, 3, 4\}$

   Ⓑ $\{5, 6, 7, 8\}$ Ⓓ $\{2, 3, 7, 8\}$

2. Solve $x^2 + 2x - 3 = 0$ by factoring.

   Ⓕ $x = -3$ and $x = 1$

   Ⓖ $x = -1$ and $x = 3$

   Ⓗ $x = 0$

   Ⓘ $x = -3$ and $x = 0$

3. Simplify $\dfrac{3a^2b^3 - 12a^4b^3 + 6a^4b^2}{3a^2b}$.

   Ⓐ $b^2 - 4a^2b^2 + 2a^2b$

   Ⓑ $a^2b - 4a^2b^2 + 2a^2b$

   Ⓒ $3b^2 - 12a^2b + 6b^2$

   Ⓓ $3ab^2 - 4a^2b + 2ab^2$

4. Which relation is not a function?

   Ⓕ $\{(1, -5), (2, 4), (1, -4)\}$

   Ⓖ $\{(1, -5), (2, 4), (3, -3)\}$

   Ⓗ $\{(1, -5), (2, 4), (3, 2)\}$

   Ⓘ $\{(1, -5), (2, 4), (3, -4)\}$

5. In the diagram, m and n are parallel.

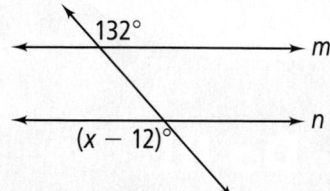

   What is the value of x?

   Ⓐ 36   Ⓒ 120

   Ⓑ 60   Ⓓ 144

6. Solve $2(1 - 2w) = 4w + 18$.

   Ⓕ -4 Ⓗ 8

   Ⓖ -2 Ⓘ 16

7. Which of the following lines is perpendicular to the line $3x + y = 2$?

   Ⓐ $y = 3x + 4$

   Ⓑ $y = \frac{1}{3}x - 2$

   Ⓒ $y = -3x + 3$

   Ⓓ $y = -\frac{1}{3}x + 1$

8. If $y = 1$, then $(x + 5) \cdot y = x + 5$. Which property supports this statement?

   Ⓕ Inverse Property of Multiplication

   Ⓖ Identity Property of Multiplication

   Ⓗ Associative Property of Addition

   Ⓘ Commutative Property of Addition

9.

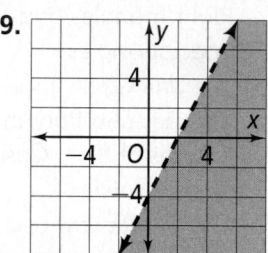

Which inequality does the graph represent?

   Ⓐ $y < 2x - 4$

   Ⓑ $y > -4x + 2$

   Ⓒ $y > 2x - 4$

   Ⓓ $y < -4x + 2$

10. The area of a trapezoid is $A = \frac{1}{2}h(b_1 + b_2)$. Solve for b_1.

   Ⓕ $b_1 = \dfrac{2A - b_2}{h}$

   Ⓖ $b_1 = \dfrac{2A - h}{b_2}$

   Ⓗ $b_1 = \dfrac{2A}{h} - b_2$

   Ⓘ $b_1 = 2A - b_2$

11. Let $\overleftrightarrow{AB}$ be parallel to $\overleftrightarrow{CD}$, with $A(-2, 3)$, $B(1, 4)$, and $C(1, 2)$. Which of the following could be the coordinates of point D?

- (A) $(4, 1)$
- (C) $(-2, 3)$
- (B) $(-2, -1)$
- (D) $(4, 3)$

12. Solve $3 \geq 4g - 5 \geq -1$.

- (F) $-\frac{3}{2} \leq g \leq 2$
- (H) $-4 \leq g \leq 8$
- (G) $-1 \leq g \leq \frac{3}{4}$
- (I) $1 \leq g \leq 2$

13. Which is *not* a solution of $5(2x + 4) \geq 2(x + 34)$?

- (A) 48
- (C) 6
- (B) 8
- (D) 3

14. Factor $6x^2 - 216$.

- (F) $6(x - 6)(x + 6)$
- (G) $(6x - 36)(6x + 36)$
- (H) $6(x - 6)$
- (I) $6(x - 36)(x + 6)$

15. Mike and Jane leave their home on bikes traveling in opposite directions on a straight road. Mike rides 5 mi/h faster than Jane. After 4 h they are 124 mi apart. At what rate does Mike ride his bike?

- (A) 5 mi/h
- (C) 18 mi/h
- (B) 13 mi/h
- (D) 31 mi/h

16. What is the point-slope form for the equation of the line in the graph?

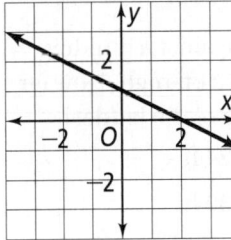

- (F) $y - 2 = \frac{3}{2}(x + 2)$
- (G) $y - 2 = \frac{1}{2}(x + 2)$
- (H) $y - 2 = -\frac{1}{2}(x + 2)$
- (I) $y - 2 = -\frac{2}{3}(x + 2)$

17. A rectangular photograph is being enlarged to poster size by making both the length and width six times as large as the original. How many times as large as the area of the original photograph is the area of the poster?

- (A) $\frac{1}{6}$
- (C) 12
- (B) 6
- (D) 36

18. A rectangle has a length of $2x + 3$ and a width of $x - 4$. Find the area of the rectangle.

- (F) $2x^2 - 12$
- (G) $2x^2 - 8x$
- (H) $2x^2 - 5x - 12$
- (I) $2x^2 - 11x - 12$

19. What is the y-intercept of the line that passes through the points $(-4, 4)$ and $(2, -5)$?

- (A) -2
- (C) $\frac{3}{2}$
- (B) $-\frac{3}{2}$
- (D) 2

20. Which of the following is equivalent to $\sqrt{2}(\sqrt{6} - 4)$?

- (F) $\sqrt{12} - 4$
- (H) $\sqrt{12} - 8$
- (G) $2\sqrt{3} - 2\sqrt{2}$
- (I) $2\sqrt{3} - 4\sqrt{2}$

21. Which of the following represents the system shown in the graph?

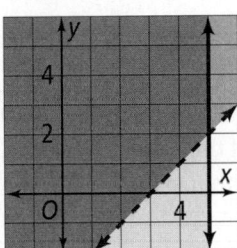

- (A) $\begin{cases} y = x - 3 \\ x \geq 5 \end{cases}$
- (C) $\begin{cases} y < x - 3 \\ x = 5 \end{cases}$
- (B) $\begin{cases} y \leq x - 3 \\ x > 5 \end{cases}$
- (D) $\begin{cases} y > x - 3 \\ x \leq 5 \end{cases}$

22. Which of the following equations represents the line that is parallel to the line $y = 5x + 2$ and that passes through the point $(1, -3)$?

- (F) $y = -5x + 2$
- (H) $y = \frac{1}{5}x - 8$
- (G) $y = 5x + 8$
- (I) $y = 5x - 8$

23. Which equation represents a line that would be perpendicular to a second line with a slope of $\frac{1}{5}$?

  (A) $y = -5x + 2$

  (B) $y = -\frac{1}{5}x + 3$

  (C) $y = 5x - 2$

  (D) $5y + x = 2$

24. $\triangle ABC$ is similar to $\triangle DEF$.

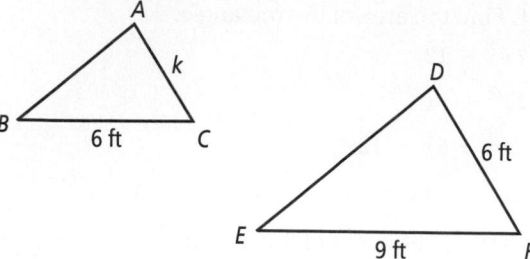

What is the value of k?

  (F) 3 ft   (H) 6 ft

  (G) 4 ft   (I) 9 ft

25. Solve the equation using the Quadratic Formula.
$$6x^2 - 10x + 3 = 0$$

  (A) $\dfrac{5 \pm \sqrt{7}}{6}$

  (B) $\dfrac{3 \pm \sqrt{5}}{6}$

  (C) -2 and 5

  (D) $\frac{3}{4}$ and $\frac{2}{3}$

26. A rectangle in the coordinate plane has vertices $(3, 2)$, $(8, 2)$, $(3, 6)$, and $(8, 6)$. Which of the following sets of vertices describes a rectangle that is congruent to this one?

  (F) $(3, -2), (3, -8), (5, -8), (5, -2)$

  (G) $(-2, -4), (-2, -8), (3, -8), (3, -4)$

  (H) $(0, 0), (5, 0), (5, 5), (0, 5)$

  (I) $(-3, 2), (1, 2), (1, 6), (-3, 6)$

27. Simplify the expression below.
$$(-6y^{-4})^5$$

  (A) $7776y^{20}$ (C) $-7776y^{20}$

  (B) $\dfrac{7776}{y^{20}}$ (D) $-\dfrac{7776}{y^{20}}$

28. What is the solution to $\dfrac{2n + 8}{3} = \dfrac{n + 7}{2}$?

  (F) -9 (H) 5

  (G) -1 (I) 13

29. Solve the system of equations below.
$$\begin{cases} 3x + y = -7 \\ 4x - y = -14 \end{cases}$$

  (A) $(-3, 2)$ (C) $(-3, -2)$

  (B) $(3, 2)$ (D) no solution

30. Which of the following is equivalent to $\dfrac{2x - 12}{x^2 - 2x - 24}$?

  (F) $\dfrac{2}{x + 4}$ (H) $\dfrac{1}{x^2 - 2}$

  (G) $\dfrac{1}{x + 2}$ (I) $\dfrac{2x - 3}{x - 6}$

31. What is (are) the solution(s) of the graphed function when the value of the function is 0?

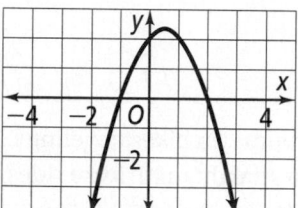

  (A) -1 and 2 (C) 2

  (B) 1 and -2 (D) 2.2

32. Which of the following is true?

  (F) $\sqrt{85} < 9$ (H) $\sqrt{\dfrac{16}{25}} > \sqrt{\dfrac{16}{4}}$

  (G) $8 < \sqrt{62}$ (I) $\sqrt{121} < \sqrt{144}$

33. A fire fighter leans a 30-ft ladder against a building in order to reach a window that is 24 ft high. How far away from the building is the base of the ladder?

  (A) 18 ft   (C) 24 ft

  (B) 20 ft   (D) 30 ft

34. What is the number of x-intercepts of the parabola with equation $y = 6x^2 - 4x - 3$?

  (F) 0   (H) 2

  (G) 1   (I) 3

Get Ready!

Skills Handbook, page 866

Adding Rational Numbers

Find each sum.

1. $6 + (-6)$ **2.** $-8 + 6$ **3.** $5.31 + (-7.40)$ **4.** $-1.95 + 10$

5. $7\frac{3}{4} + \left(-8\frac{1}{2}\right)$ **6.** $-2\frac{1}{3} + 3\frac{1}{4}$ **7.** $6\frac{2}{5} + 4\frac{3}{10}$ **8.** $-1\frac{5}{6} + 5\frac{1}{3}$

Skills Handbook, page 866

Subtracting Rational Numbers

Find each difference.

9. $-28 - 14$ **10.** $61 - (-11)$ **11.** $-16 - (-25)$ **12.** $-6.2 \div 3.6$

13. $-5\frac{2}{3} - \left(-2\frac{1}{3}\right)$ **14.** $-2\frac{1}{4} - 3\frac{1}{4}$ **15.** $2\frac{2}{3} - 7\frac{1}{3}$ **16.** $\frac{5}{2} - \frac{13}{4}$

Skills Handbook, page 866

Multiplying and Dividing Rational Numbers

Find each product or quotient.

17. $-3 \cdot 7$ **18.** $-2.1 \cdot (-3.5)$ **19.** $-\frac{2}{3} \div 4$ **20.** $-\frac{3}{8} \div \frac{5}{8}$

Skills Handbook, page 871

Using the Order of Operations

Simplify each expression.

21. $8 \cdot (-3) + 4$ **22.** $3 \cdot 4 - 8 \div 2$ **23.** $1 \div 2^2 - 0.54 + 1.26$

24. $9 \div (-3) - 2$ **25.** $5(3 \cdot 5 - 4)$ **26.** $1 - (1 - 5)^2 \div (-8)$

27. Reasoning Do the expressions $3 + 5^2 \cdot 3 \div 15$ and $(3 + 5^2) \cdot 3 \div 15$ yield the same answer? Explain.

 ## Looking Ahead Vocabulary

28. The current of a river flows north at a *constant* rate. What is the constant in the mathematical expression $4x + 5y + 3$?

29. Before signing a contract, you must review the *terms* and conditions of the contract. How many terms are there in the surface area formula below?

$$2(\ell w + wh + h\ell)$$

30. Engineers *evaluate* the efficiency of the memory and speed of a computer. What does evaluate mean in mathematics?

31. Smiling is a facial *expression* of happiness or contentment. In math, what is the expression that represents the quotient of 3 and 3 less than a number?

Expressions, Equations, and Inequalities

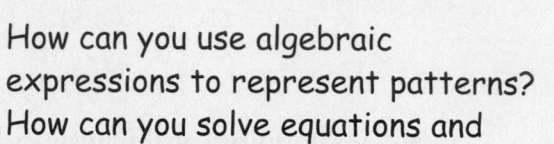
PowerAlgebra.com

Your place to get all things digital

Download videos connecting math to your world.

Math definitions in English and Spanish

The online Solve It will get you in gear for each lesson.

Interactive! Vary numbers, graphs, and figures to explore math concepts.

Download Step-by-Step Problems with Instant Replay.

Get and view your assignments online.

Extra practice and review online

You can use variables to represent the distance traveled or the time of the swimmer in the video.

How can you use algebraic expressions to represent patterns? How can you solve equations and inequalities? How can you solve absolute value equations and inequalities? You will learn how in this chapter.

Vocabulary

English/Spanish Vocabulary Audio Online:

English	Spanish
absolute value, p. 43	valor absoluto
algebraic expression, p. 5	expresión algebraica
coefficient, p. 20	coeficiente
compound inequality, p. 39	desigualdad compuesta
extraneous solution, p. 45	solución extraña
like terms, p. 21	términos semejantes
term, p. 20	término
variable, p. 5	variable

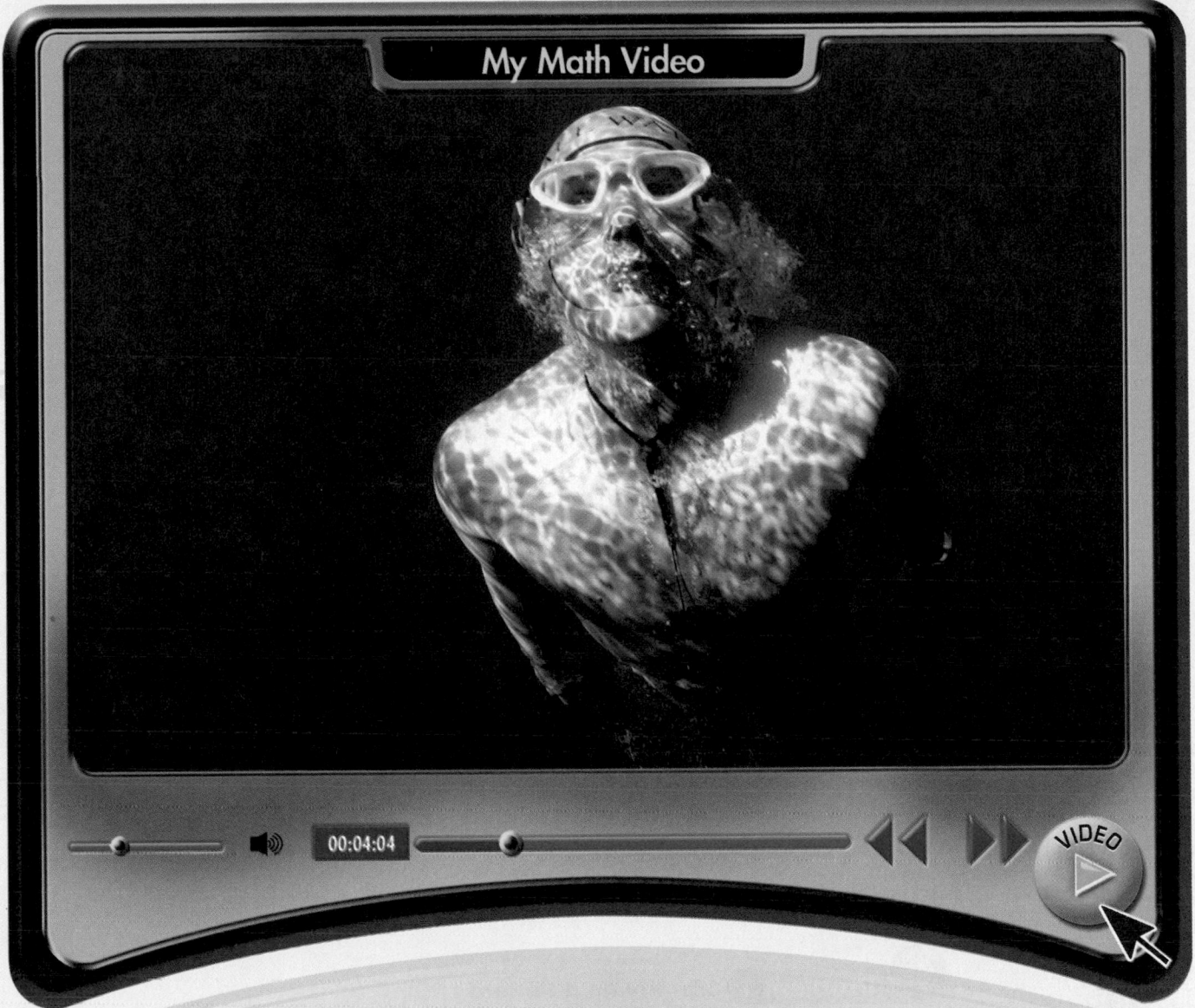

My Math Video

00:04:04

VIDEO ▶

BIGideas

1 Variable

Essential Question How do variables help you model real-world situations?

2 Properties

Essential Question How can you use the properties of real numbers to simplify algebraic expressions?

3 Solving Equations and Inequalities

Essential Question How do you solve an equation or inequality?

Chapter Preview

1-1 Patterns and Expressions

Objective To identify and describe patterns

Some video games really make you think! This one can turn your head round and round.

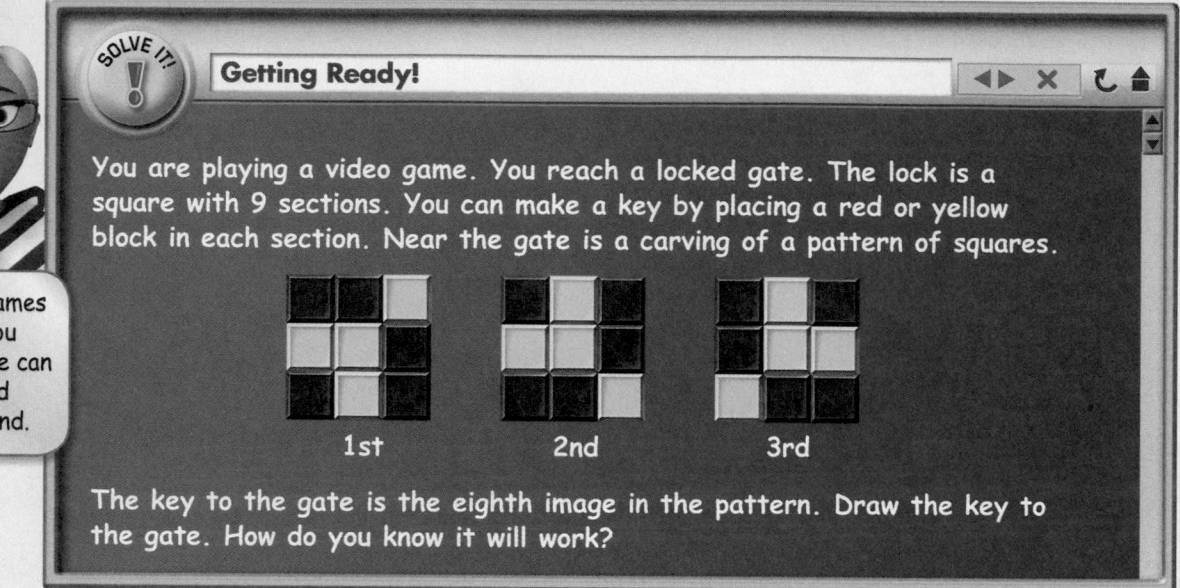

Lesson Vocabulary

- constant
- variable quantity
- variable
- numerical expression
- algebraic expression

In the Solve It, you identified and used a geometric pattern. In this lesson, you will identify patterns in pictures, tables, and graphs and describe them using numbers and variables.

Focus Question How can you describe a mathematical pattern?

Problem 1 Identifying a Pattern

Look at the figures from left to right. What is the pattern? What would the next figure in the pattern look like?

Think

How can you identify a pattern?
Look for the same type of change between consecutive figures.

The pattern shows regular polygons with the number of sides increasing by one.

The fourth figure above has six sides, so the next figure would have seven sides. This is a heptagon: .

Got It? 1. Look at the figures from left to right. What is the pattern? Draw the next figure in the pattern.

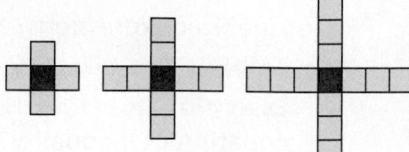

A mathematical *quantity* is anything that can be measured or counted. The *value* of the quantity is its measure or the number of items that are counted. Quantities whose values do not change are called **constants**. Quantities whose values change, or vary, are called **variable quantities**.

take note

Key Concepts   Variables and Expressions

Definition	Examples	
A **variable** is a symbol, usually a letter, that represents one or more numbers.	n	x
A **numerical expression** is a mathematical phrase that contains numbers and operation symbols.	$3 + 5$	$(8 - 2) + 5$
An **algebraic expression** is a mathematical phrase that contains one or more variables.	$3n + 5$	$(8x - 2) + 5n$

Tables are a convenient way to organize data and discover patterns. They work like an "input/output" machine. This machine takes one value as an input, processes it, and gives a value as an output. Use a process column *between* input and output columns to see how the inputs are transformed to outputs.

Problem 2 **Expressing a Pattern With Algebra**

A How many toothpicks are in the 20th figure?

Use a table. Look for a pattern that relates the figure number to the number of toothpicks.

Figure Number (Input)	Process Column	Number of Toothpicks (Output)
1	4(1)	4
2	4(2)	8
3	4(3)	12
⋮	⋮	⋮
n	■	■

To get the output, multiply the input by 4.

Pattern: Multiply the figure number by 4 to get the number of toothpicks.
So, there are $4(20) = 80$ toothpicks in the 20th figure.

Think

What would the process look like for the *n*th row?
Multiply the figure number, *n*, by 4.

B What is an algebraic expression for the number of toothpicks in the *n*th figure?

Use the pattern from part (a). There are $4n$ toothpicks in the *n*th figure.

Got It? **2. a.** How many tiles are in the 25th figure in this pattern? Show a table of values with a process column.

b. What is an algebraic expression for the number of tiles in the *n*th figure?

Problem 3 Using a Graph

Aquarium You want to set up an aquarium and need to determine what size tank to buy. The graph shows tank sizes using a rule that relates the capacity of the tank to the combined lengths of the fish it can hold.

If you want five 2-in. platys, four 1-in. guppies, and a 3-in. loach, which is the smallest capacity tank you can buy: 15-gallon, 20-gallon, or 25-gallon? Use a table to find the answer.

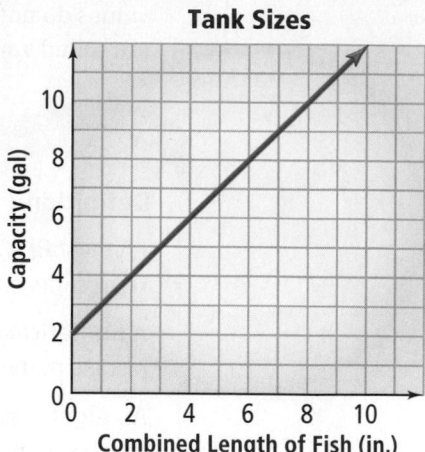

Tank Sizes

Plan

How can you use the given graph?
You can use the graph to make a table and find a pattern relating capacity and combined fish length.

Think

Choose some points on the graph.

Make a table using the input and output values shown in the ordered pairs.
Use the process column to find the pattern. Each output is 2 more than the corresponding input.

You want 5 platys, 4 guppies, and 1 loach. So, you will have a total of 17 in. of fish.
Find the output when the input is 17.

Write the answer in words.

Write

$(0, 2), (5, 7), (10, 12)$

Input	Process Column	Output
0	0 + 2	2
5	5 + 2	7
10	10 + 2	12

output = input + 2
= 17 + 2
= 19

You need to buy the 20-gal tank.

 Got It? **3.** The graph shows the total cost of platys at the aquarium shop. Use a table to answer the questions.
  a. How much do six platys cost?
  b. How much do ten platys cost?
  c. **Reasoning** Why is the graph in Problem 3 a line while the graph at the right is a set of points?

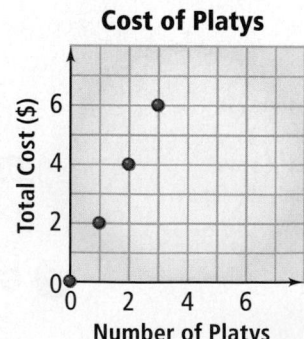

Cost of Platys

Focus Question How can you describe a mathematical pattern?

Answer Use words, tables, graphs, or algebraic expressions to describe a mathematical pattern.

Lesson Check

Do you know HOW?

Describe a rule for each pattern.

1. 35, 70, 105, 140, . . .

2.
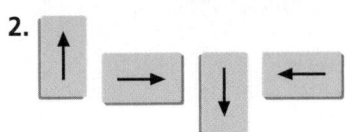

Make a table to represent each pattern. Use a process column.

3. 2, 4, 6, 8, . . .

4.

Do you UNDERSTAND?

5. Explain the strategy you use to identify a pattern.

6. **Compare and Contrast** How are tables of values like pictorial representations? How are they different?

7. **Error Analysis** Your friend looks for a pattern in the table below and claims that the output equals the input divided by 2. Is your friend correct? Explain.

Input	3	6.8	8	10	25
Output	2	3.4	4	5	12.5

Practice and Problem-Solving Exercises

A Practice

Describe each pattern using words. Draw the next likely figure in each pattern.

⬅ **See Problem 1.**

8.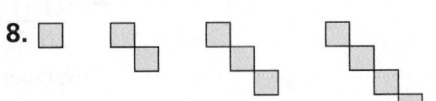

9.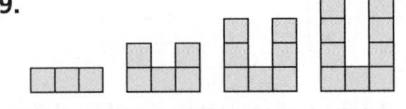

10.

11.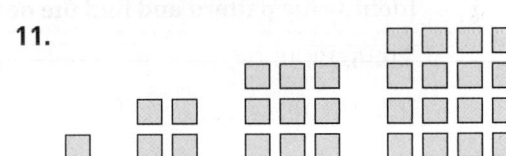

Make a table with a process column to represent each pattern. Write an expression for the number of circles in the nth figure.

⬅ **See Problem 2.**

12.

13.

Identify a pattern by making a table. Include a process column.

14.

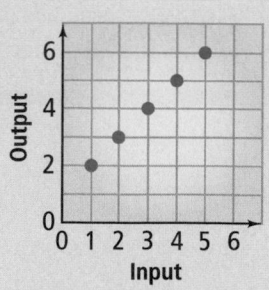

To start, list the points on the graph.

$(1, 2), (2, 3), (3, 4), (4, 5), (5, 6)$

15.

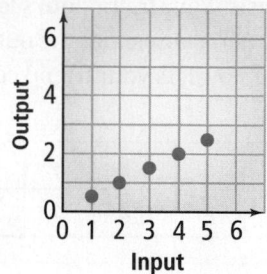

16.

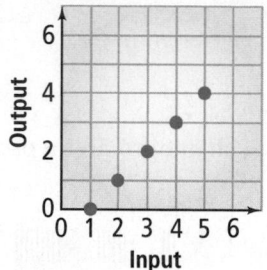

The graph shows the number of bottles of water needed for students going on a field trip.

17. How many bottles of water are needed if 5 students go?

18. How many bottles of water are needed if 20 students go?

19. How many bottles of water are needed if n students go?

Class Field Trip

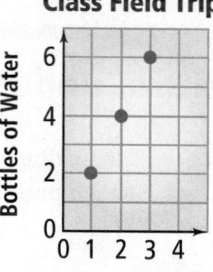

 **Apply**

Identify the pattern and find the next three numbers in the pattern.

20. 6, 12, 18, 24, . . .

21. 1, 4, 3, 6, 5, . . .

22. 3, 6, 10, 15, . . .

23. 2, 6, 10, 14, . . .

24. 1, 3, 9, 27, 81, . . .

25. 4, 20, 100, 500, . . .

26. Think About a Plan A moving company sells different sizes of boxes as shown. The extra-large box is one size larger than the third box shown. What is its volume?
 • Identify the pattern of the dimension changes.
 • What is the formula for the volume of a rectangular prism?

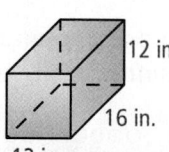

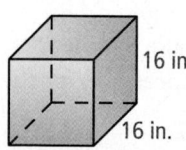

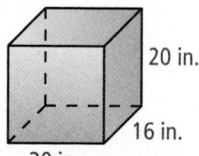

8   Chapter 1   Expressions, Equations, and Inequalities

27. Use the graph shown.
    a. Identify a pattern of the graph by making a table of the inputs and outputs.
    b. What are the outputs for inputs 6, 7, and 8?

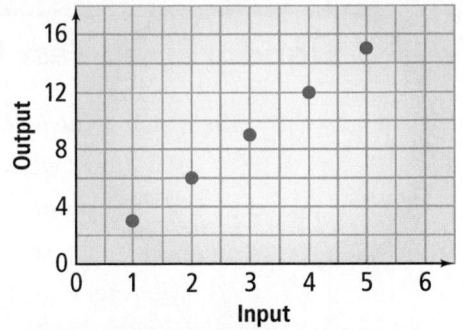

28. Collecting Jay has a rare baseball card collection. He currently owns 10 baseball cards. Each month, he purchases a new card for his collection. Write a model to represent the number of cards in Jay's collection after n months.

29. Use the figures below.

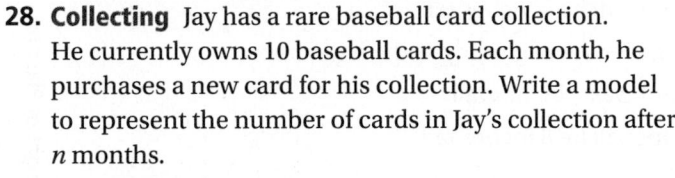

    a. Draw the next two figures.
    b. Copy and complete the table to find the number of squares in each figure.
    c. What is the number of squares in the nth figure? Explain your reasoning.

Figure (Input)	Process Column	Number of Squares (Output)
1	■	■
2	■	■
3	■	■
4	■	■
5	■	■

Copy and complete each table.

30.

Input	Output
1	5
2	9
3	13
4	17
5	■
⋮	⋮
n	■

31.

Input	Output
1	2
2	−3
3	−8
4	−13
5	■
⋮	⋮
n	■

32.

Input	Output
1	3
2	−1
3	−5
4	−9
5	■
⋮	⋮
n	■

33. Identify a pattern and draw the next three figures in the pattern.

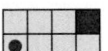

34. Open-Ended Write a rule so that for every input, the output is an even number.

Standardized Test Prep

SAT/ACT

35. Which of the following is the best statement about the graph?

Ⓐ After 4 weeks, the plant will be 7 inches tall.

Ⓑ The plant was 1 inch tall at the beginning of the experiment.

Ⓒ After 2 weeks, the plant was 3 inches tall.

Ⓓ After 6 weeks, the plant will be 8 inches tall.

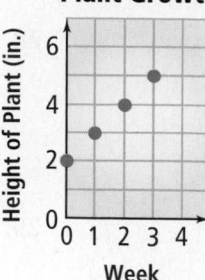

Plant Growth

36. Which is the 7th number in this pattern?

$$8, 13, 18, 23, \ldots$$

Ⓕ 28   Ⓗ 38

Ⓖ 33   Ⓘ 43

Short Response

37. Look at the pattern shown.

$$144, 72, 36, \ldots$$

a. What is a rule for the pattern?

b. What is the first non-integer number in this pattern?

Mixed Review

Simplify each expression.

See p. 868.

38. $3.6 + (-1.7)$ **39.** $1.2 - 5$ **40.** $(-3)(-9)$

41. $0(-8)$ **42.** $-2.8 \div 7$ **43.** $-35 \div (-5)$

Get Ready! **To prepare for Lesson 1-2, do Exercises 44–49.**

Write each number as a percent.

See p. 865.

44. 0.5 **45.** 0.25 **46.** $\frac{1}{3}$

47. $1\frac{2}{5}$ **48.** 1.72 **49.** 1.23

1-2 Properties of Real Numbers

Objectives To graph and order real numbers
To identify properties of real numbers

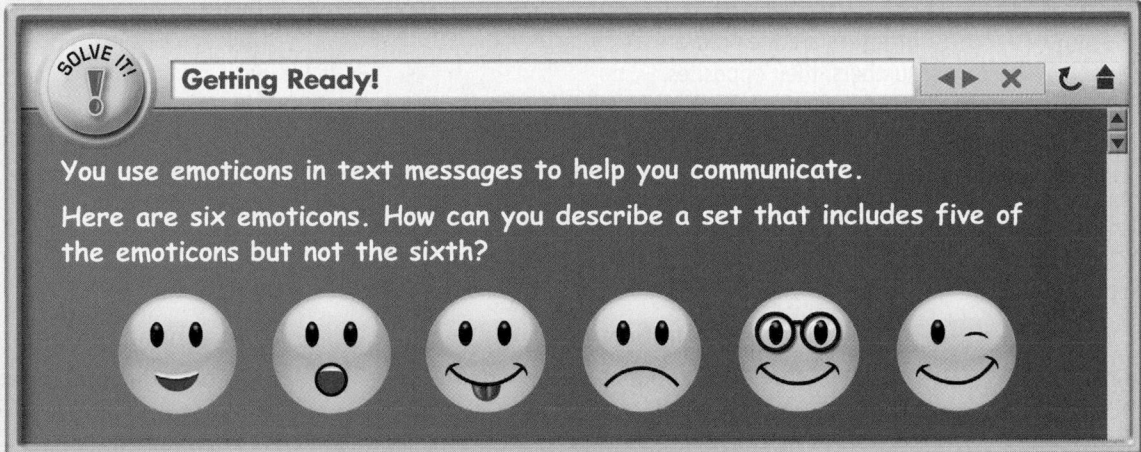

Getting Ready!

You use emoticons in text messages to help you communicate.

Here are six emoticons. How can you describe a set that includes five of the emoticons but not the sixth?

Hint
You can use a number line to compare and order numbers. A number on a number line is <u>greater than</u> all of the numbers to its left.

In the Solve It, you classified sets of emoticons. In this lesson, you will classify real numbers into special subsets that are related in particular ways.

Focus Question How are the real numbers classified?

Algebra involves operations on and relations among numbers, including real numbers and imaginary numbers. (You will learn about imaginary numbers in Chapter 4.) Rational numbers and irrational numbers form the set of real numbers.

You can graph every real number as a point on the number line.

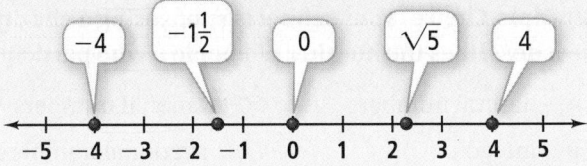

The diagram shows how subsets of the real numbers are related.

Real Numbers

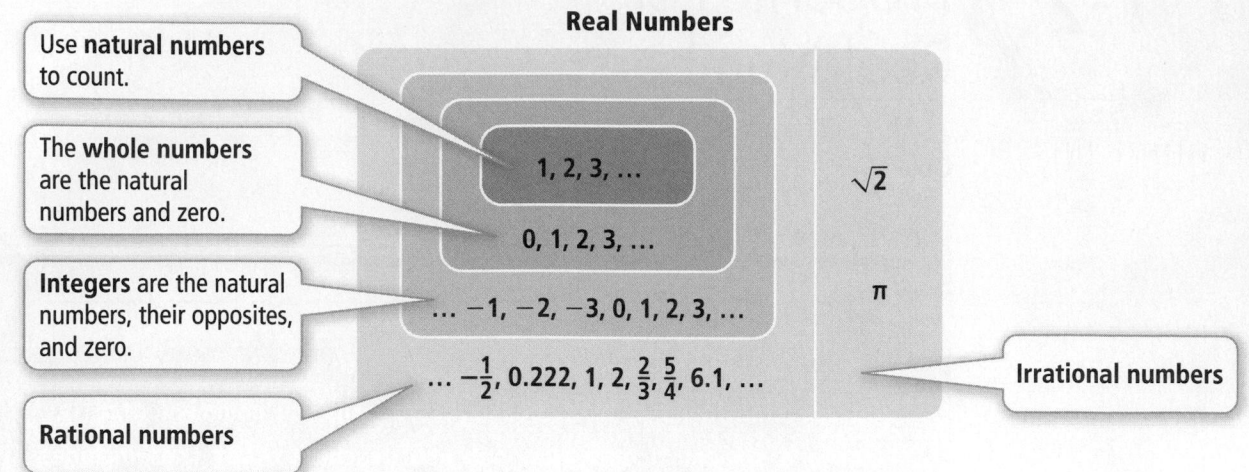

Use **natural numbers** to count.

The **whole numbers** are the natural numbers and zero.

Integers are the natural numbers, their opposites, and zero.

1, 2, 3, ...

0, 1, 2, 3, ...

... −1, −2, −3, 0, 1, 2, 3, ...

... −$\frac{1}{2}$, 0.222, 1, 2, $\frac{2}{3}$, $\frac{5}{4}$, 6.1, ...

$\sqrt{2}$

π

Irrational numbers

Rational numbers

Rational numbers
- are all numbers you can write as a quotient of integers $\frac{a}{b}$, $b \neq 0$.
- include terminating decimals. For example, $\frac{1}{8} = 0.125$.
- include repeating decimals. For example, $\frac{1}{3} = 0.\overline{3}$.

Irrational numbers
- have decimal representations that neither terminate nor repeat. For example, $\sqrt{2} = 1.414213....$
- cannot be written as quotients of integers.

You classify a variable by naming the subset of the real numbers that gives you the most information about the numbers the variable represents.

Problem 1 Classifying a Variable

Multiple Choice Your school is sponsoring a charity race. Which set of numbers best describes the number of people p who participate in the race?

(A) natural numbers   (C) rational numbers

(B) integers   (D) irrational numbers

The number of people p is a natural number. The correct answer is A.

Think

Can you eliminate any answer choices?
You can't have part of a person, so eliminate the rational and irrational numbers. The number of people can't be negative, so eliminate the integers.

Got It? **1.** In Problem 1, if each participant made a donation d of $15.50 to a local charity, which subset of real numbers best describes the amount of money raised in dollars?

Plan

How do you graph
a number on a
number line?
If the number is an
integer, determine
whether it is positive or
negative. If it's not an
integer, determine which
integer it's closest to.

 Problem 2 Graphing Numbers on the Number Line

What is the graph of the numbers $-\frac{5}{2}$, $\sqrt{2}$, and $2.\overline{6}$?

> Since $-\frac{5}{2} = -2\frac{1}{2}$, $-\frac{5}{2}$ is between -3 and -2.

> Use a calculator. $\sqrt{2} \approx 1.4$.

> Think: $2.\overline{6} = 2\frac{2}{3}$.

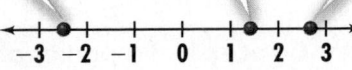

$$-3 \quad -2 \quad -1 \quad 0 \quad 1 \quad 2 \quad 3$$

 Got It? **2.** What is the graph of the numbers $\sqrt{3}$, $1.\overline{4}$, and $\frac{1}{3}$?

The number line is helpful for ordering several real numbers. It is easier to compare two numbers with one of the inequality symbols, $>$ or $<$.

 Problem 3 Comparing Real Numbers

How do $\sqrt{17}$ and 3.8 compare? Use $>$ or $<$.

Think

Why compare $\sqrt{17}$
to the square root of
a perfect square?
It makes it easier
to determine which
two integers $\sqrt{17}$ is
between.

Step 1 Approximate $\sqrt{17}$ using perfect squares.

17 is between perfect squares 16 and 25.

$\sqrt{16} = 4$ and $\sqrt{25} = 5$.

$\sqrt{16} < \sqrt{17} < \sqrt{25}$

$4 \ < \sqrt{17} < \ 5$

Step 2 Approximate 3.8 using integers.

3.8 is between 3 and 4.

$3 < 3.8 < 4$

Notice that $3.8 < 4$ and $4 < \sqrt{17}$. Therefore, $3.8 < \sqrt{17}$.

Check Use a calculator.

$\sqrt{17} \approx 4.123$

$3.8 < 4.123$ ✔

 Got It? **3. a.** How do $\sqrt{26}$ and 6.25 compare? Use $>$ or $<$.

b. **Reasoning** Let a, b, and c be real numbers such that $a < b$ and $b < c$. How do a and c compare? Explain.

Focus Question Why are the properties of real numbers important?

The properties of real numbers are relationships that are true for all real numbers except zero. Only one property excludes zero. Zero is the *additive identity* for the real numbers. For example, $2 + 0 = 2$. Zero is the only real number that has no *multiplicative inverse*. No number times 0 equals 1.

The opposite of 0 is 0.
$$0 + (-0) = 0 - 0$$
$$= 0$$
The reciprocal of 1 is 1.
$$1\left(\frac{1}{1}\right) = 1(1)$$
$$= 1$$

The **opposite** or **additive inverse** of any number a is $-a$.
The sum of a number and its opposite is 0, the additive identity.

Examples $12 + (-12) = 0$ $-7 + 7 = 0$

The **reciprocal** or **multiplicative inverse** of any nonzero number a is $\frac{1}{a}$.
The product of a number and its reciprocal is 1, the multiplicative identity.

Examples $8\left(\frac{1}{8}\right) = 1$ $-5\left(-\frac{1}{5}\right) = 1$

take note

Key Concept   Properties of Real Numbers

Let a, b, and c represent real numbers.

Property	Addition	Multiplication
Closure	$a + b$ is a real number.	ab is a real number.
Commutative	$a + b = b + a$	$ab = ba$
Associative	$(a + b) + c = a + (b + c)$	$(ab) \cdot c = a \cdot (bc)$
Identity	$a + 0 = a, 0 + a = a$ 0 is the additive identity.	$a \cdot 1 = a, 1 \cdot a = a$ 1 is the multiplicative identity.
Inverse	$a + (-a) = 0$	$a \cdot \frac{1}{a} = 1, a \neq 0$
Distributive		$a \cdot (b + c) = ab + ac$

Problem 4 Identifying Properties of Real Numbers

Plan

How can you analyze an equation?
Determine whether it
• uses addition or multiplication
• reorders or regroups the numbers
• uses an identity

Which property does the equation illustrate?

Ⓐ $\left(-\frac{2}{3}\right)\left(-\frac{3}{2}\right) = 1$

The product of the numbers is 1.

Inverse Property of Multiplication

Ⓑ $(3 \cdot 4) \cdot 5 = (4 \cdot 3) \cdot 5$

The equation reorders 3 and 4.

Commutative Property of Multiplication

 Got It? 4. a. Which property does the equation
$3(g + h) + 2g = (3g + 3h) + 2g$ illustrate?

b. Reasoning Use properties of real numbers to show that
$a + [3 + (-a)] = 3$. Justify each step of your solution.

Focus Question How are the real numbers classified?

Answer The real numbers consist of rational numbers and irrational numbers.
The rational numbers include integers, whole numbers, and natural numbers.

Focus Question Why are the properties of real numbers important?

Answer You use the properties of real numbers for all math problems that involve real numbers.

Lesson Check

Do you know HOW?

Write an example from daily life that uses each type of real number.

1. whole numbers

2. integers

3. rational numbers

Identify the property illustrated by each equation.

4. $5 + (-5) = 0$

5. $2 \cdot (4 \cdot 5) = (2 \cdot 4) \cdot 5$

Do you UNDERSTAND?

6. Vocabulary Identify another name for a reciprocal.

7. Compare and Contrast How is the Additive Identity Property similar to the Multiplicative Identity Property? How is it different?

8. Reasoning There are grouping symbols in the equation $(5 + w) + 8 = (w + 5) + 8$, but it does not illustrate the Associative Property of Addition. Explain.

9. Give an example of a number that is not a rational number. Explain why it is not rational.

Practice and Problem-Solving Exercises

 **Practice** Classify each variable according to the set of numbers that best describes its values.

◀ **See Problem 1.**

Guided Practice

To start, make a list of some numbers that could describe the number of times a ball bounces.

10. the number of times n a ball bounces

$0, 1, 2, 3, \ldots$

11. the median selling price p for a house

12. the circumference C of a circle found by using the formula $C = 2\pi r$

Graph each number on a number line.

◀ **See Problem 2.**

Guided Practice

To start, use a calculator to approximate the square root.

13. $-\sqrt{24}$

$-\sqrt{24} \approx -4.9$

14. -2

15. $2\frac{1}{2}$

16. $-4\frac{2}{3}$

17. 3.5

18. -1.4

19. $\sqrt{10}$

Compare the two numbers. Use > or <.

◀ See Problem 3.

20. $-4, -\sqrt{4}$ **21.** $-\sqrt{3}, -\sqrt{5}$ **22.** $5, \sqrt{22}$

23. $4, \sqrt{12}$ **24.** $4.7, \sqrt{26}$ **25.** $\sqrt{75}, 9$

Name the property of real numbers illustrated by each equation.

◀ See Problem 4.

26. $\pi(a + b) = \pi a + \pi b$ **27.** $-10 + 4 = 4 + (-10)$

28. $(2\sqrt{7}) \cdot \sqrt{3} = 2(\sqrt{7} \cdot \sqrt{3})$ **29.** $29 \cdot \pi = \pi \cdot 29$

30. $-\sqrt{5} + 0 = -\sqrt{5}$ **31.** $\frac{4}{7} \cdot \frac{7}{4} = 1$

 **Apply**

Estimate the numbers graphed at the labeled points.

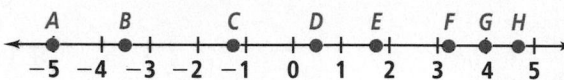

32. point A **33.** point B **34.** point C **35.** point D

36. point E **37.** point F **38.** point G **39.** point H

40. Think About a Plan A cube-shaped jewelry box has a surface area of 300 square inches. What are the dimensions of the jewelry box?
   • Write an algebraic expression to find the total surface area of a cube. What is the surface area of one side of a cube?
   • How is the side length of a square related to its area?

41. Error Analysis A student labeled the points on the number line as shown. Explain the student's error.

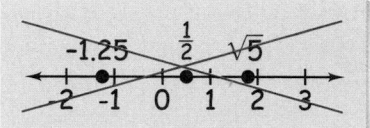

Science The formula $I = \sqrt{\frac{W}{R}}$ gives the electric current I in amperes that flows through an appliance, where W is the power in watts and R is the resistance in ohms. Which set of numbers best describes the value of I for the given values of W and R?

42. $W = 100, R = 25$ **43.** $W = 100, R = 5$ **44.** $W = 500, R = 100$

Write the numbers in decreasing order.

45. $1, -3, -\sqrt{2}, 8, \frac{1}{3}$ **46.** $\sqrt{14}, \frac{5}{2}, -\frac{9}{16}, 1, 11$ **47.** $-17, -0.06, -3\sqrt{3}, 5.73, \frac{1}{4}$

Reasoning An example is a *counterexample* to a general statement if it makes the statement false. Show that each of the following statements is false by finding a counterexample.

48. There is no integer that has a reciprocal that is an integer.

49. The product of two irrational numbers is an irrational number.

50. All square roots are irrational numbers.

51. Restaurant Five friends each ordered a sandwich and a drink at a restaurant. Each sandwich costs the same amount, and each drink costs the same amount. What are two ways to compute the bill? What property of real numbers is illustrated by the two methods?

52. Open-Ended Write an algebraic problem that requires the use of the real-number properties to solve. Then solve the problem.

Standardized Test Prep

SAT/ACT

53. Which of the following shows the numbers π, $\sqrt{8}$, and 3.5 in the correct order from greatest to least?

Ⓐ π, $\sqrt{8}$, 3.5   Ⓑ 3.5, π, $\sqrt{8}$ Ⓒ $\sqrt{8}$, π, 3.5   Ⓓ $\sqrt{8}$, 3.5, π

54. Which of the following is the best statement about the graph?

Ⓕ A 400-minute plan costs $40.

Ⓖ A 100-minute plan costs $10.

Ⓗ A 1000-minute plan costs $110.

Ⓘ A 200-minute plan costs $35.

Short Response

55. Why is the opposite of the reciprocal of 5 the same as the reciprocal of the opposite of 5?

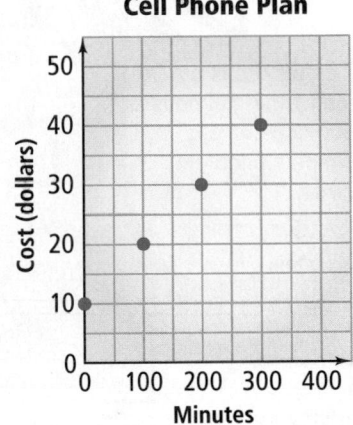

Cell Phone Plan

Mixed Review

Identify the pattern and find the next three terms in the pattern.

◀ See Lesson 1-1.

56. 4, 8, 12, 16, . . .   **57.** 8, 9, 10, 11, . . .   **58.** −4, −3, −2, −1, . . .

Get Ready!   To prepare for Lesson 1-3, do Exercises 59–64.

Use the order of operations to simplify each expression.

◀ See p. 868.

59. $3 \div 4 + 6 \div 4$

60. $5[(2 + 5) \div 3]$

61. $\dfrac{8 + 5 \times 2}{12}$

62. $(40 + 24) \div 8 - (2^2 - 1)$

63. $40 + 24 \div 8 - 2^2 - 1$

64. $(40 + 24) \div (8 - 2^2) - 1$

1-3 Algebraic Expressions

Objectives To evaluate algebraic expressions
To simplify algebraic expressions

Ten weeks is a long time! Perhaps you can solve a simpler problem first.

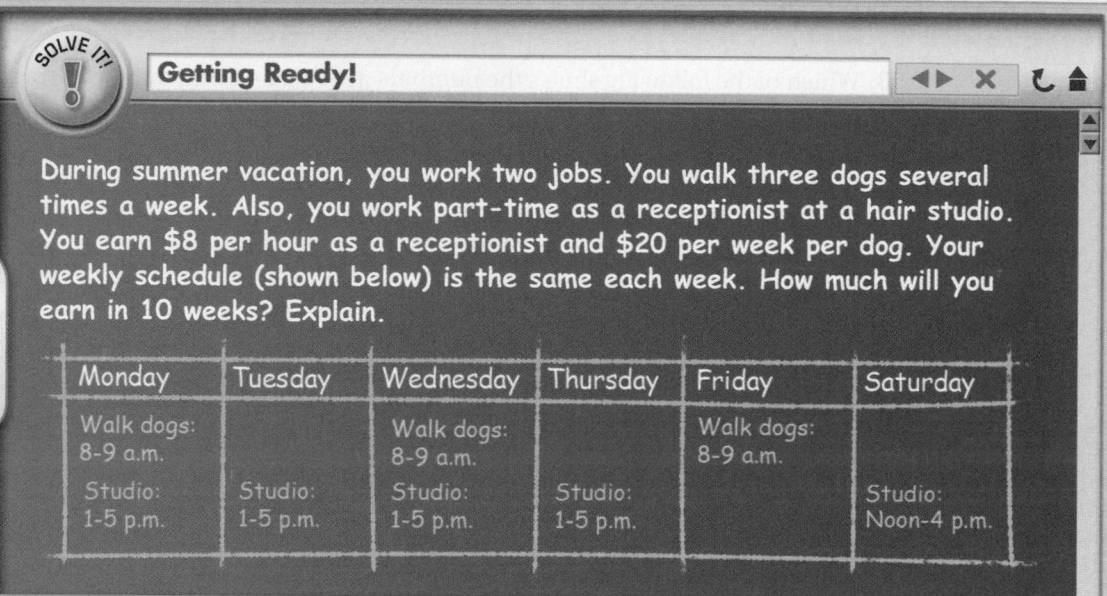

Getting Ready!

During summer vacation, you work two jobs. You walk three dogs several times a week. Also, you work part-time as a receptionist at a hair studio. You earn $8 per hour as a receptionist and $20 per week per dog. Your weekly schedule (shown below) is the same each week. How much will you earn in 10 weeks? Explain.

Monday	Tuesday	Wednesday	Thursday	Friday	Saturday
Walk dogs: 8-9 a.m.		Walk dogs: 8-9 a.m.		Walk dogs: 8-9 a.m.	
Studio: 1-5 p.m.	Studio: 1-5 p.m.	Studio: 1-5 p.m.	Studio: 1-5 p.m.		Studio: Noon-4 p.m.

Lesson Vocabulary
- evaluate
- term
- coefficient
- constant term
- like terms

The Solve It above involves both constant and variable quantities.

Focus Question How can you represent mathematical phrases and real-world situations with varying quantities?

Think

What does *seven fewer than t* mean?
Seven fewer than t means your answer will be less than *t*.

Problem 1 Modeling Words With Algebraic Expressions

Multiple Choice Which algebraic expression models the word phrase *seven fewer than a number t*?

Ⓐ $t + 7$ Ⓑ $-7t$ Ⓒ $t - 7$ Ⓓ $7 - t$

Fewer than suggests subtraction. Begin with the number *t* and subtract 7. This can be represented by the expression $t - 7$. The correct answer is C.

Got It? 1. Which algebraic expression models the word phrase *two times the sum of a and b*?

Ⓕ $a + b$ Ⓗ $2(a + b)$
Ⓖ $2a + b$ Ⓘ $a + 2b$

To model a situation with an algebraic expression, do the following:
- Identify the actions that suggest operations.
- Define one or more variables to represent the unknowns.
- Represent the actions using the variables and the operations.

 Problem 2 Modeling a Situation

Plan

How can you identify the variable?
Determine which quantity is unknown.

Saving Money You start with \$20 and save \$6 each week. What algebraic expression models the total amount you save?

Relate

starting amount	plus	amount saved	times	number of weeks

Define Let w = the number of weeks.

Write

| 20 | + | 6 | · | w |

The expression $20 + 6w$ models the situation.

✓ **Got It?** **2.** You had \$150, but you are spending \$2 each day. What algebraic expression models this situation?

To **evaluate** an algebraic expression, substitute a number for each variable in the expression. Then simplify using the order of operations.

 Problem 3 Evaluating Algebraic Expressions

Think

What operations should you start with?
Do operations that occur in grouping symbols first. Parentheses are grouping symbols.

What is the value of the expression for the given values of the variables?

Ⓐ $7(a + 4) + 3b - 8$ for $a = -4$ and $b = 5$

Write the original expression.	$7(a + 4) + 3b - 8$
Substitute the value for each variable.	$7(-4 + 4) + 3(5) - 8$
Perform operations within grouping symbols.	$7(0) + 3(5) - 8$
Multiply.	$0 + 15 - 8$
Add and subtract from left to right.	7

Ⓑ $\frac{x}{4} + y^2$ for $x = 1$ and $y = \frac{1}{2}$

Write the original expression.	$\frac{x}{4} + y^2$
Substitute the value for each variable.	$\frac{1}{4} + \left(\frac{1}{2}\right)^2$
Simplify the power.	$\frac{1}{4} + \frac{1}{4}$
Add. Reduce the fraction to lowest terms.	$\frac{2}{4} = \frac{1}{2}$

Hint

When substituting a negative value, remember to use parentheses.

✓ **Got It?** **3.** What is the value of the expression for $m = 6$ and $n = -3$?

a. $4(m - 2) + 3n + 5$ **b.** $\frac{m}{2} + n^3$

 **Problem 4** Writing and Evaluating an Expression

Sports In football, a touchdown (TD) is worth six points, an extra-point kick (EPK) one point, and a field goal (FG) three points. What algebraic expression models the total number of points that a football team scores in a game? Suppose a football team scores 3 touchdowns, 2 extra-point kicks, and 4 field goals. How many points did the team score?

Know
- Number of points each scoring play is worth
- Number of each type of score

Need
- Algebraic expression to model points scored
- Total number of points scored

Plan
- Determine the variables.
- Write an expression.
- Evaluate the expression.

Think

How many points come from touchdowns?
The number of points from touchdowns is six times the number of touchdowns.

Relate $\dfrac{\text{points}}{\text{per TD}}$ · $\boxed{\dfrac{\text{number}}{\text{of TDs}}}$ + $\dfrac{\text{points}}{\text{per EPK}}$ · $\boxed{\dfrac{\text{number}}{\text{of EPKs}}}$ + $\dfrac{\text{points}}{\text{per FG}}$ · $\boxed{\dfrac{\text{number}}{\text{of FGs}}}$

Define   Let t = number of touchdowns.
Let k = number of extra-point kicks.
Let f = number of field goals.

Write 6 · t + 1 · k + 3 · f

The expression $6t + 1k + 3f$ models the team's total score.

The football team scores 3 touchdowns, 2 extra-point kicks, and 4 field goals, so $t = 3$, $k = 2$, and $f = 4$.

Substitute the value for each variable.	$6(3) + 1(2) + 3(4)$
Multiply.	$18 + 2 + 12$
Add.	32

The team scored 32 points.

Hint

When you define variables, let w = number of two-point shots, r = number of three-point shots, and f = number of free throws.

✓ **Got It?** **4.** In basketball, teams can score by making two-point shots, three-point shots, and one-point free throws. What algebraic expression models the total number of points that a basketball team scores in a game? If a team makes 10 two-point shots, 5 three-point shots, and 7 free throws, how many points does it score in all?

An expression that is a number, a variable, or the product of a number and one or more variables is a **term**. A **coefficient** is the numerical factor of a term. A **constant term** is a term with no variables. You can add terms to form longer expressions. The expression below has three terms.

$$-4ax + 7w - 6$$

coefficients
The numerical coefficient of $-4ax$ is -4.

constant term
Think of $7w - 6$ as $7w + (-6)$.
The constant term is -6.

Like terms have the same variables raised to the same powers.

like terms   like terms

$$3x^2 + 5x^2 + 9y^3z + 2yz - 4y^3z$$

Hint

A simplified form of the above expression is
$8x^2 + 5y^3z + 2yz$

You can simplify an algebraic expression that has like terms. You combine like terms using the properties of real numbers (Lesson 1-2). An expression and its simplified form are equivalent. Their values are equal for all values of the variables.

take note

Concept Summary   Properties for Simplifying Algebraic Expressions

Let a, b, and c represent real numbers.

Definition of Subtraction	$a - b = a + (-b)$
Definition of Division	$a \div b = \frac{a}{b} = a \cdot \frac{1}{b}, b \neq 0$
Distributive Property for Subtraction	$a \cdot (b - c) = ab - ac$
Multiplication by 0	$0 \cdot a = 0$
Multiplication by −1	$-1 \cdot a = -a$
Opposite of a Sum	$-(a + b) = (-a) + (-b) = -a - b$
Opposite of a Difference	$-(a - b) = (-a) - (-b) = -a + b = b - a$
Opposite of a Product	$-(a \cdot b) = -a \cdot b = a \cdot (-b)$
Opposite of an Opposite	$-(-a) = a$

Hint

The Distributive Properties work on the right side as well:
$(b + c) \cdot a = ba + ca$
$(b - c) \cdot a = ba - ca$

Problem 5   Simplifying Algebraic Expressions

Combine like terms. What is the simplified form of each expression?

Think

Are $7x^2$ and $3y^2$ like terms?
No; they have different variables.

A $7x^2 + 3y^2 + 2y^2 - 4x^2$

Identify like terms.	$7x^2 + 3y^2 + 2y^2 - 4x^2$
Use the Commutative Property.	$7x^2 - 4x^2 + 3y^2 + 2y^2$
Use the Distributive Property.	$(7 - 4)x^2 + (3 + 2)y^2$
Combine like terms.	$3x^2 + 5y^2$

B $-(3k + m) + 2(k - 4m)$

Use the Opposite of a Sum and the Distributive Property.	$-3k - m + 2k - 8m$
Identify like terms.	$-3k - m + 2k - 8m$
Combine like terms.	$-k - 9m$

Got It? 5. Combine like terms. What is the simplified form of each expression?

     a. $-4j^2 - 7k + 5j + j^2$ **b.** $-(8a + 3b) + 10(2a - 5b)$

Focus Question How can you represent mathematical phrases and real-world situations with varying quantities?

Answer Use algebraic expressions to represent phrases or situations that have varying quantities.

Lesson Check

Do you know HOW?

Write an algebraic expression that models each word phrase.

1. the quotient of the sum of 2 and a number b, and 3

2. the sum of the product of a number k and 4, and a number m

Evaluate each algebraic expression for $x = 3$ and $y = -2$.

3. $2x - 3y$　　　**4.** $5x + y$

5. $y - x$　　　**6.** $x + 4y$

Do you UNDERSTAND?

7. Error Analysis A student simplified the expression as shown.

$$3p^2q + 2p - (5q + p - 2p^2q) = q^2p + 3p - 5q$$

Identify the errors and correct them.

8. Vocabulary Explain the difference between a constant and a coefficient.

9. Compare and Contrast How are algebraic expressions and numerical expressions alike? How are they different? Include examples to justify your reasoning.

Practice and Problem-Solving Exercises

 **Practice**　　Write an algebraic expression that models each word phrase.

 See Problem 1.

Guided Practice

To start, relate what you know.	**10.** four more than a number b
	More than means addition.
Describe what you need to find.	Begin with the number b and add 4.

11. the product of 8 and the sum of a number x and 3

12. the quotient of 2 and the difference between 5 and a number n

Write an algebraic expression that models each situation.

 **See Problem 2.**

13. The piggy bank contained $25, and $1.50 is added each day.

14. You had 250 minutes left on your cell phone, and you talk an hour each week.

Evaluate each expression for the given values of the variables.

 See Problem 3.

See Problem 3.

Guided Practice

To start, substitute the value for each variable.

15. $4a + 7b + 3a - 2b + 2a$; $a = -5$ and $b = 3$

$$4(-5) + 7(3) + 3(-5) - 2(3) + 2(-5)$$

16. $-k^2 - (3k - 5n) + 4n$; $k = -1$ and $n = -2$

17. $-5(x + 2y) + 15(x + 2y)$; $x = 7$ and $y = -7$

Physics The expression $16t^2$ models the distance in feet that an object falls during the first t seconds after being dropped. What is the distance the object falls during each time?

See Problem 4.

18. 0.25 second   **19.** 0.5 second   **20.** 2 seconds

Write an algebraic expression to model the total score in each situation. Then evaluate the expression to find the total score.

21. In the first set, the volleyball team made only 8 shots worth one point each.

22. In the last baseball game, there were two 3-run home runs and 4 hits that each scored 2 runs.

Simplify by combining like terms.

See Problem 5.

23. $5a - a$ **24.** $5 + 10s - 8s$ **25.** $2a + 3b + 4a$

26. $6r + 3s + 2s + 4r$ **27.** $0.5x - x$ **28.** $7b - (3a - 8b)$

 **Apply**

Evaluate each expression for the given value of the variable.

29. $x + 2x - x - 1$; $x = 2$ **30.** $y^2 + 3$; $y = \sqrt{7}$ **31.** $5c^3 - 6c^2 - 2c$; $c = -5$

32. Think About a Plan Tran's truck gets very poor gas mileage. If Tran pays $84 to fill his truck with gas and is able to drive m miles on a full tank, what expression shows his gas cost per mile?
- What operation does "per" indicate?
- Check your expression by substituting 200 miles for m. Does your answer make sense?

33. Reasoning Suppose you need to subtract a from b but mistakenly subtract b from a instead. How is the answer you get related to the correct answer? Explain.

> **Hint** Try several different values for a and b. Find $a - b$ and $b - a$ and identify how they are related.

Write an algebraic expression to model each situation.

34. Jobs You have a summer job at a car wash. You earn $8.50 per hour and are expected to pay a one-time fee of $15 for the uniform. If you work x hours per week, how much will you make during the first week?

35. Class Project The freshman class will be selling carnations as a class project. What is their income after they pay the florist a flat fee of $200 and sell x carnations for $2 each?

Simplify by combining like terms.

36. $-a^2 + 2b^2 + \frac{1}{4}a^2$

37. $x + \frac{x^2}{2} + 2x^2 - x$

38. $\frac{y^2}{4} + \frac{y}{3} + \frac{y^2}{3} - \frac{y}{5}$

39. $-(2x + y) - 2(-x - y)$

40. $x(3 - y) + y(x + 6)$

41. $\frac{1}{2}(x^2 - y^2) - \frac{5}{2}(x^2 - y^2)$

42. Error Analysis John simplified the expression as shown. Do you agree with his work? Explain.

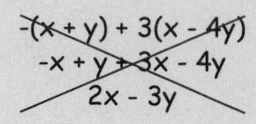

43. Open-Ended Write an example of an algebraic expression that has a nonnegative value regardless of the value of the variable.

Name the property of real numbers illustrated by the equation.

44. $2(s - t) = 2s - 2t$

45. $-[-(x - 10)] = x - 10$

46. $-(2t - 11) = 11 - 2t$

47. $-(a - b) = (-1)(a - b)$

Standardized Test Prep

SAT/ACT

48. Which expression best represents a simpler form of $4m + 3(m + n)$?

Ⓐ $7m + 3n$ Ⓑ $4m + 3mn$ Ⓒ $3m + 4n$ Ⓓ $7m^2 + 3n$

49. A driver drove 12 miles and made a pit stop. After that, the driver continued driving at a constant speed of 65 miles per hour for t hours. Which of the following represents the total distance driven?

Ⓕ $12 + 65t$ Ⓖ $65t$ Ⓗ $12t + 65$ Ⓘ $12(t + 65)$

50. What is the value of r when $s = -1$, $t = 4$, and $u = \frac{1}{5}$?

$$r = 3s^2 + 5(t - 2u)$$

Ⓐ 7 Ⓑ 15 Ⓒ 21 Ⓓ $22\frac{1}{5}$

Short Response

51. Compare $\sqrt{26}$ and 4.9. Explain your answer.

Mixed Review

Order the numbers from least to greatest.

◀ See Lesson 1-2.

52. $-1.5, -0.5, -\sqrt{2}, -1.4$

53. $-\frac{3}{8}, \frac{1}{2}, -\frac{3}{4}, -\frac{5}{6}$

54. $\sqrt{2}, -20, 0.2, \frac{1}{2}$

55. $\frac{3}{4}, -3, -0.5, -\frac{1}{4}$

Get Ready! To prepare for Lesson 1-4, do Exercises 56–59.

Simplify each expression.

◀ See Lesson 1-3.

56. $4x + 3x - 4$

57. $-\frac{p}{3} + \frac{q}{3} - \frac{2p}{3} - q$

58. $-2(4 + b) + 4(b - 5)$

59. $(k - m) - (m - k)$

Do you know HOW?

1. Draw the next figure in the pattern.

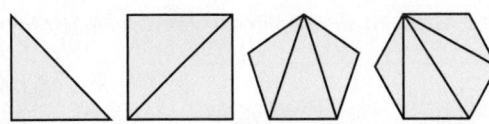

Identify a pattern and find the next number in the pattern.

2. $-405, -135, -45, -15, \ldots$

3. $\frac{2x}{3}, \frac{x}{3}, \frac{x}{6}, \frac{x}{12}, \ldots$

4. $101, 92, 83, 74, \ldots$

5. $0.4, 1.2, 3.6, 10.8, \ldots$

Name the property of real numbers illustrated by the equation.

6. $7(x - y) = 7x - 7y$

7. $\sqrt{7} \cdot 1 = \sqrt{7}$

8. $-2 \cdot \left(-\frac{1}{2}\right) = 1$

9. $2.3(3.4 \cdot 12.9) = (2.3 \cdot 3.4)(12.9)$

Write an algebraic expression to model each word phrase.

10. eight times the sum of a and b

11. four more than the product of x and y

12. six less than the quotient of d and g

13. ten less than twice the product of s and t

Simplify each expression.

14. $-x^2 + 2y - 3x^2 + 10$

15. $-2(d + 2e) + 5(3d - 8e)$

16. $-(a + 2b) + 4(a + 2b) - 2(a + 2b)$

17. $-3x + 14x + 7x^2 - 3x + 4x(x + 1)$

Identify a pattern by making a table of the inputs and outputs. Include a process column.

18. 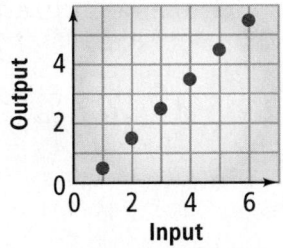   **19.**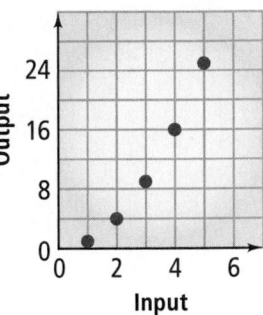

Evaluate each expression for $a = 4$, $b = -3$, and $c = 10$.

20. $7a - 5b$

21. $4a + b - 2c$

22. $a - b - c^2$

Write an algebraic expression to model each situation.

23. You have 16 tomatoes, and your tomato plants produce 5 tomatoes each day.

24. Your car's gas tank holds 25 gallons, and you use 1.5 gallons of gas each day.

Do you UNDERSTAND?

25. Writing Explain why every integer is also a rational number.

26. Reasoning What expression describes the number of squares in the nth figure?

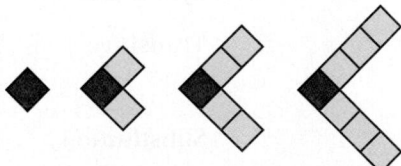

27. Reasoning Is there a Closure Property of Subtraction that applies to whole numbers? Explain.

1-4 Solving Equations

Objectives To solve equations
To solve problems by writing equations

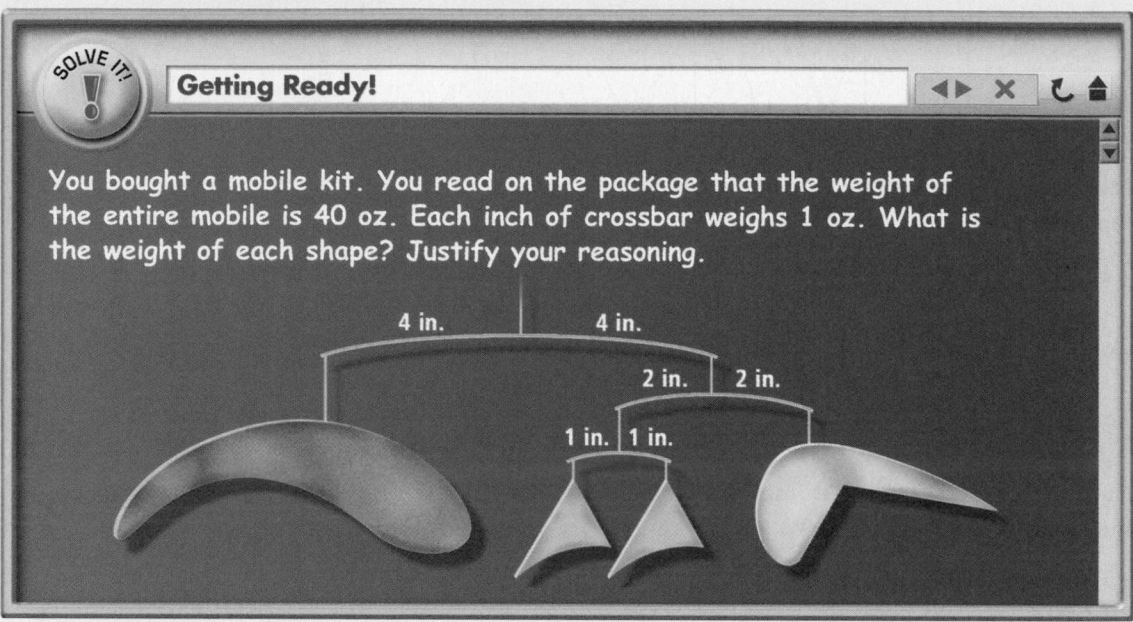

Getting Ready!

You bought a mobile kit. You read on the package that the weight of the entire mobile is 40 oz. Each inch of crossbar weighs 1 oz. What is the weight of each shape? Justify your reasoning.

4 in.   4 in.

2 in.   2 in.

1 in.   1 in.

An **equation** is a statement that two expressions are equal. In this lesson, you will model and solve problems using properties of equality and real numbers.

Focus Question What properties can you use to solve equations?

Lesson Vocabulary
- equation
- solution of an equation
- inverse operations
- identity
- literal equation

take note

Properties   Properties of Equality

Let a, b, and c represent real numbers.

Property	Definition	Example
Reflexive	$a = a$	$5 = 5$
Symmetric	If $a = b$, then $b = a$.	If $\frac{1}{2} = 0.5$, then $0.5 = \frac{1}{2}$.
Transitive	If $a = b$ and $b = c$, then $a = c$.	If $2.5 = 2\frac{1}{2}$ and $2\frac{1}{2} = \frac{5}{2}$, then $2.5 = \frac{5}{2}$.
Substitution	If $a = b$, then you can replace a with b and vice versa.	If $a = b$ and $9 + a = 15$, then $9 + b = 15$.

Properties Properties of Equality, continued

Let a, b, and c represent real numbers.

Property	Definition	Example
Addition	If $a = b$, then $a + c = b + c$.	If $x = 12$, then $x + 3 = 12 + 3$.
Subtraction	If $a = b$, then $a - c = b - c$.	If $x = 12$, then $x - 3 = 12 - 3$.
Multiplication	If $a = b$, then $a \cdot c = b \cdot c$.	If $x = 12$, then $x \cdot 3 = 12 \cdot 3$.
Division	If $a = b$, then $a \div c = b \div c$ (with $c \neq 0$).	If $x = 12$, then $x \div 3 = 12 \div 3$.

Solving an equation that contains a variable means finding all values of the variable that make the equation true. Each value is a **solution of the equation**. To find a solution, isolate the variable on one side of the equation using *inverse operations*.

Inverse operations are operations that "undo" each other. Addition and subtraction are inverse operations, as are multiplication and division.

Problem 1 Solving a One-Step Equation

Plan

How can you isolate the variable?
To isolate the variable, you have to remove the +4 from the left side of the equation.

What is the solution of $x + 4 = -12$?

Write the original equation.	$x + 4 = -12$
Use the Subtraction Property of Equality.	$x + 4 - 4 = -12 - 4$
Simplify.	$x = -16$

> Subtraction is the inverse operation of addition, so subtract 4 from each side.

Check Substitute -16 for x in the original equation. $\quad -16 + 4 \overset{?}{=} -12$

The solution checks. $\qquad\qquad\qquad\qquad\qquad -12 \quad\; = -12$ ✔

 Got It? 1. What is the solution of $12b = 18$?

Problem 2 Solving a Multi-Step Equation

Plan

How do you solve an equation with the variable on both sides?
Choose a side for the variable and remove it from the other side.

What is the solution of $-27 + 6y = 3(y - 3)$?

Write the original equation.	$-27 + 6y = 3(y - 3)$
Use the Distributive Property.	$-27 + 6y = 3y - 9$
Add 27 to each side.	$6y = 3y + 18$
Subtract 3y from each side.	$3y = 18$
Divide each side by 3.	$y = 6$

GRIDDED RESPONSE

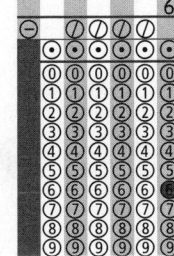

Got It? 2. What is the solution of $3(2x - 1) - 2(3x + 4) = 11x$?

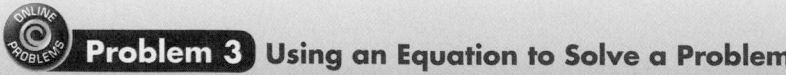
Flowers "Flower carpets" incorporate hundreds of thousands of brightly-colored flowers as well as grass, tree bark, and sometimes fountains to form intricate designs and motifs. The flower carpet shown here, from Grand Place in Brussels, Belgium, has a perimeter of 200 meters. What are the dimensions of the flower carpet?

Plan

How can you relate the dimensions to perimeter?
Use the formula for the perimeter of a rectangle.

Relate   2 · $\boxed{\text{width}}$ plus   2 · $\boxed{\text{length}}$ equals $\boxed{\text{perimeter}}$

Define   Let $\boxed{x}$ = the width.

Then $\boxed{3x}$ = the length.

Write   2 · $\boxed{x}$ +   2 · $\boxed{3x}$ = $\boxed{200}$

Write the equation.	$2x + 2 \cdot 3x = 200$
Multiply.	$2x + 6x = 200$
Combine like terms.	$8x = 200$
Divide each side by 8.	$\frac{8x}{8} = \frac{200}{8}$
Simplify.	$x = 25$
Substitute for x to find the length.	$3x = 3 \cdot 25 = 75$

The width is 25 meters. The length is 75 meters.

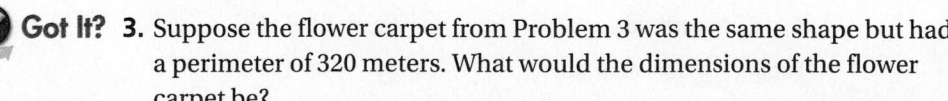 **Got It?   3.** Suppose the flower carpet from Problem 3 was the same shape but had a perimeter of 320 meters. What would the dimensions of the flower carpet be?

Focus Question Is there always exactly one solution to an equation?

An equation does not always have exactly one solution. An equation has no solution if no value of the variable makes the equation true. An equation that is true for every value of the variable is an **identity**.

Problem 4 Equations With No Solution and Identities

Think

What does it mean for an equation to be sometimes true?
An equation is sometimes true if it is true for some, but not all, values of the variable.

Is the equation *always*, *sometimes*, or *never* true?

A $11 + 3x - 7 = 6x + 5 - 3x$

| Combine like terms. | $4 + 3x = 3x + 5$ |
| Subtract $3x$ from each side. | $4 = 5$ ✗ |

Never true!

Because $4 \neq 5$, the last equation is not true.
Therefore, the original equation has no solution.

B $6x + 5 - 2x = 4 + 4x + 1$

| Combine like terms. | $4x + 5 = 4x + 5$ ✔ |

Always true!

Since $4x + 5$ always equals itself, the last equation is always true.
Therefore, the original equation is an identity.

Got It? 4. Is the equation *always*, *sometimes,* or *never* true?
   a. $7x + 6 - 4x = 12 + 3x - 8$
   b. $2x - 12 + 3x = 2(2x - 6) + x$

A **literal equation** is an equation that uses at least two letters as variables. You can solve for any variable "in terms of" the other variables.

Problem 5 Solving a Literal Equation

Plan

How do you solve a literal equation for one of its variables?
Use inverse operations to isolate the indicated variable *F*.

The equation $C = \frac{5}{9}(F - 32)$ relates temperatures in degrees Fahrenheit F and degrees Celsius C. What is F in terms of C?

Write the original equation.	$C = \frac{5}{9}(F - 32)$
Multiply each side by $\frac{9}{5}$, the reciprocal of $\frac{5}{9}$.	$\frac{9}{5}C = F - 32$
Add 32 to each side to isolate F.	$\frac{9}{5}C + 32 = F$
Use the Symmetric Property.	$F = \frac{9}{5}C + 32$

Got It? 5. **a.** The equation $K = C + 273$ relates temperatures in kelvins K and degrees Celsius C. What is C in terms of K?
   b. **Reasoning** Is the equation relating temperatures in kelvins and degrees Celsius *always, sometimes,* or *never* true? Explain your answer.

Focus Question What properties can you use to solve equations?

Answer Use the properties of equality to solve equations.

Focus Question Is there always exactly one solution to an equation?

Answer No; some equations have no solution. Some equations have infinitely many solutions.

Lesson Check

Do you know HOW?

Solve each equation.

1. $w - 15 = 8.2$

2. $\frac{x}{3} = -30$

3. $2y - 1 = y + 11$

Solve each equation for k.

4. $r - 2k = 15$

5. $6k - 2z = 12$

6. $4k + h = -2k - 14$

Do you UNDERSTAND?

7. Vocabulary Explain what it means to find a solution of an equation.

8. Reasoning Suppose you solve an equation and find that your school needs 4.3 buses for a class trip. Explain how to interpret this solution.

9. Error Analysis Find the error(s) in the steps shown. Then give the correct solution.

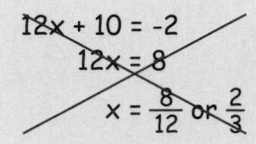

Practice and Problem-Solving Exercises

Ⓐ Practice

Solve each equation.

◀ See Problem 1.

10. $h - 12 = 6$

11. $-\frac{x}{3} = 27$

12. $4t = 48$

Solve each equation. Check your answer.

◀ See Problem 2.

To start, subtract 2 from each side.

13. $7w + 2 = 3w + 94$

$7w + 2 - 2 = 3w + 94 - 2$

14. $15 - g = 23 - 2g$

15. $5y + 1.8 = 4y - 3.2$

16. $6a - 5 = 4a + 2$

17. $4y - 8 - 2y + 5 = 0$

18. $6(n - 4) = 3n$

19. $5(2 - g) = 0$

Write an equation to solve each problem.

See Problem 3.

Guided Practice

20. **Bus Travel** Two buses leave Houston at the same time and travel in opposite directions. One bus averages 55 mi/h and the other bus averages 45 mi/h. When will they be 400 mi apart?

To start, record what you know.	Average rate of one bus: 55 mi/h
	Average rate of other bus: 45 mi/h
	Distance apart: 400 mi
Describe what you need to find.	The time each bus travels

21. **Aviation** Two planes left an airport at noon. One flew east and the other flew west at twice the speed. After 3 hours, the planes were 2700 mi apart. How fast was each plane flying?

22. **Geometry** The length of a rectangle is 3 cm greater than its width. The perimeter is 24 cm. What are the dimensions of the rectangle?

Determine whether the equation is *always*, *sometimes*, or *never* true. See Problem 4.

23. $5x + 3 - 2x = 7x + 3$

24. $2(5x + 4) = 10x + 6$

25. $\frac{2}{3}x + 4 = 2x$

26. $6x - 12 + 2x = 3 + 8x - 15$

Solve each formula for the indicated variable. See Problem 5.

27. $A = \frac{1}{2}bh$, for h

28. $s = \frac{1}{2}gt^2$, for g

29. $V = lwh$, for w

Solve each equation for x.

30. $ax + bx = c$

31. $\frac{x}{a} - 5 = b$

32. $\frac{2}{5}(x + 1) = g$

Ⓑ Apply

Solve each equation.

33. $(m - 2) - 5 = 8 - 2(m - 4)$

34. $7(a + 1) - 3a = 5 + 4(2a - 1)$

35. **Think About a Plan** The measures of an angle and its complement differ by 22°. What are the measures of the angles?
   • What is true about the sum of the measures of an angle and its complement?
   • When modeling the problem with an equation, how can you algebraically represent that the two angle measures differ by 22°?

Solve each formula for the indicated variable.

36. $R(r_1 + r_2) = r_1r_2$, for R

37. $A = \frac{1}{2}h(b_1 + b_2)$, for b_2

38. $R(r_1 + r_2) = r_1r_2$, for r_2

39. $S = 2\pi r^2 + 2\pi rh$, for h

40. **Geometry** The measure of the supplement of an angle is 20° more than three times the measure of the original angle. Find the measures of the angles.

41. Find four consecutive odd integers with a sum of 184.

42. Error Analysis Your friend says that the equations shown are two ways to write the same formula. Is your friend correct? Explain your answer.

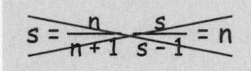

43. Rocket The first stage of a rocket burns 28 s longer than the second stage. If the total burning time for both stages is 152 s, how long does each stage burn? Write an equation to solve the problem.

Standardized Test Prep

GRIDDED RESPONSE

SAT/ACT

44. A mural made of triangular tiles has an area of 1750 square centimeters. Each triangle has a height that is 3 centimeters longer than its base of 2 centimeters. How many triangular tiles are there?

45. The table shows the population of bacteria in a petri dish at various times. If the pattern continues, what will the bacteria population be at 6:00 P.M.?

Bacteria Population				
Time	8:00 A.M.	10:00 A.M.	12:00 P.M.	2:00 P.M.
Population	100	200	400	800

46. To the nearest tenth, what is the value of t in the following equation?

$$4(t - 30) = 5 - 3t$$

47. A 10-foot-tall basketball hoop is 4 feet shorter than twice the height of a flag pole. What is the height in feet of the flag pole?

Mixed Review

Evaluate each expression for $x = -4$ and $y = 3$.

See Lesson 1-3.

48. $x - 2y + 3$

49. $x + x \div y$

50. $3x - 4y - x$

51. $x + 2y \div x$

Write an algebraic expression that models each word phrase.

See Lesson 1-3.

52. 5 more than a number x

53. the product of 16 and a number x

54. 3 times the difference of 12 and a number x

Get Ready! To prepare for Lesson 1-5, do Exercises 55–57.

State whether each inequality is *true* or *false*.

See Lesson 1-2.

55. $5 < 12$

56. $5 < -12$

57. $5 \geq 5$

Solving Inequalities

Objective To solve and graph inequalities

SOLVE IT!

Getting Ready!

You want to download some new songs on your MP3 player. Each song will use about 4.3 MB of space. The amount of storage space on your MP3 player is shown at the right. At most how many songs can you download? Explain.
(Hint: 1 GB = 1000 MB)

7.8 GB free of 19.5 GB

This is like solving an equation, but with a twist!

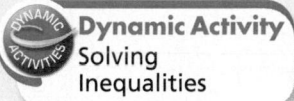

Dynamic Activity
Solving Inequalities

Phrases like "at most" and "at least" suggest that two quantities may not be equal. You can represent such a relationship with a mathematical inequality statement.

Focus Question How is solving an inequality similar to solving an equation?

take note

Key Concept Writing and Graphing Inequalities

Inequality	Word Sentence	Graph
$x > 4$	x is greater than 4.	← -1 0 1 2 3 ⊕4 5 →
$x \geq 4$	x is greater than or equal to 4.	← -1 0 1 2 3 ●4 5 →
$x < 4$	x is less than 4.	← -1 0 1 2 3 ⊕4 5 →
$x \leq 4$	x is less than or equal to 4.	← -1 0 1 2 3 ●4 5 →

In the graphs above, the point at 4 is a boundary point because it separates the graph of the inequality from the rest of the number line. An open dot at 4 means that 4 is *not* a solution of the inequality. A closed dot at 4 means that 4 *is* a solution.

 **Problem 1** Writing an Inequality From a Sentence

What inequality represents the sentence, "5 fewer than a number is at least 12."?

5 fewer than a number is at least 12.

| *Fewer* indicates subtraction. | *At least* indicates greater than or equal to. |

Translate. $x - 5 \geq 12$

 **Got It?** **1.** What inequality represents the sentence, "The quotient of a number and 3 is no more than 15."?

The properties you use for solving inequalities are similar to the properties you use for solving equations. However, when you multiply or divide each side of an inequality by a negative number, you must reverse the inequality symbol.

take note

Properties   Properties of Inequalities

Let a, b, c, and d represent real numbers.

Property	Definition	Example
Transitive	If $a > b$ and $b > c$, then $a > c$.	$5 > 3$ and $3 > 1$, so $5 > 1$
Addition	If $a > b$, then $a + c > b + c$.	$4 > 2$, so $4 + 1 > 2 + 1$
Subtraction	If $a > b$, then $a - c > b - c$.	$7 > 4$, so $7 - 3 > 4 - 3$
Multiplication	If $a > b$ and $c > 0$, then $ac > bc$.	$6 > 5$ and $3 > 0$, so $6(3) > 5(3)$
	If $a > b$ and $c < 0$, then $ac < bc$.	$3 > 2$ and $-4 < 0$, so $3(-4) < 2(-4)$
Division	If $a > b$ and $c > 0$, then $\frac{a}{c} > \frac{b}{c}$.	$9 > 3$ and $3 > 0$, so $\frac{9}{3} > \frac{3}{3}$
	If $a > b$ and $c < 0$, then $\frac{a}{c} < \frac{b}{c}$.	$12 > 6$ and $-6 < 0$, so $\frac{12}{-6} < \frac{6}{-6}$

Here's Why It Works The steps below show that if $a > b$, then $-a < -b$. Therefore, you need to reverse the inequality symbol when you multiply or divide each side of the inequality $a > b$ by -1.

Write the original inequality.	$a > b$
Subtract b from each side.	$a - b > 0$
$a - b = -b + a = -b - (-a)$	$-b - (-a) > 0$
Add $-a$ to each side.	$-b > -a$
Rewrite the inequality with $-a$ on the left side.	$-a < -b$

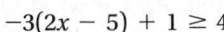 **Problem 2** Solving and Graphing an Inequality

Plan

How is solving an inequality like solving an equation?
You isolate the variable by doing the same things to each side of the inequality.

What is the solution of $-3(2x - 5) + 1 \geq 4$? Graph the solution.

Write the original inequality.	$-3(2x - 5) + 1 \geq 4$
Use the Distributive Property.	$-6x + 15 + 1 \geq 4$
Simplify.	$-6x + 16 \geq 4$
Subtract 16 from each side.	$-6x \geq -12$
Divide each side by -6. Reverse the inequality symbol.	$x \leq 2$

```
  ←——+——+——+——+——+——•——+——→
    -3  -2  -1   0   1   2   3
```

Got It? **2.** What is the solution of each inequality? Graph the solution.

   a. $2x + 10 \leq 2$ **b.** $2(4x + 1) + 3 > -3$

 Problem 3 Using an Inequality

Plan

How will an inequality help answer this question?
The cost of the first plan must be less than the cost of the second plan, so this inequality can be used to determine the number of movies.

Movie Rentals A movie rental company offers two subscription plans. You can pay $36 a month and rent as many movies as desired, or you can pay $15 a month and $1.50 to rent each movie. How many movies must you rent in a month for the first plan to cost less than the second plan?

Think

Assign a variable.

Write an expression for the cost of each plan for a month.

The first plan must cost less than the second plan.

Solve for *n*.

Write the answer in words.

Write

Let $n =$ the number of movie rentals in one month.

first plan: 36

second plan: $15 + 1.5n$

$36 < 15 + 1.5n$

$21 < 1.5n$

$14 < n$

You must rent more than 14 movies in a month for the first plan to cost less.

Got It? **3.** A digital music service offers two subscription plans. The first has a $9 membership fee and charges $1 per download. The second has a $25 membership fee and charges $.50 per download. How many songs must you download for the second plan to cost less than the first plan?

Problem 4 No Solution or All Real Numbers as a Solution

Is the inequality *always*, *sometimes*, or *never* true?

Ⓐ $-2(3x + 1) > -6x + 7$

Write the original inequality.	$-2(3x + 1) > -6x + 7$
Use the Distributive Property.	$-6x - 2 > -6x + 7$
Add $6x$ to each side.	$-2 > 7$

Think

How do you determine that an *equation* has no solution?

If you solve an equation and obtain a false statement, then the equation has no solution.

The last inequality $-2 > 7$ is false, so $-2(3x + 1) > -6x + 7$ is always false. It has no solution.

Ⓑ $5(2x - 3) - 7x \le 3x + 8$

Write the original inequality.	$5(2x - 3) - 7x \le 3x + 8$
Use the Distributive Property.	$10x - 15 - 7x \le 3x + 8$
Combine like terms.	$3x - 15 \le 3x + 8$
Subtract $3x$ from each side.	$-15 \le 8$

The inequality $-15 \le 8$ is true, so $5(2x - 3) - 7x \le 3x + 8$ is always true. All real numbers are solutions.

Ⓒ $6(2x - 1) \ge 3x + 12$

Write the original inequality.	$6(2x - 1) \ge 3x + 12$
Use the Distributive Property.	$12x - 6 \ge 3x + 12$
Subtract $3x$ from each side.	$9x - 6 \ge 12$
Add 6 to each side.	$9x \ge 18$
Divide each side by 9.	$x \ge 2$

The inequality $6(2x - 1) \ge 3x + 12$ is only true when $x \ge 2$. The inequality is sometimes true.

 Got It? **4.** Is the inequality *always*, *sometimes*, or *never* true?
   a. $4(2x - 3) < 8(x + 1)$
   b. $-2(4x - 3) - 5 \ge 9$
   c. $6(2x - 1) - 8x > 3 + 4x$

Focus Question How is solving an inequality similar to solving an equation?

Answer To solve an equation, use the properties of equality. To solve an inequality, use the properties of inequalities. For both, use inverse operations.

Lesson Check

Do you know HOW?

Write an inequality that represents each sentence.

1. Rachel's hair is at least as long as Julia's.

2. The sum of a number and 5 is less than -7.

Solve each inequality. Graph the solution.

3. $-12 \geq 24x$ **4.** $-4(3x + 2) \geq 16$

Do you UNDERSTAND?

5. Reasoning Make up an example to help explain why you must reverse the inequality symbol when you multiply or divide by a negative number.

6. Compare and Contrast Describe how the properties of inequalities are similar to the properties of equality and how they differ.

Practice and Problem-Solving Exercises

A Practice

Write the inequality that represents the sentence.

 **See Problem 1.**

7. The product of a number and 8 is at least 25.

8. Six less than a number is greater than 54.

9. The quotient of a number and 12 is no more than 6.

Solve each inequality. Graph the solution.

See Problem 2.

Guided Practice

10. $8a - 15 > 73$

To start, add 15 to each side. $8a - 15 + 15 > 73 + 15$

11. $57 - 4t \geq 13$ **12.** $-18 - 5y \geq 52$

13. $14 - 4y \geq 38$ **14.** $4(x + 3) \leq 44$

15. $4(n - 2) - 6 > 18$ **16.** $-2(w + 4) + 9 < -11$

Solve each problem by writing an inequality.

See Problem 3.

Guided Practice

17. The length of a picture frame is 3 in. greater than the width. The perimeter is less than 52 in. What are the dimensions of the frame?

To start, record what you know.

Frame length: 3 in. + width of frame
Frame perimeter: less than 52 in.

Describe what you need to find.

The length and width of the frame

18. The lengths of the sides of a triangle are in the ratio $5 : 6 : 7$. If the perimeter is less than 54 cm, what is the length of the longest side?

19. Find the lesser of two consecutive integers with a sum greater than 16.

20. The cost of a field trip is $220 plus $7 per student. If the school can spend at most $500, how many students can go on the field trip?

Is the inequality *always, sometimes,* or *never* true? ◀ See Problem 4.

21. $9(x + 2) > 9(x - 3)$

22. $6x - 13 < 6(x - 2)$

23. $-7(3x - 7) + 21x \geq 50$

24. $2(x + 6) < 30$

25. $4x - 8 > 1 + 4(x + 3)$

26. $9x + 2(2 + x) < 5 + 9x$

 **Apply**

Solve each inequality. Graph the solution.

27. $2 - 3z \geq 7(8 - 2z) + 12$

28. $6(x - 2.5) \geq 8 - 6(3.5 + x)$

29. $\frac{2}{3}(x - 12) \leq x + 8$

30. $\frac{3}{5}(x - 12) > x - 24$

31. Error Analysis A classmate solved the inequality $\frac{1}{2}(y - 16) \geq y + 2$ as shown. Prove that his answer is incorrect by checking a number that is less than -20. (Select a number that makes the computation easy.) What was his error?

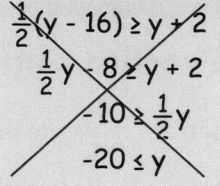

32. Writing Write a word problem that can be solved using $25 + 0.5x \leq 60$.

Justifying Steps Justify each step by identifying the property used.

33. $3x \leq 4(x - 1) - 8$

$3x \leq 4x - 4 - 8$

$3x \leq 4x - 12$

$-x \leq -12$

$x \geq 12$

34. $\frac{1}{2}(y + 3) > \frac{1}{3}(4 - y)$

$3(y + 3) > 2(4 - y)$

$3y + 9 > 8 - 2y$

$5y + 9 > 8$

$5y > -1$

$y > -0.2$

Solving Inequalities

Objective To write and solve compound inequalities

Dynamic Activity
Compound Inequalities

In Part 1 of the lesson, you learned how to solve and graph inequalities.

Connect to What You Know

Here you will use what you learned to write and solve compound inequalities.

Lesson Vocabulary
• compound inequality

Focus Question What is a compound inequality?

You can join two inequalities with the word *and* or the word *or* to form a **compound inequality**. To solve a compound inequality containing *and*, find all values of the variable that make both inequalities true.

Think

How do you graph a compound inequality with *and*?
Find the intersection of the solutions of the two inequalities.

Problem 5 Solving an *And* Inequality

What is the solution of $7 < 2x + 1$ and $3x \leq 18$? Graph the solution.

| Write the original inequalities. | $7 < 2x + 1$ | and | $3x \leq 18$ |
| Solve each inequality. | $3 < x$ | and | $x \leq 6$ |

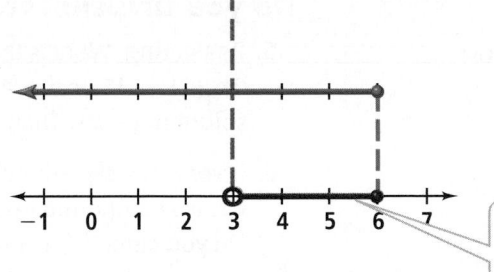

$3 < x$

$x \leq 6$

AND means that a solution makes *BOTH* inequalities true.

 Got It? **5. a.** What is the solution of $5 \leq 3x - 1$ and $2x < 12$? Graph the solution.

b. Reasoning Is the compound inequality in Problem 5 *always*, *sometimes*, or *never* true? Explain your reasoning.

You can collapse a compound *and* inequality, like $5 < x + 1$ and $x + 1 < 13$, into a simpler form: $5 < x + 1 < 13$. You read $5 < x + 1 < 13$ as "$x + 1$ is greater than 5 and less than 13."

To solve a compound inequality containing *or*, find all values of the variable that make at least one of the inequalities true.

Problem 6 Solving an *Or* Inequality

What is the solution of $7 + k \geq 6$ or $8 + k < 3$? Graph the solution.

Write the original inequalities.	$7 + k \geq 6$ or $8 + k < 3$
Use the Subtraction Property of Inequality.	$k \geq -1$ or $k < -5$

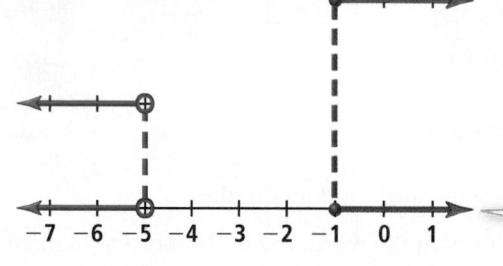

$k \geq -1$

$k < -5$

OR means that a solution makes *EITHER* inequality true.

Think

How does the solution to an *or* inequality differ from the solution to an *and* inequality?
The solution to an *or* inequality includes all solutions of either inequality, not just the solutions of both inequalities.

 Got It? **6.** What is the solution of each compound inequality? Graph the solution.
  a. $7w + 3 > 11$ or $4w - 1 < -13$ **b.** $16 < 5x + 1$ or $3x + 9 < 6$

Focus Question What is a compound inequality?
Answer A compound inequality consists of two inequalities joined by *and* or *or*.

 Lesson Check

Do you know HOW?

Write an inequality that represents each sentence.

  1. The wind speeds of tropical storms are at least 40 mi/h, but less than 74 mi/h.

  2. A discount applies to people under the age of 12 or over the age of 60.

Solve each inequality. Graph the solution.

  3. $3 < 5x - 2 < 7$

  4. $7x - 3 > 18$ or $3x - 2 \leq -2$

Do you UNDERSTAND?

  5. Reasoning What is the solution of the inequality $2x + 1 < 17$ or $x + 4 > 12$? Explain what the solution means. Then graph the solution.

  6. Error Analysis Your classmate says that you cannot write a compound inequality that has no solution. Do you agree? If so, explain why. If not, give a counterexample.

Practice and Problem-Solving Exercises

Solve each compound inequality. Graph the solution.

◀ See Problems 5 and 6.

Guided Practice

To start, simplify each inequality.

7. $2x > -10$ and $9x < 18$

$x > -5$ and $x < 2$

8. $3x \geq -12$ and $8x \leq 16$

9. $6x \geq -24$ and $9x < 54$

10. $7x > -35$ and $5x \leq 30$

11. $\frac{1}{2}x < 3$ and $5x \geq 10$

12. $4x < 16$ or $12x > 144$

13. $3x \geq 3$ or $9x < 54$

14. $8x > -32$ or $-6x \geq 48$

15. $9x \leq -27$ or $4x \geq 36$

B **Apply**

16. Think About a Plan The diagram shows the scores in seconds of a skater's first three trials in a speed-skating event. What is the maximum time she can score on her last trial so that her average time on all four trials is under 36 seconds?
- What do you need to find an average?
- What inequality can you use to model the situation?

17. Grades Your math test scores are 68, 78, 90, and 91. What is the lowest score you can earn on the next test and still achieve an average of at least 85?

18. Chemistry The pH level of a popular shampoo is between 6.0 and 6.5 inclusive. What compound inequality shows the pH levels of this shampoo? Graph the solution.

19. Geometry The sum of the lengths of any two sides of a triangle is greater than the length of the third side. In $\triangle ABC$, $BC = 4$ and $AC = 8$ AB. What can you conclude about AB?

20. Construction A contractor estimated that her expenses for a construction project would be between $700,000 and $750,000. She has already spent $496,000. How much more can she spend and remain within her estimate?

Solve each compound inequality. Graph the solution.

21. $-6 < 2x - 4 < 12$

22. $4x \leq 12$ and $-7x \leq 21$

23. $15x > 30$ or $18x < -36$

24. $11 < 3y + 2 < 20$

25. $5a - 4 > 16$ or $3a + 2 < 17$

26. $8d < -64$ and $5d > 25$

Standardized Test Prep

SAT/ACT

27. What is the solution of $1 < 2x + 3 < 9$?

   Ⓐ $-1 > x < 2$ Ⓒ $-1 < x < 2$

   Ⓑ $2 < x < 3$ Ⓓ $-1 < x < 3$

28. Which expression best represents the value of x in $y = mx + b$?

   Ⓕ $\dfrac{b - y}{m}$ Ⓗ $m(y - b)$

   Ⓖ $\dfrac{y + b}{m}$ Ⓘ $\dfrac{y - b}{m}$

29. The hourly rate of a waiter is \$4 plus tips. On a particular day, the waiter worked 8 hours and received more than \$150 in pay. Which could be the amount of tips the waiter received?

   Ⓐ \$18.75   Ⓑ \$32   Ⓒ \$118   Ⓓ \$120.75

Extended
Response

30. Solve $3(x - 2) + 8 = 12$. Identify each property of real numbers or equality you use.

Mixed Review

Simplify each expression.   ◀ **See Lesson 1-3.**

31. $(2a - 4) + (5a + 9)$ **32.** $3(x + 3y) - 5(x - y)$

33. $\frac{1}{3}(b + 12) - \frac{1}{4}(b + 12)$ **34.** $0.4(k - 0.1) + 0.5(3.3 - k)$

Get Ready!   **To prepare for Lesson 1-6, do Exercises 35–38.**

Solve each equation. Check your answers.   ◀ **See Lesson 1-4.**

35. $7x - 6(11 - 2x) = 10$ **36.** $10x - 7 = 2(13 + 5x)$

37. $4y - \frac{1}{10} = 3y + \frac{4}{5}$ **38.** $0.4x + 1.18 = -3.1(2 - 0.01x)$

1-6
PART 1

Absolute Value Equations and Inequalities

Objective To write and solve equations involving absolute value

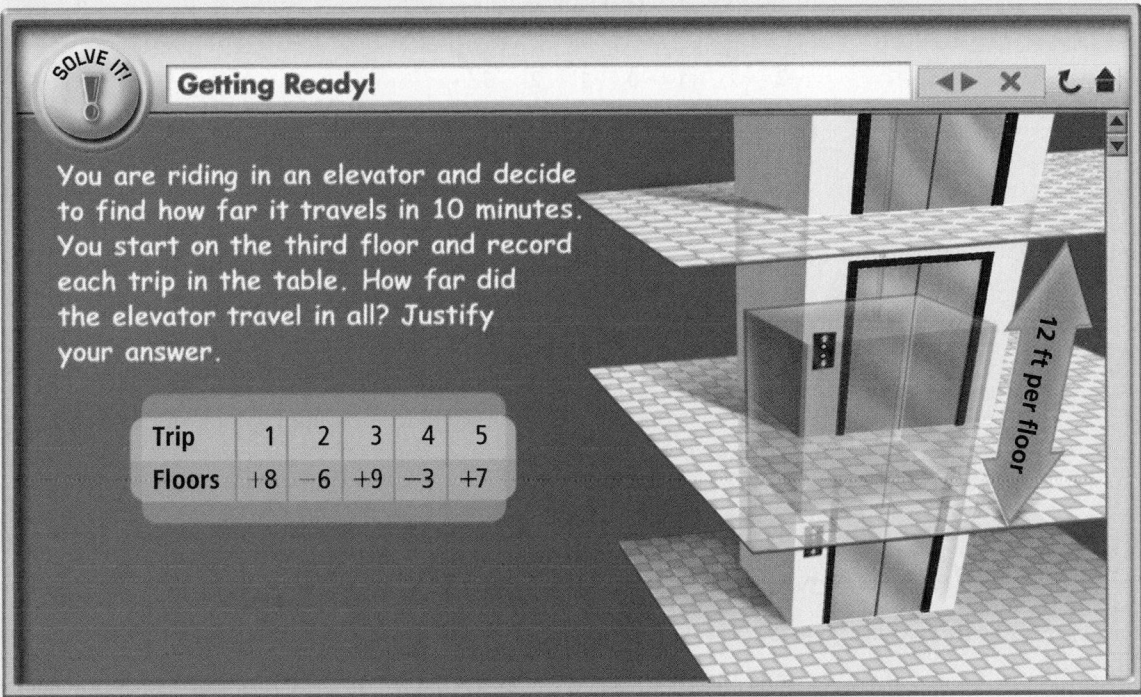

SOLVE IT!

Getting Ready!

You are riding in an elevator and decide to find how far it travels in 10 minutes. You start on the third floor and record each trip in the table. How far did the elevator travel in all? Justify your answer.

Trip	1	2	3	4	5
Floors	+8	−6	+9	−3	+7

12 ft per floor

Lesson Vocabulary
• absolute value
• extraneous solution

In the Solve It, signed numbers represent distance and direction. Sometimes, only the size of a number (its *absolute value*), not the direction, is important. An absolute value quantity is nonnegative. Since opposites have the same absolute value, an absolute value equation can have two solutions.

Focus Question How can you find the solution of an absolute value equation?

take note

Key Concept   Absolute Value

Definition	Numbers	Symbols
The **absolute value** of a real number x, written $|x|$, is its distance from zero on the number line.	$|4| = 4$ $|-4| = 4$	$|x| = x$, if $x \geq 0$ $|x| = -x$, if $x < 0$

An absolute value equation has a variable within the absolute value sign. For example, $|x| = 5$. Here, the value of x can be 5 or −5 since $|5|$ and $|-5|$ both equal 5.

Both 5 and −5 are 5 units from 0.

$$-6\ -5\ -4\ -3\ -2\ -1\ \ 0\ \ 1\ \ 2\ \ 3\ \ 4\ \ 5\ \ 6$$

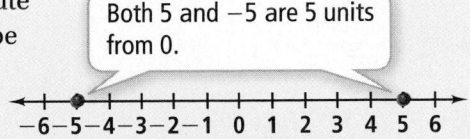

 **Problem 1** Solving an Absolute Value Equation

How is solving this equation different from solving a linear equation?
In the absolute value equation, $2x - 1$ can represent two opposite quantities.

What is the solution of $|2x - 1| = 5$? Graph the solution.

Write the original equation.	$|2x - 1| = 5$
Rewrite as two equations. $2x - 1$ could be 5 or -5.	$2x - 1 = 5$ or $2x - 1 = -5$
Add 1 to each side of both equations.	$2x = 6$ $\quad\quad$ $2x = -4$
Divide each side of both equations by 2.	$x = 3$ or $\quad$ $x = -2$

Check $|2(3) - 1| \stackrel{?}{=} 5$ $\quad\quad\quad\quad\quad\quad$ $|2(-2) - 1| \stackrel{?}{=} 5$

$\quad\quad\quad\quad$ $|6 - 1| \stackrel{?}{=} 5$ $\quad\quad\quad\quad\quad\quad\quad$ $|-4 - 1| \stackrel{?}{=} 5$

$\quad\quad\quad\quad\quad\quad$ $|5| = 5$ ✔ $\quad\quad\quad\quad\quad\quad\quad\quad$ $|-5| = 5$ ✔

✅ **Got It?** **1.** What is the solution of $|3x + 2| = 4$? Graph the solution.

Sometimes you first need to isolate the absolute value expression before rewriting as two equations.

 Problem 2 Solving a Multi-Step Absolute Value Equation

Is there a simpler way to think of this problem?
Yes. Solving $3|x + 2| - 1 = 8$ is similar to solving $3y - 1 = 8$.

What is the solution of $3|x + 2| - 1 = 8$?

Write the original equation.	$3|x + 2| - 1 = 8$
Add 1 to each side.	$3|x + 2| = 9$
Divide each side by 3.	$|x + 2| = 3$
Rewrite as two equations.	$x + 2 = 3$ or $x + 2 = -3$
Subtract 2 from each side of both equations.	$x = 1$ or $\quad$ $x = -5$

Check $3|(1) + 2| - 1 \stackrel{?}{=} 8$ $\quad\quad\quad\quad$ $3|(-5) + 2| - 1 \stackrel{?}{=} 8$

$\quad\quad\quad\quad$ $3|3| - 1 \stackrel{?}{=} 8$ $\quad\quad\quad\quad\quad\quad$ $3|-3| - 1 \stackrel{?}{=} 8$

$\quad\quad\quad\quad\quad\quad$ $8 = 8$ ✔ $\quad\quad\quad\quad\quad\quad\quad\quad$ $8 = 8$ ✔

✅ **Got It?** **2.** What is the solution of $2|x + 9| + 3 = 7$? Graph the solution.

Distance from 0 on a number line cannot be negative. Therefore, some absolute value equations, such as $|x| = -5$, have no solution. After you solve an absolute value equation, it is important to check the possible solutions. One or more of the possible solutions may be *extraneous*.

An **extraneous solution** is a solution derived from an original equation that is *not* a solution of the original equation.

 Problem 3 Checking for Extraneous Solutions

What is the solution of $|3x + 2| = 4x + 5$? Check for extraneous solutions.

Think

Can you solve this the same way as you solved Problem 1?
Yes; let $3x + 2$ equal $4x + 5$ and $-(4x + 5)$.

Write the original equation. $|3x + 2| = 4x + 5$

Rewrite as two equations. $3x + 2 = 4x + 5$ or $3x + 2 = -(4x + 5)$

Solve each equation. $-x = 3$ | $3x + 2 = -4x - 5$

$7x = -7$

$x = -3$ or $x = -1$

Check $|3(-3) + 2| \stackrel{?}{=} 4(-3) + 5$ $|3(-1) + 2| \stackrel{?}{=} 4(-1) + 5$

$|-9 + 2| \stackrel{?}{=} -12 + 5$ $|-3 + 2| \stackrel{?}{=} -4 + 5$

$|-7| \neq -7$ ✗ $|-1| = 1$ ✔

Since $x = -3$ does not satisfy the orignal equation, -3 is an extraneous solution. The only solution to the equation is $x = -1$.

 Got It?   3. What is the solution of $|5x - 2| = 7x + 14$? Check for extraneous solutions.

Focus Question   How can you find the solution of an absolute value equation?
Answer   Use the definition of absolute value. Rewrite the equation as two equations. Then solve each equation.

Lesson Check

Do you know HOW?

Solve each equation. Check your answers.

1. $|-6x| = 24$

2. $|2x + 8| - 4 = 12$

3. $|x - 2| = 4x + 8$

Do you UNDERSTAND?

4. Vocabulary   Explain what it means for a possible solution of an equation to be extraneous.

5. Reasoning   When is the absolute value of a number equal to the number itself?

Practice and Problem-Solving Exercises

Solve each equation. Check your answers.

See Problems 1 and 2.

Guided Practice

To start, rewrite the absolute value equation as two equations.

6. $|x - 3| = 9$

$x - 3 = 9$ or $x - 3 = -9$

7. $|3x| = 18$

8. $|-4x| = 32$

9. $2|3x - 2| = 14$

10. $|3x + 4| = -3$

11. $|2x - 3| = -1$

12. $|x + 4| + 3 = 17$

13. $|y - 5| - 2 = 10$

14. $|4 - z| - 10 = 1$

Solve each equation. Check for extraneous solutions.

See Problem 3.

Guided Practice

To start, rewrite as two equations.

15. $|x - 1| = 5x + 10$

$x - 1 = 5x + 10$ or $x - 1 = -(5x + 10)$

16. $|2z - 3| = 4z - 1$

17. $|3x + 5| = 5x + 2$

18. $|2y - 4| = 12$

19. $3|4w - 1| - 5 = 10$

20. $|2x + 5| = 3x + 4$

21. $|2x + 3| = 3x + 2$

Ⓑ Apply

Solve each equation.

22. $-|4 - 8b| = 12$

23. $4|3x + 4| = 4x + 8$

24. $|3x - 1| + 10 = 25$

25. $\frac{1}{2}|3c + 5| = 6c + 4$

26. $5|6 - 5x| = 15x - 35$

27. $7|8 - 3h| = 21h - 49$

28. $2|3x - 7| = 10x - 8$

29. $\frac{1}{4}|4x + 7| = 8x + 16$

Write an absolute value equation to describe each graph.

30.

$-4 \quad -2 \quad 0 \quad 2 \quad 4$

31.

$-3 \quad -2 \quad -1 \quad 0 \quad 1 \quad 2 \quad 3$

Is the absolute value equation *always*, *sometimes*, or *never* true? Explain.

32. $|x| = -6$

33. $|x| = x$

34. $|x + 2| = x + 2$

Absolute Value Equations and Inequalities

Objective To write and solve inequalities involving absolute value

In Part 1 of the lesson, you learned how to solve an absolute value equation by rewriting it as two equations.

Connect to What You Know

Here you will use similar methods to solve absolute value inequalities.

Focus Question How can you solve an absolute value inequality?

You can write an absolute value inequality as a compound inequality without absolute value symbols.

The solutions of the absolute value inequality $|x| < 5$ include values greater than -5 *and* less than 5. This is the compound inequality $x > -5$ *and* $x < 5$, which you can write as $-5 < x < 5$. So, $|x| < 5$ means x is between -5 and 5.

The graph of $|x| < 5$ is all values of x between -5 and 5.

$$-6\ -5\ -4\ -3\ -2\ -1\ \ 0\ \ 1\ \ 2\ \ 3\ \ 4\ \ 5\ \ 6$$

Problem 4 **Solving the Absolute Value Inequality $|A| < b$**

What is the solution of $|2x - 1| < 5$? Graph the solution.

Plan

Is this an *and* problem or an *or* problem?
$2x - 1$ is less than 5 and greater than -5. It is an *and* problem.

Write the original inequality.

$|2x - 1| < 5$

$2x - 1$ is greater than -5 and less than 5.

$-5 < 2x - 1 < 5$

Add 1 to each expression.

$-4 < \quad 2x \quad < 6$

Divide each part by 2.

$-2 < \quad x \quad < 3$

$$-3\ -2\ -1\ \ 0\ \ 1\ \ 2\ \ 3$$

Got It? **4.** What is the solution of $|3x - 4| \leq 8$? Graph the solution.

$|x| < 5$ means x is between -5 and 5. So, $|x| > 5$ means x is outside the interval from -5 to 5. You can say $x < -5$ *or* $x > 5$.

 Problem 5 Solving the Absolute Value Inequality $|A| \geq b$

What is the solution of $|2x + 4| \geq 6$? Graph the solution.

Think

How do you determine the boundary points?
To find the boundary points, find the solutions of the related equation.

Write the original inequality.	$|2x + 4| \geq 6$
Rewrite as a compound inequality.	$2x + 4 \leq -6$ or $2x + 4 \geq 6$
Subtract 4 from each side of both inequalities.	$2x \leq -10$ $\qquad$ $2x \geq 2$
Divide each side of both inequalities by 2.	$x \leq -5$ or $\qquad$ $x \geq 1$

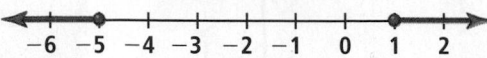

✓ **Got It?** **5. a.** What is the solution of $|5x + 10| > 15$? Graph the solution.

b. Reasoning Without solving $|x - 3| \geq 2$, describe the graph of its solution.

take note

Concept Summary Solutions of Absolute Value Statements

Symbols	Definition	Graphs
$|x| = a$	The distance from x to 0 is a units.	●────┼────● $-a$ $\quad$ 0 $\quad$ a $x = -a$ or $x = a$
$|x| < a$ $(|x| \leq a)$	The distance from x to 0 is less than a units.	⊕────┼────⊕ $-a$ $\quad$ 0 $\quad$ a $-a < x < a$ $x > -a$ and $x < a$
$|x| > a$ $(|x| \geq a)$	The distance from x to 0 is greater than a units.	◄──⊕────┼────⊕──► $-a$ $\quad$ 0 $\quad$ a $x < -a$ or $x > a$

A manufactured item's actual measurements and its target measurements can differ by a certain amount, called *tolerance*. Tolerance is one half the difference of the maximum and minimum acceptable values. You can use absolute value inequalities to describe tolerance.

Problem 6 Using an Absolute Value Inequality

Car Racing In car racing, a car must meet specific dimensions to enter a race. Officials use a template to ensure these specifications are met. What absolute value inequality describes heights of the model of race car shown within the indicated tolerance?

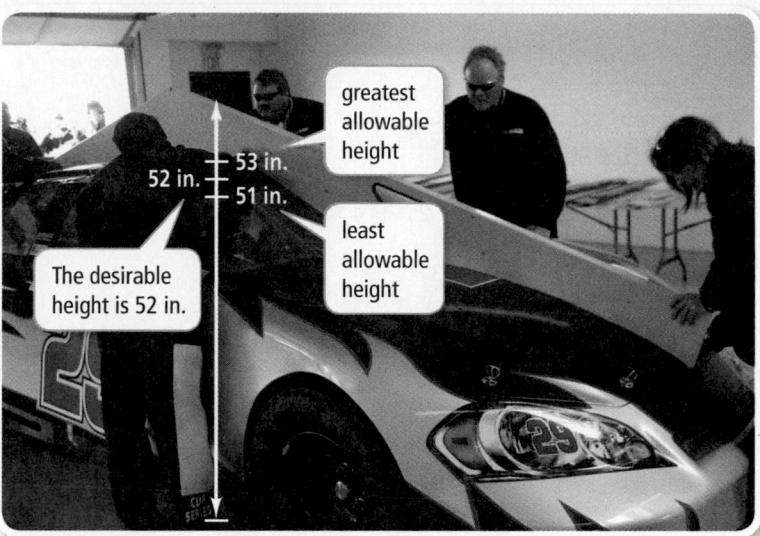

53 in. — greatest allowable height

52 in.

51 in. — least allowable height

The desirable height is 52 in.

Plan

How does *tolerance* relate to an inequality?
Tolerance allows the height to differ from a desired height by no less and no more than a small amount.

Find the tolerance.

Use *h* for the height of the race car. Write a compound inequality.

Rewrite as an absolute value inequality.

$$\frac{53 - 51}{2} = \frac{2}{2} = 1$$

$$-1 \le h - 52 \le 1$$

$$|h - 52| \le 1$$

 Got It? **6.** Suppose the least allowable height of the race car in Problem 6 was 52 in. and the desirable height was 52.5 in. What absolute value inequality describes heights of the model of race car shown within the indicated tolerance?

Focus Question How can you solve an absolute value inequality?
Answer Rewrite the inequality as a compound inequality without absolute values. Then solve the compound inequality.

Lesson Check

Do you know HOW?

Solve each inequality. Graph the solution.

1. $|2x + 2| - 5 < 15$

2. $|4x - 6| \ge 10$

3. $|3z| - 4 > 8$

Do you UNDERSTAND?

4. Open Ended Write an absolute value inequality that has no solution.

5. Compare and Contrast Describe how absolute value equations and inequalities are like linear equations and inequalities and how they differ.

Practice and Problem-Solving Exercises

See Problems 4 and 5.

A Practice

Solve each inequality. Graph the solution.

> **Guided Practice**
>
> **6.** $3|y - 9| < 27$
>
> To start, divide each side by 3. $|y - 9| < 9$

7. $|6y - 2| + 4 < 22$ **8.** $|3x - 6| + 3 < 15$

9. $|x + 3| > 9$ **10.** $\frac{1}{4}|x - 3| + 2 < 1$

11. $|x - 5| \geq 8$ **12.** $|y - 3| \geq 12$

13. $4|2w + 3| - 7 \leq 9$ **14.** $|2x + 1| \geq -9$

15. $3|2x - 1| \geq 21$ **16.** $3|5t - 1| + 9 \leq 23$

Write each compound inequality as an absolute value inequality.

See Problem 6.

> **Guided Practice**
>
> **17.** $1.3 \leq h \leq 1.5$
>
> To start, find the tolerance. $\frac{1.5 - 1.3}{2} = \frac{0.2}{2} = 0.1$

18. $27.25 \leq C \leq 27.75$ **19.** $50 \leq b \leq 55$

20. $1200 \leq m \leq 1300$ **21.** $0.1187 \leq d \leq 0.1190$

B Apply

22. Think About a Plan The circumference of a basketball for college women must be from 28.5 in. to 29.0 in. What absolute value inequality represents the circumference of the ball?
- What is the tolerance?
- What is the inequality without using absolute value?

Write an absolute value inequality to describe each graph.

23.
```
 <⊕--+--+--+--⊕->
 -4  -2   0   2   4
```

24.
```
 <--+--●--+--+--●-->
   -2  -1   0   1   2
```

25. Writing Describe the differences in the graphs of $|x| < a$ and $|x| > a$, where a is a positive real number.

26. Open-Ended Write an absolute value inequality for which every real number is a solution.

Solve each inequality. Graph the solutions.

27. $|3x - 4| + 5 \leq 27$

28. $|2x + 3| - 6 \geq 7$

29. $-2|x + 4| < 22$

30. $2|4t - 1| + 6 > 20$

31. $|3z + 15| \geq 0$

32. $|-2x + 1| > 2$

33. $\frac{1}{9}|5x - 3| - 3 \geq 2$

34. $\left|\frac{x - 3}{2}\right| + 2 < 6$

Write an absolute value inequality to represent each situation.

35. Cooking Suppose you used an oven thermometer while baking and discovered that the oven temperature varied between $+5$ and -5 degrees from the setting. If your oven is set to $350°$, let t be the actual temperature.

36. Time Workers at a hardware store take their morning break no earlier than 10 A.M. and no later than noon. Let c represent the time the workers take their break.

37. Climate A friend is planning a trip to Alaska. He purchased a coat that is recommended for outdoor temperatures from $-15°F$ to $45°F$. Let t represent the temperature for which the coat is intended.

Is the absolute value inequality *always*, *sometimes*, or *never* true? Explain.

38. $-8 > |x|$

39. $|x| + |x| \geq 2x$

40. $(|x|)^2 < x^2$

41. Error Analysis A classmate wrote the solution to the inequality $|-4x + 1| > 3$ as shown. Describe and correct the error.

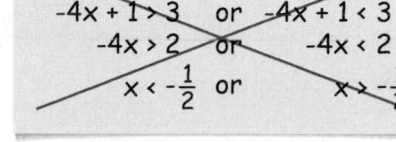

Write an absolute value inequality and a compound inequality for each length x with the given tolerance.

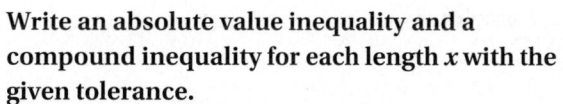

42. a length of 36.80 mm with a tolerance of 0.05 mm

43. a length of 9.55 mm with a tolerance of 0.02 mm

44. a length of 100 yd with a tolerance of 4 in.

Standardized Test Prep

SAT/ACT

45. What is the positive solution of $|3x + 8| = 19$?

46. If p is an integer, what is the least possible value of p in the following inequality?

$$|3p - 5| \leq 7$$

47. In wood shop, you have to drill a hole that is 2 inches deep into a wood panel. The tolerance for drilling a hole is described by the inequality $|t - 2| \leq 0.125$. What is the shallowest hole allowed?

48. The normal thickness of a metal structure is shown. It expands to 6.54 centimeters when heated and shrinks to 6.46 centimeters when cooled down. What is the maximum amount in cm that the thickness of the structure can deviate from its normal thickness?

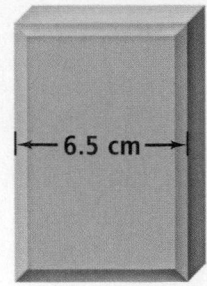

|← 6.5 cm →|

Mixed Review

Solve each inequality. Graph the solution.   ◀ See Lesson 1-5.

49. $5y - 10 < 20$ **50.** $15(4s + 1) < 23$ **51.** $4a + 6 > 2a + 14$

Describe each pattern using words. Draw the next figure in each pattern.   ◀ See Lesson 1-1.

52.
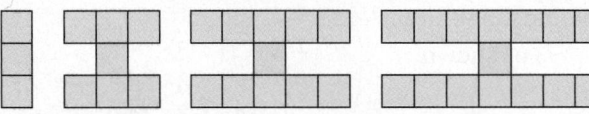

53.
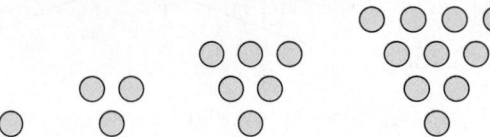

Get Ready!   To prepare for Lesson 2-1, do Exercises 54–57.

Graph each ordered pair on the coordinate plane.   ◀ See p. 870.

54. $(-4, -8)$ **55.** $(3, 6)$

56. $(0, 0)$ **57.** $(-1, 3)$

Pull It **All Together**

These problems will challenge you to pull together many concepts and skills of algebra that you have learned.

BIG idea Variables

You can use variables to represent variable quantities in real-world situations and in patterns.

BIG idea Properties

You can use the properties of real numbers to simplify algebraic expressions.

Task 1

The tables below show the same set of inputs and outputs using two different process columns.

Input	Process Column	Output
1	$2(1-1)+5$	5
2	$2(2-1)+5$	7
3	$2(3-1)+5$	9
4	▪	▪
⋮	⋮	⋮
n	▪	▪

Input	Process Column	Output
1	$2(1+1)+1$	5
2	$2(2+1)+1$	7
3	$2(3+1)+1$	9
4	▪	▪
⋮	⋮	⋮
n	▪	▪

a. Copy and complete each table. Write an algebraic expression for each rule using n.
b. Show that the two algebraic expressions are equivalent.
c. Describe a pattern using a third rule.

BIG idea Solving Equations and Inequalities

You can use properties of numbers and equality to solve an equation by finding increasingly simpler equations that have the same solution as the original equation.

Task 2

Find all possible values of a and b in the figures below, given the following conditions.
• The perimeters are equal.
• The rectangle has an area between 80 and 100 square units.
• The values of a and b are integers.

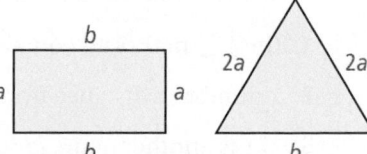

1 Chapter Review

Connecting BIG ideas and Answering Essential Questions

1 Variable
You can use variables to represent variable quantities in real-world situations and in patterns.

→ **Patterns and Expressions (Lesson 1-1)**
$$6, 12, 18, 24, \ldots \; 6n$$
$$8, 9, 10, 11, \ldots \; (n + 7)$$

→ **Algebraic Expressions (Lesson 1-3)**
$$6n$$
$$n + 7$$
$$5x - x = (5 - 1)x$$
$$a + 0 = a$$
$$h + k = k + h$$

2 Properties
The properties that apply to real numbers also apply to variables that represent them.

→ **Properties of Real Numbers (Lesson 1-2)**
$$4(6 - 1) = 4(6) - 4(1)$$
$$23 + 0 = 23$$
$$5 + 12 = 12 + 5$$

3 Solving Equations and Inequalities
You can use properties of numbers and equality (or inequality) to solve an equation (or inequality) by finding increasingly simpler equations (or inequalities) which have the same solution as the original equation (or inequality).

→ **Solving Equations and Inequalities (Lessons 1-4 and 1-5)**

$$4x - 1 = 5 \qquad\qquad 7 > -3h - 2$$
$$4x = 6 \qquad\qquad\quad 9 > -3h$$
$$x = \frac{3}{2} \qquad\qquad\; -3 < h$$

→ **Absolute Value Equations and Inequalities (Lesson 1-6)**
$$|2b + 7| = 15$$
$$2b + 7 = 15 \;\text{ or }\; 2b + 7 = -15$$
$$2b = 8 \qquad\qquad 2b = -22$$
$$b = 4 \;\text{ or }\qquad\quad b = -11$$

Chapter Vocabulary

- absolute value (p. 43)
- additive inverse (p. 14)
- algebraic expression (p. 5)
- coefficient (p. 20)
- compound inequality (p. 39)
- constant (p. 5)
- constant term (p. 20)
- equation (p. 26)

- evaluate (p. 19)
- extraneous solution (p. 45)
- identity (p. 29)
- inverse operations (p. 27)
- like terms (p. 21)
- literal equation (p. 29)
- multiplicative inverse (p. 14)

- numerical expression (p. 5)
- opposite (p. 14)
- reciprocal (p. 14)
- solution of an equation (p. 27)
- term (p. 20)
- variable (p. 5)
- variable quantity (p. 5)

Choose the correct term to complete each sentence.

1. The _?_ makes an equation true.

2. A number's distance from zero on the number line is its _?_ .

3. _?_ is another name for the multiplicative inverse of a number.

4. A pair of inequalities joined by *and* or *or* are called a _?_ .

1-1 Patterns and Expressions

Quick Review

You can represent patterns using words, diagrams, numbers, and **algebraic expressions**. You can identify a pattern by looking for the same type of change between consecutive figures or numbers. It often helps to make a table.

Example

Identify a pattern by making a table of inputs and outputs. Include a process column. 7, 14, 21, 28, 35, . . .

Input	Process Column	Output
1	$1 \cdot 7$	7
2	$2 \cdot 7$	14
3	$3 \cdot 7$	21
$\vdots$	$\vdots$	$\vdots$
n	$n \cdot 7$	$7n$

The nth output is $7n$.

Exercises

Identify a pattern and find the next three numbers in the pattern.

5. 5, 10, 15, 20, . . .   **6.** 3, 4, 5, 6, . . .

Copy and complete the table and find the output when the input is n.

7.

Input	Output
1	9
2	10
3	11
4	■
$\vdots$	$\vdots$
n	■

8.

Input	Output
1	19
2	38
3	57
4	■
$\vdots$	$\vdots$
n	■

9. Finance If you put $20 in your savings account each week, how much have you saved after n weeks?

1-2 Properties of Real Numbers

Quick Review

The natural numbers, whole numbers, integers, rational numbers, and irrational numbers are all subsets of the real numbers. You can use properties such as the ones listed below to simplify and evaluate expressions.

Commutative Properties	$-3 + 5 = 5 + (-3)$
	$2 \times 9 = 9 \times 2$
Associative Properties	$3 + (5 + 7) = (3 + 5) + 7$
	$4 \times (8 \times 11) = (4 \times 8) \times 11$
Inverse Properties	$-5 + 0 = -5$
	$12 \times 1 = 12$
Distributive Property	$5(7 + 9) = 5(7) + 5(9)$

Example

Identify the property illustrated by the equation.

$4 \cdot x = x \cdot 4$ Commutative Property of Multiplication

Exercises

Name the subset(s) of real numbers to which each number belongs.

10. 8.1π **11.** -79

12. $\sqrt{121}$ **13.** $12\frac{7}{8}$

Compare the two numbers. Use < or >.

14. $-\sqrt{60}, -8$ **15.** $5, \sqrt{32}$

Name the property of real numbers illustrated by each equation.

16. $\frac{9}{4} \cdot \frac{4}{9} = 1$

17. $\left(8 \cdot \frac{1}{3}\right) \cdot 12 = 8 \cdot \left(\frac{1}{3} \cdot 12\right)$

1-3, 1-4, and 1-5 Expressions, Equations, and Inequalities

Quick Review

You **evaluate** an algebraic expression by substituting numbers for the variables. You simplify an algebraic expression by combining **like terms**. To find the **solution of an equation** or inequality, use the properties of equality or inequality. Some **equations** and inequalities are true for all real numbers, and some have no solution.

Example

Evaluate $3(x - 4) + 2x - x^2$ for $x = 6$.

Substitute.	$3(6 - 4) + 2(6) - 6^2$
Simplify inside parentheses.	$3(2) + 2(6) - 6^2$
Multiply.	$6 + 12 - 36$
Add and subtract.	-18

Exercises

18. Evaluate $3t(t + 2) - 3t^2$ for $t = 19$.

19. Simplify $-(3a - 2b) - 3(-a - b)$.

Solve each equation. Check your answer.

20. $2x - 5 = 17$ **21.** $3(x + 1) = 9 + 2x$

Solve each inequality. Graph the solution.

22. $4 - 5z \geq 2$

23. $2(5 - 3x) < x - 4(3 - x)$

Solve each compound inequality. Graph the solution.

24. $10 \geq 7 + 3x$ and   **25.** $3 \geq 2x$ or
$\quad\quad 9 - 4x \leq 1$ $x - 4 > 2$

Write an equation to solve the problem.

26. Geometry The length and width of a rectangle are in the ratio 5 : 3. The perimeter of the rectangle is 32 cm. Find the length and width.

1-6 Absolute Value Equations and Inequalities

Quick Review

To rewrite an equation or inequality that involves the **absolute value** of an algebraic expression, you must consider both cases of the definition of absolute value.

Example

Solve $|3x - 5| = 4 + 2x$. Check for extraneous solutions.

$3x - 5 = 4 + 2x$ or $3x - 5 = -(4 + 2x)$

$x - 5 = 4$ | $3x - 5 = -4 - 2x$

                     $5x = 1$

$x = 9$ or $x = \dfrac{1}{5}$

Check $|3(9) - 5| \stackrel{?}{=} 4 + 2(9)$ $\left|3\left(\frac{1}{5}\right) - 5\right| \stackrel{?}{=} 4 + 2\left(\frac{1}{5}\right)$

        $|27 - 5| \stackrel{?}{=} 22$ $\left|\frac{3}{5} - 5\right| \stackrel{?}{=} 4 + \frac{2}{5}$

           $|22| = 22$ ✔ $\left|-\frac{22}{5}\right| = \frac{22}{5}$ ✔

Exercises

Solve each equation. Check for extraneous solutions.

27. $|2x + 8| = 3x + 7$

28. $|x - 4| + 3 = 1$

29. $3|x + 10| = 6$

30. $2|x - 7| = x - 8$

Solve each inequality. Graph the solution.

31. $|3x - 2| + 4 \leq 7$

32. $4|y - 9| > 36$

33. $|7x| + 3 \leq 21$

34. $\frac{1}{2}|x + 2| > 6$

35. The specification for a length x is 43.6 cm with a tolerance of 0.1 cm. Write the specification as an absolute value inequality.

Chapter Test

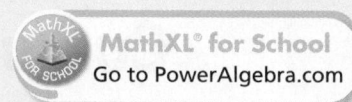

Do you know HOW?

Evaluate each expression for $x = 5$.

1. $\frac{5}{3}(3x - 6) - (6 - 4x)$

2. $3(x^2 - 4) + 7(x - 2)$

3. $x - 2x + 3x - 4x + 5x$

Simplify each expression.

4. $a^2 + a + a^2$

5. $2x + 3y - 5x + 2y$

6. $5(a - 2b) - 3(a - 2b)$

7. $3[2(x - 3) + 2] + 5(x - 3)$

Solve each equation.

8. $4y - 6 = 2y + 8$

9. $3(2z + 1) = 35$

10. $5(3w - 2) - 7 = 23$

11. $t - 2(3 - 2t) = 2t + 9$

12. $5(s - 12) - 24 = 3(s + 2)$

13. The lateral surface area of a cylinder is given by the formula $S = 2\pi rh$. Solve the equation for r.

14. Savings Briana and her sister Molly both want to buy the same model bicycle. Briana needs \$73 more before she can afford the bike. Molly needs \$65 more. If they combine their money, they will have just enough to buy one bicycle that they could share. What is the cost of the bicycle?

15. Musical There is only one freshman in the cast of a high school musical. There are 6 sophomores and 11 juniors. One third of the cast are seniors. How many seniors are in the musical?

Determine whether each equation is *always*, *sometimes*, or *never* true.

16. $2x + 7 - x = 3 + x + 4$

17. $5a - 1 - 3a = 2a + 1$

Solve each inequality or equation. Graph the solution.

18. $3x + 17 \geq 5$

19. $25 - 2x < 11$

20. $\frac{3}{8}x < -6$ or $5x > 2$

21. $2 < 10 - 4d < 6$

22. $4 - x = |2 - 3x|$

23. $5|3w + 2| - 3 > 7$

Do you UNDERSTAND?

24. Writing Describe the relationships among these sets of numbers: natural numbers, whole numbers, integers, rational numbers, irrational numbers, and real numbers.

25. Reasoning Justify each step by identifying the property used.

$$\begin{aligned} t + 5(t + 1) &= t + (5t + 5) \\ &= (t + 5t) + 5 \\ &= (1t + 5t) + 5 \\ &= (1 + 5)t + 5 \\ &= 6t + 5 \end{aligned}$$

26. Reasoning The first four figures of a pattern are shown below.

Describe the tenth figure in the pattern.

TIPS FOR SUCCESS

Some questions on tests ask you to write a short response. To get full credit for an answer, you must give the correct answer (including appropriate units, if applicable) and justify your reasoning or show your work. Read the sample question at the right. Then follow the tips to answer it.

Short Response Your school is having a bake sale to raise money for a field trip. The ingredients for each batch of bran muffins cost $3.25, and the cost for the energy to bake them is $.50. You plan to sell each batch for $5.

Write an expression to represent the total amount of money your school will have after selling n batches of muffins. Evaluate your expression for 25 batches. Show your work.

TIP 2

You need to make a profit in the bake sale in order to raise money. Consider the total sales and the cost to make the muffins. What operation do you use to find the profit?

Think it Through

It costs $3.25 + $.50 = $3.75 to bake each batch. The school makes $5 − ($3.75) = $1.25 after selling one batch. So, it makes $1.25n$ after selling n batches. It earns $1.25(25) = $31.25 after selling 25 batches. This answer is complete and earns full credit.

TIP 1

Think about the total cost to make a batch of muffins.

Vocabulary Builder

As you solve test items, you must understand the meanings of mathematical terms. Match each term with its mathematical meaning.

A. inequality

B. compound inequality

C. extraneous solution

D. expression

E. equation

I. a mathematical sentence that contains $>, <, \geq, \leq,$ or $\neq$

II. a solution of an equation derived from an original equation that is not a solution of the original equation

III. a pair of inequalities joined by *and* or *or*

IV. a mathematical sentence that contains an equals sign

V. a mathematical phrase that uses numbers, variables, and operational symbols

Multiple Choice

Read each question. Then write the letter of the correct answer on your paper.

1. Which equation represents the data in the table?

x	−2	−1	1	3	5
y	2	0	0	4	8

Ⓐ $y = -2x - 2$

Ⓑ $y = |x| + 2$

Ⓒ $y = |x| - 1$

Ⓓ $y = 2|x| - 2$

2. A model of a suspension bridge is built as shown.

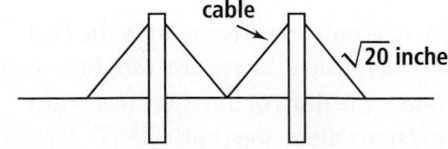

Which of the following is closest to the length of the cable?

Ⓕ 2 inches

Ⓖ 4 inches

Ⓗ 10 inches

Ⓘ 20 inches

3. Which is the graph of the inequality $|x - 2| - 3 > -2$?

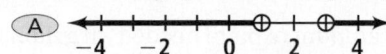

4. A worker is taking boxes of nails on an elevator. Each box weighs 54 lb, and the worker weighs 170 lb. The elevator has a weight limit of 2500 lb. Which inequality describes the number of boxes b that the worker can safely take on each trip?

(F) $54b - 170 \leq 2500$ (H) $54(b - 170) \leq 2500$

(G) $54b + 170 \leq 2500$ (I) $54(b + 170) \leq 2500$

5. Which expression is equivalent to
$-8(a - 3b) + 2(-a + 4b + 1)$?

(A) $-10a - 16b + 2$ (C) $-10a + 5b + 2$

(B) $-10a + 32b + 2$ (D) $-10a + b + 1$

6. An electric circuit is connected in series as shown. The total voltage V can be calculated by using the equation shown, where I is the total current and R is the resistance across the circuit. $\left(Hint: 1A = 1\frac{\text{volt}}{\text{ohm}}\right)$

$$V = I(R_1 + R_2 + R_3)$$

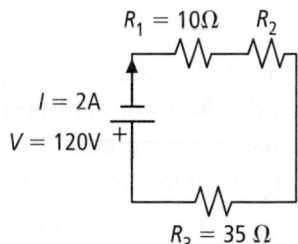

A = amperes
V = volts
Ω = ohms

What is the value of R_2?

(F) 15 Ω   (G) 45 Ω   (H) 60 Ω   (I) 75 Ω

7. Which value is a solution to $2|3x - 6| \leq 6$?

(A) -3 (B) -2 (C) -1 (D) 2

8. For which value of a does $4 = a + |x - 4|$ have no solution?

(F) -6 (G) 0   (H) 4   (I) 6

9. A rectangular solid has a volume of 81 cubic feet. If the length, width, and height are all changed to $\frac{1}{3}$ of their original size, what will be the volume of the new rectangular solid?

(A) 54 cubic feet   (C) 9 cubic feet

(B) 27 cubic feet   (D) 3 cubic feet

10. Two rectangular boxes are each 9 inches tall. Both boxes have square bases. The base edge of the larger box is 1.5 times as long as the base edge of the smaller box. Which statement is true?

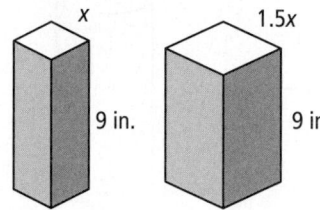

(F) The larger box holds 10.5 cubic inches more than the smaller box.

(G) The larger box holds 13.5 cubic inches more than the smaller box.

(H) The larger box holds 1.5 times as much as the smaller box.

(I) The larger box holds 2.25 times as much as the smaller box.

11. Solve $3(x - 2) + 4 \geq -3x + 1$.

(A) $x \geq -3$ (C) $x \geq \frac{3}{2}$

(B) $x \geq \frac{1}{2}$ (D) $x \leq 3$

12. A trapezoidal deck has dimensions as shown.

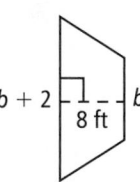

What is the longer base length if the area is 88 square feet (ft^2)?

(F) 20 ft   (G) 12 ft   (H) 10 ft   (I) 9 ft

13. Each dimension of a rectangular prism is tripled. How does the surface area of the new rectangular prism compare to the original surface area?

Ⓐ The new surface area is 12 times as great.

Ⓑ The new surface area is 9 times as great.

Ⓒ The new surface area is 6 times as great.

Ⓓ The new surface area is 3 times as great.

14. The two cylinders below have identical bases. Which statement is true?

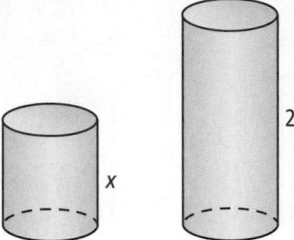

Ⓕ The shorter cylinder has one-half the surface area of the taller cylinder for all values of x.

Ⓖ The shorter cylinder has the same surface area as the taller cylinder for some values of x.

Ⓗ The shorter cylinder has one-half the volume of the taller cylinder for all values of x.

Ⓘ The shorter cylinder has the same volume as the taller cylinder for some values of x.

15. A survey was conducted to find out how customers responded to a newly released video game. Of the fifty customers who were surveyed, at least 20 customers like the game. Which of the following inequalities represents the situation?

Ⓐ $|c - 35| > 50$

Ⓑ $|c - 35| \geq 15$

Ⓒ $|c - 35| \leq 50$

Ⓓ $|c - 35| \leq 15$

16. A designer is designing a handbag. The height of the handbag must be between 16 in. and 18 in. The desirable height is 17 in. Which absolute value inequality represents the height of the handbag?

Ⓕ $|h - 16| \leq 1$ Ⓗ $|h - 17| \geq 2$

Ⓖ $|h - 17| \leq 1$ Ⓘ $|h - 18| \geq 2$

17. The graph shows the amount of paint needed (in gallons) to paint the walls (in square feet) of an office building.

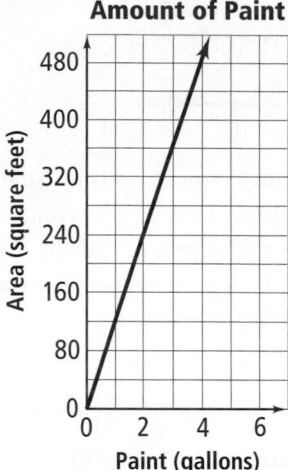

Amount of Paint

If the pattern continues, how many gallons of paint will be needed to paint 900 square feet?

18. What is the next term? 1, 4, 9, 16, . . .

19. What is the sum of the solutions of $|2x + 4| - 6 = 8$?

20. What is the value of $4x^2 + 2x - 1$ when $x = \frac{3}{4}$? Express the answer as a decimal.

Short Response

21. The cost for taking a taxi is $1.80 plus $.10 per eighth of a mile. Write an expression for the cost of a taxi ride that is n miles long. Evaluate your expression to find the cost of a ride that is 4.5 miles long. Show all work.

22. A new 10-lb dumbbell will pass inspection if it is between 9.95 lb and 10.05 lb. What is the tolerance of the weight of the dumbbell? What absolute value inequality describes acceptable weights of the dumbbell within an indicated tolerance? Show all work.

23. Without calculating $\sqrt{56}$, compare $\sqrt{56}$ and 7. Explain your answer.

Get Ready!

Lesson 1-3 ◆ Simplifying Expressions

Simplify by combining like terms.

1. $7s - s$ **2.** $3a + b + a$ **3.** $xy - y + x$

4. $0.5g + g$ **5.** $4t - (t + 3t)$ **6.** $b - 2(1 + c - b)$

7. $5f - (5d - f)$ **8.** $2(h + 2g) - (g - h)$ **9.** $-(3z - 5) + z$

10. $(2 - d)g - 3d(4 + g)$ **11.** $5v - 3(2 - v)$ **12.** $7t - 3s(2 + t) + s$

Lesson 1-4 ◆ Solving Equations

Solve each equation.

13. $4 + x = -52$ **14.** $-y + 13 = -67$ **15.** $12 = 2 - k$

16. $3x = -72$ **17.** $\frac{h}{5} = 215$ **18.** $64 = 4 + 12g$

19. $5 - 4t = 12$ **20.** $7x - 9 = x$ **21.** $3(w - 8) = 36$

22. $-10p = 2(p - 12)$ **23.** $3(2 - c) = -(c + 4)$ **24.** $7 + b = 11(b - 3)$

Lesson 1-6 ◆ Solving Absolute Value Inequalities

Solve each absolute value inequality. Graph the solution.

25. $|x - 3| < 5$ **26.** $|2a - 1| \geq 2a + 1$ **27.** $|3x + 4| > -4x - 3$

28. $|3x + 1| + 1 > 12$ **29.** $3|d - 4| \leq 13 - d$ **30.** $-\frac{1}{3}|f + 3| + 2 \geq -5$

Looking Ahead Vocabulary

31. A person's field of study is often called that person's *domain*. If your domain is American history, what topics might you be interested in?

32. When is a person's height likely to show a greater *rate of change*, from 1 to 2 years of age or from 30 to 31 years of age? Explain.

33. When you look in the mirror, you see your *reflection*. How does the image in the mirror differ from the way other people see you? How is it the same?

34. The boundaries of a country determine the limit of the country's land. How does an inequality form a *boundary* on a number line?

Functions, Equations, and Graphs

PowerAlgebra.com

Your place to get all things digital

Download videos connecting math to your world.

Math definitions in English and Spanish

The online Solve It will get you in gear for each lesson.

Interactive! Vary numbers, graphs, and figures to explore math concepts.

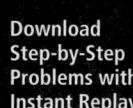
Download Step-by-Step Problems with Instant Replay.

Get and view your assignments online.

Extra practice and review online

You can use functions to model all kinds of real-world situations. A function can model something as simple as a line between two points or as complex as the curves of a roller coaster. You will learn how to work with functions in this chapter.

Vocabulary for Part A

English/Spanish Vocabulary Audio Online:

English	Spanish
direct variation, p. 74	variación directa
domain, p. 65	dominio
function, p. 66	función
linear equation, p. 82	ecuación lineal
range, p. 65	rango
relation, p. 64	relación
slope, p. 81	pendiente

My Math Video

00:04:04

VIDEO ▷

BIG ideas

1 Equivalence
Essential Question Does it matter which form of a linear equation you use?

2 Function
Essential Question How do you use transformations to help graph absolute value functions?

3. Modeling
Essential Question How can you model data with a linear function?

Chapter Preview for Part A

2-1   PART 1 **Relations and Functions**
       PART 2 **Relations and Functions**
2-2   **Direct Variation**
2-3   **Linear Functions and Slope-Intercept Form**
2-4   PART 1 **More About Linear Equations**
       PART 2 **More About Linear Equations**

2-1
PART 1

Relations and Functions

Objectives To graph relations
To identify functions

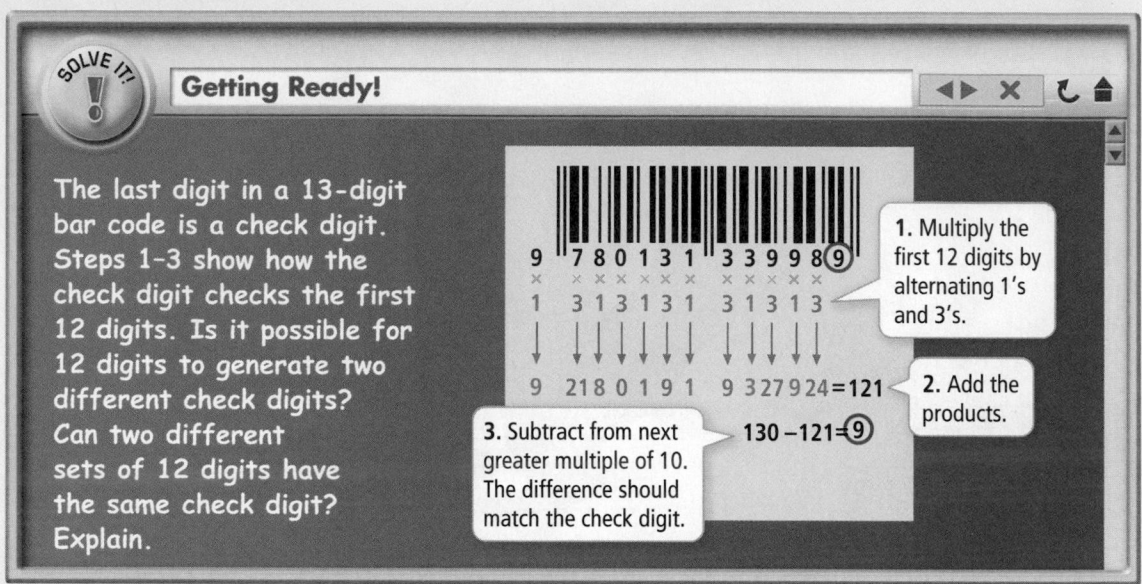

Dynamic Activity
Function Explorer

Lesson Vocabulary
• relation
• domain
• range
• function
• vertical-line test

You can use mappings to describe relationships between sets of numbers.

Focus Question What are relations and when is a relation a function?

A **relation** is a set of pairs of input and output values. You can represent a relation in four different ways as shown below.

take note

Key Concept Four Ways to Represent Relations

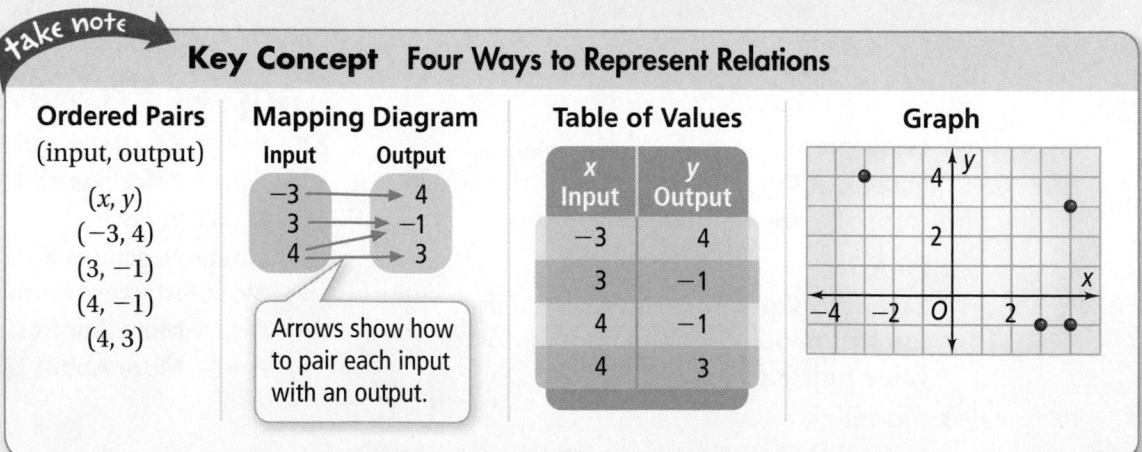

Ordered Pairs
(input, output)

(x, y)
$(-3, 4)$
$(3, -1)$
$(4, -1)$
$(4, 3)$

Mapping Diagram

Input   Output
−3 → 4
3 → −1
4 → 3

Arrows show how to pair each input with an output.

Table of Values

x Input	y Output
−3	4
3	−1
4	−1
4	3

Graph

Problem 1   Representing a Relation

Skydiving When skydivers jump out of an airplane, they experience free fall. The photos show various heights of a skydiver at different times during free fall, ignoring air resistance. How can you represent this relation in four different ways?

(0 seconds, 10,000 ft)

(8 seconds, 8976 feet)

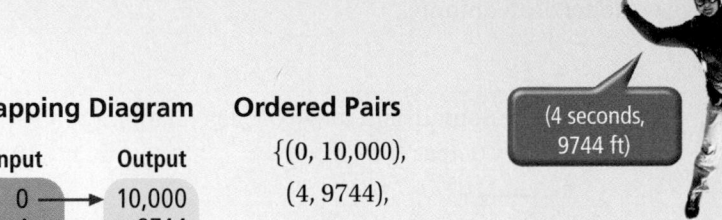

(4 seconds, 9744 ft)

(12 seconds, 7696 feet)

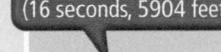

(16 seconds, 5904 feet)

Think

What is the input? The output?
The input is the time. The output is the height above the ground.

Mapping Diagram

Input		Output
0	→	10,000
4	→	9744
8	→	8976
12	→	7696
16	→	5904

Ordered Pairs

{(0, 10,000),
(4, 9744),
(8, 8976),
(12, 7696),
(16, 5904)}

Table of Values

Time (s)	Height (ft)
0	10,000
4	9744
8	8976
12	7696
16	5904

Each time value represents an input, which is paired with its corresponding output value (height).

Graph

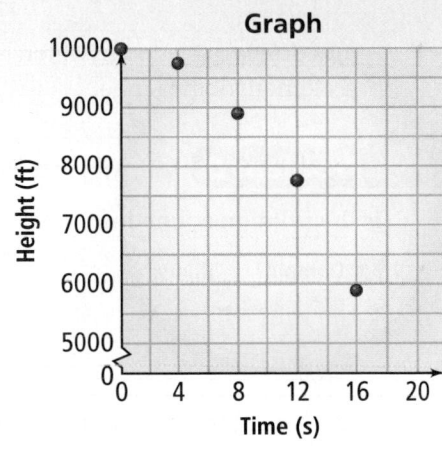

Hint

Use 1 to represent the month of January, 2 to represent February, and so on.

 Got It? **1.** The monthly average water temperature of the Gulf of Mexico in Key West, Florida varies during the year. In January, the average water temperature is 69°F, in February, 70°F, in March, 75°F, and in April, 78°F. How can you represent this relation in four different ways?

The **domain** of a relation is the set of inputs, also called *x*-coordinates, of the ordered pairs. The **range** is the set of outputs, also called *y*-coordinates, of the ordered pairs.

How can you use a
mapping diagram to
find the domain and
range?
The *input* corresponds
to the domain of the
relation. The *output*
corresponds to the range.

Problem 2 Finding Domain and Range

What are the domain and range of each relation?

A Input   Output

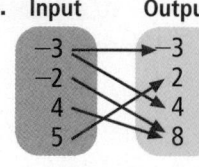

The domain is the set of all inputs.
$\{-5, -1, 3, 4\}$

The range is the set of all outputs.
$\{0, 2, 6, 7\}$

B $\{(0, 1), (1, 2), (3, 5), (4, 8), (6, 9)\}$

The domain is the set of x-coordinates.
$\{0, 1, 3, 4, 6\}$

The range is the set of y-coordinates.
$\{1, 2, 5, 8, 9\}$

✓ **Got It? 2.** What are the domain and range of each relation?

a. Input   Output

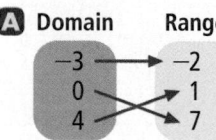

b. $\{(-3, 12), (0, 9), (2, 7), (4, 3), (9, -2)\}$

A **function** is a relation in which each element of the domain corresponds to exactly
one element of the range.

How can you use a
mapping diagram to
determine whether a
relation is a function?
A function has only one
arrow from each element
of the domain.

Problem 3 Identifying Functions

Is the relation a function?

A Domain   Range

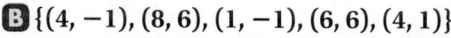

Each element in the domain corresponds
to exactly one element in the range. This
relation is a function.

B $\{(4, -1), (8, 6), (1, -1), (6, 6), (4, 1)\}$

Each x-coordinate must correspond to
only one y-coordinate. The x-coordinate
4 corresponds to -1 and 1. The relation is
not a function.

 Got It? 3. Is the relation a function?

a. Domain   Range

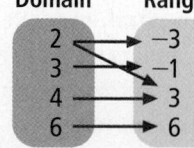

b. $\{(-7, 14), (9, -7), (14, 7), (7, 14)\}$

c. Reasoning How does a mapping diagram of a relation that is not a function
differ from a mapping diagram of a function?

You can use the *vertical-line test* to determine whether a relation is a function. The **vertical-line test** states that if any vertical line passes through more than one point on the graph of a relation, then the relation is *not* a function.

Here's Why It Works If a vertical line passes through a graph at more than one point, there is more than one value in the range that corresponds to a value in the domain. For example, the graph shows that there are two output values, y_1 and y_2, that both correspond to input value x. This relation is not a function.

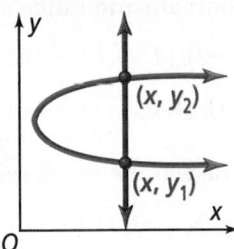

 Problem 4 Using the Vertical-Line Test

Use the vertical-line test. Which graph(s) represents a function?

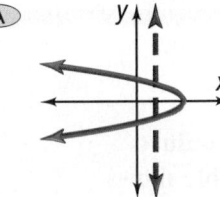 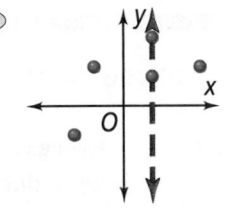

Think

Is a relation a function if it passes through the y-axis twice?

No; the y-axis is a vertical line so the relation fails the vertical-line test.

For Graphs A and C, a vertical line passes through more than one point. These graphs fail the vertical-line test and do not represent functions. Graph B passes the vertical-line test, so it represents a function.

Got It? **4.** Use the vertical-line test. Which graph(s) represents a function?

a. 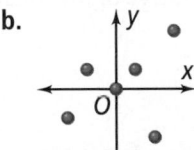 b. c.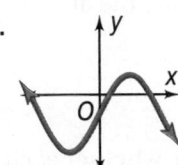

Hint

Use the edge of a sheet of paper to simulate a vertical line and move it across each graph.

Focus Question What are relations and when is a relation a function?

Answer A relation is a set of pairs of input and output values. A function is a relation in which each input corresponds with exactly one output.

Lesson Check

Do you know HOW?

List the domain and range of each relation.

1. $\{(3, -2), (4, 4), (0, -2), (4, 1), (3, 2)\}$

2. $\{(0, 4), (4, 0), (-3, -4), (-4, -3)\}$

Determine whether each relation is a function.

3. $\{(3, -8), (-9, 1), (3, 2), (-4, 1), (-11, -2)\}$

4. $\{(1, 1), (2, 0), (3, 1), (4, 3), (0, 2)\}$

Do you UNDERSTAND?

5. **Vocabulary** Can you have a relation that is not a function? Can you have a function that is not a relation? Explain.

6. **Error Analysis** Your friend writes, "In a function, every vertical line must intersect the graph in exactly one point." Explain your friend's error and rewrite the statement so that it is correct.

7. **Reasoning** Why is there no horizontal-line test for functions?

Practice and Problem-Solving Exercises

A Practice   Every year, the Rock and Roll Hall of Fame and Museum inducts legendary musicians and musical acts to the Hall. The table shows the number of inductees from 2001 to 2006.

◀ See Problems 1 and 2.

8. Represent the data using each of the following:
   a. a mapping diagram
   b. ordered pairs
   c. a graph on the coordinate plane

9. What are the domain and range of this relation?

Rock and Roll Hall of Fame Inductees

Year	Number of Inductees	Year	Number of Inductees
2001	11	2004	8
2002	8	2005	7
2003	9	2006	6

SOURCE: Rock and Roll Hall of Fame

Determine whether each relation is a function.

◀ See Problem 3.

Guided Practice

To start, identify any elements in the domain that correspond to more than one element in the range.

10.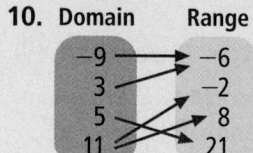

11 corresponds to -2 and 8.

11.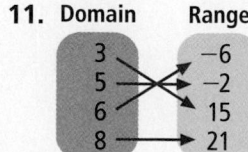

12.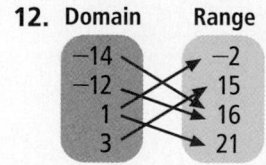

Determine whether each relation is a function.

13. $\{(3, -9), (11, 21), (121, 34), (34, 1), (23, 45)\}$

14. $\{(1, -7), (2, 10), (5, 15), (3, -4), (1, -3)\}$

15. $\{(-2, 1), (-1, -1), (0, 1), (1, -1), (2, 1)\}$

Use the vertical-line test to determine whether each graph represents a function.

See Problem 4.

16.

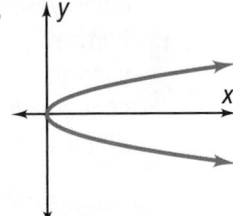

17.

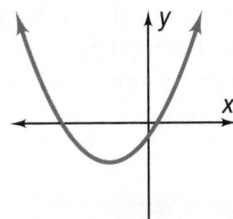

18.

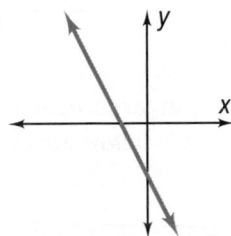

19.

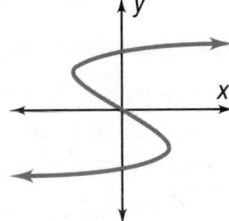

B Apply

Find the domain and range of each relation, and determine whether it is a function.

20.

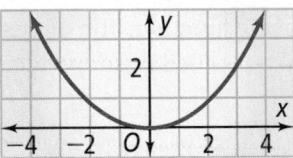

21.

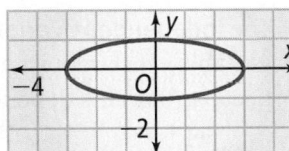

22.

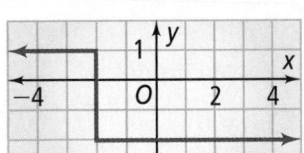

23.

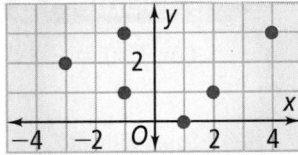

Relations and Functions

Objective To write and evaluate functions

In Part 1 of the lesson, you learned four ways to represent a function.

Connect to What You Know

Here you will learn a fifth way called function notation. You will also evaluate a function for different values.

Lesson Vocabulary
- function rule
- function notation
- independent variable
- dependent variable

Focus Question Why are function rules useful?

A **function rule** is an equation that represents an output value in terms of an input value. You can write a function rule in **function notation**. Shown below are examples of function rules.

$$y = 3x + 2 \qquad f(x) = 3x + 2 \qquad f(1) = 3(1) + 2$$

| Output | Input |

Read as "f of x" or "function f of x."

"f of 1" is the output when 1 is the input.

The **independent variable**, x, represents the input of the function. The **dependent variable**, $f(x)$, represents the output of the function. It is called the dependent variable because its value depends on the input value.

Problem 5 Using Function Notation

For $f(x) = -2x + 5$, what is the output for the given input?

Plan

How do you find the output?
Substitute the input into the function rule and simplify.

Ⓐ $x = -3$ Ⓑ $x = 0$ Ⓒ $x = \frac{1}{4}$

Substitute into the function rule.

$$f(-3) = -2(-3) + 5 \qquad f(0) = -2(0) + 5 \qquad f\left(\tfrac{1}{4}\right) = -2\left(\tfrac{1}{4}\right) + 5$$

Multiply.

$$= 6 + 5 \qquad\qquad = 0 + 5 \qquad\qquad = -\tfrac{1}{2} + 5$$

Add.

$$= 11 \qquad\qquad\quad = 5 \qquad\qquad = 4\tfrac{1}{2}$$

 Got It? 5. For $f(x) = \frac{3x - 4}{2}$, what is the output for the given input?

a. $x = 2$ **b.** $x = 1.5$ **c.** $x = -4$

To model a real-world situation using a function rule, you need to identify the dependent and independent quantities. One way to describe the dependence of a variable quantity is to use a phrase such as, "distance is a function of time." This means that distance *depends* on time.

 Problem 6 Writing and Evaluating a Function

Ticket Price Tickets to a concert are available online for $35 each plus a handling fee of $2.50. The total cost is a function of the number of tickets bought. What function rule models the cost of the concert tickets? Evaluate the function for 4 tickets.

Think

Why is *cost* the dependent quantity?
The cost depends on the number of tickets bought.

Cost is the dependent quantity and the number of tickets is the independent quantity.

Relate | Total cost | is | cost per ticket | times | number of tickets bought | plus | handling fee

Define Let t = number of tickets bought.

Let $C(t)$ = the total cost.

Write | $C(t)$ | = | 35 | · | t | + | 2.50

Write the equation. $C(t) = 35 \cdot t + 2.50$

Substitute 4 for t. $C(4) = 35 \cdot 4 + 2.50$

Simplify. $= 142.50$

The cost of 4 tickets is $142.50.

 Got It? 6. You are buying bottles of a sports drink for your softball team. Each bottle costs $1.19. What function rule models the total cost of your purchase? Evaluate the function for 15 bottles.

Focus Question Why are function rules useful?
Answer Use a function rule to find the output when given the input.

 Lesson Check

Do you know HOW?

For each function rule, identify the output for the given input.

1. $f(x) = 3x + 2$ for $x = 4$

2. $f(x) = x - 7$ for $x = 3$

3. $f(x) = 10x - 5$ for $x = 6$

4. $f(x) = 2x + 9$ for $x = 5$

Do you UNDERSTAND?

5. Vocabulary Which represents values for the dependent variable: the domain or the range?

6. Error Analysis Your teacher asked your class to find the output for $f(x) = 5x + 4$ when $x = 9$. One of your friends says the output is 1, and another friend says the output is 49. Who is correct? Explain.

Practice and Problem-Solving Exercises

A Practice

Evaluate each function for the given value of x, and write the input x and output $f(x)$ as an ordered pair.

● **See Problem 5.**

Guided Practice

To start, substitute the value of the variable.

7. $f(x) = -\frac{2x + 1}{3}$ for $x = -5$

$$f(-5) = -\frac{2(-5) + 1}{3}$$

8. $f(x) = 17x + 3$ for $x = 4$

9. $f(x) = 2x - 33$ for $x = 9$

10. $f(x) = -9x - 2$ for $x = 7$

11. $f(x) = \frac{7}{3}x - 9$ for $x = 3$

12. $f(x) = -\frac{12x}{5}$ for $x = -1$

13. $f(x) = \frac{2}{9}x - \frac{9}{2}$ for $x = 9$

Write a function rule to model the cost per month of a long-distance cell phone calling plan. Then evaluate the function for the given number of minutes.

● **See Problem 6.**

Guided Practice

To start, identify the variables.

14. Monthly service fee: $4.52
Rate: $.12 per minute
Minutes used: 250

Cost is the dependent quantity and minutes used is the independent quantity.

15. Monthly service fee: $3.12
Rate: $.18 per minute
Minutes used: 175

16. Monthly service fee: $5.15
Rate: $.10 per minute
Minutes used: 325

B Apply

17. Think About a Plan A cube is a solid figure with six square faces. If the edges of a cube have length 1.5 cm, what is the surface area of the cube?
 • What is the relationship between the length of the edges and the area of each face?
 • What is the relationship between the area of one face and the surface area of the whole cube?

18. Geometry Suppose you have a box with a 4-in. × 4-in. square base and variable height h. The surface area of this box is a function of its height. Write a function to represent the surface area. Evaluate the function for $h = 6.5$ in.

Suppose $f(x) = 2x + 5$ and $g(x) = -\frac{1}{3}x + 2$. Find each value.

19. $f(3)$

20. $g(0)$

21. $f(1)$

22. $f(-4)$

23. $g(-6)$

24. $g(7)$

25. Geometry The volume of a sphere is a function of its radius, $V = \frac{4}{3}\pi r^3$. Evaluate the function for the volume of a volleyball with radius 10.5 cm.

26. Temperature The relation between degrees Fahrenheit F and degrees Celsius C is described by the function $F = \frac{9}{5}C + 32$. In the following ordered pairs, the first element is degrees Celsius and the second element is its equivalent in degrees Fahrenheit. Find the unknown measure in each ordered pair.

    a. $(43, m)$ **b.** $(-12, n)$ **c.** $(p, 12)$ **d.** $(q, 19)$

27. Reasoning Suppose a function pairs items from set A with items from set B. You can say that the function maps *into* set B. If the function uses every item from set B, the function maps *onto* set B. Does each function below map the set of whole numbers *into* or *onto* the set of whole numbers?

    a. Function f doubles every number.
    b. Function g maps every number to 1 more than that number.
    c. Function h maps every number to itself.
    d. Function j maps every number to its square.

Standardized Test Prep

SAT/ACT

28. If $f(x) = -3x + 7$ and $g(x) = -7x + 3$, what is the value of $f(-3) - g(3)$?

    Ⓐ 40   Ⓑ 34   Ⓒ 8   Ⓓ −8

29. What is the formula for the volume of a cylinder, $V = \pi r^2 h$, solved for h?

    Ⓕ $h = \frac{r^2}{\pi V}$ Ⓖ $h = \frac{\pi V}{r^2}$ Ⓗ $h = \frac{V}{\pi r^2}$ Ⓘ $h = \frac{\pi r^2}{V}$

30. Which of the following statements are true?

    I. $-(-6) = 6$ and $-(-4) > -4$ III. $5 + 6 = 11$ or $9 - 2 = 11$
    II. $-(-4) < 4$ or $-10 > 10 - 10$ IV. $17 > 2$ or $6 < 9$

    Ⓐ I and II only   Ⓒ I, III, and IV only
    Ⓑ I, II, and III only   Ⓓ III and IV only

Short Response

31. What are the numbers 1.9, $\frac{5}{4}$, −1.2, and $\sqrt{3}$ in order from greatest to least?

Mixed Review

Solve each equation or inequality.   ◀ **See Lessons 1-4 through 1-6.**

32. $|3x + 9| = 11$ **33.** $19 + |x - 1| = 33$ **34.** $2 - 3x < 11$

35. $5x - 3 \leq 12 - 5x$ **36.** $|2x| + 4 < 7$ **37.** $4x + 6 \geq -6$

Get Ready!   **To prepare for Lesson 2-2, do Exercises 38–40.**

Solve each equation for y.   ◀ **See Lesson 1-4.**

38. $12y = 3x$ **39.** $-10y = 5x$ **40.** $\frac{3}{4}y = 15x$

Direct Variation

Objective To write and interpret direct variation equations

Getting Ready!

You are building a roof. You mark off four equal intervals from point *A* to point *B* and you place vertical posts as shown in the diagram. What are the heights at the four vertical posts? Explain.

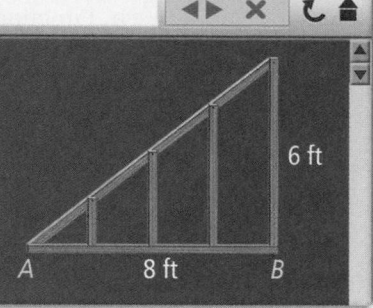

These triangles look similar to me!

The post heights in the Solve It satisfy a relationship called *direct variation*.

Lesson Vocabulary
• direct variation
• constant of variation

Focus Question When do you use direct variation?

You can write a formula for a **direct variation** function as $y = kx$, or $\frac{y}{x} = k$, where $k \neq 0$. x represents input values, and y represents output values. The formula $\frac{y}{x} = k$ says that, except for $(0, 0)$, the ratio of all output-input pairs equals the constant k, the **constant of variation**.

Problem 1 Identifying Direct Variation From Tables

For each function, determine whether y varies directly with x. If so, what is the constant of variation and the function rule?

A

x	y
1	2
3	6
4	8

B

x	y
1	4
2	8
3	11

How do you find the constant of variation?
The constant of variation is the ratio of any y-value to the corresponding x-value.

$\frac{y}{x} = \frac{2}{1} = \frac{6}{3} = \frac{8}{4} = 2,$

so y varies directly with x.

The constant of variation is 2.
The function rule is $y = 2x$.

$\frac{y}{x} = \frac{4}{1} = \frac{8}{2} \neq \frac{11}{3},$

so $\frac{y}{x}$ is *not* constant.

y does *not* vary directly with x.

Got It? **1.** For each function, determine whether y varies directly with x. If so, what is the constant of variation and the function rule?

a.

x	y
3	−21
2	−14
1	−7

b.

x	y
2	5
3	7
6	13

 Problem 2 **Identifying Direct Variation From Equations**

For each function, determine whether y varies directly with x. If so, what is the constant of variation?

A $3y = 7x$

Write the original equation. $3y = 7x$

Divide by 3 to isolate y. $\dfrac{3y}{3} = \dfrac{7x}{3}$

Simplify. $y = \dfrac{7}{3}x$

Since $y = \dfrac{7}{3}x$ is in the form $y = kx$, where $k \neq 0$, y varies directly with x.
The constant of variation is $\dfrac{7}{3}$.

Think

How is the form of this function different from the function in part A?
This function includes a nonzero constant term.

B $7y = 14x + 7$

Write the original equation. $7y = 14x + 7$

Divide by 7 to isolate y. $\dfrac{7y}{7} = \dfrac{14x + 7}{7}$

Simplify. $y = 2x + 1$

Since you cannot write the equation in the form $y = kx$, y does not vary directly with x.

 Got It? **2.** For each function, determine whether y varies directly with x. If so, what is the constant of variation?
a. $5x + 3y = 0$ **b.** $y = \dfrac{x}{9}$

In a direct variation, $\dfrac{y}{x}$ is the same for all pairs of data where $x \neq 0$.
So, $\dfrac{y_1}{x_1} = \dfrac{y_2}{x_2}$ is true for the ordered pairs (x_1, y_1) and (x_2, y_2),
where neither x_1 nor x_2 is zero.

Problem 3 Using a Proportion to Solve a Direct Variation

Suppose y varies directly with x, and $y = 9$ when $x = -15$. What is y when $x = 21$?

Know	Need	Plan
y varies directly with x. $\frac{y}{x}$ is constant.	The value of y when x is 21.	Use two forms of $\frac{y}{x}$ in a proportion.

Hint

In a proportion, the cross products are equal. So, if $\frac{a}{b} = \frac{c}{d}$, then $ad = bc$.

In a direct variation, $\frac{y}{x}$ is constant. Write a proportion. $\qquad \frac{9}{-15} = \frac{y}{21}$

Write the cross products. $\qquad 9(21) = -15(y)$

Divide each side by -15. $\qquad \dfrac{9(21)}{-15} = \dfrac{-15y}{-15}$

Simplify. $\qquad -12.6 = y$

So y is -12.6 when x is 21.

 Got It? 3. Suppose y varies directly with x, and $y = 15$ when $x = 3$. What is y when $x = 12$?

You can use the direct variation function $y = kx$ to model some situations.

 Problem 4 Using Direct Variation to Solve a Problem

A salesperson's commission varies directly with sales. For $1000 in sales, the commission is $85. What is the commission for $2300 in sales?

Think

Could you use the method in Problem 3 to solve this problem?
Yes; you could solve this problem by using the proportion $\frac{c_1}{s_1} = \frac{c_2}{s_2}$.

Step 1 Use $y = kx$ to find k.

Let $c =$ commission.

Let $s =$ sales.

$c = k \cdot s$ ← Commission varies directly with sales, so it is the dependent variable.

$85 = k \cdot 1000$

$0.085 = k$

Step 2 Write the direct variation. Find the commission when total sales is $2300.

Write the direct variation equation.	$c = ks$
Write the direct variation using the value found for k.	$c = 0.085s$
Substitute 2300 for s.	$c = 0.085 \cdot 2300$
Simplify.	$c = 195.5$

The commission for $2300 in sales is $195.50.

 Got It? 4. a. The number of Calories varies directly with the mass of cheese. If 50 grams of cheese contain 200 Calories, how many Calories are in 70 grams of cheese?

b. Reasoning If y^2 varies directly with x^2, does that mean y must vary directly with x? Explain.

The graph of a direct variation function is always a line through the origin.

 Problem 5 Graphing Direct Variation Equations

What is the graph of each direct variation equation?

Think

What x-values should you use to make a table of values?
The constant of variation is a fraction. Use multiples of the denominator for x. This ensures integer values for y.

Ⓐ $y = \frac{3}{4}x$

Make a table of x- and y-values. Graph the ordered pairs, and connect the points to show the line.

x	y
4	3
8	6
12	9

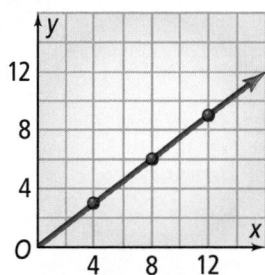

Ⓑ $y = -2x$

Make a table of x- and y-values. Graph the ordered pairs, and connect the points to show the line.

x	y
−2	4
−1	2
1	−2

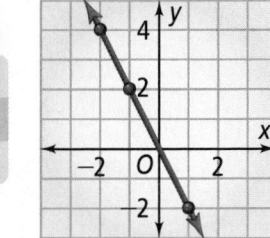

 Got It? **5.** What is the graph of each direct variation equation?

a. $y = -\frac{2}{3}x$ **b.** $y = 3x$

Focus Question When do you use direct variation?

Answer Direct variation relates quantities where the ratio of corresponding values is constant. Write a direct variation function when the ratio of each output to the corresponding input is a constant.

 Lesson Check

Do you know HOW?

1. Write a function rule for the direct variation in the table.

Identify the constant of variation.

2. $y = \frac{3}{2}x$

3. $4y - 5x = 0$

x	y
2	−1
4	−2
6	−3

Do you UNDERSTAND?

4. Vocabulary Explain what it means for two variables to be directly related.

5. Reasoning Explain why the graph of a direct variation function always passes through the origin.

6. Give an example of a function that represents a direct variation.

Practice and Problem-Solving Exercises

A Practice

For each function, determine whether y varies directly with x. If so, find the constant of variation and write the function rule.

See Problem 1.

7.

x	y
11	22
16	32
7	42

Guided Practice

To start, write the ratios of output to input.

$\frac{22}{11}, \frac{32}{16}, \frac{42}{7}$

8.

x	y
2	14
3	21
5	35

9.

x	y
27	9
30	10
60	20

10.

x	y
3	9
4	10
5	11

Determine whether y varies directly with x. If so, find the constant of variation.

See Problem 2.

11. $y = 12x$
12. $y = -2x$
13. $y = 4x + 1$
14. $y = 4x - 3$
15. $y - 6x = 0$
16. $y + 3 = -3x$

For Exercises 17–21, y varies directly with x.

See Problem 3.

Guided Practice

17. If $y = 4$ when $x = -2$, find x when $y = 6$.

To start, write a proportion.

$\frac{4}{-2} = \frac{6}{x}$

18. If $y = 6$ when $x = 2$, find x when $y = 12$.
19. If $y = 7$ when $x = 2$, find x when $y = 3$.
20. If $y = 5$ when $x = -3$, find x when $y = -1$.
21. If $y = -7$ when $x = -3$, find y when $x = 9$.

22. Distance For a given speed, the distance traveled varies directly with the time. Kate's school is 5 miles away from her home and it takes her 10 minutes to reach the school. If Josh lives 2 miles from school and travels at the same speed as Kate, how long will it take him to reach the school?

See Problem 4.

23. Conservation A dripping faucet wastes one cup of water if it drips for three minutes. The amount of water wasted varies directly with the amount of time the faucet drips. How long will it take for the faucet to waste $4\frac{1}{2}$ cups of water?

Make a table of x- and y-values and use it to graph the direct variation equation.

◀ See Problem 5.

24. $x = \left(-\frac{1}{3}\right)y$ **25.** $y = -9x$ **26.** $x = y$

 **Apply**

Determine whether y varies directly with x. If so, find the constant of variation and write the function rule.

27.

x	y
1	−2
3	−8
5	14

28.

x	y
9	6
12	8
15	10

29.

x	y
4	1
6	2
8	3

30. Think About a Plan Suppose you make a 4-minute local call using a calling card and are charged 7.6 cents. The cost of a local call varies directly with the length of the call. How much more will it cost to make a 30-minute local call?
- Which quantity is the dependent quantity?
- How does the word *more* affect the method needed to solve the problem?

Write and graph a direct variation equation whose graph passes through each point.

31. $(1, 2)$ **32.** $(-3, -7)$ **33.** $(2, -9)$

34. $(-0.1, 50)$ **35.** $(-5, -3)$ **36.** $(-3, 14)$

For Exercises 37–40, y varies directly with x.

37. If $y = \frac{1}{2}$ when $x = 4$, find y when $x = 5$.   **38.** If $y = \frac{3}{4}$ when $x = \frac{1}{2}$, find y when $x = 3$.

39. If $y = \frac{5}{3}$ when $x = \frac{3}{4}$, find x when $y = \frac{1}{2}$.   **40.** If $y = -\frac{5}{8}$ when $x = \frac{3}{2}$, find x when $y = \frac{2}{5}$.

41. Reasoning Explain why you cannot answer the following question.

y varies directly with x. If $y = 0$ when $x = 0$, what is x when $y = 13$?

Open-Ended Choose a value of k within the given range. Then write and graph a direct variation function using your value for k.

42. $0 < k < 1$ **43.** $3 < k < 4.5$ **44.** $-1 < k < -\frac{1}{2}$

45. Error Analysis Identify the error in the statement shown at the right.

> If y varies directly with x², and y = 2 when x = 4, then y = 3 when x = 9.

46. Sports The number of rotations of a bicycle wheel varies directly with the number of pedal strokes. Suppose that in the bicycle's lowest gear, 6 pedal strokes move the cyclist about 357 in. In the same gear, how many pedal strokes are needed to move 100 ft?

47. Writing Suppose you use the origin to test whether a linear equation is a direct variation function. Does this method work? Support your answer with an example.

SAT/ACT

48. A speed of 75 mi/h is equal to a speed of 110 ft/s. To the nearest mile per hour, what is the speed of an aircraft traveling at a speed of 1600 ft/s?

49. What number is a solution to both $|x - 3| = 2$ and $|9 - x| = 8$?

50. If $f(x) = 7 - 3x$ and $g(x) = 3x - 7$, what is the value of $f(1) + g(1)$?

51. Look at the pattern. How many circles are in the 6th figure of this pattern?

52. What is the solution of $4(x - 5) + x = 8x - 10 - x$?

Mixed Review

Graph each relation. Find the domain and range. ◀ See Lesson 2-1.

53. $\{(0, 1), (1, -3), (-2, -3), (3, -3)\}$

54. $\{(4, 0), (7, 0), (4, -1), (7, -1)\}$

55. $\{(1, -2), (2, -1), (4, 1), (5, 2)\}$

56. $\{(1, 7), (2, 8), (3, 9), (4, 10)\}$

Identify a pattern and find the next three numbers in the pattern. ◀ See Lesson 1-1.

57. 8, 16, 24, 32, . . .

58. 5, 3, 1, −1, . . .

59. 144, 132, 120, 108, . . .

60. 30, 45, 60, 75, . . .

Get Ready! **To prepare for Lesson 2-3, do Exercises 61–63.**

Evaluate each expression for $x = -2, 0, 1,$ and 4. ◀ See Lesson 1-3.

61. $\frac{2}{3}x + 7$

62. $3x + 1$

63. $\frac{1}{2}x - 8$

2-3 Linear Functions and Slope-Intercept Form

Objectives To graph linear equations
To write equations of lines

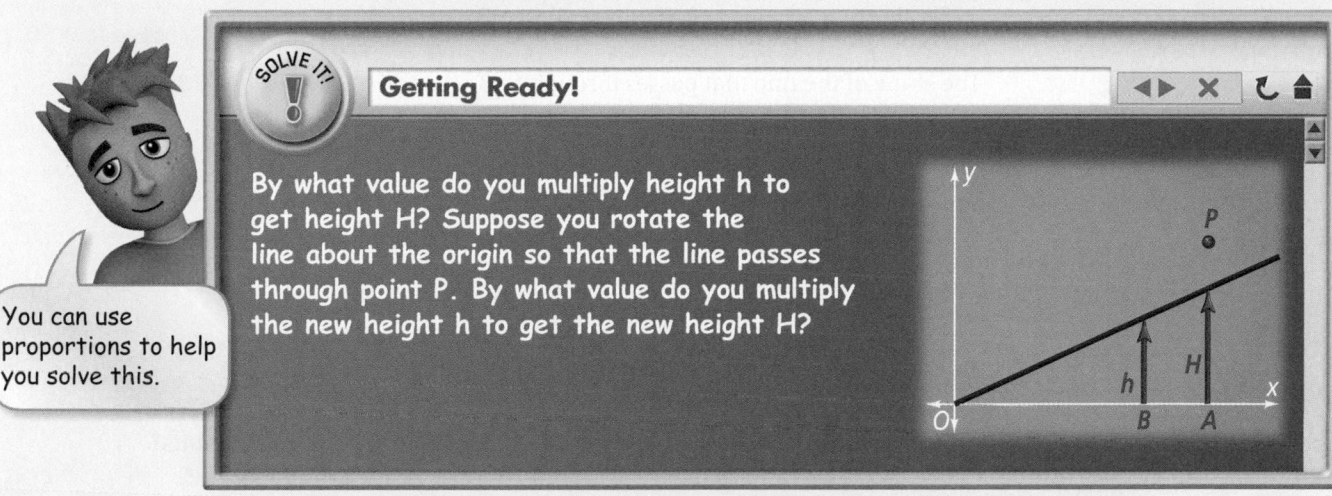

SOLVE IT!

Getting Ready!

By what value do you multiply height h to get height H? Suppose you rotate the line about the origin so that the line passes through point P. By what value do you multiply the new height h to get the new height H?

You can use proportions to help you solve this.

You can use proportions to help you solve this.

Lesson Vocabulary
- slope
- linear function
- linear equation
- *y*-intercept
- *x*-intercept
- slope-intercept form

You can describe movement in a coordinate plane by describing how far you need to move vertically and horizontally to get from one point to another point.

Focus Question What is slope-intercept form?

The **slope** of a nonvertical line is the ratio of the vertical change to the horizontal change between two points. You can calculate slope by finding the ratio of the difference in the *y*-coordinates to the difference in the *x*-coordinates for any two points on the line.

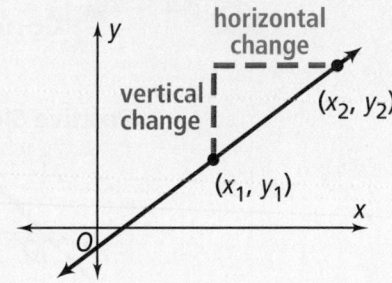

Hint

For any two points on a vertical line, $x_1 = x_2$. Using the slope formula results in division by zero, so the slope of a vertical line is undefined.

take note

Key Concept   Slope

The slope of a nonvertical line through points (x_1, y_1) and (x_2, y_2) is the ratio of the vertical change to the corresponding horizontal change.

$$\text{slope} = \frac{\text{vertical change (rise)}}{\text{horizontal change (run)}} = \frac{y_2 - y_1}{x_2 - x_1}, \text{ where } x_2 - x_1 \neq 0$$

 **Problem 1** Finding Slope

What is the slope of the line that passes through the given points?

A $(-3, 7)$ and $(-2, 4)$

Think

Does it matter which point you choose for (x_1, y_1)?

No; you can choose either point for (x_1, y_1).

Write the formula for slope. $\quad m = \dfrac{y_2 - y_1}{x_2 - x_1}$

Substitute values for (x_1, y_1) and (x_2, y_2). $\quad = \dfrac{4 - 7}{-2 - (-3)}$

Simplify. $\quad = \dfrac{-3}{1} = -3$

The slope of the line that passes through $(-3, 7)$ and $(-2, 4)$ is $\dfrac{-3}{1}$ or -3.

B $(3, 1)$ and $(-4, 1)$

Write the formula for slope. $\quad m = \dfrac{y_2 - y_1}{x_2 - x_1}$

Substitute values for (x_1, y_1) and (x_2, y_2). $\quad = \dfrac{1 - 1}{-4 - 3}$

Simplify. $\quad = \dfrac{0}{-7} = 0$

The slope of the line that passes through $(3, 1)$ and $(-4, 1)$ is $\dfrac{0}{-7}$ or 0.

Hint

Use your work for part (a) to answer part (c).

 Got It? **1.** What is the slope of the line that passes through the given points?

    a. $(5, 4)$ and $(8, 1)$ **b.** $(2, 2)$ and $(-2, -2)$

    c. Reasoning Use the slope formula to show in part (a) that it does not matter which point you choose for (x_1, y_1).

take note

Concept Summary   Slope of a Line

Positive Slope	**Negative Slope**	**Zero Slope**	**Undefined Slope**
	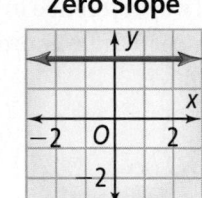	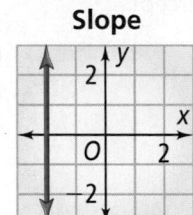	
Line rises from left to right	Line falls from left to right	Horizontal line	Vertical line

A function whose graph is a line is a **linear function**. You can represent a linear function with a **linear equation** in the form $ax + by = c$. An example of a linear equation is $y = 6x - 4$. A solution of a linear equation is any ordered pair (x, y) that makes the equation true.

A special form of a linear equation is called *slope-intercept form*.

An *intercept* of a nonvertical line is a point where a line crosses an axis. The **y-intercept** of a line is the point at which the line crosses the y-axis. The **x-intercept** of a nonhorizontal line is the point at which the line crosses the x-axis.

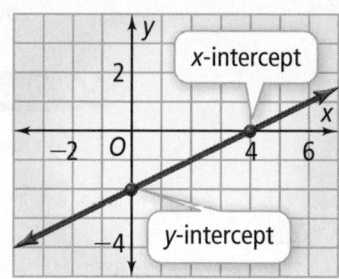

take note

Key Concept   Slope-Intercept Form

The **slope-intercept form** of an equation of a nonvertical line is $y = mx + b$, where m is the slope of the line and $(0, b)$ is the y-intercept.

Problem 2   Writing Linear Equations

What is an equation of each line?

A $m = \frac{1}{5}$ and the y-intercept is $(0, -3)$

Use the slope-intercept form. $y = mx + b$

Substitute $m = \frac{1}{5}$ and $b = -3$. $y = \frac{1}{5}x + (-3)$

Simplify. $y = \frac{1}{5}x - 3$

So, $y = \frac{1}{5}x - 3$.

B the line shown in the graph

The line crosses the y-axis at $(0, 4)$, so $b = 4$.

Use the second point $(1, 1)$ to find the slope.

Write the slope formula. $m = \frac{y_2 - y_1}{x_2 - x_1}$

Substitute. $= \frac{1 - 4}{1 - 0}$

Simplify. $= -3$

So, $y = -3x + 4$.

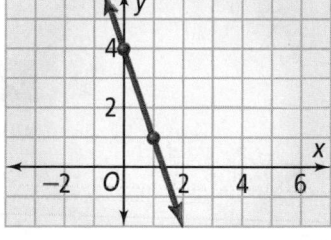

Got It? **2.** What is an equation of each line?

    a. $m = 6$, y-intercept is $(0, 5)$

    c. Reasoning Using the graph from part (b), do you get a different equation if you use $(-6, 0)$ and the y-intercept to find the slope of the line? Explain.

    b.

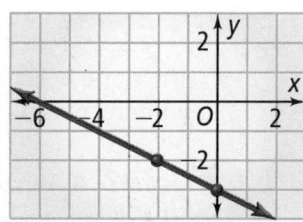

You can rewrite a linear equation in slope-intercept form by solving for y.

 Problem 3 **Writing Equations in Slope-Intercept Form**

Write each equation in slope-intercept form. What are the slope and y-intercept?

A $5x - 4y = 16$

Write the original equation.	$5x - 4y = 16$
Subtract $5x$ from each side.	$-4y = -5x + 16$
Divide each side by -4.	$\dfrac{-4y}{-4} = \dfrac{-5x}{-4} + \dfrac{16}{-4}$
Simplify. Solve for y.	$y = \dfrac{5}{4}x - 4$

The slope is $\frac{5}{4}$. The y-intercept is $(0, -4)$.

B $-\frac{3}{4}x + \frac{1}{2}y = -1$

Write the original equation.	$-\frac{3}{4}x + \frac{1}{2}y = -1$
Multiply each side by 4, the LCM of the denominators.	$-3x + 2y = -4$
Add $3x$ to each side.	$2y = 3x - 4$
Divide each side by 2.	$y = \frac{3}{2}x - 2$

The slope is $\frac{3}{2}$. The y-intercept is $(0, -2)$.

Think

Is there a way to avoid fractions in this problem?
Yes; clear the fractions by multiplying all terms by 4, the LCM of the denominators.

 Got It? **3.** Write the equation in slope-intercept form. What are the slope and y-intercept?

a. $3x + 2y = 18$ **b.** $\frac{1}{6}x + \frac{2}{3}y = 12$

 Problem 4 **Graphing a Linear Equation**

What is the graph of $-2x + y = 1$?

Know
• The equation of a line

Need
The coordinates of two points that satisfy the equation

Plan
• Write the equation in slope-intercept form.
• Plot the y-intercept.
• Use the slope to find a second point.
• Draw a line through the two points.

Write the equation in slope-intercept form.

$$-2x + y = 1$$
$$y = 2x + 1$$

The slope is 2, and the y-intercept is $(0, 1)$.

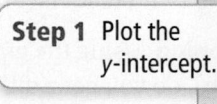

Step 1 Plot the y-intercept.

Step 2 Use the slope $\frac{2}{1}$. Go up 2 units and right 1 unit.

Step 3 Draw a line through the two points.

Hint

If the equation does not have a constant term, use b = 0.

 Got It? **4.** What is the graph of each equation?

a. $4x - 7y = 14$ **b.** $3x = 6y$

The graph shows points $(0, 1)$ and $(1, 3)$.

Focus Question What is slope-intercept form?

Answer Slope-intercept form is a special form of a linear function. Rewriting the equation of a line in slope-intercept form is useful for graphing the line.

Lesson Check

Do you know HOW?

Write each equation in slope-intercept form.

1. $x - 2y + 3 = 1$

2. $-4x + 3y = 1$

What is the slope of the line passing through each pair of points?

3. $(2, 4)$ and $(4, 2)$

4. $(-1, -3)$ and $(3, 1)$

Do you UNDERSTAND?

5. Vocabulary What is a y-intercept? How is a y-intercept different from an x-intercept?

6. Error Analysis A classmate found the slope between two points. What error did she make?

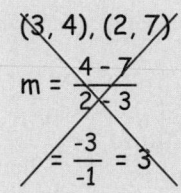

$(3, 4), (2, 7)$

$m = \dfrac{4 - 7}{2 - 3}$

$= \dfrac{-3}{-1} = 3$

Practice and Problem-Solving Exercises

 **Practice**

Find the slope of the line through each pair of points.

◀ **See Problem 1.**

Guided Practice

To start, substitute $(x_1, y_1) = (1, 6)$ and $(x_2, y_2) = (8, -1)$ into the slope formula.

7. $(1, 6)$ and $(8, -1)$

$m = \dfrac{y_2 - y_1}{x_2 - x_1} = \dfrac{(-1) - 6}{8 - 1}$

8. $(-3, 9)$ and $(0, 3)$　　　**9.** $(0, 0)$ and $(2, 6)$　　　**10.** $(-4, -3)$ and $(7, 1)$

11. $(1, 2)$ and $(2, 3)$　　　**12.** $(2, 7)$ and $(-3, 11)$　　　**13.** $(-3, 5)$ and $(4, 5)$

Write an equation for each line.

◀ **See Problem 2.**

14. $m = 3$ and the y-intercept is $(0, 2)$　　　**15.** $m = -5$ and the y-intercept is $(0, -7)$

16.
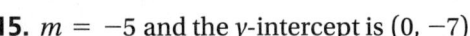
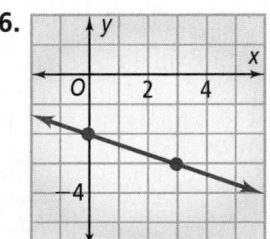

17.
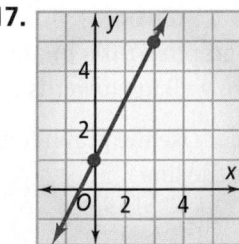

Write each equation in slope-intercept form. Then find the slope and y-intercept of each line.

◀ See Problem 3.

Guided Practice

18. $5x + y = 4$

To start, solve the equation for *y*.
Subtract 5*x* from each side.

$5x + y - 5x = 4 - 5x$

19. $-\frac{1}{2}x - y = \frac{3}{4}$ **20.** $9x - 2y = 10$ **21.** $y = 7$

Graph each equation.

◀ See Problem 4.

22. $y = 2x$ **23.** $y = -3x - 1$ **24.** $y = -4x + 5$

25. $-2x + 5y = -10$ **26.** $y + 4 = -3x$ **27.** $-y + 5 = -2x$

Ⓑ Apply

28. Think About a Plan Suppose the equation $y = 12 + 10x$ models the amount of money in your wallet, where *y* is the total in dollars and *x* is the number of weeks from today. If you graphed this equation, what would the slope represent in the situation? Explain.
   • Is the equation in slope-intercept form?
   • What units make sense for the slope?

Graph each equation.

29. $y = -\frac{1}{2}x - \frac{3}{2}$ **30.** $3y - 2x = -12$ **31.** $\frac{2}{3}x + \frac{y}{3} = -\frac{1}{3}$

32. $4x - 3y = -6$ **33.** $x = 5$ **34.** $2.4 = -3.6x - 0.4y$

Find the slope and y-intercept of each line.

35.
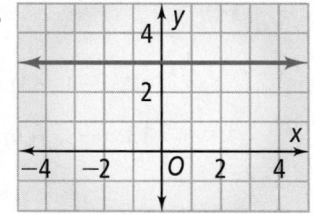

36.
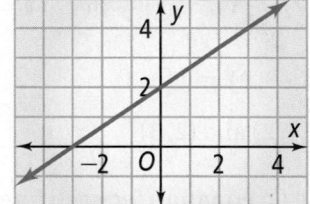

37. The equation $d = 4 - \frac{1}{15}t$ represents your distance from home *d* for each minute you walk *t*.
   a. If you graphed this equation, what would the slope represent? Explain.
   b. Are you walking towards or away from your home? Explain.

38. Reasoning Use the graph to find the slope between the following points on the line.
   a. *P* and *Q*   **b.** *Q* and *S*
   c. *S* and *P*   **d.** *R* and *Q*
   e. Make a conjecture based on your answers to parts (a)–(d).

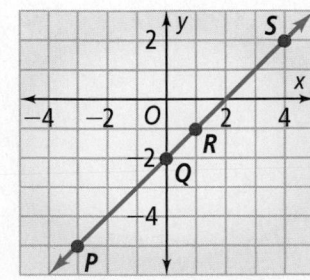

39. Error Analysis A classmate says that the graph of $3y - 2x = 5$ has a slope of 2. What mistake did he make?

Find the slope of the line through each pair of points.

40. $\left(\frac{3}{2}, -\frac{1}{2}\right)$ and $\left(-\frac{2}{3}, \frac{1}{3}\right)$ **41.** $\left(-\frac{1}{2}, -\frac{1}{2}\right)$ and $(-3, -4)$ **42.** $\left(0, -\frac{1}{2}\right)$ and $\left(\frac{7}{5}, 10\right)$

Find the slope and *y*-intercept of each line.

43. $y = 0.4 - 0.8x$ **44.** $x = -3$ **45.** $y = 0$

46. $-\frac{1}{3}x - \frac{2}{3}y = \frac{5}{3}$ **47.** $-Ax + By = -C$ **48.** $\frac{A}{D}x + \frac{B}{D}y = \frac{C}{D}$

Standardized Test Prep

SAT/ACT

49. Which equation does NOT represent a direct variation?

   Ⓐ $y - 3x = 0$ Ⓒ $\frac{y}{x} = \frac{2}{3}$

   Ⓑ $y + 2 = \frac{1}{2}x$ Ⓓ $y = \frac{x}{17}$

50. Which equation models the data in the table?

   Ⓕ $y = x^2 - 1$ Ⓗ $y = -x^2 + 3$

   Ⓖ $y = x^2 + 3$ Ⓘ $y = x^2 + 1$

x	y
1	4
2	7
3	12
4	19

51. For the formula $V = \frac{1}{3}\pi r^2 h$, which expression is equal to h?

   Ⓐ $\frac{V}{3\pi r^2}$ Ⓒ $\frac{3V}{\pi r^2}$

   Ⓑ $V - \frac{1}{3}\pi r^2$ Ⓓ $\frac{3V\pi}{r^2}$

Short Response

52. Graph the relation $\{(-2, 1), (0, 2), (-1, -1), (-2, -2)\}$. What are the domain and range?

Mixed Review

Find the domain and range of each relation, and determine whether the relation is a function.

 See Lesson 2-1.

53. 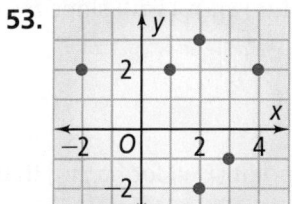   **54.** 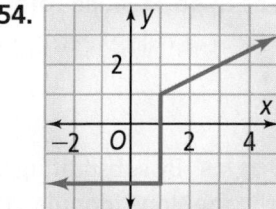   **55.**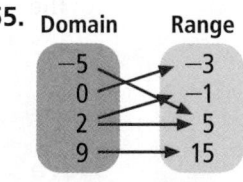

Get Ready!   **To prepare for Lesson 2-4, do Exercises 56–58.**

Evaluate each expression for $x = 0$.

◀ See Lesson 1-3.

56. $5x + 2$ **57.** $(x - 4) + 12$ **58.** $13 - 6.5x$

2-4
PART 1

More About Linear Equations

Objective To write equations of lines

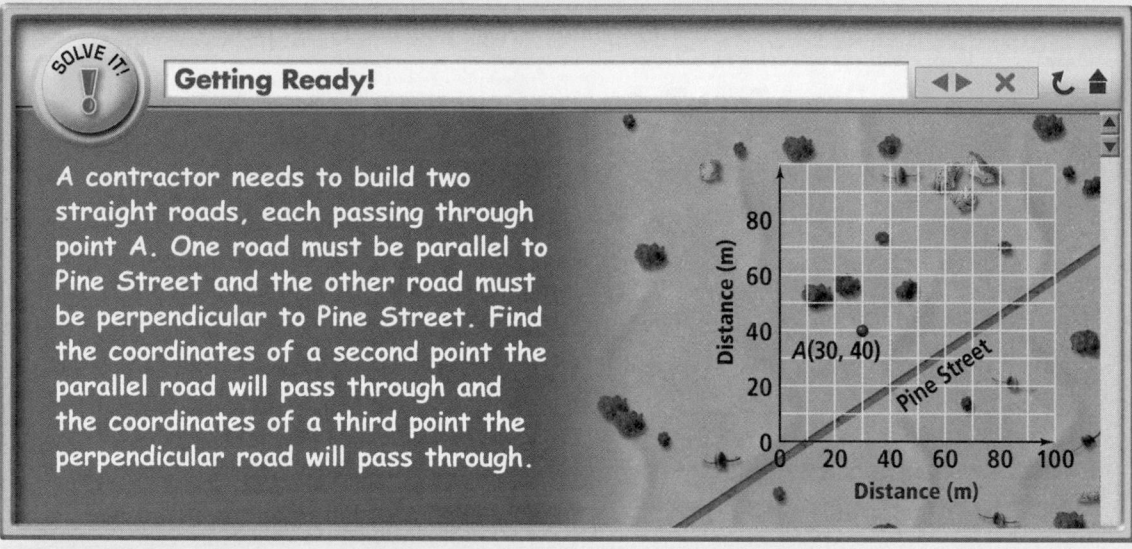

SOLVE IT!

Getting Ready!

A contractor needs to build two straight roads, each passing through point A. One road must be parallel to Pine Street and the other road must be perpendicular to Pine Street. Find the coordinates of a second point the parallel road will pass through and the coordinates of a third point the perpendicular road will pass through.

Lesson Vocabulary
- point-slope form
- standard form of a linear equation

If you travel along a line that is parallel to a given line, you will stay the same distance from the given line. If you travel along a line that is perpendicular to a given line, you will travel either toward or away from the given line along the most direct path.

Focus Question Why are there different forms for the equation of a line?

Given the slope and y-intercept, you can write the equation of a line in slope-intercept form. You can also write the equation of a line in *point-slope form*.

take note

Key Concept Point-Slope Form

The equation of a line in **point-slope form** through point (x_1, y_1) with slope m:
$$y - y_1 = m(x - x_1)$$

Here's Why It Works By substituting the general point (x, y) for (x_2, y_2) in the slope formula, you can rewrite the slope formula in point-slope form.

$$m = \frac{y_2 - y_1}{x_2 - x_1} = \frac{y - y_1}{x - x_1}$$

$$m(x - x_1) = \frac{y - y_1}{x - x_1}(x - x_1)$$

$$m(x - x_1) = y - y_1$$

$$y - y_1 = m(x - x_1)$$

Problem 1 Writing an Equation Given a Point and the Slope

A line passes through $(-4, 1)$ with slope $\frac{2}{5}$. What is the equation of the line in point-slope form?

Use point-slope form. $\qquad y - y_1 = m(x - x_1)$

Substitute $m = \frac{2}{5}$ and $(x_1, y_1) = (-4, 1)$ $\quad y - 1 = \frac{2}{5}[x - (-4)]$

Simplify. $\qquad\qquad\qquad\qquad\qquad y - 1 = \frac{2}{5}(x + 4)$

An equation for the line is $y - 1 = \frac{2}{5}(x + 4)$.

 Got It? **1.** A line passes through $(7, -1)$ with slope -3. What is the equation of the line in point-slope form?

Problem 2 Writing an Equation Given Two Points

A line passes through $(3, 2)$ and $(5, 8)$. What is an equation of the line in point-slope form?

Know	Need	Plan
Two points on a line	An equation written in point-slope form	Substitute the slope and either point into the point-slope form.

Let $(x_1, y_1) = (3, 2)$ and $(x_2, y_2) = (5, 8)$.

Substitute into the slope formula and simplify. $\quad m = \frac{8 - 2}{5 - 3} = \frac{6}{2} = 3$

Substitute into point-slope form. $\qquad\qquad y - 2 = 3(x - 3)$

 Got It? **2. a.** A line passes through $(-5, 0)$ and $(0, 7)$. What is an equation of the line in point-slope form?

b. **Reasoning** What is another equation in point-slope form of the line through the points $(-5, 0)$ and $(0, 7)$? Explain.

Another form of the equation of a line is *standard form*. Standard form sets the sum of the *x*- and *y*-terms equal to a constant. When possible, use integer values for the coefficients of *x* and *y* and the constant term.

 **Key Concept** **Standard Form of a Linear Equation**

A **standard form of a linear equation** is $Ax + By = C$, where *A*, *B*, and *C* are real numbers and *A* and *B* are not *both* zero.

Problem 3 Writing Equations in Standard Form

What is an equation of each line in standard form? Use integer coefficients.

Think

How can you rewrite the equation using only integer values? Multiply each side of the equation by the least common denominator of all fractional coefficients.

A $y = \frac{3}{4}x - 5$

Write the original equation. $\qquad\qquad y = \frac{3}{4}x - 5$

Multiply each side by 4 to clear the fractions. $\qquad\qquad 4y = 3x - 20$

Subtract $3x$ from each side. $\quad -3x + 4y = -20$

B $y = -4.2x - 5.5$

Write the original equation. $\qquad\qquad y = -4.2x - 5.5$

Multiply each side by 10 to clear the decimals. $\qquad\qquad 10y = -42x - 55$

Add $42x$ to each side. $\qquad 42x + 10y = -55$

 Got It? **3.** What is an equation of each line in standard form? Use integer coefficients.

a. $y = \frac{2}{3}x + \frac{1}{6}$ **b.** $y = 9.1x + 3.6$

take note

Concept Summary Writing Equations of Lines

Slope-Intercept Form	Point-Slope Form	Standard Form
$y = mx + b$	$y - y_1 = m(x - x_1)$	$Ax + By = C$
Use this form when you know the slope and the y-intercept.	Use this form when you know the slope and a point, or when you know two points.	A, B, and C are real numbers. A and B cannot both be zero.

Focus Question Why are there different forms for the equation of a line?

Answer Depending on what information you know about the line, use the form that is easiest to write an equation of that line.

Lesson Check

Do you know HOW?

Write an equation of each line in slope-intercept form.

1. slope -3;
through $(1, -4)$

2. slope $\frac{1}{2}$;
through $(2, 3)$

What is an equation of each line in standard form? Use integer coefficients.

3. $y = -\frac{1}{4}x + 5$

4. $y = 0.2x - 1.7$

Do you UNDERSTAND?

5. Vocabulary Tell whether each equation is in slope-intercept, point-slope, or standard form.

a. $y + 2 = -2(x - 1)$ **b.** $y = -\frac{1}{4}x + 9$

c. $-x - 2y = 1$ **d.** $y - 3 = 4x$

6. Which form would you use to write the equation of a line if you knew its slope and its x-intercept? Explain.

Practice and Problem-Solving Exercises

A Practice

Write an equation of each line in point-slope form.

 **See Problem 1.**

7. slope $= 3$; through $(1, 5)$

8. slope $= -\frac{3}{5}$; through $(-4, 0)$

9. slope $= 0$; through $(4, -2)$

10. slope $= -1$; through $(-3, 5)$

Write an equation of the line through each pair of points in point-slope form. **See Problem 2.**

Guided Practice

11. $(-10, 3)$ and $(-2, -5)$

To start, substitute $(x_1, y_1) = (-10, 3)$ and $(x_2, y_2) = (-2, -5)$ into the slope formula.

$$m = \frac{y_2 - y_1}{x_2 - x_1} = \frac{(-5) - 3}{(-2) - (-10)}$$

12. $(1, 0)$ and $(5, 5)$

13. $(-4, 10)$ and $(-6, 15)$

14. $(0, -1)$ and $(3, -5)$

Write an equation of each line in standard form with integer coefficients. **See Problem 3.**

Guided Practice

15. $y = \frac{1}{2}x - 2$

To start, multiply each side by 2 to clear the fractions.

$2y = x - 4$

16. $y = -7x - 9$

17. $y = -\frac{3}{5}x + 3$

18. $y = 4.2x + 7.9$

B Apply

Write an equation of the line through each pair of points. Use point-slope form.

19. $\left(\frac{3}{2}, -\frac{1}{2}\right)$ and $\left(-\frac{2}{3}, \frac{1}{3}\right)$

20. $\left(-\frac{1}{2}, -\frac{1}{2}\right)$ and $(-3, -4)$

21. $\left(0, \frac{1}{2}\right)$ and $\left(\frac{5}{7}, 0\right)$

22. Reasoning The definition of standard form states that A and B can't both be zero. Explain why.

23. Error Analysis A student says that the equation $3x + 2y = 6$ is a standard form of the equation $y = \frac{3}{2}x + 3$. What is the student's error?

More About Linear Equations

Objectives To write and graph the equation of a line
To write equations of parallel and perpendicular lines

In Part 1 of the lesson, you wrote equations of lines in different forms given points, slopes, and intercepts.	**Connect to What You Know**	Here you will use what you learned to graph equations and write equations of parallel and perpendicular lines.

Lesson Vocabulary
• parallel lines
• perpendicular lines

Focus Question How are the slopes of two lines related?

In Lesson 2–3, you learned how to graph an equation of a line in slope-intercept form. You can also graph an equation in standard form quickly by determining the x- and y-intercepts and then drawing the line through them.

Problem 4 Graphing an Equation Using Intercepts

What are the intercepts of $3x + 5y = 15$? Graph the equation.

Set $x = 0$ to find the y-intercept.

Substitute $x = 0$.	$3(0) + 5y = 15$
Multiply.	$5y = 15$
Solve for y.	$y = 3$

Set $y = 0$ to find the x-intercept.

Substitute $y = 0$.	$3x + 5(0) = 15$
Multiply.	$3x = 15$
Solve for x.	$x = 5$

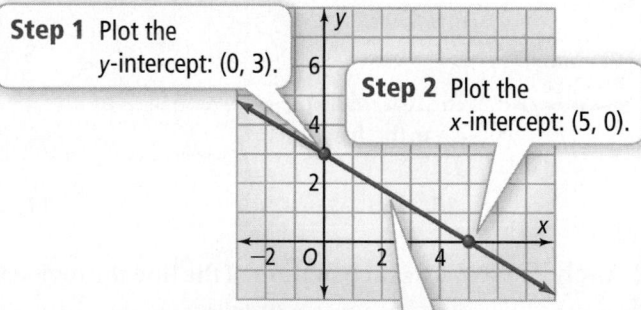

Step 1 Plot the y-intercept: (0, 3).

Step 2 Plot the x-intercept: (5, 0).

Step 3 Draw a line through the intercepts.

 Got It? **4.** What are the intercepts of $2x - 4y = 8$? Graph the equation.

Problem 5 Drawing and Interpreting a Linear Graph

Biology The number of times a cricket chirps per minute depends on the temperature. The number of chirps in 2 seconds for two temperatures are shown at the bottom right.

Think

How can you find the number of chirps in a minute given the number of chirps in 2 seconds?
There are 60 seconds in 1 minute. Multiply the number of chirps in 2 seconds by $\frac{60}{2}$ or 30.

Ⓐ What graph models the situation?

First, find the number of chirps per minute.

$40°F: 30(0) = 0 \qquad 93°F: 30(8) = 240$

Let x = temperature in degrees Fahrenheit.
Let y = number of times a cricket chirps.

Graph (40, 0) and (93, 240)
Draw a line through the points.

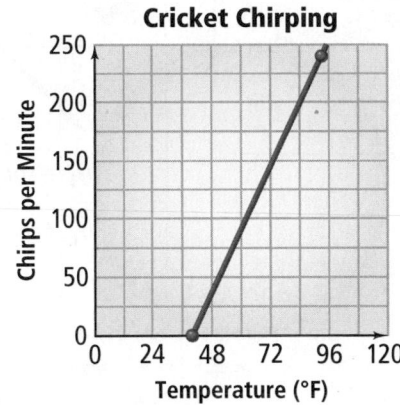

Cricket Chirping

Ⓑ What is the equation of the line in standard form?

Use the slope formula $m = \dfrac{y_2 - y_1}{x_2 - x_1}$. $\qquad m = \dfrac{240 - 0}{93 - 40}$

Subtract and simplify. $\qquad\qquad\qquad = \dfrac{240}{53} \approx 4.5$

Use point-slope form. $\qquad y - y_1 = m(x - x_1)$

Substitute one of the points: (40, 0). $\qquad y - 0 = 4.5(x - 40)$

Simplify. $\qquad\qquad\qquad\qquad y = 4.5x - 180$

Write in standard form. $\qquad\qquad 4.5x - y = 180$

Ⓒ If the temperature is 70°F, how many times would a cricket be expected to chirp in one minute?

Let $x = 70$.

Use the equation from part (b). $\qquad y = 4.5x - 180$

Substitute. $\qquad y = 4.5(70) - 180$

Simplify. $\qquad y = 135$

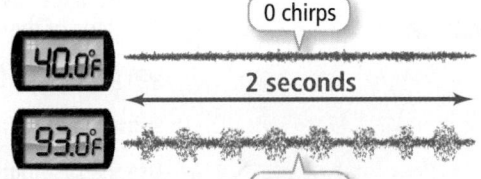

0 chirps

2 seconds

8 chirps

If the temperature is 70°F, the cricket would be expected to chirp 135 times in one minute.

Hint

On Day 0, there are 140 packs of paper. On Day 80, there are 0 packs of paper.

 Got It? **5.** The office manager of a small office ordered 140 packs of printer paper. Based on average daily use, she knows that the paper will last about 80 days.

    a. What graph represents this situation?

    b. What is the equation of the line in standard form?

    c. How many packs of printer paper should the manager expect to have after 30 days?

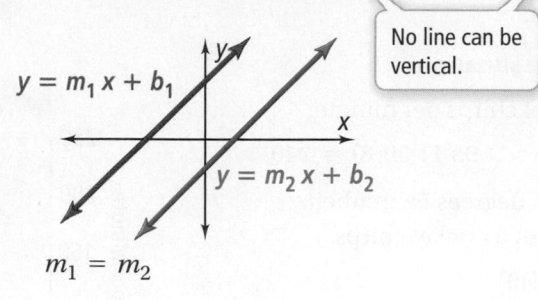

take note   Key Concepts   Parallel and Perpendicular Lines

The slopes of **parallel lines** are equal.

The slopes of **perpendicular lines** are negative reciprocals of each other.

Hint

Two numbers are <u>reciprocals</u> if their product is 1.
We say two numbers are <u>negative reciprocals</u> if their product is -1.

No line can be vertical.

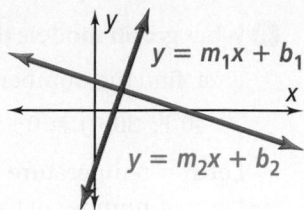

$y = m_1 x + b_1$

$y = m_2 x + b_2$

$m_1 = m_2$

$b_1 \neq b_2$

$y = m_1 x + b_1$

$y = m_2 x + b_2$

$m_1 \cdot m_2 = -1$

$m_1 = -\dfrac{1}{m_2}$

$m_2 = -\dfrac{1}{m_1}$

m_1 and m_2 are negative reciprocals of each other.

Plan

What information can you find from the given equation?
You can find the slope.

ONLINE PROBLEMS   Problem 6   Writing Equations of Parallel and Perpendicular Lines

What is the equation of each line in slope-intercept form?

A the line parallel to $y = 6x - 2$ through $(1, -3)$

Identify the slope, use point-slope form, and rewrite in slope-intercept form.

Parallel lines have the same slope. The slope of the line with equation $y = 6x - 2$ is 6.	$m = 6$
Use point-slope form.	$y - y_1 = m(x - x_1)$
Substitute 6 for m and $(1, -3)$ for (x_1, y_1).	$y - (-3) = 6(x - 1)$
Use the Distributive Property.	$y + 3 = 6x - 6$
Write in slope-intercept form.	$y = 6x - 9$

B the line perpendicular to $y = -4x + \frac{2}{3}$ through $(8, 5)$

Identify the slope, use point-slope form, and rewrite in slope-intercept form.

Think

How can you find the slope of a perpendicular line?
Slopes of perpendicular lines are negative reciprocals, so use the equation $m_1 = -\frac{1}{m_2}$.

The slopes of perpendicular lines are negative reciprocals.	$m = -\dfrac{1}{-4} = \dfrac{1}{4}$
Use point-slope form.	$y - y_1 = m(x - x_1)$
Substitute $\frac{1}{4}$ for m and $(8, 5)$ for (x_1, y_1).	$y - 5 = \frac{1}{4}(x - 8)$
Use the Distributive Property.	$y - 5 = \frac{1}{4}x - 2$
Write in slope-intercept form.	$y = \frac{1}{4}x + 3$

Got It? **6.** What is the equation of each line in slope-intercept form?
   a. the line parallel to $4x + 2y = 7$ through $(4, -2)$
   b. the line perpendicular to $y = \frac{2}{3}x - 1$ through $(0, 6)$

Focus Question How are the slopes of two lines related?

Answer The slopes of two lines in the same plane indicate how the lines are related. Two lines are parallel if they have the same slope (and different y-intercepts). Two lines are perpendicular if their slopes are negative reciprocals.

 ## Lesson Check

Do you know HOW?

1. What are the intercepts of $3x + y = 6$? Graph the equation.

Write an equation of each line in standard form.

2. the line parallel to $y = -3x + 4$ through $(0, -1)$

3. the line perpendicular to $-2x + 3y = 9$ through $(-1, -3)$

Do you UNDERSTAND?

4. Writing Explain how to graph a linear equation by using its intercepts.

5. Error Analysis Your friend says the line $y = -2x + 3$ is perpendicular to the line $x + 2y = 8$. Do you agree? Explain.

 ## Practice and Problem-Solving Exercises

 **Practice**

Guided Practice

Find the intercepts and graph each line. ◀ **See Problem 4.**

                6. $x - 4y = -4$

To start, set $x = 0$ to find the y-intercept. $0 - 4y = -4$

7. $2x + 5y = -10$ **8.** $-3x + 2y = 6$ **9.** $5x + 7y = 14$

Write and graph an equation to represent each situation. ◀ **See Problem 5.**

10. You put 15 gallons of gasoline in your car. You know that this amount of gasoline will allow you to drive about 450 miles.

11. A meal plan lets students buy $20 meal cards. Each meal card lasts about 8 days.

Write the equation of the line through each point. Use slope-intercept form.　　◀ See Problem 6.

◀ See Problem 6.

Guided Practice

12. $(1, -1)$; parallel to $y = \frac{2}{5}x - 3$

To start, identify the slope of the given line.　　$m = \frac{2}{5}$

13. $(-3, 1)$; perpendicular to $y = -\frac{2}{5}x - 4$　　**14.** $(-5, 6)$; parallel to $y = \frac{1}{3}x + 2$

15. $(-7, 10)$; parallel to $2x - 3y = -3$　　**16.** $(-2, 1)$; perpendicular to $3x + y = 1$

B Apply

Graph each equation.

17. $3x + 5y = 12$　　**18.** $2x + y = 3$　　**19.** $6y - 4x = -24$

20. $3y - x = -6$　　**21.** $-20x - 45y = 48$　　**22.** $4x - 3y = -6$

23. Think About a Plan Write an equation for the line shown here. Each interval is 1 unit.
   - What do you know from the graph?
   - Which form of the equation of a line could you use with the information you have?

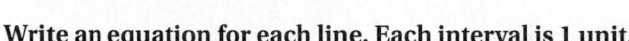

24. a. Write the point-slope form of the line that passes through $A(-3, 12)$ and $B(9, -4)$. Use point A in the equation.

   b. Write the point-slope form of the same line using point B in the equation.

   c. Rewrite each equation in standard form. What do you notice?

Write an equation for each line. Each interval is 1 unit.

25.

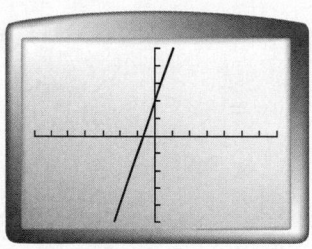

26.

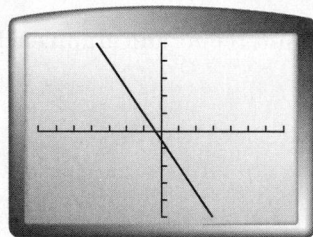

Write an equation for each line. Then graph the line.

27. $m = 0$, through $(5, -1)$　　**28.** $m = \frac{5}{6}$, through $(-4, 0)$　　**29.** $m = -\frac{3}{2}$, through $(0, -1)$

30. Reasoning Suppose lines ℓ_1 and ℓ_2 intersect at the origin. Also, ℓ_1 has slope $\frac{y}{x}$ $(x > 0, y > 0)$ and ℓ_2 has slope $-\frac{x}{y}$. Then ℓ_1 contains (x, y) and ℓ_2 contains $(-y, x)$.

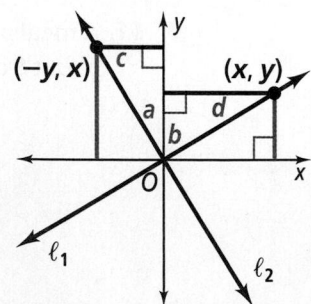

   a. Explain why the four right triangles are congruent.

   b. Complete each equation about the angle measures a, b, c, and d.
   $$a = \blacksquare \qquad c = \blacksquare$$
   $$a + c = \blacksquare \qquad b + d = \blacksquare$$

   c. What must be true about $a + b$? Why?

   d. What must be true about ℓ_1 and ℓ_2? Why?

Find the slope, if any, and the intercepts of each line.

31. $f(x) = \frac{2}{3}x + 4$ **32.** $y = -x + 1000$ **33.** $y = 0.4 - 0.8x$

34. $g(x) = 54x - 1$ **35.** $x = -3$ **36.** $y = 0$

Standardized Test Prep

SAT/ACT

37. Which line is perpendicular to the line shown in the graph?

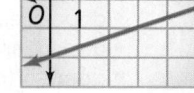

Ⓐ $-3x + y = 5$ Ⓒ $x - 3y = 0$

Ⓑ $3x + y = -1$ Ⓓ $x + 3y = -3$

38. Which line is parallel to the line $5x + 6y = 30$?

Ⓕ $5x + 9y = 30$ Ⓗ $5x + 6y = 9$

Ⓖ $9x + 6y = 30$ Ⓘ $6x + 5y = 30$

Short Response

39. What is the solution of the inequality $|x - 3| \geq 5$? Graph the solution.

Mixed Review

Find the domain and range of each relation and determine whether it is a function.

◀ See Lesson 2-1.

40. $\{(-3, 4), (-1, 2),$
$(0, -2), (1, 0), (2, 2)\}$

41.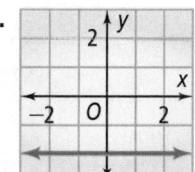

42.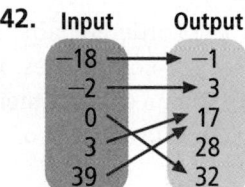

Name the property of real numbers illustrated by each equation.

◀ See Lesson 1-2.

43. $\frac{2}{5} + \frac{27}{5} \cdot \frac{5}{27} = \frac{2}{5} + 1$ **44.** $97(7) = 100(7) - 3(7)$ **45.** $21 + 19.7 - 19.7 = 21$

Get Ready! To prepare for Lesson 2-5, do Exercises 46–49.

Write the equation for each line. Use slope-intercept form.

◀ See Lesson 2-3.

46. $m = 3$ and the y-intercept is $(0, -5)$. **47.** $m = \frac{1}{2}$ and the y-intercept is $(0, 0)$.

48. $m = \frac{4}{5}$ and the y-intercept is $(0, 7)$. **49.** $m = -\frac{3}{8}$ and the y-intercept is $(0, 12)$.

Chapter Vocabulary

- constant of variation (p. 74)
- dependent variable (p. 70)
- direct variation (p. 74)
- domain (p. 65)
- function (p. 66)
- function notation (p. 70)

- function rule (p. 70)
- independent variable (p. 70)
- linear equation (p. 82)
- linear function (p. 82)
- parallel lines (p. 94)
- perpendicular lines (p. 94)

- point-slope form (p. 88)
- range (p. 65)
- relation (p. 64)
- slope (p. 81)
- slope-intercept form (p. 83)

- standard form of a linear equation (p. 89)
- vertical-line test (p. 67)
- x-intercept (p. 83)
- y-intercept (p. 83)

Choose the correct term to complete each sentence.

1. All functions are (*relations*/*domains*).

2. The graph of a function is (*always*/*sometimes*) a line.

3. The equation $y - 5 = 3(x + 2)$ is in (*point-slope*/*slope-intercept*) form.

2-1 Relations and Functions

Quick Review

A **relation** is a set of ordered pairs. The **domain** of a relation is the set of x-coordinates. The **range** is the set of y-coordinates. When each element of the domain is paired with exactly one element of the range, the relation is a **function**.

Example

Determine whether the relation is a function. Find the domain and range.

$\{(5, 0), (8, 1), (1, 3), (5, 2), (3, 8)\}$

In this relation, the x-coordinate 5 is paired with both 0 and 2. This relation is not a function.

The domain is all the x-coordinates, which is $\{1, 3, 5, 8\}$.

The range is all the y-coordinates, which is $\{0, 1, 2, 3, 8\}$.

Exercises

Determine whether each relation is a function. Find the domain and range.

4. $\{(10, 2), (-10, 2), (6, 4), (5, 3), (-6, 7)\}$

5. $\{(4, 5), (1, 5), (3, 8), (4, 6), (10, 12)\}$

6.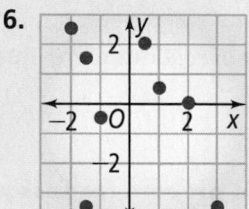

7.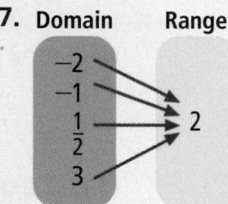

For each function, find $f(-2), f(-0.5),$ and $f(3)$.

8. $f(x) = -x + 4$

9. $f(x) = \frac{3}{8}x - 3$

2-2 Direct Variation

Quick Review

A linear equation of the form $y = kx$, $k \neq 0$, represents **direct variation**. The **constant of variation** is k. You can use proportions to solve direct variation problems.

Example

In the table, determine whether y varies directly with x. If so, what is the constant of variation and the function rule?

$\frac{6}{2} = \frac{9}{3} = \frac{24}{8} = 3$, so y varies directly with x, and the constant of variation is 3.

The function rule is $y = 3x$.

x	y
2	6
3	9
8	24

Exercises

For each function, determine whether y varies directly with x. If so, find the constant of variation and write the function rule.

10.

x	y
−2	3
1	4
2	7

11.

x	y
4	5
6	9
10	17

12.

x	y
1	1
2	2
5	5

For each function, y varies directly with x. Find each constant of variation. Then find the value of y when $x = -0.3$.

13. $y = 2$ when $x = -\frac{1}{2}$ **14.** $y = \frac{2}{3}$ when $x = 0.2$

15. $y = 7$ when $x = 2$ **16.** $y = 4$ when $x = -3$

2-3 Linear Functions and Slope-Intercept Form

Quick Review

The graph of a **linear function** is a line. You can represent a linear function with a **linear equation**. Given two points on a line, the **slope** of the line is the ratio of the change in the y-coordinates to the change in the corresponding x-coordinates. The slope is the coefficient of x when you write a linear equation in **slope-intercept form**.

Example

What is the slope of the line that passes through $(3, 5)$ and $(-1, -2)$?

Use the slope formula. $m = \frac{y_2 - y_1}{x_2 - x_1}$

Substitute and simplify. $= \frac{5 - (-2)}{3 - (-1)} = \frac{7}{4}$

Exercises

Identify the slope of the line that passes through the given points.

17. $(1, 3)$ and $(6, 1)$ **18.** $(4, 4)$ and $(-2, -3)$

19. $(3, 2)$ and $(-3, -2)$ **20.** $(5, 2)$ and $(-4, 6)$

Write an equation for each line in slope-intercept form.

21. slope $= -3$ and the y-intercept is $(0, 4)$

22. slope $= \frac{1}{2}$ and the y-intercept is $(0, 6)$

Rewrite each equation in slope-intercept form. Graph each line.

23. $4x - 2y = 3$ **24.** $-4x + 6y = 18$

25. $3y + 3x = 15$ **26.** $3y + x = 5$

2-4 More About Linear Equations

Quick Review

You can write the equation of a line in **point-slope form** when you are given either a point and the slope or two points. The **standard form of a linear equation** has the sum of the variable terms set equal to a constant. The constant term and coefficients of the variables are usually integers.

In the coordinate plane, two lines with the same slope are **parallel lines**. Two lines with slopes that are negative reciprocals of each other are **perpendicular lines**.

Example

Write an equation in standard form for the line with a slope of 2 that passes through $(1, 6)$.

Write the point-slope form for the equation of a line.	$y - y_1 = m(x - x_1)$
Substitute $m = 2$ and $(x_1, y_1) = (1, 6)$.	$y - 6 = 2(x - 1)$
Use the Distributive Property.	$y - 6 = 2x - 2$
Write in standard form.	$-2x + y = 4$

Example

What is the equation of the line perpendicular to $y = -2x + 3$ through $(4, 7)$? Write the equation in slope-intercept form.

The slope of the line is the negative reciprocal of the slope of the given line, -2.	$m = -\frac{1}{-2} = \frac{1}{2}$
Substitute $m = \frac{1}{2}$ and $(x_1, y_1) = (4, 7)$ into point-slope form.	$y - 7 = \frac{1}{2}(x - 4)$
Simplify and write in slope-intercept form.	$y = \frac{1}{2}x + 5$

Exercises

Write an equation of each line in standard form. Use integer coefficients.

27. slope $= -3$, through $(4, 0)$

28. slope $= 5$, through $(1, -1)$

29. slope $= -0.5$, through $(6, 3)$

30. slope $= \frac{2}{3}$, through $(-2, -2)$

Write an equation in point-slope form of the line through each pair of points.

31. $(0, 0)$ and $(3, -7)$

32. $(2, 3)$ and $(3, 5)$

33. $(-4, -3)$ and $(1, 2)$

34. $(2, -5)$ and $(-2, 4)$

Write the equation of the line through each point. Use slope-intercept form.

35. parallel to $y = \frac{1}{3}x - 4$, through $(1, 2)$

36. perpendicular to $y = \frac{4}{5}x - 4$, through $(-3, 4)$

37. parallel to $3x + 4y = 12$, through $(-2, -2)$

38. perpendicular to $-x + 2y = 3$, through $(1, 7)$

39. **a.** Write an equation of the line parallel to $x + 2y = 6$ through $(8, 3)$.
    b. Write an equation of the line perpendicular to $x + 2y = 6$ through $(8, 3)$.
    c. Graph the three lines on the same coordinate plane.

Do you know HOW?

Determine whether each relation is a function.

1.

x	y
3	7
4	2
3	2
5	1

2.

x	y
1	1
2	2
3	3
4	4

Find the x- and y-intercepts of each line.

3. $x - 3y = 9$

4. $y = 7x + 5$

5. $y = 6x$

6. $-4x + y = 10$

Write the equation of each line in slope-intercept form and identify the slope.

7. $2x - y = 9$

8. $4x = 2 + y$

9. $5y = -3x - 10$

10. $4x + 6y = 12$

Write an equation of each line in standard form with integer coefficients.

11. the line through $(2, 3)$ and $(4, 5)$

12. the line through $(-4, 6)$ and $(2, -2)$

13. the line through $(-4, 2)$ with slope 3

14. the line through $(1, 2)$ with slope $\frac{4}{5}$

15. a line through $(3, 1)$ with slope 0

16. a line with slope of $\frac{2}{3}$ and y-intercept $(0, 5)$

17. $2y = -4x - 12$

18. $\frac{2}{3}x + 3 = 6y - 15$

Write an equation of each line in point-slope form.

19. $(-4, 2)$ and $(-3, 5)$

20. $(0, 0)$ and $(-4, -5)$

21. $(-4, -3)$ and $(2, 7)$

Graph each equation.

22. $2y = 4x + 8$

23. $2x - 3y = 6$

24. $4y - x = 16$

For each function, determine whether y varies directly with x. If so, identify the constant of variation.

25. $2y = 3x$

26. $4y - 7x = 0$

27. $y + \frac{3}{4}x = 12$

Do you UNDERSTAND?

28. a. A group of friends is going to the movies. Each ticket costs $8.00. Write an equation to model the total cost of the group's tickets.
   b. Graph the equation. Explain what the x- and y-intercepts represent.
   c. What would the cost be for 12 tickets?
   d. Writing Could the domain include fractions? Explain.

29. Which line is perpendicular to $3x + 2y = 6$?
   Ⓐ $4x - 6y = 3$ Ⓒ $2x + 3y = 12$
   Ⓑ $y = -\frac{3}{2}x + 4$ Ⓓ $y = \frac{3}{2}x + 1$

30. Reasoning Why is the slope of a vertical line undefined?

31. Suppose $m = 25 - 0.15n$ describes the amount of money remaining m on a $25 phone card, as a function of the number of minutes of calls you make n. What are a reasonable domain and range?

CHAPTER 2 PART B

Functions, Equations, and Graphs

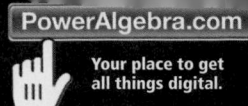

PowerAlgebra.com
Your place to get all things digital.

In Part A, you learned how to write and graph linear functions. Now you will apply what you learned to graph inequalities and transform functions.

 Vocabulary for Part B

English/Spanish Vocabulary Audio Online:

English	Spanish
absolute value function, *p. 121*	función de valor absoluto
axis of symmetry, *p. 121*	eje de simetría
linear inequality, *p. 128*	desigualdad lineal
parent function, *p. 110*	función elemental
reflection, *p. 114*	reflexión
transformation, *p. 110*	transformación
translation, *p. 110*	traslación
vertex, *p. 121*	vértice

BIG ideas

1 Equivalence
Essential Question Does it matter which form of a linear equation you use?

2 Function
Essential Question How do you use transformations to help graph absolute value functions?

3 Modeling
Essential Question How can you model data with a linear function?

Chapter Preview for Part B

2-5 Using Linear Models

Objectives To write linear equations that model real-world data
To make predictions from linear models

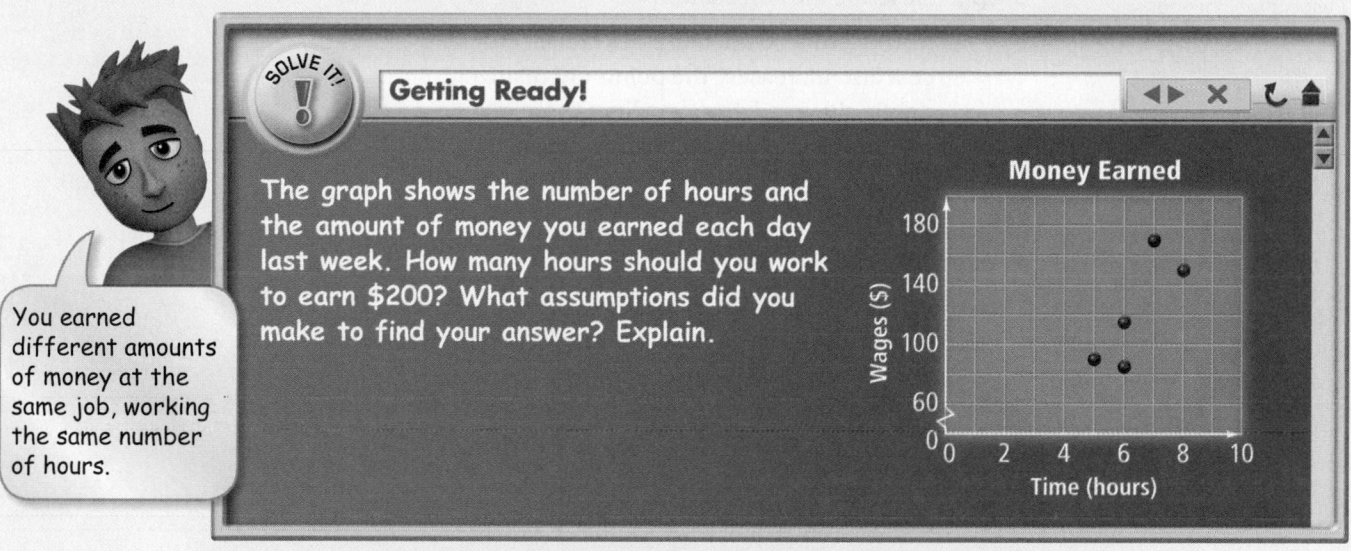

Getting Ready!

The graph shows the number of hours and the amount of money you earned each day last week. How many hours should you work to earn $200? What assumptions did you make to find your answer? Explain.

You earned different amounts of money at the same job, working the same number of hours.

Money Earned

(scatter plot with Wages ($) on the y-axis ranging 60 to 180 and Time (hours) on the x-axis ranging 0 to 10)

Lesson Vocabulary
- scatter plot
- correlation
- line of best fit
- correlation coefficient

Graphs of data pairs for a real-world situation rarely fall in a line. Their arrangement, however, can suggest a relationship that you can model with a linear function.

Focus Question Why is modeling a real-world situation with a linear equation useful?

A **scatter plot** is a graph that relates two sets of data by plotting the data as ordered pairs. You can use a scatter plot to determine the strength of the relationship, or **correlation**, between data sets. The closer the data points fall along a line with positive slope,

- the stronger the linear relationship and
- the stronger the positive correlation

between the two variables.

Strong Negative Correlation	Weak Negative Correlation	No Correlation	Weak Positive Correlation	Strong Positive Correlation

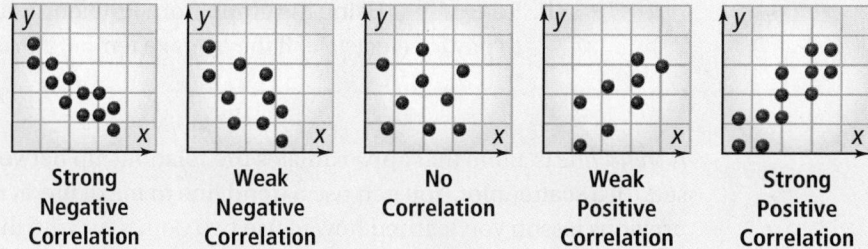

Problem 1 Using a Scatter Plot

Utilities The table lists average monthly temperatures and electricity costs for a Texas home in 2008. Make a scatter plot. How would you describe the correlation?

Plan

Which variable is the independent variable?
Temperature does not depend on the electric bill, so temperature is the independent variable.

Step 1 Make a scatter plot.

Step 2 Describe the correlation.

As the temperature increases, the electricity cost also increases. The points are relatively tightly clustered around a line. There is a strong positive correlation between temperature and electricity cost.

Average Temperatures and Electricity Costs

Month	Average Temp.	Electricity Bill
January	61°F	$150
February	58°F	$139
March	67°F	$172
April	75°F	$205
May	79°F	$170
June	83°F	$234
July	84°F	$255
August	85°F	$245
September	81°F	$210
October	76°F	$183
November	65°F	$132
December	58°F	$110

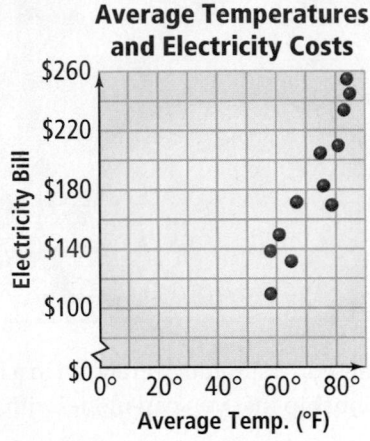

Average Temperatures and Electricity Costs

 Got It? **1. a.** The table shows the numbers of hours students spent online the day before a test and the scores on the test. Make a scatter plot. How would you describe the correlation?

Computer Use and Test Scores

Number of Hours Online	0	0	1	1	1.5	1.75	2	2	3	4	4.5	5
Test score	100	94	98	88	92	89	75	70	78	72	57	60

b. Reasoning Using the graph from Problem 1, how much would you expect to pay for electricity if the average temperature was 70°F? Explain.

A *trend line* is a line that approximates the relationship between the variables, or data sets, of a scatter plot. You can use a trend line to make predictions from the data. In the previous lesson you learned how to use two points to write the equation of a line to model a real-world problem. You can use this method to write the equation of a trend line.

Problem 2 Writing the Equation of a Trend Line

Finance The table shows the median home prices in Florida. What is the equation of a trend line that models a relationship between time and home prices? Use the equation to predict the median home price in 2020.

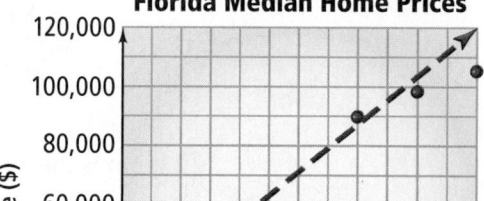

Florida Median Home Prices

Year	Median Price
1940	$23,100
1950	$40,100
1960	$58,100
1970	$57,600
1980	$89,300
1990	$98,500
2000	$105,500

Step 1 Make a scatter plot. Let $x = 0$ correspond to 1940.

Step 2 Sketch a trend line.

Step 3 Choose two points (10, 40,000) and (35, 80,000) on the trend line. Use the point-slope formula to write an equation for the line.

Find the slope. $m = \dfrac{80{,}000 - 40{,}000}{35 - 10} = 1600$

Write the equation. $y - 40{,}000 = 1600(x - 10)$

Distribute. $y - 40{,}000 = 1600x - 16{,}000$

Simplify. $y = 1600x + 24{,}000$

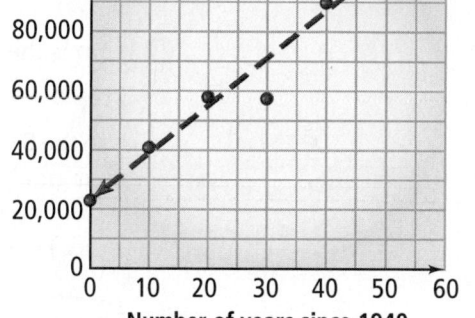

Florida Median Home Prices

Price ($) vs Number of years since 1940

Step 4 Use the equation to make a prediction. The year 2020 corresponds to $x = 80$.

Substitute $x = 80$. $y = 1600(80) + 24{,}000$

Simplify. $y = 152{,}000$

Based on the trend line, the median home price in 2020 will be around $152,000.

 Got It? **2.** The table shows median home prices in California. What is an equation for a trend line that models the relationship between time and home prices? Use the equation to predict the median home price in 2030.

California Median Home Prices							
Year	1940	1950	1960	1970	1980	1990	2000
Median Price ($)	36,700	57,900	74,400	88,700	167,300	249,800	211,500

The trend line that gives the most accurate model of related data is called the **line of best fit**. One method for finding a line of best fit is *linear regression*. You can use the **LinReg** function on your graphing calculator to find the line of best fit. The **correlation coefficient**, r, indicates the strength of the correlation. The closer r is to 1 or -1, the more closely the data resembles a line and the more accurate your model is likely to be.

 Problem 3 Finding the Line of Best Fit

Food You research the average cost of whole milk for several recent years to look for trends. The table shows your data.

Cost of Whole Milk						
Year	1998	2000	2002	2004	2006	2008
Average cost for one gallon ($)	2.65	2.89	3.00	3.01	3.20	3.77

SOURCE: U.S. Department of Agriculture

A What is the equation for the line of best fit? How accurate is your line of best fit?

Step 1

Use the **STAT** feature to enter the data in your graphing calculator. Enter the x-values (year) in **L1** and the y-values (price) in **L2**. Let 1997 = year 0.

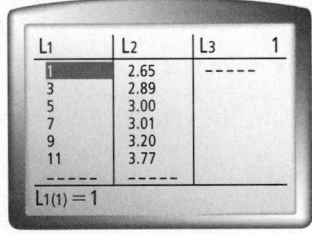

Step 2

Use **LinReg** to find the linear regression line of best fit for the data.

$$y = 0.09x + 2.53$$

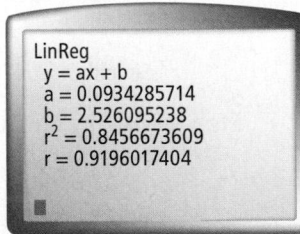

The correlation coefficient, r, is approximately 0.94. Since r is close to 1, the line of best fit is quite accurate.

Think

What factors could affect the accuracy of your prediction?
Predictions based on strongly correlated data are likely to be more reliable than predictions based on weakly correlated data.

B Based on your linear model, how much would you expect to pay for a gallon of whole milk in 2020?

Use the line of best fit.	$y = 0.09x + 2.53$
Substitute 23 for x.	$y = 0.09(23) + 2.53$
Simplify.	$y = 4.60$

In 2020, you would expect to pay about $4.60 for a gallon of whole milk.

Got It? **3.** The table lists the cost of 2% milk. Use a scatter plot to find the equation of the line of best fit. Based on your linear model, how much would you expect to pay for a gallon of 2% milk in 2025?

Cost of 2% Milk						
Year	1998	2000	2002	2004	2006	2008
Average cost for one gallon ($)	2.57	2.83	2.93	2.93	3.10	3.71

SOURCE: U.S. Department of Agriculture

Focus Question Why is modeling a real-world situation with a linear equation useful?

Answer Sometimes real-world data can be modeled with a linear equation. Then use the equation to draw conclusions about the situation.

 ## Lesson Check

Do you know HOW?

Make a scatter plot of each set of points and describe the correlation.

1. {(1.2, 1), (2.5, 6), (2.5, 7.5), (4.1, 11), (7.9, 19)}

2. {(1, 55), (2, 38), (3, 54), (4, 37), (5, 53), (6, 40), (7, 53), (8, 36)}

3. Make a scatter plot for the following set of points. Describe the correlation and sketch a trend line. {(2, 58), (6, 105), (8, 88), (8, 118), (12, 117), (16, 137), (20, 157), (20, 169)}

Do you UNDERSTAND?

4. Writing How can you determine whether there is a strong correlation between two variables x and y for a real-life situation?

5. Do you think a trend line on a graph is always the same as the line of best fit? Why or why not?

6. Compare and Contrast What is the difference between a positive correlation and a negative correlation? How might you relate positive correlation with direct variation?

Practice and Problem-Solving Exercises

A Practice Make a scatter plot and describe the correlation.  See Problem 1.

Guided Practice To start, begin plotting the points.

7. {(0, 11), (2, 8), (3, 7), (7, 2), (8, 0)}

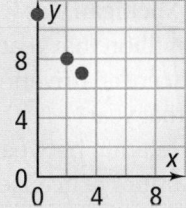

Make a scatter plot and describe the correlation.

8. **Manufacturing** The table shows the numbering system used in Europe and the United States for shoe sizes.

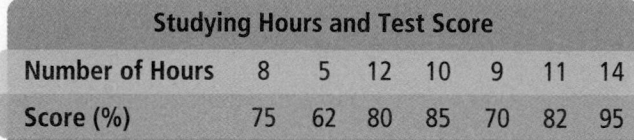

Shoe Sizes						
U.S. Size	1	3	5	7	9	11
European Size	31	34	36	39	41	44

Write the equation of a trend line.

◀ **See Problem 2.**

9. The table shows the average hours you studied before your eight math tests and your percent score on each test.

10. $\{(-15, 8), (-8, 7), (-3, 0), (0, 0), (7, -3)\}$

11. $\{(-10, 3), (-5, 1), (-1, -4), (3, -7), (12, -12)\}$

Studying Hours and Test Score							
Number of Hours	8	5	12	10	9	11	14
Score (%)	75	62	80	85	70	82	95

 12. **a. Food Production** The table below shows pork production in China from 2000 to 2007. Use a calculator to find the line of best fit.

◀ **See Problem 3.**

   b. Use your linear model to predict how many metric tons of pork will be produced in 2010.

   c. Use your linear model to predict when production is likely to reach 70,000 metric tons.

Pork Production in China								
Year	2000	2001	2002	2003	2004	2005	2006	2007
Production (metric tons)	40,475	42,010	43,413	45,331	47,177	50,254	52,407	54,491

SOURCE: USDA Foreign Agricultural Service GAIN Report

B Apply

13. **Think About a Plan** The table below shows the relationship between the production and the export of rice in Vietnam from 1985 to 2005. How much rice would you expect Vietnam to export in 2015 if the production that year is 42,250,000 tonnes?

   • How can you use a scatter plot to find a linear model?
   • How can you use your model to make a prediction?

Rice Production and Export					
Production (1000 tonnes)	15,875	19,225	24,964	32,554	35,600
Export (1000 tonnes)	59	1624	1988	3400	5100

SOURCE: International Rice Research Institute

14. **Data Analysis** The table shows population and licensed driver statistics from a recent year.
   a. Make a scatter plot.
   b. Draw a trend line.
   c. The population of Michigan was approximately 10 million that year. About how many licensed drivers lived in Michigan that year?
   d. Writing Is the correlation between population and number of licensed drivers strong or weak? Explain.

Licensed Drivers		
State	Population (millions)	Number of Drivers (millions)
Arkansas	2.8	2.0
Illinois	12.8	8.1
Kansas	2.8	2.0
Massachusetts	6.4	4.7
Pennsylvania	12.4	8.5
Texas	23.5	14.9

Reasoning For a strong correlation, people often assume that change in one quantity causes change in the second quantity. This is not always true. For each situation, predict the type of correlation you might find. Do you think that change in the first quantity causes change in the second quantity? Explain.

15. the number of ice cream cones sold and the temperature

16. the size of a car's engine and the number of passengers it is designed for

17. a person's age and the number of cassette tapes he or she owns

Standardized Test Prep

SAT/ACT

18. What is the equation of the line shown in the graph?

  Ⓐ $y = -2x + 2$ Ⓒ $y = 2x + 1$

  Ⓑ $y = 2x$ Ⓓ $y = 2x + 2$

19. Shauna drove 75 miles in 3 hours at a constant speed. How many miles did she drive in 2 hours?

  Ⓕ 25 miles   Ⓗ 75 miles

  Ⓖ 50 miles   Ⓘ 100 miles

20. Which equation does NOT represent a direct variation?

  Ⓐ $y = x$ Ⓒ $2x - y = 0$

  Ⓑ $2x - y = 5$ Ⓓ $2x - 5y = 0$

Short Response

21. The line $(y - 1) = \frac{2}{3}(x + 1)$ contains point $(a, -3)$. What is the value of a? Show your work.

Mixed Review

Graph the following linear equations.   ◀ **See Lesson 2-3.**

22. $y = -7.5x + 11$ **23.** $-\frac{2}{9}x - \frac{5}{9}y = 10$ **24.** $5x - 4y = 3$

Write the equation of each line in standard form.   ◀ **See Lesson 2-4.**

25. slope = 2; $(2, 6)$ **26.** slope = -1; $(-3, 3)$ **27.** slope = 0; $(0, 2)$

Get Ready! **To prepare for Lesson 2-6, do Exercises 28–30.**

Graph each pair of functions on the same coordinate plane.   ◀ **See Lesson 2-3.**

28. $y = -x$ **29.** $y = x + 1$ **30.** $y = -\frac{1}{4}x$

       $y = x$ $y = 2x - 1$ $y = -\frac{1}{4}x + 2$

Families of Functions

Objective To analyze transformations of functions

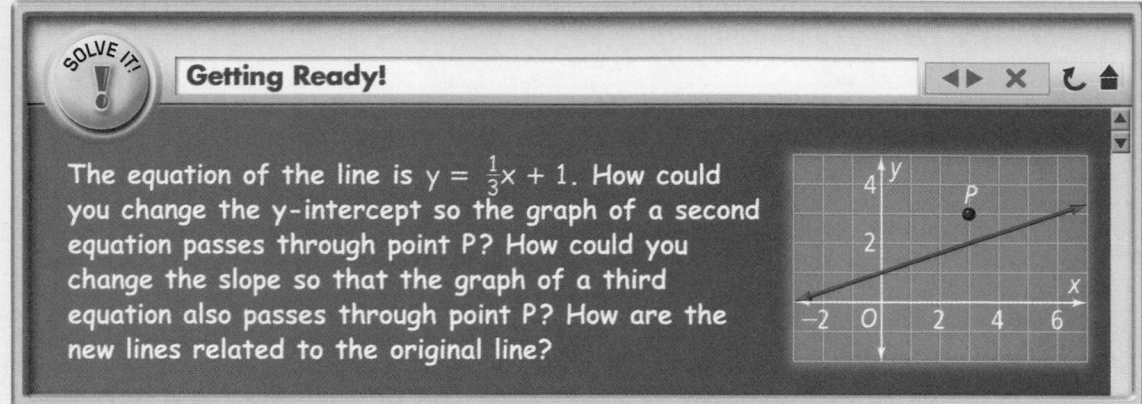

Dynamic Activity
Translating
Functions

**Lesson
Vocabulary**
• parent function
• transformation
• translation

Different non-vertical lines have different slopes, or *y*-intercepts, or both. They are graphs of different linear functions. For two such lines, you can think of one as a *transformation* of the other. In fact, you can algebraically transform the function of one line into the function of the other.

Focus Question What is a translation of a function?

The linear functions form a family of functions. Each linear function is a transformation of the function $y = x$. The function $y = x$ is the *parent* linear function.

A **parent function** is the simplest form in a set of functions that form a family. Each function in the family is a **transformation** of the parent function.

One type of transformation is a **translation**. A translation shifts the graph of the parent function horizontally, vertically, or both without changing shape or orientation. For a positive constant k and a parent function $f(x)$, $f(x) \pm k$ is a vertical translation. For a positive constant h, $f(x \pm h)$ is a horizontal translation.

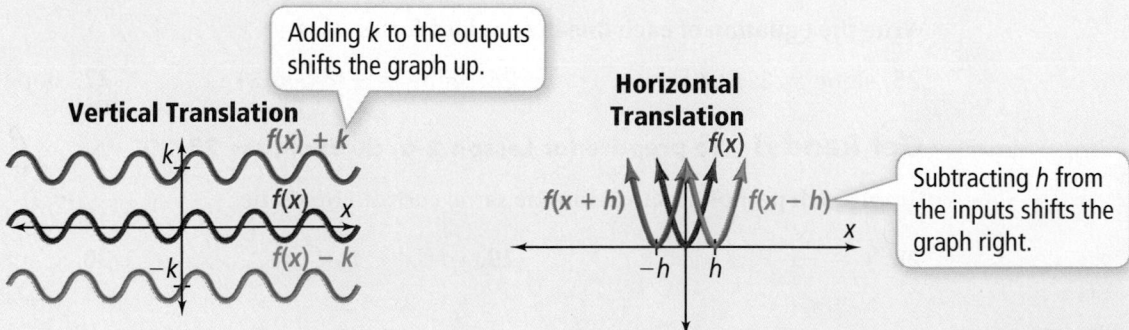

Adding *k* to the outputs shifts the graph up.

Vertical Translation

$f(x) + k$

$f(x)$

$f(x) - k$

Horizontal Translation

$f(x)$

$f(x + h)$ $f(x - h)$

Subtracting *h* from the inputs shifts the graph right.

What is one way to compare two functions?
Use a table to compare their values.

A How are the functions $y = x$ and $y = x - 2$ related? How are their graphs related?

Make a table of values.

x	y = x	y = x − 2
−2	−2	−4
−1	−1	−3
0	0	−2
1	1	−1
2	2	0

Draw their graphs.

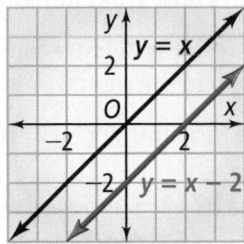

Each output for $y = x - 2$ is two less than the corresponding output for $y = x$.

The graph of $y = x - 2$ is the graph of $y = x$ translated down two units.

B What is the graph of $y = x^2$ translated up 4 units?

Translate the graph of $y = x^2$ up 4 units to get the blue parabola. The equation of the blue parabola is $y = x^2 + 4$.

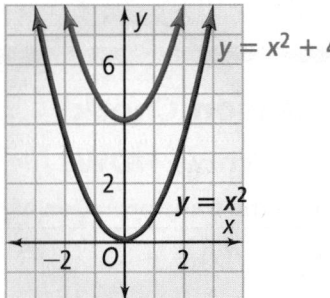

Check Every value in the $y = x^2 + 4$ column is 4 greater than the corresponding value in the $y = x^2$ column.

x	y = x²	y = x² + 4
−2	4	8
−1	1	5
0	0	4
1	1	5
2	4	8

Got It? **1. a.** How are the functions $y = 2x$ and $y = 2x - 3$ related? How are their graphs related?

b. What is the graph of $y = 3x$ translated up 2 units?

c. **Reasoning** What is the equation of the parabola $y = x^2 - 3$ after a translation up 5 units?

Problem 2 Horizontal Translation

Think

If the time of the flight is later, why do you subtract rather than add in $f(x - 2)$? The y-values of the delayed flight correspond to x-values 2 hours *earlier* than the delayed flight.

The graph shows the projected altitude $f(x)$ of an airplane scheduled to depart an airport at noon. If the plane leaves two hours late, what function represents this transformation?

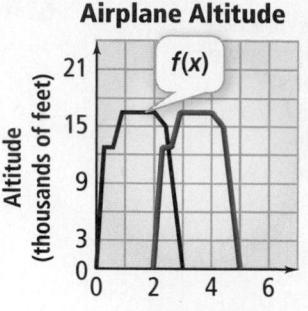

Airplane Altitude

A two-hour delay means the plane leaves at 2 P.M. This shifts the graph to the right 2 units.

The function $f(x - 2)$ represents this transformation.

Got It? 2. Suppose the flight leaves 30 minutes early. What function represents this transformation?

Focus Question What is a translation of a parent function?

Answer A translation shifts the graph of the parent function horizontally, vertically, or both without changing shape or orientation. To translate the parent function $f(x)$ horizontally, add a constant h to the input. To translate the parent function vertically, add a constant k to the output.

Lesson Check

Do you know HOW?

Describe the transformation of the parent function $f(x)$.

1. $g(x) = f(x) + 6$

2. $h(x) = f(x - 4)$

Do you UNDERSTAND?

3. Reasoning Can you give an example of a function for which a horizontal translation gives the same resulting graph as a vertical translation? Explain.

Practice and Problem-Solving Exercises

A Practice

How is each function related to $y = x$? Graph the function by translating the parent function.

 **See Problem 1.**

Guided Practice

To start, make a table of values that compares $y = x - 3$ to the parent function, $y = x$.

4. $y = x - 3$

x	y = x	y = x - 3
-2	-2	-5
-1	-1	-4
0	0	-3
1	1	-2
2	2	-1

5. $y = x + 4.5$ **6.** $y = x + 1.5$ **7.** $y = x^2 - 5$

Make a table of values for $f(x)$ after the given translation.

8. 3 units up

x	f(x)
−2	3
0	1
1	−2
3	−1

9. 1 unit down

x	f(x)
−1	1
0	0
2	−4
3	2

10. 4 units up

x	f(x)
−3	1
−1	−2
1	0
4	3

Write an equation for each vertical translation of $y = f(x)$.

11. $\frac{2}{3}$ unit down

12. 4 units up

13. 2 units up

For each function, identify the horizontal translation of the parent function, $f(x) = x^2$. Then graph the function.

◀ See Problem 2.

Guided Practice →

To start, explain how the parent function is translated.

14. $y = (x - 4)^2$

Shift the graph of $y = x^2$ to the right 4 units.

15. $y = (x + 1)^2$

16. $y = (x + 3)^2$

17. $y = (x - 6)^2$

18. The graph of the function $f(x)$ is shown at the right.
   a. Make a table of values for $f(x)$ and $f(x + 3)$.
   b. Graph $f(x)$ and $f(x + 3)$ on the same coordinate grid.

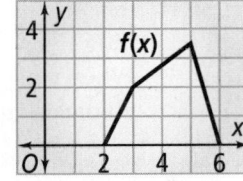

B **Apply**

19. Open-Ended Draw a figure in Quadrant I. Use a translation to move your figure into Quadrant III. Describe your translation.

Graph each pair of functions on the same coordinate plane. Describe a transformation that changes $f(x)$ to $g(x)$.

20. $f(x) = x + 1$
   $g(x) = x - 5$

21. $f(x) = x - 3$
   $g(x) = x + 1$

Families of Functions

Objective To analyze transformations of functions

In Part 1 of the lesson, you transformed parent functions using translation.

Connect to What You Know

Here you will combine what you learned with reflection, stretch, and compression of parent functions.

Focus Question What other transformations can you perform on a parent function?

A **reflection** flips the graph of a function across a line, such as the *x*- or *y*-axis. Each point on the graph of the reflected function is the same distance from the line of reflection as is the corresponding point on the graph of the original function.

When you reflect a graph in the *y*-axis, the *x*-values change sign and the *y*-values stay the same. For a function $f(x)$, the reflection in the *y*-axis is $f(-x)$.

When you reflect a graph in the *x*-axis, the *x*-values stay the same and the *y*-values change sign. For a function $f(x)$, the reflection in the *x*-axis is $-f(x)$.

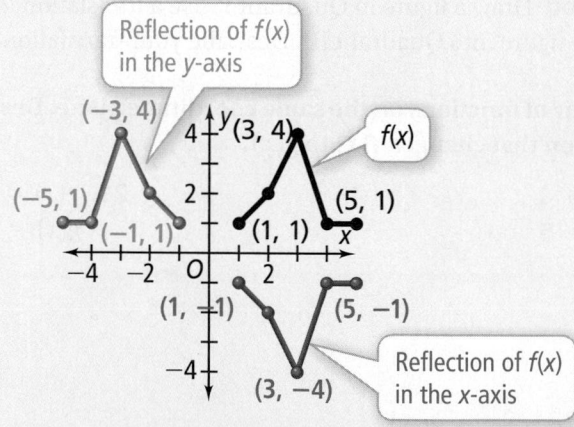

Problem 3 Reflecting a Function Algebraically

Let $g(x)$ be the reflection of $f(x) = 3x + 2$ in the y-axis. What is a function rule for $g(x)$?

Think	Write
For a reflection in the y-axis, change the sign of x.	$g(x) = f(-x)$
Evaluate $f(-x)$ and simplify.	$g(x) = f(-x)$ $\qquad = 3(-x) + 2$ $g(x) = -3x + 2$
You can check by graphing $f(x)$ and $g(x)$.	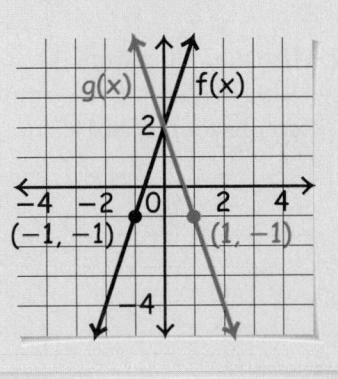

 Got It? **3.** Let $h(x)$ be the reflection of $f(x) = 3x + 2$ in the x-axis. What is a function rule for $h(x)$?

A **vertical stretch** multiplies all y-values of a function by the same factor greater than 1. A **vertical compression** reduces all y-values of a function by the same factor between 0 and 1. For a function $f(x)$ and a constant a, $y = af(x)$ is a vertical stretch when $a > 1$ and a vertical compression when $0 < a < 1$.

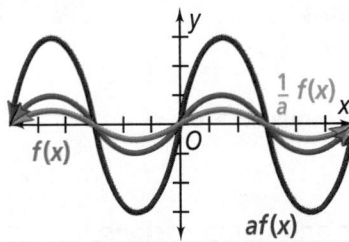

 **Problem 4** Stretching and Compressing a Function

The table at the right represents the function $f(x)$. What are the corresponding values of $g(x)$ and possible graphs for the transformation $g(x) = 3f(x)$?

x	f(x)
−5	2
−2	2
0	−3
3	1
5	−2

Think

Is this a vertical stretch or compression?
3 is greater than 1, so this is a vertical stretch.

Step 1 Multiply each value of $f(x)$ by 3 to find each corresponding value of $g(x)$.

x	f(x)	3f(x)	g(x)
−5	2	3(2)	6
−2	2	3(2)	6
0	−3	3(−3)	−9
3	1	3(1)	3
5	−2	3(−2)	−6

Step 2 Use the values from the table in Step 1. Draw simple graphs for $f(x)$ and $g(x)$.

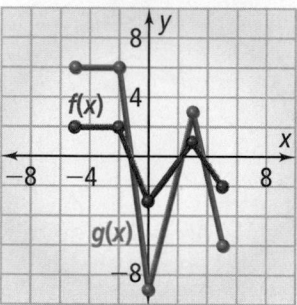

 Got It? 4. a. For the function $f(x)$ shown in Problem 4, what are the corresponding table and graph for the transformation $h(x) = \frac{1}{3}f(x)$?

   b. Reasoning If several transformations are applied to a graph, will changing the order of transformations change the resulting graph? Explain.

---

take note **Concept Summary** Transformations of $f(x)$

Vertical Translations
Translation up k units, $k > 0$
 $y = f(x) + k$
Translation down k units, $k > 0$
 $y = f(x) - k$

Horizontal Translations
Translation right h units, $h > 0$
 $y = f(x - h)$
Translation left h units, $h > 0$
 $y = f(x + h)$

Vertical Stretches and Compressions
Vertical stretch, $a > 1$
 $y = af(x)$
Vertical compression, $0 < a < 1$
 $y = af(x)$

Reflections
In the x-axis
 $y = -f(x)$
In the y-axis
 $y = f(-x)$

Problem 5 **Combining Transformations**

A The graph of $g(x)$ is the graph of $f(x) = 4x$ compressed vertically by the factor $\frac{1}{2}$ and then reflected in the y-axis. What is the function rule for $g(x)$?

Compress $f(x)$. $\frac{1}{2}(4x) = 2x$

Reflect the new function in the y-axis. $2(-x) = -2x$

The function rule is $g(x) = -2x$.

B What transformations change the graph of $f(x)$ to the graph of $g(x)$?

$$f(x) = 2x^2 \quad g(x) = 6x^2 - 1$$

$$\begin{aligned} g(x) &= 6x^2 - 1 \\ &= 3(2x^2) - 1 \\ &= 3(f(x)) - 1 \end{aligned}$$

Think

How can you write $g(x)$ in terms of $f(x)$? Factor out 3 from the $6x^2$ term.

The graph of $g(x)$ is the graph of $f(x)$ stretched vertically by a factor of 3 and then translated down 1 unit.

Got It? **5. a.** The graph of $g(x)$ is the graph of $f(x) = x$ stretched vertically by a factor of 2 and then translated down 3 units. What is the function rule for $g(x)$?

b. What transformations change the graph of $f(x) = x^2$ to the graph of $g(x) = (x + 4)^2 - 2$?

Focus Question What other transformations can you perform on a parent function?

Answer A reflection flips a function across a line, usually an axis. The equation of the reflected function changes the sign of either the inputs or outputs. Vertical stretch and compression multiply the outputs of a function by the same factor.

 Lesson Check

Do you know HOW?

Describe the transformation on the parent function $f(x)$.

1. $h(x) = 0.25f(x)$ **2.** $k(x) = f(-x)$

The graph of $f(x) = -2x$ is shown. Describe and graph each transformation.

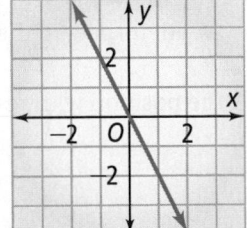

3. $g(x) = f(x + 1) - 2$

4. $h(x) = 2f(x) + 1$

Do you UNDERSTAND?

5. Compare and Contrast The graph shows $f(x) = 0.5x - 1$. Graph $g(x)$ by translating $f(x)$ up 2 units and then stretching it vertically by the factor 2.

Graph $h(x)$ by stretching $f(x)$ vertically by the factor 2 and then translating it up 2 units. Compare the graphs of $g(x)$ and $h(x)$.

6. Find a new function $g(x)$ transformed from $f(x) = -x - 2$ such that $g(x)$ is perpendicular to $f(x)$.

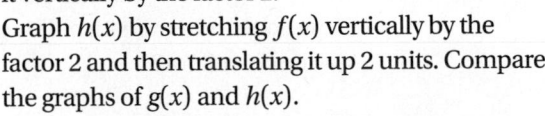

Practice and Problem-Solving Exercises

A **Practice**

Write the function rule for each function reflected in the given axis.

 **See Problem 3.**

Guided Practice

To start, change the sign of $f(x)$ for a reflection in the x-axis.

7. $f(x) = x + 1$; x-axis

$g(x) = -f(x)$

8. $f(x) = 3x$; y-axis

9. $f(x) = 2x - 4$; x-axis

Write an equation for each transformation of $y = x$.

See Problem 4.

10. vertical stretch by a factor of 4

11. vertical stretch by a factor of 2

12. vertical compression by a factor of $\frac{1}{2}$

13. vertical compression by a factor of $\frac{1}{4}$

Write the function rule $g(x)$ after the given transformations of the graph of $f(x) = 4x$.

See Problem 5.

Guided Practice

To start, translate $f(x)$ up 5 units.

14. translation up 5 units; reflection in the x-axis

$f(x) + 5 = 4x + 5$

15. vertical stretch by a factor of 3; translation down 1 unit

16. reflection in the y-axis; vertical compression by a factor of $\frac{1}{8}$

Describe the transformations of $f(x)$ that produce $g(x)$.

17. $f(x) = \frac{x}{2}$; $g(x) = -2x + 4$

18. $f(x) = 3x$; $g(x) = \frac{3x}{4} - 2$

B **Apply**

19. Error Analysis William wrote the transformations shown to describe how to change the graph of $f(x) = x^2$ to the graph of $g(x) = 2(x + 1)^2 - 3$. Explain his error and give the correct transformations.

> • ~~shift vertically 1 unit up~~
> • shift horizontally 2 units right
> • ~~shift vertically 3 units down~~

20. Think About a Plan Suppose you are playing with a yo-yo during a school talent show. The string is 3 ft long and you hold your hand 4 ft above the stage. The stage is 3.5 ft above the floor of the auditorium. Make a graph of the yo-yo's distance from the auditorium floor with respect to time during the show.
  • How could you graph the position of the yo-yo with respect to the stage, if you let time $t = 0$ when you start your routine?
  • How could you transform this graph to show the position with respect to the auditorium floor?

21. In Exercise 20, if someone started to take a video of your yo-yo routine when you were introduced, 10 seconds before you actually started, what transformation would you have to make to your graph to match their video?

Write the equations for $f(x)$ and $g(x)$. Then identify the reflection that transforms the graph of $f(x)$ to the graph of $g(x)$.

22.

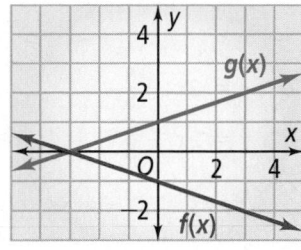

23.

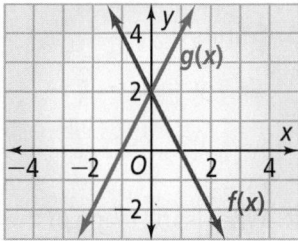

24. Open-Ended Draw a figure in Quadrant I. Use a reflection(s) to move your figure into Quadrant III. Describe your reflection(s).

25. Writing The graph of $f(x)$ is shown at the right. Suppose each transformation of $f(x)$ results in the given function.

    i. vertical translation; $g(x)$
    ii. reflection in the x-axis; $h(x)$
    iii. vertical stretch; $k(x)$
    iv. horizontal translation; $m(x)$

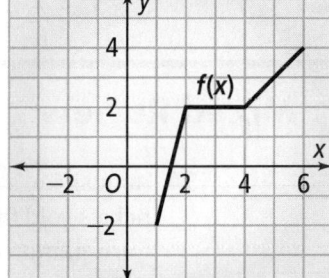

  a. Describe how the domains and ranges of the four new functions compare with the domain and range of $f(x)$.

  b. Reasoning Do you think these effects on the domain and range of the original function hold true for all functions? Explain.

Graph each pair of functions on the same coordinate plane. Describe a transformation that changes $f(x)$ to $g(x)$.

26. $f(x) = x + 1$
    $g(x) = x - 5$

27. $f(x) = -x + 3$
    $g(x) = x - 4$

28. $f(x) = x - 3$
    $g(x) = x + 1$

29. $f(x) = -x - 1$
    $g(x) = -x + 2$

Standardized Test Prep

SAT/ACT

What is an equation for each vertical translation of $y = 2x - 1$?

30. 3 units down

  Ⓐ $y = 2x - 7$ Ⓒ $y = 2x + 5$

  Ⓑ $y = 2x + 2$ Ⓓ $y = 2x - 4$

31. $\frac{3}{5}$ units up

  Ⓕ $y = 2x - \frac{2}{5}$ Ⓗ $y = 2x - \frac{8}{5}$

  Ⓖ $y = 2x - \frac{11}{5}$ Ⓘ $y = 2x + \frac{1}{5}$

32. What is the slope of the line in the graph at the right?

  Ⓐ $-\frac{5}{2}$ Ⓒ $\frac{2}{5}$

  Ⓑ $-\frac{2}{5}$ Ⓓ $\frac{5}{2}$

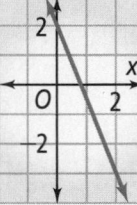

Short
Response

33. The weight of a gold bar varies directly with its volume. If a 40 cm^3 bar weighs 772 grams, how much will a 100 cm^3 bar weigh?

Mixed Review

34. A musician's manager keeps track of the ticket prices and the number of tickets sold for recent performances. Use a graphing calculator to determine the equation of the line of best fit for the given data.

See Lesson 2-5.

Ticket Prices($)	41.00	41.50	42.00	43.00	43.50	44.00	44.50	45.00	45.00	47.00
Number Sold	256	276	250	241	210	235	195	194	205	180

Solve each inequality. Graph each solution on a number line.

See Lesson 1-5.

35. $x + 7 \leq -3$ **36.** $2a + 6 > 15$ **37.** $7.5 - 3b < 12$

Get Ready!   To prepare for Lesson 2-7, do Exercises 38–40.

Solve each absolute value equation.

See Lesson 1-6.

38. $|x - 3| + 2 = 7$ **39.** $|2x + 1| - 14 = 9$ **40.** $\frac{1}{3}|5x - 3| = 6$

Objective To graph absolute value functions

Getting Ready!

You jog at a constant speed. Your jogging route takes you across the county line. Suppose you graph your distance from the county line with respect to time. What would the graph look like? Explain.

ENTERING
Jefferson
County

You'll study more graphs like this one in the lesson.

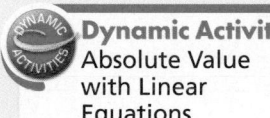
Dynamic Activity
Absolute Value with Linear Equations

Lesson Vocabulary
• absolute value function
• axis of symmetry
• vertex

There is a family of functions related to the one you represented in the Solve It.

Focus Question What is an absolute value function?

The simplest example of an **absolute value function** is $f(x) = |x|$. The graph of the absolute value of a linear function in two variables is V-shaped and symmetric about a vertical line called the **axis of symmetry**. Such a graph has either a single maximum point or a single minimum point, called the **vertex**.

take note

Key Concept Absolute Value Parent Function $f(x) = |x|$

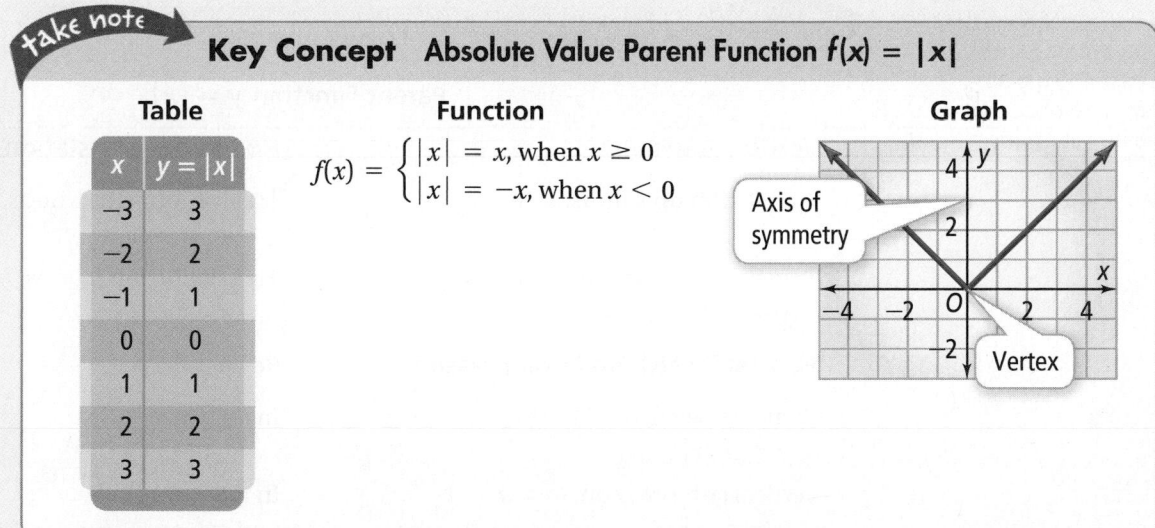

Table	
x	$y = |x|$
−3	3
−2	2
−1	1
0	0
1	1
2	2
3	3

Function

$$f(x) = \begin{cases} |x| = x, \text{ when } x \geq 0 \\ |x| = -x, \text{ when } x < 0 \end{cases}$$

Graph

Axis of symmetry

Vertex

Problem 1 Graphing an Absolute Value Function

What is the graph of the absolute value function $y = |x| - 4$? How is this graph different from the graph of the parent function $f(x) = |x|$?

Think

Make a table of values and graph the function.

Use the location of the vertex to see how to translate the parent function.
The parent function was not multiplied by a number. So, the graph of $y = |x| - 4$ is not a stretch, compression, or reflection.

Write

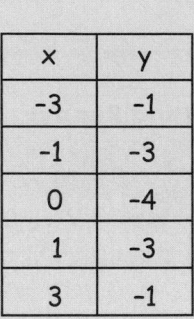

x	y
-3	-1
-1	-3
0	-4
1	-3
3	-1

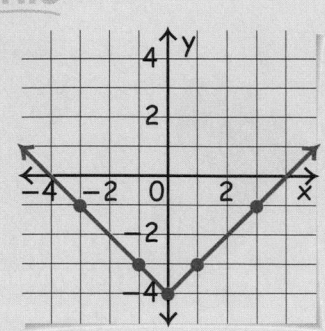

Since the vertex is at $(0, -4)$, you translated the graph of $y = |x|$ down 4 units.

 Got It? **1. a.** What is the graph of the function $y = |x| + 2$? How is this graph different from the parent function?

b. Reasoning Do transformations of the form $y = |x| + k$ affect the axis of symmetry? Explain.

Hint

The transformations you studied in Lesson 2-6 also apply to absolute value functions.

 **Key Concept** **The Family of Absolute Value Functions**

Parent Function $y = |x|$

Vertical Translation	**Horizontal Translation**
Translation up k units, $k > 0$ $y = |x| + k$	Translation right h units, $h > 0$ $y = |x - h|$
Translation down k units, $k > 0$ $y = |x| - k$	Translation left h units, $h > 0$ $y = |x + h|$
Vertical Stretch and Compression	**Reflection**
Vertical stretch, $a > 1$ $y = a|x|$	In the x-axis $y = -|x|$
Vertical compression, $0 < a < 1$ $y = a|x|$	In the y-axis $y = |-x|$

Problem 2 **Combining Translations**

Multiple Choice Which of the following is the graph of $y = |x + 2| + 3$?

Ⓐ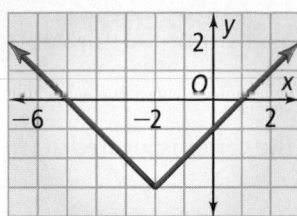

Ⓒ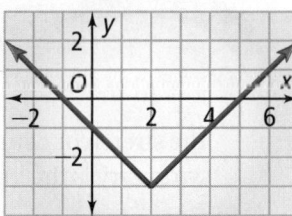

Ⓑ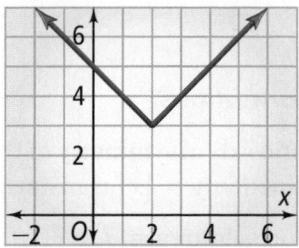

Ⓓ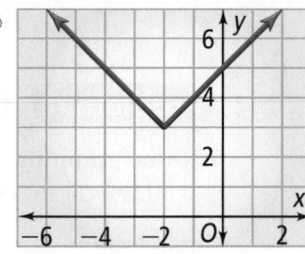

Think

Can you eliminate any answers after this comparison?
Only choices A and D show translations of $y = |x|$ to the left.

Compare $y = |x + 2| + 3$ to the parent function $y = |x|$.

    Translate the parent function left 2 units. $y = |x - (-2)| + 3$

    Translate the parent function up 3 units. $y = |x + 2| + 3$

The parent function $y = |x|$ is translated left 2 units and up 3 units. The vertex will be at $(-2, 3)$. The correct answer is D.

 Got It? **2.** What is the graph of the function $y = |x - 2| + 1$?

The right branch of the graph of $y = |x|$ has slope 1. The graph of $y = a|x|$, $a > 0$, is a stretch or compression of the graph of $y = |x|$. Its right branch has slope a. The graph of $y = -a|x|$ is a reflection of $y = a|x|$ in the x-axis and its right branch has slope $-a$.

 Problem 3 **Vertical Stretch and Compression**

What is the graph of $y = \frac{1}{2}|x|$?

The graph is a vertical compression of the graph of $f(x) = |x|$ by the factor $\frac{1}{2}$. Graph the right branch and use symmetry to graph the left branch.

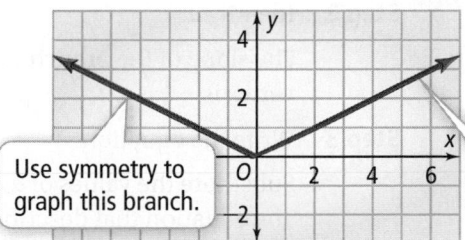

Use symmetry to graph this branch.

Starting at $(0, 0)$, graph $y = \frac{1}{2}x$.

Hint

For part (b), make a table of values to help you graph the function.

 Got It? **3.** What is the graph of each function?
    a. $y = 2|x|$ **b.** $y = -\frac{2}{3}|x|$

You can combine the equations for stretches and compressions with the equations for translations to write a general form for absolute value functions.

 take note

Key Concept General Form of the Absolute Value Function

$$y = a|x - h| + k$$

The stretch or compression factor is $|a|$, the vertex is located at (h, k), and the axis of symmetry is the line $x = h$.

 Problem 4 Identifying Transformations

Plan
To what should you compare
$y = 3|x - 2| + 4$?
Compare it to the general form,
$y = a|x - h| + k.$

Without graphing, what are the vertex and axis of symmetry of the graph of $y = 3|x - 2| + 4$? **How is the parent function** $y = |x|$ **transformed?**

Compare $y = 3|x - 2| + 4$ with the general form $y = a|x - h| + k$.

$a = 3, h = 2,$ and $k = 4.$

The vertex is $(2, 4)$ and the axis of symmetry is $x = 2$.

The parent function $y = |x|$ is translated right 2 units, vertically stretched by the factor 3, and translated up 4 units.

Check Check by graphing the equation on a graphing calculator.

Got It? **4.** What are the vertex and axis of symmetry of
$y = -2|x - 1| - 3$? How is $y = |x|$ transformed?

 Problem 5 Writing an Absolute Value Function

What is an equation of the absolute value function shown in the graph?

Think
What does the graph tell you about a?
The upside-down V-shape suggests that $a < 0$.

Step 1 Identify the vertex.

The vertex is at $(-1, 4)$, so $h = -1$ and $k = 4$.

Step 2 Identify a.

The slope of the branch to the right of the vertex is $-\frac{1}{3}$, so $a = -\frac{1}{3}$.

Step 3 Write the equation.

Substitute the values of a, h, and k into the general form $y = a|x - h| + k$.
The equation that describes the graph is $y = -\frac{1}{3}|x + 1| + 4$.

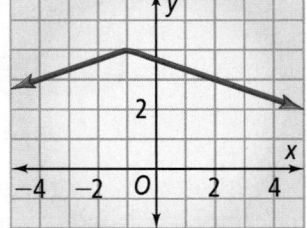

Got It? **5.** What is an equation of the absolute value function shown in the graph?

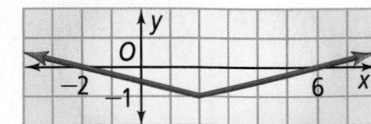

Focus Question What is an absolute value function?

Answer An absolute value function gives the distance from the line $y = 0$ for each value of $f(x)$. Write the equation of the function in the general form $y = a|x - h| + k$ to identify the transformations of the parent function $f(x) = |x|$.

Lesson Check

Do you know HOW?

Find the vertex and the axis of symmetry of the graph of each function.

1. $y = 2|x + 4| - 3$ **2.** $y = |-x - 3| + 9$

Determine if each function is a vertical stretch or vertical compression of the parent function $y = |x|$.

3. $y = -\frac{7}{2}|x|$ **4.** $y = \frac{3}{2}|x|$

Do you UNDERSTAND?

5. Is it true that without making a graph of an absolute value function, you can describe its position in the coordinate plane? Explain with an example.

6. Write two absolute value functions such that they have a common vertex in Quadrant III and one is the reflection in a horizontal line of the other.

7. Compare and Contrast How is the graph of $y = x$ different from the graph of $y = |x|$?

Practice and Problem-Solving Exercises

 **Practice**   **Make a table of values for each equation. Then graph the equation.**   **See Problems 1 and 2.**

Guided Practice

8. $y = |x| + 1$

To start, make a table of values.

x	y
−2	3
−1	2
0	1
1	2
2	3

9. $y = |x| - 1$ **10.** $y = |x| - 3$ **11.** $y = |x + 2|$

12. $y = |x - 1| + 3$ **13.** $y = |x + 6| - 1$ **14.** $y = |x - 5| + 4$

Graph each equation. Then describe the transformation from the parent function $f(x) = |x|$.   **See Problem 3.**

15. $y = 3|x|$ **16.** $y = -2|x|$ **17.** $y = -\frac{3}{4}|x|$

Without graphing, identify the vertex, axis of symmetry, and transformations from the parent function $f(x) = |x|$.

● See Problem 4.

 Guided
Practice

To start, compare the equation with the general form $y = a|x - h| + k$.

18. $y = |x + 2| - 4$

$y = 1|x - (-2)| + (-4)$

$a = 1, h = -2, k = -4$

19. $y = \frac{3}{2}|x - 6|$ **20.** $y = -|x - 5|$ **21.** $y = |x - 2| - 6$

Write an absolute value equation for each graph.

● See Problem 5.

22.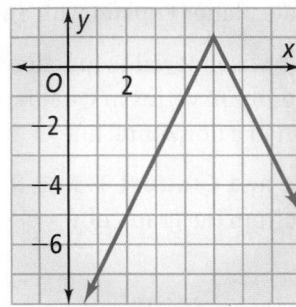

23.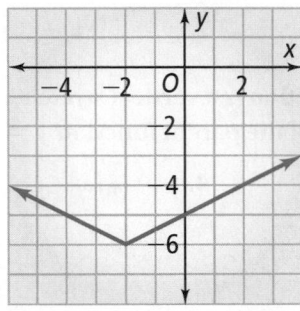

B Apply

24. Think About a Plan Graph $y = -2|x + 3| + 4$. List the x- and y-intercepts, if any.
- What is the vertex?
- What does y equal at the x-intercept(s)? What does x equal at the y-intercept(s)?

25. Graph $y = 4|x - 3| + 1$. List the vertex and the x- and y-intercepts, if any.

26. Error Analysis A classmate says that the graphs of $y = -3|x|$ and $y = |-3x|$ are identical. Graph each function and explain why your classmate is not correct.

27. Graph each pair of equations on the same coordinate grid.
  a. $y = 2|x + 1|$ and $y = |2x + 1|$ **b.** $y = 5|x - 2|$ and $y = |5x - 2|$
  c. Reasoning Explain why each pair of graphs in parts (a) and (b) are different.

28. The graphs of the absolute value functions $f(x)$ and $g(x)$ are given.
  a. Describe a series of transformations that you can use to transform $f(x)$ into $g(x)$.
  b. Reasoning If you change the order of the transformations you found in part (a), could you still transform $f(x)$ into $g(x)$? Explain.

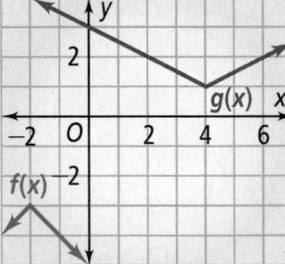

29. a. Graph the equations $y = \left|\frac{1}{2}x - 6\right| + 3$ and
    $y = -\left|\frac{1}{2}x + 6\right| - 3$ on the same set of axes.
  b. Writing Describe the similarities and differences in the graphs.

Graph each absolute value equation.

30. $y = \left|-\frac{1}{4}x - 1\right|$ **31.** $y = \left|\frac{5}{2}x - 2\right|$ **32.** $y = |3x - 6| + 1$

33. $y = -|x - 3|$ **34.** $y = 2|x + 2| - 3$ **35.** $y = 6 - |3x + 1|$

Standardized Test Prep

SAT/ACT

36. The graph shows which equation?

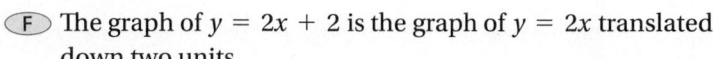

(A) $y = |3x - 1| + 2$

(B) $y = |x - 1| + 2$

(C) $y = |x - 1| - 2$

(D) $y = |3x - 3| - 2$

37. How are the graphs of $y = 2x$ and $y = 2x + 2$ related?

(F) The graph of $y = 2x + 2$ is the graph of $y = 2x$ translated down two units.

(G) The graph of $y = 2x + 2$ is the graph of $y = 2x$ translated up two units.

(H) The graph of $y = 2x + 2$ is the graph of $y = 2x$ translated to the left two units.

(I) The graph of $y = 2x + 2$ is the graph of $y = 2x$ translated to the right two units.

38. What is the equation of a line parallel to $y = x$ that passes through the point $(0, 1)$?

(A) $y = x + 1$

(B) $y = 2x + 2$

(C) $y = x - 1$

(D) $y = -x$

Short Response

39. Is $|y| = x$ a function? Explain.

Mixed Review

Write an equation for each transformation of the graph of $y = x + 2$.   ◀ See Lesson 2-6.

40. up 2 units, right 3 units

41. vertical compression by a factor of $\frac{1}{2}$, reflection in the y-axis

Find a trend line for each scatter plot. Write the equation for each trend line.   ◀ See Lesson 2-5.

42.

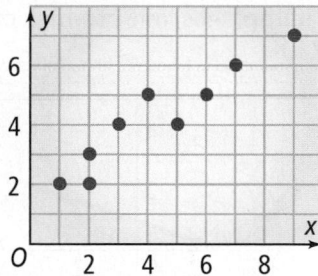

43.

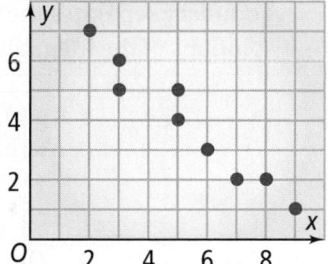

Get Ready! **To prepare for Lesson 2-8, do Exercises 44–46.**

Solve each inequality. Graph the solution on a number line.   ◀ See Lesson 1-5.

44. $12p \le 15$

45. $4 + t > 17$

46. $5 - 2t \ge 11$

2-8 Two-Variable Inequalities

Objective To graph two-variable inequalities

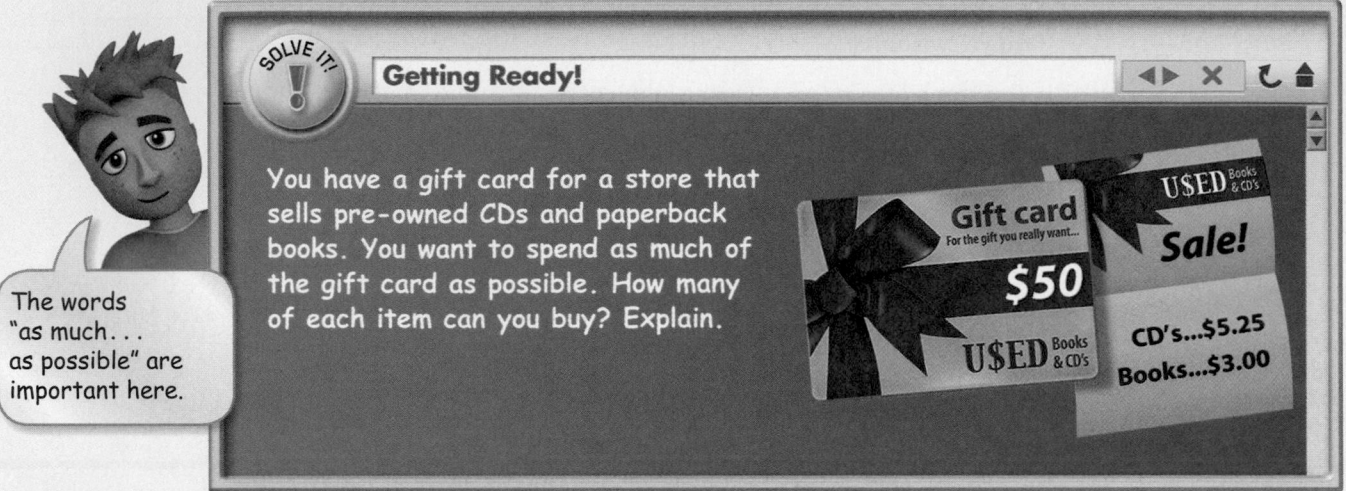

Lesson Vocabulary
- linear inequality
- boundary
- half-plane
- test point

In some situations you need to compare quantities. You can use inequalities for situations that involve these relationships: *less than, less than or equal to, greater than,* and *greater than or equal to.*

Focus Question Is graphing an inequality in two variables similar to graphing a line?

A **linear inequality** is an inequality in two variables whose graph is a region of the coordinate plane bounded by a line. This line is the **boundary** of the graph. The boundary separates the coordinate plane into two **half-planes**, one of which consists of solutions of the inequality.

Hint

A solid boundary line indicates that points on the line are solutions of the inequality. A dashed line means the points are not solutions.

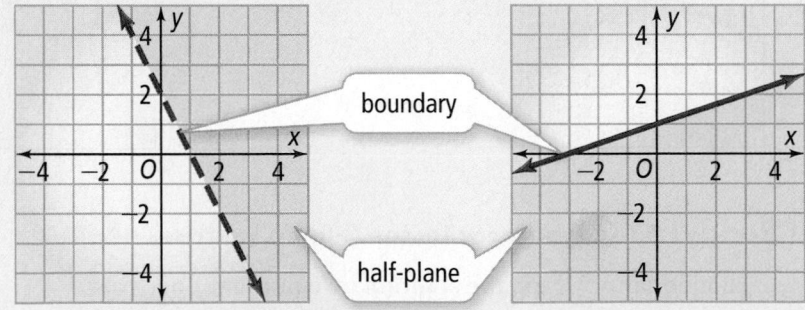

boundary

half-plane

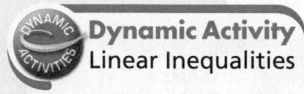
Dynamic Activity
Linear Inequalities

To determine which half-plane to shade, pick a **test point** that is *not* on the boundary. Check whether that point satisfies the inequality. If it does, shade the half-plane that includes the test point. If not, shade the other half-plane. The origin, $(0, 0)$, is usually an easy point to test, as long as it is not on the boundary.

 Problem 1 Graphing Linear Inequalities

What is the graph of each inequality?

A $y > 3x - 1$

Hint
The equation is in slope-intercept form. The line $y = 3x - 1$ has slope 3 and y-intercept $(0, -1)$.

Step 1

Graph the boundary line $y = 3x - 1$. The inequality is *greater than*. Use a dashed boundary line to show that the points on the line do not satisfy the inequality.

Step 2

Choose a test point, $(0, 0)$. Substitute $x = 0$ and $y = 0$ into $y > 3x - 1$.
$$0 > 3(0) - 1$$
$$0 > -1$$
Since $0 > -1$ is true, shade the half plane that includes $(0, 0)$.

B $y \le 3x - 1$

Think

Can you use the graph of $y > 3x - 1$ to help graph $y \le 3x - 1$?
If you shaded above the line for $y > 3x - 1$, then shade below the line for $y \le 3x - 1$.

The boundary line is again $y = 3x - 1$, but it is solid because the inequality is less than or *equal to*.

Shade the region opposite the region shaded above (for $>$) because the inequality is less than or equal to.

You can also check the point $(0, 0)$.

$$0 \le 3(0) - 1$$

$$0 \le -1$$

Since $0 \le -1$ is false, $(0, 0)$ is not part of the solution.

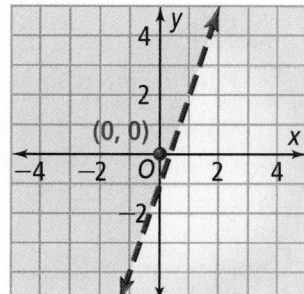

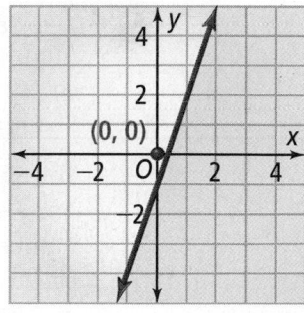

 Got It? 1. What is the graph of each inequality?

       a. $y \ge -2x + 1$ **b.** $y < -2x + 1$

You can also inspect inequalities solved for *y*, such as $y > mx + b$ to determine which half-plane to shade. Since *y* describes vertical position, the solution of $y > mx + b$ is *above* the boundary line. The solution of $y < mx + b$ is *below* the boundary line.

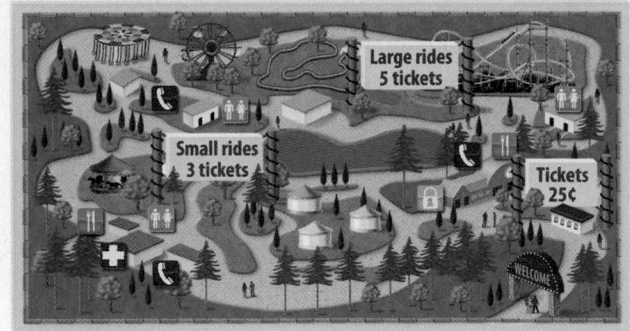

Problem 2 Using a Linear Inequality

Entertainment The map shows the number of tickets needed for small or large rides at the fair. You do not want to spend more than $15 on tickets. How many small or large rides can you ride?

Think

What are the unknowns?
The unknowns are the number of small rides and the number of large rides you can ride.

You can buy 60 tickets with $15.

Relate   the number of tickets for small rides   plus   the number of tickets for large rides   is less than or equal to   60

Define   Let x = the number of small rides.

Let y = the number of large rides.

Write $3x$ + $5y$ ≤   60

Step 1

Find the intercepts of the boundary line. Use the intercepts to graph the boundary line.

When $y = 0$, $3x + 5(0) = 60$.   When $x = 0$, $3(0) + 5y = 60$.

$$3x = 60 \qquad\qquad\qquad 5y = 60$$

$$x = 20 \qquad\qquad\qquad y = 12$$

Graph the line that connects the intercepts (20, 0) and (0, 12). Since the inequality is ≤, use a solid boundary line.

Step 2

The region above the boundary line represents an infinite number of rides. You purchased a *finite* number of tickets, so you will not be able to go on an infinite number of rides. Shade the region below the boundary line.

The number of small rides x and the number of large rides y are whole numbers. In math, such a situation is called *discrete*. All points with whole number coordinates in the shaded region represent possible combinations of small and large rides.

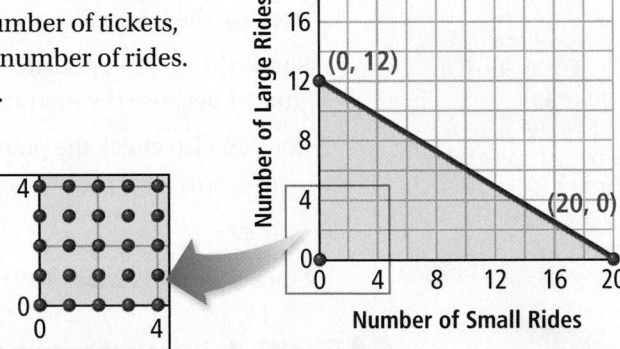

Got It? **2. a.** Suppose that you decide to spend no more than $30 for tickets. What are the possible combinations of small and large rides that you can ride now? Use a graph to find your answer.

b. Reasoning Why did the graph of the solution in Problem 2 only include Quadrant I and the positive x- and y-axes?

You can graph two-variable absolute value inequalities in the same way that you graph linear inequalities.

 Problem 3 Graphing an Absolute Value Inequality

What is the graph of $1 - y < |x + 2|$?

Know	Need	Plan
Absolute value inequality	Boundary	• Solve the inequality for y. • Graph the related equation. • Shade the solution.

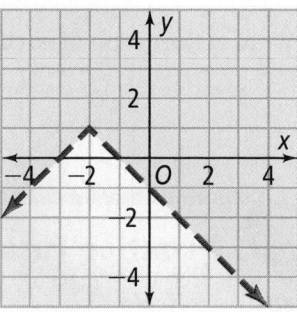

Write the original inequality. $1 - y < |x + 2|$

Subtract 1 from each side. $-y < |x + 2| - 1$

Multiply each side by -1. $y > -|x + 2| + 1$

The graph of $y = -|x + 2| + 1$ is the graph of $y = |x|$, reflected in the x-axis and translated left 2 units and up 1 unit.

Since the inequality is solved for y and $y > -|x + 2| + 1$, shade the region above the boundary.

Hint

When you multiply or divide each side of an inequality by a negative number, you must reverse the inequality symbol.

 Got It? **3.** What is the graph of $y - 4 \geq 2|x - 1|$?

You can use the forms of a line and types of transformations discussed in previous lessons to help draw the boundary graphs more quickly. You can also use them to write an inequality based on a graph.

 Problem 4 Writing an Inequality Based on a Graph

What inequality does this graph represent?

The y intercept of the boundary line is $(0, -2)$, so $b = -2$. The x-intercept of the line is $(4, 0)$. Use these two points to find the slope m.

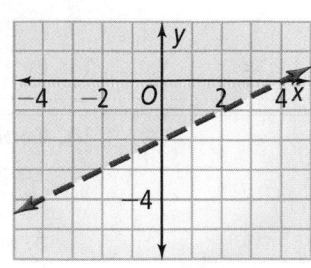

Substitute into $m = \frac{y_2 - y_1}{x_2 - x_1}$. $m = \frac{0 - (-2)}{4 - 0}$

Simplify. $= \frac{2}{4} = \frac{1}{2}$

Substitute into $y = mx + b$. $y = \frac{1}{2}x - 2$

The solution is above the boundary line, so the inequality is either $>$ or $\geq$. Since the boundary is a dashed line, the correct inequality is $y > \frac{1}{2}x - 2$.

Plan

How can you find the equation of the boundary line?
Identify its slope and y-intercept and use the form $y = mx + b$.

 Got It? **4.** What inequality does this graph represent?

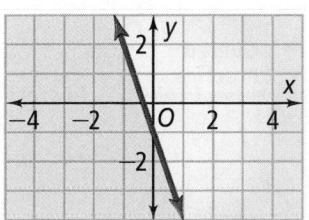

Focus Question Is graphing an inequality in two variables similar to graphing a line?

Answer Graphing an inequality is similar to graphing a line. The graph of an inequality contains all points on one side of the line. The graph may or may not include the points on the line.

Lesson Check

Do you know HOW?

What is the graph of each inequality?

1. $9y \leq 12x$ **2.** $7x + y \geq 8$

What is the graph of each absolute value inequality?

3. $y \leq |x + 1|$ **4.** $y \geq |2x - 3|$

Do you UNDERSTAND?

5. Compare and Contrast How is graphing a linear inequality in two variables different from graphing a linear equation in two variables?

6. Reasoning Is the ordered pair $\left(\frac{3}{4}, 0\right)$ a solution of $3x + y > 3$? Explain.

Practice and Problem-Solving Exercises

**Practice**   Graph each inequality.   ◀ **See Problem 1.**

Guided Practice

7. $y > 2x + 1$

To start, graph the boundary line. Use a dashed boundary because the inequality is >, and the points on the line do not satisfy the solution.

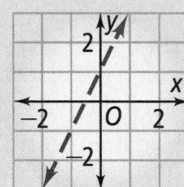

8. $y < 3$ **9.** $x \leq 0$ **10.** $y \leq x - 5$

11. $2y \geq 4x - 6$ **12.** $-y < 2x + 2$ **13.** $5 - y \geq x$

14. Cooking The time needed to roast a chicken depends on its weight. Allow at least 20 min/lb for a chicken weighing as much as 6 lb. Allow at least 15 min/lb for a chicken weighing more than 6 lb.
  a. Write two inequalities to represent the time needed to roast a chicken.
  b. Graph the inequalities.

◀ **See Problem 2.**

Graph each absolute value inequality.   ◀ **See Problem 3.**

Guided Practice

15. $y - 7 > |x + 2|$

$y = 1|x - (-2)| + 7$

To start, identify the boundary. Write the equation of the boundary in standard form $y = a|x - h| + k$.

16. $y \leq |3x| + 1$ **17.** $y \leq |4 - x|$ **18.** $y + 2 \leq \left|\frac{1}{2}x\right|$

Write an inequality for each graph. The equation for the boundary line is given.

◀ **See Problem 4.**

19. $y = -x - 2$

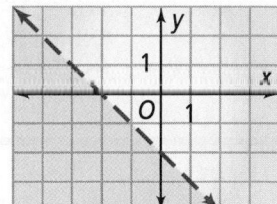

20. $5x + 3y = 9$

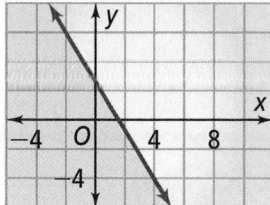

B **Apply**

Graph each inequality on a coordinate plane.

21. $5x - 2y \geq -10$

22. $2x - 5y < -10$

23. $\frac{3}{4}x + \frac{2}{3}y > \frac{5}{2}$

24. $|x - 1| > y + 7$

25. $y - |2x| \leq 21$

26. $\frac{2}{3}x + 2 \leq \frac{2}{9}y$

27. Think About a Plan The graph at the right relates the number of hours you spend on the phone to the number of hours you spend studying per week. Describe the domain for this situation. Write an inequality for the graph.
  - What is the least amount of time you can spend on the phone per week? What is the most?
  - What is the least amount of time you can spend studying per week? What is the most?
  - What is the greatest amount of time you can spend either on the phone or studying per week?

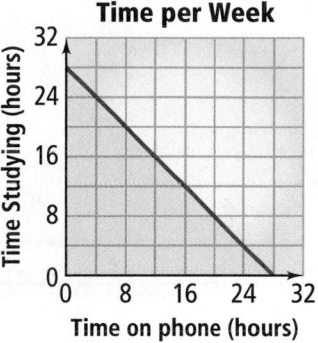

28. Reasoning You can tell from looking at the inequality $y > 5x - 3$ to shade above the boundary line to represent the solution. Can you use the same technique to show the solution of an inequality like $2x - y > 1$? Explain.

29. The graph at the right relates the amount of gas in the tank of your car to the distance you can drive.
  a. Describe the domain for this situation.
  b. Why does the graph stop?
  c. Why is only the first quadrant shown?
  d. Write an inequality for the graph.
  e. What does the coefficient of x represent?
  f. Reasoning Is every point in the solution region a solution?

Miles to Travel

30. Which graph best represents the solutions of the inequality $y \geq 2|x - 1| - 2$?

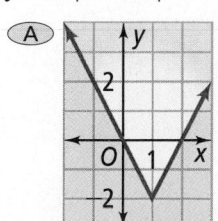
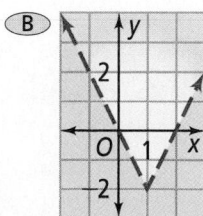
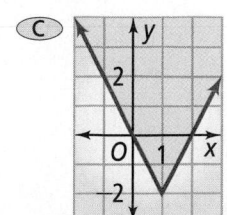
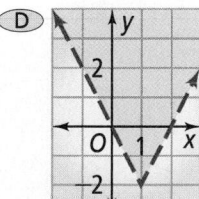

Write an inequality for each graph.

31.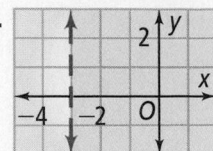

32.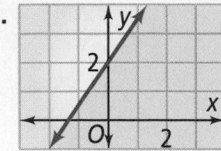

33.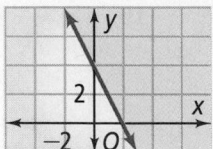

Standardized Test Prep

34. Suppose y varies directly with x. If x is 30 when y is 10, what is x when y is 9?

    Ⓐ 3   Ⓑ 27   Ⓒ 29   Ⓓ $\frac{300}{9}$

35. Which equation represents a line with slope -2 and y-intercept 3?

    Ⓕ $3y = x - 2$ Ⓖ $3y = -2x + 1$ Ⓗ $y = 2x - 3$ Ⓘ $y = -2x + 3$

36. What is the vertex of $y = |x| - 5$?

    Ⓐ $(5, 0)$ Ⓑ $(-5, 0)$ Ⓒ $(0, 5)$ Ⓓ $(0, -5)$

37. The amount of a commission is directly proportional to the amount of a sale. A realtor received a commission of $48,000 on the sale of an $800,000 house. How much would the commission be on a $650,000 house?

Mixed Review

Graph each function by translating its parent function.   ◀ **See Lesson 2-7.**

38. $y = |x| - 3$ **39.** $y = |x + 2|$ **40.** $y = |x - 1| + 5$

Determine whether y varies directly with x. If so, find the constant of variation.   ◀ **See Lesson 2-2.**

41. $y = 100x$ **42.** $5x + y = 0$ **43.** $y - 2 = 2x$

Make a scatter plot and describe the correlation.   ◀ **See Lesson 2-5.**

44. $\{(0, 6), (1, 4), (2, 4), (4, 1), (5, 0)\}$ **45.** $\{(-10, 5), (-5, -5), (-2, 0), (0, 3), (5, -2)\}$

Get Ready!   To prepare for Lesson 3-1, do Exercises 46–48.

Graph each equation. Use one coordinate plane for all three graphs.   ◀ **See Lesson 2-3.**

46. $3x - y = 2$ **47.** $3x - y = -2$ **48.** $x + 3y = -2$

2

Pull It **All Together**

To solve these problems, you will pull together concepts about equivalence, linear functions, and modeling. Show your work and justify your reasoning.

BIG idea Equivalence

You can represent a function with many different equivalent equations.

Task 1

The graph represents a function.

  a. Write the equation for the graph in standard form, point-slope form, and slope-intercept form.

  b. Which equation is the easiest to write by looking at the graph? Explain.

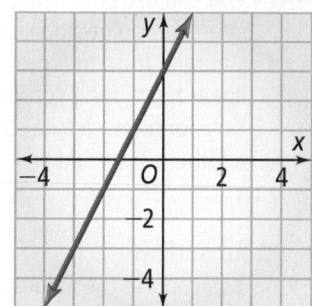

BIG idea Modeling

You can use scatter plots to model, analyze, and make predictions about certain kinds of data.

Task 2

The table at the right shows the boiling point of water at various elevations.

  a. Identify the independent and dependent quantities. Explain your choices.

  b. Make a scatter plot that models this data.

  c. Determine what kind of correlation is shown in your plot.

  d. Write an equation of the line of best fit.

  e. Use your equation to predict the temperature at which water boils at 8000 feet above sea level.

  f. At what elevation would you expect water to boil at 207°F?

Boiling Point of Water

Elevation (ft)	Boiling Point (°F)
0 (sea level)	212
1000	210.2
2000	208.4
3000	206.6
4000	204.8
5000	203

Task 3

Consider the following data: (2, 1), (4, 3), (5, 5), (7, 6), (3, 18).

  a. Exclude (3, 18) and draw trend line for the rest of the data.

  b. Use a graphing calculator to find the line of best fit for all of the points.

  c. Which linear model does a better job predicting most of the values? Explain.

② Chapter Review for Part B

Connecting BIG ideas and Answering the Essential Questions

1 Equivalence
You can use either slope-intercept, point-slope, or standard form to represent linear functions. (You can transform one version to another as needed.)

Slope-Intercept Form (Lesson 2-3)
$$y = mx + b$$
$$y = 2x - 1$$

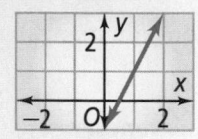

More Linear Equations (Lesson 2-4)
$$y - y_1 = m(x - x_1) \quad Ax + By = C$$
$$y - 5 = 2(x - 3) \quad 2x - y = 1$$

2 Function
You can use the values of a, h, and k in the form $y = a|x - h| + k$ to determine how the parent function $y = |x|$ has been transformed.

Families of Functions (Lesson 2-6)

$f(x) + k$	vertical translation
$f(x - h)$	horizontal translation
$af(x)$	stretch or compression
$-f(x)$	reflection in the x-axis
$f(-x)$	reflection in the y-axis

Absolute Value Functions and Graphs (Lesson 2-7)
Parent: $y = |x|$
General form:
$$y = a|x - h| + k$$
vertex: (h, k)

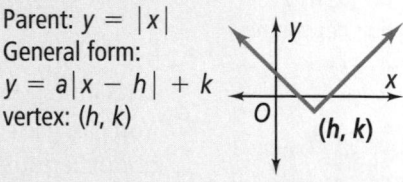

3 Modeling
You can use the equation of a trend line or line of best fit to model data that cluster in a linear pattern.

Using Linear Models (Lesson 2-5)

Positive Correlation   Trend Line

🔊 Chapter Vocabulary

- absolute value function (p. 121)
- axis of symmetry (p. 121)
- boundary (p. 128)
- correlation (p. 103)
- correlation coefficient (p. 106)
- half-plane (p. 128)
- line of best fit (p. 106)
- linear inequality (p. 128)
- parent function (p. 110)
- reflection (p. 114)
- scatter plot (p. 103)
- test point (p. 129)
- transformation (p. 110)
- translation (p. 110)
- vertex (p. 121)
- vertical compression (p. 115)
- vertical stretch (p. 115)

Choose the correct term to complete each sentence.

1. The vertex of the graph of an absolute value function is (*always*/*sometimes*) the lowest point on the graph.

2. The solution of a linear inequality in two variables is a (*half-plane*/*test point*).

3. The absolute value function $y = |x + 4|$ is symmetric about a line called the (*boundary*/*axis of symmetry*).

2-5 Using Linear Models

Quick Review

You can use a **scatter plot** to show relationships between data sets. You can make predictions using a trend line, which approximates the relationship between two data sets. The most accurate trend line is a **line of best fit**.

Example

Draw a scatter plot of the data. Is a linear model reasonable? If so, predict the value of y when $x = 9$.

$\{(0, 6), (1, 7), (2, 5), (3, 4), (4, 2), (5, 1)\}$

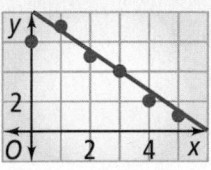

The points are close to the line $y = -\frac{4}{3}x + 8$, so a linear model is reasonable. When $x = 9$,

$y = -\frac{4}{3}(9) + 8$

$= -4$

Exercises

Draw a scatter plot of each set of data. Decide whether a linear model is reasonable. If so, describe the correlation. Then draw a trend line and write its equation. Predict the value of y when x is 15.

4. $\{(3, 5), (4, 7), (5, 9), (7, 10), (8, 10), (9, 11), (10, 13)\}$

5. $\{(6, 15.5), (7, 14.0), (8, 13.0), (9, 12.5), (10, 12.0), (11, 11.5), (12, 10.0)\}$

6.

x	0	3	6	9	12
y	17.5	35.4	50.5	60.6	66.3

2-6 Families of Functions

Quick Review

A **parent function** is the simplest form of a function in a family of functions. Each member of the family is a **transformation** of the parent function.

Translations shift the graph horizontally, vertically, or both. **Reflections** flip the graph over a line of symmetry. **Vertical stretches** and **compressions** change the shape of the graph by a factor.

Example

Write the equation of the transformation of the graph of $f(x) = x^2$ translated 3 units up, vertically stretched by a factor of 6, and reflected across the y-axis.

Translate 3 units up.	$y = x^2 + 3$
Stretch vertically.	$y = 6(x^2 + 3)$
Reflect in the y-axis.	$y = 6(-x)^2 + 18$
Simplify.	$y = 6x^2 + 18$

Exercises

Write the equation for the transformation of the graph of $y = f(x)$.

7. translated 2 units left, 7 units down

8. translated 5 units right, reflected in the x-axis

9. translated 3 units up, reflected in the y-axis

Describe the transformation(s) of the parent function $f(x)$.

10. $g(x) = f(x) - 4$

11. $h(x) = 12f(x) + 2$

12. $k(x) = -2f(-x)$

2-7 Absolute Value Functions and Graphs

Quick Review

The **absolute value function** $y = |x|$ is the parent function for the family of functions of the form $y = a|x - h| + k$. The maximum or minimum point of the graph is the **vertex** of the graph.

$y = 2|x + 3| + 1$
$a = 2, h = -3, k = 1$

- Vertex is at $(-3, 1)$
- Translated left 3 units
- Stretched by a factor of 2
- Translated up 1 unit

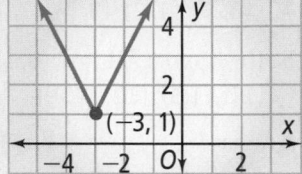

Example

Write an equation for the translation of the graph $y = |x|$ up 5 units.

Because the graph is translated up, k is positive, so the equation of the translated graph is $y = |x| + 5$.

Exercises

Write an equation for each translation of the graph of $y = |x|$.

13. up 4 units, right 2 units   **14.** vertex $(-3, 0)$

15. vertex $(5, 2)$ **16.** vertex $(4, 1)$

Graph each function.

17. $f(x) = |x| - 8$ **18.** $f(x) = 2|x - 5|$

19. $y = -\frac{1}{4}|x - 2| + 3$ **20.** $y = -2|x + 1| - 1$

Without graphing, identify the vertex and axis of symmetry of each function.

21. $y = 2|x - 4|$ **22.** $y = -|x| + 2$

2-8 Two-Variable Inequalities

Quick Review

A **linear inequality** describes a region of the coordinate plane that has a **boundary**. To graph an inequality involving two variables, first graph the boundary. Then determine which side of the boundary contains the solutions. Points on a dashed boundary are not solutions. Points on a solid boundary are solutions.

Example

Graph the inequality $y \geq 2x + 3$.

Graph the solid boundary line $y = 2x + 3$.

Since y is *greater than* $2x + 3$, shade above the boundary.

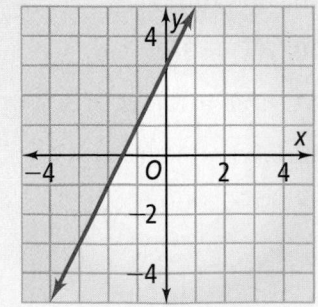

Exercises

Graph each inequality.

23. $y \geq -2$ **24.** $y < 3x + 1$

25. $y < -|x - 5|$ **26.** $y > |2x + 1|$

27. Transportation A cargo plane can transport as many as 15 regular shipping containers. One super-size container takes up the space of 3 regular containers.
   a. Write an inequality to model the number of regular and super-size containers the plane can transport.
   b. Describe the domain and range.
   c. Graph the inequality you wrote in part (a).

28. Open-Ended Write an absolute value inequality with a solid boundary that only has solutions below the x-axis.

MathXL® for School
Go to PowerAlgebra.com

Do you know HOW?

Find the domain and range. Graph each relation.

1. $\{(0, 0), (1, -1), (2, -4), (3, -9), (4, -16)\}$

2. $\{(3, 2), (4, 3), (5, 4), (6, 5), (7, 6)\}$

Determine whether each relation is a function.

3.
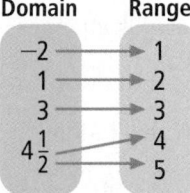

4.
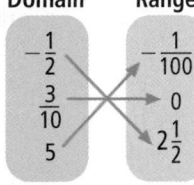

Suppose $f(x) = 2x - 5$ **and** $g(x) = |-3x - 1|$. **Find each value.**

5. $f(3)$

6. $f(1) + g(2)$

7. $g(0)$

8. $f(-1) - g(3)$

Find the slope of each line.

9. parallel to $y = 5x - 1$

10. perpendicular to $y = -2x - 4$

Write an equation of the line in standard form with the given slope through the given point.

11. slope $= -3, (0, 0)$ **12.** slope $= \frac{2}{5}, (6, 7)$

13. slope $= 4, (-2, -5)$ **14.** slope $= -0.5, (0, 6)$

Write an equation of the line in point-slope form through each pair of points.

15. $(0, 0)$ and $(-4, 7)$ **16.** $(-1, -6)$ and $(-2, 10)$

17. $(3, 0)$ and $(-1, -2)$ **18.** $(9, 5)$ and $(8, 2)$

For each direct variation, find the constant of variation. Then find the value of y when $x = -0.5$.

19. $y = 4$ when $x = 0.5$ **20.** $y = 2$ when $x = 3$

Write an equation of the line with the given slope and y-intercept. Write each equation in standard form.

21. $m = 3, b = -7$ **22.** $m = -6, b = 9$

23. $m = \frac{1}{4}, b = 11$ **24.** $m = -\frac{1}{2}, b = 4$

Graph each inequality.

25. $y \geq x + 7$ **26.** $y > 2|x + 3| - 3$

27. $4x - 3y < 2$ **28.** $y \leq -\frac{1}{2}|x + 2| - 3$

Do you UNDERSTAND?

29. Open-Ended Graph a relation that is *not* a function. Find its domain and range.

30. Writing Explain how point-slope form is related to the formula for slope.

Describe each transformation of the parent function $y = |x|$. Then graph each function.

31. $y = |x| - 4$ **32.** $y = |x - 1| - 5$

33. $y = -|x + 4| + 3$ **34.** $y = 2|x + 1|$

35. Recreation The table displays the amounts the Jackson family spent on vacations during the years 2000–2009.

Family Vacations

Year	Cost	Year	Cost
2000	$1750	2005	$2750
2001	$1750	2006	$3200
2002	$2000	2007	$2900
2003	$2200	2008	$3100
2004	$2700	2009	$3300

a. Make a scatter plot of the data.

b. Draw a trend line. Write its equation.

c. Estimate the amount the Jackson family will spend on vacations in 2015.

d. Writing Explain how to use a trend line to make a prediction.

Cumulative Test Prep

Some problems require you to use direct variation to solve for an unknown quantity. Read the question at the right. Then follow the tips to answer the sample question.

TIP 1

Some problems give more information than you need. Decide what information you need to answer the question.

A salad dressing recipe calls for $1\frac{1}{3}$ cups of buttermilk, 1 egg, $\frac{1}{2}$ cup of orange juice, and 1 tablespoon of lemon juice. Dan plans to use 2 cups of buttermilk instead. How much orange juice should he use?

Ⓐ $\frac{3}{8}$ cup

Ⓑ $\frac{3}{4}$ cup

Ⓒ $1\frac{1}{6}$ cup

Ⓓ $1\frac{1}{3}$ cup

TIP 2

Use some of the information to find k, the constant of variation in $y = kx$.

Think It Through

The ratio that shows how the amount of buttermilk changes is $k = \dfrac{2}{1\frac{1}{3}}$.

You can simplify this ratio.

$$2 \div \frac{4}{3} = \frac{2}{1} \cdot \frac{3}{4} = \frac{3}{2}$$

Use $k = \frac{3}{2}$ in the direct variation equation $y = \frac{3}{2}x$

Let x represent the original amount of orange juice.

$$y = \frac{3}{2}x = \frac{3}{2} \cdot \frac{1}{2} = \frac{3}{4}$$

The correct answer is B.

Vocabulary Builder

As you solve test items, you must understand the meanings of mathematical terms. Match each term with its mathematical meaning.

A. linear function

B. direct variation

C. range

D. translation

I. the set of all outputs, or y-coordinates, of a relation

II. a transformation that shifts a graph horizontally, vertically, or both

III. a function that can be written in the form $y = mx + b$

IV. a function that can be written in the form $y = kx$, where $k \neq 0$

Multiple Choice

Read each question. Then write the letter of the correct answer on your paper.

1. Which of the following absolute value inequalities has no solutions in Quadrant IV?

Ⓐ $y + 2 \geq |x - 3|$ Ⓒ $y - 1 > |2x + 6|$

Ⓑ $y > 3 - |5 - x|$ Ⓓ $y \leq |4x| - 7$

2. For which value of b would the equation $3|x - 2| = bx - 6$ have infinitely many solutions?

Ⓕ -6 Ⓗ -3

Ⓖ 3 Ⓘ 6

3. A meteorologist predicts the daily high and low temperatures as 91°F and 69°F. If t represents the temperature, then this situation can be described with the inequality $69 \le t \le 91$. Which of the following absolute value inequalities is an equivalent way of expressing this?

- Ⓐ $69 \le |t| \le 91$
- Ⓒ $|t - 69| \le 91$
- Ⓑ $|t - 80| \le 11$
- Ⓓ $|t - 11| \le 80$

4. What is the solution of the inequality $|x - 2| - 3 \le 2$?

- Ⓕ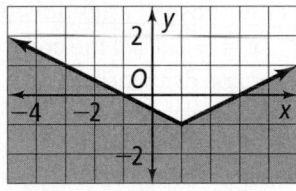
$$-8 \quad -6 \quad -4 \quad -2 \quad 0 \quad 2 \quad 4 \quad 6 \quad 8$$
- Ⓖ
$$-8 \quad -6 \quad -4 \quad -2 \quad 0 \quad 2 \quad 4 \quad 6 \quad 8$$
- Ⓗ
$$-8 \quad -6 \quad -4 \quad -2 \quad 0 \quad 2 \quad 4 \quad 6 \quad 8$$
- Ⓘ
$$-8 \quad -6 \quad -4 \quad -2 \quad 0 \quad 2 \quad 4 \quad 6 \quad 8$$

5. Which inequality best describes the graph?

- Ⓐ $y \le \frac{1}{2}|x + 1| - 1$
- Ⓑ $y \ge \frac{1}{2}|x - 1| - 1$
- Ⓒ $y \le \frac{1}{2}|x - 1| - 1$
- Ⓓ $y \ge \frac{1}{2}|x + 1| - 1$

6. Which relation is a function?

- Ⓕ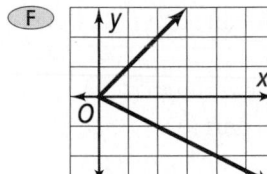
- Ⓗ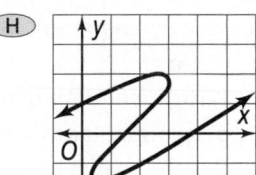
- Ⓖ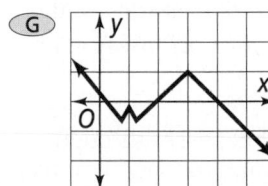
- Ⓘ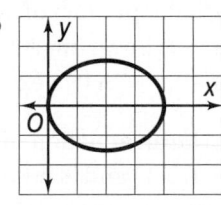

7. Which phrase does NOT describe $\sqrt{625}$?

- Ⓐ whole number
- Ⓒ irrational number
- Ⓑ integer
- Ⓓ rational number

8. Which equation is graphed?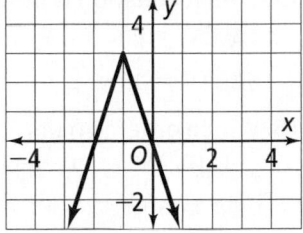

- Ⓕ $y = -3|x + 1| + 3$
- Ⓖ $y = 3|x + 1| + 3$
- Ⓗ $y = -3|x - 1| + 3$
- Ⓘ $y = 3|x + 1| - 3$

9. Which describes the translation of $y = |x - 3| + 5$?

- Ⓐ $y = |x|$ translated 3 units left and 5 units up
- Ⓑ $y = |x|$ translated 3 units right and 5 units up
- Ⓒ $y = |x|$ translated 5 units left and 3 units up
- Ⓓ $y = |x|$ translated 5 units right and 3 units up

10. Which lines are parallel?

- I. $y = -2x + 1$
- II. $y = x - 4$
- III. $y = -x + 5$
- IV. $y = 3 - 2x$

- Ⓕ I and II
- Ⓗ I and III
- Ⓖ I and IV
- Ⓘ II and III

11. Which value is in the solution set of $4 < -4x - 2 < 8$ and $3 > 4x + 2 > -10$?

- Ⓐ -2
- Ⓒ 0
- Ⓑ 3
- Ⓓ 4

12. Which is the equation of a line parallel to $5y - 2x = 6$ that passes through the point $(1, 3)$?

- Ⓕ $y - 3 = \frac{2}{5}(x - 1)$
- Ⓖ $y + 3 = \frac{2}{5}(x + 1)$
- Ⓗ $y - 3 = -\frac{2}{5}(x - 1)$
- Ⓘ $y + 3 = -\frac{2}{5}(x + 1)$

13. The line through points $(4, -8)$ and $(6, a)$ is perpendicular to $2x + 10y = 1$. What is the value of a?

- Ⓐ -5
- Ⓒ 2
- Ⓑ -2
- Ⓓ 5

14. Which line is perpendicular to $y = 2x - 4$?

   (F) $y = -2x + 4$ (H) $y = -4 - 2x$

   (G) $y = -x - 2$ (I) $y = -\frac{1}{2}x + 4$

15. Which equation is in standard form?

   (A) $x - y = 7$ (C) $y = 3x - 1$

   (B) $x = 4y + 2$ (D) $10 - 5x = 2y$

16. Which ordered pairs are solutions of $y < 2x + 3$?

   I. $(0, 2)$ II. $(-1, 1)$ III. $(2, 0)$

   (F) I only   (H) II only

   (G) I and III   (I) II and III

17. Use the Addition Property of Equality to complete the statement: If $p = q$, then $x + p =$ _____.

   (A) $p + x$ (C) $x + 0$

   (B) $x + q$ (D) $p + q$

18. Which phrase describes $\sqrt{145}$?

   (F) whole number   (H) irrational number

   (G) integer   (I) rational number

19. If a rate of speed r is constant, then distance, rate, and time are related by the direct variation equation $d = rt$, where d represents distance and t represents time. If $r = 30$ miles per hour, which of the following best describes the graph of $d = rt$?

   (A) A straight line through the point $(0, 0)$

   (B) A straight line through the point $(0, 30)$

   (C) A parabola through the point $(0, 0)$

   (D) A parabola through the point $(0, 30)$

GRIDDED RESPONSE

20. What is the slope of the line $5y + 3 = \frac{2}{5}x$?

21. A recipe for custard sauce calls for 6 eggs yolks, $\frac{2}{3}$ cup of sugar, and $1\frac{1}{2}$ cups of hot milk. Chelsea needs more sauce than the recipe yields. She plans to use 1 cup of sugar. How many cups of hot milk should she use?

22. What is the y-coordinate of the point through which the graph of every direct variation passes?

23. The line $(y - 2) = k(x + 1)$ passes through the points $L(3, 3)$ and $M(7, 4)$. Find k.

24. Matt drove at a steady speed during the first morning of his road trip. The table shows data about his driving.

Time Driving (hours)	Total Distance (miles)
1.5	87
2.25	130.5
3	174

After lunch, Matt drove an additional 232 miles at the same steady speed. How many hours did he drive after lunch?

Short Response

25. Find $f(-3)$, $f(0)$, and $f(1)$ for the function $f(x) = \frac{2}{5}x - 2$.

26. Graph $y < |x + 3|$. Identify the parent function of the boundary and describe the translation.

27. Suppose y varies directly with x, and $y = 2$ when $x = -2$. Find the constant of variation. Then find the value of x when $y = 3$.

28. Graph the relation $\{(-3, 2), (-1, 3), (0, 0), (-1, -1)\}$. Find the domain and range.

Extended Response

29. a. Write an equation of the line through $(-2, 6)$ with slope 2.

   b. Write an equation of the line through $(1, 1)$ perpendicular to the line in part (a).

   c. Graph the two lines on the same set of axes.

30. Will the product of an integer and a natural number always be an integer? Why or why not? Justify your answer with two examples.

31. Write an equation of the line that passes through $(-1, -1)$ and is perpendicular to $y = -3x + 4$. If you draw another two lines such that all four lines intersect to form a square, what would be the slopes of those two lines? Explain your reasoning.

Get Ready!

Lesson 1-3 ◆ Evaluating Algebraic Expressions

Evaluate each expression for the given values of the variables.

1. $9t + 6(2v - t) - 7v$; $t = 1$ and $v = 5$

2. $11(a + 2b) + 2(a - 2b)$; $a = -3$ and $b = 4$

3. $\frac{3}{5}d + \frac{1}{10}h - \frac{7}{10}d - \frac{4}{5}h$; $d = 5$ and $h = 10$

4. $12\left(\frac{3}{4}x - \frac{1}{2}y\right) - 6\left(\frac{1}{2}x - \frac{3}{4}y\right)$; $x = 2$ and $y = -2$

Lesson 2-3 ◆ Writing Linear Equations in Slope-Intercept Form

Write the equation of each line in slope-intercept form.

5. $2x - 4y = 10$ **6.** $3y + 9 = -6x$ **7.** $y - 5x = 16$ **8.** $-7 - y = -3x$

9. $\frac{x}{6} - \frac{5}{12}y = \frac{5}{8}$ **10.** $4x = y - 11$ **11.** $2y = -12x - 16$ **12.** $\frac{y}{9} + \frac{x}{3} = 2$

Lesson 2-3 ◆ Graphing Linear Equations

Graph each equation.

13. $3x = y - 1$ **14.** $x - 5y = 10$ **15.** $12 + 2y = 3x$ **16.** $y = 4x$

Lesson 2-8 ◆ Graphing Inequalities

Graph each inequality.

17. $4y \leq 24x$ **18.** $y \geq 2|x - 1.5|$ **19.** $x + 5y \geq 20$ **20.** $y > |x + 6| - 2$

 Looking Ahead Vocabulary

21. A *system* of mountains is a group of mountains that share similar geographic and geological features. What are some mountain systems in the United States?

22. How many books does Jeff own if he has more than 14 books? Describe the number of books that Jeff owns if you add the *constraint* that he owns fewer than his sister, who owns 19 books.

CHAPTER 3

Linear Systems

PowerAlgebra.com

Your place to get all things digital

VIDEO

Download videos connecting math to your world.

VOCABULARY

Math definitions in English and Spanish

SOLVE IT!

The online Solve It will get you in gear for each lesson.

DYNAMIC ACTIVITIES

Interactive! Vary numbers, graphs, and figures to explore math concepts.

ONLINE PROBLEMS

Download Step-by-Step Problems with Instant Replay.

ONLINE HOMEWORK

Get and view your assignments online.

MathXL FOR SCHOOL

Extra practice and review online

The cables in the video intersect at certain points, just like the graphs of linear equations might intersect.

How can you solve a system of linear equations? How can you use linear programming to solve real-world problems? How can you use a matrix to represent a system of equations? You will learn how in this chapter.

Vocabulary

English/Spanish Vocabulary Audio Online:

English	Spanish
equivalent systems, *p. 157*	sistemas equivalentes
feasible region, *p. 169*	región factible
linear system, *p. 146*	sistema lineal
matrix, *p. 184*	matriz
matrix element, *p. 184*	elemento matricial
objective function, *p. 169*	función objetiva
row operation, *p. 186*	operación de filas
system of equations, *p. 146*	sistema de ecuaciones

My Math Video

00:04:04

VIDEO
▶

BIG ideas

1 Function

Essential Question How does representing functions graphically help you solve a system of equations?

2 Equivalence

Essential Question How does writing equivalent equations help you solve a system of equations?

3 Solving Equations and Inequalities

Essential Question How are the properties of equality used in the matrix solution of a system of equations?

Chapter Preview

Objective To solve a linear system using a graph or a table

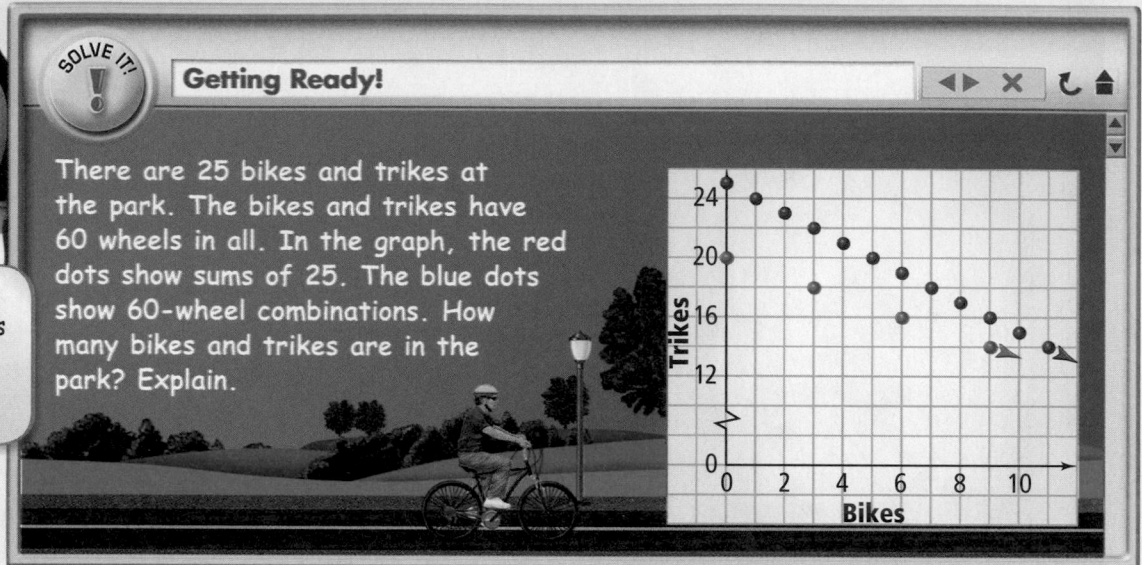

Getting Ready!

There are 25 bikes and trikes at the park. The bikes and trikes have 60 wheels in all. In the graph, the red dots show sums of 25. The blue dots show 60-wheel combinations. How many bikes and trikes are in the park? Explain.

There is just one way that 25 bikes and trikes can have a total of 60 wheels.

Lesson Vocabulary

• system of equations
• linear system
• solution of a system

When you have two or more related unknowns, you may be able to represent their relationship with a **system of equations**, which is a set of two or more equations.

Focus Question What does a solution of a system of linear equations represent?

A **linear system** consists of linear equations. A **solution of a system** is a set of values for the variables that makes all the equations true. You can solve a system of equations graphically or by using tables.

Problem 1 Using a Graph or Table to Solve a System

Think

How can you use a graph to find the solution of a system?
Find the point where the two lines intersect.

What is the solution of the system? $\begin{cases} -3x + 2y = 8 \\ x + 4y = -12 \end{cases}$

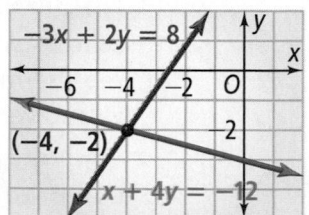

Method 1 Graph the equations. The point of intersection appears to be $(-4, -2)$.

Check Substitute the values in both equations.

$$-3x + 2y = 8 \qquad\qquad x + 4y = -12$$
$$-3(-4) + 2(-2) = 8 \qquad -4 + 4(-2) = -12$$
$$8 = 8 \checkmark \qquad\qquad -12 = -12 \checkmark$$

Both equations are true, so $(-4, -2)$ is the solution of the system.

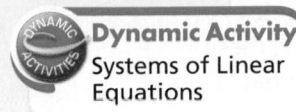
Hint

You can find the solution in the table. Look for the row where the y-values are identical.

Method 2 Use a table. Write the equations in slope-intercept form. Then enter the equations in the **Y=** screen as **Y1** and **Y2**. View the table. Adjust the x-values until you see $y_1 = y_2$.

$$-3x + 2y = 8 \qquad\qquad x + 4y = -12$$

$$2y = 3x + 8 \qquad\qquad 4y = -x - 12$$

$$\frac{2y}{2} = \frac{3x}{2} + \frac{8}{2} \qquad\qquad \frac{4y}{4} = \frac{-x}{4} - \frac{12}{4}$$

$$y_1 = \frac{3}{2}x + 4 \qquad\qquad y_2 = -\frac{1}{4}x - 3$$

X	Y1	Y2
5	-3.5	-1.75
-4	-2	-2
-3	-.5	-2.25
-2	1	-2.5
-1	2.5	-2.75
0	4	-3
1	5.5	-3.25

X = -4

When $x = -4$, both y_1 and y_2 equal -2. So $(-4, -2)$ is the solution of the system.

Got It? **1.** What is the solution of the system? Solve by making a graph and using a table.
$$\begin{cases} x - 2y = 4 \\ 3x + y = 5 \end{cases}$$

Problem 2 Using a Table to Solve a Problem

Biology The diagrams show the birth lengths and growth rates of two species of shark. If the growth rates are constant, at what age would a Spiny Dogfish and a Greenland shark be the same length?

Step 1 Define the variables and write the equation for the length of each shark.

Let x = age in years.
Let y = length in centimeters.

Length of Greenland: $y_1 = 0.75x + 37$
Length of Spiny Dogfish: $y_2 = 1.5x + 22$

Think

How can you use slope-intercept form to write each equation?
Use the growth rate for m and the length at birth for b.

Step 2 Use a table to solve the problem.

List x-values until the corresponding y-values match.

The sharks will be the same length when they are 20 years old.

Got It? **2. a.** If the growth rates continue, how long will each shark be when it is 25 years old?

b. **Reasoning** Explain why growth rates for these sharks may not continue indefinitely.

GREENLAND SHARK

Growth rate: 0.75 cm/yr
Birth length: 37 cm

SPINY DOGFISH SHARK

Growth rate: 1.5 cm/yr
Birth length: 22 cm

Shark Length in cm

Age	Greenland	Spiny Dogfish
x	$y_1 = 0.75x + 37$	$y_2 = 1.5x + 22$
15	48.25	44.5
16	49	46
⋮	⋮	⋮
20	52	52

ONLINE PROBLEMS **Problem 3** Using Linear Regression

Population The table shows the populations of the New York City and Los Angeles metropolitan regions from the census reports for 1950 through 2000. Assuming these linear trends continue, when will the populations of these regions be equal? What will that population be?

Populations of New York City and Los Angeles Metropolitan Regions (1950–2000)

	1950	1960	1970	1980	1990	2000
New York City	12,911,994	14,759,429	16,178,700	16,121,297	18,087,251	21,199,865
Los Angeles	4,367,911	6,742,696	7,032,075	11,497,568	14,531,529	16,373,645

Source: U.S. Census Bureau

Know

Population data for two regions

Need

The point in time when their populations will be the same

Plan

- Use a calculator to find linear regression models.
- Plot the models.
- Find the point of intersection.

Hint

Enter all the numbers as millions, rounded to the nearest hundred thousand. For example, enter 12,911,994 as 12.9.

Step 1 Enter the data into lists on your calculator.
   L1: number of years since 1950
   L2: New York City populations
   L3: Los Angeles populations

Step 2 Use **LinReg(ax + b)** to find lines of best fit.
   Use **L1** and **L2** for New York City.
   Use **L1** and **L3** for Los Angeles.

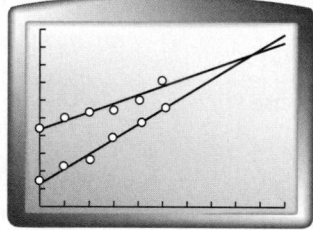

Think

What does *x* represent?
The *x*-value is the number of years *since* the zero year.

Step 3 Graph the linear regression lines.
   Use the **Intersect** feature.

The *x*-value of the point of intersection is about 87, which represents the year 2037. The data suggest that the populations of the New York City and Los Angeles metropolitan regions will each be about 25.6 million in 2037.

✔ **Got It?** **3.** The table shows the populations of the San Diego and Detroit metropolitan regions. When were the populations of these regions equal? What was that population?

Populations of San Diego and Detroit Metropolitan Regions (1950–2000)

	1950	1960	1970	1980	1990	2000
San Diego	334,387	573,224	696,769	875,538	1,110,549	1,223,400
Detroit	1,849,568	1,670,144	1,511,482	1,203,339	1,027,974	951,270

Source: U.S. Census Bureau

You can classify a system of two linear equations by the number of solutions. A system of two linear equations can have zero, one, or infinitely many solutions. The graphs of parallel lines do not intersect. So, there are no solutions. If two equations represent the same line, there are infinitely many solutions.

take note

Concept Summary   Graphical Solutions of Linear Systems

Intersecting Lines	**Coinciding Lines**	**Parallel Lines**
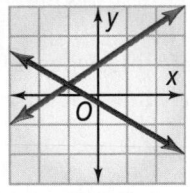	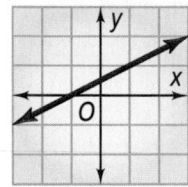	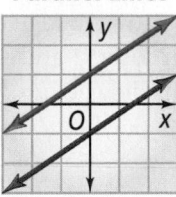
one solution	infinitely many solutions	no solution

Problem 4   Classifying a System Without Graphing

Without graphing, does the system have zero, one, or infinitely many solutions?

$$\begin{cases} 4y - 2x = 6 \\ 8y = 4x - 12 \end{cases}$$

Rewrite each equation in slope-intercept form. Compare slopes and y-intercepts.

Write the original equations. $4y - 2x = 6$ $8y = 4x - 12$

Solve for y. $y = \frac{1}{2}x + \frac{3}{2}$ $y = \frac{1}{2}x - \frac{3}{2}$

> The slopes are equal. The lines are either parallel or the same line.

Slope $= \frac{1}{2}$ Slope $= \frac{1}{2}$

> Since the y-intercepts are not equal, the lines are parallel.

y-intercept $= \frac{3}{2}$ y-intercept $= -\frac{3}{2}$

The system has no solution.

Got It? 4. Without graphing, does each system have zero, one, or infinitely many solutions?

a. $\begin{cases} -3x + y = 4 \\ x - \frac{1}{3}y = 1 \end{cases}$ b. $\begin{cases} 2x + 3y = 1 \\ 4x + y = -3 \end{cases}$ c. $\begin{cases} y = 2x - 3 \\ 6x - 3y = 9 \end{cases}$

Focus Question What does a solution of a system of linear equations represent?

Answer A solution represents values of the variables that make both equations true. To find the solution, graph the equations and find the point where the lines intersect. You can also make a table and find the value of x that makes the y-values equal.

Lesson Check

Do you know HOW?

Solve each system of equations by graphing. Check your solution.

1. $\begin{cases} y = x - 1 \\ y = -x + 3 \end{cases}$ 2. $\begin{cases} 2x + y = 4 \\ x - y = 2 \end{cases}$

3. You buy a total of 6 pens and pencils for $4. If each pen costs $1 and each pencil costs $.50, how many pens did you buy? How many pencils?

Do you UNDERSTAND?

4. Is it possible for a system of linear equations to have exactly two solutions? Explain.

5. **Open-Ended** Write a system of linear equations that has no solution.

6. **Reasoning** In a system of linear equations, the slope of one line is the negative reciprocal of the slope of the other line. Does this system have zero, one, or infinitely many solutions? Explain.

Practice and Problem-Solving Exercises

 **Practice**

Solve each system by graphing or using a table. Check your answers.

 See Problem 1.

Guided Practice

To start, graph the first equation of the system.

7. $\begin{cases} y = x - 2 \\ y = -2x + 7 \end{cases}$

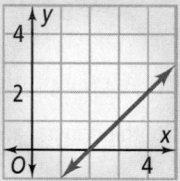

8. $\begin{cases} y = -x + 3 \\ y = \frac{3}{2}x - 2 \end{cases}$

9. $\begin{cases} 2x + 4y = 12 \\ x + y = 2 \end{cases}$

10. $\begin{cases} x = -3 \\ y = 5 \end{cases}$

11. $\begin{cases} 2x - 2y = 4 \\ y - x = 6 \end{cases}$

12. $\begin{cases} 3x + y = 5 \\ x - y = 7 \end{cases}$

13. $\begin{cases} x + 4y = 12 \\ 2x - 8y = 4 \end{cases}$

Write and solve a system of equations for each situation. Check your answers.   See Problem 2.

14. A store sells small notebooks for $8 and large notebooks for $10. If you buy 6 notebooks and spend $56, how many of each size notebook did you buy?

15. A shop has one-pound bags of peanuts for $2 and three-pound bags of peanuts for $5.50. If you buy 5 bags and spend $17, how many of each size bag did you buy?

Graphing Calculator Find linear models for each set of data. In what year will the two quantities be equal?

See Problem 3.

16.

U.S. Life Expectancy at Birth (1970–2000)

Year	1970	1975	1980	1985	1990	1995	2000
Men (years)	67.1	68.8	70.0	71.1	71.8	72.5	74.3
Women (years)	74.7	76.6	77.4	78.2	78.8	78.9	79.7

SOURCE: U.S. Census Bureau

17.

Annual U.S. Consumption of Vegetables

Year	1980	1985	1990	1995	1998	1999	2000
Broccoli (lb/person)	1.5	2.6	3.4	4.3	5.1	6.5	6.1
Cucumbers (lb/person)	3.9	4.4	4.7	5.6	6.5	6.8	6.4

SOURCE: U.S. Census Bureau

Without graphing, does each system have zero, one, or infinitely many solutions? **See Problem 4.**

Guided Practice

18. $\begin{cases} -3x + y = 4 \\ x - \frac{1}{3}y = 1 \end{cases}$

To start, rewrite each equation in slope-intercept form.

$\begin{array}{ll} -3x + y = 4 & x - \frac{1}{3}y = 1 \\ \quad y = 3x + 4 & \quad y = 3x - 3 \end{array}$

19. $\begin{cases} 7x - y = 6 \\ -7x + y = -6 \end{cases}$

20. $\begin{cases} 4x + 8y = 12 \\ x + 2y = -3 \end{cases}$

21. $\begin{cases} y = 2x - 1 \\ y = -2x + 5 \end{cases}$

22. $\begin{cases} x = 6 \\ y = -2 \end{cases}$

23. $\begin{cases} 2y = 5x + 6 \\ -10x + 4y = 8 \end{cases}$

24. $\begin{cases} x - 3y = 2 \\ 4x - 12y = 8 \end{cases}$

B Apply

Graph and solve each system.

25. $\begin{cases} 3 = 4y + x \\ 4y = -x + 3 \end{cases}$

26. $\begin{cases} y = \frac{1}{2}x + \frac{1}{2} \\ y = \frac{1}{4}x + \frac{3}{2} \end{cases}$

27. $\begin{cases} 3x + 6y - 12 = 0 \\ x + 2y = 8 \end{cases}$

28. $\begin{cases} 3x = -5y + 4 \\ 250 + 150x = 300y \end{cases}$

29. $\begin{cases} -x + 3y = 6 \\ 2x - y = 8 \end{cases}$

30. $\begin{cases} y = -\frac{1}{2}x + 8 \\ y = 2x - 6 \end{cases}$

Without graphing, does each system have zero, one, or infinitely many solutions?

31. $\begin{cases} 3x - 2y = 8 \\ 4y = 6x - 5 \end{cases}$

32. $\begin{cases} 2x + 8y = 6 \\ x = -4y + 3 \end{cases}$

33. $\begin{cases} 3m = -5n + 4 \\ n - \frac{6}{5} = -\frac{3}{5}m \end{cases}$

34. Think About a Plan You and a friend are both reading a book. You read 2 pages each minute and have already read 55 pages. Your friend reads 3 pages each minute and has already read 35 pages. Graph and solve a system of equations to find when the two of you will have read the same number of pages. Since the number of pages you have read depends on how long you have been reading, let x represent the number of minutes it takes to read y pages.
- How can you describe the relationship between x and y for you?
- How can you describe the relationship between x and y for your friend?
- How can a graph help you solve this problem?

35. Sports You can choose between two tennis courts at two university campuses to learn how to play tennis. One campus charges $25 per hour. The other campus charges $20 per hour plus a one-time registration fee of $10.
- **a.** Write a system of equations to represent the cost c for h hours of court use at each campus.
- **b. Graphing Calculator** Find the number of hours for which the costs are the same.
- **c. Reasoning** If you want to practice for a total of 10 hours, which university campus should you choose? Explain.

36. Error Analysis Your friend used a graphing calculator to solve the system of linear equations below. After using the **TABLE** feature, your friend says that the system has no solution. Explain what your friend did wrong. What is the solution of the system?

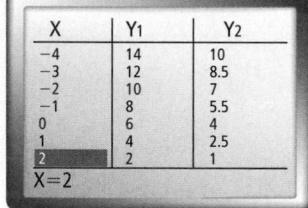

$$2x + y = 6 \qquad\qquad 3x + 2y = 8$$
$$y = 6 - 2x$$
$$y = \frac{8 - 3x}{2}$$

37. Reasoning Is it possible for a linear system with no solution to contain two lines with the same y-intercept? Explain.

38. Writing Summarize the possible relationships for the y-intercepts, slopes, and number of solutions in a system of two linear equations in two variables.

Standardized Test Prep

39. Which graph shows the solution of the following system? $\begin{cases} 4x + y = 1 \\ x + 4y = -11 \end{cases}$

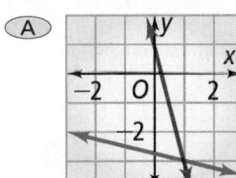

Ⓐ   Ⓑ   Ⓒ   Ⓓ

40. Which is the equation of a line that is perpendicular to the line in the graph?

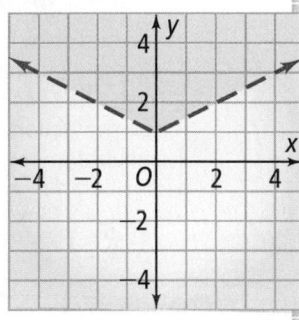

Ⓕ $y = -3x + 2$ Ⓗ $y = -\frac{1}{3}x - 4$

Ⓖ $y = \frac{1}{3}x + 5$ Ⓘ $y = 3x - 1$

41. Which inequality represents the graph at the right?

Ⓐ $y \geq \frac{1}{2}|x| + 1$ Ⓒ $y > \frac{1}{2}|x| + 1$

Ⓑ $y \leq \frac{1}{2}|x| + 1$ Ⓓ $y < \frac{1}{2}|x| + 1$

42. Amy ordered prints of a total of 6 photographs in two different sizes, 5×7 and 4×6, from an online site. She paid $7.50 for her order. The cost of a 5×7 print is $1.75 and the cost of a 4×6 print is $.25. Explain how to solve a system of equations using tables to find the number of 4×6 prints Amy ordered.

Mixed Review

Graph each inequality on a coordinate plane.

◀ See Lesson 2-8.

43. $3x - 4y \geq 16$ **44.** $-5x > 8y + 4$ **45.** $x < -4$

Solve each inequality. Check your solution.

◀ See Lesson 1-5.

46. $3n < -4(2 + n)$ **47.** $\frac{x}{3} + 5 \geq \frac{1}{6}$ **48.** $4x - 2 > \frac{1}{2}$

Find the slope of the line through each pair of points.

◀ See Lesson 2-3.

49. $(-2, -4)$ and $(1, 2)$ **50.** $(0, 0)$ and $(5, -3)$ **51.** $(1, 3)$ and $(4, 9)$

Get Ready! To prepare for Lesson 3-2, do Exercises 52 and 53.

52. What is the value of $a + b - 2c$ for $a = 3, b = 1$, and $c = -3$?

◀ See Lesson 1-3.

53. Substitute -3 for x in each of the following equations. What is the value of y?
 a. $y = 2x + 3$
 b. $y = -x + 5$
 c. $y = 3x - 1$

3-2
PART 1

Solving Systems Algebraically

Objective To solve linear systems using substitution

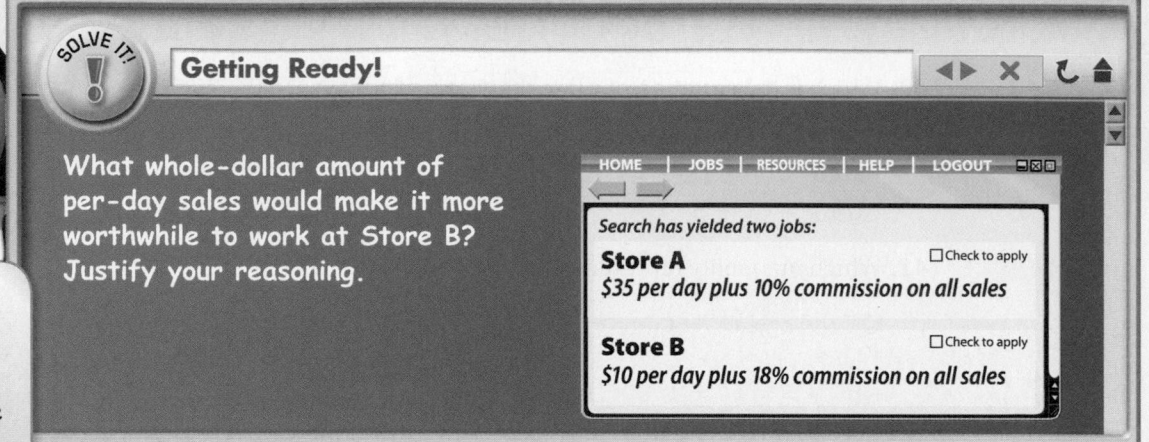

SOLVE IT!

Getting Ready!

What whole-dollar amount of per-day sales would make it more worthwhile to work at Store B? Justify your reasoning.

HOME | JOBS | RESOURCES | HELP | LOGOUT

Search has yielded two jobs:

Store A ☐ Check to apply
$35 per day plus 10% commission on all sales

Store B ☐ Check to apply
$10 per day plus 18% commission on all sales

You can draw graphs of income from each store, but the dollar amounts might be difficult to read.

Dynamic Activity
Special Types of Solutions to Linear Systems

Sometimes when you solve a system of equations by graphing, you cannot identify the exact coordinates of the point of intersection. You can solve these systems algebraically.

Focus Question When can you use substitution to solve a system?

To use the substitution method, first isolate one of the variables in one of the equations. Then substitute for that variable in the other equation and solve for the other variable.

Problem 1 Solving by Substitution

What is the solution of the system of equations? $\begin{cases} 3x + 4y = 12 \\ 2x + y = 10 \end{cases}$

Think

Which variable should you solve for first?
In the second equation, the coefficient of y is 1. It is the easiest variable to isolate.

Step 1
Solve one equation for one of the variables.

$2x + y = 10$
$\quad y = -2x + 10$

Step 2
Substitute the expression for y in the other equation. Solve for x.

$3x + 4y = 12$
$3x + 4(-2x + 10) = 12$
$3x - 8x + 40 = 12$
$-5x + 40 = 12$
$x = 5.6$

Step 3
Substitute the value for x into one of the original equations. Solve for y.

$2x + y = 10$
$2(5.6) + y = 10$
$11.2 + y = 10$
$y = -1.2$

The solution is $(5.6, -1.2)$.

 Got It? **1.** What is the solution of the system of equations? $\begin{cases} x + 3y = 5 \\ -2x - 4y = -5 \end{cases}$

Problem 2 Using Substitution to Solve a Problem

Music A music store offers piano lessons at a discount for customers buying new pianos. The cost for lessons and a one-time fee for materials (including music books, CDs, software, etc.) are shown in the advertisement. What is the cost of each lesson and the one-time fee for materials?

6 Lessons:	12 Lessons:
$300	**$480**

(Prices include one-time fee)

Relate   6 · | cost of lesson | + | one-time fee | = $300

            12 · | cost of lesson | + | one-time fee | = $480

Define   Let c = the cost of one lesson.

         Let f = the one-time fee.

Write $\begin{cases} 6 \cdot \boxed{c} + \boxed{f} = 300 \\ 12 \cdot \boxed{c} + \boxed{f} = 480 \end{cases}$

Choose one equation.	$6c + f = 300$
Solve for f in terms of c.	$f = 300 - 6c$
Substitute the expression for f into the other equation, $12c + f = 480$.	$12c + (300 - 6c) = 480$
Solve for c.	$c = 30$
Substitute the value of c into one of the equations.	$6(30) + f = 300$
Solve for f.	$f = 120$

Think

Which equation should you use to find f?
Use the equation with numbers that are easier to work with.

Check Substitute $c = 30$ and $f = 120$ into the original equations.

$6c + f = 300$	$12c + f = 480$
$6(30) + 120 \stackrel{?}{=} 300$	$12(30) + 120 \stackrel{?}{=} 480$
$180 + 120 \stackrel{?}{=} 300$	$360 + 120 \stackrel{?}{=} 480$
$300 = 300$ ✔	$480 = 480$ ✔

The cost of each lesson is $30. The one-time fee for materials is $120.

 Got It?   **2.** An online music company offers 15 downloads for $19.75 and 40 downloads for $43.50. Each price includes the same one-time registration fee. What is the cost of each download and the registration fee?

Focus Question When can you use substitution to solve a system?

Answer Use substitution when one of the equations in the system is already solved for one of the variables. You can also use substitution when it is easy to isolate a variable in one of the equations.

Lesson Check

Do you know HOW?

Solve each system by substitution.

1. $\begin{cases} 3x + 5y = 13 \\ 2x + y = 4 \end{cases}$

2. $\begin{cases} 2x - 3y = 6 \\ x + y = -12 \end{cases}$

Do you UNDERSTAND?

3. **Writing** A café sells a regular cup of coffee for $1 and a large cup for $1.50. Melissa and her friends buy 5 cups of coffee and spend a total of $6. Explain how to write and solve a system of equations to find the number of large cups of coffee they bought.

Practice and Problem-Solving Exercises

 **Practice**

Solve each system by substitution. Check your answers.

See Problem 1.

 **Guided Practice**

4. $\begin{cases} 4x + 2y = 7 \\ y = 5x \end{cases}$

$4x + 2y = 7$

$4x + 2(5x) = 7$

To start, use the second equation to substitute for y in the first equation.

5. $\begin{cases} 3c + 2d = 2 \\ d = 4 \end{cases}$

6. $\begin{cases} 4p + 2q = 8 \\ q = 2p + 1 \end{cases}$

7. $\begin{cases} x + 3y = 7 \\ 2x - 4y = 24 \end{cases}$

8. $\begin{cases} x + 6y = 2 \\ 5x + 4y = 36 \end{cases}$

9. $\begin{cases} y = 2x - 1 \\ 3x - y = -1 \end{cases}$

10. $\begin{cases} r + s = -12 \\ 4r - 6s = 12 \end{cases}$

11. **Money** A student has some $1 bills and $5 bills in his wallet. He has a total of 15 bills that are worth $47. How many of each type of bill does he have?

See Problem 2.

12. **Transportation** A youth group with 26 members is going skiing. Each of the five chaperones will drive a van or a sedan. The vans can seat seven people and the sedans can seat five people. Assuming there are no empty seats, how many of each type of vehicle could transport all 31 people to the ski area in one trip?

B **Apply**

13. **Error Analysis** Identify and correct the error shown in finding the solution of $\begin{cases} 3x - 4y = 14 \\ x + y = -7 \end{cases}$ using substitution.

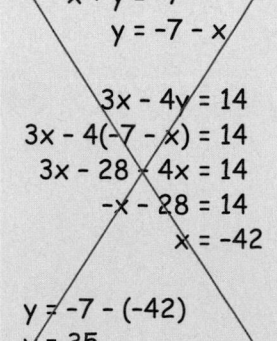

$x + y = -7$
$y = -7 - x$

$3x - 4y = 14$
$3x - 4(-7 - x) = 14$
$3x - 28 - 4x = 14$
$-x - 28 = 14$
$x = -42$

$y = -7 - (-42)$
$y = 35$

14. **Communication** Your cell phone company offers two text-messaging plans. One plan costs $.25 per text message, plus a monthly fee of $9. The other plan costs $.40 per text message with no monthly fee.
    a. For how many text messages will both plans cost the same amount?
    b. **Reasoning** If you use about 80 text messages each month, which plan should you choose? Explain.

Solve each system by substitution. Check your answers.

15. $\begin{cases} 3x = 6y \\ 2x + 8y = 4 \end{cases}$

16. $\begin{cases} 0.4x = 1 \\ 3x - 2y = 9 \end{cases}$

Solving Systems Algebraically

Objective To solve linear systems using elimination

In Part 1 of the lesson, you learned how to solve systems of equations using substitution.

Connect to What You Know

Here you will learn an alternate method to solve systems called elimination.

Focus Question When can you use elimination to solve a system of linear equations?

You can use the Addition Property of Equality to solve a system of equations. If you add a pair of additive inverses or subtract identical terms, you can eliminate a variable.

 Problem 3 Solving by Elimination

What is the solution of the system of equations? $\begin{cases} 4x + 2y = 9 \\ -4x + 3y = 16 \end{cases}$

Think

How can you use the Addition Property of Equality?
Since $-4x + 3y$ is equal to 16, you can add the same value to each side of $4x + 2y = 9$.

$$4x + 2y = 9$$
$$-4x + 3y = 16$$

One equation has $4x$, and the other has $-4x$. You can add to eliminate the variable x.

Add.	$5y = 25$
Solve for y.	$y = 5$
Choose one of the original equations.	$4x + 2y = 9$
Substitute for y.	$4x + 2(5) = 9$
Solve for x.	$4x = -1$
	$x = -\frac{1}{4}$

The solution is $\left(-\frac{1}{4}, 5\right)$.

 Got It? 3. What is the solution of the system of equations? $\begin{cases} -2x + 8y = -8 \\ 5x - 8y = 20 \end{cases}$

When you multiply each side of an equation in a system by the same nonzero number, the new system and the original system have the same solutions. The two systems are called **equivalent systems**. You can use this method to make additive inverses.

Problem 4 Solving an Equivalent System

What is the solution of the system of equations? $\begin{array}{l} ① \\ ② \end{array} \begin{cases} 2x + 7y = 4 \\ 3x + 5y = -5 \end{cases}$

Think

Multiply ① by 3 and ② by −2. This makes the x-terms opposites, and you can eliminate them.

Add ③ and ④. Solve for y.

Now that you know the value of y, use either equation to find x.

Write

① $2x + 7y = 4$ ③ $6x + 21y = 12$

② $3x + 5y = -5$ ④ $\underline{-6x - 10y = 10}$

$11y = 22$

$y = 2$

① $2x + 7(2) = 4$

$2x + 14 = 4$

$2x = -10$

$x = -5$

The solution is $(-5, 2)$.

 Got It? **4.** **a.** What is the solution of this system of equations? $\begin{cases} 3x + 7y = 15 \\ 5x + 2y = -4 \end{cases}$

b. **Reasoning** In part (a), does it matter which variable you find first? Explain.

Solving a system algebraically does not always provide a unique solution. Sometimes you get infinitely many solutions. Sometimes you get no solutions.

 Problem 5 Solving Systems Without Unique Solutions

Think

How are the two equations in this system related?

Multiplying each side of the first equation by −1 results in the second equation.

What are the solutions of the following systems? Explain.

A $\begin{cases} -3x + y = -5 \\ 3x - y = 5 \end{cases}$

$0 = 0$

Elimination gives an equation that is always true. The two equations represent the same line. This system has infinitely many solutions.

B $\begin{cases} 4x - 6y = 6 \\ -4x + 6y = 10 \end{cases}$

$0 = 16$

Elimination gives an equation that is always false. The two equations represent parallel lines. This system has no solution.

Got It? **5.** What are the solutions of the following systems? Explain.

a. $\begin{cases} -x + y = -2 \\ 2x - 2y = 0 \end{cases}$

b. $\begin{cases} 4x + y = 6 \\ 12x + 3y = 18 \end{cases}$

Focus Question When can you use elimination to solve a system of linear equations?
Answer Use elimination when the system contains a pair of additive inverses. Then add to eliminate a variable. You can also multiply one or both equations by nonzero numbers to make an equivalent system with additive inverses.

Lesson Check

Do you know HOW?

Solve each system by elimination.

1. $\begin{cases} 2x + 3y = 7 \\ -2x + 5y = 1 \end{cases}$
2. $\begin{cases} x + 2y = -1 \\ x - y = 8 \end{cases}$

3. $\begin{cases} x - y = -4 \\ 3x + 2y = 7 \end{cases}$
4. $\begin{cases} 3x + 4y = 10 \\ 2x + 3y = 7 \end{cases}$

Do you UNDERSTAND?

5. **Vocabulary** Give an example of two equivalent systems.

6. **Compare and Contrast** Explain how the substitution method of solving a system of equations differs from the elimination method.

Practice and Problem-Solving Exercises

Ⓐ Practice   Solve each system by elimination.

◀ **See Problem 3.**

Guided Practice

To start, add to eliminate the variable y.

7. $\begin{cases} x + y = 12 \\ x - y = 2 \end{cases}$

$$x + y = 12$$
$$\underline{x - y = 2}$$
$$2x \quad\quad = 14$$

8. $\begin{cases} x + 2y = 10 \\ x + y = 6 \end{cases}$
9. $\begin{cases} 3a + 4b = 9 \\ -3a - 2b = -3 \end{cases}$
10. $\begin{cases} 4x + 2y = 4 \\ 6x + 2y = 8 \end{cases}$

11. $\begin{cases} 3u + 3v = 15 \\ -2u + 3v = -5 \end{cases}$
12. $\begin{cases} 3x + 2y = 6 \\ 3x + 3 = y \end{cases}$
13. $\begin{cases} 5x - y = 4 \\ 2x - y = 1 \end{cases}$

Solve each system by elimination.

◀ **See Problems 4 and 5.**

Guided Practice

To start, write an equivalent system with additive inverses by multiplying the second equation by 2.

14. $\begin{cases} 4x - 6y = -26 \\ -2x + 3y = 13 \end{cases}$

$$\begin{cases} 4x - 6y = -26 \\ -4x + 6y = 26 \end{cases}$$

15. $\begin{cases} 9a - 3d = 3 \\ -3a + d = -1 \end{cases}$
16. $\begin{cases} 2a + 3b = 12 \\ 5a - b = 13 \end{cases}$
17. $\begin{cases} 2x - 3y = 6 \\ 6x - 9y = 9 \end{cases}$

18. $\begin{cases} 20x + 5y = 120 \\ 10x + 7.5y = 80 \end{cases}$
19. $\begin{cases} 6x - 2y = 11 \\ -9x + 3y = 16 \end{cases}$
20. $\begin{cases} 2x - 3y = -1 \\ 3x + 4y = 8 \end{cases}$

 **Apply**

21. Think About a Plan Suppose you have a part-time job delivering packages. Your employer pays you a flat rate of $9.50 per hour. You discover that a competitor pays employees $2 per hour plus $3 per delivery. How many deliveries would the competitor's employees have to make in four hours to earn the same pay you earn in a four-hour shift?

- How can you write a system of equations to model this situation?
- Which method should you use to solve the system?
- How can you interpret the solution in the context of the problem?

Solve each system.

22. $\begin{cases} 5x - 2y = -19 \\ 2x + 3y = 0 \end{cases}$

23. $\begin{cases} y = 4 - x \\ 3x + y = 6 \end{cases}$

24. $\begin{cases} 3m + 4n = -13 \\ 5m + 6n = -19 \end{cases}$

25. $\begin{cases} 5x + y = 0 \\ 5x + 2y = 30 \end{cases}$

26. $\begin{cases} 2m = -4n - 4 \\ 3m + 5n = -3 \end{cases}$

27. $\begin{cases} 7x + 2y = -8 \\ 8y = 4x \end{cases}$

28. $\begin{cases} 2m + 4n = 10 \\ 3m + 5n = 11 \end{cases}$

29. $\begin{cases} \frac{x}{3} + \frac{4y}{3} = 300 \\ 3x - 4y = 300 \end{cases}$

30. $\begin{cases} 4y = 2x \\ 2x + y = \frac{x}{2} + 1 \end{cases}$

31. Chemistry A scientist wants to make 6 milliliters of a 30% sulfuric acid solution. The solution is to be made from a combination of a 20% sulfuric acid solution and a 50% sulfuric acid solution. How many milliliters of each solution must be combined to make the 30% solution?

32. Open-Ended Write a system of equations in which both equations must be multiplied by a number other than 1 or −1 before using elimination. Solve the system.

33. Writing Explain how you decide whether to use substitution or elimination to solve a system.

34. The equation $3x - 4y = 2$ and which equation below form a system with no solutions?

Ⓐ $2y = 1.5x - 2$

Ⓒ $3x + 4y = 2$

Ⓑ $2y = 1.5x - 1$

Ⓓ $4y - 3x = -2$

For each system, choose the method of solving that seems easier to use. Explain why you made each choice. Solve each system.

35. $\begin{cases} 3x - y = 5 \\ y = 4x + 2 \end{cases}$

36. $\begin{cases} 2x - 3y = 4 \\ 2x - 5y = -6 \end{cases}$

37. $\begin{cases} 6x - 3y = 3 \\ 5x - 5y = 10 \end{cases}$

Standardized Test Prep

SAT/ACT

38. What is the slope of the line at the right?

39. What is the *x*-value of the solution of the system of equations?

$$\begin{cases} x + y = 7 \\ 3x - 2y = 11 \end{cases}$$

40. Solve $9(x + 7) - 6(x - 3) = 99$. What is the value of *x*?

41. Georgia has only dimes and quarters in her bag. She has a total of 18 coins that are worth $3. How many more dimes than quarters does she have?

42. The graph of $g(x)$ is a horizontal translation of $f(x) = 2|x + 1| + 3$, 5 units to the right. What is the *x*-value of the vertex of $g(x)$?

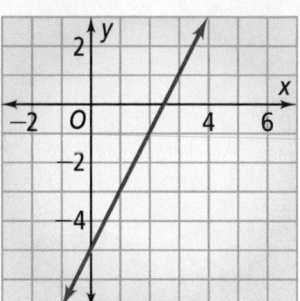

Mixed Review

Solve each system of equations by graphing. ◀ **See Lesson 3-1.**

43. $\begin{cases} y = 3x + 4 \\ 2y = 6x - 2 \end{cases}$
44. $\begin{cases} -3y = 9x + 1 \\ 6y = -18x - 2 \end{cases}$
45. $\begin{cases} 4x - y = -5 \\ -8x + 2y = 15 \end{cases}$

Use the vertical line test to determine whether each graph represents a function. ◀ **See Lesson 2-1.**

46.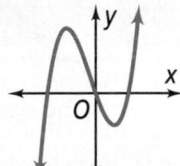
47.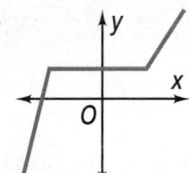
48.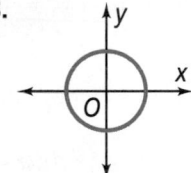

Get Ready!   **To prepare for Lesson 3-3, do Exercises 49–51.**

Solve each inequality. Graph the solution. ◀ **See Lesson 1-5.**

49. $-3(2x + 1) > 3$
50. $4x > -2$
51. $8y + 4 < 12$

3-3 Systems of Inequalities

Objective To solve systems of linear inequalities

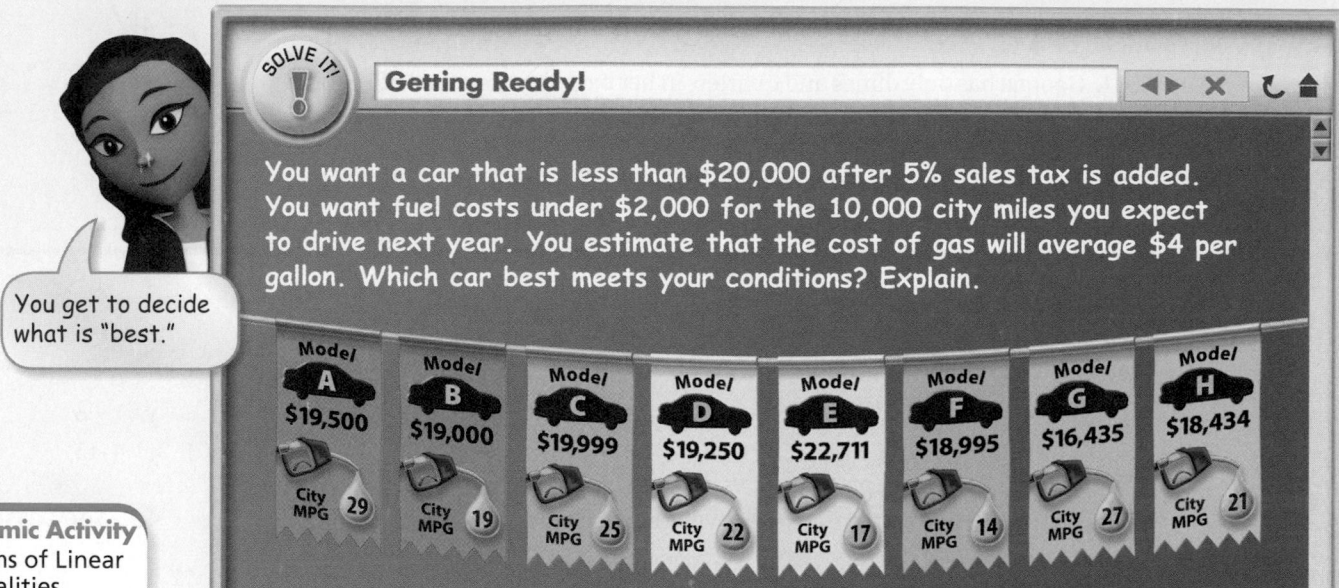

You get to decide what is "best."

Dynamic Activity
Systems of Linear Inequalities

Getting Ready!

You want a car that is less than $20,000 after 5% sales tax is added. You want fuel costs under $2,000 for the 10,000 city miles you expect to drive next year. You estimate that the cost of gas will average $4 per gallon. Which car best meets your conditions? Explain.

Model A	Model B	Model C	Model D	Model E	Model F	Model G	Model H
$19,500	$19,000	$19,999	$19,250	$22,711	$18,995	$16,435	$18,434
City MPG 29	City MPG 19	City MPG 25	City MPG 22	City MPG 17	City MPG 14	City MPG 27	City MPG 21

A solution of a system of inequalities is a solution for each inequality in the system.

Focus Question How do you know which region on a graph is the solution of a system of linear inequalities?

You can solve a system of inequalities in more than one way. Graphing the solution is usually the most appropriate method. Sometimes, you can also use a table.

Problem 1 Solving a System by Using a Table

Assume that *g* and *m* are whole numbers. What is the solution of the system of inequalities? $\begin{cases} g + m \geq 6 \\ 5g + 2m \leq 20 \end{cases}$

Make a table of whole-number values for *g* and *m* that satisfy the second inequality.

If $g = 0$, then $5(0) + 2m \leq 20$, and $m \leq 10$.
If $m = 0$, then $5g + 2(0) \leq 20$, and $g \leq 4$.

In the table, highlight each pair of values that satisfies the first inequality. The highlighted pairs are the solutions of both inequalities.

g	*m*
0	0, 1, 2, 3, 4, 5, 6, 7, 8, 9, 10
1	0, 1, 2, 3, 4, 5, 6, 7
2	0, 1, 2, 3, 4, 5
3	0, 1, 2
4	0

Plan

Which inequality should you use to build a table?
The first inequality has an infinite number of whole-number solutions. The second has a finite number of solutions. Use the second inequality.

✅ **Got It? 1.** Assume that x and y are whole numbers. What is the solution of the system of inequalities? $\begin{cases} x + y > 4 \\ 3x + 7y \le 21 \end{cases}$

You can also solve a system of linear inequalities by graphing. Recall that the graphed solution of a linear inequality is a half-plane and possibly its boundary line. For a system of two linear inequalities, the solution is the overlap of the two half-planes.

Problem 2 Solving a System by Graphing

What is the solution of the system of inequalities? $\begin{cases} 2x - y \ge -3 \\ y \ge -\frac{1}{2}x + 1 \end{cases}$

Step 1 Solve the first inequality for y to get the boundary line in slope-intercept form.

Write the original inequality.	$2x - y \ge -3$
Subtract 2x from each side.	$-y \ge -2x - 3$
Multiply each side by -1. Reverse the inequality.	$y \le 2x + 3$

Step 2 Graph each inequality. The overlap is the solution.

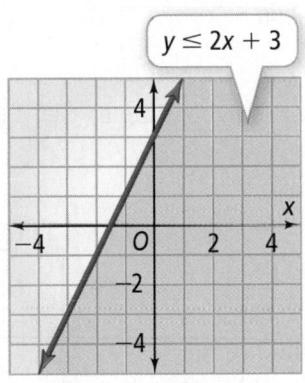
$y \le 2x + 3$

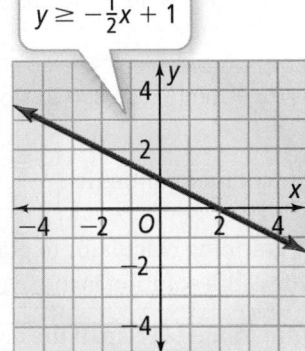
$y \ge -\frac{1}{2}x + 1$

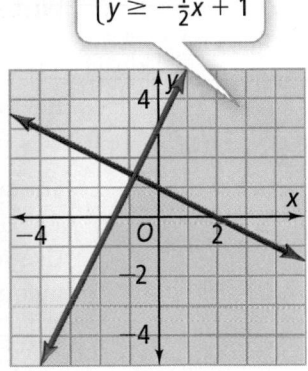
$\begin{cases} y \le 2x + 3 \\ y \ge -\frac{1}{2}x + 1 \end{cases}$

Check Pick a point in the overlap region, such as $(0, 2)$, and check it in both inequalities of the system.

$$2(0) - 2 \overset{?}{\ge} -3 \qquad 2 \overset{?}{\ge} \frac{1}{2}(0) + 1$$
$$-2 \ge -3 \; ✔ \qquad 2 \ge 1 \; ✔$$

✅ **Got It? 2.** What is the solution of the system of inequalities? $\begin{cases} x + 2y \le 4 \\ y \ge -x - 1 \end{cases}$

Sometimes, you can model a real situation with a system of linear inequalities. Solutions to real-world problems are often whole numbers. Only certain points in the overlap region will solve the problem.

 Problem 3 Using a System of Inequalities

Fundraising Your city's cultural center is sponsoring a concert to raise at least $30,000 for the city's Youth Services. Tickets are $20 for balcony seats and $30 for orchestra seats. If the center has 500 orchestra seats, how many of each type of seat must be sold?

Know
- At least $30,000 must be raised.
- There are at most 500 orchestra seats.

Need
The possible sales of balcony and orchestra seats

Plan
- Model the problem with a system of inequalities.
- Graph the inequalities on your calculator.

Relate   20 · [balcony seats] + 30 · [orchestra seats] ≥ 30,000

[orchestra seats] ≤ 500

Define   Let [x] = the number of balcony seats sold.

Let [y] = the number of orchestra seats sold.

Write   20 · [x] + 30 · [y] ≥ 30,000

[y] ≤ 500

Think

What do points in the overlap represent?
The points represent combinations of balcony and orchestra seats that have a total value of at least $30,000.

Rewrite $20x + 30y \geq 30,000$ in slope-intercept form as $y \geq -\frac{2}{3}x + 1000$.

The system of inequalities is $\begin{cases} y \geq -\frac{2}{3}x + 1000 \\ y \leq 500 \end{cases}$.

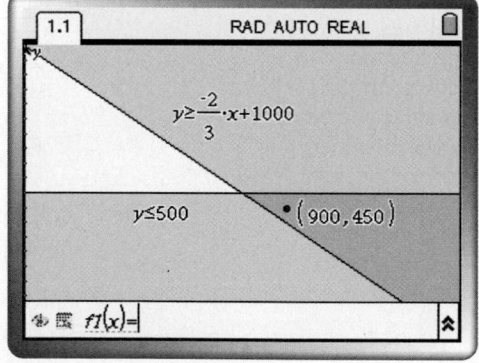

Use your graphing calculator to graph the inequalities. The solution is the overlap.

Test a point in the overlap. If the cultural center sells 900 balcony and 450 orchestra tickets, will the Youth Services meet its goal?

Hint

Remember to test the point in <u>both</u> inequalities. Points that satisfy only one inequality are not part of the solution set.

$20(900) + 30(450) \overset{?}{\geq} 30,000$ $450 \overset{?}{\leq} 500$

$18,000 + 13,500 \overset{?}{\geq} 30,000$ $450 \leq 500$ ✔

$31,500 \geq 30,000$ ✔

Because the number of seats must be a whole number, only whole-number pairs in the overlap are solutions of the problem.

 Got It? 3. A pizza parlor charges $1 for each vegetable topping and $2 for each meat topping. You want at least five toppings on your pizza. You have $10 to spend on toppings. How many of each type of topping can you get on your pizza?

Focus Question How do you know which region on a graph is the solution of a system of linear inequalities?

Answer Graph each inequality. The overlapping region is the solution of the system. To check your answer, choose a point in the region and test it in both inequalities.

Lesson Check

Do you know HOW?

Solve each system of inequalities by graphing.

1. $\begin{cases} x + y \geq 2 \\ 2x + y \leq 5 \end{cases}$

2. $\begin{cases} y > x \\ y < x + 1 \end{cases}$

3. $\begin{cases} y \geq -3x - 1 \\ y < x + 2 \end{cases}$

4. You spend no more than 3 hours each day watching TV and playing football. You play football for at least 1 hour each day. What are the possible numbers of hours you can spend on each activity in one day?

Do you UNDERSTAND?

5. **Reasoning** Is the solution of a system of linear inequalities the union or the intersection of the solutions of the two inequalities? Justify your answer.

6. **Compare and Contrast** Explain how the graphical solution of a system of inequalities is different from the graphical solution of a system of equations.

7. **Error Analysis** Describe and correct the error made in solving this system of inequalities.

$\begin{cases} y < \frac{1}{2}x - 1 \\ y \leq -3x + 3 \end{cases}$

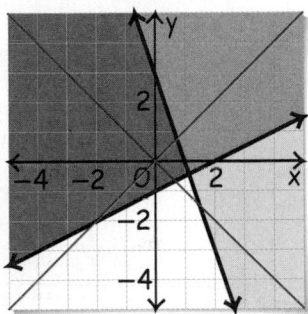

Practice and Problem-Solving Exercises

Ⓐ Practice   Find all whole number solutions of each system using a table.   ◀ **See Problem 1.**

Guided Practice

To start, make a table of values for x and y that satisfy the first inequality.

8. $\begin{cases} y + 3x \leq 8 \\ y - 3 > 2x \end{cases}$

If $x = 0$, then $y + 3(0) \leq 8$ and $y \leq 8$.

If $y = 0$, then $(0) + 3x \leq 8$ and $x \leq \frac{8}{3}$.

9. $\begin{cases} x + y < 8 \\ 3x \leq y + 6 \end{cases}$

10. $\begin{cases} y \geq x + 2 \\ 3y < -6x + 6 \end{cases}$

11. $\begin{cases} x - y \geq 1 \\ 2x + 3y \leq 21 \end{cases}$

Solve each system of inequalities by graphing.

◀ See Problem 2.

Guided
Practice →

12. $\begin{cases} y \leq 2x + 2 \\ y < -x + 1 \end{cases}$

To start, graph the first inequality.

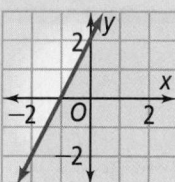

13. $\begin{cases} y > -2 \\ x < 1 \end{cases}$

14. $\begin{cases} y \leq 3x + 1 \\ -6x + 2y > 5 \end{cases}$

15. $\begin{cases} x + 2y \leq 10 \\ x + y \leq 3 \end{cases}$

16. You want to decorate a party hall with a total of at least 40 red and yellow balloons. You want a minimum of 25 yellow balloons. Write and graph a system of inequalities to model the situation.

◀ See Problem 3.

17. A gardener wants to plant at least 50 tulips and rose plants in a garden, but no more than 20 rose plants. Write and graph a system of inequalities to model the situation.

 **Apply**

18. **Think About a Plan** The food pyramid suggests that you eat 4–6 servings of fruits and vegetables a day for a healthy diet. It also says that the number of servings of vegetables should be greater than the number of servings of fruits. Find the number of servings of fruits and vegetables that could make a healthy diet. Use whole numbers only.
   • How can you write two inequalities that model the information in the problem?
   • How can you use a graph to find combinations of fruits and vegetable servings that may help in having a healthy diet?

19. **College Admissions** A college's entrance exam has two sections, a verbal section and a mathematics section. You can score a maximum of 1600 points. For admission, the college requires a math score of at least 600. Write a system of inequalities to model scores that meet the college's requirements. Then solve the system by graphing.

20. **Open-Ended** Write and graph a system of inequalities for which the solution is bounded by a dashed vertical line and a solid horizontal line.

21. **Writing** Given a system of two linear inequalities, explain how you can pick test points in the plane to determine where to shade the solution set.

Solve each system of inequalities by graphing.

22. $\begin{cases} y \leq \frac{2}{3}x + 2 \\ y \geq x + 2 \end{cases}$

23. $\begin{cases} y < x - 1 \\ y > -x + 3 \end{cases}$

24. $\begin{cases} 2x + y \leq 3 \\ y > x + 1 \end{cases}$

25. $\begin{cases} x + y < 8 \\ x \geq 0 \\ y \geq 0 \end{cases}$

26. $\begin{cases} 2y - 4x \leq 0 \\ x \geq 0 \\ y \geq 0 \end{cases}$

27. $\begin{cases} y \geq -2x + 4 \\ x > -3 \\ y \geq 1 \end{cases}$

Standardized Test Prep

28. Which system of inequalities is shown in the graph?

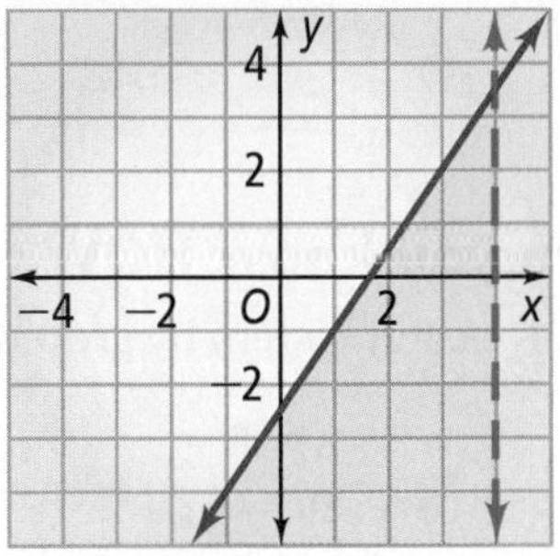

Ⓐ $\begin{cases} x \geq 4 \\ 3x - 2y > 5 \end{cases}$

Ⓒ $\begin{cases} x < 4 \\ 3x - 2y \geq 5 \end{cases}$

Ⓑ $\begin{cases} x > 4 \\ 3x - 2y \leq 5 \end{cases}$

Ⓓ $\begin{cases} x \leq 4 \\ 3x - 2y < 5 \end{cases}$

29. What is the equation of the line that passes through the point $(4, -3)$ and has slope $\frac{1}{2}$?

Ⓕ $y = \frac{1}{2}x + 3$

Ⓗ $y = \frac{1}{2}x - 5$

Ⓖ $y = \frac{1}{2}x - 1$

Ⓘ $y = x - \frac{1}{2}$

30. Which equation is a vertical translation of $y = -5x$?

Ⓐ $y = -\frac{5}{2}x$

Ⓒ $y = -10x$

Ⓑ $y = -5x + 2$

Ⓓ $y = 5x - 2$

Short Response

31. The cost of renting a pool at an aquatic center is either $30 per hour or $20 per hour with a $40 non-refundable deposit. For how many hours is the cost of renting a pool the same for both plans?

Mixed Review

Solve each system by elimination or substitution.

◀ **See Lesson 3-2.**

32. $\begin{cases} y = 3x + 1 \\ 2x - y = 8 \end{cases}$

33. $\begin{cases} 3x + y = 4 \\ 2x - 4y = 7 \end{cases}$

34. $\begin{cases} -x + 5y = 3 \\ 2x - 10y = 4 \end{cases}$

35. $\begin{cases} 2x + 4y = -8 \\ -5x + 4y = 6 \end{cases}$

36. $\begin{cases} y - 3 = x \\ 4x + y = -2 \end{cases}$

37. $\begin{cases} 2 = 4y - 3x \\ 5x = 2y - 3 \end{cases}$

Get Ready! **To prepare for Lesson 3-4, do Exercises 38–41.**

Write an ordered pair that is a solution of each system of inequalities.

◀ **See Lesson 3-3.**

38. $\begin{cases} x + y > 2 \\ 3x + 2y \leq 6 \end{cases}$

39. $\begin{cases} 2y > 4 \\ 3x + 4y \leq 14 \end{cases}$

40. $\begin{cases} x \geq 2 \\ 5x + 2y \leq 9 \end{cases}$

41. $\begin{cases} x + 3y < 6 \\ y < x \end{cases}$

Do you know HOW?

Solve each system by graphing.

1. $\begin{cases} 3x - y = 8 \\ 10 + 2y = 4x \end{cases}$

2. $\begin{cases} y + 5 = 2x \\ 3y + 6x = -3 \end{cases}$

3. $\begin{cases} 14x - 2y = 6 \\ 6y - 9x = 15 \end{cases}$

Without graphing, does each system have zero, one, or infinitely many solutions?

4. $\begin{cases} 3y + 2x = 12 \\ 36 - 9y = -6x \end{cases}$

5. $\begin{cases} -2y = 20 - 2x \\ 3y - 6x = -30 \end{cases}$

6. $\begin{cases} 15x = 10y - 20 \\ 18 + 9x = 6y \end{cases}$

Solve each system by substitution.

7. $\begin{cases} 5m - n = 7 \\ 3 + 3n = 6m \end{cases}$

8. $\begin{cases} 4y - 6 = 2x \\ y - 3x = 9 \end{cases}$

9. $\begin{cases} 3u + 8 = 4v \\ 24v = 6 - 3u \end{cases}$

Solve each system by elimination.

10. $\begin{cases} 5c - 4t = 8 \\ 14 + 4t = 3c \end{cases}$

11. $\begin{cases} 8y + 10 = 6x \\ 8y - 4x = -12 \end{cases}$

12. $\begin{cases} 11 - 2c = 3d \\ 2c - 7d = -9 \end{cases}$

Graph the solutions to each of the following systems.

13. $\begin{cases} y < 2 + 3x \\ y \geq x - 3 \end{cases}$

14. $\begin{cases} 2x + y > 7 \\ x < 4 \\ y \leq 5 \end{cases}$

Do you UNDERSTAND?

15. Which equation below combines with the equation $-4x + 6y = 3$ to form a system with an infinite number of solutions?

   Ⓐ $0.5 + x = 1.5y$

   Ⓑ $0.75 + 2x = 1.5y$

   Ⓒ $0.5 + 2x = 1.5y$

   Ⓓ $0.75 + x = 1.5y$

16. Write a system of inequalities that describes the shaded region.

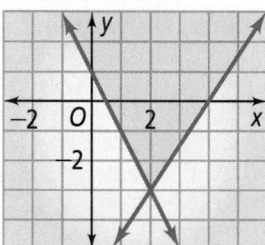

17. A refrigerator costs $503 and has an estimated annual operating cost of $92. An energy-efficient model costs $615 with an estimated annual operating cost of $64. Write a system of equations to represent this situation.
   a. What is the solution of the system?
   b. What does the solution mean?
   c. Which model would you choose for your family? Why?

18. **Writing** Explain how to classify a linear system by the number of solutions it has without graphing.

3-4 Linear Programming

Objective To solve problems using linear programming

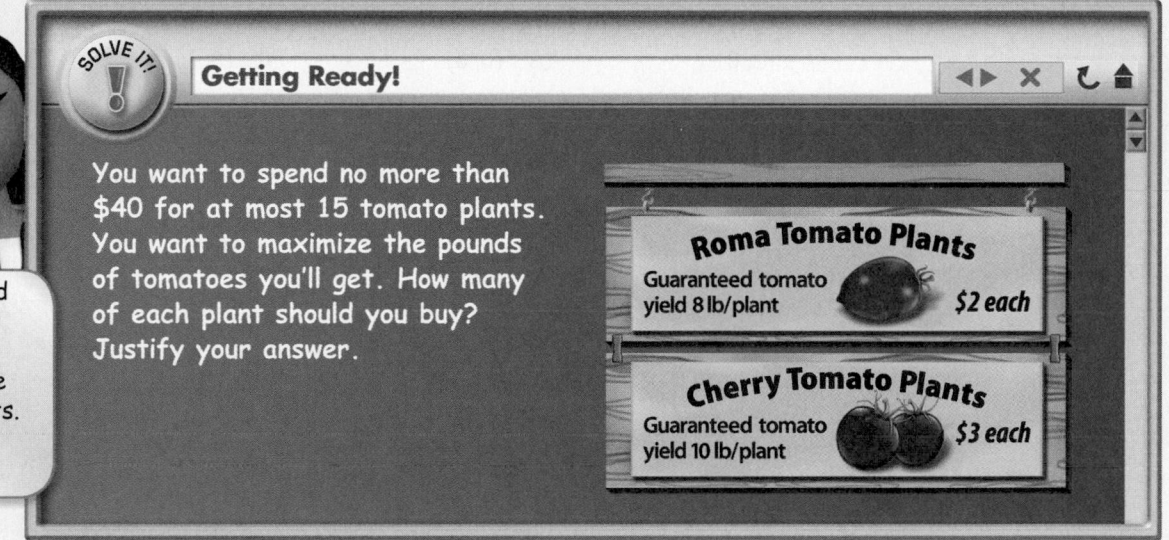

Getting Ready!

You want to spend no more than $40 for at most 15 tomato plants. You want to maximize the pounds of tomatoes you'll get. How many of each plant should you buy? Justify your answer.

Maybe I should buy only cherry tomato plants. They yield more than roma plants. On the other hand . . .

Roma Tomato Plants
Guaranteed tomato yield 8 lb/plant $2 each

Cherry Tomato Plants
Guaranteed tomato yield 10 lb/plant $3 each

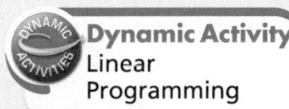
Dynamic Activity
Linear Programming

Lesson Vocabulary
• constraint
• linear programming
• feasible region
• objective function

In the Solve It, you maximized your tomato production given some limits, or **constraints**. **Linear programming** is a method for finding a minimum or maximum value of some quantity, given a set of constraints.

Focus Question How can you solve real-world problems that involve multiple linear relationships?

The constraints in a linear programming situation form a system of inequalities, like the one at the right. The graph of this system is called the **feasible region**. It contains all the points that satisfy all the constraints.

$$\begin{cases} x \geq 2 \\ y \geq 3 \\ y \leq 6 \\ x + y \leq 10 \end{cases}$$

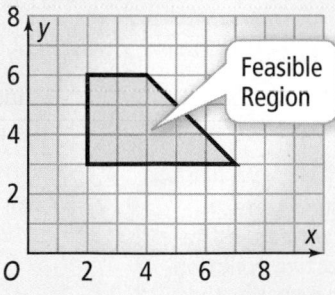

Feasible Region

The quantity you are trying to maximize or minimize is modeled with an **objective function**. Often this quantity is cost or profit. Find the point(s) within the feasible region that results in the maximum or minimum value when substituted into the objective function.

> take note

> **Key Concept** Vertex Principle of Linear Programming
>
> If there is a maximum or a minimum value of the linear objective function, it occurs at one or more vertices of the feasible region.

You can solve a problem using linear programming by testing in the objective function all of the vertices of the feasible region.

 **Problem 1** Testing Vertices

Multiple Choice What point in the feasible region maximizes P for the objective function $P = 2x + y$?

Constraints $\begin{cases} x + 2y \le 5 \\ x - y \le 2 \\ x \ge 0 \\ y \ge 0 \end{cases}$

Ⓐ (2, 0)   Ⓑ (0, 0)   Ⓒ (3, 1)   Ⓓ (1, 2)

Think

What quadrant will the feasible region be in?
The constraints $x \ge 0$ and $y \ge 0$ indicate the first quadrant.

Step 1

Graph the inequalities.

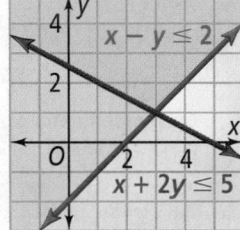

Step 2

Form the feasible region.

The maximum of P occurs at a vertex of the feasible region.

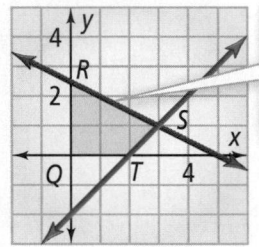

The intersections of the boundaries are the vertices of the feasible region.

Step 3

Find the coordinates of each vertex.

$Q\,(0, 0)$

$R\,(0, 2.5)$

$S\,(3, 1)$

$T\,(2, 0)$

Step 4

Evaluate P at each vertex.

$P = 2(0) + 0 = 0$

$P = 2(0) + 2.5 = 2.5$

$P = 2(3) + 1 = 7$ Maximum Value

$P = 2(2) + 0 = 4$

P has a maximum value of 7 when $x = 3$ and $y = 1$.
The correct answer is C.

Hint

Be sure to test <u>all</u> vertices in the objective function. It is possible that more than one vertex maximizes P.

 Got It? **1. a.** Use the constraints in Problem 1 with the objective function $P = x + 3y$. What values of x and y maximize P?

   b. Reasoning Can an objective function $P = ax + by + c$ have (the same) maximum value at all four vertex points Q, R, S, and T? At points R and S only? Explain using examples.

 **Problem 2** Using Linear Programming to Maximize Profit

Business You are screen-printing T-shirts and sweatshirts to sell at a blues festival and are working with the following constraints.

- You have at most 20 hours to make shirts.
- You want to spend no more than $600 on supplies.
- You want to have at least 50 items to sell.

1-Color T-shirt
Takes 10 minutes to make
Supplies cost $4
Profit $6

3-Color Sweatshirt
Takes 30 minutes to make
Supplies cost $20
Profit $20

How many T-shirts and how many sweatshirts should you make to maximize your profit? How much is the maximum profit?

Organize the information in a table.

Write the constraints and the objective function.

Constraints: $\begin{cases} 10x + 30y \leq 1200 \\ x + y \geq 50 \\ 4x + 20y \leq 600 \\ x \geq 0 \\ y \geq 0 \end{cases}$

	T-Shirts, x	Sweatshirts, y	Total
Minutes	10x	30y	1200
Number	x	y	50
Cost	4x	20y	600
Profit	6x	20y	6x + 20y

Objective Function: $P = 6x + 20y$

Hint

The last row of the table forms your objective function. Use the other rows to form your constraints.

Step 1

Graph the constraints to form the feasible region.

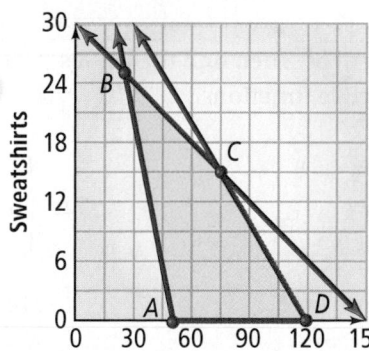

Step 2

Find the coordinates of each vertex.

$A(50, 0)$

$B(25, 25)$

$C(75, 15)$

$D(120, 0)$

Step 3

Evaluate P.

$P = 6(50) + 20(0) = 300$

$P = 6(25) + 20(25) = 650$

$P = 6(75) + 20(15) = 750$ ✔

$P = 6(120) + 20(0) = 720$

Think

How do you find the coordinates of the vertices if they are hard to read off the graph?
Solve the system of equations related to the lines that intersect to form the vertex.

You can maximize your profit by selling 75 T-shirts and 15 sweatshirts. The maximum profit is $750.

Got It? **2.** If it instead took you 20 minutes to make a sweatshirt, how many of each type of shirt should you make to maximize your profit?

Focus Question How can you solve real-world problems that involve multiple linear relationships?

Answer Use linear programming to solve real-world problems that involve multiple linear relationships. To find the maximum or minimum value of an objective function, graph the constraints of the problem. Then test the vertices of the feasible region in your objective function.

Lesson Check

Do you know HOW?

Graph each system of inequalities.

1. $\begin{cases} x + y \le 6 \\ x \ge 0 \\ y \ge 0 \end{cases}$
2. $\begin{cases} 2x - y \le 4 \\ x \ge 0 \\ y \ge 0 \end{cases}$

3. $\begin{cases} x + 2y \le 10 \\ x \ge 1 \\ y \ge 2 \end{cases}$
4. $\begin{cases} 2x + 3y \le 18 \\ 0 \le x \le 5 \\ 0 \le y \le 4 \end{cases}$

Graph each system of constraints. Then name the vertices of the feasible region.

5. $\begin{cases} x \le 5 \\ y \le 4 \\ x \ge 0 \\ y \ge 0 \end{cases}$
6. $\begin{cases} x + y \le 8 \\ y \ge 5 \\ x \ge 0 \end{cases}$

Do you UNDERSTAND?

7. Vocabulary Explain why the inequalities of a linear programming problem are called constraints. *Hint*: Use the definition of *constraint* as part of your answer.

8. Compare and Contrast What are some similarities between solving a linear programming problem and solving a system of linear inequalities? What are some differences?

9. Open-Ended Write a system of constraints whose graphs determine a trapezoid. Write an objective function and evaluate it at each vertex.

Practice and Problem-Solving Exercises

Ⓐ Practice Graph each system of constraints. Name all vertices. Then find the values of *x* and *y* that maximize or minimize the objective function. ◀ See Problem 1.

10. $\begin{cases} x + y \le 8 \\ 2x + y \le 10 \\ x \ge 0 \\ y \ge 0 \end{cases}$

Maximum for
$N = 100x + 40y$

11. $\begin{cases} x + 2y \ge 8 \\ x \ge 2 \\ y \ge 0 \end{cases}$

Minimum for
$C = x + 3y$

12. $\begin{cases} 2 \le x \le 6 \\ 1 \le y \le 5 \\ x + y \le 8 \end{cases}$

Maximum for
$P = 3x + 2y$

Use linear programming to solve the problem.

See Problem 2.

13. **Air Quality** A city wants to plant trees to absorb carbon dioxide. It has $2100 to spend on planting spruce and maple trees. The land available for planting is 45,000 ft^2. How many of each tree should the city plant to maximize carbon dioxide absorption?

Spruce and Maple Tree Data

	Spruce	Maple
Planting Cost	$30	$40
Area Required	600 ft^2	900 ft^2
Carbon Dioxide Absorption	650 lb/yr	300 lb/yr

Source: Auburn University and Anderson Associates

Guided Practice

Define the variables.

Let x = the number of spruce trees.
Let y = the number of maple trees.

Use the table to write the objective function.

Objective function: $C = 650x + 300y$

B Apply

14. **Think About a Plan** A biologist is developing two new strains of bacteria. Each sample of Type I bacteria produces four new viable bacteria, and each sample of Type II produces three new viable bacteria. Altogether, at least 240 new viable bacteria must be produced. At least 30, but not more than 60, of the original samples must be Type I. Not more than 70 of the original samples can be Type II. A sample of Type I costs $5 and a sample of Type II costs $7. How many samples of Type II bacteria should the biologist use to minimize the cost?
    - What are the unknowns?
    - What constraints do you get from each condition in the problem?
    - Are there any implicit constraints?

15. **Error Analysis** Your friend found the maximum value of $P = -x + 3y$ subject to the constraints as shown.

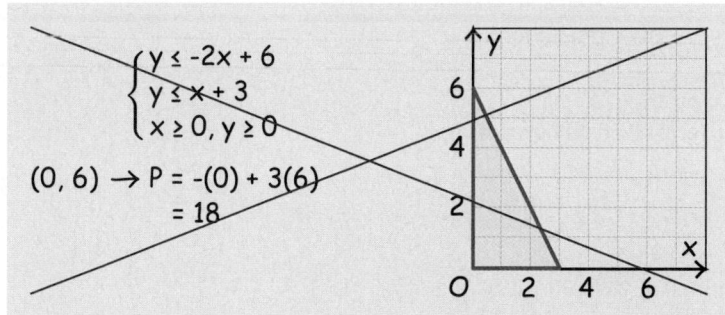

What error did your friend make? What is the correct solution?

16. **Cooking** Baking a tray of corn muffins takes 4 cups of milk and 3 cups of wheat flour. Baking a tray of bran muffins takes 2 cups of milk and 3 cups of wheat flour. A baker has 16 cups of milk and 15 cups of wheat flour. He makes $3 profit per tray of corn muffins and $2 profit per tray of bran muffins. How many trays of each type of muffin should the baker make to maximize his profit?

Graph each system of constraints. Name all vertices. Then find the values of x and y that maximize or minimize the objective function. Find the maximum or minimum value.

17. $\begin{cases} 25 \leq x \leq 75 \\ y \leq 110 \\ 8x + 6y \geq 720 \end{cases}$

   Minimum for
   $C = 8x + 5y$

18. $\begin{cases} x + y \leq 11 \\ 2y \geq x \\ x \geq 0 \\ y \geq 0 \end{cases}$

   Maximum for
   $P = 3x + 2y$

19. $\begin{cases} 2x + y \leq 300 \\ x + y \leq 200 \\ x \geq 0 \\ y \geq 0 \end{cases}$

   Maximum for
   $P = x + 2y$

Standardized Test Prep

SAT/ACT

20. Solve the equation $\frac{1}{2}(a + b) = c$ for b.

   Ⓐ $b = \frac{1}{2}c - a$ Ⓑ $b = 2a - c$ Ⓒ $b = 2c - a$ Ⓓ $b = 2ca$

21. Which is the graph of $y \leq |x - 3|$?

   Ⓕ 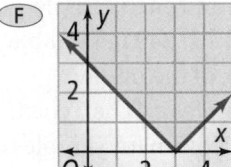   Ⓖ 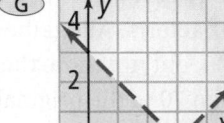   Ⓗ 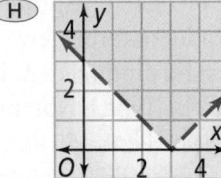   Ⓘ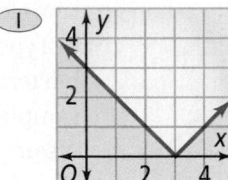

Short
Response

22. What are the vertices of the feasible region bounded by the following constraints?

   $\begin{cases} x + y \leq 3 \\ 2x + y \leq 4 \\ x \geq 0, y \geq 0 \end{cases}$

Mixed Review

Solve each system of inequalities by graphing.   ◀ See Lesson 3-3.

23. $\begin{cases} y < -2x + 8 \\ 3y \geq 4x - 6 \end{cases}$

24. $\begin{cases} x - 2y \geq 11 \\ 5x + 4y < 27 \end{cases}$

25. $\begin{cases} 2x + 6y > 12 \\ 3x + 9y \leq 27 \end{cases}$

Evaluate each expression for $a = 3$ and $b = -5$.   ◀ See Lesson 1-3.

26. $2a + b$ 27. $3(a - b)$ 28. $b(2b - a)$

Get Ready!   To prepare for Lesson 3-5, do Exercises 29–31.

Find the x- and y-intercepts of the graph of each linear equation.   ◀ See Lesson 2-4.

29. $y = 2x + 6$ 30. $2x + 9y = 36$ 31. $y = x - 1$

Concept Byte

For Use With Lesson 3-4

Linear Programming

You can solve linear programming problems using your graphing calculator.

Activity

Find the values of x and y that will maximize the objective function $P = 13x + 2y$ for the constraints at the right. What is the value of P at this maximum point?

$$\begin{cases} -3x + 2y \le 8 \\ -8x + y \ge -48 \\ x \ge 0, y \ge 0 \end{cases}$$

Step 1 Rewrite the first two inequalities to isolate y. Enter the inequalities.

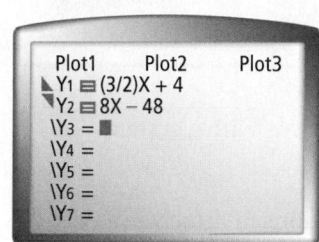

Step 2 Use the **VALUE** option of (calc) to find the upper left vertex. Press 0 (enter).

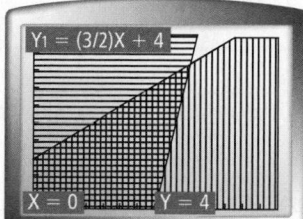

Step 3 Enter the objective function on the home screen. Press (enter) for the value of P at the vertex.

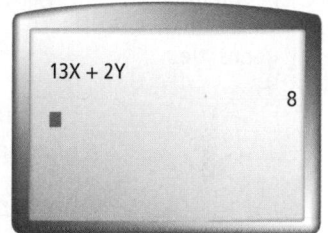

Step 4 Use the **INTERSECT** option of (calc) to find the upper right vertex. Go to the home screen and press (enter) for the value of P.

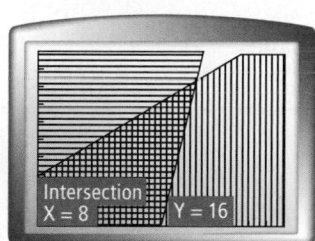

Step 5 Use the **ZERO** option of (calc) to find the lower right vertex. Go to the home screen and press (enter) for the value of P.

The objective function has a value of 0 when the vertex is at the origin. The maximum value of P is 136.

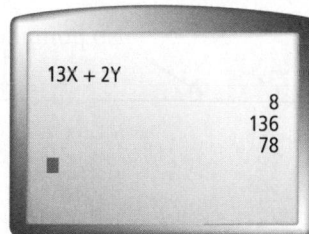

Exercises

Find the values of x and y that maximize or minimize the objective function.

1. $\begin{cases} 4x + 3y \ge 30 \\ x + 3y \ge 21 \\ x \ge 0, y \ge 0 \end{cases}$

Minimum for
$C = 5x + 8y$

2. $\begin{cases} 3x + 5y \ge 35 \\ 2x + y \le 14 \\ x \ge 0, y \ge 0 \end{cases}$

Maximum for
$P = 3x + 2y$

3. $\begin{cases} x + y \ge 8 \\ x + 5y \ge 20 \\ x \ge 0, y \ge 2 \end{cases}$

Minimum for
$C = 3x + 4y$

Systems With Three Variables

Objectives To solve systems in three variables using elimination or substitution

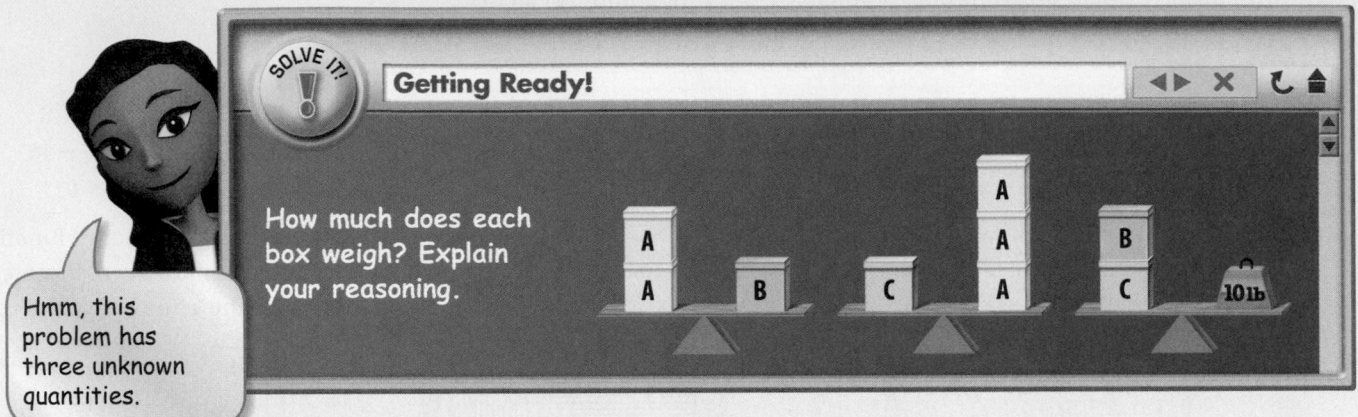

SOLVE IT!

Getting Ready!

How much does each box weigh? Explain your reasoning.

Hmm, this problem has three unknown quantities.

You can represent three relationships involving three unknowns with a system of equations.

Focus Question How is solving a system of three equations in three variables similar to solving a system of two equations in two variables?

You can represent systems of equations in three variables as graphs in three dimensions. The graph of an equation of the form $Ax + By + Cz = D$, where A, B, and C are not all zero, is a plane. You can show the solutions of a three-variable system graphically as the intersection of planes.

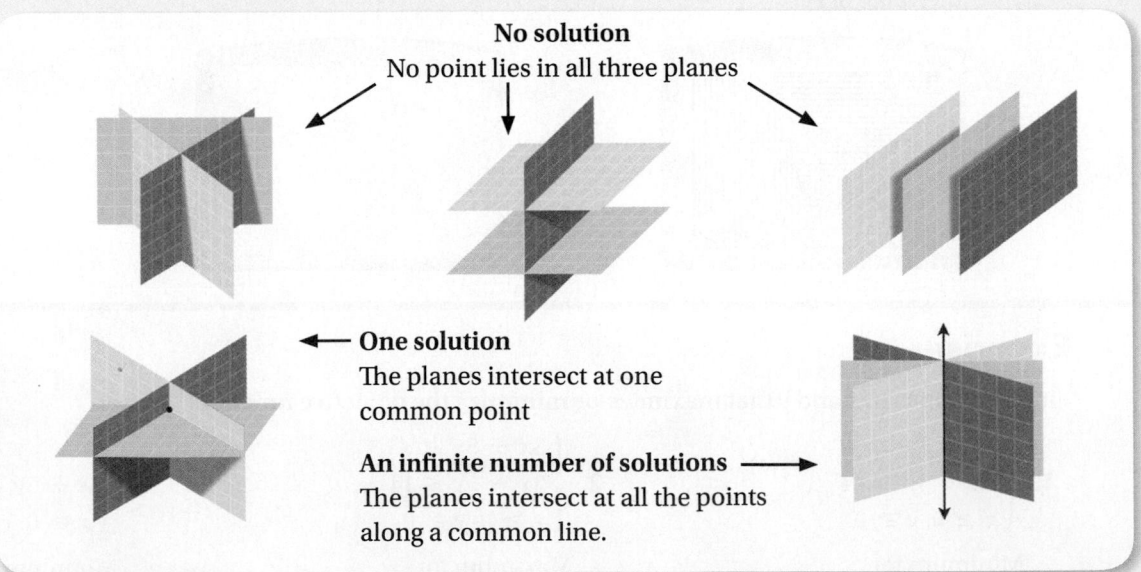

No solution
No point lies in all three planes

← **One solution**
The planes intersect at one common point

An infinite number of solutions →
The planes intersect at all the points along a common line.

You can use the elimination and substitution methods to solve a system of three equations in three variables by working with the equations in pairs. (You will use one of the equations twice.) When a single point represents the solution of a system of equations in three variables, write it as an ordered triple (x, y, z).

 Problem 1 Solving a System Using Elimination

What is the solution of the system? Use elimination. The equations are numbered to make the procedure easy to follow.

$$\text{①}\begin{cases} 2x - y + z = 4 \\ x + 3y - z = 11 \\ 4x + y - z = 14 \end{cases}\text{②}$$
$$\text{③}$$

Think

Which variable do you eliminate first?
Eliminate the variable for which the process requires the fewest steps.

Step 1 Pair the equations to eliminate z. Then you will have two equations in x and y.

Add.

$$\begin{array}{l} ① \\ ② \\ ④ \end{array}\begin{cases} 2x - y + z = 4 \\ x + 3y - z = 11 \\ \overline{3x + 2y \quad\quad = 15} \end{cases}$$

Subtract.

$$\begin{array}{l} ② \\ ③ \\ ⑤ \end{array}\begin{cases} x + 3y - z = 11 \\ 4x + y - z = 14 \\ \overline{-3x + 2y \quad\quad = -3} \end{cases}$$

Step 2 Write the two new equations as a system. Solve for x and y.

Add and solve for y.

$$\begin{array}{l} ④ \\ ⑤ \end{array}\begin{cases} 3x + 2y = 15 \\ \underline{-3x + 2y = -3} \\ \quad\quad 4y = 12 \\ \quad\quad\; y = 3 \end{cases}$$

Substitute $y = 3$ and solve for x.

$$\begin{aligned} ④ \quad 3x + 2y &= 15 \\ 3x + 2(3) &= 15 \\ 3x &= 9 \\ x &= 3 \end{aligned}$$

Think

Does it matter which equation you substitute into to find z?
No, you can substitute into any of the original three equations.

Step 3 Solve for z. Substitute the values of x and y into one of the original equations.

Use the first equation.	①	$2x - y + z = 4$
Substitute.		$2(3) - 3 + z = 4$
Simplify.		$6 - 3 + z = 4$
Solve for z.		$z = 1$

Step 4 Write the solution as an ordered triple. The solution is $(3, 3, 1)$.

 Got It? 1. What is the solution of the system? Use elimination. Check your answer in all three original equations.

$$\begin{array}{l} ① \\ ② \\ ③ \end{array}\begin{cases} x - y + z = -1 \\ x + y + 3z = -3 \\ 2x - y + 2z = 0 \end{cases}$$

You can apply the method in Problem 1 to most systems of three equations in three variables. You may need to multiply each side of an equation by the same nonzero number. Your goal is to obtain an equivalent system with coefficients that make elimination of variables easy.

Problem 2 **Solving an Equivalent System**

What is the solution of the system? Use elimination.

$$① \begin{cases} x + y + 2z = 3 \\ ② \quad 2x + y + 3z = 7 \\ ③ \quad -x - 2y + z = 10 \end{cases}$$

Think

You are trying to get two equations in x and z. Multiply ① so you can add it to ② and eliminate y. Do the same with ② and ③.

Write

$$① \begin{cases} x + y + 2z = 3 \\ ② \quad 2x + y + 3z = 7 \end{cases} \longrightarrow \begin{array}{r} -x - y - 2z = -3 \\ 2x + y + 3z = 7 \\ \hline ④ \quad x + z = 4 \end{array}$$

$$② \begin{cases} 2x + y + 3z = 7 \\ ③ \quad -x - 2y + z = 10 \end{cases} \longrightarrow \begin{array}{r} 4x + 2y + 6z = 14 \\ -x - 2y + z = 10 \\ \hline ⑤ \quad 3x + 7z = 24 \end{array}$$

Multiply ④ so you can add it to ⑤ and eliminate x.

$$④ \begin{cases} x + z = 4 \\ ⑤ \quad 3x + 7z = 24 \end{cases} \longrightarrow \begin{array}{r} -3x - 3z = -12 \\ 3x + 7z = 24 \\ \hline 4z = 12 \\ z = 3 \end{array}$$

Substitute $z = 3$ into ④. Solve for x.

$$x + 3 = 4$$
$$x = 1$$

Substitute the values for x and z into ① to find y.

$$x + y + 2z = 3$$
$$1 + y + 2(3) = 3$$
$$y = -4$$

Check the answer in the three original equations.

Check
$$1 + (-4) + 2(3) = 3 \quad ✔$$
$$2(1) + (-4) + 3(3) = 7 \quad ✔$$
$$-(1) - 2(-4) + 3 = 10 \quad ✔$$

Write the solution as an ordered triple.

The solution is $(1, -4, 3)$.

Hint

Always check your solution in all three original equations.

 Got It? **2. a.** What is the solution of the system? Use elimination.
b. Reasoning Could you have used elimination in another way? Explain.

$$① \begin{cases} x - 2y + 3z = 12 \\ ② \quad 2x - y - 2z = 5 \\ ③ \quad 2x + 2y - z = 4 \end{cases}$$

You can also use substitution to solve a system of three equations. Substitution is the best method to use when you can easily solve one of the equations for a single variable.

Problem 3 Solving a System Using Substitution

Multiple Choice What is the x-value in the solution of the system?

$$① \begin{cases} 2x + 3y - 2z = -1 \\ ② \quad x + 5y = 9 \\ ③ \quad 4z - 5x = 4 \end{cases}$$

(A) 1   (C) 6

(B) 4   (D) 10

Think

Which equation should you solve for one of its variables?
Look for an equation that has a variable with coefficient 1.

Step 1 Choose equation ②. Solve for x.

$$② \quad x + 5y = 9$$
$$x = 9 - 5y$$

Step 2 Substitute the expression for x into equations ① and ③ and simplify.

$$①\qquad\qquad 2x + 3y - 2z = -1$$
$$2(9 - 5y) + 3y - 2z = -1$$
$$18 - 10y + 3y - 2z = -1$$
$$18 - 7y - 2z = -1$$
$$④\qquad\qquad -7y - 2z = -19$$

$$③\qquad\qquad 4z - 5x = 4$$
$$4z - 5(9 - 5y) = 4$$
$$4z - 45 + 25y = 4$$
$$4z + 25y = 49$$
$$⑤\qquad 25y + 4z = 49$$

Step 3 Write the two new equations as a system. Solve for y and z.

$$④ \begin{cases} -7y - 2z = -19 \\ ⑤ \quad 25y + 4z = 49 \end{cases}$$

Multiply by 2. $-14y - 4z = -38$

Then add. $\underline{25y + 4z = 49}$

$$11y = 11$$
$$y = 1$$

Use equation ④. $④ \quad -7y - 2z = -19$

Substitute the value of y. $-7(1) - 2z = -19$

Simplify. $-2z = -12$

Solve for y. $z = 6$

Hint

Choose the equation that allows for the easiest calculations.

Step 4 Use one of the original equations to solve for x.

Use equation ②. $② \quad x + 5y = 9$

Substitute the value of y into ②. $x + 5(1) = 9$

Solve for x. $x = 4$

The solution of the system is $(4, 1, 6)$, and $x = 4$.

The correct answer is B.

Got It? **3. a.** What is the solution of the system? Use substitution.

$$① \begin{cases} x - 2y + z = -4 \\ ② \, -4x + y - 2z = 1 \\ ③ \quad 2x + 2y - z = 10 \end{cases}$$

b. Reasoning In Problem 3, was it necessary to find the value of z to solve the problem? Explain.

Problem 4 Solving a Real-World Problem

Business You manage a clothing store and budget $6000 to restock 200 shirts. You can buy T-shirts for $12 each, polo shirts for $24 each, and rugby shirts for $36 each. If you want to have twice as many rugby shirts as polo shirts, how many of each type of shirt should you buy?

Relate

T-shirts $+$ polo shirts $+$ rugby shirts $= 200$

rugby shirts $= 2 \cdot$ polo shirts

$12 \cdot$ T-shirts $+ 24 \cdot$ polo shirts $+ 36 \cdot$ rugby shirts $= 6000$

Think

How many unknowns are there?
There are three unknowns: the number of each type of shirt.

Define

Let x = the number of T-shirts.

Let y = the number of polo shirts.

Let z = the number of rugby shirts.

Write

① $\begin{cases} x + y + z = 200 \\ ② \quad z = 2 \cdot y \\ ③ \quad 12 \cdot x + 24 \cdot y + 36 \cdot z = 6000 \end{cases}$

Step 1 Since 12 is a common factor of all the terms in equation ③, write a simpler equivalent equation.

Begin with equation ③.   ③ $12x + 24y + 36z = 6000$
Divide by 12.   ④ $x + 2y + 3z = 500$

Step 2 Substitute $2y$ for z in equations ① and ④. Simplify to find equations ⑤ and ⑥.

① $x + y + z = 200$ ④ $x + 2y + 3z = 500$
$\quad x + y + (2y) = 200$ $\quad x + 2y + 3(2y) = 500$
⑤ $\qquad x + 3y = 200$ ⑥ $\qquad x + 8y = 500$

Hint

You can also solve the new system using substitution.

Step 3 Write ⑤ and ⑥ as a system. Solve for x and y.

⑤ $\begin{cases} x + 3y = 200 \\ ⑥ \quad x + 8y = 500 \end{cases}$

Multiply by -1. $-x - 3y = -200$
Then add. $\underline{\quad x + 8y = \quad 500}$
Divide by 5. $5y = \quad 300$
                             $y = \quad 60$

Use equation ⑤.   ⑤ $\quad x + 3y = 200$
Substitute the value of y. $x + 3(60) = 200$
Solve for x. $x = 20$

Step 4 Substitute the value of y into ② and solve for z.

② $z = 2y$
$\quad z = 2(60) = 120$

You should buy 20 T-shirts, 60 polo shirts, and 120 rugby shirts.

 Got It? **4.** Suppose you want to have the same number of T-shirts as polo shirts. You can buy 200 shirts with a budget of $5400. How many of each shirt should you buy?

Focus Question How is solving a system of three equations in three variables similar to solving a system of two equations in two variables?

Answer Use the same methods you used for a system of two equations in two variables: substitution and elimination.

Lesson Check

Do you know HOW?

Solve each system.

1. $\begin{cases} ① & 2y - 3z = 0 \\ ② & x + 3y = -4 \\ ③ & 3x + 4y = 3 \end{cases}$

2. $\begin{cases} ① & 3x + y - 2z = 22 \\ ② & x + 5y + z = 4 \\ ③ & x = -3z \end{cases}$

3. $\begin{cases} ① & 2x + 3y - 2z = 1 \\ ② & -x - y + 2z = 5 \\ ③ & 3x + 2y - 3z = -6 \end{cases}$

Do you UNDERSTAND?

4. **Reasoning** How do you decide whether substitution is the best method to solve a system in three variables?

5. **Error Analysis** A classmate says that the system consisting of $x = 0$, $y = 0$, and $z = 0$ has no solution. Explain the student's error.

6. The graph of a system is shown. How many solutions does this system have? Explain.

Practice and Problem-Solving Exercises

A Practice   Solve each system by elimination. Check your answers.   ◀ See Problems 1 and 2.

Guided Practice

7. $\begin{cases} ① & x - y + z = -1 \\ ② & x + y + 3z = -3 \\ ③ & 2x - y + 2z = 0 \end{cases}$

To start, pair the equations to eliminate y and add.

$$\begin{array}{ll} ① & x - y + z = -1 \\ ② & \underline{x + y + 3z = -3} \\ & 2x \quad\ + 4z = -4 \end{array} \qquad \begin{array}{ll} ② & x + y + 3z = -3 \\ ③ & \underline{2x - y + 2z = 0} \\ & 3x \quad\ + 5z = -3 \end{array}$$

8. $\begin{cases} ① & x - y - 2z = 4 \\ ② & -x + 2y + z = 1 \\ ③ & -x + y - 3z = 11 \end{cases}$

9. $\begin{cases} ① & 2x - y + z = -2 \\ ② & x + 3y - z = 10 \\ ③ & x \quad\ + 2z = -8 \end{cases}$

10. $\begin{cases} ① & a + b + c = -3 \\ ② & \quad\quad 3b - c = 4 \\ ③ & 2a - b - 2c = -5 \end{cases}$

11. $\begin{cases} ① & x - y + 2z = -7 \\ ② & y + z = 1 \\ ③ & x = 2y + 3z \end{cases}$

12. $\begin{cases} ① & x + y + 2z = 3 \\ ② & 2x + y + 3z = 7 \\ ③ & -x - 2y + z = 10 \end{cases}$

13. $\begin{cases} ① & x + 4y - 5z = -7 \\ ② & 3x + 2y + 3z = 7 \\ ③ & 2x + y + 5z = 8 \end{cases}$

Solve each system by substitution. Check your answers.   See Problems 3 and 4.

Guided Practice →

14. ① $\begin{cases} 3a + b + c = 7 \\ a + 3b - c = 13 \\ b = 2a - 1 \end{cases}$
②
③

To start, choose equation ③.
Substitute the expression for b into
equations ① and ②. Simplify.

①
$$3a + b + c = 7$$
$$3a + (2a - 1) + c = 7$$
$$3a + 2a - 1 + c = 7$$

②
$$a + 3b - c = 13$$
$$a + 3(2a - 1) - c = 13$$
$$a + 6a - 3 - c = 13$$

15. ① $\begin{cases} x + 2y + 3z = 6 \\ y + 2z = 0 \\ z = 2 \end{cases}$
②
③

16. ① $\begin{cases} 13 = 3x - y \\ 4y - 3x + 2z = -3 \\ z = 2x - 4y \end{cases}$
②
③

17. ① $\begin{cases} x + 3y - z = -4 \\ 2x - y + 2z = 13 \\ 3x - 2y - z = -9 \end{cases}$
②
③

18. ① $\begin{cases} x - 4y + z = 6 \\ 2x + 5y - z = 7 \\ 2x - y - z = 1 \end{cases}$
②
③

19. ① $\begin{cases} x + y + z = 2 \\ x + 2z = 5 \\ 2x + y - z = -1 \end{cases}$
②
③

20. ① $\begin{cases} 5x - y + z = 4 \\ x + 2y - z = 5 \\ 2x + 3y - 3z = 5 \end{cases}$
②
③

21. Manufacturing In a factory there are three machines, A, B, and C. When all three machines are working, they produce 287 bolts per hour. When only machines A and C are working, they produce 197 bolts per hour. When only machines A and B are working, they produce 202 bolts per hour. How many bolts can each machine produce per hour?

Apply

22. Think About a Plan In triangle PQR, the measure of angle Q is three times the measure of angle P. The measure of angle R is 20° more than the measure of angle P. Find the measure of each angle.
  • What are the unknowns in this problem?
  • What system of equations represents this situation?
  • Which method of solving looks easier for this problem?

23. Sports A stadium has 49,000 seats. Seats sell for $25 in Section A, $20 in Section B, and $15 in Section C. The number of seats in Section A equals the total number of seats in Sections B and C. Suppose the stadium takes in $1,052,000 from each sold-out event. How many seats does each section hold?

24. Finance A worker received a $10,000 bonus and decided to split it among three different accounts. He placed part in a savings account paying 4.5% per year, twice as much in government bonds paying 5%, and the rest in a mutual fund that returned 4%. His income from these investments after one year was $455. How much did the worker place in each account?

Solve each system using any method.

25. $\begin{cases} ① & x - 3y + 2z = 11 \\ ② & -x + 4y + 3z = 5 \\ ③ & 2x - 2y - 4z = 2 \end{cases}$

26. $\begin{cases} ① & x + 2y + z = 4 \\ ② & 2x - y + 4z = -8 \\ ③ & -3x + y - 2z = -1 \end{cases}$

27. $\begin{cases} ① & 4x - y + 2z = -6 \\ ② & -2x + 3y - z = 8 \\ ③ & 2y + 3z = -5 \end{cases}$

28. $\begin{cases} ① & 4x - y + z = -5 \\ ② & -x + y - z = 5 \\ ③ & 2x - z - 1 = y \end{cases}$

29. $\begin{cases} ① & 4a + 2b + c = 2 \\ ② & 5a - 3b + 2c = 17 \\ ③ & a - 5b = 3 \end{cases}$

30. $\begin{cases} ① & 4y + 2x = 6 - 3z \\ ② & x + z - 2y = -5 \\ ③ & x - 2z = 3y - 7 \end{cases}$

Standardized Test Prep

GRIDDED RESPONSE

31. What is the value of z in the solution of the system? $\begin{cases} ① & y = -2x + 10 \\ ② & -x + y - 2z = -2 \\ ③ & 3x - 2y + 4z = 7 \end{cases}$

32. What is the x-intercept of the line at the right after it is translated up 3 units?

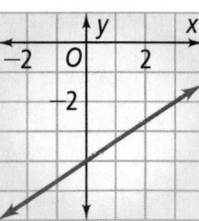

33. Suppose y varies directly with x, and $y = 15$ when $x = 10$. What is y when $x = 22$?

34. A theater has 490 seats. Seats sell for $25 on the floor, $20 in the mezzanine, and $15 in the balcony. The number of seats on the floor equals the total number of seats in the mezzanine and balcony. Suppose the theater takes in $10,520 from each sold-out event. How many seats does the mezzanine section hold?

Mixed Review

35. Maximize the objective function $P = x + 3y$ under the given constraints. At what vertex does this maximum value occur?
$\begin{cases} x + y \le 5 \\ x + 2y \le 8 \\ x \ge 0, y \ge 0 \end{cases}$
See Lesson 3-4.

Solve each inequality. Graph the solution on a number line.
See Lesson 1-5.

36. $-4x + 3 \le 9$

37. $-(x + 4) - 3 \ge 11$

38. $2(3x - 1) < x - 7$

Get Ready! To prepare for Lesson 3-6, do Exercises 39–41.

Solve each system using elimination.
See Lesson 3-2.

39. $\begin{cases} x + 4y = 12 \\ 2x - 8y = 4 \end{cases}$

40. $\begin{cases} 4x + 8y = -6 \\ 6x + 12y = -9 \end{cases}$

41. $\begin{cases} 4y - 2x = 6 \\ 8y = 4x - 12 \end{cases}$

3-6 Solving Systems Using Matrices

Objectives To represent a system of linear equations with a matrix
To solve a system of linear equations using matrices

This is not as difficult as it looks.

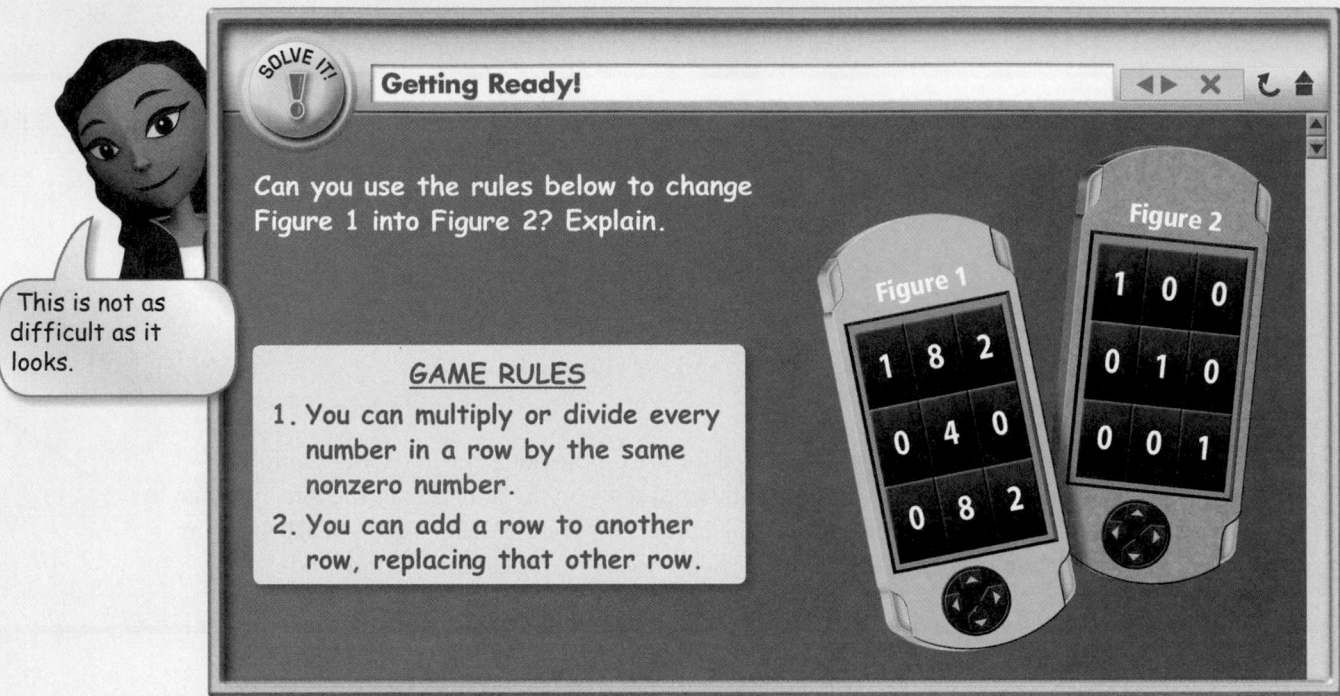

SOLVE IT! **Getting Ready!**

Can you use the rules below to change Figure 1 into Figure 2? Explain.

GAME RULES

1. You can multiply or divide every number in a row by the same nonzero number.
2. You can add a row to another row, replacing that other row.

Figure 1
1 8 2
0 4 0
0 8 2
Figure 2
1 0 0
0 1 0
0 0 1

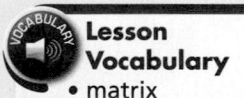

Lesson Vocabulary
- matrix
- matrix element
- row operation

An array of numbers, such as each of those suggested by the tile arrangements in the Solve It, is a *matrix*.

Focus Question Why is it helpful to use matrices to solve systems of equations?

A **matrix** is a rectangular array of numbers within brackets. The dimensions of a matrix are the numbers of rows and columns in the array.

3 columns

$$A = \begin{bmatrix} 2 & 4 & 1 \\ 6 & 5 & 3 \end{bmatrix} \quad \text{2 rows}$$

Matrix A has 2 rows and 3 columns and is a 2×3 matrix, read "2 by 3." You can write it as A or $A_{2 \times 3}$.

Each number in a matrix is a **matrix element**. You can identify a matrix element by its row and column numbers. In matrix A, a_{12} is the element in Row 1 and Column 2. The element a_{12} is 4.

 **Problem 1** Identifying a Matrix Element

Think

Does the order of the subscript numbers in a_{23} matter?
Yes. a_{23} and a_{32} are different elements.

What is element a_{23} in matrix A?

$$A = \begin{bmatrix} 4 & -9 & 17 & 1 \\ 0 & 5 & 8 & 6 \\ -3 & -2 & 10 & 0 \end{bmatrix}$$

A_{23} is in Row 2 and Column 3.

a_{23} is 8.

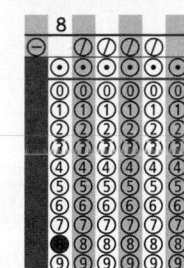

✔ **Got It?** **1. a.** What is element a_{13} in matrix A?
  b. What is element a_{31} in matrix A?

You can represent a system of equations efficiently with a matrix. Each matrix row represents an equation. The last matrix column shows the constants to the right of the equal signs. Each of the other columns shows the coefficients of one of the variables.

System of Equations
$$\begin{cases} x & + & 3y & = & 7 \\ 3x & + & y & = & -8 \end{cases}$$

x-coefficients   y-coefficients   constants

Matrix
$$\begin{bmatrix} 1 & 3 & | & 7 \\ 3 & 1 & | & -8 \end{bmatrix}$$

The 1's are coefficients of x and y.

Draw a vertical bar to replace the equal signs and separate the coefficients from the constants.

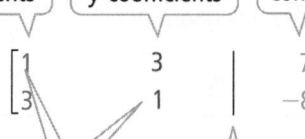 **Problem 2** Representing Systems With Matrices

How can you represent the system of equations with a matrix?

Ⓐ $\begin{cases} 2x + y = 9 \\ x - 6y = -1 \end{cases}$

The matrix $\begin{bmatrix} 2 & 1 & | & 9 \\ 1 & -6 & | & -1 \end{bmatrix}$ represents the system above.

Ⓑ $\begin{cases} x - 3y + z = 6 \\ x + 3z = 12 \\ y = -5x + 1 \end{cases}$

Think

Why is the order of elements important in a matrix?
Different orders of elements could correspond to different systems of equations.

Step 1 Write each equation in the same variable order. Line up the variables. Leave space where a coefficient is 0.

$$\begin{cases} x - 3y + z = 6 \\ x + 3z = 12 \\ 5x + y = 1 \end{cases}$$

Step 2 Write the matrix using the coefficients and constants. Notice the 1's and 0's.

$$\begin{bmatrix} 1 & -3 & 1 & | & 6 \\ 1 & 0 & 3 & | & 12 \\ 5 & 1 & 0 & | & 1 \end{bmatrix}$$

Got It? **2.** How can you represent the system of equations with a matrix?

a. $\begin{cases} -4x - 2y = 7 \\ 3x + y = -5 \end{cases}$

b. $\begin{cases} 4x - y + 2z = 1 \\ y + 5z = 20 \\ 2x = -y + 7 \end{cases}$

 Problem 3 **Writing a System From a Matrix**

What linear system of equations does this matrix represent? $\begin{bmatrix} 5 & 2 & | & 7 \\ 0 & 1 & | & 9 \end{bmatrix}$

Think

Each row shows coefficient-coefficient-constant of one equation.

Simplify. Write the system.

Write

$5x + 2y = 7$
$0x + 1y = 9$

$\begin{cases} 5x + 2y = 7 \\ y = 9 \end{cases}$

 Got It? **3.** What linear system does $\begin{bmatrix} 2 & 0 & | & 6 \\ 5 & -2 & | & 1 \end{bmatrix}$ represent?

You can use a matrix that represents a system of equations to solve the system. Use the same steps for solving by elimination. Each step is a **row operation**.

Your goal is to use row operations to get a matrix in one of the forms shown here. Notice that the first matrix represents the system $x = a, y = b$, which is the solution of a system of two equations in two unknowns. The second matrix represents the system $x = a, y = b$, and $z = c$.

$\begin{bmatrix} 1 & 0 & | & a \\ 0 & 1 & | & b \end{bmatrix}$ or $\begin{bmatrix} 1 & 0 & 0 & | & a \\ 0 & 1 & 0 & | & b \\ 0 & 0 & 1 & | & c \end{bmatrix}$

take note

Key Concept **Row Operations**

Switch any two rows.

$\begin{bmatrix} 2 & -1 & 3 \\ 3 & 2 & 5 \end{bmatrix}$ becomes $\begin{bmatrix} 3 & 2 & 5 \\ 2 & -1 & 3 \end{bmatrix}$

Hint

These steps are the same as the steps for elimination. Here, you do not have to write the variables.

Multiply a row by a constant.

$\begin{bmatrix} 3 & 2 & 5 \\ 2 & -1 & 3 \end{bmatrix}$ becomes $\begin{bmatrix} 3 & 2 & 5 \\ 2 \cdot 2 & -1 \cdot 2 & 3 \cdot 2 \end{bmatrix} = \begin{bmatrix} 3 & 2 & 5 \\ 4 & -2 & 6 \end{bmatrix}$

Add one row to another.

$\begin{bmatrix} 3 & 2 & 5 \\ 4 & -2 & 6 \end{bmatrix}$ becomes $\begin{bmatrix} 3+4 & 2-2 & 5+6 \\ 4 & -2 & 6 \end{bmatrix} = \begin{bmatrix} 7 & 0 & 11 \\ 4 & -2 & 6 \end{bmatrix}$

Combine any of these steps.

Problem 4 Solving a System Using a Matrix

Think

How is solving a
system using row
operations similar to
using elimination?
You use similar steps,
but the variables don't
appear in the matrices.

What is the solution of the system? $\begin{cases} x + 4y = -1 \\ 2x + 5y = 4 \end{cases}$

Step 1 Write the matrix for the system.

$$\begin{bmatrix} 1 & 4 & | & -1 \\ 2 & 5 & | & 4 \end{bmatrix}$$

Step 2 Multiply Row 1 by -2 and add to Row 2.

$$-2(1 \quad 4 \quad -1) = \quad -2 \quad -8 \quad 2$$
$$\underline{+ \quad 2 \quad 5 \quad 4}$$
$$ \quad 0 \quad -3 \quad 6$$

Replace Row 2 with the sum. Write the new matrix.

$$\begin{bmatrix} 1 & 4 & | & -1 \\ 0 & -3 & | & 6 \end{bmatrix}$$

Step 3 Multiply Row 2 by $-\frac{1}{3}$.

$$-\frac{1}{3}(0 \quad -3 \quad 6) = 0 \quad 1 \quad -2$$

Replace Row 2 with the product. Write the new matrix.

$$\begin{bmatrix} 1 & 4 & | & -1 \\ 0 & 1 & | & -2 \end{bmatrix}$$

Step 4 Multiply Row 2 by -4 and add to Row 1.

$$-4(0 \quad 1 \quad -2) = \quad 0 \quad -4 \quad 8$$
$$\underline{+ \quad 1 \quad 4 \quad -1}$$
$$ \quad 1 \quad 0 \quad 7$$

Replace Row 1 with the sum. Write the new matrix.

$$\begin{bmatrix} 1 & 0 & | & 7 \\ 0 & 1 & | & -2 \end{bmatrix}$$

The solution to the system is $(7, -2)$.

Check Use the original equations. $x + 4y = -1$ $2x + 5y = 4$

Substitute. $7 + 4(-2) \stackrel{?}{=} -1$ $2(7) + 5(-2) \stackrel{?}{=} 4$

Multiply. $7 + (-8) \stackrel{?}{=} -1$ $14 + (-10) \stackrel{?}{=} 4$

Simplify. $-1 = -1$ ✔ $4 = 4$ ✔

 Got It? **4. a.** What is the solution of the system? $\begin{cases} 9x - 2y = 5 \\ 3x + 7y = 17 \end{cases}$

b. Reasoning Which method, *elimination* or *substitution,* is more similar to
solving a system using row operations? Justify your reasoning.

Matrices that represent the solution of a system are in *reduced row echelon form*. Many calculators have a **rref** (reduced row echelon form) function for working with matrices. This function will do all the row operations for you. You can use **rref** to solve a system of equations.

 Problem 5 Using a Calculator to Solve a Linear System

What is the solution of the system of equations? $\begin{cases} 2a + 3b - c = 1 \\ -4a + 9b + 2c = 8 \\ -2a + 2c = 3 \end{cases}$

Think

How do you enter missing variables into a matrix?
If a variable is not present in an equation, enter its coefficient as 0 in the matrix.

Step 1 Enter the system into a calculator as a matrix.

Step 2 Apply the **rref()** function to the matrix. Show the matrix elements in fraction form if any are not integers.

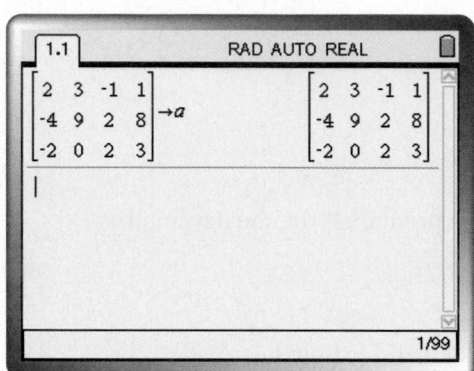

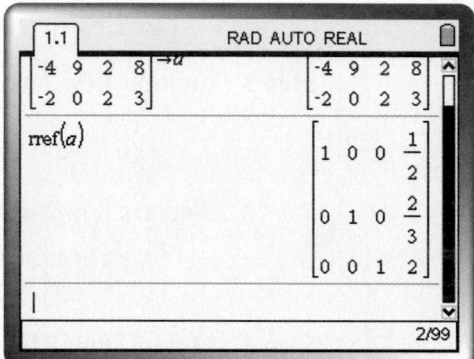

Step 3 List the solution.

The solution of the system is $a = \frac{1}{2}, b = \frac{2}{3}, c = 2$.

Hint

The calculator does not show a vertical bar separating the coefficients and the constants. Look at the last column to find the solution.

Check

$$2a + 3b - c = 1$$
$$2\left(\tfrac{1}{2}\right) + 3\left(\tfrac{2}{3}\right) - 2 \stackrel{?}{=} 1$$
$$1 + 2 - 2 \stackrel{?}{=} 1$$
$$1 = 1 \ \checkmark$$

$$-4a + 9b + 2c = 8$$
$$-4\left(\tfrac{1}{2}\right) + 9\left(\tfrac{2}{3}\right) + 2(2) \stackrel{?}{=} 8$$
$$-2 + 6 + 4 \stackrel{?}{=} 8$$
$$8 = 8 \ \checkmark$$

$$-2a + 2c = 3$$
$$-2\left(\tfrac{1}{2}\right) + 2(2) \stackrel{?}{=} 3$$
$$-1 + 4 \stackrel{?}{=} 3$$
$$3 = 3 \ \checkmark$$

 Got It? **5.** What is the solution of the system of equations?

$$\begin{cases} a + 4b + 6c = 21 \\ 2a - 2b + c = 4 \\ -8b + c = -1 \end{cases}$$

Focus Question Why is it helpful to use matrices to solve systems of equations?

Answer Solving systems using matrices is the same as solving using elimination, except you don't have to write the variables.

Lesson Check

Do you know HOW?

State the dimensions of each matrix.

1. $\begin{bmatrix} 2 \\ 5 \end{bmatrix}$

2. $\left[\begin{array}{ccc|c} 6 & 9 & 0 & 3 \\ 4 & 6 & 2 & 7 \end{array}\right]$

Write a matrix to represent each system.

3. $\begin{cases} 3a + 5b = 0 \\ a + b = 2 \end{cases}$

4. $\begin{cases} x + 3y - z = 2 \\ x + 2z = 8 \\ 2y - z = 1 \end{cases}$

Do you UNDERSTAND?

5. How many elements are in a 4×4 matrix?

6. Writing Using Matrix A in Problem 1, describe the difference in identifying element a_{21} and element a_{12}.

7. Open-Ended Write a situation that can be modeled by the matrix. $\left[\begin{array}{cc|c} 4 & 2 & 8 \\ 0 & 1 & 2 \end{array}\right]$

Practice and Problem-Solving Exercises

A Practice   Identify the indicated element.

$$A = \begin{bmatrix} 3 & 12 & 6 \\ 1 & 0 & 9 \\ 8 & 7 & 4 \end{bmatrix}$$

See Problem 1.

8. a_{32} **9.** a_{21} **10.** a_{13} **11.** a_{31}

Write a matrix to represent each system.

See Problem 2.

Guided Practice

To start, write each equation in the same variable order. Line up the variables. Leave space where a coefficient is 0.

12. $\begin{cases} 3x + 2y = 16 \\ y = 5 \end{cases}$

$\begin{cases} 3x + 2y = 16 \\ y = 5 \end{cases}$

13. $\begin{cases} x + 2y = 11 \\ 2x + 3y = 18 \end{cases}$

14. $\begin{cases} x - y + z = 0 \\ x - 2y - z = 5 \\ 2x - y + 2z = 8 \end{cases}$

15. $\begin{cases} y = 3x - 7 \\ x = 2 \end{cases}$

Write the system of equations represented by each matrix.

See Problem 3.

16. $\left[\begin{array}{cc|c} 1 & 0 & 4 \\ 0 & 1 & -6 \end{array}\right]$

17. $\left[\begin{array}{cc|c} 5 & 1 & -3 \\ -2 & 2 & 4 \end{array}\right]$

18. $\left[\begin{array}{ccc|c} 0 & 1 & 2 & 4 \\ -2 & 3 & 6 & 9 \\ 1 & 0 & 1 & 3 \end{array}\right]$

Solve the system of equations using a matrix.  **See Problems 4 and 5.**

**Guided Practice**

19. $\begin{cases} x + 3y = 5 \\ x + 4y = 6 \end{cases}$

To start, write the system as a matrix.

$\begin{bmatrix} 1 & 3 & | & 5 \\ 1 & 4 & | & 6 \end{bmatrix}$

Multiply Row 1 by -1.
Add to Row 2.

$$-1(1 \quad 3 \quad 5) = \begin{array}{rrr} -1 & -3 & -5 \\ + \quad 1 & 4 & 6 \\ \hline 0 & 1 & 1 \end{array}$$

Replace Row 2 with the sum.
Write the new matrix.

$\begin{bmatrix} 1 & 3 & | & 5 \\ 0 & 1 & | & 1 \end{bmatrix}$

20. $\begin{cases} p - 3q = -1 \\ -5p + 16q = 5 \end{cases}$

21. $\begin{cases} x + 3y = 22 \\ 2x - y = 2 \end{cases}$

22. $\begin{cases} x + 3y = 6 \\ 2x + 4y = 12 \end{cases}$

23. $\begin{cases} x + y = 5 \\ -2x + 4y = 8 \end{cases}$

Ⓑ Apply

24. Business A manufacturer sells pencils and erasers in packages. The price of a package of five erasers and two pencils is $.23. The price of a package of seven erasers and five pencils is $.41. Write a system of equations to represent this situation. Then write a matrix to represent the system.

25. Think About a Plan Last year your town invested a total of $25,000 into two separate funds. The return on one fund was 4% and the return on the other was 6%. If the town earned a total of $1300 in interest, how much money was invested in each fund?
- What variables will you use? What will they represent?
- What equations can you write to model this situation?
- How can you use a matrix to solve this system?

26. Snacks Suppose you want to fill nine 1-lb tins with a snack mix. You have $15 and plan to buy almonds for $2.45 per lb, hazelnuts for $1.85 per lb, and raisins for $.80 per lb. You want the mix to contain an equal amount of almonds and hazelnuts and twice as much of the nuts as the raisins by weight.
   a. Writing Explain how each equation at the right relates to the problem. What does each variable represent?
   b. Solve the system.
   c. How many of each ingredient should you buy?

$$\begin{cases} x + y + z = 9 \\ 2.45x + 1.85y + 0.8z = 15 \\ x + y = 2z \end{cases}$$

27. Geometry The coordinates (x, y) of a point in a plane are the solution of the system $\begin{cases} 2x + 3y = 13 \\ 5x + 7y = 31 \end{cases}$. Find the coordinates of the point.

28. Error Analysis A classmate writes the matrix at the right to represent a system and says that the solution is $x = 2$, $y = 0$. Explain your classmate's error and describe how to correct it.

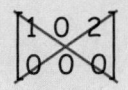

29. Paint A hardware store mixes paints in a ratio of two parts red to six parts yellow to make two gallons of pumpkin orange. A ratio of five parts red to three parts yellow makes two gallons of pepper red. A gallon of pumpkin orange sells for $25, and a gallon of pepper red sells for $28. Find the cost of 1 quart of red paint and the cost of 1 quart of yellow paint.

Standardized Test Prep

SAT/ACT

30. Which equation represents a line with a slope of $\frac{1}{2}$ and a y-intercept of $\frac{3}{4}$?

 Ⓐ $y = \frac{1}{2}x - \frac{3}{4}$ Ⓑ $y = \frac{3}{4}x - \frac{1}{2}$ Ⓒ $y = \frac{1}{2}x + \frac{3}{4}$ Ⓓ $y = \frac{3}{4}x + \frac{1}{2}$

31. Which graph best represents the solution of the inequality $y \leq 2|x - 1| - 4$?

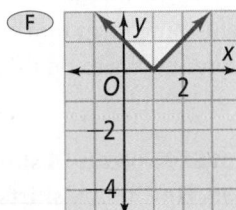
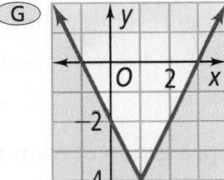
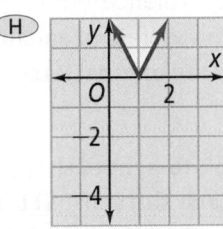
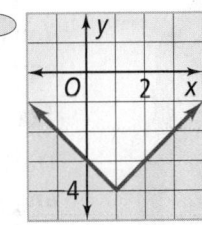

Short Response

32. At what point do the graphs of the equations $y = 7x - 3$ and $-6x + y = 2$ intersect?

Mixed Review

Solve each inequality. Graph the solution.   ◀ See Lesson 1-5.

33. $12 \geq 2(4x + 1) + 22$ **34.** $2x - (3x + 5) \leq 30$ **35.** $4x + 5 - 3x \leq 2x + 1$

Solve each equation. Check your answers.   ◀ See Lesson 1-6.

36. $|2y - 3| = 12$ **37.** $|4x| = 40$ **38.** $|2y - 4| = 16$

Get Ready!   **To prepare for Lesson 4-1, do Exercises 39 and 40.**

Write an equation for each transformation of $y = x$.   ◀ See Lesson 2-6.

39. vertical stretch by a factor of 2   **40.** vertical compression by a factor of $\frac{1}{3}$

3

Pull It **All Together**

To solve these problems, you will pull together concepts and skills related to solving a system of linear equations.

BIG idea Function

The solution of a system of two linear equations corresponds in general to the intersection of the graphs of the corresponding functions.

Task 1

You are given a linear system of two equations in two unknowns. Before solving, describe how you can mentally check whether the system has zero, one, or infinitely many solutions. In which order would you do your check? Why?

BIG idea Equivalence

You can solve a system of equations by representing the system in some form that is equivalent to the original form but easier to solve. There are different ways to do this.

Task 2

During a back-to-school shopping trip, a group of friends spent $245.86 on 14 shirts and pants. Each shirt cost $11.99. Each pair of pants cost $24.99. How many shirts and pairs of pants did the group buy?

  a. Write a system of equations to model the information in the problem.

  b. Study the system. Explain, without solving, which method you think would be most efficient for solving the system: *substitution, elimination, graphing,* or *making a table*. Explain why the other methods would be less efficient.

  c. How could you simplify the numbers used in this system to simplify the system? Does this new system change your answers to part (b)? Explain.

BIG idea Solving Equations and Inequalities

You can represent a system of equations with a matrix. Transforming the matrix to reduced row echelon form gives you an equivalent system for which the solution is obvious.

Task 3

Solve this system using a matrix. $\begin{cases} 4x + 10y = 3 \\ 7x - 2y = 2 \end{cases}$

Make three columns on your paper. In the first column, show each step, changing one matrix row at a time. In the second column, write the two equations that correspond to each matrix in the first column. In the third column, describe how you could transform each set of equations to the next.

3 Chapter Review

Connecting BIG ideas and Answering the Essential Questions

1 Function
Find a point of intersection (x, y) of the graphs of functions f and g and you have found a solution of the system $y = f(x)$, $y = g(x)$.

Solving Systems Using Tables and Graphs (Lesson 3-1)
$$\begin{cases} y = -2x + 3 \\ y = 2x - 1 \end{cases}$$
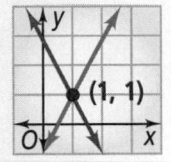
(1, 1)
The solution is (1, 1).

Systems of Inequalities and Linear Programming (Lessons 3-3 and 3-4)
$$\begin{cases} y > -2x + 3 \\ y \le 2x - 1 \end{cases}$$
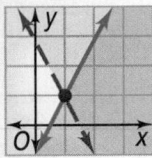

2 Equivalence
If the equations of two systems are equivalent, then a solution of the system that is easier to solve is also a solution of the more difficult system.

Solving Systems Algebraically (Lesson 3-2)
$$\begin{cases} -y = -x + 2 \\ 3y = 2x - 2 \end{cases} \rightarrow \begin{array}{r} -2y = -2x + 4 \\ 3y = 2x - 2 \\ \hline y = 2 \end{array}$$
$$3(2) = 2x - 2 \quad \rightarrow \quad x = 4$$
The solution is $x = 4$, $y = 2$.

Systems With Three Variables (Lesson 3-5)
$$\begin{cases} -2x + y + z = -3 \\ 2x - y + z = -1 \\ -2x - y - z = -1 \end{cases}$$
$x = 1$, $y = 1$, $z = -2$

3 Solving Equations and Inequalities
The matrix row operations of adding rows and multiplying a row by a constant are equivalent to addition and multiplication properties of equality.

Solving Systems Using Matrices (Lesson 3-6)
$$\begin{bmatrix} -2 & 3 & | & 1 \\ 2 & -1 & | & 1 \end{bmatrix}$$
$$\begin{bmatrix} 1 & 0 & | & 1 \\ 0 & 1 & | & 1 \end{bmatrix} \rightarrow x = 1, y = 1$$

Chapter Vocabulary

- constraint (p. 169)
- equivalent systems (p. 157)
- feasible region (p. 169)
- linear programming (p. 169)

- linear system (p. 146)
- matrix (p. 184)
- matrix element (p. 184)
- objective function (p. 169)

- row operation (p. 186)
- solution of a system (p. 146)
- system of equations (p. 146)

Fill in the blank.

1. An ordered pair that satisfies each equation in a system is a(n) _?_ .

2. _?_ is a method for finding a minimum or maximum value, given a system of limits called _?_ .

3. Performing steps called _?_ on a(n) _?_ is similar to solving a system of equations by elimination.

3-1 Solving Systems Using Tables and Graphs

Quick Review

A **system of equations** has two or more equations. Points where all the graphs intersect are solutions. A **linear system** has linear equations. A linear system with two equations in two variables can have zero, one, or infinitely many solutions.

Example

Solve the system. $\begin{cases} 3x + 2y = 4 \\ 2x - 4y = 8 \end{cases}$

Graph the equations.

The only solution, where the graphs of the lines intersect, is $(2, -1)$.

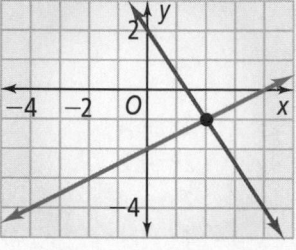

Exercises

Without graphing, classify each system of equations as having *zero*, *one*, or *infinitely many* solutions. Solve systems with one solution by graphing.

4. $\begin{cases} 6x - 2y = 2 \\ 2 + 6x = y \end{cases}$
5. $\begin{cases} 5 - y = 2x \\ 6x - 15 = -3y \end{cases}$

6. $\begin{cases} 6y + 2x = 8 \\ 12y + 4x = 4 \end{cases}$
7. $\begin{cases} 1.5 + 3x = 0.5y \\ 6 - 2y = -12x \end{cases}$

8. $\begin{cases} 2 - 0.25x = 0.5y \\ -1.5y = 1.5x - 3 \end{cases}$
9. $\begin{cases} 1 + y = x \\ x + y = 1 \end{cases}$

10. For $7.52, you purchased 8 pens and highlighters from a local bookstore. Each highlighter cost $1.09 and each pen cost $.69. How many pens did you buy?

3-2 Solving Systems Algebraically

Quick Review

To solve a system by substitution, solve one equation for a variable. Then substitute that expression into the other equation and solve for the remaining variable. To solve by elimination, add two equations with additive inverses as coefficients to eliminate one variable and solve for the other. In both cases, you solve for one of the variables and use substitution to solve for the remaining variable.

Example

Solve $\begin{cases} 10 - y = 4x \\ x = 4 + 0.5y \end{cases}$ by substitution.

Substitute for *x*. $10 - y = 4(4 + 0.5y)$

Simplify and solve for *y*. $y = -2$

Substitute into the first equation. $10 - (-2) = 4x$

Solve for *x*. $x = 3$

The solution is $(3, -2)$.

Exercises

Solve each system by substitution.

11. $\begin{cases} x - 2y = 3 \\ 3x + y = -5 \end{cases}$
12. $\begin{cases} 14x - 35 = 7y \\ -25 - 6x = 5y \end{cases}$

Solve each system by elimination.

13. $\begin{cases} 11 - 5y = 2x \\ 5y + 3 = -9x \end{cases}$
14. $\begin{cases} 2x + 3y = 4 \\ 4x + 6y = 9 \end{cases}$

15. Roast beef has 25 g of protein and 11 g of calcium per serving. A serving of mashed potatoes has 2 g of protein and 25 g of calcium. How many servings of each are needed to supply exactly 29 g of protein and 61 g of calcium?

3-3 Systems of Inequalities

Quick Review

To solve a system of inequalities by graphing, first graph the boundaries for each inequality. Then shade the region(s) of the plane containing solutions valid for both inequalities.

Example

Solve the system of inequalities by graphing.

$$\begin{cases} y > -3 \\ y \le x - 1 \end{cases}$$

Graph both inequalities and shade the region valid for both inequalities.

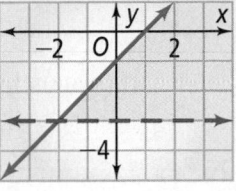

Exercises

Solve each system of inequalities by graphing.

16. $\begin{cases} y < 4x \\ 3x + y \ge 5 \end{cases}$

17. $\begin{cases} y < 2x - 4 \\ x + 5y \ge -1 \end{cases}$

18. $\begin{cases} y \le x + 2 \\ y \ge 1 + \frac{1}{4}x \end{cases}$

19. $\begin{cases} 2x + 3y > 6 \\ x \le -1 \\ y \ge 4 \end{cases}$

20. For a community breakfast, there should be at least three times as much regular coffee as decaffeinated coffee. A total of ten gallons is sufficient for the breakfast. Write and graph a system of inequalities to model the problem.

3-4 Linear Programming

Quick Review

Linear programming is used to find a minimum or maximum of an **objective function**, given **constraints** as linear inequalities. The maximum or minimum occurs at a vertex of the **feasible region**, which contains the solutions to the system of constraints.

Example

Graph the system of constraints and name the vertices. Maximize P for the objective function $P = 2x + y$.

$$\begin{cases} x \le 8 \\ y \le 5 \\ x \ge 0, y \ge 0 \end{cases}$$

Graph the inequalities and shade the feasible region.

The vertices of the feasible region are $(0, 0)$, $(0, 5)$, $(8, 5)$, and $(8, 0)$.

Evaluate the objective function at each vertex:

$2(0) + 0 = 0$ $2(0) + 5 = 5$

$2(8) + 5 = 21$ $2(8) + 0 = 16$

The maximum value occurs at $(8, 5)$.

Exercises

Graph the system of constraints. Name the vertices. Then find the values of x and y that maximize or minimize the objective function.

21. $\begin{cases} x \ge 2 \\ y \ge 0 \\ 3x + 2y \ge 12 \end{cases}$

Minimum for
$C = x + 5y$

22. $\begin{cases} 3x + 2y \le 12 \\ x + y \le 5 \\ x \ge 0, y \ge 0 \end{cases}$

Maximum for
$P = 3x + 5y$

23. A lunch stand makes $.75 profit on each chef's salad and $1.20 profit on each Caesar salad. On a typical weekday, it sells between 40 and 60 chef's salads and between 35 and 50 Caesar salads. The total number sold has never exceeded 100 salads. How many of each type should be prepared in order to maximize profit?

3-5 Systems With Three Variables

Quick Review

To solve a system of three equations, use the techniques you learned to solve a system of two equations. Either pair the equations, using one equation twice, or solve for one variable and substitute the expression into the other two equations. Then, solve the remaining system.

Example

Solve by elimination.

$$\text{①}\begin{cases} x + 2y + z = 12 \\ \text{②} \quad 2x - 3y - z = -5 \\ \text{③} \quad -3x + 2y + z = 0 \end{cases}$$

Add ① and ② to eliminate z. ④ $3x - y = 7$

Add ② and ③ to eliminate z. ⑤ $-x - y = -5$

Add -1 times ⑤ to ④ to eliminate y. $4x = 12$

Solve for x. $x = 3$

Substitute $x = 3$ into ④. $y = 2$

Substitute $x = 3$ and $y = 2$ into ① or ②. $z = 5$

The solution to the system is $(3, 2, 5)$.

Exercises

Solve each system by elimination.

24. $\begin{cases} x + y - 2z = 8 \\ 5x - 3y + z = -6 \\ -2x - y + 4z = -13 \end{cases}$

25. $\begin{cases} -x + y + 2z = -5 \\ 5x + 4y - 4z = 4 \\ x - 3y - 2z = 3 \end{cases}$

Solve each system by substitution.

26. $\begin{cases} 3x + y - 2z = 22 \\ x + 5y + z = 4 \\ x = -3z \end{cases}$

27. $\begin{cases} x + 2y + z = 14 \\ y = z + 1 \\ x = -3z + 6 \end{cases}$

3-6 Solving Systems Using Matrices

Quick Review

You can use a **matrix** to represent a system of equations. Each row represents a different equation, and the columns contain the coefficients of the variables and the constants. To solve a system using a matrix, use **row operations**, which are similar to solving the system by elimination.

Example

Solve the system using a matrix. $\begin{cases} x + 2y = 5 \\ -9y = -45 \end{cases}$

Write the matrix for the system.
$\begin{bmatrix} 1 & 2 & | & 5 \\ 0 & -9 & | & -45 \end{bmatrix}$

Multiply Row 2 by $-\frac{1}{9}$.
Replace Row 2 with the product.
$\begin{bmatrix} 1 & 2 & | & 5 \\ 0 & 1 & | & 5 \end{bmatrix}$

Multiply Row 2 by -2 and add it to Row 1.
Replace Row 1 with the sum.
$\begin{bmatrix} 1 & 0 & | & -5 \\ 0 & 1 & | & 5 \end{bmatrix}$

The solution is $(-5, 5)$.

Exercises

Solve each system using a matrix.

28. $\begin{cases} 4x - 12y = -1 \\ 6x + 4y = 4 \end{cases}$

29. $\begin{cases} 7x + 2y = 5 \\ 13x + 14y = -1 \end{cases}$

30. $\begin{cases} -5x + 3y + 4z = 2 \\ 3x - y - z = 4 \\ x - 6y - 5z = -4 \end{cases}$

31. $\begin{cases} x + y + z = 4 \\ 2x - y + z = 5 \\ x + y - 2z = 13 \end{cases}$

Do you know HOW?

Without graphing, tell how many solutions each system has. Then find the solution to each system using a graph.

1. $\begin{cases} y = 5x - 2 \\ y = x + 4 \end{cases}$

2. $\begin{cases} 3x + 2y = 9 \\ 3x + 2y = 4 \end{cases}$

Solve the system by substitution.

3. $\begin{cases} 0.3x - y = 0 \\ y = 2 + 0.25x \end{cases}$

Solve the system by elimination.

4. $\begin{cases} 4x - 2y = 3 \\ y - 2x = -\frac{3}{2} \end{cases}$

5. $\begin{cases} 3x + 4y = 9 \\ 2x + y = 6 \end{cases}$

Graph the solution of each system.

6. $\begin{cases} 2x + y < 3 \\ x < y + 3 \end{cases}$

7. $\begin{cases} x + 3 > y \\ y > 2x - 1 \end{cases}$

Graph the system of constraints. Identify all vertices. Then find the values of x and y that maximize or minimize the objective function.

8. $\begin{cases} x \le 5 \\ y \le 4 \\ x \ge 0 \\ y \ge 0 \end{cases}$

   Maximum for $P = 2x + y$

Solve each system.

9. $\begin{cases} x - y + z = 0 \\ 3x - 2y + 6z = 9 \\ -x + y - 2z = -2 \end{cases}$

10. $\begin{cases} 2x + y + z = 8 \\ x + 2y - z = -5 \\ z = 2x - y \end{cases}$

Do you UNDERSTAND?

Write a matrix that represents the system. Then solve the system. Tell what method you used and why.

11. $\begin{cases} -a + 4b + 2c = -8 \\ 3a + b - 4c = 9 \\ b = -1 \end{cases}$

12. Sales A pizza shop makes a profit of $1.50 for each small pizza and $2.15 for each large pizza. On a typical Friday, it sells between 70 and 90 small pizzas and between 100 and 140 large pizzas. The shop can make no more than 210 pizzas in a day. How many of each size pizza must be sold in order to maximize profit?

13. Investing Your parents invested $5,000 in three funds. After a year they had $5,450. The growth fund had a return rate of 12%, the income fund had a return rate of 8%, and the money market fund had a return rate of 5%. Your parents invested twice as much in the income fund as in the money market fund. How much money did they invest in each fund?

14. Writing Describe how to identify situations in which substitution may be the best method for solving a system of equations.

15. Open-Ended Write a system of constraints whose graph is a parallelogram.

3 Cumulative Test Prep

ⓉⒾⓅⓈ ⒻⓄⓇ ⓈⓊⒸⒸⒺⓈⓈ

Some problems require the selection of an appropriate representation (concrete, pictorial, graphical, verbal, or symbolic) to find a solution.

TIP 1
Make a drawing.

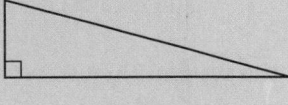

One angle of a right triangle measures 90°. The measure of the second angle is 5 times the measure of the third. What are the measures of these angles?

 (A) 30° and 60°

 (B) 30° and 150°

 (C) 15° and 75°

 (D) 20° and 100°

TIP 2
Write a system:
$$x + y + 90 = 180$$
$$x = 5y$$

Think It Through
A triangle can have only one right angle, so the other two angles must each have a measure less than 90°. Use x and y to represent the unknown angles.

$$x = 5y$$
$$5y + y + 90 = 180$$
$$6y + 90 = 180$$
$$6y = 90$$
$$y = 15, x = 75$$

The correct answer is C.

Vocabulary Builder

As you solve test items, you must understand the meanings of mathematical terms. Match each term with its mathematical meaning.

A. equivalent systems

B. absolute value

C. system of equations

D. linear inequality

I. a number's distance from zero on a number line

II. an inequality in two variables whose graph is a region of the half-plane

III. a set of two or more equations that use the same variables

IV. systems that have the same solution(s)

Multiple Choice

Read each question. Then write the letter of the correct answer on your paper.

1. Which of the following is true about the given system?
$$\begin{cases} -4y = 12 - 8x \\ y = 2x - 3 \end{cases}$$

The system has

 (A) zero solutions.

 (B) exactly one solution.

 (C) two solutions.

 (D) infinitely many solutions.

2. What is the graph of $y = -|x - 2| + 1$?

F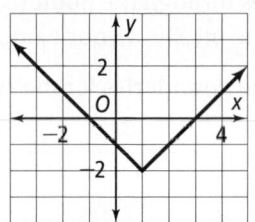

H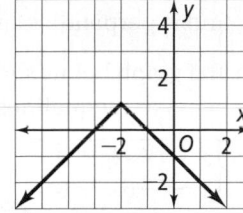

G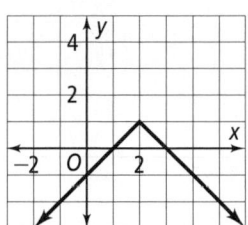

I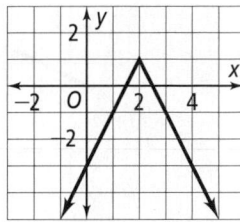

3. Which graph represents the solution of the inequality $|3x + 12| \geq 3$?

A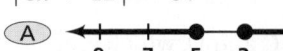

B

C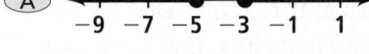

D

4. Josea wants to solve the system using substitution.
$$\begin{cases} x = -2y + 4 \\ 2x - 3y = 5 \end{cases}$$

Which of the following is the best way for Josea to proceed?

F Solve the first equation for y, then substitute into the second equation.

G Solve the second equation for y, then substitute into the first equation.

H Substitute $-2y + 4$ for x in the second equation.

I Substitute $-2y + 4$ for y in the second equation.

5. A board must be cut so that its length is 40.50 cm. The tolerance is 0.25 cm. Which inequality describes the allowable lengths for the board?

A $|x - 0.25| \leq 40.50$ C $|x - 40.50| \leq 0.25$

B $|x + 0.25| \leq 40.50$ D $|x - 0.25| \leq 40.75$

6. Which graph shows the solution to the given system?
$$\begin{cases} \frac{1}{2}x - y = 1 \\ x = 3 \end{cases}$$

F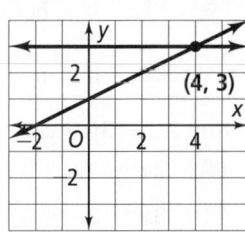

H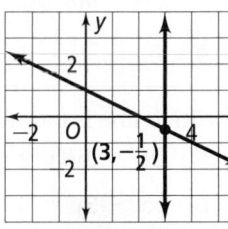

G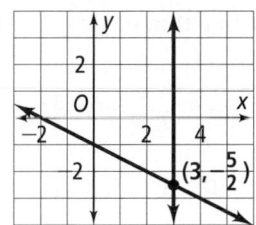

I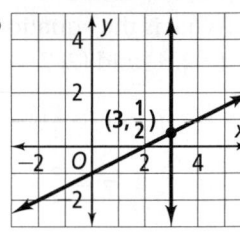

7. Consider the system below.
$$\begin{cases} 4x - 3y - 4z = 17 \\ -2x + 3y - 2z = 1 \\ 4x + 6y + 8z = 2 \end{cases}$$

Which of the following steps would NOT be used to solve the equation by elimination?

A Add the first row to 2 times the second row.

B Add the third row to 4 times the second row.

C Add the first row to the third row.

D Add the first row to the second row.

8. Which of the following inequalities does the graph represent?

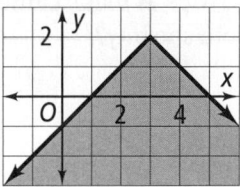

F $y \leq -|x - 3| + 2$

G $y \geq -|x - 3| + 2$

H $y \leq -|x + 3| + 2$

I $y \geq -|x + 3| + 2$

9. The formula for the area of a trapezoid is $A = \frac{h}{2}(b_1 + b_2)$. Solve this equation for b_2.

(A) $b_2 = \frac{2A}{hb_1}$ (C) $b_2 = \frac{2A}{h - b_1}$

(B) $b_2 = \frac{2A}{h} - b_1$ (D) $b_2 = \frac{2A}{h + b_1}$

10. Which line is parallel to the line $2x - 3y = 9$?

(F) $2x + 3y = 9$ (H) $3x + 2y = 9$

(G) $2x - 3y = 6$ (I) $3x - 2y = 6$

11. What is the equation of the line that passes through $(-2, 4)$ and $(2, 7)$?

(A) $y - 7 = \frac{3}{4}(x + 2)$ (C) $y - 7 = \frac{3}{4}(x - 2)$

(B) $y + 7 = \frac{3}{4}(x - 2)$ (D) $y - 2 = \frac{3}{4}(x - 7)$

GRIDDED RESPONSE

12. The nutrition label on a package of crackers shows there are 80 calories in 16 grams of crackers. How many grams are in a package labeled 100 calories?

13. A family with 4 adults and 3 children spends $47 for movie tickets at the theater. Another family with 2 adults and 4 children spends $36. What is the price of a child's ticket in dollars?

14. What is the sum of the solutions of $|5 - 3x| = x + 1$?

15. Sofia is buying party favors for her birthday party. The candles cost $1 each, the frames are $2 each, and the mugs are $2.50 each. She has $120 to spend on 75 favors. Also, she wants to buy twice as many candles as mugs. How many frames should she buy?

Short Response

16. An ice cream shop has regular mix-ins for $.50 each and premium mix-ins for $1 each. You have $2.50 to spend on mix-ins, and you want at least 4 mix-ins. How many of each type of mix-in can you get in your ice cream?

17. The equation of line m is $y = 3x - 1$. What is the equation of a line that goes through the point $(3, -2)$ and is perpendicular to line m? Show your work.

18. The graph below shows the boundaries for the system of linear inequalities.

$$\begin{cases} y \le 0.5x + 5 \\ y \le -5x - 6 \end{cases}$$

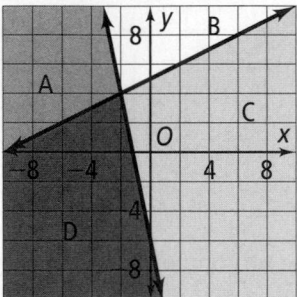

a. Of the shaded areas A, B, C and D, which area represents a solution to the first inequality but not the second?

b. Which represents a solution to the second inequality but not the first?

c. Which represents a solution to both inequalities?

d. Which represents a solution to neither inequality?

Extended Response

19. Jenna is trying to break her school's record for doing the most push-ups in ten minutes. The current record holder did 350 push-ups in ten minutes. The table shows the number of push-ups Jenna completed in the first 6 minutes.

a. Draw a scatter plot and find the line of best fit.

b. Will Jenna beat the current record? Justify your reasoning.

Time (min)	1	2	3	4	5	6
Number of push-ups	37	70	99	132	169	207

Get Ready!

Lesson 1-4 ◆ Solving Linear Equations

Solve each equation. Check your answer.

1. $9x - 16 = 8 + 5x$ 　　　　　　　　　　　　**2.** $4(y + 2) + 1 = -5(3 - 2y)$

Lesson 1-6 ◆ Solving Absolute Value Inequalities

Solve each inequality. Graph the solution.

3. $|6x - 12| + 6 < 30$ 　　　　　　　　　　**4.** $6|4y - 2| \geq 42$

Lesson 2-3 ◆ Writing and Graphing Equations in Slope-Intercept Form

Graph the line passing through the given points. Then write its equation in slope-intercept form.

5. $(1, -1)$ and $(3, 17)$ 　　　　　　　　　　**6.** $(2, 9)$ and $(6, 11)$

Lesson 2-6 ◆ Identifying Translations

Identify each horizontal and vertical translation of the parent function $y = |x|$.

7. $y = |x - 4| + 2$ 　　　　　　　　　　　　**8.** $y = |x + 10| - 3$

Lesson 3-2 ◆ Solving Systems of Equations

Solve each system of equations by substitution.

9. $\begin{cases} 2x + 6y = 14 \\ 4x - 8y = 48 \end{cases}$ 　　　　　　　　**10.** $\begin{cases} x + 2y = -18 \\ 2x - 4y = 12 \end{cases}$

Looking Ahead Vocabulary

11. A *form* is a document with blank spaces to fill in. What types of forms might you use?

12. Something is *imaginary* if it has no factual reality. What are some examples of imaginary items?

13. Many items have a specific *function*, or purpose for use. What is the function of a pencil?

Quadratic Functions and Equations

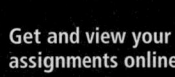

A parabola is the graph of a quadratic function. Parabolas appear all over the place. You can find them in the designs of buildings like the one on the next page.

Vocabulary for Part A

English/Spanish Vocabulary Audio Online:

English	Spanish
axis of symmetry, *p. 204*	eje de simetría
factoring, *p. 227*	descomposición factorial
greatest common factor, *p. 229*	máximo factor común de una expresión
parabola, *p. 204*	parábola
perfect square trinomial, *p. 232*	trinomio cuadrado perfecto
quadratic function, *p. 204*	función cuadrática
standard form, *p. 212*	forma normal
vertex form, *p. 204*	forma del vértice

My Math Video

00:04:04

VIDEO

BIG ideas

1 Equivalence

Essential Question What are the advantages of a quadratic function in vertex form? In standard form?

2 Function

Essential Question How is any quadratic function related to the parent quadratic function $y = x^2$?

3 Solving Equations and Inequalities

Essential Question How are the real solutions of a quadratic equation related to the graph of the related quadratic function?

Chapter Preview for Part A

4-1 **Quadratic Functions and Transformations**

4-2 PART 1 **Standard Form of a Quadratic Function**
PART 2 **Standard Form of a Quadratic Function**

4-3 **Modeling With Quadratic Functions**

4-4 PART 1 **Factoring Quadratic Expressions**
PART 2 **Factoring Quadratic Expressions**

4-1 Quadratic Functions and Transformations

Objective To identify and graph quadratic functions

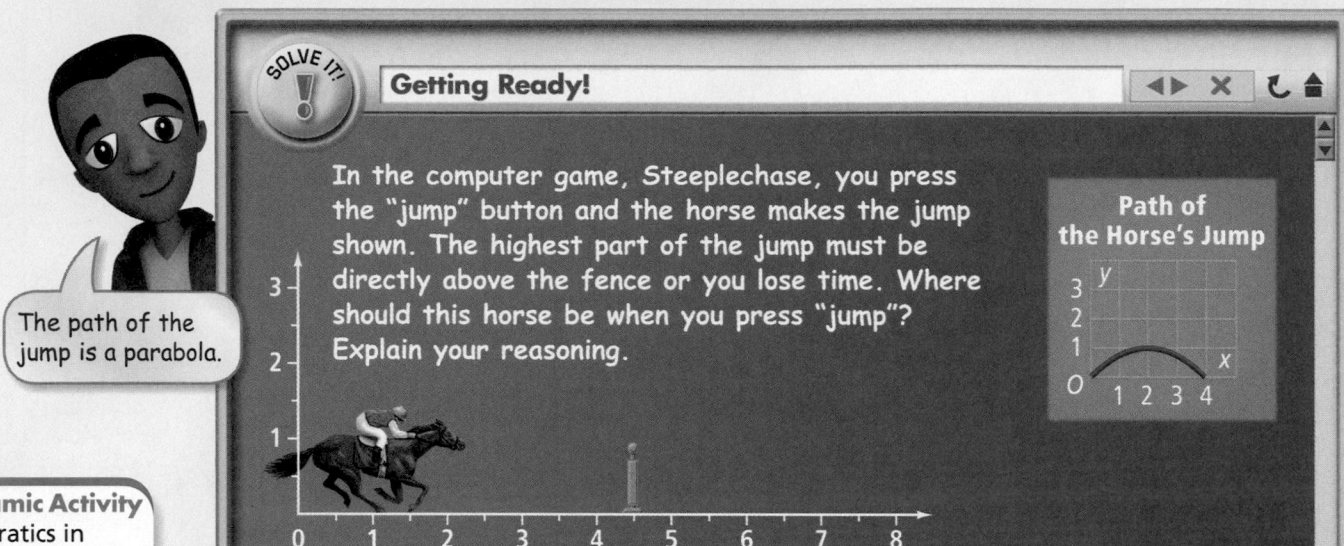

The path of the jump is a parabola.

Getting Ready!

In the computer game, Steeplechase, you press the "jump" button and the horse makes the jump shown. The highest part of the jump must be directly above the fence or you lose time. Where should this horse be when you press "jump"? Explain your reasoning.

Path of the Horse's Jump

Dynamic Activity Quadratics in Vertex Form

Lesson Vocabulary
- parabola
- quadratic function
- vertex form
- axis of symmetry
- vertex of the parabola
- minimum value
- maximum value

In the Solve It, you used the *parabolic* shape of the horse's jump. A **parabola** is the graph of a **quadratic function**, which you can write in the form $f(x) = ax^2 + bx + c$, where $a \neq 0$.

Focus Question What is the vertex form of a quadratic function?

The **vertex form** of a quadratic function is $f(x) = a(x - h)^2 + k$, where $a \neq 0$. The **axis of symmetry** is a line that vertically divides the parabola into two mirror images. The **vertex of the parabola** is the intersection of the parabola and its axis of symmetry. The equation of the axis of symmetry is $x = h$ and the vertex is (h, k).

take note

Key Concept The Parent Quadratic Function

The parent quadratic function is $f(x) = x^2$. Its graph is the parabola shown. The axis of symmetry is $x = 0$. The vertex is $(0, 0)$.

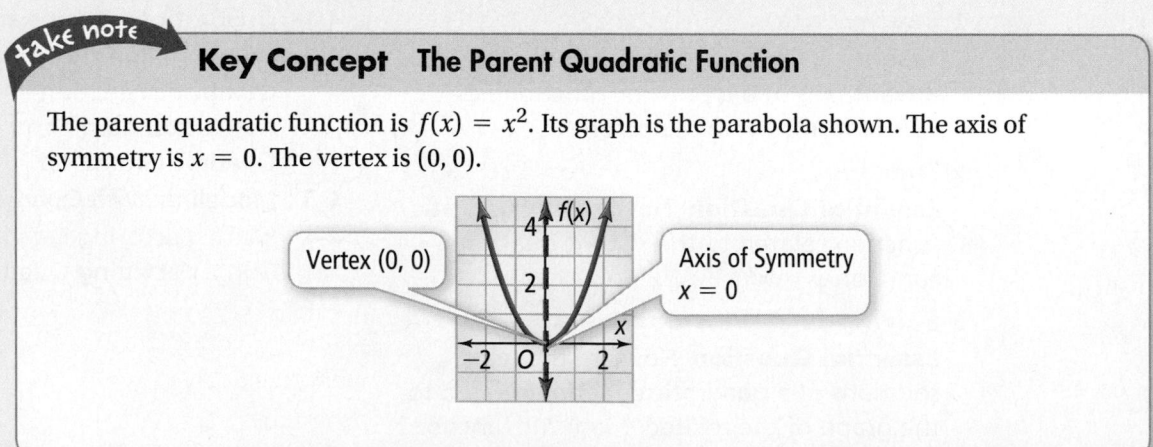

Vertex (0, 0)

Axis of Symmetry $x = 0$

Problem 1 Graphing a Function of the Form $f(x) = ax^2$

What is the graph of $f(x) = \frac{1}{2}x^2$?

Step 1 Plot the vertex $(0, 0)$. Draw the axis of symmetry, $x = 0$.

Step 2 Find and plot two points on one side of the axis of symmetry.

x	$f(x) = \frac{1}{2}x^2$	$(x, f(x))$
0	$\frac{1}{2}(0)^2 = 0$	$(0, 0)$
2	$\frac{1}{2}(2)^2 = 2$	$(2, 2)$
4	$\frac{1}{2}(4)^2 = 8$	$(4, 8)$

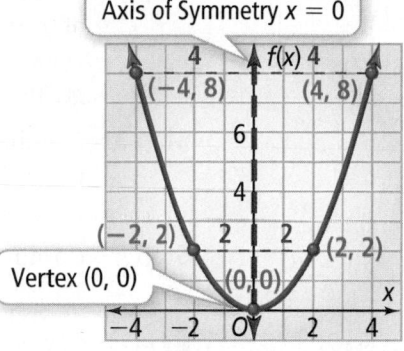

Step 3 Plot the corresponding points on the other side of the axis of symmetry.

Step 4 Sketch the curve.

Got It? **1.** What is the graph of each function?

    a. $f(x) = 2x^2$ **b.** $f(x) = -\frac{1}{3}x^2$ **c.** $f(x) = -2x^2$

    d. Reasoning What can you say about the graph of the function $f(x) = ax^2$ if a is a negative number? Explain.

The graphs of $y = ax^2$ and $y = -ax^2$ are reflections of each other in the x-axis. Increasing $|a|$ stretches the graph vertically. Decreasing $|a|$ compresses the graph vertically.

take note

Key Concept   Reflection, Stretch, and Compression

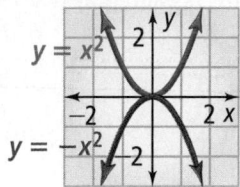
Reflection,
a and −a

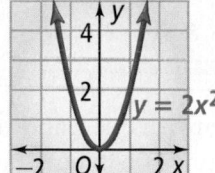
Stretch,
a > 1

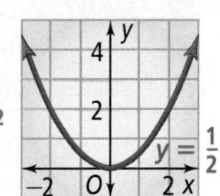
Compression,
0 < a < 1

If $a > 0$, the parabola opens upward. The y-coordinate of the vertex is the **minimum value** of the function.

If $a < 0$, the parabola opens downward. The y-coordinate of the vertex is the **maximum value** of the function.

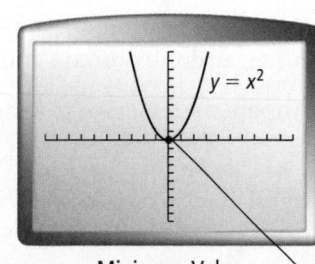
Minimum Value   Vertex

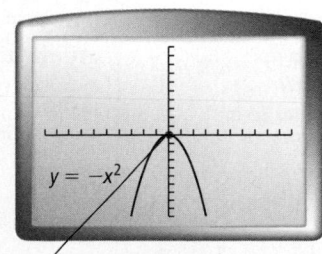
Maximum Value

Problem 2 Graphing Translations of $f(x) = x^2$

Graph each function. How is each graph a translation of the graph of $f(x) = x^2$?

Ⓐ $g(x) = x^2 - 5$

Step 1 Identify and plot the vertex, $(0, -5)$. Find the axis of symmetry, $x = 0$.

Step 2 Find and plot two points on one side of the axis of symmetry.
$g(1) = (1)^2 - 5 = -4 \rightarrow (1, -4)$
$g(2) = (2)^2 - 5 = -1 \rightarrow (2, -1)$

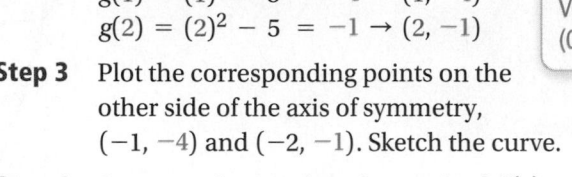

Step 3 Plot the corresponding points on the other side of the axis of symmetry, $(-1, -4)$ and $(-2, -1)$. Sketch the curve.

Think

How does $g(x)$ differ from $f(x)$?
For each value of x, the value of $g(x)$ is 5 less than the value of $f(x)$.

Step 4 Compare the graph to the graph of $f(x) = x^2$. Translate the graph of f down 5 units to get the graph of $g(x) = x^2 - 5$.

Ⓑ $h(x) = (x - 4)^2$

Step 1 Identify and plot the vertex, $(4, 0)$. Find the axis of symmetry, $x = 4$.

Step 2 Find and plot two points on one side of the axis of symmetry.
$h(2) = (2 - 4)^2 = 4 \rightarrow (2, 4)$
$h(3) = (3 - 4)^2 = 1 \rightarrow (3, 1)$

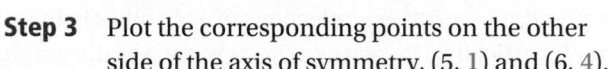

Step 3 Plot the corresponding points on the other side of the axis of symmetry, $(5, 1)$ and $(6, 4)$.

Step 4 Compare the graph to the graph of $f(x) = x^2$. Translate the graph of f to the right 4 units to get the graph of $h(x) = (x - 4)^2$.

 Got It? 2. Graph each function. How is each graph a translation of $f(x) = x^2$?
   a. $g(x) = x^2 + 3$ **b.** $h(x) = (x + 1)^2$

The vertex form of a quadratic function, $f(x) = a(x - h)^2 + k$, gives you information about the graph of f without drawing the graph.

 Problem 3 Interpreting Vertex Form

Plan

How do you use vertex form?
Compare vertex form $y = a(x - h)^2 + k$ to $y = 3(x - 4)^2 - 2$ to find values for a, h, and k.

For $y = 3(x - 4)^2 - 2$, what are the vertex, the axis of symmetry, the maximum or minimum value, and the domain and the range?

Step 1 Compare the function to vertex form: $y = a(x - h)^2 + k$
$y = 3(x - 4)^2 - 2$

Step 2 Since $h = 4$ and $k = -2$, the vertex is $(4, -2)$. The axis of symmetry is $x = 4$.

Step 3 Since $a > 0$, the parabola opens upward. The minimum value is k, or -2.

Step 4 The domain is all real numbers. There is no restriction on the value of x. Since the minimum value of the function is -2, the range is all real numbers ≥ -2.

Got It? 3. For $y = -2(x + 1)^2 + 4$, what are the vertex, axis of symmetry, the maximum or minimum value, and the domain and the range?

Hint
The vertex form of a quadratic function describes the translation of the parent function, similar to the general form of an absolute value function.

You can use the vertex form of a quadratic function, $f(x) = a(x - h)^2 + k$, to transform the graph of the parent function $f(x) = x^2$.

take note

Key Concept Translation of the Parabola

Horizontal

Vertical

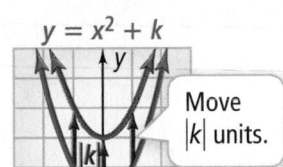

Horizontal and Vertical

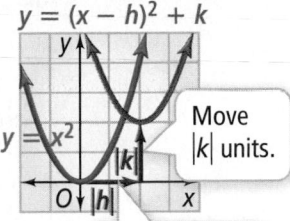

Vertex becomes $(h, 0)$.   Vertex becomes $(0, k)$.   Vertex becomes (h, k).

Problem 4 Using Vertex Form to Graph a Parabola

Plan
What do the values of a, h, and k tell you about the graph?
The graph is a stretched reflection of $y = x^2$, shifted 1 unit right and 3 units up.

A **What is the graph of $f(x) = -2(x - 1)^2 + 3$?**

Step 1   Identify the constants $a = -2$, $h = 1$, and $k = 3$. Because $a < 0$, the parabola opens downward.

Step 2   Plot the vertex $(h, k) = (1, 3)$ and draw the axis of symmetry $x = 1$.

Step 3   Find two points on the graph.

Find $f(2)$. $f(2) = -2(2 - 1)^2 + 3$

Simplify. $= 1$

Plot $(2, 1)$ and the corresponding point $(0, 1)$.

Step 4   Sketch the curve.

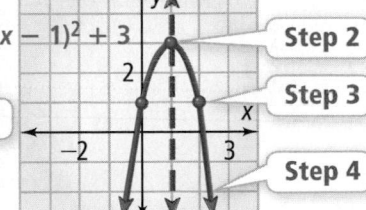

B **Multiple Choice** What steps transform the graph of $y = x^2$ to $y = -2(x + 1)^2 + 3$?

Ⓐ Stretch by the factor 2, translate to the right 1 unit and up 3 units.

Ⓑ Reflect in the x-axis, stretch by the factor 2, and translate to the right 1 unit and up 3 units.

Ⓒ Reflect in the x-axis, translate to the left 1 unit and up 3 units.

Ⓓ Stretch by the factor 2, reflect in the x-axis, and translate to the left 1 unit and up 3 units.

$|a| = 2$, so stretch by the factor 2. $a < 0$, so reflect in the x-axis. The expression $(x + 1)$ means you translate to the left 1 unit. The correct choice is D.

 Got It? 4. What steps transform the graph of $y = x^2$ to $y = 2(x + 2)^2 - 5$?

You can use the vertex form of a quadratic function to model a real-world situation.

 Problem 5 Writing a Quadratic Function in Vertex Form

Plan

What information do you need to write the quadratic function?
You need the vertex to find h and k. Then, you need the coordinates of a second point to find a.

Nature The picture shows the jump of a dolphin. What quadratic function models the path of the dolphin's jump?

Think

What is the vertex?

Choose another point, (9, 4), from the path. Substitute in the vertex form.

Solve for a.

Substitute in the vertex form.

Write

The vertex is (3, 7).
$h = 3, k = 7$

$f(x) = a(x - h)^2 + k$
$4 = a(9 - 3)^2 + 7$
$4 = 36a + 7$
$-3 = 36a$
$a = -\frac{1}{12}$

$f(x) = -\frac{1}{12}(x - 3)^2 + 7$
models the path of the dolphin's jump.

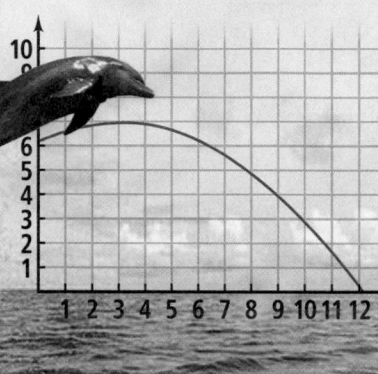

Got It? **5.** Suppose the path of the jump changes so that the axis of symmetry becomes $x = 2$ and the height stays the same. If the path of the jump also passes through the point (5, 5), what quadratic function would model this path?

Focus Question What is the vertex form of a quadratic function?

Answer The vertex form of a quadratic function is $f(x) = a(x - h)^2 + k$, where $a \neq 0$. All quadratic functions are transformations of the parent function, $f(x) = x^2$. Use vertex form to identify the transformations and graph a quadratic function.

Lesson Check

Do you know HOW?

1. Graph the function $f(x) = -3x^2$.

2. Determine whether the function
$f(x) = 0.25(2x - 15)^2 + 150$ has a
maximum or a minimum value.

3. Rewrite $y = -2x^2 + 35$ in vertex form.

Do you UNDERSTAND?

4. **Vocabulary** When does the graph of a quadratic function have a minimum value?

5. **Reasoning** Is $y = 0(x - 4)^2 + 3$ a quadratic function? Explain.

6. **Compare and Contrast** Describe the differences between the graphs of $y = (x + 6)^2$ and $y = (x - 6)^2$.

Practice and Problem-Solving Exercises

 **Practice**

Graph each function.

See Problem 1.

Guided Practice

To start, plot the vertex and draw the axis of symmetry.

7. $y = \frac{2}{5}x^2$

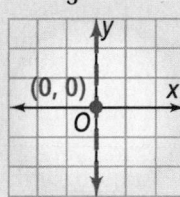

8. $y = -x^2$

9. $y = 4x^2$

10. $y = -7x^2$

Graph each function. Describe how it was translated from $f(x) = x^2$.

See Problem 2.

11. $f(x) = x^2 + 3$

12. $f(x) = (x - 2)^2$

13. $f(x) = x^2 - 6$

14. $f(x) = (x + 3)^2$

15. $f(x) = x^2 - 9$

16. $f(x) = (x + 5)^2$

Identify the vertex, the axis of symmetry, the maximum or minimum value, and the domain and the range of each function.

See Problem 3.

Guided Practice

To start, compare the function to vertex form.

17. $y = -1.5(x + 20)^2$

$y = a(x - h)^2 + k$
$y = -1.5(x - (-20))^2 + 0$

18. $f(x) = 0.1(x - 3.2)^2$

19. $f(x) = 24(x + 5.5)^2$

20. $f(x) = -(x - 4)^2 - 25$

Graph each function. Identify the axis of symmetry.   ◀ **See Problem 4.**

21. $f(x) = 2(x - 2)^2 + 5$ **22.** $y = -3(x + 7)^2 - 8$ **23.** $f(x) = -(x - 7)^2 + 10$

Write a quadratic function to model each graph.   ◀ **See Problem 5.**

24. 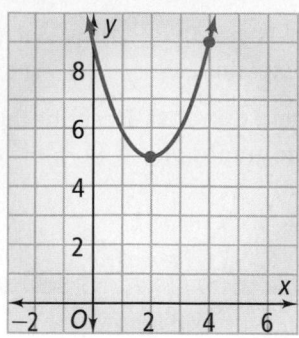   **25.** 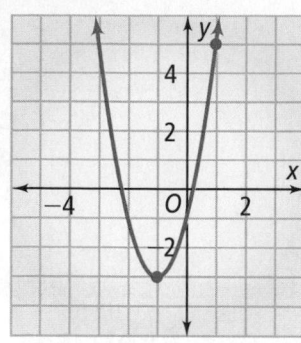   **26.**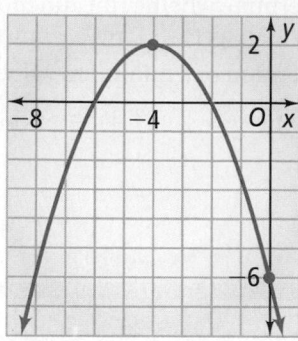

 **Apply**

27. Think About a Plan A gardener is putting a wire fence along the edge of his garden to keep animals from eating his plants. If he has 20 meters of fence, what is the largest rectangular area he can enclose?
- To find the area of a rectangle, what two quantities do you need? Choose one to be your variable and write the other in terms of this variable.
- How can a graph help you solve this problem?
- What quadratic function represents the area of the garden?

28. Manufacturing The equation for the cost in dollars of producing computer chips is $C = 0.000015x^2 - 0.03x + 35$, where x is the number of chips produced. Find the number of chips that minimizes the cost. What is the cost for that number of chips?

Describe how to transform the graph of the parent function $y = x^2$ to the graph of each function below. Graph the two functions on the same axes.

29. $y = -2(x - 1)^2$ **30.** $y = -2(x + 1)^2 + 1$ **31.** $y = 3(x - 2)^2 + 3$

32. $y = -1(x + 4)^2 + 5$ **33.** $y = -0.25x^2 + 3$ **34.** $y = 0.2(x - 12)^2 - 3$

35. Writing Describe the family of quadratic functions whose members each have $(3, 4)$ as their vertex.

36. Open-Ended Write an equation of a parabola whose graph is symmetric about $x = -10$.

Write the equation of each parabola in vertex form.

37. vertex $(1, 2)$, point $(2, -5)$ **38.** vertex $(-3, 6)$, point $(1, -2)$

39. vertex $(0, 5)$, point $(1, -2)$ **40.** vertex $\left(\frac{1}{4}, -\frac{3}{2}\right)$, point $(1, 3)$

41. Write and graph a quadratic function to represent the areas of all rectangles with a perimeter of 36 ft.

Standardized Test Prep

SAT/ACT

42. One parabola at the right has the equation $y = (x - 4)^2 + 2$. Which equation represents the second parabola?

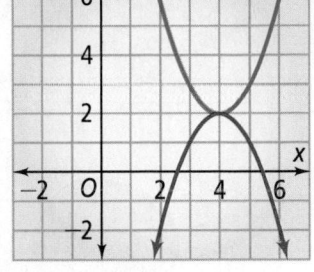

(A) $y = -(x - 4)^2 + 2$

(B) $y = (-x - 4)^2 + 2$

(C) $y = (x + 4)^2 - 2$

(D) $y = (x + 4)^2 - 2$

43. Which system has the unique solution $(1, 4)$?

(F) $\begin{cases} y = x - 3 \\ x + y = 5 \end{cases}$

(G) $\begin{cases} y = -x + 5 \\ x - y = -3 \end{cases}$

(H) $\begin{cases} x + y = 5 \\ y = -x + 3 \end{cases}$

(I) $\begin{cases} -x + y = 3 \\ 2x - 2y = -6 \end{cases}$

44. The formula for the surface area of a right circular cylinder is $S = 2\pi r h + 2\pi r^2$. What is an equivalent formula for the height of the cylinder?

(A) $h = \dfrac{S}{4\pi r}$

(B) $h = \dfrac{S}{2\pi r^2}$

(C) $h = \dfrac{S}{2\pi r} - r$

(D) $h = r - \dfrac{S}{2\pi r}$

Short Response

45. An athletic club has 225 feet of fencing to enclose a tennis court. What quadratic function can be used to find the area of the tennis court? Find the maximum area and the lengths of the sides of the resulting fence.

Mixed Review

Solve each system of equations using a matrix.

See Lesson 3-6.

46. $\begin{cases} 3x - y = 7 \\ 2x + 2y = 10 \end{cases}$

47. $\begin{cases} 2x + 5y = 10 \\ -3x + y = 36 \end{cases}$

48. $\begin{cases} 3x + y - 2z = -3 \\ x - 3y - z = -2 \\ 2x + 2y + 3z = 11 \end{cases}$

Graph each inequality.

See Lesson 2-8.

49. $y > 3x + 1$

50. $y < -x + 4$

51. $y \geq \frac{1}{2}x - 2$

Determine whether each relation is a function.

See Lesson 2-1.

52. $\{(3, 0), (2, -1), (4, 2)\}$

53. $\{(1, 2), (1, 1), (-1, 1)\}$

54. $\{(1, 2), (-1, 2), (-1, 1)\}$

Get Ready!   To prepare for Lesson 4-2, do Exercises 55–57.

Find the vertex of the graph of each function.

See Lesson 2-7.

55. $y = -2|x|$

56. $y = |-x - 1|$

57. $y = 5|x - 5|$

4-2
PART 1

Standard Form of a Quadratic Function

Objective To graph quadratic functions written in standard form

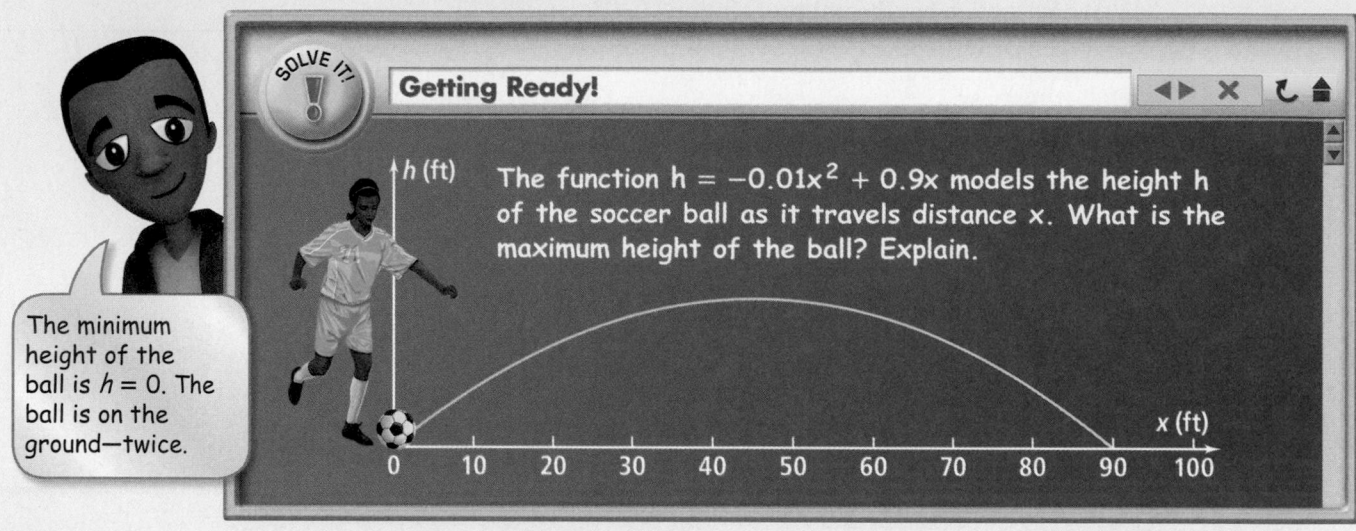

Getting Ready!

The minimum height of the ball is $h = 0$. The ball is on the ground—twice.

h (ft)

The function $h = -0.01x^2 + 0.9x$ models the height h of the soccer ball as it travels distance x. What is the maximum height of the ball? Explain.

x (ft)

0   10   20   30   40   50   60   70   80   90   100

Lesson Vocabulary
• standard form

In Lesson 4-1, you worked with quadratic functions written in vertex form. Now you will use quadratic functions in *standard form*. The **standard form** of a quadratic function is $f(x) = ax^2 + bx + c$, where $a \neq 0$.

Focus Question Why is the standard form of a quadratic function useful?

You can find information about the graph of a quadratic function (such as the vertex) easily from the vertex form. This information is "hidden" in standard form. However, standard form is easier to enter into your graphing calculator.

Problem 1 Finding the Features of a Quadratic Function

Graphing Calculator What are the vertex, the axis of symmetry, the maximum or minimum value, and the range of $y = 2x^2 + 8x - 2$?

Plan

How can you use a calculator to find the features of a quadratic function in standard form?
Graph the function. Then use the **CALC** and **TABLE** features.

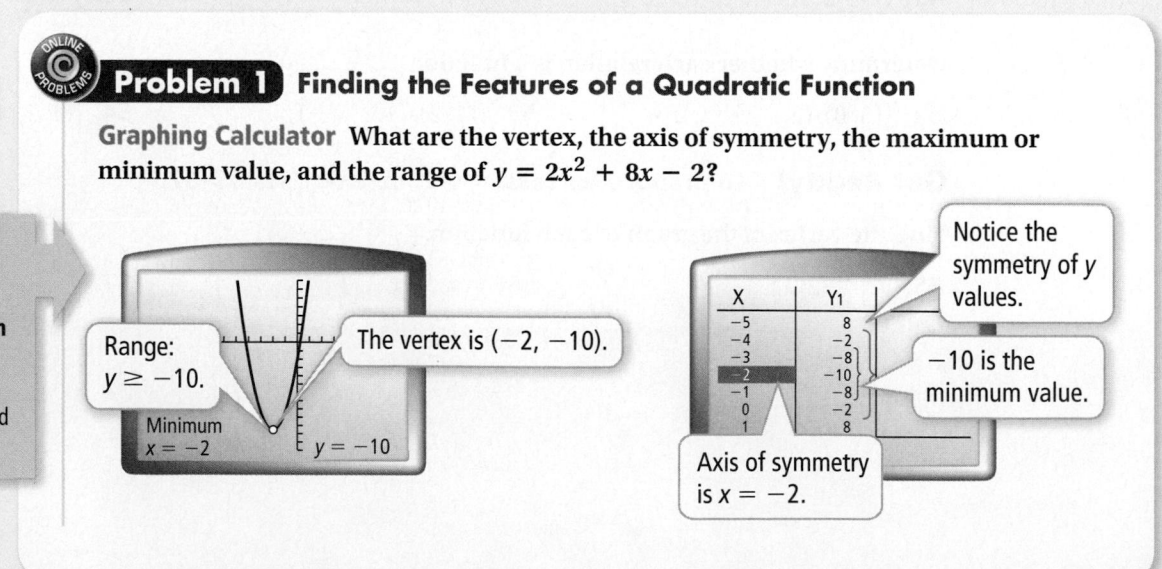

Range: $y \geq -10$.

Minimum
$x = -2$

The vertex is $(-2, -10)$.

$y = -10$

Notice the symmetry of y values.

X	Y1
−5	8
−4	−2
−3	−8
−2	−10
−1	−8
0	−2
1	8

−10 is the minimum value.

Axis of symmetry is $x = -2$.

You can find information about the quadratic function $f(x) = ax^2 + bx + c$ from the coefficients a and b, and from the constant term c.

Dynamic Activity
Quadratic
Equations in
Polynomial Form

take note

Properties   Quadratic Function in Standard Form

- The graph of $f(x) = ax^2 + bx + c, a \neq 0$, is a parabola.
- If $a > 0$, the parabola opens upward. If $a < 0$, the parabola opens downward.
- The axis of symmetry is the line $x = -\frac{b}{2a}$.
- The x-coordinate of the vertex is $-\frac{b}{2a}$. The y-coordinate of the vertex is the y-value of the function for $x = -\frac{b}{2a}$, or $y = f\left(-\frac{b}{2a}\right)$.
- The y-intercept is $(0, c)$.

$$y = ax^2 + bx + c, a > 0 \qquad y = ax^2 + bx + c, a < 0$$

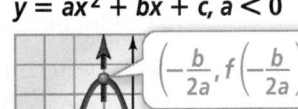

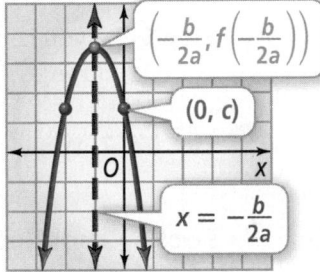

Here's Why It Works You can expand the vertex form of a quadratic function to determine properties of the graph of a quadratic function written in standard form.

Write the vertex form.	$f(x) = a(x - h)^2 + k$
Simplify the power.	$= a(x^2 - 2hx + h^2) + k$
Use the Distributive Property.	$= ax^2 - 2ahx + ah^2 + k$
Group the coefficients and constant term.	$= ax^2 + (-2ah)x + (ah^2 + k)$

Compare this result to the standard form, $f(x) = ax^2 + bx + c.$

a in standard form is the same as a in vertex form.	$a = a$	Write an equation for b.	$b = -2ah$
		Solve for h.	$-\frac{b}{2a} = h$

Since $h = -\frac{b}{2a}$, the axis of symmetry is $x = -\frac{b}{2a}$.
The vertex is $(h, k) = \left(-\frac{b}{2a}, f\left(-\frac{b}{2a}\right)\right)$.

Hint

$(x - h)^2 = (x - h)(x - h)$.
To find this product, use the Distributive Property.
$(x - h)(x - h)$
$(x - h)(x) - (x - h)(h)$
$[x(x) - h(x)] - [x(h) - h(h)]$
$x^2 - hx - hx - h^2$
$x^2 - 2hx - h^2$

Problem 2 **Graphing a Function of the Form** $y = ax^2 + bx + c$

What is the graph of $y = x^2 + 2x + 3$**?**

Step 1   Identify a, b, and c.
$a = 1, b = 2, c = 3$

Step 2   The axis of symmetry is $x = -\frac{b}{2a}$.

$$x = -\frac{2}{2(1)}$$

Lightly sketch the line $x = -1$.

Step 3   The x-coordinate of the vertex is also $-\frac{b}{2a}$, or -1.

The y-coordinate is
$y = (-1)^2 + 2(-1) + 3 = 2$.

Plot the vertex $(-1, 2)$.

Step 4   Since $c = 3$, the y-intercept is $(0, 3)$. The corresponding point is $(-2, 3)$. Plot both points.

Step 5 $a > 0$ confirms that the graph opens upward. Draw a smooth curve through the points you found in Steps 3 and 4.

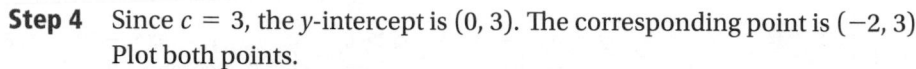

Think

How can you use the axis of symmetry?
The entire curve on one side of the axis is the mirror image of the curve on the other side.

 Got It?   **2.** What is the graph of $y = -2x^2 + 2x - 5$?

Focus Question   Why is the standard form of a quadratic function useful?

Answer   Like vertex form, it is still possible to find information about the graph of a quadratic function. However, standard form is easier to enter into your graphing calculator.

 Lesson Check

Do you know HOW?

1. Identify the vertex, axis of symmetry, and the maximum or minimum value of the parabola at the right.

Graph each function.

2. $y = x^2 - 2x + 4$

3. $y = -x^2 - 3x + 6$

Do you UNDERSTAND?

4. Error Analysis A student graphed the function $y = 2x^2 - 4x - 3$. Find and correct the error.

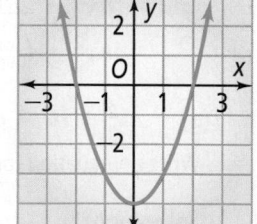

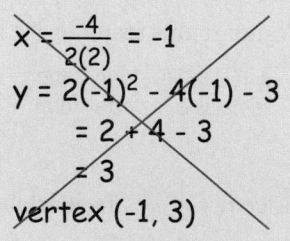

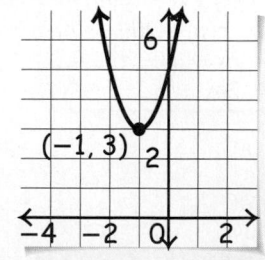

Practice and Problem-Solving Exercises

 **Practice** Identify the vertex, the axis of symmetry, the maximum or minimum value, and the range of each parabola. ◀ **See Problem 1.**

Guided Practice

To start, graph the function and use the CALC feature to find the minimum.

5. $y = x^2 + 4x + 1$

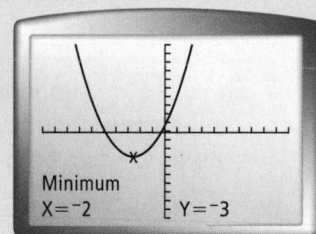

Minimum
X = -2   Y = -3

6. $y = x^2 + 2x + 1$ **7.** $y = -x^2 + 2x + 1$ **8.** $y = 3x^2 - 4x - 2$

9. $y = -2x^2 - 3x + 4$ **10.** $y = 2x^2 - 6x + 3$ **11.** $y = 2x^2 + 5$

Graph each function.   ◀ **See Problem 2.**

Guided Practice

To start, identify a, b, and c.

12. $y = -x^2 - 3x + 6$

$a = -1, b = -3, c = 6$

13. $y = x^2 + 6x + 9$ **14.** $y = 2x^2 + 4x$ **15.** $y = 4x^2 - 12x + 9$

16. $y = -6x^2 - 12x - 1$ **17.** $y = 3x^2 - 12x + 10$ **18.** $y = -4x^2 - 24x - 36$

B Apply Sketch each parabola using the given information.

19. vertex $(3, 6)$, y-intercept $(0, 2)$ **20.** vertex $(-1, -4)$, y-intercept $(0, 3)$

21. vertex $(0, 5)$, point $(1, -2)$ **22.** vertex $(2, 3)$, point $(6, 9)$

23. Physics Suppose you throw a ball over a 10-ft fence. Barely clearing the fence, the ball reaches its highest point directly above the fence and lands 10 ft from the fence. Using the fence as the axis of symmetry, write a quadratic function in standard form that models the ball's height.

Standard Form of a Quadratic Function

Objective To graph quadratic functions written in standard form

In Part 1 of the lesson, you learned about the standard form of a quadratic function.

Connect to What You Know

Here you will use what you learned to convert a quadratic equation from standard form to vertex form.

Recall that for a quadratic function $f(x) = ax^2 + bx + c$, the vertex is $\left(-\frac{b}{2a}, f\left(-\frac{b}{2a}\right)\right)$. You can use these relationships to convert between standard form and vertex form.

Focus Question When is vertex form more useful than standard form?

Problem 3 Converting Standard Form to Vertex Form

Plan

How do you find h, k, and a?
Find the vertex. This gives you h and k. The value for a is the same in both forms.

What is the vertex form of $y = 2x^2 + 10x + 7$?

Step 1 Identify a and b from the standard form equation.
$$y = 2x^2 + 10x + 7$$
$$\uparrow a \qquad \uparrow b$$

Step 2 Find the x-coordinate of the vertex, $x = -\frac{b}{2a}$.

Substitute $a = 2$ and $b = 10$. $\qquad = -\frac{10}{2(2)}$

Simplify. $\qquad = -2.5$ — This is h in vertex form.

Step 3 Find the y-coordinate of the vertex.

Write the original equation. $\qquad y = 2x^2 + 10x + 7$

Substitute $x = -2.5$. $\qquad = 2(-2.5)^2 + 10(-2.5) + 7$

Simplify. $\qquad = -5.5$ — This is k in vertex form.

The vertex is $(-2.5, -5.5)$.

Step 4 Write the equation in vertex form, $y = a(x - h)^2 + k$.

Substitute $a = 2$, $h = -2.5$, and $k = -5.5$. $\qquad y = 2[x - (-2.5)]^2 + (-5.5)$

Simplify. $\qquad y = 2(x + 2.5)^2 - 5.5$

The vertex form is $y = 2(x + 2.5)^2 - 5.5$.

 Got It? 3. What is the vertex form of $y = -x^2 + 4x - 5$?

Problem 4 Interpreting a Quadratic Graph

Length of bridge above arch

Height of arch

516 ft

Bridges The New River Gorge Bridge in West Virginia is the world's largest steel single arch bridge. You can model the arch with the function $y = -0.0005x^2 + 0.85x$, where x and y are in feet and the origin represents the left base of the supports. Approximately how high above the river is the arch? How long is the section of bridge above the arch?

Know

A function that models the arch and the vertical distance from the base of the arch supports to the water

Need

The height of the arch above the support base and the length of the bridge above the arch

Plan

Find the vertex. The y-coordinate is the height of the arch above the support base. The x-coordinate is half the distance between the supports.

Think

How can you tell that the quadratic function has a maximum value?
Since $a < 0$, the graph of the function opens downward. The function has a maximum value.

Step 1 Find the vertex of the arch.

$$x = -\frac{b}{2a} = -\frac{0.85}{2(-0.0005)} = 850$$

$$y = -0.0005(850)^2 + 0.85(850) \approx 361$$

The vertex is about (850, 361).

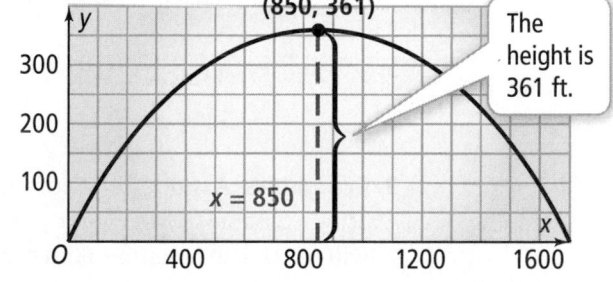

(850, 361)

The height is 361 ft.

$x = 850$

Step 2 Find the height of the arch above the base of its supports.

The y-coordinate of the vertex is the height of the arch above the base of its supports. The arch is about 361 ft above its supports.

Step 3 Find the height of the arch above the river.

The arch is about 361 ft + 516 ft = 877 ft above the river.

Step 4 Find the length of the bridge above the arch.

The x-coordinate of the vertex is half the length of the bridge above the arch. The length of that part of the bridge is about 850 ft + 850 ft = 1700 ft long.

Got It? **4. a.** The Zhaozhou Bridge in China is the oldest known arch bridge, dating to A.D. 605. You can model the support arch with the function $f(x) = -0.0011x^2 + 0.13x$, where x and y are measured in feet. Approximately how high is the arch above the base of its supports?

   b. Reasoning Why does the model in part (a) not have a constant term?

Focus Question When is vertex form more useful than standard form?

Answer Although standard form is easier to enter into a graphing calculator, the features of the quadratic function are hidden in standard form. It is easier to find information about the graph of a quadratic function from the vertex form.

Lesson Check

Do you know HOW?

Write each function in vertex form.

1. $y = x^2 - 2x + 9$

2. $y = -x^2 + 3x - 1$

Do you UNDERSTAND?

3. Compare and Contrast Explain the difference between finding the vertex of a function written in vertex form and finding the vertex of a function written in standard form.

Practice and Problem-Solving Exercises

See Problem 3.

A Practice   Write each function in vertex form.

Guided Practice

To start, identify a and b.

Find the x-coordinate of the vertex.

4. $y = x^2 - 4x + 6$

$y = 1x^2 + (-4)x + 6$

$x = -\dfrac{b}{2a} = -\dfrac{(-4)}{2(1)} = 2$

5. $y = x^2 + 2x + 5$

6. $y = 4x^2 + 7x$

7. $y = 2x^2 - 5x + 12$

8. $y = -2x^2 + 8x + 3$

9. Economics A model for a company's revenue from selling a software package is $R = -2.5p^2 + 500p$, where p is the price in dollars of the software. What price will maximize revenue? Find the maximum revenue.

See Problem 4.

 **B Apply**

10. Think About a Plan Suppose you work for a packaging company and are designing a box that has a rectangular bottom with a perimeter of 36 cm. The box must be 4 cm high. What dimensions give the maximum volume?
- How can you model the volume of the box with a quadratic function?
- What information can you get from the function to find the maximum volume?

For each function, the vertex of the function's graph is given. Find the unknown coefficients.

11. $y = x^2 + bx + c$; $(3, -4)$

12. $y = -3x^2 + bx + c$; $(1, 0)$

13. $y = ax^2 + 10x + c$; $(-5, -27)$

14. $y = c - ax^2 - 2x$; $(-1, 3)$

15. Physics The equation for the motion of a projectile fired straight up at an initial velocity of 64 ft/s is $h = 64t - 16t^2$, where h is height in feet and t is time in seconds. Find the time it takes the projectile to reach its highest point. How high will it go?

16. Landscaping A town is planning a playground. It wants to fence in a rectangular space using an existing wall. What is the greatest area it can fence in using 100 ft of donated fencing?

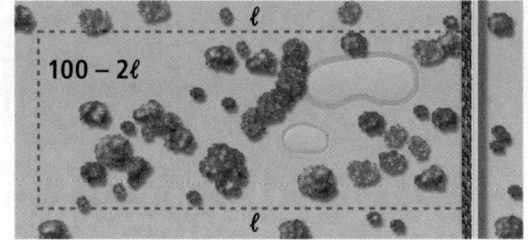

17. A student says that the graph of $y = ax^2 + bx + c$ gets wider as a increases.
  a. Error Analysis Use examples to show that the student is wrong.
  b. Writing Summarize the relationship between $|a|$ and the width of the graph of $y = ax^2 + bx + c$.

For each function, find the *y*-intercept.

18. $y = (x - 1)^2 + 2$ **19.** $y = -3(x + 2)^2 - 4$ **20.** $y = -\frac{2}{3}(x - 9)^2$

Standardized Test Prep

SAT/ACT

21. The time it takes to chalk a baseball diamond varies directly with the length of the side of the diamond. If it takes 10 minutes to chalk a little league diamond with 60-ft sides, how long will it take to chalk a major league baseball diamond with 90-ft sides?

22. What is the *x*-value of the vertex of the quadratic function $y = -5x^2 + \frac{4}{7}$?

23. Sarah works as a nanny and charges different rates for working during the week and the weekend. One week, she earned \$902.50 working 45 hours, of which 5 hours were during the weekend. The following week she earned \$1045 working 50 hours, of which 10 hours were during the weekend. What does Sarah charge per hour, in dollars, for working during the week?

Mixed Review

Solve each equation.   ◀ See Lesson 1-4.

24. $0.6(y + 2) - 0.2(2 - y) = 1$ **25.** $3(a + 4) + 2(a - 1) = a$

For each system, choose the method of solving that seems easier to use.   ◀ See Lessons 3-2 and 3-6.
Explain why you made each choice. Solve each system.

26. $\begin{cases} 3x - 5y = 26 \\ -2x - 3y = -11 \end{cases}$ **27.** $\begin{cases} y = \frac{2}{3}x - 3 \\ -x + 3y = 18 \end{cases}$ **28.** $\begin{cases} 2m + 3n = 12 \\ -5m + n = -13 \end{cases}$

Get Ready!   **To prepare for Lesson 4-3, do Exercises 29–31.**

Identify the vertex, the axis of symmetry, the maximum or minimum value, and   ◀ See Lesson 4-2.
the domain and range of each function.

29. $y = -(x - 1)^2 + 3$ **30.** $y = 3(x + 4)^2$ **31.** $y = -7(x - 4)^2 + 6$

4-3 Modeling With Quadratic Functions

Objective To model data with quadratic functions

You will have to decide where to locate the origin.

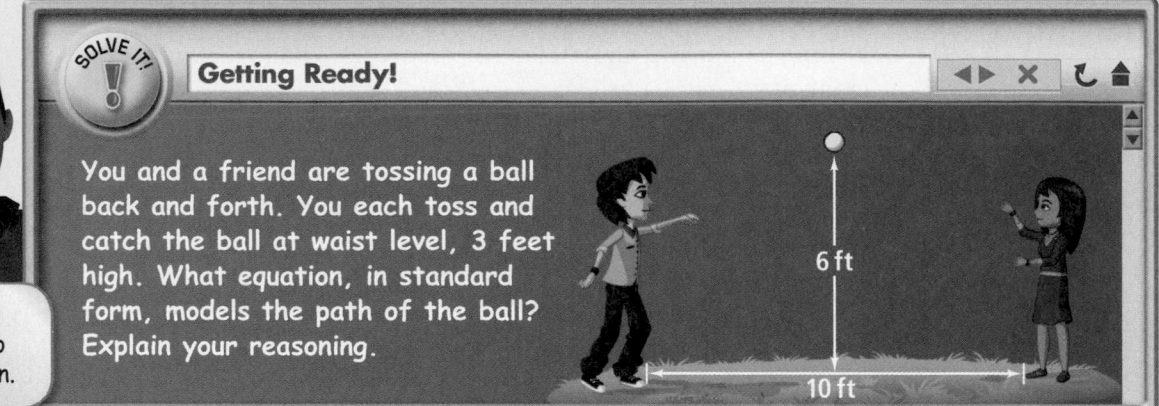

SOLVE IT!

Getting Ready!

You and a friend are tossing a ball back and forth. You each toss and catch the ball at waist level, 3 feet high. What equation, in standard form, models the path of the ball? Explain your reasoning.

6 ft

10 ft

When you know the vertex and a point on a parabola, you can use vertex form to write an equation of the parabola.

Hint

noncollinear points
Three (or more) points are noncollinear if they do not all lie on the same line.

Focus Question How can you write the equation of a parabola without knowing the vertex?

You can write an equation of a parabola through three noncollinear points (no two of which are in line vertically) by writing and solving a system of equations.

Problem 1 Writing an Equation of a Parabola

Plan

How do you use the three given points?
Use them to write a system of three equations. Solve the system to get a, b, and c.

A parabola contains the points $(0, 0)$, $(-1, -2)$, and $(1, 6)$. What is the equation of this parabola in standard form?

Substitute the (x, y) values into $y = ax^2 + bx + c$ to write a system of equations.

Write the equation.	$y = ax^2 + bx + c$
Use $(0, 0)$.	$0 = a(0)^2 + b(0) + c$ $\rightarrow$ $0 = c$
Use $(-1, -2)$.	$-2 = a(-1)^2 + b(-1) + c \rightarrow -2 = a - b + c$
Use $(1, 6)$.	$6 = a(1)^2 + b(1) + c \rightarrow 6 = a + b + c$

Since $c = 0$, the resulting system has two variables. $\begin{cases} a - b = -2 \\ a + b = 6 \end{cases}$

Use elimination. $a = 2$ and $b = 4$.

Substitute $a = 2$, $b = 4$, and $c = 0$ into standard form: $y = 2x^2 + 4x + 0$.
$y = 2x^2 + 4x$ is the equation of the parabola that contains the given points.

 Got It? **1.** What is the equation in standard form of a parabola containing the points $(0, 0)$, $(1, -2)$, and $(-1, -4)$?

Problem 2 Using a Quadratic Model

Basketball A player throws a basketball toward the hoop. The basketball follows a parabolic path through the points shown. If the center of the hoop is at (12, 10), will the ball pass through the hoop? (You can think of the units as feet.)

(4, 12)   (10, 12)

(2, 10)

Step 1 Find a quadratic model.

Substitute the *x*- and *y*-values into the standard form of a quadratic function. The result is a system of three linear equations.

Write the standard form. $y = ax^2 + bx + c$

Use (2, 10). $10 = a(2)^2 + b(2) + c$

Use (4, 12). $12 = a(4)^2 + b(4) + c$

Use (10, 12). $12 = a(10)^2 + b(10) + c$

Use one of the methods from Chapter 3. Solve. $\begin{cases} 4a + 2b + c = 10 \\ 16a + 4b + c = 12 \\ 100a + 10b + c = 12 \end{cases}$

The solution is $a = -0.125$, $b = 1.75$, and $c = 7$.

Substitute the values into the standard form of a quadratic function. An equation of the parabola is $y = -0.125x^2 + 1.75x + 7$.

Think

In terms of the quadratic model, what does it mean for the ball to pass through the hoop?
The point (12, 10) is on the parabola. That is, the point (12, 10) satisfies the quadratic equation.

Step 2 Use the quadratic model to see if the player makes the basket.

Write the equation of the model. $y = -0.125x^2 + 1.75x + 7$

Substitute $(x, y) = (12, 10)$. $10 \overset{?}{=} -0.125(12)^2 + 1.75(12) + 7$

Simplify. $10 = 10$ ✔

The point (12, 10) is on the parabola. The ball will pass through the hoop.

Hint

Check your answer to part (a) by graphing your model. Compare where the parabola is in relation to the point (5, 6).

✅ **Got It?** **2. a.** The parabolic path of a thrown ball can be modeled by the table. The top of a wall is at (5, 6). Will the ball go over the wall? If not, will it hit the wall on the way up, or the way down?

b. Reasoning What is a reasonable domain and range for the function that models the path of the ball?

x	y
1	3
2	5
3	6

When more than three data points suggest a quadratic function, you can use the quadratic regression feature of a graphing calculator to find a quadratic model.

Problem 3 Using Quadratic Regression

The table shows a meteorologist's predicted temperatures for an October day in Sacramento, California.

A What is a quadratic model for this data?

Step 1 Enter the data.

Think

How do you write times using the 24-hour clock?
Add 12 to the number of hours past noon. So, 2 P.M. is 14:00 in the 24-hour clock.

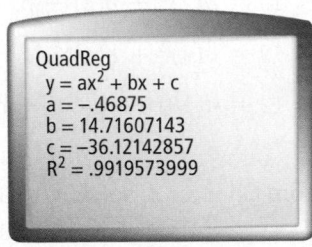

Use the 24-hour clock to represent times after noon.

Sacramento, CA

Time	Predicted Temperature (°F)
8 A.M.	52
10 A.M.	64
12 P.M.	72
2 P.M.	78
4 P.M.	81
6 P.M.	76

Step 2 Use **QuadReg**.

QuadReg
$y = ax^2 + bx + c$
$a = -.46875$
$b = 14.71607143$
$c = -36.12142857$
$R^2 = .9919573999$

Step 3 Graph the data and the function.

A quadratic model is reasonable.

A quadratic model for temperature is $y = -0.469x^2 + 14.716x - 36.121$.

B Use your model to predict the high temperature for the day. At what time does the high temperature occur?

Use the **Maximum** feature or tables.

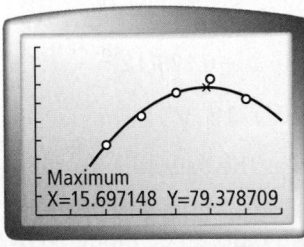

Maximum
X=15.697148 Y=79.378709

X	Y1
15.4	79.337
15.5	79.36
15.6	79.374
15.7	79.379
15.8	79.374
15.9	79.359
16	79.336

Y1 = 79.3787053571

16 represents 4 P.M. The maximum occurs at approximately 15.7, or about 3:42 P.M.

Predict the high temperature for the day to be 79.4°F at about 3:42 P.M.

Denver, CO

Time	Predicted Temperature (°F)
6 A.M.	63
9 A.M.	76
12 P.M.	86
3 P.M.	89
6 P.M.	85
9 P.M.	76

Got It? **3.** The table at the right shows a meteorologist's predicted temperatures for a summer day in Denver, Colorado. What is a quadratic model for this data? Predict the high temperature for the day. At what time does the high temperature occur?

Focus Question How can you write the equation of a parabola without knowing the vertex?

Answer If you do not know the vertex of a parabola, use standard form and three points on the parabola to write a system of three equations. Then solve the system and substitute the values of *a, b,* and *c* into standard form.

Lesson Check

Do you know HOW?

Find a quadratic function that includes each set of values.

1. $(1, 0), (2, -3), (3, -10)$

2.

x	y
-2	3.5
-1	3.5
0	7.5
1	15.5
2	27.5

3.

x	y
-2	-41.5
-1	-25.5
0	-13.5
1	-5.5

Do you UNDERSTAND?

4. Compare and Contrast How do you know whether to perform a linear regression or a quadratic regression for a given set of data?

5. Reasoning Explain how you can determine if the four points $(2, -8), (4, 3), (7, -1)$, and $(9, 5)$ lie on a single parabola.

6. Error Analysis Your classmate says he can write the equation of a quadratic function that passes through the points $(3, 4), (5, -2)$, and $(3, 0)$. Explain his error.

Practice and Problem-Solving Exercises

A Practice

Find an equation in standard form of the parabola passing through the points.  See Problem 1.

Guided Practice

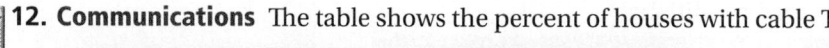

To start, substitute the (x, y) values into $y = ax^2 + bx + c$ to write a system of equations.

7. $(1, -2), (2, -2), (3, -4)$

$-2 = a(1)^2 + b(1) + c$
$-2 = a(2)^2 + b(2) + c$
$-4 = a(3)^2 + b(3) + c$

8. $(1, -2), (2, -4), (3, -4)$

9. $(1, 1), (-1, -3), (-3, 1)$

10. $(3, -6), (1, -2), (6, 3)$

11. $(-2, 9), (-4, 5), (1, 0)$

12. Communications The table shows the percent of houses with cable TV.  See Problems 2 and 3.

Cable Television Access					
Year	1985	1990	1995	2000	2005
% of Households	46	59	66	68	69

a. Find a quadratic model using 1985 as year 0, 1990 as year 5, and so on.

b. Use the model to estimate the percent of households with cable TV in 1998.

13. Physics A man throws a ball off the top of a building and records the height of the ball at different times, as shown in the table.
   a. Find a quadratic model for the data.
   b. Use the model to estimate the height of the ball at 2.5 seconds.
   c. What is the ball's maximum height?

Height of a Ball

Time (s)	Height (ft)
0	46
1	63
2	48
3	1

Ⓑ Apply   Determine whether a quadratic model exists for each set of values. If so, write the model.

14. $f(-2) = 16, f(0) = 0, f(1) = 4$

15. $f(0) = 5, f(2) = 3, f(-1) = 0$

16. $f(-1) = -4, f(1) = -2, f(2) = -1$

17. $f(-2) = 7, f(0) = 1, f(2) = 0$

18. Think About a Plan The table shows the height of a column of water as it drains from its container. Use a quadratic model of this data to estimate the water level at 30 seconds.
   • What system of equations can you use to solve this problem?
   • How can you determine if your answer is reasonable?

Water Levels

Elapsed Time (s)	Water Level (mm)
0	120
20	83
40	50

19. A parabola contains the points $(-1, 8)$, $(0, 4)$, and $(1, 2)$. Which point is also on the parabola?

Ⓐ $(2, 3)$ Ⓒ $(5, 10)$

Ⓑ $(3, 4)$ Ⓓ $(6, 14)$

20. a. Postal Rates Find a quadratic model for the data. Use 1981 as year 0.

Price of First-Class Stamp								
Year	1981	1991	1995	1999	2001	2006	2007	2008
Price (cents)	18	29	32	33	34	39	41	42

SOURCE: United States Postal Service

   b. Describe a reasonable domain and range for your model. (*Hint*: This is a discrete, real situation.)
   c. Estimation Estimate when first-class postage was 37 cents.
   d. Use your model to predict when first-class postage will be 50 cents. Explain why your prediction may not be valid.

21. Open-Ended Write three different quadratic functions, each with a graph that includes $(0, 0)$ and $(5, -1)$.

22. Road Safety The table gives the stopping distance for an automobile under certain road conditions.

Speed (mi/h)	20	30	40	50	55
Stopping Distance (ft)	17	38	67	105	127

   a. Find a linear model for the data.
   b. Find a quadratic model for the data.
   c. Writing Compare the models. Which is better? Explain.

Standardized Test Prep

SAT/ACT

23. The graph of a quadratic function has vertex $(-3, -2)$. What is the axis of symmetry?

Ⓐ $x = -3$ Ⓒ $y = -2$

Ⓑ $x = 3$ Ⓓ $y = 2$

24. Which function is NOT a quadratic function?

Ⓕ $y = (x - 1)(x - 2)$ Ⓗ $y = 3x - x^2$

Ⓖ $y = x^2 + 2x - 3$ Ⓘ $y = -x^2 + x(x - 3)$

25. Which absolute value inequality has the graph shown here?

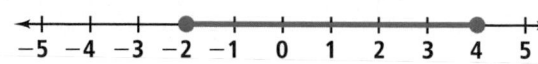

Ⓕ $|x - 1| \leq 3$ Ⓗ $|x + 1| \leq 3$

Ⓖ $|x - 1| \geq 3$ Ⓘ $|x + 1| \geq 3$

Extended
Response

26. Mark has 42 coins consisting of dimes and quarters. The total value of his coins is $6. How many of each type of coin does he have? Show all your work and explain what method you used to solve the problem.

Mixed Review

Graph each function.   See Lesson 4-2.

27. $y = x^2 - 6x - 3$ **28.** $y = 2x^2 + 9x - 4$ **29.** $y = 3x^2 - 4x + 1$

Solve each system by elimination.   See Lesson 3-2.

30. $\begin{cases} x + y = 7 \\ 5x - y = 5 \end{cases}$ **31.** $\begin{cases} 2x - 3y = -14 \\ 3x - y = 7 \end{cases}$ **32.** $\begin{cases} x - 3y = 2 \\ x - 2y = 1 \end{cases}$

For Exercises 33 and 34, y varies directly with x.   See Lesson 2-2.

33. If $y = 2$ when $x = 5$, find y when $x = 2$.   **34.** If $y = -2$ when $x = 4$, find y when $x = 7$.

Get Ready!   To prepare for Lesson 4-4, do Exercises 35–37.

Simplify by combining like terms.   See Lesson 1-3.

35. $x^2 + x + 4x - 1$ **36.** $6x^2 - 4(3)x + 2x - 3$ **37.** $4x^2 - 2(5 - x) - 3x$

Concept Byte

For Use With Lesson 4-3

Identifying Quadratic Data

You can identify perfect quadratic data when x-values are evenly spaced using the pattern in the differences between y-values.

Example

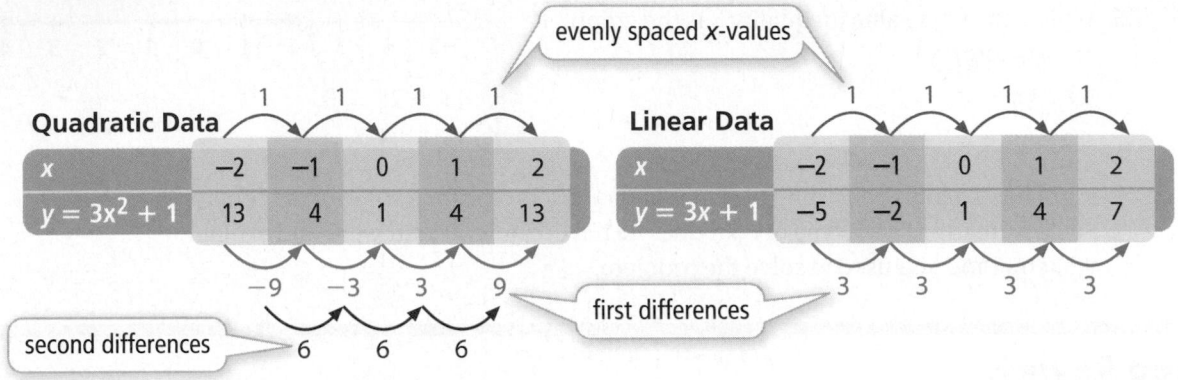

For linear data, the *first* differences of adjacent y-values are constant.
For quadratic data, the *second* differences are constant.

Exercises

Determine if each data set represents perfect quadratic data.

1.

x	y
−2	−5
−1	0
0	5
1	10
2	15

2.

x	y
1	6
2	12
3	22
4	36
5	54
6	76
7	102

3.

x	y
−2	−8
−1	−1
0	0
1	1
2	8
3	27
4	64

4.

x	y
−3	−1
−2.5	−3.75
−2	−6
−1.5	−7.75
−1	−9

5. **Reasoning** Can you use the method above to determine if a data set represents perfect linear or quadratic data if the x-values are *not* evenly spaced? Explain.

4-4
PART 1

Factoring Quadratic Expressions

Objective To find common and binomial factors of quadratic expressions

Getting Ready!

In a game, you see the two cards shown.
You get two other cards with numbers. You win if
1. the product of your two numbers equals the number on one card shown, AND
2. the sum of your two numbers equals the number on the other card shown.

What should your two cards be for you to win the game? Is there more than one answer? Explain.

I know you can win this game!

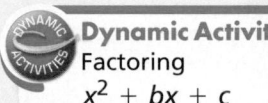

Dynamic Activity
Factoring
$x^2 + bx + c$

Lesson Vocabulary
• factoring
• greatest common factor (GCF) of an expression

A number that divides evenly into a given number is a factor of the given number. An expression that divides evenly into a given expression is a factor of the given expression. **Factoring** is rewriting an expression as a product of its factors.

Focus Question How is factoring related to the Distributive Property?

You can use the Distributive Property to multiply two binomials.

Use the Distributive Property. Distribute the first binomial to each term in the second binomial.	$(x + 4)(x + 2) = (x + 4)(x) + (x + 4)(2)$
Use the Distributive Property twice.	$= x(x) + 4(x) + x(2) + 4(2)$
Simplify.	$= x^2 + 4x + 2x + 8$
Combine like terms.	$= x^2 + 6x + 8$

To factor $x^2 + 6x + 8$, use the Distributive Property in reverse. Find two numbers with a sum of 6 and a product of 8. You can use this relationship to help you factor.

$$x^2 + 6x + 8 = (x + 4)(x + 2)$$

$4 + 2 = 6$, and $4 \cdot 2 = 8$.

Making a table of the different possible factors of the constant term may be helpful.

 **Problem 1** Factoring $ax^2 + bx + c$ when $a = \pm 1$

What is each expression in factored form?

Plan

How can you *make a table* to find factors?
Use the first row to list pairs of factors of the constant. Use the second row to find the sum of each pair of factors.

A $x^2 + 9x + 20$

Step 1 Find factors of 20 with sum 9.
Since both 20 and 9 are positive, both factors are positive.

Factors of 20	1, 20	2, 10	4, 5
Sum of factors	21	12	9

Step 2 Write the expression as the product of two binomials.

Use the factors 4 and 5. $x^2 + 9x + 20 = (x + 4)(x + 5)$

B $x^2 + 14x - 72$

Step 1 Find factors of -72 with sum 14.

Since $c < 0$, one factor is positive and the other is negative.
Since $b > 0$, the factor with greater absolute value is positive.

Factors of −72	−1, 72	−2, 36	−3, 24	−4, 18	−6, 12	−8, 9
Sum of factors	71	34	21	14	6	1

Step 2 Write the expression as a product. $x^2 + 14x - 72 = (x - 4)(x + 18)$

C $-x^2 + 13x - 12$

Step 1 Rewrite the expression to show a trinomial with leading coefficient 1.

Factor out -1. $-(x^2 - 13x + 12)$

Think

Will factoring out −1 change the answer?
No; the final factored expression will include −1 as a factor.

Step 2 Find factors of 12 with sum -13.

Since $c > 0$, both factors have the same sign.
Since $b < 0$, both factors must be negative.

Factors of 12	−1, −12	−2, −6	−3, −4
Sum of factors	−13	−8	−7

Step 3 Use the correct factors -1 and -12. Write the expression as a product.
$$-x^2 + 13x - 12 = -(x^2 - 13x + 12)$$
$$= -(x - 1)(x - 12)$$

 Got It? **1.** What is each expression in factored form?
   a. $x^2 + 14x + 40$ **b.** $x^2 - 11x + 30$ **c.** $-x^2 + 14x + 32$

The **greatest common factor (GCF) of an expression** is the common factor of the terms in the expression with the greatest coefficient and the greatest exponent. You can factor any expression that has a GCF not equal to 1.

 Problem 2 Finding Common Factors

What is the expression in factored form?

Ⓐ $6n^2 + 9n$

Factor out the GCF, $3n$.	$6n^2 + 9n = 3n(2n) + 3n(3)$
Use the Distributive Property.	$= 3n(2n + 3)$

Ⓑ $4x^2 + 20x - 56$

Factor out the GCF, 4.	$4x^2 + 20x - 56 = 4(x^2) + 4(5x) - 4(14)$
Use the Distributive Property.	$= 4(x^2 + 5x - 14)$
Factor the trinomial. Find factors of -14 with sum of 5.	$= 4(x - 2)(x + 7)$

 Got It? 2. What is the expression in factored form?

    a. $7n^2 - 21$

    b. $9x^2 + 9x - 18$

    c. $4x^2 + 8x + 12$

Plan

Should you factor out a number, a variable, or both?
Both; the two terms have numerical and variable common factors.

Focus Question How is factoring related to the Distributive Property?

Answer Factoring is rewriting an expression as a product of its factors. This process is the reverse of the Distributive Property. Use your knowledge of the Distributive Property to write a quadratic expression as a product.

 Lesson Check

Do you know HOW?

Factor each expression.

  1. $x^2 + 6x + 8$

  2. $x^2 - 13x + 12$

Find the GCF of each expression.

  3. $15x^2 - 25x$ **4.** $4a^3 + 8a^2$

  5. $18b^2 - 12b + 24$ **6.** $21h^3 + 35h^2 - 28h$

Do you UNDERSTAND?

  7. Error Analysis Your friend factored the expression $27x^2 + 21x$ as shown and found the GCF to be 3. What is his error?

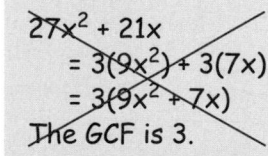

  8. Reasoning Consider the factorable quadratic trinomial $x^2 + bx + 60$, where $b > 0$. What are the possible values of b?

Practice and Problem-Solving Exercises

See Problem 1.

A Practice Factor each expression.

Guided Practice

9. $x^2 + 5x + 6$

To start, find factors of 6 with sum 5. Since both 6 and 5 are positive, both factors are positive.

Factors of 6	1, 6	2, 3
Sum of Factors	7	5

10. $x^2 + 3x + 2$ **11.** $x^2 + 7x + 10$ **12.** $x^2 + 10x + 16$

13. $y^2 + 15y + 36$ **14.** $x^2 + 22x + 40$ **15.** $x^2 - 3x + 2$

16. $-x^2 + 13x - 12$ **17.** $x^2 - 10x + 24$ **18.** $d^2 - 12d + 27$

Find the GCF of each expression. Then factor the expression completely.

See Problem 2.

Guided Practice

19. $3a^2 + 9$

To start, factor out the GCF, 3. $3(a^2) + 3(3)$

20. $4m^2 + 32$ **21.** $25b^2 - 20b$ **22.** $x^2 - 2x$

23. $5t^2 - 5t - 10$ **24.** $14y^2 + 7y - 21$ **25.** $27p^2 - 9p + 18$

B Apply Factor each expression.

26. $x^2 - 13x + 36$ **27.** $x^2 - 5x - 14$ **28.** $-x^2 - x + 20$

29. $-x^2 + 3x + 40$ **30.** $c^2 + 2c - 63$ **31.** $-t^2 + 7t + 44$

Find the GCF of each expression. Then factor the expression.

32. $y^2 - y$ **33.** $ab^2 - b$ **34.** $10x^2 - 90$

35. $3t^2 - 24t$ **36.** $2x^2 - 74x + 12$ **37.** $x^2y^2 + xy$

38. What is the factored form of $-r^2 + 11r - 18$?

  Ⓐ $-(r + 9)(r + 2)$ Ⓒ $-(r + 9)(r - 2)$

  Ⓑ $-(r - 9)(r + 2)$ Ⓓ $-(r - 9)(r - 2)$

39. Writing Explain how to factor $5x^2 + 5x - 60$ completely. Can you use similar steps to factor $-5x^2 - 5x + 60$ completely?

40. Open-Ended Write two different expressions that both have a factor of $(x + 6)$.

Factoring Quadratic Expressions

Objectives To find binomial factors of quadratic expressions
To factor special quadratic expressions

In Part 1 of the lesson, you learned to write a quadratic expression as a product of its factors.	**Connect to What You Know**	Here you will use what you learned to factor special kinds of quadratic expressions.

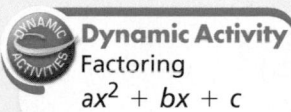

Dynamic Activity
Factoring
$ax^2 + bx + c$

Focus Question Why is it useful to recognize special quadratic expressions?

To factor a quadratic trinomial of the form $ax^2 + bx + c$ where $a \neq 1$, and there is no common factor, find factors of ac that have sum b.

Lesson Vocabulary
• perfect square trinomial
• difference of two squares

Think

How should you make your table in this case?
Use the first row to list pairs of factors of ac. Use the second row as before, to find the sum of each pair of factors.

Problem 3 Factoring $ax^2 + bx + c$ when $|a| \neq 1$

What is the expression in factored form? Check your answers.

A $2x^2 + 11x + 12$

Step 1 Since there is no common factor, find ac: $ac = 2(12) = 24$

Step 2 Since both b and ac are positive, find positive factors of 24 with sum 11.

Factors of 24	1, 24	2, 12	3, 8	4, 6
Sum of factors	25	14	11	10

Step 3 Factor the trinomial.

Write the original expression.	$2x^2 + 11x + 12$
Rewrite bx using $b = 3 + 8$.	$2x^2 + 3x + 8x + 12$
Find common factors. Factor x out of the first two terms and 4 out of the last two terms.	$x(2x + 3) + 4(2x + 3)$
Rewrite using the Distributive Property.	$(x + 4)(2x + 3)$

Check

Distribute the first binomial to each term in the second binomial.	$(x + 4)(2x + 3) = (x + 4)(2x) + (x + 4)(3)$
Use the Distributive Property twice.	$= x(2x) + 4(2x) + x(3) + 4(3)$
Simplify.	$= 2x^2 + 11x + 12$ ✔

B $4x^2 - 4x - 3$

Step 1 Since there is no common factor, find ac.

$$ac = 4(-3) = -12$$

Think

Do you need positive or negative factors?
You need one negative factor and one positive factor.

Step 2 Since $ac = -12 < 0$, find factors of ac with opposite signs.
Since $b < 0$, the factor with greater absolute value is negative.

Factors of –12	1, –12	2, –6	3, –4
Sum of factors	–11	–4	–1

Step 3 Factor the trinomial as follows.

Write the original expression.	$4x^2 - 4x - 3$
Rewrite bx using $b = 2 - 6$.	$4x^2 + 2x - 6x - 3$
Find common factors. Factor $2x$ out of the first two terms and 3 out of the last two terms.	$2x(2x + 1) - 3(2x + 1)$
Rewrite using the Distributive Property.	$(2x - 3)(2x + 1)$

Check Distribute the first binomial to each term in the second binomial.

$$(2x - 3)(2x + 1) = (2x - 3)(2x) + (2x - 3)(1)$$

Use the Distributive Property twice.

$$= 2x(2x) - 3(2x) + 2x(1) - 3(1)$$

Simplify.

$$= 4x^2 - 4x - 3 \ ✔$$

 Got It? **3.** What is the expression in factored form? Check your answers.

    a. $4x^2 + 7x + 3$ **b.** $2x^2 - 7x + 6$

    c. Reasoning Can you factor the expression $2x^2 + 2x + 2$ into a product of two binomials? Explain.

A **perfect square trinomial** is a trinomial that is the the square of a binomial. For example, $x^2 + 10x + 25$ is a perfect square trinomial because it can be factored to $(x + 5)^2$.

If $ax^2 + bx + c$ is a perfect square trinomial, then ax^2 and c are the squares of the terms of the binomial. Therefore, ax^2 and c are both positive. bx is twice the product of the terms of the binomial. If b is negative, then the binomial's terms have opposite signs.

Hint

You can rewrite $(a + b)^2$ as $(a + b)(a + b)$. Use the Distributive Property to write the square of this binomial as a perfect square trinomial.

take note

Key Concept **Factoring Perfect Square Trinomials**

$$a^2 + 2ab + b^2 = (a + b)^2 \qquad\qquad a^2 - 2ab + b^2 = (a - b)^2$$

 **Problem 4** Factoring a Perfect Square Trinomial

What is $4x^2 - 24x + 36$ in factored form?

Hint

If you don't recognize the perfect square trinomial, first try factoring out the GCF.
$4x^2 - 24x + 36 =$
$4(x^2 - 6x + 9)$

Think

Write the general form that matches the form of the expression.
Then, write the expression.

Write the first term in the form a^2.
Write the last term in the form b^2.
Write the middle term in the form $-2ab$.

Write the expression in the form $a^2 - 2ab + b^2$.

Write the expression in the factored form $(a - b)^2$.

Write

$a^2 - 2ab + b^2$
$4x^2 - 24x + 36$

$(2x)^2$
6^2
$-2(2x)(6)$

$(2x)^2 - 2(2x)(6) + 6^2$

$(2x - 6)^2$

 Got It? 4. What is $64x^2 - 16x + 1$ in factored form?

The expression $a^2 - b^2$ is the **difference of two squares**. Like a perfect square trinomial, there is a pattern to its factors.

Key Concept   Factoring a Difference of Two Squares

$$a^2 - b^2 = (a + b)(a - b)$$

 Problem 5 Factoring a Difference of Two Squares

What is $25x^2 - 49$ in factored form?

Think

How can a binomial be the product of two binomials?
When you multiply the two binomials, two of the terms are opposites and sum to 0.

Write the general form that matches the expression. Then write the expression.

Write the first term in the form a^2.
Write the second term in the form b^2.

Write the expression in the form $(a + b)(a - b)$.

$a^2 - b^2$
$25x^2 - 49$

$(5x)^2 - 7^2$

$(5x + 7)(5x - 7)$

 Got It? 5. What is $16x^2 - 81$ in factored form?

Focus Question Why is it useful to recognize special quadratic expressions?

Answer It is easier to factor a quadratic expression if you identify it as a perfect square trinomial or a difference of squares. Use the corresponding property to factor the quadratic expression.

Lesson Check

Do you know HOW?

Factor each expression.

1. $x^2 - 81$

2. $25y^2 - 36$

3. $y^2 - 6y + 9$

4. $4x^2 - 4x + 1$

Do you UNDERSTAND?

5. Vocabulary Is $4b^2 - 26b + 169$ a perfect square trinomial? Explain.

6. Compare and Contrast How is factoring a trinomial $ax^2 + bx + c^2$ when $a \neq 1$ different from factoring a trinomial when $a = 1$? How is it similar?

Practice and Problem-Solving Exercises

A Practice   Factor each expression.   ◀ **See Problem 3.**

Guided Practice

To start, since there is no common factor, find ac.

Since both b and ac are positive, both factors are positive.

7. $3x^2 + 11x + 6$

$ac = 3(6) = 18$

Factors of 18	1, 18	2, 9	3, 6
Sum of Factors	19	11	9

8. $3x^2 + 31x + 36$

9. $2x^2 - 19x + 24$

10. $5r^2 + 23r + 26$

11. $2m^2 - 11m + 15$

12. $5y^2 + 12y - 32$

13. $7x^2 - 8x - 12$

14. $2z^2 + z - 28$

15. $3x^2 + 8x - 16$

16. $28k^2 + 13k - 6$

Factor each expression.   ◀ **See Problems 4 and 5.**

Guided Practice

To start, write the general form that matches the expression. Then write the expression.

17. $t^2 - 14t + 49$

$a^2 - 2ab + b^2$

$t^2 - 14t + 7^2$

18. $x^2 + 2x + 1$

19. $k^2 - 18k + 81$

20. $4z^2 - 20z + 25$

21. $9x^2 + 48x + 64$

22. $x^2 - 4$

23. $c^2 - 64$

24. **Think About a Plan** Suppose you cut a small square from a square sheet of cardboard. Find the sides of one rectangle whose area is equal to the area of the remaining part.
    - How can you represent the remaining part as combination of rectangles with known sides?
    - Can you factor the resulting expression?

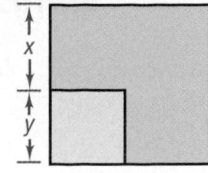

25. The area in square centimeters of a square area rug is $25x^2 - 10x + 1$. What are the dimensions of the rug in terms of x?

Factor each expression completely.

26. $9x^2 - 36$

27. $18z^2 - 8$

28. $12y^2 - 75$

29. $2a^2 - 16a + 32$

30. $64t^2 - 16$

31. $12x^2 + 36x + 27$

32. $4n^2 - 20n + 24$

33. $3x^2 - 24x - 27$

34. $18b^2 + 24b - 10$

35. $-x^2 + 5x - 4$

36. $3y^2 + 24y + 45$

37. $x^2 - y^2$

38. $4x^2 - 22x + 10$

39. $-6z^2 - 600$

40. $2x^2 - 11x + 5$

41. $9x^2 - 1$

> **Hint** If you can't spot a perfect square trinomial or difference of squares pattern, you can always use factor tables.

42. What is the factored form of $4x^2 + 15x - 4$?

   Ⓐ $(2x + 2)(2x - 2)$ Ⓒ $(4x + 1)(x - 4)$

   Ⓑ $(2x - 4)(2x + 1)$ Ⓓ $(4x - 1)(x + 4)$

43. **Error Analysis** Your friend attempted to factor an expression as shown. Find the error in your friend's work. Then factor the expression correctly.

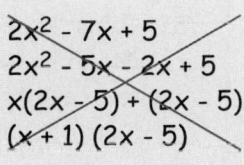

44. **Agriculture** The area in square feet of a rectangular field is $x^2 - 120x + 3500$. The width in feet is $x - 50$. What is the length, in feet?

45. **Geometry** What is the volume of the shaded pipe with outer radius R, inner radius r, and height h as shown? Express your answer in completely factored form. (*Hint:* The volume V of a cylinder with radius r and height h is $V = \pi r^2 h$.)

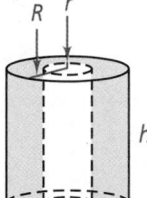

46. **Reasoning** The expression $x^2 + 5x - 24$ can be factored to the form $(x - a)(x + b)$, where $a > 0$ and $b > 0$. What is the value of $ab - a + b$?

47. **Open-Ended** Write a quadratic trinomial that you can factor, where $a \neq 1$, $ac > 0$, and $b < 0$. Factor the expression.

48. **Writing** Explain how to factor $3x^2 + 6x - 72$ completely.

Standardized Test Prep

SAT/ACT

49. How can you write $(m - 5)(m + 4) + 8$ as a product of two binomials?

Ⓐ $(m - 1)(m + 8)$

Ⓑ $(m - 4)(m + 3)$

Ⓒ $(m + 8)(m + 8)$

Ⓓ $(m - 5)(8m + 32)$

50. The graph of a quadratic function has vertex $(7, 6)$. What is the axis of symmetry?

Ⓕ $x = 6$　　　　　　　　　　　Ⓗ $x = 7$

Ⓖ $y = 6$　　　　　　　　　　　Ⓘ $y = 7$

Extended Response

51. Suppose you hit a baseball and its flight takes a parabolic path. The height of the ball at certain times appears in the table below.

Time (s)	0.5	0.75	1	1.25
Height (ft)	10	10.5	9	5.5

a. Find a quadratic model for the ball's height as a function of time.

b. Write the quadratic function in factored form.

Mixed Review

52. Find a quadratic model for the values in the table.

x	0	5	10	15	20
y	17	39	54	61	61

See Lesson 4-3.

53. Coins The combined mass of a penny, a nickel, and a dime is 9.8 g. Ten nickels and three pennies have the same mass as 25 dimes. Fifty dimes have the same mass as 18 nickels and 10 pennies. Write and solve a system of equations using a matrix to find the mass of each type of coin.

See Lesson 3-6.

Get Ready!　**To prepare for Lesson 4-5, do Exercises 54–56.**

Graph each function.

See Lesson 4-2.

54. $y = x^2 - 2x - 5$　　　　　**55.** $y = x^2 - 4x + 4$　　　　　**56.** $y = -x^2 - 3x + 8$

4 Chapter Review for Part A

 ## Chapter Vocabulary

- axis of symmetry (p. 204)
- difference of two squares (p. 233)
- factoring (p. 227)
- greatest common factor (p. 229)
- maximum value (p. 205)
- minimum value (p. 205)
- parabola (p. 204)
- perfect square trinomial (p. 232)
- quadratic function (p. 204)
- standard form (p. 212)
- vertex form (p. 204)
- vertex of the parabola (p. 204)

Choose the correct term to complete each sentence.

1. To solve an equation by factoring, the equation should first be written in (standard form/vertex form).

2. The (axis of symmetry/vertex of the parabola) is a line that divides a parabola into two mirror images.

3. The graph of the quadratic function $y = -3x^2 + 2x + 1$ has a (maximum value/minimum value).

4-1 Quadratic Functions and Transformations

Quick Review

The **vertex form** of a quadratic function is $f(x) = a(x - h)^2 + k$, where $a \neq 0$. The vertex of the **parabola** formed by a quadratic function is (h, k). The axis of symmetry is $x = h$.

If $a > 0$, k is the **minimum value** of the function.

If $a < 0$, k is the **maximum value** of the function.

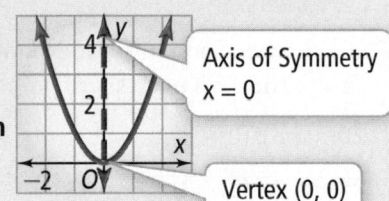

Axis of Symmetry
$x = 0$

Vertex $(0, 0)$

Example

What is the graph of the function $f(x) = 3(x - 4)^2 + 2$?

Identify a, h, and k. $a = 3, h = 4, k = 2$

Find the vertex: (h, k).   vertex: $(4, 2)$

The axis of symmetry is $x = h$.   axis of symmetry: $x = 4$

Plot the vertex and axis of symmetry. Find another point on the parabola.

$f(3) = 3(3 - 4)^2 + 2 = 5 \rightarrow (3, 5)$

Use symmetry to plot the corresponding point, $(5, 5)$.
Draw the curve.

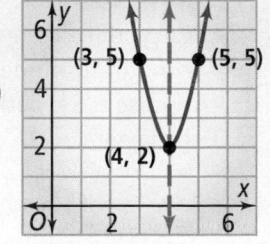

(3, 5)   (5, 5)

(4, 2)

Exercises

Identify the vertex, axis of symmetry, maximum or minimum, and domain and range of each function.

4. $f(x) = 4(x + 2)^2 - 6$

5. $f(x) = -(x - 3)^2 + 2$

6. $f(x) = 10(x - 1)^2 + 5$

7. $f(x) = 2(x + 9)^2 - 4$

Graph each function. Describe each transformation of the parent function $f(x) = x^2$.

8. $f(x) = x^2 + 4$

9. $f(x) = (x - 9)^2 + 2$

10. $f(x) = \frac{1}{2}(x + 1)^2 - 5$

4-2 Standard Form of a Quadratic Function

Quick Review

The **standard form** of a quadratic function is
$f(x) = ax^2 + bx + c$, where $a \neq 0$. When $a > 0$, the
parabola opens up. When $a < 0$, the parabola opens down.

The axis of symmetry is the line $x = -\frac{b}{2a}$. The vertex is
$\left(-\frac{b}{2a}, f\left(-\frac{b}{2a}\right)\right)$, and the y-intercept is $(0, c)$.

Example

What is the vertex of the graph of the function
$f(x) = x^2 - 6x + 8$?

Identify a, b, and c.	$a = 1, b = -6, c = 8$
Substitute to find the x-coordinate of the vertex.	$x = -\frac{b}{2a} = -\frac{-6}{2(1)} = 3$
Substitute to find the y-coordinate of the vertex.	$f(3) = (3)^2 - 6(3) + 8 = -1$

The vertex is $(3, 1)$.

Exercises

Graph each function.

11. $f(x) = x^2 + 6x + 5$ **12.** $f(x) = x^2 - 7x - 18$

13. $f(x) = x^2 - 7x + 12$ **14.** $f(x) = x^2 - 9$

Write each function in vertex form.

15. $f(x) = 4x^2 - 8x + 2$ **16.** $f(x) = x^2 - 8x + 12$

17. $f(x) = 8x^2 + 8x - 12$ **18.** $f(x) = -2x^2 - 6x + 10$

19. Physics The equation $h = -16t^2 + 32t + 9$ gives
the height of a ball, h, in feet above the ground,
at t seconds after the ball is thrown upward. How
many seconds after the ball is thrown will it reach its
maximum height? What is its maximum height?

4-3 Modeling With Quadratic Functions

Quick Review

You can use quadratic functions to model real-world data. You
can also find a quadratic function that passes through any three
noncollinear points (no two of which lie on a vertical line).

Example

**Find the equation of the parabola that passes through the
points $(-2, 8)$, $(0, -2)$, and $(1, 2)$.**

Use the standard form of a quadratic function.	$y = ax^2 + bx + c$
Substitute the (x, y) values to write a system of equations.	$\begin{cases} 8 = a(-2)^2 + b(-2) + c \\ -2 = a(0)^2 + b(0) + c \\ 2 = a(1)^2 + b(1) + c \end{cases}$
Simplify.	$\begin{cases} 4a - 2b + c = 8 \\ c = -2 \\ a + b + c = 2 \end{cases}$
Solve the system.	$a = 3, b = 1, c = -2$
Substitute a, b, and c to write the quadratic function.	$y = 3x^2 + x - 2$

Exercises

**Find an equation in standard form of the parabola that
passes through each set of points.**

20. $(0, 5), (2, -3), (-1, 12)$

21. $(2, 0), (3, -2), (1, -2)$

22. $(4, 10), (0, -18), (-2, -20)$

23. $(0, -7), (7, -14), (-3, -19)$

24. Track and Field The table
shows the height of a javelin
as it is thrown and travels
across a horizontal distance.
Use your calculator to find
a quadratic model to
represent the path of
the javelin.

Distance (m)	Height (m)
5	2
18	5
33	8
55	6
68	4
74	3

4-4 Factoring Quadratic Expressions

Quick Review

To factor an expression of the form $ax^2 + bx + c$, when $a \neq 1$, find numbers with the product ac and sum b. You can also factor an expression by finding the **greatest common factor** (GCF).

Example

Factor the expression $5x^2 + 13x + 6$.

There are no common factors. Find ac.	$ac = 5(6) = 30$
Since both b and c are positive, find positive factors of 30 with sum 13.	1, 30 2, 15 3, 10 5, 6
Write the original expression.	$5x^2 + 13x + 6$
Rewrite bx using the factors you found.	$5x^2 + 10x + 3x + 6$
Find common factors. Factor $5x$ out of the first two terms and 3 out of the last two terms.	$5x(x + 2) + 3(x + 2)$
Use the Distributive Property.	$(5x + 3)(x + 2)$

Exercises

Factor each expression.

25. $x^2 - 8x + 12$ **26.** $3x^2 + 11x - 20$

27. $-4x^2 + 14x - 6$ **28.** $x^2 + 14x + 40$

Factor each perfect square trinomial.

29. $x^2 - 14x + 49$ **30.** $9x^2 + 30x + 25$

Factor each difference of two squares.

31. $36x^2 - 16$ **32.** $25x^2 - 4$

Find the GCF of each expression. Then factor each expression.

33. $6x^2 - 24x$ **34.** $-14x^2 - 49$

Do you know HOW?

Graph each function.

1. $y = 4x^2 + 16x + 7$

2. $y = (x + 8)^2 - 3$

3. $y = -(x + 2)^2 - 7$

4. $y = -3x^2 - 2x + 1$

Identify the axis of symmetry, maximum or minimum value, and the domain and range of each function.

5. $y = -x^2 + 6x + 5$

6. $y = \frac{1}{2}(x - 6)^2 + 7$

7. $y = -3(x + 2)^2 + 1$

8. $y = 4x^2 - 8x$

9. Rewrite the equation $y = -3x^2 - 6x - 8$ in vertex form. Identify the vertex and the axis of symmetry of the graph.

Write each expression in factored form.

10. $16 - 2m^2$

11. $-x^2 + 3x$

12. $y^2 - 13y + 12$

13. $k^2 - 5k - 24$

14. $4y^2 - 9$

15. $-10n + 25 + n^2$

16. $2x^2 + 7x + 6$

Find a quadratic model in standard form for each set of values.

17. $(0, 3), (1, 10), (2, 19)$

18. $(0, 0), (1, -5), (2, 0)$

Write the equation of each parabola in vertex form.

19.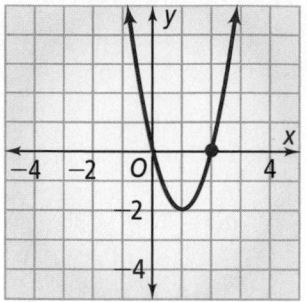

20.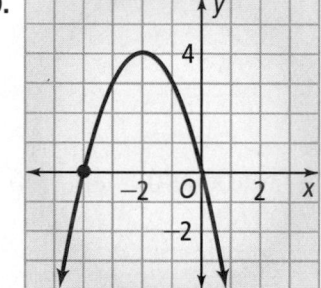

Do you UNDERSTAND?

21. Write the expression $3x^4 - 12x^3 - 36x^2$ in factored form. Explain how you know the expression is completely factored.

22. **Open-Ended** Write an equation of a parabola with vertex at $(3, 2)$. Name the axis of symmetry and the coordinates of two other points on the graph.

23. **Writing** Explain how to factor $25x^2 - 30x + 9$.

24. **Reasoning** Write the equations of two parabolas that have a common vertex and are reflections of each other across the x-axis.

25. Write the equation of a parabola in standard form and explain how to convert it to vertex form. How would you reverse the process?

26. What is the relationship between the x-intercepts of the graph of a quadratic function and the x-coordinate of the vertex of that graph? Explain how you determined your answer.

CHAPTER 4
PART B

Quadratic Functions and Equations

In Part A you learned how to write, transform, and factor quadratic functions. Now you will apply what you learned to find solutions of quadratic equations.

Vocabulary for Part B

English/Spanish Vocabulary Audio Online:

English	Spanish
completing the square, *p. 255*	completar el cuadrado
complex conjugates, *p. 272*	conjugados complejos
complex number, *p. 269*	número complejo
complex number plane, *p. 269*	plano de números complejos
discriminant, *p. 262*	discriminante
imaginary number, *p. 269*	número imaginario
Quadratic Formula, *p. 261*	Fórmula cuadrática
zero of a function, *p. 243*	cero de una función

BIG ideas

1 Equivalence
Essential Question What are the advantages of a quadratic function in vertex form? In standard form?

2 Functions
Essential Question How is any quadratic function related to the parent quadratic function $y = x^2$?

3 Solving Equations and Inequalities
Essential Question How are the real solutions of a quadratic equation related to the graph of the related quadratic function?

Chapter Preview for Part B

Algebra Review

Square Roots and Radicals

For Use With Lesson 4-5

A radical symbol $\sqrt{\ }$ indicates a square root. In general, $\sqrt{x^2} = |x|$ for all real numbers x.

Square Roots

Multiplication Property of Square Roots	Division Property of Square Roots
For any numbers $a \geq 0$ and $b \geq 0$,	For any numbers $a \geq 0$ and $b > 0$,
$\sqrt{ab} = \sqrt{a} \cdot \sqrt{b}.$	$\sqrt{\dfrac{a}{b}} = \dfrac{\sqrt{a}}{\sqrt{b}}.$

Example

Simplify each expression.

A $\sqrt{50}$

Use the Multiplication Property of Square Roots. 　　$\sqrt{50} = \sqrt{25} \cdot \sqrt{2}$

Simplify. 　　$= 5\sqrt{2}$

B $\sqrt{\dfrac{5}{11}}$

Use the Division Property of Square Roots. 　　$\sqrt{\dfrac{5}{11}} = \dfrac{\sqrt{5}}{\sqrt{11}}$

Multiply both the numerator and denominator by $\sqrt{11}$. 　　$= \dfrac{\sqrt{5}}{\sqrt{11}} \cdot \dfrac{\sqrt{11}}{\sqrt{11}}$

Use the Multiplication Property of Square Roots. 　　$= \dfrac{\sqrt{55}}{\sqrt{121}}$

Simplify. 　　$= \dfrac{\sqrt{55}}{11}$

Exercises

Simplify each radical expression.

1. $\sqrt{18}$　　　　　　　　2. $\sqrt{75}$　　　　　　　　3. $-\sqrt{32}$　　　　　　　　4. $\sqrt{\dfrac{5}{7}}$

5. $-\sqrt{\dfrac{7}{13}}$　　　　　　6. $\sqrt{\dfrac{3}{15}}$　　　　　　7. $-\sqrt{200}$　　　　　　8. $5\sqrt{320}$

9. $(2\sqrt{27})^2$　　　　　10. $-\sqrt{10^4}$　　　　11. $\sqrt{x^2 y^2}$　　　　12. $\sqrt{\dfrac{8}{x^2}}$

13. $-\sqrt{\dfrac{7x^3}{5x}}$　　　　14. $\sqrt{\dfrac{(3)^4}{12}}$　　　　15. $\sqrt{\dfrac{200}{28}}$　　　　16. $\sqrt{120x}$

4-5
PART 1

Quadratic Equations

Objectives   To solve quadratic equations by factoring
To solve quadratic equations by using a table

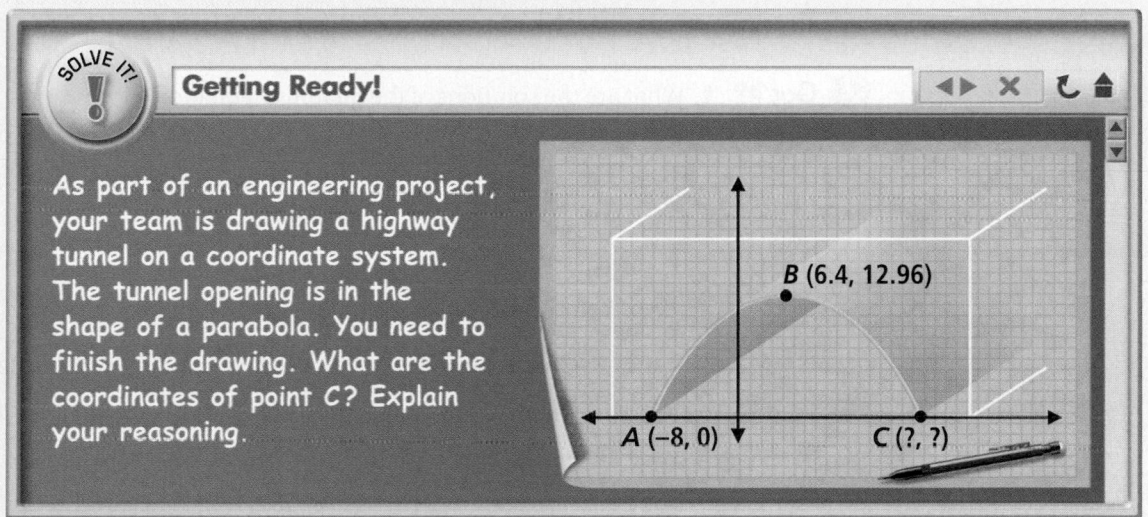

Getting Ready!

As part of an engineering project, your team is drawing a highway tunnel on a coordinate system. The tunnel opening is in the shape of a parabola. You need to finish the drawing. What are the coordinates of point C? Explain your reasoning.

B (6.4, 12.96)

A (−8, 0)   C (?, ?)

Dynamic Activity
Quadratics in
Factored Form

**Lesson
Vocabulary**
• zero of a
  function
• Zero-Product
  Property

Wherever the graph of a function $f(x)$ intersects the x-axis, $f(x) = 0$. A value of x for which $f(x) = 0$ is a **zero of the function**.

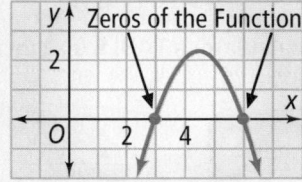

Focus Question   What are the zeros of a quadratic function?

To find the zeros of a quadratic function $y = ax^2 + bx + c$, solve the related quadratic equation $0 = ax^2 + bx + c$.

You can solve some quadratic equations in standard form by factoring the quadratic expression and using the **Zero-Product Property**.

take note

Property   Zero-Product Property

If $ab = 0$, then $a = 0$ or $b = 0$.

Example: If $(x + 7)(x − 2) = 0$, then $(x + 7) = 0$ or $(x − 2) = 0$.

Think

Problem 1 Solving a Quadratic Equation by Factoring

What are the solutions of the quadratic equation $x^2 - 5x + 6 = 0$?

Write the original equation.	$x^2 - 5x + 6 = 0$
Factor the quadratic expression.	$(x - 2)(x - 3) = 0$
Use the Zero-Product Property.	$x - 2 = 0$ or $x - 3 = 0$
Solve for x.	$x = 2$ or $x = 3$

The solutions are $x = 2$ and $x = 3$.

Hint

For part (b), move all terms to one side of the equation before factoring.

 Got It? 1. What are the solutions of the quadratic equation?

a. $x^2 - 7x + 12 = 0$ **b.** $x^2 - 18 = 3x$

You can also solve some quadratic equations using tables.

Problem 2 Solving a Quadratic Equation With Tables

What are the solutions of the quadratic equation $5x^2 + 30x + 14 = 2 - 2x$?

Step 1 Write the equation in standard form.

Write the original equation.	$5x^2 + 30x + 14 = 2 - 2x$
Add $2x$ to each side.	$5x^2 + 30x + 2x + 14 = 2 - 2x + 2x$
Simplify.	$5x^2 + 32x + 14 = 2$
Subtract 2 from each side.	$5x^2 + 32x + 14 - 2 = 2 - 2$
Simplify.	$5x^2 + 32x + 12 = 0$

Think

What should you look for in the calculator table?
Look for x-values for which $y = 0$.

Step 2 Use your calculator's **TABLE** feature to find the zeros.

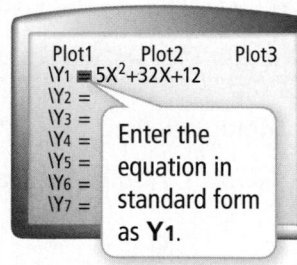

Enter the equation in standard form as **Y1**.

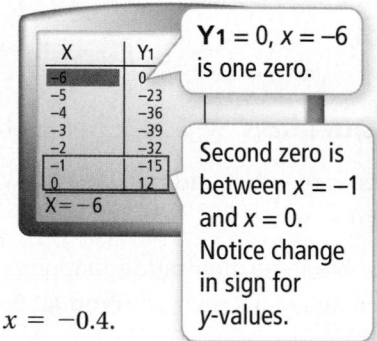

Y1 = 0, $x = -6$ is one zero.

Second zero is between $x = -1$ and $x = 0$. Notice change in sign for y-values.

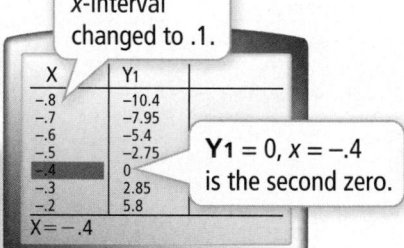

x-interval changed to .1.

Y1 = 0, $x = -.4$ is the second zero.

The solutions are $x = -6$ and $x = -0.4$.

 Got It? 2. What are the solutions of the quadratic equation $4x^2 - 14x + 7 = 4 - x$?

Focus Question What are the zeros of a quadratic function?

Answer The zeros of a quadratic function $y = ax^2 + bx + c$ are the solution(s) of $0 = ax^2 + bx + c$. To find the zeros, factor the quadratic expression into the product of two binomials. Then use the Zero-Product Property to set each factor equal to zero and solve for x.

Lesson Check

Do you know HOW?
Solve each equation by factoring.

1. $x^2 - 9 = 0$

2. $x^2 + 13x = -36$

3. $3x^2 - x - 2 = 0$

Do you UNDERSTAND?

4. Vocabulary If 5 is a zero of the function $y = x^2 + bx - 20$, what is the value of b? Explain.

5. Reasoning Using tables, how might you recognize that a quadratic equation likely has exactly one solution? No solutions?

Practice and Problem-Solving Exercises

A Practice   Solve each equation by factoring. Check your answers.   ◀ **See Problem 1.**

Guided Practice ➡

To start, factor the quadratic expression.

6. $x^2 + 6x + 8 = 0$

$(x + 2)(x + 4) = 0$

7. $x^2 + 18 = 9x$ **8.** $2x^2 - x = 3$ **9.** $x^2 - 10x + 25 = 0$

10. $2x^2 + 6x = -4$ **11.** $x^2 - 4x = 0$ **12.** $6x^2 + 4x = 0$

📟 **Graphing Calculator** Solve each equation using tables. Give each answer to at most two decimal places.   ◀ **See Problem 2.**

Guided Practice ➡

To start, enter the equation as Y1. Make a table and look for where the y-values change sign.

13. $x^2 - 11x + 24 = 0$

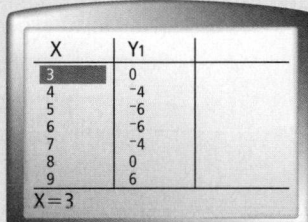

14. $x^2 + 5x + 3 = 0$ **15.** $x^2 - 7x = 11$ **16.** $2x^2 - x = 2$

17. $4x^2 = x + 3$ **18.** $5x^2 + x = 4$ **19.** $10x^2 + 3 = 11x$

B Apply

20. Error Analysis A classmate solves the quadratic equation as shown. Find and correct the error. What are the correct solutions?

$$x^2 + 5x + 6 = 2$$
$$(x + 2)(x + 3) = 2$$
$$x = -2 \text{ or } x = -3$$

21. Open-Ended Write an equation with the given solutions.
    a. 3 and 5   **b.** −3 and 2   **c.** −1 and −6

Reasoning The graphs of each pair of functions intersect. Find their points of intersection without using a calculator. (*Hint:* Solve as a system using substitution.)

22. $y = x^2$
$y = -\frac{1}{2}x^2 + \frac{3}{2}x + 3$

23. $y = x^2 - 2$
$y = 3x^2 - 4x - 2$

24. $y = -x^2 + x + 4$
$y = 2x^2 - 6$

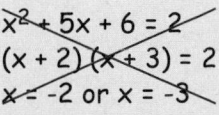

4-5
PART 2

Quadratic Equations

Objective To solve quadratic equations by graphing

In Part 1 of the lesson, you learned how to solve quadratic equations by factoring and using tables.

Connect to What You Know

Here you will learn how to solve quadratic equations using your graphing calculator.

Focus Question When is it important to solve quadratic equations using a graphing calculator?

You can also use graphing techniques to find solutions of quadratic equations.

Problem 3 Solving Quadratic Equations by Graphing

What are the solutions of the quadratic equation $2x^2 + 7x = 15$?

Write the original equation. $\qquad 2x^2 + 7x = 15$

Rewrite in standard form. $\qquad 2x^2 + 7x - 15 = 0$

Plan

How can you use a graph to find the solutions?
Find the zeros of the related quadratic function.

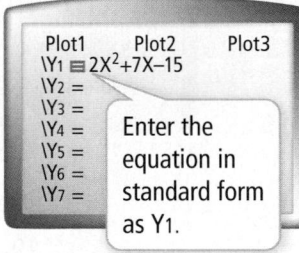

Enter the equation in standard form as Y1.

Use **ZERO** option in **CALC** feature.

Zero
X=−5   Y=0

Zero
X=1.5   Y=0

The solutions are $x = -5$ and $x = 1.5$.

 Got It? **3.** What are the solutions of the quadratic equation $x^2 + 2x - 24 = 0$?

Problem 4 Using a Quadratic Equation

Competition From the time Mark Twain wrote *The Celebrated Jumping Frog of Calaveras County* in 1865, frog-jumping competitions have been growing in popularity. The graph shows a function modeling the height of one frog's jump, where *x* is the distance, in feet, from the jump's start.

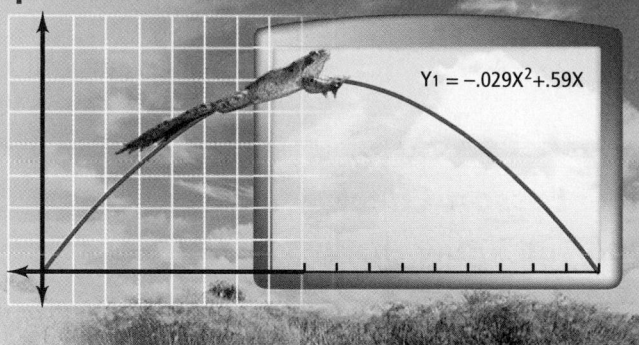

$Y1 = -.029X^2 + .59X$

Think

How can you use a graphing calculator to determine the distance?
Graph the function to locate the second zero.

A How far did the frog jump?

The height of the jump is 0 at the start and end of the jump. Find the zeros of the function. Use a graphing calculator to find the zeros of the related function $y = -0.029x^2 + 0.59x$.

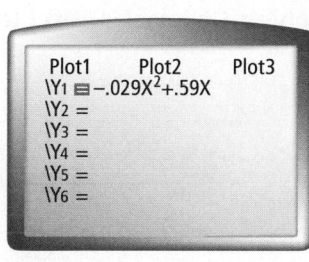

Plot1   Plot2   Plot3
\Y1 ▤ −.029X²+.59X
\Y2 =
\Y3 =
\Y4 =
\Y5 =
\Y6 =

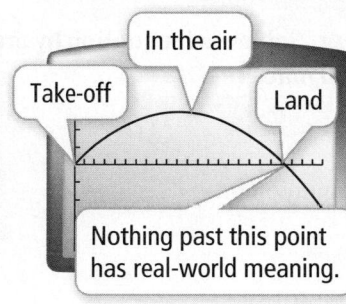

In the air

Take-off

Land

Nothing past this point has real-world meaning.

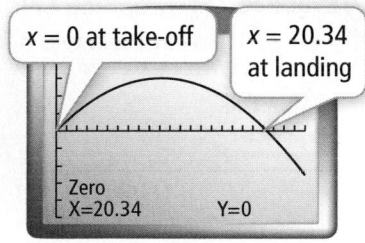

$x = 0$ at take-off

$x = 20.34$ at landing

Zero
X=20.34   Y=0

The frog jumped about 20.34 ft.

B How high did the frog jump?

The maximum height of the jump is the maximum value of the function. This occurs midway, at 10.17 ft from the start. Find *y* for $x = 10.17$.

$$y = -0.029(10.17)^2 + 0.59(10.17) \approx 3.0$$

The frog jumped to a height of about 3.0 ft.

C What is a reasonable domain and range for such a frog-jumping function?

While the function $y = -0.029x^2 + 0.59x$ has a domain of all real numbers, actual frog jumping does not allow negative values. So, a reasonable domain for frog-jumping distances is $0 \le x \le 30$. A reasonable range is $0 \le y \le 5$.

 Got It? 4. a. The function $y = -0.03x^2 + 1.60x$ models the path of a kicked soccer ball. The height is *y*, the distance is *x*, and the units are meters. How far does the soccer ball travel? How high does the soccer ball go? Describe a reasonable domain and range for the path of a soccer ball.

        b. Reasoning Are all domains and ranges reasonable for real-world situations? Explain.

Focus Question When is it important to solve quadratic equations using a graphing calculator?

Answer Some quadratic equations cannot be solved with factoring techniques. Your graphing calculator can locate the zeros of a quadratic function.

Lesson Check

Do you know HOW?

Solve by graphing.

1. $x^2 - 3x - 6 = 0$

2. $2x^2 - x - 11 = 0$

Do you UNDERSTAND?

3. Compare and Contrast When is it easier to solve a quadratic equation by graphing than to solve it by factoring?

Practice and Problem-Solving Exercises

 **Practice**  **Graphing Calculator** Solve each equation by graphing. Give each answer to at most two decimal places.

◀ **See Problem 3.**

Guided Practice

To start, write the equation in standard form.

4.
$$6x^2 = -19x - 15$$
$$6x^2 + 19x + 15 = 0$$

5. $3x^2 - 5x - 4 = 0$

6. $5x^2 - 7x - 3 = 8$

7. $6x^2 + 31x = 12$

8. $1 = 4x^2 + 3x$

9. $x^2 + 4x = 6$

10. $2x^2 - 2x - 5 = 0$

 11. Physics An object is dropped from a height of 1700 ft above the ground. The function $h = -16t^2 + 1700$ gives the object's height h in feet during the free fall at t seconds.
   a. When will the object be 1000 ft above the ground?
   b. When will the object be 940 ft above the ground?
   c. What is a reasonable domain and range for the function h?

◀ **See Problem 4.**

12. Athletics The equation $y = -0.06x^2 + 0.96x$ models the height of the winning long jump at a middle school track meet, where x is the horizontal distance, in feet, from the beginning of the jump.
   a. What was the length of the winning jump?
   b. What was the jumper's maximum height?
   c. What are a reasonable domain and range for this situation?

Apply

13. **Think About a Plan** Suppose you want to put a frame around the painting shown at the right. The frame will be the same width around the entire painting. You have 276 in.^{2} of framing material. How wide should the frame be?
    - What does 276 in.^{2} represent in this situation?
    - How can you write the dimensions of the frame using two binomials?

16 in.

|← 24 in. →|

14. The period of a pendulum is the time the pendulum takes to swing back and forth. The function $L = 0.81t^2$ relates the length L in feet of a pendulum to the time t in seconds that it takes to swing back and forth. A convention center has a pendulum that is 90 feet long. Find the period.

15. **Landscaping** Suppose you have an outdoor pool measuring 25 ft by 10 ft. You want to add a cement walkway around the pool. If the walkway will be 1 ft thick and you have 304 ft^3 of cement, how wide should the walkway be?

Solve each equation by factoring, using tables, or by graphing. If necessary, round your answer to the nearest hundredth.

16. $x^2 + 2x = 6 - 6x$

17. $6x^2 + 13x + 6 = 0$

18. $2x^2 + x - 28 = 0$

19. $2x^2 + 8x = 5x + 20$

20. $3x^2 + 7x = 9$

21. $2x^2 - 6x = 8$

22. $(x + 3)^2 = 9$

23. $x^2 + 4x = 0$

24. $x^2 = 8x - 7$

25. $x^2 - 3x = 6$

26. $4x^2 + 5x = 4$

27. $7x - 3x^2 = -10$

28. **Open Ended** Write a quadratic equation in standard form that you can solve by factoring. Then write a quadratic equation in standard form that you cannot solve by factoring.

29. **Writing** Solve the equation $x^2 - 10x + 24 = 0$ by factoring. Explain how to use the solutions to find the vertex of the graph of $y = x^2 - 10x + 24$.

Standardized Test Prep

SAT/ACT

30. What are the solutions of the equation $6x^2 + 9x - 15 = 0$?

    (A) $1, -15$ (C) $-1, -5$

    (B) $1, -\frac{5}{2}$ (D) $3, \frac{5}{2}$

31. The vertex of a parabola is $(3, 2)$. A second point on the parabola is $(1, 7)$. Which point is also on the parabola?

    (F) $(-1, 7)$ (H) $(5, 7)$

    (G) $(3, 7)$ (I) $(3, -2)$

32. For which quadratic function is -3 the constant term?

    (A) $y = (3x + 1)(-x - 3)$ (C) $f(x) = (x - 3)(x - 3)$

    (B) $y = x^2 - 3x + 3$ (D) $g(x) = -3x^2 + 3x + 9$

Short Response

33. What transformations are needed to go from the parent function $f(x) = x^2$ to the new function $g(x) = -3x^2 + 2$? Graph $g(x)$.

Mixed Review

Factor each expression.   ◀ See Lesson 4-4.

34. $16x^2 - 1$ **35.** $5x^2 - 26x + 5$ **36.** $2x^2 + 13x - 7$

Solve each system by elimination. Check your answer.   ◀ See Lesson 3-5.

37. $\begin{cases} 7x - 2y - 5z = 24 \\ -x + 3y + 4z = -10 \\ x - y - z = 4 \end{cases}$ **38.** $\begin{cases} -2x + 9y - z = 8 \\ 3x - 4y + z = -5 \\ 5x + 5y - z = -10 \end{cases}$ **39.** $\begin{cases} x - 9y + 8z = -10 \\ x + y - z = 9 \\ -x - 9z = 2 \end{cases}$

Without graphing, identify the vertex, axis of symmetry, and transformations from the parent function $f(x) = |x|$.   ◀ See Lesson 2-7.

40. $y = |x + 9| + 4$ **41.** $y = |2x - 7|$ **42.** $y = \frac{3}{4}|x| - 1$

Get Ready!   To prepare for Lesson 4-6, do Exercises 43–45.

Simplify each expression.   ◀ See Lesson 4-4.

43. $(x + 4)(x + 4) - 3$ **44.** $(2x - 1)(2x - 1)$ **45.** $(x - 3)(x - 3)$

Writing Equations From Roots

The **root** of an equation is a value that makes the equation true. You can use the Zero-Product Property to write a quadratic function from its zeros or a quadratic equation from its roots.

Activity 1

1. a. Write a nonzero linear function $f(x)$ that has a zero at $x = 3$.
   b. Write a nonzero linear function $g(x)$ that has a zero at $x = 4$.

2. a. For f and g from Exercise 1, write the product function $h(x) = f(x) \cdot g(x)$.
   b. What kind of function is $h(x)$?
   c. Solve the equation $h(x) = 0$.

Mental Math Write a quadratic equation with each pair of values as roots.

3. 5 and 3   **4.** 2.5 and 4   **5.** −4 and 4   **6.** 5 and 10   **7.** $\frac{3}{2}$ and −2

You can also use zeros or roots to write quadratic expressions in standard form.

Activity 2

8. a. Copy and complete the table. Write the product $(x - a)(x - b)$ in standard form for each pair a and b.
   b. Is there a pattern in the table? Explain.

9. a. If you know the zeros or roots, you can write a quadratic function or equation in standard form. Explain how.
   b. Demonstrate your method for each pair of values in Exercises 3–7.

a	b	$a + b$	ab	$(x - a)(x - b)$
4	5	9	20	$x^2 - 9x + 20$
−4	5	1	−20	■
4	−5	■	■	■
−4	−5	■	■	■
−9	−1	■	■	■
−2	7	■	■	■

Exercises

10. Explain how to write a quadratic equation that has −6 as its only root.

11. Describe the family of quadratic functions that have zeros at r and s. Sketch several members of the family in the coordinate plane.

Find the sum and product of the roots for each quadratic equation.

12. $2x^2 + 3x - 2 = 0$ **13.** $x^2 - 2x + 1 = 0$ **14.** $x^2 - 5x + 6 = 0$

Given the sum and product of the roots, write a quadratic equation in standard form.

15. sum = −3, product = −18   **16.** sum = 4, product = 3   **17.** sum = 2, product = $\frac{3}{4}$

Objectives To solve equations by finding square roots
To solve a perfect square trinomial equation

This suggests another way to write $(x + 3)^2$.

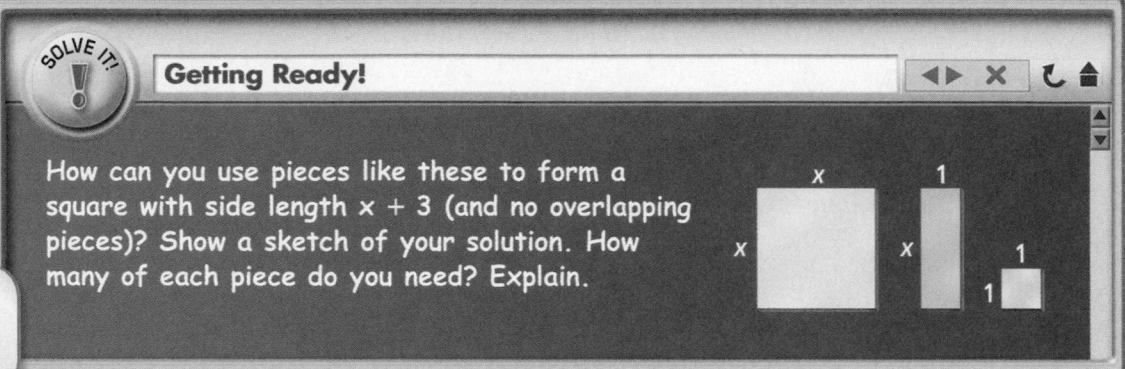

SOLVE IT!

Getting Ready!

How can you use pieces like these to form a square with side length $x + 3$ (and no overlapping pieces)? Show a sketch of your solution. How many of each piece do you need? Explain.

Forming a square with model pieces provides a useful geometric image for completing a square algebraically.

Focus Question Why is a perfect square trinomial useful?

You can solve an equation that contains a perfect square by finding square roots. The simplest of this type of equation has the form $ax^2 = c$.

Problem 1 Solving by Finding Square Roots

What is the solution of each equation?

Plan

How is solving this quadradic equation like solving a linear equation?
You isolate the variable term.

	Ⓐ $4x^2 + 10 = 46$	Ⓑ $3x^2 - 5 = 25$
Rewrite in $ax^2 = c$ form.	$4x^2 = 36$	$3x^2 = 30$
Isolate x^2.	$\frac{4x^2}{4} = \frac{36}{4}$	$\frac{3x^2}{3} = \frac{30}{3}$
Simplify.	$x^2 = 9$	$x^2 = 10$
Find square roots.	$x = \pm 3$	$x = \pm\sqrt{10}$

 Got It? **1.** What is the solution of each equation?

a. $7x^2 - 10 = 25$ **b.** $2x^2 + 9 = 13$

Problem 2 Determining Dimensions

Architecture While designing a house, an architect used windows like the one shown here. What are the dimensions of the window if it has 2766 square inches of glass?

Step 1 Find the area of each part of the window.
The area of the rectangular part is $(2x)(x) = 2x^2$ in.²
The area of the semicircular part is

$$\frac{1}{2}\pi r^2 = \frac{1}{2}\pi\left(\frac{x}{2}\right)^2 = \frac{1}{2}\pi\left(\frac{x^2}{4}\right) = \frac{\pi}{8}x^2 \text{ in.}^2.$$

Step 2 Write the equation for the total area of the window.

$$2x^2 + \frac{\pi}{8}x^2 = 2766$$

> The total amount of glass used is the sum of the areas, 2766 in.²

Step 3 Solve for x.

Write the equation in $ax^2 = c$ form.	$\left(2 + \frac{\pi}{8}\right)x^2 = 2766$
Isolate x^2.	$x^2 = \dfrac{2766}{2 + \frac{\pi}{8}}$
Find square roots. Use a calculator.	$x \approx \pm 34$

Think

Is the answer reasonable?
Yes; the rectangular part is about $30 \times 70 = 2100$ in.² This leaves enough glass for the semicircle.

Length cannot be negative. So the rectangular portion of the window is 34 in. wide by 68 in. long. The semicircular top has a radius of 17 in.

 Got It? **2.** The lengths of the sides of a rectangular window have the ratio 1.6 to 1. The area of the window is 2822.4 in.² What are the window dimensions?

Sometimes an equation shows a perfect square trinomial equal to a constant. To solve, factor the perfect square trinomial into the square of a binomial. Then find square roots.

 Problem 3 Solving a Perfect Square Trinomial Equation

What is the solution of $x^2 + 4x + 4 = 25$?

Think

Factor the perfect square trinomial.

Find square roots.

Rewrite as two equations. Solve for x.

Write

$$x^2 + 4x + 4 = 25$$
$$(x + 2)^2 = 25$$
$$x + 2 = \pm 5$$
$$x + 2 = 5 \text{ or } x + 2 = -5$$
$$x = 3 \text{ or } \qquad x = -7$$

Hint

You can also solve this equation by rewriting it in standard form and factoring.

 Got It? **3.** What is the solution of $x^2 - 14x + 49 = 25$?

Focus Question Why is a perfect square trinomial useful?

Answer Factor the perfect square trinomial as the square of a binomial. Then you can solve the quadratic equation by finding square roots.

Lesson Check

Do you know HOW?

Solve each equation by finding square roots.

1. $2x^2 = 72$

2. $6x^2 = 54$

Do you UNDERSTAND?

3. Writing Explain how to solve the equation $x^2 + 8x + 16 = 36$.

Practice and Problem-Solving Exercises

A Practice

Solve each equation by finding square roots.

◀ See Problem 1.

Guided Practice

To start, isolate x^2.

4. $5x^2 = 80$

$$\frac{5x^2}{5} = \frac{80}{5}$$

5. $x^2 - 4 = 0$

6. $9x^2 = 25$

7. $5x^2 - 40 = 0$

8. Fitness A rectangular swimming pool is 6 ft deep. One side of the pool is 2.5 times as long as the other. The amount of water needed to fill the swimming pool is 2160 cubic feet. Find the dimensions of the pool.

◀ See Problem 2.

Solve each equation.

◀ See Problem 3.

Guided Practice

To start, factor the perfect square trinomial.

9. $x^2 + 6x + 9 = 1$

$$(x + 3)^2 = 1$$

10. $x^2 - 4x + 4 = 100$

11. $x^2 - 2x + 1 = 4$

12. $4x^2 + 4x + 1 = 49$

13. $x^2 - 12x + 36 = 25$

14. $25x^2 + 10x + 1 = 9$

15. $9x^2 + 24x + 16 = 36$

B Apply

Find the value of k that would make the left side of each equation a perfect square trinomial.

16. $x^2 + kx + 25 = 0$

17. $x^2 - kx + 100 = 0$

18. $x^2 - kx + 121 = 0$

19. $x^2 + kx + 64 = 0$

20. $x^2 - kx + 81 = 0$

21. $25x^2 - kx + 1 = 0$

22. $x^2 + kx + \frac{1}{4} = 0$

23. $9x^2 - kx + 4 = 0$

24. $36x^2 - kx + 49 = 0$

Completing the Square

Objectives To solve equations by completing the square
To rewrite functions by completing the square

In Part 1 of the lesson, you learned how to solve an equation that contains a perfect square.

Connect to What You Know

Here you will learn how to rewrite an equation to contain a perfect square trinomial.

Dynamic Activity
Completing the Square

Lesson Vocabulary
• completing the square

Focus Question What is completing the square?

If $x^2 + bx$ is not part of a perfect square trinomial, you can use the coefficient b to find a constant c so that $x^2 + bx + c$ is a perfect square. When you do this, you are **completing the square**. The diagram models this process.

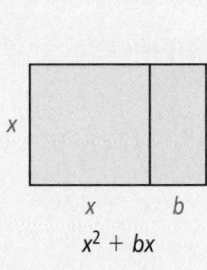

$$x^2 + bx$$

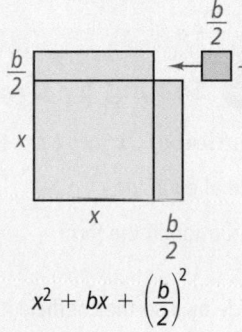

$$x^2 + bx + \left(\frac{b}{2}\right)^2$$

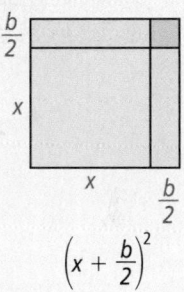

$$\left(x + \frac{b}{2}\right)^2$$

take note

Key Concept Completing the Square

You can form a perfect square trinomial from $x^2 + bx$ by adding $\left(\frac{b}{2}\right)^2$.

$$x^2 + bx + \left(\frac{b}{2}\right)^2 = \left(x + \frac{b}{2}\right)^2$$

 **Problem 4** **Completing the Square**

Think

**Why do you want
a perfect square
trinomial?**
You can factor a perfect
square trinomial as the
square of a binomial.

What value completes the square for $x^2 - 10x$? Justify your answer.

Identify $b = -10$. $x^2 - 10x$

Find $\left(\dfrac{b}{2}\right)^2$. $\left(\dfrac{b}{2}\right)^2 = \left(\dfrac{-10}{2}\right)^2 = (-5)^2 = 25$

Add the value of $\left(\dfrac{b}{2}\right)^2$ to complete the square. $x^2 - 10x + 25$

Rewrite as the square of a binomial. $x^2 - 10x + 25 = (x - 5)^2$

 Got It? 4. What value completes the square for $x^2 + 6x$?

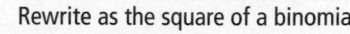 **Key Concept** **Solving an Equation by Completing the Square**

1. Rewrite the equation in the form $x^2 + bx = c$. To do this, get all terms with the
   variable on one side of the equation and the constant on the other side. Divide all
   the terms of the equation by the coefficient of x^2 (if it is not 1).

2. Complete the square by adding $\left(\dfrac{b}{2}\right)^2$ to each side of the equation.

3. Factor the trinomial.

4. Find square roots.

5. Solve for x.

 **Problem 5** **Solving by Completing the Square**

What is the solution of $3x^2 - 12x + 6 = 0$?

Write the original equation. $3x^2 - 12x + 6 = 0$

Rewrite the equation in the form
$x^2 + bx = c$. $3x^2 - 12x = -6$

Divide each side by 3 so the coefficient
of x^2 will be 1. $\dfrac{3x^2}{3} - \dfrac{12x}{3} = \dfrac{-6}{3}$

Simplify. Identify $b = -4$. $x^2 - 4x = -2$

Find $\left(\dfrac{b}{2}\right)^2 = 4$. $\left(\dfrac{b}{2}\right)^2 = \left(\dfrac{-4}{2}\right)^2 = (-2)^2 = 4$

Add 4 to each side. $x^2 - 4x + 4 = -2 + 4$

Factor the trinomial. $(x - 2)^2 = 2$

Find square roots. $x - 2 = \pm\sqrt{2}$

Solve for x. $x = 2 \pm \sqrt{2}$

Think

**How can you check
your answer?**
Check your results
on your calculator.
Replace x in the original
equation with $2 + \sqrt{2}$
and $2 - \sqrt{2}$.

 Got It? 5. What is the solution of $2x^2 - x + 3 = x + 9$?

You can complete a square to change a quadratic function to vertex form.

 Problem 6 Writing in Vertex Form

What is $y = x^2 + 4x - 6$ in vertex form? Name the vertex and y-intercept.

Write the original equation. $\qquad$ $y = x^2 + 4x - 6$

Add $\left(\frac{4}{2}\right)^2 = 2^2$ to complete the square. Also, subtract 2^2 to leave the function unchanged. $\qquad$ $y = x^2 + 4x + 2^2 - 6 - 2^2$

Factor the perfect square trinomial. $\qquad$ $y = (x + 2)^2 - 6 - 2^2$

Simplify. $\qquad$ $y = (x + 2)^2 - 10$

The vertex is $(-2, -10)$. The y-intercept is $(0, -6)$.

Check Graph the function on your graphing calculator.

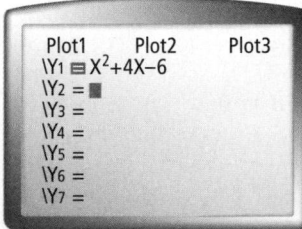 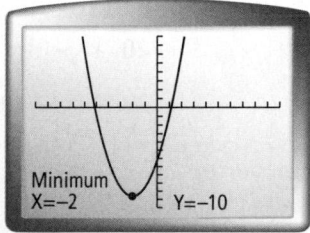 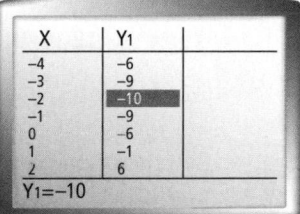

 Got It? 6. What is $y = x^2 + 3x - 6$ in vertex form? Name the vertex and y-intercept.

Think

Why do you want the equation in vertex form?
It is easier to find information about the quadratic function with vertex form.

Focus Question What is completing the square?

Answer Completing the square is a process to make a trinomial into a perfect square. Rewrite the equation in the form $x + bx = c$. Add $\left(\frac{b}{2}\right)^2$ to each side to make a perfect square trinomial. Then factor the perfect square and solve using square roots.

 Lesson Check

Do you know HOW?

Complete the square.

1. $x^2 + 2x + \blacksquare$ $\qquad$ **2.** $x^2 + 10x + \blacksquare$

3. $x^2 - 4x + \blacksquare$ $\qquad$ **4.** $x^2 + 12x + \blacksquare$

5. $x^2 + 100x + \blacksquare$ $\qquad$ **6.** $x^2 - 32x + \blacksquare$

Do you UNDERSTAND?

7. How can you rewrite the equation $x^2 + 12x + 5 = 3$ so the left side of the equation is in the form $(x + a)^2$?

8. Error Analysis Your friend completed the square and wrote the expression shown. Explain your friend's error and write the expression correctly.

$$x^2 - 14x + 36$$
$$x^2 - 14x + 49 + 36$$
$$(x - 7)^2 + 36$$

Practice and Problem-Solving Exercises

See Problem 4.

 Practice

Complete the square.

9. $x^2 + 18x + \blacksquare$ **10.** $x^2 - x + \blacksquare$ **11.** $x^2 - 24x + \blacksquare$

12. $x^2 + 20x + \blacksquare$ **13.** $m^2 - 3m + \blacksquare$ **14.** $x^2 + 4x + \blacksquare$

Solve each quadratic equation by completing the square.

See Problem 5.

Guided Practice

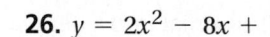

To start, rewrite the equation.
Get all terms with x on one side.

Find $\left(\dfrac{b}{2}\right)^2$.

15. $x^2 + 6x - 3 = 0$

$$x^2 + 6x = 3$$

$$\left(\dfrac{b}{2}\right)^2 = \left(\dfrac{6}{2}\right)^2 = (3)^2 = 9$$

16. $x^2 - 12x + 7 = 0$ **17.** $x^2 + 4x + 2 = 0$ **18.** $x^2 - 2x = 5$

19. $x^2 + 12 = 10x$ **20.** $x^2 - 3x = x - 1$ **21.** $x^2 + 2 = 6x + 4$

22. $2x^2 + 2x - 5 = x^2$ **23.** $4x^2 + 10x - 3 = 0$ **24.** $9x^2 - 12x - 2 = 0$

Rewrite each equation in vertex form.

See Problem 6.

Guided Practice

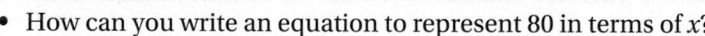

To start, add $\left(\dfrac{4}{2}\right)^2 = 2^2$ to complete the square. Also, subtract 2^2 to leave the function unchanged.

25. $y = x^2 + 4x + 1$

$$y = x^2 + 4x + 2^2 + 1 - 2^2$$

26. $y = 2x^2 - 8x + 1$ **27.** $y = -x^2 - 2x + 3$ **28.** $y = x^2 + 4x - 7$

B Apply

29. Think About a Plan The area of the rectangle shown is 80 square inches. What is the value of x?

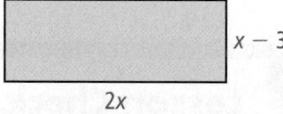

- How can you write an equation to represent 80 in terms of x?
- How can you find the value of x by completing the square?

30. Geometry The table shows some possible whole-number dimensions of rectangles with a perimeter of 100 units. Copy and complete the table.

a. Plot the points (width, area). Find a model for the data set.
b. What is another point in the data set? Use it to verify your model.
c. What is a reasonable domain for this function? Explain.
d. Find the maximum possible area. What dimensions yield this area?
e. Find a function for area in terms of width without using the table. Do you get the same model as in part (a)? Explain.

Width	Length	Area
1	49	49
2	48	$\blacksquare$
3	$\blacksquare$	$\blacksquare$
4	$\blacksquare$	$\blacksquare$
5	$\blacksquare$	$\blacksquare$

Solve each quadratic equation by completing the square.

31. $x^2 + 5x - 3 = 0$

32. $x^2 - x = 5$

33. $3x^2 - 4x = 2$

34. $5x^2 - x = 4$

35. $x^2 + \frac{3}{4}x = \frac{1}{2}$

36. $2x^2 - \frac{1}{2}x = \frac{1}{8}$

37. $3x^2 + x = \frac{2}{3}$

38. $-x^2 + 2x + 4 = 0$

39. $-x^2 - 6x = 2$

Standardized Test Prep

SAT/ACT

40. The graph of which inequality has its vertex at $\left(2\frac{1}{2}, -5\right)$?

Ⓐ $y < |2x - 5| + 5$

Ⓒ $y > |2x + 5| - 5$

Ⓑ $y < |2x + 5| - 5$

Ⓓ $y > |2x - 5| - 5$

41. Which number is a solution of $|9 - x| = 9 + x$?

Ⓕ -3

Ⓖ 0

Ⓗ 3

Ⓘ 6

42. Joanne tosses an apple seed on the ground. It travels along a parabola with the equation $y = -x^2 + 4$. Assume the seed was thrown from a height of 4 ft. How many feet away from Joanne will the apple seed land?

Ⓐ 1 ft

Ⓑ 2 ft

Ⓒ 4 ft

Ⓓ 8 ft

Extended Response

43. List the steps for solving the equation $x^2 - 9 = -8x$ by the completing the square method. Explain each step.

Mixed Review

Solve each equation by factoring. Check your answers.

See Lesson 4-5.

44. $2x^2 - 3x + 1 = 0$

45. $x^2 - 4 = -3x$

46. $16 + 22x = 3x^2$

Determine whether a quadratic model exists for each set of values. If so, write the model.

See Lesson 4-3.

47. $(-4, 3), (-3, 3), (-2, 4)$

48. $\left(-1, \frac{1}{2}\right), (0, 2), (2, 2)$

49. $(0, 2), (1, 0), (2, 4)$

Solve each system by elimination.

See Lesson 3-2.

50. $\begin{cases} 2x + y = 4 \\ 3x - y = 6 \end{cases}$

51. $\begin{cases} 2x + y = 7 \\ -2x + 5y = -1 \end{cases}$

52. $\begin{cases} 2x + 4y = 10 \\ 3x + 5y = 14 \end{cases}$

Get Ready! To prepare for Lesson 4-7, do Exercises 53 and 54.

Evaluate each expression for the given values of the variables.

See Lesson 1-3.

53. $b^2 - 4ac$; $a = 1, b = 6, c = 3$

54. $b^2 - 4ac$; $a = -5, b = 2, c = 4$

4-7 The Quadratic Formula

Objectives To solve quadratic equations using the Quadratic Formula
To determine the number of solutions by using the discriminant

SOLVE IT!

Getting Ready!

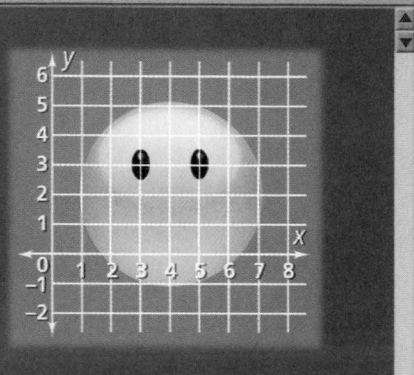

On this happy face, what quadratic function graphs a smile that
- crosses the x-axis twice?
- touches the x-axis once?
- misses the x-axis completely?

Copy and show each completed face on graph paper. Explain why each mouth meets the given condition.

You have to restrict the domain of each function to $2 \le x \le 6$.

Dynamic Activity
Roots of a Quadratic

Lesson Vocabulary
- Quadratic Formula
- discriminant

You can solve a quadratic equation $ax^2 + bx + c = 0$ in more than one way. You can find a general formula that gives values of x in terms of a, b, and c.

Focus Question Why is the Quadratic Formula important?

Here's how to rewrite $ax^2 + bx + c = 0$, where $a \ne 0$, to get the *Quadratic Formula*.

Write the original equation.	$ax^2 + bx + c = 0$
Divide each side by a.	$x^2 + \frac{b}{a}x + \frac{c}{a} = 0$
Rewrite so all terms containing x are on one side.	$x^2 + \frac{b}{a}x = -\frac{c}{a}$
Complete the square.	$x^2 + \frac{b}{a}x + \left(\frac{b}{2a}\right)^2 = \left(\frac{b}{2a}\right)^2 - \frac{c}{a}$
Factor the perfect square trinomial. Simplify.	$\left(x + \frac{b}{2a}\right)^2 = \frac{b^2 - 4ac}{4a^2}$
Find square roots.	$x + \frac{b}{2a} = \pm\sqrt{\frac{b^2 - 4ac}{4a^2}}$
Solve for x. Simplify the radical.	$x = -\frac{b}{2a} \pm \frac{\sqrt{b^2 - 4ac}}{2a}$
Simplify.	$x = \frac{-b \pm \sqrt{b^2 - 4ac}}{2a}$

Key Concept   The Quadratic Formula

To solve the quadratic equation $ax^2 + bx + c = 0$, use the **Quadratic Formula**.

$$x = \frac{-b \pm \sqrt{b^2 - 4ac}}{2a}$$

 **Problem 1**   **Using the Quadratic Formula**

What are the solutions of each equation? Use the Quadratic Formula.

A $2x^2 - x = 4$

Write the original equation.	$2x^2 - x = 4$
Write in standard form.	$2x^2 - x - 4 = 0$
Find the values of a, b, and c.	$a = 2, b = -1, c = -4$
Write the Quadratic Formula.	$x = \dfrac{-b \pm \sqrt{b^2 - 4ac}}{2a}$
Substitute for a, b, and c.	$= \dfrac{-(-1) \pm \sqrt{(-1)^2 - 4(2)(-4)}}{2(2)}$
Simplify.	$= \dfrac{1 \pm \sqrt{33}}{4}$
Write the solution.	$\dfrac{1 + \sqrt{33}}{4}$ and $\dfrac{1 - \sqrt{33}}{4}$

B $x^2 + 6x + 9 = 0$

Write the original equation.	$x^2 + 6x + 9 = 0$
Find the values of a, b, and c.	$a = 1, b = 6, c = 9$
Substitute into $\dfrac{-b \pm \sqrt{b^2 - 4ac}}{2a}$.	$x = \dfrac{-6 \pm \sqrt{6^2 - 4(1)(9)}}{2(1)}$
Simplify.	$= \dfrac{-6 \pm \sqrt{36 - 36}}{2}$
Simplify under the radical.	$= \dfrac{-6 \pm \sqrt{0}}{2}$
Write the solution.	$= -3$

Check Solve by factoring.

Write the original equation.	$x^2 + 6x + 9 = 0$
Factor the perfect square trinomial.	$(x + 3)^2 = 0$
Find square roots.	$x + 3 = 0$
Solve for x.	$x = -3$

 Got It?   **1.** What are the solutions? Use the Quadratic Formula.

     a. $x^2 + 4x = -4$ **b.** $x^2 + 4x - 3 = 0$

Plan

Should you write the equation in standard form?
Yes; write the equation in standard form to identify a, b, and c.

Think

Why is there only one solution?
When you add or subtract zero, you get the same number.

Hint

The Quadratic Formula works even when you can solve by factoring.

 **Problem 2** Applying the Quadratic Formula **GRIDDED RESPONSE**

Your school's jazz band is selling CDs as a fundraiser.
The total profit p depends on the amount x that your band charges
for each CD. The equation $p = -x^2 + 48x - 300$ models the profit
of the fundraiser. What is the least amount, in dollars, you can
charge for a CD to make a profit of $200?

Write the original equation.	$p = -x^2 + 48x - 300$
Substitute 200 for p.	$200 = -x^2 + 48x - 300$
Write the equation in standard form.	$0 = -x^2 + 48x - 500$
Find the values of a, b, and c.	$a = -1, b = 48, c = -500$
Substitute into $\dfrac{-b \pm \sqrt{b^2 - 4ac}}{2a}$.	$x = \dfrac{-48 \pm \sqrt{48^2 - 4(-1)(-500)}}{2(-1)}$
Simplify.	$x = \dfrac{-48 \pm \sqrt{304}}{-2}$
Use a calculator.	$x \approx 15.282$ or $x \approx 32.717$

To make a profit of $200, the least amount you can charge is $15.29
for each CD.

 Think

Does it make sense that two different prices can yield the same profit?
Yes; you can generate a given profit either by selling many CDs at a low price or fewer CDs at a high price.

✓ **Got It?** **2. a.** In Problem 2, what is the least amount you can charge for each CD to make a $100 profit?

       b. **Reasoning** Would a negative profit make sense in this problem? Explain.

Focus Question What is the discriminant of a quadratic equation?

A quadratic equation can have two real solutions ($x^2 = 4$), one real solution ($x^2 = 0$),
or no real solutions ($x^2 = -4$). In the Quadratic Formula, the value under the radical
symbol, $b^2 - 4ac$, tells you how many real-number solutions exist.

In Problem 1A, $b^2 - 4ac > 0$. There are two real solutions. In Problem 1B,
$b^2 - 4ac = 0$. There is only one real solution.

take note

Key Concept Discriminant

The **discriminant** of a quadratic equation in the form $ax^2 + bx + c = 0$ is the value
of the expression $b^2 - 4ac$.

$$x = \frac{-b \pm \sqrt{b^2 - 4ac}}{2a} \leftarrow \text{discriminant}$$

Discriminants and Solutions of Quadratic Equations

Value of the Discriminant	Number of Solutions for $ax^2 + bx + c = 0$	x-intercepts of Graph of Related Function $y = ax^2 + bx + c$
$b^2 - 4ac > 0$	two real solutions	two x-intercepts
$b^2 - 4ac = 0$	one real solution	one x-intercept
$b^2 - 4ac < 0$	no real solutions	no x-intercepts

ONLINE PROBLEMS

Problem 3   Using the Discriminant

Plan

Are you asked to find the solutions of the equation?
No; you want the number of real solutions. You only need to find the discriminant.

What is the number of real solutions of $-2x^2 - 3x + 5 = 0$?

Think

Find the values of a, b, and c.

Evaluate $b^2 - 4ac$.

Interpret the discriminant.

Write

$a = -2, b = -3, c = 5$

$b^2 - 4ac = (-3)^2 - 4(-2)(5)$
$= 49$

The discriminant is positive. The equation has two real solutions.

Got It?   **3.** What is the number of real solutions of each equation?
     a. $2x^2 - 3x + 7 = 0$ **b.** $x^2 = 6x + 5$

 **Problem 4** **Using the Discriminant to Solve a Problem**

Projectile Motion You hit a golf ball into the air from a height of 1 in. above the ground with an initial vertical velocity of 85 ft/s. The function $h = -16t^2 + 85t + \frac{1}{12}$ models the height, in feet, of the ball at time t, in seconds. Will the ball reach a height of 115 ft?

Plan

What value should you substitute for h?
You are trying to determine whether the ball will reach 115 ft. Replace h with 115.

Write the original equation. $\qquad h = -16t^2 + 85t + \frac{1}{12}$

Substitute 115 for h. $\qquad 115 = -16t^2 + 85t + \frac{1}{12}$

Write the equation in standard form. $\qquad 0 = -16t^2 + 85t - 114\frac{11}{12}$

Find the values of a, b, and c. $\qquad a = -16, b = 85, c = -114\frac{11}{12}$

Evaluate the discriminant. $\qquad b^2 - 4ac = 85^2 - 4(-16)\left(-114\frac{11}{12}\right)$

Simplify. $\qquad\qquad\qquad\qquad\qquad\qquad = 7225 - 7354\frac{2}{3}$

Subtract. $\qquad\qquad\qquad\qquad\qquad\qquad = -129\frac{2}{3}$

The discriminant is negative. The equation $115 = -16t^2 + 85t + \frac{1}{12}$ has no real solutions. The golf ball will not reach a height of 115 feet.

Check Graph **Y1** $= -16x^2 + 85x + \frac{1}{12}$ and **Y2** $= 115$ on a graphing calculator. The graphs of **Y1** and **Y2** do not intersect, which means there are no real solutions.

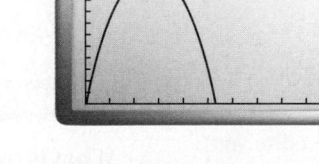

Got It? **4. Reasoning** Without solving an equation, will the golf ball in Problem 4 reach a height of 110 ft? Explain.

Focus Question Why is the Quadratic Formula important?

Answer Use the Quadratic Formula to solve any quadratic equation in standard form $0 = ax^2 + bx + c$. This formula gives values of x in terms of a, b, and c.

Focus Question What is the discriminant of a quadratic equation?

Answer The discriminant of a quadratic equation in standard form is the value of the expression $b^2 - 4ac$. Use the discriminant to find how many real-number solutions the quadratic equation has.

Lesson Check

Do you know HOW?

Solve each equation using the Quadratic Formula.

1. $x^2 - 5x - 7 = 0$

2. $x^2 + 3x - 13 = 0$

3. $2x^2 - 5x - 3 = 0$

4. $3x^2 - 4x + 3 = 0$

Find the discriminant of each quadratic equation. Determine the number of real solutions.

5. $-x^2 + 2x - 9 = 0$

6. $x^2 + 17x + 4 = 0$

7. $x^2 - 6x + 9 = 0$

Do you UNDERSTAND?

8. Reasoning For what values of k does the equation $x^2 + kx + 9 = 0$ have one real solution? Two real solutions?

9. Error Analysis Your friend concluded that because two discriminants are equal, the solutions to the two equations are the same. Explain your friend's error. Give an example of two quadratic equations that disprove this conclusion.

10. Reasoning If one quadratic equation has a positive discriminant and another quadratic equation has a discriminant equal to 0, can the two quadratic equations share a solution? If so, give two quadratic equations that meet this criterion. If not, explain why.

Practice and Problem-Solving Exercises

Ⓐ Practice

Solve each equation using the Quadratic Formula.  **See Problem 1.**

Guided Practice

To start, find the values of *a*, *b*, and *c*.

Substitute in the Quadratic Formula.

11. $x^2 - 4x + 3 = 0$

$a = 1, b = -4, c = 3$

$x = \dfrac{-(-4) \pm \sqrt{(-4)^2 - 4(1)(3)}}{2(1)}$

12. $x^2 + 8x + 12 = 0$

13. $2x^2 + 5x = 7$

14. $3x^2 + 2x - 1 = 0$

15. $x^2 = 3x - 1$

16. $3x^2 = 2(2x + 1)$

17. $x(x - 5) = -4$

Use the Quadratic Formula to answer each question.  **See Problem 2.**

18. Fundraising Your class is selling boxes of flower seeds as a fundraiser. The total profit p depends on the amount x that your class charges for each box of seeds. The equation $p = -0.5x^2 + 25x - 150$ models the profit of the fundraiser. What is the least amount, in dollars, that you can charge and still make a profit of at least $125?

Guided Practice

To start, substitute 125 for p in the equation $125 = -0.5x^2 + 25x - 150$

Then write the equation in standard form. $0 = -0.5x^2 + 25x - 275$

19. Baking Your local bakery sells more bagels when it reduces prices, but then its profit changes. The function $y = -1000x^2 + 1100x - 2.5$ models the bakery's daily profit in dollars, from selling bagels, where x is the price of a bagel in dollars. What is the greatest price the bakery can charge, in dollars, and make a profit of at least $200?

Evaluate the discriminant for each equation. Determine the number of real solutions.

◀ See Problem 3.

20. $x^2 + 4x + 5 = 0$ **21.** $x^2 - 4x - 5 = 0$ **22.** $-4x^2 + 20x - 25 = 0$

23. $-2x^2 + x - 28 = 0$ **24.** $-2x^2 + 7x = 6$ **25.** $x^2 - 12x + 36 = 0$

26. $x^2 + 8x = -16$ **27.** $3x^2 + x = -3$ **28.** $x + 2 = -3x^2$

29. Business The weekly revenue for a company is $r = -3p^2 + 60p + 1060$, where p is the price of the company's product. Use the discriminant to find whether there is a price for which the weekly revenue would be $1500.

◀ See Problem 4.

30. Physics The equation $h = 80t - 16t^2$ models the height h in feet reached in t seconds by an object propelled straight up from the ground at a speed of 80 ft/s. Use the discriminant to find whether the object will ever reach a height of 90 ft.

 **Apply**

31. Think About a Plan The area of a rectangle is 36 in.^{2}. The perimeter of the rectangle is 36 in. What are the dimensions of the rectangle to the nearest hundredth of an inch?
- How can you write an equation using one variable to find the dimensions of the rectangle?
- How can the discriminant of the equation help you solve the problem?

32. Writing Summarize how to use the discriminant to analyze the types of solutions of a quadratic equation.

Solve each equation using any method. When necessary, round real solutions to the nearest hundredth.

33. $6x^2 - 5x - 1 = 0$ **34.** $7x^2 - x - 12 = 0$ **35.** $4x^2 + 4x = 22$

36. $2x^2 - 1 = 5x$ **37.** $x^2 = 11x - 10$ **38.** $4x^2 + 4x = 3$

39. $2x^2 + 4x = 10$ **40.** $x^2 - 3x - 8 = 0$ **41.** $x^2 = 11 - 6x$

42. Air Pollution The function $y = 0.4409x^2 - 5.1724x + 99.0321$ models the emissions of carbon monoxide in the United States since 1987, where y represents the amount of carbon monoxide released in a year in millions of tons, and $x = 0$ represents the year 1987.
- **a.** How can you use a graph to estimate the year in which more than 100 million tons of carbon monoxide were released into the air?
- **b.** How can you use the Quadratic Formula to estimate the year in which more than 100 million tons of carbon monoxide were released into the air?
- **c.** Which method do you prefer? Explain why.

Without graphing, determine how many x-intercepts each function has.

43. $y = -2x^2 + 3x - 1$ **44.** $y = x^2 + 3x + 5$ **45.** $y = -x^2 + 3x + 10$

46. $y = 3x^2 - 10x + 6$ **47.** $y = -5x^2 - 4x + 3$ **48.** $y = 7x^2 - 2x + 9$

49. Sports A diver dives from a 10-m springboard. The function $f(t) = -4.9t^2 + 4t + 10$ models her height in meters above the pool at time t in seconds. At what time does she enter the water?

50. Reasoning Determine the value(s) of k for which $3x^2 + kx + 12 = 0$ has each type of solution.

    a. no real solutions   **b.** exactly one real solution   **c.** two real solutions

51. Use the discriminant to match each function with its graph.

    a. $f(x) = x^2 - 4x + 2$ **b.** $f(x) = x^2 - 4x + 4$ **c.** $f(x) = x^2 - 4x + 6$

I. 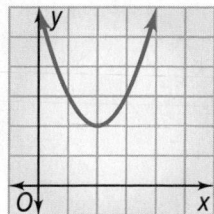   **II.** 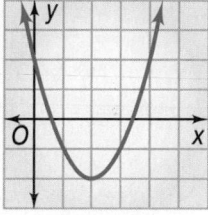   **III.**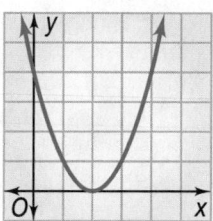

Standardized Test Prep

SAT/ACT

52. The graph of the system of inequalities $\begin{cases} y \le \frac{1}{2}x + 3 \\ y \ge 6x - 30 \\ x \ge 0 \\ y \ge 0 \end{cases}$ is shown at the right.

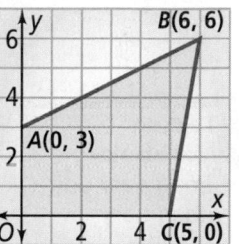

What is the maximum value of the function $P = 3x - 4y$ for the (x, y) pairs in the bounded region shown?

53. What is the y-value of the y-intercept of the quadratic function $y = 2(x + 2)^2 - 5$?

54. What is the x-value in the solution to the system $\begin{cases} 3x + y = -7 \\ 2x - 2y = -10 \end{cases}$?

55. How many different real solutions are there for $2x^2 - 3x + 5 = 0$?

Mixed Review

Solve each equation by completing the square.   ◀ See Lesson 4-6.

56. $x^2 - 8x - 20 = 0$ **57.** $2y^2 = 4y - 1$ **58.** $x^2 - 3x - 8 = 0$

Simplify by combining like terms.   ◀ See Lesson 1-3.

59. $z^2 + 8z^2 - 2z + 5z$ **60.** $4k - x - 3k + 5x$ **61.** $4y - (2y + 3x) - 5x$

Get Ready! **To prepare for Lesson 4-8, do Exercises 62–64.**

Simplify each expression. ◀ See p. 874.

62. $\sqrt{(-2)^2 + 8^2}$ **63.** $\sqrt{3^2 + 4^2}$ **64.** $\sqrt{5^2 + (-12)^2}$

4-8
PART 1

Complex Numbers

Objective To identify, graph, and perform operations with complex numbers

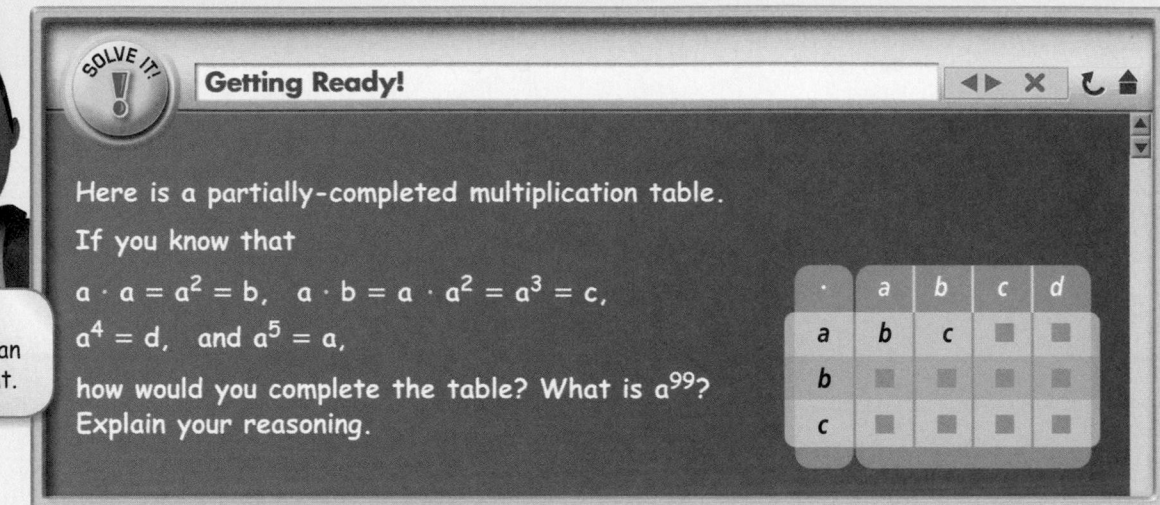

SOLVE IT!

Getting Ready!

Here is a partially-completed multiplication table.

If you know that

$a \cdot a = a^2 = b,\quad a \cdot b = a \cdot a^2 = a^3 = c,$

$a^4 = d,\quad \text{and}\quad a^5 = a,$

how would you complete the table? What is a^{99}?
Explain your reasoning.

$\cdot$	a	b	c	d
a	b	c	■	■
b	■	■	■	■
c	■	■	■	■

One of a, b, c, and d acts like an identity element.

Lesson Vocabulary
- imaginary unit
- imaginary number
- complex number
- pure imaginary number
- complex number plane
- absolute value of a complex number
- complex conjugates

In Chapter 1, you learned about different subsets of real numbers. The set of real numbers is itself a subset of a larger set of numbers, the *complex numbers*. Curiously, the complex numbers include a number like a in the Solve It. Its fifth power is itself.

Focus Question What are complex numbers?

A foundation for the complex numbers is a number whose square is -1. The **imaginary unit** i is the complex number whose square is -1.

So $\quad i^2 = -1$
and $\quad i = \sqrt{-1}.$

take note

Key Concept   Square Root of a Negative Real Number

Algebra
For any positive number a,
$\sqrt{-a} = \sqrt{-1 \cdot a} = \sqrt{-1} \cdot \sqrt{a} = i\sqrt{a}.$

Example
$\sqrt{-5} = i\sqrt{5}$

Note that $(\sqrt{-5})^2 = (i\sqrt{5})^2 = i^2(\sqrt{5})^2 = -1 \cdot 5 = -5$ (not 5).

Problem 1 Simplifying a Number Using i

Think

Is $\sqrt{-18}$ a real number?
No; there is no real number that when multiplied by itself gives -18. You must use the imaginary unit i to write $\sqrt{-18}$.

How do you write $\sqrt{-18}$ by using the imaginary unit i?

Write -18 as $-1 \cdot 18$.	$\sqrt{-18} = \sqrt{-1 \cdot 18}$
Use the Multiplication Property of Square Roots.	$= \sqrt{-1} \cdot \sqrt{18}$
Use the Definition of $i = \sqrt{-1}$.	$= i \cdot \sqrt{18}$
Simplify.	$= i \cdot 3\sqrt{2}$
Rewrite.	$= 3i\sqrt{2}$

Got It? **1.** How do you write each number in parts (a)–(c) using the imaginary unit i?

 a. $\sqrt{-12}$ **b.** $\sqrt{-25}$ **c.** $\sqrt{-7}$

 d. Reasoning Explain why $\sqrt{-64} \neq -\sqrt{64}$.

An **imaginary number** is any number of the form $a + bi$, where a and b are real numbers and $b \neq 0$. Imaginary numbers and real numbers together make up the set of *complex numbers*.

take note

Key Concept Complex Numbers

You can write a **complex number** in the form $a + bi$, where a and b are real numbers.

If $b = 0$, the number $a + bi$ is a real number.

If $a = 0$ and $b \neq 0$, the number $a + bi$ is a **pure imaginary number**.

$$\begin{array}{ccc} a & + & bi \\ \uparrow & & \uparrow \\ \text{Real} & & \text{Imaginary} \\ \text{part} & & \text{part} \end{array}$$

Complex Numbers ($a + bi$)

Real Numbers ($a + 0i$)	Imaginary Numbers ($a + bi$, $b \neq 0$)
	Pure Imaginary Numbers ($0 + bi$, $b \neq 0$)

In the **complex number plane**, the point (a, b) represents the complex number $a + bi$. To graph a complex number, locate the real part on the horizontal axis and the imaginary part on the vertical axis.

The **absolute value of a complex number** is its distance from the origin in the complex plane.

$$|a + bi| = \sqrt{a^2 + b^2}$$

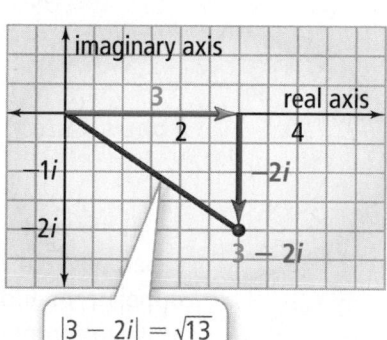

$|3 - 2i| = \sqrt{13}$

 **Problem 2** Graphing in the Complex Number Plane

What are the graph and absolute value of each number?

Ⓐ $-5 + 3i$

Step 1 Graph the number.

From the origin, move 5 units left for the real part.
Move 3 units up for the imaginary part.

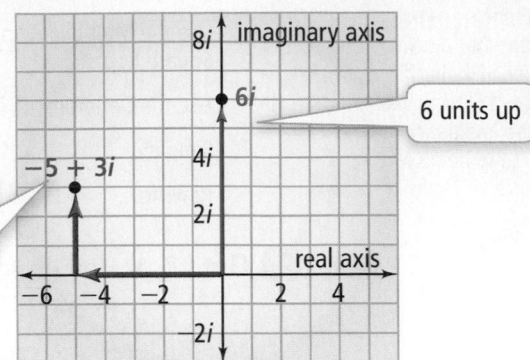

5 units left, 3 units up

6 units up

Step 2 Find the absolute value.

Use the definition of the absolute value of a complex number. $\quad |-5 + 3i| = \sqrt{(-5)^2 + 3^2}$

Simplify. $\qquad\qquad\qquad\qquad\qquad = \sqrt{34}$

Ⓑ $6i$

Step 1 Graph the number.

There is no real part. From the origin, move 6 units up.

Step 2 Find the absolute value.

Write $6i$ as $0 + 6i$. $\qquad\qquad\qquad\qquad |6i| = |0 + 6i|$

Use the definition of the absolute value of a complex number. $\qquad\qquad = \sqrt{0^2 + 6^2}$

Simplify. $\qquad\qquad\qquad\qquad\qquad = \sqrt{36}$

Find the square root. $\qquad\qquad\qquad = 6$

Think

Where is a pure imaginary number in the complex plane?
The real part of a pure imaginary number is 0. The number must be on the imaginary axis.

 Got It? **2.** What are the graph and absolute value of each number?
   a. $5 - i$ $\qquad\qquad\qquad\qquad\qquad$ **b.** $-3i$
   c. $1 + 4i$ $\qquad\qquad\qquad\qquad\quad$ **d.** 4

Focus Question How do you perform basic operations on complex numbers?

To add or subtract complex numbers, add the real parts and the imaginary parts separately. If the sum of two complex numbers is 0, or $0 + 0i$, then each number is the opposite, or additive inverse, of the other. The associative and commutative properties apply to complex numbers as well.

Problem 3 Adding and Subtracting Complex Numbers

What is each sum or difference?

Plan

How is adding complex numbers similar to adding algebraic expressions? Adding the real parts and imaginary parts separately is like adding like terms.

A $(3 + 5i) + (-2 + 4i)$

Use the commutative and associative properties.
$$3 + (-2) + 5i + 4i$$

Simplify.
$$1 + 9i$$

B $(4 - 3i) + (-4 + 3i)$

Use the commutative and associative properties.
$$4 + (-4) + (-3i) + 3i$$

Simplify.
$$0 + 0 = 0$$

$4 - 3i$ and $-4 + 3i$ are additive inverses.

C $(5 - 3i) - (-2 + 4i)$

To subtract, add the opposite.
$$5 - 3i + 2 - 4i$$

Use the commutative and associative properties.
$$5 + 2 + (-3i) - 4i$$

Simplify.
$$7 - 7i$$

 Got It? 3. What is each sum or difference?

a. $(7 - 2i) + (-3 + i)$ b. $(1 + 5i) - (3 - 2i)$

c. $(8 + 6i) - (8 - 6i)$ d. $(-3 + 9i) + (3 + 9i)$

You multiply complex numbers $a + bi$ and $c + di$ as you would multiply binomials. For imaginary parts bi and di,

$$(bi)(di) = bd(i)^2$$
$$= bd(-1)$$
$$= -bd.$$

 **Problem 4** Multiplying Complex Numbers

What is each product?

A $(3i)(-5 + 2i)$

Use the Distributive Property.
$$-15i + 6i^2$$

Substitute -1 for i^2.
$$-15i + 6(-1)$$

Simplify.
$$-6 - 15i$$

Think

How do you multiply two binomials? Multiply each term of one binomial by each term of the other binomial.

B $(4 + 3i)(-1 - 2i)$

Use the Distributive Property.
$$-4 - 8i - 3i - 6i^2$$

Substitute -1 for i^2.
$$-4 - 8i - 3i - 6(-1)$$

Simplify.
$$2 - 11i$$

C $(-6 + i)(-6 - i)$

$$36 + 6i - 6i - i^2$$

$$36 + 6i - 6i - (-1)$$

$$37$$

 Got It? 4. What is each product?

a. $(7i)(3i)$ b. $(2 - 3i)(4 + 5i)$ c. $(-4 + 5i)(-4 - 5i)$

In Problem 4(c), the product is a real number. Number pairs of the form $a + bi$ and $a - bi$ are **complex conjugates**. The product of complex conjugates is a real number.

$$(a + bi)(a - bi) = a^2 - (bi)^2$$
$$= a^2 - b^2i^2$$
$$= a^2 - b^2(-1)$$
$$= a^2 + b^2$$

You can use complex conjugates to simplify quotients of complex numbers.

 Problem 5 Dividing Complex Numbers

What is each quotient?

Plan

What is the goal?
Write the quotient in the form $a + bi$.

A $\dfrac{9 + 12i}{3i}$

B $\dfrac{2 + 3i}{1 - 4i}$

Multiply the numerator and denominator by the complex conjugate of the denominator.

$\dfrac{9 + 12i}{3i} \cdot \dfrac{-3i}{-3i}$

$\dfrac{2 + 3i}{1 - 4i} \cdot \dfrac{1 + 4i}{1 + 4i}$

Multiply.

$\dfrac{-27i - 36i^2}{-9i^2}$

$\dfrac{2 + 8i + 3i + 12i^2}{1 + 4i - 4i - 16i^2}$

Substitute -1 for i^2.

$\dfrac{-27i - 36(-1)}{-9(-1)}$

$\dfrac{2 + 8i + 3i + 12(-1)}{1 + 4i - 4i - 16(-1)}$

Simplify.

$\dfrac{36 - 27i}{9}$

$\dfrac{-10 + 11i}{17}$

Write in $a + bi$ form.

$4 - 3i$

$-\dfrac{10}{17} + \dfrac{11}{17}i$

 Got It? **5.** What is each quotient?

a. $\dfrac{5 - 2i}{3 + 4i}$

b. $\dfrac{4 - i}{6i}$

c. $\dfrac{8 - 7i}{8 + 7i}$

Focus Question What are complex numbers?
Answer The set of complex numbers includes real numbers and imaginary numbers. The basis for the complex numbers is the imaginary unit i, whose square is -1. Use an imaginary number of the form $a + bi$, where a and b are real numbers, to simplify the square root of a negative.

Focus Question How do you perform basic operations on complex numbers?
Answer To perform basic operations on complex numbers, treat the imaginary parts like variable terms of binomials. Add, subtract, or multiply as you would with algebraic expressions. To divide complex numbers, multiply numerator and denominator by the complex conjugate of the denominator and simplify.

Lesson Check

Do you know HOW?

1. Simplify $\sqrt{-75}$ by using the imaginary number i.

2. Find the absolute value of $4 - 3i$.

Simplify each expression.

3. $(4 - 2i) - (-3 + i)$

4. $(2 + i)(4 - 5i)$

Do you UNDERSTAND?

5. Vocabulary Explain the difference between the additive inverse of a complex number and a complex conjugate.

6. Error Analysis Describe and correct the error below.

$$(4 - 7i)(4 + 7i) = 16 + 28i - 28i + 49i^2$$
$$= 16 - 49$$
$$= -33$$

Practice and Problem-Solving Exercises

**Practice**

Simplify each number by using the imaginary number i.

See Problem 1.

7. $\sqrt{-4}$ **8.** $\sqrt{-7}$ **9.** $\sqrt{-15}$ **10.** $\sqrt{-81}$

Plot each complex number and find its absolute value.

See Problem 2.

11. $2i$ **12.** $5 + 12i$ **13.** $2 - 2i$ **14.** $1 - 4i$

Simplify each expression.

See Problems 3 and 4.

Guided Practice ➜

To start, group the real and imaginary parts.

15. $(2 + 4i) + (4 - i)$

$2 + 4 + 4i - i$

16. $(7 + 9i) + (-5i)$ **17.** $(12 + 5i) - (2 - i)$ **18.** $(-6 - 7i) - (1 + 3i)$

19. $(8 + i)(2 + 7i)$ **20.** $(-6 - 5i)(1 + 3i)$ **21.** $(9 + 4i)^2$

Write each quotient as a complex number.

See Problem 5.

Guided Practice ➜

To start, multiply the numerator and denominator by the complex conjugate of the denominator.

22. $\dfrac{3 - 2i}{5i}$

$\dfrac{3 - 2i}{5i} \cdot \dfrac{-5i}{-5i} = \dfrac{-15i + 10i^2}{-25i^2}$

23. $\dfrac{4 - 3i}{-1 - 4i}$ **24.** $\dfrac{i + 2}{i - 2}$ **25.** $\dfrac{4}{2 - 3i}$

**Apply**

Simplify each expression.

26. $(8i)(4i)(-9i)$ **27.** $(2 + \sqrt{-1}) + (-3 + \sqrt{-16})$

28. $2i(5 - 3i)$ **29.** $(10 + \sqrt{-9}) - (2 + \sqrt{-25})$

30. $-5(1 + 2i) + 3i(3 - 4i)$ **31.** $(3 + \sqrt{-4})(4 + \sqrt{-1})$

Objective To find complex number solutions of quadratic equations

In Part 1 of the lesson, you learned how to perform operations with complex numbers.

Connect to What You Know

Here you will use what you learned to solve quadratic equations with no real solutions.

Focus Question How are complex numbers related to the solutions of quadratic equations?

Every quadratic equation has complex number solutions. For some of these quadratic equations, the complex solutions also happen to be real numbers.

Some quadratic equations have only pure imaginary solutions.

Plan

How do you solve a quadratic equation of the form $ax^2 + c = 0$?
Use properties of equality to isolate the variable.

Problem 6 **Finding Pure Imaginary Solutions**

What are the solutions of $2x^2 + 32 = 0$?

Write the original equation. $2x^2 + 32 = 0$

Isolate x^2. $2x^2 = -32$

Divide each side by 2. $x^2 = -16$

Find square roots. $x = \pm\sqrt{-16}$

Simplify. $x = \pm 4i$

Check

Write the original equation.	$2x^2 + 32 = 0$	$2x^2 + 32 = 0$
Substitute for x.	$2(4i)^2 + 32 = 0$	$2(-4i)^2 + 32 = 0$
Simplify the exponent.	$2 \cdot 16i^2 + 32 = 0$	$2 \cdot 16i^2 + 32 = 0$
Simplify. Substitute -1 for i^2.	$-32 + 32 = 0$ ✔	$-32 + 32 = 0$ ✔

The solutions check.

 Got It? **6.** What are the solutions of each equation?

  a. $5x^2 + 20 = 0$ **b.** $x^2 + 15 = 0$

Some quadratic equations have complex solutions with both real and imaginary parts.

Problem 7 **Finding Imaginary Solutions**

What are the solutions of $2x^2 - 3x + 5 = 0$?

Think

Use the Quadratic Formula with $a = 2$, $b = -3$, and $c = 5$.

Write

$$x = \frac{-b \pm \sqrt{b^2 - 4ac}}{2a}$$

$$= \frac{-(-3) \pm \sqrt{(-3)^2 - 4(2)(5)}}{2(2)}$$

$$= \frac{3 \pm \sqrt{9 - 40}}{4}$$

Hint

The discriminant is -31. There will be no real solutions.

Simplify.

$$= \frac{3 \pm \sqrt{-31}}{4}$$

$$= \frac{3}{4} \pm \frac{\sqrt{31}}{4}i$$

Graph the associated function to check for reasonableness.

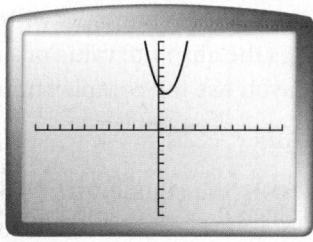

 Got It? **7.** What are the solutions of each equation?

a. $3x^2 - x + 2 = 0$ **b.** $x^2 - 4x + 5 = 0$

Focus Question How are complex numbers related to the solutions of quadratic equations?

Answer Every quadratic equation has complex number solutions. Sometimes, these complex numbers only have a real part. When a quadratic equation has no real solutions, use square roots or the Quadratic Formula to find the imaginary solutions.

 Lesson Check

Do you know HOW?

Solve each equation. Check your answers.

1. $x^2 + 16 = 0$

2. $x^2 = -7$

3. $x^2 + 36 = 0$

Do you UNDERSTAND?

4. Reasoning Explain why you can't use the graph of the related function to solve the equation $x^2 - 6x + 10 = 0$. What are the solutions of this equation?

Practice and Problem-Solving Exercises

 **Practice**

Solve each equation. Check your answer.

◀ **See Problem 6.**

Guided Practice →

5. $x^2 + 25 = 0$

To start, isolate x^2.

$x^2 = -25$

6. $2x^2 + 1 = 0$ **7.** $3s^2 + 2 = -62$ **8.** $-5x^2 - 3 = 0$

Find all solutions to each quadratic equation.

◀ **See Problem 7.**

Guided Practice →

9. $x^2 + 2x + 3 = 0$

To start, use the Quadratic Formula with $a = 1$, $b = 2$, and $c = 3$.

$x = \dfrac{-(2) \pm \sqrt{(2)^2 - 4(1)(3)}}{2(1)}$

10. $-3x^2 + x - 3 = 0$ **11.** $2x^2 - 4x + 7 = 0$ **12.** $x^2 - 2x + 2 = 0$

13. $x^2 + 5 = 4x$ **14.** $2x(x - 3) = -5$ **15.** $-5(x + 2) = x^2$

 **Apply**

16. Think About a Plan In the complex number plane, what geometric figure describes the complex numbers with absolute value 10?
- What does the absolute value of a complex number represent?
- How can you use the complex number plane to solve this problem?

17. Solve $(x + 3i)(x - 3i) = 34$.

18. Open-Ended In the equation $x^2 - 6x + c = 0$, find values of c that will give:
  a. two real solutions   **b.** two imaginary solutions   **c.** one real solution

19. A student wrote the numbers 1, 5, $1 + 3i$, and $4 + 3i$ to represent the vertices of a quadrilateral in the complex number plane. What type of quadrilateral has these vertices?

The multiplicative inverse of a complex number z is $\frac{1}{z}$ where $z \neq 0$. Find the multiplicative inverse, or reciprocal, of each complex number. Then use complex conjugates to simplify. Check each answer by multiplying it by the original number.

20. $2 + 5i$ **21.** $8 - 12i$ **22.** $a + bi$

Two complex numbers $a + bi$ and $c + di$ are equal when $a = c$ and $b = d$.
Solve each equation for x and y.

23. $2x + 3yi = -14 + 9i$ **24.** $3x + 19i = 16 - 8yi$ **25.** $-14 - 3i = 2x + yi$

Find the sum and product of the roots of each equation.

26. $x^2 - 2x + 3 = 0$ **27.** $5x^2 + 2x + 1 = 0$ **28.** $-2x^2 + 3x - 3 = 0$

For $ax^2 + bx + c = 0$, the sum of the roots is $-\frac{b}{a}$ and the product of the roots is $\frac{c}{a}$.
Find a quadratic equation for each pair of roots. Assume $a = 1$.

29. $-6i$ and $6i$ **30.** $2 + 5i$ and $2 - 5i$ **31.** $4 - 3i$ and $4 + 3i$

Standardized Test Prep

SAT/ACT

32. How can you rewrite the expression $(8 - 5i)^2$ in the form $a + bi$?

   (A) $39 + 80i$ (B) $39 - 80i$ (C) $69 + 80i$ (D) $69 - 80i$

33. How many solutions does the quadratic equation $4x^2 - 12x + 9 = 0$ have?

   (F) two real solutions   (H) two imaginary solutions

   (G) one real solution   (I) one imaginary solution

34. What are the solutions of $3x^2 - 2x - 4 = 0$?

   (A) $\dfrac{1 \pm \sqrt{13}}{3}$ (B) $\dfrac{1 \pm i\sqrt{11}}{3}$ (C) $\dfrac{-1 \pm \sqrt{13}}{3}$ (D) $\dfrac{-1 \pm i\sqrt{11}}{3}$

Short Response

35. Using factoring, what are all four solutions to $x^4 - 16 = 0$? Show your work.

Mixed Review

Solve each equation using the Quadratic Formula.   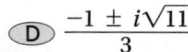 **See Lesson 4-7.**

36. $2x^2 + 3x - 4 = 0$ **37.** $4x^2 + x = 1$ **38.** $x^2 = -7x - 8$

Graph each function. Identify the axis of symmetry.   **See Lesson 4-1.**

39. $y = -2(x + 1)^2 - 3$ **40.** $y = \frac{1}{2}(x - 4)^2 + 1$ **41.** $y = 3(x - 1)^2 - 5$

Write an equation for each line.   **See Lesson 2-3.**

42. $m = 3$ and the y-intercept is -4 **43.** $m = -0.5$ and the y-intercept is -2

44. $m = -7$ and the y-intercept is 10 **45.** $m = 2$ and the y-intercept is 8

Get Ready!   **To prepare for Lesson 5-1, do Exercises 46–48.**

Simplify by combining like terms.   **See Lesson 1-3.**

46. $3q + 9q - q$ **47.** $-2ab^2 + 2a^2b + 3ab^2$ **48.** $-4y^2 + 2y + 3y^2$

Powers of Complex Numbers

You can use the rules for multiplying complex numbers to find powers of complex numbers.

Example 1

Compute and graph $(2i)^n$, for $n = 0, 1, 2,$ and 3.

n	$(2i)^n$
0	$(2i)^0 = 1$
1	$(2i)^1 = 2i$
2	$(2i)^2 = 4i^2 = 4(-1) = -4$
3	$(2i)^3 = 8i^3 = 8(i^2 \cdot i) = 8(-1 \cdot i) = -8i$

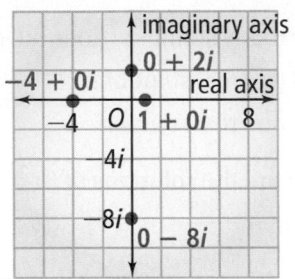

Example 2

Compute and graph $(2 - 3i)^n$, for $n = 0, 1, 2,$ and 3.

n	$(2 - 3i)^n$
0	$(2 - 3i)^0 = 1$
1	$(2 - 3i)^1 = 2 - 3i$
2	$(2 - 3i)^2 = 4 - 6i - 6i + 9i^2 = 4 - 12i + 9(-1) = -5 - 12i$
3	$(2 - 3i)^3 = -10 - 24i + 15i + 36i^2 = -10 - 9i + 36(-1) = -46 - 9i$

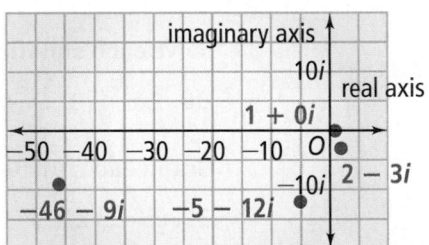

Exercises

1. Based on the graph in Example 1, predict the location of $(2i)^5$.

2. Compute and graph $(-3i)^n$ for $n = 0, 1, 2,$ and 3.

3. a. Connect the points from the graph in Example 1 with a smooth curve. Estimate $(2i)^{\frac{1}{2}}$.

   b. Use a graphing calculator to compute $(2i)^{\frac{1}{2}}$. Does it fall on the curve? Was it close to your estimate?

4. Use a graphing calculator to find values of $(2 - 3i)^n$ for $n = 0.5, 1.5,$ and 2.5. Copy the graph from Example 2 and add these points.

5. Compute and graph $(3 - 4i)^n$ for $n = 0, 1, 2,$ and 3.

Quadratic Inequalities

To solve some quadratic inequalities, relate the quadratic expression to 0 and factor. To determine the sign of each factor, use what you know about multiplying positive and negative numbers.

Example 1

Solve each inequality algebraically.

a. $2x^2 - 14x < 0$

Factor.	$2x(x - 7) < 0$
The product is negative, so the two factors must have *different* signs.	$2x > 0$ and $(x - 7) < 0$ or $2x < 0$ and $(x - 7) > 0$
Simplify.	$x > 0$ and $x < 7$, or $x < 0$ and $x > 7$
No value can be both greater than 7 *and* less than 0.	$0 < x < 7$

b. $2x^2 - 14x > 0$

Factor.	$2x(x - 7) > 0$
The product is positive, so the two factors must have the *same* sign.	$2x > 0$ and $(x - 7) > 0$, or $2x < 0$ and $(x - 7) < 0$
Simplify.	$x > 0$ and $x > 7$, or $x < 0$ and $x < 7$
A value that is greater than both 0 *and* 7 is always greater than 7. A value that is less than both 0 *and* 7 is always less than 0.	$x > 7$ or $x < 0$

You can use a table to solve inequalities by analyzing the values of y around 0.

Activity

Use the table to find the solutions of $x^2 - 6x + 5 < 0$.

1. What happens to the value of y when $0 \le x \le 6$?
2. Does this make sense when you think of the shape of the graph of $y = x^2 - 6x + 5$? Explain.
3. What x-values in the table make the inequality $x^2 - 6x + 5 < 0$ true?
4. What are the solutions of $x^2 - 6x + 5 < 0$?

x	y
0	5
1	0
2	-3
3	-4
4	-3
5	0
6	5

You can solve inequalities of the form $ax^2 + bx + c > 0$ or $ax^2 + bx + c < 0$ with $a \neq 0$ by graphing the corresponding function and seeing where the graph is above or below the x-axis.

Example 2

Find the solution sets for $\frac{1}{4}(x-2)^2 - 1 > 0$ and $\frac{1}{4}(x-2)^2 - 1 < 0$.

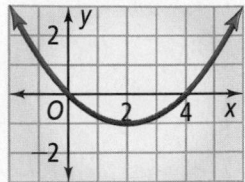
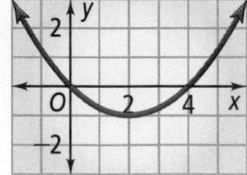

The solution set for $\frac{1}{4}(x-2)^2 - 1 > 0$ is all x-values of points on the parabola that lie above the x-axis.

$$x < 0 \text{ or } x > 4$$

The solution set for $\frac{1}{4}(x-2)^2 - 1 < 0$ is all x-values of points on the parabola that lie below the x-axis.

$$0 < x < 4$$

Example 3

Solve $-2x^2 - 8x - 6 < 0$.

Think: Since the coefficient of x^2 is less than zero, the graph of $y = -2x^2 - 8x - 6$ opens downward.

Solve: Find where $-2x^2 - 8x - 6$ equals 0.

$$-2x^2 - 8x - 6 = 0$$
$$-2(x^2 + 4x + 3) = 0$$
$$-2(x + 3)(x + 1) = 0$$
$$x = -3 \text{ or } x = -1$$

The graph of $y = -2x^2 - 8x - 6$ opens downward and crosses the x-axis at $x = -3$ and $x = -1$. The solution of $-2x^2 - 8x - 6 < 0$ is $x < -3$ or $x > -1$.

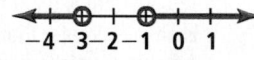

Exercises

5. Solve each inequality. Graph your solution on a number line.

    a. $x^2 < 36$ **b.** $x^2 - 9 > 0$ **c.** $x^2 < -4$ **d.** $x^2 - 3x - 18 > 0$

6. How can you use the graph of $y = 3x - 4$ to solve the linear inequality $3x - 4 < 0$? Graph the solution.

7. How can you solve the absolute value inequality $|-3x + 4| > 0$?

8. Example 2 shows two possible graphs for a quadratic inequality. What other possibilities are there?

4

Pull It **All Together**

To solve these problems, you will pull together many concepts and skills related to solving quadratic equations. Be sure to show your work and justify your reasoning.

BIG idea Equivalence and Function

The parameters a, b, c, h, and k in the standard and vertex forms of a quadratic function give information on how the graph of the function relates to the graph of the parent function $y = x^2$.

Standard form: $y = ax^2 + bx + c$ Vertex form: $y = a(x - h)^2 + k$

Task 1

Refer to the two forms shown above.

a. What information do the parameters, or combinations of parameters, provide about the graph of the quadratic function?

b. Begin with standard form. Transform it to vertex form. What are the values of h and k in terms of a, b, and c?

c. Show how the Quadratic Formula follows from your result in part (b). *Hint:* Set the expression in your vertex form equal to 0. Then solve by factoring.

BIG idea Solving Equations and Inequalities

A problem may require different types of equation solving. You should know when and how to use a graphing calculator to help you with your work.

Task 2

You shoot an arrow at a target. The parabolic path of your arrow passes through the points shown in the table.

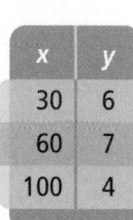

x	y
30	6
60	7
100	4

a. Find a quadratic function in standard form that models the path of your arrow. (*Hint:* The three points are (x, y)-values that satisfy $y = ax^2 + bx + c$.)

b. If the y-value represents height above the ground, for what value of x would your arrow hit the ground if you miss the target?

c. If the target bull's-eye is at $x = 100$, at what height should the bull's-eye be for your arrow to hit it?

d. If the target bull's-eye is at height $y = 2.98$, at what value of x should the bull's-eye be for the arrow to hit it?

4 | Chapter Review for Part B

Connecting BIG ideas and Answering the Essential Questions

1 Equivalence

Vertex form of a quadratic function shows the vertex of the parabola. Standard form is "calculator ready." Both forms give additional information.

→

The Different Forms of a Quadratic Function (Lessons 4-1 and 4-2)

$y = 2(x - 1)^2 + 3$ has vertex $(1, 3)$ and opens upward $(2 > 0)$.

$y = -2x^2 + 4x + 1$ has vertex with x-coordinate $-\frac{4}{2(-2)} = 1$ and opens downward $(-2 < 0)$.

Each has axis of symmetry $x = 1$.
Each is a stretch of $y = x^2$ by the factor 2.

Modeling With Quadratics (Lesson 4-3)

$y = -16x^2 + 12x + 4$ can model the height y in feet reached by the coin tossed by the referee before the game. x represents time in seconds.

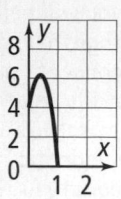

2 Function

Any quadratic function is possibly a stretch or compression, a reflection, and a translation of $y = x^2$.

→

3 Solving Equations and Inequalities

The real solutions of a quadratic equation show the zeros of the related quadratic function and the x-intercepts of its graph.

→

Helpful Aids for Solving Quadratic Equations (Lessons 4-4, 4-6, 4-8)

Factor a quadratic: $-16x^2 + 12x + 4$
$\qquad = -4(4x + 1)(x - 1)$

Complete the square: $x^2 + 4x + 1$
$= x^2 + 4x + \left(\frac{4}{2}\right)^2 + 1 - \left(\frac{4}{2}\right)^2$
$= (x + 2)^2 - 3$

Complex numbers: $x^2 + 1 = (x + i)(x - i)$ where $i = \sqrt{-1}$.

→

Solving Quadratic Equations (Lessons 4-5, 4-7)

$-16x^2 + 12x + 4 = 0 \quad \rightarrow$
$-4(4x + 1)(x - 1) = 0 \quad \rightarrow$
$x = -\frac{1}{4}$ or $x = 1$.

$-2x^2 + 4x + 1 = 0 \qquad \rightarrow$
$x = \frac{-4 \pm \sqrt{4^2 - 4(-2)(1)}}{2(-2)} \quad \rightarrow$
$x = 1 + \frac{\sqrt{6}}{2}$ or $x = 1 - \frac{\sqrt{6}}{2}$.

Chapter Vocabulary

- absolute value of a complex number (p. 269)
- completing the square (p. 255)
- complex conjugates (p. 272)
- complex number (p. 269)
- complex number plane (p. 269)
- discriminant (p. 262)
- imaginary number (p. 269)
- imaginary unit (p. 268)
- pure imaginary number (p. 269)
- Quadratic Formula (p. 261)
- zero of a function (p. 243)
- Zero-Product Property (p. 243)

Choose the correct term to complete each sentence.

1. You can use the Quadratic (Function/Formula) to solve a quadratic equation.

2. The value of $b^2 - 4ac$ for the equation $ax^2 + bx + c = 0$ is called the (discriminant/complex conjugate).

3. The number $a + bi$, where $b = 0$, is an example of a(n) (imaginary/complex) number.

4-5 Quadratic Equations

Quick Review

The zeros of a quadratic function are the solutions of the related quadratic equation. You can find the zeros from a table or from the x-intercepts of the parabola that is the graph of the function. You can also find them by factoring the standard form of a quadratic equation, $ax^2 + bx + c = 0$, and using the Zero-Product Property.

Example

Solve $2x^2 + 6x = 8$ by factoring.

Rewrite the equation in standard form.	$2x^2 + 6x - 8 = 0$
Factor out the GCF, 2.	$2(x^2 + 3x - 4) = 0$
Factor the quadratic expression.	$2(x + 4)(x - 1) = 0$
Use the Zero-Product Property.	$2(x + 4) = 0$ or $x - 1 = 0$
Solve for x.	$x = -4$ or $x = 1$

Exercises

Solve each equation by factoring.

4. $x^2 = 4x + 12$

5. $2x^2 - 3x - 14 = 0$

6. $x^2 + 2x = 8$

7. $x^2 + 7x = 18$

Solve each equation by graphing.

8. $5x^2 + 8x - 13 = 0$

9. $9 - 4x = 2x^2$

10. $x^2 - x = 1$

11. $x^2 - 2x - 4 = 0$

Solve each equation by using a table.

12. $x^2 - 6x + 8 = 0$

13. $9x - 14 = 3x^2$

14. $x^2 - 5x + 2 = 0$

15. $2x^2 - 12x = -16$

4-6 Completing the Square

Quick Review

If you cannot solve a quadratic equation by factoring, you can use **completing the square**. You write one side as a perfect square trinomial and then take square roots. You can also convert a quadratic function from standard form to vertex form by completing the square.

Example

Solve $x^2 + 6x - 7 = 0$ by completing the square.

Rewrite the equation in $x^2 + bx = c$ form.	$x^2 + 6x = 7$
Find $\left(\frac{b}{2}\right)^2$.	$\left(\frac{b}{2}\right)^2 = \left(\frac{6}{2}\right)^2 = 3^2 = 9$
Add $\left(\frac{b}{2}\right)^2$ to each side.	$x^2 + 6x + 9 = 7 + 9$
Factor and simplify.	$(x + 3)^2 = 16$
Find square roots.	$x + 3 = \pm 4$
Rewrite as two equations.	$x + 3 = 4$ or $x + 3 = -4$
Solve for x.	$x = 1$ or $x = -7$

Exercises

Solve each equation by finding square roots.

16. $4x^2 = 16$

17. $4x^2 - 20 = 0$

18. $5x^2 - 45 = 0$

19. $3x^2 = 36$

What value completes each square?

20. $x^2 - 6x$

21. $x^2 + 3x$

Solve each equation by completing the square.

22. $x^2 + 8x + 6 = 0$

23. $x^2 - 10x = 13$

24. $9x^2 + 6x + 1 = 4$

25. $x^2 - 2x + 4 = 0$

26. $x^2 + 3x = -25$

27. $4x^2 - x - 3 = 0$

4-7 The Quadratic Formula

Quick Review

You can solve a quadratic equation in the form
$ax^2 + bx + c = 0$ by using the **Quadratic Formula**,
$x = \frac{-b \pm \sqrt{b^2 - 4ac}}{2a}$.

The **discriminant** of a quadratic equation in standard
form is the value of the expression $b^2 - 4ac$. You can
use it to find the quantity and type of solutions of a
quadratic equation.

Example

Use the Quadratic Formula to solve $2x^2 - 6x = -3$.

Write the equation in standard form.	$2x^2 - 6x + 3 = 0$
Identify a, b, and c.	$a = 2, b = -6, c = 3$
Substitute a, b, and c into the Quadratic Formula.	$x = \frac{-(-6) \pm \sqrt{(-6)^2 - 4(2)(3)}}{2(2)}$
Simplify.	$x = \frac{6 \pm \sqrt{12}}{4} = \frac{3 \pm \sqrt{3}}{2}$

Exercises

Solve each equation using the Quadratic Formula.

28. $3x^2 + 5x = 8$ **29.** $x^2 = 6x - 9$

30. $x(x - 3) = 4$ **31.** $5x^2 - 7x - 3 = 0$

Determine the discriminant of each equation. How many real solutions does each equation have?

32. $4x^2 - 2x = 10$ **33.** $x^2 - 5x + 7 = 0$

34. $3x^2 + 3 = 6x$ **35.** $7 - 3x = 8x^2$

36. Gardening Margaret is planning a
rectangular garden. Its length is 4 ft less
than twice its width. Its area is 170 ft^2.
What are the dimensions of the garden?

4-8 Complex Numbers

Quick Review

A **complex number** is written in the form $a + bi$,
where a and b are real numbers, and i is equal to $\sqrt{-1}$.
If $b = 0$, $a + bi$ is a real number. If $b \neq 0$, $a + bi$ is an
imaginary number. You can use the Quadratic Formula
or completing the square to find the imaginary solutions of
quadratic equations.

Example

Use the Quadratic Formula to solve $3x^2 - 4x + 2 = 0$.

Enter a, b, and c into the Quadratic Formula.	$x = \frac{-(-4) \pm \sqrt{(-4)^2 - 4(3)(2)}}{2(3)}$
Simplify.	$x = \frac{4 \pm \sqrt{16 - 24}}{6} = \frac{4 \pm \sqrt{-8}}{6}$
Write the solutions.	$x = \frac{2}{3} \pm \frac{\sqrt{2}}{3}i$

Exercises

Simplify each expression using the imaginary unit i.

37. $\sqrt{-24}$ **38.** $\sqrt{-2} - 3$

39. $(4 + \sqrt{-25})(\sqrt{-100})$ **40.** $2\sqrt{-24} + 6$

Simplify each expression.

41. $(9 + 7i) - (6 - 2i)$ **42.** $(3 + 11i) + (10 + 9i)$

43. $(1 - 9i)(3 + 2i)$ **44.** $(3i)^2 - 3(1 + 5i)$

45. $\frac{4 - 6i}{2i}$ **46.** $\frac{2 - 3i}{1 + 5i}$

Solve each equation.

47. $x^2 + 9 = 0$ **48.** $5x^2 - 2x + 1 = 0$

49. $-x^2 + 4x = 10$ **50.** $7x^2 + 8x = -6$

Do you know HOW?

Sketch a graph of the quadratic function with the given vertex and through the given point. Then write the equation of the parabola in vertex form and describe how the function was transformed from the parent function $y = x^2$.

1. vertex $(0, 0)$, point $(-3, 3)$

2. vertex $(1, 5)$, point $(2, 1)$

Graph each quadratic function. Identify the axis of symmetry, the vertex, and the domain and the range of each function.

3. $y = x^2 - 7$

4. $y = x^2 + 2x + 6$

5. $y = -x^2 + 5x - 3$

Simplify each expression.

6. $\sqrt{-16}$

7. $4\sqrt{-9} - 2$

8. $(2 + 3i)(8 - 5i)$

9. $(-3 + 2i) - (6 + i)$

10. $\frac{4 + 2i}{2 - i}$

Factor each expression completely.

11. $x^2 + 5x - 24$

12. $2y^2 - 8y$

13. $2x^2 + 10x + 12$

14. $3x^2 + 8x - 3$

15. $9w^2 - 30w + 25$

Solve each quadratic equation.

16. $x^2 - 25 = 0$

17. $x^2 - 2x + 3 = 0$

18. $x^2 - 8x = -6$

19. $5x^2 + x + 2 = 0$

Find the additive inverse of each number.

20. $3 - 7i$

21. $-2 + i$

Evaluate the discriminant of each equation. How many real and imaginary solutions does each have?

22. $x^2 + 6x - 7 = 0$

23. $3x^2 - x + 3 = 0$

24. $-4x^2 - 4x + 1 = 0$

Do you UNDERSTAND?

25. Writing Compare graphing a number on the complex plane to graphing a point on the coordinate plane. How are they similar? How are they different?

26. Open-Ended Sketch the graph of a quadratic function $f(x) = ax^2 + bx + c$ that has no real zeros. How does this relate to the solutions of the related equation $ax^2 + bx + c = 0$?

27. Physics A model for the path of a toy rocket is given by $h = 68t - 4.9t^2$, where h is the altitude in meters and t is the time in seconds. Explain how to find both the maximum altitude of the rocket and how long it takes to reach that altitude.

Cumulative Test Prep

Some questions on tests require that you model a word problem with a quadratic function.

Roy has a 400 foot roll of wire. He wants to use it to fence in a rectangular area. What is the maximum area of the enclosed space?

- (A) 20,000 square feet
- (B) 10,000 square feet
- (C) 200 square feet
- (D) 100 square feet

TIP 1

To identify the function, use what you already know. You know that the perimeter of a rectangle is $2(\ell + w)$ and the area is $\ell \cdot w$.

TIP 2

Use the information from the problem. The perimeter is 400, so $2(\ell + w) = 400$. Solve for w: $w = 200 - \ell$.

Think It Through

Substitute for w in the area formula: $A = f(\ell) = \ell \cdot (200 - \ell)$
$$= -\ell^2 + 200\ell.$$

The maximum value is the y-coordinate of the vertex, $f\left(-\frac{b}{2a}\right) = f(100) = 10{,}000.$
So, the maximum area Roy can enclose is 10,000 square feet.

The correct answer is B.

Vocabulary Builder

As you solve test items, you must understand the meanings of mathematical terms. Match each term with its mathematical meaning.

A. axis of symmetry

B. discriminant

C. imaginary number

D. Zero-Product Property

E. parabola

F. perfect square trinomial

G. completing the square

I. value of $b^2 - 4ac$ for the equation $ax^2 + bx + c = 0$

II. If $ab = 0$, then $a = 0$ or $b = 0$.

III. line that divides a parabola into two parts that are mirror images

IV. $a + bi$, a and b are real numbers and $b \neq 0$

V. square of a binomial

VI. process of finding the last term to make a perfect square trinomial

VII. graph of a quadratic function

Multiple Choice

Read each question. Then write the letter of the correct answer.

1. Which equation is equivalent to $x^2 + 24x + 100 = -46$?

- (A) $(x + 12)^2 = -2$
- (B) $(x - 12)^2 = -2$
- (C) $(x - 12)^2 = 2$
- (D) $(x + 12)^2 = 2$

2. What is the solution of the following system of equations?

$$\begin{cases} x + y + z = 13 \\ 2x - y = 4 \\ x + z = -3 \end{cases}$$

- (F) $x = 10, y = 16, z = 13$
- (G) $x = 16, y = 28, z = -19$
- (H) $x = 10, y = 16, z = -13$
- (I) $x = -16, y = -28, z = 19$

3. What are the factors of the quadratic function graphed below?

Ⓐ $(x + 3)$ and $(x + 2)$

Ⓑ x and $(x - 6)$

Ⓒ x and $(x + 6)$

Ⓓ $(x - 3)$ and $(x + 2)$

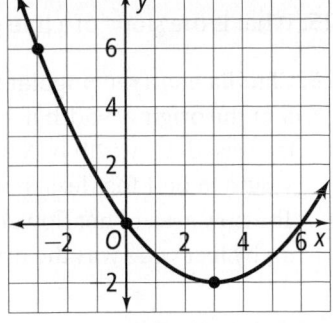

4. Which equation has $-1 \pm i$ as its solution?

Ⓕ $x^2 - 2x - 2 = 0$

Ⓖ $2x^2 - 2x - 1 = 0$

Ⓗ $2x^2 + 2x + 1 = 0$

Ⓘ $x^2 + 2x + 2 = 0$

5. Which number is equivalent to $\sqrt{-169} - 64$?

Ⓐ $8 - 13i$

Ⓒ $-64 - 13i$

Ⓑ $-64 + 13i$

Ⓓ $64 - 13i$

6. The graph of which quadratic function includes the points $(-5, 0)$ and $(-1, 0)$?

Ⓕ $y = (x + 5)^2 - 1$

Ⓖ $y = x^2 + 6x + 5$

Ⓗ $y = x^2 - 6x + 5$

Ⓘ $y = (x - 5)^2 - 1$

7. What transformation of the graph of $y = x^2$ gives the graph of $y = (x + 3)^2 - 2$?

Ⓐ 3 units left and 2 units down

Ⓑ 3 units right and 2 units up

Ⓒ 6 units right and 2 units up

Ⓓ 2 units left and 3 units down

8. What is the axis of symmetry for the graph of the quadratic equation $y = -3x^2 - 12 + 12x$?

Ⓕ $x = -2$

Ⓗ $x = 12$

Ⓖ $x = 2$

Ⓘ $x = -12$

9. What are the domain and range of the function graphed below?

Ⓐ Domain: All real numbers
Range: All real numbers ≤ 3

Ⓑ Domain: All real numbers
Range: All real numbers ≥ 3

Ⓒ Domain: All real numbers between -5 and -1
Range: All real numbers ≤ 3

Ⓓ Domain: All real numbers between -5 and -1
Range: All real numbers ≥ 3

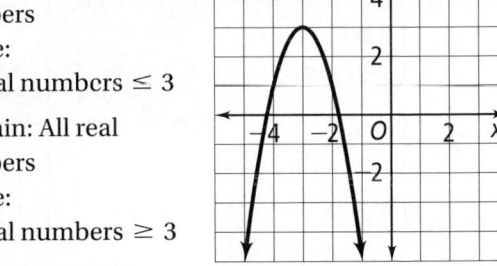

10. Which equation DOES NOT represent a direct variation?

Ⓕ $x - 5y = 0$

Ⓗ $y + 5 = 3x - 5$

Ⓖ $\frac{y}{x} = \frac{4}{3}$

Ⓘ $x = \frac{y}{-5}$

11. What is the solution of $\begin{cases} -y = 3x - 1 \\ 2y = -x - 2 \end{cases}$?

Ⓐ $x = 20, y = -11$

Ⓒ $x = -20, y = 11$

Ⓑ $x = \frac{4}{5}, y = -\frac{7}{5}$

Ⓓ $x = -\frac{4}{5}, y = \frac{7}{5}$

12. Which system of equations is graphed below?

Ⓕ $\begin{cases} y - 3 = 5x \\ y - x = 3 \end{cases}$

Ⓖ $\begin{cases} y + 3 = 5x \\ y + x = 3 \end{cases}$

Ⓗ $\begin{cases} -y + 3 = -5x \\ y + x = -3 \end{cases}$

Ⓘ $\begin{cases} y + 3 = -5x \\ -y + x = 3 \end{cases}$

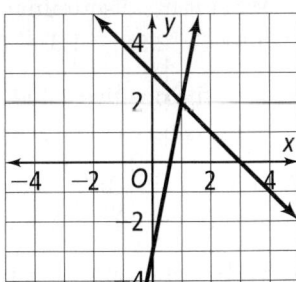

13. What is the vertex of $y = -2|x + 4| - 5$?

Ⓐ $(-2, -5)$

Ⓒ $(4, -5)$

Ⓑ $(-4, -5)$

Ⓓ $(2, -5)$

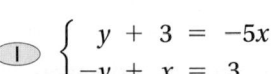

14. Which system of inequalities is graphed below?

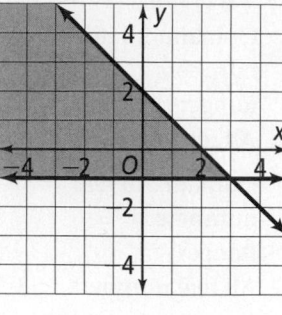

Ⓕ $\begin{cases} y \le -1 \\ y + x \ge 2 \end{cases}$

Ⓖ $\begin{cases} y \ge -1 \\ y + x \le 2 \end{cases}$

Ⓗ $\begin{cases} y < 1 \\ y + x > -2 \end{cases}$

Ⓘ $\begin{cases} y > 1 \\ y + x < -2 \end{cases}$

15. What are the solutions of $|3x - 5| = 2$?

Ⓐ $x = -1$ and $x = \frac{7}{3}$

Ⓑ $x = 1$ and $x = \frac{7}{3}$

Ⓒ $x = 1$ and $x = \frac{1}{5}$

Ⓓ $x = -1$ and $x = \frac{1}{5}$

16. The formula for the total surface area of a regular right pentagonal prism is $A = ap + pH$. Solve this equation for p.

Ⓕ $p = \frac{a + H}{A}$

Ⓗ $p = A - \frac{a}{H}$

Ⓖ $p = \frac{A}{a + H}$

Ⓘ $p = \frac{H - a}{A}$

GRIDDED RESPONSE

17. What is the discriminant of the equation $1.5x^2 - 2.5x - 1.5 = 0$?

18. Find the positive value of k that would make the expression $4x^2 + kx + 4$ a perfect square trinomial.

19. When $y = -3x^2 - 18x - 23$ is written in vertex form $y = a(x - h)^2 + k$, what is the value of k?

20. What is the value of x in the system of equations $\begin{cases} 2y = x - 2 \\ y - x = -3 \end{cases}$?

21. Line A is perpendicular to $x + 3y = 5$ and passes through the point $(-1, 1)$. What is the y-intercept of Line A?

22. What is the slope of the line that passes through $(5, 1)$ and $(-3, -2)$?

23. What is the sum of the zeros of $f(x) = x^2 - 2x - 8$?

24. A piggy bank contains $2.40 in nickels and dimes. If there are 33 coins in all, how many nickels are there?

25. What is the slope of a line parallel to $3y - 7x = 15$?

26. Claudia has a rectangular flowerbed. She decided that the original width w, in feet, was too small, so she increased the width by 3 feet. She also changed the length to be 1 foot less than twice the original width. The new area of her flowerbed is 72 square feet. How many feet wide was the original flowerbed?

Short Response

27. A swimmer swam 1000 meters downstream in 15 minutes and swam back in 30 minutes against the current. What was the rate of the swimmer in still water? How fast was the current?

28. A horticulturalist is building a fence around a rectangular garden using the side of a building for one side of the enclosure. She has 81 feet of fencing. What should the dimensions of the enclosure be so that she can maximize the garden's area?

29. Explain how you would graph $y + 4 < 2|x - 3|$ on a coordinate grid.

Extended Response

30. A hat company is designing a one-size-fits-all hat with a strap in the back that makes the hat smaller or larger. Head sizes normally range from 51 to 64 centimeters. What absolute value inequality models the different sizes of the hat? Graph the solution.

31. Robby decided to earn extra money by making and selling brownies and cookies. He had space in his oven to make at most 80 brownies and cookies. Each brownie cost $.10 to make and each cookie cost $.05 to make. He had $6 to spend on ingredients.
 a. Write a system of inequalities to represent the situation.
 b. Graph the system, choose one point in the feasible region, and explain what the point means in terms of the problem.
 c. If Robby makes a profit of $.25 on each brownie and $.20 on each cookie, how many of each dessert should he make to maximize his profit?

Get Ready!

Lesson 4-2 ◀ **Graphing Quadratic Functions**

Graph each function.

1. $f(x) = x^2 - 8x + 7$ **2.** $f(x) = -\frac{1}{2}x^2 - 4x - 4$ **3.** $f(x) = x^2 + 4x + 4$

Lesson 4-3 ◀ **Writing Equations of Parabolas**

Write in standard form the equation of the parabola passing through the given points.

4. $(-1, -6), (-3, -4), (2, 6)$ **5.** $(3, 4), (-2, 9), (2, 1)$ **6.** $(-5, -8), (4, -8), (-3, 6)$

Lesson 4-5 ◀ **Solving Quadratic Equations by Graphing**

Solve each equation by graphing. If necessary, round to the nearest hundredth.

7. $1 = 4x^2 + 3x$ **8.** $\frac{1}{2}x^2 + x - 14 = 0$ **9.** $5x^2 + 30x = 12$

Lesson 4-5 ◀ **Solving Quadratic Equations by Factoring**

Solve each equation by factoring.

10. $x^2 - x - 20 = 0$ **11.** $x^2 + 6x - 27 = 0$ **12.** $3x^2 - 9x + 6 = 0$

Lesson 4-7 ◀ **Finding the Number and Type of Solutions**

Evaluate the discriminant of each equation. Tell how many solutions each equation has and whether the solutions are real or imaginary.

13. $x^2 - 12x + 30 = 0$ **14.** $-4x^2 + 20x - 25 = 0$ **15.** $2x^2 = 8x - 8$

Looking Ahead Vocabulary

16. A *turning point* is a place where a graph changes direction. Suppose you start hiking north on a winding trail, and the trail makes a turn and heads south, and then north again. If you make a total of 3 of these 180 degree turns, in which direction will you be hiking after the last turn?

17. A *relative maximum* is the greatest value in a region. The highest point in Maine is Mt. Katahdin at 5267 ft. How might that compare to the highest point in the United States? What might the relative maximum of a graph be?

18. A contraction is a shortened form of a word or phrase. The expanded form of the contraction "don't" is "do not." You can *expand* a math phrase by multiplying it out. For example, $(x - 2)^2 = (x - 2)(x - 2) = x^2 - 4x + 4$. Expand $(2x + 1)^2$.

Polynomials and Polynomial Functions

Polynomial functions are used to model all kinds of real-world situations, like the energy produced by a turbine.

In this chapter, you will also learn theorems that will help you when working with polynomial functions and equations.

Vocabulary for Part A

English/Spanish Vocabulary Audio Online:

English	Spanish
end behavior, *p. 294*	comportamiento extremo
monomial, *p. 292*	monomio
multiplicity, *p. 304*	multiplicidad
polynomial function, *p. 293*	función polinomial
relative maximum, *p. 305*	máximo relativo
relative minimum, *p. 305*	mínimo relativo
standard form of a polynomial function, *p. 293*	forma normal de una función polinomial
synthetic division, *p. 322*	división sintética
turning point, *p. 294*	punto de giro

My Math Video

00:04:04

VIDEO

BIG ideas

1 Function

Essential Question What does the degree of a polynomial tell you about its related polynomial function?

2 Equivalence

Essential Question For a polynomial function, how are factors, zeros, and *x*-intercepts related?

3 Solving Equations and Inequalities

Essential Question For a polynomial equation, how are factors and roots related?

Chapter Preview for Part A

5-1 Polynomial Functions

Objectives To classify polynomials
To graph polynomial functions and describe end behavior

Working backwards unlocks the patterns.

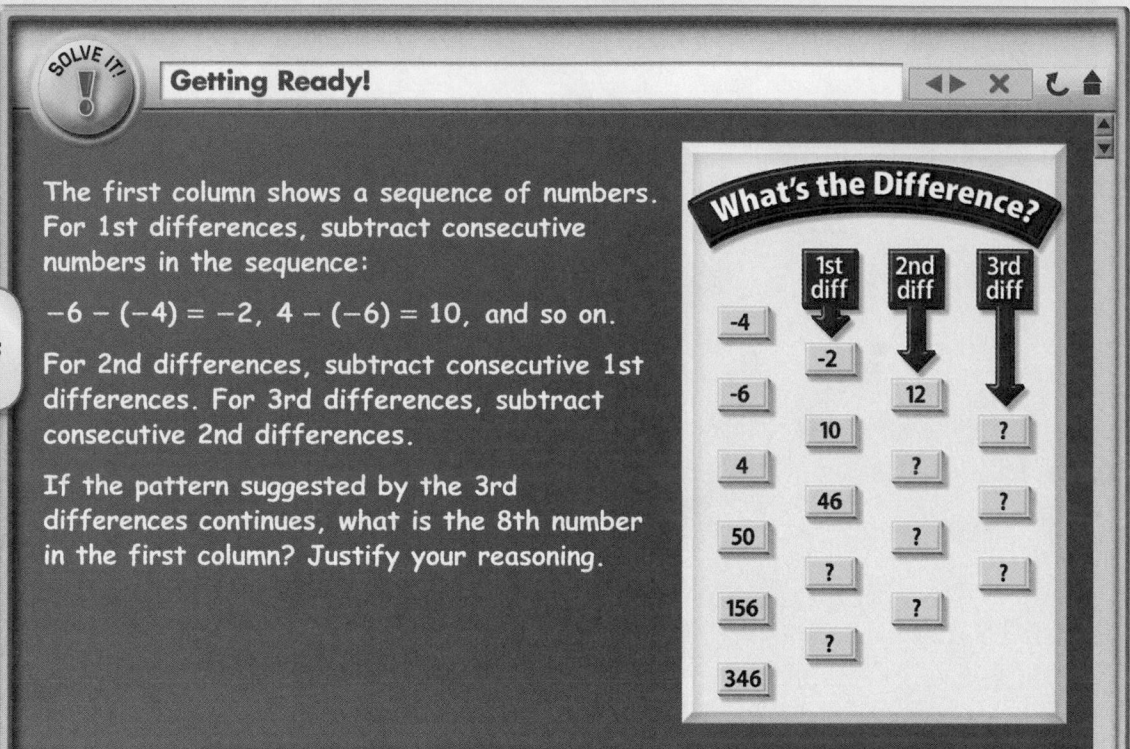

What's the Difference?

The sequence of numbers in the first column in the Solve It are values of a particular *polynomial function.* For such a sequence, you can use patterns of 1st differences, 2nd differences, 3rd differences, and so on, to learn more about the polynomial function.

Focus Question What is a polynomial function?

Lesson Vocabulary
• monomial
• degree of a monomial
• polynomial
• degree of a polynomial
• polynomial function
• standard form of a polynomial function
• turning point
• end behavior

A **monomial** is a real number, a variable, or a product of a real number and one or more variables with whole-number exponents. The **degree of a monomial** in one variable is the exponent of the variable. A **polynomial** is a monomial or a sum of monomials. The **degree of a polynomial** in one variable is the greatest degree among its monomial terms.

Monomial:

$3x^4$

The degree is 4.

Polynomial:

$2x^5 + 3x^4 - 6x + 1$

The degree is 5.

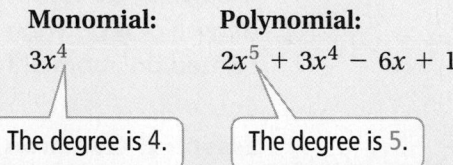

A polynomial with the variable x defines a **polynomial function** of x. The degree of the polynomial function is the same as the degree of the polynomial.

take note

Key Concept   Standard Form of a Polynomial Function

The **standard form of a polynomial function** arranges the terms by degree in descending numerical order.

A polynomial function $P(x)$ in standard form is

$$P(x) = a_n x^n + a_{n-1} x^{n-1} + \cdots + a_1 x + a_0,$$

where n is a nonnegative integer and $a_n, \ldots, a_0$ are real numbers.

$$P(x) = 4x^3 + 3x^2 + 5x - 2$$

| Cubic term | Quadratic term | Linear term | Constant term |

You can classify a polynomial by its degree or by its number of terms. Polynomials of degrees zero through five have specific names, shown in the table below.

Degree	Name Using Degree	Polynomial Example	Number of Terms	Name Using Number of Terms
0	constant	5	1	monomial
1	linear	$x + 4$	2	binomial
2	quadratic	$4x^2$	1	monomial
3	cubic	$4x^3 - 2x^2 + x$	3	trinomial
4	quartic	$2x^4 + 5x^2$	2	binomial
5	quintic	$-x^5 + 4x^2 + 2x + 1$	4	polynomial of 4 terms

ONLINE PROBLEMS

Problem 1 Classifying Polynomials

Write each polynomial in standard form. What is the classification of each polynomial by degree and number of terms?

A $3x + 9x^2 + 5$

$9x^2 + 3x + 5$

The polynomial has degree 2 and 3 terms. It is a quadratic trinomial.

B $4x - 6x^2 + x^4 + 10x^2 - 12$

$x^4 + 4x^2 + 4x - 12$

The polynomial has degree 4 and 4 terms. It is a quartic polynomial of 4 terms.

Got It? **1.** Write each polynomial in standard form. What is the classification of each polynomial by degree and number of terms?

    a. $3x^3 - x + 5x^4$ **b.** $3 - 4x^5 + 2x^2 + 10$

The degree of a polynomial function affects the shape of its graph. It determines the maximum number of **turning points**, or places where the graph changes direction. It also affects the **end behavior**, or the directions of the graph to the far left and to the far right.

For polynomial functions of degree one or greater, there are four types of end behavior as you move to the left and move to the right, away from the origin:

Up and Up	**Down and Down**	**Down and Up**	**Up and Down**
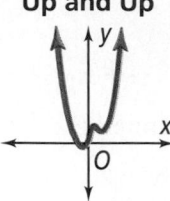	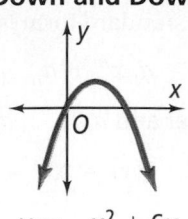	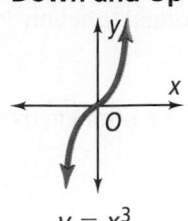	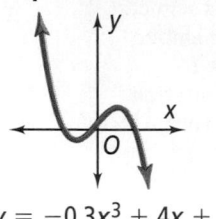
$y = x^4 - 3x^3 + 5x$	$y = -x^2 + 6x$	$y = x^3$	$y = -0.3x^3 + 4x + 2$

You can determine the end behavior of a polynomial function of degree n from the leading term ax^n of the standard form.

End Behavior of a Polynomial Function of Degree n With Leading Term ax^n (Moving Away From the Origin)

	n Even	n Odd
a **Positive**	Up and Up	Down and Up
a **Negative**	Down and Down	Up and Down

Problem 2 **Describing End Behavior of Polynomial Functions**

Consider the leading term of each polynomial function. What is the end behavior of the graph? Check your answer with a graphing calculator.

Ⓐ $y = 4x^3 - 3x$

The leading term is $4x^3$. Since n is odd and a is positive, the end behavior is down and up.

Check

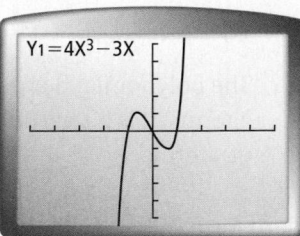

The solution checks.

Ⓑ $y = -2x^4 + 8x^3 - 8x^2 + 2$

The leading term is $-2x^4$. Since n is even and a is negative, the end behavior is down and down.

Check

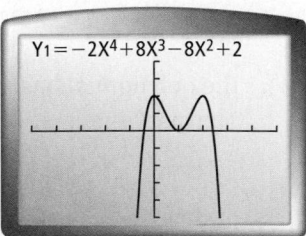

The solution checks.

✅ **Got It?** **2.** Consider the leading term of $y = -4x^3 + 2x^2 + 7$. What is the end behavior of the graph?

In general, the graph of a polynomial function of degree n (where $n \geq 1$) has at most $n - 1$ turning points. The graph of a polynomial function of odd degree has an even number of turning points. The graph of a polynomial function of even degree has an odd number of turning points. This information, combined with end behavior, determines possible shapes that the graph of a polynomial function can have.

Hint
Compare the turning point relationships with the end behavior relationships on the previous page.

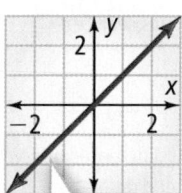

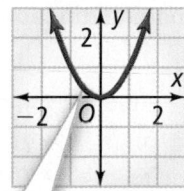

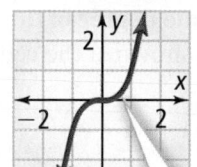

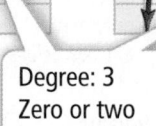

Degree: 1
Zero turning point

Degree: 2
One turning point

Degree: 3
Zero or two turning points

Problem 3 **Graphing Cubic Functions**

What is the graph of each cubic function? Describe the graph.

Ⓐ $y = \frac{1}{2}x^3$

Ⓑ $y = 2x - x^3$

Step 1 Make a table of values.

Step 1 Make a table of values.

Step 2 Plot the points and sketch the graph.

Step 2 Plot the points and sketch the graph.

Plan
How can you graph a polynomial function?
Make a table of values to help you sketch the graph near the origin. Use what you know about end behavior to sketch the graph moving out from the origin.

x	y
−2	4
−1	−0.5
0	0
1	0.5
2	4

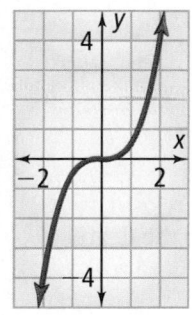

x	y
−2	4
−1	−1
0	0
1	1
2	−4

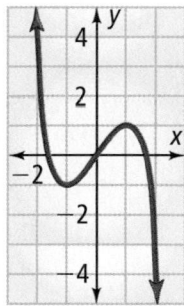

Step 3 The end behavior is down and up. There are no turning points.

Step 3 The end behavior is up and down. There are two turning points.

✅ **Got It?** **3.** What is the graph of each cubic function? Describe the graph.
   a. $y = -x^3 + 2x^2 - x - 2$ **b.** $y = x^3 - 1$

Suppose you are given a set of function outputs. You know that their corresponding inputs are an ordered set of *x*-values in which consecutive *x*-values differ by a constant. By analyzing the differences of consecutive *y*-values, it is possible to determine the least-degree polynomial function that could generate the data.

If the first differences are constant, the function is linear. If the second differences (but not the first) are constant, the function is quadratic. If the third differences (but not the second) are constant, the function is cubic, and so on.

Problem 4 Using Differences to Determine Degree

What is the degree of the polynomial function that generates the data shown at the right?

x	y
−3	−1
−2	−7
−1	−3
0	5
1	11
2	9
3	−7

Know → A set of polynomial function values

Need → Degree of the polynomial function

Plan →
• Check first differences of *y*-values.
• Check second differences, third differences, and so on until they are constant.

Think

How do you find the second differences?
Subtract the consecutive first differences.

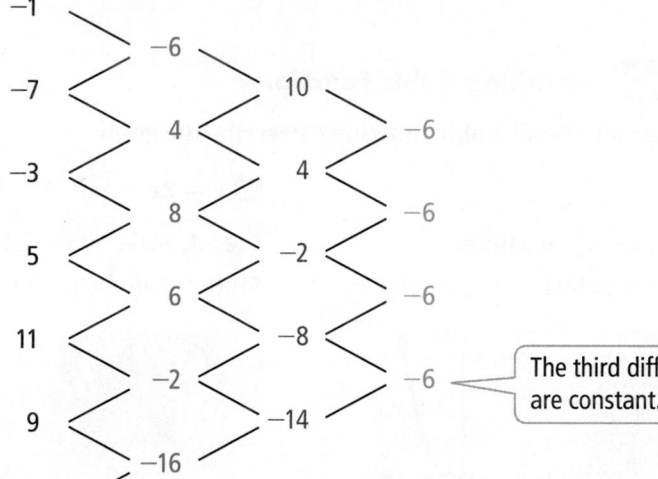

The third differences are constant.

The 3rd differences are constant, so the degree of the polynomial function is 3.

 Got It? **4. a.** What is the degree of the polynomial function that generates the data shown at the right?
b. Reasoning What is an example of a polynomial function whose fifth differences are constant but whose fourth differences are not constant?

x	y
−3	23
−2	−16
−1	−15
0	−10
1	−13
2	−12
3	29

Focus Question What is a polynomial function?

Answer A polynomial function $P(x)$ is a sum of monomial terms with the variable x classified by degree and number of terms. The algebraic form of a polynomial function and the behavior of its graph are related. Use one to find the other.

Lesson Check

Do you know HOW?

Classify each polynomial by degree and by number of terms.

1. $5x^3$

2. $6x^2 + 4x - 2$

Write each polynomial in standard form.

3. $7x + 3 + 5x^2$

4. $-3 + 9x$

Do you UNDERSTAND?

5. Vocabulary Describe the end behavior of the function $y = -2x^7 - 8x$.

6. Reasoning Can the graph of a polynomial function be a straight line? If so, give an example.

7. Error Analysis Your friend claims the graph of the function $y = 4x^3 + 4$ has only one turning point. Describe the error your friend made and give the correct number of turning points.

Practice and Problem-Solving Exercises

Ⓐ Practice Write each polynomial in standard form. Then classify it by degree and by number of terms.

◀ See Problem 1.

Guided Practice

To start, write the terms of the polynomial with their degrees in descending order.

8. $2m^2 - 3 + 7m$

$2m^2 + 7m - 3$

9. $7x + 3x + 5$

10. $5 - 3x$

11. $-x^3 + x^4 + x$

12. $-4p + 3p + 2p^2$

13. $5a^2 + 3a^3 + 1$

14. $-x^5$

15. $3 + 12x^4$

16. $7x^3 - 10x^3 + x^3$

17. $4x + 5x^2 + 8$

Determine the end behavior of the graph of each polynomial function.

◀ See Problem 2.

18. $y = -7x^3 + 8x^2 + x$

19. $y = -3x + 6x^2 - 1$

20. $y = 1 - 4x - 6x^3 - 15x^6$

21. $y = 8x^{11} - 2x^9 + 3x^6 + 4$

22. $y = -3 - 6x^5 - 9x^8$

23. $y = x^4 - 7x^2 + 3$

Describe the shape of the graph of each cubic function by determining the end behavior and number of turning points.

◀ See Problem 3.

Guided Practice

24. $y = 3x^3 - x - 3$

To start, make a table of values to help you sketch the middle part of the graph.

x	y
−1	−5
−0.5	−2.9
0	3
0.5	−3.1
1	−1

25. $y = -9x^3 - 2x^2 + 5x + 3$　　**26.** $y = 10x^3 + 9$　　　　　　**27.** $y = 3x^3$

Determine the degree of the polynomial function with the given data.

◀ See Problem 4.

28.

x	y
−2	16
−1	7
0	2
1	1
2	4

29.

x	y
−2	−15
−1	−9
0	−9
1	−9
2	−3

B Apply

30. Think About a Plan The data shows the power generated by a wind turbine. The *x* column gives the wind speed in meters per second. The *y* column gives the power generated in kilowatts. What is the degree of the polynomial function that models the data?
- What are the first differences of the *y*-values?
- What are the second differences of the *y*-values?
- When are the differences constant?

x	y
5	10
6	17.28
7	27.44
8	40.96
9	58.32

Classify each polynomial by degree and by number of terms. Simplify first if necessary.

31. $a^2 + a^3 - 4a^4$　　　　　　　　　　　**32.** $2x(3x)$

33. $(2a - 5)(a^2 - 1)$　　　　　　　　　**34.** $(-8d^3 - 7) + (-d^3 - 6)$

35. Show that the third differences of a polynomial function of degree 3 are nonzero and constant. First, use $f(x) = x^3 - 3x^2 - 2x - 6$. Then show that the third differences are nonzero and constant for $f(x) = ax^3 + bx^2 + cx + d, a \neq 0$.

36. Make a table of second differences for each polynomial function. Using your tables, make a conjecture about the second differences of quadratic functions.

    a. $y = 7x^2$ **b.** $y = 7x^2 + 1$ **c.** $y = 7x^2 + 3x + 1$

Determine the sign of the leading coefficient and the least possible degree of the polynomial function for each graph.

37. 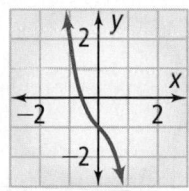   **38.** 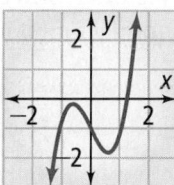   **39.**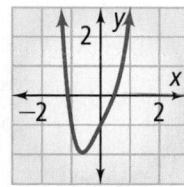

40. Open-Ended Write an equation for a polynomial function that has three turning points and end behavior up and up.

Standardized Test Prep

SAT/ACT

41. Which expression is a cubic polynomial?

     Ⓐ x^3 Ⓑ $3x + 3$ Ⓒ $2x^2 + 3x - 1$ Ⓓ $3x$

42. Which equation has $-3 \pm 5i$ as its solutions?

     Ⓕ $x^2 + 6x = -34$ Ⓖ $x^2 + 6x = -14$ Ⓗ $x^2 + 3x = 4$ Ⓘ $x^2 + 3x = 2$

43. What is the discriminant of $qx^2 + rx + s = 0$?

     Ⓐ qrs Ⓑ $q^2 - 4rs$ Ⓒ $r^2 - 4qs$ Ⓓ $s^2 - 4qr$

Short Response

44. What is a simpler form of $x^2(3x^2 - 2x) - 3x^4$? Classify the polynomial by degree and by number of terms.

Mixed Review

Find the sum or difference.   ◆ **See Lesson 4-8.**

45. $(1 - i) + (-5 + 4i)$ **46.** $(3 + 4i) - (-4 - 3i)$ **47.** $(1 + i) + (2 + 2i)$

Write an equation of each line in standard form with integer coefficients.   ◆ **See Lesson 2-4.**

48. $y = 7x + 0.4$ **49.** $y = -3x - 2.5$ **50.** $y = -\frac{2}{7}x + 4$

Get Ready!   **To prepare for Lesson 5-2, do Exercises 51–53.**

Factor each quadratic expression.   ◆ **See Lesson 4-4.**

51. $x^2 + 7x + 12$ **52.** $x^2 + 8x - 20$ **53.** $x^2 - 14x + 24$

5-2
PART 1

Polynomials, Linear Factors, and Zeros

Objectives To analyze the factored form of a polynomial
To write a polynomial function from its zeros

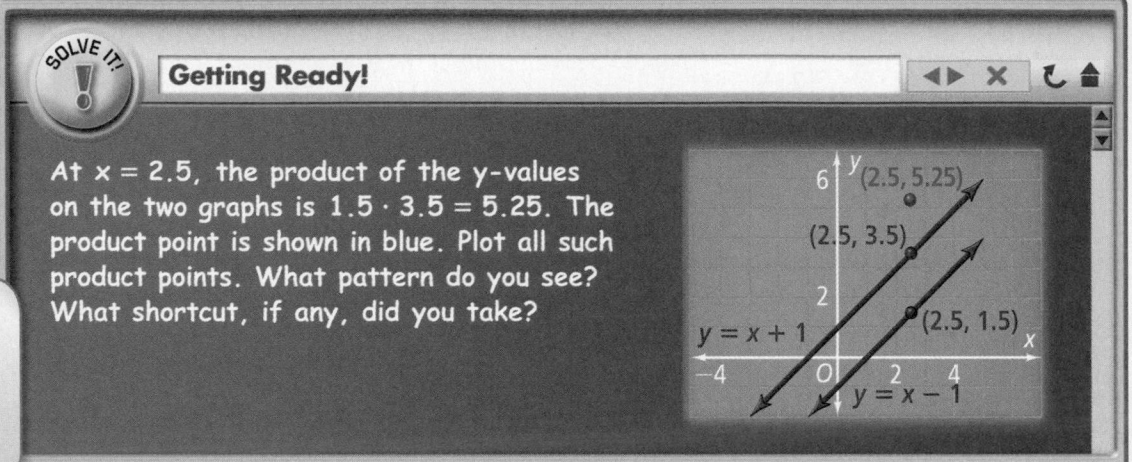

SOLVE IT!

Getting Ready!   ◄► ✕ ↺ ⬆

At x = 2.5, the product of the y-values on the two graphs is 1.5 · 3.5 = 5.25. The product point is shown in blue. Plot all such product points. What pattern do you see? What shortcut, if any, did you take?

6 y (2.5, 5.25)
(2.5, 3.5)
2
$y = x + 1$ (2.5, 1.5)
−4 O 2 4 x
$y = x − 1$

You plot <u>all</u> points based on the pattern. If you calculate for every point, you'll never get done.

Dynamic Activity
Polynomials and Linear Factors

Lesson Vocabulary
• Factor Theorem

If $P(x)$ is a polynomial function, the solutions of the related polynomial equation $P(x) = 0$ are the zeros of the function. Finding the zeros of a polynomial function will help you factor the polynomial, graph the function, and solve the related polynomial equation.

Focus Question What are the zeros of a polynomial function?

In Chapter 4, you solved a quadratic equation of the form $x^2 + bx + c = 0$ by factoring. You wrote it using *linear factors* in the form $(x − r_1)(x − r_2) = 0$. Then you applied the Zero-Product Property to find the solutions $x = r_1$ and $x = r_2$. You can solve some polynomial equations $a_n x^n + a_{n-1} x^{n-1} + \cdots + a_1 x + a_0 = 0$ in much the same way.

Plan

How do you write the factored form of a polynomial?
Write the polynomial as a product of factors. Make sure each factor cannot be factored any further.

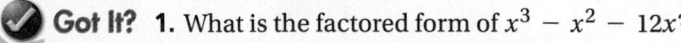

Problem 1 Writing a Polynomial in Factored Form

What is the factored form of $x^3 − 2x^2 − 15x$?

Write the original expression. $x^3 − 2x^2 − 15x$

Factor out the GCF, x. $x(x^2 − 2x − 15)$

Factor $x^2 − 2x − 15$. $x(x − 5)(x + 3)$

Check Multiply $(x − 5)(x + 3)$. $x(x − 5)(x + 3) = x(x^2 − 2x − 15)$

Use the Distributive Property. $= x^3 − 2x^2 − 15x$ ✔

✅ **Got It?** **1.** What is the factored form of $x^3 − x^2 − 12x$?

take note

Key Concepts Roots, Zeros, and x-intercepts

The following are equivalent statements about a real number b and a polynomial $P(x) = a_n x^n + a_{n-1} x^{n-1} + \cdots + a_1 x + a_0$.

- $x - b$ is a linear factor of the polynomial $P(x)$.
- b is a zero of the polynomial function $y = P(x)$.
- b is a root (or solution) of the polynomial equation $P(x) = 0$.
- b is an x-intercept of the graph of $y = P(x)$.

Problem 2 Finding Zeros of a Polynomial Function

What are the zeros of $y = (x + 2)(x - 1)(x - 3)$? Graph the function.

Know	Need	Plan
Polynomial function	• Zeros • Additional points • End behavior	• Use the Zero-Product Property to find zeros. • Find points between the zeros. • Sketch the graph.

Step 1 Use the Zero-Product Property to find the zeros.

$$(x + 2)(x - 1)(x - 3) = 0$$

$$x + 2 = 0 \quad x - 1 = 0 \quad x - 3 = 0$$

The zeros of the function are -2, 1, and 3.

Step 2 Find points on the curve for x-values between the zeros.
Evaluate $y = (x + 2)(x - 1)(x - 3)$ for $x = -1, 0,$ and 2.

$$(-1 + 2)(-1 - 1)(-1 - 3) = (1)(-2)(-4)$$
$$= 8 \qquad \rightarrow (-1, 8)$$

$$(0 + 2)(0 - 1)(0 - 3) = (2)(-1)(-3)$$
$$= 6 \qquad \rightarrow (0, 6)$$

$$(2 + 2)(2 - 1)(2 - 3) = (4)(1)(-1)$$
$$= -4 \qquad \rightarrow (2, -4)$$

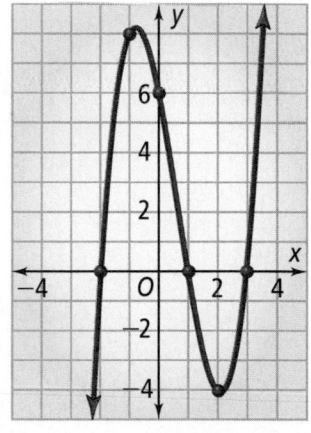

Step 3 Determine the end behavior.

The function $y = (x + 2)(x - 1)(x - 3)$ is cubic. The coefficient of x^3 is $+1$, so the end behavior is *down and up*.

Step 4 Use the zeros: $(-2, 0)$, $(1, 0)$, $(3, 0)$; the additional points: $(-1, 8)$, $(0, 6)$, $(2, -4)$; and end behavior to sketch the graph.

Got It? **2.** What are the zeros of $y = x(x - 3)(x + 5)$? Graph the function.

The Factor Theorem describes the relationship between the linear factors of a polynomial and the zeros of a polynomial.

Hint

Recall the Zero-Product Property in Chapter 4, which you used to find zeros of a quadratic equation.

take note

Theorem   Factor Theorem

The expression $x - a$ is a factor of a polynomial if and only if the value a is a zero of the related polynomial function.

Problem 3 Writing a Polynomial Function From Its Zeros

A **What cubic polynomial function in standard form has zeros −2, 2, and 3?**

Plan

How can you use the zeros to find the function?
By the Factor Theorem, a is a zero means that $x - a$ is a factor of the related polynomial.

−2, 2, and 3 are zeros.

$$\begin{array}{ccc} -2 & 2 & 3 \\ \downarrow & \downarrow & \downarrow \end{array}$$

Write a linear factor for each zero. $f(x) = (x + 2)(x - 2)(x - 3)$

Multiply $(x - 2)$ and $(x - 3)$. $= (x + 2)(x^2 - 5x + 6)$

Use the Distributive Property. $= x(x^2 - 5x + 6) + 2(x^2 - 5x + 6)$

Use the Distributive Property. $= x^3 - 5x^2 + 6x + 2x^2 - 10x + 12$

Group like terms. $= x^3 - 5x^2 + 2x^2 + 6x - 10x + 12$

Simplify. $= x^3 - 3x^2 - 4x + 12$

The cubic polynomial $f(x) = x^3 - 3x^2 - 4x + 12$ has zeros −2, 2, and 3.

B **What quartic polynomial function in standard form has zeros −2, −2, 2, and 3?**

−2, −2, 2, and 3 are zeros.

$$\begin{array}{cccc} -2 & -2 & 2 & 3 \\ \downarrow & \downarrow & \downarrow & \downarrow \end{array}$$

Write a linear factor for each zero. $g(x) = \underline{(x + 2)(x + 2)}\,\underline{(x - 2)(x - 3)}$

Multiply each pair of linear factors. $= (x^2 + 4x + 4)(x^2 - 5x + 6)$

Use the Distributive Property. $= x^2(x^2 - 5x + 6) + 4x(x^2 - 5x + 6)$
$\qquad + 4(x^2 - 5x + 6)$

Use the Distributive Property. $= x^4 - 5x^3 + 6x^2 + 4x^3 - 20x^2 + 24x$
Identify like terms. $\qquad + 4x^2 - 20x + 24$

Combine like terms. $= x^4 - x^3 - 10x^2 + 4x + 24$

The quartic polynomial $g(x) = x^4 - x^3 - 10x^2 + 4x + 24$ has zeros −2, −2, 2, and 3.

Got It? 3. a. What quadratic polynomial function has zeros 3 and −3?

b. What cubic polynomial function has zeros 3, 3, and −3?

c. Reasoning Graph both functions. How do the graphs differ? How are they similar?

Focus Question What are the zeros of a polynomial function?

Answer A zero of a polynomial function $P(x)$ is a solution of the equation $P(x) = 0$. Use the Factor Theorem to find zeros given the polynomial as the product of linear factors.

Lesson Check

Do you know HOW?

Find the zeros of each function.

1. $y = x(x - 6)$ **2.** $y = (x + 4)(x - 5)$

3. $y = (x + 12)(x - 9)(x - 7)$

4. Write a polynomial function in standard form with zeros -1, 1, and 0.

Do you UNDERSTAND?

5. Error Analysis Your friend says that to write a function that has zeros 3 and -1, you should multiply the two factors $(x + 3)$ and $(x - 1)$ to get $f(x) = x^2 + 2x - 3$. Describe and correct your friend's error.

Practice and Problem-Solving Exercises

**Practice**

Write each polynomial in factored form. Check by multiplication.

🔹 **See Problem 1.**

Guided Practice

To start, factor out the GCF, x.

6. $x^3 + 7x^2 + 10x$

$x(x^2 + 7x + 10)$

7. $x^3 - x^2 - 6x$ **8.** $x^3 - 7x^2 - 18x$ **9.** $x^3 - 4x^2 - 21x$

10. $x^3 - 36x$ **11.** $x^3 + 8x^2 + 16x$ **12.** $9x^3 + 6x^2 - 3x$

Find the zeros of each function. Then graph the function.

🔹 **See Problem 2.**

13. $y = (x - 1)(x + 2)$ **14.** $y = (x - 2)(x + 9)$ **15.** $y = x(x + 5)(x - 8)$

16. $y = (x + 1)(x - 2)(x - 3)$ **17.** $y = (x + 1)(x - 1)(x - 2)$ **18.** $y = x(x + 2)(x + 3)$

Write a polynomial function in standard form with the given zeros.

🔹 **See Problem 3.**

Guided Practice

To start, write a linear factor for each zero.

19. $x = -2, 0, 1$

$(x - (-2))(x - 0)(x - 1)$

20. $x = 5, 6, 7$ **21.** $x = -5, -5, 1$ **22.** $x = 3, 3, 3$

23. $x = 1, -1, -2$ **24.** $x = -1, -2, -3, -4$ **25.** $x = 0, 0, 2, 3$

**Apply**

Write each function in factored form. Check by multiplication.

26. $y = 3x^3 - 27x^2 + 24x$ **27.** $y = -2x^3 - 2x^2 + 40x$ **28.** $y = x^4 + 3x^3 - 4x^2$

29. Which polynomial function has zeros at -4, 3, and 5?

    Ⓐ $f(x) = (x + 4)(x + 3)(x + 5)$ Ⓒ $h(x) = (x - 4)(x - 3)(x - 5)$

    Ⓑ $g(x) = (x + 4)(x - 3)(x - 5)$ Ⓓ $k(x) = (x - 4)(x + 3)(x + 5)$

30. Writing Explain how the graph of a polynomial function can help you factor the polynomial.

5-2
PART 2

Polynomials, Linear Factors, and Zeros

Objectives To analyze the factored form of a polynomial
To identify relative maximums and minimums

In Part 1 of the lesson, you learned about factoring a polynomial function and identifying its zeros.

Connect to What You Know

Here you will explore multiple zeros and the behavior of a polynomial graph near its turning points.

Lesson Vocabulary
- multiple zero
- multiplicity
- relative maximum
- relative minimum

Focus Question When does a polynomial graph have a relative maximum and minimum?

You can write the polynomial function $f(x) = x^4 + 5x^3 + x^2 - 21x - 18$ in factored form as $f(x) = (x + 3)(x + 3)(x + 1)(x - 2)$ or $f(x) = (x + 3)^2(x + 1)(x - 2)$. The repeated linear factor $x + 3$ makes -3 a **multiple zero**.

In particular, since the linear factor $x + 3$ appears twice, you can say that -3 is a zero of **multiplicity** 2. In general, *a is a zero of multiplicity n* means that $x - a$ appears n times as a factor.

$$f(x) = (x + 3)(x + 3)(x + 1)(x - 2) \qquad f(x) = (x + 3)^2(x + 1)(x - 2)$$

multiple zero   multiplicity: 2

Key Concept   How Multiple Zeros Affect a Graph

If a is a zero of multiplicity n in the polynomial function $y = P(x)$, then the behavior of the graph at the x-intercept a will be close to linear for $n = 1$, close to quadratic for $n = 2$, close to cubic for $n = 3$, and so on.

Problem 4 Finding the Multiplicity of a Zero

What are the zeros of $f(x) = x^4 - 2x^3 - 8x^2$? What are their multiplicities? How does the graph behave at these zeros?

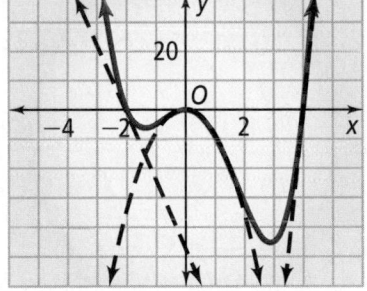

Write the original equation.	$f(x) = x^4 - 2x^3 - 8x^2$
Factor out the GCF, x^2.	$= x^2(x^2 - 2x - 8)$
Factor $(x^2 - 2x - 8)$.	$= x^2(x + 2)(x - 4)$

Think

How can you find the multiplicities?
Factor the polynomial. Find the number of times each linear factor appears.

Since $x^2 = (x - 0)^2$, the number 0 is a zero of multiplicity 2. The numbers -2 and 4 are zeros of multiplicity 1.

The graph looks close to linear at the x-intercepts -2 and 4. It resembles a parabola at the x-intercept 0.

 Got It? 4. What are the zeros of $f(x) = x^3 - 4x^2 + 4x$? What are their multiplicities? How does the graph behave at these zeros?

If the graph of a polynomial function has several turning points, the function can have a *relative maximum* and a *relative minimum*. A **relative maximum** is the value of the function at an up-to-down turning point. A **relative minimum** is the value of the function at a down-to-up turning point.

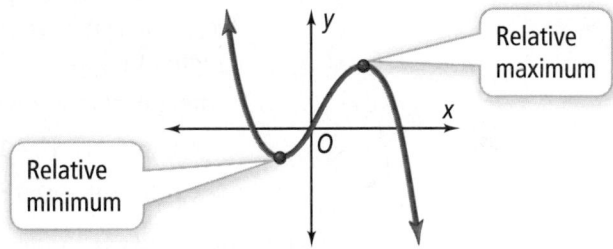

Relative maximum

Relative minimum

 Problem 5 Identifying a Relative Maximum and Minimum

What are the relative maximum and minimum of $f(x) = x^3 + 3x^2 - 24x$?

Think

How is a relative maximum different from a maximum at the vertex of a parabola?
A relative maximum is the greatest y-value in the "neighborhood" of its x-value. The maximum at the vertex of a parabola is the greatest y-value for *all* x-values.

Use a graphing calculator to find the relative maximum and the relative minimum.

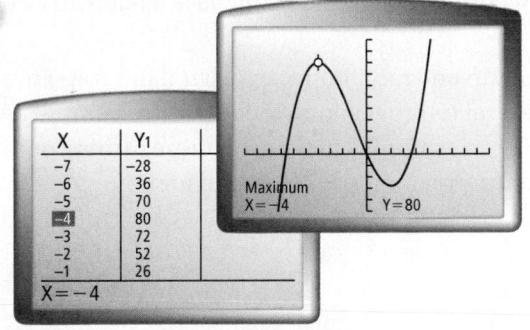

Relative maximum

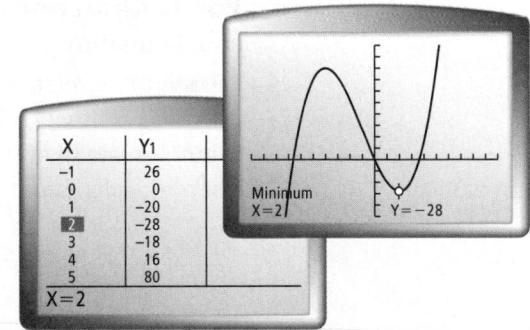

Relative minimum

The relative maximum is 80 at $x = -4$, and the relative minimum is -28 at $x = 2$.

 Got It? 5. What are the relative maximum and minimum of $f(x) = 3x^3 + x^2 - 5x$?

Problem 6 Using a Polynomial Function to Maximize Volume

Technology The length of a digital camera is 1.5 times the height. If the sum of the length, width, and height of the camera must be 6 inches, what dimensions maximize the volume of the camera?

Step 1 Define a variable.
Let $x =$ the height in inches of the camera.

Step 2 Write expressions for the length and width in terms of the height.
$$\text{length} = 1.5 \cdot \text{height} \qquad \text{width} = 6 - (\text{length} + \text{height})$$
$$= 1.5x \qquad\qquad\qquad = 6 - (1.5x + x)$$
$$= 6 - 2.5x$$

> The sum of the dimensions is 6 in.

Think

What is the formula for the volume of a "box"?
$V = \ell wh$

Step 3 Model the volume.

Substitute into $V = \ell wh$. $\qquad V = (1.5x)(6 - 2.5x)(x)$

Use the Distributive Property. $\qquad\quad = (9x - 3.75x^2)x$

Use the Distributive Property. $\qquad\quad = 9x^2 - 3.75x^3$

Step 4 Graph the polynomial function. Use the **MAXIMUM** feature to find that the maximum volume is 7.68 in.^{3} for a height of 1.6 in.

$$\text{height} = x = 1.6$$
$$\text{length} = 1.5x = 1.5\,(1.6) = 2.4$$
$$\text{width} = 6 - 2.5x = 6 - 2.5(1.6) = 2$$

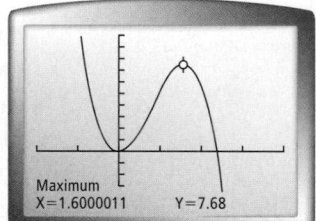

Maximum
X=1.6000011   Y=7.68

The dimensions of the camera should be 2.4 in. long by 2 in. wide by 1.6 in. high.

 Got It? 6. What is the maximum volume of the camera in Problem 6 if the sum of the dimensions is at most 4 inches?

Focus Question When does a polynomial graph have a relative maximum and minimum?

Answer A relative maximum and minimum can occur if the graph of a polynomial function has several turning points. The relative maximum and minimum are the values of the polynomial function at these turning points. Use your calculator to locate any relative maximum and minimum.

Lesson Check

Do you know HOW?

For the function $y = x(x - 4)^3(x + 4)^2$, find the multiplicity of the zero.

1. -4 **2.** 0 **3.** 4

4. Use a graphing calculator to find a relative maximum and a relative minimum of $y = x^3 + x^2 - 17x + 15$.

Do you UNDERSTAND?

5. Vocabulary Write a polynomial function h in standard form that has 3 and -5 as zeros of multiplicity 2.

6. Reasoning Can a cubic function with two turning points have two relative maximums? Explain.

Practice and Problem-Solving Exercises

Ⓐ Practice   Find the zeros of each function. State the multiplicity of multiple zeros.   ◀ See Problem 4.

Guided Practice

To start, identify the zeros.

7. $y = x(x - 1)^3$

The zeros are 0 and 1.

8. $y = 2x^3 + x^2 - x$ **9.** $y = 3x^3 - 3x$

10. $y = (x - 4)^2$ **11.** $y = (x - 2)^2(x - 1)$

12. $y = (2x + 3)(x - 1)^2$ **13.** $y = (x + 1)^2(x - 1)(x - 2)$

Find the relative maximum and relative minimum of the graph of each function.   ◀ See Problem 5.

Guided Practice

To start, use a graphing calculator. (An appropriate viewing window is $-10 \le x \le 10$ and $-5 \le y \le 25$.)

14. $f(x) = x^3 + 4x^2 - 5x$

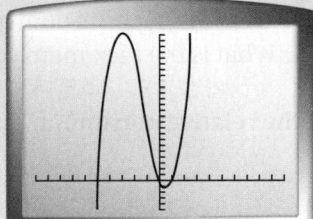

15. $f(x) = -4x^3 + 12x^2 + 4x - 12$ **16.** $f(x) = x^3 - 7x^2 + 7x + 15$

17. **Metalwork** A metalworker wants to make an open box from a sheet of metal, by cutting equal squares from each corner as shown.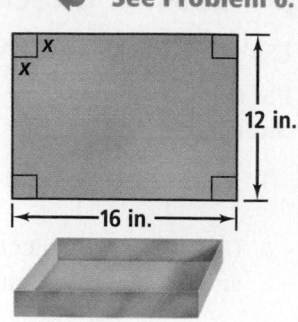

◀ See Problem 6.

    a. Write expressions for the dimensions of the open box.

    b. Write a function for the volume of the box. (*Hint:* Write the function in factored form.)

    c. Graph the function. Find the maximum volume of the box and the side length of the cut-out squares that generates this volume.

 **Apply**

18. **Think About a Plan** A storage company needs to design a new box that has twice the volume of its largest box. Its largest box is 5 ft long, 4 ft wide, and 3 ft high. The new box must be formed by increasing each dimension by the same amount. Find the increase in each dimension.

    • How can you write the dimensions of the new box as polynomial expressions?

    • How can you use the volume of the current largest box to find the volume of the new box?

19. **Carpentry** A carpenter hollowed out the interior of a block of wood as shown at the right.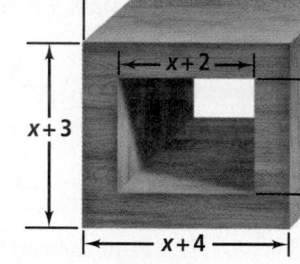

    a. Express the volume of the original block and the volume of the wood removed as polynomials in factored form.

    b. What polynomial represents the volume of the wood remaining?

20. **Geometry** A rectangular box is $2x + 3$ units long, $2x - 3$ units wide, and $3x$ units high. What is its volume, expressed as a polynomial?

21. **Measurement** The volume in cubic feet of a CD holder can be expressed as $V(x) = -x^3 - x^2 + 6x$, or, when factored, as the product of its three dimensions. The depth is expressed as $2 - x$. Assume that the height is greater than the width.

    a. Factor the polynomial to find linear expressions for the height and the width.

    b. Graph the function. Find the x-intercepts. What do they represent?

    c. What is a realistic domain for the function?

    d. What is the maximum volume of the CD holder?

Find the relative maximum, relative minimum, and zeros of each function.

22. $y = 2x^3 - 23x^2 + 78x - 72$

23. $y = 8x^3 - 10x^2 - x - 3$

24. $y = (x + 1)^4 - 1$

25. **Open-Ended** Write a polynomial function with the following features: it has three distinct zeros; one of the zeros is 1; another zero has a multiplicity of 2.

For each function, determine the zeros. State the multiplicity of any multiple zeros.

26. $f(x) = x^3 - 36x$ 27. $y = (x + 1)(x - 4)(3 - 2x)$ 28. $y = (x + 7)(5x + 2)(x - 6)^2$

Standardized Test Prep

SAT/ACT

29. The three most frequent letters in the English language are E, T, and A. They represent on average 30% of all letters. The most frequent letter, E, is 4% more frequent than the second most frequent letter, T. The combined frequency of T and A is 4% greater than the frequency of E. Approximately how many E's can you expect to encounter in a 500-letter paragraph?

  Ⓐ 49   Ⓑ 65   Ⓒ 72   Ⓓ 88

30. Which expression is the factored form of $x^3 + 2x^2 - 5x - 6$?

  Ⓕ $(x + 1)(x + 1)(x - 6)$ Ⓗ $(x + 2)(2x - 5)(x - 6)$
  Ⓖ $(x + 3)(x + 1)(x - 2)$ Ⓘ $(x - 3)(x - 1)(x + 2)$

31. A ball with a 3 in. radius has volume V_1. A second ball has a 9 in. radius and volume V_2. Which equation represents the volume of the second ball in terms of the first?

  Ⓐ $V_2 = 3V_1$ Ⓑ $V_2 = 27V_1$ Ⓒ $V_2 = V_1{}^2$ Ⓓ $V_2 = 9V_1{}^2$

Extended
Response

32. What is the polynomial function, in factored form, whose zeros are -2, 5, and 6, and whose leading coefficient is -2? Graph this function and find any relative minimums or maximums.

Mixed Review

Write each polynomial in standard form. Then classify it by degree and by number of terms.   ◀ **See Lesson 5-1.**

33. $x^2 - 1 - 3x^5 + 2x^2$ **34.** $-2x^3 - 7x^4 + x^3$ **35.** $6x + x^3 - 6x - 2$

Factor each expression.   ◀ **See Lesson 4-4.**

36. $x^2 + 5x + 4$ **37.** $x^2 - 2x - 15$ **38.** $x^2 - 12x + 36$

Get Ready!   **To prepare for Lesson 5-3, do Exercises 39–41.**

Solve each quadratic equation using any method.   ◀ **See Lesson 4-7.**

39. $x^2 + x - 6 = 0$ **40.** $2x^2 - 7x + 3 = 0$ **41.** $4x^2 - 25 = 0$

5-3
PART 1

Solving Polynomial Equations

Objective To solve polynomial equations by factoring

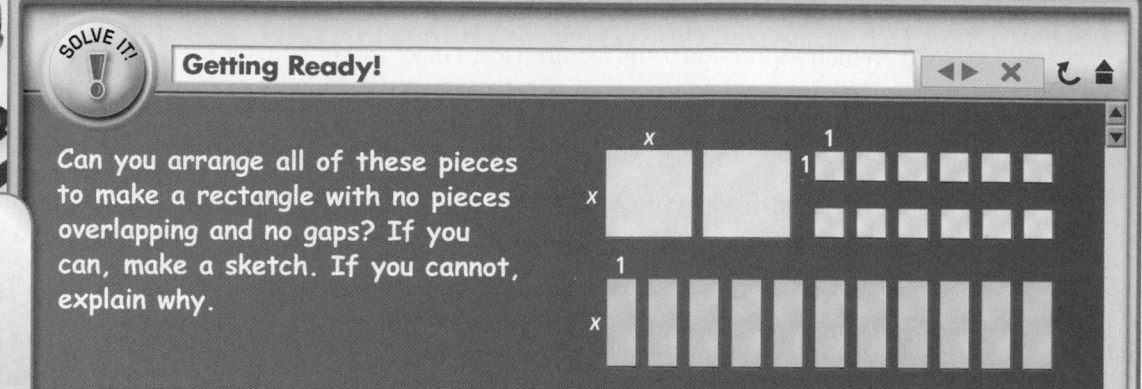

Getting Ready!

Can you arrange all of these pieces to make a rectangle with no pieces overlapping and no gaps? If you can, make a sketch. If you cannot, explain why.

I count 2 pieces with area x^2, 11 with area x, and 12 with area 1. The rectangle would have the same total area.

Lesson Vocabulary
- sum of cubes
- difference of cubes

Factoring a polynomial like $ax^2 + bx + c$ can help you solve a polynomial equation like $ax^2 + bx + c = 0$.

Focus Question How can you use factoring to solve a polynomial equation?

To solve a polynomial equation by factoring:
1. Write the equation in the form $P(x) = 0$ for some polynomial function P.
2. Factor $P(x)$. Use the Zero-Product Property to find the roots.

Problem 1 Solving Polynomial Equations Using Factors

What are the real and imaginary solutions of each polynomial equation?

Plan

What does it mean if x is a common factor of the terms in $P(x)$?
You can write $P(x)$ as $xQ(x)$, and 0 will be a solution.

A $2x^3 - 5x^2 = 3x$

Rewrite in the form $P(x) = 0$.	$2x^3 - 5x^2 - 3x = 0$
Factor out the GCF, x.	$x(2x^2 - 5x - 3) = 0$
Factor $2x^2 - 5x - 3$.	$x(2x + 1)(x - 3) = 0$
Use the Zero-Product Property.	$x = 0$ or $2x + 1 = 0$ or $x - 3 = 0$
Solve each equation for x.	$x = 0$ $\qquad$ $x = -\frac{1}{2}$ $\qquad$ $x = 3$

The solutions are 0, $-\frac{1}{2}$, and 3.

B $3x^4 + 12x^2 = 6x^3$

Think

How will the solution be similar to the solution of the equation in part (a)? Both equations have 0 as a solution, but here it will have a multiplicity of 2.

Rewrite in the form $P(x) = 0$.	$3x^4 - 6x^3 + 12x^2 = 0$
Multiply each side by $\frac{1}{3}$ to simplify.	$x^4 - 2x^3 + 4x^2 = 0$
Factor out the GCF, x^2.	$x^2(x^2 - 2x + 4) = 0$
Use the Zero-Product Property.	$x^2 = 0$ or $x^2 - 2x + 4 = 0$

Solve each equation.

Find square roots to solve $x^2 = 0$.

Use the Quadratic Formula to solve $x^2 - 2x + 4 = 0$. Substitute $a = 1, b = -2, c = 4$.

$x = 0$

$x = \dfrac{-(-2) \pm \sqrt{(-2)^2 - 4(1)(4)}}{2(1)}$

$= \dfrac{2 \pm \sqrt{-12}}{2} = \dfrac{2 \pm 2i\sqrt{3}}{2} = 1 \pm i\sqrt{3}$

The solutions are 0, $1 + i\sqrt{3}$, and $1 - i\sqrt{3}$.

 Got It? **1.** What are the real or imaginary solutions of each equation?

    a. $(x^2 - 1)(x^2 + 4) = 0$ **b.** $x^5 + 4x^3 = 5x^4 - 2x^3$

---

take note

Hint

You used many of these factoring techniques when you solved quadratic equations in Chapter 4.

Concept Summary   Polynomial Factoring Techniques

Techniques	Examples
Factoring out the GCF Factor out the greatest common factor of all the terms.	$15x^4 - 20x^3 + 35x^2$ $= 5x^2(3x^2 - 4x + 7)$
Quadratic Trinomials For $ax^2 + bx + c$, find factors with product ac and sum b.	$6x^2 + 11x - 10$ $= (3x - 2)(2x + 5)$
Perfect Square Trinomials $a^2 + 2ab + b^2 = (a + b)^2$ $a^2 - 2ab + b^2 = (a - b)^2$	$x^2 + 10x + 25 = (x + 5)^2$ $x^2 - 10x + 25 = (x - 5)^2$
Difference of Squares $a^2 - b^2 = (a + b)(a - b)$	$4x^2 - 15 = (2x + \sqrt{15})(2x - \sqrt{15})$
Factoring by Grouping $ax + ay + bx + by$ $= a(x + y) + b(x + y)$ $= (a + b)(x + y)$	$x^3 + 2x^2 - 3x - 6$ $= x^2(x + 2) + (-3)(x + 2)$ $= (x^2 - 3)(x + 2)$
Sum or Difference of Cubes $a^3 + b^3 = (a + b)(a^2 - ab + b^2)$ $a^3 - b^3 = (a - b)(a^2 + ab + b^2)$	$8x^3 + 1 = (2x + 1)(4x^2 - 2x + 1)$ $8x^3 - 1 = (2x - 1)(4x^2 + 2x + 1)$

The sum and difference of cubes are useful factoring techniques.

Here's Why It Works Factoring $a^3 + b^3 = (a + b)(a^2 - ab + b^2)$:

Add the two pairs of additive inverses as shown. $a^3 + b^3 = a^3 + a^2b - a^2b - ab^2 + ab^2 + b^3$

Factor out a^2, $-ab$, and b^2. $= a^2(a + b) - ab(a + b) + b^2(a + b)$

Factor out $(a + b)$. $= (a + b)(a^2 - ab + b^2)$

For $a^3 - b^3 = (a - b)(a^2 + ab + b^2)$, you can follow steps similar to those above, or you can factor $a^3 - b^3$ as the sum of cubes $a^3 + (-b)^3$.

Problem 2 Solving Polynomial Equations by Factoring

What are the real or imaginary solutions of each polynomial equation?

ONLINE PROBLEMS

A $x^4 - 3x^2 = 4$

Think

How can you write the polynomial in quadratic form?
Write in terms of x^2:
$(x^2)^2 - 3(x^2) - 4 = 0$,
which shows the factorable quadratic form
$a^2 - 3a - 4 = 0$.

Rewrite in the form $P(x) = 0$. $x^4 - 3x^2 - 4 = 0$

Let $a = x^2$. $a^2 - 3a - 4 = 0$

Factor. $(a - 4)(a + 1) = 0$

Replace a with x^2. $(x^2 - 4)(x^2 + 1) = 0$

Factor $x^2 - 4$ as a difference of squares. $(x + 2)(x - 2)(x^2 + 1) = 0$

It follows from the Zero-Product Property that $x = -2$, $x = 2$, or $x^2 = -1$.
Solving $x^2 = -1$ yields two imaginary roots: $x = i$ or $x = -i$.

Check Graph the related function $y = x^4 - 3x^2 - 4$.

The graph shows real zeros at $x = -2$ and $x = 2$.
It also shows three turning points.

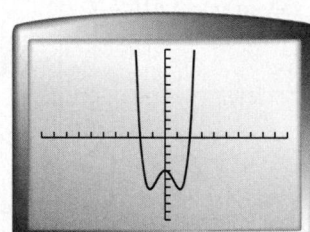

B $x^3 = 1$

Rewrite in the form $P(x) = 0$. $x^3 - 1 = 0$

Factor the difference of cubes. $(x - 1)(x^2 + x + 1) = 0$

It follows from the Zero-Product Property that $x = 1$ or $x^2 + x + 1 = 0$.
Use the Quadratic Formula to solve $x^2 + x + 1 = 0$.

$$x = \frac{-(1) \pm \sqrt{(1)^2 - 4(1)(1)}}{2(1)} = \frac{-1 \pm \sqrt{-3}}{2} = \frac{-1 \pm i\sqrt{3}}{2}$$

The three solutions of $x^3 = 1$ are 1, $-\frac{1}{2} + i\frac{\sqrt{3}}{2}$, and $-\frac{1}{2} - i\frac{\sqrt{3}}{2}$.

Hint

For part (c), rewrite the equation in the form $P(x) = 0$ and let $y = x^2$.

 Got It? 2. What are the real or imaginary solutions of each polynomial equation?
   a. $x^4 = 16$ **b.** $x^3 - 8x = 2x^2$ **c.** $x^4 - 10 = 3x^2$

Focus Question How can you use factoring to solve a polynomial equation?

Answer Write the equation in the form $P(x) = 0$, where $P(x)$ is a polynomial function. Find roots using factoring techniques, the Zero-Product Property, and the Quadratic Formula.

Lesson Check

Do you know HOW?

Factor each polynomial.

1. $x^2 - 3x - 18$ **2.** $x^3 - 27$

3. $x^3 + 3x^2 + 4x + 12$ **4.** $x^4 - 2x^2 - 8$

Solve each equation by factoring.

5. $2x^2 + 7x - 4 = 0$ **6.** $2x^3 + 2x^2 - 4x = 0$

Do you UNDERSTAND?

7. Vocabulary Identify each expression as a sum of cubes, difference of cubes, or difference of squares.

     a. $x^2 - 64$ **b.** $x^3 + 8$

     c. $x^3 - 125$ **d.** $x^2 - 81$

8. Reasoning Show two different ways to find the real roots of the polynomial equation $0 = x^6 - x^2$. Show your steps.

Practice and Problem-Solving Exercises

A Practice   Find the real or imaginary solutions of each equation by factoring.    See Problems 1 and 2.

Guided Practice

9. $x^3 + 64 = 0$

To start, write $x^3 + 64$ as a sum of cubes and factor.

$$x^3 + 4^3 = 0$$
$$(x + 4)(x^2 - 4x + 16) = 0$$

10. $x^3 - 1000 = 0$ **11.** $125x^3 - 27 = 0$ **12.** $64x^3 - 1 = 0$

13. $x^3 + 2x^2 + 5x + 10 = 0$ **14.** $6x^2 + 13x - 5 = 0$ **15.** $0 = x^3 - 27$

16. $0 = x^3 - 64$ **17.** $8x^3 = 1$ **18.** $64x^3 = -8$

19. $x^3 = 8x - 2x^2$ **20.** $x^4 - 10x^2 = -9$ **21.** $x^4 - 8x^2 = -16$

22. $x^4 - 12x^2 = 64$ **23.** $x^4 + 7x^2 = 18$ **24.** $x^4 + 4x^2 = 12$

B Apply   Solve each equation.

25. $125x^3 + 216 = 0$ **26.** $81x^3 - 192 = 0$ **27.** $x^4 - 64 = 0$

28. $27 = -x^4 - 12x^2$ **29.** $x^5 - 5x^3 + 4x = 0$ **30.** $5x^3 = 5x^2 + 12x$

31. What are the solutions of $2x^3 - 5x^2 = 12x$?

     Ⓐ $-4, -\frac{3}{2}$, and 0   Ⓑ $-4, 0$, and $\frac{3}{2}$ Ⓒ $-\frac{3}{2}, 0$, and 4   Ⓓ $0, \frac{3}{2}$, and 4

32. Writing Show how you can rewrite $\frac{m^3}{n^6} + \frac{1}{8}$ as a sum of two cubes.

Solving Polynomial Equations

Objective To solve polynomial equations by graphing

In Part 1 of the lesson, you learned how to solve polynomial equations using factoring techniques.

Connect to What You Know

Here you will learn to solve polynomial equations using the graphing features of your calculator.

Focus Question When should you solve a polynomial equation with a graphing calculator?

While factoring is an effective way to solve a polynomial equation, you can also find the real roots quickly by using a graphing calculator.

Problem 3 Finding Real Roots by Graphing

Think

Why is it helpful to graph y_1 and y_2?
The values of x for which $y_1 = y_2$ are the solutions of the original equation.

What are the real solutions of the equation $x^3 + 5 = 4x^2 + x$?

Graph $y_1 = x^3 + 5$ and $y_2 = 4x^2 + x$. Use the **INTERSECT** feature to find the x-values of the points of intersection.

These two intersection points are visible in the standard viewing window.

You must adjust the window to obtain this point of intersection.

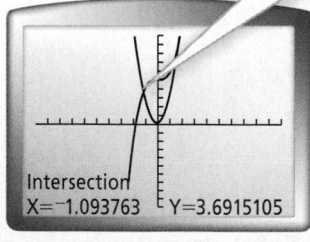
Intersection
X=-1.093763 Y=3.6915105

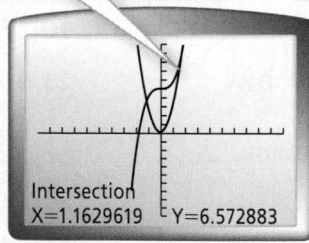
Intersection
X=1.1629619 Y=6.572883

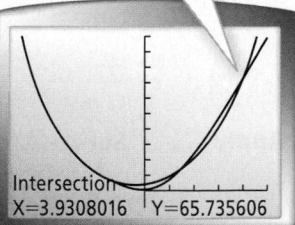
Intersection
X=3.9308016 Y=65.735606

Approximate solutions are $x = -1.09$, $x = 1.16$, and $x = 3.93$.

Hint

You can also rewrite the equation as $y = x^3 - 4x^2 - x + 5 = 0$ and use the **ZERO** feature to find all solutions.

Check Verify the solutions by showing that they satisfy the original equation. Show values of $y_1 = x^3 + 5$ and $y_2 = 4x^2 + x$ in a table. The solution checks.

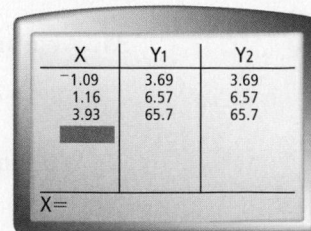

X	Y₁	Y₂
-1.09	3.69	3.69
1.16	6.57	6.57
3.93	65.7	65.7

X=

Got It? 3. What are the real solutions of the equation $x^3 + x^2 = x - 1$?

Which variable do you define first?
Stacy and Amir's ages are both compared to Una's age. Define Una's age first.

Problem 4 Modeling a Problem Situation

Stacy, Una, and Amir are close friends. Stacy is one year younger than Una. Amir is two years older than Una. If the product of their ages is 2300 more than the sum of their ages, how old is each person?

Think

Write

Define variables.

Let x = Una's age.
Stacy's age = $x - 1$.
Amir's age = $x + 2$.

Write an equation.

$$\overbrace{x + (x - 1) + (x + 2)}^{\text{Sum of ages}} + 2300 = \overbrace{x(x - 1)(x + 2)}^{\text{Product of ages}}$$

Simplify and write it in $P(x) = 0$ form.

$$3x + 2301 = x(x^2 + x - 2)$$
$$3x + 2301 = x^3 + x^2 - 2x$$
$$x^3 + x^2 - 5x - 2301 = 0$$

Only real solutions make sense, so graphing $y_1 = P(x)$ should show any real solution that exists. Use the **ZERO** feature.

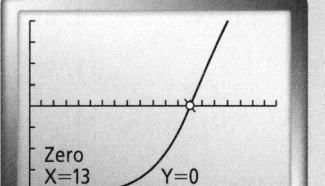

Zero
X=13   Y=0

$x = 13$

Write the answer.

Una was 13, Stacy 12, and Amir 15.

Hint

Let n represent the smallest of the three consecutive integers.

 Got It? 4. What are three consecutive integers whose product is 480 more than their sum?

Focus Question When should you solve a polynomial equation with a graphing calculator?

Answer Use a graphing calculator to solve a polynomial equation when you only need the real roots. You must use algebraic techniques to identify any complex roots.

Lesson Check

Do you know HOW?

Find the real solutions of each equation using a graphing calculator.

1. $x^3 + 13x = 10x^2$

2. $x^3 - 6x^2 + 6x = 0$

3. $12x^3 = 60x^2 + 75x$

Do you UNDERSTAND?

4. **Reasoning** Which method of solving polynomial equations does not identify the imaginary roots? Explain.

5. **Error Analysis** Your friend solved the equation $2x^3 + 6 = 2 - x$ by graphing $y_1 = 2x^3 + 6$ and $y_2 = 2 - x$ and got $x = 3.13$ for the solution. What error did she make?

Practice and Problem-Solving Exercises

A Practice Find the real solutions of each equation by graphing. ◀ **See Problem 3.**

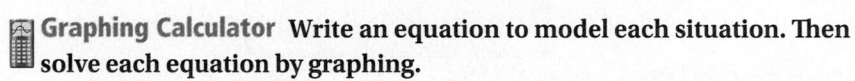

Guided Practice

6. $x^3 - 4x^2 - 7x = -10$

To start, rewrite the equation with one side equal to zero.

$x^3 - 4x^2 - 7x + 10 = 0$

7. $3x^3 - 6x^2 - 9x = 0$

8. $4x^3 - 8x^2 + 4x = 0$

9. $6x^2 = 48x$

10. $x^3 + 3x^2 + 2x = 0$

11. $2x^3 + 5x^2 = 7x$

12. $4x^3 = 4x^2 + 3x$

13. $2x^4 - 5x^3 - 3x^2 = 0$

14. $x^2 - 8x + 7 = 0$

15. $x^3 - x^2 - 16x = 20$

 **Graphing Calculator** Write an equation to model each situation. Then solve each equation by graphing. ◀ **See Problem 4.**

Guided Practice

16. The Johnson twins were born two years after their older sister. This year, the product of the three siblings' ages is exactly 4558 more than the sum of their ages. How old are the twins?

To start, relate the sum and product of the siblings' ages.

(Product of ages) = (Sum of ages) + 4558

Then define variables.

Let $x =$ the twins' ages.
The sister's age is $x + 2$.

17. The product of three consecutive integers is 210. What are the numbers?

B Apply Solve each equation.

18. $-2x^4 + 100 = 0$

19. $x^4 - 100 = 0$

20. $7x^3 = 5x^2 + 12x$

21. $x^3 + x = x^2 + 1$

22. $x^3 + x^2 + x + 1 = 0$

23. $x^3 + 1 = x^2 + x$

24. **Error Analysis** A student says that 1, 2, 3, and 4 are the zeros of a cubic polynomial function. Explain why the student is mistaken.

25. Think About a Plan The width of a plastic storage box is 1 ft longer than the height. The length is 4 ft longer than the height. The volume is 36 ft^3. What are the dimensions of the box?
- What is the formula for the volume of a rectangular prism?
- What variable expressions represent the length, height, and width?
- What equation represents the volume of the plastic storage box?

26. Geometry The width of a box is 2 m less than the length. The height is 1 m less than the length. The volume is 60 m^3. What is the length of the box?

Graph each function to find the zeros. Rewrite the function with the polynomial in factored form.

27. $y = 2x^2 + 3x - 5$ **28.** $y = x^4 - 10x^2 + 9$ **29.** $y = x^3 - 3x^2 + 4$

30. Open-Ended To solve a polynomial equation, you can use any combination of graphing, factoring, and the Quadratic Formula. Write and solve an equation to illustrate each method.

Standardized Test Prep

SAT/ACT

31. Which value is NOT a solution of the equation $x^4 - 3x^2 - 54 = 0$?

   Ⓐ -3 Ⓑ 3 Ⓒ $-3i$ Ⓓ $-i\sqrt{6}$

32. Ava drove 3 hours at 45 miles per hour. How many miles did she drive?

   Ⓕ 45 miles   Ⓖ 48 miles   Ⓗ 90 miles   Ⓘ 135 miles

33. Which polynomial has the complex roots $1 + i\sqrt{2}$ and $1 - i\sqrt{2}$?

   Ⓐ $x^2 + 2x + 3$ Ⓑ $x^2 - 2x + 3$ Ⓒ $x^2 + 2x - 3$ Ⓓ $x^2 - 2x - 3$

Short Response

34. Sam has only quarters and dimes in his pocket. He has a total of 12 coins, totaling $1.95. How many of each coin does Sam have?

Mixed Review

Write each polynomial in factored form. Check by multiplication.   ◀ See Lesson 5-2.

35. $3x^2 - 18x + 24$ **36.** $2x^4 + 6x^3 - 18x^2 - 54x$ **37.** $x^4 - 4x^3 - 5x^2$

Solve each equation by factoring. Check your answers.   ◀ See Lesson 4-5.

38. $x^2 - 4x = 12$ **39.** $x^2 + 1 = 37$ **40.** $2x^2 - 5x - 3 = 0$

Get Ready!   **To prepare for Lesson 5-4, do Exercises 41 and 42.**

Evaluate each expression for the given values of the variables.   ◀ See Lesson 1-3.

41. $\dfrac{16(x - 4)(y - 2)}{4(x - 3)y}$ for $x = 1$ and $y = -2$ **42.** $\dfrac{2(x + 5)y}{10(x - 4)(y - 2)}$ for $x = 1$ and $y = -2$

5-4
PART 1

Dividing Polynomials

Objective To divide polynomials using long division

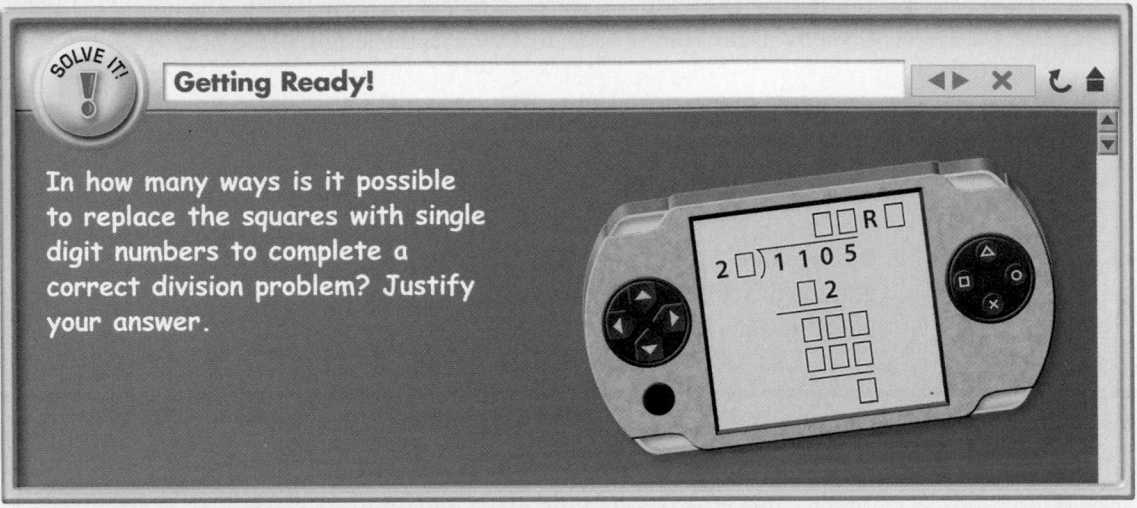

SOLVE IT!

Getting Ready!

In how many ways is it possible to replace the squares with single digit numbers to complete a correct division problem? Justify your answer.

$$\square\square \text{ R} \square$$
$$2\square\,)\overline{1\ 1\ 0\ 5}$$
$$\square\ 2$$

Long division is one of many methods you can use to divide whole numbers. You can divide polynomials using steps that are similar to the long-division steps that you use to divide whole numbers.

Focus Question How can you divide polynomials?

When you factor a polynomial, you are trying to find a divisor of the polynomial that gives a quotient (the other factor) and remainder 0. This suggests that being able to divide one polynomial by another could help you factor polynomials.

Numerical long division and polynomial long division are similar.

Hint

In polynomial long division, you must write the terms in order by degree. Write both polynomials in standard form.

Numerical Long Division

$$
\begin{array}{r}
32 \\
21\,)\overline{672} \\
\end{array}
$$

21 divides into... $21\,)\overline{672}$

...67 3 times. $\underline{63}$

21 divides into... 42

...42 2 times. $\underline{42}$

     0

Polynomial Long Division

$$
\begin{array}{r}
3x + 2 \\
2x + 1\,)\overline{6x^2 + 7x + 2} \\
\end{array}
$$

$(2x + 1)$ divides into...

...$(6x^2 + 7x)$ 3x times. $\underline{6x^2 + 3x}$

$(2x + 1)$ divides into... $4x + 2$

...$(4x + 2)$ 2 times. $\underline{4x + 2}$

     0

The remainder from each division above is 0, so 21 is a factor of 672 and $2x + 1$ is a factor of $6x^2 + 7x + 2$.

 **Problem 1** Using Polynomial Long Division

Use polynomial long division to divide $4x^2 + 23x - 16$ by $x + 5$. What is the quotient and remainder?

Divide: $\frac{4x^2}{x} = 4x$.

Multiply: $4x(x + 5) = 4x^2 + 20x$.

Subtract to get $3x$. Bring down -16.

$$
\begin{array}{r}
4x \\
x + 5 \overline{)4x^2 + 23x - 16} \\
\underline{4x^2 + 20x } \\
3x - 16
\end{array}
$$

Repeat the process of dividing, multiplying, and subtracting.

$$
\begin{array}{r}
4x + 3 \\
x + 5 \overline{)4x^2 + 23x - 16} \\
\underline{4x^2 + 20x } \\
3x - 16 \\
\underline{3x + 15} \\
-31
\end{array}
$$

Divide: $\frac{3x}{x} = 3$.

Multiply: $3(x + 5) = 3x + 15$.

Subtract to get -31.

The quotient is $4x + 3$ with remainder -31. ⟨ You can say: $4x + 3$, R -31. ⟩

Think

How can you check your result?
Show that (divisor)(quotient) + remainder = dividend.

Check

Multiply $(x + 5)$ by $(4x + 3)$. $(x + 5)(4x + 3) - 31 = (4x^2 + 3x + 20x + 15) - 31$

Simplify. $= 4x^2 + 23x - 16$ ✔

 Got It? **1.** Use polynomial long division to divide $3x^2 - 29x + 56$ by $x - 7$. What is the quotient and remainder?

---

take note

Key Concept The Division Algorithm for Polynomials

You can divide polynomial $P(x)$ by polynomial $D(x)$ to get polynomial quotient $Q(x)$ and polynomial remainder $R(x)$. The result is $P(x) = D(x)Q(x) + R(x)$.

$$
\begin{array}{r}
Q(x) \\
D(x) \overline{)P(x)} \\
\cdot \\
\cdot \\
\cdot \\
\overline{R(x)}
\end{array}
$$

If $R(x) = 0$, then $P(x) = D(x)Q(x)$ and $D(x)$ and $Q(x)$ are factors of $P(x)$.

To use long division, $P(x)$ and $D(x)$ should be in standard form with zero coefficients where appropriate.

The process stops when the degree of the remainder, $R(x)$, is less than the degree of the divisor, $D(x)$.

Hint

In numerical long division, the process stops when the remainder is less than the divisor.

Problem 2 Checking Factors

Ⓐ Is $x^2 + 1$ a factor of $3x^4 - 4x^3 + 12x^2 + 5$?

Write the division. Include 0x terms.

Divide $\frac{3x^4}{x^2} = 3x^2$. Multiply $3x^2(x^2 + 0x + 1)$.

Subtract to get $-4x^3 + 9x^2$. Bring down $+ 0x$.

Divide $\frac{-4x^3}{x^2} = -4x$. Multiply $-4x(x^2 + 0x + 1)$.

Subtract to get $9x^2 + 4x$. Bring down $+ 5$.

Divide $\frac{9x^2}{x^2} = 9$. Multiply $9(x^2 + 0x + 1)$.

Subtract to get $4x - 4$.

$$
\begin{array}{r}
3x^2 - 4x + 9 \\
x^2 + 0x + 1 \overline{)3x^4 - 4x^3 + 12x^2 + 0x + 5} \\
\underline{3x^4 + 0x^3 + 3x^2} \\
-4x^3 + 9x^2 + 0x \\
\underline{-4x^3 + 0x^2 - 4x} \\
9x^2 + 4x + 5 \\
\underline{9x^2 + 0x + 9} \\
4x - 4
\end{array}
$$

> The degree of the remainder is less than the degree of the divisor. Stop!

The remainder is not zero. $x^2 + 1$ is not a factor of $3x^4 - 4x^3 + 12x^2 + 5$.

Plan

Can you use the Factor Theorem to help answer this question?
Yes; recall that if $P(a) = 0$, then $x - a$ is a factor of $P(x)$.

Ⓑ Is $x - 2$ a factor of $P(x) = x^5 - 32$? If it is, write $P(x)$ as a product of two factors.

Step 1 Use the Factor Theorem to determine if $x - 2$ is a factor of $x^5 - 32$.

Substitute $x = 2$. $P(2) = 2^5 - 32$

Evaluate the power. $= 32 - 32$

Subtract. $= 0$

Yes; since $P(2) = 0$, $x - 2$ is a factor of $P(x)$.

Step 2 Use polynomial long division to find the other factor.

Write the division. Include terms with coefficients of 0.

Divide and multiply.
Subtract and bring down $0x^3$.

Divide and multiply.
Subtract and bring down $0x^2$.

Divide and multiply.
Subtract and bring down $0x$.

Divide and multiply.
Subtract and bring down -32.

Divide and multiply.
Subtract. The remainder is 0.

$$
\begin{array}{r}
x^4 + 2x^3 + 4x^2 + 8x + 16 \\
x - 2 \overline{)x^5 + 0x^4 + 0x^3 + 0x^2 + 0x - 32} \\
\underline{x^5 - 2x^4} \\
2x^4 + 0x^3 \\
\underline{2x^4 - 4x^3} \\
4x^3 + 0x^2 \\
\underline{4x^3 - 8x^2} \\
8x^2 + 0x \\
\underline{8x^2 - 16x} \\
16x - 32 \\
\underline{16x - 32} \\
0
\end{array}
$$

$P(x) = (x - 2)(x^4 + 2x^3 + 4x^2 + 8x + 16)$

Hint

For part (a), include the x^3 and x^2 terms even though the coefficients are zero.

✓ **Got It? 2. a.** Is $x^4 - 1$ a factor of $P(x) = x^5 + 5x^4 - x - 5$? If it is, write $P(x)$ as a product of two factors.

  b. Reasoning Use the fact that $12 \cdot 31 = 372$ to write $3x^2 + 7x + 2$ as the product of two factors.

Focus Question How can you divide polynomials?

Answer You can divide polynomials using steps that are similar to the long-division steps that you use to divide whole numbers. Given a zero of a polynomial function, use polynomial long-division to find the other zeros.

Lesson Check

Do you know HOW?

Divide.

1. $(2x^2 + 7x + 11) \div (x + 2)$

2. $(9x^3 - 15x^2 + 4x) \div (x - 3)$

Do you UNDERSTAND?

3. Reasoning A polynomial $P(x)$ is divided by a binomial $x - a$. The remainder is 0. What conclusion can you draw? Explain.

Practice and Problem-Solving Exercises

Practice — Divide using long division. Check your answers.

◄ See Problem 1.

4. $(x^2 - 3x - 40) \div (x + 5)$

Guided Practice →

To start, divide: $\frac{x^2}{x} = x$.

Then multiply: $x(x + 5) = x^2 + 5x$.

$$\begin{array}{r} x \\ x + 5 \overline{)x^2 - 3x - 40} \\ \underline{x^2 + 5x} \end{array}$$

5. $(3x^2 + 7x - 20) \div (x + 4)$

6. $(x^3 + 3x^2 - x + 2) \div (x - 1)$

7. $(2x^3 - 3x^2 - 18x - 8) \div (x - 4)$

8. $(3x^3 + 9x^2 + 8x + 4) \div (x + 2)$

9. $(9x^2 - 21x - 20) \div (x - 1)$

10. $(x^2 - 7x + 10) \div (x + 3)$

Determine whether each binomial is a factor of $x^3 + 4x^2 + x - 6$.

◄ See Problem 2.

11. $x - 3$

12. $x + 2$

13. $x + 3$

14. $x^2 + 1$

Apply

15. Reasoning When a polynomial is divided by $(x - 5)$, the quotient is $5x^2 + 3x + 12$ with remainder 7. Find the polynomial.

Divide.

16. $(2x^3 + 9x^2 + 14x + 5) \div (2x + 1)$

17. $(x^4 + 4x^3 - x - 4) \div (x^3 - 1)$

18. What is the remainder when $x^5 + 6x^3 + 2$ is divided by $x^2 - 4$?

   Ⓐ $40x - 2$

   Ⓒ $x^3 + 10x$

   Ⓑ $40x + 2$

   Ⓓ $x^3 - 10x$

Determine whether each binomial is a factor of $x^3 + x^2 - 16x - 16$.

19. $x + 2$

20. $x - 4$

21. $x + 1$

22. $x - 1$

5-4
PART 2

Dividing Polynomials

Objective To divide polynomials using synthetic division

Dynamic Activity
Synthetic
Division

In Part 1 of the lesson, you learned how to divide polynomials using the familiar method of long division.

Connect to What You Know

Here you will learn another method to divide a polynomial by a linear factor called synthetic division.

Lesson Vocabulary
• synthetic division
• Remainder Theorem

Focus Question Why is synthetic division useful?

Synthetic division simplifies the long-division process for dividing by a linear expression $x - a$. To use synthetic division, write the coefficients (including zeros) of the polynomial in standard form (omit all variables and exponents). For the divisor, use the value for x that is a solution of $x - a = 0$ (use a). This allows you to add instead of subtract.

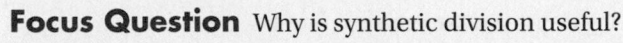

Problem 3 Using Synthetic Division

Use synthetic division to divide $x^3 - 14x^2 + 51x - 54$ by $x + 2$. What are the quotient and remainder?

Think

To divide by $x + 2$ what number do you use for the synthetic divisor?
$x + 2 = x - (-2)$, so use -2.

Step 1 Write the coefficients of the polynomial. Use -2 for the divisor.

$$-2 \mid \quad 1 \quad -14 \quad 51 \quad -54$$

Step 2 Bring down the first coefficient.

$$-2 \mid \quad 1 \quad -14 \quad 51 \quad -54$$
$$\overline{ 1}$$

Step 3 Multiply the coefficient by the divisor. Add to the next coefficient.

$$-2 \mid \quad 1 \quad -14 \quad 51 \quad -54$$
$$ -2$$
$$\overline{ 1 \quad -16}$$

Step 4 Continue multiplying and adding through the last coefficient.

$$-2 \mid \quad 1 \quad -14 \quad 51 \quad -54$$
$$ -2 \quad 32 \quad -166$$
$$\overline{ 1 \quad -16 \quad 83 \quad -220}$$

The quotient is $x^2 - 16x + 83$, R -220.

Got It? **3.** Use synthetic division to divide $x^3 - 57x + 56$ by $x - 7$. What are the quotient and remainder?

Problem 4 **Using Synthetic Division to Solve a Problem**

Crafts The polynomial $x^3 + 7x^2 - 38x - 240$ expresses the volume, in cubic inches, of the shadow box shown.

A What are the dimensions of the box? (*Hint:* The length is greater than the height (or depth).)

Use synthetic division to divide $x^3 + 7x^2 - 38x - 240$ by $x + 5$.

$$
\begin{array}{r|rrrr}
-5 & 1 & 7 & -38 & -240 \\
& & -5 & -10 & 240 \\
\hline
& 1 & 2 & -48 & 0
\end{array}
$$

Write the division.
Bring down the 1.
Multiply and add.

The quotient is $x^2 + 2x - 48$.

Next, factor the quotient.

$$x^2 + 2x - 48 = (x - 6)(x + 8)$$

So, $x^3 + 7x^2 - 38x - 240 = (x + 5)(x^2 + 2x - 48)$

$$= (x + 5)(x - 6)(x + 8)$$

The length, width, and height (or depth) of the box are $(x + 8)$ in., $(x + 5)$ in., and $(x - 6)$ in., respectively.

B If the width of the box is 15 in., what are the other two dimensions?

The width of the box is $x + 5$. So if $x + 5 = 15$, then $x = 10$.

Substitute for x to find the length and height (or depth).

Length: $x + 8 = 10 + 8 = 18$
Height: $x - 6 = 10 - 6 = 4$

The length of the box is 18 in., and the height (or depth) is 4 in.

 Got It? **4.** If the polynomial $x^3 + 6x^2 + 11x + 6$ expresses the volume, in cubic inches, of a box, and the width is $(x + 1)$ in., what are the dimensions of the box?

Plan

How can you use the picture to help solve the problem?
The picture gives the width of the box. Remember for a rectangular prism, $V = \ell wh$.

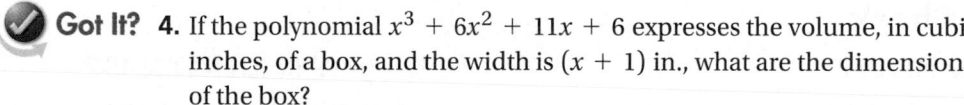

The **Remainder Theorem** provides a quick way to find the remainder of a polynomial long-division problem.

> ### Theorem   The Remainder Theorem
>
> If you divide a polynomial $P(x)$ of degree $n \geq 1$ by $x - a$, then the remainder is $P(a)$.

Here's Why It Works When you divide polynomial $P(x)$ by $D(x)$, you find
$P(x) = D(x)Q(x) + R(x)$.

Substitute $(x - a)$ for $D(x)$.	$P(x) = (x - a)Q(x) + R(x)$
Evaluate $P(a)$. Substitute a for x.	$P(a) = (a - a)Q(a) + R(a)$
Simplify.	$= R(a)$

Problem 5 Evaluating a Polynomial   GRIDDED RESPONSE

Think

Is there a way to find $P(3)$ without substituting?
Use synthetic division.
$P(3)$ is the remainder.

Given that $P(x) = x^5 - 8x^3 - x^2 + 2$, what is $P(3)$?

By the Remainder Theorem, $P(3)$ is the remainder when you divide $P(x)$ by $x - 3$.

First write $P(x)$ in standard form with 0 coefficients where appropriate.

$$P(x) = x^5 + 0x^4 - 8x^3 - x^2 + 0x + 2$$

Then use synthetic division to divide $P(x)$ by $x - 3$.

$P(3) = 20$.

$$
\begin{array}{r|rrrrrr}
3 & 1 & 0 & -8 & -1 & 0 & 2 \\
  &   & 3 & 9 & 3 & 6 & 18 \\
\hline
  & 1 & 3 & 1 & 2 & 6 & 20
\end{array}
$$

 Got It? **5.** Given that $P(x) = x^5 - 3x^4 - 28x^3 + 5x + 20$, what is $P(-4)$?

Focus Question Why is synthetic division useful?

Answer Synthetic division simplifies the process of polynomial long division. Write only the coefficients (including any 0 coefficients) and omit the variables and exponents.

 ## Lesson Check

Do you know HOW?

Divide using synthetic division.

1. $(x^3 + 5x^2 + 11x + 15) \div (x + 3)$

2. $(x^3 - x^2 - 4x + 4) \div (x - 2)$

3. $(4x^3 + 21x^2 - x - 24) \div (x + 5)$

Do you UNDERSTAND?

4. Writing Explain why it is important to have the terms of both polynomials written in descending order of degree before dividing.

5. Open-Ended Write a polynomial division that has a quotient of $x + 3$ and a remainder of 2.

Practice and Problem-Solving Exercises

See Problem 3.

A Practice

Divide using synthetic division.

Guided Practice

To start, write the coefficients of the polynomial. Use 1 for the divisor.

6. $(x^3 + 3x^2 - x - 3) \div (x - 1)$

$$\underline{1 \rfloor \quad 1 \quad 3 \quad -1 \quad -3}$$

7. $(x^3 - 4x^2 + 6x - 4) \div (x - 2)$

8. $(x^3 - 7x^2 - 7x + 20) \div (x + 4)$

9. $(x^3 - 3x^2 - 5x - 25) \div (x - 5)$

10. $(x^2 + 3) \div (x - 1)$

11. $(3x^3 + 17x^2 + 21x - 9) \div (x + 3)$

12. $(x^3 + 27) \div (x + 3)$

Use synthetic division and the given factor to completely factor each polynomial function.

See Problem 4.

13. $y = x^3 + 2x^2 - 5x - 6; (x + 1)$

14. $y = x^3 - 4x^2 - 9x + 36; (x + 3)$

15. Geometry The volume, in cubic inches, of the decorative box shown can be expressed as the product of the lengths of its sides as $V(x) = x^3 + x^2 - 6x$. What linear expressions with integer coefficients represent the length and height of the box?

x

Use synthetic division and the Remainder Theorem to find $P(a)$.

See Problem 5.

16. $P(x) = x^3 + 4x^2 - 8x - 6; a = -2$

17. $P(x) = x^3 - 7x^2 + 15x - 9; a = 3$

18. $P(x) = x^3 + 7x^2 + 4x; a = -2$

19. $P(x) = 6x^3 - x^2 + 4x + 3; a = 3$

B Apply

20. Think About a Plan Your friend multiplies $(x + 4)$ by a quadratic polynomial and gets the result $x^3 - 3x^2 - 24x + 30$. The teacher says that everything is correct except for the constant term. Find the quadratic polynomial that your friend used. What is the correct result of multiplication?

- What does the fact that all the terms except for the constant are correct tell you?
- How can polynomial division help you solve this problem?
- What is the connection between the remainder of the division and your friend's error?

Use synthetic division to determine whether each binomial is a factor of $3x^3 + 10x^2 - x - 12$.

21. $x + 3$

22. $x - 1$

23. $x + 2$

24. $x - 4$

Divide using synthetic division.

25. $(x^4 - 2x^3 + x^2 + x - 1) \div (x - 1)$

26. $(x^4 + 3x^3 + 3x^2 + 4x + 3) \div (x + 1)$

27. $(x^4 + 3x^2 + x + 4) \div (x + 3)$

28. $(x^4 - 5x^2 + 4x + 12) \div (x + 2)$

29. **Error Analysis** A student used synthetic division to divide $x^3 - x^2 - 2x$ by $x + 1$. Describe and correct the error shown.

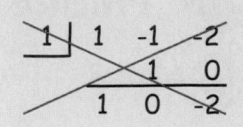

30. **Geometry** The expression $\frac{1}{3}(x^3 + 5x^2 + 8x + 4)$ represents the volume of a square pyramid. The expression $(x + 1)$ represents the height of the pyramid. What expression represents the side length of the base? (*Hint:* The formula for the volume of a pyramid is $V = \frac{1}{3}Bh$.)

Standardized Test Prep

SAT/ACT

31. What is the remainder when $x^2 - 5x + 7$ is divided by $x + 1$?

   (A) 1   (B) 3   (C) 11   (D) 13

32. What is the least degree of a polynomial that has a zero of multiplicity 3 at 1, a zero of multiplicity 1 at 0, and a zero of multiplicity 2 at 2?

   (F) 3   (G) 4   (H) 5   (I) 6

33. The equation $y = 0.17x$ represents your weight in pounds on the Moon y in relation to your weight on Earth x. If Al weighs 130 lb on Earth, what would he weigh on the Moon?

   (A) 22.1 lb   (B) 92.3 lb   (C) 130 lb   (D) 764.7 lb

Extended Response

34. The formula for the area of a circle is $A = \pi r^2$. Solve the equation for r. If the area of a circle is 78.5 cm^2, what is the radius? Use 3.14 for π.

Mixed Review

Find the real solutions of each equation by factoring.   **See Lesson 5-3.**

35. $x^3 + 2x^2 + x = 0$ 36. $2x^4 - 2x^3 + 2x^2 = 2x$ 37. $5x^5 = 125x^3$

Solve each equation using the Quadratic Formula.   **See Lesson 4-7.**

38. $x^2 + 3x - 2 = 0$ 39. $2x^2 + 4x - 4 = 0$ 40. $7x^2 - 2x - 5 = 0$

41. $x^2 - 5x = -5$ 42. $x^2 - 6x = -7$ 43. $x^2 + 7x + 11 = 0$

Find the solution of each system by graphing.   **See Lesson 3-3.**

44. $\begin{cases} y < 2x + 3 \\ y > -x \end{cases}$ 45. $\begin{cases} y > x - 4 \\ y > 4 - \frac{1}{3}x \end{cases}$ 46. $\begin{cases} y < -x + 3 \\ y > x + 1 \end{cases}$

Get Ready!   **To prepare for Lesson 5-5, do Exercises 47–49.**

Simplify each expression.   **See Lesson 4-8.**

47. $(-4i)(6i)$ 48. $(2 + i)(2 - i)$ 49. $(4 - 3i)(5 + i)$

Chapter Vocabulary

- degree of a monomial (p. 292)
- degree of a polynomial (p. 292)
- difference of cubes (p. 311)
- end behavior (p. 294)
- Factor Theorem (p. 302)
- monomial (p. 292)

- multiple zero (p. 304)
- multiplicity (p. 304)
- polynomial (p. 292)
- polynomial function (p. 293)
- relative maximum (p. 305)
- relative minimum (p. 305)

- Remainder Theorem (p. 324)
- standard form of a polynomial function (p. 293)
- sum of cubes (p. 311)
- synthetic division (p. 322)
- turning point (p. 294)

Choose the correct vocabulary word or phrase to complete each sentence.

1. A ? occurs at a down-to-up turning point.

2. The exponent of a variable in a term determines its ? .

3. The ? has terms written in descending order by degree.

4. ? is a technique that can simplify the division of polynomials.

5. The number of appearances of a zero of a polynomial function describes the ? of that zero.

5-1 Polynomial Functions

Quick Review

The **standard form of a polynomial function** is $P(x) = a_n x^n + a_{n-1} x^{n-1} + \cdots + a_1 x + a_0$, where n is a nonnegative integer and the coefficients are real numbers. You can classify a polynomial by **degree**. Its degree is the highest degree among its **monomial** term(s). The degree determines the possible number of **turning points** in the graph and the end behavior of the graph.

Example

Write the polynomial function in standard form and classify it by degree and number of terms. How many terms does it have? What are the possible numbers of turning points of the graph of $P(x)$?

$$P(x) = -4x^2 + x^4$$

Standard form arranges the terms by decreasing exponents, or $P(x) = x^4 - 4x^2$. Its degree is 4, and it has 2 terms, so $x^4 - 4x^2$ is a quartic binomial. The graph of a quartic polynomial function can have either one or three turning points.

Exercises

Write each polynomial function in standard form, classify it by degree and number of terms, and determine the end behavior of its graph.

6. $y - 12 - x^4$

7. $y = x^2 + 7 - x$

8. $y = 2x^3 - 6x + 3x^2 - x^4 + 12$

9. $y = 2x^2 + 8 - 4x + x^3$

10. $y = 10 - 3x^3 + 3x^2 + x^4$

11. If the volume of a cube can be represented by a polynomial of degree 9, what is the degree of the polynomial that represents each side length?

12. A polynomial function $P(x)$ has degree n. If n is even, is the number of turning points of the graph of $P(x)$ even or odd? What can you say about the number of turning points if n is odd?

5-2 Polynomials, Linear Factors, and Zeros

Quick Review

For any real number a and polynomial $P(x)$, if $x - a$ is a factor of $P(x)$, then a is:

- a zero of $y = P(x)$
- a root (or solution) of $P(x) = 0$, and
- an x-intercept of the graph of $y = P(x)$.

If a is a **multiple zero**, its **multiplicity** is the same as the number of times $x - a$ appears as a factor.

A turning point is a **relative maximum** or **relative minimum** of a polynomial function.

Example

Find the zeros of $y = 3x^3 - 6x^2 + 3x$, and state the multiplicity of any multiple zeros.

| Factor out the GCF, 3x. | $y = 3x(x^2 - 2x + 1)$ |
| Factor the quadratic. | $y = 3x(x - 1)(x - 1)$ |

The zeros are 1 (with multiplicity 2) and 0.

Exercises

Write a polynomial function with the given zeros.

13. $x = -1, -1, 6$ **14.** $x = -1, 0, 2$

15. $x = 1, 2, 3$ **16.** $x = -2, 1, 4$

Find the zeros of each function. State the multiplicity of any multiple zeros.

17. $y = 3x(x + 2)^3$ **18.** $y = x^4 - 8x^2 + 16$

19. $y = 4x^3 - 2x^2 - 2x$ **20.** $y = (x - 5)(x + 2)^2$

Use a graphing calculator to find the relative maximum, relative minimum, and zeros of each function.

21. $y = x^4 - 5x^3 + 5x^2 - 3$

22. $y = 5x^3 + x^2 - 9x + 4$

23. $y = x^4 - 4x - 1$

24. $y = x^3 - 3x^2 - 3x - 4$

5-3 Solving Polynomial Equations

Quick Review

One way to solve a polynomial equation is by factoring. First write the equation in the form $P(x) = 0$, where $P(x)$ is a polynomial. Then factor the polynomial, and use the Zero-Product Property to find the solutions, or roots. Real solutions and approximations of irrational solutions can also be found by using a graphing calculator. Imaginary solutions must be found using algebraic techniques.

Example

Solve $x^3 + 4x^2 = 12x$ by factoring.

Write in the form $P(x) = 0$.	$x^3 + 4x^2 - 12x = 0$
Factor the left side.	$x(x - 2)(x + 6) = 0$
Use the Zero-Product Property.	$x = 0, x - 2 = 0,$ $x + 6 = 0$
Solve each equation for x.	$x = 0, x = 2, x = -6$

The solutions are 0, 2, and −6.

Exercises

Find the real or imaginary solutions of each equation by factoring.

25. $x^2 - 11x = -24$ **26.** $4x^2 = -4x - 1$

27. $3x^3 + 3x^2 = 27x$ **28.** $2x^2 + 3 = 4x$

Find the real roots of each equation by graphing.

29. $x^4 + 3x^2 - 2x + 5 = 0$

30. $x^2 + 3 = x^3 - 5$

31. The height and width of a rectangular prism are each 2 inches shorter than the length of the prism. The volume of the prism is 40 cubic inches. Approximate the dimensions of the prism to the nearest hundredth.

5-4 Dividing Polynomials

Quick Review

You can use long division to divide a polynomial by one of its factors to find another factor. When you divide by a linear factor, you can simplify this division by writing only the coefficients of each term. This is called **synthetic division**. The **Remainder Theorem** states that $P(a)$ is the remainder when you divide $P(x)$ by $x - a$.

Example

Let $P(x) = 3x^2 - 13x + 15$. What is $P(3)$?

According to the Remainder Theorem, $P(3)$ is the remainder when you divide $P(x)$ by $x - 3$.
Use synthetic division.

Put the opposite of
the constant, 3, in the ⟶ $\underline{3}$ | 3   −13   15
divisor at the top left.

                                9   −12

                     3   −4   3

The quotient is $3x - 4$ with remainder 3, so $P(3) = 3$.

Exercises

Divide using long division. Check your answers.

32. $(x^3 + 7x^2 + 15x + 9) \div (x + 1)$

33. $(2x^3 - 7x^2 - 7x + 13) \div (x - 4)$

Determine whether each binomial is a factor of $x^3 + x^2 - 10x + 8$.

34. $x - 2$ **35.** $x - 4$

Divide using synthetic division.

36. $(x^3 + 5x^2 - x - 5) \div (x + 5)$

37. $(2x^3 + 14x^2 - 58x) \div (x + 10)$

38. $(5x^3 + 8x^2 - 60) \div (x - 2)$

Use the Remaider Theorem to determine the value of $P(a)$.

39. $P(x) = 2x^3 + 5x^2 + 7x - 4, a = -2$

40. $P(x) = x^3 - 4x^2 + 2x + 3, a = 1$

Do you know HOW?

For each polynomial function, describe the end behavior of its graph.

1. $f(x) = x^8 - 8x^4 + 6x^2$

2. $f(x) = -x^4 - x^3 + 1$

3. $f(x) = x^7 - 3x^5 - 5x^3$

4. What is the degree of the function that generates the data shown?

x	y
-3	159
-2	29
-1	-1
0	-3
1	-1
2	29
3	159

Find all solutions of each equation by factoring.

5. $x^3 - 5x^2 = 36x$

6. $27x^3 = 8$

7. $x^4 - 20x^2 + 64 = 0$

8. $x^3 + 125 = 0$

9. Use the Remainder Theorem and synthetic division to find $P(4)$ for $P(x) = 2x^4 - 3x^2 + 4x - 1$.

You have several boxes with the same dimensions. They have a combined volume of $2x^4 + 4x^3 - 18x^2 - 4x + 16$. Determine whether each binomial below could represent the number of boxes you have.

10. $x - 1$

11. $x + 2$

12. $2x + 8$

Write each polynomial in standard form. Then classify it by degree and number of terms.

13. $-2x^3 + 6 - x^3 + 5x$

14. $3(x - 1)(x + 4)$

Describe the shape of the graph of each cubic function by determining the end behavior and number of turning points.

15. $y = -5x^3$

16. $y = 3x^3 + 4x^2 + 2x - 1$

Do you UNDERSTAND?

17. You buy equal numbers of containers of strawberries, blueberries, and cherries. Cherries are $1 more per container than blueberries, which are $1 more per container than strawberries. The product of the 3 individual prices is 5 times the cost of one container of each fruit.
   a. Write a polynomial function to model the cost of your purchase.
   b. Graph to find the price of each container.
   c. **Writing** Explain how you used the graph to find the prices.

18. A cylinder has a radius of $3x - 2$ and a height of $3 - 2x$.
   a. Use 3.14 as π and graph the equation for the volume.
   b. Find the relative maximum.
   c. **Reasoning** What kind of limitation on the radius would make your answer in part (b) the maximum possible volume?

19. **Open-Ended** Write a polynomial function in factored form with at least three zeros that are negative, one of which has multiplicity 2.

Polynomials and Polynomial Functions

CHAPTER

5

PART B

In Part A, you learned about polynomial functions and graphs. Now you will apply what you learned to solve polynomial equations.

 Vocabulary for Part B

English/Spanish Vocabulary Audio Online:

English	Spanish
Binomial Theorem, *p. 348*	Teorema binomial
Conjugate Root Theorem, *p. 335*	Teorema de raíces conjugadas
expand, *p. 347*	expandir
Fundamental Theorem of Algebra, *p. 341*	Teorema fundamental de álgebra
power function, *p. 363*	función de potencia
Rational Root Theorem, *p. 332*	Teorema de la raíz racional

BIG ideas

1 Function
Essential Question What does the degree of a polynomial tell you about its related polynomial function?

2 Equivalence
Essential Question For a polynomial function, how are factors, zeros, and *x*-intercepts related?

3 Solving Equations and Inequalities
Essential Question For a polynomial equation, how are factors and roots related?

Chapter Preview for Part B

Theorems About Roots of Polynomial Equations

Objective To solve equations using the Rational Root Theorem

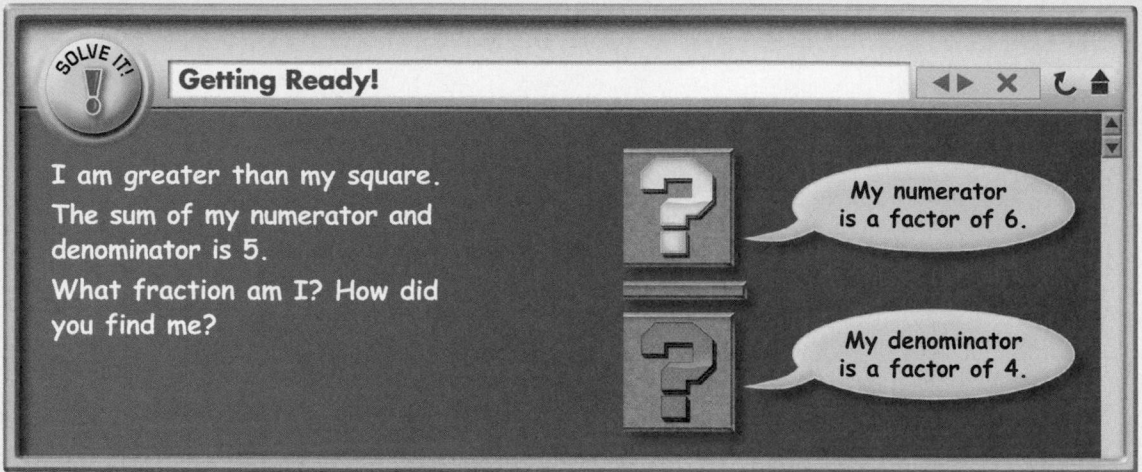

Getting Ready!

I am greater than my square.
The sum of my numerator and denominator is 5.
What fraction am I? How did you find me?

My numerator is a factor of 6.

My denominator is a factor of 4.

Lesson Vocabulary
• Rational Root Theorem

Factoring the polynomial $P(x) = a_n x^n + a_{n-1} x^{n-1} + \cdots + a_1 x + a_0$ can be challenging, especially when both a_n and a_0 have many factors.

Focus Question Why is the Rational Root Theorem important?

One way to find a root of the polynomial equation $P(x) = 0$ is to guess and check. This is usually inefficient unless there is a way to minimize the number of guesses, or possible roots. The **Rational Root Theorem** does just that.

Hint

integer factor
Factors of a number are typically only positive. The integer factors of a number include negative values.

leading coefficient
The leading coefficient is the coefficient of the first term of a polynomial written in standard form.

take note

Theorem   Rational Root Theorem

Let $P(x) = a_n x^n + a_{n-1} x^{n-1} + \cdots + a_1 x + a_0$ be a polynomial with integer coefficients. There are a limited number of possible roots of $P(x) = 0$:

• Integer roots must be factors of a_0.
• Rational roots must have reduced form $\frac{p}{q}$ where p is an integer factor of a_0 and q is an integer factor of a_n.

Factors of the leading coefficient:
$\pm 1, \pm 3, \pm 7,$ and $\pm 21.$

$$21x^2 + 29x + 10 = 0$$

$$x^2 + \frac{29}{21}x + \frac{10}{21} = 0$$

$$\left(x + \frac{2}{3}\right)\left(x + \frac{5}{7}\right) = 0$$

Factors of the constant term:
$\pm 1, \pm 2, \pm 5,$ and $\pm 10.$

The roots are $-\frac{2}{3}$ and $-\frac{5}{7}.$

Problem 1 Finding a Rational Root

What information can you get from the equation?
The equation gives you the leading coefficient and the constant term.

What are the rational roots of $2x^3 - x^2 + 2x + 5 = 0$?

The only possible rational roots have the form $\dfrac{\text{factor of constant term}}{\text{factor of leading coefficient}}$.

The constant term's factors are $\pm 1, \pm 5$. The leading coefficient's factors are $\pm 1, \pm 2$.

The only possible rational roots are $\pm 1, \pm 5, \pm\frac{1}{2}, \pm\frac{5}{2}$.

Hint

This process is similar to the tables you made to factor quadratics of the form $ax^2 + bx + c$.

The table shows the values of the function $y = P(x)$ for the possible roots. The only rational root of $2x^3 - x^2 + 2x + 5 = 0$ is -1.

x	1	-1	5	-5	$\frac{1}{2}$	$-\frac{1}{2}$	$\frac{5}{2}$	$-\frac{5}{2}$
$P(x)$	8	0	240	-280	6	$\frac{7}{2}$	35	$-\frac{75}{2}$

 Got It? 1. What are the rational roots of $3x^3 + 7x^2 + 6x - 8 = 0$?

Once you find one root, use synthetic division to factor the polynomial. Continue finding roots and dividing until you have a second-degree polynomial. Then, you can factor or use the Quadratic Formula to find the remaining roots.

Problem 2 Using the Rational Root Theorem

What are the rational roots of $15x^3 - 32x^2 + 3x + 2 = 0$?

Know	Need	Plan
The coefficients and the constant term of the polynomial	The rational roots of the polynomial equation	• Find one root. • Factor until you get a quadratic. • Use the Quadratic Formula to find the other roots.

Think

How can you find a root?
A root is a solution of the equation. Find a value that makes the equation true.

Step 1 The constant term's factors are ± 1 and ± 2. The leading coefficient's factors are $\pm 1, \pm 3, \pm 5,$ and ± 15.

Step 2 The possible rational roots are: $\pm 1, \pm 2, \pm\frac{1}{3}, \pm\frac{2}{3}, \pm\frac{1}{5}, \pm\frac{2}{5}, \pm\frac{1}{15},$ and $\pm\frac{2}{15}$.

Step 3 Test each possible rational root in the equation until you find a root.

Test 1: $15(1)^3 - 32(1)^2 + 3(1) + 2 = -12 \neq 0$

Test 2: $15(2)^3 - 32(2)^2 + 3(2) + 2 = 0$ ⟵ So 2 is a root.

Step 4 Factor the polynomial by using synthetic division:

$P(x) = (x - 2)(15x^2 - 2x - 1)$.

$$
\begin{array}{r|rrrr}
2 & 15 & -32 & 3 & 2 \\
  &   & 30 & -4 & -2 \\
\hline
  & 15 & -2 & -1 & 0
\end{array}
$$

Step 5 Since $15x^2 - 2x - 1 = (5x + 1)(3x - 1)$, the other roots are $-\frac{1}{5}$ and $\frac{1}{3}$.

Hint

Before using the Quadratic Formula, check if the expression is factorable.

The rational roots of $15x^3 - 32x^2 + 3x + 2 = 0$ are $2, -\frac{1}{5},$ and $\frac{1}{3}$.

 Got It? 2. What are the rational roots of $2x^3 + x^2 - 7x - 6 = 0$?

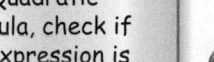

Focus Question Why is the Rational Root Theorem important?

Answer The Rational Root Theorem provides a list that includes all rational roots of the polynomial equation $P(x) = 0$. This limits your number of guesses if you try to solve by guess and check.

Lesson Check

Do you know HOW?

Use the Rational Root Theorem to list all possible rational roots for each equation.

1. $x^2 + x - 2 = 0$

2. $2x^3 - x^2 - 6 = 0$

3. $3x^4 + 2x^2 - 12 = 0$

Do you UNDERSTAND?

4. Reasoning In the statements below, r and s represent integers. Is each statement *always*, *sometimes,* or *never* true? Explain.

a. A root of the equation
$3x^3 + rx^2 + sx + 8 = 0$ could be 5.

b. A root of the equation
$3x^3 + rx^2 + sx + 8 = 0$ could be -2.

Practice and Problem-Solving Exercises

 **Practice**

Use the Rational Root Theorem to list all possible rational roots for each equation. Then find any actual rational roots.

 See Problems 1 and 2.

Guided Practice

To start, list the constant term's factors and the leading coefficient's factors.

5. $2x^3 - 5x + 4 = 0$

constant term factors: $\pm1, \pm2, \pm4$
leading coefficient factors: $\pm1, \pm2$

6. $x^3 - 4x + 1 = 0$ **7.** $x^3 + 2x - 9 = 0$ **8.** $5x^3 - 3x + 2 = 0$

9. $3x^3 + 9x - 6 = 0$ **10.** $4x^3 + 2x - 12 = 0$ **11.** $6x^3 + 2x - 18 = 0$

12. $7x^3 - x^2 + 4x + 10 = 0$ **13.** $8x^3 + 2x^2 - 5x + 1 = 0$ **14.** $10x^3 - 7x^2 + x - 10 = 0$

B Apply

Find all rational roots for $P(x) = 0$.

15. $P(x) = 2x^3 - 5x^2 + x - 1$ **16.** $P(x) = 6x^4 - 13x^3 + 13x^2 - 39x - 15$

17. $P(x) = 7x^3 - x^2 - 5x + 14$ **18.** $P(x) = 3x^4 - 7x^3 + 10x^2 - x + 12$

19. $P(x) = 6x^4 - 7x^2 - 3$ **20.** $P(x) = 2x^3 - 3x^2 - 8x + 12$

21. Error Analysis Your friend listed the possible rational roots of the equation as shown. Explain her error.

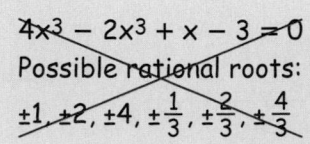

22. Which is NOT a possible rational root of $15x^3 + 6x^2 - x - 12$?

(A) -1 (B) $-\frac{4}{5}$ (C) -2 (D) $-\frac{1}{4}$

Objective To use the Conjugate Root Theorem and Descartes' Rule of Signs

In Part 1 of the lesson, you learned how to use the Rational Root Theorem to identify possible roots of a polynomial equation.

Connect to What You Know

Here you will learn how to explore roots using the Conjugate Root Theorem and Descartes' Rule of Signs.

Lesson Vocabulary
- Conjugate Root Theorem
- Descartes' Rule of Signs

Focus Question What is the Conjugate Root Theorem?

Recall from Lesson 4-8 that the complex numbers $a + bi$ and $a - bi$ are called conjugates. Similarly, the irrational numbers $a + \sqrt{b}$ and $a - \sqrt{b}$ are conjugates. If a complex number or an irrational number is a root of a polynomial equation with rational coefficients, so is its conjugate.

take note

Theorem Conjugate Root Theorem

If $P(x)$ is a polynomial with *rational* coefficients, then irrational roots of $P(x) = 0$ that have the form of $a + \sqrt{b}$ occur in conjugate pairs. If $a + \sqrt{b}$ is an irrational root with a and b rational, then $a - \sqrt{b}$ is also a root.

If $P(x)$ is a polynomial with *real* coefficients, then the complex roots of $P(x) = 0$ occur in conjugate pairs. If $a + bi$ is a complex root with a and b real, then $a - bi$ is also a root.

Problem 3 Using the Conjugate Root Theorem to Identify Roots

A quartic polynomial $P(x)$ has rational coefficients. If $\sqrt{2}$ and $1 + i$ are roots of $P(x) = 0$, what are the two other roots?

Think

Do you have real coefficients?
All rational numbers are real numbers. Therefore the rational coefficients are real coefficients.

Since $P(x)$ has rational coefficients and $0 + \sqrt{2}$ is a root of $P(x) = 0$, it follows from the Conjugate Root Theorem that $0 - \sqrt{2}$ is also a root.

Since $P(x)$ has real coefficients and $1 + i$ is a root of $P(x) = 0$, it follows that $1 - i$ is also a root.

The two other roots are $-\sqrt{2}$ and $1 - i$.

✓ **Got It?** **3.** A cubic polynomial $P(x)$ has real coefficients. If $3 - 2i$ and $\frac{5}{2}$ are two roots of $P(x) = 0$, what is one additional root?

Problem 4 **Using Conjugates to Construct a Polynomial**

Multiple Choice What cubic polynomial equation has roots -4 and $2i$?

Ⓐ $P(x) = x^3 - 2x^2 - 16x + 32$ Ⓒ $P(x) = x^3 + 4x^2 + 4x + 16$

Ⓑ $P(x) = x^3 - 4x^2 + 4x - 16$ Ⓓ $P(x) = x^3 + 4x^2 - 4x - 16$

Think

Does the Conjugate Root Theorem apply to -4?

No; the theorem does not apply because -4 is neither irrational nor imaginary.

Since $2i$ is a root, then $-2i$ is also a root.

Write the polynomial function. Use factored form.	$P(x) = (x + 2i)(x - 2i)(x + 4)$
Multiply the complex conjugates.	$= \left(x^2 - 2ix + 2ix - 4i^2\right)(x + 4)$
Add like terms. Substitute -1 for i^2.	$= \left(x^2 - 4(-1)\right)(x + 4)$
Simplify.	$= (x^2 + 4)(x + 4)$
Write in standard form.	$= x^3 + 4x^2 + 4x + 16$

The equation $x^3 + 4x^2 + 4x + 16 = 0$ has rational coefficients and has roots -4 and $2i$. The correct answer is C.

 Got It? **4.** What quartic polynomial equation has roots $2 - 3i$, 8, and 2?

Focus Question How can you find the number of real solutions of a polynomial equation?

The French mathematician René Descartes (1596–1650) recognized a connection between the roots of a polynomial equation and the $+$ and $-$ signs of the standard form.

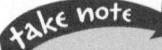 **Theorem** **Descartes' Rule of Signs**

Let $P(x)$ be a polynomial with real coefficients written in standard form.

- The number of positive real roots of $P(x) = 0$ is either equal to the number of sign changes between consecutive coefficients of $P(x)$ or is less than that by an even number.

- The number of negative real roots of $P(x) = 0$ is either equal to the number of sign changes between consecutive coefficients of $P(-x)$ or is less than that by an even number.

(In both cases, count multiple roots according to their multiplicity.)

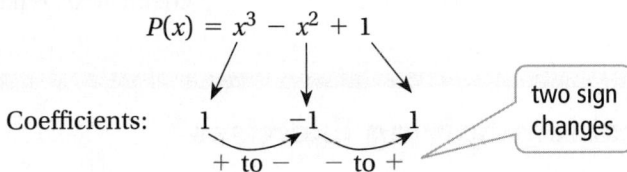

Problem 5 Using Descartes' Rule of Signs

What does Descartes' Rule of Signs tell you about the real roots of $x^3 - x^2 + 1 = 0$?

Step 1 Identify the number of positive real roots.

List the coefficients of $P(x)$. Identify the number of sign changes between consecutive coefficients.

$$P(x) = x^3 - x^2 + 1$$

Coefficients: 1   −1   1   two sign changes

+ to −   − to +

Since there are two sign changes, there are either 0 or 2 positive real roots.

Step 2 Identify the number of negative real roots.

List the coefficients of $P(-x)$. Identify the number of sign changes between consecutive coefficients.

$$P(-x) = (-x)^3 - (-x)^2 + 1$$

$$= -x^3 - x^2 + 1$$

Coefficients: −1   −1   1   one sign change

− to −   − to +

Think

Why can't there be zero negative real roots?
The number of negative roots is equal to 1 or is less than 1 by an even number. Zero is less than 1 by an odd number.

Since there is only one sign change, there is one negative real root.

Check Recall that graphs of cubic functions have zero or two turning points. Because the graph already shows two turning points, it will not change direction again. So there are no positive real roots.

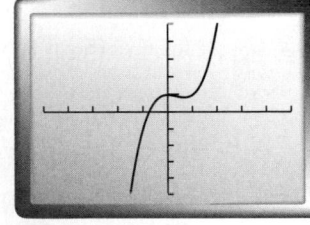

Got It? **5. a.** What does Descartes' Rule of Signs tell you about the real roots of $2x^4 - x^3 + 3x^2 - 1 = 0$?

b. **Reasoning** Can you confirm real and complex roots graphically? Explain.

Focus Question What is the Conjugate Root Theorem?
Answer The Conjugate Root Theorem allows you to identify roots in pairs. For a polynomial with rational coefficients, irrational roots occur in conjugate pairs and complex roots occur in conjugate pairs.

Focus Question How can you find the number of real solutions of a polynomial equation?
Answer Use Descartes' Rule of Signs to find the number of positive and negative real roots of a polynomial equation $P(x) = 0$. It is helpful to find out how many real roots a polynomial equation has before using the Rational Root Theorem to find the solutions.

Lesson Check

Do you know HOW?

Write a polynomial function with rational coefficients so that $P(x) = 0$ has the given roots.

1. 5 and 9

2. -4 and $2i$

Do you UNDERSTAND?

3. Vocabulary Give an example of a conjugate pair.

4. Error Analysis A student claims that $-4i$ is the only imaginary root of a polynomial equation that has real coefficients. What is the student's mistake?

Practice and Problem-Solving Exercises

A Practice

A polynomial function $P(x)$ with rational coefficients has the given roots. Find two additional roots of $P(x) = 0$.

◀ See Problem 3.

5. $-2i$ and $\sqrt{10}$

6. $14 - \sqrt{2}$ and $-6i$

7. i and $7 + 8i$

8. $-\sqrt{3}$ and $5 - \sqrt{11}$

Write a polynomial function $P(x)$ with rational coefficients so that $P(x) = 0$ has the given roots.

◀ See Problem 4.

Guided Practice

9. $-10i$

To start, use the Conjugate Root Theroem to identify a second root.	Since $-10i$ is a root, $10i$ is also a root.

10. 7 and 12

11. -9 and -15

12. $3i + 9$

13. 4, 16, and $1 + 19i$

14. $13i$ and $5 + 10i$

15. $11 - 2i$ and $8 + 13i$

What does Descartes' Rule of Signs say about the number of positive real roots and negative real roots for each polynomial function?

◀ See Problem 5.

Guided Practice

16. $P(x) = x^2 + 5x + 6$

To start, count and identify the number of sign changes in $P(x)$.	There are 0 sign changes in $P(x)$. So, there are 0 positive real roots.

17. $P(x) = 9x^3 - 4x^2 + 10$

18. $P(x) = 8x^3 + 2x^2 - 14x + 5$

B Apply

19. Think About a Plan You are building a square pyramid out of clay and want the height to be 0.5 cm shorter than twice the length of each side of the base. If you have 18 cm³ of clay, what is the greatest height you could use for your pyramid?

• How can drawing a diagram help you solve this problem?
• What is the formula for the volume of a pyramid?
• What equation can you solve to find the height of the pyramid?

> **Hint** The volume of a square pyramid with base side length s and height h is given by the formula $V = \frac{1}{3}s^2h$.

Write a polynomial function $P(x)$ with rational coefficients so that $P(x) = 0$ has the given roots.

20. -6, 3, and $-15i$

21. $4 + \sqrt{5}$ and $8i$

22. $-5 - 7i$ and $2 - \sqrt{11}$

23. Error Analysis Your friend is using Descartes' Rule of Signs to find the number of negative real roots of $x^3 + x^2 + x + 1 = 0$. Describe and correct the error.

$P(-x) = (-x)^3 + (-x)^2 + (-x) + 1$
$= -x^3 - x^2 - x + 1$
Because there is only one sign change in $P(-x)$, there must be one negative real root.

24. Reasoning A quartic equation with integer coefficients has two real roots and one imaginary root. Explain why the fourth root must be imaginary.

25. Gardening A gardener is designing a new garden in the shape of a trapezoid. She wants the shorter base to be twice the height and the longer base to be 4 feet longer than the shorter base. If she has enough topsoil to make a 60 ft^2 garden, what dimensions should she use for the garden? (*Hint:* $A = \frac{1}{2}(b_1 + b_2)h$.)

26. Open-Ended Write a quartic polynomial equation with integer coefficients that has two irrational roots and two imaginary roots.

Standardized Test Prep

GRIDDED RESPONSE

SAT/ACT

27. What is a positive root of $-5x^3 - 2x^2 + 9x + 30 = 0$?

28. What is the remainder when you divide $x^3 + 2x^2 - x - 6$ by $x - 1$?

29. A polynomial with rational coefficients has roots $-3i$ and $8 + \sqrt{7}$. What is the minimum degree of the polynomial?

30. What is the value of y in the solution of the system of equations?

31. What is the value of the greater solution of the equation $6x^2 - 17x + 5 = 0$?

Mixed Review

Divide.

See Lesson 5-4.

32. $(x^3 + 5x^2 - 3) \div (x - 1)$

33. $(7x^2 + 11x - 4) \div (x + 2)$

34. $(8x^3 + 12x^2 + 7) \div (x + 6)$

Solve.

See Lesson 4-8.

35. $7x^2 + 63 = 0$

36. $x^2 + 81 = 0$

37. $2x^2 + 288 = 0$

Get Ready! To prepare for Lesson 5-6, do Exercises 38 and 39.

Write each polynomial in standard form. Then classify it by degree and by number of terms.

See Lesson 5-1.

38. $6x^2 + 11 - 5x^4 + 9x$

39. $13x - 4x^5 + 7x^3 + 2$

The Fundamental Theorem of Algebra

Objective To use the Fundamental Theorem of Algebra to solve polynomial equations with complex solutions

SOLVE IT!

Getting Ready!

The first graph shows the three complex-number solutions of $x^3 - 1 = 0$. The second graph shows the six solutions of $x^6 - 1 = 0$. How many complex number solutions does $x^{12} - 1 = 0$ have? What are they?

These graphs are on complex planes.

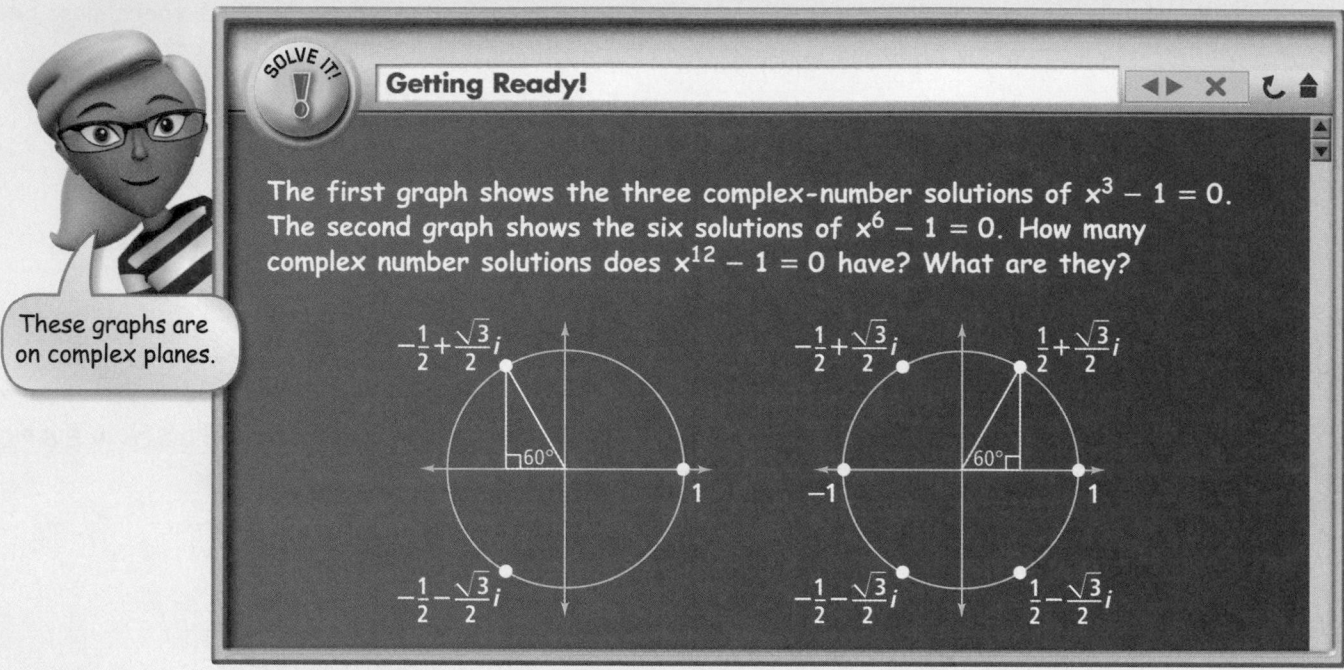

Lesson Vocabulary
• Fundamental Theorem of Algebra

You can factor any polynomial of degree n into n linear factors, but sometimes the factors will involve imaginary numbers.

Focus Question What is the Fundamental Theorem of Algebra?

It is easy to see graphically that every polynomial function of degree 1 has a single zero, the x-intercept. However, there appear to be three possibilities for polynomials of degree 2. They correspond to these three graphs:

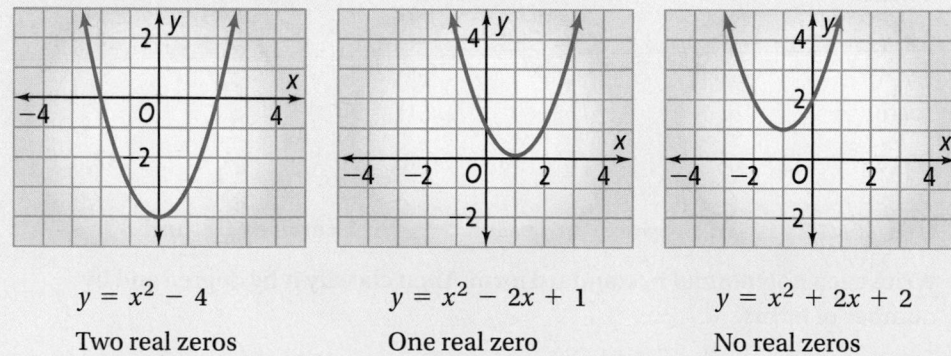

$y = x^2 - 4$

Two real zeros

$y = x^2 - 2x + 1$

One real zero

$y = x^2 + 2x + 2$

No real zeros

Hint

This is an extension of what you learned in Chapter 4 about the number of possible solutions of a quadratic equation.

However, by factoring, you can see that each related equation has two roots.

two real roots, 2 and -2	$x^2 - 4 = (x - 2)(x + 2) = 0$
a root of multiplicity *two* at 1	$x^2 - 2x + 1 = (x - 1)(x - 1) = 0$
two complex roots, $-1 + i$ and $-1 - i$	$x^2 + 2x + 2 = (x - (-1 + i))(x - (-1 - i)) = 0$

Every quadratic polynomial equation has two roots. Similarly, every cubic polynomial equation has three roots, and every polynomial of degree n has n roots.

The Fundamental Theorem of Algebra, proven by German mathematician Carl Friedrich Gauss (1777–1855), summarizes this result.

take note

Theorem   The Fundamental Theorem of Algebra

If $P(x)$ is a polynomial of degree $n \geq 1$, then $P(x) = 0$ has exactly n roots, including multiple and complex roots.

ONLINE PROBLEMS

Problem 1   Using the Fundamental Theorem of Algebra

What are all the roots of $x^5 - x^4 - 3x^3 + 3x^2 - 4x + 4 = 0$?

Know
- The polynomial equation has degree 5.
- There are 5 roots.

Need
The zeros of the function

Plan
Use the Rational Root and Factor Theorems, synthetic division, and factoring.

Step 1   The polynomial is in standard form.

The possible rational roots are $\pm 1, \pm 2, \pm 4$.

Step 2   Use synthetic division to evaluate the related polynomial function for $x = 1$. Since $P(1) = 0$, 1 is a root and $x - 1$ is a factor.

$$
\begin{array}{r|rrrrrr}
1 & 1 & -1 & -3 & 3 & -4 & 4 \\
 &   & 1 & 0 & -3 & 0 & -4 \\
\hline
 & 1 & 0 & -3 & 0 & -4 & 0 \\
\end{array}
$$

Think

How many linear factors will there be?
If there are five roots, there must be five linear factors.

Step 3   Use the results of the synthetic division to factor out $x - 1$.

Continue factoring until you have five linear factors.

$$
\begin{aligned}
x^5 - x^4 - 3x^3 + 3x^2 - 4x + 4 &= (x - 1)(x^4 - 3x^2 - 4) \\
&= (x - 1)(x^2 - 4)(x^2 + 1) \\
&= (x - 1)(x - 2)(x + 2)(x - i)(x + i)
\end{aligned}
$$

Step 4   The roots are 1, 2, -2, i, and $-i$.

By the Fundamental Theorem of Algebra, these are the only roots.

 Got It?   **1.** What are all the roots of the equation $x^4 + 2x^3 = 13x^2 - 10x$?

Problem 2 Finding All the Zeros of a Polynomial Function

What are the zeros of $f(x) = x^4 + x^3 - 7x^2 - 9x - 18$?

Step 1 Use a graphing calculator to find any real roots. The graph of $y = x^4 + x^3 - 7x^2 - 9x - 18$ shows real zeros at $x = -3$ and $x = 3$.

Think

Does the graph show all of the real roots?
Yes; the graphs of quartic functions have one or three turning points. Since the graph shows three turning points, it will not turn again to cross the *x*-axis a third time.

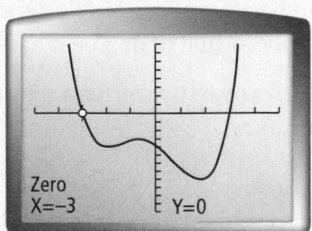
Zero
X=-3   Y=0

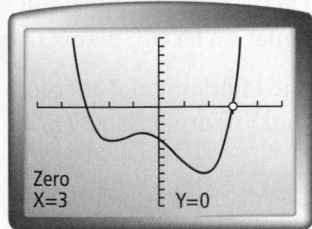
Zero
X=3   Y=0

Step 2 Factor out the linear factors $x + 3$ and $x - 3$. Use synthetic division twice.

$$
\begin{array}{r|rrrrr}
-3 & 1 & 1 & -7 & -9 & -18 \\
   &   & -3 & 6 & 3 & 18 \\
\hline
   & 1 & -2 & -1 & -6 & 0
\end{array}
\qquad
\begin{array}{r|rrrr}
3 & 1 & -2 & -1 & -6 \\
  &   & 3 & 3 & 6 \\
\hline
  & 1 & 1 & 2 & 0
\end{array}
$$

$$x^4 + x^3 - 7x^2 - 9x - 18 = (x + 3)(x^3 - 2x^2 - x - 6)$$
$$= (x + 3)(x - 3)(x^2 + x + 2)$$

Step 3 Use the Quadratic Formula. Find the complex roots of $x^2 + x + 2 = 0$.

Identify the values of *a*, *b*, and *c*. $a = 1, b = 1, c = 2$

Substitute. $\dfrac{-1 \pm \sqrt{1^2 - 4(1)(2)}}{2(1)}$

Simplify. $\dfrac{-1 \pm \sqrt{-7}}{2}$

The complex roots are $\dfrac{-1 + i\sqrt{7}}{2}$ and $\dfrac{-1 - i\sqrt{7}}{2}$.

Step 4 The four zeros of the function are $-3, 3, \dfrac{-1 + i\sqrt{7}}{2}$, and $\dfrac{-1 - i\sqrt{7}}{2}$.
By the Fundamental Theorem of Algebra, there can be no other zeros.

 **Got It?** **2. a.** What are all the zeros of the function $g(x) = 2x^4 - 3x^3 - x - 6$?

b. Reasoning A graph of
$f(x) = x^5 + 4x^4 - 3x^3 - 12x^2 - 4x - 4$
is shown at the right.
  i. Use the turning points to explain why the graph does NOT show all of the real zeros of the function.
  ii. The graph of $g(x) = f(x) + 4$ is a translation of the graph of *f* up 4 units. How many real zeros of *g* will the graph of *g* show? Explain.

Hint

For part (b), recall the possible number of turning points of a polynomial function from Lesson 5-1.

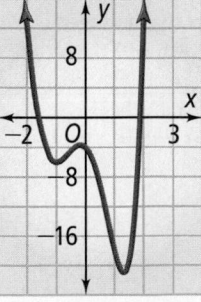

Concept Summary   The Fundamental Theorem of Algebra

Here are equivalent ways to state the Fundamental Theorem of Algebra. You can use any one of these statements to prove the others.

- Every polynomial equation of degree $n \geq 1$ has exactly n roots, including multiple and complex roots.
- Every polynomial of degree $n \geq 1$ has n linear factors.
- Every polynomial function of degree $n \geq 1$ has at least one zero.

Focus Question   What is the Fundamental Theorem of Algebra?

Answer   The Fundamental Theorem of Algebra states that for a polynomial $P(x)$ of degree $n \geq 1$, $P(x) = 0$ has exactly n roots, including any multiple and complex roots. It is useful because you can use the degree of a polynomial to determine whether you have found all possible roots.

Lesson Check

Do you know HOW?

Find the number of roots for each equation.

1. $5x^4 + 12x^3 - x^2 + 3x + 5 = 0$

2. $-x^{14} - x^8 - x + 7 = 0$

Find all the zeros for each function.

3. $y = x^3 - 5x^2 + 16x - 80$

4. $y = x^4 - 2x^3 + x^2 - 2x$

Do you UNDERSTAND?

5. Vocabulary Given a polynomial equation of degree n, explain how you determine the number of roots of the equation.

6. Open-Ended Write a polynomial function of degree 4 with rational coefficients and two complex zeros of multiplicity 2.

7. Writing Describe when to use synthetic division and when to use the Quadratic Formula to determine the linear factors of a polynomial.

Practice and Problem-Solving Exercises

 **Practice**

Without using a calculator, find all the roots of each equation.  **See Problem 1.**

Guided Practice

To start, identify the possible rational roots.

8. $x^3 - 3x^2 + x - 3 = 0$

The possible rational roots are $\pm 1, \pm 3$.

9. $x^3 + 4x^2 + x - 6 = 0$

10. $x^3 - 5x^2 + 2x + 8 = 0$

11. $x^4 + 4x^3 + 7x^2 + 16x + 12 = 0$

12. $x^4 - 4x^3 + x^2 + 12x - 12 = 0$

Find all the zeros of each function.

See Problem 2.

Guided Practice

To start, use a graphing calculator to find possible real roots.

13. $y = 2x^3 + x^2 + 1$

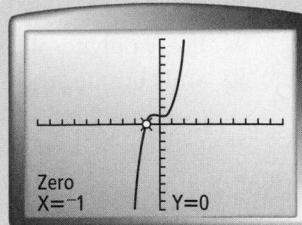

Zero
X=-1   Y=0

14. $g(x) = x^3 - 5x^2 + 5x - 4$

15. $y = x^3 - 2x^2 - 3x + 6$

16. $y = x^4 - 6x^2 + 8$

17. $f(x) = x^4 - 3x^2 - 4$

18. $y = x^3 - 3x^2 - 9x$

19. $y = x^3 + 6x^2 + x + 6$

B Apply

For each equation, state the number of complex roots, the possible number of real roots, and the possible rational roots.

20. $2x^4 - x^3 + 2x^2 + 5x - 26 = 0$

21. $x^5 - x^3 - 11x^2 + 9x + 18 = 0$

22. $-12 + x + 10x^2 + 3x^3 = 0$

23. $4x^6 - x^5 - 24 = 0$

Find all the zeros of each function.

24. $y = x^3 - 4x^2 + 9x - 36$

25. $y = 2x^3 - 3x^2 - 18x - 8$

26. $y = 3x^3 - 7x^2 - 14x + 24$

27. $y = x^3 - x^2 - 3x - 9$

28. Think About a Plan A polynomial function, $f(x) = x^4 - 5x^3 - 28x^2 + 188x - 240$, is used to model a new roller coaster section. The loading zone will be placed at one of the zeros. The function has a zero at 5. What are the possible locations for the loading zone?
  • Can you determine how many zeros you need to find?
  • How can you use polynomial division?
  • What other methods can be helpful?

29. Bridges A twist in a river can be modeled by the function $f(x) = \frac{1}{3}x^3 + \frac{1}{2}x^2 - x$, $-3 \leq x \leq 2$. A city wants to build a road that goes directly along the x-axis. How many bridges would it have to build?

30. Three roots of a polynomial equation with real coefficients are 3, $5 - 3i$, and $-3i$. Which of the following must also be a root of the equation?

I. -3 II. $5 + 3i$ III. $3i$

Ⓐ II only   Ⓒ II and III only

Ⓑ I and II only   Ⓓ I, II, and III

31. Reasoning A quartic polynomial function has zeros at 3 and $5 - i$. Can $4 + i$ also be a zero of the function? Explain your reasoning.

Determine whether each of the following statement is *always*, *sometimes*, or *never* true.

32. Polynomial functions with complex coefficients have exactly one complex zero.

33. A polynomial function that does not intercept the x-axis has complex roots only.

34. Open-Ended Write a polynomial function that has four possible rational zeros but no actual rational zeros.

35. Error Analysis Maurice says: "Every linear function has exactly one zero. It follows from the Fundamental Theorem of Algebra." Cheryl disagrees. "What about the linear function $y = 2$?" she asks. "Its graph is a line, but it has no x-intercept." Whose reasoning is incorrect? Where is the flaw?

Standardized Test Prep

SAT/ACT

36. How many roots does $f(x) = x^4 + 5x^3 + 3x^2 + 2x + 6$ have?

(A) 5   (B) 4   (C) 3   (D) 2

37. Which translation takes $y = |x + 2| - 1$ to $y = |x| + 2$?

(F) 2 units right, 3 units down   (H) 2 units left, 3 units up
(G) 2 units right, 3 units up   (I) 2 units left, 3 units down

38. What is the factored form of the expression $x^4 - 3x^3 + 2x^2$?

(A) $x^2(x - 1)(x + 2)$ (B) $x^2(x + 1)(x + 2)$ (C) $x^2(x + 1)(x - 2)$ (D) $x^2(x - 1)(x - 2)$

Short Response

39. How would you test whether $(2, -2)$ is a solution of the system? $\begin{cases} y < -2x + 3 \\ y \geq x - 4 \end{cases}$

Mixed Review

40. Find a fourth-degree polynomial equation with real coefficients that has $2i$ and $-3 + i$ as roots.   ◀ **See Lesson 5-5.**

Solve each equation using the Quadratic Formula.   ◀ **See Lesson 4-7.**

41. $x^2 - 6x + 1 = 0$ **42.** $2x^2 + 5x = -9$ **43.** $2(x^2 + 2) = 3x$

Determine whether a quadratic model exists for each set of values. If so, write the model.   ◀ **See Lesson 4-3.**

44. $f(-1) = 0, f(2) = 3, f(1) = 4$ **45.** $f(-4) = 11, f(-5) = 5, f(-6) = 3$

Get Ready!   To prepare for Lesson 5-7, do Exercises 46–48.

Write each polynomial in standard form.   ◀ **See Lesson 4-2.**

46. $(x + 1)^3$ **47.** $(x - 3)^3$ **48.** $(x + 5)^3$

Pascal's Triangle

You are standing at the corner of the grid shown at the right (point A1). You are only permitted to travel down or to the right. The only way to get to point A2 is by traveling down one unit. The only way to get to point B1 is to travel to the right one unit. There are two ways to get to point B2.

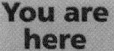

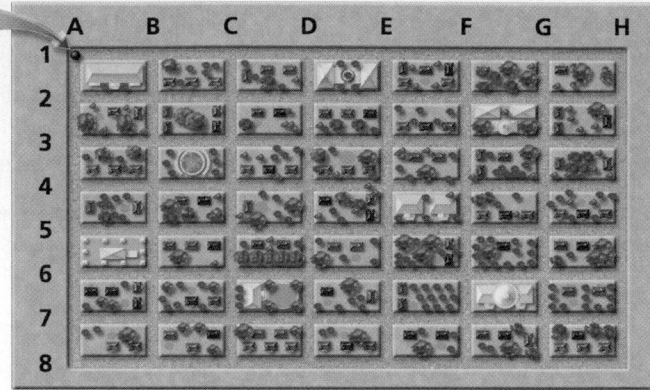

Exercises

1. What are the two different ways you can get from point A1 to point B2?

2. Copy the grid. Travel only down or to the right. In how many ways can you get from point A1 to point A3?

3. Use your copy of the grid from Exercise 2. In how many ways can you get from point A1 to point C2?

4. In how many ways can you get to point B5 from your starting point, A1?

5. Mark the number of ways you can get to each point on the grid from point A1.

6. Reasoning Describe any patterns you see in the numbers on the grid.

7. Describe how the numbers increase in each row. How can you tell the next number in each row without counting the number of paths from A1?

8. Writing The completed grid is called Pascal's Triangle. Rotate your copy of the grid 45° clockwise so that point A1 is at the top. Explain why the grid is called a triangle.

9. Find the sum of the rows of the rotated grid. (These would be diagonals in the original grid.) What pattern do you find?

5-7 The Binomial Theorem

Objectives To expand a binomial using Pascal's Triangle
To use the Binomial Theorem

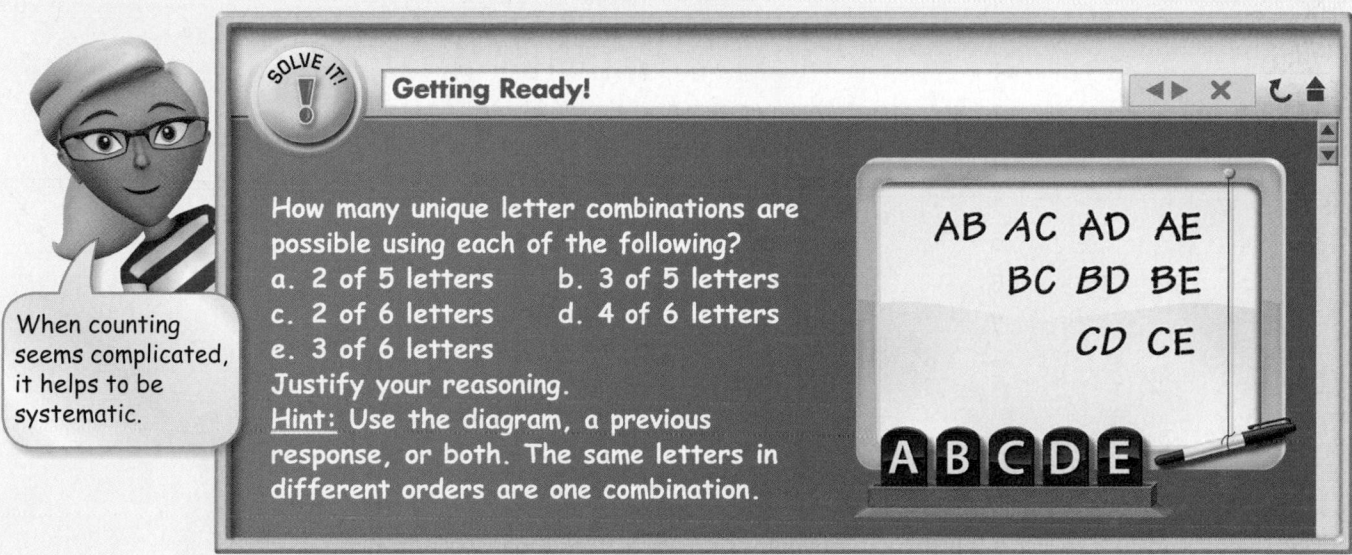

SOLVE IT!

Getting Ready!

When counting seems complicated, it helps to be systematic.

How many unique letter combinations are possible using each of the following?
a. 2 of 5 letters   b. 3 of 5 letters
c. 2 of 6 letters   d. 4 of 6 letters
e. 3 of 6 letters
Justify your reasoning.
<u>Hint:</u> Use the diagram, a previous response, or both. The same letters in different orders are one combination.

AB AC AD AE
BC BD BE
CD CE

A B C D E

Lesson Vocabulary
• expand
• Pascal's Triangle
• Binomial Theorem

There is a connection between the triangular pattern of numbers in the Solve It and the expansion of $(a + b)^n$.

Focus Question Why is the Binomial Theorem useful?

You can *expand* $(a + b)^3$ using the Distributive Property.

$(a + b)^3 = (a + b)(a + b)(a + b) = a^3 + 3a^2b + 3ab^2 + b^3$

To **expand** the power of a binomial in general, first multiply as needed. Then write the polynomial in standard form.

Consider the expansions of $(a + b)^n$ for the first few values of n:

Row	Power	Expanded Form	Coefficients Only
0	$(a + b)^0$	1	1
1	$(a + b)^1$	$1a^1 + 1b^1$	$1\ 1$
2	$(a + b)^2$	$1a^2 + 2a^1b^1 + 1b^2$	$1\ 2\ 1$
3	$(a + b)^3$	$1a^3 + 3a^2b^1 + 3a^1b^2 + 1b^3$	$1\ 3\ 3\ 1$
4	$(a + b)^4$	$1a^4 + 4a^3b^1 + 6a^2b^2 + 4a^1b^3 + 1b^4$	$1\ 4\ 6\ 4\ 1$

The "coefficients only" column matches the numbers in *Pascal's Triangle*. **Pascal's Triangle**, named for the French mathematician Blaise Pascal (1623–1662), is a triangular array of numbers in which the first and last number of each row is 1. Each of the other numbers in the row is the sum of the two numbers above it.

Hint

Remember that the first row is Row 0, not Row 1.

For example, to generate Row 5, use the sums of the adjacent elements in the row above it.

Row	Pascal's Triangle
0	1
1	1 1
2	1 2 1
3	1 3 3 1
4	1 4 6 4 1
5	1 5 10 10 5 1
6	1 6 15 20 15 6 1
7	1 7 21 35 35 21 7 1
8	1 8 28 56 70 56 28 8 1

$$1 \quad\overset{+}{\searrow}\quad 4 \quad\overset{+}{\searrow}\quad 6 \quad\overset{+}{\searrow}\quad 4 \quad\overset{+}{\searrow}\quad 1$$
$$5 \qquad 10 \qquad 10 \qquad 5$$

Problem 1 Using Pascal's Triangle

Plan

What row of Pascal's Triangle should you use for this expression?
The expression is raised to the 6th power, so use the 6th row.

What is the expansion of $(a + b)^6$? Use Pascal's Triangle.

The exponents for *a* begin with 6 and decrease to 0.

$$1a^6b^0 + 6a^5b^1 + 15a^4b^2 + 20a^3b^3 + 15a^2b^4 + 6a^1b^5 + 1a^0b^6$$

The exponents for *b* begin with 0 and increase to 6.

$$(a + b)^6 = a^6 + 6a^5b + 15a^4b^2 + 20a^3b^3 + 15a^2b^4 + 6ab^5 + b^6.$$

Got It? 1. What is the expansion of $(a + b)^8$? Use Pascal's Triangle.

The **Binomial Theorem** gives a general formula for expanding a binomial.

take note

Theorem Binomial Theorem

Hint

Note that the exponents of a and b always sum to n.

For every positive integer n,

$$(a + b)^n = P_0a^n + P_1a^{n-1}b + P_2a^{n-2}b^2 + \cdots + P_{n-1}ab^{n-1} + P_nb^n$$

where $P_0, P_1, \ldots, P_n$ are the numbers in the nth row of Pascal's Triangle.

When you use the Binomial Theorem to expand $(x - 2)^4$, $a = x$ and $b = -2$. To expand a binomial such as $(3x - 2)^5$, $a = 3x$. Remember that $a^4 = (3x)^4$, not $3x^4$.

 Problem 2 Expanding a Binomial

What is the expansion of $(3x - 2)^5$? Use the Binomial Theorem.

Think

For $(3x - 2)^5$, use the 5th row of Pascal's Triangle.

The Binomial Theorem uses a binomial sum of the form $(a + b)^n$.

Apply the Binomial Theorem with $a = 3x$ and $b = 2$.

Simplify.

Write

Pascal's Triangle

$$1$$
$$1 \quad 1$$
$$1 \quad 2 \quad 1$$
$$1 \quad 3 \quad 3 \quad 1$$
$$1 \quad 4 \quad 6 \quad 4 \quad 1$$
$$\boxed{1 \quad 5 \quad 10 \quad 10 \quad 5 \quad 1}$$

$(3x - 2)^5 = (3x + (-2))^5$

$a = 3x \qquad b = -2$

$= (3x)^5 + 5(3x)^4(-2)^1 + 10(3x)^3(-2)^2$
$\quad + 10(3x)^2(-2)^3 + 5(3x)^1(-2)^4 + 1(-2)^5$

$= 243x^5 - 810x^4 + 1080x^3 - 720x^2 + 240x - 32$

 Got It? 2. a. What is the expansion of $(2x - 3)^4$? Use the Binomial Theorem.

b. Reasoning Consider the following:

$$11^0 = 1 \qquad 11^1 = 11 \qquad 11^2 = 121 \qquad 11^3 = 1331 \qquad 11^4 = 14641$$

Why do these powers of 11 have digits that mirror Pascal's Triangle?

Hint

You can write 11 as a sum in the form $a + b$.

Focus Question Why is the Binomial Theorem useful?

Answer The Binomial Theorem provides a general formula for expanding the power of a binomial, without having to use repeated multiplication.

Lesson Check

Do you know HOW?

Use Pascal's Triangle to expand each binomial.

1. $(x + a)^3$

2. $(x - 2)^5$

3. $(2x + 4)^2$

4. $(3a - 2)^3$

Do you UNDERSTAND?

5. Vocabulary Tell whether the Binomial Theorem can expand each expression.

  a. $(2a - 6)^4$

  b. $(5x^2 + 1)^5$

  c. $(x^2 - 3x - 4)^3$

6. Writing Describe the relationship between Pascal's Triangle and the Binomial Theorem.

Practice and Problem-Solving Exercises

 **Practice**   Expand each binomial.    **See Problems 1 and 2.**

Guided Practice →

To start, identify the fourth row of Pascal's Triangle.

7. $(a + 2)^4$

     1 4 6 4 1

8. $(x - y)^3$ **9.** $(6 + a)^6$

10. $(x - 5)^3$ **11.** $(y + 1)^8$

12. $(b - 4)^7$ **13.** $(2x - y)^7$

14. $(a + 3b)^4$ **15.** $(4x + 2)^6$

16. $(4 - x)^8$ **17.** $(4x + 5)^2$

18. $(3a - 7)^3$ **19.** $(3y - 11)^4$

 **Apply**

20. Think About a Plan The side length of a cube is $\left(x^2 - \frac{1}{2}\right)$. Determine the volume of the cube.
- Rewrite the binomial as a sum.
- Consider $(a + b)^n$. Identify a and b in the given binomial.
- Which row of Pascal's Triangle can be used to expand the binomial?

21. In the expansion of $(2m - 3n)^9$, one of the terms contains m^3.
  a. What is the exponent of n in this term?
  b. What is the coefficient of this term?

Find the specified term of each binomial expansion.

22. Fourth term of $(x + 2)^5$

23. Third term of $(x - 3)^6$

24. Third term of $(3x - 1)^5$

25. Fifth term of $(a + 5b^2)^4$

26. Reasoning Explain why the coefficients in the expansion of $(x + 2y)^3$ do not match the numbers in the 3rd row of Pascal's Triangle.

27. Compare and Contrast What are the benefits and challenges of using the Binomial Theorem when expanding $(2x + 3)^2$? Using the Distributive Property? Which method would you choose when expanding $(2x + 3)^6$? Why?

Expand each binomial.

28. $(2x - 2y)^6$

29. $(x^2 + 4)^6$

30. $(x^2 - y^2)^3$

31. $(a - b^2)^5$

32. $(3x + 8y)^3$

33. $(4x - 7y)^4$

34. $(7a + 2y)^{10}$

35. $(4x^3 + 2y^2)^6$

36. $(3b - 36)^4$

37. $(5a + 2b)^3$

38. $(b^2 - 2)^8$

39. $(-2y^2 + x)^5$

40. Geometry The side length of a cube is given by the expression $(2x + 8)$. Write a binomial power for the area of a face of the cube and for the volume of the cube. Then use the Binomial Theorem to expand and rewrite the powers in standard form.

41. Writing Explain why the terms of $(x - y)^n$ have alternating positive and negative signs.

42. Error Analysis A student expands $(3x - 8)^4$ as shown below. Describe and correct the student's error.

$$(3x - 8)^4 = (3x)^4 + 4(3x)^3(-8) + 6(3x)^2(-8)^2 + 4(3x)(-8)^3 + (-8)^4$$
$$= 3x^4 - 96x^3 + 1152x^2 - 6144x + 4096$$

Standardized Test Prep

43. What is the fourth term in the expansion of $(2a + 4b)^5$?

    Ⓐ $256a^4b$ Ⓒ $2560a^2b^3$

    Ⓑ $768a^3b^2$ Ⓓ $2048ab^4$

44. Suppose y varies directly with x. If x is 30 when y is 10, what is x when y is 9?

    Ⓕ 3   Ⓗ 29

    Ⓖ 27   Ⓘ $\frac{300}{9}$

45. Which of the following is a root of $9x^2 - 30x + 25 = 0$?

    Ⓐ $x = \frac{3}{5}$ Ⓒ $x = -\frac{5}{3}$

    Ⓑ $x = \frac{5}{3}$ Ⓓ $x = -\frac{3}{5}$

46. Which expression is equivalent to $(2 - 7i) \div (2i)^3$?

    Ⓐ $\frac{7}{8} - \frac{1}{4}i$ Ⓑ $\frac{1}{4} - \frac{7}{8}i$ Ⓒ $\frac{7}{8} + \frac{1}{4}i$ Ⓓ $\frac{1}{4} + \frac{7}{8}i$

47. One company charges a monthly fee of $7.95 and $2.25 per hour for Internet access. Another company does not charge a monthly fee, but charges $2.75 per hour for Internet access. Write a system of equations to represent the cost c for t hours of access in one month for each company. Then find how many hours of use it will take for the costs to be equal.

Mixed Review

Find all the roots of each equation.   ◀ **See Lesson 5-6.**

48. $x^4 + 7x^3 + 20x^2 + 29x + 15 = 0$ **49.** $x^5 - x^4 + 10x^3 - 10x^2 + 9x - 9 = 0$

50. $2x^3 + 11x^2 + 14x + 8 = 0$ **51.** $x^4 - x^3 + 6x^2 - 13x + 7 = 0$

Simplify each expression.   ◀ **See Lesson 4-8.**

52. $(5i - 4)(-2i + 7)$ **53.** $\frac{-6 - 2i}{3 + i}$

Get Ready!   **To prepare for Lesson 5-8, do Exercises 54 and 55.**

Write each polynomial in standard form. Then classify it by degree and   ◀ **See Lesson 5-1.**
number of terms.

54. $5x^2 - x + 2x^3 + 9$ **55.** $1 + 4x - 7x^2$

Polynomial Models in the Real World

Objective To fit data to linear, quadratic, cubic, or quartic models

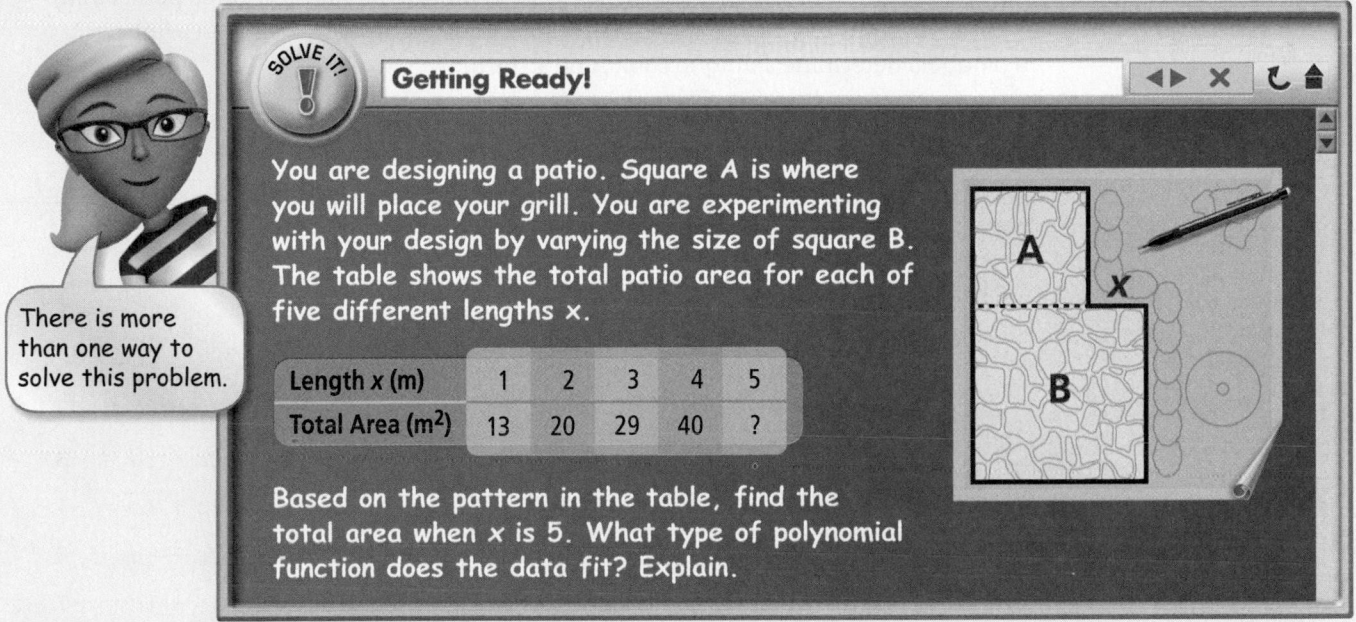

SOLVE IT!

Getting Ready!

You are designing a patio. Square A is where you will place your grill. You are experimenting with your design by varying the size of square B. The table shows the total patio area for each of five different lengths x.

There is more than one way to solve this problem.

Length x (m)	1	2	3	4	5
Total Area (m²)	13	20	29	40	?

Based on the pattern in the table, find the total area when x is 5. What type of polynomial function does the data fit? Explain.

You can use polynomial functions to model many real-world situations. The behavior of the graphs of polynomial functions of different degrees can suggest what type of polynomial will best fit a particular data set.

Focus Question How can you solve real-world situations given a particular data set?

You can use a graphing calculator to help you find functions that model data, such as the data shown in the table here.

Enter the data into your calculator and use three different regressions: **LINREG**, **QUADREG**, and **CUBICREG**.

Graph each regression function and the scatter plot of the data in the same window. For this data set, the cubic function appears to be a perfect fit.

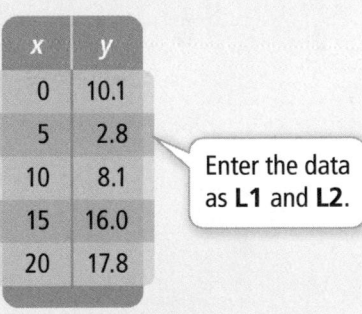

x	y
0	10.1
5	2.8
10	8.1
15	16.0
20	17.8

Enter the data as **L1** and **L2**.

Hint

Polynomial functions can be degree 0 (constant), degree 1 (linear), degree 2 (quadratic), degree 3 (cubic), and so on.

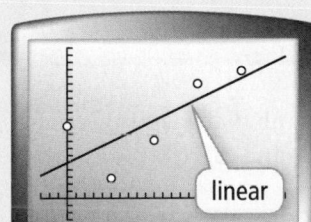

linear

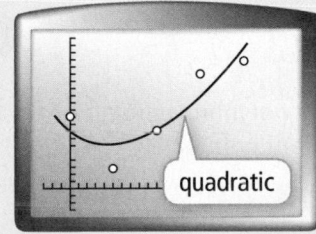

quadratic

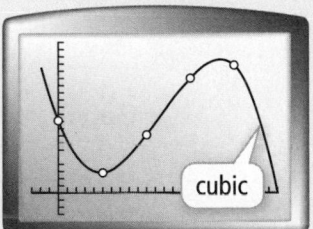

cubic

Key Concept   The $(n + 1)$ Point Principle

For any set of $n + 1$ points in the coordinate plane that pass the vertical line test, there is a unique polynomial of degree at most n that fits the points perfectly.

This principle confirms that any two points determine a unique line. Three points that are not on a line determine a unique parabola. Four points that are not on a line or a parabola determine a unique cubic, and so forth.

Problem 1   Using a Polynomial Function to Model Data

What polynomial function has a graph that passes through the four points $(0, -3)$, $(1, -1)$, $(2, 5)$, and $(-1, -7)$?

Plan

How can you use the four points to find a system of equations?
Substitute each point into a general cubic function.

Step 1   By the $(n + 1)$ Point Principle, there is a polynomial $y = ax^3 + bx^2 + cx + d$ that fits the points perfectly.

Substitute the x- and y-values of the four points to get four linear equations in four unknowns.

$$-3 = a(0)^3 + b(0)^2 + c(0) + d \quad \rightarrow \quad 0a + 0b + 0c + 1d = -3$$

$$-1 = a(1)^3 + b(1)^2 + c(1) + d \quad \rightarrow \quad 1a + 1b + 1c + 1d = -1$$

$$5 = a(2)^3 + b(2)^2 + c(2) + d \quad \rightarrow \quad 8a + 4b + 2c + 1d = 5$$

$$-7 = a(-1)^3 + b(-1)^2 + c(-1) + d \quad \rightarrow \quad -1a + 1b - 1c + 1d = -7$$

Step 2   Write the system in matrix form. Use the **RREF()** function to find the coefficient values a, b, c, and d.

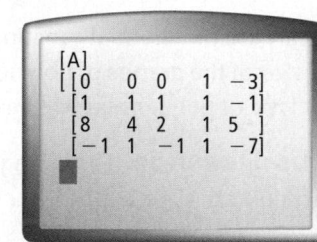
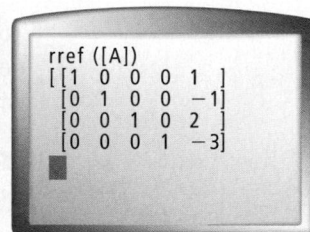

Step 3 $a = 1$, $b = -1$, $c = 2$, and $d = -3$.
The polynomial function is $y = x^3 - x^2 + 2x - 3$.

Check   Use **CUBICREG** with the four given points.

The solution checks.

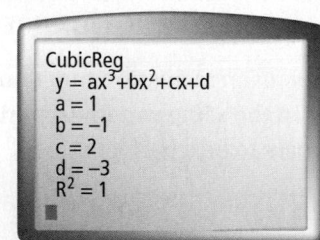
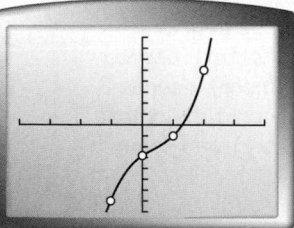

Got It?   1. What polynomial function has a graph that passes through the four points $(-2, 1)$, $(0, 5)$, $(2, 9)$, and $(3, 36)$?

Problem 2 Modeling Data

Food Production The chart shows how much milk Wisconsin dairy farms produced in 1955, 1980, and 2005. What linear model best fits the data? Use the model to estimate milk production in 2000.

Milk Production (in billions of lbs)

1955	1980	2005
16.5	22.4	22.9

Think

What data should you enter?
Enter the years, after 1900, and billions of pounds of milk produced.

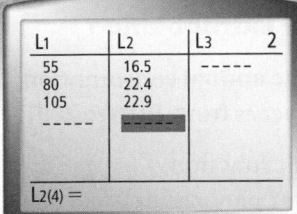

Enter the data. Let x represent years after 1900. Let y represent billions of pounds of milk.

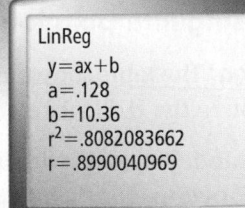

Use **LinReg** to find a linear model:
$f(x) = 0.128x + 10.36$.
Notice the value of r^2.

The closer r^2 is to 1, the better the fit.

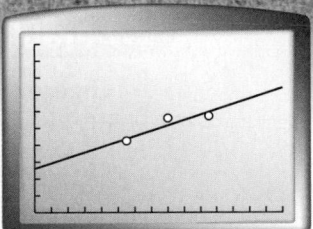

Show the scatter plot of the data and a graph of f(x).

Use the model to estimate milk production in 2000.

$$f(100) = 0.128(100) + 10.36 \approx 23.2$$

In 2000, Wisconsin produced about 23.2 billion pounds of milk.

 Got It? **2.** Use the linear model. Estimate Wisconsin milk production in 1995.

Problem 3 Comparing Models

Food Production The graph shows the quadratic model for the milk production data in Problem 2. The quadratic model fits the data points exactly because of the $(n + 1)$ Point Principle. Given that both models are good fits, which seems more likely to represent milk production over time?

Compare the shapes of the models.

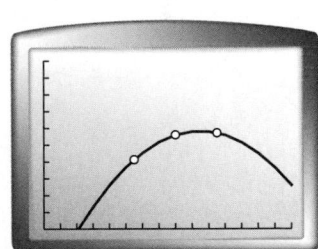

Think

Is the quadratic model reasonable?
No; the quadratic model will show milk production eventually decreasing to below zero.

Linear Model: This model continually rises.

Quadratic Model: This model has down-and-down end behavior. It shows slowing growth, a turning point, and then a decline, eventually to 0 and negative values.

Despite the R^2 value of 1 for the quadratic model, the linear model is more likely to represent milk production over time since it shows a continuing increase.

 Got It? **3.** If four data points were given, would a cubic function be the best model for the data? Explain your answer.

When deciding whether a certain model is reliable, it is important to consider the source of the data. Data generated by a law of physics or a geometric formula will have a mathematical model that fits the data and yields accurate predictions. For other data, such as sales records, you should only approximate the data close to the domain over which it was generated.

Using a model to predict a *y*-value "outside" the domain of a data set is *extrapolation*. Estimating within the domain is *interpolation*. Interpolation usually yields reliable estimates. Extrapolation becomes less reliable as you move farther away from the *x*-values of the data.

Problem 4 Using Interpolation and Extrapolation

Cheese Consumption The table shows average annual consumption of cheese per person in the U. S. for selected years from 1910 to 2001.

A Use **CUBICREG**. Model the data with a cubic function. Then graph the function along with a scatter plot of the data.

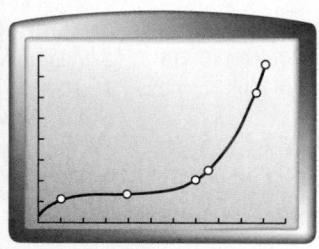

CubicReg
$y = ax^3 + bx^2 + cx + d$
$a = 9.242151\text{E}{-}5$
$b = {}^-.0095843361$
$c = .3106497055$
$d = 1.802125648$
$R^2 = .9976342$

Cheese Consumption

Year	Pounds Consumed
1910	4
1940	5
1970	8
1975	10
1995	25
2001	30

SOURCE: U.S. Department of Agriculture

Since R^2 is close to 1, the fit is good. The cubic model is approximately
$y = 0.0000924x^3 - 0.00958x^2 + 0.311x + 1.802$.

B Use the model from part (a) to estimate the U.S. cheese consumption for 1980, 2000, and 2012. In which estimate do you have the most confidence? The least confidence? Explain.

Use the cubic model from part A to estimate the cheese consumption for each year.

1980: 12.6 lb of cheese per person
2000: 29.4 lb of cheese per person
2012: 46.2 lb of cheese per person

Think

What affects your confidence in drawing conclusions from the model?
Your confidence can waver when model behavior is extreme or when there are large gaps in the data.

You can be confident in interpolating the estimates for 1980 (**Y1(80)**) and 2000 (**Y1(100)**) because the cheese consumption fits the pattern of increase shown in the table. You should have the least confidence in the extrapolated 2012 (**Y1(112)**) estimate because the cubic model increases so quickly beyond 2001.

Y1 (80)
          12.63416396
Y1 (100)
          29.44524491
Y1 (112)
          46.21454748
■

Got It? **4. a.** Use **LINREG** to find a linear model for cheese consumption. Graph it with a scatter plot.
  b. **Reasoning** Use the linear model to estimate consumption for 1980, 2000, and 2012. In which of these estimates do you have the most confidence? The least confidence? Explain.

Focus Question How can you solve real-world situations given a particular data set?

Answer Use a polynomial function to model a real-world situation. The behavior of the graphs of polynomial functions of different degrees can suggest what type of polynomial will best fit a particular data set.

Lesson Check

Do you know HOW?

Determine which type of model best fits each set of points.

1. $(-2, -1)$, $(0, 3)$, and $(2, 7)$

2. $(0, 3)$, $(3, 4)$, and $(5, 6)$

3. $(2, 3)$, $(4, 2)$, $(6, 4)$, and $(8, 5)$

4. $(-5, 6)$, $(-4, 3)$, $(0, 2)$, $(2, 4)$, and $(5, 10)$

Do you UNDERSTAND?

5. Vocabulary Explain which form of estimation, interpolation or extrapolation, is more reliable.

6. Reasoning Is it possible to write a cubic function that passes through $(0, 0)$, $(-1, 1)$, $(-2, 2)$, and $(-3, 9)$? Explain.

7. Writing The R^2 value for a quartic model is 0.94561. The R^2 value for a cubic model of the same data is 0.99817. Which model seems to show a better fit? Explain.

Practice and Problem-Solving Exercises

A Practice Find a polynomial function whose graph passes through each set of points.

 See Problem 1.

 Guided Practice

To start, substitute the *x*- and *y*-values of the points into the quadratic polynomial $y = ax^2 + bx + c$ to get three linear equations in three unknowns.

8. $(7, 13)$, $(10, -11)$, and $(0, 4)$

$$\begin{cases} 13 = a(7)^2 + b(7) + c \\ -11 = a(10)^2 + b(10) + c \\ 4 = a(0)^2 + b(0) + c \end{cases}$$

9. $(0, 5)$ and $(2, -13)$

10. $(-2, -4)$ and $(8, 1)$

11. $(-1, 8)$, $(5, -4)$, and $(7, 8)$

12. $(-1, 9)$, $(0, 6)$, $(1, 5)$, and $(2, 18)$

For each set of data, compare two models and determine which one best fits the data. Which model seems more likely to represent each set of data over time?

See Problems 2 and 3.

13.

U.S. Federal Spending

Year	Total (billions $)
1965	630
1980	1,300
1995	1,950
2005	2,650

14.

World Population

Year	Average Growth Rate (%)
1972	1.96
1982	1.73
1992	1.5
2002	1.22

15.

U.S. Homes

Year	Average Sale Price (thousands $)
1990	149
1995	158
2000	207

16.

U.S. Crude Oil and Petroleum

Month (2008)	Products Supplied (millions of barrels/day)
2	19.782
4	19.768
6	19.553

Use your models from Exercises 13–16 to make predictions.

◀ **See Problem 4.**

17. Estimate total U.S. federal spending for 1990 and 2010.

18. Estimate the average annual growth rate of the world population for 1950, 1988, and 2010.

19. Estimate the average sale price of homes sold in the United States for 1985, 1999, and 2020.

20. Estimate the number of barrels of crude oil and petroleum supplied per day for January, March, and October of 2008.

 **Apply**

Find a cubic and a quartic model for each set of values. Explain why one models the data better.

21.

x	y
−2	−25
−1	−4
0	3
2	23
3	40

22.

x	y
−2	−65
−1	−14
0	−4
1	2
2	90

358   Chapter 5 Polynomials and Polynomial Functions

Find a polynomial function whose graph passes through the points.

23. $(-14, 14)$, $(-10, 0)$, $(0, -1)$, $(8, 0)$, and $(12, 4)$

24. $(-3, -50)$, $(-2, -4)$, $(-1, 10)$, $(0, 7)$, and $(2, -23)$

25. Think About a Plan The table at the right shows the amount of carbon dioxide in the Earth's atmosphere for selected years. Predict the amount of carbon dioxide in the Earth's atmosphere in 2022. How confident are you in your prediction?
- How can you plot the data? (*Hint:* Let x equal the years after 1900.)
- What polynomial model should you use?

Year	CO$_2$ in atmosphere (ppm)
1968	324.14
1983	343.91
1998	367.68
2003	376.68
2008	385.60

Source: The Weather Channel

Find a cubic model for each set of values. Then use the regression coefficient of each model to determine whether the model is a good fit.

26. $(-5, -60)$, $(-1, -5)$, $(0, 0.5)$, $(1, 8)$, $(5, 17)$, $(10, 32)$

27. $(8, -101)$, $(-1, 10)$, $(-8, 47)$, $(-10, 59)$

28. Air Travel The table shows the percent of on-time flights for selected years. Find a polynomial function to model the data. (*Hint:* Let x equal the years after 1900.)

Year	1998	2000	2002	2004	2006
On-time Flights (%)	77.20	72.59	82.14	78.08	75.45

Source: U.S. Bureau of Transportation Statistics

29. Error Analysis The table at the right shows the number of students enrolled in a high school personal fiinance course. A student says that a cubic model would best fit the data based on the $(n + 1)$ Point Principle. Explain why a quadratic model might be more appropriate.

Year	Number of Students Enrolled
2000	50
2004	65
2008	94
2010	110

30. Writing Explain two ways to find a polynomial function to model a given set of data.

Standardized Test Prep

SAT/ACT

31. The table shows the time it takes a computer program to run, given the number of files used as input. Using a cubic model, what do you predict the run time will be if the input consists of 1000 files?

Files	Time(s)
100	0.5
200	0.9
300	3.5
400	8.2
500	14.8

32. Suppose you hit a ball and its flight follows the graph of $f(x) = -16x^2 + 20x + 3$. How many seconds will it take for the ball to hit the ground? Round your answer to the nearest second.

33. What is the multiplicity of the zeros of $y = 16x^2 - 8x + 1$?

34. What is the slope of the line shown?

35. What is the degree of the polynomial function $y = -9x^3 - 5x^2 - 2x^5 + 4x + x^4 + 1$?

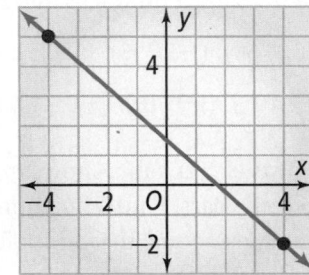

Mixed Review

Expand each binomial.   ◀ **See Lesson 5-7.**

36. $(2x + 3)^5$ **37.** $(11x - 1)^3$ **38.** $(8 - 3x)^4$

Write each compound inequality as an absolute value inequality.   ◀ **See Lesson 1-6.**

39. $7 < x < 9$ **40.** $1.7 < y < 3.9$ **41.** $500 < t < 1000$

Solve each formula for the indicated variable.   ◀ **See Lesson 1-4.**

42. $A = s^2$, for s **43.** $P = 2(l + w)$, for l **44.** $C = 2\pi r$, for r

Get Ready! **To prepare for Lesson 5-9, do Exercises 45–47.**

Graph each function.   ◀ **See Lesson 4-1.**

45. $y = -4x^2$ **46.** $y = x^2 + 3$ **47.** $y = -7x^2 - 1$

Transforming Polynomial Functions

Objective To apply transformations to graphs of polynomials

Remember how you transformed the graphs of quadratic and absolute value functions.

SOLVE IT!

Getting Ready!

The graph of the parent cubic function $f(x) = x^3$ is one of the graphs at the right. The other graph is a transformation g of the parent function. What is an equation for g? How do you know?

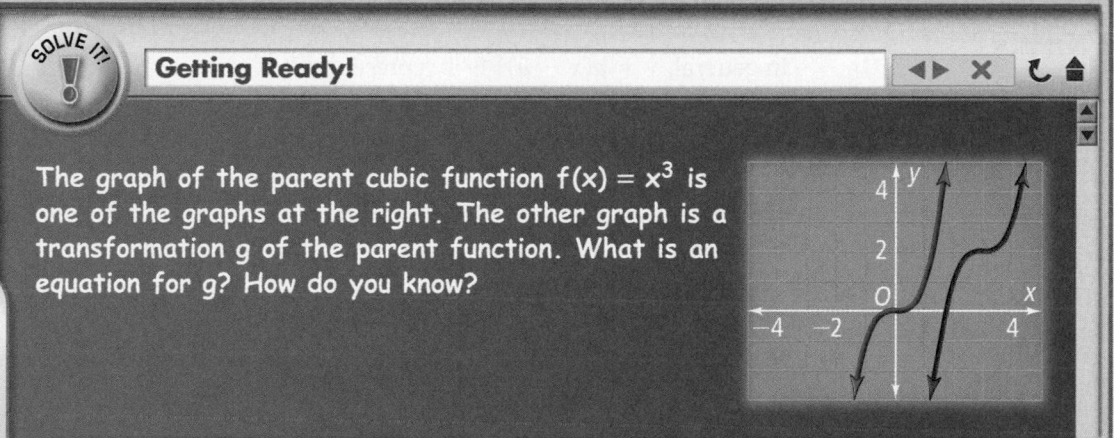

Recall that you can obtain the graph of any quadratic function from the graph of the parent quadratic function, $y = x^2$, using one or more basic transformations. You will find that this is not true for all cubic functions.

Focus Question What is a power function?

Lesson Vocabulary
- power function
- constant of proportionality

Problem 1 Transforming $y = x^3$

What is an equation of the graph of $y = x^3$ under the following sequence of transformations: a vertical compression by the factor $\frac{1}{2}$, a reflection in the x-axis, a horizontal translation 5 units to the right, and a vertical translation 2 units up?

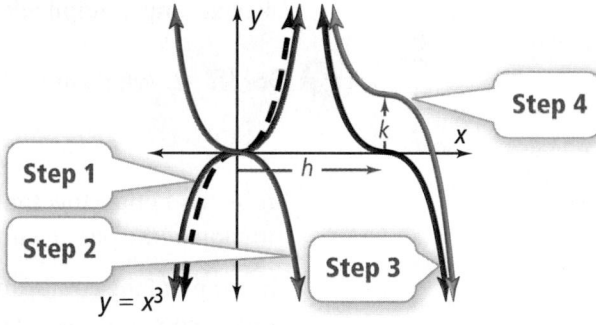

Hint
Remember when you perform transformations that order matters.

Step 1 Multiply by $\frac{1}{2}$ to compress.

$$y = x^3 \quad \rightarrow \quad y = \frac{1}{2}x^3$$

Step 2 Multiply by -1 to reflect.

$$y = \frac{1}{2}x^3 \quad \rightarrow \quad y = -\frac{1}{2}x^3$$

Step 3 Replace x with $x - 5$ to translate horizontally.

$$y = -\frac{1}{2}x^3 \quad \rightarrow \quad y = -\frac{1}{2}(x - 5)^3$$

Step 4 Add 2 to translate vertically.

$$y = -\frac{1}{2}(x - 5)^3 \quad \rightarrow \quad y = -\frac{1}{2}(x - 5)^3 + 2$$

Think

How is translating this cubic function like translating a quadratic function?
In each case you replace x with $(x - h)$ to translate h units to the right.

Got It? **1.** What is an equation of the graph of $y = x^3$ under the following sequence of transformations: a vertical stretch by the factor 2, a horizontal translation 3 units to the left, and a vertical translation 4 units down?

The graph shows $y = x^3$ and $y = -\frac{1}{2}(x - 5)^3 + 2$ from the transformations in Problem 1.

Hint
This general cubic function is similar to the vertex form of a quadratic function.

In general, $y = a(x - h)^3 + k$ represents all of the cubic functions you can obtain by stretching, compressing, or translating the cubic parent function $y = x^3$.

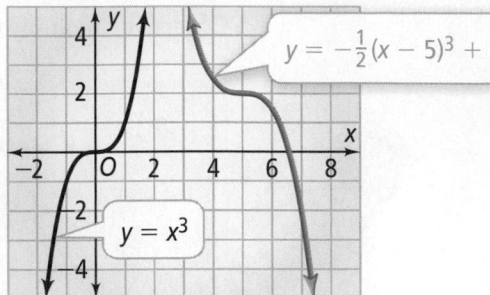

$y = -\frac{1}{2}(x - 5)^3 + 2$

$y = x^3$

Problem 2 Finding Zeros of a Transformed Cubic Function

Multiple Choice If a, h, and k are real numbers and $a \neq 0$, how many distinct real zeros does $y = -a(x - h)^3 + k$ have?

(A) 0   (B) 1   (C) 2   (D) 3

Plan
How can you find the zeros of a function?
Set the function equal to 0 and solve for x.

x is a zero means an x-intercept, so $y = 0$. $-a(x - h)^3 + k = 0$

Subtract k from each side. $-a(x - h)^3 = -k$

Divide each side by $-a$. $(x - h)^3 = \frac{k}{a}$

Take the cube root of each side. $x - h = \sqrt[3]{\frac{k}{a}}$

Solve for x. $x = \sqrt[3]{\frac{k}{a}} + h$

Disregarding multiplicities, the function has a single real zero. The correct answer is B.

Hint
Use the same steps that you used in Problem 2 to isolate the variable x.

 Got It? **2.** What are all the real zeros of the function $y = 3(x - 1)^3 + 6$?

Problems 1 and 2 together illustrate that the graph of an "offspring" function of the parent cubic function $y = x^3$ has only one x-intercept.

The graph of the cubic function $y = x^3 - 2x^2 - 5x + 6$ has three x-intercepts. You cannot obtain this function or others like it by transforming the parent cubic function $y = x^3$ using stretches, reflections, and translations.

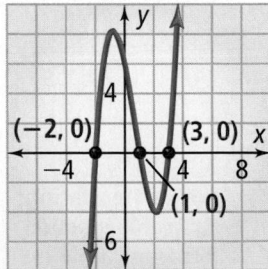

$(-2, 0)$ $(3, 0)$
$(1, 0)$

Similarly, some quartic functions are simple transformations of $y = x^4$ and some are not.

Plan

Problem 3 **Constructing a Quartic Function With Two Real Zeros**

What is a quartic function with only two real zeros, $x = 5$ and $x = 9$?

Method 1 Use transformations.

First, find a quartic with zeros at ± 2.
Translate the basic quartic 16 units down:
$y = x^4 \to y = x^4 - 16$

9 is seven units to the right of 2.
Translate right 7 units.
$y = x^4 - 16 \to y = (x - 7)^4 - 16$

A quartic function with its only real zeros at 5 and 9 is
$y = (x - 7)^4 - 16$.

$y = x^4$

$y = x^4 - 16$ $\qquad$ $y = (x - 7)^4 - 16$

Method 2 Use algebraic methods.

$$y = (x - 5)(x - 9) \cdot Q(x)$$
$$= (x - 5)(x - 9)(x^2 + 1)$$
$$= (x^2 - 14x + 45)(x^2 + 1)$$
$$= x^4 - 14x^3 + 46x^2 - 14x + 45$$

Make $Q(x)$ a quadratic with no real zeros.

Another quartic function with its only real zeros at
5 and 9 is $y = x^4 - 14x^3 + 46x^2 - 14x + 45$.

Got It? **3. a.** What is a quartic function $f(x)$ with only two real zeros, $x = 0$ and $x = 6$?
   b. Reasoning Does the quartic function $-f(x)$ have the same zeros? Explain.

Unlike the function from Method 1, the function from Method 2 cannot be found by transforming the parent quartic function. The function from Method 1 is an "offspring" of the $y = x^4$ family and belongs to a subfamily of all quartic polynomials: quartics of the form $y = a(x - h)^4 + k$. These functions also belong to another category of polynomials, and in this category you can generate families as usual.

 take note

Key Concept **Power Functions**

Definition	Examples
A **power function** is a function of the form $y = a \cdot x^b$, where a and b are nonzero real numbers.	$y = 0.5x^6$ $\qquad$ $y = \frac{1}{2}x^2$ $y = -4x^{\frac{2}{3}}$ $\qquad$ $y = x^{0.25}$

Hint

If the exponent b in $y = ax^b$ is a positive integer, the function is also a *monomial function.*

If $y = ax^b$ describes y as a power function of x, then y *varies directly with*, or is *proportional to*, the bth power of x. The constant a is the **constant of proportionality**.

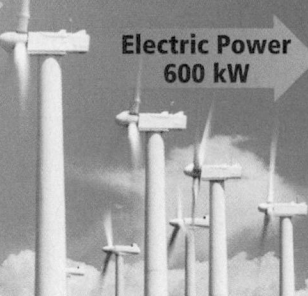

Wind
8 m/s

Electric Power
600 kW

Problem 4 Modeling With a Power Function

Wind-Generated Power Wind farms are a source of renewable energy found around the world. The power P (in kilowatts) generated by a wind turbine varies directly as the cube of the wind speed v (in meters per second). The picture shows the power output of one turbine at one wind speed. To the nearest kilowatt, how much power does this turbine generate in a 10 m/s wind?

Think

How is this problem like the direct variation you studied in Chapter 2?
With the direct variation, $y = kx$, you use a first power. Here you use a third power.

The formula for P as a power function of v is $P = a \cdot v^3$. From the picture, $P = 600$ when $v = 8$, or $600 = a \cdot 8^3$. Solve for a.

Use values of P and v to find a.	$600 = a \cdot 8^3$
Expand the power.	$600 = 512a$
Solve for a.	$a \approx 1.1719$
Use the value of a in the original formula.	$P \approx 1.1719v^3$.
Substitute 10 for v and simplify.	$P \approx 1.1719 \cdot 10^3 = 1171.9$.

This turbine generates about 1172 kW of power in a 10 m/s wind.

 Got It? **4.** Another turbine generates 210 kW of power in a 12 mi/h wind. How much power does this turbine generate in a 20 mi/h wind?

Focus Question What is a power function?

Answer A power function is a special type of polynomial function of the form $y = ax^b$, where a and b are nonzero real numbers. Unlike quadratic functions, you cannot write every polynomial function of degree $n \geq 3$ as a transformation of its parent power function, $y = x^n$.

 Lesson Check

Do you know HOW?

Find all the real zeros of each function.

1. $y = -(x + 3)^3 + 1$

2. $y = -8(x - 5)^3 - 64$

3. $y = \frac{9}{2}(x - 1)^3 + \frac{4}{3}$

Do you UNDERSTAND?

4. Vocabulary Is the function $y = 4x^3 + 5$ an example of a power function? Explain.

5. Compare and Contrast How are the graphs of $y = x^3$ and $y = 4x^3$ alike? How are they different? What transformation produces the second equation?

Practice and Problem-Solving Exercises

A **Practice**

Determine the cubic function that is obtained from the parent function $y = x^3$ after each sequence of transformations.

◀ **See Problem 1.**

Guided Practice

To start, multiply by 3 to stretch.

6. a vertical stretch by a factor of 3,
a reflection in the x-axis,
a vertical translation 2 units up, and
a horizontal translation 1 unit right

$y = 3x^3$

7. a vertical stretch by a factor of 2,
a vertical translation 4 units up, and
a horizontal translation 3 units left

8. a reflection in the y-axis,
a vertical translation 1 unit down, and
a horizontal translation 5 units left

9. a vertical stretch by a factor of 3,
a reflection in the y-axis,
a vertical translation $\frac{3}{4}$ unit up, and
a horizontal translation $\frac{1}{2}$ unit left

10. a vertical stretch by a factor of $1\frac{2}{3}$,
a reflection in the x-axis,
a vertical translation 4 units down, and
a horizontal translation 3 units right

Find all the real zeros of each function.

◀ **See Problem 2.**

11. $y = -27(x - 2)^3 + 8$

12. $y = -\frac{1}{8}(x - 7)^3 - 8$

13. $y = -3\left(x + \frac{4}{5}\right)^3 + \frac{8}{9}$

14. $y = -16(x + 3)^3 + 9$

15. $y = 4(x - 1)^3 + 10$

16. $y = 2(x + 5)^3 + 10$

Find a quartic function with the given x-values as its only real zeros.

◀ **See Problem 3.**

Guided Practice

To start, use the Factor Theorem to write the equation of a quartic with real zeros at 2 and −1 and complex zeros where $Q(x)$ has zeros.

17. $x = 2$ and $x = -1$

$y = (x - 2)(x + 1) \cdot Q(x)$

18. $x = -3$ and $x = -4$

19. $x = -1$ and $x = 3$

20. $x = 4$ and $x = 2$

21. $x = -3$ and $x = 2$

22. Cooking The number of pepperoni slices that Kim puts on a pizza varies directly as the square of the diameter of the pizza. If she puts 15 slices on a 10″ diameter pizza, how many slices should she put on a 16″ diameter pizza?

◀ **See Problem 4.**

23. Volume The amount of water that a spherical tank can hold varies directly as the cube of its radius. If a tank with radius 7.5 ft holds 1767 ft³ of water, how much water can a tank with radius 16 ft hold?

24. Think About a Plan The kinetic energy K generated by a 5 lb ball thrown with a velocity of v ft/s is represented by the formula $K = \frac{1}{2}(5)v^2$. If the ball is thrown with a velocity of 6 ft/s, how much kinetic energy is generated?
- What does 5 represent in the function?
- What number should you substitute for v?

Determine whether each function can be obtained from the parent function, $y = x^n$, using basic transformations. If so, describe the sequence of transformations.

25. $y = 3x^3$

26. $y = 2(x - 3)^2 + 5$

27. $y = x^3 - x$

28. $y = x^2 - 8x + 7$

29. $y = (x + 2)^4$

30. $y = -4x^3$

Determine the sequence of transformations that were used to change the graph of the parent function $y = x^3$ to each of the following graphs.

31.
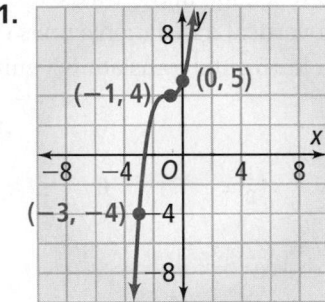

32.
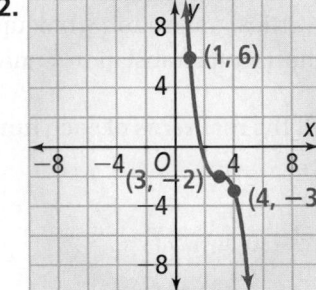

33.
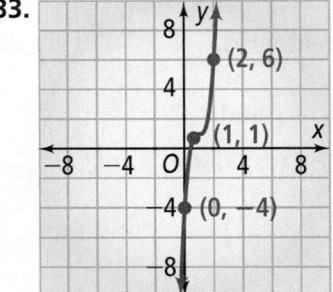

34.
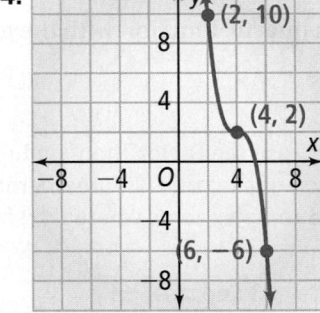

35. Physics The formula $K = \frac{1}{2}mv^2$ represents the kinetic energy of an object. If the kinetic energy of a ball is 10 lb-ft²/s² when it is thrown with a velocity of 4 ft/s, how much kinetic energy is generated if the ball is thrown with a velocity of 8 ft/s?

36. Reasoning Explain why the basic transformations of the parent function $y = x^5$ will only generate functions that can be written in the form $y = a(x - h)^5 + k$.

37. Error Analysis Your friend claims he can write any cubic polynomial as the sum of two functions: (1) a cubic monomial and (2) a transformation of $y = x^2$. Explain why your friend's claim is incorrect.

$$P(x) = \underbrace{ax^3}_{\substack{\text{cubic} \\ \text{monomial}}} + \underbrace{bx^2 + cx + d}_{\substack{\text{transformation} \\ \text{of } y = x^2}}$$

38. Reasoning Explain why some quartic polynomials cannot be written in the form $y = a(x - h)^4 + k$. Give two examples.

Standardized Test Prep

SAT/ACT

Use the graph below to answer questions 39–41.

39. Which equation does the graph at the right represent?

 Ⓐ $y = (x + 2)^2 - 1$

 Ⓑ $y = (x - 2)^2 - 1$

 Ⓒ $y = (x - 2)^2 + 1$

 Ⓓ $y = (x - 2)^4 - 1$

40. If $y = f(x)$ is an equation for the graph, what are factors of $f(x)$?

 Ⓕ $(x - 1)$ and $(x + 3)$ Ⓗ $(x + 1)$ and $(x - 3)$

 Ⓖ $(x - 1)$ and $(x - 3)$ Ⓘ $(x + 1)$ and $(x + 3)$

Short Response

41. If $y = ax^2 + bx + c$ is an equation for the graph, what type of number is its discriminant?

Mixed Review

Find a polynomial function whose graph passes through the given points. ◀ See Lesson 5-8.

42. $(-1, 4), (0, -2), (1, -2), (2, -8)$ **43.** $(-2, -17), (0, -3), (1, -5), (3, 63)$

Write an equation of each line. ◀ See Lesson 2-4.

44. slope $= -\frac{4}{5}$; through $(-1, 4)$ **45.** slope $= -3$; through $(2, -1)$

Determine whether each relation is a function. ◀ See Lesson 2-1.

46. $\{(0, -1), (-1, 3), (2, 3), (-3, 3)\}$ **47.** $\{(-4, 0), (-7, 0), (-4, 1), (-7, 1)\}$

Get Ready! **To prepare for Lesson 6-1, do Exercises 48–50.**

Write each polynomial in factored form. ◀ See Lesson 5-2.

48. $x^{10} + x^2$ **49.** $x^4 - y^4$ **50.** $81x^6y^{12} - 9x^3y^6$

Pull It **All Together**

To solve these problems, you will pull together concepts and skills related to working with polynomials and their related functions and equations.

BIG idea Function

A function is a relationship between variables in which each value of the input variable is associated with a unique value of the output variable. Some important families of functions are developed through transformations of the simplest form of the function.

Task 1

The polynomial $2x^3 + 9x^2 + 4x - 15$ represents the volume in cubic feet of a rectangular holding tank at a fish hatchery. The depth of the tank is $(x - 1)$ feet. The length is 13 feet.

a. Use synthetic division to help you factor the volume polynomial. How many linear factors should you look for? What are they?

b. Assume the length is the greatest dimension. Which linear factor represents the 13-ft length? What are the dimensions of the tank? What is its volume? What is the value of x? Do you get the same volume if you substitute the value of x into $2x^3 + 9x^2 + 4x - 15$?

BIG idea Equivalence

You can use the Binomial Theorem and properties of algebra to rewrite some powers.

Task 2

Show that the following equation is true for all values of a and b.

$$[(a - b) + 1]^5 = a^5 - 5a^4(b - 1) + 10a^3(b - 1)^2 - 10a^2(b - 1)^3 + 5a(b - 1)^4 - (b - 1)^5$$

BIG idea Solving Equations and Inequalities

A polynomial $P(x)$ of degree n, $n \geq 1$, and its related polynomial function $y = P(x)$ have n complex zeros. The zeros are identical to the n complex roots of the related polynomial equation $P(x) = 0$.

Task 3

Four of these five polynomial functions have identical zeros. The fifth has exactly two zeros in common with each of the other functions. Write this fifth function as a product of its linear factors.

$$P_1(x) = x^3 - 6x^2 + 11x - 6$$
$$P_2(x) = x^4 - 5x^3 + 7x^2 - 5x + 6$$
$$P_3(x) = x^4 - 7x^3 + 17x^2 - 17x + 6$$
$$P_4(x) = x^4 - 8x^3 + 23x^2 - 28x + 12$$
$$P_5(x) = x^4 - 9x^3 + 29x^2 - 39x + 18$$

5 Chapter Review for Part B

Connecting BIG ideas and Answering the Essential Questions

1 Function

A polynomial of degree n has n linear factors. The graph of the related function crosses the x-axis an even or odd number of times depending on whether n is even or odd.

Polynomial Functions, Zeros, and Linear Factors (Lessons 5-1 and 5-2)

$y = 2x^3 + 7x^2 - 9$ has 3 linear factors $(x + 3)$, $(2x + 3)$, $(x - 1)$, and it crosses the x-axis 3 times—at $(-3, 0)$, $(-\frac{3}{2}, 0)$, and $(1, 0)$. Its end behavior is down and up.

2 Equivalence

$(x - a)$ is a linear factor if and only if a is a zero and if and only if $(a, 0)$ is an x-intercept when a is a real number.

Theorems About Roots of Polynomial Equations (Lesson 5-5)

$P(x) = 2x^3 + 7x^2 - 9$ and $Q(x) = 2x^3 + 5x^2 + 9$ each have degree 3 so $P(x) = 0$ and $Q(x) = 0$ each have 3 complex roots.

Each has ±1, ±3, ±9, $\pm\frac{1}{2}$, $\pm\frac{3}{2}$, $\pm\frac{9}{2}$ as its possible rational roots.

$P(-3) = 0$, so $x + 3$ is a factor of $2x^3 + 7x^2 - 9$.

$Q(-3) = 0$, so $x + 3$ is a factor of $2x^3 + 5x^2 + 9$.

3 Solving Equations and Inequalities

$(x - a)$ is a linear factor if and only if a is a root of the related polynomial equation.

Solving Polynomial Equations (Lesson 5-3)

$2x^3 + 7x^2 - 9 = 0$ has factored form $(x + 3)(2x + 3)(x - 1) = 0$. It has 3 roots or solutions, $x = -3$, $x = -\frac{3}{2}$, and $x = 1$.

The Fundamental Theorem of Algebra (Lesson 5-6)

$2x^3 + 5x^2 + 9 = 0$ has factored form $(x + 3)(2x^2 - x + 3) = 0$. It has 3 roots or solutions, $x = -3$, $x = \frac{1}{4} - \frac{\sqrt{23}}{4}i$, and $x = \frac{1}{4} + \frac{\sqrt{23}}{4}i$.

Chapter Vocabulary

- Binomial Theorem (p. 348)
- Conjugate Root Theorem (p. 335)
- constant of proportionality (p. 363)
- Descartes' Rule of Signs (p. 336)
- expand a binomial (p. 347)
- Fundamental Theorem of Algebra (p. 341)
- Pascal's Triangle (p. 348)
- power function (p. 363)
- Rational Root Theorem (p. 332)

Match each vocabulary term with the description that best fits it.

1. Conjugate Root Theorem

2. Fundamental Theorem of Algebra

3. Rational Root Theorem

4. Remainder Theorem

A. determines $P(a)$ by dividing the polynomial by $x - a$

B. the degree equals the number of roots

C. minimizes guessing fraction and integer solutions

D. complex numbers as roots occur in pairs

5-5 Theorems About Roots of Polynomial Equations

Quick Review

The **Rational Root Theorem** gives a way to determine the possible roots of a polynomial equation $P(x) = 0$. If the coefficients of $P(x)$ are all integers, then every root of the equation can be written in the form $\frac{p}{q}$, where p is a factor of the constant term and q is a factor of the leading coefficient.

The **Conjugate Root Theorem** states that if $P(x)$ is a polynomial with rational coefficients, then irrational roots that have the form $a + \sqrt{b}$ and imaginary roots of $P(x) = 0$ occur in conjugate pairs. Therefore, if $a + \sqrt{b}$ is an irrational root, where a and b are rational, then $a - \sqrt{b}$ is also a root. Likewise, if $a + bi$ is a root, where a and b are real and i is the imaginary unit, then $a - bi$ is also a root.

Descartes' Rule of Signs gives a way to determine the possible number of positive and negative real roots by analyzing the signs of the coefficients. The number of positive real roots is equal to the number of sign changes in consecutive coefficients of $P(x)$, or is less than that by an even number. The number of negative real roots is equal to the number of sign changes in consecutive coefficients of $P(-x)$, or is less than that by an even number.

Example

Find the rational roots of $P(x) = 0$ if
$P(x) = 2x^3 - 4x^2 - 10x + 12$.

List the possible roots: $\pm\frac{1}{2}, \pm1, \pm\frac{3}{2}, \pm2, \pm3, \pm4, \pm6, \pm12$. Use synthetic division to test roots.

$$
\begin{array}{r|rrrr}
3 & 2 & -4 & -10 & 12 \\
  &   & 6 & 6 & -12 \\
\hline
  & 2 & 2 & -4 & 0 \\
\end{array}
$$

So $x - 3$ and $(2x^2 + 2x - 4)$ are factors of $P(x)$.
$$P(x) = (x - 3)(2x^2 + 2x - 4)$$
Factor the quadratic.
$$P(x) = 2(x - 3)(x + 2)(x - 1)$$
Solve $2(x - 3)(x + 2)(x - 1) = 0$.
$$x = 3, x = -2, \text{ or } x = 1$$
The rational roots are 3, -2, and 1.

Exercises

List the possible rational roots of $P(x)$ given by the Rational Root Theorem.

5. $P(x) = x^3 + 4x^2 - 10x + 6$

6. $P(x) = 3x^3 - x^2 - 7x + 2$

7. $P(x) = 4x^4 - 2x^3 + x^2 - 12$

8. $P(x) = 3x^4 - 4x^3 - x^2 - 7$

Find any rational roots of $P(x)$.

9. $P(x) = x^3 + 2x^2 + 4x + 21$

10. $P(x) = x^3 + 5x^2 + x + 5$

11. $P(x) = 2x^3 + 7x^2 - 5x - 4$

12. $P(x) = 3x^4 + 2x^3 - 9x^2 + 4$

A polynomial $P(x)$ has rational coefficients. Name additional roots of $P(x)$ given the following roots.

13. $1 - i$ and 5

14. $5 + \sqrt{3}$ and $-\sqrt{2}$

15. $-3i$ and $7i$

16. $-2 + \sqrt{11}$ and $-4 - 6i$

Write a polynomial function with the given roots.

17. 7 and 10

18. -3 and $5i$

19. $6 - i$

20. $3 + i$, 2, and -4

Determine the possible number of positive real zeros and negative real zeros for each polynomial function given by Descartes' Rule of Signs.

21. $P(x) = 5x^3 + 7x^2 - 2x - 1$

22. $P(x) = -3x^3 + 11x^2 + 12x - 8$

23. $P(x) = 6x^4 - x^3 + 5x^2 - x + 9$

24. $P(x) = -x^4 - 3x^3 + 8x^2 + 2x - 14$

5-6 The Fundamental Theorem of Algebra

Quick Review

The **Fundamental Theorem of Algebra** states that if $P(x)$ is a polynomial of degree n, where $n \geq 1$, then $P(x) = 0$ has exactly n roots. This includes multiple and complex roots.

Example

Use the Fundamental Theorem of Algebra to determine the number of roots for $x^4 + 2x^2 - 3 = 0$.

Because the polynomial is of degree 4, it has 4 roots.

Exercises

Find the number of roots for each equation.

25. $x^3 - 2x + 5 = 0$

26. $-x^5 - 6 = 0$

27. $5x^4 - 7x^6 + 2x^3 + 8x^2 + 4x - 11 = 0$

Find all the zeros for each function.

28. $P(x) = x^3 + 5x^2 - 4x - 2$

29. $P(x) = x^4 - 4x^3 - x^2 + 20x - 20$

30. $P(x) = x^4 - 4x^3 - 16x^2 + 21x + 18$

5-7 The Binomial Theorem

Quick Review

Rows 0–5 of **Pascal's Triangle** are shown below.

$$
\begin{array}{ccccccccccc}
 & & & & & 1 & & & & & \\
 & & & & 1 & & 1 & & & & \\
 & & & 1 & & 2 & & 1 & & & \\
 & & 1 & & 3 & & 3 & & 1 & & \\
 & 1 & & 4 & & 6 & & 4 & & 1 & \\
1 & & 5 & & 10 & & 10 & & 5 & & 1
\end{array}
$$

The **Binomial Theorem** uses Pascal's Triangle to expand binomials. For a positive integer n,

$(a + b)^n = P_0 a^n + P_1 a^{n-1}b + P_2 a^{n-2}b^2 + \cdots$
$+ P_{n-1} ab^{n-1} + P_n b^n$, where $P_0, P_1, \ldots P_n$

are the coefficients of the nth row of Pascal's Triangle.

Example

Use the Binomial Theorem to expand $(2x + 3)^3$.

Use the coefficients from Pascal's Triangle.

$(2x + 3)^3 = 1(2x)^3 + 3(2x)^2(3)$
$+ 3(2x)(3)^2 + 1(3)^3$

Simplify.

$= 8x^3 + 36x^2 + 54x + 27$

Exercises

31. How many numbers are in the 8th row of Pascal's Triangle?

32. List the numbers in the 8th row of Pascal's Triangle.

Use the Binomial Theorem to expand each binomial.

33. $(x + 9)^3$

34. $(b + 2)^4$

35. $(3a + 1)^3$

36. $(x - 5)^3$

37. $(x - 2y)^3$

38. $(3a + 4b)^5$

39. $(x + 1)^6$

40. $(2x - 1)^6$

Find the coefficient of the x^2 term in each binomial expansion.

41. $(3x + 4)^3$

42. $(ax - c)^4$

5-8 Polynomial Models in the Real World

Quick Review

You can model a data set by a polynomial function. Methods of finding a model that fits the data include the **(n + 1) Point Principle** and **regression**. Linear, quadratic, cubic, and quartic regressions can be performed on a graphing calculator. A higher R^2 value means a better fit. Once the equation that models the data is known, you can use it to make predictions.

Example

For the data set (8, 30), (10, 45), and (11, 65), predict y when x = 15.

Enter 8, 10, and 11 in **L1** and 30, 45, and 65 in **L2**. Choose **LINREG** to find the regression model $y \approx 11.071x - 60.357$. The r^2 value is about 0.928.

Now try **QUADREG**. The model is $y \approx 4.17x^2 - 67.5x + 303.3$ with an R^2 value of 1. Assuming this model makes sense in context, it fits the data better.

According to the quadratic model, $y \approx 228.3$ when $x = 15$.

Exercises

43. Write a polynomial function whose graph passes through (0, 5), (2, 10), and (1, 4). Use a regression to check your answer.

44. Find a linear, a quadratic, and a cubic model for the data. Which model best fits the data?

x	3	8	15	21
y	7	11	26	44

45. Use **CUBICREG** to model the data below. Then use the model to estimate the population in 2008. Let x be the number of years after 2000.

Year	2004	2007	2009	2010
Population	457	910	1244	1315

5-9 Transforming Polynomial Functions

Quick Review

A polynomial function can be transformed into other polynomial functions using stretches, compressions, reflections, and translations. The monomial function $y = ax^b$ is called a **power function**.

Example

This is the graph of a cubic function. Determine which sequence of transformations you can apply to the graph of the parent function $y = x^3$ to get this graph. Write an equation for the graph.

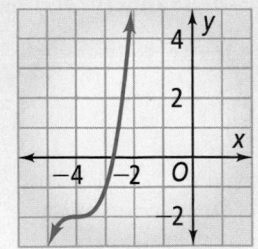

Translate 4 units left. $\quad y = x^3 \rightarrow y = (x + 4)^3$

Translate 2 units down. $\quad y = (x + 4)^3 \rightarrow y = (x + 4)^3 - 2$

Exercises

Determine the cubic function obtained from the parent function $y = x^3$ after each sequence of transformations.

46. a reflection in the x-axis, a translation 1 unit up, and a translation 2 units right

47. a vertical stretch by a factor of 6, and a translation 3 units left

48. Find a quartic function whose only real zeros are 4 and 6.

49. The parent power function $y = x^5$ is translated 3 units up and is compressed by the factor 0.3. Write an equation for the function.

Do you know HOW?

Write each polynomial function in standard form. Then classify it by degree and by number of terms and describe its end behavior.

1. $y = 3x^2 - 7x^4 + 9 - x^4$

2. $y = 2x(x^2 - 3)(x^2 + 2)$

3. $y = (t - 2)(t + 1)(t + 1)$

Write a polynomial function for each set of zeros.

4. $x = 1, 2, \frac{3}{5}$

5. $x = \sqrt{2}, -i$

6. $x = 3 + i, -1 - \sqrt{5}$

Find the quotient and remainder.

7. $(x^2 + 3x - 4) \div (x - 1)$

8. $(x^3 + 7x^2 - 5x - 6) \div (x + 2)$

9. $(2x^3 + 9x^2 + 11x + 3) \div (2x + 3)$

For each equation, state the number of complex roots, the possible number of real roots, and the possible rational roots.

10. $3x^4 + 5x^3 - 2x^2 + x - 9 = 0$

11. $x^7 - 2x^5 - 4x^3 - 2x - 1 = 0$

For each equation, find all the roots.

12. $3x^4 - 11x^3 + 15x^2 - 9x + 2 = 0$

13. $x^3 - x^2 - x - 2 = 0$

14. One x-intercept of the graph of the cubic function $f(x) = x^3 - 2x^2 - 111x - 108$ is -9. What are the other zeros?

Use synthetic division and the Remainder Theorem to find $P(a)$.

15. $P(x) = 6x^4 + 19x^3 - 2x^2 - 44x - 24$ for $a = -\frac{2}{3}$

16. $P(x) = x^4 + 3x^3 - 7x^2 - 9x + 12$ for $a = 3$

17. $P(x) = x^3 + 3x^2 - 5x - 4$ for $a = -1$

Expand each binomial.

18. $(x + z)^5$

19. $(1 - 2t)^2$

20. Graph and write the equation of the cubic function that is obtained from the parent function $y = x^3$ after this sequence of transformations: a vertical stretch by the factor 2, a reflection in the x-axis, and a translation down 3 units and right 4 units.

Do you UNDERSTAND?

21. Physics You take measurements of the distance traveled by an object that is increasing its speed at a constant rate. The distance traveled as a function of time can be modeled by a quadratic function.
  a. Write a quadratic function that models distances of 10 ft at 1 sec, 30 ft at 2 sec, and 100 ft at 4 sec.
  b. Find the zeros of the function.
  c. Reasoning Describe what each zero represents for this real-world situation.

22. Writing For the polynomial $x^6 - 64$, could you apply the Difference of Cubes? Difference of Squares? Explain your answers.

23. The number of pairs of shoes Emily buys varies directly as the square of the area of the floor of her closet. If she can fit 12 pairs of shoes when her closet was 10 square feet, how many pairs of shoes will she fit when the area of her closet floor is 18 square feet?

TIPS FOR SUCCESS

Some problems require you to simplify expressions that contain imaginary numbers.

TIP 1

When multiplying binomials, you should use the Distributive Property.

Which expression is equivalent to $(3 - 4i)(2 + i)$?

- Ⓐ $2 - 5i$
- Ⓑ $2 + 5i$
- Ⓒ $10 - 5i$
- Ⓓ $10 + 5i$

TIP 2

Recall that $i^2 = -1$.

Think It Through

$(3 - 4i)(2 + i)$
$= 6 + 3i - 8i - 4i^2$
$= 6 - 5i - 4(-1)$
$= 10 - 5i$

The correct answer is C.

Vocabulary Review

As you solve test items, you must understand the meanings of mathematical terms. Match each term with its mathematical meaning.

A. multiplicity

B. synthetic division

C. Conjugate Root Theorem

D. relative maximum

E. polynomial

I. the process of dividing a polynomial by a linear factor, omitting all variables and exponents

II. if $a + bi$ is an irrational root where a and b are real numbers, then $a - bi$ is also a root

III. a monomial or the sum of monomials

IV. the greatest y-value in a region of a graph

V. the number of times a zero is repeated in a polynomial function

Multiple Choice

Read each question. Then write the letter of the correct answer on your paper.

1. Which statement is true about this system of linear equations?

$$\begin{cases} 3x - 4y = 12 \\ 6x - 8y = 12 \end{cases}$$

- Ⓐ The solution is $(0, -1)$.
- Ⓑ The solution is $(8, 4)$.
- Ⓒ There is no solution because the lines are parallel.
- Ⓓ There are infinitely many solutions because the lines are coinciding.

2. Which of the following statements is *never* true about a quartic function?

- Ⓕ The end behavior of the function is up and up.
- Ⓖ The function has 4 zeros.
- Ⓗ The function has 4 turning points.
- Ⓘ The function has complex roots.

3. Tia deposited x dollars in a bank account that paid 4% interest. She also deposited y dollars in a bank account that paid 8% interest. The system below represents one year's interest on Tia's deposits.

$$\begin{cases} 0.04x + 0.08y = 240 \\ \quad\ 0.04x = 0.08y \end{cases}$$

Based on the solution of the system of equations, which of the following can you conclude?

Ⓐ Tia deposited $3000 in each account, and the amounts of interest earned were $240 and $120.

Ⓑ Tia deposited $3000 in each account, and the amount of interest earned in each account was $120.

Ⓒ The deposit amounts were $3000 and $1500, and the amounts of interest earned in each account were $240 and $120.

Ⓓ The deposit amounts were $3000 and $1500, and the amount of interest earned in each account was $120.

4. The total area of the parallelogram below is $4x^4 + 3x^3 - 14x^2 + 33x - 35$. Which of the following expressions best represents the length of the base of the parallelogram? (*Hint: A = bh*)

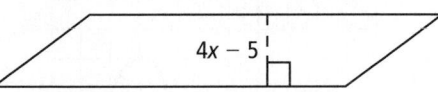

4x – 5

Ⓕ $x^3 + 2x^2 - x + 7$

Ⓖ $x^3 - 2x^2 + x - 7$

Ⓗ $4x^4 + 3x^3 - 14x^2 + 33x - 7$

Ⓘ $x^3 + 5x^2 - x + 5$

5. Which point corresponds to a zero of the function $f(x) = x^2 + 2x - 15$?

Ⓐ $(0, -15)$ Ⓒ $(-5, 0)$

Ⓑ $(5, 0)$ Ⓓ $(-3, 0)$

6. Solve the equation $x^2 + 3w = P$ for x.

Ⓕ $x = P - 3w$ Ⓗ $x = \pm\sqrt{P - 3w}$

Ⓖ $x = \pm\sqrt{\dfrac{P}{3w}}$ Ⓘ $x = \pm\sqrt{P + 3w}$

7. A bridge supported by a parabolic arch spans a stream of water 180 feet wide. There must be a clearance of at least 40 feet over a 100-foot channel in the middle of the stream. The origin is placed at water level directly below the center of the arch. Which equation best represents the situation?

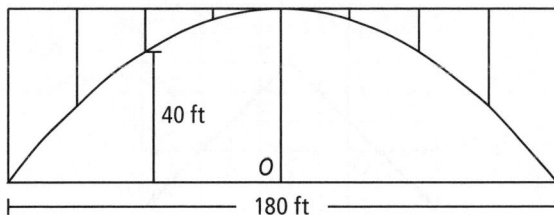

40 ft

O

180 ft

Ⓐ $y = 140(x + 180)(x - 180)$

Ⓑ $y = -\dfrac{1}{140}(x + 90)(x - 90)$

Ⓒ $y = -\dfrac{1}{140}(x + 40)(x - 40)$

Ⓓ $y = 140(x + 40)(x - 40)$

8. Sofia has $25 in her savings account. She plans to deposit between $5 and $10 each week into her account. On the graph, line m represents a deposit of exactly $5 per week and line n represents a deposit of exactly $10 per week.

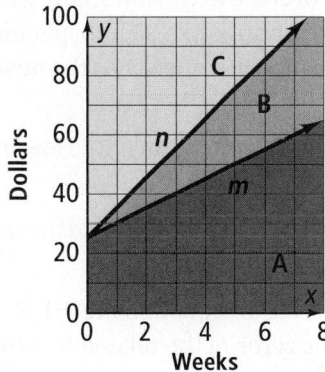

If Sofia deposits between $5 and $10 per week, which region on the graph represents all possible balances in her account?

Ⓕ A   Ⓗ C

Ⓖ B   Ⓘ A and C combined

9. Solve the absolute value inequality
$-2 |x - 3| \leq -16$.

Ⓐ $x \leq -3$ or $x \geq 4$ Ⓒ $-5 \leq x \leq 11$

Ⓑ $x \leq -5$ or $x \geq 11$ Ⓓ $-11 \leq x \leq 5$

10. Which equation does the graph represent?

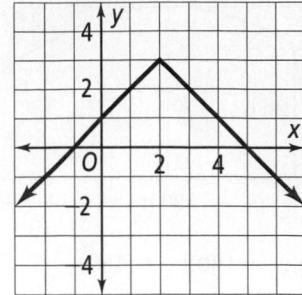

Ⓕ $y = -|x - 2| + 3$ Ⓗ $y = |x - 2| + 3$

Ⓖ $y = -|x - 3| + 2$ Ⓘ $y = |x + 2| + 3$

GRIDDED RESPONSE

11. The power created by a wind turbine varies directly as the cube of the wind speed in miles per hour. A turbine with 30% efficiency spinning in a 50 mile per hour wind can be expected to produce approximately 10,000 watts of electricity. How many watts would the same turbine produce in a 25 mile per hour wind? If necessary, round your answer to the nearest whole number.

12. One root of a cubic equation is $2i$. How many real roots does the equation have?

13. What is the value of the real part of the quotient of $(6 + 4i)$ and $(5 - i)$?

14. If the solutions of an equation are -1, 2, and 5, what is the sum of the zeros of the related function?

15. Assume y varies directly with x. If $y = -3$ when $x = -\frac{2}{5}$, what is x when y is 45?

16. What is the x-coordinate of the point where a relative maximum of $g(x) = -2x^3 + 6x^2 - 10$ occurs?

17. Using a graph, find the real zero of the function $y = 2x^3 - 2x^2 + x - 1$.

18. How many imaginary roots does $x^2 - 5x + 10 = 0$ have?

Short Response

19. The graph shows line m and point P. Write the equation of a line n that goes through point P and is perpendicular to line m. Show your work.

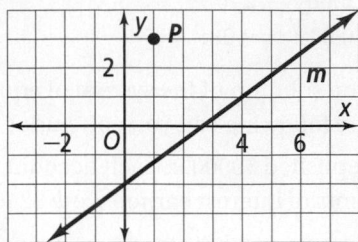

20. A cat ran around part of a telephone pole on a path modeled by the equation $y = -x^2 + 4x - 1$. Graph the cat's path in the first quadrant. If the pole is at $(2, 0)$, at what point is the cat furthest from the pole?

21. Solve the equation $x^2 - 4x = 8$ by completing the square. Explain whether you could have solved this equation by factoring or using the Quadratic Formula.

Extended Response

22. Use the graph to answer the questions below.

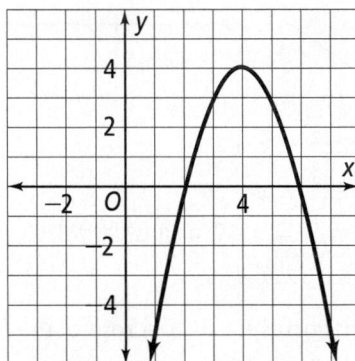

a. Describe the sequence of transformations that would take the graph of the parent function $y = x^2$ to the graph shown.

b. Identify the zeros of the function represented in the graph and explain your reasoning.

c. Write the equation of the function in the graph.

d. Explain how you could check to see that the equation is correct.

CHAPTER
6

Get Ready!

Lessons 2-1 and 4-1 ◀ **Finding the Domain and Range of Functions**

Find the domain and range of each function.

1. $\{(1, 2), (2, 3), (3, 4), (4, 5)\}$ **2.** $\{(1, 2), (2, 2), (3, 2), (4, 2)\}$

3. $f(x) = (x - 4)^2 - 8$ **4.** $f(x) = 2x^2 + 3$

Lesson 4-1 ◀ **Graphing Quadratic Functions**

Graph each function.

5. $y = 2x^2 - 4$ **6.** $y = -3(x^2 + 1)$ **7.** $y = \frac{1}{2}(x - 3)^2 + 1$

Lesson 4-4 ◀ **Multiplying Binomials**

Multiply.

8. $(3y - 2)(y - 4)$ **9.** $(7a + 10)(7a - 10)$ **10.** $(x - 3)(x + 6)(x + 1)$

Lessons 4-5 and 5-3 ◀ **Solving by Factoring**

Solve each equation by factoring.

11. $x^2 - 5x - 14 = 0$ **12.** $2x^2 - 11x + 15 = 0$ **13.** $3x^2 + 10x - 8 = 0$

14. $12x^2 - 12x + 3 = 0$ **15.** $8x^2 - 98 = 0$ **16.** $x^4 - 14x^2 + 49 = 0$

 Looking Ahead Vocabulary

17. Combining two or more elements forms composite chemical mixtures. In some cases, if you change the order in which you mix two chemicals, it can produce very different results. A *composite function* is made by combining two functions. For example, suppose you are buying a $60 shirt. There is a 50% off sale, and you have a $10 coupon. Does it make a difference which discount is applied first?

18. One-to-one relationships describe situations where people are matched with unique identifiers, such as their social security numbers. A function is a relation that matches *x* values to *y* values. What do you suppose a *one-to-one function* is?

19. In an orchestra, the principal player is chosen among all the other musicians that play a certain instrument to sit in the first chair and lead his section. In math, what do you suppose a *principal root* is?

CHAPTER 6 PART A

Radical Functions and Rational Exponents

In this chapter, you will learn how to work with radicals, whether they occur by themselves or as parts of functions or equations; whether they appear with the symbol $\sqrt{}$ or as fractional exponents. In a sense, radicals are the inverses of powers.

Mountain climbers need to be aware of air pressure, which can be calculated using fractional exponents.

Vocabulary for Part A

English/Spanish Vocabulary Audio Online:

English	Spanish
index, *p. 382*	índice
like radicals, *p. 395*	radicales semejantes
*n*th root, *p. 381*	raíz *n*-ésima
principal root, *p. 381*	raíz principal
radicand, *p. 382*	radicando
rational exponent, *p. 403*	exponente racional
rationalize the denominator, *p. 391*	racionalizar el denominador

My Math Video

00:04:04

VIDEO ▷

BIG ideas

1 Equivalence

Essential Question To simplify the *n*th root of an expression, what must be true about the expression?

2 Solving Equations and Inequalities

Essential Question When you square each side of an equation, is the resulting equation equivalent to the original?

3 Function

Essential Question How are a function and its inverse function related?

Chapter Preview for Part A

Concept Byte

For Use With Lesson 6-1

Properties of Exponents

Exponents indicate powers. The table below lists the properties of exponents. Assume that no denominator is equal to zero and that m and n are integers.

take note

Property Properties of Exponents

- $a^0 = 1, a \neq 0$
- $\dfrac{a^m}{a^n} = a^{m-n}, a \neq 0$

- $a^{-n} = \dfrac{1}{a^n}, a \neq 0$
- $(ab)^n = a^n b^n$
- $(a^m)^n = a^{mn}$

- $a^m \cdot a^n = a^{m+n}$
- $\left(\dfrac{a}{b}\right)^n = \dfrac{a^n}{b^n}, b \neq 0$

Example

Simplify and rewrite each expression using only positive exponents.

a. $(5a^3)(-3a^{-4})$

$(5a^3)(-3a^{-4}) = 5(-3)a^{(3+(-4))}$

$= -15a^{-1}$

$= \dfrac{-15}{a}$, or $-\dfrac{15}{a}$

b. $(-4x^{-3}y^5)^2$

$(-4x^{-3}y^5)^2 = (-4)^2(x^{-3})^2(y^5)^2$

$= 16x^{-6}y^{10}$

$= \dfrac{16y^{10}}{x^6}$

c. $\dfrac{4ab^6c^3}{a^5bc^3}$

$\dfrac{4ab^6c^3}{a^5bc^3} = 4a^{(1-5)}b^{(6-1)}c^{(3-3)}$

$= 4a^{-4}b^5c^0$

$= \dfrac{4b^5}{a^4}$

Exercises

Simplify each expression. Use only positive exponents.

1. $(2a^3)(5a^4)$

2. $(-3x^2)(-4x^{-2})$

3. $(3x^2y^3)^2$

4. $(3x^{-4}y^3)^2$

5. $\dfrac{4a^8}{2a^4}$

6. $\dfrac{12x^5y^3}{4x^{-1}}$

7. $\dfrac{(6x^3)^0}{3xy^2}$

8. $\left(\dfrac{2x^4}{3}\right)^3$

9. $(-4m^2n^3)(2mn)$

10. $(2x^3y^7)^{-2}$

11. $\dfrac{(3r^{-2}s^3t^0)^{-3}}{3rs}$

12. $(h^7k^3)^0$

13. $\dfrac{r^2s^4t^6}{r^3s^4t^{-6}}$

14. $\dfrac{x^2y}{4} \cdot \dfrac{16x}{y}$

15. $(s^4t)^2(st)$

16. $\left(\dfrac{1}{h^{-2}}\right)^{-1} \cdot h^3$

17. $\dfrac{1}{a^2b^{-3}}(a^2b^{-3})^{-1}$

18. $\left(\dfrac{r^{-1}s^2t^{-3}}{r^{-2}s^0t^1}\right)^{-1}$

19. Reasoning Your friend tells you that $(k^2)^{-5} = -k^{10}$. Use the properties of exponents to prove or disprove her claim.

6-1 Roots and Radical Expressions

Objective To find nth roots

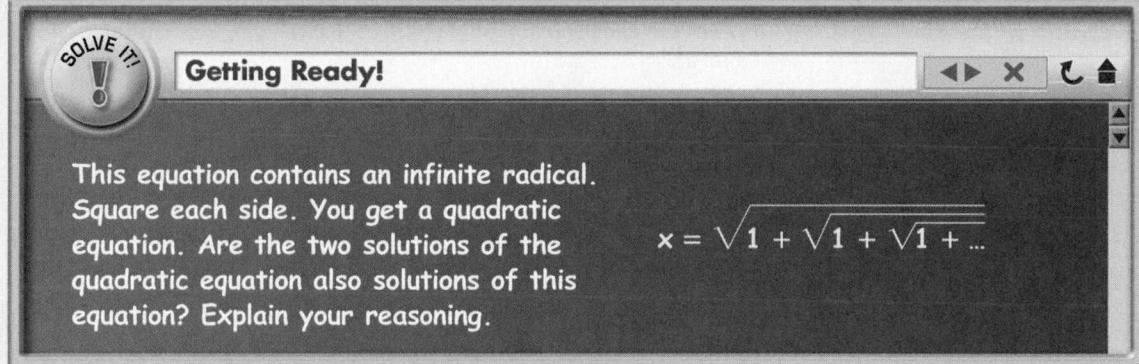

Getting Ready!

This equation contains an infinite radical. Square each side. You get a quadratic equation. Are the two solutions of the quadratic equation also solutions of this equation? Explain your reasoning.

$$x = \sqrt{1 + \sqrt{1 + \sqrt{1 + \ldots}}}$$

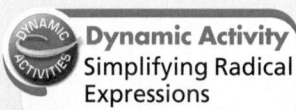

Dynamic Activity
Simplifying Radical Expressions

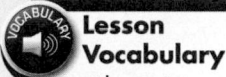

Lesson Vocabulary
• nth root
• principal root
• radicand
• index

In Chapter 5, you used the word *root* to represent a solution of an equation. For example, 2 is a root of the equation $x^3 - 8$. For such a simple power equation, you can simply refer to 2 as a cube root of 8.

Focus Question What is the nth root of a number?

Corresponding to every power, there is a root. For example, just as there are squares (second powers), there are square roots. Just as there are cubes (third powers), there are cube roots, and so on.

5 is a square root of 25.	$5^2 = 25$
5 is a cube root of 125.	$5^3 = 125$
5 is a fourth root of 625.	$5^4 = 625$
5 is a fifth root of 3125.	$5^5 = 3125$

This pattern suggests a definition of an nth root.

take note

Key Concept   The nth Root

If $a^n = b$, with a and b real numbers and n a positive integer, then a is an **nth root** of b.

If n is odd...

there is one real nth root of b, denoted in radical form as $\sqrt[n]{b}$.

If n is even...

• and b is positive, there are two real nth roots of b. The positive root is the **principal root** (or principal nth root), and its symbol is $\sqrt[n]{b}$. The negative root is its opposite, or $-\sqrt[n]{b}$.

• and b is negative, there are no real nth roots of b.

The only nth root of 0 is 0.

You use a radical sign to indicate a root. The number under the radical sign is the **radicand**. The **index** gives the degree of the root.

index   radical sign

$$\sqrt[n]{a}$$

radicand

ONLINE PROBLEMS **Problem 1** Finding All Real Roots

A What are the real cube roots of 0.008, -1000, and $\frac{1}{27}$?

Plan

How many real cube roots are there?
A cube root is the same as a third root, and 3 is odd. So there is only one real cube root of a number.

For an odd number n and real number b, there is one real root $\sqrt[n]{b}$.

Write each number b in the form a^3.	$0.008 = (0.2)^3$	$-1000 = (-10)^3$	$\frac{1}{27} = \left(\frac{1}{3}\right)^3$
Identify the cube roots.	0.2 is the only real cube root of 0.008.	-10 is the only real cube root of -1000.	$\frac{1}{3}$ is the only real cube root of $\frac{1}{27}$.

B What are the real fourth roots of 1, -0.0001, and $\frac{16}{81}$?

For an even number n and $b > 0$, there are two real roots $\sqrt[n]{b}$ and $-\sqrt[n]{b}$. Find the 4th roots of 1 and $\frac{16}{81}$.

Write each number b in the form a^4.	$1 = (1)^4$	$\frac{16}{81} = \left(\frac{2}{3}\right)^4$
Identify the principal fourth roots.	1 is a real fourth root of 1.	$\frac{2}{3}$ is a real fourth root of $\frac{16}{81}$.
Write another true equation of the form $b = a^4$.	$1 = (-1)^4$	$\frac{16}{81} = \left(-\frac{2}{3}\right)^4$
Identify the negative roots.	-1 is the other real fourth root of 1.	$-\frac{2}{3}$ is the other real fourth root of $\frac{16}{81}$.

For an even number n and $b < 0$, there are no real nth roots.

-0.0001 is negative.   There are no real fourth roots of -0.0001.

Hint

You can only find the nth root of a negative number if n is odd.

 Got It? 1. a. What are the real fifth roots of 0, -1, and 32?

b. What are the real square roots of 0.01, -1, and $\frac{36}{121}$?

c. Reasoning Explain why a negative real number b has no real nth roots if n is even.

According to the Fundamental Theorem of Algebra, $x^4 - 1 = 0$ has four roots, only two of which are real. In this chapter, the focus is on real roots only.

ONLINE PROBLEMS **Problem 2** Finding Roots

What is each real-number root?

Plan

How can you find a cube root?
Work backwards. Find a number whose cube is the radicand.

A $\sqrt[3]{-8}$

$(-2)^3 = -8$
So, $\sqrt[3]{-8} = -2$.

B $\sqrt{0.04}$

$(0.2)^2 = 0.04$
So, $\sqrt{0.04} = 0.2$.

$(-0.2)^2 = 0.04$ also, but $\sqrt{0.04}$ represents the positive square root.

C $\sqrt[4]{-1}$

There is no real root because there is no real number whose fourth power is -1.

D $\sqrt{(-2)^2}$

$\sqrt{(-2)^2} = \sqrt{4} = 2$.

Got It? **2.** What is each real-number root?

 a. $\sqrt[3]{-27}$ b. $\sqrt[4]{-81}$
 c. $\sqrt{(-7)^2}$ d. $\sqrt{-49}$

It is tempting to conclude that $\sqrt[n]{a^n} = a$ for all real numbers a, but Problem 2D shows that this is not the case. If n is even, then $\sqrt[n]{a^n}$ is nonnegative even if a itself is negative.

Hint

A simple example can help you remember to include absolute value: $\sqrt{(-5)^2} = 5$.

take note

Property *nth* Roots of *nth* Powers

For any real number a, $\sqrt[n]{a^n} = \begin{cases} a \text{ if } n \text{ is odd} \\ |a| \text{ if } n \text{ is even} \end{cases}$

It is easy to overlook this rule for simplifying radicals. It is particularly important that you remember it when the radicand contains a variable expression. You must *include* the absolute value when n is even. You must *omit* it when n is odd.

Problem 3 Simplifying Radical Expressions

Plan

How can you get started?
You're simplifying a square root, so use properties of exponents to write the *entire* radicand as a perfect square.

What is a simpler form of each radical expression?

Ⓐ $\sqrt{16x^8}$

Rewrite using perfect squares.	$\sqrt{16x^8} = \sqrt{4^2(x^4)^2}$
Use $(ab)^n = a^n b^n$.	$= \sqrt{(4x^4)^2}$
Use the definition of $\sqrt[n]{a^n}$.	$= |4x^4|$
Simplify.	$= 4x^4$

The index, 2, is even. Use absolute value symbols.

$|x^4| = x^4$ because x^4 is never negative.

Ⓑ $\sqrt[3]{a^6b^9}$

Rewrite using perfect cubes.	$\sqrt[3]{a^6b^9} = \sqrt[3]{(a^2)^3(b^3)^3}$
Use $(ab)^n = a^n b^n$.	$= \sqrt[3]{(a^2b^3)^3}$
Use the definition of $\sqrt[n]{a^n}$.	$= a^2b^3$

The index, 3, is odd. Do not use absolute value symbols.

Ⓒ $\sqrt[4]{x^8y^{12}}$

Rewrite using fourth powers.	$\sqrt[4]{x^8y^{12}} = \sqrt[4]{(x^2)^4(y^3)^4}$
Use $(ab)^n = a^n b^n$.	$= \sqrt[4]{(x^2y^3)^4}$
Use the definition of $\sqrt[n]{a^n}$.	$= |x^2y^3|$
Simplify.	$= x^2|y^3|$

The index, 4, is even. Use absolute value symbols.

$|x^2| = x^2$ because x^2 is never negative.

 Got It? **3.** What is a simpler form of each radical expression?

 a. $\sqrt{81x^4}$ b. $\sqrt[3]{a^{12}b^{15}}$ c. $\sqrt[4]{x^{12}y^{16}}$

 **Problem 4** Using a Radical Expression

Academics Some teachers adjust test scores when a test is difficult. One teacher's formula for adjusting scores is $A = 10\sqrt{R}$, where A is the adjusted score and R is the raw score. If the raw scores on one test range from 36 to 90, what is the range of the adjusted scores?

Think

You have to adjust the lowest raw score and the highest raw score. Substitute each score into the formula.

Find square roots and simplify. Use a calculator if needed.

The other adjusted scores must be between the lowest and highest adjusted scores.

Write

Lowest:
$A = 10\sqrt{R}$
$= 10\sqrt{36}$

Highest:
$A = 10\sqrt{R}$
$= 10\sqrt{90}$

$= 10(6)$
$= 60$

$\approx 10(9.487)$
$= 94.87$
≈ 95

The adjusted scores range from 60 to 95.

 Got It? **4.** In Problem 4, what are the adjusted scores for raw scores of 0 and 100?

Focus Question What is the nth root of a number?

Answer The nth root of a number is a number that when raised to the nth power gives you the original number. Write the nth root of b as $\sqrt[n]{b}$. Use the property for nth roots of nth powers to simplify radical expressions.

 Lesson Check

Do you know HOW?

Find all the real square roots of each number.

1. 25   **2.** 0.16   **3.** −64

Simplify each radical expression.

4. $\sqrt{9b^2}$ **5.** $\sqrt{a^8b^{18}}$ **6.** $\sqrt[3]{-125a^3}$

Do you UNDERSTAND?

7. Error Analysis A student said the only fourth root of 16 is 2. Describe and correct his error.

8. Vocabulary Explain the difference between a real root and a principal root.

9. Reasoning A number has only one real nth root. What can you conclude about the index n?

Practice and Problem-Solving Exercises

Ⓐ Practice

Find all the real square roots of each number.

◀ See Problem 1.

10. 225

11. 0.0049

12. $-\frac{1}{121}$

Find all the real cube roots of each number.

13. -64

14. 0.125

15. $-\frac{27}{216}$

Find each real root.

◀ See Problem 2.

Guided Practice

16. $\sqrt{0.25}$

To start, find a number whose square is equal to the radicand.

$(0.5)^2 = 0.25$

17. $\sqrt{36}$

18. $-\sqrt[3]{64}$

19. $\sqrt[3]{-27}$

Simplify each radical expression. Use absolute value symbols when needed.

◀ See Problem 3.

Guided Practice

20. $\sqrt{16x^2}$

To start, write the factors of the radicand as perfect squares.

$\sqrt{16x^2} = \sqrt{4^2 x^2}$

21. $\sqrt[3]{27y^6}$

22. $\sqrt[4]{x^8 y^{12}}$

23. $\sqrt[5]{32y^{10}}$

24. Grades In many classes, a passing test grade is 70. Using the formula $A = 10\sqrt{R}$, what raw score would a student need to get a passing grade after her score is adjusted?

◀ See Problem 4.

Ⓑ Apply

Find the two real solutions of each equation.

25. $x^2 = 100$

26. $x^4 = 1$

27. $x^2 = 0.25$

28. $x^4 = \frac{16}{81}$

29. Think About a Plan The radius of a spherical balloon can be expressed as $r = \sqrt[3]{\frac{3V}{4\pi}}$ inches, where r is the radius and V is the volume of the balloon in cubic inches. If air is pumped to inflate the balloon from 500 cubic inches to 800 cubic inches, by how many inches has the radius of the balloon increased?
  • What was the radius of the balloon originally?
  • What was the radius after inflating the balloon to 800 cubic inches?
  • How can you use the two radii to find the amount of increase?

30. Boat Building Boat builders share an old rule of thumb for sailboats. The maximum speed K in knots is 1.35 times the square root of the length L in feet of the boat's waterline.
  a. A customer is planning to order a sailboat with a maximum speed of 12 knots. How long should the waterline be?
  b. How much longer would the waterline have to be to achieve a maximum speed of 15 knots?

Simplify each radical expression. Use absolute value symbols when needed.

31. $\sqrt[3]{0.125}$ **32.** $\sqrt[3]{\dfrac{8}{216}}$ **33.** $\sqrt[4]{0.0016}$ **34.** $\sqrt[4]{\dfrac{1}{256}}$

35. Open-Ended Write three radical expressions that simplify to $-2x^2$.

Is each equation *always*, *sometimes*, or *never* true? Explain your answer.

36. $\sqrt{x^4} = x^2$ **37.** $\sqrt{x^6} = x^3$ **38.** $\sqrt[3]{x^8} = x^2$

Standardized Test Prep

SAT/ACT

39. Which equation has more than one real-number solution?

Ⓐ $x^2 = 0$ Ⓑ $x^2 = 1$ Ⓒ $x^2 = -1$ Ⓓ $x^3 = -1$

40. According to the Rational Root Theorem, which of the following is NOT a possible root of the polynomial equation $7x^5 + 3x^2 - 4x + 21 = 0$?

Ⓕ $\dfrac{1}{7}$ Ⓖ $\dfrac{1}{3}$ Ⓗ 3 Ⓘ 7

41. The fuse of a three-break firework rocket is programmed to ignite three times with 2-second intervals between the ignitions. When the rocket is shot vertically in the air, its height h in feet after t seconds is given by the formula $h(t) = -5t^2 + 70t$. At how many seconds after the shot should the firework technician set the timer of the first ignition to make the second ignition occur when the rocket is at its highest point?

Ⓐ 3 Ⓑ 9 Ⓒ 5 Ⓓ 7

Extended Response

42. Write a system of equations to find a cubic polynomial function whose graph passes through $(-3, -35)$, $(0, 1)$, $(2, 3)$, and $(4, 7)$.

Mixed Review

Determine the cubic function that is obtained from the parent function $y = x^3$ after each sequence of transformations.

 See Lesson 5-9.

43. translation up 3 units and to the left 2 units

44. vertical compression by a factor of $\dfrac{1}{2}$, translation down 2 units

Solve each equation by using the Quadratic Formula.

 See Lesson 4-7.

45. $-4x^2 + 7x - 3 = 0$ **46.** $3x^2 - 5x + 3 = 0$ **47.** $36x^2 - 132x + 121 = 0$

Get Ready! To prepare for Lesson 6-2, do Exercises 48–50.

Simplify each algebraic expression. See Lesson 1-3.

48. $\dfrac{14x^7y^9}{7x^4y^6}$ **49.** $\dfrac{3abc}{9b}$ **50.** $\dfrac{20x}{5x^3}$

6-2 PART 1

Multiplying and Dividing Radical Expressions

Objective To multiply radical expressions

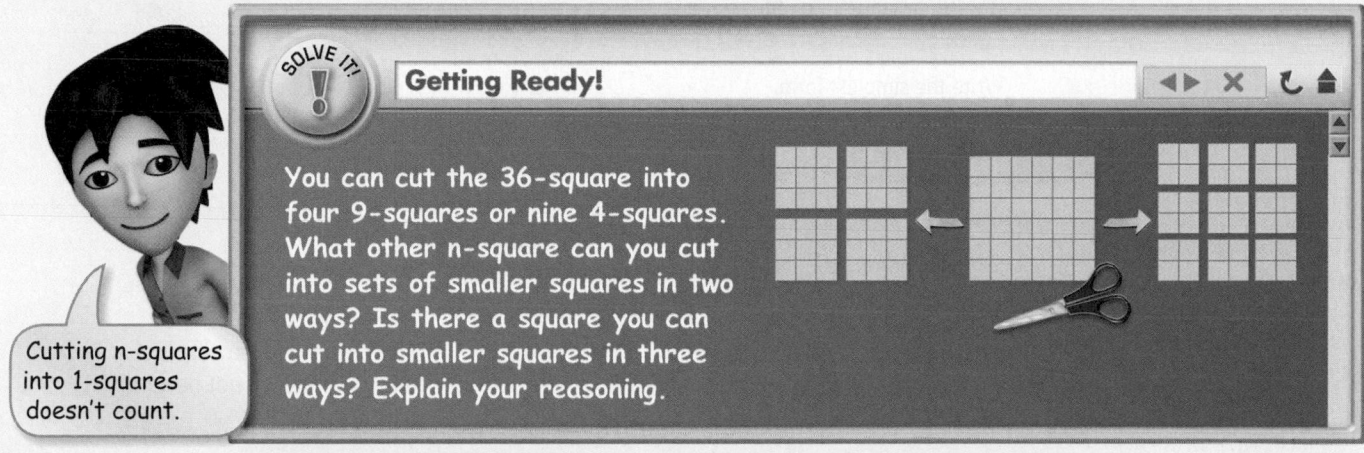

Getting Ready!

You can cut the 36-square into four 9-squares or nine 4-squares. What other n-square can you cut into sets of smaller squares in two ways? Is there a square you can cut into smaller squares in three ways? Explain your reasoning.

Cutting n-squares into 1-squares doesn't count.

Lesson Vocabulary
• Simplest form of a radical

Knowing the perfect squares greater than 1 (namely, 4, 9, 16, and so on) will help you simplify some radical expressions.

Focus Question How can you multiply radical expressions?

You can simplify the product of powers that have the same exponent. Similarly, you can simplify the product of radicals that have the same index.

Same Exponent	Same Index
$2^2 \cdot 3^2 = (2 \cdot 3)^2$	$\sqrt{2} \cdot \sqrt{3} = \sqrt{2 \cdot 3}$
$4^3 \cdot 5^3 = (4 \cdot 5)^3$	$\sqrt[3]{4} \cdot \sqrt[3]{5} = \sqrt[3]{4 \cdot 5}$

 take note

Property Combining Radical Expressions: Products

If $\sqrt[n]{a}$ and $\sqrt[n]{b}$ are real numbers, then $\sqrt[n]{a} \cdot \sqrt[n]{b} = \sqrt[n]{ab}$.

Problem 1 Multiplying Radical Expressions

Can you simplify the product of the radical expressions? Explain.

A $\sqrt{5} \cdot \sqrt{7}$

Yes. $\sqrt{5} \cdot \sqrt{7} = \sqrt{5(7)} = \sqrt{35}$

B $\sqrt[3]{6} \cdot \sqrt{2}$

No; the indexes are different. The property above does not apply.

C $\sqrt[3]{-4} \cdot \sqrt[3]{2}$

Yes. $\sqrt[3]{-4} \cdot \sqrt[3]{2} = \sqrt[3]{-4(2)} = \sqrt[3]{-8} = -2$

Plan

What allows you to use the property for multiplying radicals?
The radicals must be real numbers. The indexes must be the same.

Got It? **1.** Can you simplify the product of the radical expressions? Explain.

a. $\sqrt[4]{12} \cdot \sqrt[4]{5}$ b. $\sqrt[4]{7} \cdot \sqrt[5]{7}$ c. $\sqrt[5]{-5} \cdot \sqrt[5]{-2}$

If the radicand of $\sqrt[n]{a}$ has a perfect nth power among its factors, you can *reduce* the radical to a simpler form. If you reduce a radical as much as possible, the radical is in **simplest form**. For example, consider $\sqrt{24}$ and $\sqrt[3]{24}$.

Write the radicand as a product of factors with a perfect nth power.	$\sqrt{24} = \sqrt{4 \cdot 6}$	$\sqrt[3]{24} = \sqrt[3]{8 \cdot 3}$
Write the first factor as a power.	$= \sqrt{2^2 \cdot 6}$	$= \sqrt[3]{2^3 \cdot 3}$
Use the property of multiplying radicals.	$= \sqrt{2^2} \cdot \sqrt{6}$	$= \sqrt[3]{2^3} \cdot \sqrt[3]{3}$
Write the simplest form.	$= 2\sqrt{6}$	$= 2\sqrt[3]{3}$

Problem 2 Simplifying a Radical Expression

ONLINE PROBLEMS

Think

How do you know when you are done simplifying?
You are done when the radicand contains no perfect cube factors.

What is the simplest form of $\sqrt[3]{54x^5}$?

Find all perfect cube factors.	$\sqrt[3]{54x^5} = \sqrt[3]{3^3 \cdot 2 \cdot x^2 \cdot x^3}$
Use $\sqrt[n]{ab} = \sqrt[n]{a} \cdot \sqrt[n]{b}$.	$= \sqrt[3]{3^3 x^3} \cdot \sqrt[3]{2x^2}$
Simplify.	$= 3x\sqrt[3]{2x^2}$

The index is odd, so absolute value symbols are not needed.

Got It? 2. What is the simplest form of $\sqrt[3]{128x^7}$?

Problem 3 Simplifying a Product

ONLINE PROBLEMS

What is the simplest form of $\sqrt{12x^4y^2} \cdot \sqrt{15x^2y^3}$?

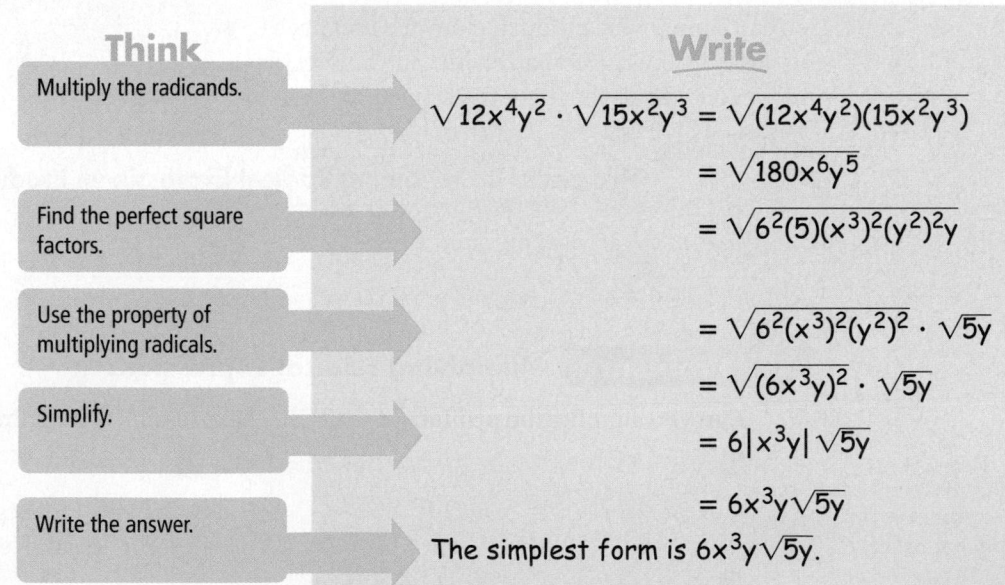

Think

Multiply the radicands.

Find the perfect square factors.

Use the property of multiplying radicals.

Simplify.

Write the answer.

Write

$\sqrt{12x^4y^2} \cdot \sqrt{15x^2y^3} = \sqrt{(12x^4y^2)(15x^2y^3)}$

$= \sqrt{180x^6y^5}$

$= \sqrt{6^2(5)(x^3)^2(y^2)^2y}$

$= \sqrt{6^2(x^3)^2(y^2)^2} \cdot \sqrt{5y}$

$= \sqrt{(6x^3y)^2} \cdot \sqrt{5y}$

$= 6|x^3y|\sqrt{5y}$

$= 6x^3y\sqrt{5y}$

The simplest form is $6x^3y\sqrt{5y}$.

Hint

Since both radicands must be real numbers, assume the variables are nonnegative. You can omit the absolute value symbols.

Got It? 3. What is the simplest form of $\sqrt{15x^5y^3} \cdot \sqrt{20xy^4}$?

Focus Question How can you multiply radical expressions?

Answer Write the product of two radicals that have the same index as a single radical expression by multiplying the radicands. You cannot use this method to multiply two radical expressions with different indexes.

Lesson Check

Do you know HOW?

Multiply, if possible. Then simplify.

1. $\sqrt{2} \cdot \sqrt{5}$

2. $\sqrt[3]{-27} \cdot \sqrt[3]{4}$

3. $\sqrt[3]{2} \cdot \sqrt[2]{7}$

4. $\sqrt{3} \cdot \sqrt{-4}$

Do you UNDERSTAND?

5. Reasoning For what values of x is $\sqrt{-4x^3}$ real? Justify your reasoning.

6. Error Analysis
Explain the error in this simplification of a radical expression.

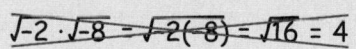

Practice and Problem-Solving Exercises

 **Practice**

Multiply, if possible. Then simplify. ◀ **See Problem 1.**

Guided Practice

7. $\sqrt{8} \cdot \sqrt{32}$

To start, identify the index of each radical.   The index of both radicals is 2.

8. $\sqrt[3]{4} \cdot \sqrt[3]{16}$

9. $\sqrt[3]{9} \cdot \sqrt[3]{-81}$

10. $\sqrt[4]{8} \cdot \sqrt[3]{32}$

Simplify. ◀ **See Problem 2.**

Guided Practice

11. $\sqrt{20x^3}$

To start, find all perfect square factors. $\sqrt{20x^3} = \sqrt{2^2 \cdot 5 \cdot x^2 \cdot x}$

12. $\sqrt[3]{81x^3}$

13. $\sqrt{200a^6b^7}$

14. $\sqrt[4]{64x^3y^6}$

Multiply and simplify. ◀ **See Problem 3.**

15. $\sqrt[3]{6} \cdot \sqrt[3]{16}$

16. $\sqrt{8x^5} \cdot \sqrt{3x}$

17. $4\sqrt{2x} \cdot 5\sqrt{6xy^2}$

18. $3\sqrt[3]{5y^3} \cdot 2\sqrt[3]{50y^4}$

19. $-\sqrt[3]{2x^2y^2} \cdot 2\sqrt[3]{15x^5y}$

20. $\sqrt[4]{81x^5y^4} \cdot \sqrt[4]{32x^3y}$

 **Apply**

Simplify each expression.

21. $\sqrt{5} \cdot \sqrt{50}$

22. $\sqrt{x^5y^5} \cdot 3\sqrt{2x^7y^6}$

23. $\sqrt{2}(\sqrt{50} + 7)$

Determine whether each expression is *always*, *sometimes*, or *never* a real number. Assume that x can be any real number.

24. $\sqrt[3]{-x^2}$

25. $\sqrt{-x^2}$

26. $\sqrt{-x}$

27. Geometry A rectangular shelf is $\sqrt{220}$ cm by $\sqrt{40}$ cm. Find its area.

Multiplying and Dividing Radical Expressions

Objective To divide radical expressions

In Part 1 of the lesson, you learned how to multiply radicals and write the product in simplest form.

Connect to What You Know

Here you will learn how to divide radical expressions, including how to rationalize a denominator.

Lesson Vocabulary
• rationalize the denominator

Focus Question How can you divide radical expressions?

Since you define division in terms of multiplication, you can extend the property for multiplying radical expressions. If the indexes are the same, you can write a quotient of roots as a root of a quotient.

Multiplying	Dividing
$\sqrt{2} \cdot \sqrt{3} = \sqrt{2 \cdot 3}$	$\dfrac{\sqrt{2}}{\sqrt{3}} = \sqrt{\dfrac{2}{3}}$
$\sqrt[3]{4} \cdot \sqrt[3]{5} = \sqrt[3]{4 \cdot 5}$	$\dfrac{\sqrt[3]{4}}{\sqrt[3]{5}} = \sqrt[3]{\dfrac{4}{5}}$

Property Combining Radical Expressions: Quotients

If $\sqrt[n]{a}$ and $\sqrt[n]{b}$ are real numbers and $b \neq 0$, then $\dfrac{\sqrt[n]{a}}{\sqrt[n]{b}} = \sqrt[n]{\dfrac{a}{b}}$.

Problem 4 Dividing Radical Expressions

What is the simplest form of each quotient?

Ⓐ $\dfrac{\sqrt{18x^5}}{\sqrt{2x^3}}$ **Ⓑ** $\dfrac{\sqrt[3]{162y^5}}{\sqrt[3]{3y^2}}$

Write the quotient of roots as the root of a quotient.

$\dfrac{\sqrt{18x^5}}{\sqrt{2x^3}} = \sqrt{\dfrac{18x^5}{2x^3}}$ $\dfrac{\sqrt[3]{162y^5}}{\sqrt[3]{3y^2}} = \sqrt[3]{\dfrac{162y^5}{3y^2}}$

Use $\dfrac{a^m}{a^n} = a^{m-n}$.

$= \sqrt{9x^2}$ $= \sqrt[3]{54y^3}$

Think

Do you need to include absolute value symbols?
No; both the divisor and dividend already require that x be nonnegative.

Rewrite using perfect nth powers.

$= \sqrt{3^2x^2}$ $= \sqrt[3]{3^3(2)y^3}$

Use $(ab)^n = a^nb^n$.

$= \sqrt{(3x)^2}$ $= \sqrt[3]{(3y)^3 \cdot 2}$

Simplify.

$= |3x|$ $= \sqrt[3]{(3y)^3} \cdot \sqrt[3]{2}$

Use the definition of $\sqrt[n]{a^n}$.

$= 3x$ $= 3y\sqrt[3]{2}$

Got It? **4. a.** What is the simplest form of $\dfrac{\sqrt{50x^6}}{\sqrt{2x^4}}$?

b. Reasoning Can you simplify the expression in Problem 4(a) by first simplifying $\sqrt{18x^5}$ and $\sqrt{2x^3}$? Explain.

Another way to simplify a radical expression is to **rationalize the denominator**. You rewrite the expression so that there are no radicals in any denominator and no fractions in any radical expression.

Hint

Multiply the numerator and denominator by $\sqrt{2}$ so the denominator becomes a whole number.

Multiply by 1.

$$\frac{1}{\sqrt{2}} = \frac{1}{\sqrt{2}}\left(\frac{\sqrt{2}}{\sqrt{2}}\right) = \frac{\sqrt{2}}{2}$$

The product of $\sqrt{2}$ and itself is a rational number, 2.

Problem 5 Rationalizing the Denominator

Multiple Choice What is the simplest form of $\sqrt[3]{\dfrac{5x^2}{12y^2z}}$?

Ⓐ $\dfrac{\sqrt[3]{90x^2yz^2}}{6yz}$ Ⓑ $\dfrac{\sqrt[3]{5x^2}}{\sqrt[3]{12y^2z}}$ Ⓒ $\dfrac{5\sqrt[3]{x^2yz^2}}{yz}$ Ⓓ $5\sqrt[3]{x^2z}$

Think

How do you choose what to multiply by?
Choose a cube root with a radicand that will make each factor of the radicand in the denominator a perfect cube.

Use the property for dividing radicals.

$$\sqrt[3]{\frac{5x^2}{12y^2z}} = \frac{\sqrt[3]{5x^2}}{\sqrt[3]{12y^2z}}$$

Factor the radicand in the denominator.

$$= \frac{\sqrt[3]{5x^2}}{\sqrt[3]{2^3 3y^2z}}$$

The radicand needs additional factors of 2, 3^2, y, and z^2 to make it a perfect cube.

Multiply the numerator and denominator by $\sqrt[3]{2 \cdot 3^2yz^2}$.

$$= \frac{\sqrt[3]{5x^2}}{\sqrt[3]{2^2 \cdot 3y^2z}} \cdot \frac{\sqrt[3]{2 \cdot 3^2yz^2}}{\sqrt[3]{2 \cdot 3^2yz^2}}$$

Use the property for multiplying radicals.

$$= \frac{\sqrt[3]{(5x^2)(2 \cdot 3^2yz^2)}}{\sqrt[3]{(2^2 \cdot 3y^2z)(2 \cdot 3^2yz^2)}}$$

Combine like factors.

$$= \frac{\sqrt[3]{90x^2yz^2}}{\sqrt[3]{2^3 \cdot 3^3y^3z^3}}$$

Use the definition of a 3rd root of a 3rd power.

$$= \frac{\sqrt[3]{90x^2yz^2}}{2 \cdot 3yz}$$

Simplify.

$$= \frac{\sqrt[3]{90x^2yz^2}}{6yz}$$

The correct answer is A.

 Got It? **5. a.** What is the simplest form of $\dfrac{\sqrt[3]{7x}}{\sqrt[3]{5y^2}}$?

b. Reasoning Which choice in Problem 5 could be eliminated immediately? Explain.

Focus Question How can you divide radical expressions?

Answer If the indexes are the same, write the quotient of roots as a root of a quotient. Then simplify the fraction in the radicand. Another way to simplify a radical expression is to rationalize the denominator.

Lesson Check

Do you know HOW?

Divide and simplify.

1. $\dfrac{\sqrt[3]{15x^2}}{\sqrt[3]{5x}}$

2. $\dfrac{\sqrt{21x^{10}}}{\sqrt{7x^5}}$

Do you UNDERSTAND?

3. **Writing** Explain how to write the expression $\sqrt[3]{\dfrac{3y}{20xy^2}}$ in simplest form.

Practice and Problem-Solving Exercises

 **Practice**

Divide and simplify.

 **See Problem 4.**

4. $\dfrac{\sqrt{500}}{\sqrt{5}}$

Guided Practice

To start, write the quotient of roots as a root of a quotient.

$\dfrac{\sqrt{500}}{\sqrt{5}} = \sqrt{\dfrac{500}{5}}$

5. $\dfrac{\sqrt{48x^3}}{\sqrt{3xy^2}}$

6. $\dfrac{\sqrt{56x^5y^5}}{\sqrt{7xy}}$

7. $\dfrac{\sqrt[3]{250x^7y^3}}{\sqrt[3]{2x^2y}}$

8. $\dfrac{\sqrt[3]{48x^3y^2}}{\sqrt[3]{6x^4y}}$

9. $\dfrac{\sqrt{20ab}}{\sqrt{45a^2b^3}}$

10. $\dfrac{\sqrt[3]{64x^5y^{10}}}{\sqrt[3]{8x^3y}}$

Rationalize the denominator of each expression.

See Problem 5.

11. $\dfrac{\sqrt{x}}{\sqrt{2}}$

Guided Practice

To start, multiply the numerator and denominator by $\sqrt{2}$ so the denominator becomes a whole number.

$\dfrac{\sqrt{x}}{\sqrt{2}} = \dfrac{\sqrt{x}}{\sqrt{2}} \cdot \dfrac{\sqrt{2}}{\sqrt{2}}$

12. $\dfrac{\sqrt{5}}{\sqrt{8x}}$

13. $\sqrt[3]{\dfrac{5}{3x}}$

14. $\dfrac{\sqrt[4]{2}}{\sqrt[4]{5}}$

15. $\dfrac{15\sqrt{60x^5}}{3\sqrt{12x}}$

16. $\dfrac{\sqrt{3xy^2}}{\sqrt{5xy^3}}$

17. $\dfrac{\sqrt[3]{12ab^3c^2}}{\sqrt[3]{10a^3bc}}$

18. **Think About a Plan** The formula $t = \sqrt{\frac{2s}{a}}$ shows the time t that any vehicle takes to travel a distance s at a constant acceleration a, starting from rest. What is the difference in time between a car accelerating at 16 m/s² and one accelerating at 25 m/s² for a distance of 200 m?
   • What is the time that a car accelerating at 16 m/s² takes to travel 200 m?
   • What is the time that a car accelerating at 25 m/s² takes to travel 200 m?

19. **Geometry** The base of a triangle is $\sqrt{18}$ cm and its height is $\sqrt{8}$ cm. Find its area.

20. **Physics** The formula $F = \frac{mv^2}{r}$ gives the centripetal force F of an object of mass m moving along a circle of radius r, where v is the tangential velocity of the object. Solve the formula for v. Rationalize the denominator.

21. **Satellites** The circular velocity v, in miles per hour, of a satellite orbiting Earth is given by the formula $v = \sqrt{\frac{1.24 \times 10^{12}}{r}}$, where r is the distance in miles from the satellite to the center of the Earth. How much greater is the velocity of a satellite orbiting at an altitude of 100 mi than the velocity of a satellite orbiting at an altitude of 200 mi? (The radius of the Earth is 3950 mi.)

Simplify each expression. Rationalize all denominators.

22. $\dfrac{\sqrt{5x^4}}{\sqrt{2x^2y^3}}$

23. $\dfrac{5\sqrt{2}}{3\sqrt{7x}}$

24. $\dfrac{1}{\sqrt[3]{9x}}$

25. **Error Analysis** A student said that the simplest form of the radical expression shown is x. Explain the student's error in this simplification.

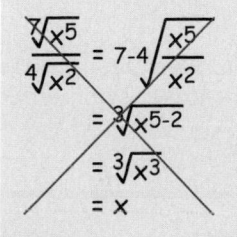

26. **Physics** The mass m of an object is $\sqrt{80}$ g and its volume V is $\sqrt{5}$ cm³. Use the formula $D = \frac{m}{V}$ to find the density D of the object.

27. **Open-Ended** Of the equivalent expressions $\sqrt{\frac{2}{3}}$, $\frac{\sqrt{2}}{\sqrt{3}}$ and $\frac{\sqrt{6}}{3}$, which do you prefer to use for finding a decimal approximation with a calculator? Justify your reasoning.

Standardized Test Prep

28. What is the simplified form of the expression $\frac{3}{\sqrt{18xy^2}}$ if x and y are positive?

    Ⓐ $\frac{\sqrt{2x}}{2xy}$

    Ⓑ $\frac{\sqrt{2y}}{2xy}$

    Ⓒ $\frac{\sqrt{54xy^2}}{2xy}$

    Ⓓ $\frac{\sqrt{27xy^2}}{2xy}$

29. Which inequality is shown by the graph at the right?

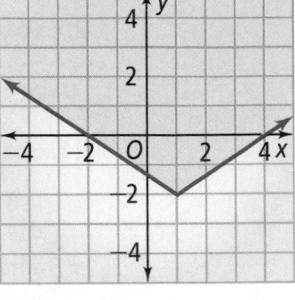

    Ⓐ $y \geq \frac{2}{3}|x - 1| - 2$

    Ⓑ $y \geq \frac{2}{3}|x - 2| - 1$

    Ⓒ $y \geq \frac{3}{2}|x - 1| - 2$

    Ⓓ $y \geq |\frac{2}{3}x - 1| - 2$

30. What are the solutions, in simplest form, of the quadratic equation $3x^2 + 6x - 5 = 0$?

    Ⓕ $\frac{-6 \pm \sqrt{96}}{6}$

    Ⓖ $\frac{-6 \pm i\sqrt{24}}{6}$

    Ⓗ $\frac{-3 \pm 2\sqrt{6}}{3}$

    Ⓘ $\frac{-3 \pm i\sqrt{6}}{3}$

31. A triangle has the dimensions shown at the right. What is the height of a triangle with equal area but a base of 36?

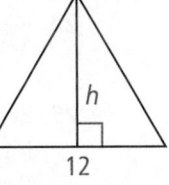

    Ⓐ $\frac{h}{3}$

    Ⓑ $\frac{2h}{3}$

    Ⓒ $2h$

    Ⓓ $3h$

32. Find the axis of symmetry of the graph of the function $y = -2x^2 - 5x + 4$. Show your work.

Mixed Review

Simplify each radical expression. Use absolute value symbols when needed.
◀ **See Lesson 6-1.**

33. $\sqrt{121a^{90}}$ **34.** $\sqrt{81c^{48}d^{64}}$ **35.** $\sqrt[3]{64a^{81}}$

Divide using synthetic division.
◀ **See Lesson 5-4.**

36. $(y^3 - 64) \div (y + 4)$ **37.** $(6a^3 + a^2 - a + 4) \div (a + 1)$

Complete each square.
◀ **See Lesson 4-6.**

38. $x^2 + 10x + \blacksquare$ **39.** $x^2 - 10x + \blacksquare$ **40.** $x^2 + 11x + \blacksquare$

Get Ready!   To prepare for Lesson 6-3, do Exercises 41–44.

Write each quotient as a complex number in the form $a + bi$.
◀ **See Lesson 4-8.**

41. $\frac{2}{3 - i}$ **42.** $\frac{5}{2 + 3i}$ **43.** $\frac{4}{4 + i}$ **44.** $\frac{-1}{7 - 5i}$

Binomial Radical Expressions

Objective To add and subtract radical expressions

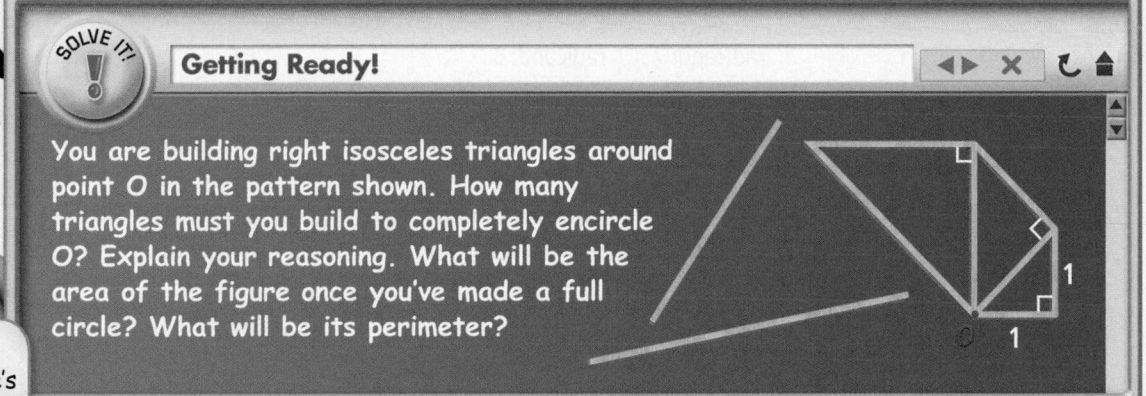

Getting Ready!

You are building right isosceles triangles around point O in the pattern shown. How many triangles must you build to completely encircle O? Explain your reasoning. What will be the area of the figure once you've made a full circle? What will be its perimeter?

1

1

One triangle's leg is another triangle's hypotenuse.

Lesson Vocabulary
• like radicals

Like radicals are radical expressions that have the same index and radicand.

Focus Question What properties of real numbers apply to radical expressions?

You can combine like radicals using properties of real numbers. Here is how you can combine like radicals using the Distributive Property.

Like Radicals With Numbers	Like Radicals With Variables
$\sqrt{2} + 3\sqrt{2} = 4\sqrt{2}$	$\sqrt{5xy} + 8\sqrt{5xy} = 9\sqrt{5xy}$
$\sqrt[3]{7} - 5\sqrt[3]{7} = -4\sqrt[3]{7}$	$\sqrt[3]{9x^2y} - 8\sqrt[3]{9x^2y} = -7\sqrt[3]{9x^2y}$

take note

Property Combining Radical Expressions: Sums and Differences

Use the Distributive Property to add or subtract like radicals.

$$a\sqrt[n]{x} + b\sqrt[n]{x} = (a + b)\sqrt[n]{x} \qquad a\sqrt[n]{x} - b\sqrt[n]{x} = (a - b)\sqrt[n]{x}$$

Combining radical expressions is different from *adding* them. The sum of any two real numbers is a real number, so you can add $\sqrt{2}$ and $\sqrt{3}$ to get the real number $\sqrt{2} + \sqrt{3}$.

However, you cannot *combine* the result into a single radical, so $\sqrt{2} + \sqrt{3} \neq \sqrt{5}$.

$$
\begin{array}{l}
\sqrt{2} \approx 1.414 \\
+ \ \sqrt{3} \approx 1.732 \\
\hline
\sqrt{2} + \sqrt{3} \approx 3.146
\end{array}
\qquad
\begin{array}{l}
\sqrt{5} \approx 2.236 \\
\\
\neq 2.236
\end{array}
$$

Problem 1 Adding and Subtracting Radicals

What is the simplified form of each expression?

Ⓐ $3\sqrt{5x} - 2\sqrt{5x}$

Think

Can you always simplify a radical sum?
No; the radicands and the indexes must be the same.

Use the Distributive Property. $3\sqrt{5x} - 2\sqrt{5x} = (3-2)\sqrt{5x}$

Simplify. $= \sqrt{5x}$

Ⓑ $6x^2\sqrt{7} + 4x\sqrt{5}$

radicand: 7   radicand: 5

The radicands are different. You cannot combine the expressions.

Ⓒ $12\sqrt[3]{7xy} - 8\sqrt[5]{7xy}$

index: 3   index: 5

The indexes are different. You cannot combine the expressions.

Got It? **1.** What is the simplified form of each expression?

a. $7\sqrt[3]{5} - 4\sqrt{5}$ **b.** $3x\sqrt{xy} + 4x\sqrt{xy}$ **c.** $17\sqrt[5]{3x^2} - 15\sqrt[3]{3x^2}$

 Problem 2 Using Radical Expressions

Architecture In the stained-glass window design, the side of each small square is 5 in. Find the perimeter of the window to the nearest tenth of an inch.

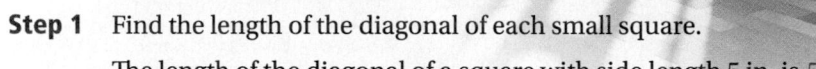

Hint

The length of the diagonal of a square with side length s is $s\sqrt{2}$.

Step 1 Find the length of the diagonal of each small square.

The length of the diagonal of a square with side length 5 in. is $5\sqrt{2}$ in.

Step 2 Find the dimensions of the entire window.

The window is 3 "diagonals" long. $3(5\sqrt{2}) = 15\sqrt{2}$

The window is 2 "diagonals" wide. $2(5\sqrt{2}) = 10\sqrt{2}$

Think

Does it make sense that you have a radical expression as the answer?
Yes; perimeter is a linear measure, and there is no squaring in the calculations.

Step 3 Find the perimeter.

Use the formula for the perimeter of a rectangle. $P = 2l + 2w$

Substitute for length and width. $= 2(15\sqrt{2}) + 2(10\sqrt{2})$

Simplify. $= 30\sqrt{2} + 20\sqrt{2}$

Combine like radicals. Use a calculator. $= 50\sqrt{2} \approx 70.7$

The perimeter of the window is about 70.7 inches.

 Got It? **2. a.** Find the perimeter of the window if the side of each small square is 6 in.

b. **Reasoning** Describe a different sequence of steps that you could use to compute the perimeter of the window.

When you have a sum or difference of radicals, you should simplify each radical so that you can find all the like radicals.

 Problem 3 **Simplifying Before Adding or Subtracting**

What is the simplest form of the expression? $\sqrt{12} + \sqrt{75} - \sqrt{3}$

Think

Simplify each radical. Factor the radicand using perfect square factors, if possible.

Use the property of multiplying radicals.

Find square roots.

These are like radicals. Combine them.

Write the solution.

Write

$$\sqrt{12} + \sqrt{75} - \sqrt{3}$$
$$= \sqrt{4 \cdot 3} + \sqrt{25 \cdot 3} - \sqrt{3}$$
$$= \sqrt{2^2 \cdot 3} + \sqrt{5^2 \cdot 3} - \sqrt{3}$$

$$= \sqrt{2^2}\sqrt{3} + \sqrt{5^2}\sqrt{3} - \sqrt{3}$$

$$= 2\sqrt{3} + 5\sqrt{3} - \sqrt{3}$$

$$= (2 + 5 - 1)\sqrt{3}$$
$$= 6\sqrt{3}$$

The simplest form is $6\sqrt{3}$.

Hint

Recall that $\sqrt{3}$ can also be written as $1 \cdot \sqrt{3}$.

 Got It? **3.** What is the simplest form of the expression? $\sqrt[3]{250} + \sqrt[3]{54} - \sqrt[3]{16}$

You can use the Distributive Property to multiply binomials that have radical expressions. Multiply each term of one binomial by each term of the other.

Problem 4 **Multiplying Binomial Radical Expressions**

Plan

How do you multiply two binomials?
Use the Distributive Property twice and simplify.
$(a + b)(c + d)$
$(a + b)c + (a + b)d$
$ac + bc + ad + bd$

What is the product of each radical expression?

A $(4 + 2\sqrt{2})(5 + 4\sqrt{2})$

Write the original expression. $(4 + 2\sqrt{2})(5 + 4\sqrt{2})$

Distribute. $20 + 10\sqrt{2} + 16\sqrt{2} + 16$

Combine like radicals. $36 + 26\sqrt{2}$

B $(3 - \sqrt{7})(5 + \sqrt{7})$

Write the original expression. $(3 - \sqrt{7})(5 + \sqrt{7})$

Distribute. $3 \cdot 5 + 3\sqrt{7} - \sqrt{7} \cdot 5 - \sqrt{7} \cdot \sqrt{7}$

Multiply and combine like radicals. $15 - 2\sqrt{7} - 7$

Simplify. $8 - 2\sqrt{7}$

 Got It? **4.** What is the product $(3 + 2\sqrt{5})(2 + 4\sqrt{5})$?

Conjugates are expressions, like $\sqrt{a} + \sqrt{b}$ and $\sqrt{a} - \sqrt{b}$, that differ only in the signs of the second terms. When a and b are rational numbers, the product of two radical conjugates is a rational number.

Problem 5 Multiplying Conjugates

What is the product $(5 - \sqrt{7})(5 + \sqrt{7})$?

Write the original expression.	$(5 - \sqrt{7})(5 + \sqrt{7})$
Distribute.	$5 \cdot 5 + 5\sqrt{7} - 5\sqrt{7} - (\sqrt{7})^2$
Simplify.	$25 - 7$
Subtract.	18

Got It? 5. What is each product?

   a. $(6 - \sqrt{12})(6 + \sqrt{12})$ **b.** $(3 + \sqrt{8})(3 - \sqrt{8})$

Sometimes a denominator is a sum or difference involving radicals. If the radical expressions are square roots, you can rationalize the denominator by multiplying the numerator and the denominator by the conjugate of the denominator.

Problem 6 Rationalizing the Denominator

How can you write the expression with a rationalized denominator?

$$\frac{3\sqrt{2}}{\sqrt{5} - \sqrt{2}}$$

The conjugate of the denominator is $\sqrt{5} + \sqrt{2}$. Multiply the numerator and denominator by $\sqrt{5} + \sqrt{2}$.	$\dfrac{3\sqrt{2}}{\sqrt{5} - \sqrt{2}} = \dfrac{3\sqrt{2}}{\sqrt{5} - \sqrt{2}} \cdot \dfrac{\sqrt{5} + \sqrt{2}}{\sqrt{5} + \sqrt{2}}$
Use the difference of squares in the denominator to multiply the conjugates.	$= \dfrac{3\sqrt{2}(\sqrt{5} + \sqrt{2})}{(\sqrt{5})^2 - (\sqrt{2})^2}$
Distribute $\sqrt{2}$ in the numerator.	$= \dfrac{3(\sqrt{2}\sqrt{5} + \sqrt{2}\sqrt{2})}{(\sqrt{5})^2 - (\sqrt{2})^2}$
Multiply the radicals in the numerator. Simplify the powers in the denominator.	$= \dfrac{3(\sqrt{10} + 2)}{5 - 2}$
Subtract in the denominator.	$= \dfrac{3(\sqrt{10} + 2)}{3}$
Simplify.	$= \sqrt{10} + 2$

Multiplying by 1 does not change the value of an expression.

Got It? 6. How can you write the expression with a rationalized denominator?

   a. $\dfrac{2\sqrt{7}}{\sqrt{3} - \sqrt{5}}$ **b.** $\dfrac{4x}{3 - \sqrt{6}}$

   c. Reasoning Suppose you were going to rationalize the denominator of $\dfrac{1 - \sqrt{8}}{2 - \sqrt{8}}$. Would you simplify $\sqrt{8}$ before or after rationalizing? Explain.

Focus Question What properties of real numbers apply to radical expressions?

Answer Use the Distributive Property to add and subtract like radicals. You can also multiply binomials that have radical expressions using the Distributive Property. If the binomials are conjugates, then the product is a rational number.

Lesson Check

Do you know HOW?

Simplify if possible.

1. $10\sqrt{6} + 2\sqrt{6}$

2. $3\sqrt{2} + 4\sqrt[3]{2}$

3. $8\sqrt{3x} - 5\sqrt{3x}$

4. $5\sqrt{3} + \sqrt{12}$

Multiply.

5. $(4 + \sqrt{3})(4 - \sqrt{3})$

6. $(5 + 2\sqrt{5})(7 + 4\sqrt{5})$

7. $(2 + 3\sqrt{2})(1 - 3\sqrt{2})$

8. $(3 + 5\sqrt{7})(3 - 5\sqrt{7})$

Do you UNDERSTAND?

9. Vocabulary Determine whether each of the following is a pair of like radicals. If so, add them.
  a. $3x\sqrt{11}$ and $3x\sqrt{10}$
  b. $2\sqrt{3xy}$ and $7\sqrt{3xy}$
  c. $12\sqrt{13y}$ and $12\sqrt{6y}$

10. Compare and Contrast How are the processes of multiplying radical expressions and multiplying polynomial expressions alike? How are the processes different?

Practice and Problem-Solving Exercises

A Practice Simplify if possible.

 See Problem 1.

> **Guided Practice**
>
> To start, determine if the expression contains like radicals.
>
> **11.** $5\sqrt{6} + \sqrt{6}$
>
> The radicands and indexes are the same, so you can combine the radicals using the Distributive Property.

12. $6\sqrt[3]{3} - 2\sqrt[3]{3}$

13. $4\sqrt{3} + 4\sqrt[3]{3}$

14. $14\sqrt{x} + 3\sqrt{y}$

15. The design of a garden path uses stone pieces shaped as squares with a side length of 15 in. Find the length of the path.

 See Problem 2.

Simplify.

See Problem 3.

> **Guided Practice**
>
> To start, factor each radicand.
>
> **16.** $6\sqrt{18} + 3\sqrt{50}$
>
> $6\sqrt{9 \cdot 2} + 3\sqrt{25 \cdot 2}$

17. $14\sqrt{20} - 3\sqrt{125}$

18. $3\sqrt[3]{81} - 2\sqrt[3]{54}$

19. $\sqrt[4]{32} + \sqrt[4]{48}$

Multiply.

See Problem 4.

20. $(3 + \sqrt{5})(1 + \sqrt{5})$

21. $(2 + \sqrt{7})(1 + 3\sqrt{7})$

22. $(3 - 4\sqrt{2})(5 - 6\sqrt{2})$

23. $(\sqrt{3} + \sqrt{5})^2$

24. $(\sqrt{13} + 6)^2$

25. $(2\sqrt{5} + 3\sqrt{2})^2$

Multiply each pair of conjugates.

See Problem 5.

26. $(5 - \sqrt{11})(5 + \sqrt{11})$

27. $(4 - 2\sqrt{3})(4 + 2\sqrt{3})$

28. $(2\sqrt{6} + 8)(2\sqrt{6} - 8)$

29. $(\sqrt{3} + \sqrt{5})(\sqrt{3} - \sqrt{5})$

Rationalize each denominator. Simplify your answer.

See Problem 6.

30. $\dfrac{4}{3\sqrt{3} - 2}$

31. $\dfrac{5 + \sqrt{3}}{2 - \sqrt{3}}$

32. $\dfrac{3 + \sqrt{8}}{2 - 2\sqrt{8}}$

 **Apply**

33. Think About a Plan The design on a parquet floor at the right is made of equilateral triangles. The side of a large triangle is 6 in., and the side of a small triangle is 3 in. Find the total area of the design to the nearest tenth of a square inch.
- How many large and how many small triangles form the design?
- Can you express the area of an equilateral triangle through its side?

Simplify.

34. $\sqrt{72} + \sqrt{32} + \sqrt{18}$

35. $\sqrt{75} + 2\sqrt{48} - 5\sqrt{3}$

36. $5\sqrt{32x} + 4\sqrt{98x}$

37. $\sqrt{75} - 4\sqrt{18} + 2\sqrt{32}$

38. $4\sqrt{216y^2} + 3\sqrt{54y^2}$

39. $3\sqrt[3]{16} - 4\sqrt[3]{54} + \sqrt[3]{128}$

40. $(1 + \sqrt{72})(5 + \sqrt{2})$

41. $(\sqrt{3} - \sqrt{7})(\sqrt{3} + 2\sqrt{7})$

42. Error Analysis Describe and correct the error made while simplifying the expression $\dfrac{3 + \sqrt{2}}{3 - \sqrt{2}}$.

$$\frac{3 + \sqrt{2}}{3 - \sqrt{2}} = \frac{3 + \sqrt{2}}{3 - \sqrt{2}} \cdot \frac{3 + \sqrt{2}}{3 + \sqrt{2}}$$

$$= \frac{3^2 + (\sqrt{2})^2}{3^2 - (\sqrt{2})^2} = \frac{9 + 2}{9 - 2} = \frac{11}{7}$$

43. Chemistry A scientist found that x grams of Metal A is completely oxidized in $2x\sqrt{3}$ seconds and x grams of Metal B is completely oxidized in $6x\sqrt{3}$ seconds. How much faster is Metal A oxidized than Metal B?

44. Reasoning Describe the possible values of a such that $\sqrt{72} + \sqrt{a}$ simplifies to a single term.

45. Geometry Show that a right triangle with legs of lengths $\sqrt{2} - 1$ and $\sqrt{2} + 1$ is similar to a right triangle with legs of lengths $6 - \sqrt{32}$ and 2.

46. Open-Ended Find two pairs of conjugates with a product of 3.

Rationalize the denominators and simplify.

47. $\dfrac{4 + \sqrt{27}}{2 - 3\sqrt{27}}$

48. $\dfrac{4 + \sqrt{6}}{\sqrt{2} + \sqrt{3}}$

49. $\dfrac{5 - \sqrt{21}}{\sqrt{3} - \sqrt{7}}$

50. $\dfrac{\sqrt{27} - \sqrt{5}}{\sqrt{15} - 3}$

51. $\dfrac{4 + \sqrt[3]{2}}{\sqrt[3]{2}}$

52. $\dfrac{4 - 2\sqrt[3]{6}}{\sqrt[3]{4}}$

Standardized Test Prep

GRIDDED RESPONSE

SAT/ACT

53. What is the value of the expression $(5 - 2\sqrt{3})(5 + 2\sqrt{3})$?

54. What is the value of z in the solution of the system of equations below?

$$\begin{cases} 2x - 3y + z = 6 \\ -x + y - 2z = -5 \\ 3x - y - 3z = -7 \end{cases}$$

55. What is the y-value of the y-intercept of the line $5x - 7y = -15$?

56. What is the slope of a line perpendicular to the line $2x + 5y = 10$?

57. What is the value of p for which the equation $x^2 - 12x + 4p = 0$ has exactly one real root?

Mixed Review

Simplify each expression. Rationalize all denominators.

◀ See Lesson 6-2.

58. $\sqrt[3]{3} \cdot \sqrt[3]{18}$

59. $\sqrt[3]{\dfrac{4}{0.5x}}$

60. $\dfrac{\sqrt{32}}{\sqrt{2}}$

61. $\sqrt[3]{2x^2} \cdot \sqrt[3]{4x}$

62. $\sqrt{7x} \cdot \sqrt{14x^3}$

63. $\sqrt{3x} \cdot \sqrt{5x}$

Find the real and imaginary solutions of each equation.

◀ See Lesson 5-3.

64. $2x^3 - 16 = 0$

65. $x^3 + 1000 = 0$

66. $125x^3 - 1 = 0$

67. $x^4 - 14x^2 + 49 = 0$

68. $25x^4 - 40x^2 + 16 = 0$

69. $81x^4 - 1 = 0$

Get Ready! To prepare for Lesson 6-4, do Exercises 70–72.

Simplify.

◀ See p. 871.

70. $(x^2)^3$

71. $(pq)^5$

72. $(2^4)(2^5)$

6-4

PART 1

Rational Exponents

Objective To use rational exponents

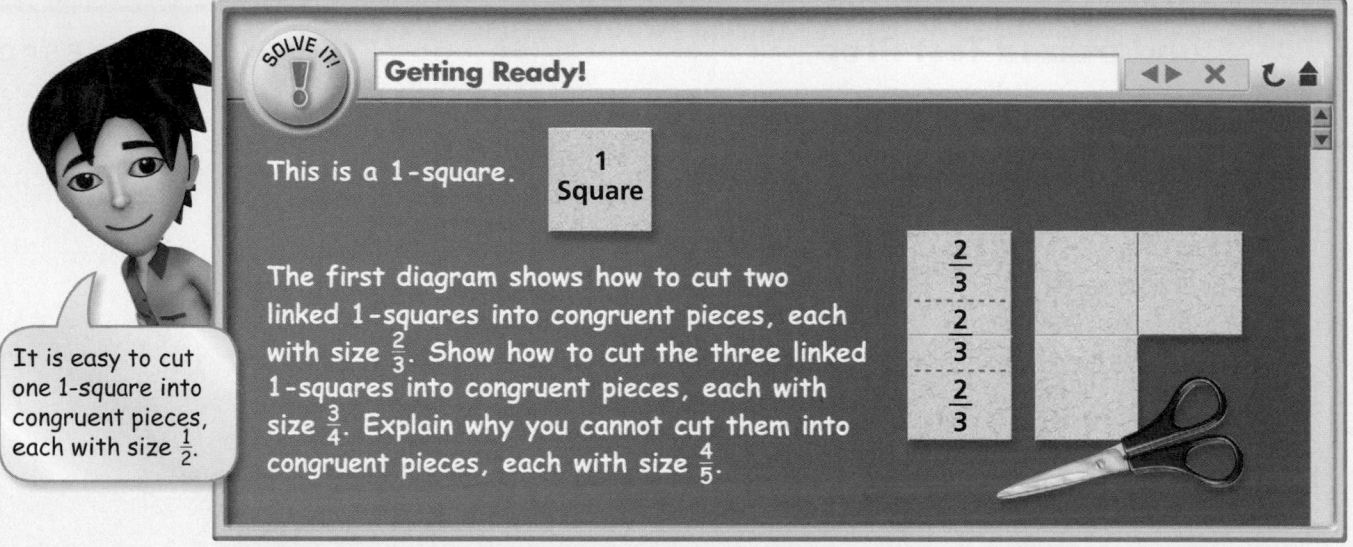

SOLVE IT!

Getting Ready!

This is a 1-square. | 1 Square |

The first diagram shows how to cut two linked 1-squares into congruent pieces, each with size $\frac{2}{3}$. Show how to cut the three linked 1-squares into congruent pieces, each with size $\frac{3}{4}$. Explain why you cannot cut them into congruent pieces, each with size $\frac{4}{5}$.

It is easy to cut one 1-square into congruent pieces, each with size $\frac{1}{2}$.

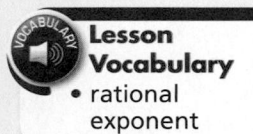

Lesson Vocabulary
- rational exponent

If $a^x = \sqrt[4]{a^3}$, then by definition, $a^x \cdot a^x \cdot a^x \cdot a^x = a^3$. By adding exponents, $a^{4x} = a^3$, so x is $\frac{3}{4}$. This suggests an alternative notation for radical expressions in which, for example, $\sqrt[4]{a^3} = a^{\frac{3}{4}}$.

Focus Question What is a rational exponent?

In general, $\sqrt[n]{x} = x^{\frac{1}{n}}$ for any positive integer n. Like the radical form, the exponent form indicates the principal root.

$$\sqrt{36} = 36^{\frac{1}{2}} \qquad \sqrt[3]{64} = 64^{\frac{1}{3}} \qquad \sqrt[4]{16} = 16^{\frac{1}{4}}$$

  Problem 1 **Simplifying Expressions With Rational Exponents**

Think

What does the denominator of the fractional exponent represent?
The denominator of the fraction is the index of the radical.

What is the simplified form of each expression?

Ⓐ $216^{\frac{1}{3}}$

Rewrite using radicals. $\qquad 216^{\frac{1}{3}} = \sqrt[3]{216}$

Simplify. $\qquad\qquad\qquad = \sqrt[3]{6^3} = 6$

Write the radicand as a perfect cube.

Ⓑ $7^{\frac{1}{2}} \cdot 7^{\frac{1}{2}}$

$7^{\frac{1}{2}} \cdot 7^{\frac{1}{2}} = \sqrt{7} \cdot \sqrt{7}$

$= 7$

Check by adding the exponents:
$7^{\frac{1}{2}} \cdot 7^{\frac{1}{2}} = 7^{\frac{1}{2} + \frac{1}{2}} = 7^1 = 7$

C $5^{\frac{1}{4}} \cdot 125^{\frac{1}{4}}$

Rewrite as radicals. $5^{\frac{1}{4}} \cdot 125^{\frac{1}{4}} = \sqrt[4]{5} \cdot \sqrt[4]{125}$

Use $\sqrt[n]{a} \cdot \sqrt[n]{b} = \sqrt[n]{ab}$. $= \sqrt[4]{5 \cdot 125}$

Multiply and rewrite the radicand. $= \sqrt[4]{625} = \sqrt[4]{5^4}$

Simplify. $= 5$

✓ Got It? **1.** What is the simplified form of each expression?

a. $64^{\frac{1}{2}}$ **b.** $11^{\frac{1}{2}} \cdot 11^{\frac{1}{2}}$ **c.** $3^{\frac{1}{2}} \cdot 12^{\frac{1}{2}}$

If $\sqrt[n]{x} = x^{\frac{1}{n}}$, it follows from the Laws of Exponents that for all real numbers
$\sqrt[n]{x^m} = (x^m)^{\frac{1}{n}} = (x^{\frac{1}{n}})^m = \left(\sqrt[n]{x}\right)^m$. This leads to the definition of a *rational exponent*.

take note

Key Concept   Rational Exponent

If the *n*th root of *a* is a real number, *m* is an integer, and $\frac{m}{n}$ is in lowest terms, then
$$a^{\frac{1}{n}} = \sqrt[n]{a} \text{ and } a^{\frac{m}{n}} = \sqrt[n]{a^m} = (\sqrt[n]{a})^m. \qquad \text{If } m \text{ is negative, } a \neq 0.$$

Problem 2 **Converting Between Exponential and Radical Form**

Think

Does the fraction $\frac{3}{7}$ first need to be simplified?
No; the fraction is already in lowest terms.

A What is $x^{\frac{3}{7}}$ in radical form?

Use the definition of a rational exponent. $x^{\frac{3}{7}} = \sqrt[7]{x^3} \text{ or } (\sqrt[7]{x})^3$

B What is $y^{-3.5}$ in radical form?

Convert the decimal exponent to a fraction. $y^{-3.5} = y^{-\frac{7}{2}}$

Use the definitions of negative exponents and rational exponents. $= \frac{1}{y^{\frac{7}{2}}} = \frac{1}{\sqrt{y^7}}$

Factor the denominator and simplify. $= \frac{1}{\sqrt{y^6 \cdot y}} = \frac{1}{y^3 \sqrt{y}} \text{ or } \frac{\sqrt{y}}{y^4}$

C What is $\sqrt{a^5}$ in exponential form?

The index is 2, so use 2 as the denominator. $\sqrt{a^5} = a^{\frac{5}{2}}$

D What is $(\sqrt[5]{b})^3$ in exponential form?

The index is 5, so use 5 as the denominator. $(\sqrt[5]{b})^3 = b^{\frac{3}{5}}$

✓ Got It? **2. a.** What are $w^{-\frac{5}{8}}$ and $x^{0.2}$ in radical form?
   b. What are $\sqrt[4]{y^3}$ and $(\sqrt[5]{z})^4$ in exponential form?

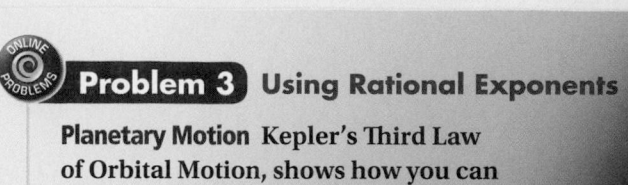

Problem 3 Using Rational Exponents

Planetary Motion Kepler's Third Law of Orbital Motion, shows how you can approximate the period P (in Earth years) it takes a planet to complete one orbit of the sun. Use the function $P = d^{\frac{3}{2}}$, where d is the distance from the planet to the sun in astronomical units (AU—about 93,000,000 miles or the distance from Earth to the sun). How many Earth years does it take Mars to orbit the sun?

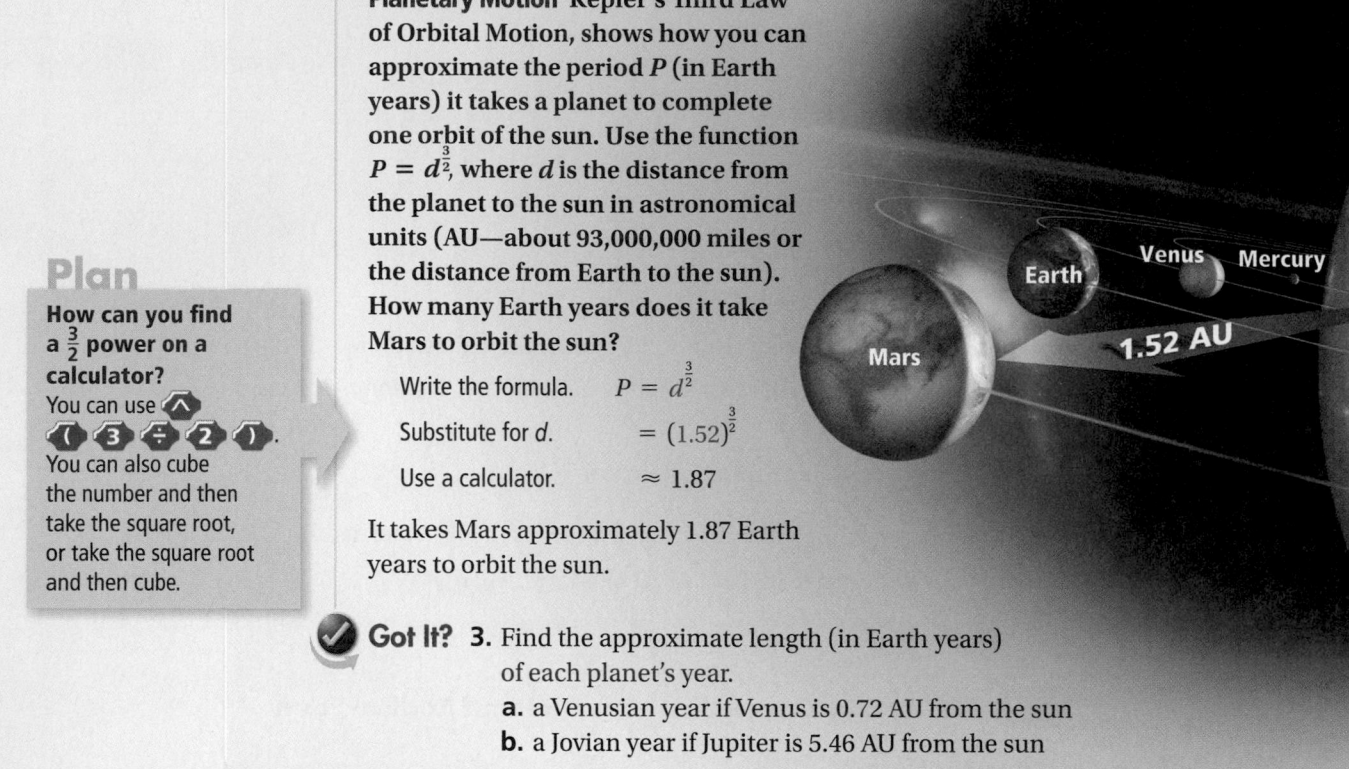

Write the formula.	$P = d^{\frac{3}{2}}$
Substitute for d.	$= (1.52)^{\frac{3}{2}}$
Use a calculator.	≈ 1.87

It takes Mars approximately 1.87 Earth years to orbit the sun.

Plan

How can you find a $\frac{3}{2}$ power on a calculator?

You can use ⌃ (3 ÷ 2) .

You can also cube the number and then take the square root, or take the square root and then cube.

Got It? **3.** Find the approximate length (in Earth years) of each planet's year.
  a. a Venusian year if Venus is 0.72 AU from the sun
  b. a Jovian year if Jupiter is 5.46 AU from the sun

Focus Question What is a rational exponent?

Answer A rational exponent is an equivalent form of a radical expression. For an nth root of a real number a and an integer m, $\sqrt[n]{a^m} = a^{\frac{m}{n}}$. You can simplify an expression using either form.

Lesson Check

Do you know HOW?

Simplify each expression.

1. $125^{\frac{1}{3}}$

2. $5^{\frac{1}{2}} \cdot 5^{\frac{1}{2}}$

3. $4^{-3.5}$

Do you UNDERSTAND?

4. Reasoning Explain why $(-64)^{\frac{1}{3}} = -64^{\frac{1}{3}}$ but $(-64)^{\frac{1}{2}} \neq -64^{\frac{1}{2}}$.

Practice and Problem-Solving Exercises

See Problem 1.

A Practice   Simplify each expression.

5. $36^{\frac{1}{2}}$ **6.** $27^{\frac{1}{3}}$ **7.** $49^{\frac{1}{2}}$

8. $10^{\frac{1}{2}} \cdot 10^{\frac{1}{2}}$ **9.** $7^{\frac{1}{2}} \cdot 21^{\frac{1}{2}}$ **10.** $3^{\frac{1}{4}} \cdot 27^{\frac{1}{4}}$

Write each expression in radical form.

See Problem 2.

Guided Practice

To start, rewrite the expression using the definition of negative exponents.

11. $y^{-\frac{9}{8}}$

$$y^{-\frac{9}{8}} = \frac{1}{y^{\frac{9}{8}}}$$

12. $x^{\frac{1}{6}}$ **13.** $x^{\frac{2}{7}}$ **14.** $y^{\frac{2}{5}}$

15. $t^{-\frac{3}{4}}$ **16.** $x^{1.5}$ **17.** $y^{1.2}$

Write each expression in exponential form.

18. $\sqrt{7x^3}$ **19.** $\sqrt{(7x)^3}$ **20.** $(\sqrt{7x})^3$

21. $\sqrt[3]{a^2}$ **22.** $(\sqrt[3]{a})^2$ **23.** $\sqrt[4]{c^2}$

Optimal Height The optimal height h of the letters of a message printed on pavement is given by the formula $h = \frac{0.00252d^{2.27}}{e}$. Here d is the distance of the driver from the letters and e is the height of the driver's eye above the pavement. All of the distances are in meters. Find h for the given values of d and e.

See Problem 3.

Guided Practice

To start, substitute the values for d and e into the formula.

24. $d = 100$ m, $e = 1.2$ m

$$h = \frac{0.00252(100)^{2.27}}{1.2}$$

25. $d = 50$ m, $e = 2.3$ m   **26.** $d = 25$ m, $e = 2.3$ m

B Apply   Simplify each number.

27. $(-343)^{\frac{1}{3}}$ **28.** $(-243)^{\frac{1}{5}}$ **29.** $32^{1.2}$

30. $64^{3.5}$ **31.** $100^{4.5}$ **32.** $25^{\frac{3}{2}}$

33. Simplify $4^{\frac{1}{2}} \cdot 4^{\frac{1}{2}}$ using the following methods. Show all your work.
   a. Use the properties of exponents.
   b. Simplify each term in the product, then multiply.
   c. Convert to radical form, then simplify.

34. Reasoning Refer to the definition of rational exponent. Explain the need for the restriction that $a \neq 0$ if m is negative.

Rational Exponents

Objective To use rational exponents

In Part 1 of the lesson, you learned how to convert between radical and exponential form.

Connect to What You Know

Here you will learn to use the properties of exponents to simplify expressions involving rational exponents.

Focus Question Why are rational exponents useful?

Properties   Properties of Rational Exponents

Hint

All the properties of integer exponents also apply to rational exponents.

Let m and n represent rational numbers. Assume that no denominator equals 0.

Property	Example	Property	Example
$a^m \cdot a^n = a^{m+n}$	$8^{\frac{1}{3}} \cdot 8^{\frac{2}{3}} = 8^{\frac{1}{3}+\frac{2}{3}} = 8^1 = 8$	$a^{-m} = \dfrac{1}{a^m}$	$9^{-\frac{1}{2}} = \dfrac{1}{9^{\frac{1}{2}}} = \dfrac{1}{3}$
$(a^m)^n = a^{mn}$	$\left(5^{\frac{1}{2}}\right)^4 = 5^{\frac{1}{2} \cdot 4} = 5^2 = 25$	$\dfrac{a^m}{a^n} = a^{m-n}$	$\dfrac{7^{\frac{3}{2}}}{7^{\frac{1}{2}}} = 7^{\frac{3}{2}-\frac{1}{2}} = 7^1 = 7$
$(ab)^m = a^m b^m$	$(4 \cdot 5)^{\frac{1}{2}} = 4^{\frac{1}{2}} \cdot 5^{\frac{1}{2}} = 2 \cdot 5^{\frac{1}{2}}$	$\left(\dfrac{a}{b}\right)^m = \dfrac{a^m}{b^m}$	$\left(\dfrac{5}{27}\right)^{\frac{1}{3}} = \dfrac{5^{\frac{1}{3}}}{27^{\frac{1}{3}}} = \dfrac{5^{\frac{1}{3}}}{3}$

You can combine radical expressions with different indexes if you convert them to expressions with rational exponents.

Problem 4 Combining Radicals

What is $\dfrac{\sqrt[4]{x^3}}{\sqrt[8]{x^2}}$ in simplest form?

Hint

The radicands are different, but both are powers of the same variable.

Think

Write the expressions using exponents.

Use the division property for exponents. Subtract the exponents.

Simplify. Write in either exponential or radical form.

Write

$$\frac{\sqrt[4]{x^3}}{\sqrt[8]{x^2}} = \frac{x^{\frac{3}{4}}}{x^{\frac{2}{8}}}$$

$$= x^{\frac{3}{4}-\frac{2}{8}} = x^{\frac{3}{4}-\frac{1}{4}}$$

$$= x^{\frac{1}{2}} \text{ or } \sqrt{x}$$

Got It? 4. What is each quotient or product in simplest form?

a. $\dfrac{\sqrt{x^3}}{\sqrt[3]{x^2}}$

b. $\sqrt{3}\left(\sqrt[4]{3}\right)$

You can simplify a number with a rational exponent using the properties of exponents or by converting the expression to a radical expression.

 Problem 5 Simplifying Numbers With Rational Exponents

What is each number in simplest form?

 **A** $16^{-2.5}$

Plan

What is the first step?
Rewrite the decimal exponent as a fraction in lowest terms.

Method 1 Use exponential form.

Convert the decimal exponent to a fraction.	$16^{-2.5} = 16^{-\frac{5}{2}}$
Write 16 as 2^4.	$= \left(2^4\right)^{-\frac{5}{2}}$
Use $(a^m)^n = a^{mn}$.	$= 2^{4\cdot-\frac{5}{2}}$
Simplify.	$= 2^{-10}$
Use the definition of a negative exponent.	$= \dfrac{1}{2^{10}}$
Evaluate the power.	$= \dfrac{1}{1024}$

Method 2 Use radical form.

Convert the decimal exponent to a fraction.	$16^{-2.5} = 16^{-\frac{5}{2}}$
Use the definition of a negative exponent.	$= \dfrac{1}{16^{\frac{5}{2}}}$
Write in radical form.	$= \dfrac{1}{\left(\sqrt{16}\right)^5}$
Find the square root.	$= \dfrac{1}{4^5}$
Evaluate the power.	$= \dfrac{1}{1024}$

B $(-32)^{\frac{4}{5}}$

Think

Does it matter that the base is negative?
No; the denominator of the exponent is odd, so there will be a real root.

Method 1 Use exponential form.

Write -32 as $(-2)^5$.	$(-32)^{\frac{4}{5}} = \left((-2)^5\right)^{\frac{4}{5}}$
Use $(a^m)^n = a^{mn}$.	$= (-2)^{5\cdot\frac{4}{5}}$
Simplify.	$= (-2)^4$
Evaluate the power.	$= 16$

Method 2 Use radical form.

Write in radical form.	$(-32)^{\frac{4}{5}} = \left(\sqrt[5]{-32}\right)^4$
Write -32 as $(-2)^5$.	$= \left(\sqrt[5]{(-2)^5}\right)^4$
Find the 5th root.	$= (-2)^4$
Evaluate the power.	$= 16$

 Got It? 5. What is each number in simplest form?

a. $32^{-\frac{3}{5}}$

b. $16^{\frac{3}{4}}$

c. $9^{-3.5}$

To write an expression with rational exponents in simplest form, write every exponent as a positive number.

 Problem 6 Writing Expressions in Simpler Form

What is each expression in simplest form?

Plan

What is the first step in simplifying a radical expression using the properties of exponents?
Rewrite the radicals using rational exponents.

A $\left(-8x\sqrt{xy}\right)^{\frac{2}{3}}$

Rewrite radicals using rational exponents. $\qquad \left(-8x\sqrt{xy}\right)^{\frac{2}{3}} = \left(-8x(xy)^{\frac{1}{2}}\right)^{\frac{2}{3}}$

Use $(ab)^n = a^n b^n$. $\qquad = (-8)^{\frac{2}{3}} \cdot x^{\frac{2}{3}} \cdot \left((xy)^{\frac{1}{2}}\right)^{\frac{2}{3}}$

Write -8 as $(-2)^3$. $\qquad = \left((-2)^3\right)^{\frac{2}{3}} \cdot x^{\frac{2}{3}} \cdot \left((xy)^{\frac{1}{2}}\right)^{\frac{2}{3}}$

Use $(a^m)^n = a^{mn}$. $\qquad = (-2)^{3 \cdot \frac{2}{3}} \cdot x^{\frac{2}{3}} \cdot (xy)^{\frac{1}{2} \cdot \frac{2}{3}}$

Simplify. $\qquad = (-2)^2 \cdot x^{\frac{2}{3}} \cdot (xy)^{\frac{1}{3}}$

Use $(ab)^n = a^n b^n$. $\qquad = (-2)^2 \cdot x^{\frac{2}{3}} \cdot x^{\frac{1}{3}} \cdot y^{\frac{1}{3}}$

Use $a^m \cdot a^n = a^{m+n}$ to combine the *x*-terms. $\qquad = (-2)^2 \cdot x^{\frac{2}{3}+\frac{1}{3}} \cdot y^{\frac{1}{3}}$

Evaluate $(-2)^2$ and add the exponents. $\qquad = 4 \cdot x^1 \cdot y^{\frac{1}{3}}$

Simplify. $\qquad = 4xy^{\frac{1}{3}}$ or $4x\sqrt[3]{y}$

B $\left(16y^{-8}\right)^{-\frac{3}{4}}$

Use $(ab)^n = a^n b^n$. $\qquad \left(16y^{-8}\right)^{-\frac{3}{4}} = 16^{-\frac{3}{4}} \cdot \left(y^{-8}\right)^{-\frac{3}{4}}$

Write 16 as $(2)^4$. $\qquad = \left(2^4\right)^{-\frac{3}{4}} \cdot \left(y^{-8}\right)^{-\frac{3}{4}}$

Use $(a^m)^n = a^{mn}$. $\qquad = 2^{4 \cdot -\frac{3}{4}} \cdot y^{-8 \cdot -\frac{3}{4}}$

Simplify. $\qquad = 2^{-3} \cdot y^6$

Use the definition of a negative exponent. $\qquad = \frac{1}{2^3} \cdot y^6$

Evaluate 2^3 and simplify. $\qquad = \frac{y^6}{8}$

Got It? 6. What is each expression in a simpler form?

a. $\left(8x^{15}\right)^{-\frac{1}{3}}$ 　　　　　　　 b. $\left(9x\sqrt[4]{y}\right)^{\frac{3}{2}}$

Focus Question Why are rational exponents useful?

Answer Use the properties of rational exponents to combine radical expressions with different indexes. All the properties of integer exponents also apply to rational exponents.

Lesson Check

Do you know HOW?

Simplify each expression.

1. $\sqrt{11}\left(\sqrt[4]{11}\right)$

2. $\dfrac{\sqrt[3]{x}}{\sqrt[6]{x^5}}$

Do you UNDERSTAND?

3. Error Analysis Explain why this simplification is incorrect.

$5(4 - 5^{\frac{1}{2}})$

$5(4) - 5(5^{\frac{1}{2}})$

$20 - 25^{\frac{1}{2}}$

15

4. Open-Ended Find a nonzero number q such that $q(1 - 2^{\frac{1}{2}})$ is a rational number. Explain.

Practice and Problem-Solving Exercises

A Practice **Find each product or quotient.** See Problem 4.

Guided Practice

5. $(\sqrt[4]{6})(\sqrt[3]{6})$

To start, rewrite the expression using exponents. $6^{\frac{1}{4}} \cdot 6^{\frac{1}{3}}$

6. $\dfrac{\sqrt[9]{y^3}}{\sqrt[3]{y^9}}$

7. $\sqrt{5} \cdot \sqrt[5]{5}$

8. $\sqrt[7]{7} \cdot \sqrt[3]{7}$

9. $\dfrac{\sqrt[6]{4}}{\sqrt[3]{4}}$

10. $\sqrt[4]{18} \cdot \sqrt{12}$

11. $\dfrac{\sqrt{6}}{\sqrt[3]{36}}$

Simplify each number. See Problem 5.

Guided Practice

12. $8^{\frac{2}{3}}$

To start, rewrite the base as a power of 2. $(2^3)^{\frac{2}{3}}$

13. $64^{\frac{2}{3}}$

14. $(-8)^{\frac{2}{3}}$

15. $(-32)^{\frac{6}{5}}$

16. $(32)^{-\frac{4}{5}}$

17. $4^{1.5}$

18. $16^{1.5}$

Write each expression in simplest form. Assume that all variables are positive.

See Problem 6.

19. $\left(x^{\frac{2}{3}}\right)^{-3}$

20. $\left(x^{-\frac{4}{7}}\right)^{7}$

21. $\left(3x^{\frac{2}{3}}\right)^{-1}$

22. $5\left(x^{\frac{2}{3}}\right)^{-1}$

23. $\left(-27x^{-9}\right)^{\frac{1}{3}}$

24. $\left(-32y^{15}\right)^{\frac{1}{5}}$

25. $\left(x^{\frac{1}{2}}y^{-\frac{2}{3}}\right)^{-6}$

26. $\left(x^{\frac{2}{3}}y^{-\frac{1}{6}}\right)^{-12}$

27. $\left(\dfrac{x^{3}}{x^{-1}}\right)^{-\frac{1}{4}}$

 **Apply**

28. Think About a Plan The ratio R of radioactive carbon to nonradioactive carbon left in a sample of an organism that died T years ago can be approximated by the formula $R = A(2.7)^{-\frac{T}{8033}}$. Here A is the ratio of radioactive carbon to nonradioactive carbon in the living organism. What percent of A is left after 2000 years? After 4000 years? After 8000 years?

- What are the known and unknown values?
- How can you use the properties of exponents to solve this problem?

29. Science A desktop world globe has a volume of about 1386 cubic inches. The radius of the Earth is approximately equal to the radius of the globe raised to the 10th power. Find the radius of the Earth. (*Hint:* Use the formula $V = \frac{4}{3}\pi r^{3}$ for the volume of a sphere.)

Simplify each expression.

30. $x^{\frac{2}{7}} \cdot x^{\frac{3}{14}}$

31. $y^{\frac{1}{2}} \cdot y^{\frac{3}{10}}$

32. $x^{\frac{3}{5}} \div x^{\frac{3}{10}}$

33. $\dfrac{x^{\frac{2}{3}}y^{-\frac{1}{4}}}{x^{\frac{1}{2}}y^{-\frac{1}{2}}}$

34. $\dfrac{x^{\frac{1}{2}}y^{-\frac{1}{3}}}{x^{\frac{3}{4}}y^{\frac{1}{2}}}$

35. $\left(\dfrac{8x^{6}}{27y^{9}}\right)^{\frac{1}{3}}$

36. Open-Ended Find three nonzero numbers a such that $a\left(4 + 5^{\frac{1}{2}}\right)$ is a rational number. Can a itself be a rational number? Explain.

37. a. Reasoning Show that $\sqrt[4]{x^{2}} = \sqrt{x}$ by using the definition of fourth root.

    b. Reasoning Show that $\sqrt[4]{x^{2}} = \sqrt{x}$ by rewriting $\sqrt[4]{x^{2}}$ in exponential form.

38. The expression $0.036m^{\frac{3}{4}}$ is used in the study of fluids. Which best represents the value of the expression for $m = 46 \times 10^{4}$?

  Ⓐ 636

  Ⓑ 1460

  Ⓒ 1660

  Ⓓ 16,600

SAT/ACT

39. What is the simplified value of $\left(\frac{1}{64}\right)^{-\frac{1}{6}}$?

40. What positive value of b makes $9x^2 - bx + 4$ a perfect square trinomial?

41. How many real roots does the cubic polynomial equation $x^3 - 7x^2 + 13x - 4 = 0$ have?

42. What is the y-value of the y-intercept of the graph of $f(x) = 4|x - 2| - 5$?

Mixed Review

Simplify. ◀ **See Lesson 6-3.**

43. $6\sqrt[3]{3} - 2\sqrt[3]{3}$

44. $3\sqrt{18} + 2\sqrt{72}$

45. $\left(\sqrt{5} - 1\right)\left(\sqrt{5} + 4\right)$

46. $\left(1 - 2\sqrt{2}\right)\left(1 + 2\sqrt{2}\right)$

47. $2\sqrt{12} - 4\sqrt{27}$

48. $\sqrt[4]{162} + 3\sqrt[4]{32}$

Factor each expression completely. ◀ **See Lesson 4-4.**

49. $4x^3 - 8x^2 + 16x$

50. $x^2 + 4x + 4$

51. $x^2 - 18x + 81$

52. $16a^2 - 9b^2$

53. $25x^2 - 40xy + 16y^2$

54. $9x^2 + 48x + 64$

Get Ready! To prepare for Lesson 6-5, do Exercises 55–60.

Solve by factoring. Check your answers. ◀ **See Lesson 4-5.**

55. $x^2 = -x + 6$

56. $x^2 = 5x + 14$

57. $2x^2 + x = 3$

58. $3x^2 - 2 = 5x$

59. $4x^2 = -8x + 5$

60. $6x^2 = 5x + 6$

Chapter Vocabulary

- index (p. 382)
- like radicals (p. 395)
- *n*th root (p. 381)

- principal root (p. 381)
- radicand (p. 382)
- rational exponent (p. 403)

- rationalize the denominator (p. 391)
- simplest form of a radical (p. 388)

Choose the correct term to complete each sentence.

1. The number under a radical sign is called the (index/radicand).

2. A radical expression can always be rewritten using a (rational exponent/principal root).

3. The expressions $\sqrt{x}$ and $\sqrt[5]{x}$ (are/are not) examples of like radicals.

6-1 Roots and Radical Expressions

Quick Review

You can simplify a radical expression by finding the roots. The **principal root** of a number with two real roots is the positive root. The principal **nth root** of b is written as $\sqrt[n]{b}$, where b is the **radicand** and n is the **index** of the radical expression.

For any real number a, $\sqrt[n]{a^n} = \begin{cases} a & \text{if } n \text{ is odd} \\ |a| & \text{if } n \text{ is even} \end{cases}$.

Example

What is the simplified form of $\sqrt{36x^6}$?

Write the factors of the radicand as perfect squares. $\sqrt{36x^6} = \sqrt{6^2(x^3)^2}$

Take the square root. Include the absolute value symbols since the index is even. $= 6|x^3|$

Exercises

Find each real root.

4. $\sqrt{25}$ **5.** $\sqrt{0.49}$

6. $\sqrt[3]{-8}$ **7.** $-\sqrt[3]{8}$

Simplify each radical expression. Use absolute value symbols when needed.

8. $\sqrt{81x^2}$ **9.** $\sqrt[3]{64x^6}$

10. $\sqrt[4]{16x^{12}}$ **11.** $\sqrt[5]{0.00032x^5}$

12. $\sqrt{\dfrac{9x^4}{36}}$ **13.** $\sqrt[3]{125x^6y^9}$

6-2 Multiplying and Dividing Radical Expressions

Quick Review

If $\sqrt[n]{a}$ and $\sqrt[n]{b}$ are real numbers, then
$(\sqrt[n]{a})(\sqrt[n]{b}) = \sqrt[n]{ab}$, and $\dfrac{\sqrt[n]{a}}{\sqrt[n]{b}} = \sqrt[n]{\dfrac{a}{b}}$ for $b \neq 0$.

To **rationalize the denominator** of an expression, rewrite it so that no denominator contains radical expressions.

Example

What is the simplest form of $\sqrt{32x^2y} \cdot \sqrt{18xy^3}$?

Write the original expression.	$\sqrt{32x^2y} \cdot \sqrt{18xy^3}$
Combine the radicands.	$= \sqrt{(32x^2y)(18xy^3)}$
Multiply.	$= \sqrt{576x^3y^4}$
Find perfect square factors.	$= \sqrt{24^2 x^2 (y^2)^2 \cdot x}$
Use the property for multiplying radicals.	$= \sqrt{(24xy^2)^2} \cdot \sqrt{x}$
Take square roots.	$= 24xy^2 \sqrt{x}$

Exercises

Multiply. Then simplify if possible.

14. $\sqrt[3]{9} \cdot \sqrt[3]{3}$ **15.** $\sqrt[3]{-7} \cdot \sqrt[3]{49}$ **16.** $\sqrt{2} \cdot \sqrt{8}$

Multiply and simplify.

17. $\sqrt{8x^2} \cdot \sqrt{2x^2}$ **18.** $5\sqrt[3]{9y^2} \cdot \sqrt[3]{24y}$

Divide and simplify.

19. $\sqrt{\dfrac{128}{8}}$ **20.** $\dfrac{\sqrt[3]{81x^5y^3}}{\sqrt[3]{3x^2}}$ **21.** $\dfrac{\sqrt[4]{162x^4}}{\sqrt[4]{2y^8}}$

Divide. Rationalize all denominators.

22. $\dfrac{\sqrt{8}}{\sqrt{6}}$ **23.** $\dfrac{\sqrt{3x^5}}{8x^2}$ **24.** $\dfrac{\sqrt[3]{6x^2y^4}}{2\sqrt[3]{5x^7y}}$

6-3 Binomial Radical Expressions

Quick Review

Like radicals have the same index and the same radicand. Use the Distributive Property to add and subtract them. Also use the Distributive Property to multiply binomial radical expressions. To rationalize a denominator that is a binomial radical expression, multiply the numerator and denominator by the conjugate of the denominator.

Example

What is the simplified form of $\sqrt{18} + \sqrt{50} - \sqrt{8}$?

Write the original expression.	$\sqrt{18} + \sqrt{50} - \sqrt{8}$
Factor the radical using perfect square factors.	$= \sqrt{3^2 \cdot 2} + \sqrt{5^2 \cdot 2} - \sqrt{2^2 \cdot 2}$
Simplify each radical.	$= 3\sqrt{2} + 5\sqrt{2} - 2\sqrt{2}$
Combine like radicals.	$= (3 + 5 - 2)\sqrt{2}$
Simplify.	$= 6\sqrt{2}$

Exercises

Add or subtract if possible.

25. $10\sqrt{27} - 4\sqrt{12}$

26. $3\sqrt{20x} + 8\sqrt{45x} - 4\sqrt{5x}$

27. $\sqrt[3]{54x^3} - \sqrt[3]{16x^3}$

Multiply.

28. $(3 + \sqrt{2})(4 + \sqrt{2})$

29. $(\sqrt{5} + \sqrt{11})(\sqrt{5} - \sqrt{11})$

30. $(10 + \sqrt{6})(10 - \sqrt{3})$

Divide. Rationalize all denominators.

31. $\dfrac{2 + \sqrt{5}}{\sqrt{5}}$ **32.** $\dfrac{3 + \sqrt{18}}{1 + \sqrt{8}}$

6-4 Rational Exponents

Quick Review

You can rewrite a radical expression with a **rational exponent**. By definition, if the nth root of a is a real number and m is an integer, then $a^{\frac{m}{n}} = \sqrt[n]{a^m} = (\sqrt[n]{a})^m$ if m is negative then $a \neq 0$. You can use rational exponents to simplify radical expressions.

Example

Multiply and simplify $\sqrt{x}\left(\sqrt[4]{x^3}\right)$.

Rewrite using rational exponents. $\sqrt{x}\left(\sqrt[4]{x^3}\right) = x^{\frac{1}{2}} \cdot x^{\frac{3}{4}}$

Use $a^m a^n = a^{m+n}$. $= x^{\frac{1}{2} + \frac{3}{4}}$

Add the exponents. $= x^{\frac{5}{4}}$

Rewrite as a radical expression. $= \sqrt[4]{x^5}$

Exercises

Simplify each expression.

33. $25^{\frac{1}{2}}$ **34.** $81^{\frac{1}{4}}$

35. $16^{\frac{1}{3}} \cdot 4^{\frac{1}{3}}$ **36.** $5^{\frac{3}{2}} \cdot 5^{\frac{1}{2}}$

Simplify each expression.

37. $\left(x^{\frac{1}{4}}\right)^4$ **38.** $\left(-8y^9\right)^{\frac{1}{3}}$

39. $\left(\sqrt{9xy^2}\right)^4$ **40.** $\left(x^{\frac{1}{6}} y^{\frac{1}{3}}\right)^{-18}$

41. $\left(\dfrac{x^4}{x^{-1}}\right)^{-\frac{1}{5}}$ **42.** $\left(\dfrac{x^{\frac{1}{3}}}{y^{-\frac{2}{3}}}\right)^9$

Do you know HOW?

Find all the real square roots of each number.

1. 100

2. 0.49

Simplify each radical expression. Use absolute value symbols when needed.

3. $\sqrt{36x^2}$

4. $\sqrt[3]{0.008y^3x^6}$

Simplify.

5. $\sqrt{50x^4y^8}$

6. $\sqrt[4]{32m^7n^9}$

Multiply and simplify.

7. $6\sqrt{4x^2} \cdot 2\sqrt{9x^2y^2}$

8. $\sqrt[3]{9} \cdot \sqrt[3]{9}$

9. $\sqrt[4]{16x^8} \cdot \sqrt[4]{x^{14}}$

Divide and simplify.

10. $\dfrac{\sqrt{36x^4}}{\sqrt{9x^6}}$

11. $\dfrac{\sqrt[3]{64x^9y^3}}{\sqrt[3]{8x^3}}$

Simplify. Rationalize all denominators.

12. $10\sqrt[3]{81} - 8\sqrt[3]{24}$

13. $\dfrac{4 + \sqrt{12}}{4 - \sqrt{12}}$

14. $\sqrt{48} - 3\sqrt{27} + 2\sqrt{75}$

15. $(3 + \sqrt{63})(1 + \sqrt{7})$

16. $\dfrac{\sqrt{x}}{\sqrt{6y^3}}$

Write each expression in exponential form.

17. $-\sqrt{17}$

18. $\sqrt[3]{y^8}$

Write each expression in radical form.

19. $m^{\frac{3}{7}}$

20. $y^{-\frac{4}{3}}$

Simplify each expression.

21. $(-27)^{\frac{2}{3}}$

22. $16^{\frac{3}{4}}$

Write each expression in simplest form.

23. $7\sqrt[3]{2x} - 3\sqrt[3]{2x}$

24. $2\sqrt{32x^2} + 3\sqrt{72x^2}$

25. $\sqrt[3]{125x^6} - \sqrt[3]{27x^6}$

26. $\sqrt[4]{7} - \sqrt[3]{7}$

27. $(\sqrt{y} - \sqrt{3})(\sqrt{y} + 2\sqrt{3})$

28. $\left(16x^{\frac{1}{4}}y^{\frac{3}{4}}\right)^{-4}$

29. $\left(\dfrac{x^{-10}}{x^5}\right)^{\frac{2}{5}}$

30. The radius of a circle can be expressed as $r = \sqrt{\dfrac{A}{\pi}}$ inches where r is the radius and A is the area of the circle. If the area of a circle is 169π in.^{2}, what is its radius?

Do you UNDERSTAND?

31. What are the real square roots of -16? Explain.

32. **Error Analysis** Identify the error in this statement.

$$\dfrac{\sqrt[3]{x}}{\sqrt[3]{y}} \cdot \dfrac{\sqrt[3]{y}}{\sqrt[3]{y}} = \dfrac{\sqrt[3]{xy}}{y}$$

33. **Reasoning** If $0^{\frac{2}{3}} = 0$, why is $0^{-\frac{2}{3}}$ undefined?

34. Given that x and y are positive integers, explain why the product of $x + \sqrt{y}$ and its conjugate will always be an integer.

35. **Reasoning** Explain why $(-8)^{\frac{1}{2}} \neq -(8)^{\frac{1}{2}}$, but $(-27)^{\frac{1}{3}} = -(27)^{\frac{1}{3}}$.

CHAPTER
6
PART B

PowerAlgebra.com
Your place to get
all things digital.

Radical Functions and Rational Exponents

In Part A, you learned to simplify expressions involving radicals and fractional exponents. Now you will apply what you learned to solve radical equations and graph radical functions.

Vocabulary for Part B

English/Spanish Vocabulary Audio Online:

English	Spanish
composite function, p. 428	función compuesta
inverse function, p. 433	función inversa
inverse relation, p. 433	relación inversa
radical equation, p. 417	ecuación radical
radical function, p. 445	función radical
square root equation, p. 417	ecuación de raíz cuadrada
square root function, p. 445	función de raíz cuadrada

BIG ideas

1 Equivalence

Essential Question To simplify the *n*th root of an expression, what must be true about the expression?

2 Solving Equations

Essential Question When you square each side of an equation, is the resulting equation equivalent to the original?

3 Functions

Essential Question How are a function and its inverse function related?

Chapter Preview for Part B

Objective To solve square root and other radical equations

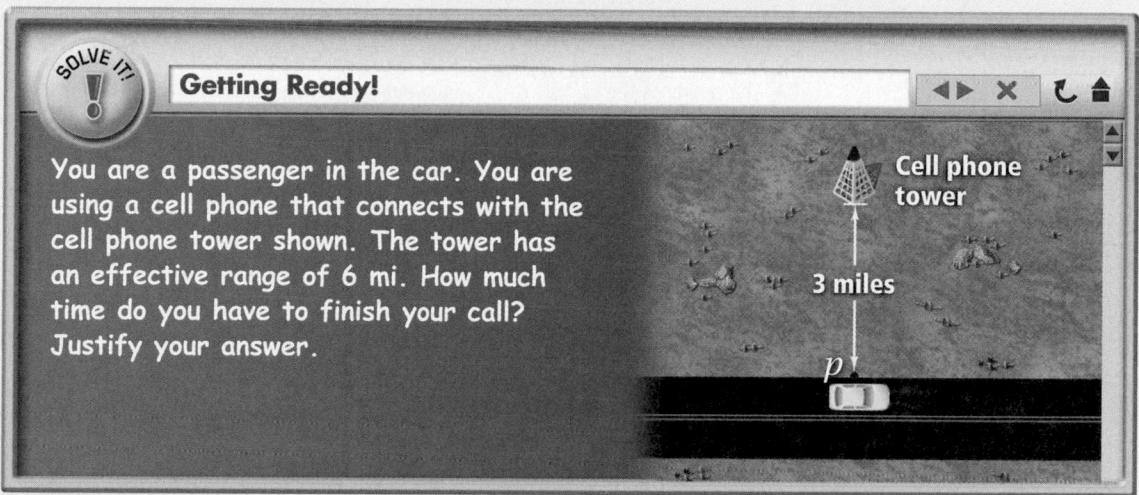

Lesson Vocabulary

• radical equation
• square root equation

A **radical equation** is an equation that has a variable in a radicand or a variable with a rational exponent. If the radical has index 2, the equation is also a **square root equation**. In this lesson, assume that all radicals and expressions with rational exponents represent real numbers.

Focus Question How can you solve radical equations?

To solve a radical equation, isolate the radical on one side of the equation. Then raise each side to the power suggested by the index.

Problem 1 Solving a Square Root Equation

What is the solution of $5 + \sqrt{3x + 4} = 10$?

Write the original equation.	$5 + \sqrt{3x + 4} = 10$
Subtract 5 from each side to isolate the radical expression.	$\sqrt{3x + 4} = 5$
Square each side.	$(\sqrt{3x + 4})^2 = 5^2$
Simplify.	$3x + 4 = 25$
Subtract 4 from each side.	$3x = 21$
Divide each side by 3.	$x = 7$

The solution is 7.

Think

Do you need to introduce a ± sign here?
No; when you take the square root of each side of an equation you do, but here you are squaring both sides of the equation.

✓ **Got It?** **1.** What is the solution of $\sqrt{4x + 1} - 5 = 0$?

To solve equations of the form $x^{\frac{m}{n}} = k$, raise each side of the equation to the power $\frac{n}{m}$, the reciprocal of $\frac{m}{n}$. If either m or n is even, then $\left(x^{\frac{m}{n}}\right)^{\frac{n}{m}} = |x|$.

Problem 2 Solving Other Radical Equations

A What is the solution of $3(x + 1)^{\frac{2}{3}} = 12$?

Know	Need	Plan
• The equation • The power of the exponential expression	Solution of the equation	• Isolate the exponential expression. • Use the inverse of the power to simplify and solve the equation.

Think

How can you get rid of the rational exponent?
Raise each side to the reciprocal power.

Write the original equation.	$3(x + 1)^{\frac{2}{3}} = 12$
Divide each side by 3.	$(x + 1)^{\frac{2}{3}} = 4$
Raise each side to the $\frac{3}{2}$ power.	$\left((x + 1)^{\frac{2}{3}}\right)^{\frac{3}{2}} = 4^{\frac{3}{2}}$
Multiply the exponents.	$(x + 1)^{\frac{6}{6}} = 4^{\frac{3}{2}}$
Use $\left(x^{\frac{m}{n}}\right)^{\frac{n}{m}} = |x|$, since $m = 2$ is even.	$|x + 1| = 8$
Write as two equations.	$x + 1 = 8$ or $x + 1 = -8$
Solve each equation for x.	$x = 7$ or $x = -9$

$$4^{\frac{3}{2}} = (\sqrt{4})^3$$
$$= (2)^3$$
$$= 8$$

Hint

To solve an absolute value equation, you need to rewrite it as two equations.

Check

Substitute the value of x in the original equation.	$3(7 + 1)^{\frac{2}{3}} \stackrel{?}{=} 12$	$3(-9 + 1)^{\frac{2}{3}} \stackrel{?}{=} 12$
Simplify inside the parentheses. Write it as a power of 3.	$3(2^3)^{\frac{2}{3}} \stackrel{?}{=} 12$	$3((-2)^3)^{\frac{2}{3}} \stackrel{?}{=} 12$
Use $(a^m)^n = a^{mn}$.	$3(2)^2 \stackrel{?}{=} 12$	$3(-2)^2 \stackrel{?}{=} 12$
Simplify.	$12 = 12$ ✔	$12 = 12$ ✔

The solutions are 7 and -9.

B What is the solution? $3\sqrt[5]{(x + 1)^3} + 1 = 25$

Think

Why is isolating the variable important?
Do not raise each side of $3\sqrt[5]{(x + 1)^3} + 1 = 25$ to the $\frac{5}{3}$ power. You will end up with a more complicated equation, not a simpler one.

Write the original equation.	$3\sqrt[5]{(x + 1)^3} + 1 = 25$
Rewrite the radical using a rational exponent.	$3(x + 1)^{\frac{3}{5}} + 1 = 25$
Subtract 1 from each side.	$3(x + 1)^{\frac{3}{5}} = 24$
Divide each side by 3.	$(x + 1)^{\frac{3}{5}} = 8$
Raise each side to the $\frac{5}{3}$ power.	$\left((x + 1)^{\frac{3}{5}}\right)^{\frac{5}{3}} = 8^{\frac{5}{3}}$
Multiply the exponents.	$(x + 1)^{\frac{15}{15}} = 8^{\frac{5}{3}}$
Use $\left(x^{\frac{m}{n}}\right)^{\frac{n}{m}} = x$, since m and n are both odd.	$x + 1 = 32$
Subtract 1 from each side.	$x = 31$

$$8^{\frac{5}{3}} = (\sqrt[3]{8})^5$$
$$= (2)^5$$
$$= 32$$

The solution is 31.

Got It? **2.** What is the solution of each equation?

    a. $2(x + 3)^{\frac{2}{3}} = 8$ **b.** $2\sqrt[5]{(x + 150)^3} - 30 = 24$

 Problem 3 Using Radical Equations

Earth Science For Meteor Crater in Arizona, the formula $d = 2\sqrt[3]{\dfrac{V}{0.3}}$ relates the diameter d of the rim (in meters) to the volume V (in cubic meters). What is the volume of Meteor Crater? (All values are approximate.)

1.2 km

Think

What is the diameter in meters?
1.2 km = 1.2 × 1000 m.

Write the equation.	$d = 2\sqrt[3]{\dfrac{V}{0.3}}$
Substitute 1200 for d.	$1200 = 2\sqrt[3]{\dfrac{V}{0.3}}$
Divide each side by 2.	$600 = \sqrt[3]{\dfrac{V}{0.3}}$
Cube each side.	$600^3 = \dfrac{V}{0.3}$
Multiply each side by 0.3.	$0.3 \cdot 600^3 = V$
Simplify.	$V = 64{,}800{,}000$

The volume of Meteor Crater is about 64,800,000 m^3.

 Got It? **3.** Suppose the diameter of a similarly shaped crater is 1 km. What is the volume of the crater? Use the formula given in Problem 3.

Focus Question How can you solve radical equations?

Answer To solve a radical equation, first isolate the radical or exponential expression. Then raise each side of the equation to either the power suggested by the index of the radical or the reciprocal of the exponent.

Lesson Check

Do you know HOW?

Solve each equation.

1. $\sqrt{4x - 23} - 3 = 2$

2. $-\sqrt[3]{x} + 3 = 0$

Do you UNDERSTAND?

3. Compare and Contrast How is solving a square root equation similar to solving an absolute value equation? How is it different?

Practice and Problem-Solving Exercises

 **Practice** Solve.

See Problem 1.

Guided Practice

4. $3\sqrt{x} + 3 = 15$

To start, subtract 3 from each side.

$3\sqrt{x} + 3 - 3 = 15 - 3$

5. $4\sqrt{x} - 1 = 3$

6. $\sqrt{x + 3} = 5$

7. $\sqrt{x + 1} = 4$

8. $\sqrt{2x - 1} = 3$

9. $\sqrt{3x + 4} = 4$

10. $\sqrt{6 - 3x} - 2 = 0$

Solve.

See Problem 2.

11. $(x + 5)^{\frac{2}{3}} = 4$

12. $(x + 2)^{\frac{2}{3}} = 9$

13. $3(x - 2)^{\frac{3}{4}} = 24$

14. $3(x + 3)^{\frac{3}{4}} = 81$

15. $(x + 1)^{\frac{3}{2}} - 2 = 25$

16. $3 + (4 - x)^{\frac{3}{2}} = 11$

17. Volume A spherical water tank holds 9000 ft³ of water. What is the diameter of the tank? $\left(\textit{Hint}: V = \frac{\pi}{6}d^3\right)$

Guided Practice

To start, substitute 9000 for V in the formula for the volume of a sphere.

$9000 = \frac{\pi}{6}d^3$

18. Hydraulics The formula $d = \sqrt{\frac{4Q}{\pi v}}$ models the diameter of a pipe where Q is the maximum flow of water in the pipe and v is the velocity of the water. What is the diameter of a pipe that allows a maximum flow of 30 ft³/min of water flowing at a velocity of 400 ft/min? Round your answer to the nearest inch.

 **Apply**

19. Mental Math What is the solution? $\sqrt{x + 11} = 4$

20. You can find the area A of a square whose side is s units with the formula $A = s^2$. What is the best estimate for the side of a square with an area of 32 m²?

    Ⓐ 4.2 m   Ⓑ 5.7 m   Ⓒ 8.0 m   Ⓓ 16 m

Solve.

21. $3\sqrt{2x} - 3 = 9$

22. $2(2x)^{\frac{1}{3}} + 1 = 5$

23. $\sqrt{2x - 1} - 3 = 0$

Solving Square Root and Other Radical Equations

Objective To solve square root and other radical equations

In Part 1 of the lesson, you learned how to solve square root and radical equations by isolating the variable.

Connect to What You Know

Here you will learn to check your solutions in the original equation to see if any are extraneous.

Focus Question Why is it important to check the solutions of a radical equation?

When you raise each side of an equation to a power, it is possible to introduce extraneous solutions. Therefore, it becomes very important that you check all solutions in the original equation.

Problem 4 Checking for Extraneous Solutions

What is the solution of $\sqrt{x+7} - 5 = x$? Check your results.

Write the original equation.	$\sqrt{x+7} - 5 = x$
Isolate the radical.	$\sqrt{x+7} = x + 5$
Square each side.	$(\sqrt{x+7})^2 = (x+5)^2$
Simplify.	$x + 7 = x^2 + 10x + 25$
Combine like terms.	$0 = x^2 + 9x + 18$
Factor.	$0 = (x+3)(x+6)$
Use the Zero-Product Property.	$x = -3 \text{ or } x = -6$

Think

How do you square a binomial?
Use the formula,
$(a+b)^2 = a^2 + 2ab + b^2$.

Check

Substitute the value of x.	$\sqrt{-3+7} - 5 \overset{?}{=} -3$	$\sqrt{-6+7} - 5 \overset{?}{=} -6$
Simplify inside the parentheses.	$\sqrt{4} - 5 \overset{?}{=} -3$	$\sqrt{1} - 5 \overset{?}{=} -6$
Find square roots.	$2 - 5 \overset{?}{=} -3$	$1 - 5 \overset{?}{=} -6$
Subtract.	$-3 = -3 \checkmark$	$-4 = -6 \times$

The only solution is -3.

false

Got It? **4. a.** What is the solution of $\sqrt{5x-1} + 3 = x$? Check your results.

b. Reasoning When should you check for extraneous solutions? Explain.

In this lesson, you have studied algebraic methods of solving square root and radical equations. In Lesson 6-8, you will study the graphs of square root functions. These graphs can help you find solutions and identify extraneous solutions.

The calculator screen shows the graphs of **Y1** = $\sqrt{(x + 7)} - 5$ and **Y2 = x.** From the graph, it is clear that -3 is a solution of $\sqrt{x + 7} - 5 = x$, and -6 is not a solution.

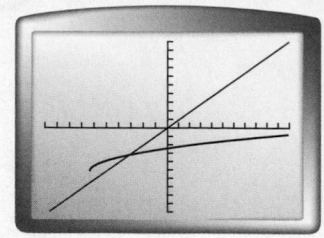

If an equation contains two radical expressions (or two terms with rational exponents), isolate one of the radicals (or one of the terms), then eliminate it (or its rational exponent). Isolate the more complicated radical expression first. In the resulting equation, simplify the expressions before you eliminate the second radical.

ONLINE PROBLEMS **Problem 5** Solving an Equation With Two Radicals

Plan
Which radical expression should you isolate first?
Isolate the more complicated radical first, $\sqrt{2x + 1}$.

What is the solution of $\sqrt{2x + 1} - \sqrt{x} = 1$?

Write the original equation.	$\sqrt{2x + 1} - \sqrt{x} = 1$
Isolate the more complicated radical.	$\sqrt{2x + 1} = \sqrt{x} + 1$
Square each side.	$(\sqrt{2x + 1})^2 = (\sqrt{x} + 1)^2$
Simplify.	$2x + 1 = x + 2\sqrt{x} + 1$
Isolate $2\sqrt{x}$.	$x = 2\sqrt{x}$
Square each side.	$x^2 = (2\sqrt{x})^2$
Simplify.	$x^2 = 4x$
Subtract $4x$ from each side.	$x^2 - 4x = 0$
Factor.	$x(x - 4) = 0$
Use the Zero-Product Property.	$x = 0 \text{ or } x = 4$

Check

Write the original equation.	$\sqrt{2x + 1} - \sqrt{x} = 1$	$\sqrt{2x + 1} - \sqrt{x} = 1$
Substitute the value of x.	$\sqrt{2(0) + 1} - \sqrt{0} \stackrel{?}{=} 1$	$\sqrt{2(4) + 1} - \sqrt{4} \stackrel{?}{=} 1$
Simplify the radicands.	$\sqrt{1} - 0 \stackrel{?}{=} 1$	$\sqrt{9} - \sqrt{4} \stackrel{?}{=} 1$
Find square roots.	$1 - 0 \stackrel{?}{=} 1$	$3 - 2 \stackrel{?}{=} 1$
Subtract.	$1 = 1$ ✔	$1 = 1$ ✔

The solutions are 0 and 4.

 Got It? 5. What is the solution of $\sqrt{5x + 4} - \sqrt{x} = 4$?

Focus Question Why is it important to check the solutions of a radical equation?
Answer You must check each solution in the original equation to see if it gives a true statement. It is possible to introduce extraneous solutions when you raise both sides of an equation to a power.

Lesson Check

Do you know HOW?

Solve. Check for extraneous solutions.

1. $5\sqrt{x} + 7 = 8$ **2.** $3\sqrt{x} = 6$

3. $5 - 2\sqrt{x} = 3$ **4.** $\sqrt[3]{x} = 8$

Do you UNDERSTAND?

5. Vocabulary Which value, 12 or 3, is an extraneous solution of $x - 6 = \sqrt{3x}$? Explain your reasoning.

Practice and Problem-Solving Exercises

A Practice

Solve. Check for extraneous solutions.

Guided Practice

To start, square each side of the equation. Simplify.

6. $\sqrt{3x + 7} = x - 1$

$$\left(\sqrt{3x + 7}\right)^2 = (x - 1)^2$$

$$3x + 7 = x^2 - 2x + 1$$

7. $(5 - x)^{\frac{1}{2}} = x + 1$ **8.** $\sqrt{11x + 3} - 2x = 0$

9. $(5x - 4)^{\frac{1}{2}} - x = 0$ **10.** $\sqrt{3x + 13} - 5 = x$

11. $(x + 3)^{\frac{1}{2}} - 1 = x$ **12.** $\sqrt{x + 7} - x = 1$

Solve. Check for extraneous solutions.

See Problem 5.

Guided Practice

To start, square each side of the equation.

13. $\sqrt{3x} = \sqrt{x + 6}$

$$\left(\sqrt{3x}\right)^2 = \left(\sqrt{x + 6}\right)^2$$

14. $(2x)^{\frac{1}{2}} = (x + 5)^{\frac{1}{2}}$ **15.** $(7x + 6)^{\frac{1}{2}} - (9 + 4x)^{\frac{1}{2}} = 0$

16. $(x + 5)^{\frac{1}{2}} - (5 - 2x)^{\frac{1}{4}} = 0$ **17.** $(x - 2)^{\frac{1}{2}} - (28 - 2x)^{\frac{1}{4}} = 0$

18. $\sqrt{5 - x} - \sqrt{x} = 1$ **19.** $\sqrt{3x + 1} - \sqrt{x + 1} = 2$

20. $\sqrt{2x + 6} - \sqrt{x - 1} = 2$ **21.** $\sqrt{3 - x} + \sqrt{x + 2} = 3$

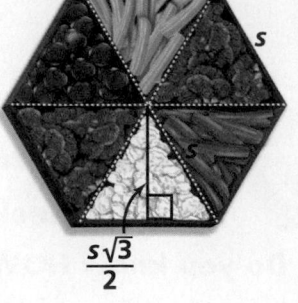

s

$\dfrac{s\sqrt{3}}{2}$

B Apply

22. **Think About a Plan** A hexagonal tray of vegetables has an area of 450 cm². What is the length of each side of the hexagon?
    - What is the area of the triangle at the bottom in terms of the side length?
    - How can you use the diagram at the right to find the formula for the area of the hexagon? (*Hint:* Six triangles make one hexagon.)

23. **Traffic Signs** A stop sign is a regular octagon, formed by cutting triangles off the corners of a square. If a stop sign measures 36 in. from top to bottom, what is the length of each side?

24. A teacher asked students why it is necessary to check for extraneous roots when squaring both sides of an equation. Which of the following answers is the best? Is this answer complete? Explain.
    - Ⓐ Because the squared equation can have negative roots.
    - Ⓑ Because squaring is multiplication, and any multiplication is a potential source of extraneous roots.
    - Ⓒ Because when you square both sides of the equation $a = b$, you add the roots of the equation $a = -b$ to the solution set.
    - Ⓓ Because any operation with an equation may result in extraneous roots.

25. **Error Analysis** A student said that 4 and 1 are the solutions of the problem shown. Describe and correct the student's error.

26. **Physics** The velocity v of an object dropped from a tall building is given by the formula $v = \sqrt{64d}$, where d is the distance the object has fallen. Solve the formula for d.

$$\sqrt{x} + 2 = x$$
$$\sqrt{x} = x - 2$$
$$(\sqrt{x})^2 = (x - 2)^2$$
$$x = x^2 - 4x + 4$$
$$0 = x^2 - 5x + 4$$
$$0 = (x - 4)(x - 1)$$

27. **Open-Ended** Write an equation that has two radical expressions and no real roots.

Solve. Check for extraneous solutions.

28. $(2x + 3)^{\frac{1}{2}} - 7 = 0$

29. $\sqrt{x^2 + 3} = x + 1$

30. $(2x + 3)^{\frac{3}{4}} - 3 = 5$

31. $2(x - 1)^{\frac{4}{3}} + 4 = 36$

32. $x^{\frac{1}{2}} - (x - 5)^{\frac{1}{2}} = 2$

33. $\sqrt{x} = \sqrt{x - 8} + 2$

34. **Reasoning** You have solved equations containing square roots by squaring each side. You were using the property that if $a = b$ then $a^2 = b^2$. Show that the following statements are *not* true for all real numbers.
    a. If $a^2 = b^2$, then $a = b$.
    b. If $a \le b$, then $a^2 \le b^2$.

Standardized Test Prep

35. What is the solution of $(x + 2)^{\frac{3}{4}} = 27$?

   Ⓐ $x = 27$ Ⓑ $x = 79$ Ⓒ $x = 81$ Ⓓ $x = 83$

36. A problem on a test asked students to solve a fifth-degree polynomial equation with real coefficients. Adam found the following roots: -11.5, $\sqrt{2}$, $\frac{2i + 6}{2}$, $-\sqrt{2}$, and $3 - i$. His teacher wrote that four of these roots are correct, and one is incorrect. Which root is incorrect?

   Ⓕ -11.5 Ⓗ $\frac{2i + 6}{2}$

   Ⓖ $\sqrt{2}$ Ⓘ $3 - i$

37. Which expression represents the solution of the equation $\frac{x}{y} = \frac{c}{a + b}$ solved for a?

   Ⓐ $\frac{c}{b} - \frac{x}{y}$ Ⓒ $\frac{yc}{x} + b$

   Ⓑ $\frac{yc}{a + b}$ Ⓓ $\frac{yc - xb}{x}$

38. To rationalize the denominator of $\sqrt[4]{\frac{4}{25}}$, by what number would you multiply the numerator and denominator of the fraction?

Mixed Review

Simplify each number.   ◀ **See Lesson 6-4.**

39. $81^{\frac{1}{4}}$ **40.** $64^{\frac{2}{3}}$ **41.** $125 \cdot 125^{\frac{1}{3}}$

42. $32 \cdot 256^{\frac{1}{2}}$ **43.** $100^{\frac{-3}{2}}$ **44.** $6^{\frac{1}{2}} \cdot 12^{\frac{1}{2}}$

Solve each equation by factoring. Check your answers.   ◀ **See Lesson 4-5.**

45. $x^2 - 7x + 12 = 0$ **46.** $x^2 - 8x + 15 = 0$ **47.** $x^2 + 9x + 20 = 0$

48. $3x^2 + 8x + 4 = 0$ **49.** $9x^2 + 15x + 4 = 0$ **50.** $4x^2 + 11x + 6 = 0$

Get Ready!   **To prepare for Lesson 6-6, do Exercises 51–56.**

Find the domain and range of each relation, and determine whether it is a function.   ◀ **See Lesson 2-1.**

51. $\{(0, -5), (2, -3), (4, -1)\}$ **52.** $\{(-1, 2), (0, 0), (1, 1)\}$ **53.** $\{(-2, -2), (0, 0), (1, 1)\}$

54. $\{(3, -1), (4, -1), (5, -1)\}$ **55.** $\{(0, 0), (1, 0), (2, 1), (2, 2)\}$ **56.** $\{(0, -2), (0, 0), (0, 2)\}$

6-6 Function Operations

Objectives To add, subtract, multiply, and divide functions
To find the composition of two functions

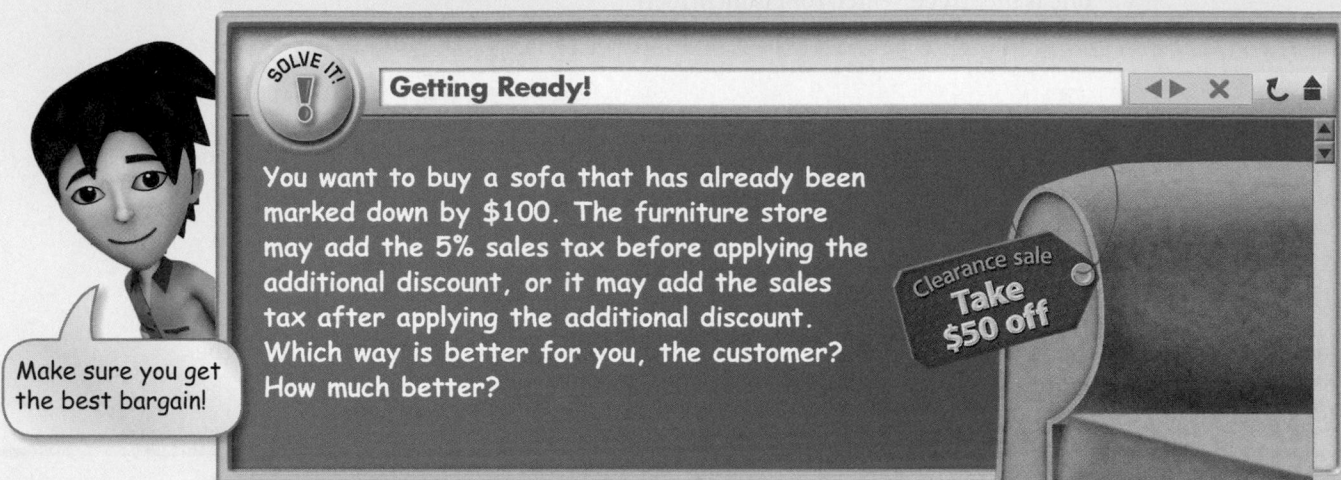

SOLVE IT!

Getting Ready!

You want to buy a sofa that has already been marked down by $100. The furniture store may add the 5% sales tax before applying the additional discount, or it may add the sales tax after applying the additional discount. Which way is better for you, the customer? How much better?

Clearance sale
Take $50 off

Make sure you get the best bargain!

The final cost of the sofa in the Solve It involves two functions: one that gives an additional discount and one that multiplies to find the sales tax.

Lesson Vocabulary
• composite function

Focus Question How are function operations different from operations on real numbers?

You can add, subtract, multiply, and divide functions based on how you perform these operations for real numbers. One difference, however, is that you must consider the domain of each function.

Hint

The function operations of addition and multiplication are commutative, just as they are for real numbers. Subtraction and division are not.

take note

Key Concepts   Function Operations

Addition	$(f + g)(x) = f(x) + g(x)$
Subtraction	$(f - g)(x) = f(x) - g(x)$
Multiplication	$(f \cdot g)(x) = f(x) \cdot g(x)$
Division	$\left(\dfrac{f}{g}\right)(x) = \dfrac{f(x)}{g(x)}, g(x) \neq 0$

The domains of the sum, difference, product, and quotient functions consist of the x-values that are in the domains of *both* f and g. Also, the domain of the quotient function does not contain any x-value for which $g(x) = 0$.

Problem 1 Adding and Subtracting Functions

Let $f(x) = 4x + 7$ and $g(x) = \sqrt{x} + x$. What are $f + g$ and $f - g$ and their domains?

Find $(f + g)(x)$.

Write the definition of $(f + g)(x)$.	$(f + g)(x) = f(x) + g(x)$
Substitute for $f(x)$ and $g(x)$.	$= (4x + 7) + (\sqrt{x} + x)$
Combine like terms.	$= 5x + \sqrt{x} + 7$

Find $(f - g)(x)$.

Write the definition of $(f - g)(x)$.	$(f - g)(x) = f(x) - g(x)$
Substitute for $f(x)$ and $g(x)$.	$= (4x + 7) - (\sqrt{x} + x)$
Combine like terms.	$= 3x - \sqrt{x} + 7$

Think

What determines the domain of g?
Because there is a square root of x, x must be ≥ 0.

The domain of f is the set of all real numbers. The domain of g is all real numbers $x \geq 0$. The domain of both $f + g$ and $f - g$ is the set of numbers common to the domains of both f and g, which is all $x \geq 0$.

 **Got It?** **1.** Let $f(x) = 2x^2 + 8$ and $g(x) = x - 3$. What are $f + g$ and $f - g$ and their domains?

Problem 2 Multiplying and Dividing Functions

Let $f(x) = x^2 - 9$ and $g(x) = x + 3$. What are $f \cdot g$ and $\frac{f}{g}$ and their domains?

Find $(f \cdot g)(x)$.

Write the definition of $(f \cdot g)(x)$.	$(f \cdot g)(x) = f(x) \cdot g(x)$
Substitute for $f(x)$ and $g(x)$.	$= (x^2 - 9)(x + 3)$
Distribute.	$= x^3 - 9x + 3x^2 - 27$
Write in standard form.	$= x^3 + 3x^2 - 9x - 27$

Find $\left(\frac{f}{g}\right)(x)$.

Write the definition of $\left(\frac{f}{g}\right)(x)$.	$\left(\frac{f}{g}\right)(x) = \dfrac{f(x)}{g(x)}$
Substitute for $f(x)$ and $g(x)$.	$= \dfrac{x^2 - 9}{x + 3}$
Factor $x^2 - 9$ as a difference of squares.	$= \dfrac{(x - 3)(x + 3)}{x + 3}$
Simplify, and restrict the domain.	$= x - 3, x \neq -3$

Think

Is the domain of $\frac{f}{g}$ the domain of $x - 3$?
No; the fraction can only be simplified and the function is only defined when $g(x) \neq -3$.

The domain of both f and g is the set of all real numbers, so the domain of $f \cdot g$ is the set of all real numbers. The domain of $\frac{f}{g}$ is all real numbers except $x \neq -3$, because $g(-3) = 0$.

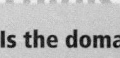 **Got It?** **2.** Let $f(x) = 3x^2 - 11x - 4$ and $g(x) = 3x + 1$. What are $f \cdot g$ and $\frac{f}{g}$ and their domains?

The diagram shows what happens when you apply one function $g(x)$ after another function $f(x)$.

The output from the first function becomes the input for the second function. When you combine two functions as in the diagram, you form a **composite function**.

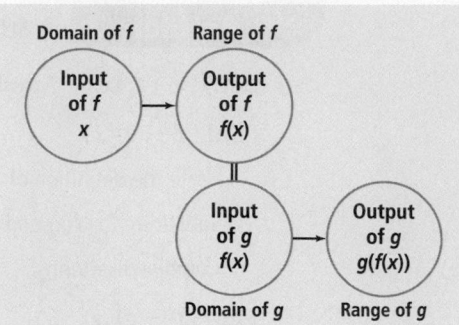

take note

Key Concept   Composition of Functions

The composition of function g with function f is written as $g \circ f$ and is defined as $(g \circ f)(x) = g(f(x))$. The domain of $g \circ f$ consists of the x-values in the domain of f for which $f(x)$ is in the domain of g.

$$(g \circ f)(x) = g(f(x))$$ **1.** Evaluate $f(x)$ first.
$$\underbrace{\quad}_{2}\underbrace{\quad}_{1}$$ **2.** Then use $f(x)$ as the input for g.

Function composition is not commutative since $f(g(x))$ does not always equal $g(f(x))$.

Problem 3   Composing Functions   GRIDDED RESPONSE

Let $f(x) = x - 5$ and $g(x) = x^2$. What is $(g \circ f)(-3)$?

Think

Which function is substituted into the other?

Use $f(x)$ as the input for g.

Method 1   Find a rule for $(g \circ f)(x)$. Then evaluate for $x = -3$.

Write the definition of $(g \circ f)(x)$.	$(g \circ f)(x) = g(f(x))$
Substitute the definition of $f(x)$.	$= g(x - 5)$
Substitute $x - 5$ for x in $g(x)$.	$= (x - 5)^2$
Substitute -3 for x to find $(g \circ f)(x)$.	$(g \circ f)(-3) = (-3 - 5)^2$
Simplify inside the parentheses.	$= (-8)^2$
Simplify.	$= 64$

Method 2   Evaluate $(g \circ f)(-3)$ directly.

Substitute -3 for x.	$(g \circ f)(-3)$
Use the definition of $(g \circ f)(x)$.	$= g(f(-3))$
Evaluate $f(-3)$.	$= g(-3 - 5)$
Simplify.	$= g(-8)$
Evaluate $g(-8)$.	$= (-8)^2$
Simplify.	$= 64$

Got It? 3. What is $(f \circ g)(-3)$ for the functions f and g defined in Problem 3?

Problem 4 Using Composite Functions

You have a coupon good for $5 off the price of any large pizza. You also get a 10% discount on any pizza if you show your student ID. How much more would you pay for a large pizza if the cashier applies the coupon first?

Know	Need	Plan
The coupon value and the discount rate.	The difference between the results of applying the discount or coupon first.	• Compose two functions in two ways. • Then find the difference in their results.

Step 1 Find functions C and D that model the cost of a large pizza.

Let $x =$ the price of a large pizza.

Cost using the coupon: $C(x) = x - 5$

Cost using the 10% discount: $D(x) = x - 0.1x = 0.9x$

Step 2 Compose the functions to apply the discount and then the coupon.

Apply the discount, $D(x)$, first. $(C \circ D)(x) = C(D(x))$

Substitute $D(x)$ into $C(x)$. $= C(0.9x)$

Simplify. $= 0.9x - 5$

Step 3 Compose the functions to apply the coupon and then the discount.

Apply the coupon, $C(x)$, first. $(D \circ C)(x) = D(C(x))$

Substitute $C(x)$ into $D(x)$. $= D(x - 5)$

Simplify. $= 0.9(x - 5) = 0.9x - 4.5$

Think

How can you find the difference between the two results?

Subtract one composition from the other.

Step 4 Subtract the composite functions to find how much more you would pay if the cashier applies the coupon first.

$$(D \circ C)(x) - (C \circ D)(x) = (0.9x - 4.5) - (0.9x - 5)$$
$$= -4.5 + 5$$
$$= 0.5$$

You pay $.50 more if the cashier applies the coupon first.

 Got It? **4.** A store is offering a 15% discount on all items. Also, employees get a 20% employee discount. Write composite functions
  a. to model taking the 15% discount and then the 20% discount.
  b. to model taking the 20% discount and then the 15% discount.
  c. Reasoning If you were an employee, which discount would you take first? Explain.

Focus Question How are function operations different from operations on real numbers?
Answer The function operations of addition, subtraction, multiplication, and division are defined only for values of x that are in the domains of *both* functions. For the composite function $(g \circ f)(x) = g(f(x))$, the domain only includes those values of x for which $f(x)$ is in the domain of g.

Lesson Check

Do you know HOW?

Let $f(x) = 3x - 2$ and $g(x) = x^2 + 1$. Perform each function operation.

1. $(f \cdot g)(x)$

2. $(f - g)(x)$

3. $(f \circ g)(x)$

4. $f(x) + g(x)$

5. $g(x) - f(x)$

6. $f(x) - g(x)$

Do you UNDERSTAND?

7. Error Analysis Your friend used some simple functions and found that $(f \circ g)(x) = (g \circ f)(x)$, and concluded that function composition is commutative. Give an example to show that your friend is mistaken.

8. Open-Ended Find two functions f and g such that $f(g(x)) = x$ for all real numbers x.

Practice and Problem-Solving Exercises

 **Practice** Let $f(x) = 7x + 5$ and $g(x) = x^2$. Perform each function operation and then find the domain of the result.

See Problems 1 and 2.

Guided Practice

9. $(f + g)(x)$

To start, write the definition of $(f + g)(x)$.
$$(f + g)(x) = f(x) + g(x)$$

Substitute for $f(x)$ and $g(x)$.
$$= (7x + 5) + x^2$$

10. $(f - g)(x)$

11. $(f \cdot g)(x)$

12. $\left(\dfrac{f}{g}\right)(x)$

13. $\left(\dfrac{g}{f}\right)(x)$

Let $f(x) = 2 - x$ and $g(x) = \frac{1}{x}$. Perform each function operation and then find the domain of the result.

14. $(f - g)(x)$

15. $(g - f)(x)$

16. $(f \cdot g)(x)$

17. $\left(\dfrac{f}{g}\right)(x)$

Let $g(x) = 2x$ and $h(x) = x^2 + 4$. Find each value.

See Problem 3.

Guided Practice

18. $(h \circ g)(1)$

To start, use the definition of composing functions to find a function rule for $(h \circ g)(x)$. Substitute the definition of $g(x)$.
$$(h \circ g)(x) = h(g(x))$$
$$= h(2x)$$

19. $(h \circ g)(-2)$

20. $(g \circ h)(-2)$

21. $(g \circ h)(0)$

Let $f(x) = x^2$ and $g(x) = x - 3$. Find each value.

22. $(g \circ f)(-2)$

23. $(f \circ g)(-2)$

24. $(g \circ f)(0)$

25. $(f \circ g)(0)$

26. $(g \circ f)(3.5)$

27. $(f \circ g)(3.5)$

28. **Sales** A computer store offers a 5% discount off the list price x for any computer  See Problem 4.
bought with cash, rather than put on credit. At the same time, the manufacturer
offers a $200 rebate for each purchase of a computer.
   a. Write a function $f(x)$ to represent the price after the cash discount.
   b. Write a function $g(x)$ to represent the price after the $200 rebate.
   c. Suppose the list price of a computer is $1500. Use a composite function to find
      the price of the computer if the discount is applied before the rebate.
   d. Suppose the list price of a computer is $1500. Use a composite function to find
      the price of the computer if the rebate is applied before the discount.

29. **Economics** Suppose the function $f(x) = 0.15x$ represents the number of U.S.
dollars equivalent to x Chinese yuan and the function $g(y) = 10.49y$ represents the
number of Mexican pesos equivalent to y U.S. dollars.
   a. Write a composite function that represents the number of Mexican pesos
      equivalent to x Chinese yuan.
   b. Find the value in Mexican pesos of an item that costs 15 Chinese yuan.

 **Apply**

30. **Think About a Plan** A craftsman makes and sells violins. The function
$I(x) = 5995x$ represents the income in dollars from selling x violins. The function
$P(y) = y - 100,000$ represents his profit in dollars if he makes an income of y
dollars. What is the profit from selling 30 violins?
   - How can you write a composite function to represent the craftsman's profit?
   - How can you use the composite function to find the profit earned when he sells
     30 violins?

Let $f(x) = 2x + 5$ and $g(x) = x^2 - 3x + 2$. Perform each function operation
and then find the domain.

31. $f(x) + g(x)$ 32. $3f(x) - 2$ 33. $-2g(x) + f(x)$

34. $f(x) - g(x) + 10$ 35. $4f(x) + 2g(x)$ 36. $f(x) \cdot g(x)$

37. $-3f(x) \cdot g(x)$ 38. $\dfrac{f(x)}{g(x)}$ 39. $\dfrac{5f(x)}{g(x)}$

40. Suppose your teacher offers to give the whole class a bonus if everyone passes
the next math test. The teacher says she will give everyone a 10-point bonus and
increase everyone's grade by 9% of their score.
   a. You earned a 75 on the test. Would you rather have the 10-point bonus first and
      then the 9% increase, or the 9% increase first and then the 10-point bonus?
   b. **Reasoning** Is this the best plan for all students? Explain.

41. **Sales** A salesperson earns a 3% bonus on weekly sales over $5000. Consider the
following functions.

$$g(x) = 0.03x \qquad\qquad h(x) = x - 5000$$

   a. Explain what each function above represents.
   b. **Reasoning** Which composition, $(h \circ g)(x)$ or $(g \circ h)(x)$, represents the
      weekly bonus? Explain.

Let $g(x) = 3x + 2$ and $f(x) = \frac{x-2}{3}$. Find each value.

42. $f(g(1))$

43. $g(f(-4))$

44. $g(f(2))$

45. $(g \circ g)(1)$

46. $(f \circ g)(-2)$

47. $(f \circ f)(0)$

For each pair of functions, find $f(g(x))$ and $g(f(x))$.

48. $f(x) = 3x, g(x) = x^2$

49. $f(x) = 3x^2 + 2, g(x) = 2x$

50. $f(x) = \frac{x-3}{2}, g(x) = 2x - 3$

Standardized Test Prep

SAT/ACT

51. Let $f(x) = x + 5$ and $g(x) = x^2 - 25$. What is the domain of $\frac{f}{g}(x)$?

Ⓐ All real numbers

Ⓒ All real numbers except -5

Ⓑ All real numbers except 5

Ⓓ All real numbers except -5 and 5

52. Let $g(x) = x - 3$ and $h(x) = x^2 + 6$. What is $(h \circ g)(1)$?

Ⓕ -14

Ⓖ 4

Ⓗ 10

Ⓘ 15

53. Which number is a solution of $|3 - 2x| < 5$?

Ⓐ -6

Ⓑ -1

Ⓒ 2

Ⓓ 4

Short Response

54. Solve the equation $-3x^2 + 5x + 4 = 0$. Show your work.

Mixed Review

Solve. Check for extraneous solutions.

◀ See Lesson 6-5.

55. $\sqrt{x^2 + 3} = x + 1$

56. $x + 8 = (x^2 + 16)^{\frac{1}{2}}$

57. $\sqrt{x^2 + 9} = x + 1$

58. $(x^2 - 9)^{\frac{1}{2}} - x = -3$

59. $\sqrt{x^2 + 12} - 2 = x$

60. $(3x)^{\frac{1}{2}} = (x + 6)^{\frac{1}{2}}$

Expand each binomial.

◀ See Lesson 5-7.

61. $(x + y)^6$

62. $(2x - y)^4$

63. $(9 - 2x)^5$

64. $(4x - y)^5$

65. $(x^2 + x)^4$

66. $(x^2 + 2y^3)^6$

Get Ready!   To prepare for Lesson 6-7, do Exercises 67–69.

Graph and solve each system.

◀ See Lesson 3-1.

67. $\begin{cases} y = x - 6 \\ y = x + 6 \end{cases}$

68. $\begin{cases} y = 0.5x + 1 \\ y = 2x - 2 \end{cases}$

69. $\begin{cases} y = \frac{x+4}{5} \\ y = 5x - 4 \end{cases}$

Inverse Relations and Functions

Objective To find the inverse of a relation or function

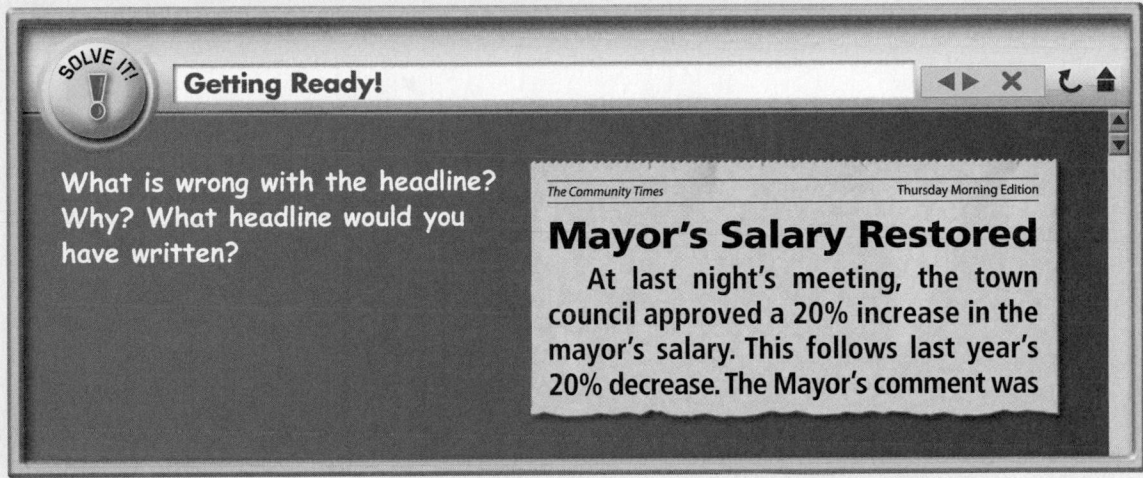

Getting Ready!

What is wrong with the headline? Why? What headline would you have written?

The Community Times   Thursday Morning Edition

Mayor's Salary Restored

At last night's meeting, the town council approved a 20% increase in the mayor's salary. This follows last year's 20% decrease. The Mayor's comment was

Lesson Vocabulary
• inverse relation
• inverse function

If a relation pairs element *a* of its domain to element *b* of its range, the **inverse relation** pairs *b* with *a*. So, if (*a*, *b*) is an ordered pair of a relation, then (*b*, *a*) is an ordered pair of its inverse. If both a relation and its inverse happen to be functions, they are **inverse functions**.

Focus Question What is the inverse of a relation?

This diagram shows a relation *r* (a function) and its inverse (not a function). The range of the relation is the domain of the inverse. The domain of the relation is the range of the inverse.

	Relation *r*			Inverse of *r*	
Domain	**Range**		**Domain**	**Range**	
1.2 →	1		1 →	1.2	
1.4 →				1.4	
1.6 →	2		2 →	1.6	
1.9 →				1.9	

Problem 1 Finding the Inverse of a Relation

Think

(0, −1) is in *s*. How do you find the corresponding pair in the inverse of *s*?
Switch the coordinates. (−1, 0) is in the inverse of *s*.

A What is the inverse of relation *s*?

Relation *s*

x	y
0	−1
2	0
3	2
4	3

Switch the *x* and *y* values to get the inverse. →

Inverse of Relation *s*

x	y
−1	0
0	2
2	3
3	4

B What are the graphs of *s* and its inverse?

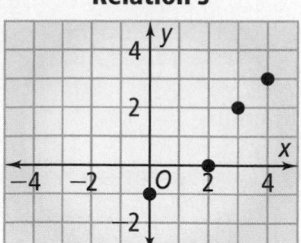

Relation s

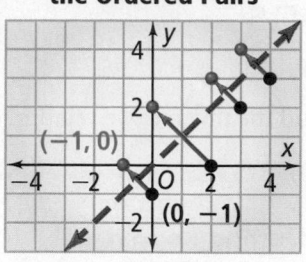

**Reversing
the Ordered Pairs**

$(-1, 0)$

$(0, -1)$

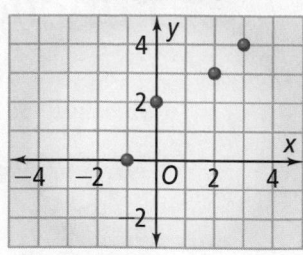

Inverse of s

 Got It? **1. a.** What are the graphs of *t* and its inverse?

b. Reasoning Is *t* a function? Is the inverse of *t* a function? Explain.

Relation t

x	y
0	−5
1	−4
2	−3
3	−3

As shown in Problem 1, the graphs of a relation and its inverse are the reflections of each other in the line $y = x$. If you describe a relation or function by an equation in *x* and *y*, you can switch *x* and *y* to get an equation for the inverse.

Problem 2 Finding an Equation for the Inverse

Think

Why do you solve for *y*?
Solve the equation for *y* to easily generate ordered pairs that are part of the inverse relation.

What is the inverse of each relation?

A $y = 4 - 3x$

Write the original equation. $\qquad\qquad y = 4 - 3x$

Switch *x* and *y*. $\qquad\qquad x = 4 - 3y$

Subtract 4 from each side. $\qquad\qquad x - 4 = -3y$

Divide each side by −3 to solve for *y*. $\qquad\dfrac{x - 4}{-3} = y$

$$\dfrac{x-4}{-3} = \dfrac{-(x-4)}{3}$$
$$= \dfrac{4-x}{3}$$

Write the inverse. $\qquad\qquad y = \dfrac{4 - x}{3}$

B $y = x^2 - 5$

Write the original equation. $\qquad\qquad y = x^2 - 5$

Switch *x* and *y*. $\qquad\qquad x = y^2 - 5$

Add 5 to each side. $\qquad\qquad x + 5 = y^2$

Find the square root of each side to solve for *y*. $\quad \pm\sqrt{x + 5} = y$

 Got It? **2.** What is the inverse of each relation?

a. $y = 2x + 8$ $\qquad\qquad\qquad$ **b.** $y = x^2 + 2$

Problem 3 Graphing a Relation and Its Inverse

Think

How would you describe the graph of $y = x^2 - 1$?
The graph of $y = x^2 - 1$ is a translation of $y = x^2$ down one unit.

What are the graphs of $y = x^2 - 1$ and its inverse, $y = \pm\sqrt{x + 1}$?

The graph of $y = x^2 - 1$ is a parabola that opens upward with vertex $(0, -1)$. The graph of the inverse is the reflection of the parabola in the line $y = x$.

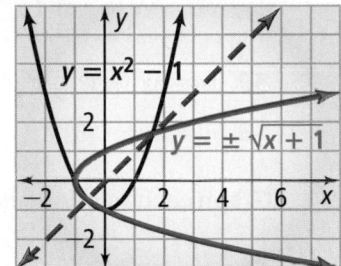

✓ **Got It?** **3.** What are the graphs of $y = 2x + 8$ and its inverse?

Focus Question What is the inverse of a relation?

Answer If a relation consists of the ordered pairs (a, b), then the inverse of the relation consists of the ordered pairs (b, a). To graph the inverse of a relation, reflect the graph of the relation in the line $y = x$.

 Lesson Check

Do you know HOW?

Find the inverse of each function. Is the inverse a function?

1. $f(x) = 4x + 3$

2. $f(x) = x^2 - 1$

3. $f(x) = (x + 1)^2$

Do you UNDERSTAND?

4. Vocabulary Does every function have an inverse that is a function? Does every relation have an inverse which is a relation?

5. Reasoning A function consists of the pairs $(2, 3)$, $(x, 4)$, and $(5, 6)$. What values, if any, may x not assume?

  **Practice and Problem-Solving Exercises**

Ⓐ **Practice** Find the inverse of each relation. Graph the given relation and its inverse.

◀ **See Problem 1.**

6.

x	y
1	0
2	1
3	0
4	2

7.

x	y
1	0
2	1
3	2
4	3

8.

x	y
0	0
1	1
2	4
3	9

Find the inverse of each function. Is the inverse a function?

← See Problem 2.

Guided Practice →

9. $y = 3x + 1$

To start, switch x and y. $x = 3y + 1$

10. $y = 2x - 1$

11. $y = 4 - 3x$

12. $y = 5 - 2x^2$

13. $y = 3x^2 - 5$

14. $y = (x - 8)^2$

15. $y = (1 - 2x)^2 + 5$

Graph each relation and its inverse.

← See Problem 3.

Guided Practice →

16. $y = 2x - 3$

To start, graph $y = 2x - 3$. This is a line with slope 2 and y-intercept -3.

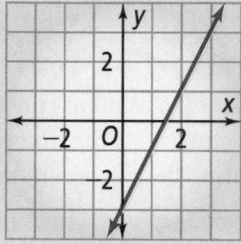

17. $y = 3 - 7x$

18. $y = -x$

19. $y = 3x^2$

20. $y = 4x^2 - 2$

21. $y = (x - 1)^2$

22. $y = (2 - x)^2$

 **Apply**

Find the inverse of each function. Is the inverse a function?

23. $f(x) = x^3$

24. $f(x) = x^4$

25. $f(x) = \frac{2x^2}{5} + 1$

26. $f(x) = 1.5x^2 - 4$

27. $f(x) = \frac{3x^2}{4}$

28. $f(x) = \sqrt{2x - 1} + 3$

29. a. Open-Ended Copy the mapping diagram at the right. Complete it by writing members of the domain and range and connecting them with arrows so that r is a function and r^{-1} is not a function.

   b. Repeat part (a) so that r is not a function and r^{-1} is a function.

Relation r

Domain   Range

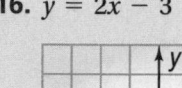

30. Reasoning To determine if the inverse of function f is also a function, you can use a *horizontal-line test*. It says that if no horizontal line intersects the graph of the function f in more than one point, then the inverse of f is a function.

   a. Explain why the horizontal-line test works.

   b. The graph of a polynomial function passes through the points $(-1, 1)$, $(0, 4)$ and $(2, 3)$. Can its inverse be a function?

6-7
PART 2

Inverse Relations and Functions

Objective To find the inverse of a relation or function

In Part 1 of the lesson, you learned how to find the inverse of a relation or function.

Connect to What You Know

Here you will learn how a function and its inverse are related and find compositions of inverse functions.

Lesson Vocabulary
• one-to-one function

Focus Question When is the inverse of a function also a function?

The inverse of a function f is denoted by f^{-1}. Read f^{-1} as "the inverse of f" or as "f inverse." The notation $f(x)$ is used for functions, but the relation f^{-1} may not even be a function.

Hint

The radicand and the principal square root cannot be negative.

Think

How could a graph help you check your answer?
You could graph f^{-1} and see whether the graph passes the vertical line test. If it does, f^{-1} is a function.

Problem 4 Finding an Inverse Function

Consider the function $f(x) = \sqrt{x - 2}$.

Ⓐ What are the domain and range of f?

The numbers $x \geq 2$ make up the domain, and the numbers $y \geq 0$ make up the range.

Ⓑ What is f^{-1}, the inverse of f?

Write the original equation.	$f(x) = \sqrt{x - 2}$
Rewrite the equation using y.	$y = \sqrt{x - 2}$
Switch x and y. Since x equals a principal square root, $x \geq 0$.	$x = \sqrt{y - 2}$
Square both sides.	$x^2 = y - 2$
Solve for y.	$y = x^2 + 2$

So, $f^{-1}(x) = x^2 + 2$, for $x \geq 0$.

Ⓒ What are the domain and range of f^{-1}?

From part (b), the domain of f^{-1} is the range of f—the numbers $x \geq 0$. Since $x^2 \geq 0$, $x^2 + 2 \geq 2$. Therefore, the numbers $y \geq 2$ make up the range of f^{-1}. Note that the range of f^{-1} is the same as the domain of f.

Ⓓ Is f^{-1} a function? Explain.

For each x in the domain ($x \geq 0$) of f^{-1}, there is only one value of y in the range. So $f^{-1}(x) = x^2 + 2$, $x \geq 0$, is a function.

Got It? 4. Let $g(x) = 6 - 4x$.

    a. What are the domain and range of g?

    b. What is the inverse of g?

    c. What are the domain and range of g^{-1}?

    d. Is g^{-1} a function? Explain.

Functions that model real-world behavior are often expressed as formulas with meaningful variables, like $A = \pi r^2$ for the area of a circle. Strictly speaking, the inverse formula would be $r = \pi A^2$, but this expresses a false relationship between A and r. It is better to leave the variables in place and solve for r as a function of A.

Original formula.
$$A = \pi r^2$$

Same formula, but inversely expressed.
$$r = \sqrt{\frac{A}{\pi}}$$

 Problem 5 Finding the Inverse of a Formula

The function $d = 4.9t^2$ represents the distance d, in meters, that an object falls in t seconds due to Earth's gravity. Find the inverse of this function. How long, in seconds, does it take for the cliff diver shown to reach the water below?

Think

Why shouldn't you interchange the variables?
Interchanging the variables leads to a false relationship between distance and time.

Write the equation.
$$d = 4.9t^2$$

Solve for t.
Do not switch the variables.
$$t^2 = \frac{d}{4.9}$$

Time must be nonnegative.
$$t = \sqrt{\frac{d}{4.9}}$$

Substitute 24 for d.
$$= \sqrt{\frac{24}{4.9}}$$

Use a calculator.
$$\approx 2.2$$

It will take about 2.2 seconds for the diver to reach the water.

24 meters

 Got It? 5. The function $d = \frac{v^2}{19.6}$ relates the distance d, in meters, that an object has fallen to its velocity v, in meters per second. Find the inverse of this function. What is the velocity of the cliff diver in meters per second as he enters the water?

Recall that each x-value in the domain of a function f corresponds to exactly one y-value in the range. For a **one-to-one function**, it is also true that each y-value in the range corresponds to exactly one x-value in the domain. A one-to-one function f has an inverse f^{-1} that is also a function. If f maps a to b, then f^{-1} must map b to a.

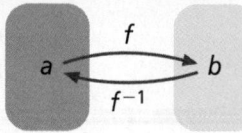

Domain of f   **Range of f**
Range of f^{-1}   **Domain of f^{-1}**

take note

Key Concept   Composition of Inverse Functions

If f and f^{-1} are inverse functions, then

$(f^{-1} \circ f)(x) = x$ and $(f \circ f^{-1})(x) = x$ for x in the domains of f and f^{-1}, respectively.

This says that the composition of a function and its inverse is essentially the identity function, $y = x$.

Problem 6   Composition of Inverse Functions

Let $f(x) = \frac{6}{x - 2}$. What is each of the following?

A $f^{-1}(x)$

Write the original equation.	$f(x) = \frac{6}{x - 2}$
Rewrite the equation using y.	$y = \frac{6}{x - 2}$
Switch x and y.	$x = \frac{6}{y - 2}$
Multiply each side by $y - 2$.	$x(y - 2) = 6$
Divide each side by x.	$y - 2 = \frac{6}{x}$
Add 2 to each side to solve for y.	$y = \frac{6}{x} + 2$

So, $f^{-1}(x) = \frac{6}{x} + 2$.

Think

Is this a function?
Yes. For each value of x, there is only one value for y.

B $(f \circ f^{-1})(2)$

Substitute 2 for x.	$(f \circ f^{-1})(2) = f(f^{-1}(2))$
Substitute in the definition of $f^{-1}(x)$.	$= f\left(\frac{6}{2} + 2\right)$
Simplify.	$= f(5)$
Substitute in the definition of $f(x)$.	$= \frac{6}{5 - 2} = 2$

C $(f^{-1} \circ f)(2)$

Substitute 2 for x.	$(f^{-1} \circ f)(2) = f^{-1}(f(2))$
Substitute in the definition of $f(x)$.	$= f^{-1}\left(\frac{6}{2 - 2}\right)$
Simplify.	$= f^{-1}\left(\frac{6}{0}\right)$

2 is not in the domain of f. Therefore $(f^{-1} \circ f)(2)$ does not exist.

$\underbrace{\qquad}$ undefined

Got It? 6. Let $g(x) = \frac{4}{x + 2}$. What is each of the following?

    a. $g^{-1}(x)$ **b.** $(g \circ g^{-1})(0)$ **c.** $(g^{-1} \circ g)(0)$

Focus Question When is the inverse of a function also a function?

Answer A function f has an inverse f^{-1} that is also a function when f is a one-to-one function. The composition of inverse functions is the identity function $y = x$.

Lesson Check

Do you know HOW?

1. For $h(x) = -\dfrac{1}{x+2}$, find:
  a. $h^{-1}(x)$
  b. $h^{-1}(4)$
  c. Value of x for which the equality $(h \circ h^{-1})(x) = x$ does not hold.

Do you UNDERSTAND?

2. Error Analysis A classmate says that $(f \circ g)^{-1}(x) = (f^{-1} \circ g^{-1})(x)$. Show that this is incorrect by finding examples of $f(x)$ and $g(x)$ for which the equation does not hold.

Practice and Problem-Solving Exercises

**Practice**

For each function, find the inverse and the domain and range of the function and its inverse. Determine whether the inverse is a function.

 **See Problem 4.**

Guided Practice

3. $f(x) = 3x + 4$

To start, identify the domain and range of f.

f is a linear function. Its domain and range are all real numbers.

4. $f(x) = 2x + 7$ **5.** $f(x) = \sqrt{x-5}$

6. $f(x) = \sqrt{x+7}$ **7.** $f(x) = \sqrt{-2x+3}$

8. $f(x) = 2x^2 + 2$ **9.** $f(x) = -x^2 + 1$

10. Temperature The formula for converting from Celsius to Fahrenheit temperatures is $F = \frac{9}{5}C + 32$.
  a. Find the inverse of the formula. Is the inverse a function?
  b. Use the inverse to find the Celsius temperature that corresponds to $25°F$.

See Problem 5.

11. Geometry The formula for the volume of a sphere is $V = \frac{4}{3}\pi r^3$.
  a. Find the inverse of the formula. Is the inverse a function?
  b. Use the inverse to find the radius of a sphere that has a volume of $35,000 \text{ ft}^3$.

For Exercises 12–15, $f(x) = 10x - 10$. **Find each value.**

◀ See Problem 6.

12. $(f^{-1} \circ f)(10)$

Guided Practice

To start, rewrite the equation for f using y.
Switch x and y.

$y = 10x - 10$
$x = 10y - 10$

13. $(f \circ f^{-1})(-10)$ **14.** $(f^{-1} \circ f)(0.2)$ **15.** $(f \circ f^{-1})(d)$

 **Apply**

16. Think About a Plan The velocity of the water that flows from an opening at the base of a tank depends on the height of water above the opening. The function $v(x) = \sqrt{2gx}$ models the velocity v in feet per second where g, the acceleration due to gravity, is about 32 ft/s² and x is the height in feet of the water. What is the depth of water when the flow is 40 ft/s? When the flow is 20 ft/s?
- How can you use inverse functions to help you find the answer?
- What restrictions are on the domain of $v(x)$? of $v^{-1}(x)$?

17. Let $f(x) = 3x^2 - 4$ and $g(x) = x - 2$. Calculate $(f \circ g^{-1})(x)$ for $x = -3$.

18. Writing Explain how you can find the range of the inverse of $f(x) = \sqrt{x - 1}$ without finding the inverse itself.

For each function, find the inverse and the domain and range of the function and its inverse. Determine whether the inverse is a function.

19. $f(x) = -\sqrt{x}$ **20.** $f(x) = \sqrt{x} + 3$

21. $f(x) = \sqrt{-x + 3}$ **22.** $f(x) = \sqrt{x + 2}$

23. $f(x) = \dfrac{x^2}{2}$ **24.** $f(x) = \dfrac{1}{x^2}$

25. $f(x) = (x - 4)^2$ **26.** $f(x) = (7 - x)^2$

27. $f(x) = \dfrac{1}{(x + 1)^2}$ **28.** $f(x) = 4 - 2\sqrt{x}$

29. $f(x) = \dfrac{3}{\sqrt{x}}$ **30.** $f(x) = \dfrac{1}{\sqrt{-2x}}$

31. Reasoning Relation r has one element in its domain and two elements in its range. Is r a function? Is the inverse of r a function? Explain.

32. Geometry Write a function that gives the length of the hypotenuse of an isosceles right triangle with side length s. Evaluate the inverse of the function to find the side length of an isosceles right triangle with a hypotenuse of 6 in.

33. Open-Ended Write a function f such that the graph of f^{-1} lies only in Quadrants III and IV.

Standardized Test Prep

34. Which pair of words make this statement FALSE?
The product of two ___(I)___ numbers is always a(n) ___(II)___ number.

Ⓐ (I) complex; (II) complex

Ⓑ (I) real; (II) complex

Ⓒ (I) rational; (II) real

Ⓓ (I) imaginary; (II) imaginary

35. If $f(x) = x + 1$ and $g(x) = x^2 - 3x - 4$, what is $(f \circ g)(x)$?

Ⓕ $x^2 - 3x - 3$ 　　　　　　　　　Ⓗ $x^2 - x$

Ⓖ $x^2 - x - 6$ 　　　　　　　　　Ⓘ $x^2 - x - 3$

36. What is the simplified form of $\left(a^{\frac{2}{3}} b^{\frac{3}{4}} \right)^2$?

Ⓐ $a^{\frac{4}{9}} b^{\frac{9}{16}}$ 　　　　　　　　　Ⓒ ab

Ⓑ $a^{\frac{4}{3}} b^{\frac{3}{2}}$ 　　　　　　　　　Ⓓ $(ab)^{\frac{17}{6}}$

37. Let $f(x) = (x + 1)^2 - 2$. Find the x- and y-intercepts of the graph of $f(x)$ and the inverse of $f(x)$. Is the inverse a function?

Mixed Review

Let $f(x) = 4x$, $g(x) = \frac{1}{2}x + 7$, and $h(x) = -2x + 4$.
Perform each function operation.

◀ **See Lesson 6-6.**

38. $(g \circ f)(x)$ 　　　　　**39.** $(h \circ g)(x)$ 　　　　　**40.** $h(x) + g(x)$

41. $f(x) \cdot g(x)$ 　　　　　**42.** $(f \circ g)(x) + h(x)$ 　　　　　**43.** $(f \circ g)(x)$

Find each real root.

◀ **See Lesson 6-1.**

44. $-\sqrt[4]{16}$ 　　　　　**45.** $\sqrt[4]{-16}$ 　　　　　**46.** $\sqrt[5]{243}$

47. $-\sqrt[5]{243}$ 　　　　　**48.** $\sqrt[5]{-243}$ 　　　　　**49.** $\sqrt[3]{0.064}$

Get Ready! **To prepare for Lesson 6-8, do Exercises 50–52.**

Graph each function.

◀ **See Lesson 4-1.**

50. $y = -x^2 - 1$ 　　　　　**51.** $y = -(x + 1)^2 + 1$ 　　　　　**52.** $y = 3x^2 + 3$

Graphing Inverses

You can graph inverses of functions on a graphing calculator by using the **DrawInv** feature or by using parametric equations. It takes more keystrokes to set up parametric equations, but once you do you can easily change from one function to another and quickly see the graphs of the new function and its inverse.

Activity

Graph $y = 0.3x^2 + 1$ and its inverse.

Method 1   Use the **DrawInv** feature.

> **Step 1**   Press **y=** and enter the equation. Press **zoom** 5 to see a graph of the function with equal x- and y-intervals.

> **Step 2**   Press **2nd** **draw** 8. You will see **DrawInv** followed by a flashing cursor. Select equation Y_1 by pressing **vars** ▷ 1 1. Press **enter** to see the graph of the function and its inverse.

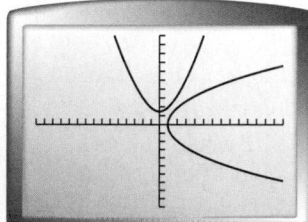

Method 2   Use parametric equations.

> **Step 1**   Set to parametric mode. Press **mode**, select **Par**, and press **2nd** **quit**.

> **Step 2**   Enter the given equation in parametric form. Press **y=** and enter the equations $X_{1T} = T$ and $Y_{1T} = .3T^2 + 1$.

> **Step 3**   Now use $X_{2T} = Y_{1T}$ and $Y_{2T} = X_{1T}$ to interchange the x- and y-values of the first parametric equation. Press **y=** and move the cursor to follow $X_{2T} =$. Select Y_{1T} by pressing **vars** ▷ 2 2. Enter the equation $Y_{2T} = X_{1T}$ in a similar fashion.

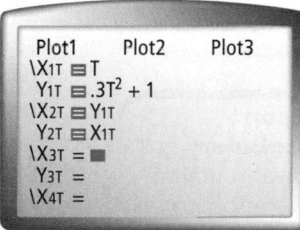

> **Step 4**   Press **zoom** 5. Adjust the **Window** so that **Tmin** and **Tmax** approximately agree with **Xmin** and **Xmax**. Press **graph** to see the graph of the function and its inverse.

Exercises

Graph each function and its inverse with a graphing calculator.
Then sketch the graphs.

1. $y = x^2 - 5$ **2.** $y = (x - 3)^2$ **3.** $y = 0.01x^4$ **4.** $y = 0.5x^3 - 3$

5. Writing   Change the parametric equation $X_{2T} = Y_{1T}$ in Method 2, Step 3 to $X_{2T} = -Y_{1T}$. Describe the graph that results.

6. Explain how once you set up parametric equations, you can change from one function to another and quickly see the graphs of the new function and its inverse.

6-8 Graphing Radical Functions

Objective To graph square root and other radical functions

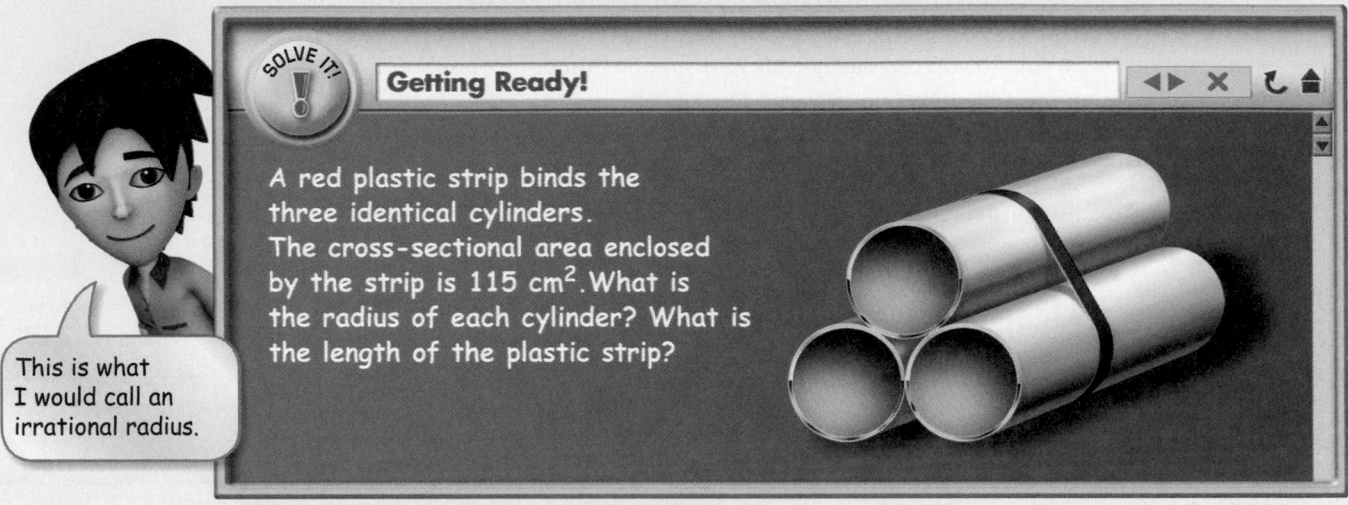

Getting Ready!

A red plastic strip binds the three identical cylinders. The cross-sectional area enclosed by the strip is 115 cm². What is the radius of each cylinder? What is the length of the plastic strip?

This is what I would call an irrational radius.

Dynamic Activity
Radical Functions

Lesson Vocabulary
• radical function
• square root function

The formula $A = \pi r^2$ shows that area is a quadratic function of the radius of a circle. The formula $r = \frac{1}{\sqrt{\pi}} \sqrt{A}$ shows that the radius of a circle is a square root function of the area.

Focus Question How is graphing a radical function similar to graphing a power function?

A horizontal line can intersect the graph of $f(x) = x^2$ in two points—where $f(-2) = f(2)$, for example. Thus, a vertical line can intersect the graph of f^{-1} in two points. f^{-1} is *not* a function because it fails the vertical line test.

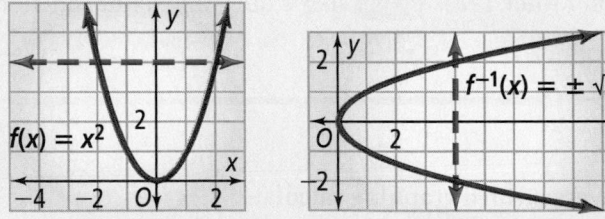

However, you can restrict the domain of f so that the inverse of the restricted function is a function.

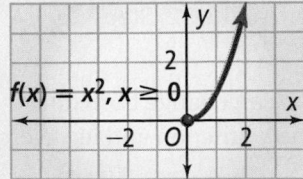

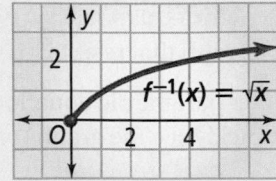

Inverses of the power functions $y = x^n$ (with domains restricted as needed) form parent functions $y = \sqrt[n]{x}$ for families of **radical functions**. In particular, $f(x) = \sqrt{x}$ is the parent for the family of **square root functions**. Members of this family have the general form $f(x) = a\sqrt{x - h} + k$.

take note

Key Concepts   Families of Radical Functions

	Square Root	**Radical**
Parent function:	$y = \sqrt{x}$	$y = \sqrt[n]{x}$
Reflection in x-axis:	$y = -\sqrt{x}$	$y = -\sqrt[n]{x}$
Stretch ($a > 1$), shrink ($0 < a < 1$) by the factor a:	$y = a\sqrt{x}$	$y = a\sqrt[n]{x}$
Translation: Horizontal by h Vertical by k	$y = \sqrt{x - h} + k$	$y = \sqrt[n]{x - h} + k$

ONLINE PROBLEMS **Problem 1** Translating a Square Root Function Vertically

Think

How is $y = \sqrt{x} + k$ related to the parent function $y = \sqrt{x}$?
It is related to the parent function in the same way that $y = f(x) + k$ is related to $y = f(x)$. It is a vertical translation of k units.

What are the graphs of $y = \sqrt{x} - 2$ and $y = \sqrt{x} + 1$?

The graph of $y = \sqrt{x} - 2$ is the graph of $y = \sqrt{x}$ shifted down 2 units.

The graph of $y = \sqrt{x} + 1$ is the graph of $y = \sqrt{x}$ shifted up 1 unit.

The domains of both functions are the set of nonnegative numbers, but their ranges differ.

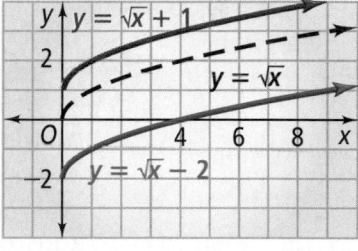

 Got It? 1. What are the graphs of $y = \sqrt{x} + 2$ and $y = \sqrt{x} - 3$?

ONLINE PROBLEMS **Problem 2** Translating a Square Root Function Horizontally

Think

How is $y = \sqrt{x - h}$ related to the parent function $y = \sqrt{x}$?
It is a horizontal translation of h units.

What are the graphs of $y = \sqrt{x + 4}$ and $y = \sqrt{x - 1}$?

The graph of $y = \sqrt{x + 4}$ is the graph of $y = \sqrt{x}$ shifted left 4 units.

The graph of $y = \sqrt{x - 1}$ is the graph of $y = \sqrt{x}$ shifted right 1 unit.

The ranges of both functions are the set of nonnegative numbers, but their domains differ.

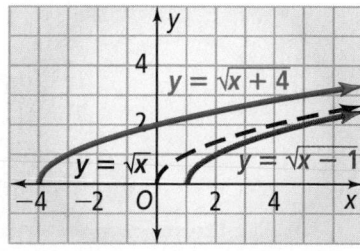

 Got It? 2. What are the graphs of $y = \sqrt{x - 3}$ and $y = \sqrt{x + 2}$?

Recall from Lesson 2-7 that for any transformation $y = af(x - h) + k$ of the parent function $f(x)$, a indicates a vertical stretch or shrink.

Similarly, for the combined transformation $y = a\sqrt{x - h} + k$, a indicates a vertical stretch ($|a| > 1$) or shrink ($0 < |a| < 1$). A negative value of a indicates a reflection in the x-axis.

Think

What would be good points to choose?
Points that have integer x- and y-coordinates.

Problem 3 Graphing a Square Root Function

What is the graph of $y = -\frac{1}{2}\sqrt{x - 3} + 1$?

Step 1 Choose several points from the parent function $y = \sqrt{x}$: $(0, 0)$, $(1, 1)$, $(4, 2)$.

Step 2 Multiply the y-coordinates by $a = -\frac{1}{2}$. This shrinks the parent graph vertically by the factor $\frac{1}{2}$ and reflects the result in the x-axis.

Step 3 The values of h and k give the horizontal and vertical translations. Translate the graph from Step 2 right 3 units and up 1 unit.

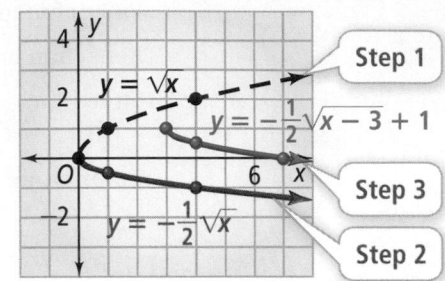

Got It? **3.** What is the graph of $y = 3\sqrt{x + 2} - 4$?

Problem 4 Solving a Radical Equation by Graphing

Multiple Choice You can model the population P of Corpus Christi, Texas, between the years 1970 and 2005 by the radical function $P(x) = 75{,}000 \sqrt[3]{x - 1950}$, where x is the year. Using this model, in what year was the population of Corpus Christi 250,000?

Think

How can you rewrite a radical function using an exponent?
You can write a radical function $y = \sqrt[n]{x}$ as $y = x^{\frac{1}{n}}$.

  Ⓐ 1980   Ⓑ 1983   Ⓒ 1987   Ⓓ 1990

For $P = 250000$, solve the equation $250000 = 75000 \sqrt[3]{x - 1950}$.

Graph **Y1 = 75000(X − 1950)^(1/3)** and **Y2 = 250000**. Adjust the window to find where the graphs intersect.

Use the **INTERSECT** feature to find the x-coordinate of the intersection.

In the year 1987, the population of Corpus Christi was 250,000. The correct answer is C.

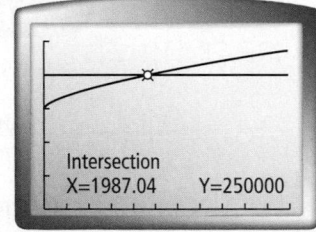

Got It? **4.** In what year was the population of Corpus Christi 275,000?

Problem 4 uses a transformation of $y = \sqrt[3]{x}$. The function $f(x) = \sqrt[3]{x}$ is the inverse of $g(x) = y^3$. Unlike $y = \sqrt{x}$, the domain and range of $f(x) = \sqrt[3]{x}$ are all real numbers.

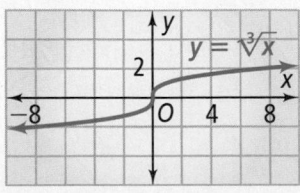

The patterns for graphing square root functions apply to other radical functions.

Problem 5 Graphing a Cube Root Function

What is the graph of $y = 2\sqrt[3]{x + 1} - 4$?

Step 1   Graph the parent function, $y = \sqrt[3]{x}$.

Step 2   Multiply the y-coordinates by 2.
This stretches the graph vertically.

Step 3   Translate the graph from Step 2,
1 unit to the left and 4 units down.

Got It? **5.** What is the graph of
$y = 3 - \frac{1}{2}\sqrt[3]{x - 2}$?

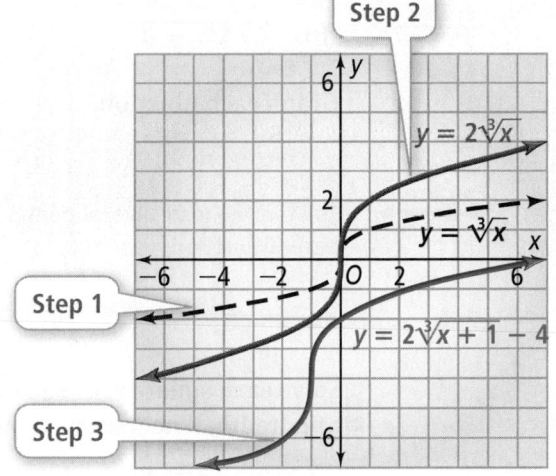

Step 2

Step 1

Step 3

$y = 2\sqrt[3]{x}$

$y = \sqrt[3]{x}$

$y = 2\sqrt[3]{x + 1} - 4$

Plan

How is
$y = a\sqrt[x]{x - h} + k$
related to its parent function?
a stretches or shrinks the parent function and h and k translate it horizontally and vertically.

Focus Question   How is graphing a radical function similar to graphing a power function?

Answer   The process for graphing a radical function is exactly the same as graphing a power function. Start by graphing the parent function $y = \sqrt[n]{x}$. Then use the general form of a radical function to identify and perform transformations on the parent function just as you did for graphs of power functions.

 Lesson Check

Do you know HOW?

Graph each function.

1. $y = -\sqrt{x} + 3$

2. $y = -\sqrt[3]{x} + 5$

3. $y = \sqrt{x - 4}$

4. $y = \sqrt[3]{x + 6}$

Do you UNDERSTAND?

5. Writing Explain the effect that a has on the graph of $y = a\sqrt{x}$. How does this compare to its effect on other functions you have studied?

6. Error Analysis Your friend states that the graph of the function $g(x) = \sqrt{-x - 1}$ is a reflection of the graph of the function $f(x) = -\sqrt{x + 1}$ in the x-axis. Describe your friend's error.

Practice and Problem-Solving Exercises

A Practice

Graph each function. ◀ **See Problems 1 and 2.**

7. $y = \sqrt{x} - 2$ **8.** $y = \sqrt{x} - 4$ **9.** $y = \sqrt{x} + 5$

10. $y = \sqrt{x - 3}$ **11.** $y = \sqrt{x + 1}$ **12.** $y = \sqrt{x + 6}$

Graph each function. ◀ **See Problem 3.**

Guided Practice

13. $y = -\sqrt{x - 1}$

To start, choose several points from the parent function, $y = \sqrt{x}$.

$(0, 0), (1, 1), (4, 2), (9, 3)$

14. $y = 3\sqrt{x}$ **15.** $y = -5\sqrt{x + 2}$ **16.** $y = 3\sqrt{x + 1} + 4$

Solve each square root equation by graphing. Round the answer to the nearest hundredth, if necessary. If there is no solution, explain why. ◀ **See Problem 4.**

17. $\sqrt{x - 3} = 12$ **18.** $\sqrt{2x - 3} = 4$ **19.** $\sqrt{2x + 5} = \sqrt{2 - x}$

20. Landscaping A sprinkler can water between 1 and 130 square yards of a lawn. The length L in inches of rotating pipe needed to water A square yards is given by the function $L = 117.75\sqrt{A}$.
   a. Graph the equation on your calculator. Make a sketch of the graph.
   b. How much area can be watered if the length of the pipe is 500, 800, or 1,300 inches long?

Graph each function. ◀ **See Problem 5.**

Guided Practice

21. $y = \sqrt[3]{x} - 4$

To start, graph the parent function, $y = \sqrt[3]{x}$.

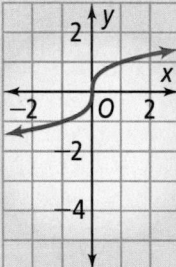

22. $y = \sqrt[3]{x + 2} - 7$ **23.** $y = -\sqrt[3]{x + 3} - 1$ **24.** $y = 2\sqrt[3]{x - 6} - 9$

25. Think About a Plan The time t in seconds for a pendulum to complete one full cycle is given by the function $t = 1.11\sqrt{l}$, where l is the length of the pendulum in feet. How long is a pendulum that takes 4.5 seconds to complete one full cycle? 6 seconds to complete one full cycle? Round your answers to the nearest hundredth.

- How can you use a graph to approximate the length of a pendulum?
- How can you check your answers algebraically?

Graph each function. Find the domain and the range.

26. $y = 4\sqrt[3]{x-2} + 1$ **27.** $y = \frac{1}{2}\sqrt{x-1} + 3$ **28.** $y = 3\sqrt[3]{x-6} + 2$

29. Suppose that a function pairs elements from set A with elements from set B. Recall that a function is called *onto* if it pairs every element in B with at least one element in A.

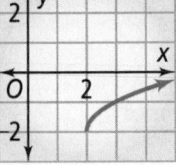

a. The graph shows a transformation of $y = \sqrt{x}$. Write the function.
b. What are the domain and range of the function?
c. For the domain, is the function onto the set of nonnegative real numbers? Explain.

30. Open-Ended Write a radical function such that for its domain, the function is onto the set of real numbers such that $y \le 3$.

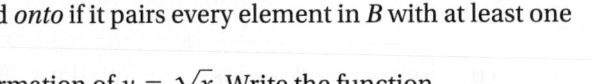**Graphing Calculator** **Solve the following radical equations.**

31. $2\sqrt{x} = \sqrt{(x+1)}$ **32.** $\sqrt{(x+3)} = 4\sqrt{(x)} - 2$ **33.** $\sqrt[3]{x-1} = \sqrt{x} - 1$

34. a. Solve $3 - \sqrt{(x-3)} = x$ algebraically.
b. Solve the equation from part (a) graphically.
c. What do you notice about your answer to part (a) compared to your answer to part (b)?

35. Electronics The size of a computer monitor is given as the length of the screen's diagonal d in inches. The equation $d = \frac{5}{6}\sqrt{3A}$ models the length of a diagonal of a monitor screen with area A in square inches.
a. Graph the equation on your calculator.
b. Suppose you want to buy a new monitor with a screen that has twice the area of your old screen. Your old screen has a diagonal of 15 inches. What will be the diagonal of your new screen?

36. Physics You can model time t, in seconds, an object takes to reach the ground falling from height H, in meters, by $t(H) = \sqrt{\frac{2H}{g}}$. The value of g is 9.81 m/s². If an object takes 7 seconds to fall to the ground, what was its initial height?

Standardized Test Prep

SAT/ACT

37. How is the graph of $y = \sqrt{x} - 5$ translated from the graph of $y = \sqrt{x}$?

  Ⓐ shifted 5 units left   Ⓒ shifted 5 units up

  Ⓑ shifted 5 units right   Ⓓ shifted 5 units down

38. Which is the composition $f(g(x))$, if $f(x) = -x - 3$ and $g(x) = 7 + 5x$?

  Ⓐ $f(g(x)) = 4x + 4$ Ⓒ $f(g(x)) = -5x - 8$

  Ⓑ $f(g(x)) = 4x - 10$ Ⓓ $f(g(x)) = -5x - 10$

39. Which polynomial cannot be factored in the real number system?

  Ⓐ $x^2 - 3x + 2$ Ⓒ $4x^2 - 1$

  Ⓑ $x^2 + 4$ Ⓓ $2x^2y - 2xy^2$

Short Response

40. How do the domains and ranges of the functions $f(x) = \sqrt{x - 1}$ and $g(x) = \sqrt{x} - 1$ compare?

Mixed Review

Find the inverse of each function. Is the inverse a function?   ◀ **See Lesson 6-7.**

41. $f(x) = \frac{2}{3}x - 3$ **42.** $f(x) = \sqrt{x + 3} - 4$ **43.** $f(x) = (2x + 1)^2$

Rationalize the denominator of each expression. Assume that all   ◀ **See Lesson 6-2.**
variables are positive.

44. $\dfrac{\sqrt{36x^3}}{\sqrt{12y}}$ **45.** $\dfrac{\sqrt[3]{x}}{\sqrt[3]{3y}}$ **46.** $\sqrt[5]{\dfrac{3x^3}{2y}}$

Solve using the Quadratic Formula.   ◀ **See Lesson 4-7.**

47. $x^2 - 9x + 15 = 0$ **48.** $3x^2 + 9x = 27$ **49.** $5x^2 + x = 3$

Get Ready!   To prepare for Lesson 7-1, do Exercises 50–52.

Evaluate each expression for the given value of x.   ◀ **See Lesson 1-3.**

50. 2^x for $x = 3$ **51.** 4^{x+1} for $x = 1$ **52.** 2^{3x+4} for $x = -1$

Pull It **All Together**

To solve these problems, you will pull together concepts and skills related to roots and radical functions.

BIG idea Solving Equations and Inequalities

Solving an equation is the process of rewriting the equation to make what it says about its variables as simple as possible.

Task 1

An environmental equipment supplier sells hemispherical holding ponds for treatment of chemical waste. The volume of a pond is $V_1 = \frac{1}{2}\left(\frac{4}{3}\pi r_1^3\right)$, where r_1 is the radius in feet. The supplier also sells cylindrical collecting tanks. A collecting tank fills completely and then drains completely to fill the empty pond. The volume of the tank is $V_2 = 12\pi r_2^2$, where r_2 is the radius of the tank.

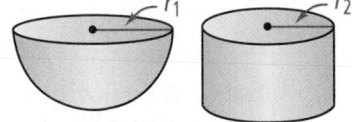

   a. Since $V_1 = V_2$, write an equation that shows r_1 as a function of r_2. Write an equation that shows r_2 as a function of r_1.

   b. You want to double the radius of the pond. How will the radius of the tank change?

BIG idea Solving Equations and Inequalities

The numbers and types of solutions vary based on the type of equation.

BIG idea Function

You can represent functions in a variety of ways (such as graphs, tables, equations, or words). Each representation is particularly useful in certain situations.

Task 2

Suppose $f(x) = \sqrt{x + 1}$.

   a. What are the domain and range of f?

   b. Find $f^{-1}(x)$. What are its domain and range? Be careful!

   c. Show that $(f \circ f^{-1})(a) = a = (f^{-1} \circ f)(a)$ for any a in the respective domains.

   d. Solve the equation $f(x) = f^{-1}(x)$. Remember to check for extraneous roots.

   e. Graph the functions f and f^{-1}. Be sure that you accurately represent the domains of each function. Interpret graphically the solutions(s) you found to the equation in part (d).

Connecting BIG ideas and Answering the Essential Questions

1 Equivalence
You can simplify the nth root of an expression that contains an nth power as a factor.

$$\sqrt[n]{x^n} = x^{\frac{n}{n}} = \begin{cases} x, n \text{ odd} \\ |x|, n \text{ even} \end{cases}$$

Radical Expressions and Rational Exponents (Lessons 6-1, 6-2 and 6-4)

$$\sqrt[3]{-8x^5}\ \sqrt[3]{x^2} = \sqrt[3]{-8x^7}$$
$$= \sqrt[3]{(-2)^3 x^6 \cdot x}$$
$$= -2x^2 \sqrt[3]{x}$$

$$(-8x^5)^{\frac{1}{3}}(x^2)^{\frac{1}{3}} = (-8x^7)^{\frac{1}{3}}$$
$$= ((-2)^3 \cdot x^6 \cdot x)^{\frac{1}{3}}$$
$$= -2x^2\, x^{\frac{1}{3}}$$

Solving Square Root Equations (Lesson 6-5)

$$x - 2 = \sqrt{x}$$
$$x^2 - 4x + 4 = x$$
$$x^2 - 5x + 4 = 0$$
$$(x - 4)(x - 1) = 0$$
$$x = 4 \text{ or } x = 1$$
$$4 - 2 = \sqrt{4}\ \checkmark$$
$$1 - 2 \neq \sqrt{1}\ \times$$

2 Solving Equations and Inequalities
When you square each side of an equation, the resulting equation may have more solutions than the original equation.

Inverse Relations and Functions (Lesson 6-7)

The inverse of $y = \sqrt{x} + 2, x \geq 0, y \geq 2$ is $x = \sqrt{y} + 2$, or $\sqrt{y} = x - 2$, or $y = (x - 2)^2, y \geq 0, x \geq 2$.

Graphing Radical Functions (Lesson 6-8)

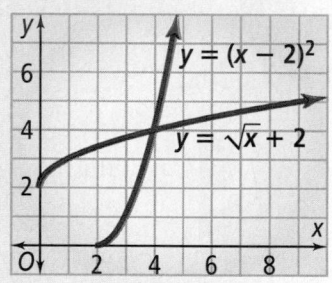

3 Function
If f and f^{-1} are inverse functions and if one maps a to b, then the other maps b to a, i.e.,

$$(f \circ f^{-1})(a) = (f^{-1} \circ f)(a)$$
$$= a.$$

Chapter Vocabulary

- composite function (p. 428)
- inverse function (p. 433)
- inverse relation (p. 433)
- one-to-one function (p. 439)
- radical equation (p. 417)
- radical function (p. 445)
- square root equation (p. 417)
- square root function (p. 445)

Choose the correct term to complete each sentence.

1. (Radical functions/Inverse functions) are of the form $f(x) = \sqrt[n]{x}$.

2. When two functions are combined so the range of one becomes the domain of the other, the resulting function is called a (square root function/composite function).

3. Reflecting the graph of function $f(x)$ in the line $y = x$ produces the graph of the (inverse relation/one-to-one function) of f.

6-5 Solving Square Root and Other Radical Equations

Quick Review

To solve a **radical equation**, you must isolate a radical expression on one side of the equation. You can then rewrite the radical expression using a rational exponent and use the reciprocal of the exponent to solve the equation.

For a rational exponent $\frac{m}{n}$ with either m or n even, $\left(x^{\frac{m}{n}}\right)^{\frac{n}{m}} = |x|$. Check all possible solutions in the original equation to eliminate extraneous solutions.

Example

What is the solution of $4(x - 2)^{\frac{2}{3}} = 16$?

Divide each side by 4.	$(x - 2)^{\frac{2}{3}} = 4$
Raise both sides to the $\frac{3}{2}$ power.	$\left((x - 2)^{\frac{2}{3}}\right)^{\frac{3}{2}} = 4^{\frac{3}{2}}$
Use the Law of Exponents.	$(x - 2)^{\frac{6}{6}} = 4^{\frac{3}{2}}$
Use $\left(x^{\frac{m}{n}}\right)^{\frac{n}{m}} = |x|$, since $m = 2$ is even.	$|x - 2| = 8$
Solve for x.	$x = 10$ or $x = -6$

Exercises

Solve each equation. Check for extraneous solutions.

4. $2 + \sqrt{x + 5} = 4$

5. $3\sqrt{2x + 6} = 18$

6. $5(3x + 1)^{\frac{1}{4}} = 10$

7. $4(3x - 3)^{\frac{2}{3}} = 36$

8. $\sqrt{3x + 3} - 1 = x$

9. $\sqrt{x + 6} + 2 = x + 6$

10. $\sqrt{5x + 1} - 2\sqrt{x} = 1$

11. $\sqrt{2x + 9} - \sqrt{x} = 3$

12. Electricity The power P, in watts, that a circular solar cell produces and the radius of the cell r in centimeters are related by the square root equation $r = \sqrt{\frac{P}{0.02\pi}}$. About how much power is produced by a cell with a radius of 12 cm?

6-6 Function Operations

Quick Review

When performing function operations, you can use the same rules you used for real numbers, but you must take into consideration the domain and range of each function. The composition of function g with function f is defined as $(g \circ f)(x) = g(f(x))$.

Example

Let $f(x) = x + 3$ and $g(x) = x^2 - 2$. What is $(g \circ f)(-2)$?

Evaluate $f(-2)$.	$g(f(-2)) = g((-2) + 3)$
Simplify.	$= g(1)$
Evaluate $g(f(-2))$.	$= (1)^2 - 2$
Simplify.	$= -1$

Therefore, $(g \circ f)(-2) = -1$.

Exercises

Let $f(x) = x - 4$ and $g(x) = x^2 - 16$. Perform each function operation and then find the domain.

13. $f(x) + g(x)$ **14.** $g(x) - f(x)$

15. $f(x) \cdot g(x)$ **16.** $\frac{g(x)}{f(x)}$

Let $g(x) = 5x - 2$ and $h(x) = x^2 + 1$. Find the value of each expression.

17. $(h \circ g)(-1)$ **18.** $(h \circ g)(0)$

19. $(g \circ h)(2)$ **20.** $(g \circ h)(a)$

21. Discounts A grocery store is offering a 50% discount off a $4.00 box of cereal. You also have a $1.00 off coupon for the same cereal. Use a composite function to show whether it is better to use the coupon before or after the store discount.

6-7 Inverse Relations and Functions

Quick Review

If (a, b) is an ordered pair of a relation, then (b, a) is an ordered pair of its **inverse relation**. If a relation or function is described by an equation in x and y, you can interchange x and y to get the inverse. The inverse of a function is denoted by f^{-1}.

Example

What is the inverse of $f(x) = \sqrt{x - 10}$?

Rewrite the equation using y.	$y = \sqrt{x - 10}$
Interchange x and y.	$x = \sqrt{y - 10}$
Square each side.	$x^2 = y - 10$
Add 10 to each side to solve for y.	$y = x^2 + 10$

$f^{-1}(x) = x^2 + 10$ for $x \geq 10$

Exercises

Find the inverse of each function. Determine whether each inverse is a function.

22. $f(x) = 2x^2 - 8$ **23.** $f(x) = 15 - 3x$

24. $f(x) = \sqrt{x + 6}$ **25.** $f(x) = (2x - 3)^2$

Graph each function and its inverse. Describe the domain and range of each.

26. $f(x) = 4x - 1$ **27.** $f(x) = (x + 3)^2$

28. $f(x) = \sqrt{x - 3}$ **29.** $f(x) = 6 - 5x^2$

30. Geometry The volume of cube is determined by the formula $V = s^3$, where s is the length of one side. Find the inverse formula. Use it to find the side length of a cube with a volume of 64 ft^3.

6-8 Graphing Radical Functions

Quick Review

The function $f(x) = \sqrt{x}$ is the parent function of the **square root function** $f(x) = a\sqrt{x - h} + k$. The graph of $f(x) = a\sqrt{x}$ is a stretch ($a > 1$) or a shrink ($0 < a < 1$) of the parent function. The graph of $f(x) = a\sqrt{x - h} + k$ is a translation h units horizontally and k units vertically of $y = a\sqrt{x}$. The graph of $f(x) = \sqrt[n]{x}$ is transformed by a, h, and k in the same way as the graph of $f(x) = \sqrt{x}$.

Example

Describe the graph of $y = 4\sqrt{x - 3} - 2$.

Compare the equation to the general form.	$y = a\sqrt{x - h} + k$
	$y = 4\sqrt{x - 3} + (-2)$

The graph of $y = 4\sqrt{x - 3} - 2$ is the graph of $y = 4\sqrt{x}$ translated 3 units to the right and 2 units down.

Exercises

Graph each function. Find the domain and range.

31. $y = \sqrt{x} - 5$

32. $y = \sqrt{x + 8}$

33. $y = 5\sqrt{x} + 9$

34. $y = -\sqrt{x - 4}$

35. $y = \sqrt[3]{x} + 10$

36. $y = -\sqrt[3]{x - 2} + 5$

Solve each equation by graphing.

37. $5 = -\sqrt{x - 3}$

38. $\sqrt{8x - 16} = 2\sqrt{x + 2}$

6 Chapter Test for Part B

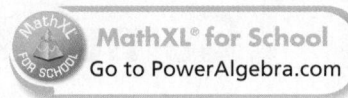
MathXL® for School
Go to PowerAlgebra.com

Do you know HOW?

Simplify each radical expression. Use absolute value symbols when needed.

1. $\sqrt{54x^3y^5}$

2. $\sqrt[3]{-0.027}$

3. $\sqrt[5]{-64x^{14}y^{20}}$

Simplify each expression. Rationalize all denominators.

4. $\sqrt{7x^3} \cdot \sqrt{14x}$

5. $\dfrac{1 - \sqrt{3x}}{\sqrt{6x}}$

6. $\sqrt{48} + 2\sqrt{27} + 5\sqrt{12}$

7. $(3 + 2\sqrt{5})(1 - \sqrt{20})$

8. $4\sqrt{7xz} + 2\sqrt{7xz}$

9. $\dfrac{5\sqrt{2}}{\sqrt{7} - \sqrt{2}}$

Simplify each expression.

10. $(125)^{-\frac{2}{3}}$

11. $x^{\frac{1}{6}} \cdot x^{\frac{1}{3}}$

12. $\left(\dfrac{8x^9y^3}{27x^2y^{12}}\right)^{\frac{2}{3}}$

13. $\sqrt{8x^5} - \sqrt{18x^5}$

Solve each equation. Check for extraneous solutions.

14. $\sqrt{x - 3} = x - 5$

15. $\sqrt{x + 4} = \sqrt{3x}$

16. $2(x - 1)^{\frac{3}{4}} = 16$

17. $\sqrt{x + 3} - 1 = x$

Let $f(x) = x - 2$ and $g(x) = x^2 - 3x + 2$. Perform each function operation and then find the domain.

18. $-2g(x) + f(x)$

19. $-f(x) \cdot g(x)$

20. $\dfrac{g(x)}{f(x)}$

Find each product or quotient.

21. $\sqrt{5}\,(\sqrt[4]{5})$

22. $\dfrac{\sqrt{x^3}}{\sqrt[5]{x^2}}$

For each pair of functions, find $(g \circ f)(x)$ and $(f \circ g)(x)$.

23. $f(x) = x^2 - 2,\ g(x) = 4x + 1$

24. $f(x) = 2x^2 + x - 7,\ g(x) = -3x - 1$

Find the inverse of each function. Is the inverse a function?

25. $f(x) = (x + 3)^2 + 1$

26. $f(x) = \sqrt{2x + 1}$

27. $g(x) = 3x^3 - 4$

28. $f(x) = \frac{1}{4}x$

Graph. Find the domain and range of each function.

29. $y = 2\sqrt{x} + 3$

30. $y = -\sqrt{2x + 3}$

31. $y = \sqrt{x + 3} - 4$

Do you UNDERSTAND?

32. **Writing** Explain why -108 has no real 6th roots.

33. **Open-Ended** Write a relation that is not a function, but whose inverse is a function.

34. **Measurement** The time t in seconds for a swinging pendulum to complete one full cycle is given by the function $t = 0.2\sqrt{l}$, where l is the length of the pendulum in centimeters. To the nearest tenth, how long is a full cycle if the pendulum is 10 cm long? 20 cm long? How long, in centimeters, is a pendulum that takes 2 seconds for one full cycle?

TIPS FOR SUCCESS

Some problems require you to find the inverse of a function.

What is the inverse of the function
$y = x^2 + 3$?

A. $y = x - 3$

B. $y = \pm\sqrt{x - 3}$

C. $y = \pm\sqrt{x^2 + 3}$

D. $y = (x - 3)^2$

TIP 2
After you interchange x and y, solve for y.

TIP 1
To find the inverse of a function, interchange x and y.

Think It Through
$y = x^2 + 3$
$x = y^2 + 3$
$x - 3 = y^2$
$\pm\sqrt{x - 3} = y$
$y = \pm\sqrt{x - 3}$
The correct answer is B.

Vocabulary Review

As you solve test items, you must understand the meanings of mathematical terms. Match each term with its mathematical meaning.

A. radicand

B. index

C. composite function

D. inverse functions

E. radical function

I. the combination of two functions such that the output from the first becomes the input for the second

II. the degree of a root in a radical expression

III. the number under the radical sign in a radical expression

IV. a function that can be written in the form $f(x) = a\sqrt[n]{x - h} + k$

V. the range of one function is the domain of the other and vice versa

Multiple Choice

Read each question. Then write the letter of the correct answer on your paper.

1. Find all the roots of $2x^4 + x^3 - 8x^2 - 4x = 0$.

A. $x = -2, x = -0.5, x = 0, x = 2$

B. $x = -2, x = -0.5, x = 2$

C. $x = -2, x = 0.5, x = 0, x = 2$

D. $x = -2, x = 0.5, x = 2$

2. Solve the equation $ax^2 + bx + c = 0$ for b.

F. $b = -cx - ax^2$

H. $b = -(cx - ax^2)$

G. $b = \frac{-c - ax^2}{x}$

I. $b = \frac{-(c - ax^2)}{x}$

3. Use the sum of cubes formula to factor $x^3 + 64$.

A. $(x + 4)(x^2 - 4x + 4)$

B. $(x + 4)(x^2 + 4x + 4)$

C. $(x + 4)(x^2 - 4x + 16)$

D. $(x + 4)(x^2 + 4x + 16)$

4. The time it takes to copy pages varies directly with the number of pages being copied. The copier at your office can copy 21 color pages per minute and 40 black and white pages per minute. Approximately how long will it take to copy 60 color pages and 35 black and white pages?

   F 0.9 minute   H 2.9 minutes

   G 2.5 minutes   I 3.7 minutes

5. Which equation is modeled by the graph?

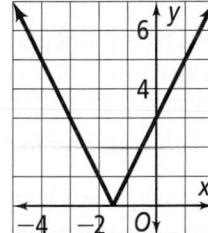

   A $y = |2x - 3|$ C $y = |2x + 3|$

   B $y = 2|x - 3|$ D $y = 2|x + 3|$

6. What are the vertex and axis of symmetry for the given parabola?

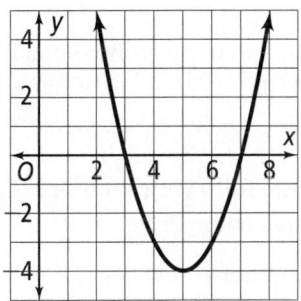

   F $(-4, 5), y = 5$ H $(5, -4), y = -4$

   G $(-4, 5), x = 5$ I $(5, -4), x = 5$

7. What is the product of $\sqrt[3]{3}$ and $\sqrt[5]{3}$?

   A $\sqrt[8]{3}$ C $\sqrt[15]{3^8}$

   B $\sqrt[8]{9}$ D $\sqrt[8]{3^{15}}$

8. Solve the equation $x^2 - 6x = 3$ by completing the square.

   F $-3 \pm 2\sqrt{3}$ H $-3 \pm 3\sqrt{2}$

   G $3 \pm 2\sqrt{3}$ I $3 \pm 3\sqrt{2}$

9. Solve $7x^2 + 196 = 0$ for x.

   A $\pm 4i\sqrt{7}$ C $\pm 2i\sqrt{7}$

   B $\pm 4\sqrt{7}$ D $\pm 2\sqrt{7}$

10. Which inequality is modeled by the line graph?

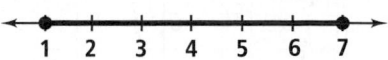

   F $k + 1 \le 7$ H $k - 4 \le 3$

   G $|k + 1| \le 7$ I $|k - 4| \le 3$

11. Which equation represents a line that contains the point $(3, 2)$ and is parallel to $y = 3x - 12$?

   A $y = \frac{1}{3}x - 7$ C $y = 3x - 3$

   B $y = 3x - 7$ D $y = \frac{1}{3}x - 3$

12. Which is the first *incorrect* step in simplifying $\sqrt[3]{x^9 y^6 z}$?

Step 1: $\sqrt[3]{x^9 y^6 z} = \sqrt[3]{x^9} \cdot \sqrt[3]{y^6} \cdot \sqrt[3]{z}$

Step 2: $= x^3 \cdot \sqrt[3]{y^6} \cdot \sqrt[3]{z}$

Step 3: $= x^3 \cdot y^3 \cdot \sqrt[3]{z}$

   F Step 1

   G Step 2

   H Step 3

   I Each step is correct.

13. A photographer is promoting three photo specials. How much does it cost for each type of print?

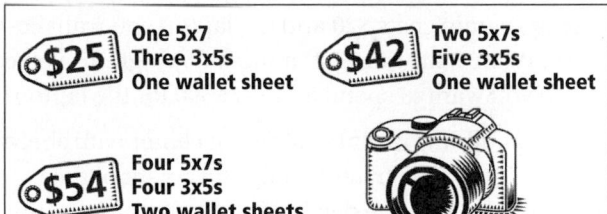

   A 5 × 7 costs \$7, 3 × 5 costs \$5, Wallet costs \$3

   B 5 × 7 costs \$11, 3 × 5 costs \$7, Wallet costs \$3

   C 5 × 7 costs \$12, 3 × 5 costs \$11, Wallet costs \$7

   D 5 × 7 costs \$7, 3 × 5 costs \$5, Wallet costs \$5

14. What is an equivalent form of $\frac{5}{2 + 2i}$?

   F $\frac{5}{4i}$ H $\frac{5 + 5i}{4}$

   G $\frac{10 - 10i}{4 - 4i}$ I $\frac{5 - 5i}{4}$

15. The graph shows a transformation of $f(x) = x^2$. What is an equation of the graph?

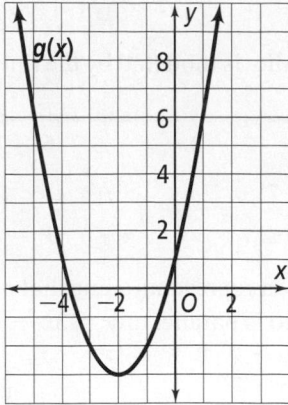

Ⓐ $g(x) = (x - 2)^2 - 3$ Ⓒ $g(x) = (x + 2)^2 - 3$

Ⓑ $g(x) = (x - 2)^2 + 3$ Ⓓ $g(x) = (x + 2)^2 + 3$

16. The total cost of $x + 2$ markers is $x^3 + 5x^2 + 2x - 8$. What is the cost of each marker?

Ⓕ $x^2 + 3x - 4$ Ⓗ $x^2 - 3x - 4$

Ⓖ $x^2 - 3x + 4$ Ⓘ $x^2 + 5x + 2$

GRIDDED RESPONSE

17. Let $g(x) = x - 3$ and $h(x) = x^2 + 6$. What is $(h \circ g)(1)$?

18. A laptop comes without any programs installed on it. Each program costs \$20 and the laptop you want costs \$319. What is the greatest number of programs you can buy if you want to spend at most \$500 for the laptop?

19. You are building an entertainment center with shelves that are x in. deep by x in. long. The height of the unit will be twice the depth. If the volume of the unit will be 8192 in.^{3}, what is the height, in inches, of the entertainment center?

20. Use Descartes' Rule of Signs to find the maximum number of positive real roots of $P(x) = 5x^4 + x^3 - 4x^2 + 3x + 1$.

21. Using the discriminant, determine the number of real roots of the equation $2x^2 + 3x = 4$.

22. What is the quotient $\dfrac{\sqrt[3]{8x^6 y^{12}}}{\sqrt{4x^4 y^8}}$?

23. What is the solution of $4 + \sqrt{3x + 5} = 7$?

24. Simplify the expression $256^{-\frac{3}{4}}$.

25. All 385 tickets for a high-school play sold in 10 days. The ticket receipts totaled \$1960. If the cost of a child's ticket was \$4 and the cost of an adult's ticket was \$6, how many adult tickets were sold?

26. What is the x-value of the x-intercept of the graph of $f(x) = x^2 + 4x + 4$?

Short Response

27. You are given that $f(x) = x^2 + 4$ and $g(x) = 3x - 1$.
  a. What are the domain and range of $f(x)$ and $g(x)$?
  b. Find $f(x) + g(x)$.
  c. What is the domain of your answer to part (b)?

28. Two friends went together. One friend bought 2 hats and 1 shirt and spent \$70, while the other friend bought 1 hat and 3 shirts and spent \$85. Use a graph to determine the costs of each shirt and hat.

29. A student found that a cubic function has zeros 16 and $1 - 2i$ with a leading coefficient of 3. What is the constant term of this polynomial function with real coefficients?

30. Describe the graph of the polynomial function $f(x) = -x^6 + 3x^5 + 4x - 10$. What is its end behavior?

Decide whether the following statements are *always*, *sometimes*, or *never* true.

31. If n is a real number, then $0^n = 0$.

32. If a and b are rational numbers, then the product of $(a + \sqrt{b})$ and its conjugate is a rational number.

Extended Response

33. An online music store is having a promotion. Customers receive a \$5 rebate if they buy any regular priced CD at \$13 each. They can also receive 15% off if they register as a store member.
  a. What functions model the two discounts?
  b. In which order should the discounts be applied for the customer to receive the greatest discount?
  c. Use part (b) to determine the amount a customer will save if she buys 5 CDs.

Get Ready!

Lesson 1-3 ◆ Evaluating Expressions

Evaluate each expression for $x = -2, 0,$ and 2.

1. 10^{x+1} **2.** $\left(\frac{3}{2}\right)^x$ **3.** -5^{x-2} **4.** $-(3)^{0.5x}$

Lesson 2-5 ◆ Using Linear Models

Draw a scatter plot and find the line of best fit for each set of data.

5. $(0, 2), (1, 4), (2, 6.5), (3, 8.5), (4, 10), (5, 12), (6, 14)$

6. $(3, 100), (5, 150), (7, 195), (9, 244), (11, 296), (13, 346), (15, 396)$

Lessons 4-1 and 5-9 ◆ Graphing Transformations

Identify the parent function of each equation. Graph each equation as a transformation of its parent function.

7. $y = (x + 5)^2 - 3$ **8.** $y = -2(x - 6)^3$

Lesson 6-4 ◆ Simplifying Rational Exponents

Simplify each expression.

9. $\left(x^{\frac{1}{5}}\right)^{10}$ **10.** $\left(-8x^3\right)^{\frac{4}{3}}$

Lesson 6-7 ◆ Finding Inverses

Find the inverse of each function. Is the inverse a function?

11. $y = 10 - 2x^2$ **12.** $y = (x + 4)^3 - 1$

Looking Ahead Vocabulary

13. In advertising, the *decay factor* describes how an advertisement loses its effectiveness over time. In math, would you expect a decay factor to increase or decrease the value of y as x increases?

14. There are many different kinds of growth patterns. Patterns that increase by a constant rate are linear. Patterns that grow *exponentially* increase by an ever-increasing rate. If your allowance doubles each week, does that represent linear growth or exponential growth?

15. The word *asymptote* comes from a Greek word meaning "not falling together." When looking at the end behavior of a function, do you expect the graph to intersect its asymptote?

CHAPTER 7

Exponential and Logarithmic Functions

PowerAlgebra.com

Your place to get all things digital

Download videos connecting math to your world.

Math definitions in English and Spanish

The online Solve It will get you in gear for each lesson.

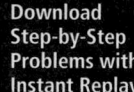

Interactive! Vary numbers, graphs, and figures to explore math concepts.

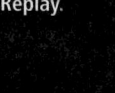

Download Step-by-Step Problems with Instant Replay.

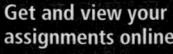

Get and view your assignments online.

Extra practice and review online

"
Logarithms provide a way to work with the inverses of exponential functions.

Exponential functions model what some might call "explosive" growth, but logarithmic values grow very slowly. Decibels are logarithms that measure sound, and when sound energy increases dramatically, the decibel values creep upward. A few extra decibels can bust your eardrums!
"

Vocabulary

English/Spanish Vocabulary Audio Online:

English	Spanish
asymptote, p. 463	asíntota
Change of Base Formula, p. 493	fórmula de cambio de base
common logarithm, p. 482	logaritmo común
exponential decay, p. 463	decremento exponencial
exponential equation, p. 498	ecuación exponencial
exponential function, p. 462	función exponencial
exponential growth, p. 463	incremento exponencial
logarithm, p. 480	logaritmo
logarithmic equation, p. 503	ecuación logarítmica
logarithmic function, p. 483	función logarítmica

My Math Video

00:04:04   VIDEO ▶

BIG ideas

1 Modeling
Essential Question How do you model a quantity that changes regularly over time by the same percentage?

2 Equivalence
Essential Question How are exponents and logarithms related?

3 Function
Essential Question How are exponential functions and logarithmic functions related?

Chapter Preview

Exploring Exponential Models

Objective To model exponential growth and decay

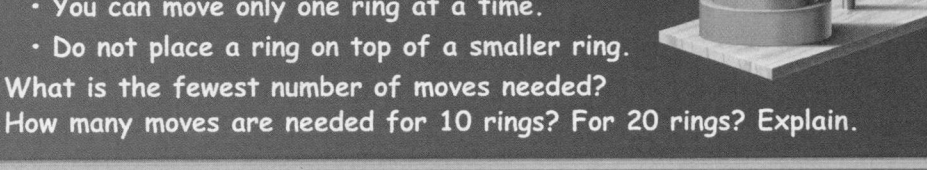

SOLVE IT!

Getting Ready!

You are to move the stack of 5 rings to another post. Here are the rules.

• A move consists of taking the top ring from one post and placing it onto another post.

• You can move only one ring at a time.

• Do not place a ring on top of a smaller ring.

What is the fewest number of moves needed?

How many moves are needed for 10 rings? For 20 rings? Explain.

This is a famous puzzle. Variations of it show up in many video games.

Lesson Vocabulary

• exponential function
• exponential growth
• exponential decay
• asymptote
• growth factor
• decay factor

The number of moves needed for additional rings in the Solve It suggests a pattern that approximates repeated multiplication. You can represent repeated multiplication with a function of the form $y = ab^x$ where b is a positive number other than 1.

Focus Question What is an exponential function?

An **exponential function** has the general form $y = ab^x$, $a \neq 0$, with $b > 0$, and $b \neq 1$. In an exponential function, the base b is a constant. The exponent x is the independent variable with domain the set of real numbers.

Plan

How does making a table help you sketch the graph?
The table shows coordinates of several points on the graph.

Problem 1 Graphing an Exponential Function

A What is the graph of $y = 2^x$?

Step 1
Make a table of values.

x	2^x	y
-4	2^{-4}	$\frac{1}{16} = 0.0625$
-3	2^{-3}	$\frac{1}{8} = 0.125$
-2	2^{-2}	$\frac{1}{4} = 0.25$
-1	2^{-1}	$\frac{1}{2} = 0.5$

x	2^x	y
0	2^0	1
1	2^1	2
2	2^2	4
3	2^3	8

Step 2
Plot and connect the points.

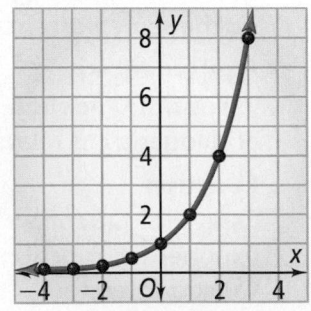

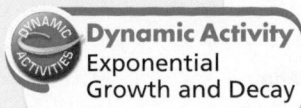
B What is the graph of $y = \left(\frac{1}{2}\right)^x$?

Step 1
Make a table of values.

x	$\left(\frac{1}{2}\right)^x$	y
-3	$\left(\frac{1}{2}\right)^{-3}$	$2^3 = 8$
-2	$\left(\frac{1}{2}\right)^{-2}$	$2^2 = 4$
-1	$\left(\frac{1}{2}\right)^{-1}$	$2^1 = 2$
0	$\left(\frac{1}{2}\right)^{0}$	$2^0 = 1$

x	$\left(\frac{1}{2}\right)^x$	y
1	$\left(\frac{1}{2}\right)^{1}$	$\frac{1}{2} = 0.5$
2	$\left(\frac{1}{2}\right)^{2}$	$\frac{1}{4} = 0.25$
3	$\left(\frac{1}{2}\right)^{3}$	$\frac{1}{8} = 0.125$
4	$\left(\frac{1}{2}\right)^{4}$	$\frac{1}{16} = 0.0625$

Step 2
Plot and connect the points.

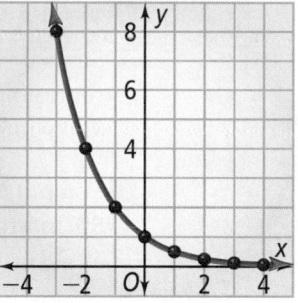

 Got It? **1.** What is the graph of each function?

    a. $y = 4^x$ **b.** $y = \left(\frac{1}{3}\right)^x$ **c.** $y = 2(3)^x$

    d. Reasoning What generalizations can you make about the domain, range, and y-intercepts of these functions?

Two types of exponential behavior are *exponential growth* and *exponential decay*.

For **exponential growth**, as the value of x increases, the value of y increases. For **exponential decay**, as the value of x increases, the value of y decreases, approaching zero.

The exponential functions shown here are *asymptotic* to the x-axis. An **asymptote** is a line that a graph approaches as x or y increases in absolute value.

> Exponential Decay
>
> Exponential Growth
>
> The x-axis is an asymptote.

Hint

Asymptote comes from the Greek word <u>asymptotos</u>, meaning "not meeting."

take note

Concept Summary   Exponential Functions

For the function $y = ab^x$,

- if $a > 0$ and $b > 1$, the function represents exponential growth.
- if $a > 0$ and $0 < b < 1$, the function represents exponential decay.

In either case, the y-intercept is $(0, a)$, the domain is all real numbers, the asymptote is $y = 0$, and the range is $y > 0$.

Problem 2 Identifying Exponential Growth and Decay

Identify each function or situation as an example of exponential growth or decay. What is the *y*-intercept?

Ⓐ $y = 12(0.95)^x$

Since $0 < b < 1$, the function represents exponential decay. The *y*-intercept is $(0, a) = (0, 12)$

Ⓑ $y = 0.25(2)^x$

Since $b > 1$, the function represents exponential growth. The *y*-intercept is $(0, a) = (0, 0.25)$.

Ⓒ **You put $1000 into a college savings account for four years. The account pays 5% interest annually.**

The amount of money in the bank grows by 5% annually. It represents exponential growth. The *y*-intercept is 1000, which is the dollar value of the initial investment.

Think

What quantity does the *y*-intercept represent?
The *y*-intercept is the amount of money at $t = 0$, which is the initial investment.

 Got It? 2. Identify each function or situation as an example of exponential growth or decay. What is the *y*-intercept?

a. $y = 3(4^x)$

b. $y = 11(0.75^x)$

c. You put $2000 into a college savings account for four years. The account pays 6% interest annually.

Hint

Growth rate refers to the value of r.
Growth factor refers to the value of b, or 1 + r.

For exponential growth $y = ab^x$, with $b > 1$, the value b is the **growth factor**. A quantity that exhibits exponential growth increases by a constant percentage each time period. The percentage increase r, written as a decimal, is the *rate of increase* or *growth rate*. For exponential growth, $b = 1 + r$.

For exponential decay, $0 < b < 1$ and b is the **decay factor**. The quantity decreases by a constant percentage each time period. The percentage decrease, r, is the *rate of decay*. For exponential decay, $b = 1 + r$, so r is a negative quantity.

take note

Key Concept Exponential Growth and Decay

You can model exponential growth or decay with this function.

Amount after t time periods

Rate of growth ($r > 0$) or decay ($r < 0$)

$$A(t) = a(1 + r)^t$$

Initial amount

Number of time periods

For growth or decay to be exponential, a quantity changes by a fixed percentage each time period.

Problem 3 Modeling Exponential Growth

You invested $1000 in a savings account at the end of 6th grade.
The account pays 5% annual interest. How much money will be
in the account after six years?

Step 1 Determine if an exponential function is a reasonable model.

The money grows at a fixed rate of 5% per year.
An exponential model is appropriate.

Step 2 Define the variables and determine the model.

Let t = the number of years since the money was invested.
Let $A(t)$ = the amount in the account after each year.

A reasonable model is $A(t) = a(1 + r)^t$.

Step 3 Use the model to solve the problem.

<table>
<tr><td>Write the model.</td><td>$A(t) = A(1 + r)^t$</td></tr>
<tr><td>Substitute $a = 1000$, $r = 0.05$, and $t = 6$.</td><td>$A(6) = 1000(1 + 0.05)^6$</td></tr>
<tr><td>Simplify inside the parentheses.</td><td>$= 1000(1.05)^6$</td></tr>
<tr><td>Simplify. Round to two decimal places.</td><td>≈ 1340.10</td></tr>
</table>

Think

What is the growth rate r?
It is the annual interest rate, written as a decimal: 5% = 0.05.

Check Use a graphing calculator to check your answer.

Graph **Y1 = 1000(1.05)^X** and find y when
x is 6.

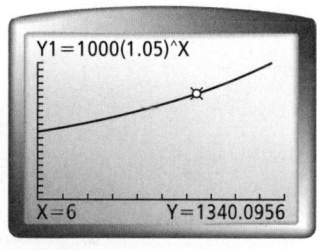

Y1=1000(1.05)^X

X=6   Y=1340.0956

The account contains $1340.10 after six years.

 Got It? 3. a. Suppose you invest $500 in a savings account that pays 3.5% annual interest.
How much will be in the account after five years?

b. Reasoning In Problem 3, would there ever be *exactly* $1300 in
the account? Explain your reasoning.

Hint

For part (b), check whether the function is continuous.

To model a discrete situation using an exponential function of the form $y = ab^x$,
you need to find the growth or decay factor b. If you know y-values for two
consecutive x-values, you can find the rate of change r using $r = \frac{y_2 - y_1}{y_1}$ and
then find b using $b = 1 + r$.

Problem 4 **Writing an Exponential Function**

Endangered Species The table shows the world population of the Iberian lynx in 2003 and 2004. If this trend continues and the population is decreasing exponentially, how many Iberian lynx will there be in 2014?

Use the general form of the exponential equation,
$y = ab^x = a(1 + r)^x$.

Step 1 Define the variables.

> Let x = the number of years since 2003.
> Let y = the population of the Iberian lynx.

Think

How can you find the value of r?
You can use the populations for two consecutive years to find r.

Step 2 Determine r.

> Use the populations for 2003 and 2004.
>
> | | |
> |---|---|
> | Write the equation for r. | $r = \dfrac{y_2 - y_1}{y_1}$ |
> | Substitute $y_1 = 150$ and $y_2 = 120$. | $= \dfrac{120 - 150}{150}$ |
> | Simplify. | $= -0.2$ |

World Population of Iberian Lynx

Year	2003	2004
Population	150	120

Step 3 Use r to determine b.

> | | |
> |---|---|
> | Write the equation for b. | $b = 1 + r$ |
> | Substitute $r = -0.2$. | $= 1 + (-0.2)$ |
> | Simplify. | $= 0.8$ |

Step 4 Write the model.

> | | |
> |---|---|
> | Write the general form of an exponential function. | $y = ab^x$ |
> | Substitute. Use the initial values $x = 0$ and $y = 150$. | $150 = a(0.8)^0$ |
> | Solve for a. | $150 = a$ |

> The model is $y = 150(0.8)^x$.

Think

How do you find the x-value corresponding to 2014?
The initial x-value corresponds to 2003, so find the difference.

Step 5 Use the model to find the population in 2014.

> For the year 2014, $x = 2014 - 2003 = 11$.
>
> | | |
> |---|---|
> | Write the model. | $y = 150(0.8)^x$ |
> | Substitute 11 for x and simplify. | $= 150(0.8)^{11} \approx 13$ |

If the 2003–2004 trend continues, there will be approximately 13 Iberian lynx in the wild in 2014.

 Got It? **4. a.** For the model in Problem 4, what will be the world population of Iberian lynx in 2020?

> **b. Reasoning** If you graphed the model in Problem 4, would it ever cross the x-axis? Explain.

Focus Question What is an exponential function?

Answer An exponential function is a function in which the independent variable is the exponent. The general form is $y = ab^x$, where $a \neq 0$, $b > 0$, and $b \neq 1$. The graph of an exponential function has a horizontal asymptote. Use an exponential function to model exponential growth or decay.

Lesson Check

Do you know HOW?

Without graphing, determine whether the function represents exponential growth or exponential decay. Then find the y-intercept.

1. $y = 10(0.45)^x$ **2.** $y = 0.75(4)^x$

3. $y = 3^x$ **4.** $y = 0.95^x$

Graph each function.

5. $A(t) = 3(1.04)^t$ **6.** $A(t) = 7(0.6)^t$

Do you UNDERSTAND?

7. Vocabulary Explain how you can tell if $y = ab^x$ represents exponential growth or exponential decay.

8. Reasoning Identify each function as *linear*, *quadratic*, or *exponential*. Explain your reasoning.
    a. $y = 3(x + 1)^2$ **b.** $y = 4(3)^x$
    c. $y = 2x + 5$ **d.** $y = 4(0.2)^x + 1$

9. Error Analysis A classmate says that the growth factor of the exponential function $y = 15(0.3)^x$ is 0.3. What is the student's mistake?

Practice and Problem-Solving Exercises

Ⓐ Practice

Graph each function.
    ◀ See Problem 1.

10. $y = 6^x$ **11.** $y = 1000(2)^x$ **12.** $y = 9(3)^x$

13. $f(x) = 2(3)^x$ **14.** $s(t) = 1.5^t$ **15.** $y = 2^{2x}$

Without graphing, determine whether the function represents exponential growth or exponential decay. Then find the y-intercept.
    ◀ See Problem 2.

16. $y = 129(1.63)^x$ **17.** $f(x) = 2(0.65)^x$ **18.** $y = 12\left(\frac{17}{10}\right)^x$

19. $y = 0.8\left(\frac{1}{8}\right)^x$ **20.** $y = 0.45(3)^x$ **21.** $y = \frac{1}{100}\left(\frac{4}{3}\right)^x$

22. Population The world population in 2000 was approximately 6.08 billion. The annual rate of increase was about 1.26%. If this rate of increase continues, what will be the approximate world population in 2050?
    ◀ See Problem 3.

23. Interest Suppose you deposit $2000 in a savings account that pays interest at an annual rate of 4%. If no money is added or withdrawn from the account, answer the following questions.
    a. How much will be in the account after 3 years?
    b. How much will be in the account after 18 years?
    c. How many years will it take for the account to contain $2500?
    d. How many years will it take for the account to contain $3000?

Write an exponential function to model each situation. Find each amount after the specified time.

◀ See Problem 4.

Guided Practice ➡

24. A population of 120,000 grows 1.2% per year for 15 years.

To start, record what you know.   Initial amount: 120,000
                                    Growth rate: 1.2%
                                    Number of time periods: 15

Then write the growth rate as a decimal.   1.2% = 0.012

25. A population of 1,860,000 decreases 1.5% each year for 12 years.

26. a. **Sports** Before a basketball game, a referee noticed that the ball seemed under-inflated. She dropped it from 6 feet and measured the first bounce as 36 inches and the second bounce as 18 inches. Write an exponential function to model the height of the ball.
    b. How high was the ball on its fifth bounce?

B Apply

27. **Think About a Plan** Your friend invested $1000 in an account that pays 6% annual interest. How much interest will your friend have after her college graduation in 4 years?
    • Is an exponential model reasonable for this situation?
    • What equation should you use to model this situation?
    • Is the solution of the equation the final answer to the problem?

For each annual rate of change, find the corresponding growth or decay factor.

28. +70%   29. −75%   30. −55%

31. −0.1%   32. +0.1%   33. +100%

34. **Oceanography** The function $y = 20(0.975)^x$ models the intensity of sunlight beneath the surface of the ocean. The output y represents the percent of surface sunlight intensity that reaches a depth of x feet. The model is accurate from about 20 feet to about 600 feet beneath the surface.
    a. Find the percent of sunlight 50 feet beneath the surface of the ocean.
    b. Find the percent of sunlight at a depth of 370 feet.

 35. **Population** The population of a certain animal species decreases at a rate of 3.5% per year. You have counted 80 of the animals in the habitat you are studying.
    a. Write a function that models the change in the animal population.
    b. Graph the function. Estimate the number of years until the population first drops below 15 animals.

36. **Business** A computer valued at $6500 depreciates at the rate of 14.3% per year.
    a. Write a function that models the value of the computer.
    b. Find the value of the computer after three years.

Standardized Test Prep

SAT/ACT

37. Which function represents the value after x years of a new delivery van that costs $25,000 and depreciates 15% each year?

Ⓐ $y = -15(25{,}000)^x$　　　　　　Ⓒ $y = 25{,}000(0.85)^x$

Ⓑ $y = 25{,}000(0.15)^x$　　　　　　Ⓓ $y = 25{,}000(1.15)^x$

38. What is $f(x) = 3x^{\frac{1}{3}}$ for $x = \frac{1}{125}$?

Ⓕ 15　　　　　Ⓖ $\frac{3}{5}$　　　　　Ⓗ $\frac{\sqrt[3]{3}}{5}$　　　　　Ⓘ $5\sqrt[3]{3}$

39. What is the simplified form of $\frac{2 + i}{2 - i}$?

Ⓐ -1　　　Ⓑ $\frac{3 + 4i}{3}$　　　Ⓒ $\frac{5 + 4i}{5}$　　　Ⓓ $\frac{3 + 4i}{5}$

40. Which graph represents the equation $y = x^2 - x - 2$?

Ⓕ 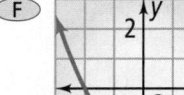　　Ⓖ 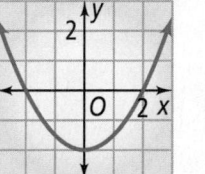　　Ⓗ 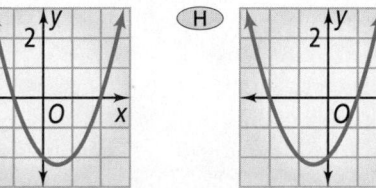　　Ⓘ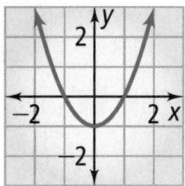

Extended Response

41. You are driving a car when a deer suddenly darts across the road in front of you. Your brain registers the emergency and sends a signal to your foot to hit the brake. The car travels a reaction distance D, in feet, during this time, where D is a function of the speed r, in miles per hour, that the car is traveling when you see the deer, given by $D(r) = \frac{11r + 5}{10}$. Find the inverse and explain what it represents. Is the inverse a function?

Mixed Review

Graph each function.　　　　　　　　　　　　　　　　　　● **See Lesson 6-8.**

42. $y = 3 - 2\sqrt{x + 2}$　　　**43.** $y = 3\sqrt[3]{2x - 1}$　　　**44.** $y = -2 + \sqrt{x}$

Factor the expression.　　　　　　　　　　　　　　　　　● **See Lesson 4-4.**

45. $8 + 27x^3$　　　**46.** $3x^2 + 11x - 4$　　　**47.** $25 - 40x + 16x^2$

Solve the system of equations using a matrix.　　　　　　● **See Lesson 3-6.**

48. $\begin{cases} x + 5y = -4 \\ x + 6y = -5 \end{cases}$　　**49.** $\begin{cases} 3a + 5b = 0 \\ a + b = 0 \end{cases}$　　**50.** $\begin{cases} -x + 2y = 0 \\ y = -2x + 3 \end{cases}$

Get Ready! To prepare for Lesson 7-2, do Exercises 51–53.

Graph each function.　　　　　　　　　　　　　　　　　　● **See Lesson 7-1.**

51. $y = 3^x$　　　**52.** $y = 0.75^x$　　　**53.** $y = 0.5(4)^x$

7-2
PART 1

Properties of Exponential Functions

Objective To explore the properties of functions of the form $y = ab^x$

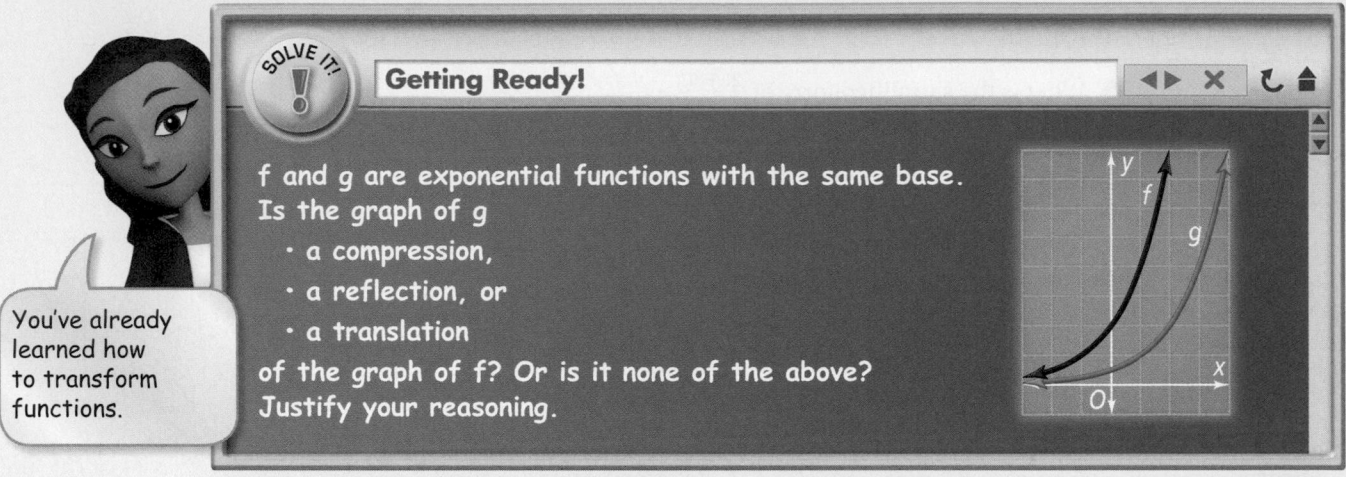

SOLVE IT!

Getting Ready!

◀▶ ✕ ↻ ⬆

f and g are exponential functions with the same base. Is the graph of g
- a compression,
- a reflection, or
- a translation

of the graph of f? Or is it none of the above? Justify your reasoning.

You've already learned how to transform functions.

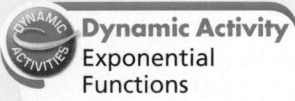

Dynamic Activity
Exponential Functions

You can apply the four types of transformations—stretches, compressions, reflections, and translations—to exponential functions.

Focus Question What are the transformations on exponential functions?

The graphs of $y = 2^x$ (in red) and $y = 3 \cdot 2^x$ (in blue) are shown. Each y-value of $y = 3 \cdot 2^x$ is 3 times the corresponding y-value of the parent function $y = 2^x$.

x	$y = 2^x$	$y = 3 \cdot 2^x$
−2	$\frac{1}{4}$	$\frac{3}{4}$
−1	$\frac{1}{2}$	$\frac{3}{2}$
0	1	3
1	2	6
2	4	12

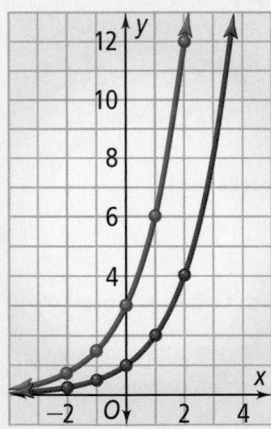

$y = 3 \cdot 2^x$ stretches the graph of the parent function $y = 2^x$ by the factor 3.

Problem 1 Graphing $y = ab^x$

Think

Which *x*-values should you use to make a table?
Use $x = 0$ and then choose both positive and negative values.

How does the graph of each function compare to the graph of the parent function?

A $y = 0.5 \cdot 2^x$

Step 1 Make a table of values.

x	$y = 2^x$	$y = 0.5 \cdot 2^x$
−2	0.25	0.125
−1	0.5	0.25
0	1	0.5
1	2	1
2	4	2

Each value is 0.5 times the corresponding value of the parent function.

Step 2 Graph the function.

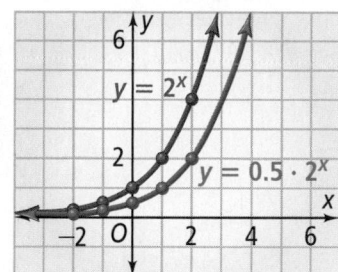

The "0.5" in $y = 0.5 \cdot 2^x$ compresses the graph of the parent function $y = 2^x$ by the factor 0.5. The domain, range, and asymptote remain unchanged. The *y*-intercept becomes 0.5.

B $y = -\frac{1}{3} \cdot 3^x$

Step 1 Make a table of values.

x	$y = 3^x$	$y = -\frac{1}{3} \cdot 3^x$
−2	$\frac{1}{9}$	$-\frac{1}{27}$
−1	$\frac{1}{3}$	$-\frac{1}{9}$
0	1	$-\frac{1}{3}$
1	3	−1
2	9	−3

Each value is $-\frac{1}{3}$ times the corresponding value of the parent function.

Step 2 Graph the function.

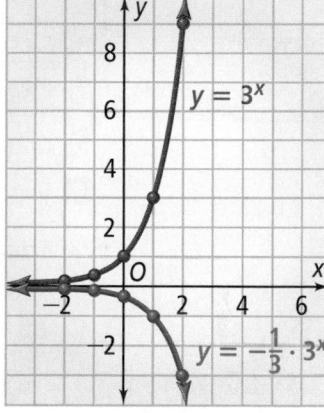

The "$-\frac{1}{3}$" in $y = -\frac{1}{3} \cdot 3^x$ reflects the graph of the parent function $y = 3^x$ across the *x*-axis and compresses it by the factor $\frac{1}{3}$. The domain and asymptote remain unchanged. The *y*-intercept becomes $-\frac{1}{3}$ and the range becomes $y < 0$.

 Got It? **1.** How does the graph of each function compare to the graph of the parent function?

a. $y = 2 \cdot 4^x$ **b.** $y = -0.5 \cdot 5^x$

Hint

You can add the exponents if the bases are the same.
$a(b^{-h} \cdot b^x) = a(b^{(-h+x)})$
$= ab^{(x-h)}$

A horizontal shift $y = ab^{(x-h)}$ is the same as the vertical stretch or compression $y = (ab^{-h})b^x$. A vertical shift $y = ab^x + k$ also shifts the horizontal asymptote from $y = 0$ to $y - k$.

Problem 2 Translating the Parent Function $y = b^x$

How does the graph of each function compare to the graph of the parent function?

Think

How is the graph of $y = 2^{(x-4)}$ different from the graph of $y = 2^x$?

The graph of $y = 2^{(x-4)}$ is a horizontal translation of $y = 2^x$ to the right 4 units.

A $y = 2^{(x-4)}$

Step 1
Make a table of values for $y = 2^x$.

x	$y = 2^x$
−2	0.25
−1	0.5
0	1
1	2
2	4

Step 2
Graph $y = 2^x$, and translate to the right 4 units.

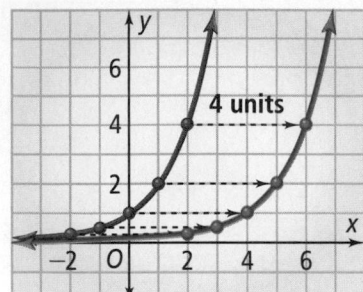

The "$(x - 4)$" in $y = 2^{(x-4)}$ translates the graph of $y = 2^x$ to the right 4 units.
The asymptote remains $y = 0$. The y-intercept becomes $\frac{1}{16}$.

Check Use a graphing calculator to graph $y = 2^{(x-4)}$. Find the y-intercept.

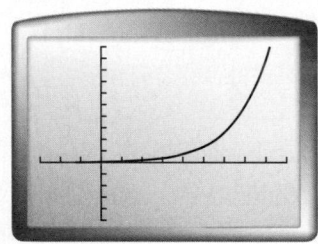

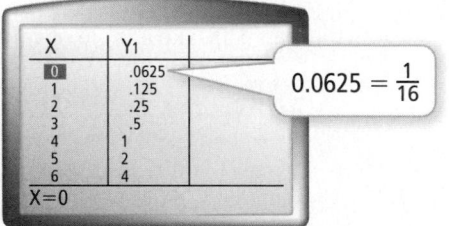

$0.0625 = \frac{1}{16}$

B $y = 20\left(\frac{1}{2}\right)^x + 10$

Step 1
Make a table of values for $y = 20\left(\frac{1}{2}\right)^x$.

Think

Where have you seen this situation before?

The graph of a function like $y = 20\left(\frac{1}{2}\right)^x + 10$ is both a stretch and a vertical translation of its parent function.

x	$y = 20 \cdot \left(\frac{1}{2}\right)^x$
−1	40
0	20
1	10
2	5
3	2.5

Step 2
Graph $y = 20\left(\frac{1}{2}\right)^x$ and translate up 10 units.

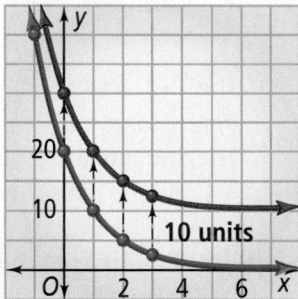

The "$+ 10$" in $y = 20\left(\frac{1}{2}\right)^x + 10$ translates the graph of $y = 20\left(\frac{1}{2}\right)^x$ up 10 units.
The asymptote becomes $y = 10$, the y-intercept becomes 30, and the range becomes $y > 10$. The domain is unchanged.

 Got It? 2. How does the graph of each function compare to the graph of the parent function?
    a. $y = 4^{(x+2)}$ **b.** $y = 5 \cdot 0.25^x + 5$

take note

Concept Summary Families of Exponential Functions

Parent function	$y = b^x$
Stretch $(\lvert a \rvert > 1)$ Compression (Shrink) $(0 < \lvert a \rvert < 1)$ Reflection $(a < 0)$ in x-axis	$y = ab^x$
Translations (horizontal by h; vertical by k)	$y = b^{(x-h)} + k$
All transformations combined	$y = ab^{(x-h)} + k$

Problem 3 Using an Exponential Model

Physics The best temperature to brew coffee is between 195°F and 205°F. Coffee is cool enough to drink at 185°F. The table shows temperature readings from a sample cup of coffee. How long does it take for a cup of coffee to be cool enough to drink? Use an exponential model.

Time (min)	Temp (°F)
0	203
5	177
10	153
15	137
20	121
25	111
30	104

Know
- Set of values
- Best serving temperature

Need
Time it takes for a cup of coffee to become cool enough to drink

Plan
Use an exponential model to find the time it takes for coffee to reach 185°F.

Think

Why does it make sense that a graph of this data would have an asymptote?
The temperature of the hot coffee will get closer and closer to room temperature as it cools, but it cannot cool below room temperature.

Step 1
Plot the data to determine if an exponential model is realistic.

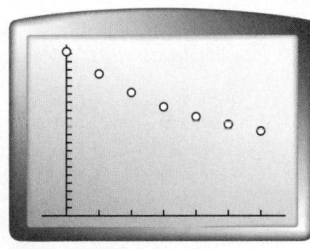

Step 2
Since room temperature is about 68°F, define **L3 = L2 − 68**.

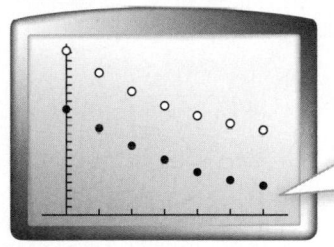

The graphing calculator exponential model assumes the asymptote is $y = 0$.

Step 3
Use **ExpReg L1, L3** to find an exponential model.

Hint

Similar to linear and quadratic regressions, an r^2 value close to 1 indicates a strong correlation.

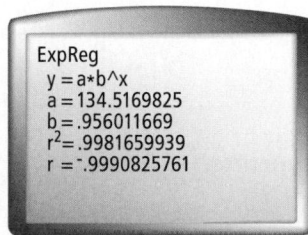

```
ExpReg
y = a*b^x
a = 134.5169825
b = .956011669
r² = .9981659939
r = ⁻.9990825761
```

Step 4
Shift $y = 134.5(0.956)^x$ up 68 units. Model the original data: $y = 134.5 \cdot 0.956^x + 68$.

X	Y₁
2.6	187.65
2.7	187.11
2.8	186.58
2.9	186.05
3	185.52
3.1	184.99
3.2	184.46

X = 3.1

The coffee takes about 3.1 min to cool to 185°F.

Got It? **3. a.** Use the exponential model. How long does it take for the coffee to reach a temperature of 100 degrees?

b. Reasoning In Problem 3, would the model of the exponential data be useful if you did not translate the data by 68 units? Explain.

Focus Question What are the transformations on exponential functions?

Answer Every exponential function can be described as a transformation of the parent exponential function, $y = b^x$. The general form is given by $y = ab^{(x-h)} + k$. The values of h and k represent translation. The factor a performs stretches, compressions, and reflections.

 ## Lesson Check

Do you know HOW?

For each function, identify the transformation from the parent function $y = b^x$.

1. $y = -2 \cdot 3^x$

2. $y = \frac{1}{2}(9)^x$

3. $y = 7^{(x-5)}$

4. $y = 5^x + 3$

Do you UNDERSTAND?

5. Error Analysis A student says that the graph of $f(x) = \left(\frac{1}{3}\right)^{x+2} + 1$ is a shift of the parent function 2 units up and 1 unit to the left. Describe and correct the student's error.

   ## Practice and Problem-Solving Exercises

A **Practice** **Graph each function.** 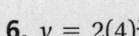 **See Problem 1.**

Guided Practice

6. $y = 2(4)^x$

To start, make a table of values.

x	$y = 4^x$	$y = 2(4)^x$
-2	$\frac{1}{16}$	$\frac{1}{8}$
-1	$\frac{1}{4}$	$\frac{1}{2}$
0	1	2
1	4	8
2	16	32

7. $y = -5^x$

8. $y = \left(\frac{1}{2}\right)^x$

9. $y = -9(3)^x$

10. $y = 3(2)^x$

11. $y = 24\left(\frac{1}{2}\right)^x$

12. $y = -\left(\frac{1}{3}\right)^x$

Graph each function as a transformation of its parent function. **See Problem 2.**

13. $y = 2^x + 5$

14. $y = 5\left(\frac{1}{3}\right)^x - 8$

15. $y = -(0.3)^{x-2}$

16. $y = -2(5)^{x+3}$

17. $y = 3(2)^{x-1} + 4$

18. $y = -2(3)^{x+1} - 5$

19. Baking A cake recipe says to bake the cake until the center is 180°F, then let the cake cool to 120°F. The table shows temperature readings for the cake.

See Problem 3.

Time (min)	Temp (°F)
0	180
5	126
10	94
15	80
20	73

a. Given a room temperature of 70°F, what is an exponential model for this data set?

b. How long does it take the cake to cool to the desired temperature?

B **Apply**

20. Assume that a is positive and $b \geq 1$. Describe the effects of $c > 0$, $c = 0$, and $c < 0$ on the graph of the function $y = ab^{cx}$.

21. Graphing Calculator Using a graphing calculator, graph each of the functions below on the same coordinate grid. What do you notice? Explain why the definition of exponential functions has the constraint that $b \neq 1$.

$$y = \left(\tfrac{1}{2}\right)^x \qquad y = \left(\tfrac{8}{10}\right)^x \qquad y = \left(\tfrac{9}{10}\right)^x \qquad y = \left(\tfrac{99}{100}\right)^x$$

The parent function for each graph below is of the form $y = ab^x$. Write the parent function. Then write a function for the translation indicated.

22.

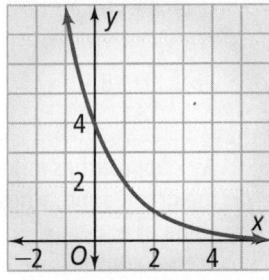

translation: left 4 units, up 3 units

23.

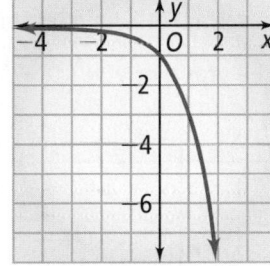

translation: right 8 units, up 2 units

24.

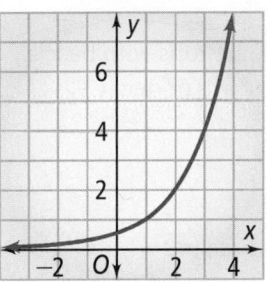

translation: right 6 units, down 7 units

25.

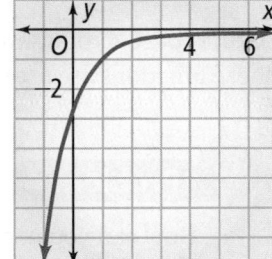

translation: left 15 units, down 1 unit

Properties of Exponential Functions

Objective To graph exponential functions that have base e

In Part 1 of the lesson, you learned how to transform exponential functions with base b.

Connect to What You Know

Here you will use what you learned to evaluate exponential functions with the natural base e.

Focus Question What is a natural base exponential function?

So far, you have worked with rational bases. Exponential functions can have irrational bases as well. One important irrational base is the number e.

The graph of $y = \left(1 + \frac{1}{x}\right)^x$ has an asymptote at $y = e$ or $y \approx 2.71828$.

x	$y = \left(1 + \frac{1}{x}\right)^x$
1	$y = 2$
10	$y \approx 2.594$
100	$y \approx 2.705$
1000	$y \approx 2.717$

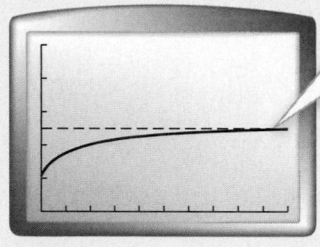

As x approaches infinity the graph approaches the value of e.

Hint
Exponential functions with base e have the same properties as other exponential functions.

Natural base exponential functions are exponential functions with base e. These functions are useful for describing *continuous* growth or decay.

Problem 4 Evaluating e^x

How can you use a graphing calculator to evaluate e^3?

Method 1 Use the e^x key.

Think

After you press the e^x key, what keys should you press?

Press **3**, **)**, and **enter**.

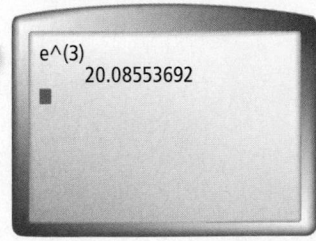

e^(3)
        20.08553692

Method 2 Use the graph of $y = e^x$.

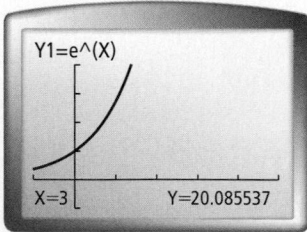

Y1=e^(X)

X=3   Y=20.085537

$e^3 \approx 20.086$.

 **Got It?** **4.** How can you use a graphing calculator to calculate e^8?

Hint

In Lesson 7-1 you studied interest that was compounded annually.

The formula for **continuously compounded interest** uses the number e.

 take note

Key Concept Continuously Compounded Interest

amount in account at time t interest rate (annual)

$$A(t) = P \cdot e^{rt}$$

Principal   time in years

Problem 5 Continuously Compounded Interest **GRIDDED RESPONSE**

Scholarships Suppose you won a contest at the start of 5th grade that deposited $3000 in an account that pays 5% annual interest compounded continuously. How much will you have in the account when you enter high school 4 years later? Express the answer to the nearest dollar.

Plan

What is the unknown?
The amount A in the account after 4 years.

Write the equation for continuously compounded interest.	$A = P \cdot e^{rt}$
Substitute values for P, r, and t.	$= 3000e^{(0.05)(4)}$
Simplify.	$= 3000e^{0.2}$
Use a calculator. Round to the nearest dollar.	≈ 3664

The amount in the account, to the nearest dollar, is $3664.
Write 3664 in the grid.

 Got It? **5.** About how much will be in the account after 4 years of high school?

Focus Question What is a natural base exponential function?

Answer A natural base exponential function is an exponential function with the irrational base $e \approx 2.71828$. Use a natural base exponential function to describe continuous growth or decay.

 Lesson Check

Do you know HOW?

Use a graphing calculator to evaluate each expression to four decimal places.

1. e^6 **2.** e^{-1} **3.** e^{10}

Do you UNDERSTAND?

4. Reasoning Is investing $2000 in an account that pays 5% annual interest compounded continuously the same as investing $1000 at 4% and $1000 at 6%, each compounded continuously? Explain.

Practice and Problem Solving Exercises

A Practice 📱 **Graphing Calculator** Use the graph of $y = e^x$ to evaluate each expression to four decimal places.

◆ **See Problem 4.**

5. e^{-2} **6.** $e^{\frac{5}{2}}$ **7.** e^e

Find the amount in a continuously compounded account for the given conditions.

◆ **See Problem 5.**

Guided Practice →

To start, write the equation for continuously compounded interest.

8. principal: $2000
annual interest rate: 5.1%
time: 3 years

$A = P \cdot e^{rt}$

9. principal: $400
annual interest rate: 7.6%
time: 1.5 years

10. principal: $950
annual interest rate: 6.5%
time: 10 years

B Apply

11. Think About a Plan A student wants to save $8000 for college in five years. How much should be put into an account that pays 5.2% annual interest compounded continuously?
- What formula should you use?
- What information do you know?
- What do you need to find?

12. Investment How long would it take to double your principal in an account that pays 6.5% annual interest compounded continuously?

13. Botany The half-life of a radioactive substance is the time it takes for half of the material to decay. Phosphorus-32 is used to study a plant's use of fertilizer. It has a half-life of 14.3 days. Write the exponential decay function for a 50-mg sample. Find the amount of phosphorus-32 remaining after 84 days.

14. Archaeology Archaeologists use carbon-14, which has a half-life of 5730 years, to determine the age of artifacts in carbon dating. Write the exponential decay function for a 24-mg sample. How much carbon-14 remains after 30 millennia?

> **Hint** A millennium is 1000 years.

15. Physics At a constant temperature, the atmospheric pressure p in pascals is given by the formula $p = 101.3e^{-0.001h}$, where h is the altitude in meters. What is p at an altitude of 500 m?

Standardized Test Prep

SAT/ACT

16. A savings account earns 4.62% annual interest, compounded continuously. After approximately how many years will a principal of $500 double?

   Ⓐ 2 years   Ⓑ 10 years   Ⓒ 15 years   Ⓓ 44 years

17. What is the inverse of the function $f(x) = \sqrt{x - 4}$?

   Ⓕ $f^{-1}(x) = x^2 - 4, x \geq 0$ Ⓗ $f^{-1}(x) = \sqrt{x + 4}$

   Ⓖ $f^{-1}(x) = x^2 + 4, x \geq 0$ Ⓘ $f^{-1}(x) = \dfrac{\sqrt{x - 4}}{x - 4}$

In Exercises 18 and 19, let $f(x) = x^2 - 4$ and $g(x) = \dfrac{1}{x + 4}$.

18. What is $(g \circ f)(x)$?

   Ⓐ $\dfrac{1}{x^2}$ Ⓑ $\dfrac{1}{x^2 - 8x + 16} - 4$ Ⓒ $\dfrac{x^2 - 4}{x + 4}$ Ⓓ $x - 4$

19. What is $(f \circ f)(3)$?

   Ⓕ 1   Ⓖ 5   Ⓗ 21   Ⓘ 77

20. What is the equation of the line shown at the right?

   Ⓐ $y = -\dfrac{4}{5}x + 2$ Ⓒ $-4x + 5y = 7$

   Ⓑ $y = \dfrac{5}{4}x - 2$ Ⓓ $4x - 5y = 15$

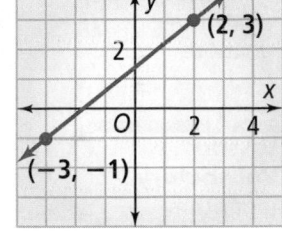

Short Response

21. How much should you invest in an account that pays 6% annual interest compounded continuously if you want exactly $8000 after four years? Show your work.

Mixed Review

Without graphing, determine whether the function represents exponential growth or exponential decay. Then find the *y*-intercept.

   ◀ See Lesson 7-1.

22. $y = 23(3.03)^x$ **23.** $f(x) = 3(5)^x$ **24.** $y = 2\left(\dfrac{3}{4}\right)^x$

Simplify.

   ◀ See Lesson 6-3.

25. $5\sqrt{5} + \sqrt{5}$ **26.** $\sqrt[3]{4} - 2\sqrt[3]{4}$ **27.** $\sqrt{75} + \sqrt{125}$

28. $\sqrt[4]{32} + \sqrt[4]{128}$ **29.** $5\sqrt{3} - 2\sqrt{12}$ **30.** $3\sqrt{63} + \sqrt{28}$

Get Ready! To prepare for Lesson 7-3, do Exercises 31–33.

Find the inverse of each function. Is the inverse a function?

   ◀ See Lesson 6-7.

31. $f(x) = 4x - 1$ **32.** $f(x) = x^7$ **33.** $f(x) = 5x^3 + 1$

7-3 Logarithmic Functions as Inverses

Objectives To write and evaluate logarithmic expressions
To graph logarithmic functions

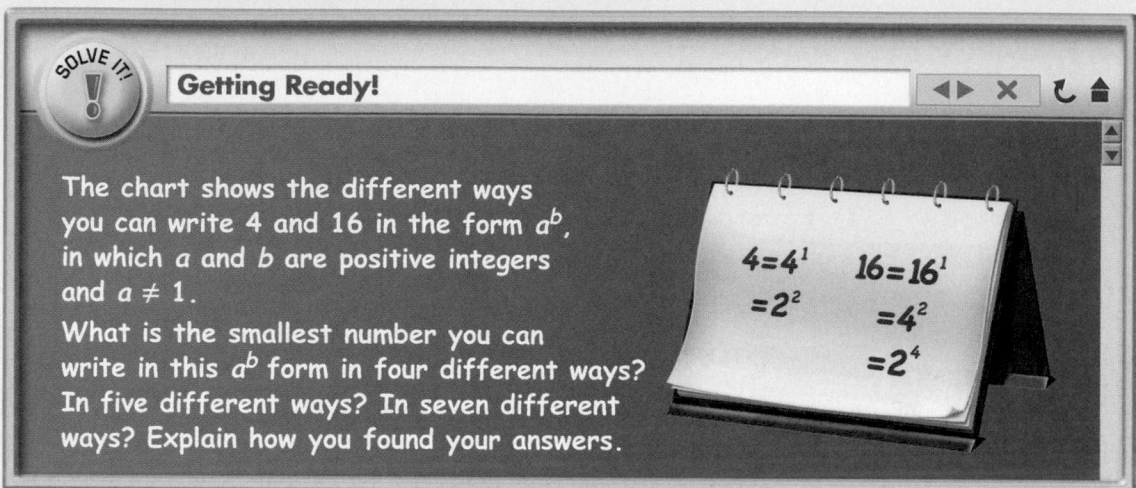

Getting Ready!

The chart shows the different ways you can write 4 and 16 in the form a^b, in which a and b are positive integers and $a \neq 1$.

What is the smallest number you can write in this a^b form in four different ways? In five different ways? In seven different ways? Explain how you found your answers.

$$4 = 4^1 \qquad 16 = 16^1$$
$$= 2^2 \qquad = 4^2$$
$$= 2^4$$

Dynamic Activity
Logarithmic
Functions

Lesson Vocabulary
• logarithm
• common logarithm
• logarithmic scale
• logarithmic function

Many even numbers can be written as power functions with base 2. In this lesson you will find ways to express all numbers as powers of a common base.

Focus Question What is a logarithm?

take note

Key Concept   Logarithm

A **logarithm** base b of a positive number x satisfies the following definition.

For $b > 0$, $b \neq 1$, $\log_b x = y$ if and only if $b^y = x$.

You can read $\log_b x$ as "log base b of x." In other words, the logarithm y is the exponent to which b must be raised to get x.

The exponent y in the expression b^y is the logarithm in the equation $\log_b x = y$. The base b in b^y and the base b in $\log_b x$ are the same. In both uses, $b \neq 1$ and $b > 0$.

Since $b \neq 1$ and $b > 0$, it follows that $b^y > 0$. Since $b^y = x$ then $x > 0$, so $\log_b x$ is defined only for $x > 0$.

You can use the definition of a logarithm to write exponential equations in logarithmic form.

 Problem 1 Writing Exponential Equations in Logarithmic Form

What is the logarithmic form of each equation?

Think

To what power do you raise 10 to get 100?
10 raised to the 2nd power equals 100.

A $100 = 10^2$

Use the definition of logarithm.

If $x = b^y$ then $\log_b x = y$.

If $100 = 10^2$ then $\log_{10} 100 = 2$.

B $81 = 3^4$

Use the definition of logarithm.

If $x = b^y$ then $\log_b x = y$.

If $81 = 3^4$ then $\log_3 81 = 4$.

Got It? **1.** What is the logarithmic form of each equation?

     a. $36 = 6^2$ **b.** $1 = 3^0$ **c.** $\frac{8}{27} = \left(\frac{2}{3}\right)^3$

You can use the exponential form to help you evaluate logarithms.

 Problem 2 Evaluating a Logarithm

Multiple Choice What is the value of $\log_8 32$?

    Ⓐ $\frac{3}{5}$ Ⓑ $\frac{5}{3}$ Ⓒ 3   Ⓓ 5

Plan

How can you use the definition of logarithm to help you find the value of $\log_8 32$?
If $\log_b x = y$ then $x = b^y$, so to what power must you raise 8 to get 32?

Use the definition of logarithm.	$\log_b x = y$
Write a logarithmic equation.	$\log_8 32 = y$
Use the definition of a logarithm to write an exponential equation.	$32 = 8^y$
Write each side using base 2.	$2^5 = (2^3)^y$
Use the Power Property of Exponents.	$2^5 = 2^{3y}$
Since the bases are the same, the exponents must be equal.	$5 = 3y$
Solve for y.	$\frac{5}{3} = y$

Since $8^{\frac{5}{3}} = 32$, then $\log_8 32 = \frac{5}{3}$.
The correct answer is B.

Got It? **2.** What is the value of each logarithm?

     a. $\log_5 125$ **b.** $\log_4 32$ **c.** $\log_{64} \frac{1}{32}$

A **common logarithm** is a logarithm with base 10. You can write a common logarithm $\log_{10} x$ simply as $\log x$, without showing the 10.

Many measurements of physical phenomena have such a wide range of values that the reported measurements are logarithms (exponents) of the values, not the values themselves. When you use the logarithm of a quantity instead of the quantity, you are using a **logarithmic scale**. The Richter scale is a logarithmic scale. It gives logarithmic measurements of earthquake magnitude.

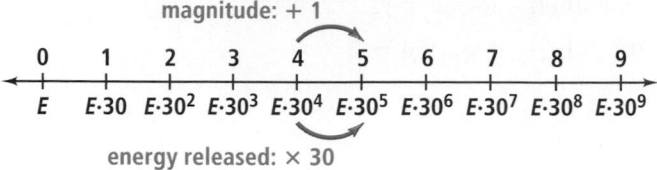

The Richter Scale

magnitude: + 1

0	1	2	3	4	5	6	7	8	9
E	$E \cdot 30$	$E \cdot 30^2$	$E \cdot 30^3$	$E \cdot 30^4$	$E \cdot 30^5$	$E \cdot 30^6$	$E \cdot 30^7$	$E \cdot 30^8$	$E \cdot 30^9$

energy released: × 30

Problem 3 Using a Logarithmic Scale

In December 2004, an earthquake with magnitude 9.3 on the Richter scale hit off the northwest coast of Sumatra. The diagram shows the magnitude of an earthquake that hit Sumatra in March 2005. The formula $\log \frac{I_1}{I_2} = M_1 - M_2$ compares the intensity levels of earthquakes where I is the intensity level determined by a seismograph, and M is the magnitude on a Richter scale. How many times more intense was the December earthquake than the March earthquake?

THAILAND

Magnitude 8.7

MALAYSIA

Epicenter, March 2005

Sumatra

INDONESIA

Write the formula. $\qquad \log \frac{I_1}{I_2} = M_1 - M_2$

Substitute $M_1 = 9.3$ and $M_2 = 8.7$. $\qquad \log \frac{I_1}{I_2} = 9.3 - 8.7$

Simplify. $\qquad \log \frac{I_1}{I_2} = 0.6$

Apply the definition of common logarithm. $\qquad \frac{I_1}{I_2} = 10^{0.6}$

Use a calculator. $\qquad \approx 4$

The December earthquake was about 4 times as strong as the one in March.

Think

What is the base of this logarithm?
This is the common logarithm. It has base 10.

Got It? **3.** In 1995, an earthquake in Mexico registered 8.0 on the Richter scale. In 2001, an earthquake of magnitude 6.8 shook Washington state. How many times more intense was the 1995 earthquake than the 2001 earthquake?

Focus Question What is the relationship between exponential functions and logarithmic functions?

A **logarithmic function** is the inverse of an exponential function. The graph shows $y = 10^x$ and its inverse $y = \log x$. Note that $(0, 1)$ and $(1, 10)$ are on the graph of $y = 10^x$, and that $(1, 0)$ and $(10, 1)$ are on the graph of $y = \log x$.

Hint

Recall that the graphs of inverse functions are reflections of each other in the line $y = x$.

You can graph $y = \log_b x$ as the inverse of $y = b^x$. Because $y = b^x$ and $y = \log_b x$ are inverse functions, their compositions map a number a to itself. In other words, $b^{\log_b a} = a$ for $a > 0$ and $\log_b b^a = a$ for all a.

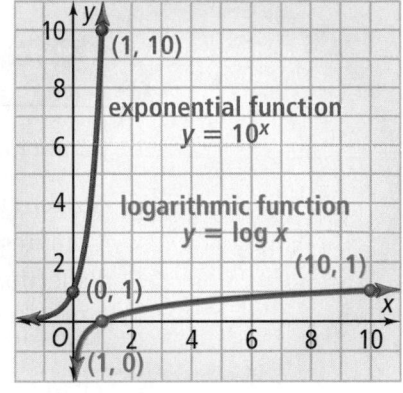

Problem 4 Graphing a Logarithmic Function

What is the graph of $y = \log_3 x$? Describe the domain and range and identify the y-intercept and the asymptote.

$y = \log_3 x$ is the inverse of $y = 3^x$.

Step 1 Graph $y = 3^x$.

Step 2 Reflecting across the line $y = x$ produces the inverse of $y = 3^x$.

Step 3 Choose a few points on $y = 3^x$ and reverse their coordinates. Plot these new points and graph $y = \log_3 x$.

The domain is $x > 0$. The range is all real numbers. There is no y-intercept. The vertical asymptote is $x = 0$.

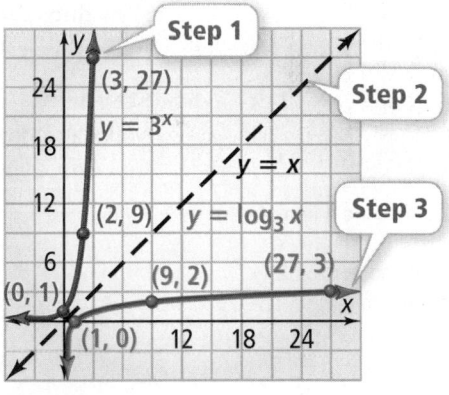

Think

How are the domain and range of $y = 3^x$ and $y = \log_3 x$ related?

Since they are inverse functions, the domain and range of $y = \log_3 x$ are the same as the *range* and *domain* of $y = 3^x$.

✓ **Got It?** **4. a.** What is the graph of $y = \log_4 x$? Describe the domain, range, y-intercept, and asymptotes.

   b. Reasoning Suppose you use the table shown to help you graph $y = \log_2 x$. (Recall that if $y = \log_2 x$, then $2^y = x$.) Copy and complete the table. Explain your answers.

x	$2^y = x$	y
-1	$2^y = -1$	▦
0	$2^y = 0$	▦
1	$2^y = 1$	▦
2	$2^y = 2$	▦

The function $y = \log_b x$ is the parent for a function family. You can graph $y = \log_b(x - h) + k$ by translating the graph of the parent function, $y = \log_b x$, horizontally by h units and vertically by k units. The value of a in $y = a \log_b x$ indicates a stretch, a compression, and possibly a reflection.

 take note

Concept Summary   Families of Logarithmic Functions

Parent function	$y = \log_b x,\ b > 0,\ b \neq 1$
Stretch $(\lvert a \rvert > 1)$ Compression (Shrink) $(0 < \lvert a \rvert < 1)$ Reflection $(a < 0)$ in x-axis	$y = a \log_b x$
Translations (horizontal by h; vertical by k)	$y = \log_b(x - h) + k$
All transformations combined	$y = a \log_b(x - h) + k$

Problem 5 Translating $y = \log_b x$

Think

How is the function $y = \log_4(x - 2) + 6$ similar to other functions you have seen?

Recall that the graph of $y = f(x - h) + k$ is a vertical and horizontal translation of the parent function, $y = f(x)$.

How does the graph of $y = \log_4(x - 2) + 6$ compare to the graph of the parent function?

Step 1
Make a table of values for the parent function. Use the definition of logarithm.

x	$\log_4 x = y \longrightarrow 4^y = x$	y
$\frac{1}{16}$	$4^{-2} = \frac{1}{16}$	-2
$\frac{1}{4}$	$4^{-1} = \frac{1}{4}$	-1
1	$4^0 = 1$	0
4	$4^1 = 4$	1
16	$4^2 = 16$	2

Step 2
Graph the parent function. Shift the graph to the right 2 units and up 6 units to graph $y = \log_4(x - 2) + 6$.

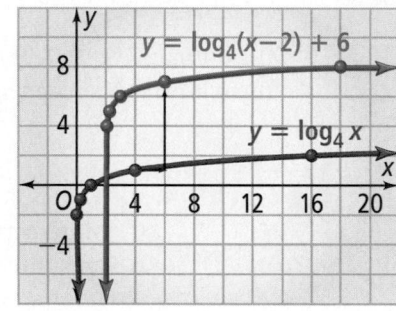

Because $y = \log_4(x - 2) + 6$ translates the graph of the parent function to the right 2 units, the asymptote changes from $x = 0$ to $x = 2$. The domain changes from $x > 0$ to $x > 2$. The range remains all real numbers.

Got It? **5.** How does the graph of each function compare to the graph of the parent function?

a. $y = \log_2(x - 3) + 4$ **b.** $y = 5 \log_2 x$

Focus Question What is a logarithm?

Answer A logarithm y is the exponent to which base b must be raised to get a number x. So, $\log_b x = y$ if and only if $b^y = x$.

Focus Question What is the relationship between exponential functions and logarithmic functions?

Answer Because the exponential function $y = b^x$ is one-to-one, its inverse is a function. The logarithmic function $y = \log_b x$ is the inverse of the exponential function $y = b^x$. The graphs of these functions are reflections of each other in the line $y = x$.

Lesson Check

Do you know HOW?

Write each equation in logarithmic form.

1. $25 = 5^2$ **2.** $64 = 4^3$

3. $243 = 3^5$ **4.** $25 = 5^2$

Evaluate each logarithm.

5. $\log_2 8$ **6.** $\log_9 9$

7. $\log_7 49$ **8.** $\log_2 \frac{1}{4}$

Do you UNDERSTAND?

9. Vocabulary Determine whether each logarithm is a common logarithm.

     a. $\log_2 4$ **b.** $\log 64$ **c.** $\log_{10} 100$ **d.** $\log_5 5$

10. Reasoning Explain how you could use an inverse function to graph the logarithmic function $y = \log_6 x$.

11. Compare and Contrast Compare the graph of $y = \log_2 (x + 4)$ to the graph of $y = \log_2 x$. How are the graphs alike? How are they different?

Practice and Problem-Solving Exercises

 **Practice** Write each equation in logarithmic form.  **See Problem 1.**

> **Guided Practice**
>
> To start, write the definition of logarithm.
>
> **12.** $49 = 7^2$
>
> If $x = b^y$, then $\log_b x = y$.

13. $10^3 = 1000$ **14.** $625 = 5^4$ **15.** $\frac{1}{10} = 10^{-1}$

16. $4 = \left(\frac{1}{2}\right)^{-2}$ **17.** $\left(\frac{1}{3}\right)^3 = \frac{1}{27}$ **18.** $10^{-2} = 0.01$

Evaluate each logarithm.   **See Problem 2.**

> **Guided Practice**
>
> To start, write the logarithmic equation.
>
> **19.** $\log_2 16$
>
> $\log_2 16 = x$

20. $\log_4 2$ **21.** $\log_8 8$ **22.** $\log_4 8$

23. $\log_2 8$ **24.** $\log_{49} 7$ **25.** $\log_5 (-25)$

26. $\log_2 2^5$ **27.** $\log 10,000$ **28.** $\log_5 125$

Seismology In 1812, an earthquake of magnitude 7.9 shook New Madrid, Missouri. Compare the intensity level of that earthquake to the intensity level of each earthquake below.

See Problem 3.

29. magnitude 7.7 in San Francisco, California, in 1906

30. magnitude 9.5 in Valdivia, Chile, in 1960

31. magnitude 3.2 in Charlottesville, Virginia, in 2001

Graph each function on the same set of axes.

See Problem 4.

32. $y = \log_2 x$

33. $y = 2^x$

34. $y = \log_{\frac{1}{2}} x$

35. $y = \left(\frac{1}{2}\right)^x$

Describe how the graph of each function compares with the graph of the parent function, $y = \log_b x$.

See Problem 5.

36. $y = \log_5 x + 1$

37. $y = \log_7 (x - 2)$

38. $y = \log_4 (x + 2) - 1$

Apply

39. **Think About a Plan** The pH of a substance equals $-\log[H^+]$, where $[H^+]$ is the concentration of hydrogen ions, and it ranges from 0 to 14. A pH level of 7 is neutral. A level greater than 7 is basic, and a level less than 7 is acidic. The table shows the hydrogen ion concentration $[H^+]$ for selected foods. Is each food basic or acidic?
    • How can you find the pH value of each food?
    • What rule can you use to determine if the food is basic or acidic?

Approximate [H⁺] of Foods

Food	$[H^+]$
Apple juice	3.2×10^{-4}
Buttermilk	2.5×10^{-5}
Cream	2.5×10^{-7}
Ketchup	1.3×10^{-4}
Shrimp sauce	7.9×10^{-8}
Strained peas	1.0×10^{-6}

40. **Chemistry** Find the concentration of hydrogen ions in seawater, if the pH level of seawater is 8.5.

Write each equation in exponential form.

41. $\log_2 128 = 7$

42. $\log 0.0001 = -4$

43. $\log_6 6 = 1$

44. $\log_4 1 = 0$

45. $\log_2 \frac{1}{2} = -1$

46. $\log_3 \frac{1}{9} = -2$

Find the greatest integer that is less than the value of the logarithm. Use your calculator to check your answers.

47. $\log 5$

48. $\log 0.08$

49. $\log 17.52$

50. **Error Analysis** Find the error in the following evaluation of $\log_{27} 3$. Then evaluate the logarithm correctly.

$$x = \log_{27} 3$$
$$x^3 = 27$$
$$\sqrt[3]{x^3} = \sqrt[3]{27}$$
$$x = 3$$
$$\log_{27} 3 = 3$$

51. **Writing** Explain why the base b in $y = \log_b x$ cannot equal 1.

52. **Open-Ended** Write a logarithmic function of the form $y = \log_b x$. Find its inverse function. Graph both functions on one set of axes.

Find the inverse of each function.

53. $y = \log_4 x$

54. $y = \log_{10} x$

55. $y = \log_2 2x$

56. $y = \log(x + 1)$

57. $y = \log 10x$

58. $y = \log(x - 6)$

Graph each logarithmic function.

59. $y = \log 2x$

60. $y = 2\log_2 x$

61. $y = \log_4(2x + 3)$

Find the domain and the range of each function.

62. $y = \log_5 x$

63. $y = 3\log x$

64. $y = 2\log(x - 2)$

Standardized Test Prep

SAT/ACT

65. Which is the logarithmic form of the exponential equation $2^3 = 8$?

   Ⓐ $\log_8 2 = 3$ Ⓑ $\log_8 3 = 2$ Ⓒ $\log_3 8 = 2$ Ⓓ $\log_2 8 = 3$

66. Dan will begin advertising his video production business online pay-per-click method, which charges $30 as an initial fee, plus a fixed amount each time the ad is clicked. Dan estimates that with the cost of 8 cents per click, his ad will be clicked about 150 times per day. Which expression represents Dan's total estimated cost of advertising, in dollars, after x days?

   Ⓕ $(30 + 0.08x)150$ Ⓖ $360x$ Ⓗ $30 + 1200x$ Ⓘ $30 + 12x$

67. Which translation takes $y = |x|$ to $y = |x + 3| - 1$?

   Ⓐ 3 units right, 1 unit down   Ⓒ 3 units left, 1 unit down

   Ⓑ 3 units right, 1 unit up   Ⓓ 3 units left, 1 unit up

Short
Response

68. What is the expression $\sqrt[3]{(\sqrt{a})^7}$ written as a variable raised to a single rational exponent?

Mixed Review

Graph each function.   ◀ See Lesson 7-2.

69. $y = 5^x - 100$

70. $y = -10(4)^{x+2}$

71. $y = -27(3)^{x-1} + 9$

Factor each expression.   ◀ See Lesson 4-4.

72. $4x^2 - 8x + 3$

73. $4b^2 - 100$

74. $5x^2 + 13x - 6$

Get Ready!   **To prepare for Lesson 7-4, do Exercises 75–77.**

Evaluate each expression for the given value of the variable.   ◀ See Lesson 1-3.

75. $x^2 - x$; $x = 2$

76. $x^3 \cdot x^5$; $x = 2$

77. $\dfrac{x^8}{x^{10}}$; $x = 2$

Fitting Curves to Data

Example 1

Which type of function models the data best—linear, logarithmic, or exponential?

Connect the points with a smooth curve. Since the points do not fall along a line, the function is not linear. The graph appears to approach a horizontal asymptote, so an exponential function models the data best.

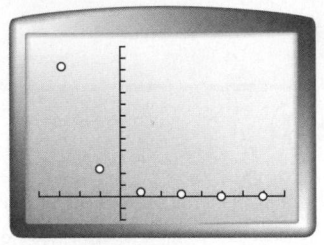 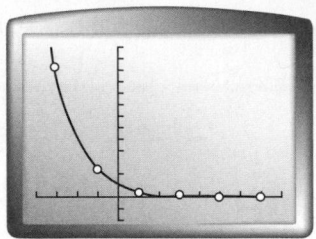

Example 2

Which type of function models the data best—quadratic, logarithmic, or cubic?

Step 1 Press (stat) (enter) to enter the data in lists.

Step 2 Use the (stat plot) feature to draw a scatter plot.

Step 3 If you connect the points with a smooth curve, the end behavior of the graph is up and up. The graph is not cubic or logarithmic, so the quadratic function best models the data.

x	y
0	14
1	7.5
2	4
3	1.8
4	1.8
5	3.9

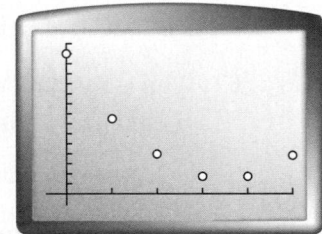

Exercises

1. Which type of function best models the data shown in the graphing-calculator screen—*linear*, *quadratic*, *logarithmic*, *cubic*, or *exponential*?

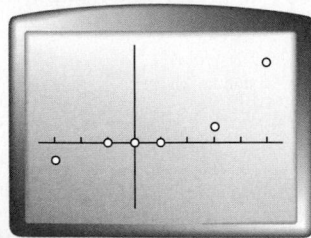

2. Which type of function best models the data in the table—*linear*, *quadratic*, *logarithmic*, *cubic*, or *exponential*?

3. **Reasoning** Could you use a different model for the data in Exercises 1 and 2? Explain.

x	y
−1	0
1	1.4
3	2.09
5	2.53
7	2.81
9	3.12

Example 3

The table shows the number of bacteria in a culture after the given number of hours. Find a good model for the data. Based on the model, how many bacteria will be in the culture after an additional ten hours?

Hour	Bacteria
1	2205
2	2270
3	2350
4	2653
5	3052
6	3417
7	3890
8	4522
9	5107
10	5724

Step 1   Press (stat) (enter) to enter the data in lists. Use the (stat plot) feature to draw a scatter plot.

Step 2   Notice from the scatter plot that the data appears exponential. Find the equations for the best-fitting exponential function. Press (stat) ▷ **0** to use the **ExpReg** feature.

$$y = 1779.404(1.121)^x$$

Step 3   Graph the function. Press (y=) (clear) (vars) **5** ▷ ▷ (enter) to enter the **ExpReg** results. Press (graph) to display the function and the scatter plot together. Press (zoom) **9** to automatically adjust the window.

Step 4   In 10 more hours, there will be approximately $y = 1779.404(1.121)^{20} \approx 17{,}474$ bacteria in the culture.

Exercises

Use a graphing calculator to find the exponential or quadratic function that best fits each set of data. Graph each function.

4.

x	y
−1	4.9
0	3.8
1	5.0
2	8.1
3	13.3
4	70.2

5.

x	y
−3	0.1
−1	0.4
1	1.6
3	6.4
5	25.6
7	102.4

6.

x	y
1	3.5
2	2.11
3	1.30
4	0.73
5	0.28
6	0.08

7. Writing   In Exercise 6, the function appears to level off. Explain why.

8. Find a quadratic model for the data in Exercise 6. Compare the graphs of the quadratic and exponential models for this data. Predict the y-values for both models when $x = -2$. Discuss the differences if any between the predictions.

Do you know HOW?

Determine whether each function is an example of exponential growth or decay. Then find the y-intercept.

1. $y = 100(0.25)^x$ **2.** $y = \frac{7}{8}(18)^x$

Graph each function. Then find the domain, range, and y-intercept.

3. $y = -4(2)^x$ **4.** $y = 8(0.25)^x$

5. Investment Suppose you deposit $600 into a savings account that pays 3.9% annual interest. How much will you have in the account after 3 years if no money is added or withdrawn?

6. Depreciation The initial value of a car is $25,000. After one year, the value of the car is $21,250. Write an exponential function to model the expected value of the car. Estimate the value of the car after 5 years.

Graph each function as a transformation of its parent function. Write the parent function.

7. $y = 3^x - 2$ **8.** $y = \frac{1}{2}(5)^{x-1} + 4$

9. $y = -(0.5)^{x+3}$ **10.** $y = -6\left(\frac{3}{4}\right)^x - 10$

Evaluate each expression to four decimal places.

11. e^5 **12.** $e^{\frac{3}{2}}$

Find the amount in a continuously compounded account for the given conditions.

13. principal: $500; annual interest rate: 4.9%; time: 2.5 years

14. principal: $6000; annual interest rate: 6.8%; time: 10 years

Write each equation in logarithmic form.

15. $10^4 = 10,000$ **16.** $8 = \left(\frac{1}{2}\right)^{-3}$

Evaluate each logarithm.

17. $\log_8 64$ **18.** $\log_{\frac{1}{5}} 625$

Graph each logarithmic function. Find the domain and range.

19. $y = \log_5 (x - 1)$ **20.** $y = 4 \log x + 5$

21. Crafts For glass to be shaped, its temperature must stay above 1200°F. The temperature of a piece of glass is 2200°F when it comes out of the furnace. The table shows temperature readings for the glass. Write an exponential model for this data set and then find how long it takes for the piece of glass to cool to 1200°F.

Time (min)	Temp (°F)
0	2200
5	1700
10	1275
15	1000
20	850
25	650

Do you UNDERSTAND?

22. Error Analysis A student claims the y-intercept of the graph of the function $y = ab^x$ is the point $(0, b)$. What is the student's mistake? What is the actual y-intercept?

23. Writing Without graphing, how can you tell whether an exponential function represents exponential growth or exponential decay?

24. Compare and Contrast Compare the graph of $y = \log_3 (x + 1)$ to the graph of its inverse $y = 3^x - 1$. How are the graphs alike? How are they different?

25. Vocabulary Explain how the continuously compounded interest formula differs from the annually compounded interest formula.

7-4 | Properties of Logarithms

Objective To use the properties of logarithms

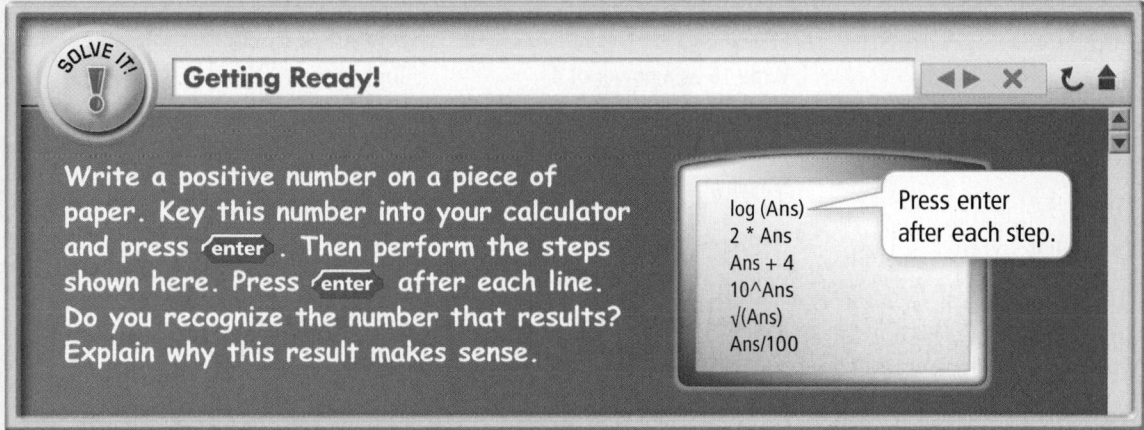

SOLVE IT!

Getting Ready!

Write a positive number on a piece of paper. Key this number into your calculator and press ⟨enter⟩. Then perform the steps shown here. Press ⟨enter⟩ after each line. Do you recognize the number that results? Explain why this result makes sense.

log (Ans)
2 * Ans
Ans + 4
10^Ans
√(Ans)
Ans/100

Press enter after each step.

Lesson Vocabulary
- Change of Base Formula

You can derive the properties of logarithms from the corresponding properties of exponents.

Focus Question How are the properties of logarithms similar to the properties of exponents?

Here's Why It Works You can use a product property of exponents to derive a product property of logarithms.

Hint

Because logarithmic functions and exponential functions are inverses, $\log_b b^a = a$

Let $x = \log_b m$ and $y = \log_b n$.

Use the definition of logarithm.	$m = b^x$ and $n = b^y$
Write mn as a product of powers.	$mn = b^x \cdot b^y$
Use the Product Property of Exponents.	$mn = b^{x+y}$
Use the definition of logarithm.	$\log_b mn = x + y$
Substitute for x and y.	$\log_b mn = \log_b m + \log_b n$

take note

Properties   Properties of Logarithms

For any positive numbers m, n, and b where $b \neq 1$, the following properties apply.

Product Property	$\log_b mn = \log_b m + \log_b n$
Quotient Property	$\log_b \frac{m}{n} = \log_b m - \log_b n$
Power Property	$\log_b m^n = n \log_b m$

 **Problem 1** Simplifying Logarithms

What is each expression written as a single logarithm?

Ⓐ $\log_4 32 - \log_4 2$

Write the original expression.	$\log_4 32 - \log_4 2$
Use the Quotient Property of Logarithms.	$\log_4 \frac{32}{2}$
Divide.	$\log_4 16$
Write 16 as a power of 4.	$\log_4 4^2$
Use the Power Property of Logarithms.	$2\log_4 4$
Simplify.	2

Ⓑ $6\log_2 x + 5\log_2 y$

Think

What must you do with the numbers that multiply the logarithms?
Apply the Power Property of Logarithms.

Write the original expression.	$6\log_2 x + 5\log_2 y$
Use the Power Property of Logarithms.	$\log_2 x^6 + \log_2 y^5$
Use the Product Property of Logarithms.	$\log_2 x^6 y^5$

Got It? **1.** What is each expression written as a single logarithm?

    a. $\log_4 5x + \log_4 3x$ **b.** $2\log_4 6 - \log_4 9$

You can expand a single logarithm to involve the sum or difference of two or more logarithms.

 Problem 2 Expanding Logarithms

What is each logarithm expanded?

Ⓐ $\log \frac{4x}{y}$

Use the Quotient Property of Logarithms.	$\log \frac{4x}{y} = \log 4x - \log y$
Use the Product Property of Logarithms.	$= \log 4 + \log x - \log y$

Ⓑ $\log_9 \frac{x^4}{729}$

Think

Can you apply the Power Property of Logarithms first?
No; the fourth power applies only to x.

Use the Quotient Property of Logarithms.	$\log_9 \frac{x^4}{729} = \log_9 x^4 - \log_9 729$
Use the Power Property of Logarithms.	$= 4\log_9 x - \log_9 729$
Write 729 as a power of 9.	$= 4\log_9 x - \log_9 9^3$
Simplify.	$= 4\log_9 x - 3$

Got It? **2.** What is each logarithm expanded?

    a. $\log_3 \frac{250}{37}$ **b.** $\log_3 9x^5$

Focus Question Why is the Change of Base Formula useful?

Hint

You can evaluate any logarithm using your calculator.

The ▭log▭ key on a calculator finds $\log_{10}$ of a number. To evaluate a logarithm with any base, use the **Change of Base Formula**.

Property   Change of Base Formula

For any positive numbers m, b, and c, with $b \neq 1$ and $c \neq 1$,

$$\log_b m = \frac{\log_c m}{\log_c b}.$$

Here's Why It Works

Multiply $\log_b m$ by $\dfrac{\log_c b}{\log_c b} = 1$. $\qquad \log_b m = \dfrac{(\log_b m)(\log_c b)}{(\log_c b)}$

Use the Power Property of Logarithms. $\qquad\qquad = \dfrac{\log_c b^{\log_b m}}{\log_c b}$

Use $b^{\log_b m} = m$. $\qquad\qquad\qquad\qquad\qquad = \dfrac{\log_c m}{\log_c b}$

Problem 3   Using the Change of Base Formula

What is the value of each expression?

Ⓐ $\log_{81} 27$

Think

What common base has powers that equal 27 and 81?
3 is a common base.
$3^3 = 27$ and $3^4 = 81$.

Method 1 Use a common base.

Use the Change of Base Formula. $\qquad \log_{81} 27 = \dfrac{\log_3 27}{\log_3 81}$

Simplify. $\qquad\qquad\qquad\qquad\qquad\qquad = \dfrac{3}{4}$

Method 2 Use a calculator and base 10.

Use the Change of Base Formula. $\qquad \log_{81} 27 = \dfrac{\log 27}{\log 81}$

Use a calculator. $\qquad\qquad\qquad\qquad\qquad = 0.75$

Ⓑ $\log_5 36$

Write the original expression. $\qquad\qquad\qquad \log_5 36$

> There is no common base for 36 and 5.

Think

What would be a reasonable result?
$5^2 = 25$ and $5^3 = 125$, so $\log_5 36$ should be between 2 and 3.

Use the Change of Base Formula and base 10. $\qquad = \dfrac{\log 36}{\log 5}$

Use a calculator to evaluate. $\qquad\qquad\qquad \approx 2.23$

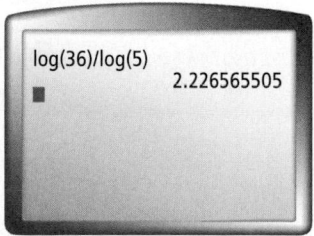

Got It? **3.** Use the Change of Base Formula. What is the value of each expression?

        a. $\log_8 32$ **b.** $\log_4 18$

Problem 4 Using a Logarithmic Scale

Chemistry The pH of a substance equals $-\log[H^+]$, where $[H^+]$ is the concentration of hydrogen ions. $[H^+_a]$ for household ammonia is 10^{-11}. $[H^+_v]$ for vinegar is 6.3×10^{-3}. What is the difference of the pH levels of ammonia and vinegar?

Think

Write the equation for pH.

Write the difference of the pH levels.

Substitute values for $[H^+_v]$ and $[H^+_a]$.

Use the Product Property of Logarithms, and simplify.

Use a calculator.

Write the answer.

Write

$$pH = -\log[H^+]$$

$$(-\log[H^+_a]) - (-\log[H^+_v])$$
$$= -\log[H^+_a] + \log[H^+_v]$$
$$= \log[H^+_v] - \log[H^+_a]$$

$$= \log(6.3 \times 10^{-3}) - \log 10^{-11}$$

$$= \log 6.3 + \log 10^{-3} - \log 10^{-11}$$
$$= \log 6.3 - 3 + 11$$

$$\approx 8.8$$

The pH level of ammonia is about 8.8 greater than the pH level of vinegar.

Hint

$\log 10^x = x$ for all values of x because a common logarithm has a base of 10.

 Got It? **4. Reasoning** Suppose the hydrogen ion concentration for Substance A is twice that for Substance B. Which substance has the greater pH level? What is the greater pH level minus the lesser pH level? Explain.

Focus Question How are the properties of logarithms similar to the properties of exponents?

Answer The properties of logarithms are derived from the properties of exponents. Use the Product, Quotient, and Power Properties to simplify or expand logarithms.

Focus Question Why is the Change of Base Formula useful?

Answer The Change of Base Formula allows you to write a logarithmic expression in one base as an equivalent logarithmic expression in another base (usually base 10). Use the Change of Base Formula to evaluate logarithmic expressions with a calculator.

Lesson Check

Do you know HOW?

Write each expression as a single logarithm.

1. $\log_4 2 + \log_4 8$ **2.** $\log_6 24 - \log_6 4$

Expand each logarithm.

3. $\log_3 \frac{x}{y}$ **4.** $\log m^2 n^5$ **5.** $\log_2 \sqrt{x}$

Do you UNDERSTAND?

6. State which property or properties need to be used to write each expression as a single logarithm.
     a. $\log_4 5 + \log_4 5$ **b.** $\log_5 4 - \log_5 6$

7. Reasoning If $\log x = 5$, what is the value of $\frac{1}{x}$?

8. Open-Ended Write $\log 150$ as a sum or difference of two logarithms. Simplify if possible.

Practice and Problem-Solving Exercises

 **Practice**

Write each expression as a single logarithm.    **See Problem 1.**

Guided Practice

To start, use the Quotient Property of Logarithms.

     9. $\log_2 9 - \log_2 3$

     $\log_2 9 - \log_2 3 = \log_2 \frac{9}{3}$

10. $\log 7 + \log 2$ **11.** $5 \log 3 + \log 4$ **12.** $\log 8 - 2 \log 6 + \log 3$

Expand each logarithm.   **See Problem 2.**

Guided Practice

To start, use the Product Property of Logarithms.

     13. $\log x^3 y^5$

     $\log x^3 y^5 = \log x^3 + \log y^5$

14. $\log_3 (2x)^2$ **15.** $\log_3 7(2x - 3)^2$ **16.** $\log 10 m^4 n^{-2}$

Use the Change of Base Formula to evaluate each expression.   **See Problem 3.**

17. $\log_2 9$ **18.** $\log_{12} 20$ **19.** $\log_7 30$

20. $\log_5 10$ **21.** $\log_3 54$ **22.** $\log_3 33$

23. Science The concentration of hydrogen ions in household dish detergent is 10^{-12}. What is the pH level of household dish detergent?   **See Problem 4.**

 **Apply**

24. Think About a Plan The loudness in decibels (dB) of a sound is defined as $10 \log \frac{I}{I_0}$, where I is the intensity of the sound in watts per square meter (W/m^2). I_0, the intensity of a barely audible sound, is equal to 10^{-12}W/m^2. Town regulations require the loudness of construction work not to exceed 100 dB. Suppose a construction team is blasting rock for a roadway. One explosion has an intensity of $1.65 \times 10^{-2} \text{W/m}^2$. Is this explosion in violation of town regulations?
- Which physical value do you need to calculate to answer the question?
- What values should you use for I and I_0?

25. Construction The foreman of a construction team puts up a sound barrier that reduces the intensity of their noise by 50%. By how many decibels is the noise reduced? Use the formula $L = 10 \log \frac{I}{I_0}$ to measure loudness. (*Hint:* Find the difference between the expression for loudness for intensity I and the expression for loudness for intensity $0.5I$.)

Use the properties of logarithms to evaluate each expression.

26. $\log_2 4 - \log_2 16$

27. $\log_3 27 - 2\log_3 3$

28. $\log_6 12 + \log_6 3$

29. $\log_4 48 - \frac{1}{2}\log_4 9$

Determine if each statment is *true* or *false*. Justify your answer.

30. $\log_2 4 + \log_2 8 = 5$

31. $\log_3 \frac{3}{2} = \frac{1}{2}\log_3 3$

32. $\log(x - 2) = \frac{\log x}{\log 2}$

33. $(\log x)^2 = \log x^2$

Write each logarithmic expression as a single logarithm.

34. $\frac{1}{2}(\log_x 4 + \log_x y) - 3\log_x z$

35. $x\log_4 m + \frac{1}{y}\log_4 n - \log_4 p$

36. Error Analysis Explain why the expansion at the right of $\log_4 \sqrt{\frac{t}{s}}$ is incorrect. Then do the expansion correctly.

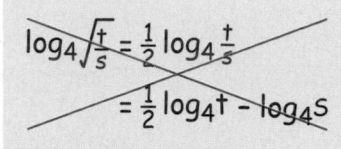

$$\log_4 \sqrt{\frac{t}{s}} = \frac{1}{2}\log_4 \frac{t}{s}$$
$$= \frac{1}{2}\log_4 t - \log_4 s$$

37. Reasoning Can you expand $\log_3(2x + 1)$? Explain.

38. Writing Explain why $\log(5 \cdot 2) \neq \log 5 \cdot \log 2$.

Expand each logarithm.

39. $\log \sqrt{\frac{2x}{y}}$

40. $\log \frac{s\sqrt{7}}{t^2}$

41. $\log \left(\frac{2\sqrt{x}}{5}\right)^3$

42. $\log \frac{m^3}{n^4 p^{-2}}$

43. $\log 4\sqrt{\frac{4r}{s^2}}$

44. $\log_4 \frac{\sqrt{x^5 y^7}}{zw^4}$

Write each logarithm as the quotient of two common logarithms. Do not simplify the quotient.

45. $\log_7 2$

46. $\log_5 140$

47. $\log_4 3x$

Astronomy The apparent brightness of stars is measured on a logarithmic scale called magnitude, in which lower numbers mean brighter stars. The relationship between the ratio of apparent brightness of two objects and the difference in their magnitudes is given by the formula $m_2 - m_1 = -2.5 \log\frac{b_2}{b_1}$, where m is the magnitude and b is the apparent brightness.

Capella
$m = 0.1$

48. How many times brighter is a magnitude 1.0 star than a magnitude 2.0 star?

49. The star Rigel has a magnitude of 0.12. How many times brighter is Capella than Rigel?

Standardized Test Prep

SAT/ACT

50. Which expression is NOT equivalent to $\sqrt[6]{16r^2}$?

  Ⓐ $\left(16r^2\right)^{\frac{1}{6}}$ Ⓑ $4r^{\frac{1}{3}}$ Ⓒ $(4r)^{\frac{1}{3}}$ Ⓓ $\sqrt[3]{4r}$

51. Assume that there are no more turning points beyond those shown. Which graph CANNOT be the graph of a fourth degree polynomial?

Ⓕ 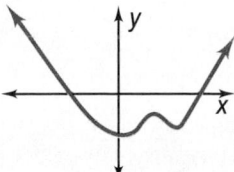   Ⓗ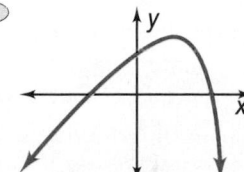

Ⓖ 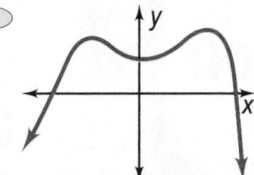   Ⓘ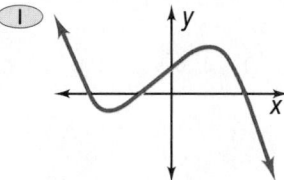

52. A florist is arranging a bouquet of daisies and tulips. He wants twice as many daisies as tulips in the bouquet. If the bouquet contains 24 flowers, how many daisies are in the bouquet?

  Ⓐ 8 daisies   Ⓑ 12 daisies   Ⓒ 16 daisies   Ⓓ 24 daisies

Short Response

53. Use the properties of logarithms to write log 18 in four different ways. Name each property you use.

Mixed Review

Write each equation in logarithmic form.   ◀ **See Lesson 7-3.**

54. $49 = 7^2$ **55.** $\frac{1}{4} = 8^{-\frac{2}{3}}$ **56.** $5^{-3} = \frac{1}{125}$

Solve. Check for extraneous solutions.   ◀ **See Lesson 6-5.**

57. $\sqrt[3]{y^4} = 16$ **58.** $\sqrt[3]{7x} - 4 = 0$ **59.** $2\sqrt{w-1} = \sqrt{w+2}$

Write a polynomial function with rational coefficients and the given roots.   ◀ **See Lesson 5-5.**

60. $\sqrt{3}, -5$ **61.** $-i, 4i$ **62.** $-\sqrt{7}, 1 + 2i$

Get Ready!   To prepare for Lesson 7-5, do Exercises 63–65.

Evaluate each logarithm.   ◀ **See Lesson 7-3.**

63. $\log_{12} 144$ **64.** $\log_4 64$ **65.** $\log_{64} 4$

7-5 PART 1

Exponential and Logarithmic Equations

Objective To solve exponential equations

SOLVE IT!

Getting Ready! ◄► ✕ ↻ ⌂

You are a winner on a TV game show. Which prize would you choose? Explain.

Make sure you win the most money.

Prize A
$10,000
per week

Prize B
1¢ today,
2¢ tomorrow,
4¢ the next day,
and so on,
doubling each day

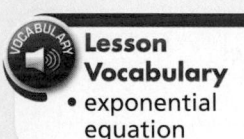
Lesson Vocabulary
• exponential equation

Any equation that contains an expression of the form b^{cx}, such as $a = b^{cx}$, where the exponent includes a variable is an **exponential equation**.

Focus Question How can you solve exponential equations?

Problem 1 Solving an Exponential Equation—Common Base

Multiple Choice What is the solution of $16^{3x} = 8$?

Ⓐ $x = \frac{1}{4}$ Ⓑ $x = \frac{3}{7}$ Ⓒ $x = 1$ Ⓓ $x = 4$

Plan

What common base is appropriate?
2 because 16 and 8 are both powers of 2.

Write the original equation.	$16^{3x} = 8$
Rewrite each side with a common base.	$(2^4)^{3x} = 2^3$
Use the Power Property of Exponents.	$2^{12x} = 2^3$
Since the bases are the same, their exponents are equal.	$12x = 3$
Solve for x and simplify.	$x = \frac{1}{4}$

The correct answer is A.

Hint

Remember to check your answer using substitution.

 Got It? **1.** What is the solution of $27^{3x} = 81$?

When the bases are not the same, you can solve an exponential equation by taking the logarithm of each side of the equation. If m and n are positive numbers and $m = n$, then $\log m = \log n$.

 Problem 2 Solving an Exponential Equation—Different Bases

What is the solution of $15^{3x} = 285$?

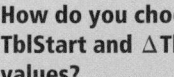
Think

Which property of logarithms will help isolate x?
The rule $\log a^x = x \log a$ moves x out of the exponent position.

Write the original equation.	$15^{3x} = 285$
Take the logarithm base 10 of each side.	$\log 15^{3x} = \log 285$
Use the Power Property of Logarithms.	$3x \log 15 = \log 285$
Divide each side by 3 log 15 to isolate x.	$x = \dfrac{\log 285}{3 \log 15}$
Use a calculator to evaluate.	$x \approx 0.6958$

Check $15^{3x} = 285$

$$15^{3(0.6958)} \approx 285.0840331 \approx 285 \checkmark$$

 Got It? **2. a.** What is the solution of $5^{2x} = 130$?

b. Reasoning Why can't you use the same method you used in Problem 1 to solve Problem 2?

 Problem 3 Solving an Exponential Equation With a Graph or Table

What is the solution of $4^{3x} = 6000$?

Method 1 Solve using a graph.

Use a graphing calculator. Graph the equations $Y_1 = 4^{3x}$ and $Y_2 = 6000$.

Adjust the window to find the point of intersection. The solution is $x \approx 2.09$.

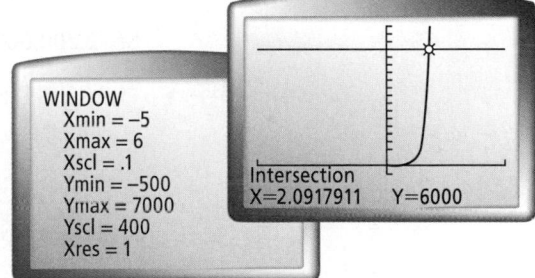

Method 2 Solve using a table.

Use the table feature of a graphing calculator. Enter $Y_1 = 4^{3x}$.

Think

How do you choose TblStart and △Tbl values?
Start with 0 and 1, respectively. Adjust both values as you close in on the solution.

Use the **TABLE SETUP** and **△Tbl** features to locate the x-value that gives the y-value closest to 6000. The solution is $x \approx 2.09$.

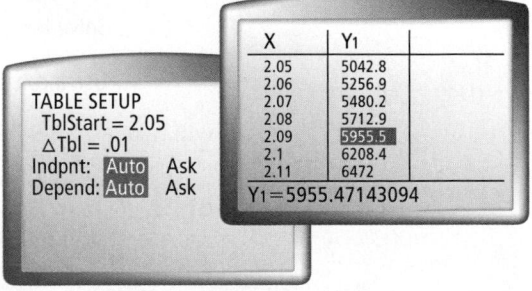

 Got It? **3.** What is the solution of each exponential equation? Check your answer.

a. $7^{4x} = 800$ **b.** $5.2^{3x} = 400$

 **Problem 4** Modeling With an Exponential Equation

Resource Management Wood is a sustainable, renewable, natural resource when you manage forests properly. Your lumber company has 1,200,000 trees. You plan to harvest 7% of the trees each year. How many years will it take to harvest half of the trees?

Know
• Number of trees
• Rate of decay

Need
Number of years it takes to harvest 600,000 trees

Plan
• Write an exponential equation.
• Use logarithms to solve the equation.

Think

What equation should you use to model this situation?
Since you are planning to harvest 7% of the trees each year, you should use $y = ab^x$, where b is the decay factor.

Step 1 Is an exponential model reasonable for this situation?

Yes, you are harvesting a fixed percentage each year.

Step 2 Define the variables and determine the model.

Let $n =$ the number of years it takes to harvest half of the trees.

Let $T(n) =$ the number of trees remaining after n years.

A reasonable model is $T(n) = ab^n$.

Step 3 Use the model to write an exponential equation.

a is the initial number of trees. $\qquad\qquad\qquad$ $a = 1{,}200{,}000$

$T(n)$ is half of the initial number of trees, or $\frac{1}{2}a$. $\quad T(n) = 600{,}000$

r is the rate of decay. $\qquad\qquad\qquad\qquad\qquad$ $r = -7\% = -0.07$

b is the decay factor. $\qquad\qquad\qquad\qquad$ $b = 1 + r = 1 + (-0.07) = 0.93$

So, $1{,}200{,}000(0.93)^n = 600{,}000$.

Step 4 Solve the equation. Use logarithms.

Write the original equation. $\qquad\qquad$ $1{,}200{,}000(0.93)^n = 600{,}000$

Isolate the term with n. $\qquad\qquad\qquad$ $0.93^n = \dfrac{600{,}000}{1{,}200{,}000}$

Take the logarithm of each side. $\qquad\quad$ $\log 0.93^n = \log 0.5$

Use the Power Property of Logarithms. $\quad$ $n \log 0.93 = \log 0.5$

Solve for n. $\qquad\qquad\qquad\qquad\qquad$ $n = \dfrac{\log 0.5}{\log 0.93}$

Use a calculator to evaluate. $\qquad\qquad$ $n \approx 9.55$

It will take about 9.55 years to harvest half of the original trees.

 Got It? 4. How many years will it take to harvest half of the trees if you harvest 5% instead of 7% each year?

Focus Question How can you solve exponential equations?

Answer Use logarithms, a graph, or a table to solve exponential equations.

Lesson Check

Do you know HOW?

Solve each equation.

1. $3^x = 9$

2. $2^x = 8$

3. $2^{y+1} = 25$

Do you UNDERSTAND?

4. Reasoning Is it possible for an exponential equation to have no solutions? If so, give an example. If not, explain why.

Practice and Problem-Solving Exercises

A Practice   Solve each equation.   ◀ See Problem 1.

> **Guided Practice**
>
> To start, rewrite each side with a common base.
>
> **5.** $3^{2x} = 27$
>
> $3^{2x} = 3^3$

6. $4^{3x} = 64$

7. $5^{3x} = \dfrac{1}{125}$

8. $2^{5x+1} = 32$

9. $3^{-2x+2} = 81$

10. $2^{3x} = 4^{x+1}$

11. $3^{x+2} = 27^{2x}$

Solve each equation. Round to the nearest ten-thousandth. Check your answers.   ◀ See Problem 2.

> **Guided Practice**
>
> To start, take the logarithm of each side.
>
> **12.** $2^x = 3$
>
> $\log 2^x = \log 3$

13. $4^x = 19$

14. $8 + 10^x = 1008$

15. $5 - 3^x = -40$

16. $9^{2y} = 66$

17. $25^{2x+1} = 144$

18. $2^{3x-4} = 5$

🖩 **Graphing Calculator** Solve by graphing. Round to the nearest ten-thousandth.   ◀ See Problem 3.

19. $4^{7x} = 250$

20. $5^{3x} = 500$

21. $6^x = 4565$

Use a table to solve each equation. Round to the nearest hundredth.

22. $2^{x+3} = 512$

23. $3^{x-1} = 72$

24. $5^{2x} = 56$

25. The equation $y = 6.72(1.014)^x$ models the world population y, in billions of people, x years after the year 2000. Find the year in which the world population is about 8 billion.   ◀ See Problem 4.

 **Apply**

26. Consider the equation $2^{\frac{x}{3}} = 80$.

    a. Solve the equation by taking the logarithm base 10 of each side.

    b. Solve the equation by taking the logarithm base 2 of each side.

    c. Writing Compare your result in parts (a) and (b). What are the advantages of each method? Explain.

27. As a town gets smaller, the population of its high school decreases by 6% each year. The senior class has 160 students now. In how many years will it have about 100 students? Write an equation. Then solve the equation without graphing.

Mental Math Solve each equation.

28. $2^x = \frac{1}{2}$ **29.** $3^x = 27$ **30.** $10^x = \frac{1}{100}$ **31.** $25^x = \frac{1}{5}$

32. Reasoning The graphs of $y = 2^{3x}$ and $y = 3^{x+1}$ intersect at approximately (1.1201, 10.2692). What is the solution of $2^{3x} = 3^{x+1}$?

33. Demography The table below lists the states with the highest and lowest population growth rates. Determine in how many years each event can occur. Use the model $P = P_0(1 + r)^x$, where P_0 is population from the table, as of July, 2007; x is the number of years after July, 2007, P is the projected population and r is the growth rate.

    a. Population of Idaho exceeds 2 million.

    b. Population of Michigan decreases by 1 million.

    c. Population of Nevada doubles.

State	Growth rate (%)	Population (in thousands)	State	Growth rate (%)	Population (in thousands)
1. Nevada	2.93	2,565	46. New York	0.08	19,298
2. Arizona	2.81	6,339	47. Vermont	0.08	621
3. Utah	2.55	2,645	48. Ohio	0.03	11,467
4. Idaho	2.43	1,499	49. Michigan	−0.30	10,072
5. Georgia	2.17	9,545	50. Rhode Island	−0.36	1,058

SOURCE: U.S. Census Bureau

Solve each equation. If necessary, round to the nearest ten-thousandth.

34. $8^x = 444$ **35.** $9^{2x} = 42$ **36.** $12^{4-x} = 20$

37. $5^{3x} = 125$ **38.** $4^{3x} = 77.2$ **39.** $7^x - 1 = 371$

Exponential and Logarithmic Equations

Objective To solve logarithmic equations

| In Part 1 of the lesson, you learned how to solve exponential equations using logarithms. | **Connect to What You Know** | Here you will learn to solve logarithmic equations using exponents. |

Lesson Vocabulary
- logarithmic equation

Focus Question How can you solve logarithmic equations?

A **logarithmic equation** is an equation that includes one or more logarithms involving a variable.

Problem 5 Solving a Logarithmic Equation

Plan

How do you convert between log form and exponential form?
Use the rule: $\log a = b$ if and only if $a = 10^b$.

What is the solution of $\log (4x - 3) = 2$?

Method 1 Solve using exponents.

Write the original equation.	$\log (4x - 3) = 2$
Write in exponential form.	$4x - 3 = 10^2$
Simplify.	$4x = 103$
Solve for x.	$x = \frac{103}{4} = 25.75$

Hint

You can also solve using a table. First, let $Y_1 = \text{LOG} (4x - 3)$. Then use **TABLE SETUP** to find the x-value that corresponds to a y-value of 2.

Method 2 Solve using a graph.

Graph the equations $Y_1 = \text{LOG} (4x - 3)$ and $Y_2 = 2$. Find the point of intersection. The solution is $x = 25.75$.

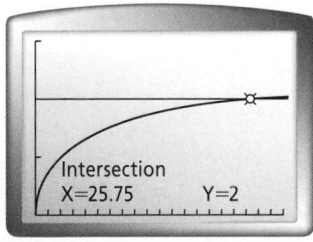

Intersection
X=25.75   Y=2

 Got It? **5.** What is the solution of $\log (3 - 2x) = -1$? Solve using both exponents and a graph.

Sometimes you need to use the properties of logarithms before you can rewrite a logarithmic equation in exponential form.

 Problem 6 Using Logarithmic Properties to Solve an Equation

What is the solution of $\log(x - 3) + \log x = 1$?

Write the original equation.	$\log(x - 3) + \log x = 1$
Use the Product Property of Logarithms.	$\log((x - 3)x) = 1$
Write in exponential form.	$(x - 3)x = 10^1$
Use the Distributive Property.	$x^2 - 3x = 10$
Write as a quadratic equation in standard form.	$x^2 - 3x - 10 = 0$
Factor the trinomial.	$(x - 5)(x + 2) = 0$
Solve for x.	$x = 5$ or $x = -2$

Think

What is the domain of the logarithm function?
Logs are defined only for positive numbers. The log of a negative number is undefined.

Check

Write the equation.	$\log(x - 3) + \log(x) = 1$	$\log(x - 3) + \log x = 1$
Substitute.	$\log(5 - 3) + \log 5 = 1$	$\log(-2 - 3) + \log(-2) = 1$
Simplify.	$\log 2 + \log 5 = 1$	$\log(-5) + \log(-2) = 1$ ✗
Use a calculator.	$0.3101 + 0.6990 = 1$ ✔	

undefined

The solution is $x = 5$.

 Got It? **6.** What is the solution of $\log 6 - \log 3x = -2$?

Focus Question How can you solve logarithmic equations?

Answer Use exponents to solve logarithmic equations. Solve a logarithmic equation by rewriting it in exponential form and using the properties of logarithms and exponents. You can also use a graph or table.

 Lesson Check

Do you know HOW?

Solve each equation.

1. $\log 4x = 2$

2. $\log x - \log 2 = 3$

3. $2 \log x = -1$

Do you UNDERSTAND?

4. Error Analysis Describe and correct the error made in solving the equation.

$$\log_2 x = 2 \log_3 9$$
$$\log_2 x = \log_3 9^2$$
$$x = 9^2$$
$$x = 81$$

Practice and Problem-Solving Exercises

See Problem 5.

Practice

Guided Practice

Solve each equation. Check your answers.

5. $\log 2x = -1$

To start, write the equation in exponential form.

$2x = 10^{-1}$

6. $\log (3x + 1) = 2$ **7.** $\log x + 4 = 8$ **8.** $\log 6x - 3 = -4$

9. $3 \log x = 1.5$ **10.** $2 \log (x + 1) = 5$ **11.** $\log (5 - 2x) = 0$

Solve each equation.

See Problem 6.

Guided Practice

12. $\log x - \log 3 = 8$

To start, use the Quotient Property of Logarithms.

$\log \frac{x}{3} = 8$

13. $\log x + \log 5 = 2$ **14.** $\log 2x + \log x = 11$ **15.** $2 \log x + \log 4 = 2$

16. $\log 5 - \log 2x = 1$ **17.** $3 \log x - \log 6 + \log 2.4 = 9$ **18.** $\log (7x + 1) = \log (x - 2) + 1$

Apply

19. Think About a Plan An earthquake of magnitude 9.1 occurred in 2004 in the Indian Ocean near Indonesia. It was about 74,900 times as strong as the greatest earthquake ever to hit Texas. Find the magnitude of the Texas earthquake. (Remember that an increase of 1.0 on the Richter scale means an earthquake is 30 times stronger.)
- Can you write an exponential or logarithmic equation?
- How does the solution of your equation help you find the magnitude?

20. Seismology An earthquake of magnitude 7.7 occurred in 2001 in Gujarat, India. It was 4900 times as strong as the greatest earthquake ever to hit Pennsylvania. What is the magnitude of the Pennsylvania earthquake? (*Hint:* Refer to the Richter scale on page 482.)

Acoustics In Exercises 21 and 22, the loudness measured in decibels (dB) is defined by loudness $= 10 \log \frac{I}{I_0}$, where I is the intensity and $I_0 = 10^{-12}$ W/m^2.

21. The human threshold for pain is 120 dB. Instant perforation of the eardrum occurs at 160 dB.
   a. Find the intensity of each sound.
   b. How many times as intense is the noise that will perforate an eardrum as the noise that causes pain?

22. The noise level inside a convertible driving along the freeway with its top up is 70 dB. With the top down, the noise level is 95 dB.
   a. Find the intensity of the sound with the top up and with the top down.
   b. By what percent does leaving the top up reduce the intensity of the sound?

Solve each equation. If necessary, round to the nearest ten-thousandth.

23. $\frac{1}{2}\log x + \log 4 = 2$ **24.** $4\log_3 2 - 2\log_3 x = 1$ **25.** $\log_8(2x - 1) = \frac{1}{3}$

26. $\log(5x - 4) = 3$ **27.** $\log 4 + 2\log x = 6$ **28.** $\log_7 3x = 3$

Mental Math Solve each equation.

29. $\log_9 3 = x$ **30.** $\log_4 64 = x$ **31.** $\log_8 2 = x$ **32.** $\log_7 343 = x$

33. Open-Ended Write and solve a logarithmic equation.

34. Reasoning If $\log 12^{0.5x} = \log 143.6$, then $12^{0.5x} = \underline{\ ?\ }$.

Standardized Test Prep

SAT/ACT

35. The graph at the right shows the translation of the graph of the parent function $y = |x|$ down 2 units and 3 units to the right. What is the area of the shaded triangle in square units?

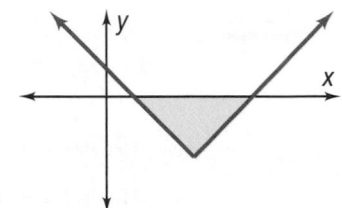

36. What does x equal if $\log(1 + 3x) = 3$?

37. Using the change of base formula, what is the value of x for which $\log_9 x = \log_3 5$?

38. The polynomial $x^4 + 3x^3 + 16x^2 - 19x + 8$ is divided by the binomial $x - 1$. What is the coefficient of x^2 in the quotient?

39. What positive value of b makes $x^2 + bx + 81$ a perfect square trinomial?

Mixed Review

Expand each logarithm.   ◀ **See Lesson 7-4.**

40. $\log 2x^3 y^{-2}$ **41.** $\log_3 \frac{x}{y}$ **42.** $\log_3 \sqrt{9x}$

Let $f(x) = 3x$ and $g(x) = x^2 - 1$. Perform each function operation.   ◀ **See Lesson 6-6.**

43. $(g - f)(x)$ **44.** $(f \circ g)(x)$ **45.** $(g \circ f)(x)$

Find all the zeros of each function.   ◀ **See Lesson 5-6.**

46. $y = x^3 - x^2 + x - 1$ **47.** $f(x) = x^4 - 16$ **48.** $f(x) = x^4 - 5x^2 + 6$

Get Ready! To prepare for Lesson 8-1, do Exercises 49 and 50.

For Exercises 49 and 50, y varies directly with x.   ◀ **See Lesson 2-2.**

49. If $y = 4$ when $x = 2$, find y when $x = 5$.   **50.** If $y = 5$ when $x = 1$, find y when $x = 3$.

Using Logarithms for Exponential Models

You can transform an exponential function into a linear function by taking the logarithm of each side. Since linear models are easy to recognize, you can then determine whether an exponential function is a good model for a set of values.

Write the general form of an exponential function.	$y = ab^x$
Take the logarithm of each side.	$\log y = \log ab^x$
Use the Product Property and the Power Property.	$\log y = \log a + x(\log b)$

If $\log b$ and $\log a$ are constants, then $\log y = (\log b)x + \log a$ is a linear equation in slope-intercept form when you plot the points as $(x, \log y)$.

Activity

Determine whether an exponential function is a good model for the values in the table.

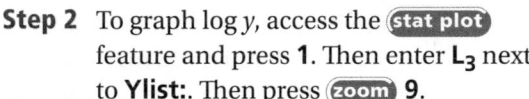

x	0	2	4	6	8	10
y	0.5	2	7.8	32	127.9	511.7

Step 1 Enter the values into $\boxed{\text{stat}}$ lists L_1 and L_2. To enter the values of $\log y$, place the cursor in the heading of L_3 and press $\boxed{\text{log}}$ L_2 $\boxed{\text{enter}}$.

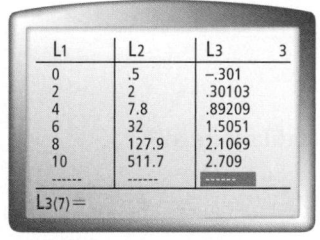

Step 2 To graph $\log y$, access the $\boxed{\text{stat plot}}$ feature and press **1**. Then enter L_3 next to **Ylist:**. Then press $\boxed{\text{zoom}}$ **9**.

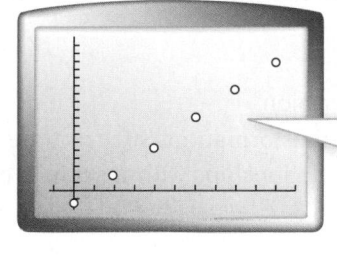

The points $(x, \log y)$ lie on a line, so an exponential model is appropriate.

Step 3 Press $\boxed{\text{stat}}$ $\triangleright$ **0** $\boxed{\text{enter}}$ to find the exponential function $y = 0.5(2)^x$.

Exercises

For each set of values, determine whether an exponential function is a good model. If so, find the exponential function.

1.

x	1	3	5	7	9
y	6	22	54	102	145

2.

x	−1	0	1	2	3
y	40.2	19.8	9.9	5.1	2.5

3. Writing Explain how you could determine whether a logarithmic function is a good model for a set of data.

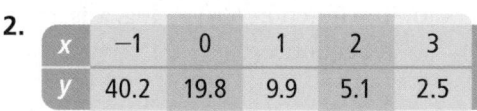

Pull It **All Together**

To solve these problems, you will pull together concepts and skills related to exponential functions and logarithms.

BIG idea Modeling

You can represent many real-world mathematical problems algebraically. An algebraic model can lead to an algebraic solution.

Task 1

Suppose you invest a dollars to earn an annual interest rate of r percent (as a decimal). After t years, the value of the investment with interest compounded yearly is $A(t) = a(1 + r)^t$. The value with interest compounded continuously is $A(t) = a \cdot e^{rt}$.

   a. Explain why you can call $e^r - 1$ the effective annual interest rate for the continuous compounding.
   b. Suppose you can earn interest at some rate between 0% and 5%. Use your knowledge of the exponential function to explain why continuous compounding does not give you much of an investment advantage.
   c. For each situation find the unknown quantity, such that continuous compounding gives you a $1 advantage over annually compounded interest.
   - How much must you invest for 1 year at 2%?
   - At what interest rate must you invest $1000 for 1 year?
   - For how long must you invest $1000 at 2%?

BIG idea Function

You can use transformations such as translations, reflections, and dilations to understand relationships within a family of functions.

Task 2

$f(x) = b^x$ and $g(x) = \log_b x$ are inverse functions. Explain why each of the following is true.
   a. The translation $f_1(x) = b^{x-h}$ of f is equivalent to a vertical stretch or compression of f.
   b. The inverse of $f_1(x) = b^{x-h}$ is equivalent to a translation of g.
   c. The inverse of $f_1(x) = b^{x-h}$ is not equivalent to a vertical stretch or compression of g.
   d. The function $h(x) = \log_c x$ is a vertical stretch or compression of g or of its reflection $-g$.

Connecting BIG ideas and Answering the Essential Questions

1 Modeling
The function $y = ab^x$, $a > 0$, $b > 1$, models exponential growth. $y = ab^x$ models exponential decay if $0 < b < 1$.

Exponential Models (Lesson 7-1)
The population P is 1000 at the start. In each time period,

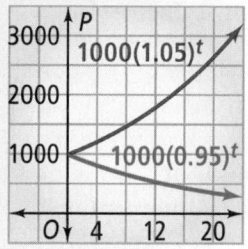

- P grows by 5%. $P = 1000(1.05)^t$
- P shrinks by 5%. $P = 1000(0.95)^t$

Properties of Logarithms (Lesson 7-4)
$$b^a b^c = b^{a+c}$$
$$\log_b mn = \log_b m + \log_b n$$
$$\frac{b^a}{b^c} = b^{a-c}$$
$$\log_b \frac{m}{n} = \log_b m - \log_b n$$
$$\log_b m^n = n \log_b m$$
$$\log_n m = \frac{\log_b m}{\log_b n}$$

2 Equivalence
Logarithms are exponents. In fact, $\log_b a = c$ if and only if $b^c = a$.

3 Function
The exponential function $y = b^x$ and the logarithmic function $y = \log_b x$ are inverse functions.

Logarithmic Functions as Inverses (Lesson 7-3)
- $y = 2^x$
- $y = \log_2 x$
- $y = 2^{x-1}$
- $y = (\log_2 x) + 1$

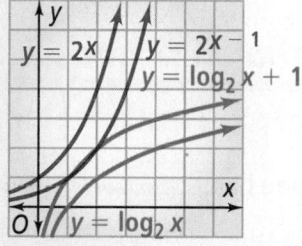

Exponential and Logarithmic Equations (Lesson 7-5)
$$5^{x+3} = 16$$
$$\log 5^{x+3} = \log 16$$
$$(x + 3)\log 5 = \log 16$$
$$(x + 3) = \frac{\log 16}{\log 5}$$
$$x = \frac{\log 16}{\log 5} - 3$$

Chapter Vocabulary

- asymptote (p. 463)
- Change of Base Formula (p. 493)
- common logarithm (p. 482)
- continuously compounded interest (p. 477)
- decay factor (p. 464)
- exponential decay (p. 463)
- exponential equation (p. 498)
- exponential function (p. 462)
- exponential growth (p. 463)
- growth factor (p. 464)
- logarithm (p. 480)
- logarithmic equation (p. 503)
- logarithmic function (p. 483)
- logarithmic scale (p. 482)
- natural base exponential function (p. 476)

Fill in the blanks.

1. There are two types of exponential functions. For __?__, as the value of x increases, the value of y decreases, approaching zero. For __?__, as the value of x increases, the value of y increases.

2. As x or y increases in absolute value, the graph may approach a(n) __?__.

3. A(n) __?__ with a base e is a(n) __?__.

4. $A = Pe^{rt}$ is known as the __?__ formula.

5. A __?__ uses base 10.

7-1 Exploring Exponential Models

Quick Review

The general form of an **exponential function** is $y = ab^x$, where x is a real number, $a \neq 0$, $b > 0$, and $b \neq 1$. When $b > 1$, the function models **exponential growth**, and b is the **growth factor**. When $0 < b < 1$, the function models **exponential decay**, and b is the **decay factor**. The y-intercept is $(0, a)$.

Example

Determine whether $y = 2(1.4)^x$ is an example of exponential growth or decay. Then, find the y-intercept.

Since $b = 1.4 > 1$, the function represents exponential growth.

Since $a = 2$, the y-intercept is $(0, 2)$.

Exercises

Determine whether each function is an example of exponential growth or decay. Then, find the y-intercept.

6. $y = 5^x$

7. $y = 2(4)^x$

8. $y = 0.2(3.8)^x$

9. $y = 3(0.25)^x$

10. $y = \frac{25}{7}\left(\frac{7}{5}\right)^x$

11. $y = 0.0015(10)^x$

12. $y = 2.25\left(\frac{1}{3}\right)^x$

13. $y = 0.5\left(\frac{1}{4}\right)^x$

Write a function for each situation. Then find the value of each function after five years. Round to the nearest dollar.

14. A \$12,500 car depreciates 9% each year.

15. A baseball card bought for \$50 increases 3% in value each year.

7-2 Properties of Exponential Functions

Quick Review

Exponential functions can be translated, stretched, compressed, and reflected.

The graph of $y = ab^{x-h} + k$ is the graph of the parent function $y = b^x$ stretched or compressed by a factor $|a|$, reflected across the x-axis if $a < 0$, and then translated h units horizontally and k units vertically.

The **continuously compounded interest formula** is $A = Pe^{rt}$, where P is the principal, r is the annual interest rate, and t is time in years.

Example

How does the graph of $y = -3^x + 1$ compare to the graph of the parent function?

The parent function is $y = 3^x$.

Since $a = -1$, the graph is reflected across the x-axis.

Since $k = 1$, it is then translated up 1 unit.

Exercises

How does the graph of each function compare to the graph of the parent function?

16. $y = 5(2)^{x+1} + 3$

17. $y = -2\left(\frac{1}{3}\right)^{x-2}$

Find the amount in a continuously compounded account for the given conditions.

18. principal: \$1000
annual interest rate: 4.8%
time: 2 years

19. principal: \$250
annual interest rate: 6.2%
time: 2.5 years

Evaluate each expression to four decimal places.

20. e^{-3}

21. e^{-1}

22. e^5

23. $e^{-\frac{1}{2}}$

7-3 Logarithmic Functions as Inverses

Quick Review

If $x = b^y$, then $\log_b x = y$. The **logarithmic function** is the inverse of the exponential function, so the graphs of the functions are reflections of each other in the line $y = x$. Logarithmic functions can be translated, stretched, compressed, and reflected, as represented by $y = a \log_b(x - h) + k$, similarly to exponential functions.

When $b = 10$, the logarithm is called a **common logarithm**, which you can write as $\log x$.

Example

Write $5^{-2} = 0.04$ in logarithmic form.

If $y = b^x$, then $\log_b y = x$.

$y = 0.04$, $b = 5$ and $x = -2$.

So, $\log_5 0.04 = -2$.

Exercises

Write each equation in logarithmic form.

24. $6^2 = 36$ **25.** $2^{-3} = 0.125$

26. $3^3 = 27$ **27.** $10^{-3} = 0.001$

Evaluate each logarithm.

28. $\log_2 64$ **29.** $\log_3 \frac{1}{9}$

30. $\log 0.00001$ **31.** $\log_2 1$

Graph each logarithmic function.

32. $y = \log_3 x$ **33.** $y = \log x + 2$

34. $y = 3 \log_2(x)$ **35.** $y = \log_5(x + 1)$

How does the graph of each function compare to the graph of the parent function?

36. $y = 3 \log_4(x + 1)$ **37.** $y = \log_3(x - 5) + 3$

7-4 Properties of Logarithms

Quick Review

For any positive numbers, m, n, and b where $b \neq 1$, each of the following statements is true. Each can be used to rewrite a logarithmic expression.

- $\log_b mn = \log_b m + \log_b n$ Product Property
- $\log_b \frac{m}{n} = \log_b m - \log_b n$ Quotient Property
- $\log_b m^n = n \log_b m$ Power Property

Example

Write $2 \log_2 y + \log_2 x$ as a single logarithm. Identify any properties used.

Write the expression.	$2 \log_2 y + \log_2 x$
Use the Power Property.	$\log_2 y^2 + \log_2 x$
Use the Product Property.	$\log_2 xy^2$

Exercises

Write each expression as a single logarithm. Identify any properties used.

38. $\log 8 + \log 3$ **39.** $\log_2 5 - \log_2 3$

40. $4 \log_3 x + \log_3 7$ **41.** $\log x - \log y$

42. $\log 5 - 2 \log x$ **43.** $3 \log_4 x + 2 \log_4 x$

Expand each logarithm. State the properties of logarithms used.

44. $\log_4 x^2 y^3$ **45.** $\log 4s^4 t$

46. $\log_3 \frac{2}{x}$ **47.** $\log(x + 3)^2$

48. $\log_2(2y - 4)^3$ **49.** $\log \frac{z^2}{5}$

Use the Change of Base Formula to evaluate each expression.

50. $\log_2 7$ **51.** $\log_3 10$

7-5 Exponential and Logarithmic Equations

Quick Review

An equation in the form $b^{cx} = a$, where the exponent includes a variable, is called an **exponential equation**. You can solve exponential equations by taking the logarithm of each side of the equation. An equation that includes one or more logarithms involving a variable is called a **logarithmic equation**.

Example

Solve $6^{2x} = 75$. **Round your answer to the nearest ten-thousandth.**

Write the original equation.	$6^{2x} = 75$
Take the logarithm of each side.	$\log 6^{2x} = \log 75$
Use the Power Property.	$2x \log 6 = \log 75$
Divide each side by 2 log 6.	$x = \dfrac{\log 75}{2 \log 6}$
Use a calculator to evaluate.	$x \approx 1.2048$

Exercises

Solve each equation. Round to the nearest ten-thousandth.

52. $25^{2x} = 125$

53. $3^x = 36$

54. $7^{x-3} = 25$

55. $5^x + 3 = 12$

56. $\log 3x = 1$

57. $\log_2 4x = 5$

58. $\log x = \log 2x^2 - 2$

59. $2 \log_3 x = 5$

Solve by graphing. Round to the nearest ten-thousandth.

60. $5^{2x} = 20$

61. $3^{7x} = 160$

62. $6^{3x+1} = 215$

63. $0.5^x = 0.12$

64. A culture of 10 bacteria is started, and the number of bacteria will double every hour. In about how many hours will there be 3,000,000 bacteria?

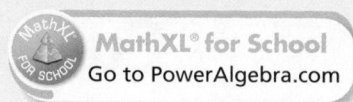

Do you know HOW?

Determine whether each function is an example of exponential growth or decay. Then find the y-intercept.

1. $y = 3(0.25)^x$

2. $y = 2(6)^{-x}$

3. $y = 0.1(10)^x$

4. $y = 3e^x$

Describe how the graph of each function is related to the graph of its parent function. Then find the domain, range, and asymptotes.

5. $y = 3^x + 2$

6. $y = \left(\frac{1}{2}\right)^{x+1}$

7. $y = -(2)^{x+2}$

Write each equation in logarithmic form.

8. $5^4 = 625$

9. $e^0 = 1$

Evaluate each logarithm.

10. $\log_2 8$

11. $\log_7 7$

12. $\log_5 \frac{1}{125}$

13. $\log_{11} 1$

Graph each logarithmic function. Compare each graph to the graph of its parent function. List each function's domain, range, y-intercept, and asymptotes.

14. $y = \log_3 (x - 1)$

15. $y = \frac{1}{2}\log_3 (x + 2)$

16. $y = 1 - \log_2 x$

Write each logarithmic expression as a single logarithm.

17. $\log_2 4 + 3 \log_2 9$

18. $3 \log a - 2 \log b$

Expand each logarithm.

19. $\log_7 \frac{a}{b}$

20. $\log 3x^3y^2$

Use the properties of logarithms to evaluate each expression.

21. $\log_9 27 - \log_9 9$

22. $2 \log 5 + \log 40$

Solve each equation.

23. $(27)^{3x} = 81$

24. $3^{x-1} = 24$

25. $\log (x - 2) = 1$

26. $2 \log x = -4$

Use the Change of Base Formula to rewrite each expression using common logarithms.

27. $\log_3 16$

28. $\log_2 10$

29. $\log_7 8$

30. $\log_4 9$

Do you UNDERSTAND?

31. Writing Show that solving the equation $3^{2x} = 4$ by taking the common logarithm of each side is equivalent to solving it by taking the logarithm with base 3 of each side.

32. Open-Ended Give an example of an exponential function that models exponential growth and an example of an exponential function that models exponential decay.

33. Investment You put $1500 into an account that pays 7% annual interest compounded continuously. How long will it be before you have $2000 in your account?

TIPS FOR SUCCESS

Some problems ask you to find lengths of arcs or areas of sectors. Read the question at the right. Then follow the tips to answer the sample question.

Let $f(x) = \pi x^2$ represent the area of a circle with radius x. Let $g(x) = \frac{60x}{360}$ represent the area of a 60° sector of a circle with area x. A circle with radius 6 centimeters has a sector measuring 60°. What is the area of this sector $(g \circ f)(x)$?

Ⓐ 6π cm²

Ⓑ 12π cm²

Ⓒ 24π cm²

Ⓓ 36π cm²

TIP 1

Draw a diagram

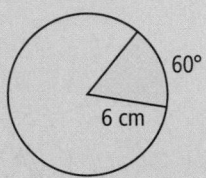

60°

6 cm

TIP 2

Find $f(x)$ first.

$f(x) = \pi x^2$

$\quad = \pi \cdot 6^2$

$\quad = 36\pi$

Think It Through

$$g(x) = \frac{60x}{360}$$

$$(g \circ f)(x) = \frac{60(36\pi)}{360}$$

$$= \frac{36\pi}{6}$$

$$= 6\pi$$

The correct answer is A.

Vocabulary Builder

As you solve problems, you must understand the meanings of mathematical terms. Match each term with its mathematical meaning.

A. growth factor

B. asymptote

C. logarithmic function

D. exponential equation

I. the inverse of an exponential function

II. a line that a graph approaches as x or y increases in absolute value

III. the value of b in $y = ab^x$, when $b > 1$

IV. an equation of the form $b^{cx} = a$, where the exponent includes a variable

Multiple Choice

Read each question. Then write the letter of the correct answer on your page.

1. The population of a town is modeled by the equation $P = 16{,}581e^{0.02t}$ where P represents the population t years after 2000. According to the model, what will the population of the town be in 2020?

Ⓐ 16,916   Ⓒ 20,252

Ⓑ 17,258   Ⓓ 24,736

2. If $i = \sqrt{-1}$, then which expression is equal to $9i(13i)$?

Ⓕ -117 Ⓗ 117

Ⓖ $117i$ Ⓘ $-117i$

3. Which expression is equivalent to $\log_5 32$?

Ⓐ $\log 5 + \log 32$

Ⓑ $\log 5 - \log 32$

Ⓒ $(\log 5)(\log 32)$

Ⓓ $\dfrac{\log 32}{\log 5}$

4. The table shows the height of a ball that was tossed into the air. Which equation best models the relationship between time t and the height of the ball h?

Time (seconds)	0	0.25	0.5	0.75
Height (feet)	4	10.5	15	17.5

- **F** $h = 26t + 4$
- **G** $h = -16t^2 + 30t + 4$
- **H** $h = 4t^2$
- **I** $h = -16t^2 + 4$

5. Which is the graph of $y = 3^x$?

- **A**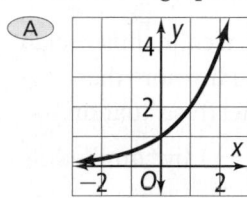
- **C**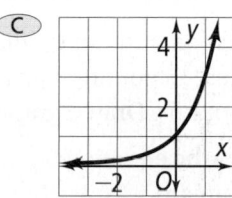
- **B**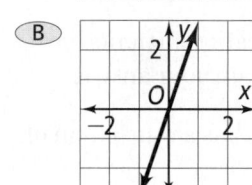
- **D**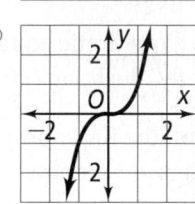

6. Which exponential function is equivalent to $y = \log_3 x$?

- **F** $y = 3^x$
- **H** $y = x^3$
- **G** $y = \frac{x}{3}$
- **I** $x = 3^y$

7. Simplify $\left(\dfrac{3x^{\frac{1}{2}}y^4}{x^2y^3}\right)^2$.

- **A** $\dfrac{3y^2}{x^3}$
- **C** $\dfrac{9y^2}{x^3}$
- **B** $3x^3y^2$
- **D** $9x^3y^2$

8. Solve the mass energy equivalence formula $e = mc^2$ for c.

- **F** $c = e^2m$
- **H** $c = \sqrt{\left(\frac{e}{m}\right)}$
- **G** $c = \sqrt{\left(\frac{m}{e}\right)}$
- **I** $c = \sqrt{(e - m)}$

9. What is the quotient of $(x^3 + 2x^2 - x + 6) \div (x + 3)$?

- **A** $x^2 + 5x + 14$, R 42
- **C** $x^3 + 5x^2 + 14x + 42$
- **B** $x^2 - x + 2$
- **D** $x^2 + x - 2$

10. On a certain night, a restaurant employs x servers at \$25 per hour and y bus persons at \$8 per hour. The total hourly cost for the restaurant's 12 employees that night is \$249. The following system of equations can be used to find the number of servers and the number of bus persons at work.

$$\begin{cases} 25x + 8y = 249 \\ x + y = 12 \end{cases}$$

Based on the solution of the system of equations, which of the following can you conclude?

- **F** Fewer than 2 bus persons were working.
- **G** More than ten servers were working.
- **H** 50% of the people working were bus persons.
- **I** 75% of the people working were servers.

11. Which polynomial equation has the real roots of $-3, 1, 1,$ and $\frac{3}{2}$?

- **A** $x^4 - \frac{1}{2}x^3 - \frac{13}{2}x^2 + \frac{21}{2}x - \frac{9}{2} = 0$
- **B** $x^4 - \frac{1}{2}x^3 - \frac{17}{2}x^2 - 10x - \frac{9}{2} = 0$
- **C** $x^4 + x^3 - 5x^2 + 3x - \frac{3}{2} = 0$
- **D** $(x - 3)(x + 1)(x + 1)\left(x + \frac{3}{2}\right) = 0$

12. What is the factored form of $2x^3 + 5x^2 - 12x$?

- **F** $x(2x - 3)(x + 4)$
- **G** $(2x^2 - 3)(x + 4)$
- **H** $x(2x + 4)(x - 3)$
- **I** $(2x - 4)(x + 3)$

13. Simplify $5\sqrt[3]{x^2} + 3\sqrt[3]{x^2}$.

- **A** $8\sqrt[3]{x^2}$
- **B** $8\sqrt[6]{x^2}$
- **C** $8\sqrt[3]{x^4}$
- **D** $8\sqrt[6]{x^4}$

14. What is the equation of the function graphed below?

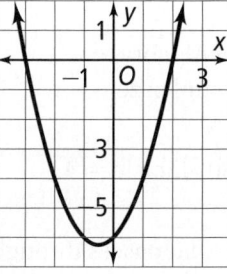

- **F** $y = (x + 2)(x - 3)$
- **H** $y = (x + 3)(x - 2)$
- **G** $y = (x - 6)^2$
- **I** $y = (x - 1)(x + 5)$

15. Which graph shows $y = -\sqrt{x + 3} + 2$, a transformation of the radical parent function $y = \sqrt{x}$?

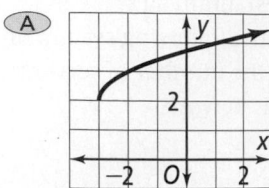 A

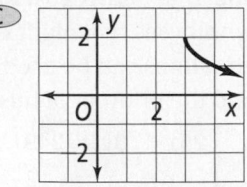 C

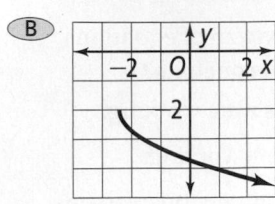 B

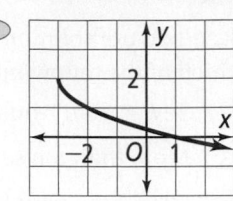 D

16. Which function would have a graph whose end behavior is up and up?

F $f(x) = x^3 + 1$ H $f(x) = 5x^2 - 7$

G $f(x) = -2x^4$ I $f(x) = -3x$

GRIDDED RESPONSE

17. What is the solution of the equation $\log_9 x = \log_6 x$?

18. A savings account pays 4.62% annual interest, compounded continuously. After approximately how many years will a principal of $500 double?

19. The graph of a polynomial has x-intercepts at $(-3, 0)$, $(-1, 0)$, and $(1, 0)$. What is the least possible degree of the polynomial?

20. Evaluate $\log_4 8$.

21. Solve $4^{2x} = 32$.

22. How many different real solutions are there for the equation $4x^2 = -4x - 4$?

23. Use the Fundamental Theorem of Algebra to determine the total number of complex zeros of $f(x) = x^2 - 3x^5 + 4x - x^7 - 44$.

24. y varies directly with x and $y = 30$ when $x = 4$. What is y when $x = 7$?

25. What is the y-intercept of the line that passes through the point $(-2, 7)$ and is parallel to $y = 3x + 5$?

26. What is the solution of $\sqrt{x + 2} = x$?

27. Simplify $9^{\frac{5}{2}}$.

28. What is the x-intercept of $f(x) = x^3 - x^2 + 1$? Round the answer to the nearest hundredth.

Short Response

29. What are the domain and range of the parabola?

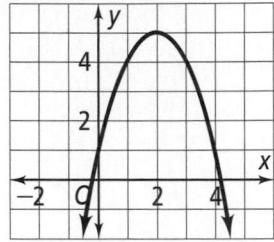

30. To use an outdoor toddler swing, a child must weigh at least 15 pounds, and can weigh no more than 35 pounds. Draw a graph to model this situation.

31. Solve the equation $0 = x^2 + 3x - 1$ by completing the square.

32. Can a quadratic equation with real coefficients have exactly one imaginary root? Explain your answer.

33. Graph the function $y = -3(2)^{x+1}$ as a translation of its parent function.

Extended Response

34. A transformation of the parent absolute value function is shown in the graph.

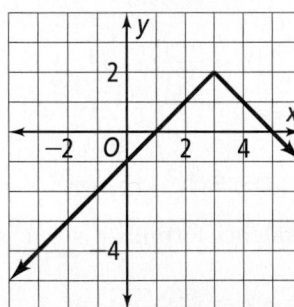

a. What is the transformation from the parent function $y = |x|$?

b. Draw the graph of the transformed function after reflecting it across the y-axis and translating it 4 units down.

Get Ready!

CHAPTER 8

Lesson 2-2   ◆ Using Direct Variation

For each direct variation, find the constant of variation. Then find the value of y when $x = -3$.

1. $y = 4$ when $x = 3$

2. $y = 1$ when $x = -1.5$

3. $y = -5$ when $x = \frac{3}{2}$

4. $y = -16$ when $x = 7$

Lesson 4-4   ◆ Factoring Quadratic Expressions

Factor each expression.

5. $x^2 + x - 6$

6. $4x^2 + 17x + 15$

7. $9x^2 - 25$

8. $x^2 - 12x + 36$

9. $3x^2 + 10x + 8$

10. $x^2 - 5x + 6$

Lesson 4-5   ◆ Solving Quadratic Equations

Solve each equation.

11. $x^2 + 7x - 8 = 0$

12. $\frac{1}{4}x^2 + \frac{7}{2}x = -12$

13. $3x^2 = 18x - 24$

14. $9x^2 + 6x = 0$

15. $4x^2 + 16 = 34x$

16. $x^2 - 13x - 30 = 0$

Looking Ahead Vocabulary

17. If you need to drive 30 miles, you have many options. For instance, you can drive 15 miles per hour for 2 hours, 30 miles per hour for 1 hour, or 60 miles per hour for half an hour. Notice that when you double your speed, it takes half as much time to get to your destination. Mathematicians describe this kind of relationship as an *inverse variation*. Why do you suppose they use the word *inverse* to describe it?

18. Suppose you are hiking on a trail and find that the bridge over the river has been washed out, making a gap or *discontinuity* in the trail. Graphs can have gaps too. Sketch what you think a graph with a discontinuity might look like.

Rational Functions

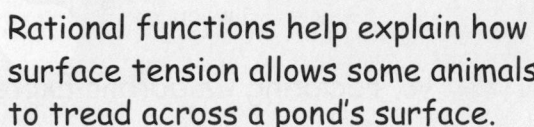

Rational functions help explain how surface tension allows some animals to tread across a pond's surface.

How can you graph rational functions and solve rational equations? You will learn how in this chapter.

Vocabulary

English/Spanish Vocabulary Audio Online:

English	Spanish
combined variation, p. 523	variación combinada
complex fraction, p. 559	fracción compleja
continuous graph, p. 539	gráfica continua
discontinuous graph, p. 539	gráfica discontinua
inverse variation, p. 520	variación inversa
joint variation, p. 523	variación conjunta
point of discontinuity, p. 539	punto de discontinuidad
rational equation, p. 565	ecuación racional
rational expression, p. 548	expresión racional
rational function, p. 538	función racional
reciprocal function, p. 530	función recíproca

My Math Video

00:04:04

VIDEO

BIG ideas

1 **Proportionality**
   Essential Question Are two quantities inversely proportional if an increase in one corresponds to a decrease in the other?

2 **Function**
   Essential Question What kinds of asymptotes are possible for a rational function?

3 **Equivalence**
   Essential Question Are a rational expression and its simplified form equivalent?

Chapter Preview

Objectives To recognize and use inverse variation
To use joint and other variations

Getting Ready!

You have 20 bags of mulch. You plan to spread the mulch from all the bags to make a rectangular layer that is 3-in. thick. How many square feet can you cover? If ℓ and w represent the length and width of the rectangle in feet, what equation relates ℓ and w? Justify your reasoning.

Mulch is a ground cover that helps keep moisture in the soil.

Lesson Vocabulary
- inverse variation
- combined variation
- joint variation

Among all rectangles with a given area, the longer the length of one side, the shorter the length of an adjacent side.

Focus Question What is inverse variation?

Recall that direct variation has the form $y = kx$, where $k \neq 0$. **Inverse variation** can have the form $xy = k$, $y = \frac{k}{x}$, or $x = \frac{k}{y}$, where $k \neq 0$. When two quantities vary inversely, as one quantity increases, the other decreases proportionally. For both inverse and direct variation, k is the constant of variation.

Problem 1 Identifying Direct and Inverse Variations

Is the relationship between the variables a *direct variation*, an *inverse variation*, or *neither*? Write function models for the direct and inverse variations.

Think

How can you tell if the quantities vary directly or inversely?
If the product of corresponding x- and y-values is constant, they vary inversely. If the ratio of corresponding x- and y-values is constant, they vary directly.

A

x	y
2	15
4	7.5
10	3
15	2

As x increases, y decreases. This might be an inverse relationship. A plot confirms that an inverse relationship is possible. Test to see whether xy is constant.

$2 \cdot 15 = 30$ $4 \cdot 7.5 = 30$
$10 \cdot 3 = 30$ $15 \cdot 2 = 30$

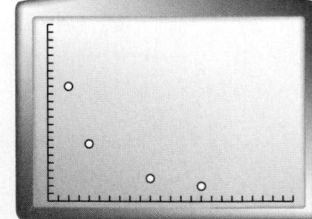

The product of each pair is 30, so $xy = 30$ and y varies inversely with x. The constant of variation is 30. The function model is $y = \frac{30}{x}$.

B

x	y
2	10
4	8
10	3
15	1.5

The table and graph suggest that an inverse relationship is possible. Test to see whether the products of x and y are constant.

$2 \cdot 10 = 20, 4 \cdot 8 = 32, 10 \cdot 3 = 30$, and $15 \cdot 1.5 = 22.5$

Since the products are not constant, the relationship is not an inverse variation.

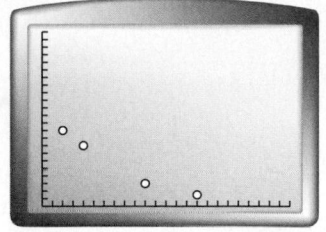

Dynamic Activity
Direct and Inverse Variation

C

x	y
2	6
4	12
10	30
15	45

As x increases, y increases. A quick plot confirms a direct variation is possible. Each y-value is 3 times the corresponding x-value. y varies directly with x. The constant of variation is 3. The function is $y = 3x$.

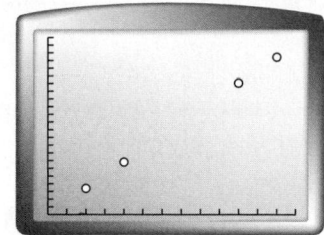

Got It? **1.** Is the relationship between the variables a *direct variation*, an *inverse variation*, or *neither*? Write function models for the direct and inverse variations.

a.

x	y
0.2	8
0.5	20
1.0	40
1.5	60

b.

x	y
0.2	40
0.5	16
1.0	8.0
2.0	4.0

c.

x	y
0.5	40
1.2	12
2	10
2.5	6

Problem 2 Determining an Inverse Variation

Suppose x and y vary inversely, and $x = 4$ when $y = 12$. Graph the inverse variation. What is the value of y when $x = 10$?

Step 1
Write a function model.

Write the general form for inverse variation. $y = \frac{k}{x}$

Substitute for x and y. $12 = \frac{k}{4}$

Solve for k. $k = 48$

The function is $y = \frac{48}{x}$.

Step 3
Find y when $x = 10$.

Substitute 10 for x and simplify. $y = \frac{48}{10} = 4.8$

$y = 4.8$ when $x = 10$.

Step 2
Make a table of values. Sketch a graph.

x	y
3	16
4	12
6	8
8	6
12	4
16	3

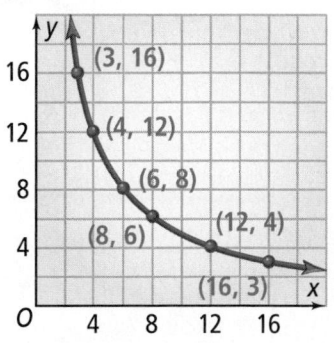

✔ **Got It?** **2.** Suppose x and y vary inversely, and $x = 8$ when $y = -7$.
Graph the inverse variation. What is the value of y when $x = 2$?

Problem 3 **Modeling an Inverse Variation**

Your math class has decided to pick up litter each weekend in a local park. Each week there is approximately the same amount of litter. The table shows the number of students who worked each of the first four weeks of the project and the time needed for the pickup.

Park Cleanup Project

Number of students (n)	3	5	12	17
Time in minutes (t)	85	51	21	15

Think

Can you still use inverse variation to model the data if $12 \times 21 = 252$?
Often, you cannot describe real-world data exactly with a function rule. But 252 is close enough to 255 for inverse variation to still be a good model.

Ⓐ What function models the data?

Step 1 Investigate the data. The more students who help, the less time the cleanup takes. An inverse variation seems appropriate.

If this is an inverse variation, then $nt = k$. From the table, nt (or **L1•L2**) is almost always 255.

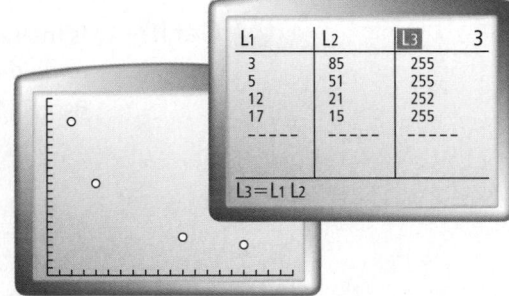

Step 2 Determine the model.

$$t = \frac{255}{n}$$

Ⓑ How many students should there be to complete the project in at most 30 minutes each week?

Use the model from part A. $nt = 255$

Substitute 30 for t. $n(30) = 255$

Solve for n and simplify. $n = \dfrac{255}{30} = 8.5$

There should be at least 9 students to do the job in at most 30 minutes.

Hint

If n and t vary inversely, their product is a constant.

✔ **Got It?** **3.** After a major storm, your math class volunteers to remove debris from yards. The table shows the time t in minutes that it takes a group of n students to remove the debris from an average-sized yard.

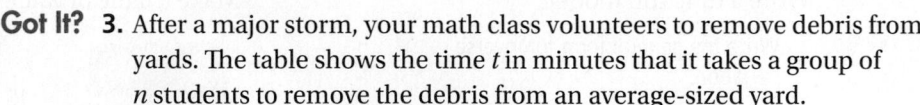

Number of students (n)	1	3	5	14
Time in minutes (t)	225	75	45	16

a. What function models the time needed to clear the debris from an average-sized yard relative to the number of students who do the work?

b. How many students should there be to clear debris from an average-sized yard in at most 25 minutes?

Focus Question What is combined variation?

You have seen many variation formulas in geometry. Some, like the formula for the perimeter of a square, are simple direct variations. Others, like the volume of a cone, relate three or more variables.

When one quantity varies with respect to two or more quantities, you have a **combined variation**. When one quantity varies directly with two or more quantities, you have **joint variation**.

take note

Key Concept   Combined Variations

Combined Variation	Equation Form
z varies jointly with x and y.	$z = kxy$
z varies jointly with x and y and inversely with w.	$z = \dfrac{kxy}{w}$
z varies directly with x and inversely with the product wy.	$z = \dfrac{kx}{wy}$

Problem 4   Using Combined Variation

Plan

How can you write the model?
Write the constant of variation and direct variation variable in the numerator. Write the inverse variation variable in the denominator.

Multiple Choice The number of bags of grass seed n needed to reseed a yard varies directly with the area a to be seeded and inversely with the weight w of a bag of seed. If it takes two 3-lb bags to seed an area of 3600 ft^2, how many 3-lb bags will seed 9000 ft^2?

   Ⓐ 3 bags   Ⓑ 4 bags   Ⓒ 5 bags   Ⓓ 6 bags

Step 1
Use the given information to write the variation equation.

n varies directly with a and inversely with w.	$n = \dfrac{ka}{w}$
Substitute for n, a, and w.	$2 = \dfrac{3600k}{3}$
Solve for k.	$\dfrac{(2)(3)}{3600} = k$
Multiply and simplify.	$k = \dfrac{6}{3600} = \dfrac{1}{600}$

The variation equation is $n = \dfrac{a}{600w}$.

Step 2
Use the equation to find the number of bags for 9000 ft^2.

Use the combined variation equation.	$n = \dfrac{a}{600w}$
Substitute for a and w.	$n = \dfrac{9000}{600 \cdot 3}$
Multiply.	$= \dfrac{9000}{1800}$
Simplify.	$= 5$

You need five 3-lb bags to seed 9000 ft^2. The correct answer is C.

Hint

The general form for a joint variation is $z = kxy$.

Got It? **4.** The number of bags of mulch you need to cover a planting area varies jointly with the area to be mulched a in square feet and the depth of the mulch d in feet. If you need 10 bags to mulch 120 ft^2 to a depth of 3 in., how many bags do you need to mulch 200 ft^2 to a depth of 4 in.?

Problem 5 Applying Combined Variation

Physics Gravitational potential energy *PE* is a measure of energy. *PE* varies directly with an object's mass *m* in kg and its height *h* in meters above the ground. Physicists use *g* to represent the constant of variation, which is gravity.

The skateboarder in the photo has a mass of 58 kg and a potential energy of 2273.6 joules. What is the gravitational potential energy of a 65-kg skateboarder on the halfpipe shown?

HEIGHT 4 M

Know

- The mass of each skateboarder
- The height of each skateboarder
- The potential energy of the first skateboarder

Need

The potential energy of the second skateboarder

Plan

- Write the variation for potential energy.
- Use the known information to find *g*.
- Then find the potential energy of the second skateboarder.

Step 1 Write the formula for potential energy. Potential energy varies directly with mass and height. $PE = gmh$

Step 2 Use the given data to find *g*.

Use the potential energy formula. $PE = gmh$

Substitute 2273.6 for *PE*, 58 for *m*, and 4 for *h*. $2273.6 = g(58)(4)$

Solve for *g*. $9.8 = g$

Plan

Can you use the same value of *g* for different situations? The value of *g* is constant on Earth. Potential energy calculations for situations on the moon would use a different value of *g*.

Step 3 Use the formula to find the potential energy of the second skateboarder.

Use the potential energy formula. $PE = 9.8mh$

Evaluate for $m = 65$ and $h = 4$. $= 9.8(65)(4)$

Simplify. $= 2548$

The second skateboarder has 2548 joules of potential energy.

Hint

Refer to the formula for potential energy from Problem 5.

 Got It? **5. a.** How much potential energy would a 41-kg diver have standing on a 10-m diving platform?

b. Reasoning An 80-kg diver stands on a 6-m diving platform. At what height should a 40-kg diver stand to have equal potential energy? Do you need to find the potential energy of either diver to solve this? Explain your reasoning.

Focus Question What is inverse variation?

Answer Inverse variation relates quantities whose product is constant. Use an inverse variation function when one quantity increases and the other decreases proportionally.

Focus Question What is combined variation?

Answer Combined variation occurs when one quantity varies with respect to two or more quantities. Use combined variation when you want to relate three or more variables. The variables can vary directly and/or inversely.

Lesson Check

Do you know HOW?

Is the relationship between the variables in each table a *direct variation,* an *inverse variation,* or *neither*? Write equations to model the direct and inverse variations.

1.

x	y
1	6
3	2
12	0.5
15	0.4

2.

u	v
−3	−15
5	25
6	30
16	80

Do you UNDERSTAND?

3. Compare and Contrast Describe the difference between direct variation and inverse variation.

4. Writing Describe how the variables in the given equation are related.

$$p = \frac{kqrt}{s}$$

5. Error Analysis A student described the relationship between the variables in the equation below as *d* varies directly with *r* and inversely with *t.* Correct the error in relating the variables.

$$d = \frac{k\sqrt[3]{r}}{t^2}$$

Practice and Problem-Solving Exercises

A **Practice**

Is the relationship between the values in each table a *direct variation,* an *inverse variation,* or *neither*? Write equations to model the direct and inverse variations.

◀ See Problem 1.

6.

x	y
3	15
8	40
10	50
22	110

7.

x	y
3	14
5	8.4
7	6
10.5	4

8.

x	y
0.5	1
2.1	4.2
3.5	7
11	22

Suppose that x and y vary inversely. Write a function that models each inverse variation. Graph the function and find y when $x = 10$.

◀ See Problem 2.

Guided Practice →

9. $x = 1$ when $y = 11$

To start, write the general form for inverse variation.

$y = \frac{k}{x}$

10. $x = -13$ when $y = 100$　　11. $x = 1$ when $y = 1$　　12. $x = 1$ when $y = 5$

13. $x = 1.2$ when $y = 3$　　14. $x = 20$ when $y = -4$　　15. $x = 5$ when $y = -\frac{1}{3}$

16. **Fundraising** In a bake sale, you recorded the number of muffins sold and the amount of sales in a table as shown.
    a. What is a function that relates the sales and the number of muffins?
    b. How many muffins would you have to sell to make at least $250.00 in sales?

◀ See Problem 3.

Number of muffins (m)	Sales (s)
5	$12.50
8	$20.00
13	$32.50
20	$50.00

Use combined variation to solve each problem.

◀ See Problem 4.

17. **Painting** The number of buckets of paint n needed to paint a fence varies directly with the total area a of the fence and inversely with the amount of paint p in a bucket. It takes three 1-gallon buckets of paint to paint 72 square feet of fence. How many 1-gallon buckets will be needed to paint 90 square feet of fence?

Guided Practice →

To start, record what you know.　　n varies directly with a and inversely with p.

Then write the combined variation.　　$n = \frac{ka}{p}$

18. **Health** A person's body mass index (BMI) varies directly with his or her weight in pounds and inversely with the square of his or her height in inches. A student with a height of 68 in. and a weight of 150 lb has a BMI of 22.8. What is the BMI of a student with a height of 61 in. and a weight of 115 lb?

19. **Potential Energy** On Earth with a gravitational acceleration g, the potential energy stored in an object varies directly with its mass m and its vertical height h. What is the equation of the potential energy of a 2-kg skateboard that is sliding down a ramp?

◀ See Problem 5.

B **Apply**

20. **Think About a Plan** The table shows data about how the life span s of a mammal relates to its heart rate r. The data can be modeled by an equation of the form $rs = k$. Estimate the life span of a cat with a heart rate of 126 beats/min.
    • How can you estimate a constant of the inverse variation?
    • What expression would you use to find the life span?

Heart Rate and Life Span

Mammal	Heart rate (beats/min)	Life span (min)
Mouse	634	1,576,800
Rabbit	158	6,307,200
Lion	76	13,140,000

Source: *The Handy Science Answer Book*

21. Physics The force F of gravity on a rocket varies directly with its mass m and inversely with the square of its distance d from Earth. Write a model for this combined variation.

22. The spreadsheet shows data that can be modeled by an equation of the form $PV = k$. Estimate P when $V = 62$.

23. Chemistry The formula for Ideal Gas Law is $PV = nRT$, where P is the pressure in kilopascals (kPA), V is the volume in liters (L), T is the temperature in Kelvin (K), n is the number of moles of gas, and $R = 8.314$ is the universal gas constant.

    a. What volume is needed to store 5 moles of helium gas at 350 K under the pressure 190 kPA?

    b. A 10-L cylinder is filled with hydrogen gas to a pressure of 5,000 kPA. The temperature of the gas is 300 K. How many moles of hydrogen gas are in the cylinder?

	A	B
1	P	V
2	140.00	100
3	147.30	95
4	155.60	90
5	164.70	85
6	175.00	80
7	186.70	75

Write the function that models each variation. Find z when $x = 4$ and $y = 9$.

24. z varies directly with x and inversely with y. When $x = 6$ and $y = 2$, $z = 15$.

25. z varies jointly with x and y. When $x = 2$ and $y = 3$, $z = 60$.

26. z varies inversely with the product of x and y. When $x = 2$ and $y = 4$, $z = 0.5$.

Each pair of values is from a direct variation. Find the missing value.

27. $(2, 5), (4, y)$ **28.** $(4, 6), (x, 3)$ **29.** $(3, 7), (8, y)$

Each ordered pair is from an inverse variation. Find the constant of variation.

30. $(6, 3)$ **31.** $(0.9, 4)$ **32.** $\left(\frac{3}{8}, \frac{2}{3}\right)$

Each pair of values is from an inverse variation. Find the missing value.

33. $(2, 5), (4, y)$ **34.** $(4, 6), (x, 3)$ **35.** $(3, 7), (8, y)$

Standardized Test Prep

SAT/ACT

36. Which equation represents inverse variation between x and y?

- **A** $x = \dfrac{y}{z}$
- **B** $x = -\dfrac{15z}{y}$
- **C** $z = -\dfrac{15y}{x}$
- **D** $xz = 5y$

37. How can you rewrite the expression $(8 - 5i)^2$ in the form $a + bi$?

- **F** $39 + 80i$
- **G** $39 - 80i$
- **H** $89 + 80i$
- **I** $89 - 80i$

38. The height of a ball thrown straight up from the ground with a velocity of 96 ft/s is given by the quadratic function $h(t) = -16t^2 + 96t$. What is the maximum height the ball reaches?

- **A** 6 ft
- **B** 128 ft
- **C** 144 ft
- **D** 160 ft

39. Which expression is NOT equivalent to $\sqrt[6]{81x^4y^8}$?

- **F** $\left(3xy^2\right)^{\frac{2}{3}}$
- **G** $(3x)^{\frac{2}{3}}y^{\frac{4}{3}}$
- **H** $\left(3x^2y^2\right)^{\frac{1}{3}}$
- **I** $\sqrt[3]{9x^2y^4}$

Short Response

40. What is the inverse of $y = 4x^2 + 5$? Is the inverse a function?

Mixed Review

Solve each equation.

See Lesson 7-5.

41. $3^{2x} = 6561$

42. $7^x - 2 = 252$

43. $\log 3x = 4$

Multiply and simplify.

See Lesson 6-2.

44. $-5\sqrt{6x} \cdot 3\sqrt{6x^3}$

45. $3\sqrt[3]{2x^2} \cdot 7\sqrt[3]{32x^4}$

46. $\sqrt{5x^3} \cdot \sqrt{40xy^7}$

Simplify each radical expression. Use absolute value bars where they are needed.

See Lesson 6-1.

47. $\sqrt{x^{10}y^{100}}$

48. $\sqrt[3]{-64a^3b^6}$

49. $\sqrt[4]{64m^8n^4}$

Get Ready! To prepare for Lesson 8-2, do Exercises 50–55.

Graph each equation. Then describe the transformation of the parent function $f(x) = |x|$.

See Lesson 2-7.

50. $y = |x| + 2$

51. $y = |x + 2|$

52. $y = |x| - 3$

53. $y = |x - 3|$

54. $y = |x + 4| - 5$

55. $y = |x - 10| + 7$

Graphing Rational Functions

You can use your graphing calculator to graph *rational functions* and other members of the reciprocal function family. It is sometimes preferable to use the **DOT** plotting mode rather than **CONNECTED** plotting mode. The **CONNECTED** mode can join branches of a graph that should be separated. Try both modes to get the best graph.

Example

Graph $y = \dfrac{4}{x - 3} - 1.5$.

Step 1 Press the (mode) key. Scroll down to highlight the word **DOT**. Then press (enter).

Step 2 Enter the function. Use parentheses to enter the denominator accurately.

Step 3 Graph the function.

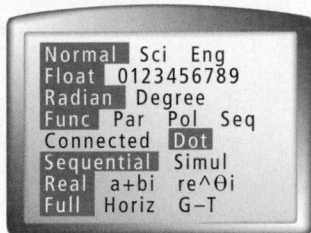

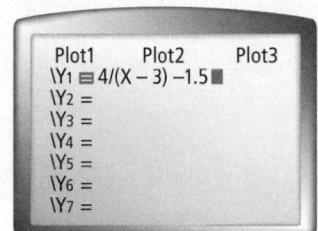

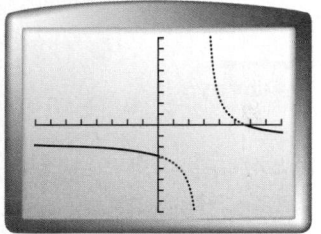

Exercises

1. **a.** Graph the parent reciprocal function $y = \frac{1}{x}$.
   b. Examine both negative and positive values of x. Describe what happens to the y-values as x approaches zero.
   c. What happens to the y-values as x increases? As x decreases?

2. **a.** Change the mode on your calculator to **CONNECTED**. Graph the function from the example.
   b. Press (trace) and trace the function. What happens between $x \approx 2.8$ and $x \approx 3.2$?
   c. **Reasoning** How does your graph differ from the graph in the example? Explain the differences.

Use a graphing calculator to graph each function. Then sketch the graph.

3. $y = \dfrac{7}{x}$

4. $y = \dfrac{3}{x + 4} - 2$

5. $y = \dfrac{x + 2}{(x + 1)(x + 3)}$

6. $y = \dfrac{4x + 1}{x - 3}$

7. $y = \dfrac{2}{x - 2}$

8. $y = \dfrac{1}{x + 2} + 3$

9. $y = \dfrac{2x}{x + 3}$

10. $y = \dfrac{x^2}{x^2 - 5}$

11. $y = \dfrac{20}{x^2 + 5}$

8-2 The Reciprocal Function Family

Objectives To graph reciprocal functions
To graph translations of reciprocal functions

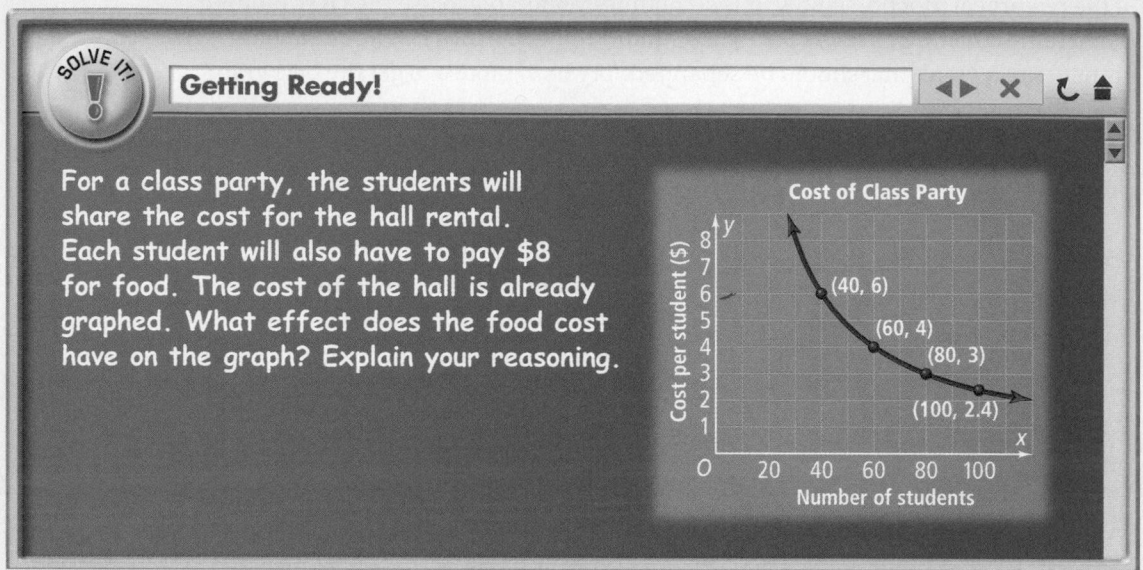

SOLVE IT!

Getting Ready! ◀▶ ✕ ↻ ⬆

For a class party, the students will share the cost for the hall rental. Each student will also have to pay $8 for food. The cost of the hall is already graphed. What effect does the food cost have on the graph? Explain your reasoning.

Cost of Class Party

(graph with points (40, 6), (60, 4), (80, 3), (100, 2.4); y-axis: Cost per student ($), x-axis: Number of students)

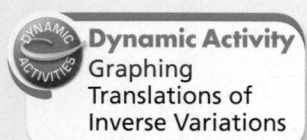

Dynamic Activity
Graphing
Translations of
Inverse Variations

Lesson Vocabulary
• reciprocal function
• branch

Functions that model inverse variation have the form $f(x) = \frac{a}{x}$, where $x \neq 0$.

They belong to a family whose parent is the **reciprocal function** $f(x) = \frac{1}{x}$, where $x \neq 0$.

Focus Question What are reciprocal functions?

take note ➤

Key Concept General Form of the Reciprocal Function Family

The general form of a member of the reciprocal function family is $y = \frac{a}{x - h} + k$, where $x \neq h$.

The inverse variation functions, $y = \frac{a}{x}$, are stretches, shrinks, and reflections of the parent reciprocal function, depending on the value of a.

The graph of the parent reciprocal function, $y = \frac{1}{x}$, is shown at the right.

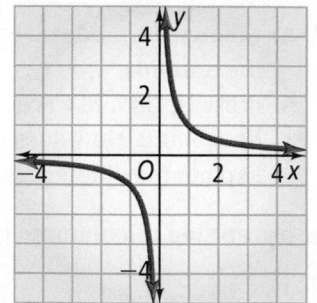

Problem 1 Graphing an Inverse Variation Function

What is the graph of $y = \frac{8}{x}$, $x \neq 0$? Identify the x- and y-intercepts and the asymptotes of the graph. Also, state the domain and range of the function.

Think

What values should you choose for x?
Choose values of x that divide nicely into 8. Make a table of points that are easy to graph.

Step 1
Make a table of values that includes positive and negative values of x.

x	y	x	y
-16	$-\frac{1}{2}$	$\frac{1}{2}$	16
-8	-1	1	8
-4	-2	2	4
-2	-4	4	2
-1	-8	8	1
$-\frac{1}{2}$	-16	16	$\frac{1}{2}$

Step 2
Graph the points from the table.

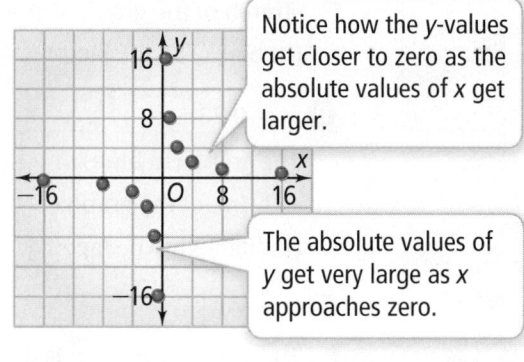

Notice how the y-values get closer to zero as the absolute values of x get larger.

The absolute values of y get very large as x approaches zero.

Step 3
Connect the points with a smooth curve.

x cannot be zero, so there is no y-intercept.
The numerator is never zero, so y is never 0.
There is no x-intercept.

The x-axis is a horizontal asymptote.
The y-axis is a vertical asymptote.
Knowing the asymptotes provides you with the basic shape of the graph.

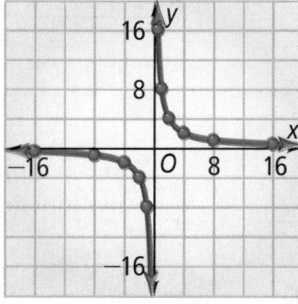

The domain is the set of all real numbers except $x = 0$.
The range is the set of all real numbers except $y = 0$.

Got It? **1. a.** What is the graph of $y = \frac{12}{x}$? Identify the x- and y-intercepts and the asymptotes of the graph. Also, state the domain and range of the function.

  b. Reasoning Would the function $y = \frac{6}{x}$ have the same domain and range as $y = \frac{8}{x}$ or $y = \frac{12}{x}$? Explain.

Hint

The graph of the function in Problem 1 might look like two separate graphs, but it is defined by a single function.

Each part of the graph of a reciprocal function is called a **branch**. The branches of the parent function $y = \frac{1}{x}$ are in Quadrants I and III. Stretches and compressions of the parent function remain in the same quadrants. Reflections are in Quadrants II and IV.

Problem 2 Identifying Reciprocal Function Transformations

For each given value of a, how do the graphs of $y = \frac{1}{x}$ and $y = \frac{a}{x}$ compare? What is the effect of a on the graph?

Hint

For each x-value, the y-value for $y = \frac{6}{x}$ is stretched 6 times as far from the x-axis as the y-value for $y = \frac{1}{x}$.

Think

How does the negative sign affect the graph?
The y-values have signs that are opposite those in part A. The graph in A reflects across the x-axis.

A $a = 6$

The graph (in red) of $y = \frac{6}{x}$ is a stretch of the graph of $y = \frac{1}{x}$ (in black) by the factor 6.

B $a = 0.25$

The graph (in blue) of $y = \frac{0.25}{x}$ is a shrink of the graph of $y = \frac{1}{x}$ (in black) by the factor $\frac{1}{4}$.

C $a = -6$

The graph of $y = \frac{-6}{x}$ is the stretch by the factor 6 in part A followed by a reflection across the x-axis.

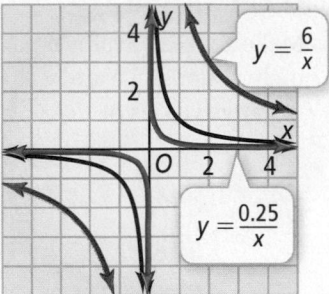

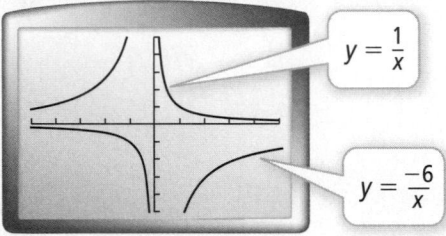

Got It? **2.** For each given value of a, how do the graphs of $y = \frac{1}{x}$ and $y = \frac{a}{x}$ compare? What is the effect of a on the graph?

a. $a = \frac{1}{2}$ **b.** $a = 2$ **c.** $a = -\frac{1}{2}$

You can translate a reciprocal function horizontally or vertically just as you can other functions.

take note

Key Concept   The Reciprocal Function Family

Parent function	$y = \frac{1}{x}, x \neq 0$
Stretch $(\lvert a \rvert > 1)$ Compression (Shrink) $(0 < \lvert a \rvert < 1)$ Reflection $(a < 0)$ in x-axis	$y = \frac{a}{x}, x \neq 0$
Translation (horizontal by h; vertical by k) with vertical asymptote $x = h$; horizontal asymptote $y = k$	$y = \frac{1}{x - h} + k; x \neq h$
All transformations combined	$y = \frac{a}{x - h} + k; x \neq h$

When you graph a translated reciprocal function, a good first step is to draw the asymptotes.

 Problem 3 Graphing a Translation

Think

How do you find the asymptotes?
Translate the asymptotes of $y = \frac{1}{x}$ (the axes) 4 units left and 6 units down.

What is the graph of $y = \frac{1}{x + 4} - 6$? Identify the domain and range.

Step 1 Draw the asymptotes (red).

For, $y = \frac{1}{x + 4} - 6$, $h = -4$ and $k = -6$.
The vertical asymptote is $x = -4$.
The horizontal asymptote is $y = -6$.

Step 2 Translate the graph of $y = \frac{1}{x}$.

The graph of $y = \frac{1}{x}$ contains the points $(1, 1)$ and $(-1, -1)$.
Translate these points 4 units to the left and 6 units down to $(-3, -5)$ and $(-5, -7)$, respectively. Draw the branches through these points (blue).

The domain is the set of all real numbers except $x = -4$. The range is the set of all real numbers except $y = -6$.

 Got It? 3. What is the graph of $y = \frac{1}{x - 2} + 4$? Identify the domain and range.

If you know the asymptotes of the graph of a reciprocal function and the value of a, you can write the equation of the function.

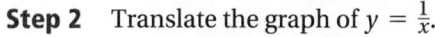 **Problem 4** Writing the Equation of a Transformation

Multiple Choice This graph is a translation of the graph of $y = \frac{2}{x}$. What is an equation for the function?

Ⓐ $y = \frac{2}{x + 3} + 4$ Ⓒ $y = \frac{2}{x - 3} + 4$

Ⓑ $y = \frac{2}{x + 3} - 4$ Ⓓ $y = \frac{2}{x - 3} - 4$

Plan

How can you get started?
Identify the asymptotes of the graph.

The asymptotes are $x = -3$ and $y = 4$. Thus, $h = -3$ and $k = 4$.

Write the general form. $y = \frac{a}{x - h} + k$

Substitute for a, h, and k. $y = \frac{2}{x - (-3)} + 4$

Simplify. $y = \frac{2}{x + 3} + 4$

The correct choice is A.

Hint

Use a graphing calculator to check. Remember to use parentheses around the denominator.

 Got It? 4. This graph is a translation of the graph of $y = \frac{2}{x}$. What is an equation for the function?

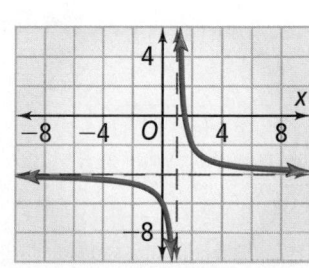

Problem 5 Using a Reciprocal Function

Clubs The rowing club is renting a 57-passenger bus for a day trip. The cost of the bus is $750. Five passengers will be chaperones. If the students who attend share the bus cost equally, what function models the cost per student *C* with respect to the number of students *n* who attend? What is the domain of the function? How many students must ride the bus to make the cost per student no more than $20?

Know
- The bus holds 57 passengers.
- The bus costs $750.
- Five riders are chaperones who pay nothing for the bus.

Need
- A function for the cost per student
- The number of students needed so that the cost does not exceed $20 per student

Plan
- Write a reciprocal function for the situation.
- Graph the function and solve an inequality using the $20 limit.

Step 1 Write a function.

To share the cost equally, divide by the number of students who attend. $C = \frac{750}{n}$

The function that models the cost per student is $C(n) = \frac{750}{n}$.

Step 2 Identify the domain.

The bus has a capacity of 57 passengers and there will be 5 chaperones. The maximum number of students is $57 - 5 = 52$.

The domain is the set of integers from 1 to 52.

Think

Is the domain $n \le 52$? No. The domain is the possible numbers of students, so only positive integers make sense.

Step 3 Use a graphing calculator to solve the inequality $\frac{750}{n} \le 20$.

Let **Y1** $= \frac{750}{x}$ and **Y2 = 20**.

Adjust the window dimensions to get a closer look at the graph. Use the **intersect** feature.

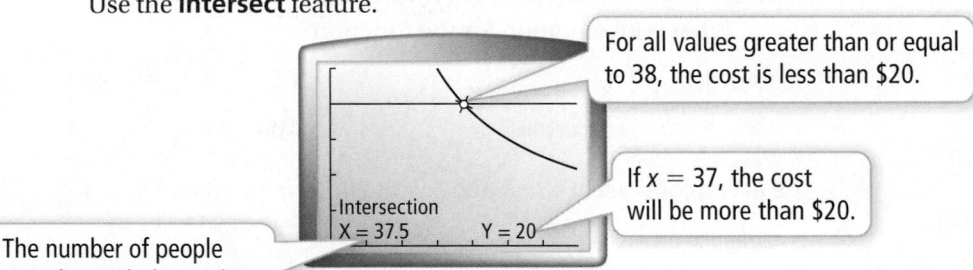

For all values greater than or equal to 38, the cost is less than $20.

If $x = 37$, the cost will be more than $20.

Intersection
X = 37.5   Y = 20

The number of people must be a whole number.

At least 38 students must ride the bus.

Got It? **5.** The junior class is renting a laser tag facility with a capacity of 325 people. The cost for the facility is $1200. The party must have 13 adult chaperones.
  a. If the students who attend share the facility cost equally, what function models the cost per student *C* with respect to the number of students *n* who attend?
  b. What is the domain of the function?
  c. How many students must attend to make the cost per student no more than $7.50?

Hint

For part (c), let **Y1** be the function you wrote for part (a) and let **Y2** be 7.50.

Focus Question What are reciprocal functions?

Answer A reciprocal function is a function with the independent variable in the denominator of a fraction. All reciprocal functions can be written in the form $y = \frac{a}{x - h} + k$ as transformations of the parent function, $y = \frac{1}{x}$. Use a reciprocal function to model inverse variation.

Lesson Check

Do you know HOW?

1. Graph the equation $y = \frac{3}{x}$.

Describe the transformation from the graph of $y = \frac{1}{x}$ to the graph of the given function.

2. $y = \frac{1}{x} + 5$

3. $y = \frac{-4}{x}$

4. What are the asymptotes of the graph of $y = \frac{5}{x + 2} - 7$?

Do you UNDERSTAND?

5. Vocabulary What transformation changes the graph of $y = \frac{1}{x}$ into the graph of $y = \frac{1}{2x}$?

6. Write an equation of the reflection of the graph $y = \frac{1}{x}$ in the x-axis.

7. Writing Explain how you can tell if a function $y = \frac{a}{x}$ is a stretch or compression of the parent function $y = \frac{1}{x}$.

Practice and Problem-Solving Exercises

Ⓐ Practice

Graph each function. Identify the x- and y-intercepts and the asymptotes of the graph. Also, state the domain and the range of the function.

◀ See Problem 1.

8. $y = \frac{2}{x}$

9. $y = \frac{-3}{x}$

10. $y = -\frac{10}{x}$

11. $y = \frac{10}{x}$

Graphing Calculator Graph the equations $y = \frac{1}{x}$ and $y = \frac{a}{x}$ using the given value of a. Then identify the effect of a on the graph.

◀ See Problem 2.

12. $a = 2$

13. $a = -4$

14. $a = 0.5$

15. $a = 0.75$

Sketch the asymptotes and the graph of each function. Identify the domain and range.

◀ See Problem 3.

Guided Practice

To start, compare the equation to general form to identify h and k.

16. $y = \frac{1}{x} - 3$

$y = \frac{a}{x - h} + k$

$y = \frac{1}{x - 0} + (-3)$

17. $y = \frac{-2}{x} - 3$

18. $y = \frac{1}{x - 2} + 5$

19. $y = \frac{1}{x - 3} + 4$

20. $y = \frac{2}{x + 6} - 1$

21. $y = \frac{1}{x} - 2$

22. $y = \frac{-8}{x + 5} - 6$

Write an equation for the translation of $y = \frac{2}{x}$ that has the given asymptotes.

◀ See Problem 4.

23. $x = 0$ and $y = 4$

24. $x = -2$ and $y = 3$

25. $x = 4$ and $y = -8$

26. **Construction** The weight P in pounds that a beam can safely carry is inversely proportional to the distance D in feet between the supports of the beam. For a certain type of wooden beam, $P = \frac{9200}{D}$. What distance between supports is needed to carry 1200 lb?

 **See Problem 5.**

See Problem 5.

B **Apply**

27. **Think About a Plan** A high school decided to spend $750 on student academic achievement awards. At least 5 awards will be given, they should be equal in value, and each award should not be less than $50. Write and sketch a function that models the relationship between the number a of awards and the cost c of each award. What are the domain and range of the function?
    • Which equation describes the relationship between a and c?
    • What information can you use to determine the domain and range?

28. **Open-Ended** Write an equation for a horizontal translation of $y = \frac{2}{x}$. Then write an equation for a vertical translation of $y = \frac{2}{x}$. Identify the horizontal and vertical asymptotes of the graph of each function.

Sketch the graph of each function.

29. $xy = 3$ 30. $xy + 5 = 0$ 31. $5xy = 2$ 32. $10xy = -4$

33. The formula $p = \frac{69.1}{a + 2.3}$ models the relationship between atmospheric pressure p in inches of mercury and altitude a in miles.

Use the data shown with the photo. At which location does the model predict the pressure to be about 23.93 in. of mercury? (*Hint:* 1 mi = 5280 ft.)

Ⓐ Sahara Desert

Ⓑ Kalahari Desert

Ⓒ Mt. Kilimanjaro

Ⓓ Vinson Massif

Sahara Desert average alt. 1500 ft

Kalahari Desert average alt. 3100 ft

Mt. Kilimanjaro alt. 19,340 ft

Vinson Massif alt. 16,680 ft

📟 **Graphing Calculator** Graph each pair of functions. Find the approximate point(s) of intersection.

34. $y = \frac{6}{x - 2}, y = 6$ 35. $y = -\frac{1}{x - 3} - 6, y = 6.2$ 36. $y = \frac{3}{x + 1}, y = -4$

37. **a. Gasoline Mileage** Suppose you drive an average of 10,000 miles each year. Your gasoline mileage (mi/gal) varies inversely with the number of gallons of gasoline you use each year. Write and graph a model for your average mileage m in terms of the gallons g of gasoline used.
    b. After you begin driving on the highway more often, you use 50 gal less per year. Write and graph a new model to include this information.
    c. Calculate your old and new mileage assuming that you originally used 400 gal of gasoline per year.

Standardized Test Prep

SAT/ACT

38. What is an equation for the translation of $y = \frac{2}{x}$ that has asymptotes at $x = 3$ and $y = -5$?

(A) $y = \frac{2}{x-3} - 5$ (B) $y = \frac{2}{x+3} + 5$ (C) $y = \frac{2}{x+5} - 3$ (D) $y = \frac{2}{x-5} + 3$

39. The graph at the right shows which inequality?

(F) $y < -2.5x + 5$ (H) $-2.5x + y < 5$

(G) $2.5x + y \geq 5$ (I) $5x + y \leq 5$

40. If p and q vary inversely, and $p = 10$ when $q = -4$, what is q when $p = -2$?

(A) 20   (C) $-\frac{4}{5}$

(B) $\frac{4}{5}$ (D) -20

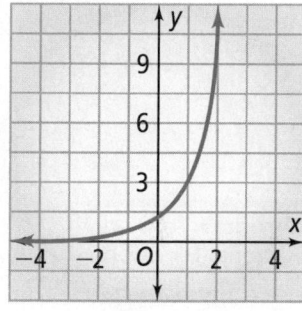

41. Which equation represents the inverse of the graph at the right?

(F) $y = \log_3 x$ (H) $y = \log_x 3$

(G) $x = \log_3 y$ (I) $x = \log_y 3$

Short Response

42. What is b if the graph of $y = 27b^x$ includes the point $(-1, 81)$?

Mixed Review

Suppose that x and y vary inversely. Write a function that models each inverse variation and find y when $x = -5$.   ◀ **See Lesson 8-1.**

43. $x = 2$ when $y = 12$ **44.** $x = 25$ when $y = 2$ **45.** $x = 12$ when $y = 4$

Without graphing, determine whether the function represents exponential growth or exponential decay. Then find the y-intercept.   ◀ **See Lesson 7-1.**

46. $y = 3(4)^x$ **47.** $y = 0.1(2)^x$ **48.** $y = 5(0.8)^x$

Multiply.   ◀ **See Lesson 6-3.**

49. $(5\sqrt{3} - 2)^2$ **50.** $(4 + 2\sqrt{3})(6 - 3\sqrt{3})$ **51.** $(\sqrt{3} + \sqrt{5})(\sqrt{3} - \sqrt{5})$

Get Ready!   To prepare for Lesson 8-3, do Exercises 52–54.

Factor each expression.   ◀ **See Lesson 4-4.**

52. $x^2 + 6x - 27$ **53.** $2x^2 + x - 28$ **54.** $2x^2 - 19x + 24$

8-3 Rational Functions and Their Graphs

Objectives To identify properties of rational functions
To graph rational functions

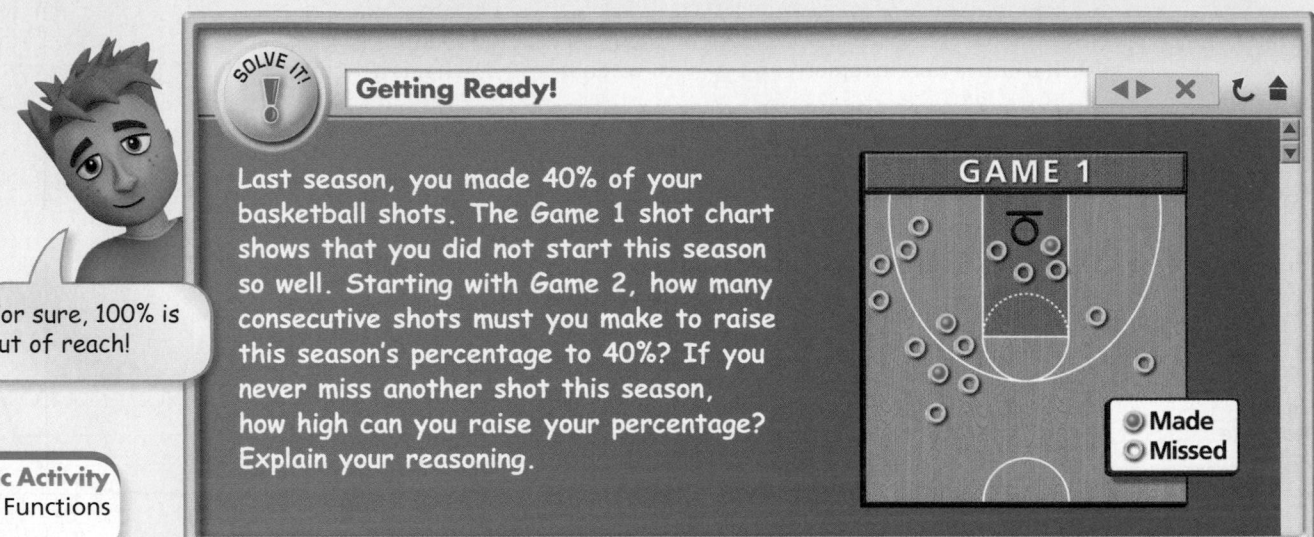

Getting Ready!

Last season, you made 40% of your basketball shots. The Game 1 shot chart shows that you did not start this season so well. Starting with Game 2, how many consecutive shots must you make to raise this season's percentage to 40%? If you never miss another shot this season, how high can you raise your percentage? Explain your reasoning.

For sure, 100% is out of reach!

GAME 1

○ Made
○ Missed

Dynamic Activity
Rational Functions

Lesson Vocabulary
• rational function
• continuous graph
• discontinuous graph
• point of discontinuity
• removable discontinuity
• non-removable discontinuity

You use a ratio of polynomial functions to form a *rational function*, like $y = \frac{x+3}{x+16}$.

Focus Question What is a rational function?

A **rational function** is a function that you can write in the form $f(x) = \dfrac{P(x)}{Q(x)}$

where $P(x)$ and $Q(x)$ are polynomial functions. The domain of $f(x)$ is all real numbers except those values for which $Q(x) = 0$.

Here are graphs of three rational functions:

$$y = \frac{x^2}{x^2 + 1}$$

$$y = \frac{(x+3)(x+2)}{(x+2)}$$

$$y = \frac{x+4}{x-2}$$

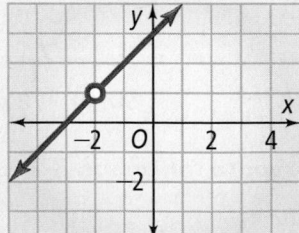

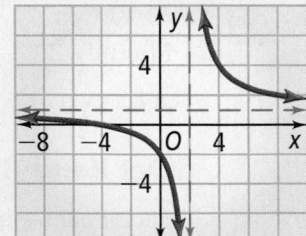

For the first rational function, $y = \frac{x^2}{x^2 + 1}$, there is no value of x that makes the denominator 0. The graph is a **continuous graph** because it has no jumps, breaks, or holes. You can draw the graph and your pencil never leaves the paper.

For $y = \frac{(x + 3)(x + 2)}{x + 2}$, $x \neq -2$ For $y = \frac{x + 4}{x - 2}$, $x \neq 2$. The second and third graphs are **discontinuous graphs**.

take note

Key Concept   Point of Discontinuity

If a is a real number for which the denominator of a rational function $f(x)$ is zero, then a is not in the domain of $f(x)$. The graph of $f(x)$ is not continuous at $x = a$ and the function has a **point of discontinuity** at $x = a$.

The graph of $y = \frac{(x + 3)(x + 2)}{x + 2}$ has a **removable discontinuity** at $x = -2$. The hole in the graph is called a removable discontinuity because you could make the function continuous by redefining it at $x = -2$ so that $f(-2) = 1$.

The graph of $y = \frac{x + 4}{x - 2}$ has a **non-removable discontinuity** at $x = 2$. There is no way to redefine the function at 2 to make the function continuous.

The discontinuity caused by $(x - a)$ in the denominator is removable if the numerator also has $(x - a)$ as a factor.

Hint

When you look for discontinuities, it is helpful to factor the numerator and denominator as a first step. The factors of the denominator will reveal the points of discontinuity.

ONLINE PROBLEMS

Problem 1 Finding Points of Discontinuity

What are the domain and points of discontinuity of each rational function? Are the points of discontinuity *removable* or *non-removable*? What are the x- and y-intercepts?

A $y = \dfrac{x + 3}{x^2 - 4x + 3}$

Step 1 Factor (if possible) to identify the domain.

$$y = \frac{x + 3}{x^2 - 4x + 3} = \frac{x + 3}{(x - 1)(x - 3)}$$

The function is undefined where $x - 1 = 0$ and where $x - 3 = 0$, at $x = 1$ and $x = 3$. The domain of the function is the set of all real numbers except $x = 1$ and $x = 3$.

Step 2 Identify the points of discontinuity.

There are non-removable points of discontinuity at $x = 1$ and $x = 3$.

Step 3 Identify the x- and y-intercepts.

The x-intercept occurs where y equals 0, at $x = -3$.

To find the y-intercept, let $x = 0$ and simplify.

$y = 0$ when the numerator of y equals zero.

$$y = \frac{0 + 3}{(0 - 1)(0 - 3)} = \frac{3}{(-1)(-3)} = \frac{3}{3} = 1$$

Think

Are the discontinuities removable?
There are no common factors in the numerator and denominator. Any discontinuity is non-removable.

B $y = \dfrac{x-5}{x^2+1}$

Step 1 Factor (if possible) to identify the domain.

You cannot factor the numerator or the denominator. Also, no values of x make the denominator 0. The domain is all real numbers, so there are no discontinuities.

Step 2 Identify the x- and y-intercepts.

The x-intercept occurs where the numerator equals 0, at $x = 5$.

To find the y-intercept, let $x = 0$ and simplify: $y = \dfrac{0-5}{0^2+1} = \dfrac{-5}{1} = -5$

C $y = \dfrac{x^2 - 3x - 4}{x - 4}$

Step 1 Factor (if possible) to identify the domain. $\quad y = \dfrac{x^2 - 3x - 4}{x - 4} = \dfrac{(x-4)(x+1)}{(x-4)}$

The function is undefined where $x - 4 = 0$, at $x = 4$. The domain is all real numbers except $x = 4$.

Step 2 Identify the points of discontinuity.

Notice that the graph is identical to the graph of $y = x + 1$, except at $x = 4$, where there is a removable discontinuity.

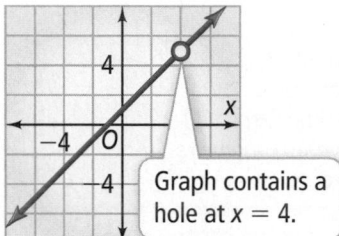

Graph contains a hole at $x = 4$.

You can "remove" this discontinuity by redefining a piecewise function using the domain and the x-value of the discontinuity. At $x = 4$, $y = x + 1 = 4 + 1 = 5$. Remove the discontinuity by redefining the function as shown at the right:

$$y = \begin{cases} \dfrac{x^2 - 3x - 4}{x - 4}, & \text{if } x \neq 4 \\ 5, & \text{if } x = 4 \end{cases}$$

Step 3 Identify the x- and y-intercepts.

The x-intercept occurs where the numerator factor $x + 1 = 0$, at $x = -1$.

To find the y-intercept, let $x = 0$ and simplify.

$y = \dfrac{0^2 - 3 \cdot 0 - 4}{0 - 4} = \dfrac{0 - 0 - 4}{-4} = \dfrac{-4}{-4} = 1$

Think

When is the denominator zero?
x^2 is at least 0, so $x^2 + 1$ is always greater than 0.

Think

Is there also an x-intercept at $x = 4$?
No; although $x = 4$ is a zero of the numerator, it is not in the domain.

✅ **Got It?**

1. What are the domain and points of discontinuity of the rational function? Are the points of discontinuity *removable* or *non-removable*? What are the x- and y-intercepts of the rational function?

a. $y = \dfrac{1}{x^2 - 16}$ **b.** $y = \dfrac{x^2 - 1}{x^2 + 3}$ **c.** $y = \dfrac{x + 1}{x^2 + 3x + 2}$

Hint

An <u>asymptote</u> is a line that a graph approaches as x or y increases in absolute value.

If a rational function has a non-removable discontinuity at $x = a$, the graph has a vertical asymptote at $x = a$.

Key Concept   **Vertical Asymptotes of Rational Functions**

The graph of the rational function $f(x) = \dfrac{P(x)}{Q(x)}$ has a vertical asymptote at each real zero of $Q(x)$ if $P(x)$ and $Q(x)$ have no common zeros. If $P(x)$ and $Q(x)$ have $(x - a)^m$ and $(x - a)^n$ as factors, respectively and $m < n$, then $f(x)$ also has a vertical asymptote at $x = a$.

Plan

How can you locate a vertical asymptote?
Find factors $x - a$ of the denominator that have no matching factor in the numerator. $x = a$ is a vertical asymptote.

 Problem 2 Finding Vertical Asymptotes

What are the vertical asymptotes for the graph of $y = \dfrac{(x + 1)}{(x - 2)(x - 3)}$?

Since 2 and 3 are roots of the denominator and neither is a root of the numerator, the lines $x = 2$ and $x = 3$ are vertical asymptotes.

 Got It? 2. What are the vertical asymptotes for the graph of $y = \dfrac{x - 2}{(x - 1)(x + 3)}$?

While the graph of a rational function can have any number of vertical asymptotes, it can have no more than one horizontal asymptote.

take note

Key Concept   Horizontal Asymptote of a Rational Function

To find the horizontal asymptote of the graph of a rational function, compare the degree of the numerator m to the degree of the denominator n.

If $m < n$, the graph has horizontal asymptote $y = 0$ (the x-axis).

If $m > n$, the graph has no horizontal asymptote.

If $m = n$, the graph has horizontal asymptote $y = \dfrac{a}{b}$ where a is the coefficient of the term of greatest degree in the numerator and b is the coefficient of the term of greatest degree in the denominator.

 Problem 3 Finding Horizontal Asymptotes

What is the horizontal asymptote for the graph of each rational function?

Plan

How can you find the horizontal asymptote when the numerator and denominator have equal degree?
Find the quotient, q, of the leading coefficients of the numerator and denominator. $y = q$ is the horizontal asymptote.

Ⓐ $y = \dfrac{2x}{x - 3}$

The degree of the numerator and denominator are the same.

$y = \dfrac{2x}{x - 3}$ ← degree: 1
   ← degree: 1

The horizontal asymptote is $y = \dfrac{2}{1}$, or $y = 2$.

Ⓑ $y = \dfrac{x - 2}{x^2 - 2x - 3}$

The degree of the numerator is less than the degree of the denominator.

$y = \dfrac{x - 2}{x^2 - 2x - 3}$ ← degree: 1
   ← degree: 2

The horizontal asymptote is $y = 0$.

Ⓒ $y = \dfrac{x^2}{2x - 5}$

The degree of the numerator is greater than the degree of the denominator.

$y = \dfrac{x^2}{2x - 5}$ ← degree: 2
   ← degree: 1

There is no horizontal asymptote.

 Got It? 3. What is the horizontal asymptote for each rational function?

a. $y = \dfrac{-2x + 6}{x - 5}$ 　　　　 **b.** $y = \dfrac{x - 1}{x^2 + 4x + 4}$ 　　　　 **c.** $y = \dfrac{x^2 + 2x - 3}{x - 2}$

Focus Question What information is useful for graphing a rational function?

 Problem 4 Graphing Rational Functions

What is the graph of the rational function $y = \dfrac{x^2 + x - 12}{x^2 - 4}$?

How can you graph this function?
Find the horizontal and vertical asymptotes and the x- and y-intercepts. Look for holes and find additional points to help get a better sense of the graph.

Think

Write

Identify the degrees of the numerator and denominator.

$y = \dfrac{x^2 + x - 12}{x^2 - 4}$ ← degree: 2 ← degree: 2

The degrees are the same.

horizontal asymptote: $y = \dfrac{1}{1} = 1$

Factor the numerator and the denominator. Identify holes or vertical asymptotes.

$y = \dfrac{(x + 4)(x - 3)}{(x + 2)(x - 2)}$

There are no common factors, so there are no holes. There are vertical asymptotes at the zeros of the denominator.

vertical asymptotes: $x = -2$ and $x = 2$

Find the x- and y-intercepts. The x-intercepts occur where $y = 0$. The y-intercepts occur where $x = 0$.

$y = 0$ when the numerator equals zero.

x-intercepts: $(-4, 0)$ and $(3, 0)$

Substitute $x = 0$.

$y = \dfrac{(0 + 4)(0 - 3)}{(0 + 2)(0 - 2)} = \dfrac{(4)(-3)}{(2)(-2)} = \dfrac{-12}{-4} = 3$

y-intercept: $(0, 3)$

Find a few more points on the graph.

More points on the graph:

$\left(-3, -\dfrac{6}{5}\right), (-1, 4), \left(1, \dfrac{10}{3}\right)$ and $\left(4, \dfrac{2}{3}\right)$

Graph the asymptotes. Then plot the intercepts and additional points. Use the points to sketch the graph.

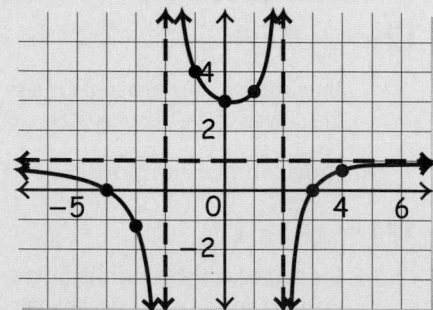

 Got It? **4.** What is the graph of the rational function $y = \dfrac{x + 3}{x^2 - 6x + 5}$?

Problem 5 Using a Rational Function

GRIDDED RESPONSE

Chemistry You work in a pharmacy that mixes different concentrations of saline solutions for its customers. The pharmacy has a supply of two concentrations, 0.5% and 2%. The function $y = \frac{(100)(0.02) + x(0.005)}{100 + x}$ gives the concentration of the saline solution after adding x milliliters of the 0.5% solution to 100 milliliters of the 2% solution. How many milliliters of the 0.5% solution must you add for the combined solution to have a concentration of 0.9%?

Plan

How can you use a calculator to solve the problem?
Graph
$y = \frac{(100)(0.02) + x(0.005)}{100 + x}$
and $y = 0.009$ in the calculator and find the point of intersection.

Step 1 Use a graphing calculator to graph $\mathbf{Y1} = \frac{(100)(0.02) + x(0.005)}{100 + x}$ and $\mathbf{Y2} = 0.009$.

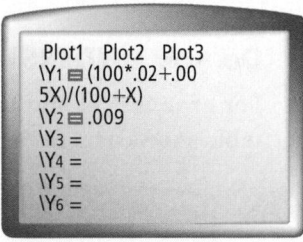 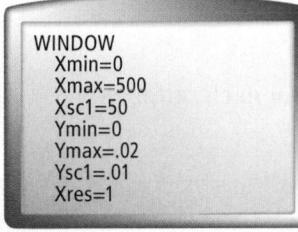 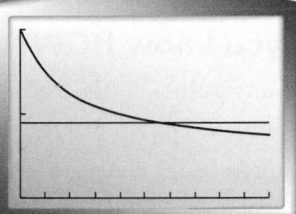

Step 2 Find the point of intersection of the two functions.

Graphic Solution

Table Solution

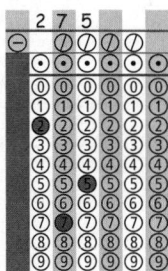

You should add 275 mL of the 0.5% solution to get a 0.9% solution.
Write 275 in the grid.

Check Write the original function.

$$y = \frac{(100)(0.02) + x(0.005)}{100 + x}$$

Substitute 275 for x.

$$y \stackrel{?}{=} \frac{(100)(0.02) + (275)(0.005)}{100 + 275}$$

Simplify.

$$y \stackrel{?}{=} \frac{2 + 1.375}{375}$$

Use a calculator.

$$y = 0.009 \ ✔$$

✅ **Got It?** **5. a.** You want to mix a 10% orange juice drink with 100% pure orange juice to make a 40% orange juice drink. The function $y = \frac{(2)(1.0) + x(0.1)}{2 + x}$ gives the concentration y of orange juice in the drink after you add x gallons of the 10% drink to 2 gallons of pure juice. How much of the 10% drink must you add to get a drink that is 40% juice?

b. Reasoning If you wanted a drink that is 80% juice, would you need to add half as much as your answer in part (a)? Explain.

Hint

For part (a), convert 40% to a decimal, 0.4. Define $Y2 = 0.4$.

Focus Question What is a rational function?

Answer A rational function is a function whose numerator and denominator are both polynomials. If a function has a polynomial in its denominator, its graph has a gap at each zero of the polynomial. The gap could be a one-point hole, or it could be the location of a vertical asymptote.

Focus Question What information is useful for graphing a rational function?

Answer Find the asymptotes and intercepts of a rational function to make a reasonable graph.

Lesson Check

Do you know HOW?

Find any points of discontinuity for each rational function.

1. $y = \dfrac{x + 5}{x^2 + 9x + 20}$

2. $y = \dfrac{x^2 + 2x}{x^2 - 7x - 18}$

3. $y = \dfrac{x - 1}{(x + 1)^2}$

4. $y = \dfrac{x^2 - x - 2}{3x^2 - 7x + 2}$

Find the vertical asymptotes of the graph of each rational function.

5. $y = \dfrac{x - 3}{x + 5}$

6. $y = \dfrac{x - 3}{x^2 + 5x + 6}$

7. $y = \dfrac{2x + 2}{x^2 - 1}$

8. $y = \dfrac{x^2 + 2x + 3}{x^2 + 2x - 3}$

Sketch the graph of each rational function.

9. $y = \dfrac{3x}{x - 4}$

10. $y = \dfrac{x + 3}{(x - 1)(x - 6)}$

Do you UNDERSTAND?

For Exercises 11 and 12, use the following table. The table shows data for a rational function.

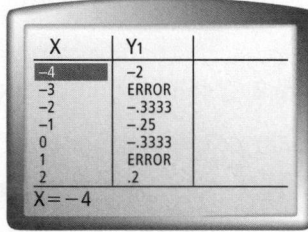

X	Y1
-4	-2
-3	ERROR
-2	-.3333
-1	-.25
0	-.3333
1	ERROR
2	.2

X=-4

11. What do the **Y1** entries for **X = −3** and **X = 1** tell you about the rational function?

12. Reasoning Assume that there are no more **ERROR** values in the **Y1** column. What is the lowest possible degree of the denominator? Explain how you know.

Practice and Problem-Solving Exercises

 **Practice** Find the domain, points of discontinuity, and x- and y- intercepts of each rational function. Determine whether the discontinuities are removable or non-removable.  **See Problem 1.**

Guided Practice

To start, factor the numerator and denominator if possible.

13. $y = \dfrac{2x^2 + 5}{x^2 - 2x}$

$y = \dfrac{2x^2 + 5}{x(x - 2)}$

14. $y = \dfrac{x^2 + 2x}{x^2 + 2}$

15. $y = \dfrac{3x - 3}{x^2 - 1}$

16. $y = \dfrac{6 - 3x}{x^2 - 5x + 6}$

Find the vertical asymptotes and holes for the graph of each rational function. 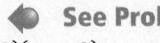 **See Problem 2.**

17. $y = \dfrac{x + 5}{x + 5}$

18. $y = \dfrac{x + 3}{(2x + 3)(x - 1)}$

19. $y = \dfrac{(x + 3)(x - 2)}{(x - 2)(x + 1)}$

Find the horizontal asymptote of the graph of each rational function.  **See Problem 3.**

See Problem 3.

Guided Practice

To start, identify the degree of the numerator and denominator.

20. $y = \dfrac{5}{x + 6}$

$y = \dfrac{5}{x + 6}$ ← degree: 0
← degree: 1

21. $y = \dfrac{x + 1}{x + 5}$

22. $y = \dfrac{x^2 + 2}{2x^2 - 1}$

23. $y = \dfrac{5x^3 + 2x}{2x^5 - 4x^3}$

Sketch the graph of each rational function. **See Problem 4.**

24. $y = \dfrac{x^2 - 4}{3x - 6}$

25. $y = \dfrac{4x}{x^3 - 4x}$

26. $y = \dfrac{x + 4}{x - 4}$

27. $y = \dfrac{x(x + 1)}{x + 1}$

28. $y = \dfrac{x + 6}{(x - 2)(x + 3)}$

29. $y = \dfrac{3x}{(x + 2)^2}$

30. Pharmacology Use the rational function given in Problem 5. How many milliliters of the 0.5% solution must be added to the 2% solution to get a 0.65% solution? **See Problem 5.**

B Apply

Find the vertical and horizontal asymptotes, if any, of the graph of each rational function.

31.

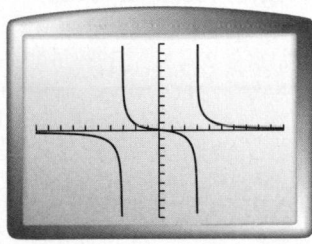

32.

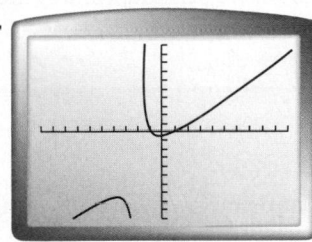

33.

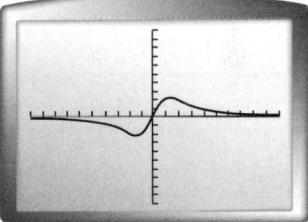

34. Think About a Plan A basketball player has made 21 of her last 30 free throws—a percentage of 70%. How many more consecutive free throws does she need to raise her free throw percentage to 75%?
- How can you model the player's free throw percentage as a rational function?
- How can a graph help you answer this question?

Hint Let x = the number of additional free throws needed.

35. Grades A student earns an 82% on her first test. How many consecutive 100% test scores does she need to bring her average up to 95%? Assume that each test has equal impact on the average grade.

36. Business CDs can be manufactured for $.19 each. The development cost is $210,000. The first 500 discs are samples and will not be sold.
- **a.** Write a function for the average cost of a disc that is not a sample. Graph the function.
- **b.** What is the average cost if 5000 discs are produced? If 15,000 discs are produced?
- **c.** How many discs must be produced to bring the average cost under $10?
- **d.** What are the vertical and horizontal asymptotes of the graph of the function?

37. Writing Describe the conditions that will produce a rational function with a graph that has no vertical asymptotes.

38. Error Analysis A student listed the asymptotes of the function $y = \dfrac{x^2 - 3x + 2}{x^2 + 6x + 5}$ as shown at the right. Explain the student's error. What are the correct asymptotes?

vertical asymptotes:
~~x = 1, x = 2~~
horizontal asymptotes:
~~y = -1, y = -5~~

Sketch the graph of each rational function.

39. $y = \dfrac{2x + 3}{x - 5}$

40. $y = \dfrac{x^2 + 6x + 9}{x + 3}$

41. $y = -\dfrac{x}{(x - 1)^2}$

Standardized Test Prep

GRIDDED RESPONSE

SAT/ACT

42. What is $\log 33{,}000 - \log 99 + \log 30$?

43. Suppose z varies directly with x and inversely with y. If z is 1.5 when x is 9 and y is 4, what is z when x is 6 and y is 0.5?

44. What is the y-coordinate of the vertex of the parabola $y = -3(x - 4)^2 + 5$?

45. What is the real solution of $54x^3 - 16 = 0$ written as a fraction?

46. Using the Change of Base Formula, what is the value of $\log_7 15$ rounded to the nearest hundredth?

Mixed Review

Sketch the asymptotes and the graph of each equation. Identify the domain and range.

◀ See Lesson 8-2.

47. $y = \dfrac{3}{x} + 4$

48. $y = \dfrac{2}{x + 3}$

49. $y = \dfrac{5}{x - 7} - 3$

Find the inverse of each function. Determine if the inverse is a function.

◀ See Lesson 6-7.

50. $y = 2x - 3$

51. $y = 2x^2$

52. $y = \dfrac{1}{x + 2}$

Solve each inequality. Graph the solution.

◀ See Lesson 1-5.

53. $6a - 17 < 47$

54. $5(x - 11) + 13 \geq 47$

55. $6 + y < 3y - 2$

Get Ready! To prepare for Lesson 8-4, do Exercises 56–58.

Factor each expression.

◀ See Lesson 4-4.

56. $2x^2 - 3x + 1$

57. $4x^2 - 9$

58. $5x^2 + 6x + 1$

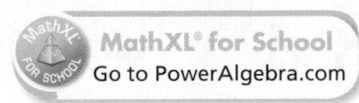
Do you know HOW?

If $z = 30$ when $x = 3$ and $y = 2$, write the function that models the relationship.

1. z varies jointly with x and y.

2. z varies directly with x and inversely with y.

3. z varies inversely with the product of x and y.

Is the relationship between the values in the table a *direct variation*, an *inverse variation*, or *neither*?

4.

x	y
22	104
35	174
48	239
54	269

5.

x	y
15	2.4
18	2
20	1.8
45	0.8

Suppose that x and y vary inversely. Write a function that models the inverse variation.

6. $x = 13$ when $y = 17$

7. $x = -12$ when $y = 4$

8. $x = -52$ when $y = \frac{1}{4}$

Explain how the graph of y_2 is related to the graph of y_1.

9. $y_1 = \frac{4}{x}$ and $y_2 = \frac{9}{x}$

10. $y_1 = \frac{1}{x}$ and $y_2 = \frac{1}{x} + 5$

11. $y_1 = \frac{1}{x-1} + 2$ and $y_2 = \frac{1}{x+1} - 2$

Find any holes and vertical or horizontal asymptotes for the graph of each rational function.

12. $y = \dfrac{1}{x^2 + 3x - 10}$

13. $y = \dfrac{x + 2}{(x + 2)(x - 3)}$

14. $y = \dfrac{x - 1}{x^2 - 2x + 1}$

15. $y = \dfrac{5x - 2}{x + 2}$

Sketch the graph of each rational function. Then identify the domain and range.

16. $y = \frac{-2}{x}$

17. $y = \frac{5}{x + 3} - 4$

18. $y = \frac{x^2 - 9}{2x + 6}$

19. $y = \frac{3x}{x^3 - x}$

20. $y = \frac{x + 3}{x - 3}$

21. $y = \frac{x^2 - 2x}{x - 2}$

Do you UNDERSTAND?

Open-Ended Write a rational function with the given characteristics.

22. a vertical asymptote at $x = 8$ and a horizontal asymptote at $y = 0$

23. a vertical asymptote at $x = -4$ and a horizontal asymptote at $y = 3$

24. a hole at $x = -5$ and a vertical asymptote at $x = 2$

25. Reasoning How many inverse variation functions have $(2, 3)$ as a solution?

26. Reasoning The graph of an inverse variation function contains the point (a, b). Using a and b, identify 3 other points on the graph.

27. Reasoning Graph the equations $y = \frac{x^2 + x - 6}{x^2 - 5x + 6}$ and $y = \frac{x + 3}{x - 3}$. Are they equivalent? Explain.

Rational Expressions

Objectives To simplify rational expressions
To multiply and divide rational expressions

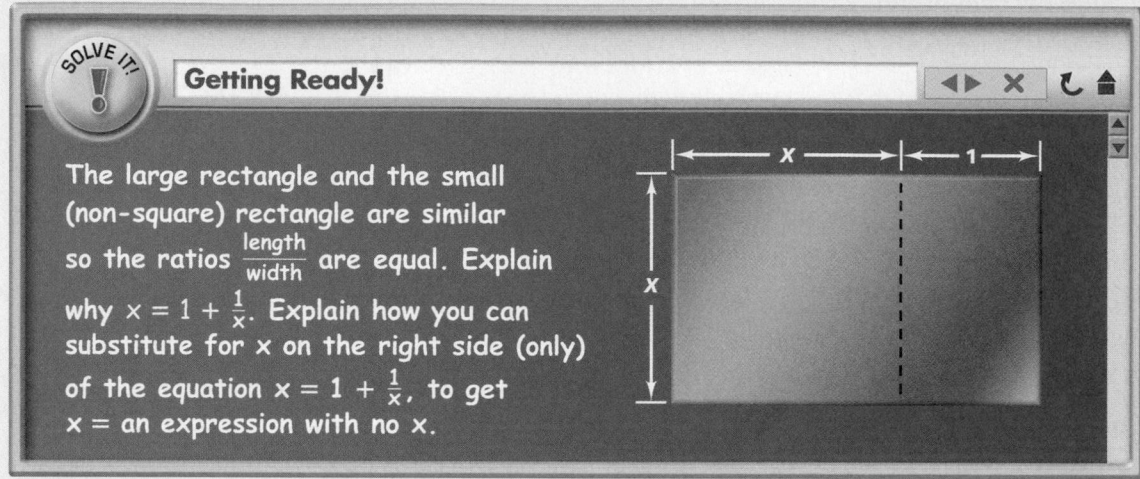

Getting Ready!

The large rectangle and the small (non-square) rectangle are similar so the ratios $\frac{length}{width}$ are equal. Explain why $x = 1 + \frac{1}{x}$. Explain how you can substitute for x on the right side (only) of the equation $x = 1 + \frac{1}{x}$, to get $x = $ an expression with no x.

Lesson Vocabulary
• rational expression
• simplest form

The expression $1 + \frac{1}{x}$ in the Solve It is equivalent to the *rational expression* $\frac{x+1}{x}$. A **rational expression** is the quotient of two polynomials. You will find that, at different times, it is helpful to think of rational expressions as ratios, as fractions, or as quotients.

Focus Question How is multiplying and dividing rational expressions similar to multiplying and dividing fractions?

A rational expression is in **simplest form** when its numerator and denominator are polynomials that have no common factors.

In simplest form	Not in simplest form
$\frac{x+1}{x-1}, \frac{x^2+3x+2}{x+3}$	$\frac{x}{x^2}, \frac{3(x-3)}{x-3}, \frac{x^2-x-6}{x^2+x-2}$

Hint

You used the same method to simplify numerical fractions.
$\frac{12}{80} = \frac{3 \cdot 4}{4 \cdot 20} = \frac{3}{20}$

You simplify a rational expression by dividing out the common factors in the numerator and the denominator. Factoring the numerator and denominator will help you identify the common factors.

A rational expression and any simplified form must have the same domain in order to be equivalent.

$$\frac{x^2-x-6}{x^2+x-2} = \frac{(x-3)(x+2)}{(x-1)(x+2)} \text{ and } \frac{x-3}{x-1}, x \neq -2, \text{ are equivalent.}$$

In the example above, you must exclude -2 from the domain of $\frac{x-3}{x-1}$ because -2 is not in the domain of $\frac{x^2-x-6}{x^2+x-2}$. Note that this restriction is not clear from the simplified expression $\frac{x-3}{x-1}$.

Problem 1 Simplifying a Rational Expression

What is $\frac{x^2 + 7x + 10}{x^2 - 3x - 10}$ in simplest form? State any restrictions on the variable.

Factor the numerator and denominator. $\frac{x^2 + 7x + 10}{x^2 - 3x - 10} = \frac{(x + 2)(x + 5)}{(x + 2)(x - 5)}$

Divide out common factors. $= \frac{\cancel{(x + 2)}(x + 5)}{\cancel{(x + 2)}(x - 5)}$

Simplify. $= \frac{x + 5}{x - 5}$

Think

Is there more than one restriction?
Yes, before you divided the common factors out, $(x + 2)$ was one of the factors of the denominator so $x \neq -2$.

The simplified form is $\frac{x + 5}{x - 5}$ for $x \neq 5$ and $x \neq -2$. The restriction $x \neq -2$ is not clear from the simplified form, but is needed to prevent the denominator of the original expression from being zero.

 Got It? **1.** What is the rational expression in simplest form? State any restrictions on the variables.

a. $\frac{24x^3y^2}{-6x^2y^3}$ **b.** $\frac{x^2 + 2x - 8}{x^2 - 5x + 6}$ **c.** $\frac{12 - 4x}{x^2 - 9}$

You can use what you know about simplifying rational expressions when you multiply and divide them.

 Problem 2 Multiplying Rational Expressions

What is the product $\frac{x^2 + x - 6}{x - 5} \cdot \frac{x^2 - 25}{x^2 + 4x + 3}$ in simplest form? State any restrictions on the variable.

Plan

How is multiplying rational expressions like multiplying fractions?
To multiply rational expressions, you multiply the numerators and multiply the denominators.

Write the original expression. $\frac{x^2 + x - 6}{x - 5} \cdot \frac{x^2 - 25}{x^2 + 4x + 3}$

Factor all polynomials. $= \frac{(x + 3)(x - 2)}{x - 5} \cdot \frac{(x + 5)(x - 5)}{(x + 3)(x + 1)}$

Divide out common factors. $= \frac{\cancel{(x + 3)}(x - 2)}{\cancel{x - 5}} \cdot \frac{(x + 5)\cancel{(x - 5)}}{\cancel{(x + 3)}(x + 1)}$

Simplify. $= \frac{(x - 2)(x + 5)}{x + 1}$

The product is $\frac{(x - 2)(x + 5)}{x + 1}$ for $x \neq -3, x \neq -1$, and $x \neq 5$. The restrictions $x \neq -3$ and $x \neq 5$ are not clear from the simplified form, but are needed to prevent the denominators in the original product from being zero.

 Got It? **2.** What is the product $\frac{2x - 8}{x^2 - 16} \cdot \frac{x^2 + 5x + 4}{x^2 + 8x + 16}$ in simplest form? State any restrictions on the variable.

To divide rational expressions, you multiply by the reciprocal of the divisor, just as you do when you divide rational numbers.

 Problem 3 **Dividing Rational Expressions**

Plan

How do you start?
Think of division
as multiplying by
the reciprocal.

What is the quotient $\dfrac{2-x}{x^2+2x+1} \div \dfrac{x^2+3x-10}{x^2-1}$ in simplest form? State any restrictions on the variable.

Think

Write the expression.

To divide, you multiply by the reciprocal.

Factor the numerators and denominators to find common factors.

Factor -1 from $(2-x)$ to get $(x-2)$.

Divide out common factors.

Rewrite the remaining factors.

Identify the restrictions from the denominator of the simplest form and from any other denominator used.

Write

$$\dfrac{2-x}{x^2+2x+1} \div \dfrac{x^2+3x-10}{x^2-1}$$

$$= \dfrac{2-x}{x^2+2x+1} \cdot \dfrac{x^2-1}{x^2+3x-10}$$

$$= \dfrac{2-x}{(x+1)(x+1)} \cdot \dfrac{(x+1)(x-1)}{(x+5)(x-2)}$$

$$= \dfrac{-1(x-2)}{(x+1)(x+1)} \cdot \dfrac{(x+1)(x-1)}{(x+5)(x-2)}$$

$$= \dfrac{-1\cancel{(x-2)}}{\cancel{(x+1)}(x+1)} \cdot \dfrac{\cancel{(x+1)}(x-1)}{(x+5)\cancel{(x-2)}}$$

$$= \dfrac{-1(x-1)}{(x+1)(x+5)}$$

$$x \neq -1, \, x \neq -5, \, x \neq 1, \text{ and } x \neq 2$$

✓ **Got It?** **3. a.** What is the quotient $\dfrac{x^2+5x+4}{x^2+x-12} \div \dfrac{x^2-1}{2x^2-6x}$ in simplest form? State any restrictions on the variable.

b. Reasoning Without doing the calculation, what is greatest number of restrictions the quotient $\dfrac{x^2+8x+7}{x^2-x-12} \div \dfrac{x^2+2x-8}{x^2+13x+24}$ could have? Explain.

Hint

For part (b), recall
that the greatest
possible number of
zeros of a quadratic
function is 2.

Construction Your community is building a park. It wants to fence in a play space for toddlers. It wants the maximum area for a given amount of fencing. Which shape, a square or a circle, provides a more efficient use of fencing?

Step 1 One measure of efficiency is the ratio $\frac{\text{area fenced}}{\text{fencing used}}$, or $\frac{\text{area}}{\text{perimeter}}$.

Find this ratio for both shapes.

	Square	**Circle**
Define area A and perimeter P.	Area $\;\;\;\;\rightarrow A = s^2$ Perimeter $\rightarrow P = 4s$	Area $\;\;\;\;\rightarrow A = \pi r^2$ Perimeter $\rightarrow P = 2\pi r$
Express s and r in terms of a common variable, P.	$s = \frac{P}{4}$	$r = \frac{P}{2\pi}$
Write the ratios.	$\frac{\text{Area}}{\text{Perimeter}} = \frac{s^2}{P}$	$\frac{\text{Area}}{\text{Perimeter}} = \frac{\pi r^2}{P}$
Substitute for s and r.	$= \frac{\left(\frac{P}{4}\right)^2}{P}$	$= \frac{\pi\left(\frac{P}{2\pi}\right)^2}{P}$
Simplify.	$= \frac{P^2}{16} \cdot \frac{1}{P} = \frac{P}{16}$	$= \frac{\pi P^2}{4\pi^2} \cdot \frac{1}{P} = \frac{P}{4\pi}$

Step 2 Compare the ratios. Which has the greater ratio?

Since $\frac{P}{4\pi} > \frac{P}{16}$, a circle provides a more efficient use of fencing.

 Got It? **4.** Which shape of play space provides for a more efficient use of fencing, a square or an equilateral triangle?

Focus Question How is multiplying and dividing rational expressions similar to multiplying and dividing fractions?

Answer Multiply and divide rational expressions as you would multiply and divide fractions. Restrict the domain to ensure the original expression is never undefined.

✓ Lesson Check

Do you know HOW?

Simplify each rational expression. State any restrictions on the variables.

1. $\frac{4z - 12}{8z + 24}$　　**2.** $\frac{3x - 3}{x^2 - x}$

Multiply or divide. State any restrictions on the variables.

3. $\frac{x^2 + 3x - 10}{x^2 + 4x - 12} \cdot \frac{3x + 18}{x + 3}$

4. $\frac{x^2 - 7x + 10}{x^2 - 8x + 15} \div \frac{4 - x^2}{x^2 + 3x - 18}$

Do you UNDERSTAND?

5. Vocabulary Is the equation $y = \frac{x + 1}{x^2 + 1}$ in simplest form? Explain how you can tell.

6. Error Analysis A student claims that $x = 2$ is the only solution of the equation $\frac{x}{x - 2} = \frac{2}{x - 2}$. Is the student correct? Explain.

7. Reasoning The width of the rectangle is $\frac{a + 10}{3a + 24}$. Write an expression for the length of the rectangle in simplest form.

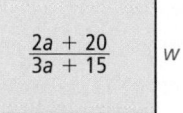

$\frac{2a + 20}{3a + 15}$ ⎤ w

ℓ

Practice and Problem-Solving Exercises

A Practice

Simplify each rational expression. State any restrictions on the variables.

See Problem 1.

8. $-\dfrac{5x^3y}{15xy^3}$

9. $\dfrac{2x}{4x^2 - 2x}$

10. $\dfrac{6c^2 + 9c}{3c}$

11. $\dfrac{49 - z^2}{z + 7}$

12. $\dfrac{x^2 + 8x + 16}{x^2 - 2x - 24}$

13. $\dfrac{12 - x - x^2}{x^2 - 8x + 15}$

Multiply. State any restrictions on the variables.

See Problem 2.

Guided Practice

To start, factor all polynomials.

14. $\dfrac{x^2 - 4}{x^2 - 1} \cdot \dfrac{x + 1}{x^2 + 2x}$

$\dfrac{(x - 2)(x + 2)}{(x - 1)(x + 1)} \cdot \dfrac{x + 1}{x(x + 2)}$

15. $\dfrac{2x^4}{10y^{-2}} \cdot \dfrac{5y^3}{4x^3}$

16. $\dfrac{8y - 4}{10y - 5} \cdot \dfrac{5y - 15}{3y - 9}$

17. $\dfrac{2x + 12}{3x - 9} \cdot \dfrac{6 - 2x}{3x + 8}$

18. $\dfrac{x^2 - 5x + 6}{x^2 - 4} \cdot \dfrac{x^2 + 3x + 2}{x^2 - 2x - 3}$

Divide. State any restrictions on the variables.

See Problem 3.

Guided Practice

To start, rewrite the division as multiplication by the reciprocal.

19. $\dfrac{7x}{4y^3} \div \dfrac{21x^3}{8y}$

$\dfrac{7x}{4y^3} \cdot \dfrac{8y}{21x^3}$

20. $\dfrac{3x^3}{5y^2} \div \dfrac{6y^{-3}}{5x^{-5}}$

21. $\dfrac{6x + 6y}{y - x} \div \dfrac{18}{5x - 5y}$

22. $\dfrac{x^2}{x^2 + 2x + 1} \div \dfrac{3x}{x^2 - 1}$

23. $\dfrac{y^2 - 5y + 6}{y^3} \div \dfrac{y^2 + 3y - 10}{4y^2}$

24. **Industrial Design** A storage tank will have a circular base of radius r and a height of r. The tank can be either cylindrical or hemispherical (half a sphere).

See Problem 4.

a. Write and simplify an expression for the ratio of the volume of the hemispherical tank to its surface area (including the base). For a sphere, $V = \frac{4}{3}\pi r^3$ and $SA = 4\pi r^2$.

b. Write and simplify an expression for the ratio of the volume of the cylindrical tank to its surface area (including the bases). For a cylinder, $V = \pi r^2 h$ and $SA = 2\pi r^2 + 2\pi rh$.

c. Compare the ratios of volume to surface area for the two tanks.

d. Compare the volumes of the two tanks.

25. Architecture An architecture firm is designing a new office building in the shape of a cylinder. The company wants the maximum volume for a given surface area. The cylinder will either have a circular base with radius r and a height $2r$, or a circular base with radius $2r$ and a height r.

   a. Write and simplify an expression for the ratio of the volume to the surface area for a building with a circular base of radius r and height $2r$.

   b. Write and simplify an expression for the ratio of the volume to the surface area for a building with a circular base of radius $2r$ and height r.

   c. Compare the ratios of volume to surface area for the two buildings. Which building will be more efficient?

 **Apply**

Simplify each rational expression. State any restrictions on the variables.

26. $\dfrac{x^2 - 5x - 24}{x^2 - 7x - 30}$

27. $\dfrac{2y^2 + 8y - 24}{2y^2 - 8y + 8}$

28. $\dfrac{xy^3 - 9xy}{12xy^2 + 12xy - 144x}$

29. $\dfrac{(x^2 - x)^2}{x(x - 1)^{-2}(x^2 + 3x - 4)}$

30. $\dfrac{2x + 6}{(x - 1)^{-1}(x^2 + 2x - 3)}$

31. $\dfrac{54x^3y^{-1}}{3x^{-2}y}$

32. Think About a Plan A cereal company wants to use the most efficient packaging for their new product. They are considering a cylindrical-shaped box and a cube-shaped box. Compare the ratios of the volume to the surface area of the containers to determine which packaging will be more efficient.

   • How can you measure the cereal box's efficiency?

   • What formulas will you need to use to solve this problem?

Multiply or divide. State any restrictions on the variables.

33. $\dfrac{6x^3 - 6x^2}{x^4 + 5x^3} \div \dfrac{3x^2 - 15x + 12}{2x^2 + 2x - 40}$

34. $\dfrac{2x^2 - 6x}{x^2 + 18x + 81} \cdot \dfrac{9x + 81}{x^2 - 9}$

35. $\dfrac{x^2 - x - 2}{2x^2 - 5x + 2} \div \dfrac{x^2 - x - 12}{2x^2 + 5x - 3}$

36. $\dfrac{2x^2 + 5x + 2}{4x^2 - 1} \cdot \dfrac{2x^2 + x - 1}{x^2 + x - 2}$

37. Reasoning Write a simplified expression for the area of the rectangle at the right. State all restrictions on a.

38. Manufacturing A toy company is considering a cube or sphere-shaped container for packaging a new product. The height of the cube would equal the diameter of the sphere. Compare the volume-to-surface area ratios of the containers. Which packaging will be more efficient? (*Hint*: For a sphere, $SA = 4\pi r^2$.)

$\dfrac{4a + 4}{a + 3}$

$\dfrac{3a + 9}{2a - 6}$

39. Open-Ended Write three rational expressions that simplify to $\dfrac{x}{x + 1}$.

Decide whether the given statement is *always*, *sometimes*, or *never* true.

40. Rational expressions are undefined for values of the variables that make the denominator 0.

41. Restrictions on variables change when a rational expression is simplified.

Standardized Test Prep

SAT/ACT

42. Which function is graphed at the right?

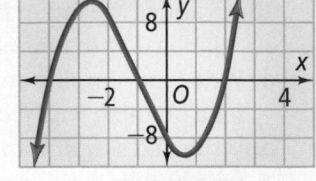

  Ⓐ $y = (x + 4)(x - 1)(x + 2)$

  Ⓑ $y = (x - 4)(x - 1)(x + 2)$

  Ⓒ $y = (x - 4)(x + 1)(x - 2)$

  Ⓓ $y = (x + 4)(x + 1)(x - 2)$

43. Which function generates the table of values at the right?

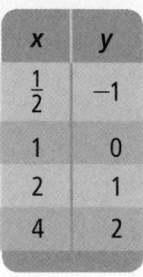

x	y
$\frac{1}{2}$	-1
1	0
2	1
4	2

  Ⓕ $y = \log_{\frac{1}{2}} x$

  Ⓖ $y = -\log_2 x$

  Ⓗ $y = \log_2 x$

  Ⓘ $y = \left(\frac{1}{2}\right)^x$

44. Which expression equals $\dfrac{x}{x^2 - 2x - 3} \cdot \dfrac{2x - 6}{x^2 - 4x + 3}$?

  Ⓐ $\dfrac{2x - 1}{(x - 1)(x + 3)(x + 1)}$

  Ⓒ $\dfrac{2x}{(x - 1)(x + 1)(x - 3)}$

  Ⓑ $\dfrac{2x + 1}{(x - 1)(x + 1)(x - 3)}$

  Ⓓ $\dfrac{2x}{(x + 3)(x - 1)(x + 1)}$

Short Response

45. What is the solution of the equation $3^{-x} = \frac{1}{243}$?

Mixed Review

Find the vertical asymptotes and holes for the graph of each rational function.   ◀ See Lesson 8-3.

46. $y = \dfrac{x - 3}{x - 3}$

47. $y = \dfrac{x - 1}{(3x + 2)(x + 1)}$

48. $y = \dfrac{(x - 4)(x + 5)}{(x + 3)(x - 4)}$

Evaluate each logarithm.   ◀ See Lesson 7-3.

49. $\log_4 64$

50. $\log_2 \dfrac{1}{32}$

51. $\log_{16} 8$

Solve. Check for extraneous solutions.   ◀ See Lesson 6-5.

52. $\sqrt{x} - 3 = 4$

53. $\sqrt{x + 1} - 5 = 8$

54. $\sqrt{5x - 3} = \sqrt{2x + 3}$

Get Ready!   To prepare for Lesson 8-5, do Exercises 55–57.

Add or subtract.   ◀ See p. 866.

55. $\dfrac{5}{19} + \dfrac{7}{38}$

56. $\dfrac{7}{24} - \dfrac{5}{36}$

57. $\dfrac{11}{12} - \dfrac{7}{45}$

8-5
PART 1

Adding and Subtracting Rational Expressions

Objective To add and subtract rational expressions

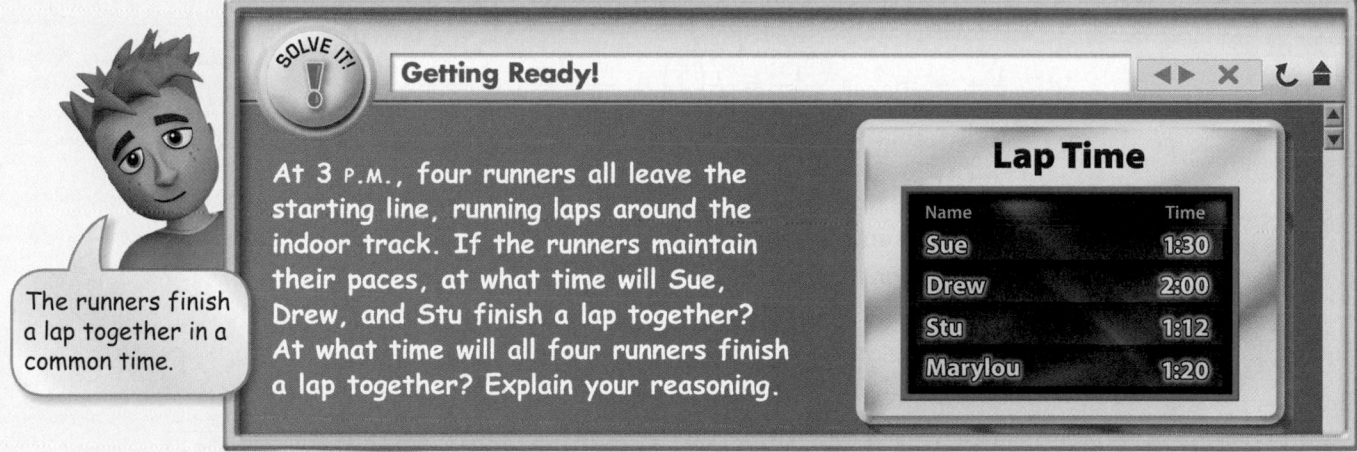

Getting Ready!

At 3 P.M., four runners all leave the starting line, running laps around the indoor track. If the runners maintain their paces, at what time will Sue, Drew, and Stu finish a lap together? At what time will all four runners finish a lap together? Explain your reasoning.

Lap Time

Name	Time
Sue	1:30
Drew	2:00
Stu	1:12
Marylou	1:20

The runners finish a lap together in a common time.

You use common multiples of polynomials to add and subtract rational expressions, just as you use common multiples of numbers to add and subtract fractions.

Hint
You can use any common denominator, but it is often easiest to use the LCM of the denominators.

Focus Question How do you add and subtract rational expressions?

To add or subtract rational expressions, first find the least common multiple (LCM) of the denominators. To find the LCM of several expressions, factor the expressions (numbers or polynomials) completely. The LCM is the product of the prime factors, each raised to the greatest power that occurs in any of the expressions.

Plan
How do you determine the exponent of each factor for the LCM?
Use the exponent from the expression that has that factor to the greatest power.

Problem 1 Finding the Least Common Multiple

What is the LCM of $12x^2y(x^2 + 2x + 1)$ and $18xy^3(x^2 + 5x + 4)$?

Step 1 Find the prime factors of each expression.

Write the expression.	$12x^2y(x^2 + 2x + 1)$	$18xy^3(x^2 + 5x + 4)$
Factor the trinomial.	$= 12x^2y(x + 1)(x + 1)$	$= 18xy^3(x + 1)(x + 4)$
Factor completely.	$= 2^2 \cdot 3x^2y(x + 1)^2$	$= 2 \cdot 3^2xy^3(x + 1)(x + 4)$

Step 2 Identify the greatest power of each factor that occurs in either expression.

$$12x^2y(x^2 + 2x + 1) = 2^2 \cdot 3 \cdot x^2 \cdot y \cdot (x + 1)^2$$
$$18xy^3(x^2 + 5x + 4) = 2 \cdot 3^2 \cdot x \cdot y^3 \cdot (x + 1) \cdot (x + 4)$$

Step 3 Write the product of the factors you identified above.

$$2^2 \cdot 3^2 \cdot x^2 \cdot y^3 \cdot (x + 1)^2 \cdot (x + 4)$$

The LCM is $2^2 \cdot 3^2x^2y^3(x + 1)^2(x + 4)$, or $36x^2y^3(x + 1)^2(x + 4)$.

Got It? **1.** What is the LCM of each pair of expressions?

      a. $2x + 4$ and $x^2 - x - 6$

      b. $x^2 + 3x - 4$, $x^2 + 2x - 8$, and $x^2 - 4x + 4$

The LCM of the denominators of two rational expressions is also the Least Common Denominator (LCD). You can use the LCD to add or subtract the rational expressions.

Recall how you used the LCD to add fractions.

$$\frac{1}{8} + \frac{1}{10} = \frac{1}{2^3} + \frac{1}{2 \cdot 5} = \frac{1}{2^3}\left(\frac{5}{5}\right) + \frac{1}{2 \cdot 5}\left(\frac{2^2}{2^2}\right) = \frac{5}{40} + \frac{4}{40} = \frac{9}{40}$$

 Problem 2 **Adding Rational Expressions**

What is the sum of the two rational expressions in simplest form? State any restrictions on the variable. $\dfrac{x}{x - 1} + \dfrac{2x - 1}{x^2 - 3x + 2}$

Plan

How does the LCD help you simplify this sum?
The LCD is $(x - 1)(x - 2)$. Multiply the first expression by $\frac{x - 2}{x - 2}$ to get a common denominator.

Write the original expression.

$$\frac{x}{x - 1} + \frac{2x - 1}{x^2 - 3x + 2}$$

Factor the denominators.

$$= \frac{x}{x - 1} + \frac{2x - 1}{(x - 1)(x - 2)}$$

Rewrite each expression with the LCD.

$$= \frac{x}{x - 1} \cdot \frac{x - 2}{x - 2} + \frac{2x - 1}{(x - 1)(x - 2)}$$

Simplify the first expression.

$$= \frac{x^2 - 2x}{(x - 1)(x - 2)} + \frac{2x - 1}{(x - 1)(x - 2)}$$

Add the numerators. Combine like terms.

$$= \frac{x^2 - 2x + 2x - 1}{(x - 1)(x - 2)}$$

Simplify the numerator.

$$= \frac{x^2 - 1}{(x - 1)(x - 2)}$$

Factor the numerator. Divide out the common factors.

$$= \frac{\cancel{(x - 1)}(x + 1)}{\cancel{(x - 1)}(x - 2)}$$

Write the equivalent expression in simplest form.

$$= \frac{x + 1}{x - 2}, x \neq 1$$

The sum of the expressions is $\frac{x + 1}{x - 2}$ for $x \neq 1$ and $x \neq 2$.

Hint

For part (c), think about the different common denominators you could use to find the sum $\frac{5}{12} + \frac{9}{16}$.

 Got It? **2.** What is the sum of the two rational expressions in simplest form? State any restrictions on the variable.

    a. $\dfrac{x + 1}{x - 1} + \dfrac{-2}{x^2 - x}$ **b.** $\dfrac{x}{x^2 - 4} + \dfrac{1}{x + 2}$

    c. **Reasoning** Is it possible to add the rational expressions in Problem 2 by finding a common denominator, but not the *least* common denominator? Explain.

Problem 3 Subtracting Rational Expressions

What is the difference of the two rational expressions in simplest form? State any restrictions on the variable. $\dfrac{x+2}{x^2-2x} - \dfrac{x+2}{2x-4}$

Think

Write the original expression. Factor the denominators to find the LCD.

Rewrite each expression with the LCD.

Simplify the numerators and subtract.

Factor the numerator and divide out the common factors.

Write the answer. State any restrictions on the domain.

Write

$$\dfrac{x+2}{x^2-2x} - \dfrac{x+2}{2x-4}$$

$$= \dfrac{x+2}{x(x-2)} - \dfrac{x+2}{2(x-2)}$$

The LCD is $2x(x-2)$.

$$= \dfrac{x+2}{x(x-2)} \cdot \dfrac{2}{2} - \dfrac{x+2}{2(x-2)} \cdot \dfrac{x}{x}$$

$$= \dfrac{2(x+2)}{2x(x-2)} - \dfrac{x(x+2)}{2x(x-2)}$$

$$= \dfrac{2x+4}{2x(x-2)} - \dfrac{x^2+2x}{2x(x-2)}$$

$$= \dfrac{2x+4-(x^2+2x)}{2x(x-2)}$$

$$= \dfrac{2x+4-x^2-2x}{2x(x-2)}$$

$$= \dfrac{-x^2+4}{2x(x-2)}$$

$$= \dfrac{-(x^2-4)}{2x(x-2)}$$

$$= \dfrac{-(x-2)(x+2)}{2x(x-2)}$$

$$= \dfrac{-(x+2)}{2x}$$

The difference is $\dfrac{-(x+2)}{2x}$ for $x \neq 2$ and $x \neq 0$.

Hint

Multiplying by $\frac{2}{2}$ did not introduce any restrictions on the variable because $\frac{2}{2}$ is defined for all values of x.

Got It? **3.** What is the difference of the two rational expressions in simplest form? State any restrictions on the variable.

a. $\dfrac{x+3}{x-2} - \dfrac{6x-7}{x^2-3x+2}$

b. $\dfrac{x-1}{x+5} - \dfrac{x+3}{x^2+6x+5}$

Focus Question How do you add and subtract rational expressions?

Answer Add and subtract rational expressions just as you would add and subtract fractions. Rewrite the expressions using the LCM of the denominators. Remember to include any restrictions on the variable.

Lesson Check

Do you know HOW?

Simplify each sum or difference. State any restrictions on the variables.

1. $\dfrac{a + 11}{3a - 5} + \dfrac{a - 21}{3a - 5}$

2. $\dfrac{1}{x^2 - 4} + \dfrac{6}{x + 2}$

3. $\dfrac{m}{3m + 6} - \dfrac{4m}{m + 2}$

4. $\dfrac{b - 4}{b^2 + 2b - 8} - \dfrac{b + 2}{b^2 - 16}$

Do you UNDERSTAND?

5. Open-Ended Write two rational expressions that simplify to $\dfrac{x + 1}{x - 5}$.

6. Writing Explain how to find the least common multiple of two polynomials.

Practice and Problem-Solving Exercises

 **Practice**

Find the least common multiple of each pair of polynomials.

◀ **See Problem 1.**

Guided Practice

To start, completely factor each expression.

7. $9(x + 2)(2x - 1)$ and $3(x + 2)$

$3^2 \cdot (x + 2) \cdot (2x - 1)$ and $3 \cdot (x + 2)$

8. $x^2 - 1$ and $x^2 + 2x + 1$

9. $x^2 - 32x - 10$ and $2x + 10$

Simplify each sum or difference. State any restrictions on the variables.

◀ **See Problems 2 and 3.**

Guided Practice

To start, factor the denominators and identify the LCD.

10. $\dfrac{5y + 2}{xy^2} + \dfrac{2x - 4}{4xy}$

$\dfrac{5y + 2}{x \cdot y^2} + \dfrac{2x - 4}{4 \cdot x \cdot y}$ The LCD is $4xy^2$.

11. $\dfrac{d - 3}{2d + 1} + \dfrac{d - 1}{2d + 1}$

12. $\dfrac{-2}{x} - \dfrac{1}{x}$

13. $\dfrac{-5y}{2y - 1} - \dfrac{y + 3}{2y - 1}$

14. $\dfrac{5x}{x^2 - 9} + \dfrac{2}{x + 4}$

15. $\dfrac{y}{2y + 4} - \dfrac{3}{y + 2}$

16. $\dfrac{x}{3x + 9} - \dfrac{8}{x^2 + 3x}$

 **Apply**

Add or subtract. Simplify where possible. State any restrictions on the variables.

17. $\dfrac{3}{4x} - \dfrac{2}{x^2}$

18. $\dfrac{3}{x + 1} + \dfrac{x}{x - 1}$

19. $\dfrac{4}{x^2 - 9} + \dfrac{7}{x + 3}$

20. $\dfrac{5x}{x^2 - x - 6} - \dfrac{4}{x^2 + 4x + 4}$

21. $3x + \dfrac{x^2 + 5x}{x^2 - 2}$

22. $\dfrac{5y}{y^2 - 7y} - \dfrac{4}{2y - 14} + \dfrac{9}{y}$

23. Writing Explain how factoring is used when adding or subtracting rational expressions. Include an example in your explanation.

Adding and Subtracting Rational Expressions

Objective To add and subtract rational expressions

In Part 1 of the lesson, you learned how to add and subtract rational expressions using the LCD.

Connect to What You Know

Here you will use what you learned to simplify complex fractions.

Lesson Vocabulary
• complex fraction

Focus Question What is a complex fraction?

A **complex fraction** is a rational expression that has at least one fraction in its numerator or denominator or both. Here are some examples.

$$\frac{\frac{1}{x} + \frac{1}{y}}{\frac{1}{xy}} \qquad \frac{\frac{x+3}{2}}{\frac{2}{x-4}} \qquad \frac{\frac{x+3}{x^2-2x+1} + \frac{x}{x^2-3x+2}}{\frac{x}{x^2-4x+4} - \frac{2}{x^2-4}}$$

Sometimes you can simplify a complex fraction by multiplying the numerator and denominator by the LCD of all the rational expressions. Consider a numerical example:

$$\frac{\frac{1}{2} + \frac{2}{3}}{\frac{1}{3}} = \frac{\left(\frac{1}{2} + \frac{2}{3}\right) \cdot 6}{\frac{1}{3} \cdot 6} = \frac{\frac{1}{2} \cdot 6 + \frac{2}{3} \cdot 6}{\frac{1}{3} \cdot 6} = \frac{3+4}{2} = \frac{7}{2}$$

You can also simplify this complex fraction by combining the fractions in the numerator and those in the denominator.

$$\frac{\frac{1}{2} + \frac{2}{3}}{\frac{1}{3}} = \frac{\frac{1}{2} \cdot \frac{3}{3} + \frac{2}{3} \cdot \frac{2}{2}}{\frac{1}{3}} = \frac{\frac{3}{6} + \frac{4}{6}}{\frac{1}{3}} = \frac{\frac{7}{6}}{\frac{1}{3}}$$

Hint

To divide a fraction by another fraction, multiply the first fraction by the reciprocal of the second fraction.

Then divide the new numerator by the new denominator.

$$\frac{7}{6} \div \frac{1}{3} = \frac{7}{6} \cdot \frac{3}{1} = \frac{21}{6} = \frac{7}{2}$$

Problem 4 Simplifying a Complex Fraction

Think

What is the LCD of $\frac{1}{x}$, $\frac{x}{y}$, and $\frac{1}{y}$?

The LCD of the rational expressions is xy.

What is the simplest form of the complex fraction? $\dfrac{\frac{1}{x} + \frac{x}{y}}{\frac{1}{y} + 1}$

Method 1 Multiply both the numerator and the denominator by the LCD of all the rational expressions and simplify the result.

Multiply the numerator and the denominator by xy.

$$\frac{\frac{1}{x} + \frac{x}{y}}{\frac{1}{y} + 1} = \frac{\left(\frac{1}{x} + \frac{x}{y}\right) \cdot xy}{\left(\frac{1}{y} + 1\right) \cdot xy}$$

Use the Distributive Property.

$$= \frac{\frac{1}{x} \cdot xy + \frac{x}{y} \cdot xy}{\frac{1}{y} \cdot xy + 1 \cdot xy}$$

Simplify.

$$= \frac{y + x^2}{x + xy}$$

Method 2 Combine the expressions in the numerator and those in the denominator. Then multiply the new numerator by the reciprocal of the new denominator.

Write equivalent expressions with common denominators.

$$\frac{\frac{1}{x} + \frac{x}{y}}{\frac{1}{y} + 1} = \frac{\frac{1}{x} \cdot \frac{y}{y} + \frac{x}{y} \cdot \frac{x}{x}}{\frac{1}{y} + 1 \cdot \frac{y}{y}}$$

> The LCD of the fractions in the numerator is xy.

Multiply.

$$= \frac{\frac{y}{xy} + \frac{x^2}{xy}}{\frac{1}{y} + \frac{y}{y}}$$

> The LCD of the fractions in the denominator is y.

Add.

$$= \frac{\frac{y + x^2}{xy}}{\frac{1 + y}{y}}$$

Divide the numerator fraction by the denominator fraction.

$$= \frac{y + x^2}{xy} \div \frac{1 + y}{y}$$

Multiply by the reciprocal.

$$= \frac{y + x^2}{xy} \cdot \frac{y}{1 + y}$$

Divide out the common factor, y.

$$= \frac{\cancel{y}(y + x^2)}{x\cancel{y}(1 + y)}$$

Simplify.

$$= \frac{y + x^2}{x(1 + y)}$$

Use the Distributive Property.

$$= \frac{y + x^2}{x + xy}$$

 Got It? **4.** What is the simplest form of the complex fraction?

a. $\dfrac{x}{\frac{1}{x} + \frac{1}{y}}$

b. $\dfrac{\frac{x-2}{x} + \frac{2}{x+1}}{\frac{3}{x-1} - \frac{1}{x+1}}$

c. Reasoning Which method from Problem 4 is easier to use? Explain.

 **Problem 5** Using Rational Expressions to Solve a Problem

Fuel Economy A woman drives an SUV that gets 10 mi/gal (mpg). Her husband drives a hybrid that gets 60 mpg. Every week, they travel the same number of miles. They want to improve their combined mpg. They have two options on how they can improve it.

Option 1: They can tune the SUV and increase its mileage by 1 mpg and keep the hybrid as it is.

Option 2: They can buy a new hybrid that gets 80 mpg and keep the SUV as it is.

Which option will give them a better combined mpg?

Think

The combined gas mileage is total miles divided by total gallons.

Define a variable and describe each option.

Write the variable expressions for each option. The gallons used by each vehicle are $\frac{miles}{mpg}$.

Find the LCD of the fractions in each expression. Multiply the numerator and denominator by the LCD.

Distribute and simplify.

Round the ratios and compare them.

Write

$$\text{combined mpg} = \frac{\text{SUV miles} + \text{Hybrid miles}}{\text{SUV gallons} + \text{Hybrid gallons}}$$

Let x = number of miles each drives in a week

Option 1	Option 2
Tuned SUV gets 11 mpg. Hybrid gets 60 mpg.	SUV gets 10 mpg. New Hybrid gets 80 mpg.

$$\frac{x + x}{\frac{x}{11} + \frac{x}{60}} \qquad \frac{x + x}{\frac{x}{10} + \frac{x}{80}}$$

$$\left(\frac{2x}{\frac{x}{11} + \frac{x}{60}}\right) \cdot \left(\frac{660}{660}\right) \qquad \left(\frac{2x}{\frac{x}{10} + \frac{x}{80}}\right) \cdot \left(\frac{80}{80}\right)$$

$$\frac{(2x)(660)}{\left(\frac{x}{11}\right)(660) + \left(\frac{x}{60}\right)(660)} \qquad \frac{(2x)(80)}{\left(\frac{x}{10}\right)(80) + \left(\frac{x}{80}\right)(80)}$$

$$= \frac{1320x}{60x + 11x} \qquad = \frac{160x}{8x + x}$$

$$= \frac{1320x}{71x} \qquad = \frac{160x}{9x}$$

$$\approx 18.6 \text{ mpg} \qquad \approx 17.8 \text{ mpg}$$

Option 1 gives the better combined mpg.

 Got It? **5.** Suppose Option 3 is to buy a new hybrid that will get double the mileage of the present hybrid. The SUV mileage stays the same. Which of the three options will give the best combined mpg?

Focus Question What is a complex fraction?

Answer A complex fraction is a rational expression that has at least one fraction in its numerator or denominator or both. To simplify a complex fraction, multiply the numerator and the denominator by the LCD of all the rational expressions. You can also simplify by first combining the fractions in the numerator and the fractions in the denominator and then dividing.

Lesson Check

Do you know HOW?

Simplify each complex fraction.

1. $\dfrac{\frac{1}{x}}{\frac{2}{y}}$

2. $\dfrac{\frac{1}{3}}{\frac{3}{b}}$

Do you UNDERSTAND?

3. **Error Analysis** Describe and correct the error made in simplifying the complex fraction.

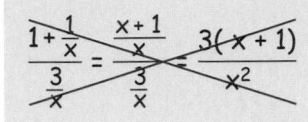

$$\frac{1 + \frac{1}{x}}{\frac{3}{x}} = \frac{\frac{x+1}{x}}{\frac{3}{x}} = \frac{3(x+1)}{x^2}$$

Practice and Problem-Solving Exercises

A Practice   Simplify each complex fraction.

◀ See Problem 4.

4. $\dfrac{1 - \frac{1}{4}}{2 - \frac{3}{5}}$

Guided Practice

To start, multiply the numerator and the denominator by the LCD of all the rational expressions.

$$\frac{\left(1 - \frac{1}{4}\right) \cdot 20}{\left(2 - \frac{3}{5}\right) \cdot 20}$$

5. $\dfrac{\frac{2}{x+y}}{3}$

6. $\dfrac{\frac{-2}{x}}{\frac{2}{x}}$

7. $\dfrac{1}{1 + \frac{x}{y}}$

8. $\dfrac{3}{\frac{2}{x} + y}$

9. $\dfrac{\frac{2}{x+y}}{\frac{5}{x+y}}$

10. $\dfrac{12}{\frac{3}{x} + \frac{6}{y}}$

11. $\dfrac{-3}{\frac{5}{x} + y}$

12. $\dfrac{\frac{3}{x-4}}{1 - \frac{2}{x-4}}$

13. $\dfrac{\frac{2}{x+4} + 2}{1 + \frac{3}{x+4}}$

14. Your car gets 25 mi/gal around town and 30 mi/gal on the highway.

 **See Problem 5.**

    a. If 50% of the miles you drive are on the highway and 50% are around town, what is your overall average miles per gallon?

    b. If 60% of the miles you drive are on the highway and 40% are around town, what is your overall average miles per gallon?

 **Apply**

15. Think About a Plan For the image of the overhead projector to be in focus, the distance d_i from the projector lens to the image, the projector lens focal length f, and the distance d_o from the transparency to the projector lens must satisfy the thin-lens equation $\frac{1}{f} = \frac{1}{d_i} + \frac{1}{d_o}$. What is the focal length of the projector lens if the transparency placed 4 in. from the projector lens is in focus on the screen located 8 ft from the projector lens?

- Can you write the equation for the unknown variable?
- What units would you use for the focal length of the lens?

16. Optics To read small font, you use a magnifying lens with the focal length 3 in. How far from the magnifying lens should you place the page if you want to hold the lens at 1 foot from your eyes? Use the thin-lens equation from Exercise 15.

Simplify each sum or difference. State any restrictions on the variables.

17. $\dfrac{-3x}{x^2 - 9} + \dfrac{4}{2x - 6}$

18. $\dfrac{5x}{x^2 - x - 6} + \dfrac{4}{x^2 + 4x + 4}$

19. $\dfrac{2x}{x^2 - x - 2} - \dfrac{4x}{x^2 - 3x + 2}$

20. Open-Ended Write two complex fractions that simplify to $\frac{x - 2}{x + 4}$.

Simplify each complex fraction.

21. $\dfrac{\frac{2}{x} + \frac{3}{y}}{\frac{-5}{x} + \frac{7}{y}}$

22. $\dfrac{1 + \frac{2}{x}}{2 + \frac{3}{2x}}$

23. $\dfrac{\frac{1}{xy} - \frac{1}{y^2}}{\frac{1}{x^2 y} - \frac{1}{xy^2}}$

24. Harmony The harmonic mean of two numbers a and b equals $\dfrac{2}{\frac{1}{a} + \frac{1}{b}}$. As you vary the length of a violin or guitar string, its pitch changes. If a full-length string is 1 unit long, then many lengths that are simple fractions produce pitches that harmonize, or sound pleasing together. The harmonic mean relates two lengths that produce harmonious sounds. Find the harmonic mean for each pair of string lengths.

    a. 1 and $\frac{1}{2}$

    c. $\frac{3}{4}$ and $\frac{3}{5}$

    b. $\frac{3}{4}$ and $\frac{1}{2}$

    d. $\frac{1}{2}$ and $\frac{1}{4}$

> **Hint** Remember that for $b \neq 0$, $\frac{1}{b}$ is the reciprocal of b. So, if $b = \frac{3}{4}$, then $\frac{1}{b} = \frac{4}{3}$.

SAT/ACT

25. Which expression equals $\dfrac{5x}{x^2 - 9} - \dfrac{4x}{x^2 + 5x + 6}$?

Ⓐ $\dfrac{7x}{(x-3)(x+3)(x+2)}$

Ⓒ $\dfrac{x^2 + 22x}{(x-3)(x+3)(x+2)}$

Ⓑ $\dfrac{x^2 - 2x}{(x-3)(x+3)(x+2)}$

Ⓓ $\dfrac{9x^2 - 2x}{(x-3)(x+3)(x+2)}$

26. Which of the relationships is represented by the graph at the right?

Ⓕ $y = \log_4(x - 1) + 5$

Ⓖ $y = \log_4(x - 1) - 2$

Ⓗ $y = \log_4(x + 2) - 2$

Ⓘ $y = \log_4(x - 1) - 1$

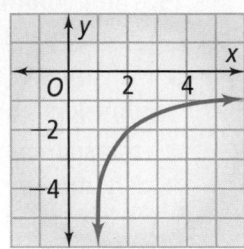

27. What is the simpler form of $\dfrac{\frac{2}{x} - 5}{\frac{6}{x} - 3}$?

Ⓐ $\dfrac{2 - 5x}{6 - 3x}$

Ⓑ $\dfrac{2 + 5x}{6 - 3x}$

Ⓒ $\dfrac{2x - 5}{6x + 3}$

Ⓓ $\dfrac{6 + 3x}{2 - 5x}$

28. What word makes the statement "The domain and range of a(n) _____ function is the set of all real numbers" *sometimes* true?

Ⓕ polynomial

Ⓗ exponential

Ⓖ logarithmic

Ⓘ quadratic

Short Response

29. What is the least common denominator for the rational expressions $\dfrac{1}{x^2 - 5x - 6}$ and $\dfrac{1}{x^2 - 12x + 36}$? Show your work.

Mixed Review

Divide. State any restrictions on the variable.   ◀ **See Lesson 8-4.**

30. $\dfrac{3x^2 - 9x}{x - 2} \div \dfrac{x^2 - 9}{4x - 8}$

31. $\dfrac{3x - 6}{12x - 24} \div \dfrac{x^2 - 5x + 6}{3x^2 - 12}$

32. $\dfrac{5x + 15}{10x - 10} \div \dfrac{x^2 + 6x + 9}{3x^2 - 3}$

Write each logarithmic expression as a single logarithm.   ◀ **See Lesson 7-4.**

33. $\log_3 y + 4 \log_3 t$

34. $7 \log p + 2 \log q$

35. $\log_5 x - \frac{1}{5} \log_5 y$

Let $f(x) = x^2 + 1$ and $g(x) = 3x$. Evaluate each expression.   ◀ **See Lesson 6-6.**

36. $(g \circ f)(-3)$

37. $(f \circ g)(-3)$

38. $(g \circ f)\left(\frac{1}{2}\right)$

Get Ready!   **To prepare for Lesson 8-6, do Exercises 39–41.**

Solve each equation. Check your answers.   ◀ **See Lesson 1-4.**

39. $-3(x - 4) = 2(x + 8)$

40. $0.2(x + 8) - 3.4 = 2.4$

41. $\frac{x}{2} + \frac{x}{3} = 15$

8-6 Solving Rational Equations

Objectives To solve rational equations
To use rational equations to solve problems

A straight path is the shortest distance between two points.

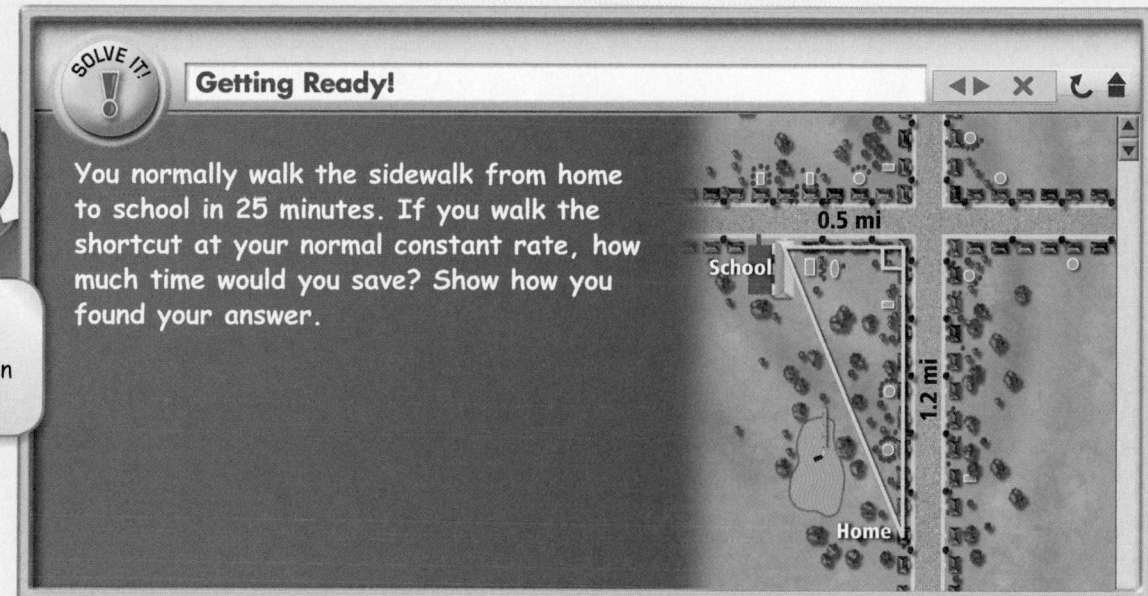

SOLVE IT!

Getting Ready!

You normally walk the sidewalk from home to school in 25 minutes. If you walk the shortcut at your normal constant rate, how much time would you save? Show how you found your answer.

0.5 mi

School

1.2 mi

Home

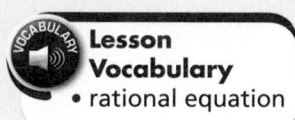

Lesson Vocabulary
• rational equation

Sometimes you can solve a problem using a proportion—an equation involving two rational expressions set equal to each other.

Focus Question How is solving a rational equation similar to solving a polynomial equation?

A **rational equation** contains at least one rational expression. You can make it easier to solve a rational equation if you first clear the equation of denominators. Multiply each side of the equation by the LCD of the rational expressions in the equation.

Rational Equation

$$\frac{x}{x+1} + \frac{x}{x-1} = \frac{2}{x^2-1}$$

Not a Rational Equation

$$x + \frac{1}{2} = \frac{2}{3}$$

Hint

Recall that an extraneous solution is a solution of the derived equation, but not a solution of the original equation.

Any time you multiply each side of an equation by an algebraic expression, it is possible to introduce extraneous solutions. You must check all solutions in the original equation to confirm that they are indeed solutions.

Problem 1 Solving a Rational Equation

What are the solutions of the rational equation?

Ⓐ $\dfrac{x}{x-3} + \dfrac{x}{x+3} = \dfrac{2}{x^2-9}$

Think

Factor the denominators to find the LCD.

Multiply each side by the LCD to clear denominators.

Now distribute, simplify, and solve.

Check whether $x = 1$ or $x = -1$ is extraneous. Use the original equation.

Write the solutions.

Write

$$\dfrac{x}{x-3} + \dfrac{x}{x+3} = \dfrac{2}{x^2-9}$$

$$\dfrac{x}{x-3} + \dfrac{x}{x+3} = \dfrac{2}{(x-3)(x+3)}$$

$$(x-3)(x+3)\left[\dfrac{x}{x-3} + \dfrac{x}{x+3}\right] = (x-3)(x+3)\dfrac{2}{(x-3)(x+3)}$$

$$x(x+3) + x(x-3) = 2$$
$$x^2 + 3x + x^2 - 3x = 2$$
$$x^2 + 3x + x^2 - 3x = 2$$
$$2x^2 = 2$$
$$x^2 = 1, \text{ so } x = \pm 1$$

$$\dfrac{1}{1-3} + \dfrac{1}{1+3} \stackrel{?}{=} \dfrac{2}{(1)^2 - 9} \qquad\qquad \dfrac{-1}{-1-3} + \dfrac{-1}{-1+3} \stackrel{?}{=} \dfrac{2}{(-1)^2 - 9}$$

$$-\dfrac{1}{2} + \dfrac{1}{4} = -\dfrac{1}{4} \checkmark \qquad\qquad\qquad \dfrac{1}{4} + -\dfrac{1}{2} = -\dfrac{1}{4} \checkmark$$

The solutions are $x = 1$ and $x = -1$.

Ⓑ $\dfrac{x-1}{x^2+3x+2} + \dfrac{2x}{x+2} = \dfrac{x-1}{x+1}$

$$\dfrac{x-1}{x^2+3x+2} + \dfrac{2x}{x+2} = \dfrac{x-1}{x+1}$$

The LCD is $(x+2)(x+1)$.

$$(x+2)(x+1)\left[\dfrac{x-1}{(x+2)(x+1)} + \dfrac{2x}{x+2}\right] = (x+2)(x+1)\left(\dfrac{x-1}{x+1}\right)$$

$$(x-1) + 2x(x+1) = (x+2)(x-1)$$

$$2x^2 + 3x - 1 = x^2 + x - 2$$

$$x^2 + 2x + 1 = 0$$

$$(x+1)(x+1) = 0, \text{ so } x = -1$$

Think

How is this rational equation related to a quadratic equation?
Multiplying each side of the equation by the LCD of the rational expressions turns it into a quadratic equation.

The solution $x = -1$ is extraneous because the original equation restricts x so that $x \neq -2$ and $x \neq -1$. There is no solution to this equation.

 Got It? **1.** What are the solutions of the rational equation?

a. $\dfrac{x-1}{x+2} = \dfrac{x^2+2x-3}{x+2}$

b. $\dfrac{x}{x+1} + \dfrac{3}{x+4} = \dfrac{x+3}{x+4}$

Problem 2 Using Rational Equations

Flight A flight across the U.S. takes longer east to west than it does west to east. Assume that winds are constant in the eastward direction. When flying westward, the headwind decreases the airplane's speed. When flying eastward, the tailwind increases its speed. The time for the round trip shown at the right is $7\frac{3}{4}$ h. If the airplane cruises at 480 mi/h in still air, what is the speed of the wind?

1850 mi

Chicago

San Francisco

Let x = the wind speed.

$$\text{Rate} \times \text{Time} = \text{Distance, so Time} = \frac{\text{Distance}}{\text{Rate}}$$

	Distance	Rate	Time
Going west to east	1850	480 + x	$\frac{1850}{480 + x}$
Going east to west	1850	480 − x	$\frac{1850}{480 - x}$

Total time = Time west to east + Time east to west

$$7.75 = \frac{1850}{480 + x} + \frac{1850}{480 - x}$$

> Multiply both sides by the LCD, $(480 + x)(480 - x)$.

$$(480 + x)(480 - x)7.75 = (480 + x)(480 - x)\frac{1850}{480 + x} + (480 + x)(480 - x)\frac{1850}{480 - x}$$

$$7.75(480 + x)(480 - x) = 1850(480 - x) + 1850(480 + x)$$

$$1{,}785{,}600 - 7.75x^2 = 888{,}000 - 1850x + 888{,}000 + 1850x$$

$$-7.75x^2 = -9600$$

$$x^2 = \frac{-9600}{-7.75}$$

$$x \approx \pm 35$$

Think

If you substitute 35 for *x* will the equation check exactly?
No; since 35 is an approximation, it is likely that the values will be nearly equal, but probably not equal.

Check $7.75 = \frac{1850}{480 + x} + \frac{1850}{480 - x}$

$$7.75 \stackrel{?}{=} \frac{1850}{480 + 35} + \frac{1850}{480 - 35}$$

$$7.75 \approx 3.6 + 4.2 \checkmark$$

Wind speed is positive, so $x \approx 35$. The west-to-east wind speed is about 35 mi/h.

Got It? **2. a.** You ride your bike to a store, 4 mi away, to pick up things for dinner. When there is no wind, you ride at 10 mi/h. Today your trip to the store and back took 1 hour. What was the speed of the wind today?

b. Reasoning Explain why there is no difference between the travel time to and from the store when there is no wind.

You can also use a graphing calculator to solve a rational equation.

 Problem 3 Using a Graphing Calculator to Solve a Rational Equation

What are the solutions of the rational equation? Use a graphing calculator to solve.

$$\frac{2}{x+2} + \frac{x}{x-2} = 1$$

Plan

How do the graphs of the two sides of the equation help you find solutions?
The x-values of the points of intersection are the solutions to the equation.

Enter one side of the equation as Y_1. Enter the other side as Y_2.

There appears to be only one intersection point, at $x = 0$.

$Y_1 = Y_2$ when $x = 0$.

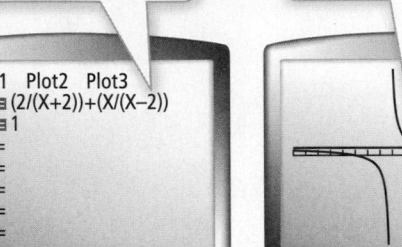

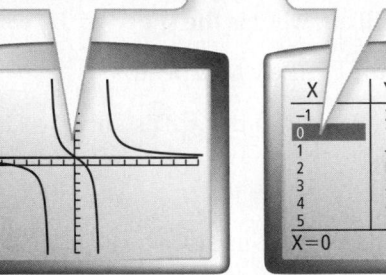

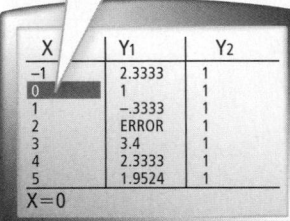

The solution is $x = 0$.

Check Write the original equation. $\frac{2}{x+2} + \frac{x}{x-2} = 1$

Substitute $x = 0$. $\frac{2}{0+2} + \frac{0}{0-2} \stackrel{?}{=} 1$

Simplify. $1 + 0 = 1$ ✔

 Got It? **3.** What are the solutions of the rational equation $\frac{x+2}{1-2x} = 5$? Use a graphing calculator to solve.

Focus Question How is solving a rational equation similar to solving a polynomial equation?

Answer Multiply each side of a rational equation by the LCD of the rational expressions in the equation to rewrite it as a polynomial equation. Then use the techniques for solving polynomial equations to find solutions. Because you multiplied each side of an equation by an algebraic expression, you must check for extraneous solutions.

Lesson Check

Do you know HOW?

Solve each equation. Check each solution.

1. $\frac{4}{x-2} = \frac{x-1}{x-2}$

2. $\frac{2a+1}{6} + \frac{a}{2} = \frac{a-1}{3}$

3. $\frac{2}{n} + \frac{n+2}{n+1} = \frac{-2}{n^2+n}$

4. Flight If the speed of an airplane is 350 mi/h with a tail wind of 40 mi/h, what is the speed of the plane in still air?

Do you UNDERSTAND?

5. Error Analysis Describe and correct the error made in solving the equation.

$$\frac{5}{x} + \frac{9}{7} = \frac{28}{x}$$
$$\frac{14}{x+7} = \frac{28}{x}$$
$$14x = 28(x+7)$$
$$14x = 28x + 196$$
$$-196 = 14x$$
$$-14 = x$$

6. Open-Ended Write a rational equation using expressions that have $x^2 - 9$ as their LCD.

7. Reasoning Describe two methods you can use to check whether a solution is extraneous.

Practice and Problem-Solving Exercises

A Practice

Solve each equation. Check each solution.

◀ **See Problem 1.**

See Problem 1.

Guided Practice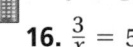

To start, multiply each side by the LCD, 6.

8. $\frac{2x}{3} - \frac{1}{2} = \frac{2x+5}{6}$

$6 \cdot \left(\frac{2x}{3} - \frac{1}{2}\right) = 6 \cdot \frac{2x+5}{6}$

9. $\frac{1}{4} - x = \frac{x}{8}$

10. $\frac{y}{5} + \frac{y}{2} = 7$

11. $\frac{1}{x} + \frac{x}{2} = \frac{x+4}{2x}$

12. $\frac{3}{2x} - \frac{5}{3x} = 2$

13. $\frac{2}{y} + \frac{1}{2} = \frac{5}{2y}$

14. $\frac{1}{4x} - \frac{3}{4} = \frac{7}{x}$

15. Transportation The speed s of an airplane is given by $s = \frac{d}{t}$, where d represents the distance and t is the time.

◀ **See Problem 2.**

See Problem 2.

  a. A plane flies 700 miles from New York to Chicago at a speed of 360 mi/h. Find the time for the trip.

  b. On the return trip from Chicago to New York, a tail wind helps the plane move faster. The total flying time for the round trip is 3.5 h. Find the speed x of the tail wind.

Graphing Calculator Solve each equation. Check each solution.

◀ **See Problem 3.**

See Problem 3.

16. $\frac{3}{x} = 5$

17. $\frac{2}{x-1} = 4$

18. $\frac{3x-1}{x+2} = 7$

19. $\frac{2}{x} = \frac{x}{2}$

20. $\frac{2}{x+3} = \frac{x-3}{2}$

21. $\frac{2}{x-1} + \frac{3}{x+1} = 4$

B Apply

Solve each equation for the given variable.

22. $m = \frac{2E}{V^2}$ for E

23. $\frac{c}{E} - \frac{1}{mc} = 0$ for E

24. $\frac{m}{F} = \frac{1}{a}$ for F

25. $\frac{1}{c} - \frac{c}{a^2 - b^2} = 0$ for c

26. $\frac{\ell}{T^2} = \frac{g}{4\pi^2}$ for T

27. $\frac{q}{m} = \frac{2V}{B^2 r^2}$ for B

28. **Think About a Plan** You and a classmate have volunteered to contact every member of your class by phone to inform them of an upcoming event. You can complete the calls in six days if you work alone. Your classmate can complete them in four days. How long will it take to complete the calls working together?
    * If N is the total number of calls, what expression represents the number of calls that you can make per day? What expression represents the number of calls your friend can make per day?
    * What is the expression for the number of days needed to make N calls if you are working together?

29. **Storage** One pump can fill a tank with oil in 4 hours. A second pump can fill the same tank in 3 hours. If both pumps are used at the same time, how long will they take to fill the tank?

30. **Teamwork** You can stuff envelopes twice as fast as your friend. Together, you can stuff 6750 envelopes in 4.5 hours. How long would it take each of you working alone to complete the job?

31. **Grades** On the first four tests of the term your average is 84%. You think you can score 96% on each of the remaining tests. How many consecutive test scores of 96% would you need to bring your average up to 90% for the term?

32. **Error Analysis** Describe and correct the error made in solving the equation shown on the right.

33. **Fuel Economy** Suppose you drive an average of 15,000 miles per year, and your car gets 24 miles per gallon. Suppose gasoline costs $3.60 a gallon.
    a. How much money do you spend each year on gasoline?
    b. You plan to trade in your car for one that gets x more miles per gallon. Write an expression to represent the new yearly cost of gasoline.
    c. Write an expression to represent your total savings on gasoline per year.
    d. Suppose you can save $600 a year with the new car. How many miles per gallon does the new car get?

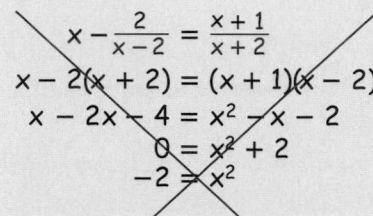

There is no square root of a negative number, so the equation has no solution.

Solve each equation. Check each solution.

34. $\frac{15}{x} + \frac{9x - 7}{x + 2} = 9$

35. $\frac{2}{x + 2} - \frac{1}{x} = \frac{-4}{x(x + 2)}$

36. $\frac{1}{b + 1} + \frac{1}{b - 1} = \frac{2}{b^2 - 1}$

37. $c - \frac{c}{3} + \frac{c}{5} = 26$

38. $\frac{1}{x - 5} = \frac{x}{x^2 - 25}$

39. $\frac{k}{k + 1} + \frac{k}{k - 2} = 2$

40. $\frac{5}{x^2 - 7x + 12} - \frac{2}{3 - x} = \frac{5}{x - 4}$

41. $\frac{2}{x + 3} - \frac{3}{4 - x} = \frac{2x - 2}{x^2 - x - 12}$

42. Woodworking A tapered cylinder is made by decreasing the radius of a rod continuously as you move from one end to the other. The rate at which it tapers is the taper per foot. You can calculate the taper per foot using the formula $T = \frac{24(R - r)}{L}$. The lengths R, r, and L are measured in inches.

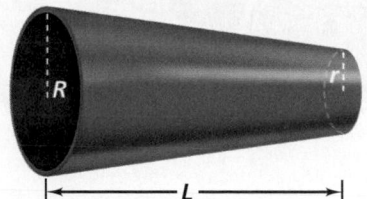

a. Solve this equation for L.
b. What is L for $T = 0.75, 0.85,$ and 0.95, if $R = 4$ in.; $r = 3$ in.?

43. Writing Write and solve a problem that can be modeled by a rational equation.

Standardized Test Prep

44. What is the solution of $x + \frac{1}{x} = -2$?

Ⓐ $1, -1$ Ⓑ 0 only   Ⓒ $-\frac{1}{2}$ only   Ⓓ -1 only

45. Which of the following is equivalent to $\frac{6\sqrt{24}}{2\sqrt{3}}$?

Ⓕ $2\sqrt{2}$ Ⓖ $3\sqrt{2}$ Ⓗ $5\sqrt{2}$ Ⓘ $6\sqrt{2}$

46. An investment of $750 will be worth $1500 after 12 years of continuous compounding at a fixed interest rate. What is that interest rate?

Ⓐ 2.00% Ⓑ 5.78% Ⓒ 6.93% Ⓓ 200%

47. A librarian orders 48 fiction and nonfiction books for the school library. A fiction book costs $15 and a nonfiction book costs $20. The total cost of the order was $900. How many nonfiction books did the librarian order? Show your work.

Mixed Review

Simplify each difference.   See Lesson 8-5.

48. $\frac{3y + 1}{4y + 4} - \frac{2y + 7}{2y + 2}$

49. $\frac{5x}{2y + 4} - \frac{6}{y^2 + 2y}$

50. $\frac{x + 1}{2x - 2} - \frac{2x}{x^2 + 2x - 3}$

Solve each equation.   See Lesson 7-5.

51. $\log_{10} 0.001 = x$

52. $\log_3 27 = 3x + 6$

53. $\log_{0.5}(x + 1) = 3$

Find the inverse of each function. Is the inverse a function?   See Lesson 6-7.

54. $y = 5 - 2x$

55. $y = x^2 + 1$

56. $y = x^3 - 4$

Get Ready!   To prepare for Lesson 9-1, do Exercises 57–62.

Identify the pattern and find the next three terms.   See Lesson 1-1.

57. $1, 3, 5, 7, \ldots$

58. $-2, -4, -6, -8, \ldots$

59. $0.2, 1, 5, 25, 125, \ldots$

60. $50, 45, 40, 35, \ldots$

61. $16, 32, 64, \ldots$

62. $-3, -7, -11, -15, \ldots$

Pull It **All Together**

To solve these problems, you will pull together concepts and skills related to rational expressions, functions, and equations.

BIG idea Proportionality

Inverse proportionality involves a relationship in which the products of two quantities remain constant as the corresponding values of the quantities change.

Task 1

Rectangle R has varying length ℓ and width w but a constant perimeter of 4 ft.

   a. Express the area A as a function of ℓ. What do you know about this function?
   b. For what values of ℓ and w will the area of R be greatest? Give an algebraic argument. Give a geometric argument.

Task 2

Rectangle R has varying length ℓ and width w but a constant area of 4 ft^2.

   a. Express the perimeter P as a function of ℓ. What kind of function is P? What is its domain?
   b. Describe the asymptotic behavior of P. What can you say about R because of this behavior? Could you have made a similar statement about R in Task 1?
   c. For what values of ℓ and w will the perimeter of R be least? Give a calculator-based argument. Give a geometric argument.

BIG idea Function

You can represent functions in a variety of ways (such as graphs, tables, equations, or words). Each representation is particularly useful in certain situations.

Task 3

Describe the discontinuities of $f(x) = \frac{x^2 + x - 6}{x^2 - 5x + 6}$. Find an equivalent form for f that shows how the graph of f is related to the graph of $y = \frac{1}{x}$. Describe the relationship. **(You do not have to draw the graphs, but you can if you wish.)**

BIG idea Equivalence

You can use symbols to represent an equation in an unlimited number of ways, where all equations have the same solution.

Task 4

Solve $x - 1 = \sqrt{\dfrac{x^4 - 2x^3}{x^2 - 4}}$.

Connecting **BIG** ideas and Answering the Essential Questions

1 Proportionality

Quantities x and y are inversely proportional only if growing x by the factor k ($k > 1$) means shrinking y by the factor $\frac{1}{k}$.

Inverse Variation (Lesson 8-1)

Are ℓ and w inversely proportional?

$A = \ell w$
$P = 2\ell + 2w$

- for a constant area—yes
- for a constant perimeter—no

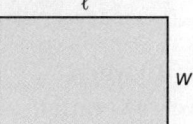

The Reciprocal Function Family (Lesson 8-2)

$A(\ell) = \frac{5}{\ell}$ is a stretch of the graph of $A(\ell) = \frac{1}{\ell}$ by a factor of 5.

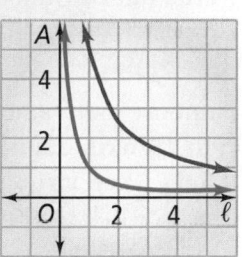

2 Function

A rational function may have no asymptotes, one horizontal or oblique asymptote, and any number of vertical asymptotes.

Rational Functions and Their Graphs (Lesson 8-3)

Asymptotes:

For $y = \frac{2x^2}{x^2 - 9}$

horizontal: $y = 2$

vertical: $x = \pm 3$

For $y = \frac{2x^3 + 6x^2}{x^2 + 1}$

oblique: $y = 2x + 6$.

$y = \frac{x^4 + 5}{x^2 + 1}$ has no asymptotes.

Solving Equations Involving Rational Expressions (Lessons 8-4, 8-5, and 8-6)

$\frac{2x^2}{x^2 - 9} = \frac{x - 6}{x - 3} + \frac{18}{x^2 - 9}$

$\frac{2x^2}{x^2 - 9} = \frac{(x - 6)(x + 3)}{(x - 3)(x + 3)} + \frac{18}{x^2 - 9}$

$2x^2 = x^2 - 3x - 18 + 18$

$x^2 + 3x = 0$

$x(x + 3) = 0$

$x = 0 \checkmark$ or $x = -3$ ✗

3 Equivalence

$f(x) = \frac{x + a}{x^2 - a^2}$, $x \neq \pm a$,

and $g(x) = \frac{1}{x - a}$, $x \neq \pm a$, are equivalent.

Chapter Vocabulary

- branch (p. 531)
- combined variation (p. 523)
- complex fraction (p. 559)
- continuous graph (p. 539)
- discontinuous graph (p. 539)
- inverse variation (p. 520)
- joint variation (p. 523)
- non-removable discontinuity (p. 539)
- point of discontinuity (p. 539)
- rational equation (p. 565)
- rational expression (p. 548)
- rational function (p. 538)
- reciprocal function (p. 530)
- removable discontinuity (p. 539)
- simplest form (p. 548)

Choose the correct term to complete each sentence.

1. When the numerator and denominator of a rational expression are polynomials with no common factors, the rational expression is in   ? .

2. If a quantity varies directly with one quantity and inversely with another, it is a(n)   ? .

3. A(n)   ?   has a fraction in its numerator, denominator, or both.

4. If a is a zero of the polynomial denominator of a rational function, the function has a(n)   ?   at $x = a$.

5. A(n)   ?   of the graph of a rational function is one of the continuous pieces of its graph.

8-1 Inverse Variation

Quick Review

An equation in two variables of the form $y = \frac{k}{x}$ or $xy = k$, where $k \neq 0$, is an **inverse variation** with a *constant of variation k*. **Joint variation** describes when one quantity varies directly with two or more other quantities.

Example

Suppose that x and y vary inversely, and $x = 10$ when $y = 15$. Write a function that models the inverse variation. Find y when $x = 6$.

$y = \frac{k}{x}$

$15 = \frac{k}{10}$, so $k = 150$.

The inverse variation is $y = \frac{150}{x}$.

When $x = 6$, $y = \frac{150}{6} = 25$.

Exercises

6. Suppose that x and y vary inversely, and $x = 30$ when $y = 2$. Find y when $x = 5$.

Write a direct or inverse variation equation for each relation.

7.

x	y
3	24
4	18
8	9

8.

x	y
5	30
7	42
9	54

Write the function that models each relationship. Find z when $x = 4$ and $y = 8$.

9. z varies jointly with x and y. When $x = 2$ and $y = 2$, $z = 7$.

10. z varies directly with x and inversely with y. When $x = 5$ and $y = 2$, $z = 10$.

8-2 The Reciprocal Function Family

Quick Review

The graph of a **reciprocal function** has two parts called **branches**. The graph of $y = \frac{k}{x - b} + c$ is a translation of $y = \frac{k}{x}$ by b units horizontally and c units vertically. It has a vertical asymptote at $x = b$ and a horizontal asymptote at $y = c$.

Example

Graph the equation $y = \frac{3}{x - 2} + 1$. Identify the x- and y-intercepts and the asymptotes of the graph.

$b = 2$, so the vertical asymptote is $x = 2$.

$c = 1$, so the horizontal asymptote is $y = 1$.

Translate $y = \frac{3}{x}$ two units to the right and one unit up.

When $y = 0$, $x = -1$.
The x-intercept is $(-1, 0)$.

When $x = 0$, $y = -\frac{1}{2}$.
The y-intercept is $(0, -\frac{1}{2})$.

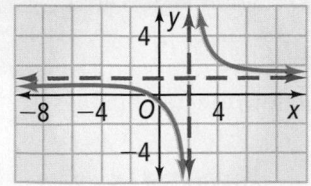

Exercises

Graph each equation. Identify the x- and y-intercepts and the asymptotes of the graph.

11. $y = \frac{1}{x}$

12. $y = \frac{-2}{x^2}$

13. $y = \frac{-1}{x} - 4$

14. $y = \frac{2}{x + 3} - 1$

Write an equation for the translation of $y = \frac{4}{x}$ that has the given asymptotes.

15. $x = 0, y = 3$

16. $x = 2, y = 2$

17. $x = -3, y = -4$

18. $x = 4, y = -3$

8-3 Rational Functions and Their Graphs

Quick Review

The **rational function** $f(x) = \frac{P(x)}{Q(x)}$ has a **point of discontinuity** for each real zero of $Q(x)$.

If $P(x)$ and $Q(x)$ have

- no common factors, then $f(x)$ has a vertical asymptote when $Q(x) = 0$.
- a common real zero a, then there is a hole or a vertical asymptote at $x = a$.
- degree of $P(x) <$ degree of $Q(x)$, then there is a horizontal asymptote at $y = 0$.
- degree of $P(x) =$ degree of $Q(x)$, then there is a horizontal asymptote at $y = \frac{a}{b}$, where a and b are the coefficients of the terms of greatest degree in $P(x)$ and $Q(x)$, respectively.
- degree of $P(x) >$ degree of $Q(x)$, then there is no horizontal asymptote.

Example

Find any points of discontinuity for the graph of the rational function $y = \frac{2.5}{x + 7}$. Describe any vertical or horizontal asymptotes and any holes.

There is a vertical asymptote at $x = -7$ and a horizontal asymptote at $y = 0$.

Exercises

Find any points of discontinuity for each rational function. Sketch the graph. Describe any vertical or horizontal asymptotes and any holes.

19. $y = \dfrac{x - 1}{(x + 2)(x - 1)}$

20. $y = \dfrac{x^3 - 1}{x^2 - 1}$

21. $y = \dfrac{2x^2 + 3}{x^2 + 2}$

22. The start-up cost of a company is \$150,000. It costs \$.17 to manufacture each headset. Graph the function that represents the average cost of a headset. How many must be manufactured to result in a cost of less than \$5 per headset?

8-4 Rational Expressions

Quick Review

A **rational expression** is in **simplest form** when its numerator and denominator are polynomials that have no common factors.

Example

Simplify the rational expression. State any restrictions on the variable.

$$\frac{2x^2 + 7x + 3}{x - 4} \cdot \frac{x^2 - 16}{x^2 + 8x + 15}$$

$$= \frac{(2x + 1)(x + 3)}{x - 4} \cdot \frac{(x - 4)(x + 4)}{(x + 3)(x + 5)}$$

$$= \frac{(2x + 1)(x + 4)}{x + 5}, \ x \neq -5, \ x \neq -3, \text{ and } x \neq 4$$

Exercises

Simplify each rational expression. State any restrictions on the variable.

23. $\dfrac{x^2 + 10x + 25}{x^2 + 9x + 20}$

24. $\dfrac{x^2 - 2x - 24}{x^2 + 7x + 12} \cdot \dfrac{x^2 - 1}{x - 6}$

25. $\dfrac{4x^2 - 2x}{x^2 + 5x + 4} \div \dfrac{2x}{x^2 + 2x + 1}$

26. What is the ratio of the volume of a sphere to its surface area?

8-5 Adding and Subtracting Rational Expressions

Quick Review

To add or subtract rational expressions with different denominators, rewrite each expression with the LCD. A fraction that has a fraction in its numerator or denominator or in both is called a **complex fraction**. Sometimes you can simplify a complex fraction by multiplying the numerator and denominator by the LCD of all the rational expressions.

Example

Simplify the complex fraction. $\dfrac{\frac{1}{x} + 3}{\frac{5}{y} + 4}$

$$\frac{\frac{1}{x} + 3}{\frac{5}{y} + 4} = \frac{\left(\frac{1}{x} + 3\right) \cdot xy}{\left(\frac{5}{x} + 4\right) \cdot xy}$$

$$= \frac{\frac{1}{x} \cdot xy + 3 \cdot xy}{\frac{5}{x} \cdot xy + 4 \cdot xy}$$

$$= \frac{y + 3xy}{5y + 4xy}$$

Exercises

Simplify the sum or difference. State any restrictions on the variable.

27. $\dfrac{3x}{x^2 - 4} + \dfrac{6}{x + 2}$

28. $\dfrac{1}{x^2 - 1} - \dfrac{2}{x^2 + 3x}$

Simplify the complex fraction.

29. $\dfrac{2 - \frac{2}{x}}{3 - \frac{1}{x}}$

30. $\dfrac{\frac{1}{x + y}}{4}$

Lesson 8-6 Solving Rational Equations

Quick Review

Solving a **rational equation** often requires multiplying each side by an algebraic expression. This may introduce extraneous solutions—solutions that solve the derived equation but not the original equation. Check all possible solutions in the original equation.

Example

Solve the equation. Check your solution.

$$\frac{1}{2x} - \frac{2}{5x} = \frac{1}{2}$$

$$10x\left(\frac{1}{2x} - \frac{2}{5x}\right) = 10x\left(\frac{1}{2}\right)$$

$$5 - 4 = 5x$$

$$x = \frac{1}{5}$$

Check $\dfrac{1}{2\left(\frac{1}{5}\right)} - \dfrac{2}{5\left(\frac{1}{5}\right)} = \dfrac{5}{2} - 2 = \dfrac{1}{2}$ ✔

Exercises

Solve each equation. Check your solutions.

31. $\dfrac{1}{x} = \dfrac{5}{x - 4}$

32. $\dfrac{2}{x + 3} - \dfrac{1}{x} = \dfrac{-6}{x(x + 3)}$

33. $\dfrac{1}{2} + \dfrac{x}{6} = \dfrac{18}{x}$

34. You travel 10 mi on your bicycle in the same amount of time it takes your friend to travel 8 mi on his bicycle. If your friend rides his bike 2 mi/h slower than you ride your bike, find the rate at which each of you is traveling.

Do you know HOW?

Write a function that models each variation.

1. $x = 2$ when $y = -8$, and y varies inversely with x.

2. $x = 0.2$ and $y = 3$ when $z = 2$, and z varies jointly with x and y.

3. $x = \frac{1}{3}$, $y = \frac{1}{5}$, and $r = 3$ when $z = \frac{1}{2}$, and z varies directly with x and inversely with the product of r^2 and y.

Is the relationship between the values in each table a *direct variation*, an *inverse variation*, or *neither*? Write equations to model any direct or inverse variations.

4.
x	y
3	6
5	8
7	10
9	12

5.
x	y
4	32
8	16
16	8
32	4

Write and graph an equation of the translation of $y = \frac{7}{x}$ that has the given asymptotes.

6. $x = 1$; $y = 2$

7. $x = -3$; $y = -2$

For each rational function, identify any holes or horizontal or vertical asymptotes of the graph.

8. $y = \frac{x + 1}{x - 1}$

9. $y = \frac{x + 3}{x + 3}$

10. $y = \frac{x - 2}{(x + 1)(x - 2)}$

11. $y = \frac{2x^2}{x^2 - 4x}$

12. $y = \frac{1}{x + 2} - 3$

13. $y = \frac{x^2 + 5}{x - 5}$

Simplify each complex fraction.

14. $\dfrac{\frac{2}{x}}{1 - \frac{1}{y}}$

15. $\dfrac{3 - \frac{3}{x}}{\frac{1}{2} - \frac{1}{x}}$

Simplify each rational expression. State any restrictions on the variable.

16. $\dfrac{x^2 + 7x + 12}{x^2 - 9}$

17. $\dfrac{(x + 3)(2x - 1)}{x(x + 4)} \div \dfrac{(-x - 3)(2x + 1)}{x}$

18. $\dfrac{x^2 - 1}{x^2 + 2x - 3} - \dfrac{x + 1}{x + 3}$

19. $\dfrac{x(x + 4)}{x - 2} + \dfrac{x - 1}{x^2 - 4}$

Solve each equation. Check your solutions.

20. $\dfrac{x}{2} = \dfrac{x + 1}{4}$

21. $\dfrac{3}{x - 1} = \dfrac{4}{3x + 2}$

22. $\dfrac{3x}{x + 1} = 0$

23. $\dfrac{3}{x + 1} = \dfrac{1}{x^2 - 1}$

24. $\dfrac{1}{x} + \dfrac{1}{3} = \dfrac{6}{x^2}$

25. $\dfrac{1}{x} + \dfrac{x}{x + 2} = 1$

26. Your neighbor can seal your driveway in 4 hours. Working together, you and your neighbor can seal it in 2.3 hours. How long would it take you to seal it working alone?

Do you UNDERSTAND?

27. **Vocabulary** Describe a situation that represents an inverse variation.

28. **Compare and Contrast** How is simplifying rational expressions similar to simplifying fractions? How is it different?

29. **Writing** When does a discontinuity result in a vertical asymptote? When does it result in a hole in the graph?

30. **Open-Ended** Write a function whose graph has a hole, a vertical asymptote, and a horizontal asymptote.

31. **Reasoning** State any restrictions on the variable in the complex fraction. $\dfrac{\frac{x - 3}{x + 4}}{\frac{x^2 - 1}{x}}$

Some problems ask you to find the lateral area or the (total) surface area of a three-dimensional figure. Read the sample question at the right. Then follow the tips to answer the question.

TIP 1

Use the formula for the lateral area of a cone:
$S = \pi r \ell$.

What is the approximate lateral area of the cone shown below?

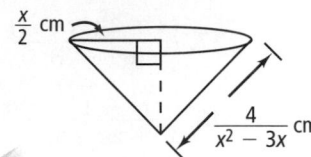

$\frac{x}{2}$ cm

$\frac{4}{x^2 - 3x}$ cm

A $\quad\dfrac{3}{x + 3}$

C $\quad\dfrac{3}{x - 3}$

B $\quad\dfrac{6}{x - 3}$

D $\quad\dfrac{6}{x + 3}$

TIP 2

Use the information from the diagram for the values you need in the formula.

Think It Through

radius: $r = \dfrac{x}{2}$

slant height: $\ell = \dfrac{4}{x^2 - 3x}$

$S = \pi r \ell$

$\quad = \pi\left(\dfrac{x}{2}\right)\left(\dfrac{4}{x^2 - 3x}\right)$

$\quad = \dfrac{2\pi}{x - 3}$

Since $\pi \approx 3$, the correct answer is B.

Vocabulary Builder

As you solve test items, you must understand the meanings of mathematical terms. Match each term with its mathematical meaning.

A. joint variation

B. branch

C. point of discontinuity

D. inverse variation

E. reciprocal function

I. a point where the graph of a function breaks into branches

II. each piece of a discontinuous graph

III. a relation represented by an equation of the form $y = \dfrac{k}{x}$ or $xy = k$, where $k \neq 0$

IV. a function that can be written in the form $f(x) = \dfrac{a}{x - h} + k$, where $a \neq 0$

V. one variable varies directly with two or more other variables

Multiple Choice

Read each question. Then write the letter of the correct answer on your paper.

1. Which expression equals $\dfrac{5x}{x^2 - 9} - \dfrac{4x}{x^2 + 5x + 6}$?

A $\quad\dfrac{7x}{(x - 3)(x + 3)(x + 2)}$

B $\quad\dfrac{x^2 - 2x}{(x - 3)(x + 3)(x + 2)}$

C $\quad\dfrac{x^2 + 22x}{(x - 3)(x + 3)(x + 2)}$

D $\quad\dfrac{9x^2 - 2x}{(x - 3)(x + 3)(x + 2)}$

2. If x is a real number, for what values of x is the equation $\dfrac{2x - 8}{4x^{-1}} = \dfrac{x^2 - 4x}{2}$ true?

F all values of x

G some values of x

H no values of x

I impossible to determine

3. What is the equation of the line that goes through the point $(-3, 2)$ and is parallel to the line shown in the graph below?

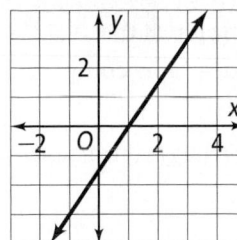

- Ⓐ $y + 3 = 1.5(x - 2)$
- Ⓑ $y + 2 = 1.5(x - 3)$
- Ⓒ $y - 3 = 1.5(x - 2)$
- Ⓓ $y - 2 = 1.5(x + 3)$

4. Which expression is a simpler form of the complex fraction $\dfrac{\frac{1}{x} + \frac{3}{y}}{\frac{2}{xy}}$?

- Ⓕ $\dfrac{3xy}{2}$
- Ⓗ $\dfrac{3}{2}$
- Ⓖ $\dfrac{3x + y}{2xy}$
- Ⓘ $\dfrac{3x + y}{2}$

5. Which is the first *incorrect* step in simplifying $\log_9 243$?

Step 1: $\log_9 243 = x$

Step 2: $\qquad 9^x = 243$

Step 3: $\qquad x = 243 \div 9$

Step 4: $\qquad = 27$

- Ⓐ Step 1
- Ⓒ Step 3
- Ⓑ Step 2
- Ⓓ Step 4

6. Which is/are the solution(s) of the equation $\sqrt{2x + 2} = 2x - 4$?

- Ⓕ $x = 3.5$ and $x = 1$
- Ⓖ $x = 3.5$ and $x = -1$
- Ⓗ $x = 3.5$
- Ⓘ $x = 1$

7. Which is the simplest form of the expression?
$4\sqrt{18x^4} - 3\sqrt{72x^4}$

- Ⓐ $-6x^2\sqrt{2}$
- Ⓒ -6
- Ⓑ $-6x^2$
- Ⓓ none of the above

8. Ana and Matthew each worked out the same problem, as shown below. Which statement is true of their solutions?

Ana's Work

$$\frac{a^{\frac{2}{3}}b^{\frac{4}{3}}}{\sqrt[3]{a^5 b}} = \frac{a^{\frac{2}{3}}b^{\frac{4}{3}}}{a^{\frac{3}{5}}b}$$
$$= a^{\frac{2}{3} - \frac{3}{5}}b^{\frac{4}{3} - 1}$$
$$= a^{\frac{10}{15} - \frac{9}{15}}b^{\frac{4}{3} - \frac{3}{3}}$$
$$= a^{\frac{1}{15}}b^{\frac{1}{3}}$$

Matthew's work

$$\frac{a^{\frac{2}{3}}b^{\frac{4}{3}}}{\sqrt[3]{a^5 b}} = \frac{a^{\frac{2}{3}}b^{\frac{4}{3}}}{a^{\frac{5}{3}}b^{\frac{1}{3}}}$$
$$= a^{\frac{2}{3} - \frac{5}{3}}b^{\frac{4}{3} - \frac{1}{3}}$$
$$= a^{-1}b^1$$
$$= \frac{b}{a}$$

- Ⓕ Ana is correct.
- Ⓖ Matthew is correct.
- Ⓗ Both answers are incorrect.
- Ⓘ Both answers are correct.

9. If $i = \sqrt{-1}$, what is the value of $-i^4$?

- Ⓐ i
- Ⓒ 1
- Ⓑ $-i$
- Ⓓ -1

10. What is the range of the graph shown below?

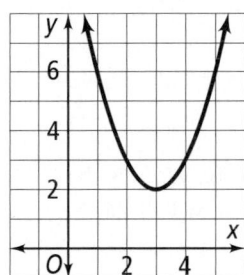

- Ⓕ $x \geq 3$
- Ⓗ $x \geq 2$
- Ⓖ $y \geq 3$
- Ⓘ $y \geq 2$

11. Given the equation $y = \log_x n$ where $n > 0$ and $y < 0$, which statement is valid for real values of x?

- Ⓐ $x < 0$
- Ⓒ $x \geq 0$
- Ⓑ $x \leq 0$
- Ⓓ $x > 0$

12. Which expression represents the solution to $4^x = 13$?

F $\dfrac{\log 13}{\log 4}$

G $\log_4 + \log_{13}$

H $\dfrac{\log 4}{\log 13}$

I $\log_{13} 4$

13. If $f(x) = x^2$ and $g(x) = x - 1$, which statement is true?

A $(f \circ g)(x) \geq (g \circ f)(x)$ for all values of x.

B $(f \circ g)(x) \leq (g \circ f)(x)$ for all values of x.

C $(f \circ g)(x) = (g \circ f)(x)$ only for $x = 1$.

D $(f \circ g)(x) \neq (g \circ f)(x)$ for any value of x.

14. If $g(x) = x^2 - 4$ and $h(x) = 4x - 6$, which expression is equal to $\left(\dfrac{g}{h}\right)(x)$?

F $\dfrac{4x - 6}{x^2 - 4}$

G $\dfrac{x^2 - 2}{4x - 3}$

H $x^2 - 4 - (4x - 6)$

I $\dfrac{(x + 2)(x - 2)}{2(2x - 3)}$

GRIDDED RESPONSE

15. Suppose that x and y vary inversely. What is the constant of variation if $x = 12$ when $y = 4$?

16. Solve for x: $\dfrac{5}{2x - 2} = \dfrac{15}{x^2 - 1}$.

17. Solve for x: $\log(x - 3) = 3$.

18. What is the x-coordinate of the solution of the system of equations?
$$\begin{cases} 2x + y = 6 \\ y - 3 = x \end{cases}$$

19. What is the remainder when $x^4 - 3x^2 + 7x + 3$ is divided by $x - 2$?

20. The product of three consecutive even integers is -2688. What is the value of the largest integer?

21. What is the smallest zero of $f(x) = 2x^5 - 4x^2 + 3x + 7$? Round your answer to the nearest hundredth.

22. What number do you add to each side of the equation when you solve $x^2 + 5x = 4$ by completing the square?

23. How many real roots does $y = x^2 - 3x + 7$ have?

Short Response

24. Sketch the graph of $y = \dfrac{x - 2}{(x - 2)(x - 1)}$.

25. Solve the inequality $|2x - 5| < 9$. Graph the solution.

26. Solve $2x^2 - 11 = 12x$.

27. Solve the equation $\dfrac{2g^2}{d} - c = 3x$ for g. Show your work.

28. Factor $x^3 - 12x^2 + 35x$ completely.

29. Explain how you know that the graph of $f(x) = -x^4 - 3x + 7$ does not have up and down end behavior.

30. Graph $y = 3^{x+2} - 5$.

Extended Response

31. Explain how to find an equation for the translation of $y = \dfrac{3}{x}$ that has asymptotes at $x = -13$ and $y = 5$.

32. What is the inverse of $y = x^2 + 15$? Is the inverse a function? Explain.

33. A third-degree polynomial equation with rational coefficients has roots -4 and $-4i$. If the leading coefficient of the equation is $\frac{3}{2}$, what is the equation? Show your work.

34. Graph $y + 2 < |x - 4|$. How did you decide where to shade and whether the boundary was a dashed or a solid line?

Get Ready!

CHAPTER 9

Lesson 2-1 ◆ **Evaluating Functions**

For each function, find $f(1), f(2), f(3),$ and $f(4)$.

1. $f(x) = 2x + 7$
2. $f(x) = 5x - 4$

3. $f(x) = 0.2x + 0.7$
4. $f(x) = -5x + 3$

5. $f(x) = 4x - \frac{2}{3}$
6. $f(x) = -3x - 9$

Lesson 1-1 ◆ **Identifying Mathematical Patterns**

Identify a pattern and find the next three numbers in the pattern.

7. $9, 4, -1, -6, \ldots$
8. $1, 2, 4, 8, \ldots$

9. $18, 9, 10, 1, 2, \ldots$
10. $7, 10, 13, 16, \ldots$

Lesson 8-5 ◆ **Simplifying Complex Fractions**

Simplify each complex fraction.

11. $\dfrac{1 - \frac{1}{3}}{\frac{1}{2}}$
12. $\dfrac{\frac{1}{3} + \frac{1}{6}}{\frac{2}{3}}$
13. $\dfrac{1}{1 - \frac{2}{5}}$
14. $\dfrac{1 - \frac{3}{8}}{2 + \frac{1}{4}}$

 ## Looking Ahead Vocabulary

15. Think of a function and evaluate the function for the input numbers 1, 2, 3, 4, and 5. List the five outputs in order. This list is a *sequence* of numbers. The sequence can be infinitely long.

16. Use a linear function to generate a sequence of five numbers. Beginning with the second number, subtract the number that precedes it. Continue doing this until you have found all four differences. Are the results the same? If so, you have discovered that your sequence has a *common difference*.

17. Now use an exponential function to define your sequence. Instead of subtracting, divide each number by the number that precedes it. Do this until you find all four quotients. Are these four results the same? If so, you have discovered that your sequence has a *common ratio*.

Sequences and Series

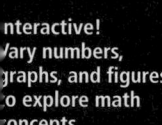
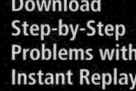
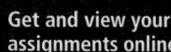
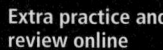

Arithmetic and geometric sequences are types of patterns. What patterns do you see in these terraced rice fields? You will learn about all kinds of sequences in this chapter.

 ## Vocabulary

English/Spanish Vocabulary Audio Online:

English	Spanish
arithmetic sequence, *p. 592*	progresión aritmética
arithmetic series, *p. 607*	serie aritmética
common difference, *p. 592*	diferencia común
common ratio, *p. 600*	razón común
converge, *p. 617*	convergir
diverge, *p. 617*	divergir
explicit formula, *p. 585*	fórmula explícita
geometric sequence, *p. 600*	progresión geométrica
geometric series, *p. 614*	serie geométrica
limits, *p. 610*	límites
recursive formula, *p. 586*	formula recursiva

My Math Video

00:04:04

VIDEO ▷

BIG ideas

1 Variable
Essential Questions How can you
represent the terms of a sequence explicitly?
How can you represent them recursively?

2 Equivalence
Essential Question What are equivalent
explicit and recursive definitions for an
arithmetic sequence?

3 Modeling
Essential Questions How can you model
a geometric sequence? How can you model
its sum?

Chapter Preview

9-1 Mathematical Patterns

Objectives To identify mathematical patterns found in a sequence
To use a formula to find the *n*th term of a sequence

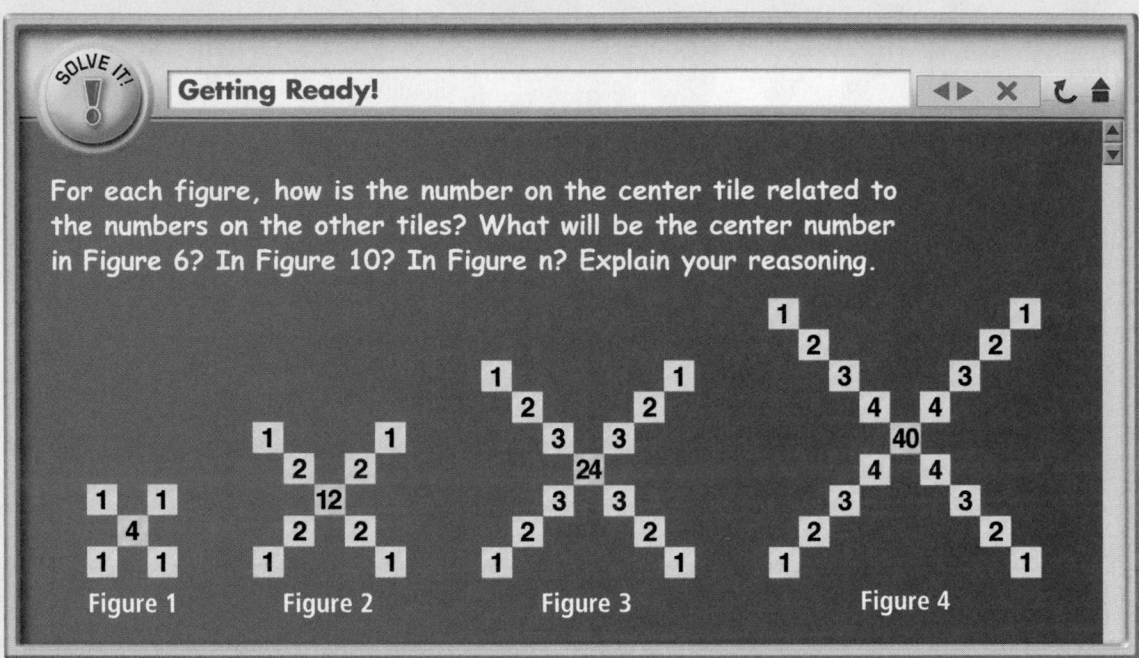

Getting Ready!

For each figure, how is the number on the center tile related to the numbers on the other tiles? What will be the center number in Figure 6? In Figure 10? In Figure n? Explain your reasoning.

Figure 1   Figure 2   Figure 3   Figure 4

Lesson Vocabulary
- sequence
- term
- explicit formula
- recursive formula

Sometimes you can easily state a rule to describe a pattern. At other times, you have to do a bit of work to find a rule.

Focus Question What is a sequence?

A **sequence** is an ordered list of numbers. Each number in a sequence is a **term** of the sequence. You can represent a term of a sequence by using a variable with a subscript number to indicate its position in the sequence. For example, a_5 is the fifth term in the sequence $a_1, a_2, a_3, a_4, \ldots$.

The subscripts of sequence terms are often positive integers starting with 1. If so, you can generalize a term as a_n, the *n*th term in the sequence.

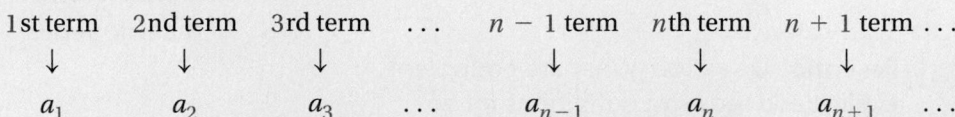

1st term	2nd term	3rd term	$\ldots$	$n-1$ term	nth term	$n+1$ term $\ldots$
$\downarrow$	$\downarrow$	$\downarrow$		$\downarrow$	$\downarrow$	$\downarrow$
a_1	a_2	a_3	$\ldots$	a_{n-1}	a_n	a_{n+1} $\ldots$

An **explicit formula** describes the nth term of a sequence using the number n.

For example, in the sequence 2, 4, 6, 8, 10, . . . , the nth term is twice the value of n. You write this as $a_n = 2n$. The table shows how to find a_n by substituting the value of n into the explicit formula.

n	nth term
1	$a_1 = 2(1) = 2$
2	$a_2 = 2(2) = 4$
3	$a_3 = 2(3) = 6$
4	$a_4 = 2(4) = 8$

Problem 1 Generating a Sequence Using an Explicit Formula

A sequence has an explicit formula $a_n = 3n - 2$. What are the first 10 terms of this sequence?

Plan

How does the explicit formula help you find the value of a term?
Replace n in the formula with the number of the term. Simplify to find the value of the term.

Write the formula. $a_n = 3n - 2$

Substitute 1 for n. $a_1 = 3(1) - 2$

Simplify. $= 1$

Substitute 2 for n. $a_2 = 3(2) - 2$

Simplify. $= 4$

You can use a table to organize your work for the remaining terms.

n	a_n
3	$a_3 = 3(3) - 2 = 7$
4	$a_4 = 3(4) - 2 = 10$
5	$a_5 = 3(5) - 2 = 13$
6	$a_6 = 3(6) - 2 = 16$
7	$a_7 = 3(7) - 2 = 19$
8	$a_8 = 3(8) - 2 = 22$
9	$a_9 = 3(9) - 2 = 25$
10	$a_{10} = 3(10) - 2 = 28$

Substitute 3 for n and simplify.

And so on.

The first ten terms are 1, 4, 7, 10, 13, 16, 19, 22, 25, 28.

Got It? **1.** A sequence has an explicit formula $a_n = 12n + 3$. What is term a_{12} in the sequence?

Sometimes you can see the pattern in a sequence by comparing each term after the first term to the one that came before it. For example, in the sequence 133, 130, 127, 124, . . . , each term is equal to three less than the previous term.

A recursive definition for this sequence contains two parts.
(a) an initial condition (the value of the first term): $a_1 = 133$
(b) a **recursive formula** (relates each term to the one before it): $a_n = a_{n-1} - 3$, for $n > 1$

Problem 2 Writing a Recursive Definition for a Sequence

The number of blocks in a two-dimensional pyramid is a sequence that follows a recursive formula. Look at the picture below. What is a recursive definition for the sequence?

  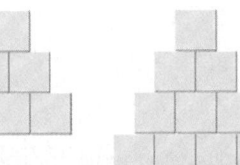  

Think

Count the number of blocks in each pyramid.

Subtract consecutive terms to find out what happens from one term to the next.

Use n to express the relationship between successive terms.

To write a recursive definition, state the initial condition and the recursive formula.

Write

1, 3, 6, 10, 15, 21

$a_2 - a_1 = 3 - 1 = 2$
$a_3 - a_2 = 6 - 3 = 3$
$a_4 - a_3 = 10 - 6 = 4$
$a_5 - a_4 = 15 - 10 = 5$
$a_6 - a_5 = 21 - 15 = 6$

$a_n - a_{n-1} = n$

$a_1 = 1$ and $a_n = a_{n-1} + n$.

 Got It? 2. What is a recursive definition for each sequence?
  a. 1, 2, 6, 24, 120, 720, . . .
  b. 1, 5, 14, 30, 55, . . .

Recursive definitions can be very helpful when you look at a small section of a sequence. However, if you want to know both a_3 and a_{5000} of a sequence, an explicit formula is often more useful.

 Problem 3 Writing an Explicit Formula for a Sequence

Plan

Why do you use the explicit formula to find a_{100}?
Because starting with a_1, it would take 99 iterations of the formula to get a_{100} using the recursive formula.

What is the 100th term of the pyramid sequence in Problem 2?

Step 1 Find an explicit formula.

Consider different ways of expressing the terms of the pyramid sequence.

a_1	a_2	a_3	a_4	a_5	$\ldots$	a_n
1	$1 + 2$	$1 + 2 + 3$	$1 + 2 + 3 + 4$	$1 + 2 + 3 + 4 + 5$	$\ldots$	$1 + 2 + \ldots + n$
1	3	6	10	15	$\ldots$	■

So, you can write the nth term of the pyramid sequence as the sum of the first n positive integers.

$$a_n = 1 + 2 + 3 + \cdots + (n - 2) + (n - 1) + n$$

You can also write the nth term as follows.

$$a_n = n + (n - 1) + (n - 2) + \cdots + 3 + 2 + 1$$

Hint

Remember that addition is commutative. You can reverse the order of the terms without changing the sum.

Now add the two previous equations as shown to get the following result:

$$a_n = \quad 1 \quad + \quad 2 \quad + \quad 3 \quad + \cdots + (n - 2) + (n - 1) + \quad n$$
$$a_n = \quad n \quad + (n - 1) + (n - 2) + \cdots + \quad 3 \quad + \quad 2 \quad + \quad 1$$
$$\overline{2a_n = (n + 1) + (n + 1) + (n + 1) + \cdots + (n + 1) + (n + 1) + (n + 1)}$$

$$2a_n = n \cdot (n + 1) \quad \text{There are } n \text{ terms. Every term is } (n + 1).$$

$$a_n = \tfrac{1}{2}n(n + 1) \quad \text{Solve for } a_n.$$

The explicit formula for this sequence is $a_n = \tfrac{1}{2}n(n + 1)$.

Step 2 Use the explicit formula to find the 100th term.

Write the formula. $a_n = \tfrac{1}{2}n(n + 1)$

Substitute 100 for n. $a_{100} = \tfrac{1}{2}(100)(100 + 1)$

Add. $= \tfrac{1}{2}(100)(101)$

Simplify. $= 5050$

The 100th term is 5050.

 Got It? **3. a.** What is an explicit formula for the sequence 0, 3, 8, 15, 24, . . . ? What is the 20th term?

b. Reasoning Why is using an explicit formula often more efficient than using a recursive definition?

Problem 4 Using Formulas to Find Terms of a Sequence

Finance Pierre began the year with an unpaid balance of $300 on his credit card. Because he had not read the credit card agreement, he did not realize that the company charged 1.8% interest each month on his unpaid balance, in addition to a $29 penalty in any month he might fail to make a minimum payment. Pierre ignored his credit card bill for 4 consecutive months before finally deciding to pay off the balance. What did he owe after 4 months of non-payment?

Step 1 Write a recursive definition.
Initial condition: $a_0 = 300$ (Use a_0 so that a_1 represents the balance after 1 month.)
Recursive formula: $a_n = 1.018 \cdot a_{n-1} + 29$, for $n > 1$

Think

Why is it helpful to change FLOAT to 2?
This problem involves money, so real-world solutions will have only 2 decimal places.

Step 2 Use a calculator. In the **MODE** menu, change the digit display from **FLOAT** to 2.

Step 3 Use a calculator. Enter 300. Then enter the recursive formula **1.018ANS+29** and press **enter** for the balance after one month.

Step 4 Press **enter** three more times until the calculator shows the balance after 4 months.

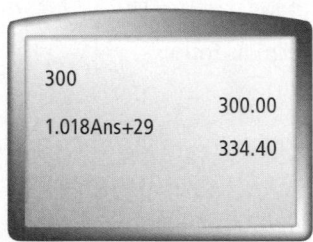

After 4 months, Pierre owes $441.36.

 Got It? **4.** Suppose the credit card company allowed Pierre to continue making no payments. After how many months would his balance exceed $1000?

Focus Question What is a sequence?

Answer A sequence is an ordered list of numbers, called terms. To find the nth term of a sequence, use either an explicit formula or a recursive definition.

 Lesson Check

Do you know HOW?

Find the first five terms of each sequence.

1. $a_n = 5n - 3$

2. $a_n = n^2 - 2n$

3. What is a recursive definition for the sequence 3, 6, 12, 24, . . . ?

4. What is an explicit formula for the sequence 5, 8, 11, 14, . . . ?

Do you UNDERSTAND?

5. Vocabulary Explain the difference between an explicit formula and a recursive definition. Give an example of each.

6. Error Analysis A student writes that $a_n = 3n + 1$ is an explicit formula for the sequence 1, 4, 7, 10, ... Explain the student's error and write a correct explicit formula for the sequence.

Practice and Problem-Solving Exercises

A Practice **Find the first six terms of each sequence.** ◀ See Problem 1.

Guided Practice

7. $a_n = -5n + 1$

To start, substitute 1 for n.
Simplify.

$a_1 = -5(1) + 1$
$\quad = -4$

8. $a_n = \frac{1}{2}n$

9. $a_n = n^2 + 1$

10. $a_n = 3n^2 - n$

11. $a_n = 2^n - 1$

12. $a_n = \frac{1}{2}n^3 - 1$

13. $a_n = (-3)^n$

Write a recursive definition for each sequence. ◀ See Problem 2.

Guided Practice

14. $80, 77, 74, 71, 68, \ldots$

To start, look for simple addition
or multiplication patterns to relate
consecutive terms.

$77 - 80 = -3$
$74 - 77 = -3$
$71 - 74 = -3$
$68 - 71 = -3$

15. $4, 8, 16, 32, 64, \ldots$

16. $0, 3, 7, 12, 18, \ldots$

17. $1, 4, 7, 10, 13, \ldots$

18. $100, 10, 1, 0.1, 0.01, \ldots$

19. $\frac{1}{2}, \frac{1}{4}, \frac{1}{8}, \frac{1}{16}, \frac{1}{32}, \ldots$

20. $4, -8, 16, -32, 64, \ldots$

Write an explicit formula for each sequence. Find the tenth term. ◀ See Problem 3.

21. $4, 5, 6, 7, 8, \ldots$

22. $3, 7, 11, 15, 19, \ldots$

23. $-2\frac{1}{2}, -2, -1\frac{1}{2}, -1, \ldots$

24. $1, 4, 9, 16, \ldots$

25. $\frac{1}{2}, \frac{1}{3}, \frac{1}{4}, \frac{1}{5}, \frac{1}{6}, \ldots$

26. $\frac{1}{2}, -\frac{1}{4}, \frac{1}{8}, -\frac{1}{16}, \ldots$

Find the eighth term of each sequence.

27. $-2, -1, 0, 1, 2, \ldots$

28. $43, 41, 39, 37, 35, \ldots$

29. $40, 20, 10, 5, \frac{5}{2}, \ldots$

30. $6, 1, -4, -9, \ldots$

31. $\frac{1}{2}, \frac{1}{4}, \frac{1}{8}, \frac{1}{16}, \frac{1}{32}, \ldots$

32. $\frac{3}{4}, -\frac{3}{2}, 3, -6, \ldots$

33. Exercise You walk 1 mile the first day of your training, 1.2 miles the second day, ◀ See Problem 4.
1.6 miles the third day, and 2.4 miles the fourth day. If you continue this pattern,
how many miles do you walk the seventh day?

B Apply **Determine whether each formula is *explicit* or *recursive*. Then find the first five terms of each sequence.**

34. $a_n = 2a_{n-1} + 3$, where $a_1 = 3$

35. $a_n = (n - 5)(n + 5)$

36. $a_n = -3a_{n-1}$, where $a_1 = -2$

37. $a_n = -4n^2 - 2$

38. Think About a Plan You invested money in a company and each month you receive a payment for your investment. Over the first four months, you received $50, $52, $56, and $62. If this pattern continues, how much do you receive in the tenth month?
- What pattern do you see between consecutive terms?
- Can you write a recursive or explicit formula to describe the pattern?
- How can you use your formula to find the amount you receive in the tenth month?

39. Entertainment Suppose you are building a tower of cards with levels as displayed below. Copy and complete the table, assuming the pattern continues.

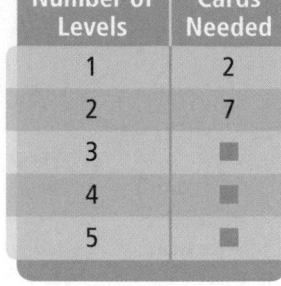

Number of Levels	Cards Needed
1	2
2	7
3	■
4	■
5	■

Find the next two terms in each sequence. Write a formula for the nth term. Identify each formula as *explicit* or *recursive*.

40. $5, 8, 11, 14, 17, \ldots$ **41.** $3, 6, 12, 24, 48, \ldots$ **42.** $1, 8, 27, 64, 125, \ldots$

43. $4, 16, 64, 256, 1024, \ldots$ **44.** $49, 64, 81, 100, 121, \ldots$ **45.** $-1, 1, -1, 1, -1, 1, \ldots$

46. $-16, -8, -4, -2, \ldots$ **47.** $-75, -68, -61, -54, \ldots$ **48.** $21, 13, 5, -3, \ldots$

49. Geometry Suppose you are stacking boxes in levels that form squares. The numbers of boxes in successive levels form a sequence. The figure at the right shows the top four levels as viewed from above.
  a. How many boxes of equal size would you need for the next lower level?
  b. How many boxes of equal size would you need to add three levels?
  c. Suppose you are stacking a total of 285 boxes. How many levels will you have?

Use the given rule to write the 4th, 5th, 6th, and 7th terms of each sequence.

50. $a_n = (n + 1)^2$ **51.** $a_n = \dfrac{n^2}{n + 1}$ **52.** $a_n = \dfrac{n + 1}{n + 2}$

53. a. Open-Ended Write four terms of a sequence of numbers that you can describe both recursively and explicitly.
  b. Write a recursive definition and an explicit formula for your sequence.
  c. Find the 20th term of the sequence by evaluating one of your formulas. Use the other formula to check your work.

Standardized Test Prep

SAT/ACT

54. Scientists determine an object is moving at the rate of $(5 - \sqrt{2})$ ft/s. How many seconds will it take the object to travel 125 ft? Round the answer to the nearest tenth of a second.

55. What is the solution of $\sqrt{4x - 23} - 3 = 2$?

56. Using a calculator, what is the solution of $1080 = 15^{3x - 4}$? Round the answer to the nearest hundredth.

57. Using the change of base formula, what is the solution of $\log_5 x = \log_3 20$? Round the answer to the nearest tenth.

58. The battery power available to operate a deep space probe is given by the formula $P = 42e^{-0.005t}$, where P is power in watts and t is time in years. For how many years can the probe run if it requires 35 watts? Round the answer to the nearest tenth of a year.

Mixed Review

Solve each equation. Check the solution.

See Lesson 8-6.

59. $\dfrac{y}{y + 1} = \dfrac{2}{3}$

60. $\dfrac{4}{2a} = \dfrac{5}{a + 6}$

61. $\dfrac{3}{b + 2} = \dfrac{6}{b - 1}$

Find the slope of the line that passes through the two points.

See Lesson 2-3.

62. $(4, 5)$ and $(1, 8)$

63. $(-3, -3)$ and $(2, 2)$

64. $(1, 3)$ and $(4, 9)$

Get Ready! To prepare for Lesson 9-2, do Exercises 65–67.

Identify the pattern and find the next three terms.

See Lesson 1-1.

65. $10, 8, 6, 4, 2, 0, \ldots$

66. $100, 117, 134, 151, 168, \ldots$

67. $\dfrac{5}{7}, \dfrac{8}{7}, \dfrac{11}{7}, 2, \ldots$

9-2 Arithmetic Sequences

Objective To define, identify, and apply arithmetic sequences

Getting Ready!

To train for a 10-km race 10 weeks from now, you are planning to run the same distance each day for one week. After that, you will increase your distance by an equal amount from week to week. By how much must you increase each week to complete your chart? Explain.

Training Schedule

Week 1	Week 2	Week 3	Week 4	Week 5
4 km				

Week 6	Week 7	Week 8	Week 9	Week 10
			10 k	

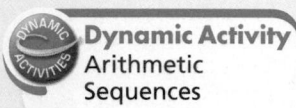

Dynamic Activity
Arithmetic Sequences

Lesson Vocabulary
- arithmetic sequence
- common difference
- arithmetic mean

It sometimes is helpful to represent a situation with a sequence of numbers. There are different types of numerical sequences.

Focus Question What is an arithmetic sequence?

An **arithmetic sequence** is a sequence where the difference between consecutive terms is constant. This difference is the **common difference**.

take note

Key Concept Arithmetic Sequence

An arithmetic sequence with a starting value a and common difference d is a sequence of the form

$$a, a + d, a + 2d, a + 3d, \ldots$$

A recursive definition for this sequence has two parts:

initial condition $a_1 = a$

recursive formula $a_n = a_{n-1} + d$, for $n > 1$

An explicit definition for this sequence is a single formula:

$a_n = a + (n - 1)d$, for $n \geq 1$

Problem 1 Identifying Arithmetic Sequences

Plan

How do you know whether a sequence is arithmetic?
The differences between consecutive terms in an arithmetic sequence are the same.

Is the sequence an arithmetic sequence?

Ⓐ 3, 6, 9, 12, 15, ...

Find the differences between consecutive terms.

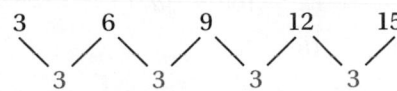

The sequence has a common difference of 3. This sequence is an arithmetic sequence.

Ⓑ 1, 4, 9, 16, 25, ...

Find the differences between consecutive terms.

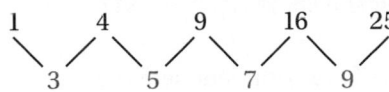

The differences are not the same. This sequence is not an arithmetic sequence.

 Got It? **1.** Is the sequence an arithmetic sequence?

   a. 2, 4, 8, 16, . . .   **b.** 1, 5, 9, 13, 17, . . .

Problem 2 Analyzing Arithmetic Sequences

Ⓐ What is the 100th term of the arithmetic sequence that begins 6, 11, ...?

Step 1 Identify the common difference.

The first term a is 6. The second term is 11.
The common difference d is $11 - 6 = 5$.

Step 2 Identify the 100th term.

Use the explicit formula. $a_n = a + (n - 1)d$

Substitute 100 for n, 6 for a, and 5 for d. $a_{100} = 6 + (100 - 1)5$

Simplify. $a_{100} = 501$

The 100th term is 501.

**What do you need to
find the second term
given the first term?**
You need to know the
common difference of
the arithmetic sequence.

B What are the second and third terms of the arithmetic sequence 100, ■, ■, 82, ...?

Step 1 Identify the common difference.

There are 3 common differences
between 100 and 82.

| | | | 100 ■ ■ 82 |

Write an equation. $82 = 100 + 3d$

Isolate the variable term. $-18 = 3d$

Solve for d. $-6 = d$

Step 2 Identify the missing terms.

Find the second term. $100 + (-6) = 94$

Find the third term. $94 + (-6) = 88$

The second and third terms are 94 and 88.

Got It? **2. a.** What is the 46th term of the arithmetic sequence that begins 3, 5, 7, . . . ?

b. What are the second and third terms of this arithmetic sequence?
80, ■, ■, 125, . . .

The **arithmetic mean**, or average, of two numbers x and y is $\frac{x + y}{2}$.

In an arithmetic sequence, the middle term of any three consecutive terms is
the arithmetic mean of the other two terms.

Problem 3 Using the Arithmetic Mean ········· GRIDDED RESPONSE

**To use the formula
for arithmetic mean,
what are x and y?**
x is 15 and y is 59.

What is the missing term of the arithmetic sequence . . . , 15, ■, 59, . . . ?

Use the formula for the arithmetic
mean to find the missing term.

$$\text{arithmetic mean} = \frac{x + y}{2}$$

Substitute 15 for x and 59 for y.

$$= \frac{15 + 59}{2}$$

Simplify.

$$= \frac{74}{2} = 37$$

The missing term is 37.

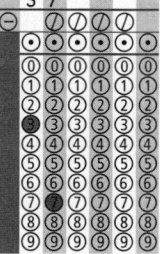

Got It? **3. a.** The 9th and 11th terms of an arithmetic sequence are 132 and 98.
What is the 10th term?

b. **Reasoning** If you know the 5th and 6th terms of an arithmetic
sequence, how can you find the 7th term using the arithmetic mean?

Problem 4 Using an Explicit Formula for an Arithmetic Sequence

Sports Arena The number of seats in the first 13 rows in a section of an arena form an arithmetic sequence. Rows 1 and 2 are shown in the diagram below. How many seats are in Row 13?

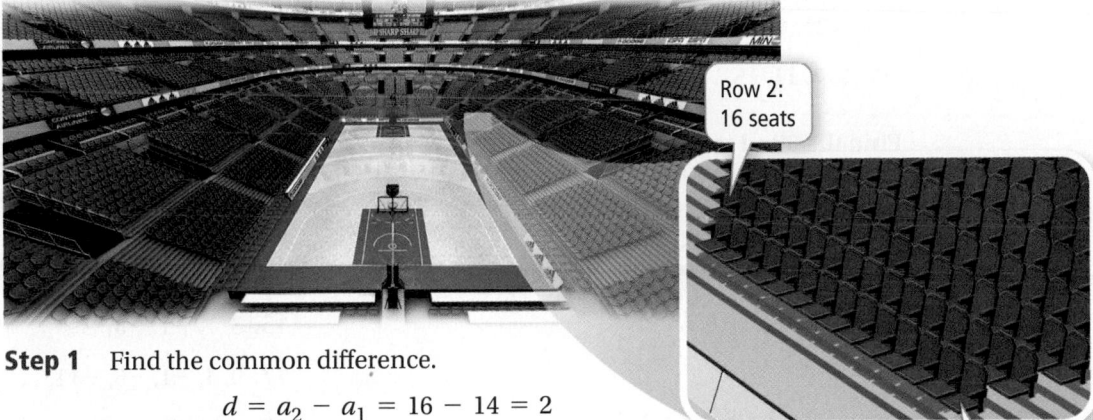

Row 2: 16 seats

Row 1: 14 seats

Plan

What two terms should you use to find the common difference?
Use the consecutive terms given.

Step 1 Find the common difference.

$$d = a_2 - a_1 = 16 - 14 = 2$$

Step 2 Write an explicit formula for the arithmetic sequence.

Use the explicit formula. $a_n = a + (n - 1)d$

Substitute 13 for n, 14 for a, and 2 for d. $a_{13} = 14 + (13 - 1)2$

Simplify. $= 38$

There are 38 seats in Row 13.

 Got It? **4.** The number of seats in the first 16 rows in a curved section of another arena form an arithmetic sequence. If there are 20 seats in Row 1 and 23 seats in Row 2, how many seats are in Row 16?

Focus Question What is an arithmetic sequence?

Answer In an arithmetic sequence, the difference between any two consecutive terms is constant. You can build an arithmetic sequence by adding the same number to each term.

 Lesson Check

Do you know HOW?

Find the tenth term of each arithmetic sequence.

1. 2, 8, 14, 20, . . .   **2.** 15, 23, 31, . . .

Find the missing term of each arithmetic sequence.

3. . . . 4, ■, 22 . . .   **4.** . . . 25, ■, 53 . . .

Do you UNDERSTAND?

5. Vocabulary Explain what it means for a sequence to be an arithmetic sequence.

6. Open-Ended Give an example of a sequence that is not an arithmetic sequence.

Practice and Problem-Solving Exercises

 **Practice**

Determine whether each sequence is arithmetic. If so, identify the common difference.

See Problem 1.

7. 10, 20, 30, 40, . . .

8. 1, 1, 2, 3, 5, 8, . . .

9. −21, −18, −15, −12, . . .

10. 97, 86, 75, 64, . . .

11. 3, 7, 11, 15, . . .

12. 100, 10, 1, 0.1, . . .

Find the 32nd term of each sequence.

See Problem 2.

Guided Practice

To start, identify the common difference.

13. 34, 37, 40, 43, . . .

$37 - 34 = 3$

14. −9, −8.7, −8.4, . . .

15. 3, 1, −1, −3, . . .

16. 23, 30, 37, 44, . . .

17. 9, 4, −1, −6, −11, . . .

18. 13, 17, 21, 25, . . .

19. 0.1, 0.5, 0.9, 1.3, . . .

Find the missing term of each arithmetic sequence.

See Problem 3.

Guided Practice

To start, use the formula for the arithmetic mean.

20. −15, ■, 1, . . .

$$\text{arithmetic mean} = \frac{x + y}{2}$$

21. 14, ■, 28, . . .

22. . . . 5, ■, 21, . . .

23. 103, ■, −119, . . .

24. . . . 98, ■, 66, . . .

25. 25, ■, −10, . . .

26. . . . 65, ■, −60, . . .

27. Savings A student deposits the same amount of money into her bank account each week. At the end of the second week she has $30 in her account. At the end of the third week she has $45 in her account. How much will she have in her bank account at the end of the ninth week?

See Problem 4.

B Apply

Find the 17th term of each sequence.

28. $a_{16} = 18, d = 5$

29. $a_{16} = 21, d = -3$

30. $a_{18} = -5, d = 12$

31. $a_{18} = 32, d = -4$

32. $a_{16} = \frac{1}{5}, d = \frac{1}{2}$

33. $a_{18} = -9, d = -11$

34. Think About a Plan The arithmetic mean of the monthly salaries of two employees is $3210. One employee earns $3470 per month. What is the monthly salary of the other employee?

• What is the given information and what is the unknown?

• What equation can you use to find the other monthly salary?

Find the arithmetic mean a_n of the given terms.

35. $a_{n-1} = 7, a_{n+1} = 1$

36. $a_{n-1} = 21, a_{n+1} = 5$

37. $a_{n-1} = -19, a_{n+1} = -21$

38. $a_{n-1} = 4, a_{n+1} = -3$

39. $a_{n-1} = 0.3, a_{n+1} = 1.9$

40. $a_{n-1} = 9, a_{n+1} = -11$

41. Error Analysis A student claims that the next term of the arithmetic sequence 0, 2, 4, . . . is 8. Explain and correct the student's error.

Write an explicit and a recursive formula for each sequence.

42. 0, 6, 12, 18, 24, . . .

43. $-5, -4, -3, -2, -1, \ldots$

44. $-4, -8, -12, -16, -20, \ldots$

45. $-5, -3.5, -2, -0.5, 1, \ldots$

46. $-32, -20, -8, 4, 16, \ldots$

47. 27, 15, 3, -9, -21, . . .

48. Reasoning What information do you need to find a term of a sequence using an explicit formula?

49. Writing Describe some advantages and some disadvantages of a recursive formula and an explicit formula. When is it appropriate to use each formula?

50. Transportation Suppose a trolley stops at a certain intersection every 14 min. The first trolley of the day gets to the stop at 6:43 A.M. How long do you have to wait for a trolley if you get to the stop at 8:15 A.M.? At 3:20 P.M.?

Find the missing terms of each arithmetic sequence.

51. $2, a_2, a_3, a_4, -22, \ldots$

52. $10, a_2, a_3, a_4, -11.6, \ldots$

53. $1, a_2, a_3, a_4, -35, \ldots$

54. $\ldots \frac{13}{5}, a_6, a_7, a_8, \frac{37}{5}, \ldots$

55. $17, a_2, a_3, a_4, 17, \ldots$

56. $660, a_2, a_3, a_4, 744, \ldots$

> **Hint** The arithmetic mean of the first and fifth terms is the third term.

57. Income The arithmetic mean of the monthly salaries of two people is $4475. One person earns $3895 per month. What is the monthly salary of the other person?

58. Reasoning Suppose you turn the water on in an empty bathtub with vertical sides. After 20 s, the water has reached a level of 1.15 in. You then leave the room. You want to turn the water off when the level in the bathtub is 8.5 in. How many minutes later should you return? (*Hint:* Begin by identifying two terms of an arithmetic sequence.)

59. a. Graphing Calculator Use your calculator to generate an arithmetic sequence with a common difference of -7. How could you use a calculator to find the 6th term? The 8th term? The 20th term?

    b. Reasoning Explain how your answer to part (a) relates to the explicit formula $a_n = a_1 + (n - 1)d$.

SAT/ACT

60. The equation $X(t) = t^4 - 5t^2 + 6$ gives the position of a comet relative to a fixed point, measured in millions of miles, at time t, measured in days. Solve the equation $X(t) = 0$. At what times is the position zero?

    Ⓐ 2, 3

    Ⓑ −2, −3

    Ⓒ $\sqrt{2}, \sqrt{3}$

    Ⓓ $\pm\sqrt{2}, \pm\sqrt{3}$

61. Simplify $\dfrac{3 - \frac{1}{x}}{\frac{1}{2x} - 5}$.

    Ⓕ $\dfrac{6x - 2}{1 - 10x}$

    Ⓖ $\dfrac{3x - 1}{1 - 10x}$

    Ⓗ $\dfrac{4}{1 - 10x}$

    Ⓘ $\dfrac{3x - 1}{1 - 5x}$

Extended
Response

62. What are all the solutions of $\dfrac{3}{x^2 - 1} + \dfrac{4x}{x + 1} = \dfrac{1.5}{x - 1}$? Show your work.

Mixed Review

Determine whether each formula is *explicit* or *recursive*. Then find the first five terms of each sequence.

◀ See Lesson 9-1.

63. $a_1 = -2, a_n = a_{n-1} - 5$ **64.** $a_n = 3n(n + 1)$ **65.** $a_n = n^2 - 1$

Write an equation in point-slope form for each pair of points.

◀ See Lesson 2-4.

66. $(0, 3)$ and $(3, 11)$ **67.** $(4, 6)$ and $(10, 30)$ **68.** $(1, 10)$ and $(5, 42)$

69. Geometry The formula for volume V of a sphere with radius r is $V = \frac{4}{3}\pi r^3$. Find the radius of a sphere as a function of its volume. Rationalize the denominator.

◀ See Lesson 6-2.

Get Ready!   **To prepare for Lesson 9-3, do Exercises 70–72.**

Find the next term in each sequence.

◀ See Lesson 9-1.

70. 2, 4, 8, 16, . . .   **71.** 1, 5, 25, 125, . . .   **72.** −1, −3, −9, −27, . . .

Do you know HOW?

Find the first five terms of each sequence.

1. $a_n = 3n + 1$

2. $a_n = -2n - 1$

3. $a_n = n^2 + 2n$

4. $a_n = 3a_{n-1}$, where $a_1 = 2$

5. $a_n = 5 - a_{n-1}$, where $a_1 = 1$

6. $a_n = a_{n-1} + 2n$, where $a_1 = 1$

Write a recursive definition for each sequence.

7. $2, -4, 8, -16, \ldots$

8. $1, 4, 7, 10, \ldots$

9. $4, 2, 5, 1, 6, \ldots$

Write an explicit formula for each sequence.

10. $2, 4, 8, 16, \ldots$

11. $5, 2, -1, -4, \ldots$

12. $2, 5, 10, 17, \ldots$

Find the ninth and tenth terms of each arithmetic sequence.

13. $1, 8, 15, 22, \ldots$

14. $4, 10, 16, 22, \ldots$

15. $6, 3, 0, -3, \ldots$

Determine whether each sequence is arithmetic. If so, identify the common difference.

16. $1, 3, 9, 27, \ldots$

17. $11, 22, 33, 44, \ldots$

18. $1, -1, -3, -5, -7, \ldots$

19. $0, 2, 5, 9, 14, \ldots$

Find the missing term of each arithmetic sequence.

20. $\ldots, 3, \blacksquare, 17, \ldots$

21. $\ldots, 25, \blacksquare, -15, \ldots$

22. $\ldots, -3, \blacksquare, 8, \ldots$

23. $\ldots, 66, \blacksquare, 48, \ldots$

Find the missing terms of each arithmetic sequence.

24. $4, a_2, a_3, a_4, 32, \ldots$

25. $10, a_2, a_3, a_4, -20, \ldots$

26. $5, a_2, a_3, a_4, 35, \ldots$

Do you UNDERSTAND?

27. Open-Ended Write the first four terms of an arithmetic sequence with a common difference of 3 and a third term of 10. Then write both a recursive definition and an explicit formula for this sequence.

28. Investments You invested money in a fund and each month you receive a payment for your investment. Over the first four months, you received $50, $52, $55, and $59. If this pattern continues, how much will you receive in the tenth month?
  a. Write a formula to describe this sequence.
  b. Identify your formula as explicit or recursive.
  c. Writing Explain the difference between an explicit formula and a recursive formula. Use your formula from part (a) as part of your explanation.

29. Open-Ended Write the first five terms of a sequence that is not an arithmetic sequence. Then give both an explicit and recursive formula to describe this sequence.

30. Sports A tennis club charges players a $20 court fee plus a $10 hourly charge with a 5-hour maximum. A posted list of the total charges for 1, 2, 3, 4, or 5 hours forms an arithmetic sequence. What is the first term and what is the common difference?

Geometric Sequences

Objective To define, identify, and apply geometric sequences

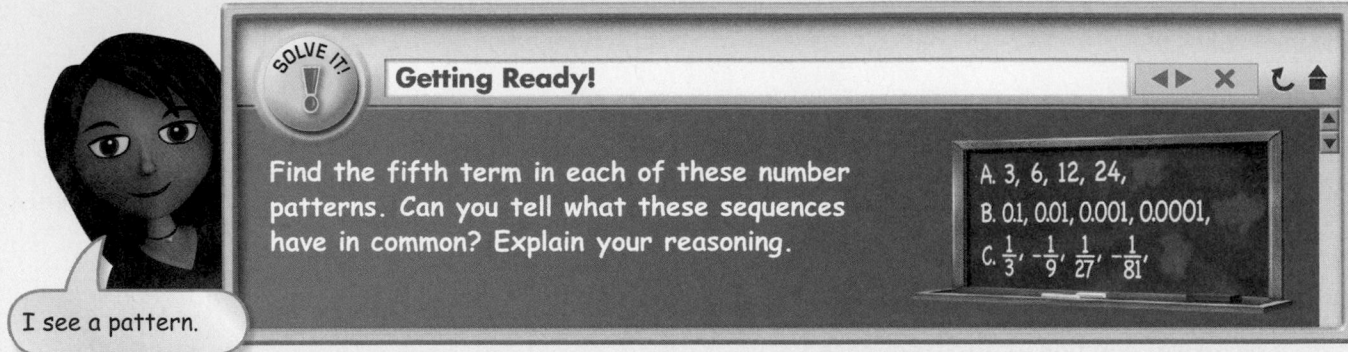

I see a pattern.

Getting Ready!

Find the fifth term in each of these number patterns. Can you tell what these sequences have in common? Explain your reasoning.

A. 3, 6, 12, 24,

B. 0.1, 0.01, 0.001, 0.0001,

C. $\frac{1}{3}, -\frac{1}{9}, \frac{1}{27}, -\frac{1}{81},$

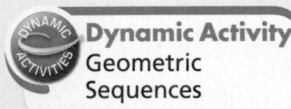

Dynamic Activity
Geometric
Sequences

You build a *geometric sequence* by multiplying each term by a constant.

Focus Question What is a geometric sequence?

Lesson Vocabulary
- geometric sequence
- common ratio
- geometric mean

take note

Key Concept Geometric Sequence

A **geometric sequence** with a starting value a and a **common ratio** r is a sequence of the form

$$a, ar, ar^2, ar^3, \ldots$$

A recursive definition for the sequence has two parts:

initial condition $a_1 = a$

recursive formula $a_n = a_{n-1} \cdot r$, for $n > 1$

An explicit definition for this sequence is a single formula:

$a_n = a_1 \cdot r^{n-1}$, for $n \geq 1$

Problem 1 Identifying Geometric Sequences

Think

How do you find the ratios between consecutive terms?
Divide the second term by the first term, then the third term by the second term, and so on.

Is the sequence geometric? If it is, what are a_1 and r?

Ⓐ 3, 6, 12, 24, 48, ...

Find the ratios between consecutive terms.

The common ratio is 2.

3   6   12   24   48

$$\frac{6}{3} = \frac{12}{6} = \frac{24}{12} = \frac{48}{24} = 2$$

This sequence is geometric with $a_1 = 3$ and $r = 2$.

B 3, 6, 9, 12, 15, ...

Find the ratios between consecutive terms.

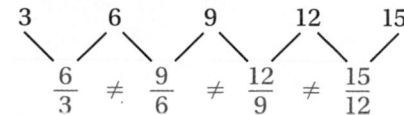

$$\frac{6}{3} \neq \frac{9}{6} \neq \frac{12}{9} \neq \frac{15}{12}$$

The ratios are different. With no common ratio, this sequence is not geometric.

C $3^5, 3^{10}, 3^{15}, 3^{20}, \ldots$

Use the properties of exponents to simplify the ratios of consecutive terms.

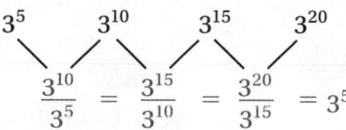

$$\frac{3^{10}}{3^5} = \frac{3^{15}}{3^{10}} = \frac{3^{20}}{3^{15}} = 3^5$$

The common ratio is 3^5. This sequence is geometric with $a_1 = 3^5$ and $r = 3^5$.

Hint

As soon as you find two ratios that are not equal, you can conclude the sequence is not geometric.

 Got It? 1. Is the sequence geometric? If it is, what are a_1 and r?

    a. 2, 4, 8, 16, ...   **b.** 1, 5, 9, 13, 17, ...   **c.** $2^3, 2^7, 2^{11}, 2^{15}, \ldots$

Problem 2   Analyzing Geometric Sequences

What are the indicated terms of the geometric sequence?

A the 10th term of the geometric sequence 4, 12, 36, ...

The first term a_1 is 4. The common ratio r is $12 \div 4 = 3$.

Use the explicit formula.	$a_n = a_1 r^{n-1}$
Substitute 10 for n, 4 for a_1, and 3 for r.	$a_{10} = 4 \cdot 3^{10-1}$
Simplify.	$a_{10} = 78{,}732$

The 10th term is 78,732.

Plan

What do you need to find the second term given the first term?
You need the common ratio.

B the second and third terms of the geometric sequence 2, ■, ■, −54, ...

Step 1   Identify the common ratio.

The first term a_1 is 2. The fourth term a_4 is −54.

Use the explicit formula.	$a_n = a_1 r^{n-1}$
Substitute 4 for n and 2 for a_1.	$a_4 = 2r^{4-1}$
Substitute −54 for a_4. Simplify.	$-54 = 2r^3$
Divide each side by 2.	$-27 = r^3$
Solve for r.	$-3 = r$

Step 2   Identify the missing terms.

Find the second term.	$2 \cdot (-3) = -6$
Find the third term.	$-6 \cdot (-3) = 18$

The second and third terms are −6 and 18.

 Got It? 2. a. What is the 8th term of the geometric sequence that begins 2, 10, ...?

    b. What are the second and third terms of this geometric sequence?

       120, ■, ■, 15, ...

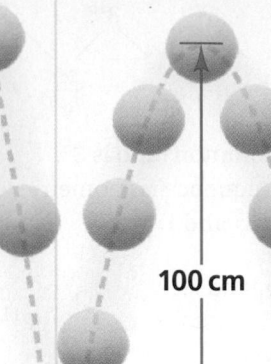

Problem 3 Using a Geometric Sequence

Physics When a ball bounces, the heights of consecutive bounces form a geometric sequence. What are the heights of the 4th and 5th bounces?

100 cm

49 cm

Think

The heights of the first and third bounces are given in the picture.

Use the explicit formula to relate a_1 to a_3, and to find r.

Hint

r must be positive since the bounces are above the floor.

Solve for r.

To find a_4 and a_5, build the sequence recursively, starting from a_3.

Write the answer.

Write

$a_1 = 100$
$a_3 = 49$

$a_n = a_1 r^{n-1}$
$a_3 = a_1 r^{3-1}$
$49 = 100r^2$

$100r^2 = 49$
$r = \sqrt{\dfrac{49}{100}} = \dfrac{7}{10}$

$a_n = a_{n-1} \cdot r$
$a_4 = a_3 \cdot r = 49 \cdot \dfrac{7}{10} = 34.3$
$a_5 = a_4 \cdot r = 34.3 \cdot \dfrac{7}{10} \approx 24$

The heights are 34.3 cm and 24 cm.

 Got It? 3. a. Reasoning To find the height of the 10th bounce, would you use the recursive or the explicit formula? Explain.

b. What are the heights of the 6th and 10th bounces?

In a geometric sequence, the square of the middle term of any three consecutive terms is equal to the product of the other two terms. For example, examine the sequence 2, −6, 18, −54, . . . , as shown here.

$$(-6)^2 = 2 \cdot 18 = 36$$

$$2, -6, 18, -54, \ldots$$

$$18^2 = (-6)(-54) = 324$$

In an arithmetic sequence, recall that the middle term of any three consecutive terms is the arithmetic mean of the other two terms.

The **geometric mean** of two positive numbers x and y is $\sqrt{xy}$. By definition, the geometric mean is positive.

For a geometric sequence a_1, ■, a_3, …, there are two possible values for the missing term. The geometric mean is one possible value. The opposite of the geometric mean is the other.

Multiple Choice What are the possible values of the missing term of the geometric sequence?

48, ■, 3, . . .

(A) ±4   (B) ±9   (C) ±12   (D) ±20

Find the geometric mean of 48 and 3.

Use the formula for the geometric mean to find a possible value for the missing term.   geometric mean $= \sqrt{xy}$

Substitute 48 for x and 3 for y. $= \sqrt{48 \cdot 3}$

Simplify. $= \sqrt{144}$

$= 12$

The possible values for the missing term are the geometric mean and its opposite, or ±12. The correct answer is C.

 Got It? **4.** The 9th and 11th terms of a geometric sequence are 45 and 80. What are possible values for the 10th term?

Hint

The sequence at the right is an example of why you must consider two possible values for the missing term.

Think

Why would this question ask for "possible values" rather than "the value"?
The geometric mean and its opposite are both possible values.

Focus Question What is a geometric sequence?

Answer In a geometric sequence, the ratio of any term (after the first) to its preceding term is a constant value. You can build a geometric sequence by multiplying each term by a constant.

Lesson Check

Do you know HOW?

Determine whether each sequence is geometric. If so, find the common ratio.

1. 5, 10, 15, . . .

2. 10, 20, 40, . . .

Find the seventh term of each geometric sequence.

3. 1, −3, 9, . . .

4. 100, 20, 4, . . .

Do you UNDERSTAND?

5. Error Analysis To find the third term of the geometric sequence 5, 10, ■, ■, 80, your friend says that there are two possible answers—the geometric mean of 5 and 80, and its opposite. Explain your friend's error.

6. Compare and Contrast How is finding a missing term of a geometric sequence using the geometric mean similar to finding a missing term of an arithmetic sequence using the arithmetic mean? How is it different?

Practice and Problem-Solving Exercises

 **Practice**

Determine whether each sequence is geometric. If so, find the common ratio.   ◀ **See Problem 1.**

7. 1, 2, 4, 8, . . .

8. 1, 2, 3, 4, . . .

9. 1, −2, 4, −8, . . .

10. −1, 1, −1, 1, . . .

11. 7, 0.7, 0.07, 0.007, . . .

12. −1, −6, −36, −216, . . .

Find the eighth term of each geometric sequence.   ◀ **See Problem 2.**

Guided Practice

To start, identify the common ratio.

13. 3, 9, 27, . . .

$$\frac{9}{3} = 3$$

14. −3, 6, −12, . . .

15. 24, −6, $\frac{3}{2}$, . . .

16. −30, 7.5, −1.875, . . .

17. Science When radioactive substances decay, the amount remaining will form a geometric sequence when measured over constant intervals of time. The table shows the amount of Np-240, a radioactive isotope of Neptunium, initially and after 2 hours. What are the amounts left after 1 hour, 3 hours, and 4 hours?   ◀ **See Problem 3.**

Hours Elapsed	0	1	2	3	4
Grams of Np-240	1244	■	346	■	■

Find the missing term of each geometric sequence. It could be the geometric mean or its opposite.   ◀ **See Problem 4.**

Guided Practice

To start, use the formula for the geometric mean.

18. 5, ■, 911.25, . . .

geometric mean = $\sqrt{xy}$

19. $\frac{2}{5}$, ■, $\frac{8}{45}$, . . .

20. 3, ■, 0.75, . . .

21. 5, ■, 2.8125, . . .

 **Apply**

Write an explicit formula for each sequence. Then generate the first five terms.

22. $a_1 = 1, r = 0.5$

23. $a_1 = 100, r = -20$

24. $a_1 = 7, r = 1$

25. $a_1 = 1024, r = 0.5$

26. $a_1 = 4, r = 0.1$

27. $a_1 = 10, r = -1$

Identify each sequence as *arithmetic, geometric,* or *neither.* Then find the next two terms.

28. $45, 90, 180, 360, \ldots$

29. $25, 50, 75, 100, \ldots$

30. $3, -3, 3, -3, \ldots$

31. $-5, 10, -20, 40, \ldots$

32. $2, 1, 0.5, 0.25, \ldots$

33. $1, 4, 9, 16, \ldots$

Find the missing terms of each geometric sequence.

34. $972, \blacksquare, \blacksquare, \blacksquare, 12, \ldots$

35. $2.5, \blacksquare, \blacksquare, \blacksquare, 202.5, \ldots$

36. $12.5, \blacksquare, \blacksquare, \blacksquare, 5.12, \ldots$

37. $-4, \blacksquare, \blacksquare, \blacksquare, -30\frac{3}{8}, \ldots$

> **Hint** The geometric mean of the first and fifth terms is the third term. Some terms might be negative.

38. Think About a Plan Suppose a balloon is filled with 5000 cm^3 of helium. It then loses one fourth of its helium each day. How much helium will be left in the balloon at the start of the tenth day?
- How can you write a sequence of numbers to represent this situation?
- Is the sequence arithmetic, geometric, or neither?
- How can you write a formula for this sequence?

39. Athletics During your first week of training for a marathon, you run a total of 10 miles. You increase the distance you run each week by twenty percent. How many miles do you run during your twelfth week of training?

40. a. Open-Ended Choose two positive numbers. Find their geometric mean.
  b. Find the common ratio for a geometric sequence that includes the terms from part (a) as its first three terms.
  c. Find the 9th term of the geometric sequence from part (b).
  d. Find the geometric mean of the term from part (c) and the first term of your sequence. What term of the sequence have you just found?

For the geometric sequence 3, 12, 48, 192, . . . , find the indicated term.

41. 17th term

42. 20th term

43. nth term

Find the 10th term of each geometric sequence.

44. $a_9 = 8, r = \frac{1}{2}$

45. $a_9 = -5, r = -\frac{1}{2}$

46. $a_9 = -\frac{1}{3}, r = \frac{1}{2}$

47. Writing Describe the similarities and differences between a common difference and a common ratio.

SAT/ACT

48. What is the common ratio in the geometric sequence 4, 10, 25, 62.5, . . . ?

A 0.4

B 2.5

C 15

D 25

49. The first term of a geometric sequence is 1 and its common ratio is 6. What is the sixth term?

F 31

G 3176

H 7776

I 46,656

50. Determine by inspection the end behavior of the graph of $y = -2x^3 + 5x - 4$.

A falls to the left, falls to the right: ($\swarrow$, $\searrow$)

B falls to the left, rises to the right: ($\swarrow$, $\nearrow$)

C rises to the left, falls to the right: ($\nwarrow$, $\searrow$)

D rises to the left, rises to the right: ($\nwarrow$, $\nearrow$)

51. What are the asymptotes of the graph of $y = \frac{10}{x-5}$?

F $x = 0, y = 5$

G $x = 5, y = 0$

H $x = 5, y = 10$

I $x = 10, y = 5$

Mixed Review

Write an explicit and a recursive formula for each arithmetic sequence.   ◀ See Lesson 9-2.

52. $-3, 0, 3, 6, \ldots$ **53.** $17, 8, -1, \ldots$ **54.** $-2, -13, -24, \ldots$

Expand each binomial.   ◀ See Lesson 5-7.

55. $(a + 5)^4$ **56.** $(x - 9)^3$ **57.** $(2x + y)^5$ **58.** $(b^2 - 3)^6$

Find the vertical asymptotes and holes for the graph of each rational function.   ◀ See Lesson 8-3.

59. $y = \frac{x-3}{x+3}$ **60.** $y = \frac{x-3}{x+1}$

61. $y = \frac{x-3}{x(x-1)}$ **62.** $y = \frac{x(x+3)}{(x-3)(x+3)}$

Get Ready!   To prepare for Lesson 9-4, do Exercises 63–65.

Write a recursive formula for each sequence.   ◀ See Lesson 9-1.

63. $1, 3, 6, 10, \ldots$ **64.** $1, 4, 9, 16, \ldots$ **65.** $1, 5, 14, 30, \ldots$

Arithmetic Series

Objective To define arithmetic series and find their sums

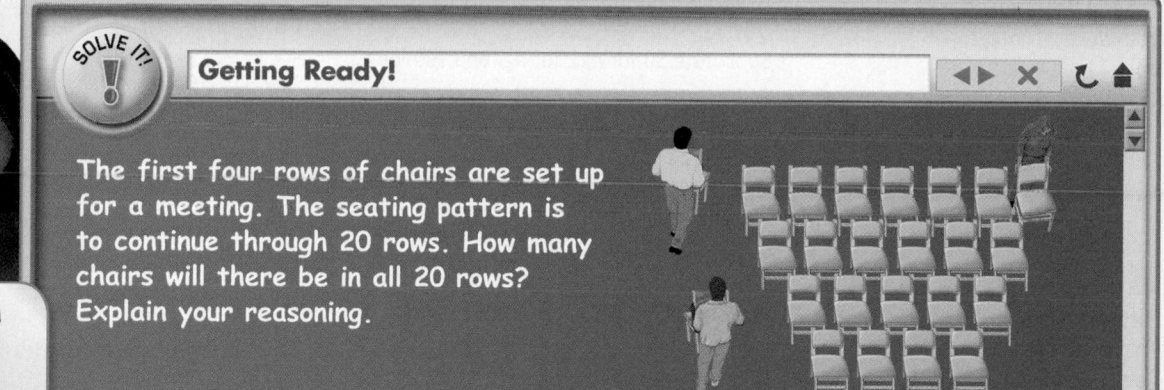

SOLVE IT!

Getting Ready!

The first four rows of chairs are set up for a meeting. The seating pattern is to continue through 20 rows. How many chairs will there be in all 20 rows? Explain your reasoning.

You will learn an easier way to find the sum in this lesson.

Lesson Vocabulary
- series
- finite series
- infinite series
- arithmetic series
- limits

Just as you found formulas for terms of sequences, you can find formulas for the sums of the terms of sequences.

Focus Question What is an arithmetic series?

A **series** is the indicated sum of the terms of a sequence. A **finite series**, like a finite sequence, has a first term and a last term, while an **infinite series** continues without end.

Finite sequence	**Finite series**
6, 9, 12, 15, 18	$6 + 9 + 12 + 15 + 18$ (The sum is 60.)

Infinite sequence	**Infinite series**
3, 7, 11, 15, . . .	$3 + 7 + 11 + 15 + . . .$

An **arithmetic series** is a series whose terms form an arithmetic sequence (as shown above). When a series has a finite number of terms, you can use a formula involving the first and last term to evaluate the sum.

take note

Property   Sum of a Finite Arithmetic Series

The sum S_n of a finite arithmetic series $a_1 + a_2 + a_3 + \cdots + a_n$ is

$$S_n = \frac{n}{2}(a_1 + a_n)$$

where a_1 is the first term, a_n is the nth term, and n is the number of terms.

Problem 1 Finding the Sum of Finite Arithmetic Series

Think

How many even integers are there from 2 to 100?

Double 1, 2, 3,..., 50, and you get 2, 4, 6,..., 100, the even integers from 2 to 100. There are 50 even integers.

What is the sum of each finite arithmetic series?

Ⓐ $2 + 4 + 6 + \cdots + 100$

This series is the sum of the even integers from 2 to 100. The first term is 2, the last (and 50th) term is 100, and the common difference is 2.

Use the sum formula.	$S_n = \frac{n}{2}(a_1 + a_n)$
Substitute 50 for n, 2 for a_1, and 100 for a_n.	$S_{50} = \frac{50}{2}(2 + 100)$
Simplify.	$= 25(102)$
Multiply.	$= 2550$

The sum is 2550.

Ⓑ $7 + 11 + 15 + \cdots + 223$

Step 1 Find the number of terms in the series.

The first term is 7, the last term is 223, and the constant difference is $11 - 7 = 4$.

Use the explicit formula.	$a_n = a + (n - 1)d$
Substitute 223 for a_n, 7 for a, and 4 for d.	$223 = 7 + (n - 1)4$
Use the Distributive Property.	$223 = 7 + 4n - 4$
Isolate the variable term.	$220 = 4n$
Solve for n.	$55 = n$

There are 55 terms in the series.

Step 2 Find the sum of the series.

Use the sum formula.	$S_n = \frac{n}{2}(a_1 + a_n)$
Substitute 55 for n, 7 for a_1, and 223 for a_n.	$S_{55} = \frac{55}{2}(7 + 223)$
Simplify.	$= \frac{55}{2}(230)$
Multiply.	$= 6325$

The sum is 6325.

Hint

Before you can use the sum formula, you need to use the explicit formula for an arithmetic sequence to find the number of terms n.

 Got It? **1.** What is the sum of the finite arithmetic series?

    a. $1 + 3 + 5 + \cdots + 99$

    b. $4 + 9 + 14 + \cdots + 134$

    c. Reasoning Will the sum of a sequence of even numbers always be an even number? Will the sum of a sequence of odd numbers always be an odd number? Explain.

Problem 2 Using the Sum of a Finite Arithmetic Series

Bonus A company pays a $10,000 bonus to salespeople at the end of their first 50 weeks if they make 10 sales in their first week, and then improve their sales numbers by two each week thereafter. One salesperson qualified for the bonus with the minimum possible number of sales. How many sales did the salesperson make in week 50? In all 50 weeks?

Know
- The number of sales in the first week
- The increase in sales each week after the first week

Need
- The number of sales in the 50th week
- The total number of sales in all 50 weeks

Plan
- Write a formula for the sequence.
- Use the formula to find the number of sales in the 50th week.
- Find the sum of the sales for all 50 weeks.

Think

Write

The first week sales were 10.
Sales increased by 2 each week.

$a_1 = 10 \qquad d = 2$

The sequence is arithmetic. Use the explicit formula to find the sales in week 50.

$a_n = a_1 + (n - 1)d$

Substitute 50 for n, 10 for a_1, and 2 for d. Then simplify.

$$a_{50} = 10 + (50 - 1)2$$
$$= 10 + (49)2$$
$$= 10 + 98$$
$$= 108$$

Use the formula for S_n to find the total sales for all 50 weeks.

$S_n = \frac{n}{2}(a_1 + a_n)$

Substitute 50 for n, 10 for a_1, and 108 for a_{50}. Then simplify.

$$S_{50} = \frac{50}{2}(10 + 108)$$
$$= 25(118) = 2950$$

Write the answer in words.

The salesperson made 108 sales in week 50 and 2950 sales in all 50 weeks.

 Got It? **2.** The company in Problem 2 has an alternative bonus plan. It pays a $5000 bonus if a new salesperson makes 10 sales in the first week and then improves by *one* sale per week each week thereafter. One salesperson qualified for this bonus with the minimum number of sales. How many sales did the salesperson make in week 50? In all 50 weeks?

You can use the Greek capital letter sigma, Σ, to indicate a sum. With it, you use *limits* to indicate how many terms you are adding. **Limits** are the least and greatest values of n in the series. You write the limits below and above the Σ to indicate the first and last terms of the series.

For example, you can write the series $3^2 + 4^2 + 5^2 + \cdots + 108^2$ as $\displaystyle\sum_{n=3}^{108} n^2$.

Upper limit: the series ends with $n = 108$.

$$\displaystyle\sum_{n=3}^{108} n^2$$ The explicit formula for each term is n^2.

Lower limit: the series begins with $n = 3$.

To find the number of terms in a series written in Σ form, subtract the lower limit from the upper limit and add 1.

The number of terms in the series above is $108 - 3 + 1 = 106$.

Problem 3 Writing a Series in Summation Notation

Multiple Choice What is summation notation for the series?
$7 + 11 + 15 + \cdots + 203 + 207$

A $\displaystyle\sum_{n=1}^{51}(4n + 3)$
B $\displaystyle\sum_{n=1}^{50}(4n + 3)$
C $\displaystyle\sum_{n=1}^{50}(7n)$
D $\displaystyle\sum_{n=1}^{51}(7n)$

The sequence $7, 11, 15, \ldots, 203, 207$ is arithmetic with first term $a_1 = 7$ and common difference $d = 4$.

Use the explicit formula for an arithmetic sequence.	$a_n = a_1 + (n - 1)d$
Substitute 7 for a_1, and 4 for d.	$a_n = 7 + (n - 1)4$
Simplify.	$= 4n + 3$

An explicit formula for the nth term is $4n + 3$.

Use the explicit formula to find the value of n for the term 207.	$a_n = 4n + 3$
Substitute 207 for a_n.	$207 = 4n + 3$
Isolate the variable term.	$204 = 4n$
Solve for n.	$51 = n$

The upper limit is 51. You can write the series as $\displaystyle\sum_{n=1}^{51}(4n + 3)$.
The correct answer is A.

Plan

What do you need to write a series in summation notation?
You need an explicit formula for the nth term and the lower and upper limits.

✓ **Got It?** **3.** What is summation notation for the series?
  a. $-5 + 2 + 9 + 16 + \cdots + 261 + 268$
  b. $500 + 490 + 480 + \cdots + 20 + 10$

Focus Question What is an arithmetic series?

Answer An arithmetic series is a series whose terms form an arithmetic sequence. You can find the sum of a finite arithmetic series using a formula involving the first term, the last term, and the number of terms.

Lesson Check

Do you know HOW?

Find the sum of each finite arithmetic series.

1. $4 + 7 + 10 + 13 + 16 + 19 + 22$

2. $10 + 20 + 30 + \cdots + 110 + 120$

Write each arithmetic series in summation notation.

3. $3 + 6 + 9 + 12 + 15 + 18 + 21$

4. $1 + 5 + 9 + \cdots + 41 + 45$

Do you UNDERSTAND?

5. Vocabulary What is the difference between an arithmetic sequence and an arithmetic series?

6. Error Analysis A student writes the arithmetic series $3 + 8 + 13 + \cdots + 43$ in summation notation as $\sum_{n=3}^{8}(3 + 5n)$. Describe and correct the error.

7. Reasoning Is more than one arithmetic series with four terms whose sum is 44 possible? Explain.

Practice and Problem-Solving Exercises

A Practice

Find the sum of each finite arithmetic series. ◀ **See Problem 1.**

Guided Practice

To start, identify what you know.

8. $8 + 9 + 10 + \cdots + 15$

The first term is 8, the last (and 8th) term is 15, and the common difference is 1.

9. $5 + 6 + 7 + \cdots + 11$

10. $1 + 4 + 7 + \cdots + 31$

11. $7 + 14 + 21 + \cdots + 105$

12. $1 + 4 + 9 + \cdots + 81$

13. $(-3) + (-6) + (-9) + \cdots + (-30)$

14. $105 + 97 + 89 + \cdots + (-71)$

15. Grades A student has taken three math tests so far this semester. His scores for the first three tests were 75, 79, and 83. ◀ **See Problem 2.**
  a. Suppose his test scores continue to improve at the same rate. What will be his grade on the sixth (and final) test?
  b. What will be his total score for all six tests?

Write each arithmetic series in summation notation. ◀ **See Problem 3.**

16. $4 + 8 + 12 + 16 + 20$

17. $7 + 9 + 11 + \cdots + 21$

18. $5 + 8 + 11 + \cdots + 38$

19. $100 + 90 + 80 + \cdots + 10$

 **Apply**

20. Think About a Plan A meeting room is set up with 16 rows of seats. The number of seats in a row increases by two with each successive row. The first row has 12 seats. What is the total number of seats?
- How can you find the number of seats in each row using an explicit formula?
- What is the number of seats in the 16th row?
- How can you find the sum of the seats in 16 rows?

Determine whether each list is a *sequence* or a *series* and *finite* or *infinite*.

21. 1, 2, 4, 8, 16, 32, . . .

22. 1, 0.5, 0.25, 0.125, 0.0625

23. $-0.5 - 0.25 - 0.125 - \ldots$

24. 2.3 + 4.6 + 9.2 + 18.4

Each sequence has eight terms. Evaluate each related series.

25. $\frac{1}{2}, \frac{3}{2}, \frac{5}{2}, \ldots, \frac{15}{2}$

26. 1, −1, −3, . . . , −13

27. 5, 13, 21, . . . , 61

28. −3.5, −1.25, 1, . . . , 12.25

29. 1765, 1414, 1063, . . . , −692

30. −13, −14.5, −16, . . . , −23.5

31. Architecture In a 20-row theater, the number of seats in a row increases by three with each successive row. The first row has 18 seats.
- **a.** Write an arithmetic series to represent the number of seats in the theater.
- **b.** Find the total seating capacity of the theater.
- **c.** Front-row tickets for a concert cost $60. After every 5 rows, the ticket price goes down by $5. What is the total amount of money generated by a full house?

32. a. Grocery A supermarket displays cans in a triangle. Write an explicit formula for the sequence of the number of cans.
- **b.** Use summation notation to write the related series for a triangle with 10 cans in the bottom row.
- **c.** Suppose the triangle had 17 rows. How many cans would be in the 17th row?
- **d. Reasoning** Could the triangle have 110 cans? 140 cans? Explain.

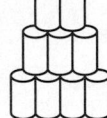

Evaluate each series to the given term.

33. 2 + 4 + 6 + 8 + . . . ; 10th term

34. −5 − 25 − 45 − . . . ; 9th term

35. a. Open-Ended Write two explicit formulas for arithmetic sequences.
- **b.** Write the first five terms of each related series.
- **c.** Use summation notation to rewrite each series.
- **d.** Evaluate each series.

Standardized Test Prep

SAT/ACT

36. Which expression represents the series $14 + 20 + 26 + 32 + 38 + 44 + 50$?

Ⓐ $\displaystyle\sum_{n=2}^{8}(7n - 1)$ Ⓑ $\displaystyle\sum_{n=3}^{8}(6n - 4)$ Ⓒ $\displaystyle\sum_{n=3}^{9}(6n - 4)$ Ⓓ $\displaystyle\sum_{n=8}^{14}(n + 6)$

37. What is the common ratio in the geometric sequence $\frac{9}{2}, 3, 2, \frac{4}{3}, \ldots$?

Ⓕ $\frac{3}{2}$ Ⓖ $\frac{9}{2}$ Ⓗ $\frac{2}{3}$ Ⓘ $\frac{27}{2}$

38. Which expression is NOT equivalent to $\sqrt[4]{4n^2}$?

Ⓐ $\left(4n^2\right)^{\frac{1}{4}}$ Ⓒ $\left(2|n|\right)^{\frac{1}{2}}$

Ⓑ $2n^{\frac{1}{2}}$ Ⓓ $\sqrt{2|n|}$

39. The graph shows the inverse of which function?

Ⓕ $y = 3x$ Ⓗ $y = 3^x$

Ⓖ $y = -3^{2x}$ Ⓘ $y = 2^{3x}$

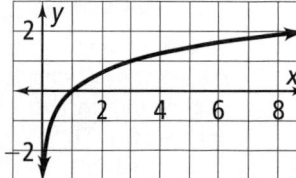

Short Response

40. Solve the equation $x^2 + 10x + 40 = 5$ by completing the square.

Mixed Review

Write an explicit formula for each geometric sequence. Then find the first three terms.   ◀ See Lesson 9-3.

41. $a_1 = 1, r = 2$ **42.** $a_1 = -1, r = -1$ **43.** $a_1 = 3, r = \frac{3}{2}$

Simplify each rational expression. State any restrictions on the variable.   ◀ See Lesson 8-4.

44. $\dfrac{x^2 + 4x + 3}{x^2 - 3x - 4}$ **45.** $\dfrac{c^2 - 8c + 12}{c^2 - 11c + 30}$ **46.** $\dfrac{3z^4 + 36z^3 + 60z^2}{3z^3 - 3z^2}$

Get Ready! To prepare for Lesson 9-5, do Exercises 47–49.

Find the common ratio for each geometric sequence.   ◀ See Lesson 9-3.

47. $90, -30, 10, \ldots$ **48.** $64, 48, 36, \ldots$ **49.** $-9, 4.5, -2.25, \ldots$

9-5 Geometric Series

Objective To define geometric series and find their sums

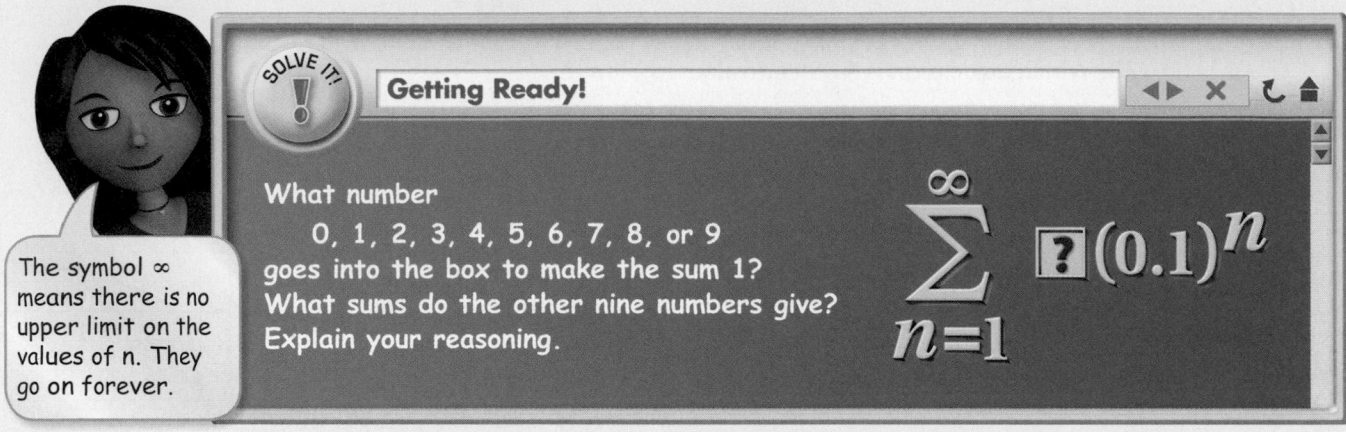

The symbol ∞ means there is no upper limit on the values of n. They go on forever.

Getting Ready!

What number
  0, 1, 2, 3, 4, 5, 6, 7, 8, or 9
goes into the box to make the sum 1?
What sums do the other nine numbers give?
Explain your reasoning.

$$\sum_{n=1}^{\infty} \boxed{?}(0.1)^n$$

Lesson Vocabulary
- geometric series
- converge
- diverge

You can write any whole number that has the same digit in every place as the sum of the terms of a geometric sequence. For example,

$$4444 = 4(10)^0 + 4(10)^1 + 4(10)^2 + 4(10)^3$$

You can write any rational number as an infinite repeating decimal.
For example, $\frac{47}{90} = 0.5222\ldots$.

Therefore, you can write any rational number as a number plus the sum of an infinite geometric sequence.

$$0.5222\ldots = 0.5 + 2(0.1)^2 + 2(0.1)^3 + 2(0.1)^4 + \ldots$$

Focus Question What is a geometric series?

A **geometric series** is the sum of the terms of a geometric sequence.

take note

Key Concept   Sum of a Finite Geometric Series

The sum S_n of a finite geometric series $a_1 + a_1r + a_1r^2 + \cdots + a_1r^{n-1}, r \neq 1$, is

$$S_n = \frac{a_1(1 - r^n)}{1 - r}$$

where a_1 is the first term, r is the common ratio, and n is the number of terms.

Problem 1 Finding the Sums of Finite Geometric Series

What is the sum of the finite geometric series?

Plan

What do you need to find the sum?
You need the first term, the common ratio, and the number of terms in the series.

A $3 + 6 + 12 + 24 + \cdots + 3072$

The first term is 3. The common ratio is $\frac{6}{3} = 2$. The nth term is 3072.

Find the value of n.

Use the explicit formula. $\qquad\qquad\qquad a_n = a_1 r^{n-1}$

Substitute 3 for a_1, 2 for r, and 3072 for a_n. $\quad 3072 = 3 \cdot 2^{n-1}$

Divide each side by 3. $\qquad\qquad\qquad 1024 = 2^{n-1}$

1024 is 2^{10}, so $n - 1 = 10$ and $n = 11$.

Use the sum formula. $\qquad\qquad\qquad S_n = \dfrac{a_1(1 - r^n)}{1 - r}$

Substitute 3 for a_1, 2 for r, and 11 for n. $\quad S_{11} = \dfrac{3(1 - 2^{11})}{1 - 2}$

Simplify. $\qquad\qquad\qquad\qquad\qquad = 6141$

The sum of the series is 6141.

B $4 + 2 + 1 + \frac{1}{2} + \cdots + \frac{1}{128}$

The first term is 4. The common ratio is $\frac{2}{4} = \frac{1}{2}$. The nth term is $\frac{1}{128}$.

Find the value of n.

Use the explicit formula. $\qquad\qquad\qquad a_n = a_1 r^{n-1}$

Substitute 4 for a_1, $\frac{1}{2}$ for r, and $\frac{1}{128}$ for a_n. $\quad \dfrac{1}{128} = 4\left(\dfrac{1}{2}\right)^{n-1}$

Divide each side by 4. $\qquad\qquad\qquad \dfrac{1}{512} = \left(\dfrac{1}{2}\right)^{n-1}$

$\frac{1}{512}$ is $\left(\frac{1}{2}\right)^9$, so $n - 1 = 9$ and $n = 10$.

Use the sum formula. $\qquad\qquad\qquad S_n = \dfrac{a_1(1 - r^n)}{1 - r}$

Substitute 4 for a_1, $\frac{1}{2}$ for r, and 10 for n. $\quad S_{10} = \dfrac{4\left(1 - \left(\frac{1}{2}\right)^{10}\right)}{1 - \frac{1}{2}}$

Simplify. Use a calculator. $\qquad\qquad\qquad \approx 8$

The sum of the series is approximately 8.

Got It? **1.** What is the sum of the finite geometric series?

    a. $-15 + 30 - 60 + 120 - 240 + 480$

    b. $5 - 10 + 20 - 40 + \cdots - 2560$

The Soldier's Reasonable Request A famous story involves a soldier who rescues his king in battle. The king grants him any prize "within reason" from the riches of the kingdom. The soldier asks for a chessboard with a single kernel of wheat on the first square, two kernels of wheat on the second square, then four, then eight, and so on for all 64 squares of the chessboard. The king decides that the request is reasonable.

Problem 2 Using the Geometric Series Formula

According to the story above, how many total kernels of wheat did the soldier request?

Know	Need	Plan
The amount of wheat in the first 4 squares	The total amount of wheat	• Find the common ratio • Use the sum formula to find the total amount of wheat.

Step 1 Identify the first term, common ratio, and the number of terms.

$$a_1 = 1, r = 2, n = 64$$

Step 2 Use the sum formula.

Write the sum formula. $\quad S_n = \dfrac{a_1(1 - r^n)}{1 - r}$

Substitute for a_1, r, and n. $\quad S_{64} = \dfrac{1(1 - 2^{64})}{1 - 2}$

Simplify. $\quad = 2^{64} - 1$

Write in scientific notation. $\quad \approx 1.845 \times 10^{19}$

The soldier requested approximately 1.845×10^{19} kernels of wheat.

 Got It? **2.** To save money for a vacation, you set aside $100. For each month thereafter, you plan to set aside 10% more than the previous month. How much money will you save in 12 months?

The Rest of the Story A bushel of wheat contains about a million kernels. The total US output of wheat in a recent year was just over 2.1 billion bushels. How many years of production at that level would it take the United States to produce enough wheat to satisfy the soldier's "reasonable" request?

In Problem 2, you found that the terms of a geometric series grow rapidly when the common ratio is greater than 1. Likewise, they diminish rapidly when the common ratio is between 0 and 1. In fact, they diminish so rapidly that the infinite geometric series actually has a finite sum.

take note

Key Concept   Infinite Geometric Series

An infinite geometric series with first term a_1 and common ratio $|r| < 1$ has a finite sum S.

$$S = \frac{a_1}{1 - r}.$$

An infinite geometric series with $|r| \geq 1$ does not have a finite sum.

To say that an infinite series $a_1 + a_2 + a_3 + \ldots$ has a sum means that the *sequence of partial sums* $S_1 = a_1, S_2 = a_1 + a_2, S_3 = a_1 + a_2 + a_3, \ldots,$ $S_n = a_1 + a_2 + \cdots + a_n, \ldots$ **converges** to a number S as n gets very large.

When an infinite series does not converge to a sum, the series **diverges**. An infinite geometric series with $|r| \geq 1$ diverges.

 Problem 3 Analyzing Infinite Geometric Series

Does the series *converge* or *diverge*? If it converges, what is the sum?

Ⓐ $1 + \frac{1}{2} + \frac{1}{4} + \ldots$

The common ratio is $\frac{1}{2} \div 1 = \frac{1}{2}$. Since $|r| = \left|\frac{1}{2}\right| < 1$, the series converges.

Use the sum formula. $S = \dfrac{a_1}{1 - r}$

Substitute 1 for a_1 and $\frac{1}{2}$ for r. $= \dfrac{1}{1 - \frac{1}{2}}$

Simplify. $= \dfrac{1}{\frac{1}{2}} = 2$

The sum is 2.

Think

When does an infinite geometric series converge?
An infinite geometric series converges when the absolute value of the common ratio is less than 1.

B $\frac{2}{3} - \frac{5}{6} + \frac{25}{24} - \frac{125}{96} + \cdots$

The common ratio is $-\frac{5}{6} \div \frac{2}{3} = -\frac{15}{12} = -\frac{5}{4}$.

Since $|r| = \left|-\frac{5}{4}\right| = \frac{5}{4} > 1$, the series diverges.

Got It? **3.** Does the infinite series *converge* or *diverge*? If it converges, what is the sum?

  a. $\frac{1}{2} + \frac{3}{4} + \frac{9}{8} + \cdots$ **b.** $\frac{1}{3} - \frac{1}{9} + \frac{1}{27} - \frac{1}{81} + \cdots$

  c. Reasoning Will an infinite geometric series either converge or diverge? Explain.

Focus Question What is a geometric series?

Answer A geometric series is the sum of the terms of a geometric sequence. Find the sum of a finite geometric series using the first term, the number of terms, and the common ratio. You can also find the sum of an infinite geometric series if the common ratio $|r| < 1$.

 Lesson Check

Do you know HOW?

Evaluate each finite geometric series.

1. $\frac{1}{5} + \frac{1}{10} + \frac{1}{20} + \frac{1}{40} + \frac{1}{80}$

2. $9 - 6 + 4 - \frac{8}{3} + \frac{16}{9}$

Determine whether each infinite geometric series *diverges* or *converges*.

3. $1 - \frac{1}{6} + \frac{1}{36} - \frac{1}{216} + \cdots$

4. $\frac{1}{64} + \frac{1}{32} + \frac{1}{16} + \cdots$

Do you UNDERSTAND?

5. Error Analysis A classmate uses the formula for the sum of an infinite geometric series to evaluate $1 + 1.1 + 1.21 + 1.331 + \cdots$ and gets -10. What error did your classmate make?

6. Writing Explain how you can determine whether an infinite geometric series has a sum.

7. Compare and Contrast How are the formulas for the sum of a finite arithmetic series and the sum of a finite geometric series similar? How are they different?

Practice and Problem-Solving Exercises

 **Practice**

Evaluate the sum of the finite geometric series.   ◀ See Problem 1.

Guided Practice

To start, use the explicit formula for a geometric sequence with $a_1 = 1$, $r = 2$ and $a_n = 128$.

8. $1 + 2 + 4 + 8 + \cdots + 128$

$$a_n = a_1 r^{n-1}$$
$$128 = 1 \cdot 2^{n-1}$$

9. $4 + 12 + 36 + 108 + \cdots + 972$

10. $3 + 6 + 12 + 24 + \cdots + 768$

11. $-5 - 10 - 20 - 40 - \cdots - 2560$

12. $1 - 3 + 9 - 27 + \cdots - 2187$

13. Financial Planning In March, a family starts saving for a vacation they are planning for the end of August. The family expects the vacation to cost $1375. They start with $125. Each month they plan to deposit 20% more than the previous month. Will they have enough money for their trip? If not, how much more do they need?   ◀ See Problem 2.

Determine whether each infinite geometric series *diverges* or *converges*. If the series converges, state the sum.   ◀ See Problem 3.

Guided Practice

To start, find the common ratio.

14. $1 + \frac{1}{4} + \frac{1}{16} + \ldots$

$$\frac{1}{4} \div 1 = \frac{1}{4}$$

15. $1 - \frac{1}{2} + \frac{1}{4} - \ldots$

16. $4 + 2 + 1 + \ldots$

17. $1 + 2 + 4 + \ldots$

18. $6 + 18 + 54 + \ldots$

19. $-54 - 18 - 6 - \ldots$

20. $1 - 1 + 1 - \ldots$

Evaluate each infinite geometric series.

21. $1.1 + 0.11 + 0.011 + \ldots$

22. $3 + 1 + \frac{1}{3} + \frac{1}{9} + \ldots$

23. $3 - 2 + \frac{4}{3} - \frac{8}{9} + \ldots$

 **Apply**

24. Think About a Plan The height a ball bounces is less than the height of the previous bounce due to friction. The heights of the bounces form a geometric sequence. Suppose a ball is dropped from one meter and rebounds to 95% of the height of the previous bounce. What is the total distance traveled by the ball when it comes to rest?
- Does the problem give you enough information to solve the problem?
- How can you write the general term of the sequence?
- What formula should you use to calculate the total distance?

Determine whether each series is *arithmetic* or *geometric*. Then evaluate the finite series for the specified number of terms.

25. $2 + 4 + 8 + 16 + \ldots$; $n = 10$

26. $2 + 4 + 6 + 8 + \ldots$; $n = 20$

27. $-5 + 25 - 125 + 625 - \ldots$; $n = 9$

28. $6.4 + 8 + 10 + 12.5 + \ldots$; $n = 7$

29. $1 + 2 + 3 + 4 + \ldots$; $n = 1000$

30. $81 + 27 + 9 + 3 + \ldots$; $n = 200$

31. Communications Many companies use a telephone chain to notify employees of a closing due to bad weather. Suppose a company's CEO calls three people. Then each of these people calls three others, and so on.
   a. Make a diagram to show the first three stages in the telephone chain. How many calls are made at each stage?
   b. Write the series that represents the total number of calls made through the first six stages.
   c. How many employees have been notified after stage six?

32. Graphing Calculator The graph models the sum of the first n terms in a geometric series with $a_1 = 20$ and $r = 0.9$.
   a. Write the first four sums of the series.
   b. Use the graph to evaluate the series to the 47th term.
   c. Write and evaluate the formula for the sum of the series.
   d. Graph the formula using the window values shown. Use the graph to verify your answer to part (b).

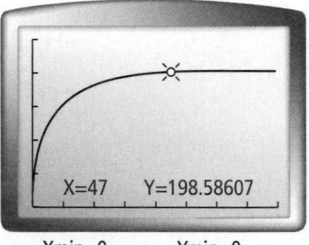

X=47   Y=198.58607

Xmin=0   Ymin=0
Xmax=94   Ymax=250
Xscl=10   Yscl=50

33. Open-Ended Write an infinite geometric series that converges to 3. Use the formula to evaluate the series.

34. Physics Because of friction and air resistance, each swing of a pendulum is a little shorter than the previous one. The lengths of the swings form a geometric sequence. Suppose the first swing of a pendulum has a length of 100 cm and the return swing is 99 cm.
   a. On which swing will the arc first have a length less than 50 cm?
   b. What is the total distance traveled by the pendulum when it comes to rest?

35. Writing Suppose you are to receive an allowance each week for the next 26 weeks. Would you rather receive (a) $1000 per week or (b) $.02 the first week, $.04 the second week, $.08 the third week, and so on for the 26 weeks? Justify your answer.

36. The sum of an infinite geometric series is twice its first term.
   a. Error Analysis A student says the common ratio of the series is $\frac{3}{2}$. What is the student's error?
   b. Find the common ratio of the series.

Standardized Test Prep

SAT/ACT

37. Solve $\sqrt{x} + \sqrt{2x} = 2$. Check for extraneous solutions.

38. Evaluate the infinite geometric series $\frac{2}{5} + \frac{4}{25} + \frac{8}{125} + \dots$. Enter your answer as a fraction.

39. Use $\log_5 2 \approx 0.43$ and $\log_5 7 \approx 1.21$ and the properties of logarithms to approximate $\log_5 \sqrt{14}$ without using a calculator.

40. Use a calculator to solve the equation $7^{2x} = 75$. Round the answer to the nearest hundredth.

41. Use the Change of Base Formula and your calculator to solve $\log_9 x = \log_6 15$. Round the answer to the nearest tenth.

Mixed Review

Evaluate each series to the given term.

◀ See Lesson 9-4.

42. $12.5 + 15 + 17.5 + 20 + 22.5 + \dots$; 7th term

43. $-100 - 95 - 90 - 85 - \dots$; 11th term

Add or subtract. Simplify where possible.

◀ See Lesson 8-5.

44. $\frac{7}{2c} - \frac{2}{c^2}$

45. $\frac{5}{y+3} + \frac{15}{y-3}$

46. $\frac{4}{x^2-36} + \frac{x}{x-6}$

Use the properties of logarithms to evaluate each expression.

◀ See Lesson 7-4.

47. $\log_2 \frac{1}{8} + \log_2 8$

48. $\log_{15} 25 + \log_{15} 9$

49. $3 \log_9 3 - \frac{1}{4} \log_9 81$

Pull It **All Together**

To solve these problems, you will pull together concepts and skills related to sequences and series.

BIG idea Variable

You can represent quantities using variables and algebraic expressions.

Task 1

The sum S_n of a finite arithmetic series of n terms is $S_n = \frac{n}{2}(a_1 + a_n)$ where a_1 is the first term and a_n is the nth term.

a. Show that $S_n = na_1 + \frac{n(n-1)}{2}d$ by replacing a_n with its value in terms of a_1, n, and d in the above formula.

b. Explain why $S_n = na_1 + \frac{n(n-1)}{2}d$ makes sense by explaining how you can extract each of na_1 and $\frac{n(n-1)}{2}d$ from the sum
$a_1 + (a_1 + d) + (a_1 + 2d) + \cdots + (a_1 + (n-1)d)$.

BIG idea Equivalence

You can represent any *function* in an unlimited number of ways, where all representations have the same domain and the same pairing of inputs with outputs.

Task 2

A sequence is a function with domain the natural numbers $1, 2, 3, \ldots$.
Using function notation, you can write the sequence $a_n = a_1 + (n-1)d$ as $a(n) = a_1 + (n-1)d$ and the sequence $a_n = a_1 r^{n-1}$ as $a(n) = a_1 r^{n-1}$.

a. Is $a(n) = a_1 + (n-1)d$ a linear function? Explain. If not, how can you adjust its definition so that it is a linear function? What is the slope?

b. What type of function does $a(n) = a_1 r^{n-1}$ suggest? To what family of functions does this function belong? Explain how it is related to the parent function of that family. Draw its graph.

c. What type of function is suggested by the sum sequence $S(n) = \frac{a_1(1-r^n)}{1-r}$? By $S(n) = \frac{n}{2}(a_1 + a(n))$? Explain each answer.

BIG idea Modeling

You can represent many real-world mathematical problems algebraically. These representations can lead to algebraic solutions.

Task 3

Each of these sequence or series formulas involves four quantities. For each formula, describe the four quantities. Then explain how you can find the fourth quantity if you know the values of the other three.

a. $a_n = a_1 + (n-1)d$

b. $S_n = \frac{n}{2}(a_1 + a_n)$

c. $a_n = a_1 r^{n-1}$

d. $S_n = \frac{a_1(1-r^n)}{1-r}$

Connecting BIG ideas and Answering the Essential Questions

1 Variable

You can define a sequence
- by describing its nth term with a formula using n.
- by stating its first term and a formula that relates the $n - 1$ and nth terms.

2 Equivalence

$a_n = a + (n - 1)d$ and $a_1 = a$, $a_n = a_{n-1} + d$ for $n > 1$ define the same arithmetic sequence, $a, a + d, a + 2d, \ldots$

3 Modeling

You can model a geometric sequence explicitly or recursively. The sum of its first n terms is $\frac{a_1(1 - r^n)}{1 - r}$.

Mathematical Patterns and Arithmetic Sequences (Lessons 9-1 and 9-2)

$a_n = 2 - \frac{3}{4}(n - 1)$ and $a_1 = 2$, so

$a_n = a_{n-1} - \frac{3}{4}$ represent the arithmetic

sequence $2, \frac{5}{4}, \frac{2}{4}, -\frac{1}{4}, -1, \ldots$

Mathematical Patterns and Geometric Sequences (Lessons 9-1 and 9-3)

$a_n = 2\left(-\frac{1}{2}\right)^{n-1}$ and $a_1 = 2$, so

$a_n = \left(-\frac{1}{2}\right)a_{n-1}$ represents the geometric

sequence $2, -1, \frac{1}{2}, -\frac{1}{4}, \frac{1}{8}, \ldots$

Arithmetic Series (Lesson 9-4)

The sum $S_n = a_1 + a_2 + \cdots + a_n$ of an arithmetic series is $S_n = \frac{n}{2}(a_1 + a_n)$. The sum

$S_6 = 2 + \frac{5}{4} + \frac{2}{4} - \frac{1}{4} - 1 - \frac{7}{4}$

$= 3\left(2 - \frac{7}{4}\right) = \frac{3}{4}$.

Geometric Series (Lesson 9-5)

$S_n = \frac{a_1(1 - r^n)}{1 - r}$ is the sum of the

first n terms of a geometric series. If the series is infinite with $|r| < 1$, the sum is $S = \frac{a_1}{1 - r}$.

For the geometric series,

$a_1 = 2$, $a_n = \left(-\frac{1}{2}\right)a_{n-1}$,

$S_6 = \frac{2\left(1 - \left(-\frac{1}{2}\right)^6\right)}{1 - \left(-\frac{1}{2}\right)}$, or $\frac{21}{16}$, and

$S = \frac{2}{1 - \left(-\frac{1}{2}\right)} = \frac{4}{3}$.

Chapter Vocabulary

- arithmetic mean (p. 594)
- arithmetic sequence (p. 592)
- arithmetic series (p. 607)
- common difference (p. 592)
- common ratio (p. 600)
- converge (p. 617)

- diverge (p. 617)
- explicit formula (p. 585)
- finite series (p. 607)
- geometric mean (p. 603)
- geometric sequence (p. 600)
- geometric series (p. 614)

- infinite series (p. 607)
- limits (p. 610)
- recursive formula (p. 586)
- sequence (p. 584)
- series (p. 607)
- term (p. 584)

Choose the vocabulary term that correctly completes each sentence.

1. When you use Σ to write a series, you can use ___?___ to indicate how many terms you are adding.

2. An ordered list of terms is a ___?___ .

3. If an infinite geometric series ___?___ , then it must have a sum.

4. There is a constant ___?___ between consecutive terms in a geometric sequence.

5. A formula that expresses the nth term of a sequence in terms of n is a(n) ___?___ .

9-1 Mathematical Patterns

Quick Review

A **sequence** is an ordered list of numbers called **terms**.

A recursive definition gives the first term and defines the other terms using a **recursive formula** that relates each term after the first term to the one before it.

An **explicit formula** expresses the nth term of a sequence in terms of n, where n is a positive integer.

Example

A sequence has an explicit formula $a_n = n^2$. What are the first three terms of this sequence?

Substitute 1 for n and evaluate.	$a_1 = (1)^2 = 1$
Substitute 2 for n and evaluate.	$a_2 = (2)^2 = 4$
Substitute 3 for n and evaluate.	$a_3 = (3)^2 = 9$

The first three terms are 1, 4, and 9.

Exercises

Find the first five terms of each sequence.

6. $a_n = -2n + 3$

7. $a_n = -n^2 + 2n$

8. $a_n = 2a_{n-1} - 1$, where $a_1 = 2$

9. $a_n = \frac{1}{2} a_{n-1}$, where $a_1 = 20$

Write a recursive definition for each sequence.

10. 5, 22, 39, 56, . . .   **11.** $-2, 7, 16, 25, . . .$

Write an explicit formula for each sequence.

12. 1, 4, 7, 10, . . .   **13.** $4, 1.5, -1, -3.5, . . .$

9-2 Arithmetic Sequences

Quick Review

In an **arithmetic sequence**, the constant difference between consecutive terms is called the **common difference**.

For an arithmetic sequence, a is the first term, a_n is the nth term, n is the number of the term, and d is the common difference.

An explicit formula is $a_n = a + (n - 1)d$.

A recursive definition is $a_{n+1} = a_n + d$, with $a_1 = a$.

The **arithmetic mean** of two numbers x and y is the average of the two numbers $\frac{x + y}{2}$.

Example

What is the missing term of the arithmetic sequence 11, ■, 27, . . . ?

Use the formula for the arithmetic mean.	arithmetic mean $= \frac{x + y}{2}$
Substitute 11 for x and 27 for y.	$= \frac{11 + 27}{2}$
Simplify.	$= \frac{38}{2} = 19$

The missing term is 19.

Exercises

Determine whether each sequence is arithmetic. If so, identify the common difference and find the 32nd term of the sequence.

14. 2, 4, 7, 10, . . .   **15.** 3, 18, 33, 48, . . .

16. 7, 10, 13, 16, . . .   **17.** 2, 5, 9, 14, . . .

Find the missing term(s) of each arithmetic sequence.

18. 1, ■, 9, . . .   **19.** 104, ■, 99, . . .

20. -1, ■, 11, . . .   **21.** -4.6, ■, -5.2, . . .

22. -13, ■, ■, ■, -3, . . .   **23.** 2, ■, ■, ■, -0.4, . . .

Write an explicit formula for each arithmetic sequence.

24. $-2, 7, 16, 25, . . .$ **25.** 62, 59, 56, 53, . . .

9-3 Geometric Sequences

Quick Review

In a **geometric sequence**, the ratio of consecutive terms is constant. This ratio is the **common ratio**. For a geometric sequence, a is the first term, a_n is the nth term, n is the number of the term, and r is the common ratio.

An explicit formula is $a_n = a \cdot r^{n-1}$.

A recursive definition is $a_n = a_{n-1} \cdot r$, with $a_1 = a$.

The geometric mean of two positive numbers x and y is $\sqrt{xy}$.

Example

What is the sixth term of the geometric sequence that begins 2, 6, 18, ... ?

The first term a is 2. The common ratio r is $6 \div 2 = 3$.

Use the explicit formula.	$a_n = ar^{n-1}$
Substitute 6 for n, 2 for a, and 3 for r.	$a_6 = 2 \cdot 3^{6-1}$
Simplify.	$= 486$

The sixth term is 486.

Exercises

Determine whether each sequence is geometric. If so, identify the common ratio and find the next two terms.

26. $1, \frac{1}{2}, \frac{1}{4}, \frac{1}{8}, \ldots$

27. $1, 3, 5, 7, \ldots$

28. $3, 3.6, 4.32, 5.184, \ldots$

Find the missing term(s) of each geometric sequence.

29. $3, \blacksquare, 12, \ldots$

30. $0.004, \blacksquare, 0.4, \ldots$

31. $-20, \blacksquare, \blacksquare, \blacksquare, -1.25, \ldots$

Write an explicit formula for each geometric sequence.

32. $1, 2, 4, 8, \ldots$

33. $25, 5, 1, \frac{1}{5}, \ldots$

Use an explicit formula to find the 10th term of each geometric sequence.

34. $5, 10, 20, 40, \ldots$ **35.** $-3, 6, -12, 24, \ldots$

9-4 Arithmetic Series

Quick Review

A **series** is the expression for the sum of the terms of a sequence. An **arithmetic series** is the sum of the terms of an arithmetic sequence. The sum S_n of the first n terms of an arithmetic series is $S_n = \frac{n}{2}(a_1 + a_n)$.

Example

What is the sum of the arithmetic series?

$2 + 5 + 8 + 11 + 14 + 17 + 20$

The first term is 2, and the last (and 7th) term is 20.

Use the sum formula.	$S_n = \frac{n}{2}(a_1 + a_n)$
Substitute 7 for n, 2 for a_1, and 20 for a_n.	$S_7 = \frac{7}{2}(2 + 20)$
Simplify.	$= 77$

Exercises

Use summation notation to write each arithmetic series for the specified number of terms. Then evaluate the sum.

36. $10 + 7 + 4 + \ldots ; n = 5$

37. $50 + 55 + 60 + \ldots ; n = 7$

38. $6 + 7.4 + 8.8 + \ldots ; n = 11$

39. $21 + 19 + 17 + \ldots ; n = 8$

9-5 Geometric Series

Quick Review

A **geometric series** is the sum of the terms of a geometric sequence. The sum S_n of the first n terms of a geometric series is $S_n = \frac{a_1(1 - r^n)}{1 - r}, r \neq 1$.

When an infinite series has a finite sum, the series **converges**. When the series does not converge, the series **diverges**.

For an infinite geometric series, when $|r| < 1$, the series converges to $S = \frac{a_1}{1 - r}$. When $|r| \geq 1$, the series diverges.

Example

What is the sum of the geometric series?

$5 + 10 + 20 + 40 + 80 + 160$

The first term is 5, and common ratio is $10 \div 5 = 2$.

There are 6 terms.

Use the sum formula.　　　　$S_n = \frac{a_1(1 - r^n)}{1 - r}$

Substitute 6 for n, 5 for a_1, and 2 for r.　　$S_6 = \frac{5(1 - 2^6)}{1 - 2}$

Simplify.　　　　　　　　$= 315$

The sum is 315.

Exercises

Evaluate each finite series for the specified number of terms.

40. $1 + 2 + 4 + \ldots; n = 5$

41. $80 - 40 + 20 - \ldots; n = 8$

42. $12 + 2 + \frac{1}{3} + \ldots; n = 4$

Determine whether each infinite geometric series *converges* or *diverges*. If the series converges, state the sum.

43. $150 + 30 + 6 + \ldots$

44. $2.2 + 2.42 + 2.662 + \ldots$

45. $-10 - 20 - 40 - \ldots$

46. $\frac{2}{3} + \frac{4}{9} + \frac{8}{27} + \ldots$

Do you know HOW?

Write a recursive definition and an explicit formula for each sequence. Then find a_{12}.

1. 7, 13, 19, 25, 31, . . .

2. 10, 20, 40, 80, 160, . . .

Determine whether each sequence is *arithmetic, geometric,* or *neither*. Then find the tenth term.

3. 23, 27, 31, 35, 39, . . .

4. −12, −5, 2, 9, 16, . . .

5. −5, 15, −45, 135, −405, . . .

6. $\frac{1}{4}$, 1, 4, 16, . . .

Find the missing term of each arithmetic sequence.

7. 4, ■, 12, . . .   **8.** −11, ■, 23, . . .

Determine whether each sequence is *arithmetic* or *geometric*. Then identify the common difference or common ratio.

9. 1620, 540, 180, 60, 20, . . .

10. 78, 75, 72, 69, 66, 63, 60, . . .

11. $\frac{3}{32}, \frac{3}{16}, \frac{3}{8}, \frac{3}{4}, \frac{3}{2}$, 3, 6, . . .

a_1 is the first term of a sequence, r is the common ratio, and d is the common difference. Write the first five terms.

12. $a_1 = 2, r = -2$ **13.** $a_1 = 3, d = 7$

14. $a_1 = -100, r = \frac{1}{5}$ **15.** $a_1 = 19, d = -4$

Find the missing term of each geometric sequence.

16. 2, ■, 0.5, . . .   **17.** 2, ■, 8, . . .

Find the sum of each infinite geometric series.

18. 0.5 + 0.05 + 0.005 + . . .

19. $1 - \frac{1}{2} + \frac{1}{4} - \ldots$

20. $6 + 5 + \frac{25}{6} + \ldots$

Determine whether each series is *arithmetic* or *geometric*. Then evaluate the finite series for the specified number of terms.

21. 2 + 7 + 12 + . . . ; $n = 8$

22. 5000 + 1000 + 200 + . . . ; $n = 5$

23. 1 + 0.01 − 0.98 − . . . ; $n = 5$

24. 2 + 6 + 18 + . . . ; $n = 6$

Do you UNDERSTAND?

25. You have saved $50. Each month you add $10 more to your savings.
  a. Write an explicit formula to model the amount you have saved after n months.
  b. How much have you saved after six months?

26. Open-Ended Write an arithmetic sequence. Then write an explicit formula for it.

27. Reasoning How can you tell if a geometric series converges or diverges? Include examples of both types of series. Evaluate the series that converges.

28. A diamond is purchased for $2500. Suppose its value increases 5% each year.
  a. What is the value of diamond after 8 years?
  b. Writing Explain how you can write an explicit formula for a geometric sequence to answer the question.

Read the question at the right. Then follow the tips to answer the sample question.

TIP 1

Find where y = 0. These are the x-intercepts of the graph.

TIP 2

Check your solutions in the original equation.

The graph below shows the quadratic function $y = 2x^2 + 2x - 4$. Use the graph to find the solutions of $2x^2 + 2x - 4 = 0$.

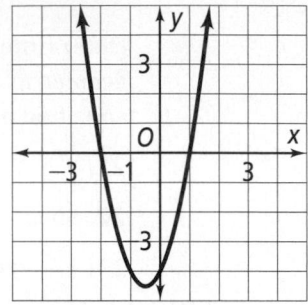

Ⓐ −4 and 0   Ⓒ −1 and 2

Ⓑ −2 and 1   Ⓓ 2 and −1

Think It Through

The x-intercepts of the graph are at $x = -2$ and $x = 1$.

Substitute to verify your answers.

$$2(-2)^2 + 2(-2) - 4$$
$$= 2(4) - 4 - 4$$
$$= 0$$
$$2(1)^2 + 2(1) - 4$$
$$= 2 + 2 - 4$$
$$= 0$$

The correct answer is B.

Vocabulary Builder

As you solve test items, you must understand the meanings of mathematical terms. Match each term with its mathematical meaning.

A. recursive formula

B. limit

C. explicit formula

D. sequence

I. a formula that expresses the nth term in terms of n

II. an ordered list of numbers

III. the least or greatest integer value of n in a series

IV. a formula that gives the first term in a sequence and defines the other terms by relating each term to the one before it

Multiple Choice

Read each question. Then write the letter of the correct answer on your paper.

1. What is the solution set of the equation $(2x - 4)(x + 6) = 0$?

Ⓐ $\{-4, 6\}$ Ⓒ $\{2, -6\}$

Ⓑ $\{-4, 6\}$ Ⓓ $\{-2, -6\}$

2. What are the first five terms of the sequence $a_n = 2n - 1$?

Ⓕ 0, 1, 2, 3, 4   Ⓗ 2, 4, 6, 8, 10

Ⓖ 1, 3, 5, 7, 9   Ⓘ 3, 5, 7, 9, 11

3. What is the common ratio in a geometric series if $a_2 = \frac{2}{5}$ and $a_5 = \frac{16}{135}$?

Ⓐ $\frac{2}{5}$ Ⓒ $\frac{6}{65}$

Ⓑ $\frac{2}{3}$ Ⓓ $\frac{8}{27}$

4. The total area of a sheet of paper can be represented by $27x^3 + 64y^3$. Which factors could represent the length times the width?

- Ⓕ $(3x + 4y)(3x^2 + 4y^2)$
- Ⓖ $(3x + 4y)(9x^2 - 12xy + 16y^2)$
- Ⓗ $(3x - 4y)(9x^2 - 12xy + 16y^2)$
- Ⓘ $(3x + 4y)(3x^2 - 3xy + 4y^2)$

5. The graph below shows the quadratic function $y = x^2 + 2x - 3$. Use the graph to find all the solutions of $x^2 + 2x - 3 = 0$.

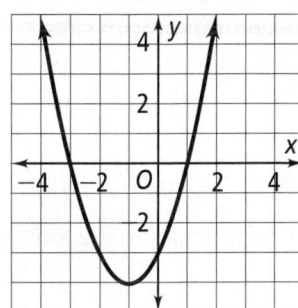

- Ⓐ -3
- Ⓑ -1
- Ⓒ -3 and 1
- Ⓓ 3 and -1

6. The table shows ordered pairs that satisfy the equation $y = -x^2 + 2x + 15$.

x	−3	0	2	3	5
y	0	15	15	12	0

Based on this table, what is the solution set of the equation $-x^2 + 2x + 15 = 0$?

- Ⓕ $\{0, 15\}$
- Ⓖ $\{-3, 15\}$
- Ⓗ $\{5, 0\}$
- Ⓘ $\{-3, 5\}$

7. What is the product of $\frac{x^2 + 5x + 4}{(x - 1)(x + 1)}$ and $\frac{x^2 - 5x + 6}{x - 2}$?

- Ⓐ $\frac{x^2 + 7x + 12}{x - 1}$ for $x \ne 1$
- Ⓑ $\frac{x^2 + x - 12}{x - 1}$ for $x \ne -1, 1,$ or 2
- Ⓒ $\frac{x^2 + x - 12}{x - 1}$ for $x \ne 1$
- Ⓓ $\frac{x^2 + 7x + 12}{x - 1}$ for $x \ne -1, 1,$ or 2

8. What is the sum of the infinite geometric series $\frac{1}{4} + \frac{1}{16} + \frac{1}{64} + \frac{1}{256} + \dots$?

- Ⓕ $\frac{1}{4}$
- Ⓖ $\frac{1}{3}$
- Ⓗ $\frac{1}{2}$
- Ⓘ 3

9. If $f(x) = 4x^4 - 9$ and $g(x) = 2x^2 + 3$, what is $\left(\frac{f}{g}\right)(x)$?

- Ⓐ $2x^2 - 3$
- Ⓑ $2x + 3$
- Ⓒ $2x - 3$
- Ⓓ $2x^2 + 3$

10. Marisol wants to start saving money for college. She sees the advertisement below in her local newspaper.

> Start a savings account today and earn
> **4.7% annual interest!**
> **Bonus Offer:** After one year, an additional
> **$50** will be added to your account!

For x dollars in this savings account, $I(x) = 1.047x$ is the value of the account after one year. $B(x) = x + 50$ is the value of the account after the one-year bonus. $(B \circ I)(x)$ models the value of this account after one year of investment time and the one-year bonus. Marisol opens a savings account by depositing $120. What is the value of the account after one year?

- Ⓕ $175.64
- Ⓖ $182.58
- Ⓗ $226.40
- Ⓘ $249.90

11. What is the area of the parallelogram below?

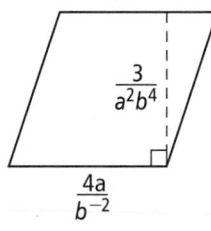

- Ⓐ $\frac{12}{ab^2}$
- Ⓑ $\frac{3}{ab^2}$
- Ⓒ $\frac{12b^2}{a}$
- Ⓓ $\frac{3b^5}{4a^3}$

12. If $\log 5 \approx 0.69897$ and $\log 6 \approx 0.77815$, what is the approximate value of $\log 150$?

   Ⓕ 0.34188

   Ⓖ 0.38017

   Ⓗ 1.20412

   Ⓘ 2.17609

13. What is $\dfrac{4x^2 - 1}{2x^2 - 5x - 3} \cdot \dfrac{x^2 - 6x + 9}{2x^2 + 5x - 3}$?

   Ⓐ 1

   Ⓑ $x + 3$

   Ⓒ $x - 3$

   Ⓓ $\dfrac{x - 3}{x + 3}$

14. Which is the factored form of $0.81p^2 - 0.09$?

   Ⓕ $(0.9p + 0.045)(0.9p - 0.045)$

   Ⓖ $(0.9p + 0.3)(0.9p - 0.3)$

   Ⓗ $(0.9p + 0.03)(0.9p - 0.03)$

   Ⓘ $(0.9p + 0.81)(0.9p - 0.81)$

15. Which arithmetic sequence does NOT include the term 33?

   Ⓐ 1, 5, 9, 13, . . .

   Ⓑ 3, 9, 15, . . .

   Ⓒ 1, 11, 21, . . .

   Ⓓ 85, 72, 59, . . .

16. The graph shows a transformation of which parent function?

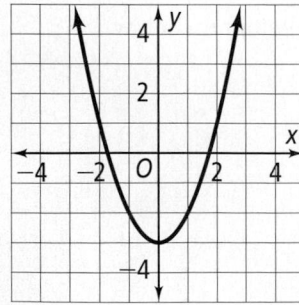

   Ⓕ $y = x$ Ⓗ $y = |x|$

   Ⓖ $y = x^2$ Ⓘ $y = \frac{1}{x}$

GRIDDED RESPONSE

17. What is the sum of the following finite geometric series?

$1 + 4 + 16 + 64 + 256$

18. What is the sum of the following finite arithmetic series?

$14 + 20 + 26 + 32 + 38 + 44 + 50$

19. What is the value of $\log_4 256$?

20. Rita works a part-time job at a clothing store and earns \$7 per hour. Juan works at another clothing store and earns \$6 per hour plus a 10% commission on sales. How many sales, in dollars, would Juan have to make in two hours to earn the same amount as Rita in a two-hour shift?

21. Let $f(x) = x + 1$ and $g(x) = x^2$. What is $(g \circ f)(2)$?

22. What is the slope of a line perpendicular to the line $y = -\frac{1}{2}x + 5$?

Short Response

23. What is the graph and absolute value of $-3 + 2i$?

24. What is an equation of the line passing through points $(3, 5)$ and $(7, 1)$?

25. Write an explicit formula for the geometric sequence for which $a_1 = 6$ and $r = \frac{1}{2}$. Then generate the first five terms.

26. The 30th term of a finite arithmetic series is 4.4. The sum of the first 30 terms is 78. What is the first term of the series?

27. What is the inverse of $y = \sqrt{x - 5}$?

Extended Response

28. Use the properties of logarithms to write log 45 in four different ways. Name each property you use.

29. In a geometric sequence, $a_1 = 2$ and $a_5 = 162$. Explain how to use the geometric mean to find the missing terms a_2, a_3, and a_4.

30. What are all the solutions to $27x^4 + 8x = 0$? Show your work.

Get Ready!

Lesson 4-1 ◀) **Graphing Quadratic Functions**

Graph each function.

1. $y = -x^2$

2. $y = \frac{1}{3}x^2$

3. $y = 2x^2 + 5$

4. $y = x^2 + 6x + 8$

Lesson 4-3 ◀) **Identifying Quadratic Functions**

Determine whether each function is *linear* or *quadratic*. Identify the quadratic, linear, and constant terms.

5. $y = 6x - x^2 + 1$

6. $f(x) = -2(3 + x)^2 + 2x^2$

7. $y = 2x - y - 13$

8. $y = 4x(7 - 2x)$

9. $g(x) = -2x^2 - 3(x - 2)$

10. $y = x - 2(x + 5)$

Lesson 4-6 ◀) **Completing the Square**

Complete the square.

11. $x^2 + 8x +$ ■

12. $x^2 - 5x +$ ■

13. $x^2 + 14x +$ ■

Rewrite each equation in vertex form. Then graph the function.

14. $y = x^2 + 6x + 7$

15. $y = 2x^2 - 4x + 10$

16. $y = -3x^2 + x$

Lesson 4-1 ◀) **Graphing Quadratic Functions in Vertex Form**

Graph each function.

17. $y = 2(x - 3)^2 + 1$

18. $y = -1(x + 7)^2 - 4$

Lesson 2-7 ◀) **Graphing Absolute Value Functions**

Graph each function.

19. $y = 2|x|$

20. $y = |x| + 2$

Looking Ahead Vocabulary

21. The word *radius* is a Latin word for the spoke of a wheel. It is also the source of the word "radio" because electromagnetic rays radiate from a radio in every direction. Why do you think mathematicians use the term radius to label any line segment from the center of a circle to any point on the circle?

22. In geometry, you learned that a *vertex* is typically a corner or point where two lines intersect. The four corners of a square are called vertices. Using this information, what can you conclude about the vertex of a parabola?

CHAPTER 10

Quadratic Relations and Conic Sections

In this chapter you will learn how to work with curves that you can trace along the surface of a cone. These curves are called <u>conic sections</u>.

People can manufacture these curves to make beautiful architecture, as shown on the next page.

 ## Vocabulary

English/Spanish Vocabulary Audio Online:

English	Spanish
center of a circle, *p. 649*	centro de un círculo
circle, *p. 649*	círculo
conic section, *p. 634*	sección cónica
directrix, *p. 641*	directriz
ellipse, *p. 658*	elipse
hyperbola, *p. 666*	hipérbola
radius, *p. 649*	radio
standard form of an equation of a circle, *p. 650*	forma normal de la ecuación de un círculo

00:04:04

BIG ideas

1 Modeling

Essential Question What is the intersection of a cone and a plane parallel to a line along the side of the cone?

2 Equivalence

Essential Question What is the graph of $\frac{x^2}{9} + \frac{y^2}{9} = 1$?

3 Coordinate Geometry

Essential Question What is the difference between the algebraic representations of ellipses and hyperbolas?

Chapter Preview

10-1 Exploring Conic Sections

Objective To graph and identify conic sections

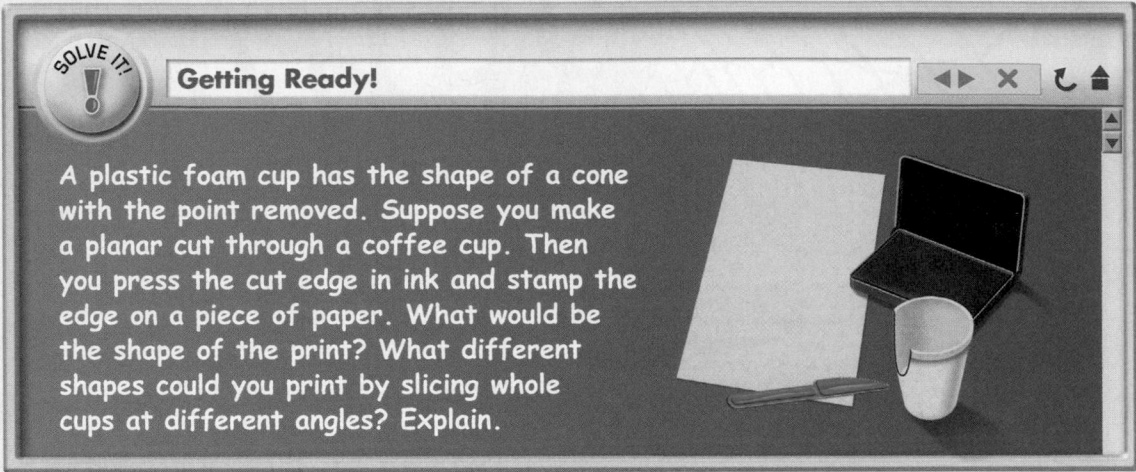

SOLVE IT!

Getting Ready!

A plastic foam cup has the shape of a cone with the point removed. Suppose you make a planar cut through a coffee cup. Then you press the cut edge in ink and stamp the edge on a piece of paper. What would be the shape of the print? What different shapes could you print by slicing whole cups at different angles? Explain.

Lesson Vocabulary
• conic section

In Chapter 4, you studied parabolas. Geometrically, a parabola has the shape of a cross section of a cone that you cut in a particular way. Parabolas form a family of curves that belong to a larger family known as *conic sections*.

Focus Question What is a conic section?

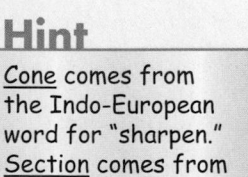

Hint

<u>Cone</u> comes from the Indo-European word for "sharpen." <u>Section</u> comes from the word for "cut."

take note

Key Concept   Conic Sections

A **conic section** is a curve you get by intersecting a plane and a double cone. By changing the inclination of the plane, you can get a circle, a parabola, an ellipse, or a hyperbola.

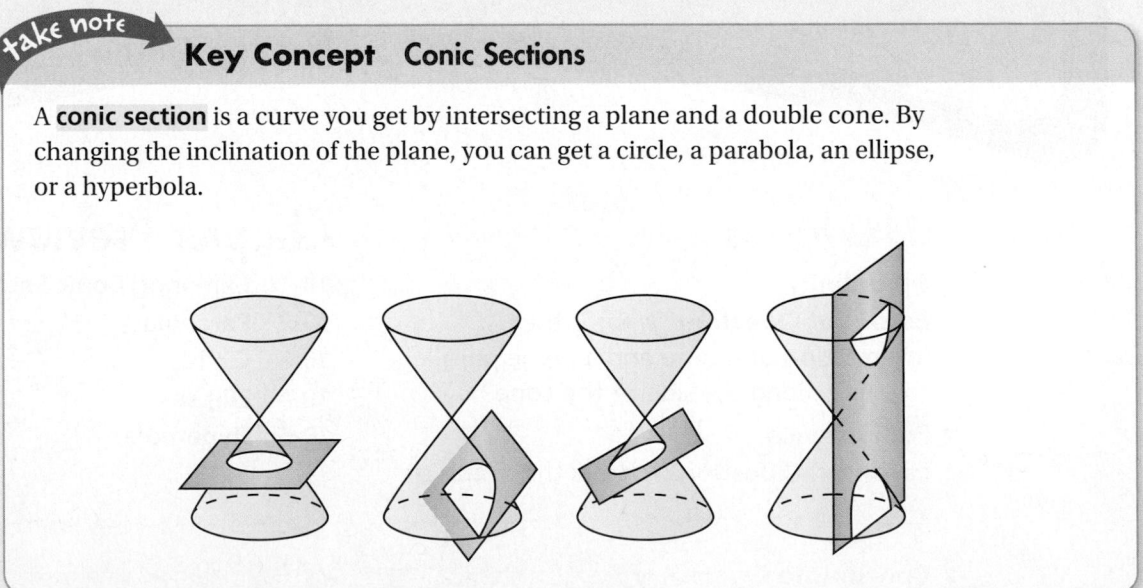

You can use lines of symmetry to graph a conic section.

 Problem 1 Graphing a Circle

What is the graph of $x^2 + y^2 = 25$? What are its lines of symmetry? What are the domain and range?

Know	Need	Plan
An equation	The lines of symmetry of the graph, the domain and range of the relation	• Plot points and connect them with a smooth curve. • Look for lines of symmetry on the graph. • Determine the domain and range.

Think

Can you find values of *x* and *y* that satisfy the equation?
Yes; find the *x*- and *y*-intercepts. Then look for other values of *x* and *y* that make the calculations easy.

Make a table of values. Plot the points and connect them with a smooth curve.

x	y
−5	0
−4	±3
−3	±4
0	±5
3	±4
4	±3
5	0

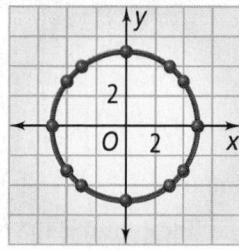

The graph is a circle with radius 5. Its center is the origin.
Every line through the center is a line of symmetry.

The domain is the set of real numbers x with $-5 \le x \le 5$.
The range is the set of real numbers y with $-5 \le y \le 5$.

 Got It? **1. a.** What is the graph of $x^2 + y^2 = 9$? What are its lines of symmetry? What are the domain and range?

   b. Reasoning In Problem 1, why is there no point on the graph with x-coordinate 6?

Its many lines of symmetry make a circle a special kind of an *ellipse*. In general, an ellipse has only two lines of symmetry.

 Problem 2 Graphing an Ellipse

Think

What values should you substitute for *x*? Substitute both positive and negative values for *x*.

What is the graph of $9x^2 + 16y^2 = 144$? What are its lines of symmetry? What are the domain and range?

Step 1 Make a table of values. Plot the points and connect them with a smooth curve.

x	y
−4	0
−3	±2
0	±3
3	±2
4	0

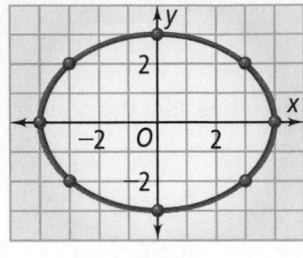

Step 2 Identify lines of symmetry.

The graph is an ellipse. The center is the origin.
The ellipse has two lines of symmetry: the *x*-axis and the *y*-axis.

Step 3 Identify the domain and range.

The domain is the set of real numbers *x* with $-4 \leq x \leq 4$.
The range is the set of real numbers *y* with $-3 \leq y \leq 3$.

 Got It? **2.** What is the graph of $2x^2 + y^2 = 18$? What are its lines of symmetry? What are the domain and range?

You are probably familiar with the conic sections explored in Problems 1 and 2, the circle and the ellipse. You should also recall the parabola from your work with quadratic functions in Chapter 4. You probably have not encountered the last conic section, the hyperbola. It is unique because it consists of two separate curves called branches.

Hint

You will learn more about hyperbolas in Lesson 10-5.

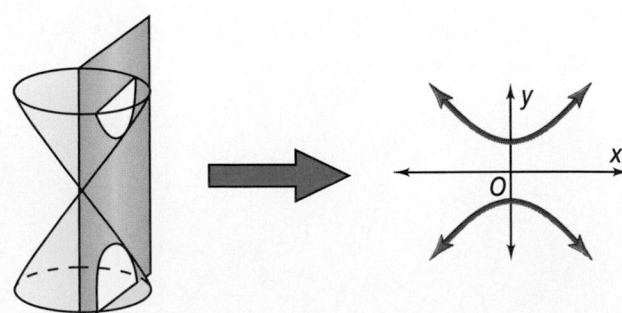

Problem 3 Graphing a Hyperbola

What is the graph of $x^2 - y^2 = 9$? What are its lines of symmetry? What are the domain and range?

Make a table of values.

x	−5	−4	−3	−2	−1	0	1	2	3	4	5
y	±4	±2.6	0	—	—	—	—	—	0	±2.6	±4

Think

How will you know which points to connect?
Plot enough points so you see a pattern. Only connect points if you know that the points between them satisfy the equation.

Plot the points and connect them with smooth curves.

The graph is a hyperbola that consists of two branches. Its center is the origin. It has two lines of symmetry: the x-axis and the y-axis.

The domain is the set of real numbers x with $x \leq -3$ or $x \geq 3$. The range is the set of real numbers.

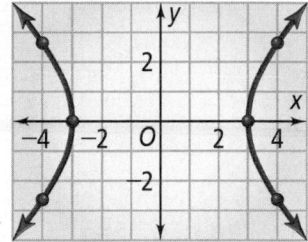

 Got It? **3.** What is the graph of $x^2 - y^2 = 16$? What are its lines of symmetry? What are the domain and range?

Focus Question What is a conic section?

Answer A conic section is a curve that is formed by the intersection of a plane and a double cone. The four types of conic sections are circles, parabolas, ellipses, and hyperbolas.

 Lesson Check

Do you know HOW?

Graph each equation. Find the lines of symmetry, the domain, and the range.

1. $x^2 + 4y^2 = 36$

2. $4x^2 - 9y^2 = 36$

Identify the domain and range.

3.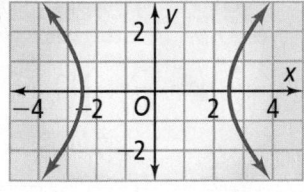

4.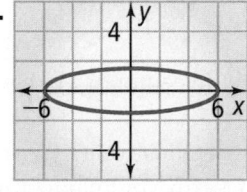

Do you UNDERSTAND?

5. Vocabulary Identify the type of conic section graphed.

a.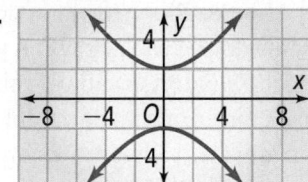

b.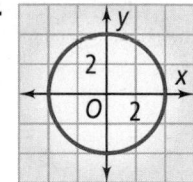

6. Compare and Contrast How is the domain of an ellipse different from the domain of a hyperbola?

Practice and Problem-Solving Exercises

 **Practice**

Graph each equation. Identify the conic section and describe the graph and its lines of symmetry. Then find the domain and range.

◀ See Problems 1, 2, and 3.

 **Guided Practice**

7. $3y^2 - x^2 = 25$

To start, make a table of values.

x	y
−3	±3.37
−2	±3.11
−1	±2.94
0	±2.89
1	±2.94
2	±3.11
3	±3.37

8. $2x^2 + y^2 = 36$

9. $x^2 + y^2 = 16$

10. $3y^2 - x^2 = 9$

11. $4x^2 + 25y^2 = 100$

12. $x^2 + y^2 = 49$

13. $x^2 - y^2 + 1 = 0$

14. $x^2 - 2y^2 = 4$

15. $6x^2 + 6y^2 = 600$

16. $x^2 + y^2 - 4 = 0$

17. $6x^2 + 24y^2 - 96 = 0$

18. $4x^2 + 4y^2 - 20 = 0$

19. $x^2 + 9y^2 = 1$

B **Apply**

Graph each equation. Describe the graph and its lines of symmetry. Then find the domain and range.

20. $9x^2 - y^2 = 144$

21. $11x^2 + 11y^2 = 44$

22. $-8x^2 + 32y^2 - 128 = 0$

23. $25x^2 + 16y^2 - 320 = 0$

24. Think About a Plan The light emitted from a lamp with a shade forms a shadow on the wall. How can you turn the lamp in relation to the wall so that the shadow cast by the shade forms a parabola and a circle?
- How can a drawing or model help you solve this problem?
- Can you form a hyperbola and an ellipse? If so, explain how.

25. a. Writing Describe the relationship between the center of a circle and the axes of symmetry of the circle.
b. Make a Conjecture Where is the center of an ellipse or a hyperbola located in relation to the axes of symmetry? Verify your conjecture with examples.

Graph each circle with the given radius or diameter so that the center is at the origin. Then write the equation for each graph.

26. radius 6

27. radius $\frac{1}{2}$

28. diameter 8

29. diameter 2.5

Mental Math Each given point is on the graph of the given equation. Use symmetry to find at least one more point on the graph.

30. $(2, -4)$, $y^2 = 8x$

31. $(-\sqrt{2}, 1)$, $x^2 + y^2 = 3$

32. $(2, 2\sqrt{2})$, $x^2 + 4y^2 = 36$

33. $(-2, 0)$, $9x^2 + 9y^2 - 36 = 0$

34. $(-3, -\sqrt{51})$, $6y^2 - 9x^2 - 225 = 0$

35. $(0, \sqrt{7})$, $x^2 + 2y^2 = 14$

36. Sound An airplane flying faster than the speed of sound creates a cone-shaped pressure disturbance in the air. This is heard by people on the ground as a sonic boom. What is the shape of the path on the ground?

37. Open-Ended Describe any other figures you can see that can be formed by the intersection of a plane and another shape, such as a sphere.

Standardized Test Prep

SAT/ACT

38. Which expression can be simplified to $\frac{x-1}{x-3}$?

Ⓐ $\frac{x^2 - x - 6}{x^2 - x - 2}$

Ⓑ $\frac{x^2 - 2x + 1}{x^2 + 2x - 3}$

Ⓒ $\frac{x^2 - 3x - 4}{x^2 - 7x + 12}$

Ⓓ $\frac{x^2 - 4x + 3}{x^2 - 6x + 9}$

39. Which product is NOT equal to 13?

Ⓕ $(4 + \sqrt{3})(4 - \sqrt{3})$

Ⓗ $(6 + \sqrt{23})(6 - \sqrt{23})$

Ⓖ $(5 - 2\sqrt{3})(5 + 2\sqrt{3})$

Ⓘ $(7 - \sqrt{6})(7 + \sqrt{6})$

40. Which function represents exponential growth?

Ⓐ $y = 35x^{1.35}$

Ⓑ $y = 35 \cdot (0.35)^x$

Ⓒ $y = 35 \cdot (1.35)^x$

Ⓓ $y = 35 \div (1.35)^x$

Short Response

41. What is an explicit formula for the sequence 4, 9, 16, 25, 36, ...? What is the ninth term in this sequence?

Mixed Review

Determine whether each geometric series *diverges* or *converges*. If the series converges, state the sum.

◆ See Lesson 9-5.

42. $1 + 3 + 9 + \cdots$

43. $1 + \frac{4}{3} + \frac{16}{9} + \cdots$

44. $\frac{1}{2} + \frac{1}{4} + \frac{1}{8} + \ldots$

Expand each binomial.

◆ See Lesson 5-7.

45. $(x - y)^3$

46. $(p + q)^6$

47. $(x - 2)^4$

Get Ready! To prepare for Lesson 10-2, do Exercises 48–50.

Make a table of values for each equation. Then graph the equation.

◆ See Lesson 2-7.

48. $y = |x| + 3$

49. $y = |x - 2|$

50. $y = |x + 1| - 4$

Concept Byte

For Use With Lesson 10-1

Graphing Conic Sections

You can use your graphing calculator to graph relations that are not functions.

Example

Graph the ellipse $\frac{x^2}{16} + \frac{y^2}{9} = 1$.

Step 1 Solve the equation for y.

$$\frac{x^2}{16} + \frac{y^2}{9} = 1$$

$$\frac{y^2}{9} = 1 - \frac{x^2}{16}$$

$$y^2 = 9\left(1 - \frac{x^2}{16}\right)$$

$$y = \pm 3\sqrt{1 - \frac{x^2}{16}}$$

Step 2 Enter the equations as Y_1 and Y_2.

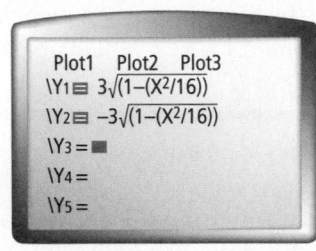

Plot1 Plot2 Plot3
\Y1 = 3√(1−(X²/16))
\Y2 = −3√(1−(X²/16))
\Y3 = ■
\Y4 =
\Y5 =

Step 3 Select a square window.

ZOOM MEMORY
1: ZBOX
2: Zoom In
3: Zoom Out
4: ZDecimal
5: ZSquare
6: ZStandard
7↓ZTrig

Step 4 Graph.

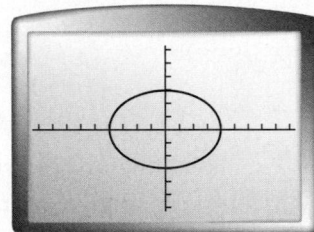

Exercises

Graph each conic section.

1. $x^2 + y^2 = 25$

2. $4x^2 + y^2 = 16$

3. $9x^2 - 16y^2 = 144$

4. $x^2 - y^2 = 3$

5. $\frac{x^2}{4} - \frac{y^2}{9} = 1$

6. $x^2 + \frac{y^2}{4} = 16$

7. a. Graph $y = \sqrt{\frac{81}{4} - x^2}$ and $y = -\sqrt{\frac{81}{4} - x^2}$.
   b. Estimate the x-intercepts and find the y-intercepts.
   c. Adjust the window to $-9.3 \le x \le 9.5$. What are the x-intercepts?
   d. What conic section does the graph represent?

Graph each conic section. Find the x- and y-intercepts.

8. $4x^2 + y^2 = 25$

9. $x^2 + y^2 = 30$

10. $9x^2 - 4y^2 = 72$

11. Reasoning Which conic sections can you graph using only one equation? Explain.

10-2 Parabolas

Objective To write the equation of a parabola and to graph parabolas

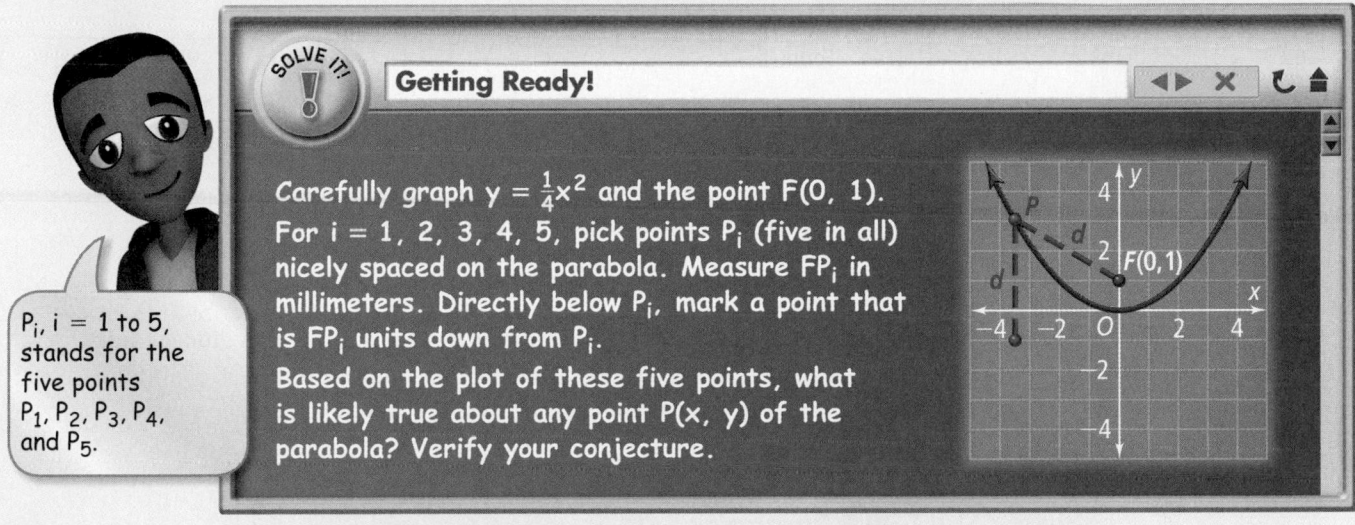

Getting Ready!

Carefully graph $y = \frac{1}{4}x^2$ and the point $F(0, 1)$. For $i = 1, 2, 3, 4, 5$, pick points P_i (five in all) nicely spaced on the parabola. Measure FP_i in millimeters. Directly below P_i, mark a point that is FP_i units down from P_i.

Based on the plot of these five points, what is likely true about any point $P(x, y)$ of the parabola? Verify your conjecture.

P_i, $i = 1$ to 5, stands for the five points $P_1, P_2, P_3, P_4,$ and P_5.

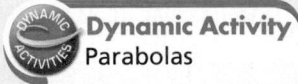

Dynamic Activity Parabolas

From Chapter 4, you know that a parabola has a vertex and an axis of symmetry. A parabola also has other special characteristics.

Focus Question What are the focus and directrix of a parabola?

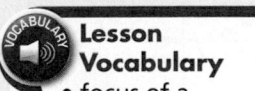

Lesson Vocabulary
• focus of a parabola
• directrix
• focal length

Key Concept Parabola

Definition

A parabola is the set of all points in a plane that are the same distance from a fixed line and a fixed point not on the line.

The fixed point is called the **focus of a parabola**.

The fixed line is called the **directrix**.

The distance between the vertex and the focus is the **focal length** of the parabola.

Graph

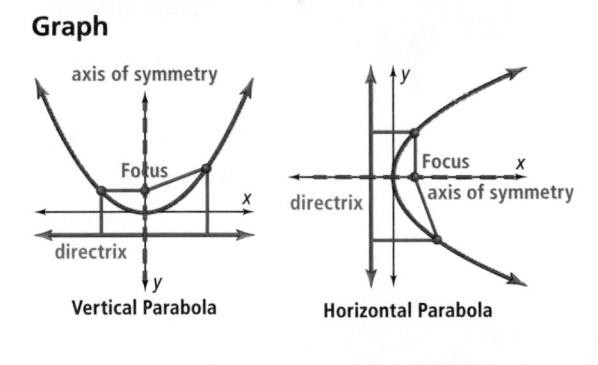

In this lesson, you will consider vertical parabolas (each of which has a vertical axis of symmetry and a horizontal directrix) and horizontal parabolas (each of which has a horizontal axis of symmetry and a vertical directrix).

You can find the equation of a vertical parabola with its vertex at the origin by using the geometric definition. If the focus is the point $(0, c)$, the directrix is the line with equation $y = -c$.

Here's Why It Works Any point (x, y) on the parabola must be equidistant from the focus and the directrix. Use the Distance Formula.

Hint

The distance between two points (x_1, y_1) and (x_2, y_2) is $\sqrt{(x_2 - x_1)^2 + (y_2 - y_1)^2}$.

Use the Distance Formula.	$\sqrt{(x - 0)^2 + (y - c)^2} = \sqrt{(x - x)^2 + (y - (-c))^2}$
Square each side.	$x^2 + (y - c)^2 = 0^2 + (y + c)^2$
Expand.	$x^2 + y^2 - 2cy + c^2 = y^2 + 2cy + c^2$
Subtract y^2 and c^2 from each side.	$x^2 - 2cy = 2cy$
Add $2cy$ to each side.	$x^2 = 4cy$
Write in standard quadratic form.	$y = \frac{1}{4c}x^2$

Note that the equation has the expected quadratic form $y = ax^2$ for a vertical parabola with vertex at $(0, 0)$. The coefficient $a = \frac{1}{4c}$ determines both the focus $(0, c)$ and the directrix $y = -c$. This is the key to shifting between the algebraic and geometric representations of a parabola.

Problem 1 **Parabolas with Equation $y = ax^2$**

A **What is an equation of the parabola with vertex at the origin and focus $(0, 2)$?**

The focus is directly above the vertex. This is a vertical parabola with vertex at the origin. The focus is $(0, c)$, so $c = 2$.

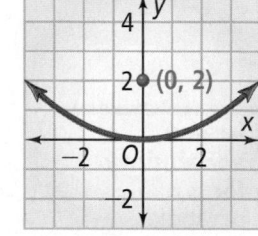

Write the standard form.	$y = \frac{1}{4c}x^2$
Substitute 2 for c.	$= \frac{1}{4(2)}x^2$
Simplify.	$= \frac{1}{8}x^2$

Plan

How can you tell if this is a vertical or a horizontal parabola?
The focus and the vertex are on the axis of symmetry. They both lie on the y-axis so the parabola is vertical.

B **What are the vertex, focus, and directrix of the parabola with equation $y = -\frac{1}{12}x^2$?**

This is a vertical parabola. The vertex is at the origin and $a = -\frac{1}{12}$. Find c.

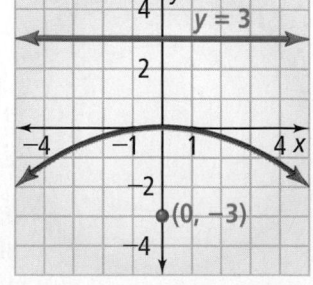

Write the equation relating a and c.	$a = \frac{1}{4c}$
Substitute $-\frac{1}{12}$ for a.	$-\frac{1}{12} = \frac{1}{4c}$
Write the cross products.	$4c = -12$
Divide each side by 4.	$c = -3$

Think

What does the sign of a tell you about the graph?
Since a is negative, the parabola opens downward.

Since $c = -3$ and the vertex is at the origin, you can conclude that the focus is the point $(0, -3)$ and the directrix is the line with equation $y = 3$.

Got It? **1. a.** What is an equation of the parabola with vertex $(0, 0)$ and focus $(0, -1.5)$?

b. What are the focus and directrix of the parabola with equation $y = \frac{x^2}{4}$?

c. Reasoning How does the distance of the focus from the vertex affect the shape of a parabola?

The quadratic equation $x = ay^2$ determines a *horizontal parabola* with vertex at $(0, 0)$. The coefficient $a = \frac{1}{4c}$ determines both the focus $(c, 0)$ and the directrix $x = -c$.

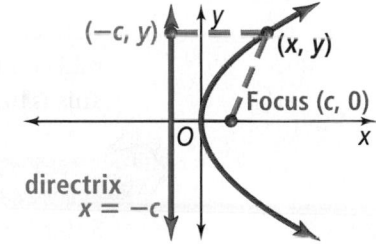

Problem 2 **Parabolas with Equation $x = ay^2$**

A What is an equation of a parabola with vertex at the origin and directrix $x = 1.25$?

Plan

How can you tell if this is a vertical or a horizontal parabola?
The directrix is parallel to the y-axis, so this is a horizontal parabola.

The directrix lies directly to the right of the vertex. The parabola is horizontal. The directrix has equation $x = -c$, so $c = -1.25$.

Write the general equation of a horizontal parabola. $x = \frac{1}{4c}y^2$

Substitute -1.25 for c. $= \frac{1}{4(-1.25)}y^2$

Simplify. $= -\frac{1}{5}y^2$

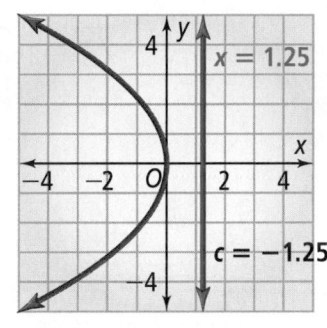

Check for Reasonableness

The graph is reasonable since it opens in the negative direction and $a < 0$.

B What are the vertex, focus, and directrix of the parabola with equation $x = 0.75y^2$?

Think

What does the sign of a tell you about the graph?
Since a is positive, the parabola opens to the right.

This is a horizontal parabola. The vertex is at the origin and $a = 0.75$. Find c.

Write the equation relating a and c. $a = \frac{1}{4c}$

Substitute $0.75 = \frac{3}{4}$ for a. $\frac{3}{4} = \frac{1}{4c}$

Write the cross products. $12c = 4$

Divide each side by 12 and simplify. $c = \frac{4}{12} = \frac{1}{3}$

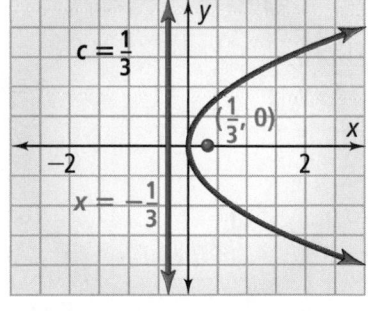

Since $c = \frac{1}{3}$ and the vertex is at the origin, you can conclude that the focus is the point $\left(\frac{1}{3}, 0\right)$ and the directrix is the line with equation $x = -\frac{1}{3}$.

 Got It? **2. a.** What is an equation of the parabola with vertex at the origin and directrix $x = -\frac{5}{2}$?

b. What are the vertex, focus, and directrix of the parabola with equation $x = -4y^2$?

The geometry of a parabola implies a very important reflective property that gives real-world meaning to the word "focus."

As the diagram of a *parabolic reflector* shows, lines from the focus reflect off the parabola along lines parallel to the axis of symmetry. This is how a flashlight works.

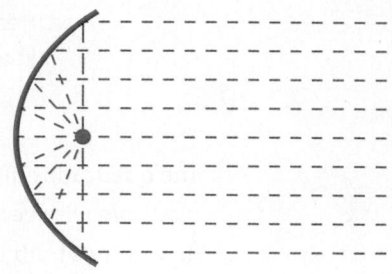

Conversely, lines parallel to the axis of symmetry reflect off the parabola directly into the focus. This is how a satellite dish works.

 Problem 3 Using Parabolas to Solve Problems

Solar Reflector The parabolic solar reflector pictured has a depth of 2 feet at the center. How far from the vertex is the focus? (What is the focal length?)

Think

What is the shape of the solar reflector?
A cross section is part of a parabola and is 8 ft across.

Graph the parabola in a coordinate system with vertex $(0, 0)$.
The vertical parabola has the form $y = \frac{1}{4c}x^2$.
Substitute one of the points: $(4, 2)$.

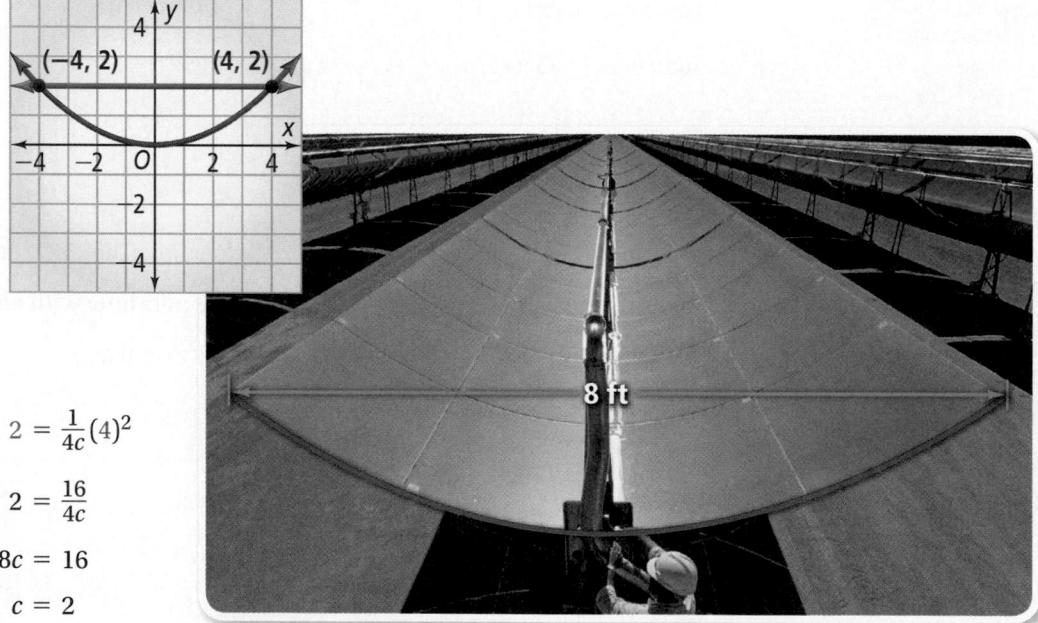

$2 = \frac{1}{4c}(4)^2$

$2 = \frac{16}{4c}$

$8c = 16$

$c = 2$

Therefore, the focus is at $(0, 2)$, 2 ft from the vertex.
The focal length is 2 ft.

 Got It? **3.** The mirrored reflector of a flashlight is 8 cm across and 4 cm deep. How far from the vertex should the light bulb be positioned?

In Chapter 4, you studied how to translate a parabola with vertex $(0, 0)$ to one with vertex (h, k). For such a translation, all of the other features—axis of symmetry, focus, and directrix—translate along with the parabola and its vertex.

take note

Key Concept Transformations of a Parabola

Vertical Parabola	Vertex (0, 0)	Vertex (h, k)
Equation	$y = \frac{1}{4c}x^2$	$y = \frac{1}{4c}(x - h)^2 + k$
Focus	$(0, c)$	$(h, k + c)$
Directrix	$y = -c$	$y = k - c$

Horizontal Parabola	Vertex (0, 0)	Vertex (h, k)
Equation	$x = \frac{1}{4c}y^2$	$x = \frac{1}{4c}(y - k)^2 + h$
Focus	$(c, 0)$	$(h + c, k)$
Directrix	$x = -c$	$x = h - c$

ONLINE PROBLEMS

Problem 4 Analyzing a Parabola

What are the vertex, focus, and directrix of the parabola with equation $y = x^2 - 4x + 8$?

Know
The equation of the parabola

Need
- vertex
- focus
- directrix

Plan
- Find c, h, and k.
- Use these values to find the vertex, focus, and directrix.

First, complete the square to get the equation in vertex form.

Think

How can you change the equation to an equivalent form?
Subtract the same value outside the parentheses that you added inside the parentheses.

Write the original equation.	$y = x^2 - 4x + 8$
Add $\left(\frac{1}{2} \cdot -4\right)^2$ inside parentheses; subtract it outside.	$y = (x^2 - 4x + 4) + 8 - 4$
Factor and simplify.	$y = (x - 2)^2 + 4$

Next, compare the resulting equation to the vertex form of a vertical parabola.

Write the general form.	$y = \frac{1}{4c}(x - h)^2 + k$
Write the vertex form.	$y = 1 \cdot (x - 2)^2 + 4$

Note that, in this case, $\frac{1}{4c} = 1$, so $c = 0.25$.

The vertex (h, k) is $(2, 4)$. The focus $(h, k + c)$ is $(2, 4.25)$.
The directrix $y = k - c$ is $y = 3.75$.

Hint

To complete the square for $x^2 + bx$, you need to find the value of $\left(\frac{b}{2}\right)^2$.

✓ **Got It? 4.** What are the vertex, focus, and directrix of the parabola with equation $y = x^2 + 8x + 18$?

Problem 5 **Writing an Equation of a Parabola**

Multiple Choice Which is an equation of the parabola with vertex $(3, 7)$ and focus $(5, 7)$?

Ⓐ $x = \frac{1}{4}(y - 7)^2 + 3$

Ⓒ $x = \frac{1}{8}(y - 7)^2 + 3$

Ⓑ $y = \frac{1}{8}(x - 7)^2 + 3$

Ⓓ $x = \frac{1}{8}(y + 7)^2 - 3$

Plan

How do you determine which equation to use?
Use the focus and the vertex to determine the orientation of the parabola.

The focus is to the right of the vertex, so the parabola is horizontal.
Use the equation. $x = \frac{1}{4c}(y - k)^2 + h$.

The vertex (h, k) is $(3, 7)$ and the focus $(h + c, k)$ is $(5, 7)$.
So, $h = 3$, $k = 7$, and $c = 2$.

Substitute into the general equation and simplify.

$$x = \frac{1}{4(2)}(y - 7)^2 + 3$$

$$= \frac{1}{8}(y - 7)^2 + 3$$

The correct answer is C.

 Got It? **5.** What is an equation of the parabola with vertex $(1, 4)$ and focus $(1, 6)$?

Focus Question What are the focus and directrix of a parabola?

Answer Each point of a parabola is equidistant from a fixed point called the focus and a fixed line (not containing the focus) called the directrix. Use the focus and directrix to write the equation of a parabola given its graph.

 Lesson Check

Do you know HOW?

Write an equation of a parabola with the given information.

1. vertex $(0, 0)$, focus $\left(0, \frac{1}{2}\right)$

2. vertex $(3, 2)$, focus $(4, 2)$

Find the vertex, focus, and the directrix of each parabola.

3. $x = \frac{1}{16}y^2$

4. $y = x^2 + 6x + 5$

Do you UNDERSTAND?

5. Vocabulary If the vertex of a parabola is 3 units from the focus, how far is the focus from the directrix?

6. Error Analysis The vertex of a parabola is at the origin, one unit away from the focus. A student concludes that the equation is $y = \frac{1}{4}x^2$. Identify at least two ways in which the student's equation might be in error.

Practice and Problem-Solving Exercises

A **Practice**

Write an equation of a parabola with vertex at the origin and the given focus. 🔵 **See Problem 1.**

7. focus at $(6, 0)$ **8.** focus at $(0, -4)$ **9.** focus at $(-1, 0)$

Identify the vertex, the focus, and the directrix of the parabola with the given equation. Then sketch the graph of the parabola. 🔵 **See Problems 1 and 2.**

Guided Practice

10. $y = -\frac{1}{8}x^2$

To start, identify the orientation and vertex of the parabola.

This is a vertical parabola with vertex at $(0, 0)$.

11. $y = 4x^2$ **12.** $x = y^2$ **13.** $x = \frac{1}{2}y^2$

Write an equation of a parabola with vertex at the origin and the given directrix. 🔵 **See Problem 2.**

14. directrix $x = -3$ **15.** directrix $y = 5$ **16.** directrix $x = 9$

17. Optics A cross section of a flashlight reflector is a parabola. The bulb is located at the focus. Suppose the bulb is located $\frac{1}{4}$ in. from the vertex of the reflector. Model a cross section of the reflector by writing an equation of a parabola that opens upward and has its vertex at the origin. What is an advantage of this parabolic design? 🔵 **See Problem 3.**

Identify the vertex, the focus, and the directrix of the parabola with the given equation. Then sketch the graph of the parabola. 🔵 **See Problem 4.**

Guided Practice

18. $y = x^2 + 4x + 3$

To start, complete the square by adding and subtracting $\left(\frac{b}{2}\right)^2 = \left(\frac{4}{2}\right)^2 = 4$.

$y = (x^2 + 4x + 4) + 3 - 4$

19. $y = x^2 - 6x + 11$ **20.** $y = x^2 - 2x - 4$ **21.** $y = 2x^2 + 4x - 2$

Write an equation of a parabola with the given vertex and focus. 🔵 **See Problem 5.**

22. vertex $(4, 1)$; focus $(6, 1)$ **23.** vertex $(0, 3)$; focus $(-8, 3)$

24. vertex $(-5, 4)$; focus $(-5, 0)$ **25.** vertex $(7, 2)$; focus $(7, -2)$

B **Apply**

26. Think About a Plan In some solar collectors, a mirror with a parabolic cross section is used to concentrate sunlight on a pipe, which is located at the focus of the mirror as shown in the diagram. What is an equation of the parabola that models the cross section of the mirror?

- What information can you get from the diagram?
- What information do you need to be able to write an equation that models the cross section of the mirror?

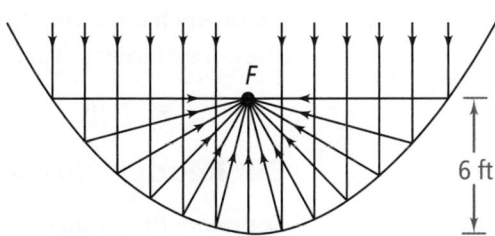

27. Sound Broadcasters use a parabolic microphone on football sidelines to pick up field audio for broadcasting purposes. A certain parabolic microphone has a reflector dish with a diameter of 28 inches and a depth of 14 inches. If the receiver of the microphone is located at the focus of the reflector dish, how far from the vertex should the receiver be positioned?

Identify the vertex, the focus, and the directrix of a parabola with each equation. Then sketch a graph of the parabola with the given equation.

28. $y^2 - 25x = 0$

29. $x^2 = -4y$

30. $(x - 2)^2 = 4y$

31. $-8x = y^2$

32. $y^2 - 6x = 18$

33. $x^2 + 24y - 8x = -16$

Write an equation of a parabola with vertex at (1, 1) and the given information.

34. directrix $y = -\frac{1}{2}$

35. directrix $x = \frac{3}{2}$

36. focus at $(1,0)$

37. Writing Explain how to find the distance from the focus to the directrix of the parabola $x = 2y^2$.

Standardized Test Prep

SAT/ACT

38. What is the equation of a parabola with vertex at the origin and focus at $\left(0, \frac{5}{2}\right)$?

   Ⓐ $x = -\frac{1}{10}y^2$ Ⓑ $x = \frac{1}{10}y^2$ Ⓒ $x = -\frac{1}{10}x^2$ Ⓓ $y = \frac{1}{10}x^2$

39. Use the information in the graph to find the equation for the graph.

   Ⓕ $y^2 + 6x = 0$ Ⓗ $x^2 + 6y = 0$

   Ⓖ $y^2 - 6x = 0$ Ⓘ $x^2 - 6y = 0$

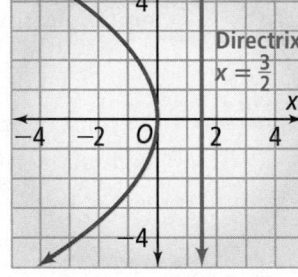

40. What is the fifth term in the expansion of $(a - 5b)^7$?

   Ⓐ $35a^3b^4$ Ⓒ $625a^3b^4$

   Ⓑ $-175a^3b^4$ Ⓓ $21{,}875a^3b^4$

Extended Response

41. Use the properties of logarithms to write log 12 in four different ways. Name each property you use.

Mixed Review

Graph each equation. Identify the conic section and describe the graph and its lines of symmetry. Then find the domain and range.

               ◀ See Lesson 10-1.

42. $x^2 + y^2 = 64$

43. $x^2 + 9y^2 = 9$

44. $4x^2 - 9y^2 = 36$

Get Ready! To prepare for Lesson 10-3, do Exercises 45–47.

Complete the square.

               ◀ See Lesson 4-6.

45. $x^2 - 2x + \blacksquare$

46. $x^2 + 10x + \blacksquare$

47. $x^2 - 6x + \blacksquare$

10-3 Circles

Objectives To write and graph the equation of a circle
To find the center and radius of a circle and use them to graph the circle

You've seen these shapes before.

SOLVE IT!

Getting Ready!

In your backyard, there is a square-shaped bare patch in the middle of the grass. You want to put a circular pond in that patch. You also want a circular feeder pond at its upper right as shown in the drawing. What is the radius of the pond? What is the radius of the feeder pond? Explain.

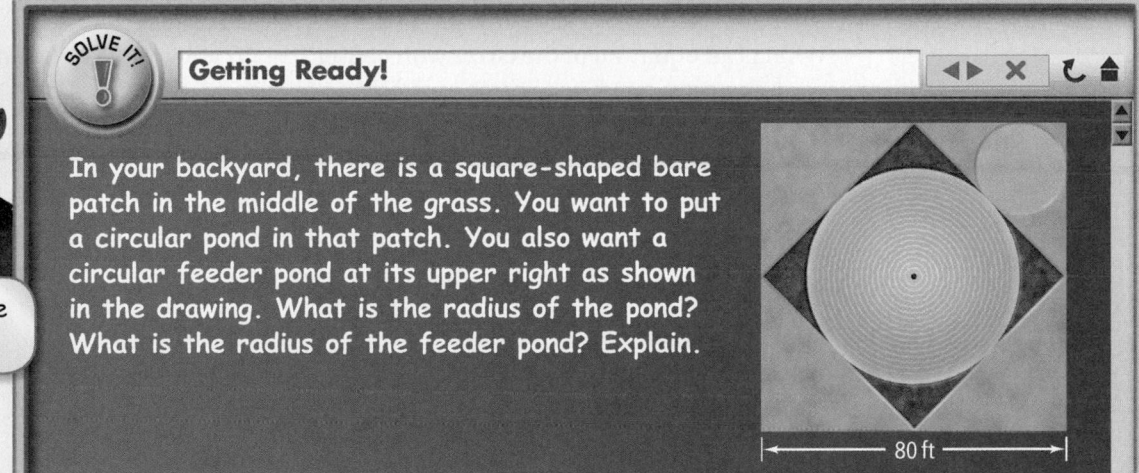

80 ft

Dynamic Activity
Circles in the Coordinate Plane

Lesson Vocabulary
• circle
• center of a circle
• radius
• standard form of an equation of a circle

A **circle** is the set of all points in a plane that are a distance r from a given point, the **center of a circle**. The distance r is the **radius** of the circle. The use of *distance* in these definitions makes the Distance Formula

$d = \sqrt{(x_2 - x_1)^2 + (y_2 - y_1)^2}$ a useful tool for describing a circle in the coordinate plane.

circle
center

Focus Question How is the equation of a circle related to its graph?

An equation of a circle with center $(0, 0)$ and radius r in the coordinate plane is $x^2 + y^2 = r^2$. Not every circle has its center at the origin. Suppose a circle with radius r has center (h, k). Then r is the distance from (h, k) to any point (x, y) on the circle.

| Use the Distance Formula. | $r = \sqrt{(x - h)^2 + (y - k)^2}$ |
| Square each side. | $r^2 = (x - h)^2 + (y - k)^2$ |

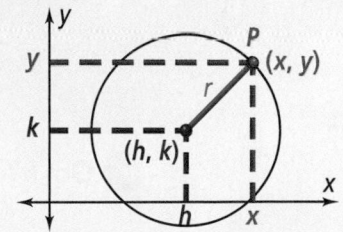

Key Concept   Standard Form of an Equation of a Circle

The **standard form of an equation of a circle** with center (h, k) and radius r is $(x - h)^2 + (y - k)^2 = r^2$.

You can use the center and the radius of a circle to write an equation for the circle.

 Problem 1 **Writing an Equation of a Circle**

What is an equation of the circle with center $(-4, 3)$ and radius 4? Check your answer.

Plan

How do you know which equation to use?
Since this circle is not centered at the origin, use the standard form equation.

Use the standard form. $(x - h)^2 + (y - k)^2 = r^2$

Substitute -4 for h, 3 for k, and 4 for r. $(x - (-4))^2 + (y - 3)^2 = 4^2$

Simplify. $(x + 4)^2 + (y - 3)^2 = 16$

An equation of the circle is $(x + 4)^2 + (y - 3)^2 = 16$.

Check   Solve the equation for y.

Write the equation. $(x + 4)^2 + (y - 3)^2 = 16$

Subtract $(x + 4)^2$ from each side. $(y - 3)^2 = 16 - (x + 4)^2$

Find the square root of each side. $y - 3 = \pm\sqrt{16 - (x + 4)^2}$

Add 3 to each side. $y = \pm\sqrt{16 - (x + 4)^2} + 3$

Enter both functions into your graphing calculator.

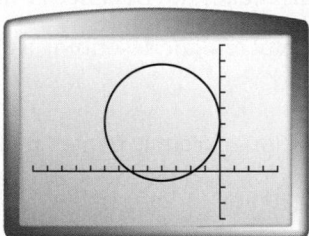

The graph shows a circle with center $(-4, 3)$ and radius 4. ✔

 Got It?   **1.** What is an equation of the circle with center $(5, -2)$ and radius 8? Check your answer.

You can use the standard form of an equation of a circle to graph a circle.

 Problem 2 **Using Translations to Write an Equation**

What is an equation for the translation of $x^2 + y^2 = 9$ by 4 units left and 3 units up? Draw the graph.

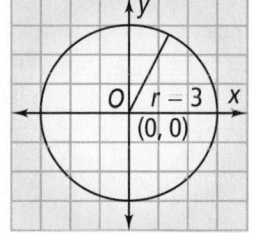

Know

An equation that is translated 4 units left and 3 units up

Need

The equation and graph of the translation

Plan

• Use the standard form to write the equation of the translation.
• Graph the translation.

Step 1 Write the equation of the translation.

Write the original equation.	$x^2 + y^2 = 9$
Translate 4 units left and 3 units up.	$(x - (-4))^2 + (y - 3)^2 = 9$
Simplify.	$(x + 4)^2 + (y - 3)^2 = 3^2$

Think

How does the translation help you draw the graph?
Use the translation to determine the new center coordinates.

Step 2 Graph the equation of the translation.

The radius is 3.

 Got It? 2. What is an equation for each translation? Draw the graph.
  a. $x^2 + y^2 = 1$; left 5 units and down 3 units
  b. $x^2 + y^2 = 9$; right 2 units and up 3 units

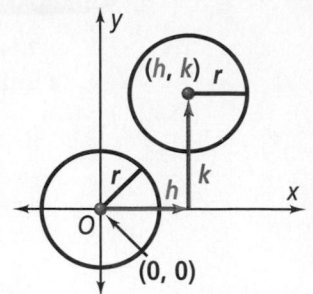

Key Concept Transforming a Circle

You can use the parameter r to stretch or shrink the unit circle $x^2 + y^2 = 1$ to the circle $x^2 + y^2 = r^2$ with radius r.

You can use the parameters h and k to translate the circle $x^2 + y^2 = r^2$ with center $(0, 0)$ to the circle $(x - h)^2 + (y - k)^2 = r^2$ with center (h, k).

Problem 3 Using a Graph to Write an Equation

Multiple Choice Which equation models the circular irrigation field?

Ⓐ $(x - 450)^2 + (y - 500)^2 = 160{,}000$

Ⓒ $(x - 450)^2 + (y - 500)^2 = 400$

Ⓑ $(x + 500)^2 + (y + 450)^2 = 160{,}000$

Ⓓ $(x + 450)^2 + (y + 500)^2 = 400$

According to the photograph, this circular irrigation field has radius 400 and center at the point $(450, 500)$.

Plan

What information do you need to write an equation for the circle?

You need the center and radius of the circle.

Use the standard form. $(x - h)^2 + (y - k)^2 = r^2$

Substitute the values of h, k, and r from the photograph. $(x - 450)^2 + (y - 500)^2 = 400^2$

Simplify. $(x - 450)^2 + (y - 500)^2 = 160{,}000$

The correct answer is A.

✓ **Got It? 3. a.** What is an equation of the circle for a circular irrigation field that has radius 12 and center $(7, -10)$?

b. Reasoning Will the graph of every equation of the form $(x - h)^2 + (y - k)^2 = r^2$, where h, k, and r are real numbers, be a circle? Explain your reasoning.

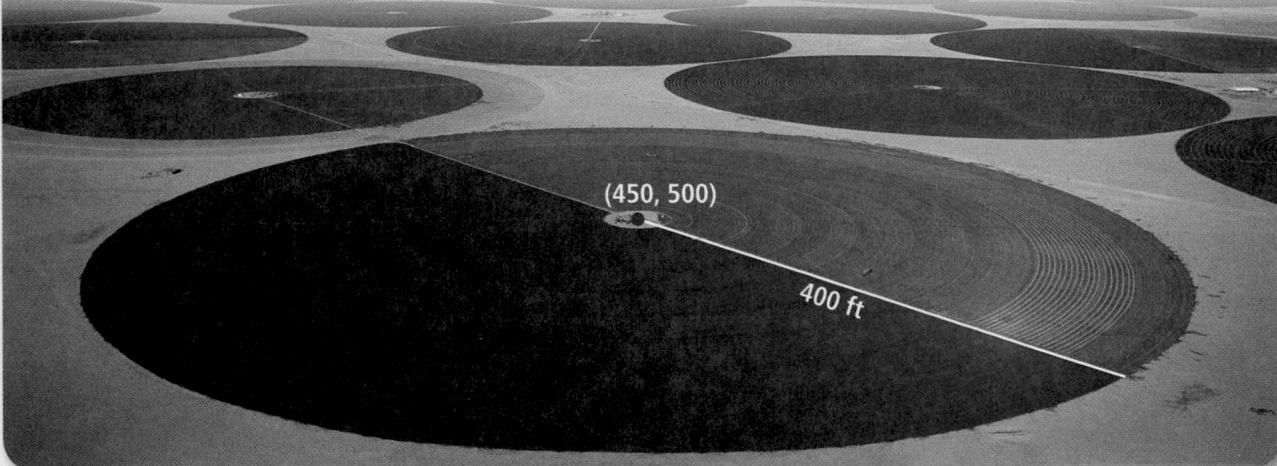

(450, 500)

400 ft

You can find the center and radius of a circle by rewriting the equation in standard form. In some cases, you may need to complete the square.

 Problem 4 Finding the Center and Radius

What are the center and radius of the circle with the given equation?

Plan

What do you need to do to the equation to find the center and radius of the circle?
Write the equation in standard form.

A $(x - 16)^2 + (y + 9)^2 = 144$

Rewrite the equation in standard form. $\quad (x - 16)^2 + (y - (-9))^2 = 12^2$

Identify h, k, and r. $\qquad\qquad h = 16 \quad k = -9 \quad r = 12$

The center of the circle is $(16, -9)$. The radius is 12.

B $x^2 + y^2 + 8x - 10y = 8$

Set up to complete the squares. $\qquad (x^2 + 8x) + (y^2 - 10y) = 8$

Complete the squares and balance the equation. $\qquad (x^2 + 8x + 16) + (y^2 - 10y + 25) = 8 + 16 + 25$

Simplify. $\qquad\qquad\qquad\qquad (x + 4)^2 + (y - 5)^2 = 49$

Rewrite in standard form. $\qquad\qquad (x - (-4))^2 + (y - 5)^2 = 7^2$

Identify h, k, and r. $\qquad\qquad h = -4 \quad k = 5 \quad r = 7$

The center of the circle is $(-4, 5)$. The radius is 7.

Got It? **4.** What are the center and radius of the circle with the given equation?
a. $(x + 8)^2 + (y + 3)^2 = 121$ **b.** $x^2 + y^2 - 6x + 14y = 8$

You can use the center and the radius to graph a circle.

 Problem 5 Graphing a Circle Using Center and Radius

Plan

What information do you need to graph a circle?
You need the center and radius of the circle.

What is the graph of $(x + 1)^2 + (y - 3)^2 = 25$?

Step 1 Identify the center and radius.

Write the original equation. $\quad (x + 1)^2 + (y - 3)^2 = 25$

Rewrite the equation in standard form. $\quad (x - (-1))^2 + (y - 3)^2 = 5^2$

Identify h, k, and r. $\quad h = -1 \quad k = 3 \quad r = 5$

Step 2 Plot the center, $(-1, 3)$.

Step 3 Draw a circle of radius 5.

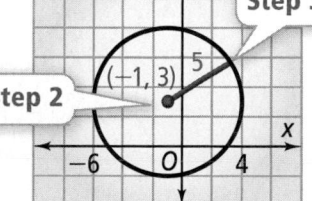

Got It? **5.** What is the graph of $(x - 4)^2 + (y + 2)^2 = 49$?

Focus Question How is the equation of a circle related to its graph?

Answer The standard form of the equation of a circle with center (h, k) and radius r is $(x - h)^2 + (y - k)^2 = r^2$. Use the graph of a circle to write its equation, or use the equation of a circle to draw its graph.

Lesson Check

Do you know HOW?

Use the given information to write an equation of a circle.

1. center at $(-1, -5)$, radius 2

2. center at $(0, 0)$, radius 6

Write an equation for each translation.

3. $x^2 + y^2 = 121$; up 3 units

4. $x^2 + y^2 = 16$; left 5 units and down 3 units

Do you UNDERSTAND?

5. Error Analysis A student claims that the circle $(x + 7)^2 + (y - 7)^2 = 8$ is a translation of the circle $x^2 + y^2 = 8$, 7 units right and 7 units down. What is the student's mistake?

6. Reasoning Let $P(x, y)$ be any point on the circle with center $(0, 0)$ and radius r. Prove that $x^2 + y^2 = r^2$ is an equation for the circle.

Practice and Problem-Solving Exercises

 **Practice**

Write an equation of a circle with the given center and radius. Check your answers.

◀ See Problem 1.

7. center $(0, 0)$, radius 10

8. center $(-4, -6)$, radius 7

9. center $(2, 3)$, radius 4.5

10. center $(-6, 10)$, radius 1

11. center $(1, -3)$, radius 10

12. center $(-1.5, -3)$, radius 2

Write an equation for each translation.

◀ See Problem 2.

Guided Practice →

To start, translate left 1 unit.

13. $x^2 + y^2 = 81$; left 1 unit and up 3 units

$(x - (-1))^2 + y^2 = 81$

14. $x^2 + y^2 = 9$; down 1 unit

15. $x^2 + y^2 = 25$; right 2 units and down 4 units

16. $x^2 + y^2 = 100$; down 5 units

17. $x^2 + y^2 = 49$; right 3 units and up 2 units

Write an equation for each circle. Each interval represents one unit.

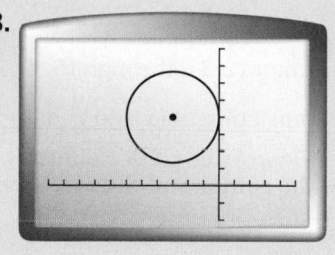

18.

See Problem 3.

Guided Practice

To start, identify the values of h, k, and r from the graph.

$h = -3$ $k = 4$ $r = 3$

19.

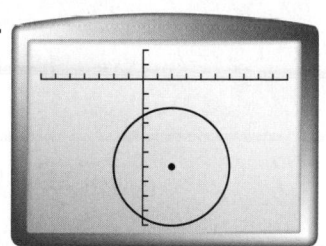

20.

For each equation, find the center and radius of the circle.

See Problem 4.

21. $(x - 1)^2 + (y - 1)^2 = 1$

22. $(x - 3)^2 + (y + 1)^2 = 36$

23. $x^2 + (y + 3)^2 = 25$

24. $(x + 6)^2 + y^2 = 121$

Use the center and the radius to graph each circle.

See Problem 5.

25. $(x + 4)^2 + (y - 4)^2 = 4$

26. $(x - 6)^2 + y^2 = 64$

27. $(x - 7)^2 + (y - 1)^2 = 100$

28. $x^2 + (y + 4)^2 = 144$

 **Apply**

29. Think About a Plan Three gears of radii 6 in., 4 in., and 2 in. mesh with each other in a motor assembly as shown at the right. What is the equation of each circle in standard form?
- How can the diagram of the gears in the coordinate plane help you solve this problem?
- How can you write an equation for each circle?

30. Open-Ended Write two functions that together represent a circle.

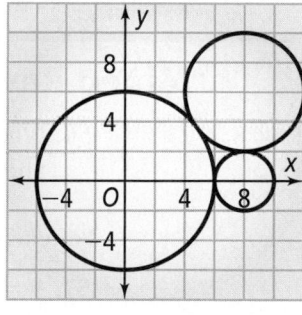

Write the equation of the circle that passes through the given point and has a center at the origin.

31. $(0, 4)$

32. $(0, -3)$

33. $(4, -3)$

34. $(-2, 3)$

35. $(1, -5)$

36. $(-6, -4)$

Hint Use the Distance Formula to find the radius.

37. Machinery Three gears, A, B, and C, mesh with each other in a motor assembly. Gear A has a radius of 4 in., B has a radius of 3 in., and C has a radius of 1 in. If the largest gear is centered at $(-7, 0)$, the smallest gear is centered at $(4, 0)$, and Gear B is centered at the origin, what is the equation of each circle in standard form?

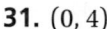

Use the given information to write an equation of the circle.

38. radius 7, center $(-6, 13)$

39. center $(1, -2)$, through $(0, 1)$

40. center $(2, 1)$, through $(6, 4)$

41. center $(6, 4)$, through $(2, 1)$

42. translation of $(x - 1)^2 + (y + 3)^2 = 36$, 2 units left and 4 units down

Find the center and the radius of each circle.

43. $x^2 + y^2 = 2$

44. $x^2 + (y + 1)^2 = 5$

45. $(x + 5)^2 + y^2 = 18$

46. $(x + 2)^2 + (y + 4)^2 = 50$

47. $(x + 3)^2 + (y - 5)^2 = 38$

48. $x^2 + 2x + 1 + y^2 = 4$

49. $x^2 + y^2 - 6x - 2y + 4 = 0$

50. $x^2 + y^2 - 4y - 16 = 0$

Standardized Test Prep

GRIDDED RESPONSE

SAT/ACT

51. What is the radius of the circle with equation $(x + 5)^2 + (y - 3)^2 = 144$?

52. Find the positive zero of the function $y = x^2 + 2x - 5$ by graphing. Enter your answer as a decimal to the nearest hundredth.

53. What is the distance between $T(9, -5)$ and the center of the circle with equation $(x - 6)^2 + (y + 1)^2 = 10$?

54. What is the common ratio in a geometric series if $a_2 = \frac{2}{5}$ and $a_5 = \frac{16}{135}$? Enter your answer as a fraction.

55. Evaluate the sum $\sum_{n=1}^{3} \left(\frac{1}{n + 1} \right)^2$. Enter your answer as a decimal to the nearest hundredth.

Mixed Review

56. What is an equation of a parabola opening left with vertex $(0, 0)$ and focus $(-3, 0)$?

See Lesson 10-2.

For each rational function, find any points of discontinuity.

See Lesson 8-3.

57. $y = \frac{2}{x + 1}$

58. $y = \frac{1}{x^2 - 5x + 6}$

59. $y = \frac{2x - 1}{x^2 + 4}$

Evaluate each logarithm.

See Lesson 7-3.

60. $\log_2 16$

61. $\log_5 25$

62. $\log_3 \frac{1}{27}$

63. $\log 10,000$

64. $\log_{36} 6$

65. $\log_{100} 100$

Get Ready!   To prepare for Lesson 10-4, do Exercises 66–68.

Solve each equation.

See Lesson 5-3.

66. $x^2 + 11x = -18$

67. $m^5 - 256m = 0$

68. $p^4 + 32 = 12p^2$

Do you know HOW?

Graph each equation. Identify the conic section and describe the graph and its lines of symmetry. Then find the domain and range.

1. $y^2 - 2x^2 = 16$

2. $3x^2 + 3y^2 - 12 = 0$

3. $9x^2 - 25y^2 = 225$

4. $36 - 4x^2 - 9y^2 = 0$

Identify the vertex, focus, and directrix of each parabola. Then graph the parabola.

5. $y = 3x^2$

6. $x = 4(y + 2)^2$

7. $y + 1 = (x - 3)^2$

Write an equation for the parabola with the given vertex and focus.

8. vertex $(-5, 4)$; focus $(-5, 0)$

9. vertex $(7, 2)$; focus $(7, -2)$

10. vertex $(0, 0)$; focus $(-7, 0)$

11. vertex $(2, 4)$; focus $(1, 4)$

12. Write an equation that models the graph below.

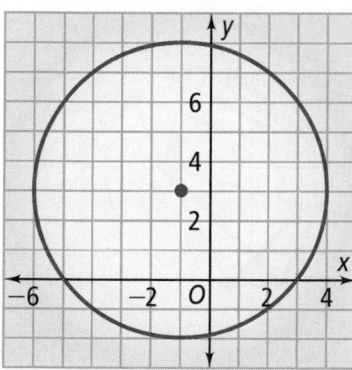

Write an equation in standard form of the circle with the given center and radius.

13. center $(-6, 3)$, radius 8

14. center $(1, 1)$, radius 1.5

Do you UNDERSTAND?

Determine whether each point lies on the graph of the conic section with the given equation.

15. $x^2 + y^2 = 36$
   a. $(-6, 0)$
   b. $(-2, -\sqrt{3})$
   c. $(0, \sqrt{2})$

16. $4x^2 - y^2 - 4 = 0$
   a. $(-1, 0)$
   b. $(2, 2)$
   c. $(1, 0)$

17. Writing Suppose that $x^2 = 4py$ and $y = ax^2$ represent the same parabola. Explain how a and p are related.

Reasoning Without graphing, describe how each graph differs from the graph of $y = x^2$.

18. $y = 2x^2$

19. $y = -x^2$

20. $y = x^2 + 2$

21. $y = \frac{1}{3}x^2$

22. A circle has center $(0, 0)$ and radius 1. Write an equation that represents the translation of the circle 7 units left and 8 units up. Then graph the equation.

Write the standard form of the equation of the circle that passes through the given point and whose center is at the origin.

23. $(-6, 0)$

24. $(0, 5)$

25. $(-11, -11)$

26. $(-8, 14)$

Ellipses

Objectives To write the equation of an ellipse
To find the foci of an ellipse
To graph an ellipse

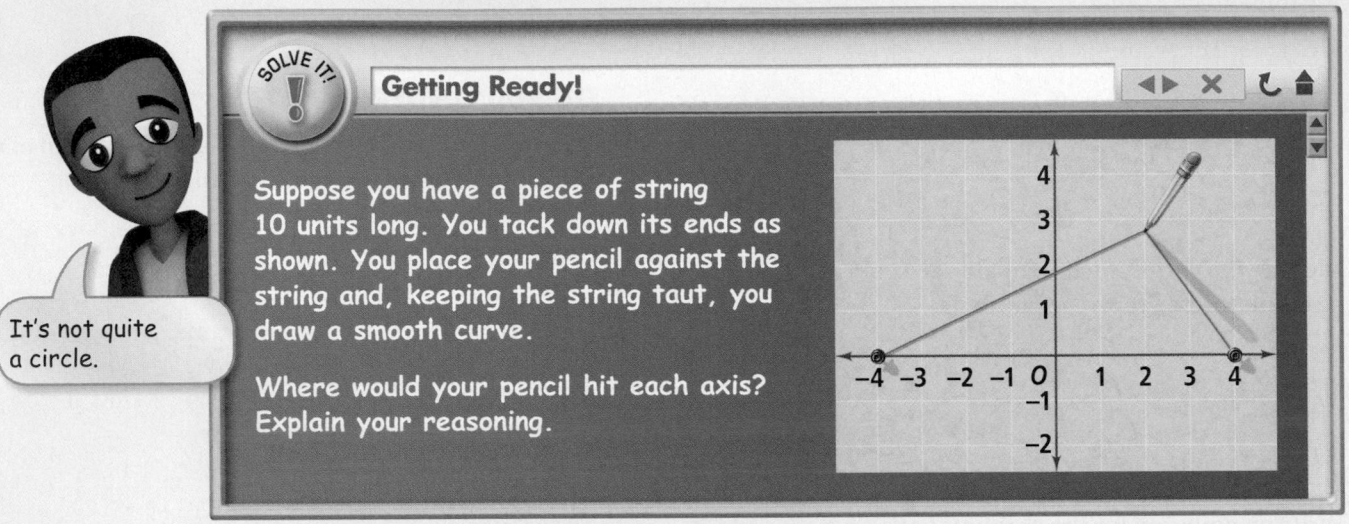

It's not quite a circle.

SOLVE IT!

Getting Ready!

Suppose you have a piece of string 10 units long. You tack down its ends as shown. You place your pencil against the string and, keeping the string taut, you draw a smooth curve.

Where would your pencil hit each axis? Explain your reasoning.

Points on the smooth curve in the Solve It have a total distance of 10 units to the points $(-4, 0)$ and $(4, 0)$. In fact, all of the points on the smooth curve have a total distance of 10 units to the two fixed points. You can describe this smooth curve with an equation.

Focus Question What is an ellipse?

Lesson Vocabulary
- ellipse
- focus of an ellipse
- major axis
- center of an ellipse
- minor axis
- vertices of an ellipse
- co-vertices of an ellipse

take note

Key Concept   Ellipse

Definition
An **ellipse** is a set of all points P in a plane such that the sum of the distances from P to two fixed points, F_1 and F_2, is a constant k. A **focus of an ellipse** (plural: foci) is one of the two fixed points.

Symbols
$PF_1 + PF_2 = k$, where $k > F_1F_2$.

Graph

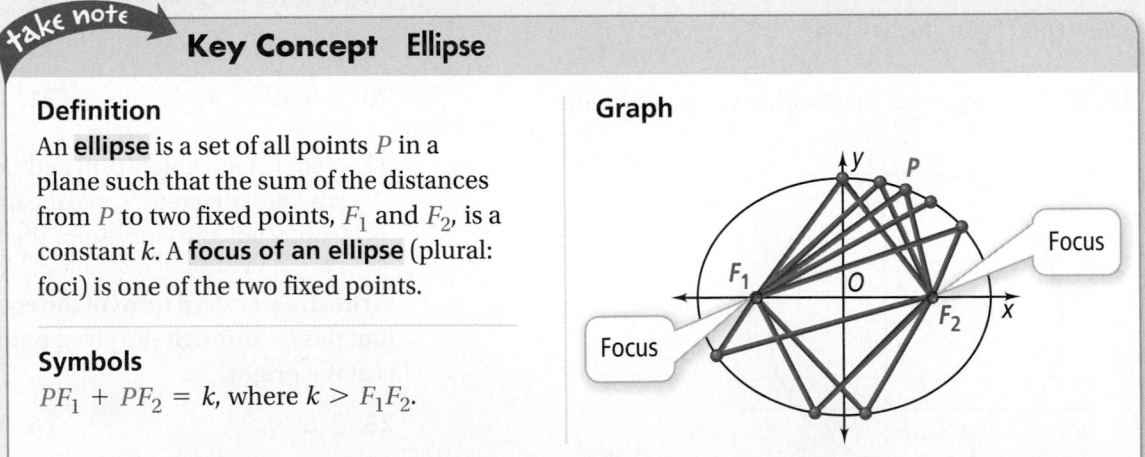

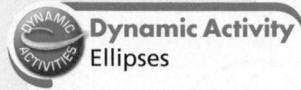
The **major axis** is the segment that contains the foci and has its endpoints on the ellipse. Its midpoint is the **center of the ellipse**. The **minor axis** is perpendicular to the major axis at the center. The **vertices of an ellipse** (singular: *vertex*) are the endpoints of the major axis. The **co-vertices of an ellipse** are the endpoints of the minor axis.

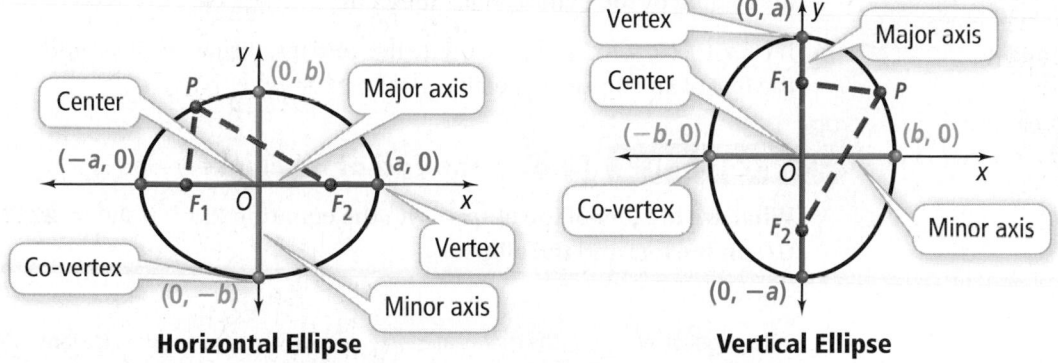

Horizontal Ellipse   **Vertical Ellipse**

take note

Key Concept   Properties of Ellipses with Center (0, 0)

	Horizontal Ellipses	Vertical Ellipses
Standard Equation	$\frac{x^2}{a^2} + \frac{y^2}{b^2} = 1, a > b > 0$	$\frac{x^2}{b^2} + \frac{y^2}{a^2} = 1, a > b > 0$
Major Axis	horizontal	vertical
Vertices	$(\pm a, 0)$	$(0, \pm a)$
Co-vertices	$(0, \pm b)$	$(\pm b, 0)$
Foci	$(\pm c, 0)$ on x-axis	$(0, \pm c)$ on y-axis

The length of the major axis is $2a$ and the length of the minor axis is $2b$.
For any point P on an ellipse, $PF_1 + PF_2 = 2a$.

Problem 1   Writing an Equation of an Ellipse

What is an equation in standard form of an ellipse centered at the origin with a vertex at $(-6, 0)$ and a co-vertex at $(0, 3)$?

Since one vertex is at $(-6, 0)$, the other vertex is at $(6, 0)$. The major axis is horizontal.
Since one co-vertex is $(0, 3)$, the other co-vertex is $(0, -3)$. The minor axis is vertical.
So $a = 6, b = 3, a^2 = 36$, and $b^2 = 9$.

Write the standard form of a horizontal ellipse. $\frac{x^2}{a^2} + \frac{y^2}{b^2} = 1$

Substitute for a^2 and b^2. $\frac{x^2}{36} + \frac{y^2}{9} = 1$

Think

What is the orientation of the ellipse?
Since the vertices $(-6, 0)$ and $(6, 0)$ are aligned horizontally, the ellipse is horizontal.

 Got It?   1. What is the equation in standard form of an ellipse centered at the origin with a vertex at $(0, 5)$ and a co-vertex at $(2, 0)$?

Since the co-vertex $P(0, b)$ is on the ellipse, $PF_1 + PF_2 = 2a$. If you denote the distance from each focus to the center of the ellipse by c, then a, b, and c are the lengths of the sides of a right triangle, as shown in the ellipse at the right. Thus, the distances from the center to each vertex, to each co-vertex, and to each focus are related by the Pythagorean Theorem.

If $(\pm a, 0)$, $(0, \pm b)$, and $(\pm c, 0)$ are the vertices, the co-vertices, and the foci of an ellipse, respectively, then $c^2 = a^2 - b^2$.

Problem 2 Finding the Foci of an Ellipse

What are the foci of the ellipse with the equation $25x^2 + 9y^2 = 225$? Graph the foci and the ellipse.

Know	Need	Plan
The equation of an ellipse	The coordinates of the vertices, co-vertices, and foci	• Write the equation in standard form to find a^2 and b^2. Use $c^2 = a^2 - b^2$ to find c. • Use a, b, and c to draw the ellipse.

Step 1 Write the equation in standard form.

Write the original equation.	$25x^2 + 9y^2 = 225$
Divide each side by 225.	$\dfrac{25x^2}{225} + \dfrac{9y^2}{225} = 1$
Simplify.	$\dfrac{x^2}{9} + \dfrac{y^2}{25} = 1$

Step 2 Identify the foci.

Identify a^2 and b^2 from the standard equation for a vertical ellipse.	$a^2 = 25$ and $b^2 = 9$
Find the value of c.	$c^2 = a^2 - b^2$
Substitute 25 for a^2 and 9 for b^2.	$c^2 = 25 - 9$
Simplify.	$c^2 = 16$
Find square roots.	$c = \pm 4$

The foci are $(0, 4)$ and $(0, -4)$.

Step 3 Plot points for the vertices, co-vertices, and foci. Then, graph the ellipse.

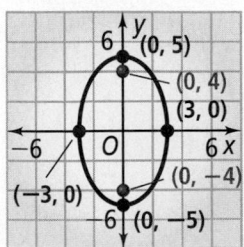

Got It? **2. a.** What are the coordinates of the foci of the ellipse with the equation $36x^2 + 100y^2 = 3600$? Graph the ellipse.

        b. Reasoning What happens to the foci as c gets closer to 0? What would the graph of an ellipse be if $c = 0$?

Like parabolas, ellipses have an important reflective property related to their foci: Any line emanating from one focus of an ellipse will reflect off the ellipse directly into the other focus. This property is related to the two-focus definition of an ellipse and is shown in the picture.

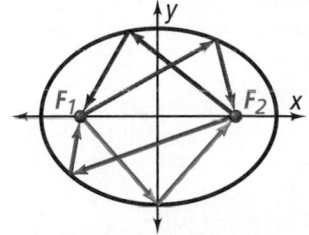

 Problem 3 **Using the Foci of an Ellipse**

Whispering Gallery A room with an elliptical ceiling (called an *ellipsoid*, since it is 3-dimensional) forms a "whispering gallery." Thanks to the reflective property of the ellipse, a whispered message at one focus can be heard clearly by someone standing across the room at the other focus. If the elliptical ceiling has a major axis of 120 feet and a minor axis of 72 feet, how far apart are the foci?

Plan

How can you find the distance between foci, given the major and minor axes?
Find the values of a and b. Then, use a^2 and b^2 to solve for c. The distance between the foci is $2c$.

The major axis has length $2a = 120$, so $a = 60$.
The minor axis has length $2b = 72$, so $b = 36$.

$$c = \sqrt{a^2 - b^2}$$
$$= \sqrt{60^2 - 36^2}$$
$$= 48$$

Thus, the foci are $2c = 96$ feet apart.

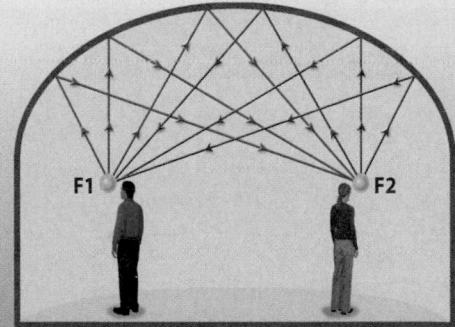

 Got It? **3.** How far apart are the foci of an ellipse with a major axis of 26 ft and a minor axis of 10 ft?

Problem 4 Using the Foci of an Ellipse

What is the standard form equation of the ellipse shown?

The foci are on the x-axis, so the major axis is horizontal.

Since $c = 5$ and $a = 8$, $c^2 = 25$ and $a^2 = 64$.

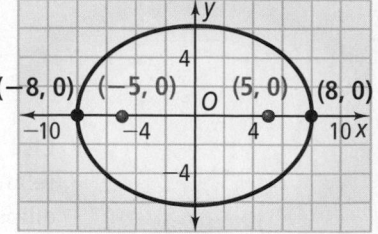

Relate the values of a, b, and c.	$c^2 = a^2 - b^2$
Substitute.	$25 = 64 - b^2$
Solve.	$b^2 = 39$
Write the standard form of a horizontal ellipse.	$\dfrac{x^2}{a^2} + \dfrac{y^2}{b^2} = 1$
Substitute.	$\dfrac{x^2}{64} + \dfrac{y^2}{39} = 1$

Got It? **4.** What is the standard form equation of an ellipse with foci at $(0, \pm\sqrt{17})$ and co-vertices at $(\pm6, 0)$?

Focus Question What is an ellipse?

Answer An ellipse is the set of all points P such that the sum of the distances from two fixed points F_1 and F_2 (the foci of the ellipse) is a given constant k.

Lesson Check

Do you know HOW?

1. What is an equation in standard form of an ellipse with co-vertices $(0, \pm6)$ and major axis with length 16?

2. What are the coordinates of the foci of an ellipse with the equation $4x^2 + 25y^2 = 100$?

3. What is an equation in standard form of an ellipse centered at the origin with vertices $(\pm13, 0)$ and foci $(\pm12, 0)$?

4. How far apart are the foci of an ellipse with a major axis of 32 ft and minor axis of 14 ft?

Do you UNDERSTAND?

5. **Error Analysis** A student claims that an equation of the ellipse shown is $\dfrac{x^2}{41} + \dfrac{y^2}{29} = 1$. Describe the student's error. What is the correct equation in standard form of the ellipse?

6. **Reasoning** Explain why a circle is a special case of an ellipse.

Practice and Problem-Solving Exercises

 **Practice**

Write an equation of an ellipse in standard form with center at the origin and with the given vertex and co-vertex listed respectively.

◀ **See Problem 1.**

Guided Practice

To start, identify both vertices and co-vertices.

7. $(4, 0), (0, 3)$
Vertices: $(4, 0)$ and $(-4, 0)$
Co-vertices: $(0, 3)$ and $(0, -3)$

8. $(2, 0), (0, 1)$ **9.** $(3, 0), (0, -1)$ **10.** $(0, 6), (1, 0)$

11. $(0, -7), (4, 0)$ **12.** $(-6, 0), (0, 5)$ **13.** $(0, 5), (-3, 0)$

Find the foci for each equation of an ellipse. Then graph the ellipse.

◀ **See Problem 2.**

Guided Practice

To start, write the equation in standard form.

14. $x^2 + 4y^2 = 16$
$$\frac{x^2}{16} + \frac{y^2}{4} = 1$$

15. $\frac{x^2}{4} + \frac{y^2}{9} = 1$ **16.** $\frac{x^2}{9} + \frac{y^2}{25} = 1$ **17.** $\frac{x^2}{81} + \frac{y^2}{49} = 1$

18. $\frac{x^2}{25} + \frac{y^2}{16} = 1$ **19.** $\frac{x^2}{64} + \frac{y^2}{100} = 1$ **20.** $3x^2 + y^2 = 9$

Find the distance between the foci of an ellipse. The lengths of the major and minor axes are listed respectively.

◀ **See Problem 3.**

21. 40 and 24 **22.** 10 and 8 **23.** 16 and 10

24. 20 and 16 **25.** 18 and 14 **26.** 8 and 6

Write an equation of an ellipse for the given foci and co-vertices.

◀ **See Problem 4.**

27. foci $(\pm 5, 0)$, co-vertices $(0, \pm 8)$ **28.** foci $(0, \pm 4)$, co-vertices $(\pm 2, 0)$

29. Miniature Golf The figure at the right represents a miniature golf green. The green is elliptical with the tee at one focus and the hole at the other.
  a. How far is the hole from the tee?
  b. Knowing that the border is elliptical, how should you aim your putt from the tee?

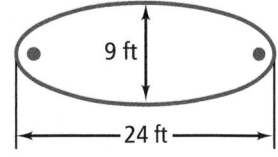

Ⓑ Apply **Find the foci for each equation of an ellipse.**

30. $4x^2 + 9y^2 = 36$ **31.** $16x^2 + 4y^2 = 64$

32. $36x^2 + 4y^2 = 144$ **33.** $25x^2 + 24y^2 = 600$

34. Think About a Plan The open area south of the White House is known as the Ellipse, or President's Park South. It is 902 ft wide and 1058 ft long. Assume the origin is at the center of the President's Park South. What is the equation of the ellipse in standard form?
- How does the length and width of the ellipse relate to the equation?
- What does the center at the origin tell you?
- How can you write the equation of the ellipse in standard form?

35. The eccentricity of an ellipse is a measure of how nearly circular it is. Eccentricity is defined as $\frac{c}{a}$, where c is the distance from the center to a focus and a is the distance from the center to a vertex.
- **a.** Find the eccentricity of an ellipse with foci $(\pm 9, 0)$ and vertices $(\pm 10, 0)$.
- **b.** Find the eccentricity of an ellipse with foci $(\pm 1, 0)$ and vertices $(\pm 10, 0)$.
- **c.** Describe the shape of an ellipse that has an eccentricity close to 0.
- **d.** Describe the shape of an ellipse that has an eccentricity close to 1.

Write an equation for each ellipse.

36. 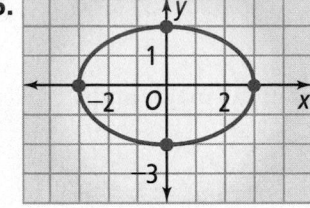   **37.**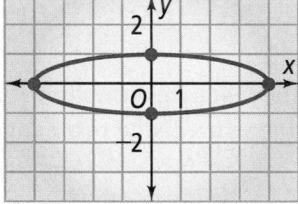

38. Open-Ended Find a real-world design that uses ellipses. Place a coordinate grid over the design and write an equation of the ellipse.

39. Aerodynamics Scientists used the Transonic Tunnel at NASA Langley Research Center, Virginia, to study the dynamics of air flow. The elliptical opening of the Transonic Tunnel is 82 ft wide and 58 ft high. What is an equation of the ellipse?

Write an equation of an ellipse in standard form with center at the origin and with the given characteristics.

40. focus $(1, 0)$, width 4   **41.** $a = 5$, $b = 2$, width 10

42. vertex $(-11, 0)$, co-vertex $(0, 9)$ **43.** focus $(-5, 0)$, co-vertex $(0, -12)$

44. $c^2 = 68$, vertex $(0, -18)$ **45.** focus $(2, 0)$, x-intercept 4

46. focus $(0, -5)$, y-intercept 8   **47.** focus $(3, 0)$, x-intercept -6

Standardized Test Prep

48. Which equation is represented by the circle shown?

    Ⓐ $(x - 1)^2 + (y + 2)^2 = 4$ Ⓒ $(x + 2)^2 + (y - 1)^2 = 4$

    Ⓑ $(x + 1)^2 + (y - 2)^2 = 4$ Ⓓ $(x - 2)^2 + (y + 1)^2 = 4$

49. What is the center of the circle with equation $(x + 3)^2 + (y - 2)^2 = 49$?

    Ⓕ $(3, -2)$ Ⓖ $(-3, 2)$ Ⓗ $(3, 2)$ Ⓘ $(-3, -2)$

50. The graph of which equation contains all the points in the table below?

x	-4	-2	0	2	4
y	0	$\pm\sqrt{3}$	± 2	$\pm\sqrt{3}$	0

    Ⓐ $x^2 + 4y^2 = 16$ Ⓑ $4x^2 + 16y^2 = 144$ Ⓒ $4x^2 + 25y^2 = 64$ Ⓓ $9x^2 + 4y^2 = 81$

51. Find the horizontal asymptote of $y = \frac{5x + 7}{x + 3}$ by dividing the numerator by the denominator. Explain your steps.

Mixed Review

Write an equation of a circle with the given center and radius.   ◀ **See Lesson 10-3.**

52. center $(1, -5)$, radius 3   **53.** center $(-2, 4)$, radius 9

Simplify each expression. State any restrictions on the variable.   ◀ **See Lesson 8-4.**

54. $\dfrac{3x}{6x^2 - 9x^5}$ **55.** $\dfrac{x^2 - 36}{x^2 + 5x - 6}$ **56.** $\dfrac{x^2 - 3x - 10}{x^3 + 8}$

Write each expression as a single logarithm.   ◀ **See Lesson 7-4.**

57. $\log 3 + \log 5$ **58.** $\log_3 12 - \log_3 2$ **59.** $3 \log 2 - \log 4$

Get Ready!   **To prepare for Lesson 10-5, do Exercises 60 and 61.**

Write an equation of a line in slope-intercept form using the given information.   ◀ **See Lesson 2-3.**

60. $m = 2$ and the y-intercept is 4   **61.** passes through $(3, 1)$ and $(9, 3)$

Hyperbolas

Objectives To graph hyperbolas
To find and use the foci of a hyperbola

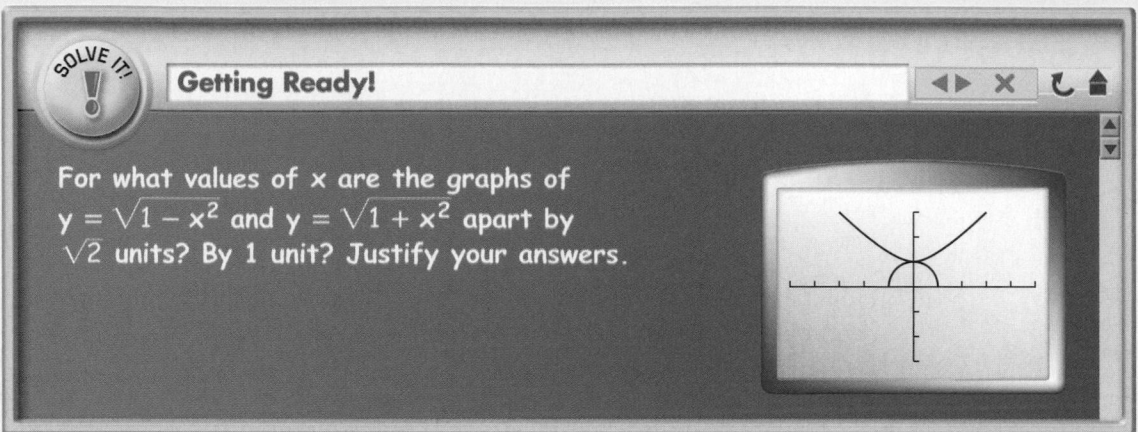

Getting Ready!

For what values of x are the graphs of
$y = \sqrt{1 - x^2}$ and $y = \sqrt{1 + x^2}$ apart by
$\sqrt{2}$ units? By 1 unit? Justify your answers.

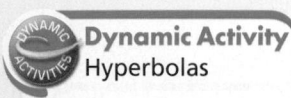

Dynamic Activity
Hyperbolas

Lesson Vocabulary

- hyperbola
- focus of the hyperbola
- vertex of a hyperbola
- transverse axis
- axis of symmetry
- center of a hyperbola
- conjugate axis

In the Solve It, you saw the top halves of two different conic sections. You can complete each conic section by graphing $y = -\sqrt{1 - x^2}$ and $y = -\sqrt{1 + x^2}$ respectively.

Recall from Lesson 10-1, that you can get a variety of conic sections by slicing the double cone with a plane. Changing the angle at which the plane slices the double cone determines the shape of the curve and whether or not the plane will slice both cones. If the plane is parallel to the axis of the double cone, it slices both cones and the result is a *hyperbola*.

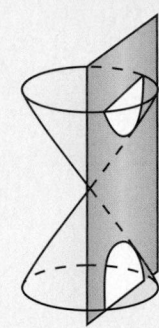

Focus Question What is a hyperbola?

take note

Key Concept Hyperbola

A **hyperbola** is the set of points P in a plane such that the absolute value of the difference between the distances from
P to two fixed points F_1 and F_2 is a constant k.

$$|PF_1 - PF_2| = k, \text{ where } k < F_1F_2$$

Each fixed point F is a **focus of the hyperbola**.

Since F_1 and F_2 are the foci of the hyperbola, the long and short segments in each of the two colored paths differ in length by k.

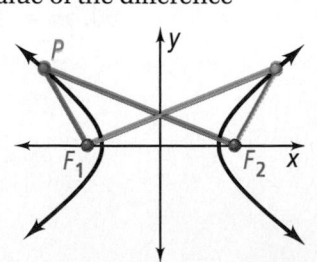

A hyperbola consists of two smooth branches. The turning point of each branch is a **vertex of the hyperbola**. The segment connecting the two vertices is the **transverse axis**, which lies on the **axis of symmetry**. The two foci also lie on the axis of symmetry. The **center of the hyperbola** is the midpoint between the two vertices, which also is the midpoint between the two foci.

Just as for an ellipse, if the foci are $(\pm c, 0)$, the distance between the two foci is $2c$. If the vertices are $(\pm a, 0)$, the distance between the two vertices is $2a$.

Since vertex P is on the hyperbola, it must satisfy the equation $|PF_1 - PF_2| = k$, but you can also see that

$$|PF_1 - PF_2| = |[2a + (c - a)] - (c - a)|$$
$$= |2a + c - a - c + a|$$
$$= |2a| = 2a$$

Therefore, $k = 2a$.

Hint

Recall that an asymptote is a line that a graph approaches but never intersects.

In a standard hyperbola, c is related to a and b by the equation $c^2 = a^2 + b^2$. The length of the **conjugate axis** is $2b$. The transverse and conjugate axes determine a rectangle that lies between the vertices, and the diagonals of that central rectangle determine the asymptotes of the hyperbola. The branches of the hyperbola approach the asymptotes.

take note

Key Concept   Properties of Hyperbolas with Center (0, 0)

Horizontal Hyperbola

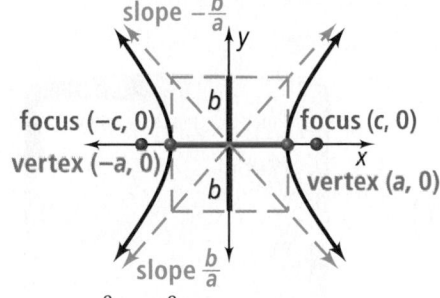

Equation: $\dfrac{x^2}{a^2} - \dfrac{y^2}{b^2} = 1$

Transverse axis: Horizontal

Vertices: $(\pm a, 0)$

Foci: $(\pm c, 0)$, where $c^2 = a^2 + b^2$

Asymptotes: $y = \pm\dfrac{b}{a}x$

Vertical Hyperbola

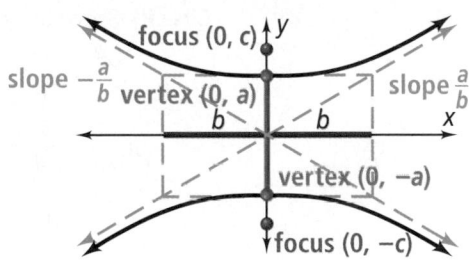

Equation: $\dfrac{y^2}{a^2} - \dfrac{x^2}{b^2} = 1$

Transverse axis: Vertical

Vertices: $(0, \pm a)$

Foci: $(0, \pm c)$, where $c^2 = a^2 + b^2$

Asymptotes: $y = \pm\dfrac{a}{b}x$

Because of symmetry, for both the ellipse and a hyperbola, the value of c is half the distance between the two foci.

 Problem 1 Writing and Graphing the Equation of a Hyperbola

A hyperbola centered at $(0, 0)$ has vertices $(\pm 4, 0)$ and one focus $(5, 0)$.

A What is the standard-form equation of the hyperbola?

First, find a, b, and c. The vertices are $(\pm 4, 0)$, so $a = 4$. One focus is $(5, 0)$, so $c = 5$.

The transverse axis is horizontal. Use $c^2 = a^2 + b^2$ to find b: $5^2 = 4^2 + b^2$, so $b = 3$.

Then write the equation of a horizontal hyperbola in standard form $\dfrac{x^2}{a^2} - \dfrac{y^2}{b^2} = 1$.

Substitute values for a and b. $\dfrac{x^2}{4^2} - \dfrac{y^2}{3^2} = 1$

Simplify. $\dfrac{x^2}{16} - \dfrac{y^2}{9} = 1$

Think

Is the transverse axis horizontal or vertical?
The vertices and focus are on a horizontal line. The transverse axis is horizontal.

B Sketch the hyperbola. Use a graphing calculator to check.

Step 1 Draw the horizontal transverse axis, vertices, and central rectangle. This rectangle shares a center with the hyperbola and in this case has a height of $2b$ and a width of $2a$. If the hyperbola were vertical, the dimensions would be reversed.

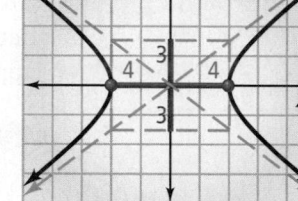

Step 2 Extend the diagonals of the rectangle to show the asymptotes.

Step 3 Sketch the branches from the vertices.

Check Solve for y.

$$\dfrac{x^2}{16} - \dfrac{y^2}{9} = 1$$

$$\dfrac{y^2}{9} = \dfrac{x^2}{16} - 1$$

$$y^2 = 9\left(\dfrac{x^2}{16} - 1\right)$$

$$y = \pm 3\sqrt{\dfrac{x^2}{16} - 1}$$

Hint

The central rectangle guides the drawing of the graph.

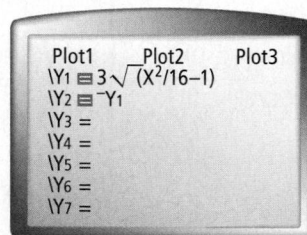

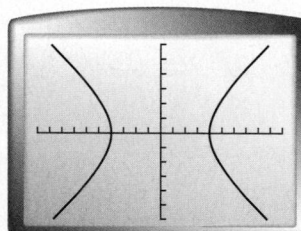

 Got It? **1. a.** What is the standard-form equation of the hyperbola with vertices $(0, \pm 4)$ and foci $(0, \pm 5)$?

b. Sketch the hyperbola. Use a graphing calculator to check.

c. Reasoning Under what circumstances are the asymptotes of the graph of a hyperbola perpendicular?

 **Problem 2** Analyzing a Hyperbola from Its Equation

What are the vertices, foci, and asymptotes of the hyperbola with equation $9y^2 - 7x^2 = 63$? Sketch the graph.

Think

Write the original equation.

In standard form, the right side must be 1. Divide each side by 63.

Simplify. Since y^2 has the positive coefficient, the hyperbola is vertical. The vertices and foci are on the y-axis.

Compare to $\frac{y^2}{a^2} - \frac{x^2}{b^2} = 1$ to find a^2 and b^2.

Find c^2. Use $c^2 = a^2 + b^2$.

You know a, b, and c. You can answer the questions and draw the graph. $\sqrt{7} \approx 2.65$

Write

$$9y^2 - 7x^2 = 63$$

$$\frac{9y^2}{63} - \frac{7x^2}{63} = 1$$

$$\frac{y^2}{7} - \frac{x^2}{9} = 1$$

$$a^2 = 7 \text{ and } b^2 = 9$$
$$a = \pm\sqrt{7} \quad b = \pm 3$$

$$c^2 = 7 + 9, \text{ so } c = \pm\sqrt{7 + 9}$$
$$c = \pm 4$$

Vertices: $(0, \pm\sqrt{7})$, Foci: $(0, \pm 4)$.

Slopes of asymptotes: $m = \pm\dfrac{\sqrt{7}}{3}$

Asymptotes: $y = \pm\dfrac{\sqrt{7}}{3}x$

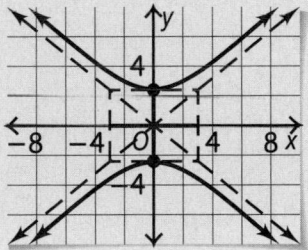

Hint
Use a graphing calculator to check your graph. Define $Y1 = \sqrt{(7(X^2/9+1))}$ and $Y2 = -Y1$.

 Got It? **2.** What are the vertices, foci, and asymptotes of the hyperbola with equation $9x^2 - 4y^2 = 36$? Sketch a graph.

The *reflection property of a hyperbola* is important in optics. As with an ellipse, the reflection property of a hyperbola involves both foci, but only one branch reflects. Any ray on the *external side* of a branch directed at its internal focus will reflect off the branch toward the *external focus*.

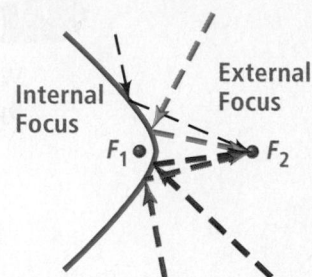

Internal Focus

External Focus

Problem 3 Modeling with a Hyperbola

Communications The graph shows a 2-dimensional view of a satellite dish. The focus is located at F_1 but the receiving device is located on the bottom of the dish at the point F_2. The rays are reflected by the first reflector (the black curve), toward F_1 and then reflected by the second reflector (the blue curve) toward F_2.

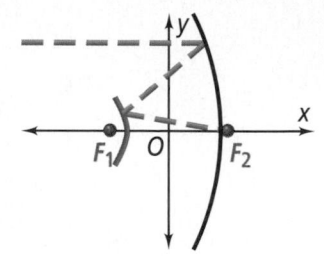

Think

What information does the diagram give you?
It helps you see the relative positions of the reflectors and foci.

A What kind of curve is the second reflector? How can you tell?

The second reflector is a hyperbola because it reflects rays aimed at its internal focus toward its external focus.

B The vertex of the second reflector is 3 in. from F_1 and 21 in. from F_2. What is an equation for the second reflector? Assume the conic is horizontal and centered at the origin.

Step 1 Determine the standard-form equation of the conic.
The conic is a horizontal hyperbola centered at the origin.

$$\frac{x^2}{a^2} - \frac{y^2}{b^2} = 1$$

Step 2 Find c.

The distance between the foci is $3 + 21 = 24$ in.
Since c is half this distance, $c = 12$.

Step 3 Find a.

The distance from the internal focus to the vertex of the reflector is 3 in.
So, $c - a = 12 - a = 3$ and $a = 9$.

Step 4 Use c and a to find b^2.

Relate a^2, b^2, and c^2. $b^2 = c^2 - a^2$

Substitute. $= 12^2 - 9^2$

Simplify. $= 63$

Step 5 Use a^2 and b^2 to write the equation.

An equation is $\frac{x^2}{81} - \frac{y^2}{63} = 1$.

 Got It? **3.** Suppose the vertex of the second reflector in Problem 3 were 4 in. from F_1 and 18 in. from F_2. What is the equation for the second reflector? Assume the conic is horizontal and centered at the origin.

Focus Question What is a hyperbola?

Answer A hyperbola is the set of points P such that the absolute value of the difference between the distances from P to two fixed points F_1 and F_2 (the foci of the hyperbola) is a constant k.

Lesson Check

Do you know HOW?

Find the vertices and foci of each equation. Write the slopes of the asymptotes. Then graph the equation.

1. $\dfrac{x^2}{36} - \dfrac{y^2}{25} = 1$ 2. $\dfrac{y^2}{16} - \dfrac{x^2}{25} = 1$

3. $4y^2 - x^2 = 16$ 4. $16x^2 - 25y^2 = 400$

5. What is an equation of a hyperbola with vertices $(\pm 5, 0)$ and focus $(7, 0)$?

Do you UNDERSTAND?

6. **Compare and Contrast** How is graphing a hyperbola like graphing an ellipse? How is it different?

7. **Error Analysis** Your friend says that a graph must be a vertical hyperbola because the larger denominator is under the y^2 term. What error did your friend make?

Practice and Problem-Solving Exercises

 **Practice**

Write an equation of a hyperbola with the given values, foci, or vertices. Assume that the transverse axis is horizontal.

 **See Problem 1.**

Guided Practice

To start, write the equation of a horizontal hyperbola in standard form.

8. $a = 3, b = 4$
$$\dfrac{x^2}{a^2} - \dfrac{y^2}{b^2} = 1$$

9. $a = -12, c = 13$ 10. $b = 9, c = 10$

11. foci $(\pm 13, 0)$, vertices $(\pm 12, 0)$ 12. foci $(\pm 3, 0)$, vertices $(\pm 2, 0)$

Find the vertices, foci, and asymptotes of each hyperbola. Then sketch the graph.

See Problem 2.

Guided Practice

To start, identify the location of the vertices and foci.

13. $\dfrac{y^2}{81} - \dfrac{x^2}{16} = 1$

y^2 has the positive coefficient. The hyperbola is vertical. The vertices and foci are on the y-axis.

14. $\dfrac{x^2}{121} - \dfrac{y^2}{144} = 1$ 15. $\dfrac{y^2}{25} - \dfrac{x^2}{100} = 1$

16. $81y^2 - 9x^2 = 729$ 17. $4y^2 - 25x^2 = 100$

18. $36x^2 - 8y^2 = 288$ 19. $14y^2 - 28x^2 = 448$

20. Satellite Dish The diagram at the right models a satellite dish and the small reflector inside it. Suppose F_1 and F_2 are 7 meters apart, and F_1 is 1 meter from the vertex of the small reflector. What equation best models the small reflector?

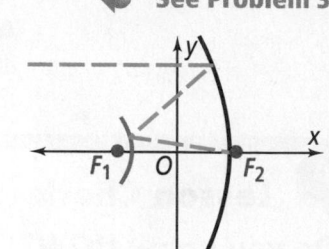

See Problem 3.

B **Apply**

21. Think About a Plan The path that Voyager 2 made around Jupiter followed one branch of a hyperbola. Find an equation that models the path of Voyager 2 around Jupiter, given that $a = 2{,}184{,}140$ km and $c = 2{,}904{,}906.2$ km. Use the horizontal model.
- What information do you need to write the equation?
- How can you use the given information to find the information you need?

Write an equation of a hyperbola with the given foci and vertices.

22. foci $(\pm5, 0)$, vertices $(\pm3, 0)$

23. foci $(0, \pm13)$, vertices $(0, \pm5)$

24. foci $(0, \pm2)$, vertices $(0, \pm1)$

25. foci $(\pm\sqrt{5}, 0)$, vertices $(\pm2, 0)$

Write an equation of a hyperbola from the given information. Assume the center of each hyperbola is $(0, 0)$.

26. Transverse axis is vertical and is 9 units; central rectangle is 9 units by 4 units

27. Perimeter of central rectangle is 16 units; vertices are $(0, 3)$ and $(0, -3)$

Graphing Calculator Solve each equation for y. Graph each relation on your graphing calculator. Use the TRACE feature to locate the vertices.

28. $x^2 - 2y^2 = 4$

29. $3x^2 - y^2 = 2$

30. Comets The path of a comet around the sun followed one branch of a hyperbola. Find an equation that models its path around the sun, given that $a = 40$ million miles and $c = 250$ million miles. Use the horizontal model.

31. Open-Ended Choose two points on an axis to be the vertices of a hyperbola. Choose two other points on the same axis to be the foci. Write the equation of your hyperbola and draw its graph.

Graph each equation.

32. $5x^2 - 12y^2 = 120$

33. $16x^2 - 20y^2 = 560$

34. Error Analysis On a test, a student found that the foci of the hyperbola with equation $\frac{y^2}{100} - \frac{x^2}{21} = 1$ were $(0, \pm\sqrt{79})$. The teacher credited the student three points out of a possible five. What did the student do right? What did the student do wrong?

Standardized Test Prep

SAT/ACT

35. The graph of $\frac{x^2}{16} - \frac{y^2}{4} = 1$ is a hyperbola. Which set of equations represents the asymptotes of the hyperbola's graph?

Ⓐ $y = \frac{1}{2}x, y = -\frac{1}{2}x$ Ⓒ $x = \frac{1}{2}y, x = -\frac{1}{2}y$

Ⓑ $y = 2x, y = -2x$ Ⓓ $y = \frac{1}{4}x, y = -\frac{1}{4}x$

36. Simplify $\dfrac{\frac{1}{y} - \frac{1}{x}}{\frac{1}{xy} - 1}$.

Ⓕ $-\dfrac{y - x}{xy - 1}$ Ⓖ $\dfrac{x - y}{1 - xy}$ Ⓗ $\dfrac{x + y}{1 + xy}$ Ⓘ $x + y$

37. How is the graph of $y = 4 \cdot \left(\frac{1}{2}\right)^{x-3}$ translated from the graph of $y = 4 \cdot \left(\frac{1}{2}\right)^{x}$?

Ⓐ 3 units right   Ⓑ 3 units left   Ⓒ 3 units down   Ⓓ 3 units up

Short Response

38. Using sigma notation, what is an expression for the sum of a 6-term arithmetic sequence with first term of 3 and a common difference of 4? What is the sum?

Mixed Review

Find the foci for each equation of an ellipse. Then graph the ellipse.   ◀ See Lesson 10-4.

39. $\frac{x^2}{34} + \frac{y^2}{25} = 1$ **40.** $3x^2 + 2y^2 = 6$ **41.** $25x^2 + 16y^2 - 1600$

Solve each equation. Check your answers.   ◀ See Lesson 7-5.

42. $8^{2x} = 4$ **43.** $\log 8x = 3$ **44.** $2\log_3 x - \log_3 4 = 2$

Get Ready!   To prepare for Lesson 11-1, do Exercises 45 and 46.

Evaluate each expression for the given value of the variable.   ◀ See Lesson 1-3.

45. $x + 5x - x - 9;\ x = -2$ **46.** $(n - 4)^2 + n;\ n = 5$

Pull It **All Together**

To solve these problems, you will pull together concepts and skills related to conic sections.

BIG idea Modeling

You can represent many real-world mathematical problems algebraically.

TASK 1

Imagine a plane and a cone intersecting to form a parabola.

   a. Explain why the plane has to intersect the axis of the cone.
   b. Imagine the plane moving so that it keeps the same angle, but its point of intersection with the axis moves in the direction of the apex of the cone and eventually passes through the apex. Describe what happens to the parabola and write equations that describe how the parabola changes.

BIG idea Equivalence

You can represent any relationship in an infinite number of ways, where each representation has the same domain and the same pairing of inputs with outputs.

TASK 2

You can define an ellipse using a cone, a set of points, or algebra. For each kind of definition, explain how to describe a circle as a special case of an ellipse.

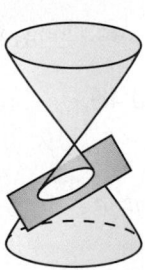

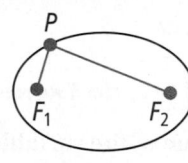

$$PF_1 + PF_2 = k$$

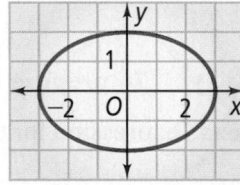

$$\frac{x^2}{9} + \frac{y^2}{4} = 1$$

BIG idea Coordinate Geometry

You can use a coordinate system to represent and analyze geometric relationships.

TASK 3

The focus of the hyperbola $\frac{x^2}{a^2} - \frac{y^2}{b^2} = 1$ is c_h units from $(0, 0)$. Imagine the ellipse inscribed in the central rectangle of the hyperbola. Its focus is c_e units from $(0, 0)$. How far apart are the foci $(c_e, 0)$ and $(c_h, 0)$? Give the distance in terms of a and b.

⑩ Chapter Review

Connecting **BIG** ideas and Answering the Essential Questions

1 Modeling
The intersection of a cone and a plane parallel to the side of a cone is a parabola.

➤

Parabolas (Lesson 10-2)
Centered at the origin,
- a parabola has equation $y = ax^2$, or $x = ay^2$.

2 Equivalence
$\frac{x^2}{9} + \frac{y^2}{9} = 1$ is an equation of a circle centered at the origin with radius 3. Multiply each side by 9 to get $x^2 + y^2 = 9$.

➤

Circles (Lesson 10-3)
Centered at the origin,
- a circle with radius r has equation $x^2 + y^2 = r^2$.

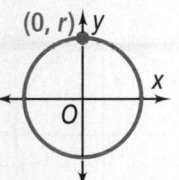

3 Coordinate Geometry
The x^2 and y^2 terms of the algebraic form of an ellipse are both positive. For a hyperbola, one term is negative.

➤

Ellipses and Hyperbolas (Lessons 10-4 and 10-5)
Centered at the origin,
- an ellipse has equation $\frac{x^2}{a^2} + \frac{y^2}{b^2} = 1$
- a hyperbola has equation $\frac{x^2}{a^2} - \frac{y^2}{b^2} = 1$ or $\frac{y^2}{a^2} - \frac{x^2}{b^2} = 1$.

Chapter Vocabulary

- axis of symmetry (p. 667)
- center of a circle (p. 649)
- center of an ellipse (p. 659)
- center of a hyperbola (p. 667)
- circle (p. 649)
- conic section (p. 634)
- conjugate axis (p. 667)
- co-vertices of an ellipse (p. 659)

- directrix (p. 641)
- ellipse (p. 658)
- focal length (p. 641)
- focus of a parabola (p. 641)
- foci of an ellipse (p. 658)
- foci of a hyperbola (p. 666)
- hyperbola (p. 666)
- major axis (p. 659)

- minor axis (p. 659)
- radius (p. 649)
- standard form of an equation of a circle (p. 650)
- transverse axis (p. 667)
- vertices of an ellipse (p. 659)
- vertices of a hyperbola (p. 667)

Fill in the blanks.

1. In the definition of a parabola, a point on the curve is equidistant from the focus and the ⎯?⎯ .

2. The vertices of an ellipse are on its ⎯?⎯ .

3. $(x - h)^2 + (y - k)^2 = r^2$ is the ⎯?⎯ .

4. The distance from a point on a circle to its center is the ⎯?⎯ of the circle.

5. The vertices of a hyperbola are on its ⎯?⎯ .

10-1 Exploring Conic Sections

Quick Review

A **conic section** is formed by the intersection of a plane and a double cone. Circles, ellipses, parabolas, and hyperbolas are all conic sections.

Example

Graph the equation $x^2 + y^2 = 9$. Identify the conic section and the domain and range.

Plot points that satisfy the equation. Connect them with a smooth curve.

The graph is a circle with center $(0, 0)$ and radius 3.

The domain is $-3 \le x \le 3$.

The range is $-3 \le y \le 3$.

Exercises

Graph each equation. Identify the conic section, any lines of symmetry, and the domain and range.

6. $\dfrac{x^2}{49} + \dfrac{y^2}{121} = 1$

7. $x^2 + y^2 = 4$

8. $\dfrac{x^2}{25} - \dfrac{y^2}{4} = 1$

9. $x = 2y^2 + 5$

Identify the center and domain and range of each graph.

10.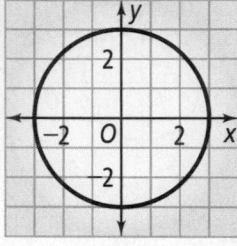

11.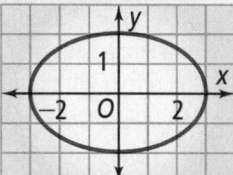

10-2 Parabolas

Quick Review

In a plane, a parabola is the set of all points that are the same distance, c, from a fixed point, the **focus**, and a fixed line, the **directrix**.

For $y = ax^2$, if $a > 0$, the parabola opens up, and has focus $(0, c)$ and directrix $y = -c$; if $a < 0$, the parabola opens down, and has focus $(0, -c)$ and directrix $y = c$.

For $x = ay^2$, if $a > 0$, the parabola opens right, and has focus $(c, 0)$ and directrix $x = -c$; if $a < 0$, the parabola opens left, and has focus $(-c, 0)$ and directrix $x = c$. In all cases, $a = \dfrac{1}{4c}$.

Example

Write an equation of a parabola that opens up, with vertex at the origin and focus 1 unit from the vertex.

Since the parabola opens up, use $y = ax^2$. Since the focus is 1 unit from the vertex, $c = 1$.

$$a = \frac{1}{4c} = \frac{1}{4(1)} = \frac{1}{4}$$

An equation for the parabola is $y = \frac{1}{4}x^2$.

Exercises

Write an equation of a parabola with vertex at the origin and the given focus.

12. $(5, 0)$ **13.** $(0, -5)$ **14.** $(0, 6)$

Write an equation of a parabola that opens up, with vertex at the origin and a focus as described.

15. focus is 2.5 units from the vertex

16. focus is $\frac{1}{12}$ of a unit from the vertex

Write an equation of a parabola with the given focus and directrix.

17. focus: $(0, 3)$; directrix: $y = -1$

18. focus: $(-2, 0)$; directrix: $x = 4$

Find the focus and the directrix of the graph of each equation. Sketch the graph.

19. $y = 5x^2$ **20.** $x = 2y^2$ **21.** $x = -\frac{1}{8}y^2$

10-3 Circles

Quick Review

In a plane, a **circle** is the set of all points that are a given distance, the **radius**, r, from a given point, the **center**, (h, k).

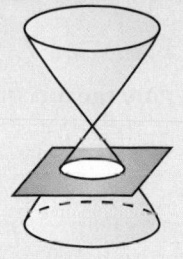

Example

Write an equation in standard form of a circle with center $(-3, 4)$ and radius 2.

Use the standard form of the equation of a circle. Substitute -3 for h, 4 for k, and 2 for r.

$$(x - h)^2 + (y - k)^2 = r^2$$
$$(x - (-3))^2 + (y - 4)^2 = 2^2$$
$$(x + 3)^2 + (y - 4)^2 = 4$$

An equation for the circle is $(x + 3)^2 + (y - 4)^2 = 4$.

Exercises

Write an equation in standard form of a circle with the given center and radius.

22. center $(0, 0)$; radius 4

23. center $(8, 1)$; radius 5

Write an equation for each translation of $x^2 + y^2 = r^2$ with the given radius.

24. left 3 units, up 2 units; radius 10

25. right 5 units, down 3 units; radius 8

Find the center and the radius of each circle. Graph each circle. Describe the translation from center $(0, 0)$.

26. $(x - 1)^2 + y^2 = 64$

27. $(x + 7)^2 + (y + 3)^2 = 49$

10-4 Ellipses

Quick Review

An **ellipse** is the set of all points P, where the sum of the distances between P and two fixed points, the **foci**, is constant. The **major axis** contains the foci, and its endpoints are the **vertices of the ellipse**. For $a > b$, there are two standard forms of ellipses centered at the origin. If $\frac{x^2}{a^2} + \frac{y^2}{b^2} = 1$, the major axis is horizontal with vertices $(\pm a, 0)$, foci $(\pm c, 0)$, and co-vertices $(0, \pm b)$. If $\frac{x^2}{b^2} + \frac{y^2}{a^2} = 1$, the major axis is vertical with vertices $(0, \pm a)$, foci $(0, \pm c)$, and co-vertices $(\pm b, 0)$.
In either case, $c^2 = a^2 - b^2$.

Example

Write an equation of an ellipse with foci $(\pm 5, 0)$ and co-vertices $(0, \pm 3)$.

Since the foci are $(\pm 5, 0)$, the major axis is horizontal. Since $c = 5$ and $b = 3$, $c^2 = 25$ and $b^2 = 9$. Using the equation $c^2 = a^2 - b^2$, $a^2 = 34$.
An equation of the ellipse is $\frac{x^2}{34} + \frac{y^2}{9} = 1$.

Exercises

Write an equation of an ellipse centered at the origin, satisfying the given conditions.

28. foci $(\pm 1, 0)$; co-vertices $(0, \pm 4)$

29. vertex $(0, \sqrt{29})$; co-vertex $(-5, 0)$

30. focus $(0, 1)$; vertex $(0, \sqrt{10})$

31. foci $(\pm 2, 0)$; co-vertices $(0, \pm 6)$

32. Write an equation of an ellipse centered at the origin with height 8 units and width 16 units.

33. Find the foci of the graph of $\frac{x^2}{4} + \frac{y^2}{9} = 1$. Graph the ellipse.

10-5 Hyperbolas

Quick Review

A **hyperbola** is the set of all points P such that the absolute value of the difference of the distances from P to two fixed points, the **foci**, is constant. There are two standard forms of hyperbolas centered at the origin. If $\frac{x^2}{a^2} - \frac{y^2}{b^2} = 1$, the asymptotes are $y = \pm\frac{b}{a}x$, the **transverse axis** is horizontal with vertices $(\pm a, 0)$, and the foci are $(\pm c, 0)$. If $\frac{y^2}{a^2} - \frac{x^2}{b^2} = 1$, the asymptotes are $y = \pm\frac{a}{b}x$, the transverse axis is vertical with vertices $(0, \pm a)$, and the foci are $(0, \pm c)$. In either case, $c^2 = a^2 + b^2$.

Example

Find the foci of the graph of $\frac{x^2}{25} - \frac{y^2}{9} = 1$.

The equation is in the form $\frac{x^2}{a^2} - \frac{y^2}{b^2} = 1$, so the transverse axis is horizontal; $a^2 = 25$ and $b^2 = 9$.

Using the Pythagorean Theorem to find c,
$c = \sqrt{25 + 9} = \sqrt{34} \approx 5.8$.
The foci, $(\pm c, 0)$, are approximately $(5.8, 0)$ and $(-5.8, 0)$.

Exercises

Find the foci of each hyperbola. Graph the hyperbola.

34. $\dfrac{x^2}{36} - \dfrac{y^2}{225} = 1$

35. $\dfrac{y^2}{400} - \dfrac{x^2}{169} = 1$

36. $\dfrac{x^2}{121} - \dfrac{y^2}{81} = 1$

Write an equation of a hyperbola with the given foci and vertices.

37. foci $(\pm 17, 0)$, vertices $(\pm 8, 0)$

38. foci $(0, \pm 25)$, vertices $(0, \pm 7)$

39. Find an equation that models the hyperbolic path of a spacecraft around a planet if $a = 107{,}124$ km and $c = 213{,}125.9$ km.

Do you know HOW?

Graph each equation. Identify the conic section and describe the graph and its lines of symmetry. Then find the domain and range.

1. $36 - 9x^2 - 4y^2 = 0$

2. $9x^2 - 4y^2 - 36 = 0$

3. $x^2 + 4y^2 = 4$

4. $4x^2 + 36 = 9y^2$

Identify the focus and the directrix of the graph of each equation.

5. $y = 3x^2$

6. $x = -2y^2$

7. $x + 5y^2 = 0$

8. $9x^2 - 2y = 0$

Write an equation of a parabola with its vertex at the origin and the given characteristics.

9. focus at $(0, -2)$

10. focus at $(3, 0)$

11. directrix $x = 7$

12. directrix $y = -1$

For each equation, find the center and radius of the circle. Graph the circle.

13. $(x - 2)^2 + (y - 3)^2 = 36$

14. $(x + 5)^2 + (y + 8)^2 = 100$

15. $(x - 1)^2 + (y + 7)^2 = 81$

16. $(x + 4)^2 + (y - 10)^2 = 121$

Write an equation of an ellipse for each given height and width. Assume that the center of the ellipse is $(0, 0)$.

17. height 10 units; width 16 units

18. height 2 units; width 12 units

19. height 9 units; width 5 units

Find the foci of each ellipse. Then graph the ellipse.

20. $x^2 + \dfrac{y^2}{49} = 1$ **21.** $4x^2 + y^2 = 4$

Find the foci of each hyperbola. Then graph the hyperbola.

22. $\dfrac{x^2}{64} - \dfrac{y^2}{4} = 1$ **23.** $y^2 - \dfrac{x^2}{225} = 1$

Write an equation of an ellipse centered at the origin with the given characteristics.

24. horizontal major axis of length 8; minor axis of length 6

25. vertical major axis of length 12; minor axis of length 10

Write an equation of a hyperbola with the given characteristics.

26. vertices $(\pm 3, 0)$; foci $(\pm 5, 0)$

27. vertices $(0, \pm 5)$; foci $(0, \pm 7)$

Do you UNDERSTAND?

28. Reasoning Suppose you graph a conic section that has two foci and a range of all real numbers. What type of conic section did you graph? Explain.

29. Reasoning What shape is an ellipse whose height and width are equal?

30. Open-Ended Write an equation of a hyperbola whose transverse axis is on the x-axis.

T·I·P·S F·O·R S·U·C·C·E·S·S

Read the question at the right. Then follow the tips to answer the multiple choice question.

TIP 1

Read the labels on the axes to understand the meaning of a point on the graph.

A stone falls from a 56-foot cliff. The graph shows the height of the stone h, in feet, after t seconds. In about how many seconds does the stone reach the ground?

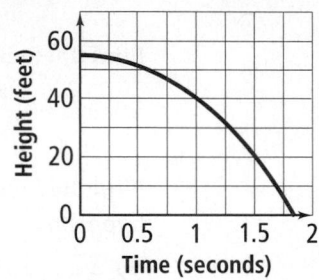

Time (seconds)

Ⓐ 0.9 second   Ⓒ 1.5 seconds

Ⓑ 1.0 second   Ⓓ 1.9 seconds

TIP 2

Use the graph to determine when $h = 0$.

Think It Through

Find the point where the graph crosses the horizontal axis.

The graph crosses the horizontal axis at about $(1.9, 0)$. So the stone reaches the ground in about 1.9 seconds.

The correct answer is D.

Vocabulary Builder

As you solve test items, you must understand the meanings of mathematical terms. Match each term with its mathematical meaning.

A. conic section

B. hyperbola

C. directrix

D. ellipse

E. circle

I. a set of points P in a plane such that the absolute value of the difference between the distances from P to two fixed points F_1 and F_2 is a constant k

II. a set of points P in a plane such that the sum of the distances from P to two fixed points F_1 and F_2 is a constant k

III. the set of all points in a plane that are a distance r from a given point

IV. a curve formed by the intersection of a plane and a double cone

V. the fixed line equidistant with the focus from each point on a parabola

Multiple Choice

Read each question. Then write the letter of the correct answer on your paper.

1. The graph of $\frac{x^2}{21} - \frac{y^2}{4} = 1$ is a hyperbola. Which set of coordinates represents the foci?

Ⓐ $(0, 5)$ and $(0, -5)$

Ⓑ $(5, 0)$ and $(0, -5)$

Ⓒ $(0, 5)$ and $(-5, 0)$

Ⓓ $(5, 0)$ and $(-5, 0)$

2. If the equation $y = 4x$ is graphed, which of the following values of x would produce a point on the x-axis?

Ⓕ 3   Ⓗ 1

Ⓖ 0   Ⓘ 4

3. An acrobat landed on a teeterboard and launched his partner into the air. The graph below shows the height *h* of the partner, in yards, at *t* seconds after the launch.

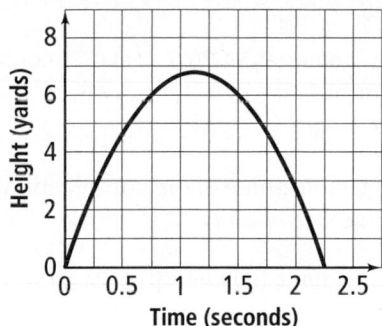

Which value is the best approximation of the maximum height of the partner?

- (A) 6.0 yards
- (C) 6.8 yards
- (B) 6.4 yards
- (D) 7.2 yards

4. The bacteria in a petri dish are growing exponentially with time, as shown in the table below.

Bacteria Growth

Day	Bacteria
0	50
1	150
2	450

Which of the following equations expresses the number of bacteria *y* present on day *x*?

- (F) $y = (3)^x$
- (G) $y = 50 + (3)^x$
- (H) $y = 50 \cdot (3)^x$
- (I) $y = 150 \cdot (3)^x$

5. A truck driver traveled 120 miles in 2.5 hours. How far can he drive in 2 hours?

- (A) 48 miles
- (C) 96 miles
- (B) 72 miles
- (D) 144 miles

6. Alexandra dives from a 30-foot board into a swimming pool. The graph below shows her height *h*, in feet, *t* seconds after jumping.

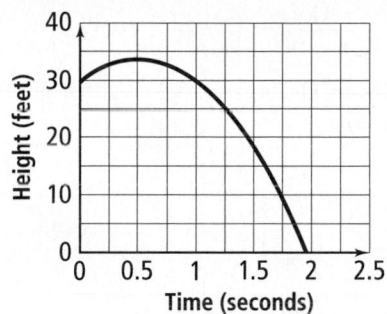

After leaving the board, in how many seconds is Alexandra at the height of 30 feet again?

- (F) 0.5 second
- (H) 1.5 seconds
- (G) 1 second
- (I) 2 seconds

7. What is the standard form of the equation of the conic section given below?

$$25x^2 - 49y^2 - 1225 = 0$$

- (A) $\dfrac{x^2}{49} - \dfrac{y^2}{25} = 1$
- (B) $\dfrac{x^2}{49} + \dfrac{y^2}{25} = 1$
- (C) $25x^2 - 49y^2 = 1225$
- (D) $49x^2 - 25y^2 = 1$

8. Owen threw a ball straight up into the air from an initial height of 5 feet. The graph below shows the height *h* of the ball, in feet, at *t* seconds after Owen threw it. Of the following times, when was the ball closest to the ground?

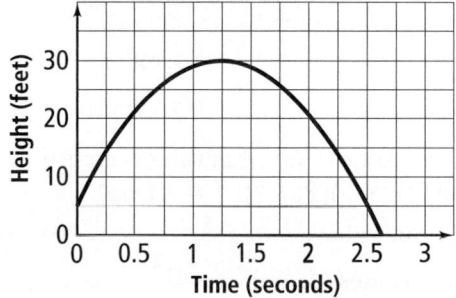

- (F) 0.6 second
- (H) 1.6 seconds
- (G) 1 second
- (I) 2 seconds

9. Which is the first *incorrect* step in simplifying?

$$\frac{4}{(x-1)^{-1}(x^2+3x-4)}$$

Step 1: $\dfrac{4(x-1)}{x^2+3x-4}$

Step 2: $\dfrac{4(x-1)}{(x+4)(x-1)}$

Step 3: $\dfrac{4(x-1)}{(x+4)(x-1)} \div \dfrac{x-1}{x-1}$

Step 4: $\dfrac{4}{x+4} \div \dfrac{4}{4} = \dfrac{1}{x}$

   Ⓐ Step 1   Ⓒ Step 3

   Ⓑ Step 2   Ⓓ Step 4

10. Which of the following is the graph of the quadratic parent function?

Ⓕ 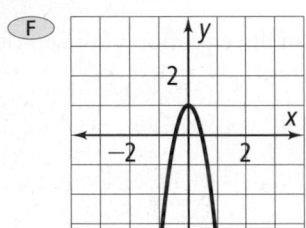   Ⓗ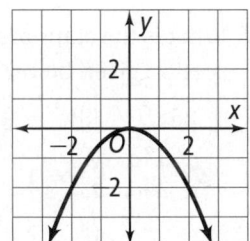

Ⓖ 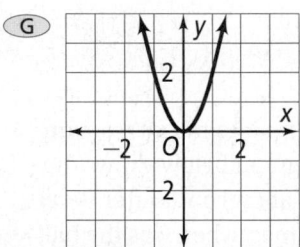   Ⓘ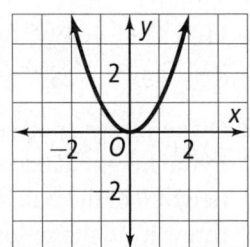

11. Which conic section is represented by the equation $x^2 + y^2 = 6x - 14y - 9$?

   Ⓐ circle   Ⓒ ellipse

   Ⓑ parabola   Ⓓ hyperbola

12. If x is a real number, for what values of x is the equation $(3x - 6)(x - 2)^{-1} = 3$ true?

   Ⓕ all values of x

   Ⓖ some values of x

   Ⓗ no values of x

   Ⓘ impossible to determine

13. What is the value of $\dfrac{1 - \frac{1}{8}}{2 - \frac{3}{4}}$?

14. A copy center charges \$4.26 to make 71 copies. At that rate, how much will the copy center charge for 165 copies?

15. What is the y-coordinate of the y-intercept of the line with equation $-6x - 2y = 7$?

16. What is the distance between $(-3, 2)$ and $(5, -4)$?

Short Response

17. Write an explicit formula for the geometric sequence for which $a_1 = -5$ and $r = 3$. Then generate the first five terms.

18. Write the expression $\dfrac{35x^3}{24} \div \dfrac{5x}{16}$ in simplest form.

19. Find the zeros of the function $y = x^2 - 2x$. Show your work.

Extended Response

20. Suppose you put \$10,000 in an account that pays 6.5% annual interest compounded continuously. How much will be in the account after one year? After five years?

21. Explain how to graph $y = \sqrt{x} - 3$ by translating the graph of $y = \sqrt{x}$.

22. Find a nonzero value for k such that the equation $kx^2 - 10x + 25 = 0$ has one solution. Show your work.

23. Explain when the function $y = a \cdot b^x$ models exponential growth and when it models exponential decay.

Get Ready!

Skills Handbook, page 865

Finding Percent

Write each number as a percent.

1. $\frac{5}{6}$

2. $\frac{7}{36}$

3. $\frac{48}{52}$

4. 0.3056

Skills Handbook, page 868

Simplifying Expressions

Simplify each expression.

5. $8 \cdot 7 \cdot 6 \cdot 5 \cdot 4$

6. $\frac{52 \cdot 51 \cdot 50}{3 \cdot 2 \cdot 1}$

7. $\frac{5 \cdot 4 \cdot 3 \cdot 2 \cdot 1}{3 \cdot 2 \cdot 1 \cdot 2 \cdot 1}$

Lesson 5-7

Expanding Binomials

Use Pascal's Triangle to expand each binomial.

8. $(a + b)^5$

9. $(j + 3k)^3$

10. $(m + 0.7)^2$

11. $(2 + t)^4$

12. $(m + n)^2$

13. $(x + 3y)^4$

Lesson 6-1

Finding Real Roots

Find the real square roots of each number.

14. $\frac{1}{100}$

15. $\frac{1}{400}$

16. $\frac{1}{196}$

17. $\frac{1}{4}$

18. $\frac{1}{9}$

19. $\frac{1}{576}$

Looking Ahead Vocabulary

20. In a history class, students may learn about history through a *simulation*. How do you think simulations might be used in a math class?

21. When you describe the likelihood that it will rain tomorrow given that it rained today, you are giving a *conditional probability*. What is the condition in this situation?

22. When you give a value to represent the typical data value in a data set, you are giving a *measure of central tendency* of the data set. What value do you think best represents the following data set? Explain.

$\{1, 3, 3, 3, 4, 10, 20, 30, 40\}$

Probability and Statistics

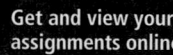

In this chapter you will learn about probability and statistics.

What's the probability of scoring in soccer on a penalty kick? Do statistics from past games help you decide? How do you apply theoretical and experimental probabilities? How can you compare data sets? You will learn how in this chapter.

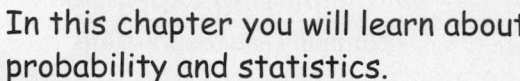

Vocabulary for Part A

English/Spanish Vocabulary Audio Online:

English	Spanish
combination, *p. 690*	combinación
conditional probability, *p. 711*	probabilidad condicional
experimental probability, *p. 695*	probabilidad experimental
mutually exclusive events, *p. 705*	sucesos mutuamente excluyentes
permutation, *p. 687*	permutación
simulation, *p. 696*	simulación
theoretical probability, *p. 698*	probabilidad teórica

My Math Video

00:04:04

VIDEO

BIG ideas

1 Probability
Essential Question What is the difference between a permutation and a combination?

2 Probability
Essential Question What is the difference between experimental and theoretical probability?

3 Data Collection and Analysis
Essential Question How are measures of central tendency different from standard deviation?

Chapter Preview for Part A

11-1
PART 1

Permutations and Combinations

Objectives To use the Fundamental Counting Principle
To count permutations

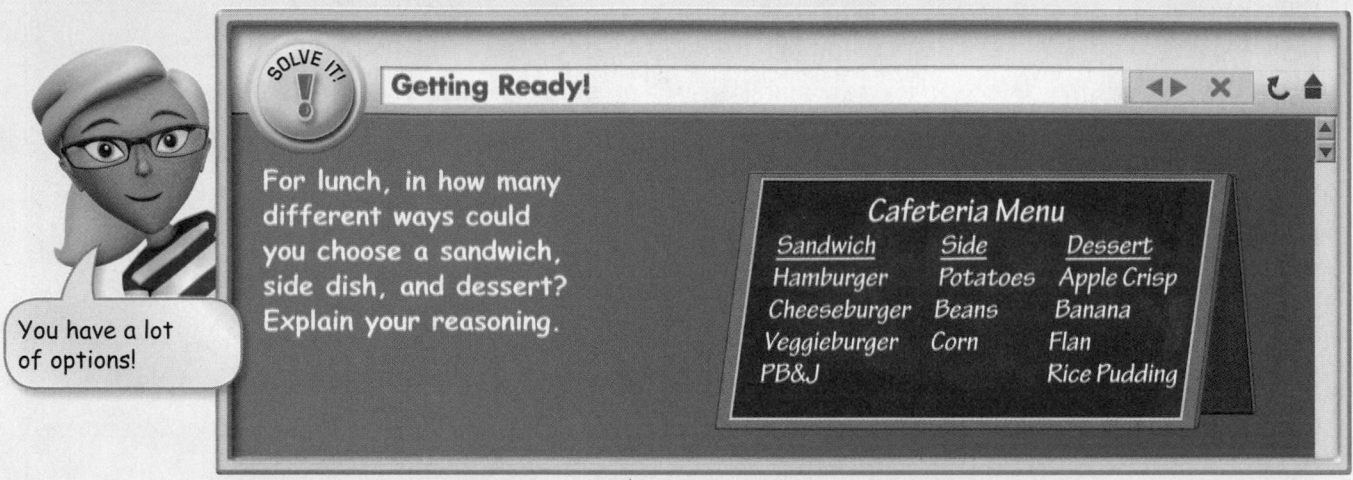

You have a lot of options!

Getting Ready!

For lunch, in how many different ways could you choose a sandwich, side dish, and dessert? Explain your reasoning.

Cafeteria Menu

Sandwich	Side	Dessert
Hamburger	Potatoes	Apple Crisp
Cheeseburger	Beans	Banana
Veggieburger	Corn	Flan
PB&J		Rice Pudding

Lesson Vocabulary
- Fundamental Counting Principle
- permutation
- *n* factorial

It is fairly easy to count the ways you can pick items from a short list. But, sometimes there are so many choices that counting the possibilities is impractical.

Focus Question What is a permutation?

The **Fundamental Counting Principle** describes the method of using multiplication to count the number of ways certain things can happen.

> *take note*
>
> **Key Concept** **Fundamental Counting Principle**
>
> If event M can occur in m ways and is followed by event N that can occur in n ways, then event M followed by event N can occur in $m \cdot n$ ways.
>
> **Example** 3 pairs of pants and 2 shirts give $3 \cdot 2 = 6$ possible outfits.

Hint

This diagram assumes you choose the pants first. You could instead choose a shirt first and obtain 2 groups of 3 outfits, or $2 \cdot 3 = 6$ outfits.

Here's Why It Works Making a tree diagram, you can see that there are 3 groups of 2 outfits, or $3 \cdot 2 = 6$ outfits.

You can extend the Fundamental Counting Principle to three or more events.

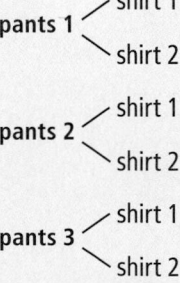

pants 1 — shirt 1 / shirt 2

pants 2 — shirt 1 / shirt 2

pants 3 — shirt 1 / shirt 2

 **Problem 1** Using the Fundamental Counting Principle

Motor Vehicles The photos show Maryland license plates in 2004 and 1912. How many more 2004-style license plates were possible than 1912-style plates?

Think

How many digits are in our number system? How many letters are in our alphabet?
There are 10 digits and 26 letters.

The 2004 license plates had places for three letters and three digits.

Number of possible 2004 license plates:

$26 \cdot 26 \cdot 26 \cdot 10 \cdot 10 \cdot 10 = 17{,}576{,}000$

The 1912 license plates had places for four digits.

Number of possible 1912 license plates:

$10 \cdot 10 \cdot 10 \cdot 10 = 10{,}000$

Find the difference. $17{,}576{,}000 - 10{,}000 = 17{,}566{,}000$

There were 17,566,000 more 2004-style license plates possible than 1912-style plates.

 Got It? **1.** In 1966, one type of Maryland license plate had two letters followed by four digits. How many of this type of license plate were possible?

A **permutation** is an arrangement of items in a particular order. Suppose you want to find the number of ways to order three items. There are 3 ways to choose the first item, 2 ways to choose the second, and 1 way to choose the third. By the Fundamental Counting Principle, there are $3 \cdot 2 \cdot 1 = 6$ permutations.

Hint

A special case is zero factorial:
$0! = 1$

Using *factorial* notation, you can write $3 \cdot 2 \cdot 1$ as 3!, read "three factorial." For any positive integer n, **n factorial** is $n! = n \cdot (n-1) \cdot \ldots \cdot 3 \cdot 2 \cdot 1$.

 **Problem 2** Finding the Number of Permutations of n Items

Plan

What strategy can you use to help you see how to solve?
Act it out and you will see how many options you have at each step.

In how many ways can you file 12 folders, one after another, in a drawer?

Use the Fundamental Counting Principle to count the number of permutations of 12 items. There are 12 ways to select the first folder, 11 ways to select the next folder, and so on. The total number of permutations is

$12! = 12 \cdot 11 \cdot \ldots \cdot 2 \cdot 1 = 479{,}001{,}600.$

There are 479,001,600 ways to file 12 folders in a drawer.

 Got It? **2.** In how many ways can you arrange 8 shirts on hangers in a closet?

Sometimes you are interested in the number of permutations possible ordering just a few objects from a set at a time. You can still use the Fundamental Counting Principle or factorial notation.

Key Concept Number of Permutations

The number of permutations of n items of a set arranged r items at a time is

$$_nP_r = \frac{n!}{(n-r)!} \text{ for } 0 \le r \le n.$$

Example $_{10}P_4 = \frac{10!}{(10-4)!} = \frac{10!}{6!} = 5040$

Problem 3 Finding $_nP_r$

Track Ten students are in a race. First, second, and third places will win medals. In how many ways can 10 runners finish first, second, and third (no ties allowed)?

Method 1 Use the Fundamental Counting Principle.

$$10 \cdot 9 \cdot 8 = 720$$

Method 2 Use the permutation formula.

There are $n = 10$ runners to arrange $r = 3$ at a time.

Use the formula for permutations.	$_nP_r = \frac{n!}{(n-r)!}$
Substitute 10 for n and 3 for r.	$_{10}P_3 = \frac{10!}{(10-3)!}$
Subtract in the denominator. Then, rewrite 10! to find common factors.	$= \frac{10!}{7!} = \frac{10 \cdot 9 \cdot 8 \cdot 7!}{7!}$
Remove the common factors and simplify.	$= 10 \cdot 9 \cdot 8 = 720$

There are 720 ways that 10 runners can finish in first, second, and third places.

Got It? **3. a.** In how many ways can 15 runners finish first, second, and third?

b. Reasoning In Problem 3, is the number of ways for runners to finish first, second, and third the same as the number of ways to finish eighth, ninth, and tenth? Explain.

Focus Question What is a permutation?

Answer A permutation is an arrangement of items in a particular order. Use the permutation formula to quickly count the number of ways to order n items r at a time.

Lesson Check

Do you know HOW?

Evaluate each expression.

1. $_6P_3$ **2.** $_9P_4$ **3.** $_5P_2$

Do you UNDERSTAND?

4. Open-Ended Describe a situation in which the number of outcomes is given by $_9P_2$.

Practice and Problem-Solving Exercises

A Practice

Guided Practice

See Problem 1.

Use the Fundamental Counting Principle to solve each problem.

5. To make an entry code, you need to first choose a letter and then choose three single-digit numbers. How many different entry codes are possible?

To start, record what you know.	Number of letters: 26
	Number of digits: 10
Describe what you need to find.	The number of codes possible using one letter and three digits

6. The prom committee has four sites available for the banquet and three sites for the dance. How many arrangements are possible for the banquet and dance?

Evaluate each expression.

See Problem 2.

7. 5! **8.** 10! **9.** 5!3!

10. $\frac{12!}{6!}$ **11.** $\frac{10!}{7!3!}$ **12.** $\frac{15!}{10!5!}$

13. Automobiles You should rotate tires on a car at regular intervals.
    a. In how many ways can four tires be arranged on a car?
    b. If a spare tire is included, how many arrangements are possible?

Evaluate each expression.

See Problem 3.

Guided Practice

14. $_8P_1$

To start, write the formula for permutations. $_nP_r = \frac{n!}{(n-r)!}$

15. $_8P_2$ **16.** $_8P_3$ **17.** $_8P_4$

18. $_3P_2$ **19.** $_7P_4$ **20.** $_9P_6$

21. Scheduling Fifteen students ask to visit a college admissions counselor. Each scheduled visit includes one student. In how many ways can ten time slots be assigned?

B Apply

Assume a and b are positive integers. Determine whether each statement is _true_ or _false_. If it is true, explain why. If it is false, give a counterexample.

22. $a! + b! = b! + a!$ **23.** $a!(b!c!) = (a!b!)c!$ **24.** $(a+b)! = a! + b!$

25. $(ab)! = a!b!$ **26.** $(a!)! = (a!)^2$ **27.** $(a!)^b = a^{(b!)}$

28. Writing In how many ways is it possible to arrange the two numbers a and b in an ordered pair? Explain why such a pair is called an _ordered_ pair.

11-1
PART 2

Permutations and Combinations

Objectives To count permutations
To count combinations

In Part 1 of the lesson, you learned how to find the number of arrangements of items when order is important.

Connect to What You Know

Here you will learn to find the number of ways to select items when order does not matter.

Lesson Vocabulary
• combination

Focus Question What is a combination?

In Problem 3, you found the number of ways that 10 runners can finish in first, second, and third places. Suppose instead that the three runners who finish first, second, and third in a race advance to a championship race. In this case, the order in which the first three runners cross the finish line does not matter. A selection in which order does not matter is called a **combination**.

As with permutations, you can use a formula to find the number of combinations of n items chosen r at a time.

Hint

The formula for combinations is similar to the formula for permutations. This formula has an additional factorial in the denominator.

take note

Key Concept Number of Combinations

The number of combinations of n items of a set chosen r items at a time is

$$_nC_r = \frac{n!}{r!(n-r)!} \text{ for } 0 \le r \le n.$$

Example $_5C_3 = \frac{5!}{3!(5-3)!} = \frac{5!}{3! \cdot 2!} = \frac{120}{6 \cdot 2} = 10$

Problem 4 Finding $_nC_r$

What is $_{13}C_4$, the number of combinations of 13 items taken 4 at a time?

Think **Write**

Write the formula for the number of combinations.

$$_nC_r = \frac{n!}{r!(n-r)!}$$

Substitute 13 for n and 4 for r. Subtract in the denominator.

$$_{13}C_4 = \frac{13!}{4!(13-4)!}$$

$$= \frac{13!}{4! \cdot 9!}$$

Hint

Similar to how you simplified expressions for the number of permutations, you can always find and remove common factors.

Write out the factors of the numerator until you get a common factor of the denominator.

$$= \frac{13 \cdot 12 \cdot 11 \cdot 10 \cdot 9!}{4! \cdot 9!}$$

Write out the factors of the denominator. Remove common factors and simplify.

$$= \frac{13 \cdot \overset{}{12} \cdot 11 \cdot \overset{5}{10}}{\overset{}{4} \cdot \overset{}{3} \cdot \overset{}{2} \cdot 1}$$

$$= 13 \cdot 11 \cdot 5 = 715$$

Write the answer in words.

There are 715 combinations of 13 items taken 4 at a time.

 Got It? **4.** What is the value of each expression?

  a. $_8C_3$ **b.** $_9C_2$ **c.** $_{15}C_5$

Problem 5 Identifying Whether Order is Important

For each situation, determine whether you should use a permutation or combination. What is the answer to each question?

Plan

How will you solve?
If order is important, use the formula $_nP_r = \frac{n!}{(n-r)!}$. If order is not important, use the formula $_nC_r = \frac{n!}{r!(n-r)!}$.

A A chemistry teacher divides his class into eight groups. Each group submits one drawing of the molecular structure of water. He will select four of the drawings to display. In how many different ways can he select the drawings?

Write the formula for combinations.

$$_nC_r = \frac{n!}{r!(n-r)!}$$

There is no reason why order is important. Use a combination.

Substitute 8 for n and 4 for r.

$$_8C_4 = \frac{8!}{4!(8-4)!}$$

Subtract in the denominator.

$$= \frac{8!}{4! \cdot 4!}$$

Rewrite to show common factors.

$$= \frac{8 \cdot 7 \cdot 6 \cdot 5 \cdot 4!}{4 \cdot 3 \cdot 2 \cdot 1 \cdot 4!}$$

Simplify.

$$= \frac{8 \cdot 7 \cdot 6 \cdot 5}{4 \cdot 3 \cdot 2 \cdot 1} = 70$$

There are 70 ways to select the drawings.

B You will draw winners from a total of 25 tickets in a raffle. The first ticket wins
$100. The second ticket wins $50. The third ticket wins $10. In how many different
ways can you draw the three winning tickets?

The values of the tickets depend on the order in which you draw them.
Order is important. Use a permutation.

Write the formula for permutations.	$_nP_r = \dfrac{n!}{(n-r)!}$
Substitute 25 for n and 3 for r.	$_{25}P_3 = \dfrac{25!}{(25-3)!}$
Subtract in the denominator.	$= \dfrac{25!}{22!}$
Rewrite to show common factors.	$= \dfrac{25 \cdot 24 \cdot 23 \cdot 22!}{22!}$
Simplify.	$= 25 \cdot 24 \cdot 23 = 13{,}800$

There are 13,800 ways you can draw the winning tickets.

Hint

When determining
whether to use
a permutation or
combination, you
must decide whether
order is important.

Got It? **5.** In Problem 5(a), in how many ways can the teacher select and arrange the
four drawings from left to right on the wall?

Focus Question What is a combination?

Answer A combination is a selection of items for which order does not matter. Use
the combination formula to find the number of groups of n items chosen r at a time.

 Lesson Check

Do you know HOW?

Evaluate each expression.

1. $_5C_2$ **2.** $_7C_5$ **3.** $_4C_3$

4. Sports How many different nine-player batting
orders can be chosen from a baseball team of 16?

Do you UNDERSTAND?

5. Vocabulary Explain the difference between
permutations and combinations.

6. Open-Ended Describe a situation in which the
number of outcomes is given by $_4C_2$.

Practice and Problem-Solving Exercises

See Problem 4.

 **Practice**

Evaluate each expression.

Guided Practice

7. $_6C_2$

To start, write the formula for combinations.

$$_nC_r = \frac{n!}{r!(n-r)!}$$

8. $_8C_5$ **9.** $_4C_4$ **10.** $_7C_3$

11. $3(_5C_4)$ **12.** $_6C_2 + _6C_3$ **13.** $\dfrac{_7C_4}{_9C_4}$

14. Awards There are eight swimmers in a competition where the top three swimmers advance. In how many ways can three swimmers advance?

For each situation, determine whether to use a permutation or a combination. Then solve the problem.

See Problem 5.

15. How many different teams of 11 players can be chosen from a soccer team of 16?

16. Suppose you find seven equally useful articles related to the topic of your research paper. In how many ways can you choose five articles to read?

17. A salad bar offers eight choices of toppings for a salad. In how many ways can you choose four toppings?

B **Apply**

18. Think About a Plan You and your friends are picking up videos at a video store. You have selected 7 videos but will only have time to watch 3 videos together. How many different ways can you select the 3 videos to watch?
- Does the order in which the videos are selected make a difference?
- What formula should you use?

19. Security A car door lock has a five-button keypad. Each button has two numerals. The entry code 21914 uses the same button sequence as the code 11023. How many different five-button patterns are possible? You can use a button more than once.

A 120   B 720   C 3125   D 5555

20. Consumer Issues A consumer magazine rates televisions by identifying two levels of price, five levels of repair frequency, three levels of features, and two levels of picture quality. How many different ratings are possible?

21. Reasoning Determine whether the statement $_nC_r = _nP_r$ is *always*, *sometimes*, or *never* true. Explain your reasoning.

22. There are 3!, or 6, arrangements of 3 objects. Consider the number of clockwise arrangements possible for objects placed in a loop, without a beginning or end.

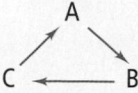 ABC, BCA, and CAB are all parts of one possible clockwise loop arrangement of the letters A, B, and C.

a. Find the number of clockwise loop arrangements possible for letters A, B, and C.
b. Use the diagram at the right to help find the number of loop arrangements possible for A, B, C, and D.
c. Write an expression for the number of clockwise loop arrangements for n objects.

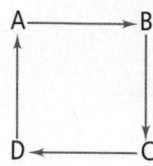

Standardized Test Prep

23. What is the value of $_7C_2$?

   (A) 2520   (B) 49   (C) 42   (D) 21

24. What are all the solutions of $\frac{3}{x^2-1} + \frac{4x}{x+1} = \frac{1.5}{x-1}$?

   (F) 1, −1   (G) 1, 0.375   (H) 0.375   (I) 0.375, 3

25. Use a calculator to solve $-x^2 - 3x + 7 = 0$. Round to the nearest hundredth.

   (A) −0.76, 4.76   (B) 0.76, 5.76   (C) −1.54, 4.54   (D) −4.54, 1.54

26. What is the center of the circle with equation $(x - 5)^2 + (y + 1)^2 = 81$?

   (F) (5, 1)   (G) (5, −1)   (H) (−5, 1)   (I) (−5, −1)

Mixed Review

Find the foci of each hyperbola. Draw the graph.   ◀ See Lesson 10-5.

27. $\frac{x^2}{49} - \frac{y^2}{36} = 1$ **28.** $8y^2 - 6x^2 = 72$ **29.** $4y^2 - 100x^2 = 400$

Factor each expression completely.   ◀ See Lesson 4-4.

30. $4x^2 - 8x + 4$ **31.** $-x^2 - 6x - 9$ **32.** $3x^2 - 75$

Get Ready! To prepare for Lesson 11-2, do Exercises 33–35.

Simplify each expression.   ◀ See Lesson 11-1.

33. $10 \cdot 9 \cdot 8 \cdot 7 \cdot 6$ **34.** $\frac{4 \cdot 3 \cdot 2}{6 \cdot 5}$ **35.** $\frac{7 \cdot 6 \cdot 5 \cdot 4 \cdot 3 \cdot 2 \cdot 1}{4 \cdot 3 \cdot 2 \cdot 1}$

11-2 Probability
PART 1

Objective To find the probability of an event using experimental and simulation methods

Thinking of all possible outcomes can be a challenge!

◀▶ ✕ ↻ ▲

Getting Ready!

In a probability experiment, you fold an index card slightly off center, as shown at the right. Then you drop the card from a height of several feet. What outcomes are possible? Which do you think is most likely to occur? Explain your reasoning.

Dynamic Activity
Geometric Probability

Probability measures how likely it is for an event to occur. The probability of an impossible event is 0 (or 0%). The probability of a certain event is 1 (or 100%). Other events have probabilities between 0 and 1 (or between 0% and 100%).

Focus Question How can you find the probability that a given event occurs?

Lesson Vocabulary
• experimental probability
• simulation

When you gather data from observations, you can calculate an *experimental probability*. Each observation is called an experiment or a trial.

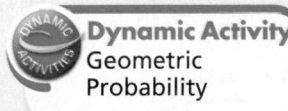

Key Concept Experimental Probability

experimental probability of event: $P(\text{event}) = \dfrac{\text{number of times the event occurs}}{\text{number of trials}}$

Problem 1 Finding Experimental Probability

Think

What is a trial? What is an event?
A trial is a vehicle parking in the lot. An event is the vehicle being a truck.

Gridded Response Of the 60 vehicles in a teachers' parking lot today, 15 are pickup trucks. What is the experimental probability that a vehicle in the lot is a pickup truck?

Use the formula. $P(\text{pickup truck}) = \dfrac{\text{number of pickup trucks}}{\text{number of vehicles}}$

Substitute and simplify. $= \dfrac{15}{60} = 0.25$

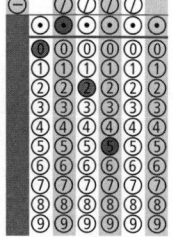

The probability that a vehicle in the lot is a pickup truck is 0.25, or 25%.

Got It? 1. A softball player got a hit in 20 of her last 50 times at bat. What is the experimental probability that she will get a hit in her next at bat?

Sometimes actual trials are difficult or unreasonable to conduct. In these situations, you can estimate the experimental probability of an event by using a simulation. A **simulation** is a model of the event.

 Problem 2 Using a Simulation

Testing On a multiple-choice test, each item has 4 choices, but only one choice is correct. How can you simulate guessing the answers? What is the probability that you will pass the test by guessing at least 6 of 10 answers correctly?

Plan

How do you simulate guessing one out of four?
You can pick at random from four numbers, specifying that one of them will be the "correct" answer.

Think

Randomly generate 1, 2, 3, or 4 ten times. Let 1 represent a correct guess. Then 2, 3, and 4 represent incorrect guesses.

Write

Enter **RANDINT** (1, 4, 10) on a graphing calculator. Press **enter** to get 10 outcomes.

The 10 outcomes represent 10 guesses on one test. Take the test a total of 20 times.

3431421212 ← Three 1's. You score 30% on the test.

Take the test 19 more times.

3242431421	4114113144	3431433434
4412432243	4141441132	2131241131
2143224113	1234312221	(2111311214)
4433323314	3242243214	4314424244
3322213323	2232224422	3233222413
4112411124	2442122233	3314222333
	3223334334	

Hint

A score of 60% is equivalent to six 1's out of 10 guesses.

Look for tests that show a score of at least 60%.

Only one test has 6 or more correct answers.

Use the probability formula.

$$P(\text{passing}) = \frac{\text{number of passing tests}}{\text{number of tests taken}}$$
$$= \frac{1}{20} = 0.05 = 5\%$$

 Got It? **2.** In Problem 2, what is the probability of passing if a passing score is 50% or better?

Focus Question How can you find the probability that a given event occurs?

Answer Gather data from observations or simulations to find the experimental probability of an event.

Lesson Check

Do you know HOW?

1. What is the probability a quarterback will complete his next pass if he has completed 30 of his last 40 passes?

2. What is the probability a quarterback will complete his next pass if he has completed 36 of his last 45 passes?

Do you UNDERSTAND?

3. **Writing** List three ways you could simulate answering a true-false question.

4. **Reasoning** Why is a simulation better the more times you perform it?

Practice and Problem-Solving Exercises

 **Practice**

Find each experimental probability.

 See Problem 1.

Guided Practice

5. A class tossed coins and recorded 161 heads and 179 tails. What is the experimental probability of heads? Of tails?

To start, write the formula for experimental probability.

$$P(\text{heads}) = \frac{\text{number of heads}}{\text{number of tosses}}$$

6. A class rolled number cubes. Their results are shown in the table. What is the experimental probability of rolling each number?

Number	1	2	3	4	5	6
Occurrences	42	44	45	44	47	46

 **Graphing Calculator** For Exercises 7–9, define a simulation by telling how you represent correct answers, incorrect answers, and the quiz. Use your simulation to find each experimental probability.

See Problem 2.

7. If you guess the answers at random, what is the probability of getting at least two correct answers on a five-question true-or-false quiz?

8. If you guess the answers at random, what is the probability of getting at least three correct answers on a five-question true-or-false quiz?

9. A five-question multiple-choice quiz has five choices for each answer. What is the probability of correctly guessing at random exactly one correct answer? Exactly two correct answers? Exactly three correct answers? (*Hint:* You could let any two digits represent correct answers, and the other digits represent wrong answers.)

 **Apply**

10. a. **Sports** Out of four games, team A has won one game and team B has won three games in a championship series. What is the experimental probability that team A wins the next game? That team B wins the next game?

b. **Reasoning** Do you think that experimental probability is a good predictor of the winner of the next game? Explain.

11-2
PART 2

Probability

Objective To find the probability of an event using theoretical methods

In Part 1 of the lesson, you learned how to find experimental probability based on observations and simulations.

Connect to What You Know

Here you will find probabilities based on the number and likelihood of outcomes in a sample space.

Lesson Vocabulary
- sample space
- equally likely outcomes
- theoretical probability

Focus Question What is theoretical probability?

The set of all possible outcomes to an experiment or activity is a **sample space**. When each outcome in a sample space has the same chance of occurring, the outcomes are **equally likely outcomes**.

For one roll of a standard number cube, there are six equally likely outcomes in the sample space. You can calculate *theoretical probability* as a ratio of outcomes.

take note

Key Concept Theoretical Probability

If a sample space has n equally likely outcomes and an event A occurs in m of these outcomes, then the **theoretical probability** of event A is $P(A) = \frac{m}{n}$.

Sample space: n outcomes

Event A: m outcomes

Problem 3 Finding Theoretical Probability

What is the theoretical probability of each event?

A getting a 5 on one roll of a standard number cube

There are six equally likely outcomes: 1, 2, 3, 4, 5, and 6. A 5 occurs in only one way.

$$P(5) = \frac{1}{6}$$

Plan

How many outcomes are there?
Each cube has six numbers on it, so there are
$6 \cdot 6 = 36$ outcomes.

B getting a sum of 5 on one roll of two standard number cubes

There are 36 possible equally likely outcomes. The favorable outcomes are those with a sum of 5.

$$P(\text{sum } 5) = \frac{4}{36} = \frac{1}{9}$$

Got It? **3. a.** What is the theoretical probability of getting a sum that is an odd number on one roll of two standard number cubes?

        b. **Reasoning** Without calculating the probability, is it more likely to get an even or odd number on one roll of a standard number cube? Explain.

It can be easier to use *combinatorics* to find theoretical probability rather than listing and counting all the equally likely outcomes. Combinatorics include the Fundamental Counting Principle and other ways to count permutations and combinations.

 Problem 4 **Finding Probability Using Combinatorics**

What is the theoretical probability of being dealt exactly two 7's in a 5-card hand from a standard 52-card deck?

Plan

Should you use permutations or combinations?
Order does not matter. Use combinations.

Step 1 Find the number of ways to get a hand with exactly two 7's.

A hand with exactly 2 sevens also has exactly 3 non-sevens.

Find the number of ways to choose exactly 2 sevens from 4 possible sevens.	$_4C_2$
Find the number of ways to choose exactly 3 non-sevens from the 48 remaining cards.	$_{48}C_3$
The product is the number of ways to get exactly 2 sevens.	$_4C_2 \cdot {}_{48}C_3$

Step 2 Find the number of possible 5-card hands.

Find the number of ways to choose exactly 5 cards from 52 possible cards.	$_{52}C_5$

Step 3 Find the probability.

Use the formula for probability.
$$P(\text{hand with two 7's}) = \frac{\text{number of hands with two 7's}}{\text{total number of possible hands}}$$

Substitute.
$$= \frac{_4C_2 \cdot {}_{48}C_3}{_{52}C_5}$$

Simplify.
$$= \frac{103{,}776}{2{,}598{,}960}$$

Use a calculator.
$$\approx 0.0399$$

The probability of a 5-card hand with exactly two 7's is about 0.04, or 4%.

 Got It? **4.** What is the theoretical probability of being dealt all four 7's in a 5-card hand?

Sometimes you can use areas to find a theoretical probability.

Problem 5 Finding Geometric Probability

Geometry A batter's strike zone depends on the height and stance of the batter. What is the geometric probability that a baseball thrown at random within the batter's strike zone, as shown in the figure below, will be a high-inside strike (one of the hardest pitches to hit)?

Think

What are the favorable outcomes? All outcomes?
Favorable outcomes are points in the high-inside region. All outcomes are points in the strike zone.

Use the formula for probability.

$$P(\text{high-inside strike}) = \frac{\text{area of high-inside strike zone}}{\text{area of total strike zone}}$$

Substitute.

$$= \frac{4 \cdot 6}{17 \cdot 22}$$

Use a calculator.

$$\approx 0.064$$

For a baseball thrown at random in the batter's strike zone, the probability that it will be a high-inside strike is about 6.4%.

 Got It? **5.** Suppose a batter's strike zone is 15 in.-by-20 in. and the high-inside strike zone is 3 in.-by-5 in. What is the probability that a baseball thrown at random within the strike zone will be a high-inside strike?

Focus Question What is theoretical probability?

Answer The theoretical probability of an event A is $P(A) = \frac{m}{n}$, where the sample space has n equally likely outcomes and the event A occurs in m of the outcomes.

Lesson Check

Do you know HOW?

Find the theoretical probability of each event when rolling a standard number cube.

1. $P(3)$ 　　　　　 **2.** $P(2 \text{ or } 4)$

Do you UNDERSTAND?

3. Vocabulary Explain the difference between experimental probability, theoretical probability, and geometric probability.

Practice and Problem-Solving Exercises

A Practice 　A jar contains 30 red marbles, 50 blue marbles, and 20 white marbles. You pick one marble from the jar at random. Find each theoretical probability. 　　🔵 **See Problem 3.**

Guided Practice →

To start, find the total number of outcomes. 　　　　**4.** $P(\text{red})$

$30 + 50 + 20 = 100$

5. $P(\text{blue})$ 　　　　　　　　　　　　　**6.** $P(\text{not blue})$

7. $P(\text{not white})$ 　　　　　　　　　　**8.** $P(\text{red or blue})$

A bag contains 36 red blocks, 48 green blocks, 22 yellow blocks, and 19 purple blocks. You pick one block from the bag at random. Find each theoretical probability.

9. $P(\text{green})$ 　　　　　　　　　　　　**10.** $P(\text{purple})$

11. $P(\text{not yellow})$ 　　　　　　　　　 **12.** $P(\text{green or yellow})$

13. $P(\text{yellow or not green})$ 　　　　　 **14.** $P(\text{purple or not red})$

15. Games A group of 30 students from your school is part of the audience for a TV game show. The total number of people in the audience is 150. What is the theoretical probability of 3 students from your school being selected as contestants out of 9 possible contestant spots? 　　🔵 **See Problem 4.**

See Problem 5.

Geometry Suppose that a dart lands at random on the dartboard shown at the right. Find each theoretical probability.

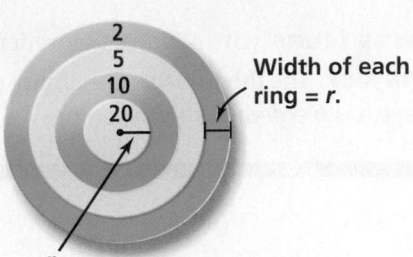

Width of each ring = r.

Guided Practice

To start, find the area of the bull's eye region.

16. The dart lands in the bull's eye.

$$A = \pi r^2$$

17. The dart lands in a green region.

18. The dart scores at least 10 points.

19. The dart scores fewer than 10 points.

B Apply

20. Think About a Plan Suppose you roll two standard number cubes. What is the theoretical probability of getting a sum of 7?
  • What is the sample space?
  • How many outcomes are there?

In a class of 147 students, 95 are taking math (M), 73 are taking science (S), and 52 are taking both math and science. One student is picked at random. Find each probability.

21. P(taking math or science or both)

22. P(not taking math)

23. P(taking math but not science)

24. P(taking neither math nor science)

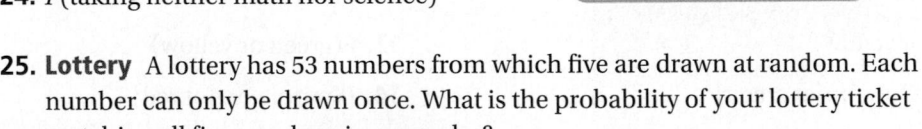

25. Lottery A lottery has 53 numbers from which five are drawn at random. Each number can only be drawn once. What is the probability of your lottery ticket matching all five numbers in any order?

26. Writing Explain what you would need to know to determine the theoretical probability of a five-digit postal ZIP code ending in 1.

Standardized Test Prep

SAT/ACT

27. What is the theoretical probability of getting a 2 or a 3 when rolling a standard number cube?

(A) $\frac{1}{2}$ (B) $\frac{1}{3}$ (C) $\frac{1}{4}$ (D) $\frac{1}{6}$

28. Which expression is equivalent to $\left(n^{\frac{3}{2}} \div n^{-\frac{1}{6}} \right)^{-3}$?

(F) n^{27} (G) n^{-27} (H) n^{-4} (I) n^{-5}

29. How can you rewrite the equation $x^2 + 12x + 5 = 3$ so the left side of the equation is in the form $(x + a)^2$?

(A) $(x - 6)^2 = 28$ (C) $(x + 6)^2 = 39$

(B) $(x + 6)^2 = 34$ (D) $(x + 12)^2 = -2$

30. How many ways are there to select 25 books from a collection of 27 books?

(F) 702   (G) 5.4×1027 (H) 351   (I) 675

Short Response

31. Use the center and radius to graph the circle with equation $(x + 4)^2 + (y - 2)^2 = 16$.

Mixed Review

Evaluate each expression.

● **See Lesson 11-1.**

32. $_5P_2$ **33.** $_7P_4$ **34.** $_5C_3$ **35.** $_{10}C_8$

Add or subtract. Simplify where possible.

● **See Lesson 8-5.**

36. $\dfrac{5}{a^2 b} - \dfrac{7a}{5b^2}$ **37.** $\dfrac{3}{p} + \dfrac{7}{q}$ **38.** $\dfrac{x}{x - 5} + \dfrac{x}{5 - x}$

Get Ready!   To prepare for Lesson 11-3, do Exercises 39–41.

A bag contains 24 green marbles, 22 blue marbles, 14 yellow marbles, and 12 red marbles. Suppose you pick one marble at random. What is each probability?

● **See Lesson 11-2.**

39. $P(\text{yellow})$ **40.** $P(\text{not blue})$ **41.** $P(\text{green or red})$

11-3 Probability of Multiple Events

Objectives To find the probability of the event A and B
To find the probability of the event A or B

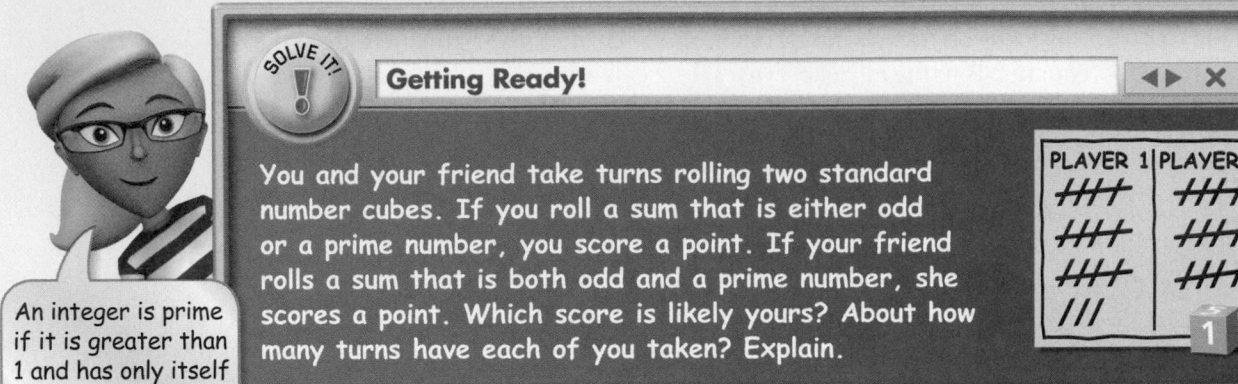

An integer is prime if it is greater than 1 and has only itself and 1 as positive integer factors.

Getting Ready!

You and your friend take turns rolling two standard number cubes. If you roll a sum that is either odd or a prime number, you score a point. If your friend rolls a sum that is both odd and a prime number, she scores a point. Which score is likely yours? About how many turns have each of you taken? Explain.

You can find the probabilities of multiple events occurring by using the probabilities of the individual events.

Focus Question How do you find the probability of multiple events?

Before you can find the probability of two events occurring together, you have to decide whether one event occurring affects the other event. When the occurrence of one event affects how a second event can occur, the events are **dependent events**. Otherwise, the events are **independent events**.

Lesson Vocabulary
• dependent events
• independent events
• mutually exclusive events

Problem 1 Classifying Events

Is each pair of events dependent or independent?

Think

What must you ask yourself?
Does the first event have an effect on the outcome of the second event?

A Roll a number cube. Then spin a spinner.

The two events do not affect each other.
They are independent.

B Pick one flash card, then another from a stack of 30 flash cards.

Picking the first card affects the possible outcomes of picking the second card.
The events are dependent.

 Got It? 1. You select a coin at random from your pocket. You replace the coin and select again. Are your selections independent events? Explain.

Multiply to find the probability that two independent events will both occur.

Dynamic Activity
Independent and
Dependent Events

take note

> **Key Concept**   Probability of *A* and *B*
>
> If *A* and *B* are independent events, then $P(A \text{ and } B) = P(A) \cdot P(B)$.

 Problem 2 Finding the Probability of Independent Events

Think

Is it important that you don't look?
Yes; probability is based on random events. It is not random if you look.

Picnic At a picnic there are 10 diet drinks and 5 regular drinks. There are also 8 bags of fat-free chips and 12 bags of regular chips. If you grab a drink and a bag of chips without looking, what is the probability that you get a diet drink and fat-free chips?

Event *A* = picking a diet drink   Event *B* = picking fat-free chips

A and *B* are independent. Picking a drink has no effect on picking the chips.

Use the formula.	$P(A \text{ and } B) = P(A) \cdot P(B)$
Write the probability of each event.	$= \dfrac{\text{number of diet drinks}}{\text{total number of drinks}} \cdot \dfrac{\text{number of bags of fat-free chips}}{\text{total number of bags of chips}}$
Substitute.	$= \dfrac{10}{15} \cdot \dfrac{8}{20}$
Simplify and use a calculator.	$= \dfrac{4}{15} \approx 0.267$

Hint

The probability that <u>both</u> events occur is always less than or equal to the probability of each individual event.

The probability that you get a diet drink and fat-free chips is about 0.267, or 26.7%.

 Got It? 2. In Problem 2, what is the probability that you get a regular drink and regular chips?

Two events that cannot happen at the same time are **mutually exclusive events**.
If *A* and *B* are mutually exclusive events, then $P(A \text{ and } B) = 0$.

 Problem 3 Mutually Exclusive Events

Think

Can you roll a 2 and a 3 at the same time?
No; only one number comes up on one roll of one number cube.

You roll a standard number cube. Are the events mutually exclusive? Explain.

A rolling a 2 and a 3

You cannot roll a 2 and 3 at the same time. These events are mutually exclusive.

B rolling an even number and a multiple of 3

The even numbers on a number cube are 2, 4, and 6. The multiples of 3 on a number cube are 3 and 6. There is one possible outcome that is both an even number *and* a multiple of 3, namely 6. These events are not mutually exclusive.

 Got It? 3. You roll a standard number cube. Are the events mutually exclusive? Explain.
   a. rolling an even number and rolling a prime number
   b. rolling an even number and rolling a number less than 2

To find the probability of either event A or event B occurring, you need to determine whether events A and B are mutually exclusive.

Key Concept **Probability of A or B**

$P(A \text{ or } B) = P(A) + P(B) - P(A \text{ and } B)$

If A and B are mutually exclusive events, then $P(A \text{ or } B) = P(A) + P(B)$.

Problem 4 **Finding Probability for Mutually Exclusive Events**

Languages At your high school, a student can take one foreign language each term. About 37% of the students take Spanish. About 15% of the students take French. What is the probability that a student chosen at random is taking Spanish or French?

Know	Need	Plan
• The percentages of students taking Spanish or French • Students can take one foreign language at a time.	The probability that a student is taking Spanish or French	Use the correct formula for $P(A \text{ or } B)$.

One foreign language each term means a student cannot take both Spanish and French. The events are mutually exclusive.

$P(A \text{ or } B) = P(A) + P(B)$ for mutually exclusive events.

$P(\text{Spanish or French}) = P(\text{Spanish}) + P(\text{French})$

Substitute. $\approx 0.37 + 0.15$

Simplify. $= 0.52$

The probability that a student chosen at random is taking Spanish or French is about 0.52, or about 52%.

Hint

Remember that 37% can be written as a decimal, 0.37, or as a fraction, $\frac{37}{100}$.

 Got It? **4. a.** In Problem 4, about 9% of the students take Mandarin Chinese. What is the probability that a student chosen at random is taking Spanish, French, or Mandarin Chinese?

b. Reasoning Without knowing the number of students in the school in Problem 4, can you determine which language most students take? Explain.

When events A and B are *not* mutually exclusive, $P(A)$ and $P(B)$ may have common outcomes. You need to subtract the probability of these common outcomes to find $P(A \text{ or } B)$.

 Problem 5 **Finding Probability**

Multiple Choice Suppose you reach into the dish and select a token at random. What is the probability that the token is round or green?

Ⓐ $\frac{2}{9}$ Ⓑ $\frac{3}{9}$ Ⓒ $\frac{6}{9}$ Ⓓ $\frac{8}{9}$

Think

Are the events mutually exclusive?
No; it is possible to have a round *and* green token.

These events are not mutually exclusive.
Use the formula $P(A \text{ or } B) = P(A) + P(B) - P(A \text{ and } B)$.

Write the formula. $P(\text{round or green})$
$$= P(\text{round}) + P(\text{green}) - P(\text{round and green})$$

Hint

The probability that <u>either</u> event occurs is always greater than or equal to the probability of each individual event.

Determine the probability for each type of token and substitute.

5 round tokens   3 green tokens   2 round and green tokens

$$= \frac{5}{9} + \frac{3}{9} - \frac{2}{9}$$

9 tokens in all

Simplify. $= \frac{6}{9}$

The probability of selecting a round or green token is $\frac{6}{9}$, or $\frac{2}{3}$. The correct answer is C.

 Got It? **5.** Suppose you select a token at random from the dish above. What is each probability?
     a. the token is square or red   **b.** the token is green or square

Focus Question How do you find the probability of multiple events?
Answer If A and B are independent events, then $P(A \text{ and } B) = P(A) \cdot P(B)$ and $P(A \text{ or } B) = P(A) + P(B) - P(A \text{ and } B)$.

 Lesson Check

Do you know HOW?

A and B are independent events. Find $P(A \text{ and } B)$.

1. $P(A) = \frac{1}{6}$, $P(B) = \frac{2}{5}$ **2.** $P(A) = \frac{9}{20}$, $P(B) = \frac{3}{4}$

C and D are mutually exclusive events. Find $P(C \text{ or } D)$.

3. $P(C) = \frac{2}{5}$, $P(D) = \frac{3}{5}$ **4.** $P(C) = \frac{1}{2}$, $P(D) = \frac{3}{8}$

5. Events A and B are not mutually exclusive. If $P(A) = \frac{1}{2}$, $P(B) = \frac{1}{4}$, and $P(A \text{ and } B) = \frac{1}{8}$, find $P(A \text{ or } B)$.

Do you UNDERSTAND?

6. Vocabulary Explain the difference between independent events and mutually exclusive events.

7. Error Analysis The weather forecast for the weekend is a 30% chance of rain on Saturday and a 70% chance of rain on Sunday. Your friend says that means there is a 100% chance of rain this weekend. What error did your friend make?

8. Open-Ended Describe two events that are mutually exclusive.

Practice and Problem-Solving Exercises

Ⓐ Practice   Classify each pair of events as *dependent* or *independent*.   ◀ **See Problem 1.**

9. A month is selected at random; a number from 1 to 30 is selected at random.

10. A month is selected at random; a day of that month is selected at random.

11. A letter of the alphabet is selected at random; one of the remaining letters is selected at random.

Q and *R* are independent events. Find $P(Q \text{ and } R)$.   ◀ **See Problem 2.**

Guided Practice
→ To start, write the formula for the probability of independent events.

12. $P(Q) = \frac{1}{4}, P(R) = \frac{2}{3}$

$P(Q \text{ and } R) = P(Q) \cdot P(R)$

13. $P(Q) = \frac{12}{17}, P(R) = \frac{3}{8}$ **14.** $P(Q) = 0.6, P(R) = 0.9$

15. Reading Suppose you have five books in your book bag. Three are novels, one is a biography, and one is a poetry book. Today you grab one book out of your bag without looking, and return it later. Tomorrow you do the same thing. What is the probability that you grab a novel both days?

Two fair number cubes are rolled. State whether the events are mutually exclusive. Explain your reasoning.   ◀ **See Problem 3.**

16. The sum is a prime number; the sum is less than 4.

17. The numbers are equal; the sum is odd.

S and *T* are mutually exclusive events. Find $P(S \text{ or } T)$.   ◀ **See Problem 4.**

Guided Practice
→ To start, write the formula for the probability of mutually exclusive events.

18. $P(S) = \frac{5}{8}, P(T) = \frac{1}{8}$

$P(S \text{ or } T) = P(S) + P(T)$

19. $P(S) = \frac{3}{5}, P(T) = \frac{1}{3}$ **20.** $P(S) = 12\%, P(T) = 27\%$

21. Population About 30% of the U.S. population is under 20 years old. About 17% of the population is over 60. What is the probability that a person chosen at random is under 20 or over 60?

A standard number cube is tossed. Find each probability. See Problem 5.

22. $P(3 \text{ or odd})$

23. $P(\text{even or less than } 4)$

24. $P(\text{odd or greater than } 2)$

25. $P(\text{odd or prime})$

 **Apply**

26. Think About a Plan A multiple-choice test has four choices for each answer. Suppose you make a random guess on three of the ten test questions. What is the probability that you will answer all three correctly?
- Is each guess a dependent event or an independent event?
- What is the probability that a random guess on one question will yield the correct answer?

27. Suppose a number from 1 to 100 is selected at random. What is the probability that a multiple of 4 or 5 is chosen?

Statistics The graph at the right shows the types of jobs held by people in the U.S. Find each probability.

28. A person is in a service occupation.

29. A person is in service or sales and office.

30. A person is neither in service nor in sales and office.

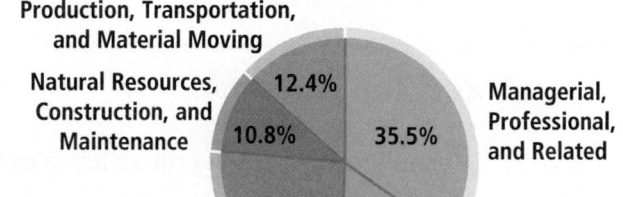

U.S. Employment, by Occupation

Source: U.S. Census Bureau

A jar contains four blue marbles and two red marbles. Suppose you choose a marble at random, and do not replace it. Then you choose a second marble. Find the probability of each event.

31. You select a blue marble and then a red marble.

32. You select a red marble and then a blue marble.

33. One of the marbles you select is blue and the other is red.

34. Both of the marbles you select are red.

For each set of probabilities, determine if the events A and B are mutually exclusive.

35. $P(A) = \frac{1}{2}, P(B) = \frac{1}{3}, P(A \text{ or } B) = \frac{2}{3}$

36. $P(A) = \frac{1}{6}, P(B) = \frac{3}{8}, P(A \text{ or } B) = \frac{13}{24}$

Standardized Text Prep

SAT/ACT

37. A bag contains 5 red marbles, 1 blue marble, 3 yellow marbles, and 2 green marbles. One marble is drawn from the bag. What is the probability that the marble is red or yellow?

38. What is the theoretical probability of getting a 1 or 6 when rolling a standard number cube?

39. The first term of an arithmetic series is 123. The common difference is 12 and the sum 1320. How many terms are in the series?

40. What is the slope of the graph of the equation $6x - 18y = -24$?

41. What is the radius of the circle with equation $x^2 - 4x + y^2 - 21 = 0$?

42. How many five-letter permutations can you form from the letters of the word COMPUTER?

Mixed Review

Find the theoretical probability of each event when rolling a standard number cube.

◀ **See Lesson 11-2.**

43. $P(5)$ **44.** $P(\text{an even number})$ **45.** $P(\text{less than 4})$

Solve each equation. Check each solution.

◀ **See Lesson 8-6.**

46. $\frac{1}{2} - x = \frac{x}{6}$ **47.** $\frac{2}{2x - 1} = \frac{x}{3}$ **48.** $\frac{3}{2x} - \frac{2}{3x} = 5$

Solve each equation. Check your answers.

◀ **See Lesson 7-5.**

49. $\log 2x = 3$ **50.** $\log x + \log 2 = 6$ **51.** $\log x^2 + 1 = 5$

Get Ready!   To prepare for Lesson 11-4, do Exercises 52–54.

A spinner has four equal sections that are red, blue, green, and yellow. Find each probability for two spins.

◀ **See Lesson 11-3.**

52. $P(\text{blue, then blue})$ **53.** $P(\text{red, then yellow})$ **54.** $P(\text{not yellow, then green})$

Conditional Probability

Objectives To find conditional probabilities
To use tables and tree diagrams to determine conditional probabilities

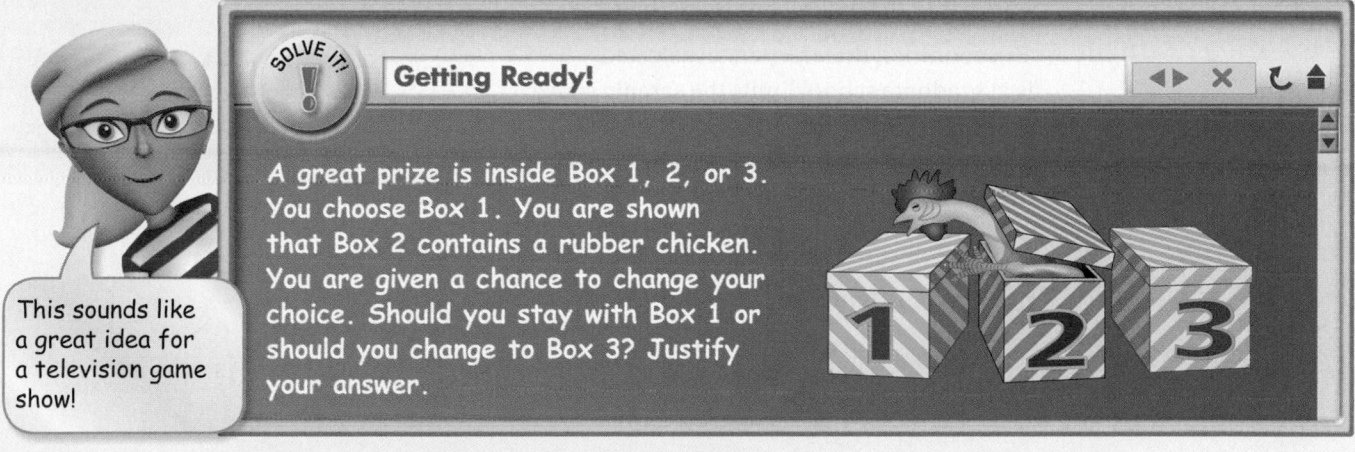

SOLVE IT!

Getting Ready!

A great prize is inside Box 1, 2, or 3. You choose Box 1. You are shown that Box 2 contains a rubber chicken. You are given a chance to change your choice. Should you stay with Box 1 or should you change to Box 3? Justify your answer.

This sounds like a great idea for a television game show!

Lesson Vocabulary
• conditional probability

The probability that an event, *B*, will occur given that another event, *A*, has already occurred is called a **conditional probability**. You can use conditional probability when two events are dependent.

Focus Question How do you find conditional probability?

You write the conditional probability of event *B*, given that event *A* occurs, as $P(B \mid A)$. You read $P(B \mid A)$ as "the probability of event *B*, given event *A*."

For example, suppose you select a tile from those shown and get a circle. You want to know the probability that the circle you have selected is orange.

You can describe the above as "the probability the tile is orange, given that it is a circle" and represent it as $P(\text{orange} \mid \text{circle})$. Of the 5 tiles that are circles, 2 are orange. So, $P(\text{orange} \mid \text{circle}) = \frac{2}{5}$.

Tables and tree diagrams can help you find conditional probabilities.

 **Problem 1** Finding Conditional Probability

Education The table shows students by gender at two- and four-year colleges, and graduate schools, in 2005. You pick a student at random.

Think

What's the condition?
The student is at a graduate school.

Student Genders

	Males (in thousands)	Females (in thousands)
Two-year colleges	1866	2462
Four-year colleges	4324	5517
Graduate schools	1349	1954

SOURCE: U.S. Census Bureau

A What is P(female | graduate school)?

The condition that the person selected is at graduate school limits the sample space. There are $1349 + 1954 = 3303$ thousand students at graduate schools. Of those 3303 thousand students, 1954 thousand are female.

$$P(\text{female | graduate school}) = \frac{1954}{3303} \approx 0.59$$

B What is P(female)?

$$P(\text{F}) = \frac{\text{total number of females}}{\text{total number of students}} = \frac{2462 + 5517 + 1954}{1866 + 2462 + 4324 + 5517 + 1349 + 1954}$$

$$= \frac{9933}{17,472} \approx 0.57$$

 Got It? **1. a.** In Problem 1, what is P(four-year | male)?

b. Reasoning Without calculating, given a student is enrolled in a four-year college is it more likely for the student to be male or female? Explain.

 **Problem 2** Conditional Probability in Statistics

Multiple Choice Americans recycle increasing amounts through municipal waste collection. The table shows the collection data for 2007. What is the probability that a sample of recycled waste is paper?

Ⓐ 16%   Ⓒ 33%

Ⓑ 28%   Ⓓ 57%

Think

What's the condition?
The waste sample has to be recycled waste.

Municipal Waste Collected (millions of tons)

Material	Recycled	Not Recycled
Paper	45.2	37.8
Metal	7.2	13.6
Glass	3.2	10.4
Plastic	2.1	28.6
Other	21.7	46.3

SOURCE: U.S. Environmental Protection Agency

The given condition is that the waste is *recycled*. A favorable outcome is that the recycled waste is paper.

$$P(\text{paper | recycled}) = \frac{45.2}{45.2 + 7.2 + 3.2 + 2.1 + 21.7}$$

$$\approx 0.57$$

The probability that the recycled waste is paper is about 57%. The correct answer is D.

 Got It? **2. a.** What is the probability that a sample of recycled waste is plastic?

b. What is the probability that a sample of recycled waste is glass?

You can also use a formula to find conditional probability.

Key Concept   Conditional Probability

For any two events A and B with $P(A) \neq 0$,

$$P(B \mid A) = \frac{P(A \text{ and } B)}{P(A)}$$

Hint

Recall the formula
$P(A \text{ and } B) =$
    $P(A) \cdot P(B)$

Using the formula above, you can calculate a conditional probability from other probabilities.

Problem 3 Using the Conditional Probability Formula

Market Research A utility company asked 50 of its customers whether they pay their bills online or by mail. What is the probability that a customer pays the bill online, given that the customer is male?

Bill Payment

	Online	By Mail
Male	12	8
Female	24	6

Think

To use the formula, you need $P(\text{male and online})$ and $P(\text{male})$.

Write the formula for conditional probability.

Substitute and simplify.

Write the answer in words.

Write

$P(\text{male and online}) = \frac{12}{50}$ $P(\text{male}) = \frac{20}{50}$

$P(\text{online} \mid \text{male}) = \dfrac{P(\text{male and online})}{P(\text{male})}$

$= \dfrac{\frac{12}{50}}{\frac{20}{50}}$

$= \dfrac{12}{20} = \dfrac{3}{5} = 0.6$

The probability that a customer pays online, given that the customer is male, is 0.6, or 60%.

Got It? **3.** Researchers asked shampoo users whether they apply shampoo directly to the head, or indirectly using a hand. What is the probability that a respondent applies shampoo directly to the head, given that the respondent is female?

Applying Shampoo

	Directly Onto Head	Into Hand First
Male	2	18
Female	6	24

Another way to write the formula for conditional probability $P(B \mid A) = \frac{P(A \text{ and } B)}{P(A)}$ is $P(A \text{ and } B) = P(A) \cdot P(B \mid A)$.

You can use this rule along with a tree diagram to find probabilities of dependent events.

 **Problem 4** **Using a Tree Diagram**

Education A school system compiled the following information from a survey it sent to people who were juniors 10 years earlier.

- 85% of the students graduated from high school.
- Of the students who graduated from high school, 90% are happy with their present jobs.
- Of the students who did not graduate from high school, 60% are happy with their present jobs.

What is the probability that a member of the junior class 10 years ago graduated from high school and is happy with his or her present job?

Make a tree diagram to help organize the information.

Let G = graduated, NG = not graduated, H = happy with present job, and NH = not happy with present job.

Think

What are the branches at each point?
The tree first branches at "graduated" and "not graduated." Each of these paths branches at "happy" and "not happy."

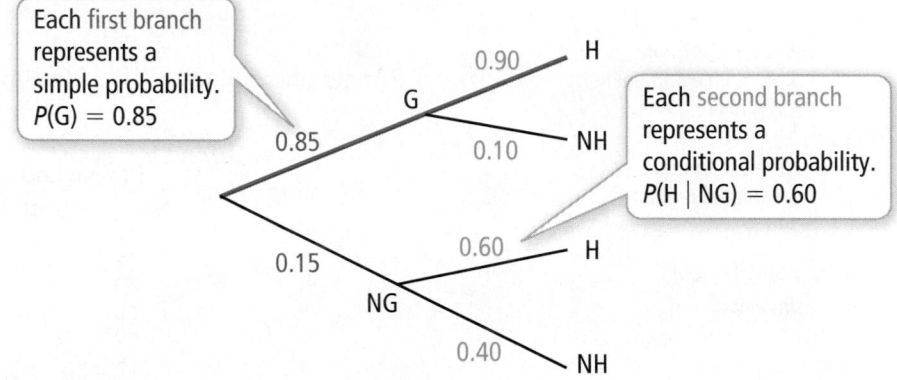

The blue highlighted path represents $P(G \text{ and } H)$.

Use the formula for conditional probability.	$P(G \text{ and } H) = P(G) \cdot P(H \mid G)$
Substitute.	$= 0.85 \cdot 0.90$
Simplify.	$= 0.765$

Hint

Follow the path along the graduated branch then the happy with present job branch.

The probability that a person from the junior class 10 years ago graduated and is happy with his or her present job is 0.765, or 76.5%.

 Got It? **4.** What is the probability that a student from the junior class 10 years ago in Problem 4 did not graduate and is happy with his or her present job?

Focus Question How do you find conditional probability?

Answer For any two events A and B with $P(A) \neq 0$, the conditional probability of event B, given that event A occurs is $P(B \mid A) = \dfrac{P(A \text{ and } B)}{P(A)}$. Use conditional probability when two events are dependent.

Lesson Check

Do you know HOW?

A card is drawn from a standard deck of cards. Find each probability, given that the card drawn is black.

1. $P(\text{club})$
2. $P(4)$
3. $P(\text{diamond})$

4. The probability that a car has two doors, given that it is red is 0.6. The probability that a car has two doors *and* is red is 0.2. What is the probability that a car is red?

Do you UNDERSTAND?

5. **Reasoning** Using the tree diagram in Problem 4, explain why the probabilities on each pair of branches must add up to 1.

6. **Open-Ended** Describe a situation in which you would use conditional probability to find the answer.

7. **Compare and Contrast** How are the Fundamental Counting Principle and tree diagrams alike? How are they different?

Practice and Problem-Solving Exercises

 **Practice**   Use the table to find each probability.   **See Problem 1.**

Characteristics of Job Applicants

		Has Experience	
		Yes	No
Has High School Diploma	Yes	54	27
	No	5	4

 **Guided Practice**

To start, find the total number of job applicants with a diploma.

8. $P(\text{has diploma})$
$54 + 27 = 81$

9. $P(\text{has diploma and experience})$

10. $P(\text{has no diploma} \mid \text{has experience})$

Use the table to find each probability.   **See Problem 2.**

11. $P(\text{The degree is a bachelor's.})$

12. $P(\text{The recipient is female, given that the degree is an associate's.})$

13. $P(\text{The degree is } not \text{ an associate's, given that the recipient is male.})$

Projected Number of Degree Recipients in 2010 (thousands)

Degree	Male	Female
Associate's	245	433
Bachelor's	598	858

SOURCE: U.S. National Center for Education Statistics

Use the survey results for Exercises 14 and 15.

◀ See Problem 3.

14. Find the probability that a respondent has a pet, given that the respondent has had a pet.

15. Find the probability that a respondent has never had a pet, given that the respondent does not have a pet now.

> 39% have a pet now and have had a pet.
>
> 61% do not have a pet now.
>
> 86% have had a pet.
>
> 14% do not have a pet now and have never had a pet.

Make a tree diagram to find each conditional probability.

◀ See Problem 4.

16. Sports A football team has a 70% chance of winning when it doesn't snow, but only a 40% chance of winning when it snows. Suppose there is a 50% chance of snow. Find the probability that the team will win.

17. The results of a survey are given below. Find P(a female respondent is left-handed) and P(a respondent is both male and right-handed).
- Of all the respondents, 17% are male.
- Of the male respondents, 33% are left-handed.
- Of female respondents, 90% are right-handed.

 **Apply**

18. Suppose A and B are independent events, with $P(A) = 0.60$ and $P(B) = 0.25$. Find each probability.
  a. $P(A \text{ and } B)$ **b.** $P(A \mid B)$
  c. What do you notice about $P(A)$ and $P(A \mid B)$?
  d. Reasoning One way to describe A and B as independent events is *The occurrence of B has no effect on the probability of A.* Explain how the answer to part (c) illustrates this relationship.

19. Think About a Plan A math teacher gives her class two tests. 60% of the class passes both tests and 80% of the class passes the first test. What percent of those who pass the first test also pass the second test?
- What conditional probability are you looking for?
- How can a tree diagram help you solve this problem?

Weather Use probability notation to describe the chance of each event. Let S, C, W, and R represent sunny, cloudy, windy, and rainy weather, respectively.

20. sunny and windy weather   **21.** rainy weather if it is windy

22. Transportation You can take Bus 65 or Bus 79. You take the first bus that arrives. The probability that Bus 65 arrives first is 75%. There is a 40% chance that Bus 65 picks up passengers along the way. There is a 60% chance that Bus 79 picks up passengers. Your bus picked up passengers. What is the probability that it was Bus 65?

The tree diagram relates snowfall and school closings. Find each probability. Let H, L, O, and C represent heavy snowfall, light snowfall, schools open, and schools closed, respectively.

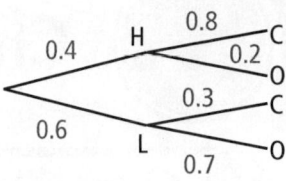

23. $P(\text{H and O})$ **24.** $P(\text{H} \mid \text{C})$ **25.** $P(\text{L} \mid \text{O})$

Standardized Test Prep

Use the table for Exercises 26 and 27. A school library classifies its books as hardback or paperback, fiction or nonfiction, and illustrated or non-illustrated.

		Illustrated	Non-Illustrated
Hardback	Fiction	420	780
	Nonfiction	590	250
Paperback	Fiction	150	430
	Nonfiction	110	880

SAT/ACT

26. What is the probability that a book selected at random is a paperback, given that it is illustrated?

   Ⓐ $\dfrac{260}{3610}$ Ⓑ $\dfrac{150}{1270}$ Ⓒ $\dfrac{260}{1270}$ Ⓓ $\dfrac{110}{150}$

27. What is the probability that a book selected at random is nonfiction, given that it is a non-illustrated hardback?

   Ⓕ $\dfrac{250}{2040}$ Ⓖ $\dfrac{780}{1030}$ Ⓗ $\dfrac{250}{1030}$ Ⓘ $\dfrac{250}{780}$

28. Which of the following expressions is equivalent to $3(n - 3)(n + 4)$?

   Ⓐ $3n^2 + 3n - 36$ Ⓒ $3n^2 - 3n - 36$

   Ⓑ $3n^2 - 3n + 36$ Ⓓ $3n^2 - 36$

Short Response

29. What is the sample space for spinning the spinner twice? Are all the outcomes equally likely?

Mixed Review

Q and R are independent events. Find $P(Q \text{ and } R)$.   ◀ See Lesson 11-3.

30. $P(Q) = \frac{3}{4};\ P(R) = \frac{4}{9}$ **31.** $P(Q) = \frac{17}{20};\ P(R) = \frac{5}{19}$

Write an equation of a parabola with the given vertex and focus.   ◀ See Lesson 10-2.

32. vertex $(5, 2)$; focus $(6, 2)$ **33.** vertex $(-2, 3)$; focus $(-2, 6)$

Get Ready!   **To prepare for Lesson 11-5, do Exercises 34 and 35.**

Order each set of values from least to greatest. Then find the middle value.   ◀ See Lesson 1-2.

34. 0.2   0.3   0.6   1.2   0.7   0.9   0.8   **35.** 11   23   15   17   21   18   21

Chapter Vocabulary

- combination (p. 690)
- conditional probability (p. 711)
- dependent events (p. 704)
- equally likely outcomes (p. 698)
- experimental probability (p. 695)
- Fundamental Counting Principle (p. 686)
- independent events (p. 704)
- mutually exclusive events (p. 705)
- *n* factorial (*n*!) (p. 687)
- permutation (p. 687)
- sample space (p. 698)
- simulation (p. 696)
- theoretical probability (p. 698)

Choose the correct term to complete each sentence.

1. A (*combination/permutation*) is an arrangement of items in a particular order.

2. (*Conditional/Theoretical*) probability refers to the probability that an event will occur given that another event has already occurred.

3. You can use a (*sample space/simulation*) to model an event when it is difficult or unreasonable to conduct numerous trials.

4. Two events that cannot occur at the same time are called (*dependent/mutually exclusive*) events.

11-1 Permutations and Combinations

Quick Review

If event M can occur in m ways and event N can occur in n ways, then M followed by N can occur in $m \cdot n$ ways. The notation **$n!$ (n factorial)** means $n \cdot (n - 1) \cdot \ldots \cdot 3 \cdot 2 \cdot 1$. The number of ways to choose r items from a set of n items, without regard to order, is $_nC_r = \frac{n!}{r!(n-r)!}$. The number of ways to choose r items from a set of n items and place those items in some order is $_nP_r = \frac{n!}{(n-r)!}$.

Example

A vacationer making travel preparations chooses 3 books from a shelf containing 15 books. How many ways are there to choose 3 books without regard to order? How many ways are there to choose one book for the trip to the destination, one for the stay, and one for the homeward trip?

Ignoring order, there are $_{15}C_3 = \frac{15!}{3!12!} = 455$ ways to choose 3 books.

There are $_{15}P_3 = \frac{15!}{12!} = 2730$ ways to choose 3 books to read in a particular order.

Exercises

Evaluate each of the following.

5. $3!$

6. $9!$

7. $\frac{4!}{2!}$

8. $\frac{5!}{2!2!}$

9. $_7C_2$

10. $_4C_3 + {}_6C_5$

11. $_6P_2$

12. $_4P_3 + {}_6P_5$

13. Camping On a camping trip, you bring 12 items for 4 dinners. For each dinner, you use 3 items. In how many ways can you choose the 3 items for the first dinner? For the second? For the third? For the fourth?

14. Advertising A newspaper ad includes a telephone number 1-555-DIAL VSW. How many 7-letter arrangements are possible for the phone number using the 26 letters of the alphabet if no letter is used more than once? Express your answer using scientific notation.

11-2 Probability

Quick Review

Experimental probability is based on successes during repeated trials, while **theoretical probability** is based on number of occurrences in a **sample space** of equally likely outcomes. When an actual event cannot easily be repeated through numerous trials, you can use a **simulation** to obtain an experimental probability.

Example

What is the probability that a person chosen at random was born on a Thursday?

Since a random person had an equal chance of being born on any one of the 7 days of the week, the probability that the person was born on a Thursday is $\frac{1}{7}$.

Exercises

15. How many possible outcomes are there when a standard number cube is rolled three times?

16. You flipped a coin 70 times and recorded 23 heads. What is the experimental probability of flipping tails?

Find the probability of each event.

17. A fair number cube rolls a 13.

18. A number picked at random from the numbers 1 through 15 is prime.

19. Writing Suppose you have 20 tiles with the numbers 1 through 20. The theoretical probability that a tile chosen at random is a 5 is $\frac{1}{20}$. If you pick a tile randomly, 20 times, replacing the chosen tile each time, will you get a 5 exactly once? Explain.

11-3 Probability of Multiple Events

Quick Review

For any events A and B,
$P(A \text{ or } B) = P(A) + P(B) - P(A \text{ and } B)$.

When the occurrence of one event affects how a second event can occur, the events are **dependent**.

When A and B are **independent**,
$P(A \text{ and } B) = P(A) \cdot P(B)$. For **mutually exclusive events**, $P(A \text{ and } B) = 0$, so $P(A \text{ or } B) = P(A) + P(B)$.

Example

You roll a standard number cube. Are the following events mutually exclusive: rolling a 1 and rolling an even number? Explain.

You cannot roll a 1 and an even number at the same time. The events are mutually exclusive.

Exercises

Classify each pair of events as *dependent* or *independent*.

20. A student in your algebra class is selected at random. One of the remaining students is then selected at random.

21. You select a number 1 through 6 by tossing a standard number cube. You select a second number by tossing the number cube again.

Calculate each probability, given that $P(A) = 0.3$, $P(B) = 0.7$, and A and B are independent.

22. $P(A \text{ and } B)$

23. $P(A \text{ or } B)$

11-4 Conditional Probability

Quick Review

The probability that event B will occur, given that A has already occured, is the **conditional probability**

$$P(B \mid A) = \frac{P(A \text{ and } B)}{P(A)}.$$

Example

A standard number cube is rolled twice. If the first number rolled is a and the second is b, find $P(a$ is even and $b > 2)$ and $P(b$ is even $\mid b > 3)$.

Number cube rolls are independent events.

$P(a \text{ is even and } b > 2) = P(a \text{ is even}) \cdot P(b > 2)$

$$= \frac{1}{2} \cdot \frac{2}{3} = \frac{1}{3}$$

$P(b \text{ is even} \mid b > 3) = \dfrac{P(b > 3 \text{ and } b \text{ is even})}{P(b > 3)}$

$$= \frac{P(4 \text{ or } 6)}{P(4 \text{ or } 5 \text{ or } 6)}$$

$$= \frac{\frac{2}{6}}{\frac{3}{6}} = \frac{2}{3}$$

Exercises

Calculate each probability, given that $P(A) = 0.3$, $P(B) = 0.7$, and A and B are independent.

24. $P(A \mid B)$

25. $P(B \mid A)$

Calculate each probability, given that $P(A) = 0.5$, $P(B) = 0.4$, and $P(A \text{ and } B) = 0.1$.

26. $P(A \mid B)$

27. $P(B \mid A)$

28. $P(A \text{ and } B \mid A \text{ or } B)$

Do you know HOW?

Evaluate each expression.

1. $4!$

2. $6!$

3. $\frac{5!}{3!}$

4. $\frac{6!}{4!2!}$

5. $_7C_3$

6. $_9C_8$

7. $_5P_2$

8. $_{11}P_9$

9. $_4C_4$

10. $_4P_4$

Indicate whether each situation involves a combination or permutation. Then solve.

11. How many ways are there to select 5 actors from a troupe of 9 to improvise a scene?

12. How many different 3-student study groups can be formed from a class of 15?

13. Your teacher is looking for a new apartment. There are 5 apartments available. In how many ways can your teacher inspect the apartments?

Suppose you select a number at random from the sample space {5, 6, 7, 8, 9, 10, 11, 12, 13, 14}. Find each probability.

14. $P(7)$

15. $P(5 \text{ or } 13)$

16. $P(\text{greater than } 10)$

17. $P(\text{multiple of } 30)$

18. $P(\text{less than } 7 \text{ or greater than } 10)$

19. $P(\text{greater than } 6 \text{ and less than } 12)$

20. $P(\text{integer})$

21. $P(\text{less than } 10 \mid \text{less than } 13)$

22. $P(\text{greater than } 8 \mid \text{less than } 11)$

23. $P(\text{greater than } 7 \mid \text{greater than } 12)$

Two standard number cubes are tossed. State whether the events are mutually exclusive. Then find $P(A \text{ or } B)$.

24. A means their sum is 12; B means both are odd.

25. A means they are equal; B means their sum is a multiple of 3.

Do you UNDERSTAND?

26. Vocabulary Explain the difference between experimental probability and theoretical probability.

27. Suppose you select a number at random from the set $\{90, 91, 92, \ldots, 99\}$. Event A is selecting a multiple of 2. Event B is selecting a multiple of 3.
  a. Writing Are events A and B mutually exclusive? Are they independent? Explain your answers.
  b. Find $P(A)$ and $P(B)$.
  c. Find $P(A \text{ and } B)$.
  d. Find $P(A \text{ or } B)$.
  e. Find $P(A \mid B)$ and $P(B \mid A)$.

28. Reasoning Let F and G be mutually exclusive events. Event F occurs more frequently than event G. Write the following in order from least to greatest: $P(F)$, $P(G)$, $P(F \text{ or } G)$, $P(G \mid F)$.

29. Error Analysis For two events A and B, a student calculates the probabilities shown. Explain how you can tell that the student made a mistake.

$$P(A \text{ and } B) = 0.35$$
$$P(A \mid B) = 0.29$$

30. Open-Ended Your teacher selects at random two days out of every five days to give a "pop" quiz. Define a simulation to find the experimental probability that you will get a pop quiz on two consecutive days. Then use your simulation to find the probability.

Probability and Statistics

In Part A, you learned to calculate permutations, combinations, and probability. Now you will analyze data using measures of central tendency and variation.

 Vocabulary for Part B

English/Spanish Vocabulary Audio Online:

English	Spanish
mean, *p. 723*	media
measure of central tendency, *p. 723*	medida de tendencia central
median, *p. 723*	mediana
mode, *p. 723*	moda
normal distribution, *p. 752*	distribución normal
outlier, *p. 724*	valor extremo
sample, *p. 738*	muestra
standard deviation, *p. 732*	desviación típica

BIG ideas

1 Probability
Essential Question What is the difference between a permutation and a combination?

2 Probability
Essential Question What is the difference between experimental and theoretical probability?

3 Data Collection and Analysis
Essential Question How are measures of central tendency different from standard deviation?

Chapter Preview for Part B

Analyzing Data

Objectives To calculate measures of central tendency
To draw and interpret box-and-whisker plots

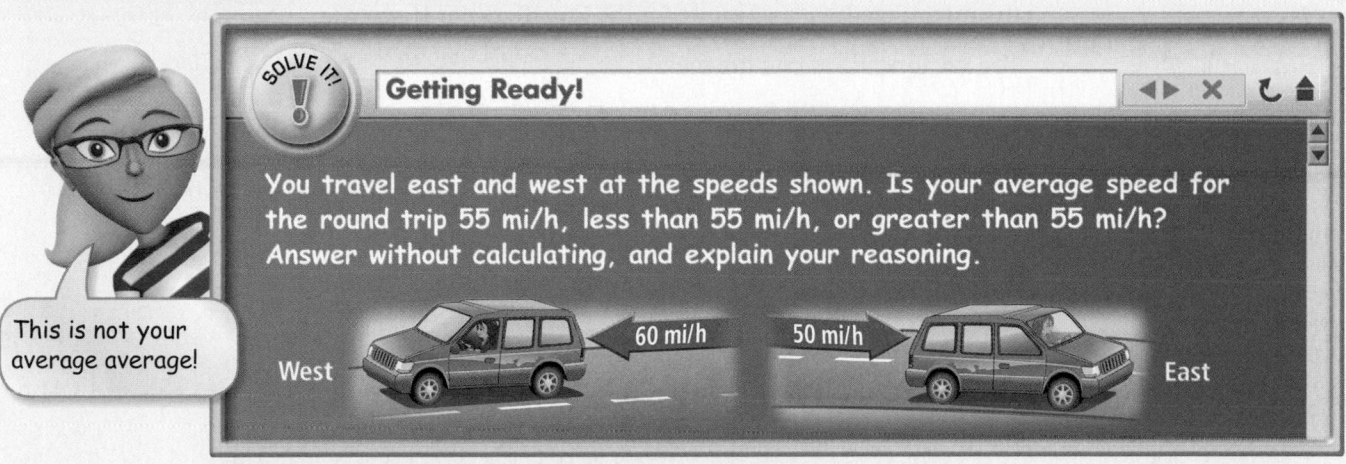

Getting Ready!

You travel east and west at the speeds shown. Is your average speed for the round trip 55 mi/h, less than 55 mi/h, or greater than 55 mi/h? Answer without calculating, and explain your reasoning.

West   60 mi/h   50 mi/h   East

This is not your average average!

Dynamic Activity
Box-and-Whisker Plots

Lesson Vocabulary
- measure of central tendency
- mean
- median
- mode
- bimodal
- outlier
- range of a set of data
- quartile
- interquartile range
- box-and-whisker plot
- percentile

People often refer to the mean as the *average*. The mean is only one of the measures considered the average, a measure of the center of a set of data.

Focus Question How can you compare and describe sets of data?

Statistics is the study, analysis, and interpretation of data. One way to analyze data is by finding a *measure of central tendency*. A **measure of central tendency** indicates the "middle" of a data set. The *mean, median,* and *mode* are the most common measures of central tendency.

take note

Key Concepts **Measures of Central Tendency**

Measure	Definition	Example, using 1, 2, 3, 3, 4, 5, 5, 9
Mean	$\dfrac{\text{sum of the data values}}{\text{number of data values}}$	$\dfrac{1 + 2 + 3 + 3 + 4 + 5 + 5 + 9}{8} = 4$
Median	for a data set listed in order: the middle value for an odd number of data values; the mean of the two middle values for an even number of data values	For 1, 2, 3, 3, 4, 5, 5, 9, the middle two values are 3 and 4. The median is the mean of these values: $\dfrac{3 + 4}{2} = 3.5$.
Mode	the most frequently occurring value(s)	Two modes: In 1, 2, 3, 3, 4, 5, 5, 9, both 3 and 5 occur twice.

Hint

If a data set has more than two modes, then the modes are probably not statistically useful.

A **bimodal** data set has two modes. If no value occurs more frequently than any other, then there is no mode.

 Problem 1 Finding Measures of Central Tendency

Career The frequency table shows the number of job offers received by each student within two months of graduating with a mathematics degree from a small college. What are the mean, median, and mode for the job offers per student?

Job Offers	0	1	2	3	4
Students	2	2	4	5	2

Use the formula to find the mean.

Think

How do you find the total number of job offers?
Add the products of each number of job offers and the number of students who received that many job offers.

Write the formula. The symbol $\bar{x}$, read "x bar," represents the mean.

$$\bar{x} = \frac{\text{sum of the data values}}{\text{number of data values}}$$

Substitute.

$$= \frac{2(0) + 2(1) + 4(2) + 5(3) + 2(4)}{15}$$

Simplify.

$$= \frac{33}{15} = 2.2$$

The mean is 2.2.

List the data set in order to find the median.

List each value the number of times it occurs. Arrange them in order.

$$0, 0, 1, 1, 2, 2, 2, 2, 3, 3, 3, 3, 3, 4, 4$$
$$\uparrow$$
$$2$$

Identify the middle value.

Hint

Remember median as the middle and mode as the most.

The median is 2.

Identify repeated values to find the mode(s).

The mode is the number of job offers received by the greatest number of students.

$$0, 0, 1, 1, 2, 2, 2, 2, \underline{3, 3, 3, 3, 3}, 4, 4$$
$$\uparrow$$
$$3$$

Five students received 3 job offers each.

The mode is 3.

 Got It? 1. The frequency table shows the number of trees in the yard of each house on one street. What are the mean, median, and mode for the trees per yard?

Trees	3	4	5	6	7	8
Yards	1	5	7	4	1	2

Hint

An outlier can significantly affect the mean of a data set. Discard any outliers before calculating the mean.

An **outlier** is a value that is substantially different from the rest of the data set. If the data is arranged in order, outliers can occur at the "ends." Sometimes an outlier is an important part of the data. At other times it can be misleading because it affects measures of central tendency.

Problem 2 Identifying an Outlier

Multiple Choice **Which is an outlier for this data set: 56 65 73 59 98 65 59?**

Ⓐ 42 Ⓑ 65 Ⓒ 98 Ⓓ 59

Think

What should you do first?
Put the numbers in order.

Order the data. 56 59 59 65 65 73 98

Find differences between adjacent values. 3 0 6 0 8 25

This difference is significantly larger than the others. The value 98 is an outlier.

The correct answer is C.

Got It? **2.** Suppose the values in Problem 2 are the data for the situations below. Would you discard the outlier? Explain.

a. water temperature of a lake at seven locations

b. the number of customers in a restaurant each night in one week

The **range of a set of data** is the difference between the greatest and least values. If you order data from least value to greatest value, the median divides the data into two parts. The median of each part divides the data further and you have four parts in all. The values separating the four parts are **quartiles**. The **interquartile range** is the difference between the third and first quartiles.

For example, consider the ordered data set: 56 61 68 73 79 83 86

The median is the middle number, 73. The median is also the value of the second quartile, Q_2. 56 61 68 (73) 79 83 86

The median of the set of numbers *below* the median is the value of the first quartile: $Q_1 = 61$. 56 (61) 68 (73) 79 83 86

The median of the set of numbers *above* the median is the value of the third quartile: $Q_3 = 83$. 56 (61) 68 (73) 79 (83) 86

The range is the difference between the greatest and least values. $86 - 56 = 30$

The interquartile range is the difference between Q_3 and Q_1. $83 - 61 = 22$

A *box-and-whisker plot* uses minimum and maximum values, the median, and the first and third quartiles to display the spread, or variability, in a data set.

take note

Key Concept Box-and-Whisker Plot

Definition

A **box-and-whisker plot** is a way to display data that uses

- quartiles to bound the center box and
- the minimum and maximum values to form the whiskers.

Graph

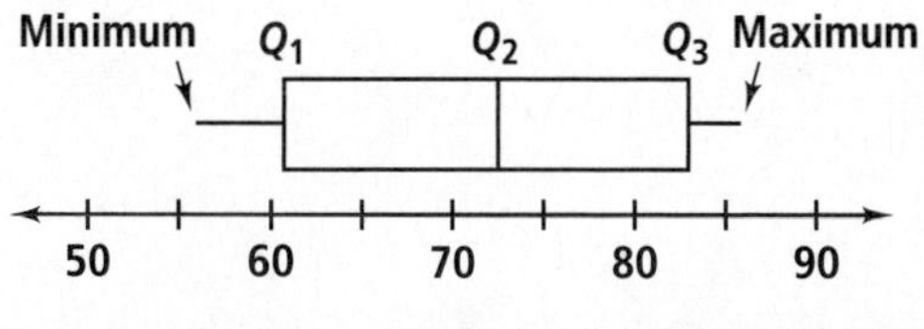

Problem 3 Comparing Data Sets

Temperature The table shows average monthly water temperatures for four locations on the Gulf of Mexico. How can you compare the 12 water temperatures from St. Petersburg with the 12 water temperatures from Key West?

Gulf of Mexico Eastern Coast Water Temperatures (°F)

Location	J	F	M	A	M	J	J	A	S	O	N	D
St. Petersburg, Florida	62	64	68	74	80	84	86	86	84	78	70	64
Key West, Florida	69	70	75	78	82	85	87	87	86	82	76	72
Dauphin Island, Alabama	51	53	60	70	75	82	84	84	80	72	62	56
Grand Isle, Louisiana	61	61	64	70	77	83	85	85	83	77	70	65

SOURCE: National Oceanographic Data Center

Know → Water temperatures near the two cities

Need → The means, medians, modes, ranges, and interquartile ranges

Plan → Order the data. Find the means, medians, modes, minimums, maximums, quartiles, range, and interquartile range.

St. Petersburg:

Find the mean.

$$\bar{x} = \frac{62 + 64 + 64 + 68 + 70 + 74 + 78 + 80 + 84 + 84 + 86 + 86}{12}$$

$$= \frac{900}{12} = 75$$

Find the mode(s). 64, 84, and 86

Find the range. Mininum: 62; Maximum: 86
Range: $86 - 62 = 24$

> Median (Q_2) = 76

Order the data and find the median and quartiles.

62 64 (64 68) 70 (74 78) 80 (84 84) 86 86

> Median of lower part (Q_1) = 66

> Median of upper part (Q_3) = 84

Hint
For an even number of data values, the median is the mean of the two middle values.

Find the interquartile range. $Q_3 - Q_1 = 84 - 66$
$= 18$

St. Petersburg

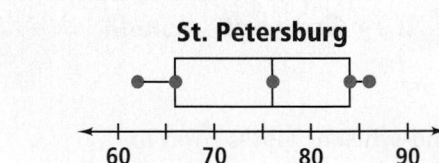

Key West:

Find the mean.

$$\bar{x} = \frac{69 + 70 + 72 + 75 + 76 + 78 + 82 + 82 + 85 + 86 + 87 + 87}{12}$$

$$= \frac{949}{12} \approx 79.1$$

Think

What location has a greater range in water temperature?
The range of water temperatures at St. Petersburg is 6°F greater than the range at Key West.

Find the mode(s).   82 and 87

Find the range.   Minimum: 69; Maximum: 87
Range: 87 − 69 = 18

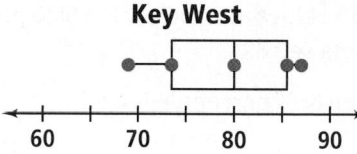

Order the data and find the median and quartiles.   69 70 72 75 76 78 82 82 85 86 87 87

Median $(Q_2) = 80$

Median of lower part $(Q_1) = 73.5$ Median of upper part $(Q_3) = 85.5$

Find the interquartile range. $Q_3 - Q_1 = 85.5 - 73.5 = 12$

Key West

The range and the interquartile range show the temperatures varying less at Key West than at St. Petersburg. Also, the temperatures at Key West are generally higher.

Got It? **3.** How can you compare the 12 water temperatures in Problem 3 from Dauphin Island with the 12 water temperatures from Grand Isle?

Problem 4 **Using a Box-and-Whisker Plot**

How can you use a graphing calculator box-and-whisker plot to find quartiles for the water temperature data of St. Petersburg from Problem 3?

Think

What about the appearance of a box-and-whisker plot might suggest an outlier?
If a "whisker" is much longer than the box, it's endpoint may be an outlier.

Step 1 For St. Petersburg, use **STAT EDIT** to enter the temperature data in **L1**.

Step 2 In **STAT PLOT**, select a box-and-whisker plot. Enter **L1** for the St. Petersburg data. Enter the window values. Draw the box-and-whisker plot.

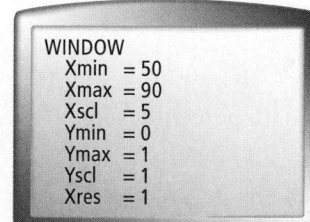
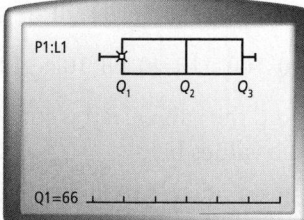

Step 3 Use **TRACE** to find the quartiles: $Q_1 = 66$, $Q_2 = 76$, and $Q_3 = 84$.

Got It? **4. a.** How can you use graphing calculator box-and-whisker plots to find water temperature quartiles for other Gulf Coast sites from Problem 3 and Got It 3?

b. **Reasoning** Is a box-and-whisker plot a useful graphical display for data with an outlier? Explain.

A **percentile** is a number from 0 to 100 that you can associate with a value x from a data set. It shows the percent of the data that are less than or equal to x. For example, if x is at the 63rd percentile, then 63% of the data are less than or equal to x.

 Problem 5 **Finding Percentiles**

Testing Here is an ordered list of midterm test scores for a Spanish class. What value is at the 65th percentile?

41	54	61	65	67	73	74
77	77	77	79	80	82	88
89	93	97	98	98	100	

Plan

What should you do first to find percentiles?
Make sure the data is in order.

Of these 20 values, 65% fall at or below the value at the 65th percentile.

Find 65% of 20. $20 \cdot 65\% = 20 \cdot 0.65 = 13$

So, there are 13 values at or below the 65% percentile. Count to find the 13th value in the ordered data set: 82.

The value at the 65% percentile is 82.

 Got It? **5.** What is the value at each percentile for the data in Problem 5?
a. 55th percentile   **b.** 95th percentile

Focus Question How can you compare and describe sets of data?
Answer Use the different measures of central tendency, as well as the range and interquartile range to compare and describe sets of data. Find the mean, median, and mode(s), and take any outliers into consideration.

 Lesson Check

Do you know HOW?

Identify the outlier in the data set. Then find the mean, median, and mode of the data set both when the outlier is included and when it is not.

1. 16 19 21 18 18 54 20 22 23 17

2. 90 100 110 40 98 102 112 90 92

3. Find the values at the 40th and 80th percentiles for the values below.

58 53 35 60 58 42 57 60 43 44 51 49 58

Do you UNDERSTAND?

4. Error Analysis A student found the median of the data set below. Explain and correct the student's error.

Score	80	85	90	95
Frequency	6	4	10	1

Median: $\dfrac{85 + 90}{2} = \dfrac{175}{2} = 87.5$

Practice and Problem-Solving Exercises

A Practice

Find the mean, median, and mode of each set of values.

🔹 See Problem 1.

5. Time spent on Internet per day (in minutes): 75 68 43 120 65 180 95 225 140

6.

Age (years)	13	14	15	16	17	18	19
Frequency	7	12	18	9	5	4	2

Identify the outlier of each set of values.

🔹 See Problem 2.

7. 3.4 4.5 2.3 5.9 9.8 3.3 2.1 3.0 2.9

8. 17 21 19 10 15 19 14 0 11 16

9. Weather The table shows average monthly temperatures of two cities. How can you compare the temperatures?

🔹 See Problem 3.

	J	F	M	A	M	J	J	A	S	O	N	D
Jacksonville, Florida	52.4	55.2	61.1	67.0	73.4	79.1	81.6	81.2	78.1	69.8	61.9	55.1
Austin, Texas	48.8	52.8	61.5	69.9	75.6	81.3	84.5	84.8	80.2	71.1	60.9	51.6

Make a box-and-whisker plot for each set of values.

🔹 See Problem 4.

Guided Practice ➡

10. 12 11 15 12 19 20 19 14 18 15 16

To start, order the data.   11 12 12 14 15 15 16 18 19 19 20

11. 120 145 133 105 117 150 130 136 128

Find the values at the 30th and 90th percentiles for each data set.

🔹 See Problem 5.

12. 6283 5700 6381 6274 5700 5896 5972 6075 5993 5581

13. 7 12 3 14 17 20 5 3 17 4 13 2 15 9 15 18 16 9 1 6

B Apply

Identify the outlier in each data set. Then find the mean, median, and mode of the data set both when the outlier is included and when it is not.

14. 87 104 381 215 174 199 233 186 142 228 9 53 117 129

15. 49 57.5 58 49.2 62 22.2 67 52.1 77 99.9 80 51.7 64

16. Think About a Plan Use the water temperature data for the eastern coast of the Gulf of Mexico during the summer months, as shown in the graph below. Find the quartiles by graphing a box-and-whisker plot of the data.

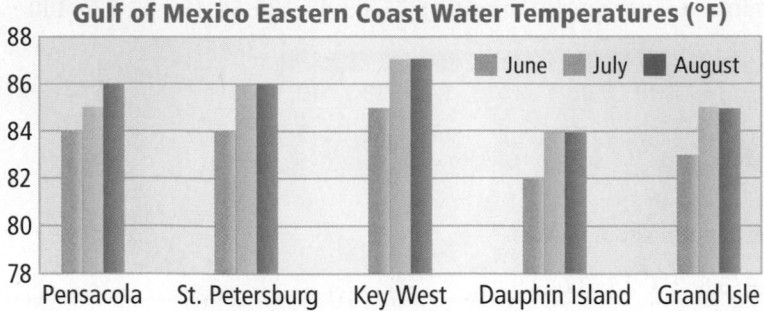

Gulf of Mexico Eastern Coast Water Temperatures (°F)

- What information can you get from the graph?
- How can you use that information to make a box-and-whisker plot?
- How can you find the quartiles using your box-and-whisker plot?

17. Meteorology On May 3, 1999, 59 tornadoes hit Oklahoma in the largest tornado outbreak ever recorded in the state. Sixteen of these were classified as strong (F2 or F3) or violent (F4 or F5).
a. Make a box-and-whisker plot of the data for length of path.
b. Identify the outliers. Remove them from the data set and make a revised box-and-whisker plot.
c. Writing How does the removal of the outliers affect the box-and-whisker plot? How does it affect the median of the data set?

For Exercises 18–20, use the set of values below.
1 1 1 1 1 1 2 3 5 8 13 21 34 55 89 89 89 89 89 89

18. At what percentile is 1?   **19.** At what percentile is 34?

20. Error Analysis A student claims that 89 is at the 70th percentile. Explain the student's error.

21. Advertising An electronics store placed an ad in the newspaper showing flat-screen TVs for sale. The ad says "Our flat-screen TVs average $695." The prices of the flat-screen TVs are $1200, $999, $1499, $895, $695, $1100, $1300, and $695.
a. Find the mean, median, and mode of the prices.
b. Which measure is the store using in its ad? Why did they choose it?
c. As a consumer, which measure would you want to see advertised? Explain your reasoning.

22. The table displays the frequency of scores for one Calculus class on the Advanced Placement Calculus exam. The mean of the exam scores is 3.5.
a. What is the value of f in the table?
b. What is the mode of all of the exam scores?
c. What is the median of all of the exam scores?

Major Tornadoes in Oklahoma, May 3, 1999

Length of Path (miles)	Intensity
6	F3
9	F3
4	F2
37	F5
7	F2
12	F3
8	F2
7	F2
15	F4
39	F4
1	F2
22	F3
15	F3
8	F2
13	F3
2	F2

SOURCE: National Oceanic & Atmospheric Administration

Score	1	2	3	4	5
Frequency	1	3	f	12	3

Standardized Test Prep

SAT/ACT

23. Use a calculator to solve $2x^2 - 7x - 5 = 0$. Round answers to the nearest hundredth.

Ⓐ $-1.56, -4.44$ Ⓑ $-5.44, 1.56$ Ⓒ $-0.61, 4.11$ Ⓓ $-5.56, -1.44$

24. Which function generates the table of values at the right?

Ⓕ $y = 27\left(\frac{2}{3}\right)^x$

Ⓖ $y = 6\left(\frac{4}{3}\right)^x$

Ⓗ $y = \left(\frac{8}{3}\right)^x$

Ⓘ $y = 6\left(\frac{3}{4}\right)^x$

x	y
−2	$\frac{27}{8}$
−1	$\frac{9}{2}$
0	6
1	8
2	$\frac{32}{3}$

25. A homeroom class consists of 6 boys whose last name begins with S, 8 boys whose last name begins with T, 4 girls whose last name begins with S, and 11 girls whose last name begins with T. A student is chosen at random from the class. What is the probability that the student is a girl or has a last name that begins with S?

Ⓐ $\frac{18}{29}$

Ⓑ $\frac{21}{29}$

Ⓒ $\frac{23}{29}$

Ⓓ $\frac{25}{29}$

Short Response

26. In a library, the probability that a book is a hardback, given that it is illustrated, is 0.40. The probability that a book is hardback *and* illustrated is 0.20. Find the probability that a book is illustrated.

Mixed Review

Of all the respondents to a survey, 59% are girls. Of the girls, 61% read horror stories. Of the boys, 49% read horror stories. Find each probability.

◀ See Lesson 11-4.

27. P(boy and reads horror stories)

28. P (reads horror stories)

Determine whether each sequence is arithmetic. If it is, identify the common difference.

◀ See Lesson 9-2.

29. $16, 7, -2, \ldots$

30. $34, 51, 68, \ldots$

31. $2, 2.2, 2.22, \ldots$

Get Ready!   To prepare for Lesson 11-6, do Exercises 32–34.

Find all real square roots of each number.

◀ See Lesson 6-1.

32. 256

33. 0.0081

34. $\frac{121}{16}$

11-6 Standard Deviation

Objectives To find the standard deviation and variance of a set of values
To apply standard deviation and variance

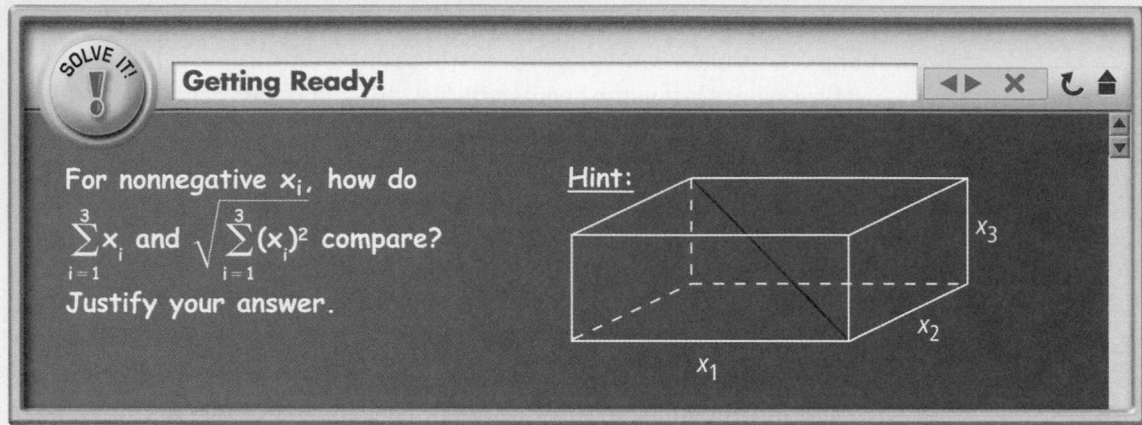

Getting Ready!

For nonnegative x_i, how do

$$\sum_{i=1}^{3} x_i \text{ and } \sqrt{\sum_{i=1}^{3} (x_i)^2} \text{ compare?}$$

Justify your answer.

Hint:

Lesson Vocabulary
• measure of variation
• variance
• standard deviation

You learned about summation notation in Chapter 9. To find the mean of a data set, you add the data values and divide by the number of data values. You can use summation to measure how data deviates from the mean.

Focus Question What are standard deviation and variance?

In the previous lesson you studied range and interquartile range. Each of these is a **measure of variation**. A measure of variation describes how the data in a data set are spread out.

Variance and **standard deviation** are measures showing how much data values deviate from the mean. The Greek letter σ (sigma) represents standard deviation. σ^2 (sigma squared) is the variance.

take note

Key Concepts Finding Variance and Standard Deviation

To find the standard deviation, σ, follow these five steps:

1. Find the mean, $\bar{x}$, of the n values in a data set.
2. Find the difference, $x - \bar{x}$, between each value x and the mean.
3. Square each difference, $(x - \bar{x})^2$.
4. Find the average (mean) of these squares. This is the variance.

$$\sigma^2 = \frac{\sum (x - \bar{x})^2}{n}$$

5. Take the square root of the variance. This is the standard deviation.

$$\sigma = \sqrt{\frac{\sum (x - \bar{x})^2}{n}}$$

Problem 1 Finding Variance and Standard Deviation

What are the mean, variance, and standard deviation of these values?
6.9 8.7 7.6 4.8 9.0

Step 1 Find the mean.

Use the formula and simplify. $\bar{x} = \dfrac{6.9 + 8.7 + 7.6 + 4.8 + 9.0}{5} = 7.4$

Think

How can you organize your work?
Use a table to record the values.

Step 2 Find the variance.

Make a table. Use the columns shown.

x	$\bar{x}$	$x - \bar{x}$	$(x - \bar{x})^2$
6.9	7.4	−0.5	0.25
8.7	7.4	1.3	1.69
7.6	7.4	0.2	0.04
4.8	7.4	−2.6	6.76
9.0	7.4	1.6	2.56
		Sum:	11.30

Find the difference between each value and the mean. Square the differences.

Add the squares of the differences.

Write the formula for variance. $\sigma^2 = \dfrac{\sum(x - \bar{x})^2}{n}$

Subtitute and simplify. $= \dfrac{11.30}{5} = 2.26$

Step 3 Find the standard deviation.

Use the formula. Subtitute and simplify. $\sigma = \sqrt{\sigma^2} = \sqrt{2.26} \approx 1.5$

The mean is 7.4. The variance is 2.26. The standard deviation is about 1.5.

 Got It? **1.** What are the mean, variance, and standard deviation of these values?
52 63 65 77 80 82

 Problem 2 Using a Calculator to Find Standard Deviation

Meteorology The table displays the number of U.S. hurricane strikes by decade from the years 1851 to 2000. What are the mean and standard deviation for this data set?

Decade	1	2	3	4	5	6	7	8	9	10	11	12	13	14	15
Strikes	19	15	20	22	21	18	21	13	19	24	17	14	12	15	14

SOURCE: National Hurricane Center

Think

How do you know you are entering all the data values?
The calculator value for *n* should match the number of table values.

Use **STAT EDIT** to enter the data in list **L1**.

In **STAT CALC** select the **1– Var Stats** option.

The mean is 17.6, and the standard deviation is about 3.5.

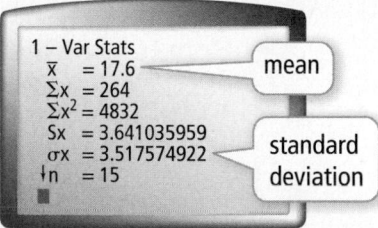

1 – Var Stats
$\bar{x}$ = 17.6 ← mean
Σx = 264
Σx^2 = 4832
Sx = 3.641035959
σx = 3.517574922 ← standard deviation
↓n = 15

✓ **Got It?** **2. Meteorology** The table displays the number of hurricanes in the Atlantic Ocean from 1992 to 2006. What are the mean and standard deviation?

Year	1	2	3	4	5	6	7	8	9	10	11	12	13	14	15
Number	4	4	3	11	10	3	10	8	8	9	4	7	9	14	5

SOURCE: National Hurricane Center

In a data list, every value falls within some number of standard deviations of the mean. For example, if the mean is 50 and the standard deviation is 10, then a value x, where $40 \leq x \leq 60$, is within one standard deviation of the mean.

Problem 3 **Using Standard Deviation to Describe Data**

Meteorology Use the U.S. hurricane-strike data from Problem 2. Within how many standard deviations from the mean do all of the values fall?

Know

The data values, their mean, and their standard deviation

Need

The number of standard deviations from the mean that include all the data

Plan

- Draw a number line.
- Plot the data values and the mean.
- Mark off intervals of 3.5 on either side of the mean.

Think

What is a good way to tell which values lie within each σ interval?

Plotting the values on a number line makes it easy to see the σ intervals.

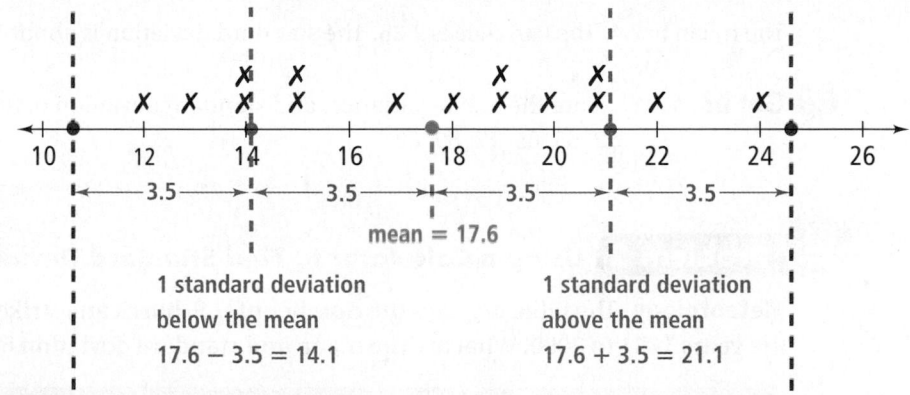

mean = 17.6

1 standard deviation below the mean
17.6 − 3.5 = 14.1

1 standard deviation above the mean
17.6 + 3.5 = 21.1

2 standard deviations below the mean
17.6 − 2(3.5) = 10.6

2 standard deviations above the mean
17.6 + 2(3.5) = 24.6

All of the values fall within two standard deviations of the mean. Hurricane watchers can expect that the number of U.S. hurricane strikes in a decade will probably fall within two standard deviations of the 15-decade mean.

✓ **Got It?** **3. Meteorology** Use the Atlantic Ocean hurricane data from Got It 2.

    a. Within how many standard deviations of the mean do all of the values fall?

    b. Reasoning How might the U.S. Federal Emergency Management Agency (FEMA) use this information?

Focus Question What are standard deviation and variance?

Answer Standard deviation and variance are measures of how the data values of a data set vary from the mean. The standard deviation is the square root of the variance. Use variance to describe how spread out a set of data is.

Lesson Check

Do you know HOW?

1. Find the mean, variance, and standard deviation for the data set.

5, 15, 9, 3, 12, 8, 13, 6, 18, 11

2. Within how many standard deviations of the mean do all of the data values fall?

12, 17, 15, 13, 9, 10, 12, 10, 15, 17

Do you UNDERSTAND?

3. Vocabulary Explain the difference between *measures of central tendency* and *measures of variation*.

4. Compare and Contrast Three data sets each have a mean of 70. Set A has a standard deviation of 10. Set B has a standard deviation of 5. Set C has a standard deviation of 20. Compare and contrast these 3 sets.

Practice and Problem-Solving Exercises

 **Practice** Find the mean, variance, and standard deviation for each data set.

 **See Problem 1.**

Guided Practice

To start, find the mean of the data.

5. 78 90 456 673 111 381 21

$$\bar{x} = \frac{78 + 90 + 456 + 673 + 111 + 381 + 21}{7}$$

$$\approx 258.57$$

6. 13 15 17 18 12 21 10   **7.** 12 3 2 4 5 7   **8.** 60 40 35 45 39

 Graphing Calculator Find the mean and the standard deviation.

See Problem 2.

9. The Dow Jones Industrial average for the first 12 weeks of 1988:

1911.31	1956.07	1903.51	1958.22	1910.48	1983.26
2014.59	2023.21	2057.86	2034.98	2087.37	2067.14

10. The Dow Jones Industrial average for the first 12 weeks of 2008:

12800.18	12606.30	12099.3	12207.17	12743.19	12182.13
12348.21	12381.02	12266.39	11893.69	11951.09	11972.25

Determine the whole number of standard deviations from the mean that include all data values.

◀ See Problem 3.

11. The mean price of the nonfiction books on a best-sellers list is $25.07; the standard deviation is $2.62.
$26.95, $22.95, $24.00, $24.95, $29.95, $19.95, $24.95, $24.00, $27.95, $25.00

12. The mean length of Beethoven's nine symphonies is 37 minutes; the standard deviation is 12 minutes.
27 min, 30 min, 47 min, 35 min, 30 min, 40 min, 35 min, 22 min, 65 min

 **Apply**

13. Think About a Plan Use the data for daily energy usage of a small town during ten days in June. Find the mean and the standard deviation of the data. How many values in the data set fall within one standard deviation from the mean? Within two standard deviations? Within three standard deviations?

51.8 MWh	53.6 MWh	54.7 MWh	51.9 MWh	49.3 MWh
52.0 MWh	53.5 MWh	51.2 MWh	60.7 MWh	59.3 MWh

- How is the mean of the data set used in the formula for standard deviation?
- How can a table help you find the standard deviation?
- How can a graph help you decide how many standard deviations a data value is from the mean?

Income Use the chart at the right for Exercises 14–16.

14. Find the mean income for each year.

15. Writing Use the standard deviation for each year to describe how farm income varied from 2001 to 2002.

16. For 2001, the farm incomes of which states are not within one standard deviation of the mean?

17. Energy The data for daily energy usage of a small town during ten days in January is shown.

83.8 MWh	87.1 MWh	92.5 MWh	80.6 MWh	82.4 MWh
77.6 MWh	78.9 MWh	78.2 MWh	81.8 MWh	80.1 MWh

a. Find the mean and the standard deviation of the data.
b. How many values in the data set fall within one standard deviation from the mean? Within two standard deviations? Within three standard deviations?

Farm Income in Midwestern States (millions of dollars)

State	2001	2002
Iowa	10,653	10,834
Kansas	7979	7862
Minnesota	7537	7478
Missouri	4723	4402
Nebraska	9221	9589
North Dakota	2938	3223
South Dakota	3897	3779

SOURCE: U.S. Department of Agriculture

18. Error Analysis One of your friends says that the data below fall within three standard deviations from the mean. Your other friend disagrees, saying that the data fall within six standard deviations from the mean. With whom do you agree? Explain.

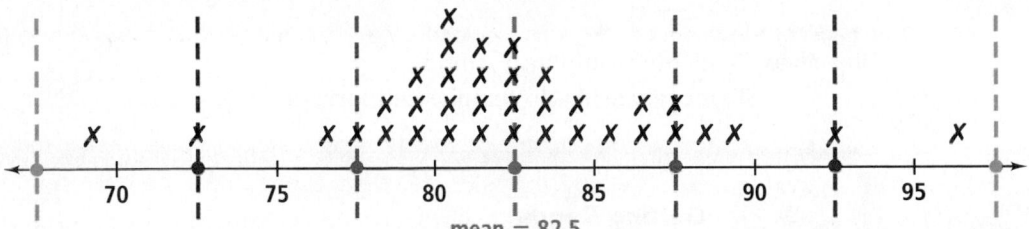

mean = 82.5

Standardized Test Prep

GRIDDED RESPONSE

SAT/ACT

For Exercises 19–20, use the following bowling scores for six members of a bowling team: 175, 210, 180, 195, 208, 196.

19. What is the mean of the scores?

20. What is the standard deviation of the scores?

21. The 30th term of a finite arithmetic series is 4.4. The sum of the first 30 terms is 78. What is the value of the first term of the series?

22. What is the probability of NOT getting a five when rolling a number cube? Write your answer as a fraction reduced to lowest terms.

Mixed Review

Make a box-and-whisker plot for each set of values.   ◀ **See Lesson 11-5.**

23. 25, 25, 30, 35, 45, 45, 50, 55, 60, 60   **24.** 20, 23, 25, 36, 37, 38, 39, 50, 52, 55

Find the center and the radius of each circle.   ◀ **See Lesson 10-3.**

25. $(x - 2)^2 + (y + 1)^2 = 36$ **26.** $(x - 1)^2 + (y - 1)^2 = 4$

Get Ready!   To prepare for Lesson 11-7, do Exercises 27–29.

Simplify each radical expression.   ◀ **See Lesson 6-1.**

27. $\dfrac{1}{\sqrt{4}}$ **28.** $-\dfrac{1}{\sqrt{9}}$ **29.** $\dfrac{1}{\sqrt{36}}$

11-7 Samples and Surveys

Objectives To identify sampling methods
To recognize bias in samples and surveys

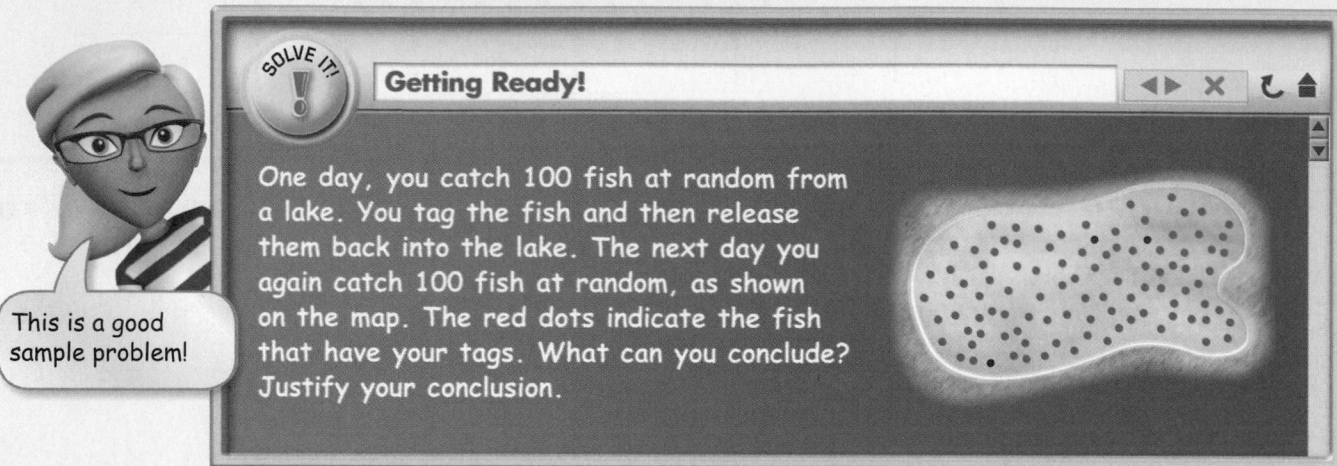

This is a good sample problem!

Getting Ready!

One day, you catch 100 fish at random from a lake. You tag the fish and then release them back into the lake. The next day you again catch 100 fish at random, as shown on the map. The red dots indicate the fish that have your tags. What can you conclude? Justify your conclusion.

A **population** is all the members of a set. A **sample** is part of a population. If you determine a sample carefully, it can give a good estimate of the total population.

Focus Question How can you collect unbiased data in a sample?

Suppose you want to know what percent of all voters in your city favor a tax increase to pay for school improvements. It would be too difficult to ask an opinion of every voter. Instead, you select a sample of the voters to estimate the percentage who favor the idea.

You can define different types of samples by the methods used to select them.

Lesson Vocabulary
- population
- sample
- convenience sample
- self-selected sample
- systematic sample
- random sample
- bias
- observational study
- controlled experiment
- survey

take note

Key Concepts Sampling Types and Methods

For a **convenience sample**, select any members of the population who are conveniently and readily available.

For a **self-selected sample**, select only members of the population who volunteer for the sample.

For a **systematic sample**, order the population in some way, and then select from it at regular intervals.

In a **random sample**, all members of the population are equally likely to be chosen.

A sample has a *bias* when a part of a population is overrepresented or underrepresented. A **bias** is a systematic error introduced by the sampling method.

 **Problem 1** Analyzing Sampling Methods

Public Opinion A newspaper wants to find out what percent of the city population favors a property tax increase to raise money for local parks. What is the sampling method used for each situation? Does the sample have a bias? Explain.

A A newspaper article on the tax increase invites readers to call the paper and express their opinions.

This is a self-selected sample. It might have a bias, depending on who calls the newspaper. The people who call may overrepresent or underrepresent some views. For example, some property owners who are against the tax might organize a campaign to get friends and neighbors to call in.

B A reporter interviews people leaving the city's largest park.

This is a convenience sample, since it is convenient for the reporter to stay in one place. Because the location is near a park, the sample may overrepresent park supporters and the results will have a bias.

C A survey service calls every 50th listing from the local phone book.

This is a systematic sample because the phone listing is ordered alphabetically. The regular sampling interval is every 50 listings. This sample may have a bias if there is some link between people who are listed (or not listed) in a phone book and people who pay property taxes.

 Got It? **1. a.** To survey the eating habits of the community, employees of a local television station interview people visiting a food court in the mall. What sampling method are they using? Does the sample have a bias? Explain.

   b. Reasoning A poll of every person in the population is a *census*. What is a situation that requires a census instead of a sample?

One way to collect sample information is to perform a study.

 **Key Concepts** **Study Methods**

In an **observational study**, you measure or observe members of a sample in such a way that they are not affected by the study.

In a **controlled experiment**, you divide the sample into two groups. You impose a treatment on one group but not on the other "control" group. Then you compare the effect on the treated group to the control group.

In a **survey**, you ask every member of the sample a set of questions.

Hint

A survey question should be clear, precise, and fair so that everyone hears the same question.

A poorly written survey question can introduce bias. An unbiased survey question *avoids*:

- combining two or more issues
- using double negatives
- overlapping answer choices
- words that cause strong reactions (a *loaded* question)
- suggesting that you want a particular answer (a *leading* question)

 Problem 2 Analyzing Survey Questions

Is the survey question biased? Explain.

Plan

How do you tell whether a survey question is biased?
Look for unclear wording, strong words, suggestive wording, and combined questions.

A Do you think farmers should use poison to control insects on crops?

There is bias because the question is loaded. Using the term "poison" instead of "pesticide" could cause a strong reaction from respondents.

B Don't you agree that most childcare workers are underpaid?

There is bias because the question is leading. It suggests that you want a certain answer, that childcare workers are underpaid.

C Do you think teachers should communicate frequently with students and their parents about class grades?

There is bias because the question asks about two issues: teachers communicating with students and teachers communicating with parents.

Got It? 2. Is the survey question biased? Explain.
- **a.** Do you think the cafeteria food is nutritional and tasty?
- **b.** How would you rate the performance of the highly effective student council?

 Problem 3 Designing a Survey

Think

How do you think of a survey question that has no bias?
Keep it simple. The simplest question is likely to be the least biased.

Sports During the 2008 Olympic Games, a U.S. swimmer won more gold medals than any Olympic swimmer before. What sampling method could you use to find the percent of students in your school who recognize that swimmer from a photograph? What is a survey question that is likely to yield unbiased information?

A possible sampling method is to question every 10th student entering school in the morning. This is a systematic sampling. It usually contains the least bias. A possible unbiased survey question is, "Who is pictured in this photograph?".

Got It? 3. **a.** What sampling method could you use to find the percent of residents in your neighborhood who recognize the governor of your state by name? What is a survey question that is likely to yield unbiased information?
- **b.** For the scenario described in Problem 3, suppose you asked members of your school's swim team the survey question "Who is this world-famous swimmer?". Why are this sampling method and question not appropriate?

Focus Question How can you collect unbiased data in a sample?

Answer Choose your sampling method carefully. Systematic samples and random samples are more likely to produce results that represent the entire population. Avoid biased survey questions by using simple, clear language.

Lesson Check

Do you know HOW?

1. To investigate a community's reading habits, a newspaper conducts a poll from a table near the exit of a history museum.
   a. What is the sampling method?
   b. Does the sampling method have any bias? Explain.

2. A survey asks, "Aren't handmade gifts always better than tacky purchased gifts?" Does this survey question have any bias? Explain.

Do you UNDERSTAND?

3. **Vocabulary** What is the difference between a population and a sample? Give an example of each.

4. **Writing** What does it mean to have an unbiased sample? Why does it matter?

5. **Reasoning** Would a large or small sample tend to give a better estimate of how the total population feels about a topic? Explain.

Practice and Problem-Solving Exercises

 **Practice**

Identify the sampling method. Then identify any bias in each method.

 See Problem 1.

Guided Practice →

6. A supermarket wants to find the percent of shoppers who use coupons. A manager interviews every shopper entering the greeting card aisle.

   To start, identify the type of sample.   This is a convenience sample.

7. A maintenance crew wants to estimate how many of 3000 air filters in an office building need replacing. The crew examines five filters chosen at random on each floor of the building.

8. The student government wants to find out how many students have after-school jobs. A pollster interviews students selected at random as they board buses at the end of the school day.

Identify any bias in each survey question.

 **See Problem 2.**

9. Do you feel that you spend too much time each week doing academic homework and household chores?

10. Do you prefer reading exciting historical novels or dull autobiographies?

11. Don't you agree that the wrestling team doesn't get enough coverage in the school newspaper?

12. a. Energy What sampling method could you use to find the percent of adults in your community who support building more nuclear power plants? See Problem 3.

    b. What is an example of a survey question that is likely to yield unbiased information?

 **Apply**

A university researcher is studying the effect of watching television on residents of the city. Describe a sampling method that can be used for each population.

13. all teenagers   **14.** all homeowners

15. all women over the age of 21   **16.** all children under the age of 13

17. Think About a Plan An online advertisement asks you to participate in a survey. The survey asks how much time you spend online each week. What sampling method is the survey using? Identify any bias in the sampling method.
- What population is likely to see the survey?
- What population is likely to respond to the survey?

Suppose you are conducting a survey about careers. Write a survey question using each of the following biases.

18. leads people to a particular response   **19.** does not provide enough information

20. combines two or more issues   **21.** is too wordy or confusing

22. a. Data Collection Write a survey question to find out the number of students at your school who plan to continue their education after high school.
    b. Describe the sampling method you would use.
    c. Conduct your survey.

23. Entertainment A magazine publisher mails a survey to every tenth person on a subscriber list that is alphabetized by last name. The survey asks for three favorite leisure-time activities. What sampling method is the survey using? Identify any bias in the sampling method.

Margin of Error When you take a random sample of size n from a large population, the sample has a *margin of error* of approximately $\pm \frac{1}{\sqrt{n}}$. Approximate the margin of error for each sample.

24. In 2007, the U.S. Mint began issuing one-dollar coins featuring the images of the nation's Presidents. In a survey, 76% of 2431 U.S. adults opposed using one-dollar coins. (SOURCE: *The Harris Poll #41, April 14, 2008*. Copyright © 2008 Harris Interactive, Inc.)

25. In 2008, tax rebate checks were sent to many American tax payers. In a poll, 45% of 2529 U.S. adults said they felt the rebate program would help stimulate the U.S. economy. (SOURCE: Rebate Checks: No Economic Stimulus, September 10, 2008. Copyright © 2008 Harris Interactive, Inc.)

Standardized Test Prep

SAT/ACT

26. To determine the most popular brands of tea consumed by Americans, a survey is conducted in a busy downtown location at lunchtime. Which of the following is NOT a potential bias in the sampling method?

Ⓐ Urban office employees are not representative of the general population.

Ⓑ The results could be influenced by national brand teas available in the area.

Ⓒ A lunchtime survey does not reflect peoples' tastes at other times of the day.

Ⓓ The survey must include call-in and online responses.

27. Which is the equation for the graph of the circle at the right?

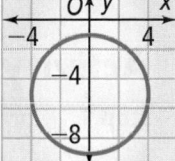

Ⓕ $x^2 + (y - 5)^2 = 16$

Ⓗ $(x - 5)^2 + y^2 = 16$

Ⓖ $x^2 + (y + 5)^2 = 16$

Ⓘ $(x + 5)^2 + y^2 = 16$

28. A bag contains 5 red marbles, 1 blue marble, 3 yellow marbles, and 2 green marbles. One marble is drawn from the bag, the color is noted, and then the marble is replaced. The experiment is repeated. What is the probability that the first marble drawn is red and the second marble drawn is not red?

Ⓐ 1   Ⓑ $\frac{1}{2}$ Ⓒ $\frac{30}{121}$ Ⓓ $\frac{1}{11}$

Short Response

29. What is the sum of the infinite geometric sequence? Show your work.

$$\frac{2}{5}, \frac{4}{25}, \frac{8}{125}, \cdots$$

Mixed Review

Find the mean and the standard deviation for each data set.   ◆ See Lesson 11-6.

30. 0, 1, 1, 1, 2, 2, 2, 3, 3, 4, 5, 10

31. 1, 1, 2, 2, 3, 4, 5, 6, 8, 9, 10, 10, 12

Find the inverse of each function. Is the inverse a function?   ◆ See Lesson 6-7.

32. $f(x) = 2x + 5$

33. $f(x) = x^2$

34. $f(x) = 3\sqrt{x}$

Get Ready!   To prepare for Lesson 11-8, do Exercises 35–37.

Evaluate each expression.   ◆ See Lesson 11-1.

35. $_4C_2$

36. $_3C_3$

37. $_5C_2$

Concept Byte | Describing Data

For Use With Lesson 11-7

ACTIVITY

Suppose you want to know the mean number of letters in the last names of everyone listed in your local phone book. You could count the letters in every last name, but that is not very practical. Instead, you could approximate this mean by taking a *sample* of last names and finding the mean number of letters in only those names.

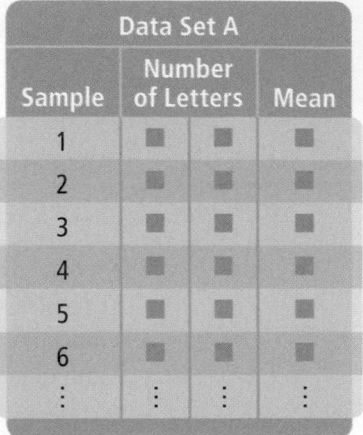

Data Set A		
Sample	Number of Letters	Mean
1	■	■
2	■	■
3	■	■
4	■	■
5	■	■
6	■	■
⋮	⋮	⋮

Activity 1

Step 1 Copy the table at the right. Extend the table to go to Sample 20.

Step 2 Without looking, open a phone book to a random page. Place your index finger on the page, still without looking. Then, count the number of letters in the name closest to the tip of your finger. Record this number in the table in the first blank space for Sample 1. Close the phone book.

Step 3 Repeat Step 2 and record this number in the table in the second blank space for Sample 1. These two numbers make up one sample. Find the mean and record it in the table.

Step 4 Collect a total of 20 samples by repeating Steps 2 and 3.

Step 5 Copy the grid at the right and use the means from Data Set A to make a bar graph.

Step 6 Make a second table with space for 10 numbers in each of the 20 samples. Label this table Data Set B.

Step 7 Repeat Steps 2 and 3, but now select 10 names for each sample. Record the data in the second table.

Step 8 Copy the grid again and use the means in Data Set B to make a bar graph.

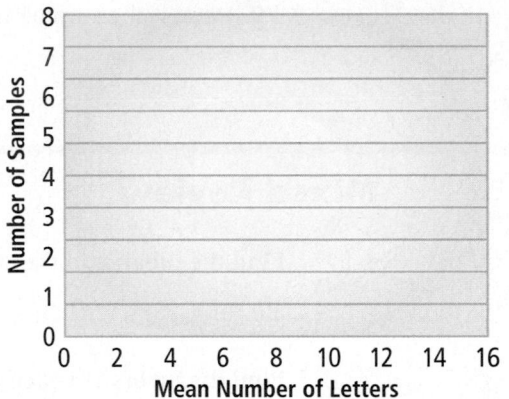

1. Does the graph of Data Set A or the graph of Data Set B show more variation?

2. Which data set has a greater range?

3. Which data set has a greater standard deviation?

4. The *Law of Large Numbers* states that the variation in the means of repeated samples decreases as the sample size increases. Do your results support this law?

5. **Compare and Contrast** Compare your results with those of another student in the class. How are they the same? How are they different?

6. **Reasoning** Suppose you conduct this experiment by collecting all of the samples from one page of the phone book. Predict how this sampling technique might affect your results.

11-8 Binomial Distributions

Objective To find binomial probabilities and to use binomial distributions

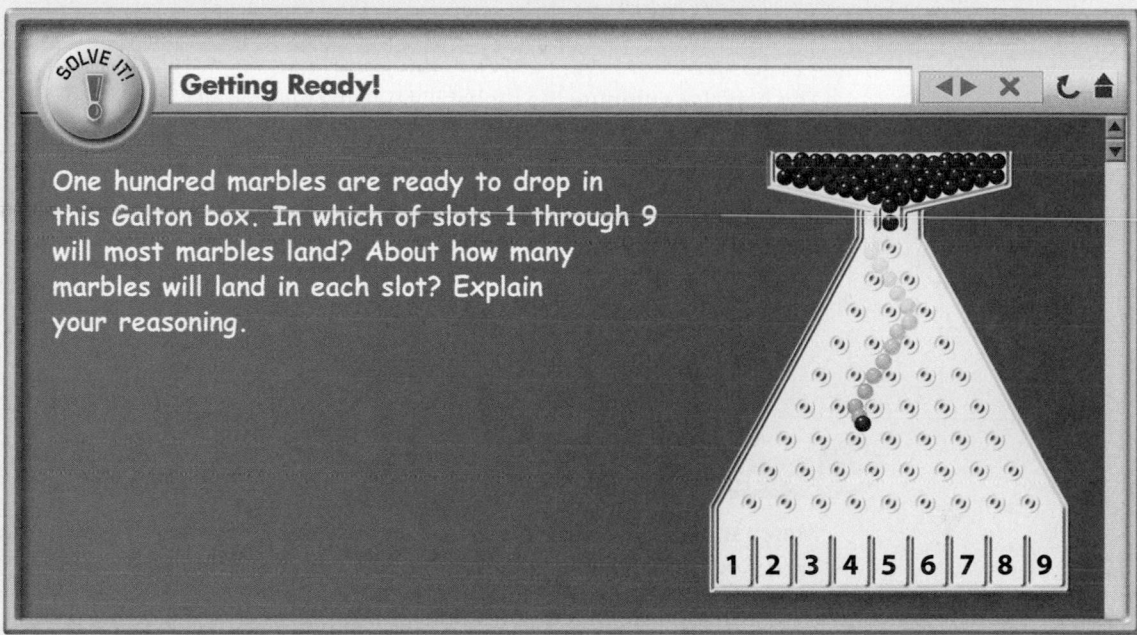

Getting Ready!

One hundred marbles are ready to drop in this Galton box. In which of slots 1 through 9 will most marbles land? About how many marbles will land in each slot? Explain your reasoning.

1 2 3 4 5 6 7 8 9

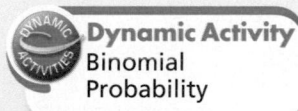

Dynamic Activity
Binomial
Probability

**Lesson
Vocabulary**
- binomial experiment
- binomial probability
- Binomial Theorem
- probability distribution

At each level of a Galton box, a marble can take one of two possible paths.

Focus Question What is binomial probability?

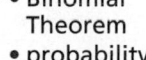

Key Concept Binomial Experiment

A **binomial experiment** has these important features:
- There are a fixed number of trials.
- Each trial has two possible outcomes.
- The trials are independent.
- The probability of each outcome is constant throughout the trials.

Hint

Recall from Lesson 11-4 that you can use a tree diagram to find probabilities.

The tree diagram on the following page shows different outcomes and probabilities for a basketball player shooting two free throws. It is known that this player is a good shooter, having hit (*H*) about 90% of the free throws so far this season.

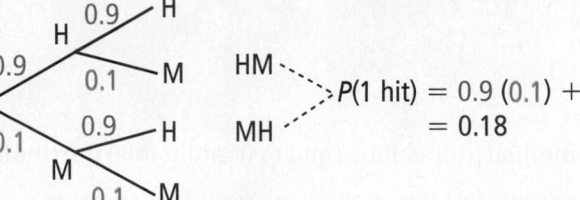

Hint

The basketball player shoots 2 free throws—each independent of the other (ignoring pressure). The player will succeed on 0, 1, or 2 of them.

HH $\qquad$ $P(2 \text{ hits}) = 0.9^2 = 0.81$

H: Hits (makes) a shot
M: Misses a shot

HM $\qquad$
$\qquad$ $P(1 \text{ hit}) = 0.9\,(0.1) + 0.1(0.9)$
MH $\qquad$ $\qquad\qquad = 0.18$

MM $\qquad$ $P(0 \text{ hits}) = 0.1^2 = 0.01$

You can also compute the probabilities using the formula for *binomial probability*.

take note

Key Concept   Binomial Probability

Suppose you have n repeated independent trials, each with a probability of success p and a probability of failure q (with $p + q = 1$). Then the **binomial probability** of x successes in the n trials can be found using the following formula.

$$P(x) = {}_nC_x\,p^x q^{n-x}$$

Problem 1   Using a Formula to Find Probabilities

Merchandising As part of a promotion, a store is giving away scratch-off cards. Each card has a 40% chance of awarding a prize. Suppose you have five cards. Find the probability that exactly four of the five cards will reveal a prize.

Know
- The number of trials n
- The number of successes x
- The probability of success p

Need
- The probability of failure q
- The probability of picking exactly 4 winning cards

Plan
- Determine that this is binomial probability.
- Find the probability of failure q.
- Use the formula for binomial probability.

Determine if this a binomial experiment:
- The situation involves 5 repeated trials—5 cards selected at random.
- Each trial has two possible outcomes: A card is a winner or it is not.
- The probability of success is constant, 0.4, throughout the trials.
- The trials are independent. The outcome of scratching one card does not affect the probability of any of the other cards revealing a prize.

This is a binomial experiment with $n = 5$, $x = 4$, $p = 0.4$, and $q = 1 - p = 0.6$.

Think

How can you find $_nC_x$ using your calculator?
$$_nC_x = \frac{n!}{x!(n-x)!}$$
On a graphing calculator, use **MATH** and $_nC_r$ in the **PRB** menu.

Write the formula for binomial probability. $\qquad P(x) = {}_nC_x\,p^x q^{n-x}$

Substitute. $\qquad\qquad\qquad\qquad\qquad\qquad P(4) = {}_5C_4(0.4)^4(0.6)^1$

Evaluate $_5C_4$ and simplify. $\qquad\qquad\qquad\qquad = 5(0.4)^4(0.6)^1 \approx 0.08$

The probability is about 8% that exactly 4 of the five cards will reveal a prize.

Got It? **1.** In Problem 1, what is the probability that the number of cards that reveal a prize is 0? 1? 2? 3? 5?

Hint

Be careful not to confuse elements of Pascal's Triangle P_i with probability $P(x)$ or permutations $_nP_r$.

The Binomial Theorem (Lesson 5-7) says that for every positive integer n,

$$(a + b)^n = P_0a^n + P_1a^{n-1}b + P_2a^{n-2}b^2 + \cdots + P_{n-1}ab^{n-1} + P_nb^n$$

where $P_0, P_1, \ldots, P_n$ are the numbers in the nth row of Pascal's Triangle.

For that row, it is possible to show that $P_i = {_nC_i}$.

```
        1                                    ₀C₀
      1   1                              ₁C₀    ₁C₁
    1   2   1         ───────▶        ₂C₀    ₂C₁    ₂C₂
  1   3   3   1                    ₃C₀    ₃C₁    ₃C₂    ₃C₃
1   4   6   4   1               ₄C₀    ₄C₁    ₄C₂    ₄C₃    ₄C₄
```

So, you can restate the **Binomial Theorem** using combinations.

---

take note

Key Concept Binomial Theorem

For every positive integer n,

$$(a + b)^n = {_nC_0}a^n + {_nC_1}a^{n-1}b + {_nC_2}a^{n-2}b^2 + \cdots + {_nC_{n-1}}ab^{n-1} + {_nC_n}b^n$$

Problem 2 Expanding Binomials

Use the Binomial Theorem to solve.

Ⓐ What is the binomial expansion of $(x + y)^5$?

Use the Binomial Theorem with $a = x$, $b = y$, and $n = 5$.

Write the expansion. $(x + y)^5 = {_5C_0}x^5 + {_5C_1}x^4y + {_5C_2}x^3y^2 + {_5C_3}x^2y^3 + {_5C_4}xy^4 + {_5C_5}y^5$

Substitute for the $_nC_i$. $= x^5 + 5x^4y + 10x^3y^2 + 10x^2y^3 + 5xy^4 + y^5$

Think

Which $_4C_i$ do you use in the third term?
You use $_4C_0$, not $_4C_1$, for the first term. Therefore, use $_4C_2$ in the third term.

Ⓑ What is the third term of $(2x - 3y)^4$?

The third term of the binomial expansion is $_4C_2a^{4-2}b^2$.

Substitute $a = 2x$ and $b = -3y$. $_4C_2a^{4-2}b^2 = {_4C_2}(2x)^2(-3y)^2$

Evaluate $_4C_2$. $= 6(4x^2)(9y^2)$

Simplify. $= 216x^2y^2$

 Got It? **2.** What is the binomial expansion of $(3x + y)^4$?

A **probability distribution** is a function that gives the probability of each outcome in a sample space. To find the full probability distribution for a binomial experiment, use the Binomial Theorem to expand the binomial $(p + q)^n$. For example, suppose you guess on four questions of a five-choice multiple-choice test. For four questions, $n = 4$, $P(\text{guessing correctly}) = \frac{1}{5}$, so $p = 0.2$, and $q = 0.8$.

Hint
The full probability distribution for a binomial experiment must sum to 1, or 100%.

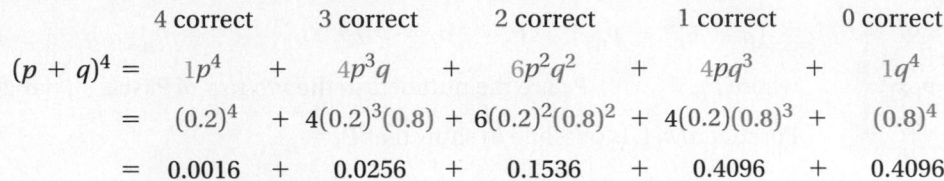

You can display the distribution of binomial probabilities as a graph.

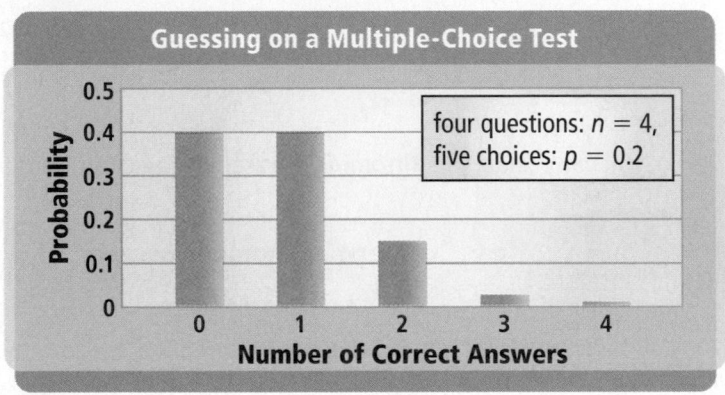

Guessing on a Multiple-Choice Test

four questions: $n = 4$,
five choices: $p = 0.2$

Probability / Number of Correct Answers

 Problem 3 Applying Binomial Probability

Manufacturing Each hour at a cell phone factory, Quality Control (QC) tests the durability of four randomly selected phones. If more than one fails, QC rejects the entire production for that hour. If in one hour, 95% of the phones made are acceptable, what is the probability that QC rejects that hour's phone production?

Think

What is a "success" in one trial of this binomial experiment?
Success in this experiment means that a phone fails the test.

Write the binomial expansion of $(p + q)^n$ with $n = 4$, $p = 0.05$, and $q = 0.95$.

4 fail   3 fail   2 fail   1 fail   0 fail

$(p + q)^4 = p^4q^0 + 4p^3q^1 + 6p^2q^2 + 4p^1q^3 + p^0q^4$

$= (0.05)^4 + 4(0.05)^3(0.95)^1 + 6(0.05)^2(0.95)^2 + 4(0.05)^1(0.95)^3 + (0.95)^4$

$\approx 0.000006 + 0.000475 + 0.013538 + 0.171475 + 0.814506$

Probability (4, 3, or 2 phones fail) $\approx 0.000006 + 0.000475 + 0.013538$

≈ 0.014019

There is about a 1.4% chance that QC will reject the phones produced in the last hour.

Got It? 3. A multiple-choice quiz has five questions. Each question has four answer choices. If you guess every answer, what is the probability of getting at least three correct?

Focus Question What is binomial probability?

Answer For n independent trials, each with a probability of success p and probability of failure q, the binomial probability of x successes is $P(x) = {}_nC_x p^x q^{n-x}$. Use binomial probability to model situations with two possible outcomes.

Lesson Check

Do you know HOW?

Find the probability of x successes in n trials for the given probability of success p on each trial.

1. $x = 2, n = 6, p = 0.4$ **2.** $x = 6, n = 9, p = 0.5$

Find the indicated term of each binomial expansion.

3. fourth term of $(c + d)^6$ **4.** second term of $(x - 2y)^5$

5. What is the probability of 2 successes in 4 trials of an experiment if the probability of success of one trial is 0.3?

Do you UNDERSTAND?

6. Vocabulary Explain how flipping a coin 10 times meets all of the conditions for a binomial experiment.

7. Error Analysis A student finds the fifth term of the binomial expansion $(j - k)^7$. Describe and correct the error the student made.

$$
{}_nC_5 a^{(n-5)} b^5 = {}_7C_5 j^2 (-k)^5
$$
$$
= -21 j^2 k^5
$$

Practice and Problem-Solving Exercises

A Practice Find the probability of x successes in n trials for the given probability of success p on each trial.

◆ **See Problem 1.**

Guided Practice

To start, identify the probability of failure q.

8. $x = 3, n = 8, p = 0.3$
$q = 1 - p$
$= 1 - 0.3 = 0.7$

9. $x = 5, n = 10, p = 0.5$ **10.** $x = 5, n = 10, p = 0.1$

11. Battery Life A calculator contains four batteries. With normal use, each battery has a 90% chance of lasting for one year. What is the probability that all four batteries will last a year?

Expand each binomial.

◆ **See Problem 2.**

12. $(m + 5n)^3$ **13.** $(4c - d)^4$

Find the indicated term of each binomial expansion.

Guided Practice

To start, write the second term of the binomial expansion of $(a + b)^7$.

14. second term of $(2g + 2h)^7$
${}_7C_1 a^{(7-1)} b^1 = {}_7C_1 a^6 b$

15. fifth term of $(x - y)^5$ **16.** eighth term of $(3x - y)^8$

Use the binomial expansion of $(p + q)^n$ to calculate each binomial distribution. ◀ **See Problem 3.**

17. $n = 6, p = 0.3$ **18.** $n = 6, p = 0.5$

 **Apply**

19. Think About a Plan One survey found that 80% of respondents eat corn on the cob in circles rather than from side to side. Assume that this sample accurately represents the population. What is the probability that, out of five people you know, at least two of them eat corn on the cob in circles?
- How can you find the probability that one person eats corn on the cob in circles?
- How does a probability distribution help you solve the problem?

20. Weather A scientist hopes to launch a weather balloon on one of the next three mornings. For each morning, there is a 40% chance of suitable weather. What is the probability that there will be at least one morning with suitable weather?

Marketing A fruit company guarantees that 90% of the pineapples it ships will ripen within four days of delivery. Find each probability for a case containing 12 pineapples.

21. All 12 are ripe within four days.   **22.** At least 10 are ripe within four days.

Sociology A study shows that 50% of people in a community watch television during dinner. Suppose you select 10 people at random from this population. Find each probability.

23. P(exactly 5 of the 10 people watch television during dinner)

24. P(exactly 6 of the 10 people watch television during dinner)

25. P(at least 5 of the 10 people watch television during dinner)

26. Writing Explain how a binomial experiment is related to a binomial expansion.

27. Quality Control A company claims that 99% of its cereal boxes have at least as much cereal by weight as the amount stated on the box.
- **a.** At a quality control checkpoint, one box out of a random sample of ten boxes falls short of its stated weight. What is the probability of this happening due to chance variation in box weights?
- **b. Reasoning** Suppose three of ten boxes fail to have the claimed weight. What would you conclude? Explain.

28. Genetics About 11% of the general population is left-handed. At a school with an average class size of 30, each classroom contains four left-handed desks. Does this seem adequate? Justify your answer.

29. Open-Ended Describe a binomial experiment that can be solved using the expression $_7C_2(0.6)^2(0.4)^5$.

30. Graph each probability distribution for $(p + q)^3$.
- **a.** $p = 0.9, q = 0.1$ **b.** $p = 0.45, q = 0.55$
- **c. Compare and Contrast** How are the graphs in parts (a) and (b) similar? How are they different?

Standardized Test Prep

SAT/ACT

31. A survey shows that 60% of adults floss their teeth every day. In a random sample of ten adults, what is the probability that exactly six adults floss every day?

    Ⓐ 11%   Ⓑ 25%   Ⓒ 60%   Ⓓ 100%

32. Which of the statements about the following equation is correct?

$$\frac{b^2 - 4b + 3}{b - 3} = b - 1$$

    Ⓕ The equation is always true.

    Ⓖ The equation is true, except when $b = 3$.

    Ⓗ The equation is never true.

    Ⓘ The equation is true when $b = 3$.

33. Which is the inverse of $f(x) = (x - 3)^2$?

    Ⓐ $f^{-1}(x) = \dfrac{x^2}{(3x - 1)^2}$ Ⓒ $f^{-1}(x) = \dfrac{1}{(3x - 1)^2}$

    Ⓑ $f^{-1}(x) = \pm\sqrt{x} + 3$ Ⓓ $f^{-1}(x) = \pm\sqrt{x - 3}$

34. If $\log 4 \approx 0.60206$ and $\log 5 \approx 0.69897$, what is the approximate value of $\log 80$?

    Ⓕ 0.2534   Ⓖ 0.2914   Ⓗ 1.903   Ⓘ 11.1835

Extended Response

35. In a geometric sequence, $a_1 = 3$ and $a_4 = 192$. Explain how to find a_2 and a_3.

Mixed Review

Identify any bias in each survey question.   ◀ See Lesson 11-7.

36. Do you agree that replacing that dog park with a beautiful new library would be better for our town?

37. Do you agree with the amendments to Proposition 39?

Find the vertices, foci, and asymptotes of each hyperbola.   ◀ See Lesson 10-5.

38. $\dfrac{y^2}{49} - \dfrac{x^2}{25} = 1$ **39.** $4y^2 - 9x^2 = 36$ **40.** $64y^2 - 36x^2 = 576$

A standard number cube is tossed. Find each probability.   ◀ See Lesson 11-3.

41. $P(2 \text{ or greater than } 3)$ **42.** $P(6 \text{ or even})$ **43.** $P(\text{prime or } 1)$

Get Ready!   **To prepare for Lesson 11-9, do Exercises 44–47.**

Find the mean and standard deviation for each data set.   ◀ See Lessons 11-5 and 11-6.

44. 16, 20, 28, 25, 26, 33, 27, 22, 29, 18   **45.** 81, 78, 79, 80, 76, 88, 83, 90, 87, 76

46. 8.5, 7.9, 8.2, 9.0, 8.3, 9.1, 9.2   **47.** 23.5, 22.4, 25.6, 26.8, 28.1, 22.3, 24.5

11-9 Normal Distributions

Objective To use a normal distribution

The function equation must be true for every value of x.

Getting Ready!

Even and odd functions are defined as follows.

Even function: $f(x) = f(-x)$

Odd function: $-f(x) = f(-x)$

Which is the graph of an even function? Of an odd function? Justify your answers.

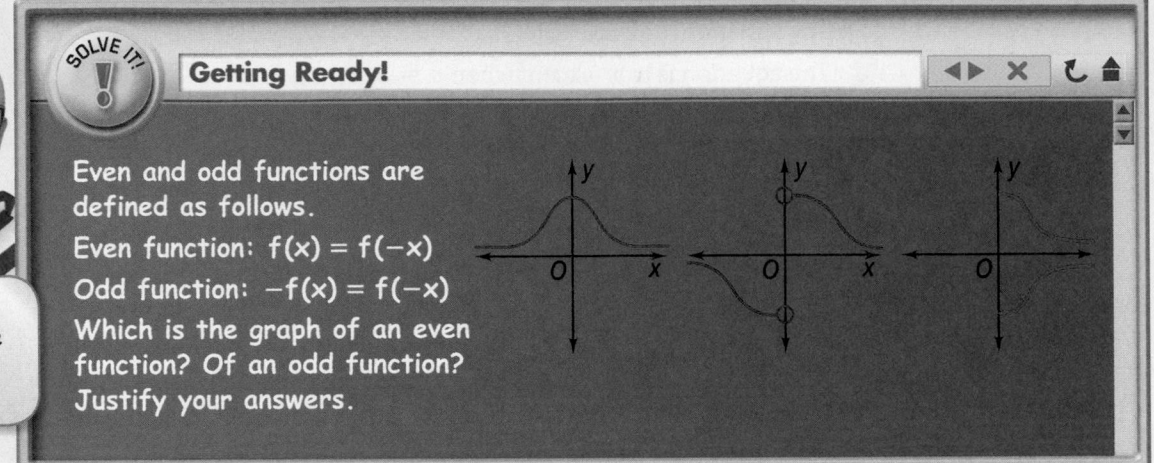

Lesson Vocabulary

• discrete probability distribution
• continuous probability distribution
• normal distribution

A **discrete probability distribution** has a finite number of possible events, or values. The binomial probability distribution you studied in the preceding lesson is a discrete probability distribution.

The events for a **continuous probability distribution** can be any value in an interval of real numbers. If a data set is large, the distribution of its discrete values approximates a continuous distribution.

Focus Question What is a normal distribution?

A **normal distribution** has data that vary randomly from the mean. The graph of a normal distribution is called a normal curve.

Key Concept Normal Distribution

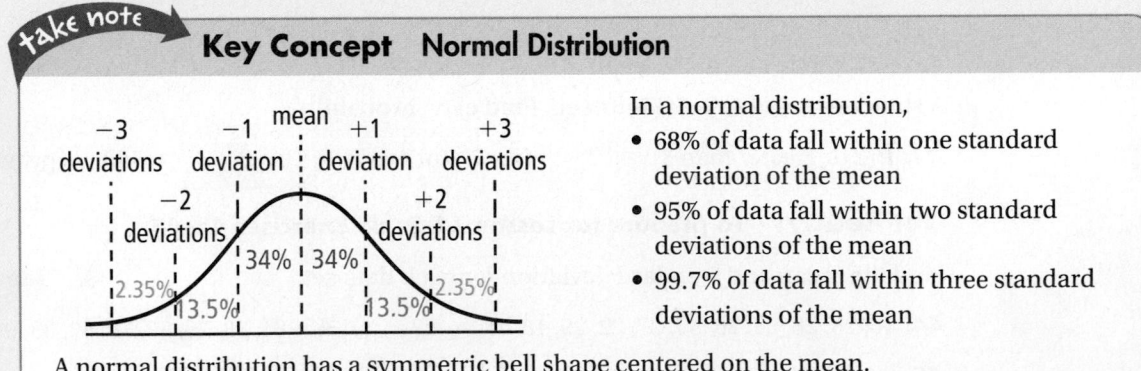

In a normal distribution,
• 68% of data fall within one standard deviation of the mean
• 95% of data fall within two standard deviations of the mean
• 99.7% of data fall within three standard deviations of the mean

A normal distribution has a symmetric bell shape centered on the mean.

Sometimes an extraordinary factor affects data that would otherwise be normally distributed. A coin, for example, may be somehow weighted unevenly so that heads tends to come up more frequently than tails. In such a case, the data set could have a distribution that is *skewed*, an asymmetric curve where one end stretches out further than the other end.

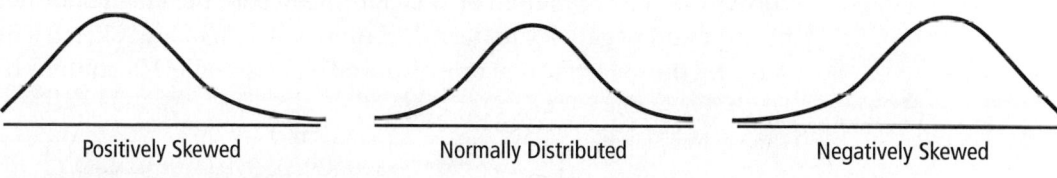

Positively Skewed   Normally Distributed   Negatively Skewed

Problem 1 **Analyzing Normally Distributed Data**

Zoology The bar graph gives the weights of a population of female brown bears. The red curve shows how the weights are normally distributed about the mean, 115 kg. Approximately what percent of female brown bears weigh between 100 and 129 kg?

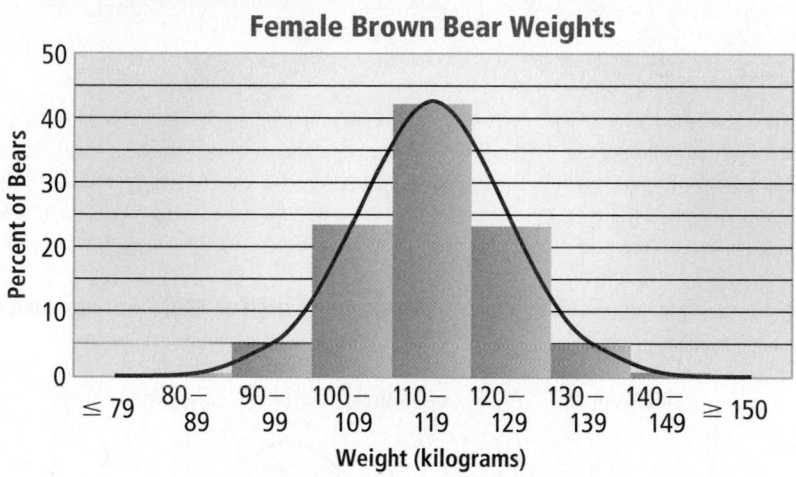

Female Brown Bear Weights

Estimate and add the percents for the intervals 100–109, 110–119, and 120–129.

$$23 + 42 + 23 = 88$$

About 88% of female brown bears weigh between 100 and 129 kg.

Got It? **1. a.** Approximately what percent of female brown bears in Problem 1 weigh less than 120 kg?

b. The standard deviation in the weights of female brown bears is about 10 kg. Approximately what percent of female brown bears have weights that are within 1.5 standard deviations of the mean?

When data are normally distributed, you can sketch the graph of the distribution because a normal curve has a symmetric bell shape.

Problem 2 Sketching a Normal Curve

Zoology For a population of male European eels, the mean body length and one positive and negative standard deviation is shown below. Sketch a normal curve showing the eel lengths at one, two, and three standard deviations from the mean.

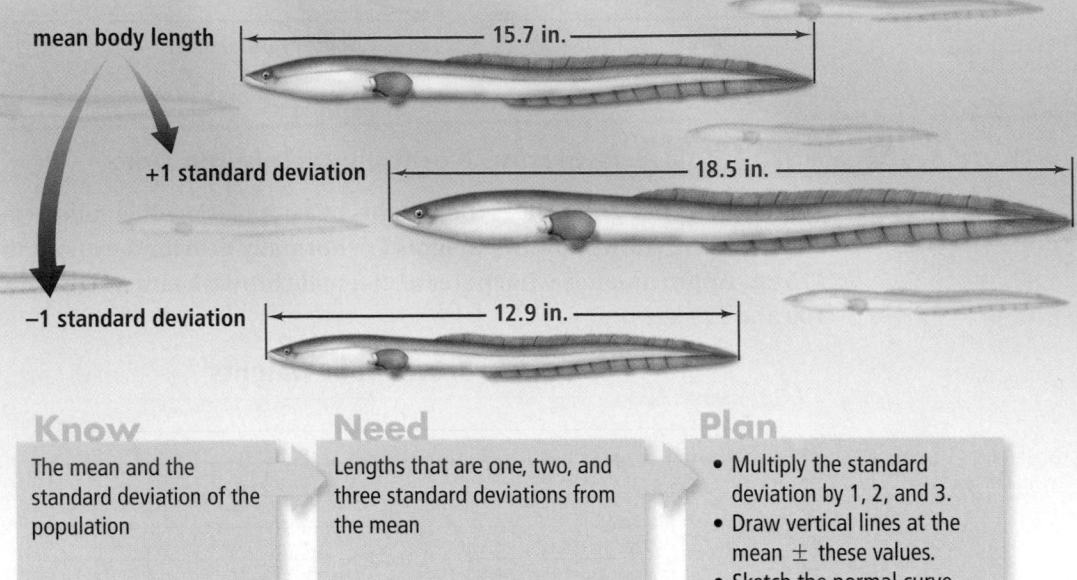

mean body length — 15.7 in.

+1 standard deviation — 18.5 in.

−1 standard deviation — 12.9 in.

Know

The mean and the standard deviation of the population

Need

Lengths that are one, two, and three standard deviations from the mean

Plan

- Multiply the standard deviation by 1, 2, and 3.
- Draw vertical lines at the mean ± these values.
- Sketch the normal curve.

Think

How high do you draw the curve? Unless you actually label the vertical scale, the height of the curve doesn't matter.

Distribution of Body Lengths for Male European Eels

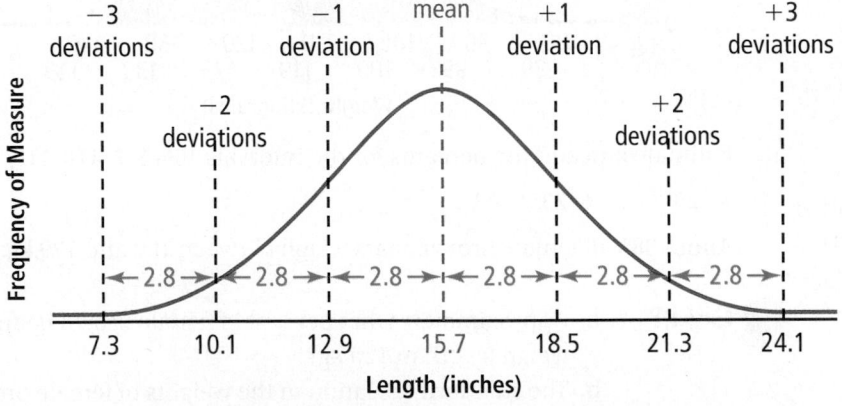

Frequency of Measure

−3 deviations | −2 deviations | −1 deviation | mean | +1 deviation | +2 deviations | +3 deviations

←2.8→←2.8→←2.8→←2.8→←2.8→←2.8→

7.3   10.1   12.9   15.7   18.5   21.3   24.1

Length (inches)

✓ **Got It?** **2.** For a population of female European eels, the mean body length is 21.1 in. The standard deviation is 4.7 in. Sketch a normal curve showing eel lengths at one, two, and three standard deviations from the mean.

When you show a probability distribution as a bar graph, the height of the bar indicates probability. For a normal distribution, however, the area between the curve and an interval on the x-axis represents probability.

 Problem 3 Analyzing a Normal Distribution

The heights of adult American males are approximately normally distributed with mean 69.5 in. and standard deviation 2.5 in.

Ⓐ What percent of adult American males are between 67 in. and 74.5 in. tall?

Step 1 Draw a normal curve.

Step 2 Label the mean, 69.5.

Step 3 Divide the graph into sections that are one standard-deviation, or 2.5 in., wide.

Step 4 Label the percentages for each section.

Because the graph is a normal distribution, each section within one standard deviation has a probability of 34%. Similarly, each section from one standard deviation to two standard deviations has a probability of 13.5%. Each outermost section has a probability of 2.35%.

Think

How do you divide the graph of the distribution?
Draw vertical lines at intervals that are one standard deviation wide, on both sides of the mean.

Distribution of Heights—Adult American Males

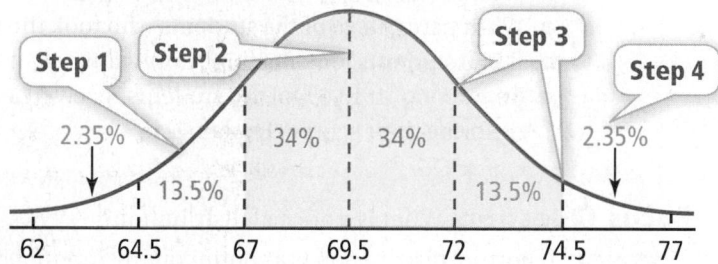

Step 5 Find the probability between 67 and 74.5.

Use the percentages to calculate probability.

$$P(67 < \text{height} < 74.5) = 0.34 + 0.34 + 0.135$$

Simplify.

$$= 0.815$$

About 82% of adult American males are between 67 in. and 74.5 in. tall.

B In a group of 2000 adult American males, about how many would you expect to be taller than 6 ft (or 72 in.)?

Because the graph is symmetric about the mean, the right half of the distribution contains 50% of the data. If you subtract everything between 69.5 in. and 72 in. from the right half, only the part of the distribution that is greater than 72 in. remains.

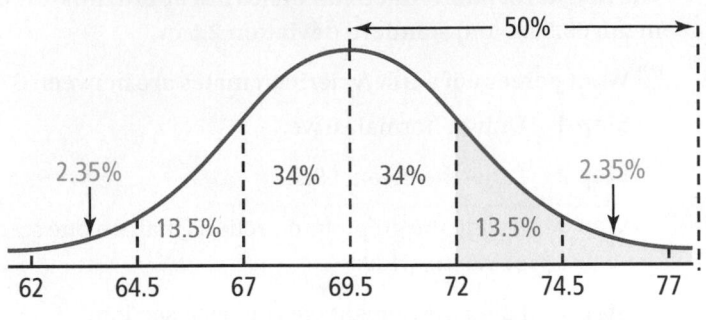

Distribution of Heights—Adult American Males

$$P(\text{height} > 72) = 0.50 - 0.34 = 0.16$$

You would expect about 16% of the 2000 adult American males to be taller than 72 in. You would expect about $0.16 \cdot 2000 = 320$ to be over 6 ft tall.

 Got It? **3.** The scores on the Algebra 2 final are approximately normally distributed with a mean of 150 and a standard deviation of 15.
    a. What percentage of the students who took the test scored above 180?
    b. If 250 students took the final, approximately how many scored above 135?
    c. **Reasoning** If 13.6% of the students received a B on the final, how can you describe their scores? Explain.

Focus Question What is a normal distribution?

Answer A normal distribution is a continuous distribution whose data vary randomly from the mean. The graph of a normal distribution is a symmetric bell-shaped curve centered on the mean. Use the percentage for each interval to calculate probability.

Lesson Check

Do you know HOW?

1. Use the graph from Problem 1. What is the approximate percent of female brown bears weighing at least 100 kg?

2. Draw a curve to represent a normally distributed experiment that has a mean of 180 and a standard deviation of 15. Label the x-axis and indicate the probabilities.

3. The scores on an exam are normally distributed, with a mean of 85 and a standard deviation of 5. What percent of the scores are from 85 to 95?

Do you UNDERSTAND?

4. **Vocabulary** Why is a normal distribution "normal"?

5. **Compare and Contrast** How do the mean and median compare in a normal distribution?

6. **Reasoning** What is the effect on a normal distribution if each data value increases by 10? Justify your answer.

Practice and Problem-Solving Exercises

A Practice

Biology The heights of men in a survey are distributed normally about the mean. Use the graph to the right for Exercises 7–10.

◀ **See Problem 1.**

7. About what percent of men aged 25 to 34 are 69–71 in. tall?

8. About what percent of men aged 25 to 34 are less than 70 in. tall?

9. Suppose the survey included data on 100 men. About how many would you expect to be 69–71 in. tall?

10. The mean of the data is 70, and the standard deviation is 2.5. Approximately what percent of men are within one standard deviation of the mean height?

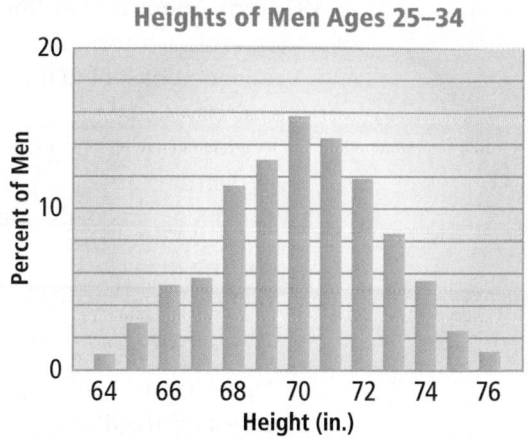

Sketch a normal curve for each distribution. Label the *x*-axis values at one, two, and three standard deviations from the mean.

◀ **See Problem 2.**

Guided Practice

To start, sketch a normal curve and label the mean.

11. mean = 45, standard deviation = 5

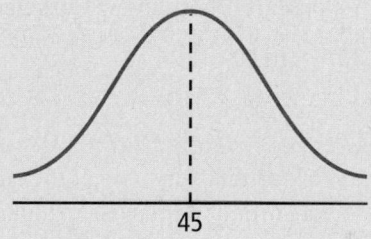

45

12. mean = 45, standard deviation = 2

13. mean = 45, standard deviation = 3.5

A set of data has a normal distribution with a mean of 50 and a standard deviation of 8. Find the percent of data within each interval.

◀ **See Problem 3.**

14. from 42 to 58

15. greater than 34

16. less than 50

Apply

17. **a.** From the table at the right, select the set of values that appears to be distributed normally.
   b. Using the set you chose in part (a), make a histogram of the values.
   c. Sketch a normal curve over your graph.

18. **Think About a Plan** The numbers of paper clips per box in a truckload of boxes are normally distributed, with a mean of 100 and a standard deviation of 5. Find the probability that a box will *not* contain between 95 and 105 clips.
   • How should you label the vertical lines on the graph of the normal distribution?
   • Which parts of the graph are *not* between 95 and 105 clips?

19. **Writing** In a class of 25, one student receives a score of 100 on a test. The grades are distributed normally, with a mean of 78 and a standard deviation of 5. Do you think the student's score is an outlier? Explain.

20. **Agriculture** To win a prize, the diameter of a tomato must be greater than 4 in. The diameters of a crop of tomatoes grown in a special soil are normally distributed, with a mean of 3.2 in. and a standard deviation of 0.4 in. What is the probability that a tomato grown in the special soil will be a winner?

Set 1	Set 2	Set 3
1	5	5
10	7	6
5	7	9
19	7	1
2	4	1
7	11	5
1	7	11
7	7	1
2	7	10
10	9	4
6	7	2
9	7	8

A normal distribution has a mean of 100 and a standard deviation of 10. Find the probability that a value selected at random is in the given interval.

21. from 80 to 100

22. from 90 to 120

23. at most 110

24. at least 80

25. **Weather** The table at the right shows the number of tornadoes that were recorded in the U.S. in 2008.
   a. Draw a histogram to represent the data.
   b. Does the histogram approximate a normal curve? Explain.

26. **Error Analysis** In a set of data, the value 332 is 3 standard deviations from the mean and the value 248 is 1 standard deviation from the mean. A classmate claims that there is only one possible mean and standard deviation for this data set. Do you agree? Explain.

27. **Reasoning** Jake and Elena took the same standardized test, but with different groups of students. They both received a score of 87. In Jake's group, the mean was 80 and the standard deviation was 6. In Elena's group, the mean was 76 and the standard deviation was 4. Did either student score in the top 10% of his or her group? Explain.

Month	Tornadoes
1	84
2	147
3	129
4	189
5	461
6	294
7	93
8	101
9	111
10	21
11	20
12	40

Standardized Test Prep

SAT/ACT

28. For a daily airline flight between two cities, the number of pieces of checked luggage has a mean of 380 and a standard deviation of 20. On what percent of the flights would you expect from 340 to 420 pieces of checked luggage?

    Ⓐ 34%   Ⓑ 47.5%   Ⓒ 68%   Ⓓ 95%

29. A jar contains 37 pennies, 53 nickels, 29 dimes, and 21 quarters. A coin is drawn at random from the jar. What is the probability that the coin drawn is NOT a quarter?

    Ⓕ $\dfrac{56{,}869}{2{,}744{,}000}$ Ⓖ $\dfrac{3}{20}$ Ⓗ $\dfrac{3}{17}$ Ⓘ $\dfrac{17}{20}$

30. A multiple-choice quiz contains five questions, each with three answer choices. You select all five answer choices at random. What is the best estimate of the probability that you will get at least four answers correct?

    Ⓐ 4.1%   Ⓑ 4.5%   Ⓒ 13.2%   Ⓓ 46.1%

Short Response

31. Distribution A has 50 data values with mean 40 and standard deviation 2.4. Distribution B has 30 data values with mean 40 and standard deviation 2.8. Which distribution has more data values at or below 40? Show your work.

Mixed Review

Find the probability of x successes in n trials for the given probability of success p on each trial.

See Lesson 11-8.

32. $x = 4, n = 7, p = 0.2$ **33.** $x = 2, n = 9, p = 0.4$ **34.** $x = 6, n = 10, p = 0.3$

Graph each equation. Identify the conic section and describe the graph and its lines of symmetry. Then find the domain and range.

See Lesson 10-1.

35. $x^2 + y^2 = 64$ **36.** $x^2 - y^2 = 9$ **37.** $9x^2 + 25y^2 = 225$

Get Ready! To prepare for Lesson 12-1, do Exercises 38–40.

Write an equation for each horizontal translation of $y = x - 2$. Then graph each translation.

See Lesson 2-6.

38. 1 unit right   **39.** 2 units left   **40.** $\frac{3}{4}$ unit left

11

Pull It **All Together**

To solve these problems, you will pull together concepts and skills related to probability and statistics.

BIG idea Probability

Various counting methods (such as permutations and combinations) can help you analyze situations and develop theoretical probabilities.

Task 1

Suppose you have n items from which you choose r at a time. Explain why you must divide the number of permutations $\frac{n!}{(n-r)!}$ by $r!$ to find the number of combinations $\frac{n!}{r!(n-r)!}$.

Task 2

Suppose you stack three identical number cubes. It is possible to have no sides, two sides, or all four sides of the stack showing all the same number. (Note that if one side of a stack shows all the same number, then the opposite side must as well.)

How many ways are there to stack three standard number cubes so that at least two sides of the stack show all the same number? If you can rotate a stack so that it is the same as another, count them as the same arrangement.

0 sides

2 sides

4 sides

BIG idea Data Collection and Analysis

Standard measures that describe data from a real-world situation can help you make estimates or decisions about the situation, or predictions about future occurrences.

Task 3

Show all of your work and explain your steps.

a. Find the mean and standard deviation of the sums you should get when you roll two standard number cubes.

b. Suppose you can replace one number cube with a nonstandard number cube, where any of the numbers 1 through 6 can appear on multiple faces. How can you arrange the numbers on the nonstandard cube so that the mean of the rolls is the same as that of two standard number cubes, but the standard deviation is as large as possible? What is this value?

Chapter Review for Part B

Connecting **BIG** ideas and Answering the Essential Questions

1 Probability
A combination is a collection. A permutation is an ordered collection.

Permutations and Combinations (Lesson 11-1)
For n items chosen r at a time, $0 \le r \le n$,

• $_nP_r = \dfrac{n!}{(n-r)!}$ • $_nC_r = \dfrac{n!}{r!(n-r)!}$

Probability of Multiple Events and Conditional Probability (Lessons 11-3 and 11-4)
If A and B are independent events,
• $P(A \text{ and } B) = P(A) \cdot P(B)$
• $P(A \text{ or } B) = P(A) + P(B)$
The probability of event B, given event A is $P(B \mid A) = \dfrac{P(A \text{ and } B)}{P(A)}$.

2 Probability
You base experimental probability on *past*—and theoretical probability on *possible*—occurrences.

Probability (Lesson 11-2)
Experimental probability:

$P(\text{event}) = \dfrac{\text{number of times the event occurs}}{\text{number of trials}}$

Theoretical probability: For n equally likely outcomes, if event A occurs in m of these outcomes, then $P(A) = \dfrac{m}{n}$.

3 Data Collection and Analysis
Standard deviation describes how spread out data is from the mean of the data.

Analyzing Data and Standard Deviation (Lessons 11-5 and 11-6)
• $\bar{x}$, the mean,   • σ, standard deviation,

$= \dfrac{\sum x}{n}$ $= \sqrt{\dfrac{\sum (x - \bar{x})^2}{n}}$

Binomial Distributions and Normal Distributions (Lessons 11-8 and 11-9)
In a normal distribution, about 68% (95%) of data are within one (two) standard deviation(s) of the mean.

Chapter Vocabulary

- bias (p. 739)
- bimodal (p. 724)
- binomial experiment (p. 745)
- binomial probability (p. 746)
- Binomial Theorem (p. 747)
- box-and-whisker plot (p. 725)
- continuous probability distribution (p. 752)

- controlled experiment (p. 739)
- convenience sample (p. 738)
- discrete probability distribution (p. 752)
- interquartile range (p. 725)
- mean (p. 723)
- measure of central tendency (p. 723)
- measure of variation (p. 732)

- median (p. 723)
- mode (p. 723)
- normal distribution (p. 752)
- observational study (p. 739)
- outlier (p. 724)
- percentile (p. 728)
- population (p. 738)
- probability distribution (p. 748)
- quartile (p. 725)

- random sample (p. 738)
- range of a set of data (p. 725)
- sample (p. 738)
- self-selected sample (p. 738)
- standard deviation (p. 732)
- survey (p. 739)
- systematic sample (p. 738)
- variance (p. 732)

Fill in the blanks.

1. A(n) __?__ is part of a population.

2. A(n) __?__ has a value substantially different from other data in the set.

3. A function that gives the probability of each event in a sample space is a(n) __?__ .

4. The __?__ is the simplest measure of variation.

11-5 Analyzing Data

Quick Review

You can use **measures of central tendency** to analyze data. The **mean**, $\overline{x}$, equals the sum of the values divided by the number of values. The **median** is the middle value of a data set in numerical order. The **mode** is the most frequently occurring value. A data value substantially different from the rest of the data is an **outlier**. A **box-and-whisker plot** summarizes information about the **range**, the median, and the first and third **quartiles** of a data set.

Example

Find the mean, median, mode, and range of the following set of numbers, and identify any outliers.

   3, 3, 4, 6, 19

The mean is $\frac{3 + 3 + 4 + 6 + 19}{5} = 7$.

The median is the middle data value, which is 4.

The mode is 3, which occurs twice.

The range is $19 - 3 = 16$.

The value 19 is very different from the others and is an outlier.

Exercises

5. Identify the outlier of this set of values.

   17, 15, 16, 15, 9, 18, 16

Find the mean, median, and mode for each set of values.

6. 1, 1, 3, 3, 5, 5, 6, 7, 9, 9, 9, 10, 10

7. 0, 3, 3, 7, 7, 8, 21, 22, 25

8. 8, 9, 11, 12, 13, 15, 16, 18, 18, 18, 27

9. 11, 6, 9, 4, 19, 10, 15, 2

Find the range, Q_1, and Q_3 for each set of values.

10. 25, 25, 30, 35, 45, 45, 50, 55, 60, 60

11. 20, 23, 25, 36, 37, 38, 39, 50, 52, 55

12. 36, 36, 48, 65, 75, 82, 92, 101

11-6 Standard Deviation

Quick Review

The range of a data set is one **measure of variation**, used to describe the spread of data. Another measure of variation is the **standard deviation**, defined as

$$\sigma = \sqrt{\frac{\sum(x - \overline{x})^2}{n}}$$

where $\overline{x}$ is the mean of the data set and n is the number of values. The **variance** is σ^2.

Example

Find the mean, variance, and standard deviation for the following data values: 1, 3, 4, 6, 8, 11, 23.

The mean is $\overline{x} = \frac{1 + 3 + 4 + 6 + 8 + 11 + 23}{7} = 8$.
The sum of the squares of the differences is
$(-7)^2 + (-5)^2 + (-4)^2 + (-2)^2 + 0^2 + 3^2 + 15^2 = 328$.
So the variance is $\sigma^2 = \frac{328}{7} \approx 46.9$, and the standard deviation is $\sigma \approx \sqrt{46.9} \approx 6.8$.

Exercises

For each pair of data sets, which is likely to have the greater standard deviation?

13. heights of three people
    heights of twenty people

14. ages of thirty college students
    ages of thirty high school students

15. gas mileages of eighteen sport utility vehicles
    gas mileages of eighteen automobiles of various types

Find the mean and the standard deviation for each set of values.

16. 1, 1, 2, 2, 3, 4, 5, 6, 8, 9, 10, 10, 12, 20

17. 15, 17, 19, 20, 14, 23, 12

18. 3.1, 4.5, 7.8, 7.9, 8.0, 9.6, 11.6

11-7 Samples and Surveys

Quick Review

A **sample** is part of a **population**. For a **random sample**, all members of the population are equally likely to be chosen. A **bias** is a systematic error introduced by the sampling method.

Example

Identify any bias in the survey question "Do you think the school day should be extended even longer than it already is?". Explain.

There is bias because the question is leading. It implies that the school day is already too long and should not be extended.

Exercises

Determine if each of the following is a random sample. Explain your answer.

19. The first 50 names in the telephone directory

20. Twelve jurors chosen through examination by opposing lawyers

21. Two class representatives chosen by drawing names from a hat

22. Five newspapers picked on the basis of circulation size

23. The city council is trying to determine if the city's residents support the building of a new parking garage. They poll 200 people at the local bus station. Identify any bias in the sampling method.

11-8 Binomial Distributions

Quick Review

A **binomial experiment** has repeated independent trials with each trial having two possible outcomes. In a binomial experiment with probability of success p and of failure q (so $p + q = 1$), the probability of exactly x successes in n trials is $_nC_x p^x q^{n-x}$. This value is the **binomial probability**. The **Binomial Theorem** says that for every positive integer n, $(a + b)^n = {}_nC_0 a^n + {}_nC_1 a^{n-1}b + {}_nC_2 a^{n-2}b^2 + \cdots + {}_nC_{n-1}ab^{n-1} + {}_nC_n b^n$.

Example

In a binomial experiment, the probability of success is 0.8 for each trial. Find the probability of exactly 4 successes in 7 trials.

$p = 0.8, q = 0.2, x = 4$, and $n = 7$

$P(4) = {}_7C_4(0.8)^4(0.2)^3$

$\quad\quad = \frac{7!}{3!4!}(0.8)^4(0.2)^3$

$\quad\quad \approx 0.115$

The probability of 4 successes in 7 trials is about 0.115.

Exercises

For each of the following binomial experiments, state the value of p, the probability of success.

24. A series of coin flips, where success is "heads."

25. A series of number cube rolls, where success is "2 or 4."

In a binomial trial, the probability of success is 0.6 for each trial. Find the probability of each of the following.

26. 13 successes in 24 trials

27. 9 successes in 20 trials

28. 9 successes in 15 trials

29. 6 failures in 12 trials

Use the Binomial Theorem to write each of the following.

30. the third term in the expansion of $(a + b)^7$

31. the sixth term in the expansion of $(a + b)^8$

11-9 Normal Distributions

Quick Review

A **discrete probability distribution** has a finite number of possible values, while the values for a **continuous probability distribution** are all the values on some interval of real numbers. A **normal distribution** shows data that vary from the mean in a random, continuous manner. The pattern they form is a bell-shaped curve called a normal curve. When a data set follows the normal curve, about 68% of the data fall within one standard deviation of the mean, about 95% fall within two standard deviations, and about 99.7% fall within three standard deviations.

Example

Sketch a curve for a normal distribution with mean 10 and standard deviation 4. Label the *x*-axis at one, two, and three standard deviations from the mean.

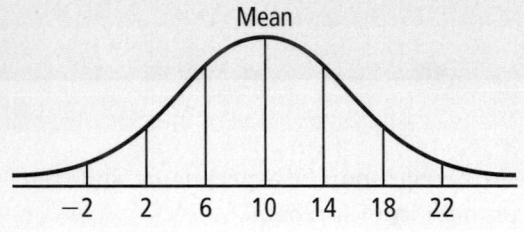

Mean

−2   2   6   10   14   18   22

Exercises

For each of the following, state whether the probability distribution would be *discrete* or *continuous*.

32. distance from an arrow's impact point to the center of the bullseye

33. shoe sizes on a softball team

34. price of a gallon of premium unleaded gasoline at a randomly selected gas station

35. time a customer spends on hold during a call to a computer manufacturer's tech support

36. Auto Maintenance Suppose the time required for an auto shop to do a tune-up is normally distributed, with a mean of 102 minutes and a standard deviation of 18 minutes. What is the probability that a tune-up will take more than two hours? Under 66 minutes?

Do you know HOW?

Evaluate each expression.

1. $6!$
2. $_7C_3$
3. $_{11}P_9$

Q and R are independent events. Find $P(Q \text{ and } R)$.

4. $P(Q) = 0.5$, $P(R) = 0.4$

5. $P(Q) = \frac{1}{3}$, $P(R) = \frac{3}{8}$

Use the table below for Exercises 6–8.

Age of Respondent	Number of Groups	
	0–4	5 or more
< 30	7	18
≥ 30	12	12

6. Find $P(5 \text{ or more})$.

7. Find $P(5 \text{ or more } | \text{ age } <30)$.

8. Find $P(\text{age} \geq 30 \mid 0-4)$.

Two standard number cubes are tossed. State whether the events are mutually exclusive.

9. One of the numbers is 1 less than the other. The sum is odd.

10. The sum is greater than 10. Six is one of the numbers.

11. Find Q_1 and Q_3 for this set of values:
36, 38, 42, 47, 51, 56, 62, 69, 70, 74.

12. Open-Ended Write a set of values that has a range of 10, a mean of 86, and a mode of 85.

A set of data has a normal distribution with a mean of 29 and a standard deviation of 4. Find the percent of data within each interval.

13. from 25 to 33
14. greater than 29

A newspaper wants to take a poll about which candidate voters prefer for President. Identify any bias in each sampling method.

15. The newspaper interviews people at a political debate.

16. The newspaper calls people selected at random from the local telephone book.

17. At a high school, 30% of the students buy class rings. You select five students at random. Find $P(\text{exactly two buy rings})$ and $P(\text{at least two buy rings})$.

Do you UNDERSTAND?

18. Indicate whether each situation involves a combination or a permuation.
   a. A team of 6 chosen from a class of 36
   b. An 8-digit code chosen for a lock

19. A data set is normally distributed with a mean of 37 and a standard deviation of 8.1. Sketch a normal curve for the distribution. Label the x-axis values at one, two, and three standard deviations from the mean.

20. Open-Ended A student guesses the answers to three questions on a true-false test. Design and describe a simulation to find the probability that the student guesses at least one of the questions correctly.

21. Writing Describe how a situation can have more than one sample space. Include an example.

22. Airline Ticket Pricing The table contains information from a study of the prices of comparable airline tickets. Which sample most likely was greater in size, A or B? Explain.

Sample	Standard deviation
A	$10.81
B	$3.97

TIPS FOR SUCCESS

Some questions on standardized tests ask you to use data analysis concepts like mean, outlier, and percentile. Read the question at the right. Then follow the tips to answer the sample question.

Find the third quartile for the data set.

2 6 8 5 9 3 5 7 1 8 4 4 5

- Ⓐ 6.5
- Ⓑ 7
- Ⓒ 7.5
- Ⓓ 8

TIP 1

If necessary, rewrite the data values in order, from least to greatest.

TIP 2

Make sure you clearly understand the definition of the concept you are applying. The third quartile is the median of the upper half of the data, not including the median.

Think It Through

In order, the data values are as follows.

1 2 3 4 4 5 5 5 6 7 8 8 9

The upper half of the data contains the values 5 6 7 8 8 9

The median of the upper half is $\frac{7 + 8}{2} = 7.5$.

The correct answer is C.

Vocabulary Review

As you solve test items, you must understand the meanings of mathematical terms. Match each term with its mathematical meaning.

A. normal distribution

B. standard deviation

C. quartile

D. median

E. mutually exclusive events

I. one of three values that separate a finite data set into 4 equal parts

II. a measure of how much the values in a data set vary from the mean

III. the middle value of an ordered data set

IV. shows data that vary randomly from the mean in a bell-shaped curve

V. events that cannot happen at the same time

Multiple Choice

Read each question. Then write the letter of the correct answer on your paper.

1. A and B are mutually exclusive events. $P(A) = \frac{1}{3}$ and $P(B) = \frac{1}{2}$. What is $P(A \text{ or } B)$?

- Ⓐ $\frac{1}{6}$
- Ⓒ $\frac{5}{6}$
- Ⓑ $\frac{2}{3}$
- Ⓓ 1

2. Which of the following relationships is best represented by the graph at the right?

- Ⓕ $y = -2^x$
- Ⓖ $y = 2(3)^{-x}$
- Ⓗ $y = -2(3)^x$
- Ⓘ $y = (-6)^x$

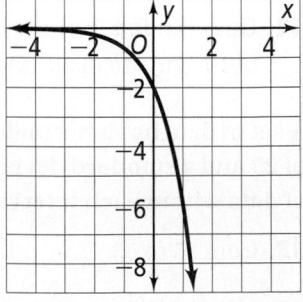

3. Which relation is *not* a function?

Ⓐ $\{(-1, 2), (-2, 2), (-3, 2), (-4, 2)\}$

Ⓑ $\{(2, 1), (3, 2), (4, 3), (3, 1)\}$

Ⓒ $\{(0, 1), (2, 1), (3, -1), (-1, 2)\}$

Ⓓ $\{(4, 2), (-3, 2), (-2, 1), (-4, 1)\}$

4. What is the vertex of the graph of $y = 2x^2 - 4x + 5$?

Ⓔ $(1, 5)$ Ⓗ $(1, 3)$

Ⓕ $(3, 1)$ Ⓘ $(5, 0)$

5. Which equation has $2 - \sqrt{3}$ as one of its solutions?

Ⓐ $x^2 + 4x + 1 = 0$

Ⓑ $x^2 - 4x + 1 = 0$

Ⓒ $x^2 + 4x - 1 = 0$

Ⓓ $x^2 - 4x - 1 = 0$

6. The equation for the circle below is $x^2 + y^2 = 9$. If the graph is translated one unit up and two units to the left, what is the new equation?

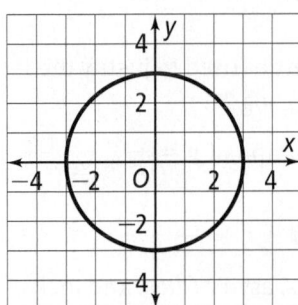

Ⓔ $(x - 1)^2 + (y + 2)^2 = 9$

Ⓕ $(x + 1)^2 + (y - 2)^2 = 9$

Ⓗ $(x - 2)^2 + (y + 1)^2 = 9$

Ⓘ $(x + 2)^2 + (y - 1)^2 = 9$

7. In six basketball games, you scored the following points per game. What is the approximate standard deviation of points scored?

8 11 14 7 12 18

Ⓐ 1.0   Ⓒ 4.0

Ⓑ 2.0   Ⓓ 5.0

8. Which sequence has a common difference of 3?

 I. $a_n = a_{n-1} - 3, a_1 = 2$

 II. $a_n = 3$

 III. $a_n = a_{n-1} + 3, a_1 = -7$

 IV. $a_n = n^2 + 3$

Ⓔ I only   Ⓗ II only

Ⓕ III only   Ⓘ II and IV

9. Which number completes the square for $x^2 - 3x$?

Ⓐ 9   Ⓒ $-\frac{9}{2}$

Ⓑ $-\frac{3}{2}$ Ⓓ $\frac{9}{4}$

10. What are the solutions to $9x^2 + 4 = 0$?

Ⓔ ± 2 Ⓗ $\pm\frac{2}{3}$

Ⓕ $\pm\frac{2}{3}i$ Ⓘ $\pm\sqrt{\frac{2}{3}}$

11. If $f(x) = x^2 - 1$ and $g(x) = |2x + 3|$, which has the greatest value?

Ⓐ $f(g(3))$ Ⓒ $g(f(-1))$

Ⓑ $g(f(2))$ Ⓓ $f(g(10))$

12. If $f(x) = 2x^2$ and $g(x) = 3(x + 1)$, what is $f(x) + g(x)$?

Ⓔ $2x^2 + 3x + 1$

Ⓕ $2x^2 + 3x + 3$

Ⓗ $2x^2 + 3x - 3$

Ⓘ $5x^3 + 3$

13. The first term of an arithmetic series is 123. The common difference is 12 and the sum is 1113. How many terms are in the series?

Ⓐ 7   Ⓒ 9

Ⓑ 8   Ⓓ 10

14. In the equation $y = 2x^2 - x - 21$, which is a value of x when $y = 0$?

Ⓔ -21 Ⓗ 3

Ⓕ $1\frac{1}{2}$ Ⓘ $3\frac{1}{2}$

15. Students were asked in a survey whether they had been to a movie theater in the last month. The table below shows the results.

	Yes	No
Male	35	17
Female	28	20

What is the probability that a student did not go to a movie in the last month, given that the student is a male?

- Ⓐ $\frac{17}{52}$
- Ⓒ $\frac{52}{37}$
- Ⓑ $\frac{37}{52}$
- Ⓓ $\frac{17}{37}$

16. Which expression simplifies to 15?

- Ⓕ $(5 + \sqrt{3})(5 - \sqrt{3})$
- Ⓖ $(2\sqrt{3} - 1)(2\sqrt{3} + 1)$
- Ⓗ $(6 + 3\sqrt{2})(6 - 3\sqrt{2})$
- Ⓘ $(2\sqrt{6} - 3)(2\sqrt{6} + 3)$

17. What is the coefficient of x^2y^4 in the expansion of $(x + 2y)^6$?

- Ⓐ 15
- Ⓒ 160
- Ⓑ 60
- Ⓓ 240

GRIDDED RESPONSE

18. What is the maximum value of the objective function $P = 3x + 4y$ within the feasible region described by the constraints at the right?

$\begin{cases} x \geq 0, \ y \geq 0 \\ x + y \leq 4 \\ 2x + y \leq 5 \end{cases}$

19. What is the discriminant of $2x^2 - 5x + 3 = 0$?

20. What is the sum of the solutions to the equation $x^2 = 2x + 15$?

21. Solve $\log_7 x = \log_3 10$. Round your answer to the nearest tenth.

22. Evaluate $\sum\limits_{n=1}^{8} \frac{3n}{2}$.

23. For a school play, six 9th graders and six 10th graders volunteer to be ushers. If two ushers are chosen at random by drawing names from a bowl, what is the probability that both ushers will be 10th graders? Write your answer as a fraction.

24. What is the radius of the circle with equation $x^2 - 6x + y^2 - 4y - 12 = 0$? If necessary, round your answer to the nearest hundredth.

25. Suppose x and y vary inversely and $x = 4$ when $y = 9$. What is x when $y = 12$?

Short Response

26. An employer is selecting 4 out of 30 workers as employees of the month.
   a. Does this situation involve a combination or a permutation? Explain.
   b. How many different selections are possible?

27. Solve the equation $\frac{x}{6} = \frac{x + 4}{9}$. Check your solution. Show your work.

28. State the property or properties used to justify the identity $9 \log 3 - 3 \log 9 = \log 27$.

29. Find all asymptotes of the graph of $y = \frac{3x^2 + 1}{x^2 + 2x - 3}$.

Extended Response

30. Find the vertices, intercepts, asymptotes, and foci of the hyperbola $\frac{x^2}{16} - \frac{y^2}{9} = 1$.

31. Is the series $10,000 + 1000 + 100 + 10 + \ldots$ *arithmetic* or *geometric*? Find the sum of the first eight terms.

32. Find the mean, median, and mode for the following set of values.

13 12 15 18 14 16 18 12 13 14 14 17 15 8 17 16
12 16 14 15 13 13 17 15 14 18 16 12 12 13

Then make a box-and-whisker plot.

Get Ready!

Lesson 1-3
Evaluating Expressions

Evaluate $ad - bc$ for the given values of the variables.

1. $a = -1, b = -2, c = 5, d = 4$

2. $a = \frac{1}{2}, b = -1, c = -\frac{2}{3}, d = 2$

3. $a = 2, b = \frac{1}{2}, c = \frac{1}{4}, d = -\frac{1}{8}$

4. $a = -\frac{1}{3}, b = \frac{1}{2}, c = \frac{1}{4}, d = -\frac{2}{3}$

Lesson 3-6
Identifying Matrix Elements

Identify the indicated element.

$$A = \begin{bmatrix} 2 & -1 & 3 \\ 5 & 7 & -9 \\ 4 & 11 & 21 \end{bmatrix}$$

5. a_{23}　　　　**6.** a_{32}　　　　**7.** a_{13}

Lessons 3-2
and 3-6
Solving Systems of Equations

Solve each system.

8. $\begin{cases} -2x + y = -5 \\ 4x + y = -2 \end{cases}$

9. $\begin{cases} 4x - y = -2 \\ -\frac{1}{2}x - y = 1 \end{cases}$

10. $\begin{cases} 3x + y = 5 \\ -x + y = 2 \end{cases}$

11. $\begin{cases} x + y + z = 10 \\ 2x - y = 5 \\ y - z = 15 \end{cases}$

12. $\begin{cases} -x + y + 2z = 16 \\ 2x - 2y - 2z = -16 \\ x + y = 0 \end{cases}$

13. $\begin{cases} -2x + 3y + z = 1 \\ x - 3z = 7 \\ -y + z = -5 \end{cases}$

 ## Looking Ahead Vocabulary

14. The local museum store sells books, postcards, and gifts. There are different prices for museum members and nonmembers. At the end of each month, the numbers of items sold in each category are recorded in a table, or *matrix.* Make a sketch of what one of these might look like for one month.

15. Suppose you have the twelve tables, one for each month, of the museum's sales in the previous problem. These can be combined using *matrix addition* to determine the total number of items sold in each category during the year. Describe how this is done. Use several examples like the one you made in the previous problem to see if your method works.

CHAPTER 12

Matrices

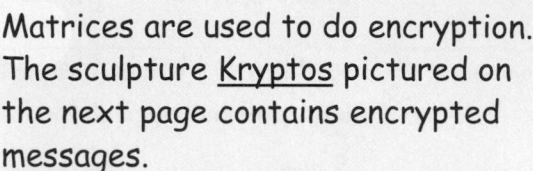

PowerAlgebra.com

Your place to get all things digital

VIDEO

Download videos connecting math to your world.

VOCABULARY

Math definitions in English and Spanish

SOLVE IT!

The online Solve It will get you in gear for each lesson.

DYNAMIC ACTIVITIES

Interactive! Vary numbers, graphs, and figures to explore math concepts.

ONLINE PROBLEMS

Download Step-by-Step Problems with Instant Replay.

ONLINE HOMEWORK

Get and view your assignments online.

MathXL FOR SCHOOL

Extra practice and review online

Matrices are used to do encryption. The sculpture <u>Kryptos</u> pictured on the next page contains encrypted messages.

How can you add, subtract, and multiply arrays of numbers? How can you use a matrix to represent and solve systems of equations? And how can you use matrices to find areas of geometric figures? You will learn how in this chapter.

Vocabulary

English/Spanish Vocabulary Audio Online:

English	Spanish
coefficient matrix, *p. 801*	matriz de coeficientes
determinant, *p. 790*	determinante
equal matrices, *p. 775*	matrices equivalentes
matrix equation, *p. 773*	ecuación matricial
scalar multiplication, *p. 781*	multiplicación escalar
square matrix, *p. 789*	matriz cuadrada
variable matrix, *p. 801*	matriz variable
zero matrix, *p. 775*	matriz cero

My Math Video

00:04:04

VIDEO

BIG ideas

1 Data Representation

Essential Question How can you use a matrix to organize data?

2 Modeling

Essential Question How can you use a matrix equation to model a real-world situation?

Chapter Preview

12-1 Adding and Subtracting Matrices

Objectives To add and subtract matrices
To solve matrix equations

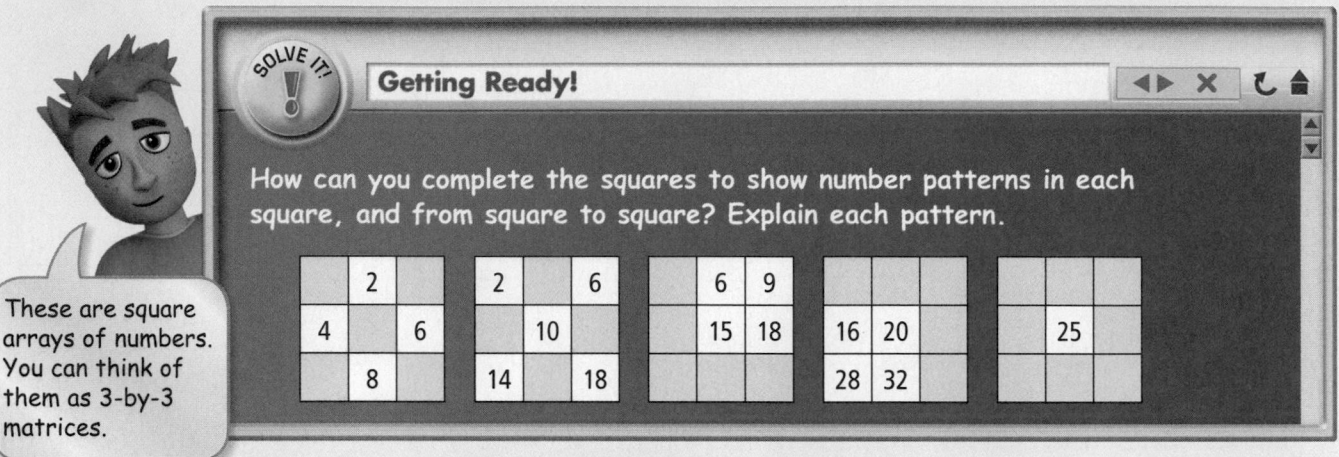

SOLVE IT!

Getting Ready!

How can you complete the squares to show number patterns in each square, and from square to square? Explain each pattern.

These are square arrays of numbers. You can think of them as 3-by-3 matrices.

Lesson Vocabulary
- corresponding elements
- matrix equation
- zero matrix
- equal matrices

In Lesson 3-6, you solved a system of equations by expressing it as a single matrix. Now you will learn how to work with more than one matrix at a time.

Focus Question When can you add and subtract matrices?

Recall that the *dimensions* of a matrix are the numbers of rows and columns. A matrix with 2 rows and 3 columns is a 2×3 matrix. Each number in a matrix is a *matrix element*. In matrix A, a_{12} is the element in row 1 and column 2.

Sometimes you want to combine matrices to get new information. You can combine two matrices with equal dimensions by adding or subtracting the *corresponding elements*. **Corresponding elements** are elements in the same position in each matrix.

take note

Key Concept   Matrix Addition and Subtraction

To add matrices A and B with the same dimensions, add corresponding elements. Similarly, to subtract matrices A and B with the same dimensions, subtract corresponding elements.

$$A = \begin{bmatrix} a_{11} & a_{12} \\ a_{21} & a_{22} \end{bmatrix} \qquad B = \begin{bmatrix} b_{11} & b_{12} \\ b_{21} & b_{22} \end{bmatrix}$$

$$A + B = \begin{bmatrix} a_{11} + b_{11} & a_{12} + b_{12} \\ a_{21} + b_{21} & a_{22} + b_{22} \end{bmatrix} \qquad A - B = \begin{bmatrix} a_{11} - b_{11} & a_{12} - b_{12} \\ a_{21} - b_{21} & a_{22} - b_{22} \end{bmatrix}$$

Problem 1 **Adding and Subtracting Matrices**

Given $C = \begin{bmatrix} 3 & 2 & 4 \\ -1 & 4 & 0 \end{bmatrix}$ and $D = \begin{bmatrix} 1 & 4 & 3 \\ -2 & 2 & 4 \end{bmatrix}$, what are the following?

Think

To add matrices, they need to have the same dimensions. What are the dimensions of C? Matrix C has 2 rows and 3 columns. It is a 2×3 matrix.

A $C + D$

Write the matrix addition.

$$\begin{bmatrix} 3 & 2 & 4 \\ -1 & 4 & 0 \end{bmatrix} + \begin{bmatrix} 1 & 4 & 3 \\ -2 & 2 & 4 \end{bmatrix}$$

Add corresponding elements.

$$= \begin{bmatrix} 3+1 & 2+4 & 4+3 \\ -1+(-2) & 4+2 & 0+4 \end{bmatrix}$$

Simplify each sum.

$$= \begin{bmatrix} 4 & 6 & 7 \\ -3 & 6 & 4 \end{bmatrix}$$

B $C - D$

Write the matrix subtraction.

$$\begin{bmatrix} 3 & 2 & 4 \\ -1 & 4 & 0 \end{bmatrix} - \begin{bmatrix} 1 & 4 & 3 \\ -2 & 2 & 4 \end{bmatrix}$$

Subtract corresponding elements.

$$= \begin{bmatrix} 3-1 & 2-4 & 4-3 \\ -1-(-2) & 4-2 & 0-4 \end{bmatrix}$$

Simplify each difference.

$$= \begin{bmatrix} 2 & -2 & 1 \\ 1 & 2 & -4 \end{bmatrix}$$

 Got It? 1. Given $A = \begin{bmatrix} -12 & 24 \\ -3 & 5 \\ -1 & 10 \end{bmatrix}$ and $B = \begin{bmatrix} -3 & 1 \\ 2 & -4 \\ -1 & 5 \end{bmatrix}$, what are the following?

a. $A + B$

b. $A - B$

c. Reasoning Is matrix addition commutative? Explain.

A **matrix equation** is an equation in which the variable is a matrix. You can use the addition and subtraction properties of equality to solve a matrix equation. An example of a matrix equation is shown below.

Hint

You can only add two matrices if they have the same dimensions. Matrix A must be a 3×3 matrix.

$$\begin{bmatrix} 1 & 0 & 12 \\ 3 & 5 & 9 \\ 7 & 8 & -2 \end{bmatrix} + A = \begin{bmatrix} 8 & 11 & 9 \\ -5 & 5 & 2 \\ 10 & 7 & 8 \end{bmatrix}$$

Problem 2 Solving a Matrix Equation

Sports The first table shows the teams with the four best records halfway through their season. The second table shows the full season records for the same four teams. Which team had the best record during the second half of the season?

Records for the First Half of the Season

Team	Wins	Losses
Team 1	30	11
Team 2	29	12
Team 3	25	16
Team 4	24	17

Records for Season

Team	Wins	Losses
Team 1	53	29
Team 2	67	15
Team 3	58	24
Team 4	61	21

Know
- Records for the first half of the season
- Records for the full season

Need
Records for the second half of the season

Plan
- Use the equation first half records + second half records = season records.
- Solve the matrix equation.

Step 1 Write 4×2 matrices to show the information from the two tables. The rows should represent the teams. The columns should represent the wins and losses.

Let A = the first half records.
Let B = the second half records.
Let F = the final records.

$$A = \begin{bmatrix} 30 & 11 \\ 29 & 12 \\ 25 & 16 \\ 24 & 17 \end{bmatrix} \quad F = \begin{bmatrix} 53 & 29 \\ 67 & 15 \\ 58 & 24 \\ 61 & 21 \end{bmatrix}$$

Think

What are the dimensions of matrix *B*?
Matrix B will have 4 rows and 2 columns. It is a 4×2 matrix.

Step 2 Solve $A + B = F$ for B and substitute.

$B = F - A$

$$B = \begin{bmatrix} 53 & 29 \\ 67 & 15 \\ 58 & 24 \\ 61 & 21 \end{bmatrix} - \begin{bmatrix} 30 & 11 \\ 29 & 12 \\ 25 & 16 \\ 24 & 17 \end{bmatrix} = \begin{bmatrix} 53-30 & 29-11 \\ 67-29 & 15-12 \\ 58-25 & 24-16 \\ 61-24 & 21-17 \end{bmatrix} = \begin{bmatrix} 23 & 18 \\ 38 & 3 \\ 33 & 8 \\ 37 & 4 \end{bmatrix}$$

Team 2 had the best record (**38 wins** and **3 losses**) during the second half of the season.

Got It? 2. If $B = \begin{bmatrix} 1 & 6 & -1 \\ 2 & 6 & 1 \\ -1 & -2 & 4 \end{bmatrix}$, $C = \begin{bmatrix} 2 & 0 & 0 \\ -1 & -3 & 6 \\ 2 & 3 & -1 \end{bmatrix}$, and $A - B = C$, what is A?

For $m \times n$ matrices, the additive identity matrix is the **zero matrix** O, or $O_{m \times n}$, with all elements zero. The *opposite*, or *additive inverse*, of an $m \times n$ matrix A is $-A$. Each element of $-A$ is the opposite of the corresponding element of A.

Problem 3 Using Identity and Opposite Matrices

What are the following sums?

A $\begin{bmatrix} 1 & 2 \\ 5 & -7 \end{bmatrix} + \begin{bmatrix} 0 & 0 \\ 0 & 0 \end{bmatrix}$

Add corresponding elements. $\begin{bmatrix} 1 & 2 \\ 5 & -7 \end{bmatrix} + \begin{bmatrix} 0 & 0 \\ 0 & 0 \end{bmatrix} = \begin{bmatrix} 1 + 0 & 2 + 0 \\ 5 + 0 & -7 + 0 \end{bmatrix}$

Simplify. $= \begin{bmatrix} 1 & 2 \\ 5 & -7 \end{bmatrix}$

Think

How is this like adding real numbers?
Adding the zero matrix results in the original matrix. Adding opposite matrices gives you the zero matrix.

B $\begin{bmatrix} 2 & 8 \\ -3 & 0 \end{bmatrix} + \begin{bmatrix} -2 & -8 \\ 3 & 0 \end{bmatrix}$

Add corresponding elements. $\begin{bmatrix} 2 & 8 \\ -3 & 0 \end{bmatrix} + \begin{bmatrix} -2 & -8 \\ 3 & 0 \end{bmatrix} = \begin{bmatrix} 2 + (-2) & 8 + (-8) \\ -3 + 3 & 0 + 0 \end{bmatrix}$

Simplify. $= \begin{bmatrix} 0 & 0 \\ 0 & 0 \end{bmatrix}$

 Got It? 3. What are the following sums?

a. $\begin{bmatrix} 14 & 5 \\ 0 & -2 \end{bmatrix} + \begin{bmatrix} -14 & -5 \\ 0 & 2 \end{bmatrix}$ **b.** $\begin{bmatrix} 0 & 0 & 0 \\ 0 & 0 & 0 \end{bmatrix} + \begin{bmatrix} -1 & 10 & -5 \\ 0 & 2 & -3 \end{bmatrix}$

take note

Properties Properties of Matrix Addition

If A, B, and C are $m \times n$ matrices, then

Example	Property
$A + B$ is an $m \times n$ matrix	**Closure Property of Addition**
$A + B = B + A$	**Commutative Property of Addition**
$(A + B) + C = A + (B + C)$	**Associative Property of Addition**
There is a unique $m \times n$ matrix O such that $O + A = A + O = A$	**Additive Identity Property**
For each A, there is a unique opposite, $-A$, such that $A + (-A) = O$	**Additive Inverse Property**

Hint

You can use the definition of equal matrices to find unknown values in a matrix equation.

Equal matrices have the same dimensions and equal corresponding elements.

For example, $\begin{bmatrix} 0.25 & 1.5 \\ -3 & \frac{4}{5} \end{bmatrix}$ and $\begin{bmatrix} \frac{1}{4} & 1\frac{1}{2} \\ -3 & 0.8 \end{bmatrix}$ are equal matrices.

You can use the definition of equal matrices to find unknown values in matrix elements.

 Problem 4 Finding Unknown Matrix Values

Multiple Choice What values of x and y make the equation true?

$$\begin{bmatrix} 3x + 1 & 9 \\ 10 & 2y - 1 \end{bmatrix} = \begin{bmatrix} 16 & 9 \\ 10 & -5 \end{bmatrix}$$

Ⓐ $x = 3, y = 5$ ⓒ $x = 5, y = -2$
Ⓑ $x = \frac{17}{3}, y = 5$ Ⓓ $x = 5, y = -3$

Plan

How can you solve the equation?
For the two matrices to be equal, the corresponding elements must be equal.

Identify corresponding elements that contain unknowns.

$$\begin{bmatrix} 3x + 1 & 9 \\ 10 & 2y - 1 \end{bmatrix} = \begin{bmatrix} 16 & 9 \\ 10 & -5 \end{bmatrix}$$

Set corresponding elements equal. $3x + 1 = 16$ $2y - 1 = -5$

Isolate the variable term. $3x + 1 - 1 = 16 - 1$ $2y - 1 + 1 = -5 + 1$

Simplify. $3x = 15$ $2y = -4$

Solve for x and y. $x = 5$ $y = -2$

The correct answer is C.

 Got It? 4. What values of x and y make the following equations true?

a. $\begin{bmatrix} x + 3 & -2 \\ y - 1 & x + 1 \end{bmatrix} = \begin{bmatrix} 9 & -2 \\ 2y + 5 & 7 \end{bmatrix}$

b. $\begin{bmatrix} 12 & -3 \\ 3x & 0 \end{bmatrix} - \begin{bmatrix} 10 & -4 \\ x & 2y + 6 \end{bmatrix} = \begin{bmatrix} 2 & 1 \\ 8 & 4y + 12 \end{bmatrix}$

Focus Question When can you add or subtract matrices?

Answer You can only add or subtract matrices that have the same dimensions. To add two matrices, add corresponding elements. To subtract two matrices, subtract corresponding elements.

 Lesson Check

Do you know HOW?

Find each sum or difference.

1. $\begin{bmatrix} 1 & -1 \\ 2 & 3 \end{bmatrix} + \begin{bmatrix} 0 & 2 \\ -4 & 5 \end{bmatrix}$

2. $\begin{bmatrix} 5 & -3 & 7 \\ -1 & 0 & 8 \end{bmatrix} - \begin{bmatrix} 4 & 6 & -1 \\ 2 & 1 & 0 \end{bmatrix}$

3. What is the solution of this matrix equation?

$\begin{bmatrix} 6 & 1 \\ 4 & -2 \end{bmatrix} + X = \begin{bmatrix} 3 & 5 \\ -1 & 9 \end{bmatrix}$

Do you UNDERSTAND?

4. Vocabulary Are the two matrices equal? Explain.

$\begin{bmatrix} \frac{1}{2} & \frac{3}{8} \\ 0.2 & \sqrt[3]{27} \end{bmatrix}$ and $\begin{bmatrix} 0.5 & 0.375 \\ \frac{1}{5} & 3 \end{bmatrix}$

5. Error Analysis Describe and correct the error made in subtracting the two matrices.

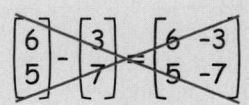

Practice and Problem-Solving Exercises

A) Practice Find each sum or difference. ◀ See Problem 1.

Guided Practice

To start, subtract corresponding elements.

6. $\begin{bmatrix} 2 & 1 & 2 \\ 1 & 2 & 1 \end{bmatrix} - \begin{bmatrix} 2 & 3 & 2 \\ 3 & 2 & 3 \end{bmatrix}$

$\begin{bmatrix} 2-2 & 1-3 & 2-2 \\ 1-3 & 2-2 & 1-3 \end{bmatrix}$

7. $\begin{bmatrix} 6.4 & -1.9 \\ -6.4 & 0.8 \end{bmatrix} + \begin{bmatrix} -2.5 & -0.4 \\ 5.8 & 8.3 \end{bmatrix}$

8. $\begin{bmatrix} 1.5 & -1.9 \\ 0 & 4.6 \end{bmatrix} - \begin{bmatrix} 8.3 & -3.2 \\ 2.1 & 5.6 \end{bmatrix}$

Solve each matrix equation. ◀ See Problem 2.

Guided Practice

To start, use the Addition Property of Equality to isolate the variable matrix.

9. $X - \begin{bmatrix} 1 & 4 \\ -2 & 3 \end{bmatrix} = \begin{bmatrix} 5 & -2 \\ 1 & 0 \end{bmatrix}$

$X = \begin{bmatrix} 5 & -2 \\ 1 & 0 \end{bmatrix} + \begin{bmatrix} 1 & 4 \\ -2 & 3 \end{bmatrix}$

10. $X + \begin{bmatrix} 6 & 1 \\ -2 & 3 \end{bmatrix} = \begin{bmatrix} 2 & 0 \\ -3 & 1 \end{bmatrix}$

11. $\begin{bmatrix} 2 & 1 & -1 \\ 0 & 2 & 1 \end{bmatrix} - X = \begin{bmatrix} 11 & 3 & -13 \\ 15 & -9 & 8 \end{bmatrix}$

Find each sum. ◀ See Problem 3.

12. $\begin{bmatrix} 2 & -3 & 4 \\ 5 & 6 & -7 \end{bmatrix} + \begin{bmatrix} 0 & 0 & 0 \\ 0 & 0 & 0 \end{bmatrix}$

13. $\begin{bmatrix} 6 & -3 \\ -7 & 2 \end{bmatrix} + \begin{bmatrix} -6 & 3 \\ 7 & -2 \end{bmatrix}$

Find the value of each variable. ◀ See Problem 4.

14. $\begin{bmatrix} 2 & 2 \\ -1 & 6 \end{bmatrix} - \begin{bmatrix} 4 & -1 \\ 0 & 5 \end{bmatrix} = \begin{bmatrix} x & y \\ -1 & z \end{bmatrix}$

15. $\begin{bmatrix} 2 & 4 \\ 8 & 4.5 \end{bmatrix} = \begin{bmatrix} 4x - 6 & -10t + 5 \\ 4x & 15t + 1.5x \end{bmatrix}$

B) Apply Find each matrix sum or difference if possible. If not possible, explain why.

$A = \begin{bmatrix} 3 & 4 \\ 6 & -2 \\ 1 & 0 \end{bmatrix} \quad B = \begin{bmatrix} -3 & 1 \\ 2 & -4 \\ -1 & 5 \end{bmatrix} \quad C = \begin{bmatrix} 1 & 2 \\ -3 & 1 \end{bmatrix} \quad D = \begin{bmatrix} 5 & 1 \\ 0 & 2 \end{bmatrix}$

16. $A + B$ **17.** $B + D$ **18.** $C - D$

19. Think About a Plan The table shows the number of beach balls produced during one shift at two manufacturing plants. Plant 1 has two shifts per day and Plant 2 has three shifts per day. Write matrices to represent one day's total output at the two plants. Then find the difference between daily production totals at the two plants.

- How can you use the number of shifts to find the total daily production totals at each plant?
- What matrix equation can you use to solve this problem?

Beach Ball Production Per Shift

	1-color		3-color	
	Plastic	Rubber	Plastic	Rubber
Plant 1	500	700	1300	1900
Plant 2	400	1200	600	1600

Solve each equation for each variable.

20. $\begin{bmatrix} 4b+2 & -3 & 4d \\ -4a & 2 & 3 \\ 2f-1 & -14 & 1 \end{bmatrix} = \begin{bmatrix} 11 & 2c-1 & 0 \\ -8 & 2 & 3 \\ 0 & 3g-2 & 1 \end{bmatrix}$

21. $\begin{bmatrix} 4c & 2-d & 5 \\ -3 & -1 & 2 \\ 0 & -10 & 15 \end{bmatrix} = \begin{bmatrix} 2c+5 & 4d & g \\ -3 & h & f-g \\ 0 & -4c & 15 \end{bmatrix}$

22. Sports The modern pentathlon is a grueling all-day competition. Each member of a team competes in five events: target shooting, fencing, swimming, horseback riding, and cross-country running. Here are scores for the U.S. women at the 2004 Olympic Games.

a. Write two 5×1 matrices to represent each woman's scores for each event.

b. Find the total score for each athlete.

U.S. Women's Pentathlon Scores, 2004 Olympics

Event	Anita Allen	Mary Beth Iagorashvili
Shooting	952	760
Fencing	720	832
Swimming	1108	1252
Riding	1172	1144
Running	1044	1064

SOURCE: Athens 2004 Olympic Games

23. Data Analysis Refer to the table.

a. Add two matrices to find the total number of people participating in each activity.

b. Subtract two matrices to find the difference between the numbers of males and females in each activity.

c. Reasoning In part (b), does the order of the matrices matter? Explain.

24. Writing Given a matrix A, explain how to find a matrix B such that $A + B = 0$.

U.S. Participation (millions) in Selected Leisure Activities

Activity	Male	Female
Movies	59.2	65.4
Exercise Programs	54.3	59.0
Sports Events	40.5	31.1
Home Improvement	45.4	41.8

SOURCE: U.S. National Endowment for the Arts

Standardized Test Prep

SAT/ACT

25. What is the sum $\begin{bmatrix} 5 & 7 & 3 \\ -1 & 0 & -4 \end{bmatrix} + \begin{bmatrix} -7 & 4 & 2 \\ 1 & -2 & -3 \end{bmatrix}$?

Ⓐ The matrices cannot be added.

Ⓒ $\begin{bmatrix} 12 & 3 & 1 \\ -2 & 2 & -1 \end{bmatrix}$

Ⓑ $\begin{bmatrix} -2 & 11 & 5 \\ 0 & -2 & -7 \end{bmatrix}$

Ⓓ $\begin{bmatrix} -35 & 28 & 6 \\ -1 & 0 & 12 \end{bmatrix}$

26. Which arithmetic sequence includes the term 27?

I. $a_1 = 7, a_n = a_{n-1} + 5$ II. $a_n = 3 + 4(n-1)$ III. $a_n = 57 - 6n$

Ⓕ I only   Ⓖ I and II only   Ⓗ II and III only   Ⓘ I, II, and III

27. Which equation is graphed at the right?

Ⓐ $(x + 3)^2 + (y - 2)^2 = 25$

Ⓑ $(x - 2)^2 + (y + 3)^2 = 25$

Ⓒ $(x + 2)^2 + (y - 3)^2 = 25$

Ⓓ $(x - 3)^2 + (y + 2)^2 = 25$

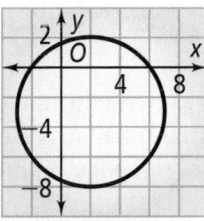

Short Response

28. For a daily airline flight to Denver, the numbers of checked pieces of luggage are normally distributed with a mean of 380 and a standard deviation of 20. What number of checked pieces of luggage is 3 standard deviations above the mean?

Mixed Review

A set of data with a mean of 62 and a standard deviation of 5 is normally distributed. Find the percent of data within each interval.

⬅ See Lesson 11-9.

29. from 57 to 67   **30.** greater than 52   **31.** from 62 to 72

Find the slope and y-intercept of each line.

⬅ See Lesson 2-3.

32. $y = 2x - 6$ **33.** $3y = 6 + 2x$ **34.** $y = 5x$

Get Ready!   To prepare for Lesson 12-2, do Exercises 35 and 36.

Find each sum.

⬅ See Lesson 12-1.

35. $\begin{bmatrix} 3 & 5 \\ 2 & 8 \end{bmatrix} + \begin{bmatrix} 3 & 5 \\ 2 & 8 \end{bmatrix} + \begin{bmatrix} 3 & 5 \\ 2 & 8 \end{bmatrix}$

36. $\begin{bmatrix} -4 \\ 7 \end{bmatrix} + \begin{bmatrix} -4 \\ 7 \end{bmatrix} + \begin{bmatrix} -4 \\ 7 \end{bmatrix} + \begin{bmatrix} -4 \\ 7 \end{bmatrix} + \begin{bmatrix} -4 \\ 7 \end{bmatrix}$

Working with Matrices

You can use a graphing calculator to work with matrices. First you need to know how to enter a matrix into the calculator.

Example 1

Enter matrix $A = \begin{bmatrix} -3 & 4 \\ 7 & -5 \\ 0 & -2 \end{bmatrix}$ into your graphing calculator.

Select the **EDIT** option of the (matrix) feature to edit matrix **[A]**. Specify a 3 × 2 matrix by pressing **3** (enter) **2** (enter). Enter the matrix elements one row at a time, pressing (enter) after each element. Then use the (quit) feature to return to the main screen.

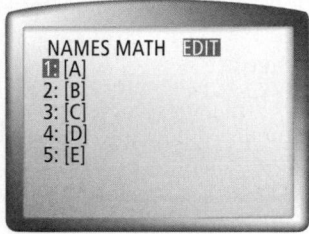 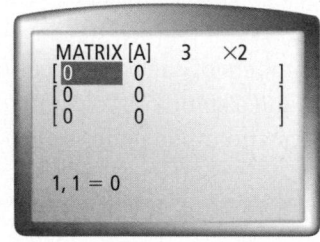 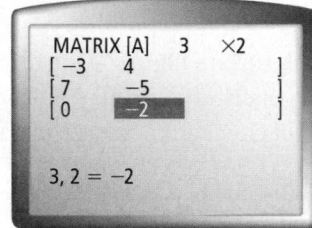

Example 2

Given $A = \begin{bmatrix} -3 & 4 \\ 7 & -5 \\ 0 & -2 \end{bmatrix}$ and $B = \begin{bmatrix} 10 & -7 \\ 4 & -3 \\ -12 & 11 \end{bmatrix}$, find $A + B$ and $A - B$.

Enter both matrices in the calculator. Use the **NAMES** option of the (matrix) feature to select each matrix. Press (enter) to see the sum. Repeat the corresponding steps to find the difference $A - B$.

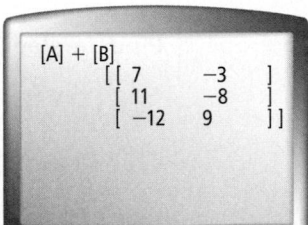

Exercises

Find each sum or difference.

1. $\begin{bmatrix} 0 & -3 \\ 5 & -7 \end{bmatrix} - \begin{bmatrix} -5 & 3 \\ 4 & 10 \end{bmatrix}$

2. $\begin{bmatrix} 3 & 5 & -7 \\ 0 & -2 & 0 \end{bmatrix} - \begin{bmatrix} -1 & 6 & 2 \\ -9 & 4 & 0 \end{bmatrix}$

3. $\begin{bmatrix} 3 \\ 5 \end{bmatrix} - \begin{bmatrix} -6 \\ 7 \end{bmatrix}$

4. $\begin{bmatrix} 3 & 5 & -8 \end{bmatrix} + \begin{bmatrix} -6 & 4 & 1 \end{bmatrix}$

5. $\begin{bmatrix} 17 & 8 & 0 \\ 3 & -5 & 2 \end{bmatrix} - \begin{bmatrix} 4 & 6 & 5 \\ 2 & -2 & 9 \end{bmatrix}$

6. $\begin{bmatrix} -9 & 6 & 4 \end{bmatrix} + \begin{bmatrix} -3 & 8 & 4 \end{bmatrix}$

12-2 Matrix Multiplication

Objective To multiply matrices using scalar and matrix multiplication

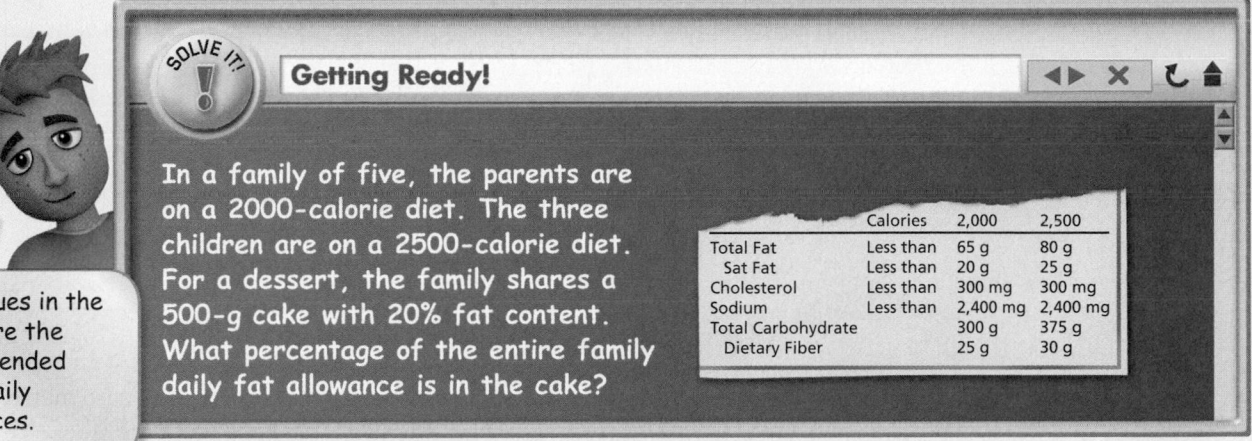

Getting Ready!

In a family of five, the parents are on a 2000-calorie diet. The three children are on a 2500-calorie diet. For a dessert, the family shares a 500-g cake with 20% fat content. What percentage of the entire family daily fat allowance is in the cake?

Calories		2,000	2,500
Total Fat	Less than	65 g	80 g
Sat Fat	Less than	20 g	25 g
Cholesterol	Less than	300 mg	300 mg
Sodium	Less than	2,400 mg	2,400 mg
Total Carbohydrate		300 g	375 g
Dietary Fiber		25 g	30 g

The values in the chart are the recommended 100% daily allowances.

 **Lesson Vocabulary**
- scalar
- scalar multiplication

In the Solve It, you may have found the sum of products. Finding the sum of products is essential to matrix multiplication.

Focus Question How do you find the product of two matrices?

Before you learn how to multiply two matrices, you should learn a simpler type of multiplication. This type of multiplication allows you to *scale*, or resize, the elements of a matrix.

$$3\begin{bmatrix} 5 & -1 \\ 3 & 7 \end{bmatrix} = \begin{bmatrix} 3(5) & 3(-1) \\ 3(3) & 3(7) \end{bmatrix} = \begin{bmatrix} 15 & -3 \\ 9 & 21 \end{bmatrix}$$

The real number factor (such as 3 in the example above) is a **scalar**. Multiplication of a matrix A by a scalar c is **scalar multiplication**. To find the resulting matrix cA, you multiply each element of A by c.

Hint
This process is similar to the Distributive Property of Real Numbers.

take note **Key Concept** Scalar Multiplication

To multiply a matrix by a scalar c, multiply each element of the matrix by c.

$$A = \begin{bmatrix} a_{11} & a_{12} & a_{13} \\ a_{21} & a_{22} & a_{23} \end{bmatrix} \quad cA = \begin{bmatrix} ca_{11} & ca_{12} & ca_{13} \\ ca_{21} & ca_{22} & ca_{23} \end{bmatrix}$$

Problem 1 Using Scalar Products

If $A = \begin{bmatrix} 2 & 8 & -3 \\ -1 & 5 & 2 \end{bmatrix}$ and $B = \begin{bmatrix} -1 & 0 & 5 \\ 0 & 3 & -2 \end{bmatrix}$, what is $4A + 3B$?

Think

What operation should you do first?
You should first multiply by the scalars, 4 and 3.

Substitute matrices A and B.

$$4A + 3B = 4\begin{bmatrix} 2 & 8 & -3 \\ -1 & 5 & 2 \end{bmatrix} + 3\begin{bmatrix} -1 & 0 & 5 \\ 0 & 3 & -2 \end{bmatrix}$$

Multiply each element of A by 4.
Multiply each element of B by 3.

$$= \begin{bmatrix} 8 & 32 & -12 \\ -4 & 20 & 8 \end{bmatrix} + \begin{bmatrix} -3 & 0 & 15 \\ 0 & 9 & -6 \end{bmatrix}$$

Add corresponding elements.

$$= \begin{bmatrix} 5 & 32 & 3 \\ -4 & 29 & 2 \end{bmatrix}$$

✔ **Got It?** **1.** Using matrices A and B from Problem 1, what is $3A - 2B$?

---

take note

Properties Scalar Multiplication

If A and B are $m \times n$ matrices, c and d are scalars, and O is the $m \times n$ zero matrix, then

Example	Property
cA is an $m \times n$ matrix	**Closure Property**
$(cd)A = c(dA)$	**Associative Property of Multiplication**
$c(A + B) = cA + cB$ $(c + d)A = cA + dA$	**Distributive Properties**
$1 \cdot A = A$	**Multiplicative Identity Property**
$0 \cdot A = O$ and $cO = O$	**Multiplicative Properties of Zero**

Problem 2 Solving a Matrix Equation With Scalars

Think

Where have you seen problems that look like this before?
You saw problems like this when you solved one variable equations like $2x + 3(5) = 20$.

What is the solution of $2X + 3\begin{bmatrix} 2 & -1 \\ 3 & 4 \end{bmatrix} = \begin{bmatrix} 8 & 5 \\ 11 & 0 \end{bmatrix}$?

Multiply by the scalar 3.

$$2X + \begin{bmatrix} 6 & -3 \\ 9 & 12 \end{bmatrix} = \begin{bmatrix} 8 & 5 \\ 11 & 0 \end{bmatrix}$$

Use the Subtraction Property of Equality to isolate the variable matrix.

$$2X = \begin{bmatrix} 8 & 5 \\ 11 & 0 \end{bmatrix} - \begin{bmatrix} 6 & -3 \\ 9 & 12 \end{bmatrix}$$

Subtract corresponding elements.

$$2X = \begin{bmatrix} 2 & 8 \\ 2 & -12 \end{bmatrix}$$

Multiply each side by $\frac{1}{2}$ and simplify.

$$X = \frac{1}{2}\begin{bmatrix} 2 & 8 \\ 2 & -12 \end{bmatrix} = \begin{bmatrix} 1 & 4 \\ 1 & -6 \end{bmatrix}$$

✔ **Got It?** **2.** What is the solution of $3X - 2\begin{bmatrix} -1 & 5 \\ 7 & 0 \end{bmatrix} = \begin{bmatrix} 17 & -13 \\ -7 & 0 \end{bmatrix}$?

Not all pairs of matrices can be multiplied to obtain a product. If you *can* multiply a pair of matrices, the product is also a matrix.

take note

Key Concept Matrix Multiplication

To find element c_{ij} of the product matrix AB, multiply each element in the ith row of A by the corresponding element in the jth column of B. Then add the products.

$$AB = \begin{bmatrix} a_{11} & a_{12} \\ a_{21} & a_{22} \end{bmatrix} \begin{bmatrix} b_{11} & b_{12} \\ b_{21} & b_{22} \end{bmatrix} = \begin{bmatrix} a_{11}b_{11} + a_{12}b_{21} & a_{11}b_{12} + a_{12}b_{22} \\ a_{21}b_{11} + a_{22}b_{21} & a_{21}b_{12} + a_{22}b_{22} \end{bmatrix}$$

Problem 3 Multiplying Matrices

Think

What relationship must exist between the numbers of elements in a row of *A* and a column of *B*?
They must be equal.

If $A = \begin{bmatrix} 2 & 1 \\ -3 & 0 \end{bmatrix}$ and $B = \begin{bmatrix} -1 & 3 \\ 0 & 4 \end{bmatrix}$, what is AB?

Step 1 Multiply the elements in the first row of *A* by the elements in the first column of *B*. Add the products, and place the sum in the first row, first column of *AB*.

$$\begin{bmatrix} 2 & 1 \\ -3 & 0 \end{bmatrix} \begin{bmatrix} -1 & 3 \\ 0 & 4 \end{bmatrix} = \begin{bmatrix} -2 & \_\_ \\ \_\_ & \_\_ \end{bmatrix}$$ $2(-1) + 1(0) = -2$

Step 2 Multiply the elements in the first row of *A* by the elements in the second column of *B*. Add the products, and place the sum in the first row, second column of *AB*.

$$\begin{bmatrix} 2 & 1 \\ -3 & 0 \end{bmatrix} \begin{bmatrix} -1 & 3 \\ 0 & 4 \end{bmatrix} = \begin{bmatrix} -2 & 10 \\ \_\_ & \_\_ \end{bmatrix}$$ $2(3) + 1(4) = 10$

Step 3 Multiply the elements in the second row of *A* by the elements in the first column of *B*. Add the products, and place the sum in the second row, first column of *AB*.

$$\begin{bmatrix} 2 & 1 \\ -3 & 0 \end{bmatrix} \begin{bmatrix} -1 & 3 \\ 0 & 4 \end{bmatrix} = \begin{bmatrix} -2 & 10 \\ 3 & \_\_ \end{bmatrix}$$ $(-3)(-1) + 0(0) = 3$

Step 4 Multiply the elements in the second row of *A* by the elements in the second column of *B*. Add the products, and place the sum in the second row, second column of *AB*.

$$\begin{bmatrix} 2 & 1 \\ -3 & 0 \end{bmatrix} \begin{bmatrix} -1 & 3 \\ 0 & 4 \end{bmatrix} = \begin{bmatrix} -2 & 10 \\ 3 & -9 \end{bmatrix}$$ $(-3)(3) + 0(4) = -9$

The product $\begin{bmatrix} 2 & 1 \\ -3 & 0 \end{bmatrix} \begin{bmatrix} -1 & 3 \\ 0 & 4 \end{bmatrix}$ is $\begin{bmatrix} -2 & 10 \\ 3 & -9 \end{bmatrix}$.

Got It? 3. If $A = \begin{bmatrix} 2 & -1 \\ 3 & 4 \end{bmatrix}$ and $B = \begin{bmatrix} -3 & 1 \\ 0 & 2 \end{bmatrix}$, what are the following products?

a. AB **b.** BA

c. Reasoning Is matrix multiplication commutative? Explain.

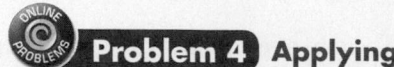 **Problem 4** **Applying Matrix Multiplication**

Sports In 1966, Washington and New York (Giants) played the highest scoring game in National Football League history. The table summarizes the scoring. A touchdown (TD) is worth 6 points, a field goal (FG) is worth 3 points, a safety (S) is worth 2 points, and a point after touchdown (PAT) is worth 1 point. Using matrix multiplication, what was the final score?

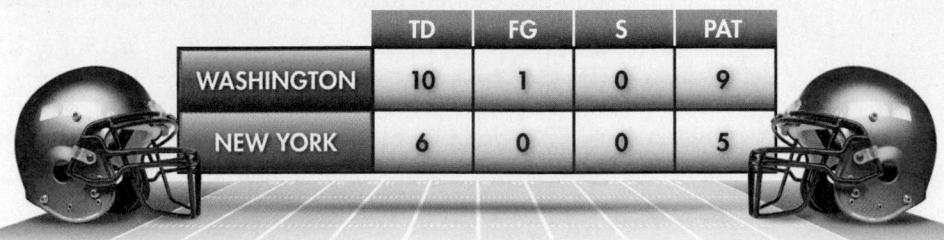

	TD	FG	S	PAT
WASHINGTON	10	1	0	9
NEW YORK	6	0	0	5

Know
- The number of each type of score
- The point value of each score

Need
The scoring summary and point values as matrices

Plan
Multiply the matrices to find each team's final score.

Think

What is the meaning of each number in matrix P?
They are the point values for each type of score.

Step 1 Enter the information in matrices.

$$S = \begin{bmatrix} 10 & 1 & 0 & 9 \\ 6 & 0 & 0 & 5 \end{bmatrix} \qquad P = \begin{bmatrix} 6 \\ 3 \\ 2 \\ 1 \end{bmatrix}$$

Step 2 Use matrix multiplication. The final score is the product SP.

Write the matrix multiplication.
$$SP = \begin{bmatrix} 10 & 1 & 0 & 9 \\ 6 & 0 & 0 & 5 \end{bmatrix} \begin{bmatrix} 6 \\ 3 \\ 2 \\ 1 \end{bmatrix}$$

Multiply and simplify.
$$= \begin{bmatrix} 10(6) + 1(3) + 0(2) + 9(1) \\ 6(6) + 0(3) + 0(2) + 5(1) \end{bmatrix} = \begin{bmatrix} 72 \\ 41 \end{bmatrix}$$

Step 3 Interpret the product matrix.

The first row of SP shows scoring for Washington, so the final score was Washington 72, New York 41.

Got It? **4.** There are three ways to score in a basketball game: three-point field goals, two-point field goals, and one-point free throws. In 1994, suppose a high school player scored 36 two-point field goals and 28 free throws. In 2006, suppose a high school player scored 7 three-point field goals, 21 two-point field goals, and 18 free throws. Using matrix multiplication, how many points did each player score?

You can multiply two matrices A and B only if the number of columns of A is equal to the number of rows of B.

Property Dimensions of a Product Matrix

If A is an $m \times n$ matrix and B is an $n \times p$ matrix,
then the product matrix AB is an $m \times p$ matrix.

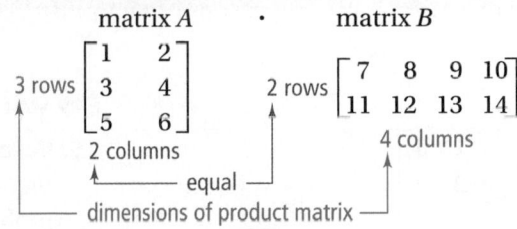

The product matrix AB is a 3×4 matrix.

Problem 5 Determining Whether Product Matrices Exist

Does either product AB or BA exist?

$$A = \begin{bmatrix} -2 & 1 \\ 3 & -2 \\ 0 & 1 \end{bmatrix} \qquad B = \begin{bmatrix} -1 & 0 & 2 & 1 \\ 2 & 0 & 0 & 3 \end{bmatrix}$$

Think

How can you tell if a product matrix exists without computing it?
Compare the dimensions of the matrices.

AB

$(3 \times 2)(2 \times 4) \; \rightarrow \; 3 \times 4$ product matrix

equal

BA

$(2 \times 4)(3 \times 2) \; \rightarrow \;$ no product

not equal

Product AB exists.

Got It? 5. Do the following products exist?

$$A = \begin{bmatrix} 1 & 4 \\ -3 & 5 \end{bmatrix} \qquad B = \begin{bmatrix} -1 & 1 \end{bmatrix} \qquad C = \begin{bmatrix} 4 & 2 & 0 \\ 1 & 3 & 5 \end{bmatrix}$$

a. AB **b.** BA **c.** AC **d.** CA **e.** BC

Hint

Matrix multiplication of square (n × n) matrices shares some properties of real number multiplication.

Properties Matrix Multiplication

If A, B, and C are $n \times n$ matrices, and O is the $n \times n$ zero matrix, then

Example	Property
AB is an $n \times n$ matrix	**Closure Property**
$(AB)C = A(BC)$	**Associative Property of Multiplication**
$A(B + C) = AB + AC$ $(B + C)A = BA + CA$	**Distributive Property**
$OA = AO = O$	**Multiplicative Property of Zero**

Focus Question How do you find the product of two matrices?

Answer The product of two matrices A and B is the matrix AB. To find element c_{ij} of AB, multiply each element in the ith row of A by the corresponding element of the jth column of B. Then add the products. Not all pairs of matrices can be multiplied.

Lesson Check

Do you know HOW?

Let $A = \begin{bmatrix} 3 & -1 \\ 2 & 0 \end{bmatrix}$ and $B = \begin{bmatrix} 1 & 3 \\ -2 & 2 \end{bmatrix}$.

Find each of the following.

1. $2A$

2. $3B - 2A$

3. AB

4. BA

Do you UNDERSTAND?

5. Vocabulary Which type of multiplication, *scalar* or *matrix*, can help you with a repeated matrix addition problem? Explain.

6. Error Analysis Your friend says there is a right order and a wrong order when multiplying A (a 2×4 matrix) and B (a 3×6 matrix). Explain your friend's error.

Practice and Problem-Solving Exercises

A Practice   Use matrices A, B, C, and D. Find each product, sum, or difference.   ◀ See Problem 1.

$$A = \begin{bmatrix} 3 & 4 \\ 6 & -2 \\ 1 & 0 \end{bmatrix} \qquad B = \begin{bmatrix} -3 & 1 \\ 2 & -4 \\ -1 & 5 \end{bmatrix} \qquad C = \begin{bmatrix} 1 & 2 \\ -3 & 1 \end{bmatrix} \qquad D = \begin{bmatrix} 5 & 1 \\ 0 & 2 \end{bmatrix}$$

7. $3A$

8. $-3C$

9. $-D$

10. $A - 2B$

11. $4C + 3D$

12. $2A - 5B$

Solve each matrix equation. Check your answers.   ◀ See Problem 2.

Guided Practice

To start, use the subtraction property of equality to isolate the variable matrix.

13. $4X + \begin{bmatrix} 1 & 3 \\ -7 & 9 \end{bmatrix} = \begin{bmatrix} -3 & 11 \\ 5 & -7 \end{bmatrix}$

$4X = \begin{bmatrix} -3 & 11 \\ 5 & -7 \end{bmatrix} - \begin{bmatrix} 1 & 3 \\ -7 & 9 \end{bmatrix}$

14. $3\begin{bmatrix} 2 & 0 \\ -1 & 5 \end{bmatrix} - 2X = \begin{bmatrix} -10 & 5 \\ 0 & 17 \end{bmatrix}$

15. $\frac{1}{2}X + \begin{bmatrix} 4 & -3 \\ 12 & 1 \end{bmatrix} = \begin{bmatrix} 2 & 1 \\ 1 & 2 \end{bmatrix}$

Find each product.

◀ See Problem 3.

Guided Practice →

To start, find the element in the first row, first column of the product matrix.

16. $\begin{bmatrix} -3 & 4 \\ 5 & 2 \end{bmatrix}\begin{bmatrix} 1 & 0 \\ 2 & -3 \end{bmatrix}$

$\begin{bmatrix} -3 & 4 \\ 5 & 2 \end{bmatrix}\begin{bmatrix} 1 & 0 \\ 2 & -3 \end{bmatrix} \rightarrow (-3)(1) + (4)(2) = 5$

17. $\begin{bmatrix} 1 & 0 \\ 2 & -3 \end{bmatrix}\begin{bmatrix} -3 & 4 \\ 5 & 2 \end{bmatrix}$

18. $\begin{bmatrix} 0 & 2 \\ -4 & 0 \end{bmatrix}\begin{bmatrix} 0 & 2 \\ -4 & 0 \end{bmatrix}$

19. $\begin{bmatrix} -3 & 5 \end{bmatrix}\begin{bmatrix} -3 \\ 5 \end{bmatrix}$

20. $\begin{bmatrix} -3 & 5 \end{bmatrix}\begin{bmatrix} -3 & 0 \\ 5 & 0 \end{bmatrix}$

21. $\begin{bmatrix} -3 & 5 \end{bmatrix}\begin{bmatrix} 0 & -3 \\ 0 & 5 \end{bmatrix}$

22. $\begin{bmatrix} 0 & -3 \\ 0 & 5 \end{bmatrix}\begin{bmatrix} -3 & 0 \\ 5 & 0 \end{bmatrix}$

23. Business A florist makes three special floral arrangements. One uses three lilies. The second uses three lilies and four carnations. The third uses four daisies and three carnations. Lilies cost $2.15 each, carnations cost $.90 each, and daisies cost $1.30 each.
◀ See Problem 4.
  a. Write a matrix to show the number of each type of flower in each arrangement.
  b. Write a matrix to show the cost of each type of flower.
  c. Find the matrix showing the cost of each floral arrangement.

Determine whether the product exists.

◀ See Problem 5.

$F = \begin{bmatrix} 2 & 3 \\ 6 & 9 \end{bmatrix}$ $G = \begin{bmatrix} -3 & 6 \\ 2 & -4 \end{bmatrix}$ $H = \begin{bmatrix} -5 \\ 6 \end{bmatrix}$ $J = \begin{bmatrix} 0 & 7 \end{bmatrix}$

24. FG **25.** GF **26.** HG **27.** JH

Apply

28. Think About a Plan A hardware store chain sells hammers for $3, flashlights for $5, and lanterns for $7. The store manager tracks the daily purchases at three of the chain's stores in a 3×3 matrix. What is the total gross revenue from the flashlights sold at all three stores?
  • How can you use matrix multiplication to solve this problem?
  • What does the product matrix represent?

Number of Items Sold

	Store A	Store B	Store C
Hammers	10	9	8
Flashlights	3	14	6
Lanterns	2	5	7

29. Sports Two teams are competing in a two-team track meet. Points for individual events are awarded as follows: 5 points for first place, 3 points for second place, and 1 point for third place. Points for team relays are awarded as follows: 5 points for first place and no points for second place.
  a. Use matrix operations to determine the score in the track meet.
  b. Who would win if the scoring was changed to 5 points for first place, 2 points for second place, and 1 point for third place in each individual event and 5 points for first place and 0 points for second place in a relay?

	Individual Events			Relays	
Team	First	Second	Third	First	Second
West River	8	5	2	8	5
River's Edge	6	9	12	6	9

30. Writing Suppose A is a 2×3 matrix and B is a 3×2 matrix with elements not all being equal. Are AB and BA equal? Explain your reasoning. Include examples.

Use matrices D, E, and F. Perform the indicated operations if they are defined. If an operation is not defined, label it *undefined*.

$$D = \begin{bmatrix} 1 & 2 & -1 \\ 0 & 3 & 1 \\ 2 & -1 & -2 \end{bmatrix} \qquad E = \begin{bmatrix} 2 & -5 & 0 \\ 1 & 0 & -2 \\ 3 & 1 & 1 \end{bmatrix} \qquad F = \begin{bmatrix} -3 & 2 \\ -5 & 1 \\ 2 & 4 \end{bmatrix}$$

31. DE

32. $-3F$

33. $(DE)F$

34. $D(EF)$

35. $(E - D)F$

36. $(DD)E$

Standardized Test Prep

SAT/ACT

37. Which product is NOT defined?

Ⓐ $\begin{bmatrix} -1 \\ 2 \end{bmatrix} [-1 \quad 2]$ Ⓑ $\begin{bmatrix} -1 & 2 \\ -1 & 2 \end{bmatrix} [-1 \quad 2]$ Ⓒ $\begin{bmatrix} -1 & 2 \\ -1 & 2 \end{bmatrix} \begin{bmatrix} 2 & -1 \\ 2 & -1 \end{bmatrix}$ Ⓓ $[-1 \quad 2] \begin{bmatrix} -1 \\ 2 \end{bmatrix}$

38. What is the geometric mean of 8 and 18?

Ⓕ 12   Ⓖ 13   Ⓗ 26   Ⓘ 36

39. The random number table simulates an experiment where you toss a coin 90 times. Even digits represent heads and odd digits represent tails. What is the experimental probability, to the nearest percent, of the coin coming up heads?

Ⓐ 45%   Ⓑ 50%   Ⓒ 54%   Ⓓ 56%

Random Number Table		
31504	51648	40613
79321	80927	42404
15594	84675	68591
34178	00460	31754
49676	58733	00884
85400	72294	22551

40. Four percent of the tenants in an apartment building live alone. Suppose five tenants are selected randomly. Which expression represents $P(\text{all live alone})$?

Ⓕ $(0.04)^5$ Ⓖ $(0.4)^5$ Ⓗ $(0.96)^5$ Ⓘ $(5)^{0.04}$

Short Response

41. Explain how to find an equation for the ellipse, centered at the origin, that is 50 units wide and 40 units high.

Mixed Review

Add or subtract. 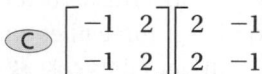 **See Lesson 12-1.**

42. $\begin{bmatrix} -1 & 2 \\ 0 & 17 \end{bmatrix} - \begin{bmatrix} 32 & 14 \\ 6 & -10 \end{bmatrix}$

43. $\begin{bmatrix} 0 & -1 & 5 \\ 6 & 10 & 12 \end{bmatrix} + \begin{bmatrix} 9 & -5 & 7 \\ -4 & 10 & 0 \end{bmatrix}$

Get Ready! To prepare for Lesson 12-3, do Exercises 44 and 45.

Simplify each group of expressions. 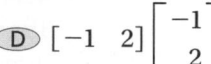 **See p. 868.**

44. a. $3(4)$ **b.** $2(6)$ **c.** $3(4) - 2(6)$

45. a. $3(-4)$ **b.** $2(-6)$ **c.** $3(-4) - 2(-6)$

12-3
PART 1

Determinants and Inverses

Objective To find the determinant of a matrix

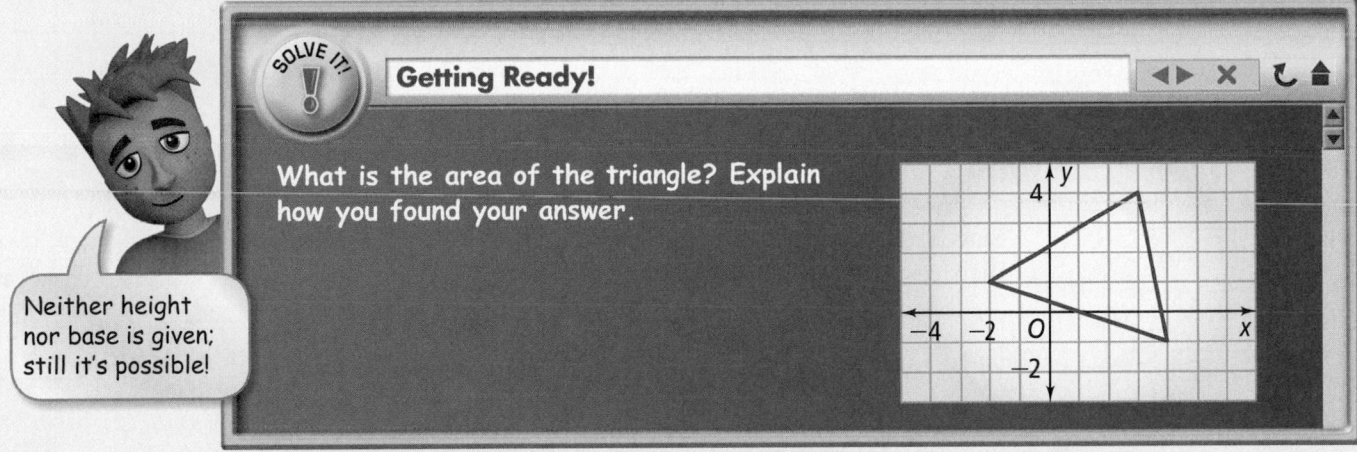

Lesson Vocabulary
- square matrix
- multiplicative identity matrix
- multiplicative inverse matrix
- determinant

Hint

main diagonal
The main diagonal of a square matrix are the entries that run from the top left corner to the bottom right corner.

This lesson will prepare you to use matrices to solve problems, including how to find the area of a triangle with vertices anywhere in the coordinate plane.

Focus Question What are multiplicative identity matrices and multiplicative inverse matrices?

A **square matrix** is a matrix with the same number of rows and columns. While there is a multiplicative identity matrix for any square matrix, not all square matrices have multiplicative inverses.

take note

Key Concepts   Identity and Multiplicative Inverse Matrices

For an $n \times n$ matrix, the **multiplicative identity matrix** is an $n \times n$ matrix I, or I_n with 1's along the main diagonal and 0's elsewhere.

$$I_2 = \begin{bmatrix} 1 & 0 \\ 0 & 1 \end{bmatrix}, \quad I_3 = \begin{bmatrix} 1 & 0 & 0 \\ 0 & 1 & 0 \\ 0 & 0 & 1 \end{bmatrix}, \quad \text{and so forth.}$$

If A and B are square matrices and $AB = BA = I$, then B is the **multiplicative inverse matrix** of A, written A^{-1}.

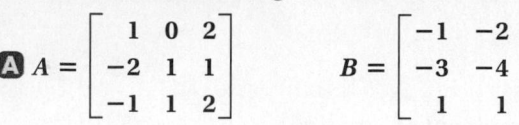

Problem 1 Determining Whether Matrices are Inverses

Think

How do you determine whether A and B are inverses?
Find AB and BA. Both products must equal I for the matrices to be inverses.

For each of the following, are matrices A and B inverses?

A $A = \begin{bmatrix} 1 & 0 & 2 \\ -2 & 1 & 1 \\ -1 & 1 & 2 \end{bmatrix}$ $B = \begin{bmatrix} -1 & -2 & 2 \\ -3 & -4 & 5 \\ 1 & 1 & -1 \end{bmatrix}$

Since $AB = I$ and $BA = I$, matrices A and B are inverses.

```
1.b                    RAD AUTO REAL
[ 1  0  2][ -1  -2  2]           [ 1  0  0]
[-2  1  1]·[ -3  -4  5]          [ 0  1  0]
[-1  1  2][  1   1 -1]           [ 0  0  1]

[ -1  -2  2][ 1  0  2]           [ 1  0  0]
[ -3  -4  5]·[-2  1  1]          [ 0  1  0]
[  1   1 -1][-1  1  2]           [ 0  0  1]
                                        2/99
```

Hint
Once you find that $AB \neq I$ (or $BA \neq I$) you can conclude that the matrices are not inverses, without having to find the other product.

B $A = \begin{bmatrix} 2 & 4 \\ 2 & 2 \end{bmatrix}$ $B = \begin{bmatrix} 2 & 5 \\ -1 & -3 \end{bmatrix}$

Since $AB \neq I$ (and $BA \neq I$), matrices A and B are not inverses.

```
1.c                    RAD AUTO REAL
[ 2  4]·[ 2  5]                  [ 0  -2]
[ 2  2] [-1 -3]                  [ 2   4]

[ 2  5]·[ 2  4]                  [ 14  18]
[-1 -3] [ 2  2]                  [ -8 -10]

|
                                        2/99
```

Got It? **1.** For each of the following, are matrices A and B inverses?

a. $A = \begin{bmatrix} 1 & 1 \\ 5 & 4 \end{bmatrix}$ $B = \begin{bmatrix} -4 & 1 \\ 5 & -1 \end{bmatrix}$ **b.** $A = \begin{bmatrix} 3 & 2 \\ 5 & 4 \end{bmatrix}$ $B = \begin{bmatrix} 2 & -1 \\ -\dfrac{5}{2} & \dfrac{3}{2} \end{bmatrix}$

c. Reasoning Does the matrix $\begin{bmatrix} 0 & 0 \\ 0 & 0 \end{bmatrix}$ have an inverse? Explain.

Every square matrix with real-number elements has a certain number associated with it. The number is called its *determinant*. Given $A = \begin{bmatrix} a & b \\ c & d \end{bmatrix}$,

Write	**Read**	**Evaluate**
↓	↓	↓
det A	the determinant of A	$\det \begin{bmatrix} a & b \\ c & d \end{bmatrix} = ad - bc$

take note

Key Concept Determinant of a 2 × 2 Matrix

The **determinant** of a 2 × 2 matrix $\begin{bmatrix} a & b \\ c & d \end{bmatrix}$ is $\det \begin{bmatrix} a & b \\ c & d \end{bmatrix} = ad - bc$.

take note ▶

Key Concept   Determinant of a 3 × 3 Matrix

The determinant of a 3×3 matrix $\begin{bmatrix} a_1 & b_1 & c_1 \\ a_2 & b_2 & c_2 \\ a_3 & b_3 & c_3 \end{bmatrix}$ is

$$a_1b_2c_3 + b_1c_2a_3 + c_1a_2b_3 - (a_3b_2c_1 + b_3c_2a_1 + c_3a_2b_1)$$

Visualize the pattern this way:

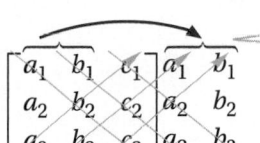

a copy of the first two columns

ONLINE PROBLEMS **Problem 2** **Evaluating the Determinants of Matrices**

What are the following determinants?

A $\det \begin{bmatrix} 3 & -1 \\ 2 & 5 \end{bmatrix}$

Use the formula. $\det \begin{bmatrix} 3 & -1 \\ 2 & 5 \end{bmatrix} = (3)(5) - (-1)(2)$

Simplify. $= 15 - (-2) = 17$

Think

What can you do first to evaluate a 3 × 3 determinant?
Copy the first two columns to the right of the matrix.

$\begin{bmatrix} 1 & 0 & -2 \\ 0 & 4 & -1 \\ 3 & 5 & 2 \end{bmatrix} \begin{matrix} 1 & 0 \\ 0 & 4 \\ 3 & 5 \end{matrix}$

B $\det \begin{bmatrix} 1 & 0 & -2 \\ 0 & 4 & -1 \\ 3 & 5 & 2 \end{bmatrix}$

Use the formula. $= [(1)(4)(2) + (0)(-1)(3) + (-2)(0)(5)] - [(3)(4)(-2) + (5)(-1)(1) + (2)(0)(0)]$

Multiply. $= 8 + 0 + 0 - (-24 - 5 + 0)$

Simplify. $= 8 - (-29) = 37$

Check Use a graphing calculator.

 Got It?   **2.** What are the following determinants?

a. $\begin{bmatrix} 3 & 6 \\ 2 & 5 \end{bmatrix}$ **b.** $\begin{bmatrix} 1 & 0 & 3 \\ 2 & 4 & 6 \\ 5 & -1 & 3 \end{bmatrix}$

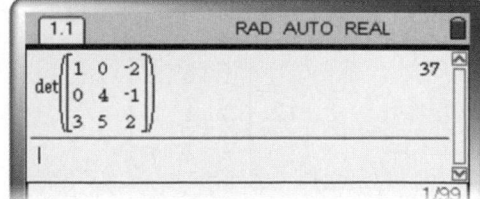

Focus Question What are multiplicative identity matrices and multiplicative inverse matrices?

Answer Multiplicative identity matrices are square matrices with 1's along the main diagonal and 0's elsewhere. The product of a square matrix and its multiplicative inverse matrix is a multiplicative identity matrix.

Lesson Check

Do you know HOW?

Evaluate the determinant of each matrix.

1. $\begin{bmatrix} 4 & -1 \\ 8 & 2 \end{bmatrix}$

2. $\begin{bmatrix} 1 & 0 & 0 \\ -1 & 2 & 3 \\ 4 & -1 & 2 \end{bmatrix}$

Do you UNDERSTAND?

3. Error Analysis What mistake did the student make when finding the determinant of $\begin{bmatrix} 2 & 5 \\ -3 & 1 \end{bmatrix}$?

$\det \begin{bmatrix} 2 & 5 \\ -3 & 1 \end{bmatrix} = (2)(1) + (-3)(5) = 2 - 15 = -13$

Practice and Problem-Solving Exercises

A Practice

Determine whether the matrices are multiplicative inverses.

⬥ **See Problem 1.**

4. $\begin{bmatrix} 3 & 2 \\ 4 & 3 \end{bmatrix}, \begin{bmatrix} 3 & -2 \\ -4 & 3 \end{bmatrix}$

5. $\begin{bmatrix} -3 & 7 \\ -2 & 5 \end{bmatrix}, \begin{bmatrix} -5 & 7 \\ -2 & 3 \end{bmatrix}$

6. $\begin{bmatrix} 1 & 2 & -1 \\ -1.5 & -3 & 1.75 \\ 0 & -1 & 0.5 \end{bmatrix}, \begin{bmatrix} 1 & 0 & 2 \\ 3 & 2 & -1 \\ 6 & 4 & 0 \end{bmatrix}$

7. $\begin{bmatrix} 2 & 2 & 2 \\ -2 & 2 & -2 \\ -2 & -2 & -2 \end{bmatrix}, \begin{bmatrix} 2 & 2 & 2 \\ -2 & 2 & -2 \\ -2 & -2 & -2 \end{bmatrix}$

Evaluate the determinant of each matrix.

⬥ **See Problem 2.**

8. $\begin{bmatrix} 7 & 2 \\ 0 & -3 \end{bmatrix}$

Guided Practice

To start, write the formula for the determinant of a 2 × 2 matrix.

$\det \begin{bmatrix} a & b \\ c & d \end{bmatrix} = ad - bc$

9. $\begin{bmatrix} 6 & 2 \\ -6 & -2 \end{bmatrix}$

10. $\begin{bmatrix} -1 & 3 \\ 5 & 2 \end{bmatrix}$

11. $\begin{bmatrix} 5 & 3 \\ -2 & 1 \end{bmatrix}$

12. $\begin{bmatrix} 1 & 2 & 5 \\ 3 & 1 & 0 \\ 1 & 2 & 1 \end{bmatrix}$

13. $\begin{bmatrix} 1 & 4 & 0 \\ 2 & 3 & 5 \\ 0 & 1 & 0 \end{bmatrix}$

14. $\begin{bmatrix} -2 & 4 & 1 \\ 3 & 0 & -1 \\ 1 & 2 & 1 \end{bmatrix}$

B Apply

Evaluate each determinant.

15. $\begin{bmatrix} 4 & 5 \\ -4 & 4 \end{bmatrix}$

16. $\begin{bmatrix} -3 & 10 \\ 6 & 20 \end{bmatrix}$

17. $\begin{bmatrix} 4 & 6 & -1 \\ 2 & 3 & 2 \\ 1 & -1 & 1 \end{bmatrix}$

18. $\begin{bmatrix} -3 & 2 & -1 \\ 2 & 5 & 2 \\ 1 & -2 & 0 \end{bmatrix}$

19. Writing Evaluate the determinant of each matrix. Describe any patterns.

a. $\begin{bmatrix} 1 & 2 & 3 \\ 1 & 2 & 3 \\ 1 & 2 & 3 \end{bmatrix}$

b. $\begin{bmatrix} -1 & -2 & -3 \\ -3 & -2 & -1 \\ -1 & -2 & -3 \end{bmatrix}$

c. $\begin{bmatrix} 1 & 2 & 3 \\ 2 & 3 & 1 \\ 1 & 2 & 3 \end{bmatrix}$

d. $\begin{bmatrix} -1 & 2 & -3 \\ 2 & -3 & -1 \\ -1 & 2 & -3 \end{bmatrix}$

12-3
PART 2

Determinants and Inverses

Objective To find the inverse of a matrix

In Part 1 of the lesson, you learned when two matrices are inverses and how to find a determinant.

Connect to What You Know

Here you will relate determinants to inverse matrices and explore real-world applications.

Lesson Vocabulary
• singular matrix

Focus Question Why is the determinant of a matrix useful?

It is sometimes easy to calculate the area of a triangle in the coordinate plane by using the formula $A = \frac{1}{2}bh$.

For the triangle shown here, the length of the base is the difference in the x-coordinates: $6 - 2 = 4$. The height is the difference in the y-coordinates: $4 - 1 = 3$. The area of the triangle is $\frac{1}{2}(4)(3) = 6$ square units.

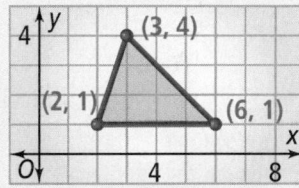

For other triangles, the lengths of the base and height are not obvious from its graph. You can use determinants to help you find the area of a triangle given only its vertices.

Hint

Since all polygons can be divided into triangles, you can use this method to find the area of any polygon.

take note

Key Concept Area of a Triangle

The area of a triangle with vertices (x_1, y_1), (x_2, y_2), and (x_3, y_3) is

$$\text{Area} = \frac{1}{2} \cdot \det A, \text{ where } A = \begin{bmatrix} x_1 & y_1 & 1 \\ x_2 & y_2 & 1 \\ x_3 & y_3 & 1 \end{bmatrix}$$

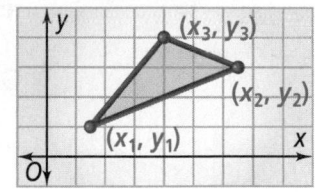

Problem 3 Finding the Area of a Polygon

Land One factor in flood safety along a levee is the area that will absorb water should the levee break. The coordinates shown are in miles. What is the area in the pictured California community?

(1.4, 2.0)

(1.9, 0.4)

(0, 0)

Write the matrix for the area formula.

$$A = \begin{bmatrix} x_1 & y_1 & 1 \\ x_2 & y_2 & 1 \\ x_3 & y_3 & 1 \end{bmatrix}$$

Substitute coordinates.

$$= \begin{bmatrix} 0 & 0 & 1 \\ 1.9 & 0.4 & 1 \\ 1.4 & 2.0 & 1 \end{bmatrix}$$

Think

Why must you use absolute value?
A determinant can be positive or negative. Area must be positive.

Write the area formula. $\text{Area} = \frac{1}{2} \cdot \det A$

Use a calculator to evaluate. $= 1.62$

The area of the triangle is 1.62 mi².

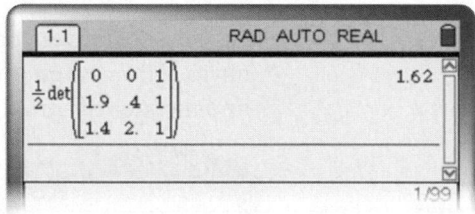

Check for Reasonableness The area is approximately one-half the area of a 1.9 by 2 rectangle. Thus, an area of about 1.6 units² is reasonable.

 Got It? **3.** What is the area of the triangle with the given vertices?

　　　a. $(1, 3), (-3, 0), (5, 0)$ 　　　　　　**b.** $(1, 3), (5, 8), (9, -1)$

The determinant of a matrix can help you determine whether the matrix has an inverse. If an inverse matrix exists, you can use the determinant to find the inverse.

Key Concept Inverse of a 2 × 2 Matrix

Let $A = \begin{bmatrix} a & b \\ c & d \end{bmatrix}$.

If det $A = 0$, then A is a **singular matrix** and has no inverse.

If det $A \neq 0$, then the inverse of A, written A^{-1}, is

$$A^{-1} = \frac{1}{\det A}\begin{bmatrix} d & -b \\ -c & a \end{bmatrix} = \frac{1}{ad - bc}\begin{bmatrix} d & -b \\ -c & a \end{bmatrix}.$$

Hint

You switch the elements on the main diagonal. You change the sign on the other diagonal.

Problem 4 **Finding the Inverse of a Matrix**

Does the matrix $A = \begin{bmatrix} -3 & 6 \\ -1 & 3 \end{bmatrix}$ have an inverse? If it does, what is A^{-1}?

Think

Evaluate det A. If *det A* ≠ 0, the matrix has an inverse.

Write the formula for A^{-1}.

You know det $A = -3$. In matrix A, $a = -3$, $b = 6$, $c = -1$, and $d = 3$.

Multiply by the scalar and simplify the fractions.

Write

det $A = ad - bc$

$= (-3)(3) - (6)(-1)$

$= -9 - (-6)$

$= -9 + 6$

$= -3$

det $A \neq 0$, so A has an inverse.

$A^{-1} = \frac{1}{\det A}\begin{bmatrix} d & -b \\ -c & a \end{bmatrix}$

$= \frac{1}{-3}\begin{bmatrix} 3 & -6 \\ 1 & -3 \end{bmatrix}$

$= \begin{bmatrix} \frac{3}{-3} & \frac{-6}{-3} \\ \frac{1}{-3} & \frac{-3}{-3} \end{bmatrix}$

$= \begin{bmatrix} -1 & 2 \\ -\frac{1}{3} & 1 \end{bmatrix}$

Hint

You can check your answer using a graphing calculator. Either verify that $AA^{-1} = I$ or evaluate A^{-1} directly.

Got It? **4.** Does the matrix have an inverse? If so, what is it?

a. $A = \begin{bmatrix} 4 & 2 \\ 3 & 2 \end{bmatrix}$

b. $B = \begin{bmatrix} 2 & 5 \\ -4 & -10 \end{bmatrix}$

c. $C = \begin{bmatrix} 7 & 4 \\ 5 & 3 \end{bmatrix}$

Problem 5 Encoding and Decoding With Matrices

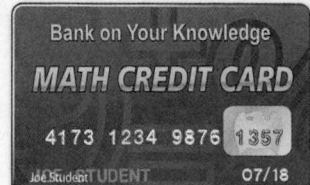
Bank on Your Knowledge
MATH CREDIT CARD
4173 1234 9876 1357
Joe Student STUDENT   07/18

A How can you use matrix multiplication with matrix C to encode the account number from the credit card?

$$C = \begin{bmatrix} 2 & -1 \\ 3 & 5 \end{bmatrix}$$

Plan

What size matrix should you use for the card information?
Since the coding matrix has two columns, the information matrix must have two rows, so they can be multiplied CA.

Step 1 Place the card information in a matrix with appropriate dimensions for multiplication by the coding matrix.

$$A = \begin{bmatrix} 4 & 1 & 7 & 3 & 1 & 2 & 3 & 4 \\ 9 & 8 & 7 & 6 & 1 & 3 & 5 & 7 \end{bmatrix}$$

Step 2 Multiply the coding matrix and the information matrix to encode the information. Use a calculator.

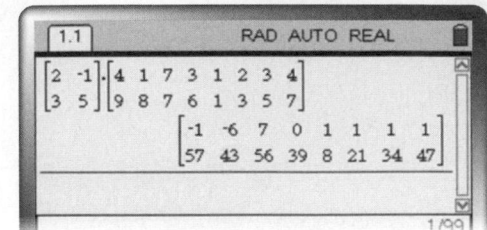
1.1   RAD AUTO REAL
$\begin{bmatrix} 2 & -1 \\ 3 & 5 \end{bmatrix} \cdot \begin{bmatrix} 4 & 1 & 7 & 3 & 1 & 2 & 3 & 4 \\ 9 & 8 & 7 & 6 & 1 & 3 & 5 & 7 \end{bmatrix}$
$\begin{bmatrix} -1 & -6 & 7 & 0 & 1 & 1 & 1 & 1 \\ 57 & 43 & 56 & 39 & 8 & 21 & 34 & 47 \end{bmatrix}$
1/99

$$CA = \begin{bmatrix} 2 & -1 \\ 3 & 5 \end{bmatrix} \begin{bmatrix} 4 & 1 & 7 & 3 & 1 & 2 & 3 & 4 \\ 9 & 8 & 7 & 6 & 1 & 3 & 5 & 7 \end{bmatrix}$$

$$= \begin{bmatrix} -1 & -6 & 7 & 0 & 1 & 1 & 1 & 1 \\ 57 & 43 & 56 & 39 & 8 & 21 & 34 & 47 \end{bmatrix}$$

Step 3 The coded account number is $-1, -6, 7, 0, 1, 1, 1, 1, 57, 43, 56, 39, 8, 21, 34, 47$.

B How do you use a decoding matrix to recover the account number?

The decoding matrix is the inverse of the encoding matrix C. Use a calculator to find C^{-1}.

$$C^{-1} = \begin{bmatrix} \dfrac{5}{13} & \dfrac{1}{13} \\ -\dfrac{3}{13} & \dfrac{2}{13} \end{bmatrix}$$

Multiply the coded information by C^{-1}. Use a calculator.

$$\begin{bmatrix} \dfrac{5}{13} & \dfrac{1}{13} \\ -\dfrac{3}{13} & \dfrac{2}{13} \end{bmatrix} \begin{bmatrix} -1 & -6 & 7 & 0 & 1 & 1 & 1 & 1 \\ 57 & 43 & 56 & 39 & 8 & 21 & 34 & 47 \end{bmatrix} = \begin{bmatrix} 4 & 1 & 7 & 3 & 1 & 2 & 3 & 4 \\ 9 & 8 & 7 & 6 & 1 & 3 & 5 & 7 \end{bmatrix}$$

Got It? **5. a.** How can you use matrix multiplication and the coding matrix $\begin{bmatrix} 4 & 8 \\ -2 & 4 \end{bmatrix}$ to encode the credit card account number in Problem 5?

b. How can you use a decoding matrix to recover the credit card number?

Focus Question Why is the determinant of a matrix useful?

Answer You can use the determinant of a matrix to find the area of a triangle. You can also use the determinant to find the inverse of a matrix, if one exists.

Lesson Check

Do you know HOW?

Find the inverse of each matrix, if it exists.

1. $\begin{bmatrix} 4 & 2 \\ 10 & 5 \end{bmatrix}$

2. $\begin{bmatrix} 5 & 2 \\ 7 & 3 \end{bmatrix}$

Do you UNDERSTAND?

3. Reasoning Explain why a 2×3 matrix does not have a multiplicative inverse.

Practice and Problem-Solving Exercises

Ⓐ Practice

4. Use the map to determine the approximate area of the Bermuda Triangle.

◆ **See Problem 3.**

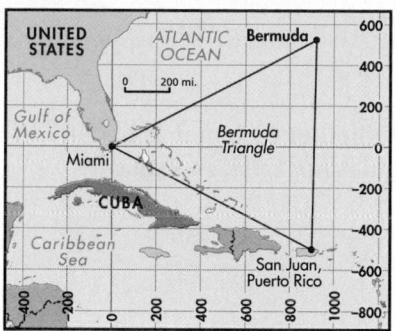

Determine whether each matrix has an inverse. If an inverse matrix exists, find it.

◆ **See Problem 4.**

5. $\begin{bmatrix} 2 & -1 \\ 1 & 0 \end{bmatrix}$

Guided Practice

To start, find the determinant of the matrix.

$\det \begin{bmatrix} 2 & -1 \\ 1 & 0 \end{bmatrix} = (2)(0) - (-1)(1) = 1$

6. $\begin{bmatrix} 2 & 3 \\ 1 & 1 \end{bmatrix}$

7. $\begin{bmatrix} 2 & 3 \\ 2 & 4 \end{bmatrix}$

8. $\begin{bmatrix} 1 & 3 \\ 2 & 0 \end{bmatrix}$

9. $\begin{bmatrix} 6 & -8 \\ -3 & 4 \end{bmatrix}$

10. Use the coding matrix $C = \begin{bmatrix} 2 & -1 \\ 3 & 5 \end{bmatrix}$ to encode the phone number (555) 358-0001.

◆ **See Problem 5.**

Ⓑ Apply

11. Think About a Plan Use matrices to find the area of the figure.
- What shapes do you know how to find the area of?
- Can the polygon be broken into these shapes?
- How many shapes will you need to break the polygon into?

12. Writing Suppose $A = \begin{bmatrix} a & b \\ c & d \end{bmatrix}$ has an inverse. In your own words, describe how to switch or change the elements of A to write A^{-1}.

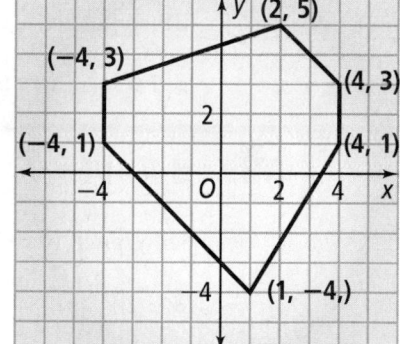

13. Geometry Use matrices to find the area of the figure at the right. Check your result by using standard area formulas.

14. Error Analysis A student wrote $\begin{bmatrix} 1 & \frac{1}{2} \\ \frac{1}{3} & \frac{1}{4} \end{bmatrix}$ as the inverse of $\begin{bmatrix} 1 & 2 \\ 3 & 4 \end{bmatrix}$.

What mistake did the student make? Explain your reasoning.

Evaluate each determinant.

15. $\begin{bmatrix} -\frac{1}{2} & 2 \\ -2 & 8 \end{bmatrix}$

16. $\begin{bmatrix} 6 & 9 \\ 3 & 6 \end{bmatrix}$

17. $\begin{bmatrix} 0 & 2 & -3 \\ 1 & 2 & 4 \\ -2 & 0 & 1 \end{bmatrix}$

18. $\begin{bmatrix} 5 & 1 & 0 \\ 0 & 2 & -1 \\ -2 & -3 & 1 \end{bmatrix}$

Determine whether each matrix has an inverse. If an inverse matrix exists, find it. If it does not exist, explain why.

19. $\begin{bmatrix} 1 & 4 \\ 1 & 3 \end{bmatrix}$

20. $\begin{bmatrix} -3 & 11 \\ 2 & -7 \end{bmatrix}$

21. $\begin{bmatrix} 2 & 0 \\ 0 & 2 \end{bmatrix}$

> **Hint** Use the formula to find the inverses of the 2 × 2 matrices. Use a calculator to find the inverses of the 3 × 3 matrices.

22. $\begin{bmatrix} -2 & 1 & -1 \\ 2 & 0 & 4 \\ 0 & 2 & 5 \end{bmatrix}$

23. $\begin{bmatrix} 2 & 0 & -1 \\ -1 & -1 & 1 \\ 3 & 2 & 0 \end{bmatrix}$

24. $\begin{bmatrix} 0 & 0 & 2 \\ 1 & 4 & -2 \\ 3 & -2 & 1 \end{bmatrix}$

25. **Reasoning** For what value of x will matrix A have no inverse? $A = \begin{bmatrix} 1 & 2 \\ 3 & x \end{bmatrix}$

26. **Open Ended** Write a 2 × 2 matrix that has an inverse. Use the matrix to encode your telephone number (including the area-code).

Standardized Test Prep

GRIDDED RESPONSE

SAT/ACT

27. What is the determinant of $\begin{bmatrix} -2 & -3 \\ 5 & 0 \end{bmatrix}$?

28. If $A = \begin{bmatrix} 4 & 2 \\ -3 & -1 \end{bmatrix}$, and the inverse of A is $x \begin{bmatrix} -1 & -2 \\ 3 & 4 \end{bmatrix}$, what is the value of x? Enter your answer as a fraction.

29. What is the value of $\frac{6!}{8!}$? Give your answer as a fraction in simplest terms.

30. If $\log(7y - 5) = 2$, what is the value of y?

Mixed Review

Solve each matrix equation.

◀ See Lesson 12-2.

31. $2 \begin{bmatrix} -1 & 3 \\ -2 & 0 \end{bmatrix} - 3X = \begin{bmatrix} -8 & -9 \\ -7 & -3 \end{bmatrix}$

32. $2X + 3 \begin{bmatrix} 4 & -6 \\ 8 & -3 \end{bmatrix} = \begin{bmatrix} -8 & 20 \\ -16 & 5 \end{bmatrix}$

Evaluate each expression.

◀ See Lesson 11-1.

33. $6!$

34. $9!$

35. $\frac{15!}{5!}$

36. $\frac{12!}{6!3!}$

Get Ready! To prepare for Lesson 12-4, do Exercises 37 and 38.

Solve each system.

◀ See Lesson 3-5.

37. $\begin{cases} x = 5 \\ x - y + z = 5 \\ x + y - z = -5 \end{cases}$

38. $\begin{cases} x - y - z = 9 \\ 3x + 2z = 12 \\ x = y - 2z \end{cases}$

12-4
PART 1

Inverse Matrices and Systems

Objective To solve matrix equations using matrix inverses and multiplication

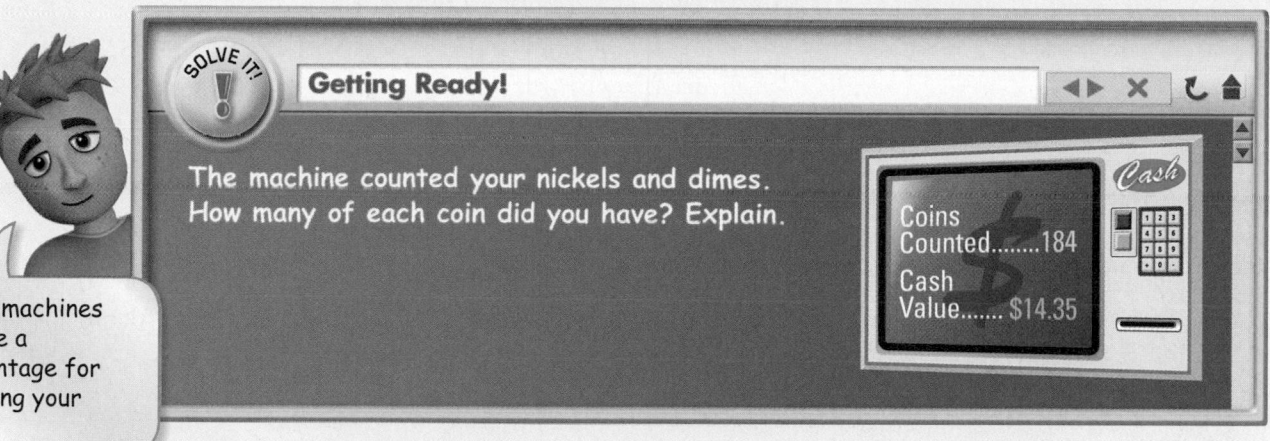

Getting Ready!

The machine counted your nickels and dimes. How many of each coin did you have? Explain.

Coins Counted.......184
Cash Value........ $14.35

Some machines charge a percentage for counting your coins.

In Chapter 3, you used row operations on a matrix to solve a system of equations. Now you will solve systems by solving a matrix equation.

Lesson Vocabulary
• coefficient matrix
• variable matrix
• constant matrix

Focus Question How can you solve a matrix equation of the form $AX = B$?

If matrix A has an inverse, you can use it to solve the matrix equation $AX = B$. Multiply each side of the equation by A^{-1} *on the left* to find X.

Write the matrix equation.	$AX = B$
Multiply each side by A^{-1}.	$A^{-1}AX = A^{-1}B$
$A^{-1}A = I$, the identity matrix.	$IX = A^{-1}B$
$IX = X$	$X = A^{-1}B$

Hint

Remember that matrix multiplication is <u>not</u> commutative.

Notice that you cannot multiply AX by A^{-1} on the *left* and multiply B by A^{-1} on the *right*.

Suppose $A = \begin{bmatrix} 2 & 5 \\ 1 & 3 \end{bmatrix}$, $A^{-1} = \begin{bmatrix} 3 & -5 \\ -1 & 2 \end{bmatrix}$, and $B = \begin{bmatrix} 2 & 2 \\ 1 & 1 \end{bmatrix}$. Solve $AX = B$ for X.

Correct

$A^{-1}AX = A^{-1}B$

$X = \begin{bmatrix} 3 & -5 \\ -1 & 2 \end{bmatrix}\begin{bmatrix} 2 & 2 \\ 1 & 1 \end{bmatrix} = \begin{bmatrix} 1 & 1 \\ 0 & 0 \end{bmatrix}$

Check

$AX = \begin{bmatrix} 2 & 5 \\ 1 & 3 \end{bmatrix}\begin{bmatrix} 1 & 1 \\ 0 & 0 \end{bmatrix} = \begin{bmatrix} 2 & 2 \\ 1 & 1 \end{bmatrix} = B$ ✔

Incorrect

$A^{-1}AX = BA^{-1}$

$X = \begin{bmatrix} 2 & 2 \\ 1 & 1 \end{bmatrix}\begin{bmatrix} 3 & -5 \\ -1 & 2 \end{bmatrix} = \begin{bmatrix} 4 & -6 \\ 2 & -3 \end{bmatrix}$

Check

$AX = \begin{bmatrix} 2 & 5 \\ 1 & 3 \end{bmatrix}\begin{bmatrix} 4 & -6 \\ 2 & -3 \end{bmatrix} = \begin{bmatrix} 18 & -27 \\ 10 & -15 \end{bmatrix}$ ✗

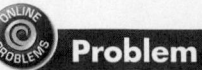 **Problem 1** Solving Matrix Equations Using an Inverse Matrix

Think

How do you know the equation has a solution?
Check det A. If det $A \neq 0$, you can solve the equation.

What is the solution of each matrix equation?

A $\begin{bmatrix} 5 & 3 \\ 3 & 2 \end{bmatrix} X = \begin{bmatrix} 1 \\ -3 \end{bmatrix}$

Step 1 Evaluate det A and find A^{-1}.

$$\det A = ad - bc = (5)(2) - (3)(3) = 1$$

$$A^{-1} = \frac{1}{\det A}\begin{bmatrix} d & -b \\ -c & a \end{bmatrix} = \frac{1}{1}\begin{bmatrix} 2 & -3 \\ -3 & 5 \end{bmatrix} = \begin{bmatrix} 2 & -3 \\ -3 & 5 \end{bmatrix}$$

Step 2 Multiply each side of the equation by A^{-1}.

Think

Does it matter if you multiply by A^{-1} on the left or right side of A?
Even though $A^{-1}A = AA^{-1} = I$, you must multiply each side of the equation by A^{-1} on the left.

$$\begin{bmatrix} 2 & -3 \\ -3 & 5 \end{bmatrix}\begin{bmatrix} 5 & 3 \\ 3 & 2 \end{bmatrix} X = \begin{bmatrix} 2 & -3 \\ -3 & 5 \end{bmatrix}\begin{bmatrix} 1 \\ -3 \end{bmatrix}$$

$$\begin{bmatrix} (2)(5) + (-3)(3) & (2)(3) + (-3)(2) \\ (-3)(5) + (5)(3) & (-3)(3) + (5)(2) \end{bmatrix} X = \begin{bmatrix} (2)(1) + (-3)(-3) \\ (-3)(1) + (5)(-3) \end{bmatrix}$$

$$\begin{bmatrix} 1 & 0 \\ 0 & 1 \end{bmatrix} X = \begin{bmatrix} 11 \\ -18 \end{bmatrix}$$

$$X = \begin{bmatrix} 11 \\ -18 \end{bmatrix}$$

Check

Method 1 Use paper and pencil.

$$\begin{bmatrix} 5 & 3 \\ 3 & 2 \end{bmatrix} X \stackrel{?}{=} \begin{bmatrix} 1 \\ -3 \end{bmatrix}$$

$$\begin{bmatrix} 5 & 3 \\ 3 & 2 \end{bmatrix}\begin{bmatrix} 11 \\ -18 \end{bmatrix} \stackrel{?}{=} \begin{bmatrix} 1 \\ -3 \end{bmatrix}$$

$$\begin{bmatrix} (5)(11) + (3)(-18) \\ (3)(11) + (2)(-18) \end{bmatrix} \stackrel{?}{=} \begin{bmatrix} 1 \\ -3 \end{bmatrix}$$

$$\begin{bmatrix} 1 \\ -3 \end{bmatrix} = \begin{bmatrix} 1 \\ -3 \end{bmatrix} ✔$$

Method 2 Use a calculator.

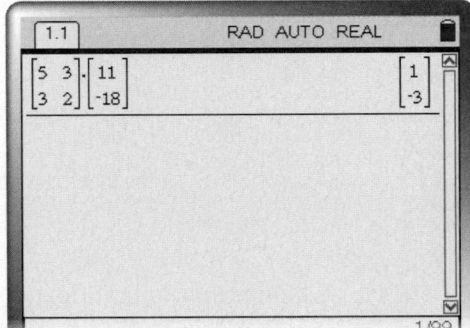

B $\begin{bmatrix} 3 & -9 \\ -2 & 6 \end{bmatrix} X = \begin{bmatrix} 2 \\ 5 \end{bmatrix}$

Evaluate det A.

$$\det A = (3)(6) - (-2)(-9) = 18 - 18 = 0$$

Since det $A = 0$, matrix A does not have an inverse. The equation has no solution.

 Got It? 1. What is the solution of each matrix equation?

a. $\begin{bmatrix} 4 & 3 \\ 2 & 2 \end{bmatrix} X = \begin{bmatrix} -5 \\ 2 \end{bmatrix}$ **b.** $\begin{bmatrix} 7 & 5 \\ 4 & 3 \end{bmatrix} X = \begin{bmatrix} -3 & 0 \\ 1 & 4 \end{bmatrix}$ **c.** $\begin{bmatrix} 2 & 3 \\ 4 & 6 \end{bmatrix} X = \begin{bmatrix} 3 \\ -7 \end{bmatrix}$

You can write a system of equations as a matrix equation $AX = B$, using a **coefficient matrix**, a **variable matrix**, and a **constant matrix**.

Hint

In Chapter 3, you represented a system of equations using only one matrix.

System of Equations

$$\begin{cases} 2x + 3y = 1 \\ 5x - 2y = 13 \end{cases}$$

Matrix Equation

$$\begin{bmatrix} 2 & 3 \\ 5 & -2 \end{bmatrix}\begin{bmatrix} x \\ y \end{bmatrix} = \begin{bmatrix} 1 \\ 13 \end{bmatrix}$$

coefficient matrix, A — variable matrix, X — constant matrix, B

Problem 2 Writing Systems as Matrix Equations

What is the matrix equation that corresponds to each system?

A $\begin{cases} 4x + 7y = 6 \\ -5x + 3y = 1 \end{cases}$

Step 1 Identify the coefficient, variable, and constant matrices.

coefficient matrix, A variable matrix, X constant matrix, B

$$\begin{bmatrix} 4 & 7 \\ -5 & 3 \end{bmatrix} \qquad \begin{bmatrix} x \\ y \end{bmatrix} \qquad \begin{bmatrix} 6 \\ 1 \end{bmatrix}$$

Step 2 Write the matrix equation.

$$\begin{bmatrix} 4 & 7 \\ -5 & 3 \end{bmatrix}\begin{bmatrix} x \\ y \end{bmatrix} = \begin{bmatrix} 6 \\ 1 \end{bmatrix}$$

B $\begin{cases} 3a + 5b - 12c = 6 \\ 7b + 2c = 8 \\ 5a = 3c + 1 \end{cases}$

Plan

How is this system different from the one in part A?
There are three variables. Some terms have coefficients of 0 and the third equation has a variable on the right side of the = sign.

Step 1 Rewrite the system so the variables are in the same order in each equation. Leave spaces for variables with coefficients of 0.

$$\begin{cases} 3a + 5b - 12c = 6 \\ 7b + 2c = 8 \\ 5a = 3c + 1 \end{cases} \rightarrow \begin{cases} 3a + 5b - 12c = 6 \\ 7b + 2c = 8 \\ 5a - 3c = 1 \end{cases}$$

Step 2 Identify the coefficient, variable, and constant matrices.

coefficient matrix, A variable matrix, X constant matrix, B

$$\begin{bmatrix} 3 & 5 & -12 \\ 0 & 7 & 2 \\ 5 & 0 & -3 \end{bmatrix} \qquad \begin{bmatrix} a \\ b \\ c \end{bmatrix} \qquad \begin{bmatrix} 6 \\ 8 \\ 1 \end{bmatrix}$$

Step 3 Write the matrix equation.

$$\begin{bmatrix} 3 & 5 & -12 \\ 0 & 7 & 2 \\ 5 & 0 & -3 \end{bmatrix}\begin{bmatrix} a \\ b \\ c \end{bmatrix} = \begin{bmatrix} 6 \\ 8 \\ 1 \end{bmatrix}$$

Got It? **2.** What is the matrix equation that corresponds to each system?

a. $\begin{cases} 3x - 7y = 8 \\ 5x + y = -2 \end{cases}$ **b.** $\begin{cases} x + 3y + 5z = 12 \\ -2x + y - 4z = -2 \\ 7x - 2y = 7 \end{cases}$ **c.** $\begin{cases} 2x + 3 = 8y \\ -x + y = -4 \end{cases}$

Focus Question How can you solve a matrix equation of the form $AX = B$?

Answer If matrix A has an inverse, you can solve the matrix equation $AX = B$ by multiplying both sides of the equation (in the same order) by A^{-1}. So, $X = A^{-1}B$.

 ## Lesson Check

Do you know HOW?

Write each system as a matrix equation.

1. $\begin{cases} -6x + 3y = 8 \\ 4x - 2y = 10 \end{cases}$

2. $\begin{cases} 2x + 3y = 12 \\ x - 2y + z = 9 \\ 6y - 4z = 8 \end{cases}$

Do you UNDERSTAND?

3. Reasoning Explain how to write the matrix equation $\begin{bmatrix} -2 & 3 \\ 4 & 1 \end{bmatrix}\begin{bmatrix} p \\ q \end{bmatrix} = \begin{bmatrix} 2 \\ -5 \end{bmatrix}$ as a system of linear equations.

Practice and Problem-Solving Exercises

A) Practice Solve each matrix equation. If an equation cannot be solved, explain why. ◀ **See Problem 1.**

4. $\begin{bmatrix} 12 & 7 \\ 5 & 3 \end{bmatrix} X = \begin{bmatrix} 2 & -1 \\ 3 & 2 \end{bmatrix}$

Guided Practice

To start, find the determinant of the coefficient matrix.

$\det\begin{bmatrix} 12 & 7 \\ 5 & 3 \end{bmatrix} = (12)(3) - (7)(5) = 1$

5. $\begin{bmatrix} 5 & 1 & 4 \\ 2 & -3 & -5 \\ 7 & 2 & -6 \end{bmatrix} X = \begin{bmatrix} 5 \\ 2 \\ 5 \end{bmatrix}$

6. $\begin{bmatrix} 0 & -4 \\ 0 & -1 \end{bmatrix} X = \begin{bmatrix} 0 \\ 4 \end{bmatrix}$

7. $\begin{bmatrix} 6 & 10 & 13 \\ 4 & -2 & 7 \\ 0 & 9 & -8 \end{bmatrix} X = \begin{bmatrix} 84 \\ 18 \\ 56 \end{bmatrix}$

Write each system as a matrix equation. Identify the coefficient matrix, the variable matrix, and the constant matrix. ◀ **See Problem 2.**

8. $\begin{cases} x + y = 5 \\ x - 2y = -4 \end{cases}$

9. $\begin{cases} y = 3x - 7 \\ x = 2 \end{cases}$

10. $\begin{cases} x + 3y - z = 2 \\ x + 2z = 8 \\ 2y - z = 1 \end{cases}$

B) Apply Solve each matrix equation. If the coefficient matrix has no inverse, write *no unique solution.*

11. $\begin{bmatrix} 1 & 1 \\ 1 & 2 \end{bmatrix}\begin{bmatrix} x \\ y \end{bmatrix} = \begin{bmatrix} 8 \\ 10 \end{bmatrix}$

12. $\begin{bmatrix} 2 & -3 \\ -4 & 6 \end{bmatrix}\begin{bmatrix} a \\ b \end{bmatrix} = \begin{bmatrix} 1 \\ -2 \end{bmatrix}$

13. $\begin{bmatrix} 2 & 1 \\ 4 & 3 \end{bmatrix}\begin{bmatrix} x \\ y \end{bmatrix} = \begin{bmatrix} 10 \\ -2 \end{bmatrix}$

12-4
PART 2

Inverse Matrices and Systems

Objective To solve systems of equations using matrix inverses and multiplication

In Part 1 of the lesson, you learned how to represent a system of equations using a matrix equation.

Connect to What You Know

Here you will learn to solve a system of equations using a matrix equation and inverse matrices.

Focus Question How can you solve a system of equations using a related matrix equation?

If the coefficient matrix has an inverse, you can use it to find a unique solution to a system of equations.

In Part 1 of the lesson, you wrote the system of equations $\begin{cases} 2x + 3y = 1 \\ 5x - 2y = 13 \end{cases}$ as the matrix equation $AX = B$, or $\begin{bmatrix} 2 & 3 \\ 5 & -2 \end{bmatrix}\begin{bmatrix} x \\ y \end{bmatrix} = \begin{bmatrix} 1 \\ 13 \end{bmatrix}$. The determinant of the coefficient matrix, A, is $(2)(-2) - (3)(5) = -19 \neq 0$, so the system has a unique solution, $A^{-1}B$. To find it, first find A^{-1}.

$$A^{-1} = \frac{1}{\det A}\begin{bmatrix} -2 & -3 \\ -5 & 2 \end{bmatrix} = -\frac{1}{19}\begin{bmatrix} -2 & -3 \\ -5 & 2 \end{bmatrix} = \begin{bmatrix} \frac{2}{19} & \frac{3}{19} \\ \frac{5}{19} & -\frac{2}{19} \end{bmatrix}$$

Now find $A^{-1}B$.

$$X = A^{-1}B$$

$$\begin{bmatrix} x \\ y \end{bmatrix} = \begin{bmatrix} \frac{2}{19} & \frac{3}{19} \\ \frac{5}{19} & -\frac{2}{19} \end{bmatrix}\begin{bmatrix} 1 \\ 13 \end{bmatrix} = \begin{bmatrix} \frac{41}{19} \\ -\frac{21}{19} \end{bmatrix}$$

Hint

Always check your solutions in the original system of equations.

Check

Write the original equations.	$2x + 3y = 1$	$5x - 2y = 13$
Substitute.	$2\left(\frac{41}{19}\right) + 3\left(-\frac{21}{19}\right) \overset{?}{=} 1$	$5\left(\frac{41}{19}\right) - 2\left(-\frac{21}{19}\right) \overset{?}{=} 13$
Multiply.	$\frac{82}{19} - \frac{63}{19} \overset{?}{=} 1$	$\frac{205}{19} + \frac{42}{19} \overset{?}{=} 13$
Simplify.	$\frac{19}{19} = 1$ ✔	$\frac{247}{19} = 13$ ✔

So, the solution is $x = \frac{41}{19}$ and $y = -\frac{21}{19}$.

Problem 3 Solving a System of Two Equations

What is the solution of the system $\begin{cases} 5x - 4y = 4 \\ 3x - 2y = 3 \end{cases}$? Solve using matrices.

Think

Write the system as a matrix equation. Write the coefficient, variable, and constant matrices.

First, find A^{-1}.

Since det $A = 2$, A^{-1} exists.

Multiply each side of the matrix equation by A^{-1} on the left.

Solve for $\begin{bmatrix} x \\ y \end{bmatrix}$ and check.

Write

$$A \quad X = B$$

$$\begin{bmatrix} 5 & -4 \\ 3 & -2 \end{bmatrix} \begin{bmatrix} x \\ y \end{bmatrix} = \begin{bmatrix} 4 \\ 3 \end{bmatrix}$$

$$A^{-1} = \frac{1}{\det A} \begin{bmatrix} -2 & 4 \\ -3 & 5 \end{bmatrix}$$

$$= \frac{1}{(5)(-2) - (3)(-4)} \begin{bmatrix} -2 & 4 \\ -3 & 5 \end{bmatrix}$$

$$= \frac{1}{2} \begin{bmatrix} -2 & 4 \\ -3 & 5 \end{bmatrix}$$

$$= \begin{bmatrix} -1 & 2 \\ -\frac{3}{2} & \frac{5}{2} \end{bmatrix}$$

$$\begin{bmatrix} -1 & 2 \\ -\frac{3}{2} & \frac{5}{2} \end{bmatrix} \begin{bmatrix} 5 & -4 \\ 3 & -2 \end{bmatrix} \begin{bmatrix} x \\ y \end{bmatrix} = \begin{bmatrix} -1 & 2 \\ -\frac{3}{2} & \frac{5}{2} \end{bmatrix} \begin{bmatrix} 4 \\ 3 \end{bmatrix}$$

$$\begin{bmatrix} x \\ y \end{bmatrix} = \begin{bmatrix} (-1)(4) + (2)(3) \\ \left(-\frac{3}{2}\right)(4) + \left(\frac{5}{2}\right)(3) \end{bmatrix} = \begin{bmatrix} 2 \\ \frac{3}{2} \end{bmatrix}$$

The solution is $x = 2$, $y = \frac{3}{2}$.

$5(2) - 4\left(\frac{3}{2}\right) = 4$ ✔

$3(2) - 2\left(\frac{3}{2}\right) = 3$ ✔

 Got It? **3.** What is the solution of each system of equations? Solve using matrices.

a. $\begin{cases} 9x + 2y = 3 \\ 3x + y = -6 \end{cases}$

b. $\begin{cases} 4x - 6y = 9 \\ -10x + 15y = 8 \end{cases}$

Hint

The lines represented by this system are parallel.

The system $\begin{cases} -6x + 3y = 8 \\ 4x - 2y = 10 \end{cases}$ has coefficient matrix A with det $A = 0$. There is no inverse matrix and the system has no unique solution. Recall that this means the system either has no solutions (graphs represent parallel lines in the 2×2 case) or infinitely many solutions (graphs represent coinciding lines in the 2×2 case).

You can use a graphing calculator to solve a system of three equations.

 Problem 4 Solving a System of Three Equations

Multiple Choice On a new exercise program, your friend plans to do a run-jog-walk routine every other day for 40 min. She would like to burn 310 calories during each session. The table shows how many calories a person your friend's age and weight burns per minute of each type of exercise.

Calories Burned

Running (8 mi/h)	Jogging (5 mi/h)	Walking (3.5 mi/h)
12.5 cal/min	7.5 cal/min	3.5 cal/min

If your friend plans on jogging twice as long as she runs, how many minutes should she exercise at each rate?

Ⓐ run 10, jog 5, walk 25   Ⓒ run 5, jog 10, walk 25

Ⓑ run 30, jog 15, walk 5   Ⓓ run 10, jog 20, walk 10

Step 1 Define the variables.

Let x = number of minutes running.
Let y = number of minutes jogging.
Let z = number of minutes walking.

Think

How many equations do you need to solve this problem?
Since there are three variables you need three equations.

Step 2 Write a system of equations for the problem.

$$\begin{cases} 12.5x + 7.5y + 3.5z = 310 \\ x + y + z = 40 \\ 2x = y \end{cases} \rightarrow \begin{cases} 12.5x + 7.5y + 3.5z = 310 \\ x + y + z = 40 \\ 2x - y + 0z = 0 \end{cases}$$

Step 3 Write the system as a matrix equation.

$$\begin{bmatrix} 12.5 & 7.5 & 3.5 \\ 1 & 1 & 1 \\ 2 & -1 & 0 \end{bmatrix} \begin{bmatrix} x \\ y \\ z \end{bmatrix} = \begin{bmatrix} 310 \\ 40 \\ 0 \end{bmatrix}$$

Step 4 Use a calculator. Solve for the variable matrix.

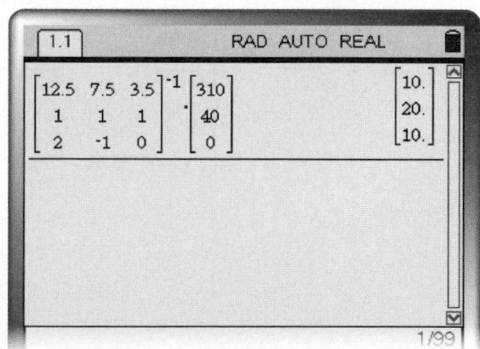

Step 5 Interpret the solution.

Your friend should run for 10 min, jog for 20 min, and walk for 10 min.

The correct answer is D.

 Got It? **4.** After following her exercise program from Problem 4 for a month, your friend plans to increase the calories she burns with each session. She still wants to exercise for 40 min every other day, but now she wants to burn 460 calories during each session. If she only runs and jogs, how many minutes of each exercise type should she do now?

Focus Question How can you solve a system of equations using a related matrix equation?

Answer You can solve a system of equations by first writing it as a matrix equation $AX = B$, where A is the coefficient matrix, X is the variable matrix, and B is the constant matrix. Then, find A^{-1} (if it exists) and compute $A^{-1}B$ to get the solution.

Lesson Check

Do you know HOW?

Solve each system using a matrix equation. Check your answer.

1. $\begin{cases} x + 2y = 11 \\ x + 4y = 17 \end{cases}$

2. $\begin{cases} 2x - 3y = 6 \\ x + y = -12 \end{cases}$

Do you UNDERSTAND?

3. Error Analysis A student is trying to use the matrix equation below to solve a system of equations. What error did the student make? What matrix equation should the student use?

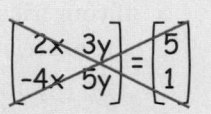

Practice and Problem-Solving Exercises

 **Practice**

See Problem 3.

Solve each system of equations using a matrix equation. Check your answers.

4. $\begin{cases} x + 3y = 5 \\ x + 4y = 6 \end{cases}$

Guided Practice To start, write the system as a matrix equation.

$$\begin{bmatrix} 1 & 3 \\ 1 & 4 \end{bmatrix}\begin{bmatrix} x \\ y \end{bmatrix} = \begin{bmatrix} 5 \\ 6 \end{bmatrix}$$

5. $\begin{cases} 300x - y = 130 \\ 200x + y = 120 \end{cases}$

6. $\begin{cases} x + 5y = -4 \\ x + 6y = -5 \end{cases}$

7. $\begin{cases} 2x + 3y = 12 \\ x + 2y = 7 \end{cases}$

8. $\begin{cases} 2x + 3y = 5 \\ x + 2y = 6 \end{cases}$

9. $\begin{cases} x + y + z = 4 \\ 4x + 5y = 3 \\ y - 3z = -10 \end{cases}$

10. $\begin{cases} 9y + 2z = 18 \\ 3x + 2y + z = 5 \\ x - y = -1 \end{cases}$

11. Fitness Your classmate is starting a new fitness program. He is planning to ride his bicycle 60 minutes every day. He burns 7 Calories per minute bicycling at 11 mph and 11.75 Calories per minute bicycling at 15 mph. How long should he bicycle at each speed to burn 600 calories per hour?

 See Problem 4.

 **Apply**

12. Think About a Plan Suppose you want to fill nine 1-lb tins with a snack mix. You plan to buy almonds for $2.45/lb, peanuts for $1.85/lb, and raisins for $.80/lb. You want the mix to contain twice as much nuts as raisins by weight. If you spend exactly $15, how much of each ingredient should you buy?
  • How many equations do you need to represent this situation?
  • How can you represent this system using a matrix equation?

13. Nutrition Suppose you are making a trail mix for your friends and want to fill three 1-lb bags. Almonds cost $2.25/lb, peanuts cost $1.30/lb, and raisins cost $.90/lb. You want each bag to contain twice as much nuts as raisins by weight. If you spent $4.45, how much of each ingredient did you buy?

Solve each system.

14. $\begin{cases} -3x + 4y = 2 \\ x - y = -1 \end{cases}$

15. $\begin{cases} x + 2y = 10 \\ 3x + 5y = 26 \end{cases}$

16. $\begin{cases} x = 5 - y \\ 3y = z \\ x + z = 7 \end{cases}$

17. $\begin{cases} -x = -4 - z \\ 2y = z - 1 \\ x = 6 - y - z \end{cases}$

18. $\begin{cases} x + y + z = 4 \\ 4x + 5y = 4 \\ y - 3z = -9 \end{cases}$

19. $\begin{cases} x + y + z = 4 \\ 4x + 5y = 3 \\ y - 3z = -10 \end{cases}$

20. Coordinate Geometry The coordinates (x, y) of a point in a plane are the solution of the system $\begin{cases} 2x + 3y = 13 \\ 5x + 7y = 31 \end{cases}$. Find the coordinates of the point.

21. Geometry A rectangle is twice as long as it is wide. The perimeter is 840 ft. Find the dimensions of the rectangle.

22. Reasoning Substitute each point, $(-3, 5)$ and $(2, -1)$, into the slope-intercept form of a linear equation to write a system of equations. Then use the system to find the equation of the line containing the two points. Explain your reasoning.

Solve each system using matrices. If the coefficient matrix has no inverse, write *no unique solution*.

23. $\begin{cases} 20x + 5y = 240 \\ y = 20x \end{cases}$

24. $\begin{cases} 20x + 5y = 145 \\ 30x - 5y = 125 \end{cases}$

25. $\begin{cases} y = 2000 - 65x \\ y = 500 + 55x \end{cases}$

26. $\begin{cases} y = \frac{2}{3}x - 3 \\ y = -x + 7 \end{cases}$

27. $\begin{cases} 3x + 2y = 10 \\ 6x + 4y = 16 \end{cases}$

28. $\begin{cases} x + 2y + z = 4 \\ y = x - 3 \\ z = 2x \end{cases}$

SAT/ACT

29. Which matrix equation represents the system $\begin{cases} 2x - 3y = -3 \\ -5x + y = 14 \end{cases}$?

Ⓐ $\begin{bmatrix} x \\ y \end{bmatrix} \begin{bmatrix} 2 & -3 \\ -5 & 1 \end{bmatrix} = \begin{bmatrix} -3 \\ 14 \end{bmatrix}$

Ⓒ $\begin{bmatrix} 2 & -3 \\ -5 & 1 \end{bmatrix} \begin{bmatrix} -3 \\ 14 \end{bmatrix} = \begin{bmatrix} x \\ y \end{bmatrix}$

Ⓑ $\begin{bmatrix} 2 & -3 \\ -5 & 1 \end{bmatrix} \begin{bmatrix} x \\ y \end{bmatrix} = \begin{bmatrix} -3 \\ 14 \end{bmatrix}$

Ⓓ $\begin{bmatrix} -3 \\ 14 \end{bmatrix} \begin{bmatrix} x & y \end{bmatrix} = \begin{bmatrix} 2 & -3 \\ -5 & 1 \end{bmatrix}$

30. What is the value of x if $17 \cdot 10^{4x} = 85$?

Ⓕ $\frac{5}{4}$

Ⓖ $\frac{\log 85}{17 \cdot \log 4}$

Ⓗ $\frac{\log 5}{4}$

Ⓘ $\frac{\log 85 - \log 17}{\log 4}$

31. A set of data is normally distributed with a mean of 44 and a standard deviation of 3.2. Which statements are NOT true?

  I. 68% of the values are between 37.6 and 50.4

  II. 13.5% of the values are less than 40.8

  III. 5% of the values are lower than 37.6 or higher than 50.4

Ⓐ I and II only

Ⓒ II and III only

Ⓑ I and III only

Ⓓ I, II, and III

Short Response

32. How can you write the three equations below as a matrix equation for a system? Explain your steps.

$$2x - 3y + z + 10 = 0$$
$$x + 4y = 2z + 11$$
$$-2y + 3z + 7 = 3x$$

Mixed Review

Evaluate the determinant of each matrix.

See Lesson 12-3.

33. $\begin{bmatrix} -1 & 3 & 7 \\ 5 & -4 & -2 \\ 0 & 2 & 10 \end{bmatrix}$

34. $\begin{bmatrix} 17 & 0 & 0 \\ 0 & 17 & 0 \\ 0 & 0 & 17 \end{bmatrix}$

35. $\begin{bmatrix} -3 & 0 & 5 \\ 5 & -3 & 2 \\ -3 & -5 & -2 \end{bmatrix}$

Find the mean, variance, and standard deviation for each data set.

See Lesson 11-6.

36. 29, 35, 44, 25, 36, 30, 40, 33, 38

37. 5.2, 6.0, 3.5, 4.4, 2.5, 3.0, 4.6

38. 14 m, 18 m, 22 m, 28 m, 15 m, 21 m

39. 71 mi, 60 mi, 82 mi, 30 mi, 44 mi

Get Ready! To prepare for Lesson T-1, do Exercises 40–42.

Solve each proportion.

See p. 867.

40. $\frac{x}{7} = \frac{28}{49}$

41. $\frac{10}{14} = \frac{15}{x}$

42. $\frac{21}{10} = \frac{x}{25}$

Pull It **All Together**

12

To solve these problems, you will pull together concepts and skills related to matrices.

BIG idea Data Representation

You can represent data in a variety of ways.

TASK 1

The first matrix represents inventory (how many there are) of four types of objects. The second matrix is a price matrix. The third matrix is the product of the first two matrices. Give an example of real inventory and real prices for which the product matrix makes sense. Explain the meaning of the product.

$$\begin{bmatrix} a_1 & a_2 \\ b_1 & b_2 \end{bmatrix} \begin{bmatrix} p_1 \\ p_2 \end{bmatrix} = \begin{bmatrix} r_1 \\ r_2 \end{bmatrix}$$

BIG idea Modeling

You can represent many real-world mathematical problems algebraically. These representations can lead to algebraic solutions.

TASK 2

Suppose the matrix equation $AX = B$ represents the system $\begin{cases} a_1x + a_2y = b_1 \\ a_3x + a_4y = b_2 \end{cases}$ and det $A = 0$. Show that the system has either infinitely many solutions or no solutions. (*Hint:* First show that a_3 and a_4 are proportional to a_1 and a_2.)

Connecting **BIG** ideas and Answering the Essential Questions

1 Data Representation
You can organize data in a matrix in exactly the same way that you organize data in a rectangular table.

Adding, Subtracting, and Multiplying Matrices (Lessons 12-1 and 12-2)
To add or subtract matrices, add or subtract corresponding elements.

To multiply two matrices:

$$\begin{bmatrix} a & b \\ c & d \end{bmatrix}\begin{bmatrix} e & f \\ g & h \end{bmatrix} = \begin{bmatrix} ae + bg & af + bh \\ ce + dg & cf + dh \end{bmatrix}$$

Inverse Matrices and Systems (Lesson 12-4)
The matrix equation $AX = B$ represents a system of linear equations.

  A is the coefficient matrix,
  X is the variable matrix,
  B is the constant matrix.

If det $A \neq 0$, then multiply each side by A^{-1} to find X.

$$A^{-1}AX = A^{-1}B$$
$$X = A^{-1}B$$

2 Modeling
If you can model a real-world situation with a system of equations, you can represent the system with a matrix equation.

Determinants and Inverses (Lesson 12-3)
Let A be an $n \times n$ matrix. If det $A \neq 0$, then A^{-1} exists and $AA^{-1} = A^{-1}A = I_n$ (the $n \times n$ identity matrix).

Chapter Vocabulary

- coefficient matrix (p. 801)
- constant matrix (p. 801)
- corresponding elements (p. 772)
- determinant (p. 790)
- equal matrices (p. 775)
- matrix equation (p. 773)
- multiplicative identity matrix (p. 789)
- multiplicative inverse matrix (p. 789)
- scalar (p. 781)
- scalar multiplication (p. 781)
- singular matrix (p. 795)
- square matrix (p. 789)
- variable matrix (p. 801)
- zero matrix (p. 775)

Choose the correct term to complete each sentence.

1. If corresponding elements of matrices are equal, the matrices are __?__.

2. The additive identity of a matrix is the __?__.

3. A(n) __?__ consists of a coefficient matrix, a variable matrix, and a constant matrix.

4. An $n \times n$ matrix is called a(n) __?__.

12-1 Adding and Subracting Matrices

Quick Review

To perform matrix addition or subtraction, add or subtract the **corresponding elements** in the matrices.

Two matrices are **equal matrices** when they have the same dimensions and corresponding elements are equal. This principle is used to solve a **matrix equation**.

Example

If $A = \begin{bmatrix} 2 & 1 & -2 \\ 1 & 4 & 3 \\ -2 & -1 & 5 \end{bmatrix}$ and $B = \begin{bmatrix} 1 & -2 & 4 \\ -3 & -2 & 1 \\ 0 & 0 & 5 \end{bmatrix}$,

what is $A + B$?

$A + B = \begin{bmatrix} 2+1 & 1+(-2) & -2+4 \\ 1+(-3) & 4+(-2) & 3+1 \\ -2+0 & -1+0 & 5+5 \end{bmatrix}$

$= \begin{bmatrix} 3 & -1 & 2 \\ -2 & 2 & 4 \\ -2 & -1 & 10 \end{bmatrix}$

Exercises

Find each sum or difference.

5. $\begin{bmatrix} 1 & 2 & -5 \\ 3 & -2 & 1 \end{bmatrix} + \begin{bmatrix} -2 & 7 & -3 \\ 1 & 2 & 5 \end{bmatrix}$

6. $\begin{bmatrix} 0 & 2 \\ -4 & -1 \end{bmatrix} - \begin{bmatrix} -5 & 6 \\ -9 & -1 \end{bmatrix}$

Solve each matrix equation.

7. $\begin{bmatrix} 2 & -6 & 8 \end{bmatrix} + \begin{bmatrix} -1 & -2 & 4 \end{bmatrix} = X$

8. $\begin{bmatrix} 7 & -1 \\ 0 & 8 \end{bmatrix} + X = \begin{bmatrix} 4 & 9 \\ -3 & 11 \end{bmatrix}$

Find the value of each variable.

9. $\begin{bmatrix} x-5 & 9 \\ 4 & t+2 \end{bmatrix} = \begin{bmatrix} -7 & w+1 \\ 8-r & 1 \end{bmatrix}$

10. $\begin{bmatrix} -4+t & 2y \\ r & w+5 \end{bmatrix} = \begin{bmatrix} 2t & 11 \\ -2r+12 & 9 \end{bmatrix}$

12-2 Matrix Multiplication

Quick Review

To obtain the product of a matrix and a **scalar**, multiply each matrix element by the scalar. Matrix multiplication uses both multiplication and addition. The element in the ith row and the jth column of the product of two matrices is the sum of the products of each element of the ith row of the first matrix and the corresponding element of the jth column of the second matrix. The first matrix must have the same number of columns as the second matrix has rows.

Example

If $A = \begin{bmatrix} 1 & -3 \\ -2 & 0 \end{bmatrix}$ and $B = \begin{bmatrix} 1 & 4 \\ 0 & 2 \end{bmatrix}$, what is AB?

$AB = \begin{bmatrix} (1)(1) + (-3)(0) & (1)(4) + (-3)(2) \\ (-2)(1) + (0)(0) & (-2)(4) + (0)(2) \end{bmatrix}$

$= \begin{bmatrix} 1 & -2 \\ -2 & -8 \end{bmatrix}$

Exercises

Use matrices A, B, C, and D to find each product, sum, or difference, if possible. If an operation is not defined, label it _undefined_.

$A = \begin{bmatrix} 6 & 1 & 0 & 8 \\ -4 & 3 & 7 & 11 \end{bmatrix}$ $\qquad B = \begin{bmatrix} 1 & 3 \\ -2 & 4 \end{bmatrix}$

$C = \begin{bmatrix} -2 & 1 \\ 4 & 0 \\ 2 & 2 \\ 1 & 1 \end{bmatrix}$ $\qquad D = \begin{bmatrix} 5 & -2 \\ 3 & 6 \end{bmatrix}$

11. $3A$ **12.** $B - 2A$

13. AB **14.** BA

15. $AC - BD$ **16.** $4B - 3D$

12-3 Determinants and Inverses

Quick Review

A **square matrix** with 1's along its main diagonal and 0's elsewhere is the **multiplicative identity matrix**, I. If A and X are square matrices such that $AX = I$, then X is the **multiplicative identity matrix** of A, A^{-1}.

You can use a calculator to find the inverse of a matrix. You can find the inverse of a 2×2 matrix

$A = \begin{bmatrix} a & b \\ c & d \end{bmatrix}$ by using its **determinant**.

$$A^{-1} = \frac{1}{\det A}\begin{bmatrix} d & -b \\ -c & a \end{bmatrix} = \frac{1}{ad - bc}\begin{bmatrix} d & -b \\ -c & a \end{bmatrix}$$

Example

What is the determinant of $\begin{bmatrix} 2 & -3 \\ 3 & -4 \end{bmatrix}$?

$$\det\begin{bmatrix} 2 & -3 \\ 3 & -4 \end{bmatrix} = (2)(-4) - (-3)(3)$$

$$= -8 - (-9) = 1$$

Exercises

Evaluate the determinant of each matrix and find the inverse, if possible.

17. $\begin{bmatrix} 6 & 1 \\ 0 & 4 \end{bmatrix}$

18. $\begin{bmatrix} 5 & -2 \\ 10 & -4 \end{bmatrix}$

19. $\begin{bmatrix} 10 & 1 \\ 8 & 5 \end{bmatrix}$

20. $\begin{bmatrix} 1 & 0 & 2 \\ -1 & 0 & 1 \\ -1 & -2 & 0 \end{bmatrix}$

12-4 Inverse Matrices and Systems

Quick Review

You can use inverse matrices to solve some matrix equations and systems of equations. When equations in a system are in standard form, the product of the **coefficient matrix** and the **variable matrix** equals the **constant matrix**. You solve the equation by multiplying both sides of the equation by the inverse of the coefficient matrix. If that inverse does not exist, the system does not have a unique solution.

Example

What is the matrix equation that corresponds to the following system? $\begin{cases} 2x - y = 12 \\ x + 4y = 15 \end{cases}$

Identify $A = \begin{bmatrix} 2 & -1 \\ 1 & 4 \end{bmatrix}$, $X = \begin{bmatrix} x \\ y \end{bmatrix}$, and $B = \begin{bmatrix} 12 \\ 15 \end{bmatrix}$.

The matrix equation is $AX = B$ or $\begin{bmatrix} 2 & -1 \\ 1 & 4 \end{bmatrix}\begin{bmatrix} x \\ y \end{bmatrix} = \begin{bmatrix} 12 \\ 15 \end{bmatrix}$.

Exercises

Use an inverse matrix to solve each equation or system.

21. $\begin{bmatrix} 3 & 5 \\ 6 & 2 \end{bmatrix} X = \begin{bmatrix} -2 & 6 \\ 4 & 12 \end{bmatrix}$

22. $\begin{cases} x - y = 3 \\ 2x - y = -1 \end{cases}$

23. $\begin{bmatrix} 4 & 1 \\ 2 & 1 \end{bmatrix}\begin{bmatrix} x \\ y \end{bmatrix} = \begin{bmatrix} 10 \\ 6 \end{bmatrix}$

24. $\begin{bmatrix} -6 & 0 \\ 7 & 1 \end{bmatrix} X = \begin{bmatrix} -12 & -6 \\ 17 & 9 \end{bmatrix}$

25. $\begin{cases} x + 2y = 15 \\ 2x + 4y = 30 \end{cases}$

26. $\begin{cases} a + 2b + c = 14 \\ b = c + 1 \\ a = -3c + 6 \end{cases}$

Do you know HOW?

Find each sum or difference.

1. $\begin{bmatrix} 4 & 7 \\ -2 & 1 \end{bmatrix} - \begin{bmatrix} -9 & 3 \\ 6 & 0 \end{bmatrix}$

2. $\begin{bmatrix} 4 & -5 & 1 \\ 10 & 7 & 4 \\ 21 & -9 & -6 \end{bmatrix} + \begin{bmatrix} -7 & -10 & 4 \\ 17 & 0 & 3 \\ -2 & -6 & 1 \end{bmatrix}$

Find each product.

3. $\begin{bmatrix} 2 & 6 \\ 1 & 0 \end{bmatrix}\begin{bmatrix} -1 & 5 \\ 3 & 1 \end{bmatrix}$

4. $2\begin{bmatrix} -8 & 5 & -1 \\ 0 & 9 & 7 \end{bmatrix}$

5. $\begin{bmatrix} 0 & 3 \\ -4 & 9 \end{bmatrix}\begin{bmatrix} -4 & 6 & 1 & 3 \\ 9 & -8 & 10 & 7 \end{bmatrix}$

Solve each equation for x and y.

6. $\begin{bmatrix} -3 + 2x & 2 \\ 4 & -7y \end{bmatrix} = \begin{bmatrix} x - 4 & 2 \\ 4 & -35 \end{bmatrix}$

7. $\begin{bmatrix} 2x & 3 \\ -3 & -7x + y \end{bmatrix} = \begin{bmatrix} 3x + 2 & 3 \\ -3 & -4x \end{bmatrix}$

Find the determinant of each matrix.

8. $\begin{bmatrix} 1 & 0 & 0 \\ 0 & 1 & 0 \\ 0 & 0 & 1 \end{bmatrix}$

9. $\begin{bmatrix} 2 & 3 & 0 \\ -1 & 1 & 0 \\ 4 & 2 & 1 \end{bmatrix}$

10. $\begin{bmatrix} 8 & -3 \\ 2 & 9 \end{bmatrix}$

11. $\begin{bmatrix} \frac{1}{2} & -3 \\ 1 & 0 \end{bmatrix}$

Find the inverse of each matrix, if it exists.

12. $\begin{bmatrix} 3 & 8 \\ -7 & 10 \end{bmatrix}$

13. $\begin{bmatrix} 0 & -5 \\ 9 & 6 \end{bmatrix}$

14. $\begin{bmatrix} 3 & 1 & 0 \\ 1 & -1 & 2 \\ 1 & 1 & 1 \end{bmatrix}$

15. $\begin{bmatrix} 1 & 1 & 2 \\ 2 & 1 & 3 \\ 2 & 1 & 1 \end{bmatrix}$

Solve each matrix equation.

16. $\begin{bmatrix} 3 & -8 \\ 10 & 5 \end{bmatrix} - X = \begin{bmatrix} 2 & 8 \\ -1 & 12 \end{bmatrix}$

17. $\begin{bmatrix} 3 & 2 \\ -1 & 5 \end{bmatrix}X = \begin{bmatrix} -10 & -11 \\ 26 & -36 \end{bmatrix}$

18. $2X - \begin{bmatrix} -2 & 0 \\ 1 & 4 \end{bmatrix} = \begin{bmatrix} 5 & 10 \\ -15 & 9 \end{bmatrix}$

Find the area of each triangle with the given vertices.

19. vertices at $(2, 3), (-3, -1), (0, 4)$

20. vertices at $(-2, -3), (5, 0), (-1, 4)$

Do you UNDERSTAND?

21. Open-Ended Write a matrix that has no inverse.

22. Writing Explain how to determine whether two matrices can be multiplied and what the dimensions of the product matrix will be.

23. Reasoning Suppose the product of two matrices has dimensions 4×3. If one of the matrices in the multiplication has dimensions 4×5, what are the dimensions of the other matrix?

24. Sales A store sells three kinds of pencils and the first matrix below shows the prices, in dollars, for each type. The second matrix shows the quantity sold for each type. Explain how you can find the total sales using the two matrices.

$$\begin{array}{c} \text{Type } A \quad B \quad C \\ [3 \quad 4 \quad 2] \end{array} \qquad \begin{array}{cc} & \text{Type} \\ \begin{array}{c} A \\ B \\ C \end{array} & \begin{bmatrix} 20 \\ 10 \\ 15 \end{bmatrix} \end{array}$$

25. Shopping A local store is having a special promotion where all movies sell at the same price and all video games sell at another. Suppose you buy 5 movies and 4 video games for $97.50 and your friend buys 3 movies and 6 video games for $103.50. Write a matrix equation to describe the purchases. Then solve the matrix equation to find the price of a movie and the price of a video game.

End-of-Course Assessment
to Prepare for the ADP Algebra 2 Test

This practice test is designed to help you prepare for the American Diploma Project (ADP) Algebra 2 Test.

Complete the following items *without* a calculator. For multiple choice items, write the letter of the correct response on your paper. For all other items, show or explain your work.

1. The graph of a quadratic function $f(x)$ is shown below.

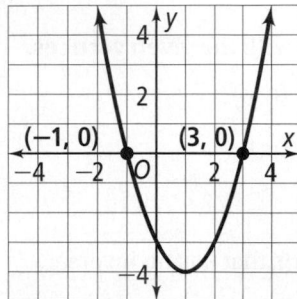

Use the graph to solve $f(x) < 0$.

  Ⓐ $-1 < x < 3$ Ⓒ $x < -1$ or $x > 3$

  Ⓑ $-1 \le x \le 3$ Ⓓ $x \le -1$ or $x > 3$

2. Newton's Law of Universal Gravitation is $F = \dfrac{Gm_1m_2}{r^2}$. Solve this equation for r.

  Ⓕ $r = \sqrt{\dfrac{F}{Gm_1m_2}}$ Ⓗ $r = \dfrac{F}{2Gm_1m_2}$

  Ⓖ $r = \sqrt{\dfrac{Gm_1m_2}{F}}$ Ⓘ $r = \dfrac{Gm_1m_2}{2F}$

3. Let $f(x) = x^3 - 4x^2 + 9x$ and let $g(x) = 6x^3 + x^2 - 5x - 12$. What is $f(x) - g(x)$?

  Ⓐ $-5x^3 - 5x^2 + 14x + 12$

  Ⓑ $-5x^3 - 3x^2 + 4x - 12$

  Ⓒ $7x^3 - 3x^2 + 4x - 12$

  Ⓓ $-5x^4 - 5x^3 + 14x^2 + 12x$

4. Let $f(x) = x - 3$ and let $g(x) = 2x^2 - 6$. What is $g(f(x))$?

  Ⓕ $2x^2 - 9$ Ⓗ $2x^2 - 12x + 12$

  Ⓖ $2x^2 - 12$ Ⓘ $2x^3 - 6x^2 - 6x + 18$

5. Let $f^{-1}(x) = 2x + 3$. What is the solution of $f(x) = f^{-1}(x)$?

  Ⓐ $x = -1$ or $x = -2$ Ⓒ $(x, y) = (-1, -2)$

  Ⓑ $x = -3$ Ⓓ $(x, y) = (-3, -3)$

6. Which is a simpler form of $\dfrac{\sqrt{5}}{3 - \sqrt{2}}$?

  Ⓕ $\dfrac{\sqrt{10}}{3\sqrt{2} - 2}$ Ⓗ $\dfrac{3\sqrt{5} - \sqrt{10}}{7}$

  Ⓖ $\dfrac{5}{3\sqrt{5} - 10}$ Ⓘ $\dfrac{3\sqrt{5} + \sqrt{10}}{7}$

7. Suppose that $\sqrt[4]{n} = 2$. What is $n^{-\frac{1}{2}}$?

  Ⓐ -8 Ⓒ $\dfrac{1}{8}$

  Ⓑ -4 Ⓓ $\dfrac{1}{4}$

8. What is the quotient $\dfrac{2 + 5i}{4 + 3i}$ written in standard form?

  Ⓕ $\dfrac{1}{2} + \dfrac{5}{3}i$ Ⓗ $-\dfrac{7}{7} + \dfrac{26}{7}i$

  Ⓖ $\dfrac{8}{25} - \dfrac{12}{25}i$ Ⓘ $\dfrac{23}{25} + \dfrac{14}{25}i$

9. Multiply $\dfrac{x^3}{x^2 - 4} \cdot \dfrac{5x + 10}{10x}$.

  Ⓐ $\dfrac{5x}{4}$ Ⓒ $\dfrac{x^2}{2(x + 2)}$

  Ⓑ $\dfrac{x^2}{2(x - 2)}$ Ⓓ $\dfrac{5^3}{10(x - 2)}$

10. Which is a simpler form of the complex fraction $\dfrac{\frac{1}{b} + c}{b + \frac{1}{c}}$?

  Ⓕ 1 Ⓗ $\left(\dfrac{1}{b} + c\right)^2$

  Ⓖ $\dfrac{c}{b}$ Ⓘ $(1 + c)(b + 1)$

11. What is the sum of the x-intercepts of the graph of the quadratic function $y = x^2 - 4x - 12$?

  Ⓐ 6 Ⓒ -1

  Ⓑ 4 Ⓓ -4

12. What is an equation of a parabola with the following characteristics?

Axis of symmetry: $x = -3$

Range: all real numbers less than or equal to 4

- Ⓕ $y = -(x - 4)^2 - 3$
- Ⓖ $y = (x - 4)^2 - 3$
- Ⓗ $y = -(x + 3)^2 + 4$
- Ⓘ $y = (x + 3)^2 + 4$

13. The graph of a degree 4 polynomial function with integer zeros is shown below.

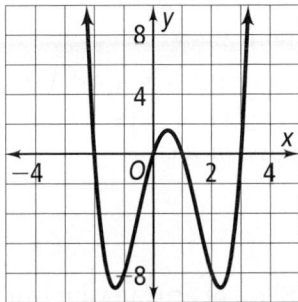

What is the equation of the polynomial function?

- Ⓐ $y = x^4 - 6x^3 + 11x^2 - 6x$
- Ⓑ $y = x^4 - 2x^3 - 5x^2 + 6x$
- Ⓒ $y = x^4 - 2x^3 + x^2 + 3x$
- Ⓓ $y = x^4 + 2x^3 - 5x^2 - 6x$

14. Which function is best represented by the graph below?

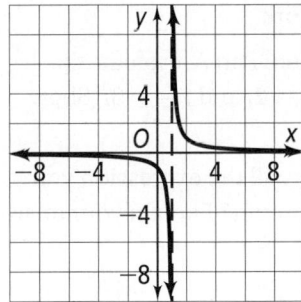

- Ⓕ $y = \dfrac{1}{x - 1}$
- Ⓗ $y = \dfrac{x}{x - 1}$
- Ⓖ $y = \dfrac{1}{x + 1}$
- Ⓘ $y = \dfrac{x}{x + 1}$

15. How many distinct real roots does the equation $x^4 + 3x^3 - 4x = 0$ have?

- Ⓐ 1
- Ⓒ 3
- Ⓑ 2
- Ⓓ 4

16. Which function best represents the graph?

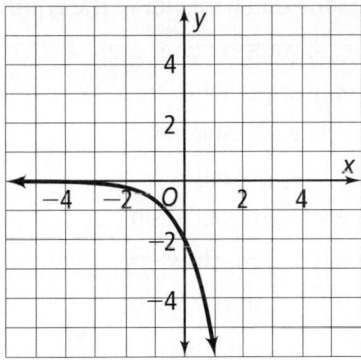

- Ⓕ $f(x) = 2 \cdot 3^{-x}$
- Ⓖ $f(x) = -2 \cdot 3^x$
- Ⓗ $f(x) = 2 \cdot 3^x$
- Ⓘ $f(x) = -2 \cdot 3^{-x}$

17. Which system is represented by the graph below?

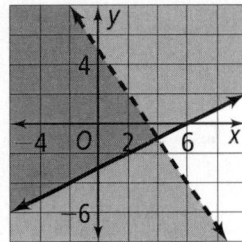

- Ⓐ $\begin{cases} 2y + 6 \geq x \\ y < -\frac{3}{2}x + 5 \end{cases}$
- Ⓒ $\begin{cases} 2y - 6 \geq x \\ y < -\frac{3}{2}x + 5 \end{cases}$
- Ⓑ $\begin{cases} 2y + 6 \geq x \\ y > -\frac{3}{2}x + 5 \end{cases}$
- Ⓓ $\begin{cases} 2y + 6 \geq x \\ -y < \frac{3}{2}x + 5 \end{cases}$

18. The graph of a rational function is shown below.

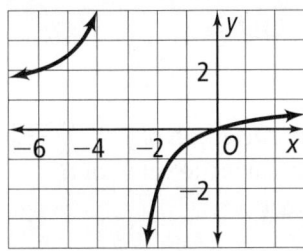

Which function best represents the graph?

- Ⓕ $f(x) = \dfrac{3}{x - 1}$
- Ⓗ $f(x) = \dfrac{3x}{x - 1}$
- Ⓖ $f(x) = \dfrac{1}{x + 3}$
- Ⓘ $f(x) = \dfrac{x}{x + 3}$

19. Consider the exponential function $f(x) = ab^x$. If $a < 0$ and $0 < b < 1$, what is the end behavior of the graph?

Ⓐ as x approaches $-\infty$, y approaches $-\infty$
as x approaches ∞, y approaches 0

Ⓑ as x approaches $-\infty$, y approaches ∞
as x approaches ∞, y approaches 0

Ⓒ as x approaches $-\infty$, y approaches 0
as x approaches ∞, y approaches $-\infty$

Ⓓ as x approaches $-\infty$, y approaches 0
as x approaches ∞, y approaches ∞

20. If $f(x) = (x + 2)^2 - 1$, restrict the domain of f so that its inverse is also a function.

Ⓕ $x \geq -2$ Ⓗ $x \geq 0$
Ⓖ $x \geq -1$ Ⓘ $x \geq 2$

21. Solve $\frac{3}{2x + 10} + \frac{5}{4} = \frac{7}{x + 5}$ for x.

Ⓐ $-\frac{50}{11}$ Ⓒ $-\frac{9}{5}$
Ⓑ $-\frac{34}{10}$ Ⓓ $-\frac{3}{5}$

22. Solve $\sqrt{x - 2} - 7 = -4$ for x.

Ⓕ 5   Ⓗ 18
Ⓖ 11   Ⓘ 25

23. What is the value of x if $\sqrt[5]{b^3} = b^x$?

Ⓐ $\frac{3}{5}$ Ⓒ 3
Ⓑ $\frac{5}{3}$ Ⓓ 15

24. What is the x-coordinate of the vertex of the graph of $f(x) = 2x^2 + 4x - 6$?

Ⓕ -6 Ⓗ 1
Ⓖ -1 Ⓘ 4

25. The horizontal asymptote of the graph of $y = \frac{4x - 4}{2x - 6}$ is $y = t$ for a real number t. What is the value of t?

Ⓐ 1   Ⓒ 3
Ⓑ 2   Ⓓ 4

26. Graph $f(x) = |2x + 6| - 1$.

27. The graph of $y = x^2$ is shown below.

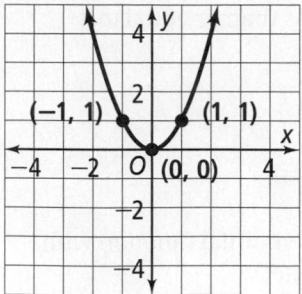

Use transformations to graph $y = -x^2 - 3$.

28. Consider the graph of the function $f(x) = 2(4)^x$. Explain how the graph of the function $g(x) = -2(4)^x + 3$ can be obtained from the graph of $f(x)$.

29. Let $f(x) = \frac{4}{x - 1}$.

Part A: Determine $f^{-1}(x)$. Show or explain your work.

Part B: Find $f(f^{-1}(x))$ and $f^{-1}(f(x))$. Show your work.

Part C: How are the domain and range of f and f^{-1} related?

30. Consider this expression: $\left(\frac{r^{3m}}{r^{-m}t^{4n}}\right)^{\frac{1}{n}} \cdot \left(\frac{r^{\frac{1}{n}}}{t^{\frac{2}{m}}}\right)^{-m}$

Part A: Simplify the expression so that r and t are only written once. Show your work.

Part B: Using your answer from Part A, evaluate the expression when $m = 1$, $n = 2$, and $t = -3i$. Show your work.

Part C: For what values of r will the expression you found in Part B be a real number? Explain your answer.

You may use a calculator with the following items. For multiple choice items, write the letter of the correct response on your paper. For all other items, show or explain your work.

31. Solve $|x + 2| \geq 5$.

  (A) $x \geq 3$ (C) $x \leq 3$ or $x \geq 7$

  (B) $-7 \leq x \leq 3$ (D) $x \leq -7$ or $x \geq 3$

32. Which equation shows an inverse variation?

  (F) $y = 5x$ (H) $6 = \frac{x}{y}$

  (G) $xy - 4 = 0$ (I) $y = -4$

33. What are all the complex solutions of $x^2 - 4x = -5$?

  (A) $-1, 5$

  (B) $1, 3$

  (C) $2 + i, 2 - i$

  (D) $2 + 3i, 2 - 3i$

34. The length of a rectangle is $2x^2 - 4x + 1$. The width is $3x - 5$. Which polynomial represents the area of the rectangle?

  (F) $6x^3 + 22x^2 + 23x + 5$

  (G) $6x^3 - 22x^2 + 23x - 5$

  (H) $3x^3 - 11x^2 + 11.5x - 2.5$

  (I) $2x^2 - x - 4$

35. Simplify $\dfrac{r^{\frac{1}{2}}}{r^{-\frac{1}{4}}}$.

  (A) $-r^{\frac{1}{4}}$ (C) $r^{\frac{1}{8}}$

  (B) $-r^2$ (D) $r^{\frac{3}{4}}$

36. The graph of a quadratic function, $y = ax^2 + bx + c$ passes through the points shown. What is the axis of symmetry of the parabola?

  (F) $x = -2$

  (G) $x = -1$

  (H) $x = 1$

  (I) $x = 2$

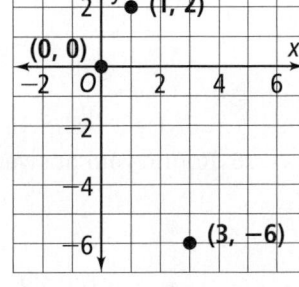

37. What is the end behavior of the graph of the polynomial function $f(x) = -2x^5 + x^4 + 3x^3 - x + 1$?

  (A) down and down

  (B) down and up

  (C) up and down

  (D) up and up

38. $500 is invested in an account with 1.5% interest compounded continuously. The equation $A(x) = 500(1.015)^x$ can be used to find the balance in the account after x years. To the nearest year, in how many years will the account have a balance of $817?

  (F) 2 years   (H) 72 years

  (G) 33 years   (I) 109 years

39. The graph of the exponential equation $y = 2^x$ is reflected in the x-axis and translated down 1 unit. What is the equation of the resulting graph?

  (A) $y = 2^{-x-1}$

  (B) $y = -2^{x-1}$

  (C) $y = 2^{-x} - 1$

  (D) $y = -2^x - 1$

40. The function $C(x) = \dfrac{10}{2x^2 + 1}$ can be used to find the concentration $C(x)$ in mg/L of a certain drug in the bloodstream of a patient x hours after an injection. In approximately how many hours after an injection will the concentration of the drug be 1.3 mg/L?

  (F) 0.5 h   (H) 1.8 h

  (G) 0.7 h   (I) 2.3 h

41. The half-life of radium-226 is about 1600 years. After 4000 years what percentage of a sample of radium-226 remains?

  (A) 2.5%   (C) 40.0%

  (B) 17.7%   (D) 75.8%

42. Solve $8.2(3^{2x-4}) - 11 = 557.1$. Round your answer to the nearest tenth.

  (F) 1.8   (H) 3.5

  (G) 2.9   (I) 3.9

43. An exponential function is represented in the table below.

x	f(x)
−2	12
−1	6
0	3
1	1.5

Which equation best represents the function?

- Ⓐ $f(x) = 3(2^{-x})$
- Ⓒ $f(x) = 2^{-x} + 3$
- Ⓑ $f(x) = 3(2^x)$
- Ⓓ $f(x) = 2^x + 3$

44. What is the range of the graph of $f(x) = -ab^x$ if $a > 0$ and $b > 1$?

- Ⓕ $f(x) \le 0$
- Ⓗ $f(x) \ge a$
- Ⓖ $f(x) \le a$
- Ⓘ All real numbers

45. The characteristics of function $f(x) = ax^n$ are shown below.

Domain: All real numbers

Range: $f(x) \le 0$

Symmetric with respect to the y-axis

What must be true about the values of a and n?

- Ⓐ $a < 0$ and n is even
- Ⓒ $a > 0$ and n is even
- Ⓑ $a < 0$ and n is odd
- Ⓓ $a > 0$ and n is odd

46. A train leaves a city traveling due north. A car leaves the city at the same time traveling due west. The car is traveling 15 mi/h faster than the train. After 2 h they are approximately 150 mi apart. What is the speed of the train?

- Ⓕ 30 mi/h
- Ⓗ 60 mi/h
- Ⓖ 45 mi/h
- Ⓘ 75 mi/h

47. A high school sold 800 tickets for a soccer game. Three types of tickets were sold: adult, student, and child. There were four times as many adult tickets sold as child tickets, and there were 62 more student tickets sold than adult tickets. How many adult tickets were sold?

- Ⓐ 82
- Ⓒ 328
- Ⓑ 123
- Ⓓ 384

48. The equation $x^2 - 0.8x + c = 0$ has one real solution. Use the discriminant to find the value of c.

- Ⓕ 0.4
- Ⓖ 0.8
- Ⓗ 0.12
- Ⓘ 0.16

49. Let $f(x) = 3x + 5$ and let $g(x) = x^2 + 2x$. What is $f(-3) \cdot g(-3)$?

- Ⓐ −32
- Ⓑ −12
- Ⓒ 9
- Ⓓ 60

50. The volume of a square pyramid with a height equal to four less than the length of a side of the base is given by $V(x) = \frac{1}{3}(x^3 + 8x^2 + 16x)$ where x is the height in cm. If the length of a side of the base is 9 cm, what is the volume of the pyramid?

- Ⓕ 135 cm³
- Ⓗ 507 cm³
- Ⓖ 405 cm³
- Ⓘ 1521 cm³

51. A quadratic function is represented in the table below.

x	f(x)
1	−13
2	−3
3	3
4	5
5	3

Which equation best represents the function?

- Ⓐ $f(x) = -2(x - 4)^2 + 5$
- Ⓑ $f(x) = -2(x - 3)^2 + 3$
- Ⓒ $f(x) = 2(x - 4)^2 + 5$
- Ⓓ $f(x) = 2(x - 3)^2 + 3$

52. Find the x-value of the solution to the following system of equations.

$$\begin{cases} 3x + y = -3 \\ 2y - z = 6 \\ x + y - 2z = 1 \end{cases}$$

- Ⓕ −2
- Ⓗ $\frac{3}{5}$
- Ⓖ −1
- Ⓘ 3

53. Solve: $4(3^x) = 26$. Round your answer to the nearest tenth.

- Ⓐ 0.3
- Ⓒ 1.7
- Ⓑ 1.3
- Ⓓ 2.2

54. The amount of cesium-137 remaining after x years in an initial sample of 200 milligrams can be found using the equation $C(x) = 200e^{-0.02295x}$. In approximately how many years will the sample contain 120 milligrams of cesium-137?

   F 13   **G** 22   **H** 26   **I** 39

55. Graph the solution set of the following system of inequalities.

$$\begin{cases} x - 3y \leq 6 \\ 2x + y > 5 \end{cases}$$

56. Simplify the expression below. Show your work.

$$\sqrt{16x^2 + 48x + 36}$$

57. What is the vertex of the graph of $f(x) = a|bx - 1| + c$? Explain your answer.

58. Find the solution set for $x^2 - 4 > 0$.

59. A company produces two types of doghouses, regular and deluxe. A regular doghouse requires 7 hours to build and 3 hours to paint. A deluxe doghouse requires 11 hours to build and 4 hours to paint. The company employs 5 builders and 2 painters. Each employee can work a maximum of 40 hours.

Part A: Write a system of inequalities that can be used to find the number of each type of doghouse built in a week. Define the variables you use in your system.

Part B: Graph the solution set of your system of inequalities from Part A. Label each line in your graph.

Part C: How many of each type of doghouse can be built in one week if each employee works exactly 40 hours? Show your work.

60. Consider the function $f(x) = \frac{1}{x}$.

Part A: Graph $f(x)$.

Part B: Explain how the graph of $g(x) = \frac{4}{x + 2}$ compares to the graph of $f(x)$.

Part C: What is the horizontal asymptote (if any) of the graph of $g(x)$?

Part D: What is the vertical asymptote of the graph of $g(x)$? Explain how this relates to the domain of $g(x)$.

The following items cover topics from the ADP modules: Data and Statistics, Probability, Logarithmic Functions, Matrices, Conic Sections, and Sequences and Series.

You may use a calculator with these items.

61. Consider the recursive model shown below.

$$\begin{cases} a_1 = 5 \\ a_{n+1} = a_n - 7 \end{cases}$$

What is an explicit formula for this sequence?

   A $a_n = 5 + 7(n - 1)$

   B $a_n = 5n - 7(n - 1)$

   C $a_n = -7 + 5(n - 1)$

   D $a_n = 5 - 7(n - 1)$

62. An arch in the shape of the upper half of an ellipse supports a bridge that spans a distance of 80 ft. The maximum height of the arch is 30 ft. To the nearest tenth of a foot, what is the height of the arch 28 ft from the center of the ellipse?

   F 14.4 ft   **H** 28.1 ft

   G 21.4 ft   **I** 29.7 ft

63. A scientist wants to study the effects of a new medication on acne. Which type of study would give the most reliable results?

   A Controlled experiment

   B Observational study

   C Survey

   D Random sample

64. Suppose scores on an entry exam are normally distributed. The exam has a mean score of 140 and a standard deviation of 20. What is the probability that a person who takes the test will score between 120 and 160?

   F 14%   **H** 68%

   G 40%   **I** 95%

65. If $\log_b 4 \approx 1.2$ and $\log_b 5 \approx 1.4$, what is the approximate value of $\log_b 80$?

   A 2.3   **C** 3.8

   B 2.6   **D** 4.0

66. Which parabola has focus $(3, 0)$ and directrix $x = -3$?

- F $y = \frac{1}{12}x^2$
- H $y = -\frac{1}{3}x^2$
- G $x = \frac{1}{12}y^2$
- I $x = \frac{1}{3}y^2$

67. What is the determinant of the matrix below?

$$\begin{bmatrix} 1 & 3 & -1 \\ 1 & 2 & 1 \\ -2 & -5 & -4 \end{bmatrix}$$

- A -8
- C 0
- B -4
- D 4

68. Write the expression below as a single logarithm.

$4 \log_3 x + \log_3 y - 2 \log_3 z$

- F $\log_3 \dfrac{x^4 y}{z^2}$
- H $\log_3 (4x + y - 2z)$
- G $\dfrac{\log_3 x^4 y}{\log_3 z^2}$
- I $\log_3 (x^4 + y - z^2)$

69. A computer manufacturing company sampled two different parts and tested for defects. The results are shown in the table below.

	Part A	Part B
Defective	14	33
Not defective	266	312

What is the probability that if a Part B is randomly chosen, it is defective?

- A 5.28%
- C 9.57%
- B 5.71%
- D 10.58%

70. Which equation represents a circle with center $(-3, 8)$ and radius 12?

- F $(x - 8)^2 + (y + 3)^2 = 144$
- G $(x - 8)^2 - (y + 3)^2 = 144$
- H $(x + 3)^2 + (y - 8)^2 = 144$
- I $(x - 3)^2 - (y - 8)^2 = 144$

71. Which of the following numbers is an outlier for the given data set?

3, 7, 19, 2, 6, 8, 5, 8

- A 6.5
- B 8
- C 16
- D 19

72. What is the 30th term of the sequence
7, 16, 25, 34, . . . ?

- F 261
- H 270
- G 268
- I 277

73. Which is the best indicator of the accuracy of a line of best fit?

- A The y-intercept of the line of best fit
- B The number of points below the line of best fit
- C The distance of the points from the line of best fit
- D The absolute value of the slope of the line of best fit

74. A fair coin is tossed 4 times. What is the probability that it lands heads up at least 3 times?

- F 18.75%
- G 25%
- H 31.25%
- I 75%

75. An employee's initial salary is \$30,000. The person receives a 5% raise at the end of each year. What is the formula for the term s_n which represents the salary at the beginning of the nth year?

- A $s_n = 30,000 + 1.05n$
- B $s_n = 30,000 + 5(n - 1)$
- C $s_n = 30,000(1.05)^{n-1}$
- D $s_n = 30,000(1.05)^n$

76. Use the Change of Base Formula to approximate the value of $\log_2 3.2$ to the nearest tenth.

- F 0.2
- G 0.8
- H 1.7
- I 9.2

77. If $B = \begin{bmatrix} -2 & 1 \\ 4 & -1 \end{bmatrix}$, what is B^{-1}?

- A $\begin{bmatrix} -0.5 & 1 \\ 0.25 & -1 \end{bmatrix}$
- C $\begin{bmatrix} 2 & -1 \\ -4 & 1 \end{bmatrix}$
- B $\begin{bmatrix} 0.5 & 0.5 \\ 2 & 1 \end{bmatrix}$
- D $\begin{bmatrix} 4 & -1 \\ -2 & 1 \end{bmatrix}$

78. A multiple choice test has 8 questions with 4 options per question. What is the probability of getting exactly 3 answers correct by guessing?

- F 0.00371
- H 0.21875
- G 0.20764
- I 0.37500

79. The magnitude M of an earthquake can be found using the equation $M(x) = \log\left(\frac{x}{0.001}\right)$ where x represents the seismograph reading of the earthquake in mm. An earthquake has a magnitude of 6.2. What is the seismograph reading of the earthquake in mm?

(A) 0.0062   (B) 0.0008   (C) 1.014   (D) 1584.9

80. A teacher's grading scale is shown below:

Item	Percent of Total Grade
Homework	5%
Quizzes	10%
Tests 1, 2, 3	20% each
Final Exam	25%

Sally's grade in the class was an 88. She earned a 97 on homework, 95 on quizzes, 85 on Test 1, 79 on Test 2 and 93 on Test 3. What was Sally's Final Exam grade?

(F) 22   (G) 66   (H) 79   (I) 89

81. There are 15 runners in a semifinal race where the top three runners advance to the finals. In how many ways can three runners advance?

(A) 6   (B) 455   (C) 910   (D) 2730

82. The first term of a finite arithmetic series is 123. The common difference is 12 and the sum is 1539. How many terms are in the series?

(F) 7   (G) 8   (H) 9   (I) 10

83. Multiply $\begin{bmatrix} 4 & -1 \\ 0 & 5 \end{bmatrix} \cdot \begin{bmatrix} 1 & 3 \\ -6 & 1 \end{bmatrix}$

(A) $\begin{bmatrix} 4 & 14 \\ -24 & 11 \end{bmatrix}$ (C) $\begin{bmatrix} 10 & -30 \\ 11 & 5 \end{bmatrix}$

(B) $\begin{bmatrix} 4 & -3 \\ 0 & 5 \end{bmatrix}$ (D) $\begin{bmatrix} 10 & 11 \\ -30 & 5 \end{bmatrix}$

84. Consider the data set: 15, 20, 25, 25, 35, 60, 65.

Part A: Find the mean, median, and mode.

Part B: Find the range and interquartile range.

Part C: Make a box-and-whisker plot for the data.

85. Solve for x to the nearest hundredth. Show or explain your work.

$2 \log 4x + 5 = 8$

86. A pendulum initially swings through an arc that is 20 inches long. On each swing, the length of the arc is 0.85 of the previous swing.

Part A: Write a recursive model of geometric decay to represent the sequence of lengths of the arc of each swing. Let $p_1 = 20$.

Part B: Rewrite your model from Part A using an explicit formula.

Part C: What is the approximate total distance the pendulum swings after 11 swings? Show your work.

Part D: What is the total distance, approximately, that the pendulum has swung when it stops? Show your work.

87. A dietician wants to prepare a meal with 24 g of protein, 27 g of fat, and 20 g of carbohydrates using the three foods shown in the table.

Food	Protein	Fat	Carbohydrates
A	2 g/oz	3 g/oz	4 g/oz
B	3 g/oz	3 g/oz	1 g/oz
C	3 g/oz	3 g/oz	2 g/oz

Part A: Set up a matrix equation for the data.

Part B: Solve the matrix equation.

Part C: How many ounces of each food are needed? Show your work or explain your answer.

88. Consider the following system of equations.

$$\begin{cases} x + 2z = -1 \\ y - 2z = 2 \\ 2x + y + z = 1 \end{cases}$$

Part A: Represent the system of equations using the matrix equation $AX = B$.

Part B: Find the determinant of the matrix A.

Part C: Solve the equation from Part A. If it cannot be solved, use your result from Part B to explain why.

89. An ellipse centered at the origin has a horizontal major axis of length 4 and a vertical minor axis of length 2.

Part A: What is the equation of the ellipse in standard form?

Part B: Identify the foci of the ellipse.

Part C: Explain how to use your work from Parts A and B to find the equation and foci of the ellipse centered at the origin with a vertical major axis of length 4 and horizontal minor axis of length 2.

Trigonometry Concepts

Sometimes you can't measure things using a ruler or tape measure. Maybe you want to measure the distance across a lake or the height of a building. In this section you will use trigonometric ratios to solve measurement problems.

Table of Contents

BIG ideas

1 Function
Essential Question If you know the value of sin θ, how can you find the values of the other trigonometric ratios?

2 Modeling
Essential Question How can you model periodic behavior?

3 Equivalence
Essential Question How do you verify that a trigonometric equation is an identity?

T-1 Right Triangles and Trigonometric Ratios

Objective To find lengths of sides in a right triangle
To find measures of angles in a right triangle

Lesson Vocabulary
• trigonometric ratios

You can use *trigonometric ratios* to relate angle measures to the lengths of certain line segments. You can then use these relationships to solve algebraic equations.

Focus Question What are the trigonometric ratios of a right triangle?

The **trigonometric ratios** for a right triangle are the six different ratios of the sides of a right triangle. These ratios do not depend on the size of the right triangle. They depend only on the measures of the acute angles in the triangle.

take note

Key Concept   Trigonometric Ratios for a Right Triangle

If θ is an acute angle of a right triangle, x is the length of the adjacent leg, y is the length of the opposite leg, and r is the length of the hypotenuse, then the trigonometric ratios of θ are as follows.

$$\text{sine } \theta = \frac{\text{opposite}}{\text{hypotenuse}} \qquad \text{cosecant } \theta = \frac{\text{hypotenuse}}{\text{opposite}}$$

$$\text{cosine } \theta = \frac{\text{adjacent}}{\text{hypotenuse}} \qquad \text{secant } \theta = \frac{\text{hypotenuse}}{\text{adjacent}}$$

$$\text{tangent } \theta = \frac{\text{opposite}}{\text{adjacent}} \qquad \text{cotangent } \theta = \frac{\text{adjacent}}{\text{opposite}}$$

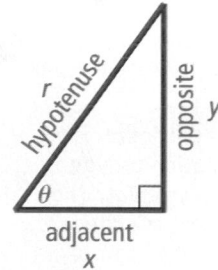

Hint

Notice that the ratios in the second column are the <u>reciprocals</u> of the ratios in the first column.

Using the side lengths from the right triangle above, you can write the trigonometric ratios as follows. (The abbreviation of each ratio is given.)

$$\text{sine } \theta \rightarrow \sin \theta = \frac{y}{r} \qquad \text{cosecant } \theta \rightarrow \csc \theta = \frac{r}{y}$$

$$\text{cosine } \theta \rightarrow \cos \theta = \frac{x}{r} \qquad \text{secant } \theta \rightarrow \sec \theta = \frac{r}{x}$$

$$\text{tangent } \theta \rightarrow \tan \theta = \frac{y}{x} \qquad \text{cotangent } \theta \rightarrow \cot \theta = \frac{x}{y}$$

Hint

For a right triangle, these ratios are defined for <u>both</u> acute angles, in terms of their respective opposite and adjacent sides.

Problem 1 Identifying Trigonometric Ratios

Right triangle *XYZ* is shown.
What is the value of each trigonometric ratio?

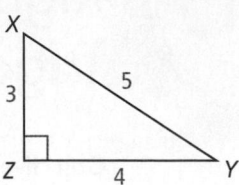

Ⓐ sin *X*

Look at the relationships in the diagram.

Think

How is the leg adjacent to ∠*Y* related to ∠*X*?
The leg adjacent to ∠*Y* is the same as the leg opposite ∠*X*.

Use the definition of sin *X* and substitute.

$$\sin X = \frac{\text{length of leg opposite } \angle X}{\text{length of hypotenuse}} = \frac{4}{5}$$

Ⓑ sec *Y*

$$\sec Y = \frac{\text{length of hypotenuse}}{\text{length of leg adjacent to } \angle Y} = \frac{5}{4}$$

Ⓒ cot *Y*

$$\cot Y = \frac{\text{length of leg adjacent to } \angle Y}{\text{length of leg opposite } \angle Y} = \frac{4}{3}$$

 Got It? **1.** For right triangle *XYZ* from Problem 1, what is the value of each trigonometric ratio?

  a. cos *Y* **b.** csc *Y* **c.** tan *X*

In right triangle trigonometry, the value of one trigonometric ratio determines the values of the others.

 Problem 2 Finding Trigonometric Ratios

Think

What additional information do you need to calculate the trigonometric ratios?
You need the length of the third side.

In $\triangle ABC$, $\angle C$ is a right angle and $\sin A = \frac{5}{13}$. What are cos *A*, cot *A*, and sin *B*?

Step 1 Draw a diagram to display the known information.

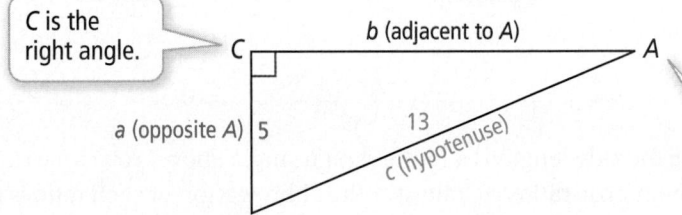

C is the right angle.

Since $\sin A = \frac{5}{13}$, use $\sin A = \frac{\text{opposite } A}{\text{hypotenuse}}$ to label known side lengths.

Step 2 Find the missing side length.

Write the Pythagorean Theorem.	$c^2 = a^2 + b^2$
Substitute.	$13^2 = 5^2 + b^2$
Simplify.	$169 = 25 + b^2$
Subtract.	$144 = b^2$
Solve for *b*.	$12 = b$

Step 3 Write the ratios.

$$\cos A = \frac{\text{adjacent } A}{\text{hypotenuse}} = \frac{12}{13}$$

$$\cot A = \frac{\text{adjacent } A}{\text{opposite } A} = \frac{12}{5}$$

$$\sin B = \frac{\text{opposite } B}{\text{hypotenuse}} = \frac{12}{13}$$

The side opposite ∠*B* is the same as the side adjacent to ∠*A*.

 Got It? **2.** In $\triangle DEF$, $\angle D$ is a right angle and $\tan E = \frac{3}{4}$. What are sin *E* and sec *F*?

There are many applications of right-triangle trigonometry. Most involve degree measure and require the use of a calculator.

 Problem 3 Finding Distance

The large glass pyramid at the Louvre in Paris has a square base. The angle formed by each face and the ground is 49.7°. How high is the pyramid?

Look at the photograph. The distance from the midpoint of a side of the square base to the "center" of the base (directly below the top of the pyramid) is half the length of a side of the base, or $\frac{1}{2}(35) = 17.5$ m.

Use $\tan \theta = \dfrac{\text{opposite}}{\text{adjacent}}$. $\tan 49.7° = \dfrac{x}{17.5}$

Solve for x. $x = 17.5 \cdot \tan 49.7°$

Use a calculator. $x \approx 20.6$

The pyramid is about 20.6 m high.

49.7°

35m

 Got It? **3.** What is each distance for the Louvre pyramid?
      a. from the midpoint of a side of the base to the top, along a lateral face
      b. from a corner of the base to the top

Focus Question What are the trigonometric ratios of a right triangle?

Answer There are six trigonometric ratios of an acute angle of a right triangle. These ratios are relationships between different side lengths of the triangle. You can use trigonometric ratios to find missing side lengths of a right triangle.

 Lesson Check

Do you know HOW?

Use the diagram for Exercises 1–3.

1. Write ratios for $\sin 57°$, $\cos 57°$, and $\tan 57°$.

2. If $a = 10$, what is b?

3. Find the values of $\sin 33°$, $\cos 33°$, and $\tan 33°$ as fractions and as decimals. Round to the nearest tenth.

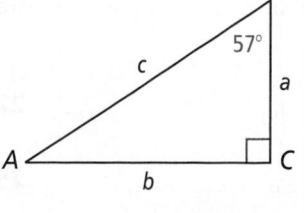

Do you UNDERSTAND?

4. Error Analysis Your friend drew a diagram and made the conclusion shown. What is his error?

5. Writing In a right triangle, the length of the shortest side is 6.3 m. The sine of the angle opposite that side is $\frac{3}{5}$. Explain how to find the tangent of the angle opposite the shortest side.

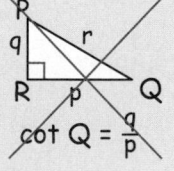

$\cot Q = \dfrac{q}{p}$

Practice and Problem-Solving Exercises

A Practice In △ABC, find each value.

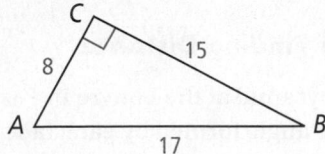

See Problem 1.

Guided Practice

6. sin A

To start, write the formula for the sine of angle A.

$$\sin A = \frac{\text{leg opposite } \angle A}{\text{hypotenuse}}$$

7. sec A   **8.** cot A   **9.** csc B   **10.** sec B   **11.** tan B

In △GHI, ∠H is a right angle, GH = 40, and cos G = $\frac{40}{41}$. Draw a diagram and find each value.

See Problem 2.

12. sin G   **13.** sin I   **14.** cot G

15. csc G   **16.** cos I   **17.** sec H

Use trigonometric ratios to solve each problem.

See Problem 3.

Guided Practice

18. You want to build a bicycle ramp that is 10 ft long and makes a 30° angle with the ground. What would be the height of the ramp?

To start, draw a diagram to represent this situation.

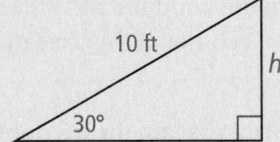

19. Indirect Measurement In 1915, the tallest flagpole in the world stood in San Francisco.

   a. When the sun was 55° above the ground, the length of the shadow cast by this flagpole was 210 ft. Find the height of the flagpole to the nearest foot.

   b. What was the length of the shadow when the sun was 34° above the ground?

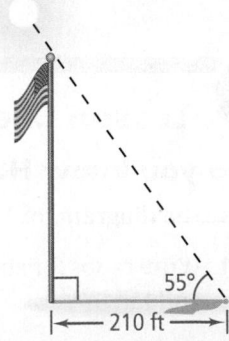

B Apply Sketch a right triangle with θ as the measure of one acute angle. Find the other five trigonometric ratios of θ.

20. sin θ = $\frac{3}{8}$ **21.** cos θ = $\frac{7}{20}$ **22.** cos θ = $\frac{1}{5}$

23. tan θ = $\frac{24}{7}$.   **24.** sec θ = $\frac{16}{9}$ **25.** sin θ = 0.35

26. **Construction** A radio tower has supporting cables attached to it at points 100 ft above the ground. Write a model for the length d of each supporting cable as a function of the angle θ that it makes with the ground. Then find d when $\theta = 60°$ and when $\theta = 50°$.

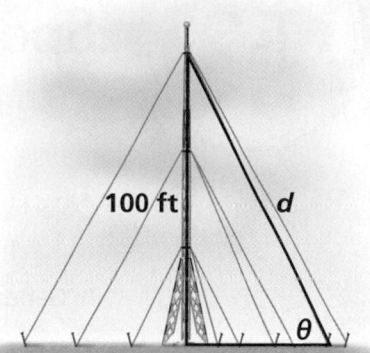

27. **Geometry** An altitude inside a triangle is 5 m long and forms 36° and 42° angles with two of the sides. Find the area of the triangle.

28. **Indirect Measurement** You are 330 ft from the base of a building. The angles of elevation to the top and bottom of a flagpole on top of the building are 55° and 53°. Find the height of the flagpole.

In $\triangle ABC$, $\angle C$ is a right angle. Two measures are given. Find the remaining sides and angles. Round your answers to the nearest tenth.

29. $a = 7, b = 10$ 30. $m\angle A = 52°, c = 10$

> **Hint** The <u>angle of elevation</u> is the angle between a horizontal line (usually the ground) and a person's line of sight, looking up or down at an object.

Standardized Test Prep

SAT/ACT

31. In $\triangle XYZ$, $\angle Z$ is a right angle and $\tan X = \frac{8}{15}$. What is $\sin Y$?

    Ⓐ $\frac{8}{17}$ Ⓑ $\frac{15}{17}$ Ⓒ $\frac{17}{15}$ Ⓓ $\frac{15}{8}$

32. What is the center of the circle with equation $(x + 3)^2 + (y - 2)^2 = 49$?

    Ⓕ $(3, -2)$ Ⓖ $(-3, 2)$ Ⓗ $(3, 2)$ Ⓘ $(-3, -2)$

Short Response

33. Find the measures of the acute angles of a right triangle, to the nearest tenth, if the legs are 135 cm and 95 cm.

Mixed Review

Solve each system of equations. Check your answers.

◀ See Lesson 12-4.

34. $\begin{cases} 3x + 2y = 5 \\ -x + y = -5 \end{cases}$

35. $\begin{cases} x + 4y + 3z = 3 \\ 2x - 5y - z = 5 \\ 3x + 2y - 2z = -3 \end{cases}$

36. $\begin{cases} x + y + z = -1 \\ y + 3z = -5 \\ x + z = -2 \end{cases}$

Get Ready!   To prepare for Lesson T-2, do Exercises 37–39.

◀ See p. 874.

Find the missing length in each right triangle.

37.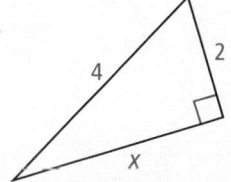

38.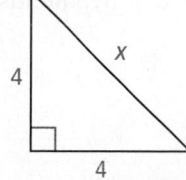

39.

Special Angles

Objectives To use the properties of 45°-45°-90° and 30°-60°-90° triangles

To find the trigonometric ratios of 30°, 45°, and 60° angles

In Geometry, you learned about two special types of right triangles: 45°-45°-90° and 30°-60°-90° triangles.

Focus Question What are the properties of special right triangles?

take note

Key Concepts   Special Right Triangles

Hint

The relationships between sides of special right triangles are related to the Pythagorean Theorem.

45°-45°-90° triangles

In a 45°-45°-90° triangle, both legs are congruent and the length of the hypotenuse is $\sqrt{2}$ times the length of a leg.

$$\text{hypotenuse} = \sqrt{2} \cdot \text{leg}$$

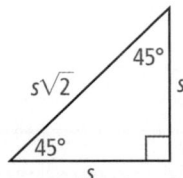

30°-60°-90° triangles

In a 30°-60°-90° triangle, the length of the hypotenuse is twice the length of the shorter leg. The length of the longer leg is $\sqrt{3}$ times the length of the shorter leg.

$$\text{hypotenuse} = 2 \cdot \text{shorter leg}$$

$$\text{longer leg} = \sqrt{3} \cdot \text{shorter leg}$$

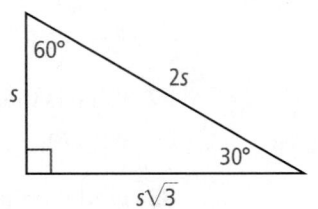

You can use these properties to find missing side lengths in special right triangles.

Problem 1 Finding Side Lengths in 45°-45°-90° Triangles

What is the value of each variable?

A

Think

How is length of the hypotenuse related to the length of a leg?
The length of the hypotenuse is $\sqrt{2}$ times the length of a leg.

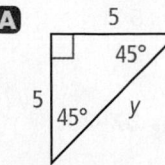

Relate the side lengths.	$\text{hypotenuse} = \sqrt{2} \cdot \text{leg}$
Substitute.	$y = \sqrt{2} \cdot 5$
Simplify.	$y = 5\sqrt{2}$

B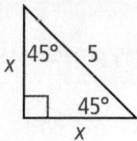

Relate the side lengths.	hypotenuse $= \sqrt{2} \cdot$ leg
Substitute.	$5 = \sqrt{2} \cdot x$
Divide each side by $\sqrt{2}$.	$x = \dfrac{5}{\sqrt{2}}$
Rationalize the denominator and simplify.	$= \dfrac{5}{\sqrt{2}} \cdot \dfrac{\sqrt{2}}{\sqrt{2}} = \dfrac{5\sqrt{2}}{2}$

> Multiplying by 1 does not change the value of an expression.

 Got It? 1. What is the value of each variable?

a. 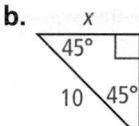

b.

Hint

The length of a leg is the length of the hypotenuse <u>divided by</u> $\sqrt{2}$.

Plan

Which is the known side length?
You know the length of the longer leg.

 Problem 2 **Finding Side Lengths in 30°-60°-90° Triangles**

What are the missing side lengths in this triangle?

Step 1 Find the length of the shorter leg.

Relate the side lengths.	longer leg $= \sqrt{3} \cdot$ shorter leg
Substitute.	$4 = \sqrt{3} \cdot z$
Solve for z.	$z = \dfrac{4}{\sqrt{3}}$
Simplify.	$z = \dfrac{4}{\sqrt{3}} \cdot \dfrac{\sqrt{3}}{\sqrt{3}} = \dfrac{4\sqrt{3}}{3}$

The length of the shorter leg is $\dfrac{4\sqrt{3}}{3}$ units.

Step 2 Find the length of the hypotenuse.

Relate the side lengths.	hypotenuse $= 2 \cdot$ shorter leg
Substitute.	$w = 2 \cdot z$
Substitute for z.	$= 2 \cdot \dfrac{4\sqrt{3}}{3}$
Simplify.	$= \dfrac{2 \cdot 4\sqrt{3}}{3} = \dfrac{8\sqrt{3}}{3}$

The length of the hypotenuse is $\dfrac{8\sqrt{3}}{3}$ units.

Got It? 2. What are the missing side lengths in this triangle?

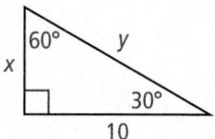

Problem 3 Finding Missing Legs Given the Hypotenuse

What are the values of *a* and *b*?

Find the length of the shorter leg, *a*.

Relate the side lengths.	hypotenuse = 2 · shorter leg
Substitute.	$24 = 2 \cdot a$
Solve for *a*.	$a = 12$

The length of the shorter leg is 12 units, so $a = 12$.

Find the length of the longer leg, *b*.

Relate the side lengths.	longer leg = $\sqrt{3}$ · shorter leg.
Substitute.	$b = \sqrt{3} \cdot 12$
Simplify.	$= 12\sqrt{3}$

The length of the longer leg is $12\sqrt{3}$ units, so $b = 12\sqrt{3}$.

 Got It? 3. What are the values of *a* and *b*?

You can extend the relationships explored in Problems 1–3 to find the trigonometric ratios for the special angles 30°, 45°, and 60°. For each type of special right triangle, let the hypotenuse have a length of 1 unit. Then find the lengths of the legs as shown below.

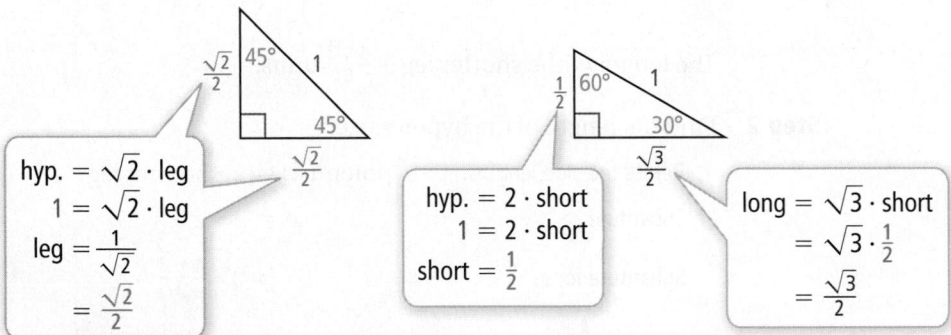

Think

Which leg should you find first?
The hypotenuse is given in terms of the shorter leg, and so is the longer leg. Find the length of leg *a* first.

Using the diagrams on the previous page, you can apply the definitions of each trigonometric ratio.

Hint

Recall the six trigonometric ratios:

$\sin \theta = \dfrac{OPP}{HYP}$

$\cos \theta = \dfrac{ADJ}{HYP}$

$\tan \theta = \dfrac{OPP}{ADJ}$

$\csc \theta = \dfrac{HYP}{OPP}$

$\sec \theta = \dfrac{HYP}{ADJ}$

$\cot \theta = \dfrac{ADJ}{OPP}$

Key Concepts Trigonometric Ratios of Special Angles

θ	30°	45°	60°
$\sin \theta$	$\dfrac{1}{2}$	$\dfrac{\sqrt{2}}{2}$	$\dfrac{\sqrt{3}}{2}$
$\cos \theta$	$\dfrac{\sqrt{3}}{2}$	$\dfrac{\sqrt{2}}{2}$	$\dfrac{1}{2}$
$\tan \theta$	$\dfrac{\sqrt{3}}{3}$	1	$\sqrt{3}$
$\csc \theta$	2	$\sqrt{2}$	$\dfrac{2\sqrt{3}}{3}$
$\sec \theta$	$\dfrac{2\sqrt{3}}{3}$	$\sqrt{2}$	2
$\cot \theta$	$\sqrt{3}$	1	$\dfrac{\sqrt{3}}{3}$

Focus Question What are the properties of special right triangles?

Answer In a 45°-45°-90° triangle, both legs are congruent and the length of the hypotenuse is $\sqrt{2}$ times the length of a leg. In a 30°-60°-90° triangle, the length of the hypotenuse is twice the length of the shorter leg. The length of the longer leg is $\sqrt{3}$ times the length of the shorter leg. Use the properties of special right triangles as a shortcut to determine side lengths without using the Pythagorean Theorem.

Lesson Check

Do you know HOW?

Find each value of x.

1.
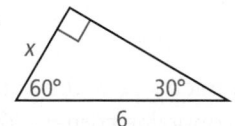
45° 45° x
7

2.
x
60° 30°
6

Do you UNDERSTAND?

3. **Error Analysis** A classmate drew a 30°-60°-90° triangle with a hypotenuse of 5 in. She concluded that the length of the shorter leg of the triangle is $\dfrac{5\sqrt{2}}{2}$ in. Do you agree? Explain.

Practice and Problem-Solving Exercises

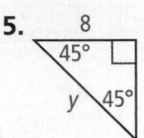 **Practice**   Find the value of each variable.

◀ See Problem 1.

4. w, 60, $45°$, $45°$, z

5. 8, $45°$, $45°$, y, x

6. 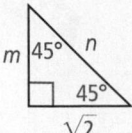 m, $45°$, n, $45°$, $\sqrt{2}$

Find the value of each variable.

◀ See Problems 2 and 3.

7.
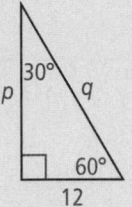
p, $30°$, q, $60°$, 12

Guided Practice →

To start, write the relationship between the hypotenuse and the shorter leg.

hypotenuse $= 2 \cdot$ shorter leg

8. 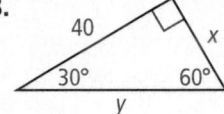 40, x, $30°$, $60°$, y

9. 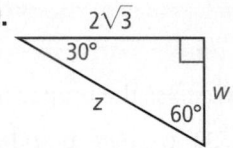 $2\sqrt{3}$, $30°$, z, $60°$, w

10. 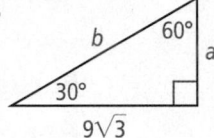 b, $60°$, a, $30°$, $9\sqrt{3}$

 **Apply**

11. Air Travel A conveyor belt moves luggage from the ground outside the airport up to an entrance into the baggage claim area. The conveyor belt moves at a rate of 100 ft/min. How many seconds does it take for a suitcase to go from the ground to the entrance?

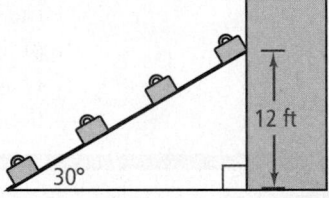
12 ft
30°

Geometry Find the value of each variable.

12. 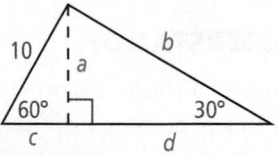 10, b, a, $60°$, $30°$, c, d

13. 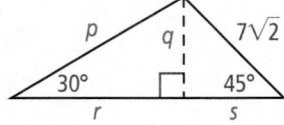 p, q, $7\sqrt{2}$, $30°$, $45°$, r, s

14. 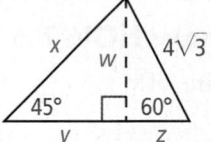 x, w, $4\sqrt{3}$, $45°$, $60°$, y, z

15. Recreation A city park is in the shape of a square. Each side of the park is 300 ft in length, and sidewalks across the park join opposite corners. To the nearest foot, how long is each diagonal sidewalk?

Hint An isosceles right triangle is always a 45°-45°-90° triangle.

Use the given information to find the missing side length(s) in each 45°-45°-90° triangle. Rationalize any denominators.

16. leg 2 cm

17. hypotenuse $\sqrt{3}$ ft

18. leg $2\sqrt{5}$ m

Use the given information to find the missing side lengths in each
30°-60°-90° triangle. Rationalize any denominators.

19. shorter leg 3 in.   **20.** longer leg 1 cm   **21.** hypotenuse $2\sqrt{2}$ ft

22. longer leg $\sqrt{5}$ cm   **23.** hypotenuse $3\sqrt{2}$ m   **24.** shorter leg $\sqrt{3}$ cm

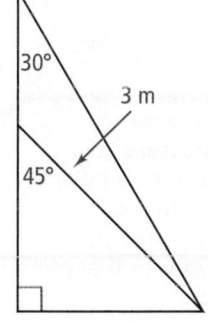

25. Tree Planting To ensure that a young tree stays upright in a windy area, a gardener
placed a 3 m brace against the tree at a 45° angle. Then, at the same spot on the
ground, she placed a second, longer brace to make a 30° angle with the trunk of
the tree.
   a. How long is the longer brace? Round to the nearest tenth of a meter.
   b. About how much higher does the longer brace reach than the shorter brace?

26. Open Ended Write a real-world problem that you can solve using a
30°-60°-90° triangle with a 15-ft hypotenuse. Show your solution.

SAT/ACT

27. A right isosceles triangle has a hypotenuse of length 36 mm. What is the length of
each leg?

   Ⓐ $36\sqrt{2}$ mm   Ⓑ $24\sqrt{3}$ mm   Ⓒ $18\sqrt{2}$ mm   Ⓓ $12\sqrt{3}$ mm

28. A ladder rests against a building. The ladder is 14 ft long and forms an angle of 76.5°
with the ground. Which statement is NOT true?

   Ⓕ The bottom of the ladder is 13.6 ft from the base of the building.

   Ⓖ The bottom of the ladder is 3.3 ft from the base of the building.

   Ⓗ The top of the ladder touches the building 13.6 ft from the ground.

   Ⓘ The ladder forms an angle of 13.5° with the building.

Short Response

29. How can you use the arithmetic mean to find the missing terms in the arithmetic
sequence 15, ■, ■, ■, 47, . . . ?

Mixed Review

In $\triangle ABC$, $\angle C$ is a right angle. Two measures are given. Find the remaining
sides and angles. Round answers to the nearest tenth.

◀ **See Lesson T-1.**

30. $m\angle A = 34.2°$, $b = 5.7$ **31.** $m\angle B = 17.2°$, $b = 8.3$ **32.** $m\angle B = 8.3°$, $c = 20$

Get Ready! **To prepare for Lesson T-3, do Exercises 33–35.**

Write an equation of the circle that passes through the given point and
has its center at the origin. (*Hint:* Use the distance formula to find the radius.)

◀ **See Lesson 10-3.**

33. $(0, 1)$ **34.** $\left(\frac{\sqrt{3}}{2}, \frac{1}{2}\right)$ **35.** $\left(\frac{\sqrt{2}}{2}, \frac{\sqrt{2}}{2}\right)$

T-3 The Unit Circle

Objectives To work with angles in standard position

To find coordinates of points on the unit circle

An angle in the coordinate plane is in **standard position** when the vertex is at the origin and one ray is on the positive *x*-axis. The ray on the *x*-axis is the **initial side** of the angle. The other ray is the **terminal side** of the angle.

The measure of an angle in standard position is the amount of rotation from the initial side to the terminal side.

Standard Position

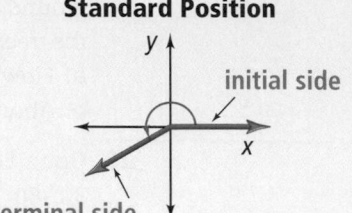

Focus Question How is the unit circle related to trigonometric ratios?

The measure of an angle is positive when the rotation from the initial side to the terminal side is in the counterclockwise direction. The measure is negative when the rotation is clockwise.

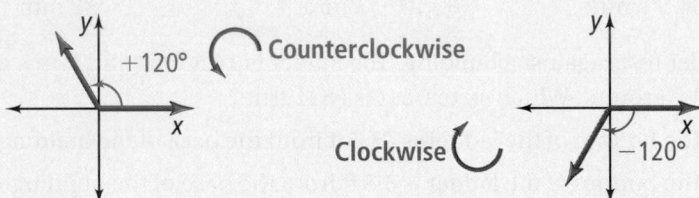

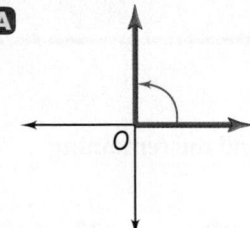 **Problem 1** **Measuring Angles in Standard Position**

What is the measure of each angle?

A

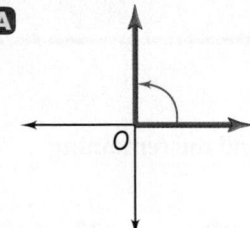

B

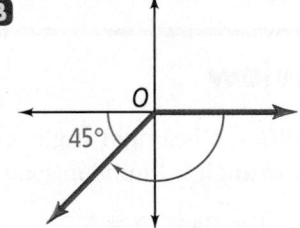

Think

How many degrees are in a circle?
There are 360° in a circle, 180° in half of a circle, and 90° in a quarter of a circle.

This angle is a counterclockwise rotation that makes a right angle, so its measure is 90°.

This angle is a clockwise rotation that goes 45° beyond a right angle, so its measure is −135°.

Got It? **1.** What is the measure of the angle shown?

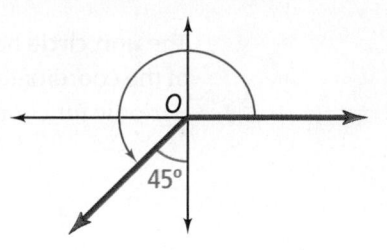

Hint

Quadrantal angles (0°, 90°, 180°, 270°, and 360° angles) do not have reference angles.

An angle in standard position with a terminal side not on an axis has an associated *reference angle*. The **reference angle** is the acute angle formed by the terminal side of an angle in standard position and the *x*-axis. A reference angle corresponds to a right triangle, as shown in the diagram at the right.

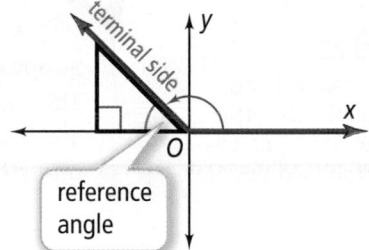

reference angle

Problem 2 **Sketching Angles in Standard Position**

What is a sketch of each angle in standard position? Identify the reference angle.

Ⓐ 36°

Ⓑ 315°

Think

What is the initial side of the angle?
In standard position, the initial side is always the positive *x*-axis.

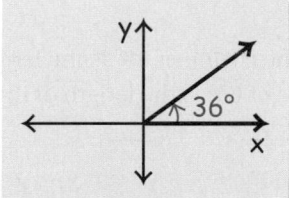

36° Counterclockwise

The reference angle is the angle itself: 36°.

315° Counterclockwise

The reference angle is $360° - 315° = 45°$.

Ⓒ −150°

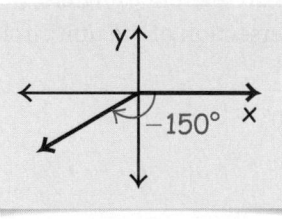

150° Clockwise

The reference angle is $180° - 150° = 30°$.

Got It? **2.** What is a sketch of each angle in standard position? Identify the reference angle.

a. 85°   **b.** −320°   **c.** 140°

The **unit circle** has a radius of 1 unit and its center at the origin of the coordinate plane. Points on the unit circle are related to periodic functions.

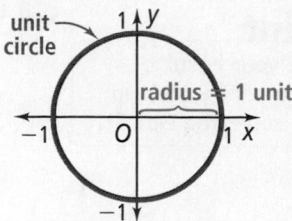

take note

Key Concepts   Cosine and Sine of an Angle

Hint

You can use the symbol θ for the measure of an angle in standard position.

Suppose an angle in standard position has measure θ. The cosine of θ ($\cos \theta$) is the x-coordinate of the point at which the terminal side of the angle intersects the unit circle. The sine of θ ($\sin \theta$) is the y-coordinate.

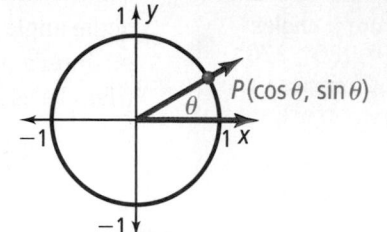

Problem 3 Finding Cosines and Sines of Angles

What are $\cos \theta$ and $\sin \theta$ for each angle?

A $\theta = 60°$

Hint

In a 30°-60°-90° triangle, the shorter leg is half the hypotenuse. The longer leg is $\sqrt{3}$ times the shorter leg.

Sketch the angle in standard position. The cosine of 60° is the length of the shorter leg of the triangle. The sine of 60° is the length of the longer leg.

$$x = \cos 60° \qquad\qquad y = \sin 60°$$
$$\quad = \text{length of shorter leg} \qquad = \text{length of longer leg}$$
$$\quad = \frac{1}{2} \qquad\qquad\qquad\quad = \frac{\sqrt{3}}{2}$$

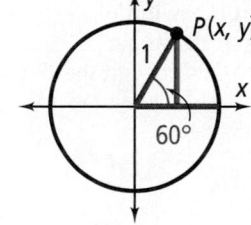

B $\theta = 90°$

Think

Does every angle have a reference angle?

No; an angle whose terminal side is on an axis does not have a reference angle.

Since a 90° angle in standard position has no reference angle, use the coordinates of the point at the intersection of the unit circle and the terminal side.

$$x = \cos 90° \qquad\qquad y = \sin 90°$$
$$\quad = 0 \qquad\qquad\qquad = 1$$

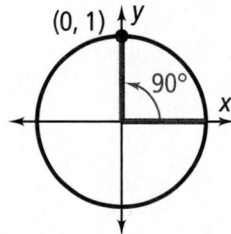

 Got It? **3.** What are $\cos \theta$ and $\sin \theta$ for each angle?

    a. $\theta = 30°$ **b.** $\theta = 360°$ **c.** $\theta = 540°$

Hint

Refer to the chart of trigonometric ratios for 30°, 45°, and 60° angles from Lesson T-2.

You can find the exact value of sine and cosine for angles that are multiples of 30° or 45° using their corresponding reference angles.

 Problem 4 Finding Exact Values of Cosine and Sine

What are the cosine and sine of each angle?

Ⓐ $\theta = -120°$

Know	Need	Plan
An angle	The *x*- and *y*-coordinates of the point where the angle intersects the unit circle	• Sketch the angle on the unit circle. • Use the angle to draw a right triangle with one leg on the *x*-axis. • Find the lengths of the legs. • Identify the coordinates.

Step 1 Sketch an angle of −120° in standard position. Also sketch a unit circle and the point of intersection with the terminal side of the angle.

Step 2 Use the reference angle to sketch the associated 30°-60°-90° triangle.

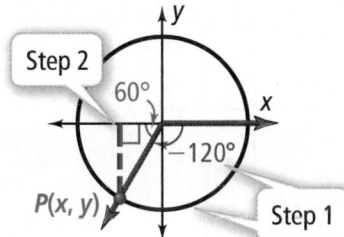

Hint

Refer to Lesson T-2 for the side relationships in special right triangles.

Step 3 Find the lengths of the legs of the triangle.

The hypotenuse is the radius of the unit circle.	hypotenuse $= 1$
The shorter leg is half the hypotenuse.	shorter leg $= \frac{1}{2}$
The longer leg is $\sqrt{3}$ times the shorter leg.	longer leg $= \sqrt{3} \cdot \frac{1}{2} = \frac{\sqrt{3}}{2}$

Step 4 Identify the coordinates.

Since the point lies in Quadrant III, both the *x*- and *y*-coordinates are negative. The shorter leg lies along the *x*-axis, so $\cos(-120°) = -\frac{1}{2}$, and $\sin(-120°) = -\frac{\sqrt{3}}{2}$.

Ⓑ $\theta = 135°$

Sketch a 135° angle in standard position to determine the point $P(x, y)$ on the unit circle. Find the reference angle and sketch the associated right triangle.

The hypotenuse of the triangle has length 1, so the legs have length $\frac{\sqrt{2}}{2}$. Since point *P* is in Quadrant II, the *x*-coordinate is negative and the *y*-coordinate is positive.

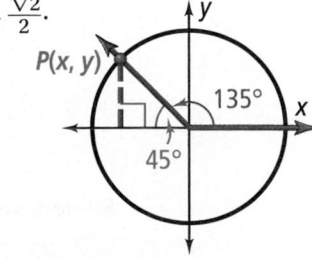

Think

How are the side lengths related in a 45°-45°-90° triangle?

The length of a leg is $\frac{\sqrt{2}}{2}$ times the length of the hypotenuse.

$$x = \cos 135°$$
$$= -(\text{length of leg})$$
$$= -\frac{\sqrt{2}}{2}$$

$$y = \sin 135°$$
$$= \text{length of leg}$$
$$= \frac{\sqrt{2}}{2}$$

Got It? 4. What are the cosine and sine of the angle?

    a. $\theta = 330°$ **b.** $\theta = -30°$

    c. Reasoning For an angle θ, can $\cos \theta$ equal $\sin \theta$? Explain.

Focus Question How is the unit circle related to trigonometric ratios?

Answer The sine and cosine ratios are related to the point where the terminal side of an angle in standard position intersects the unit circle. If θ represents the angle, then $\sin \theta$ is the y-coordinate of the point and $\cos \theta$ is the x-coordinate.

Lesson Check

Do you know HOW?

Find the measure of each angle in standard position.

1.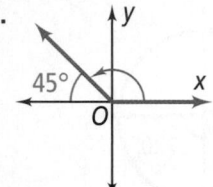

2.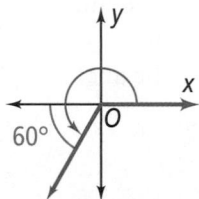

Do you UNDERSTAND?

3. Open-Ended Find a reference angle for $\theta = 1485°$.

4. Error Analysis On a test, a student wrote that a $310°$ angle in standard position has the same terminal side as a $50°$ angle. Describe and correct the student's error.

Practice and Problem-Solving Exercises

 **Practice**   Find the measure of each angle in standard position.   ◀ **See Problem 1.**

5.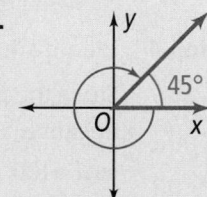

Guided Practice →

To start, identify whether the measure of the angle is positive or negative.

The rotation is clockwise, so the angle measure is negative.

6. 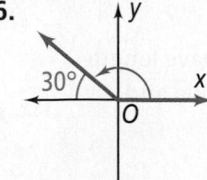   **7.** 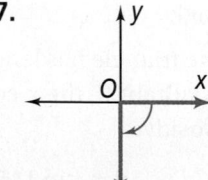   **8.**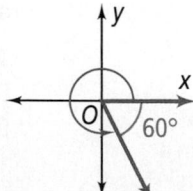

Sketch each angle in standard position. Then determine the reference angle.   ◀ **See Problem 2.**

9. $40°$ **10.** $-130°$ **11.** $-270°$ **12.** $120°$

Find the cosine and sine of each angle. ◀ See Problem 3.

13. 45°   **14.** 30°   **15.** 180°

Find the exact values of the cosine and sine of each angle. ◀ See Problem 4.

16. 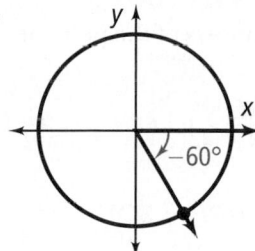   **17.** 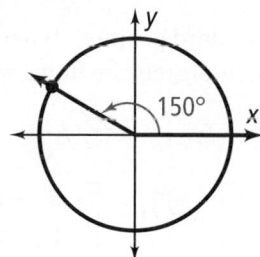   **18.**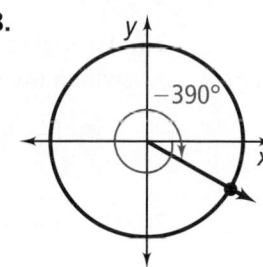

19. −240°   **20.** 315°   **21.** −30°

 **Apply**   📟 **Graphing Calculator** For each angle θ, find the values of $\cos \theta$ and $\sin \theta$. Round your answers to the nearest hundredth.

22. −95°   **23.** −10°   **24.** 154°   **25.** 210°

26. Time On an analog clock, the minute hand has moved 128° from 12 o'clock. What number will it pass next?

Determine the quadrant or axis where the terminal side of each angle lies.

27. 150°   **28.** 210°   **29.** 540°   **30.** −60°

31. Time The time is 2:46 P.M. What is the measure of the angle that the minute hand swept through since 2:00 P.M.?

32. a. Copy and complete the chart at the right.
 b. Suppose you know that $\cos \theta$ is negative and $\sin \theta$ is positive. In which quadrant does the terminal side of the angle lie?
 c. Writing Summarize how the quadrant in which the terminal side of an angle lies affects the sign of the sine and cosine of that angle.

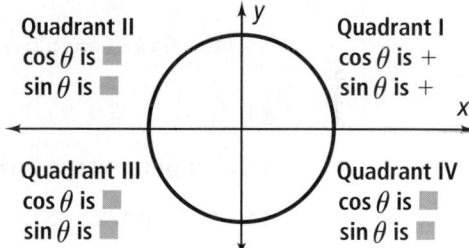

33. a. Graphing Calculator Use a calculator to find the value of each expression: cos 40°, cos 400°, and cos (−320°).
 b. Reasoning What do you notice about the values you found in part (a)? Explain.

Standardized Test Prep

SAT/ACT

34. An angle drawn in standard position has a terminal side that passes through the point $(\sqrt{2}, -\sqrt{2})$. What is one possible measure of the angle?

    (A) 45°   (B) 225°   (C) 315°   (D) 330°

35. An angle of 120° is in standard position. What are the coordinates of the point at which the terminal side intersects the unit circle?

    (F) $\left(\frac{1}{2}, \frac{\sqrt{3}}{2}\right)$ (G) $\left(-\frac{1}{2}, \frac{\sqrt{3}}{-2}\right)$ (H) $\left(\frac{-\sqrt{3}}{2}, \frac{1}{2}\right)$ (I) $\left(-\frac{1}{2}, \frac{\sqrt{3}}{2}\right)$

36. Given $P = \begin{bmatrix} 4 & 3 & -2 \\ -1 & 0 & 5 \end{bmatrix}$ and $Q = \begin{bmatrix} 3 & -2 & -5 \\ -1 & -2 & -1 \end{bmatrix}$, what is $2P - 3Q$?

    (A) $\begin{bmatrix} 1 & -5 & 3 \\ 0 & -2 & 6 \end{bmatrix}$ (B) $\begin{bmatrix} 17 & 0 & 19 \\ -5 & 6 & 7 \end{bmatrix}$ (C) $\begin{bmatrix} -1 & 12 & 11 \\ 1 & 6 & 13 \end{bmatrix}$ (D) $\begin{bmatrix} 1 & 5 & 3 \\ 0 & 2 & 6 \end{bmatrix}$

Short Response

37. Use an angle in standard position to find the exact value of $[\sin(-135°)]^2 + [\cos(-135°)]^2$. Show your work.

Mixed Review

Find the value of each variable.   ◀ See Lesson T-2.

38.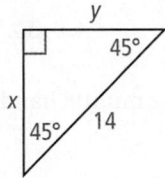

39.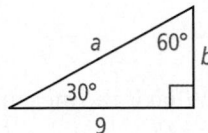

40.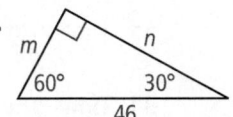

Find the foci of each hyperbola. Draw the graph.   ◀ See Lesson 10-5.

41. $\frac{y^2}{16} - \frac{x^2}{4} = 1$ **42.** $\frac{y^2}{25} - \frac{x^2}{100} = 1$ **43.** $\frac{x^2}{36} - \frac{y^2}{49} = 1$

Write in point-slope form an equation of the line through each pair of points.   ◀ See Lesson 2-4.

44. $(0, 1)$ and $(2, -5)$ **45.** $(-9, 3)$ and $(-4, -4)$ **46.** $(1, 8)$ and $(7, 2)$

Get Ready!   **To prepare for Lesson T-4, do Exercises 47–49.**

Find the area of a circle with the given radius or diameter. Use 3.14 for π.   ◀ See p. 869.

47. radius 4 in.   **48.** radius 8 mi   **49.** diameter 3.4 ft

Degrees and Radian Measure

Objectives To use radian measure for angles
To find the length of an arc of a circle

In the past, you have used degrees to measure angles. In certain functions, angles are often measured in larger units called *radians*.

Focus Question What is a radian?

A **central angle** of a circle is an angle with a vertex at the center of a circle. An **intercepted arc** is the portion of the circle with endpoints on the sides of the central angle.

A **radian** is the measure of a central angle that intercepts an arc with length equal to the radius of the circle. Radians, like degrees, measure the amount of rotation from the initial side to the terminal side of an angle.

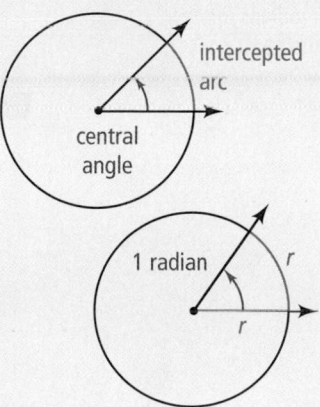

---

take note

Key Concept Proportion Relating Radians and Degrees

You can use the proportion $\frac{d°}{180°} = \frac{r\,\text{radians}}{\pi\,\text{radians}}$ to convert between radians and degrees.

Here's Why It Works Suppose you continued marking intercepted arcs of length r around a circle. Because the circumference of a circle is $2\pi r$, a circle can be divided into $\frac{2\pi r}{r} = 2\pi$ arcs of length r. Therefore, there are 2π radians in any circle, including the unit circle, the top half of which is shown here. Since 2π radians $= 360°$, it follows that π radians $= 180°$. This equality leads to the following *conversion factors* for radian measure and degree measure.

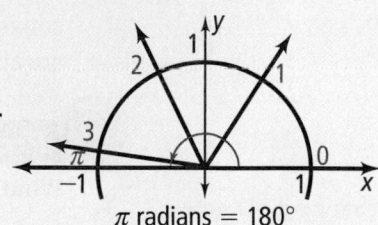

π radians $= 180°$

---

take note

Key Concept Converting Between Radians and Degrees

To convert degrees to radians, multiply by $\frac{\pi\,\text{radians}}{180°}$.

To convert radians to degrees, multiply by $\frac{180°}{\pi\,\text{radians}}$.

Hint

You can use conversion factors and dimensional analysis to convert between angle measurement systems.

 Problem 1 Using Dimensional Analysis

Think

How do you know which conversion factor to use?
Because radians are in the numerator, use the conversion factor with radians in the denominator.

Ⓐ What is the degree measure of an angle of $-\frac{3\pi}{4}$ radians?

Multiply by the conversion factor $\frac{180°}{\pi \text{ radians}}$.

$$-\frac{3\pi}{4} \text{ radians} = -\frac{3\pi}{4} \text{ radians} \cdot \frac{180°}{\pi \text{ radians}}$$

Divide out common factors and units.

$$= -\frac{3\pi}{\underset{1}{4}} \text{ radians} \cdot \frac{\overset{45}{180°}}{\pi \text{ radians}}$$

Simplify.

$$= -3 \cdot 45° = -135°$$

An angle of $-\frac{3\pi}{4}$ radians measures $-135°$.

Ⓑ What is the radian measure of an angle of $27°$?

Multiply by the conversion factor $\frac{\pi \text{ radians}}{180°}$.

$$27° = 27° \cdot \frac{\pi \text{ radians}}{180°}$$

Divide out common factors and units.

$$= \overset{3}{27°} \cdot \frac{\pi \text{ radians}}{\underset{20}{180°}}$$

Simplify.

$$= 3 \cdot \frac{\pi \text{ radians}}{20} = \frac{3\pi}{20} \text{ radians}$$

An angle of $27°$ measures $\frac{3\pi}{20}$ radians.

 **Got It? 1.** What is the degree measure of each angle expressed in radians? What is the radian measure of each angle expressed in degrees? (Express radian measures in terms of π.)

a. $\frac{\pi}{2}$ radians   **b.** $225°$ **c.** 2 radians   **d.** $150°$

Although you can find the sine and cosine of angles in radian measure by converting the radian measure to degrees, this step is unnecessary if you are able to think in radians.

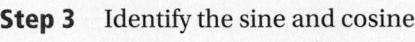 **Problem 2** Finding Cosine and Sine of a Radian Measure

Think

What kind of angle is π?
It is a straight angle.

What are the exact values of $\cos \frac{\pi}{4}$ and $\sin \frac{\pi}{4}$?

Step 1 Draw the angle on the unit circle.

$$\frac{\pi}{4} = \frac{1}{4}\pi = \frac{1}{4} \text{ of a straight angle, or } 45°$$

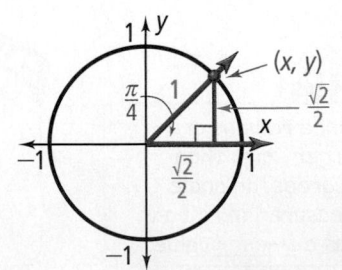

Step 2 Complete a $45°$-$45°$-$90°$ triangle.

Since the hypotenuse has length 1, both legs have length $\frac{\sqrt{2}}{2}$.

Step 3 Identify the sine and cosine.

The point (x, y) is in Quadrant I, so x and y are positive.

$$x = \cos\frac{\pi}{4} = \frac{\sqrt{2}}{2} \qquad y = \sin\frac{\pi}{4} = \frac{\sqrt{2}}{2}$$

If an angle has no units, it is measured in radians.

 Got It? **2.** What are the exact values of $\cos \frac{7\pi}{6}$ and $\sin \frac{7\pi}{6}$?

If you know the radius and the measure in radians of a central angle, you can find the length of the intercepted arc.

take note

Key Concept **Length of an Intercepted Arc**

For a circle of radius r and a central angle of measure θ (in radians), the length s of the intercepted arc is $s = r\theta$.

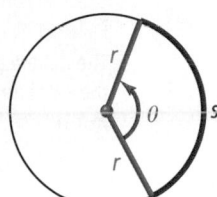

Here's Why It Works The length of the intercepted arc is the same fraction of the circumference of the circle as the central angle is of 2π. So, $\frac{\theta}{2\pi} = \frac{s}{C}$.

Write the proportion.	$\frac{\theta}{2\pi} = \frac{s}{C}$
Substitute $2\pi r$ for C.	$\frac{\theta}{2\pi} = \frac{s}{2\pi r}$
Write the cross products.	$2\pi r\theta = 2\pi s$
Divide out common factors.	$2\not\pi r\theta = 2\not\pi s$
Simplify.	$s = r\theta$

Problem 3 **Finding the Length of an Arc**

Think

What units will the length of the arc have?
Because the radius is in inches, the arc length will also be in inches.

Use the circle at the right. What is length s to the nearest tenth?

Use the formula.	$s = r\theta$
Substitute 3 for r and $\frac{5\pi}{6}$ for θ.	$= 3 \cdot \frac{5\pi}{6}$
Simplify.	$= \frac{5\pi}{2}$
Use a calculator.	≈ 7.9

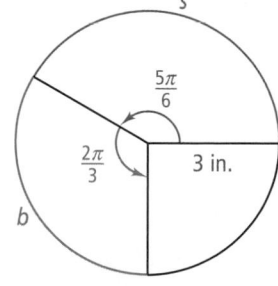

The arc has a length of about 7.9 in.

 Got It? **3. a.** What is length b in Problem 3 to the nearest tenth?

b. Reasoning If the radius of the circle doubled, how would the arc length change?

 **Problem 4** Using Radian Measure to Solve a Problem

Weather Satellite A weather satellite in a circular orbit around Earth completes one orbit every 2 h. How far does the satellite travel in 1 h?

Know

- A complete satellite orbit is 2 h.
- The radius of the Earth is 6400 km.
- The height of the orbit is 2600 km.

Need

The distance that the satellite travels in 1 h

Plan

- Find the angle the satellite travels in 1 h.
- Use the formula for arc length, $s = r\theta$.

2600 km

the center of Earth

6400 km

Not to scale

Step 1 Find the angle through which the satellite travels in 1 h.

$$\theta = \frac{1}{2} \cdot 2\pi = \pi$$

Step 2 Find the length of the arc.

 **Think**

What value should you use for r?
Use the sum of the Earth's radius and the height of the orbit.

Write the formula for arc length.	$s = r\theta$
Substitute.	$= (6400 + 2600)\pi$
Simplify.	$= 9000\pi$
Use a calculator.	$\approx 28{,}274$

The satellite travels about 28,000 km in 1 h.

 Got It? **4.** Suppose the satellite orbited 3600 km above Earth's surface and completes an orbit every 4 h. How far would the satellite travel in 1 h?

Focus Question What is a radian?

Answer A radian is the measure of a central angle that intercepts an arc with length equal to the radius of the circle. Use the relationship $180° = \pi$ radians to convert units. Use the formula $s = r\theta$ as a shortcut to calculate arc length given the radius and the central angle.

Lesson Check

Do you know HOW?

1. Find the radian measure of an angle of 300°.

2. Find the degree measure of an angle of $\frac{3\pi}{4}$ radians.

3. Find the length a.

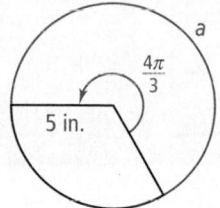

Do you UNDERSTAND?

4. **Vocabulary** The radius of a circle is 9 cm. A central angle intercepts an arc that is 9 cm. What is the measure of the central angle in radians?

5. **Reasoning** A certain baker believes that a perfect slice of pie has a central angle of 1 radian. How many "perfect" slices can he get out of one pie?

Practice and Problem-Solving Exercises

A Practice

Write each measure in radians. Express your answer in terms of π and as a decimal rounded to the nearest hundredth.

See Problem 1.

6. $-300°$ 7. $150°$ 8. $-90°$ 9. $20°$

Write each measure in degrees. Round your answer to the nearest degree, if necessary.

Guided Practice

To start, multiply by the conversion factor $\frac{180°}{\pi \text{ radians}}$.

10. 3π radians

3π radians $\cdot \dfrac{180°}{\pi \text{ radians}}$

11. $\frac{11\pi}{10}$ radians   12. $-\frac{2\pi}{3}$ radians   13. -3 radians

The measure θ of an angle in standard position is given. Find the exact values of $\cos\theta$ and $\sin\theta$ for each angle measure.

See Problem 2.

14. $\frac{\pi}{6}$ 15. $\frac{\pi}{3}$ 16. $-\frac{\pi}{4}$

17. $\frac{2\pi}{3}$ 18. $-\frac{\pi}{2}$ 19. $\frac{7\pi}{6}$

Use each circle to find the length of the indicated arc. Round your answer to the nearest tenth.

See Problem 3.

20. 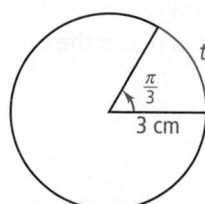   21. 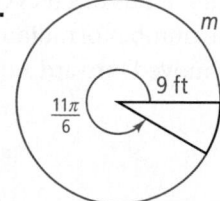   22.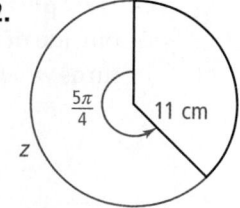

Find the length of each arc.

23.

24.

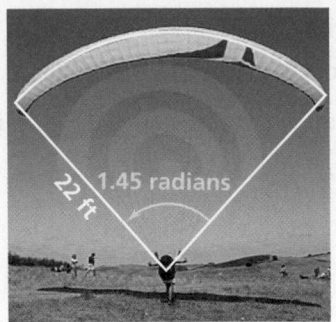

25. **Space** A geostationary satellite is positioned 35,800 km above Earth's surface. It takes 24 h to complete one orbit. The radius of Earth is about 6400 km.   ◀ **See Problem 4.**
   a. What distance does the satellite travel in 1 h? 3 h? 2.5 h? 25 h?
   b. **Reasoning** After how many hours has the satellite traveled 200,000 km?

B **Apply**

26. **Automobiles** Suppose a windshield wiper arm has a length of 22 in. and rotates through an angle of 110°. What distance does the tip of the wiper travel as it moves once across the windshield?

27. **Geography** The 24 lines of longitude that approximate the 24 standard time zones are equally spaced around the equator.
   a. Suppose you use 24 central angles to divide a circle into 24 equal arcs. Express the measure of each angle in degrees and in radians.
   b. The radius of the equator is about 3960 mi. About how wide is each time zone at the equator?
   c. The radius of the Arctic Circle is about 1580 mi. About how wide is each time zone at the Arctic Circle?

Determine the quadrant or axis where the terminal side of each angle lies.

28. $\frac{4\pi}{3}$

29. $-\frac{5\pi}{4}$

30. $-\pi$

Draw an angle in standard position with each given measure. Then find the values of the cosine and sine of the angle.

31. $\frac{7\pi}{4}$

32. $-\frac{2\pi}{3}$

33. $\frac{5\pi}{2}$

34. **Open-Ended** Draw an angle in standard position. Draw a circle with its center at the vertex of the angle. Find the measure of the angle in radians and degrees.

35. **Transportation** Suppose the radius of a bicycle wheel is 13 in. (measured to the outside of the tire). Find the number of radians through which a point on the tire turns when the bicycle has moved forward a distance of 12 ft.

36. Error Analysis A student wanted to rewrite $\frac{9\pi}{4}$ in degrees. The screen shows her calculation. What error did the student make?

9*π/4*360/2*π
 3997.189782

37. Music A CD with diameter 12 cm spins in a CD player. Calculate how much farther a point on the outside edge of the CD travels in one revolution than a point 1 cm closer to the center of the CD.

Standardized Test Prep

SAT/ACT

38. Which pairs of measurements represent the same angle measures?

 I. $240°, \frac{7\pi}{6}$ II. $135°, \frac{3\pi}{4}$ III. $150°, \frac{5\pi}{6}$

 (A) I and II only   (B) I and III only   (C) II and III only   (D) I, II, and III

39. What is the exact value of $\cos\frac{5\pi}{4}$?

 (F) $-\frac{\sqrt{3}}{2}$ (G) $-\frac{\sqrt{2}}{2}$ (H) $-\frac{1}{2}$ (I) $\frac{\sqrt{2}}{2}$

40. Two arcs have the same length. One arc is intercepted by an angle of $\frac{3\pi}{2}$ in a circle of radius 15 cm. If the radius of the other circle is 25 cm, what central angle intercepts the arc?

 (A) $\frac{3\pi}{2}$ (B) $\frac{9\pi}{10}$ (C) $\frac{5\pi}{2}$ (D) $\frac{5\pi}{3}$

Short Response

41. For a central angle of one radian, describe the relationship between the radius of the circle and the length of the arc.

Mixed Review

Sketch each angle in standard position.   ◀ **See Lesson T-3.**

42. $15°$ **43.** $-75°$ **44.** $150°$ **45.** $-270°$

Find the mean and the standard deviation for each set of values.   ◀ **See Lesson 11-6.**

46. 12 13 15 9 16 5 18 16 12 11 15   **47.** 21 29 35 26 25 28 27 51 24 34

Get Ready!   To prepare for Lesson T-5, do Exercises 48–51.

In $\triangle PQR$, find each value.   ◀ **See Lesson T-1.**

48. $\cos P$ **49.** $\tan Q$

50. $\tan P$ **51.** $\sin Q$

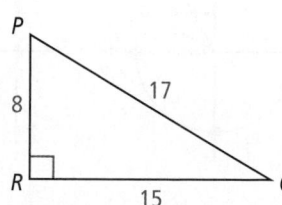

T-5 Graphs of Sine, Cosine, and Tangent Functions

Objectives To identify properties of the sine, cosine, and tangent functions
To graph sine, cosine, and tangent functions

Dynamic Activity
The Sine Curve
The Cosine Curve
The Tangent Curve

Recall that for an angle in standard position with measure θ, the point at which the terminal side of the angle intersects the unit circle has coordinates $(\cos\theta, \sin\theta)$. You can use these relationships to define and graph *sine* and *cosine functions*.

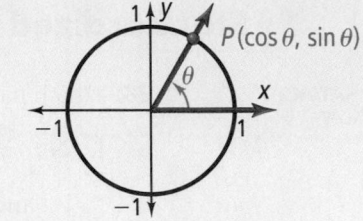

Focus Question What are the graphs of sine and cosine functions?

Lesson Vocabulary
• sine function
• cosine function
• periodic function
• cycle
• period
• amplitude
• tangent function

The **sine function**, $y = \sin\theta$, matches the measure θ of an angle in standard position with the y-coordinate of a point on the unit circle. This point is where the terminal side of the angle intersects the unit circle.

Although you can graph the sine function in radians or degrees, use radians unless degrees are specified. The graph of the sine function for $0 \le \theta \le 2\pi$ is shown below. Notice that the graph will repeat the same pattern of y-values if you continue moving around the unit circle.

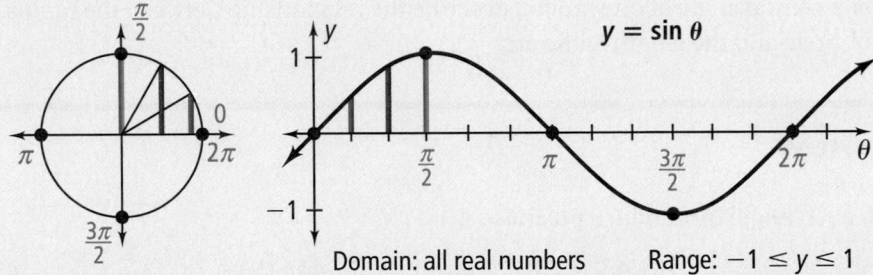

Domain: all real numbers   Range: $-1 \le y \le 1$

The **cosine function**, $y = \cos\theta$, matches θ with the x-coordinate of the point of intersection of the terminal side of angle θ and the unit circle. The symmetry of the set of points $(x, y) = (\cos\theta, \sin\theta)$ on the unit circle guarantees that the graphs of sine (above) and cosine (below) are translations of each other.

Hint

The graph of $y = \cos\theta$ is a translation of $y = \sin\theta$ either left or right $\frac{\pi}{2}$ units.

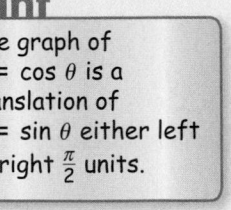

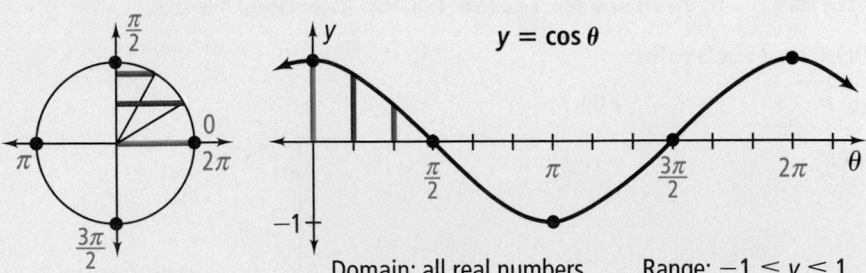

Domain: all real numbers   Range: $-1 \le y \le 1$

The graph of a sine function is called a sine curve. Similarly, the graph of a cosine function is called a cosine curve. Since the pattern of *y*-values repeat over time, sine and cosine functions are examples of *periodic functions*.

Hint

A cycle may begin at any point on the graph of the function.

A **periodic function** is a function that repeats a pattern of *y*-values (outputs) at regular intervals. One complete pattern is called a **cycle**. The **period** of a function is the horizontal length of one cycle. By varying the period, you can get different sine and cosine curves.

Problem 1 Finding Periods of Sine and Cosine Curves

How many cycles occur in the graph? What is the period of the function?

A

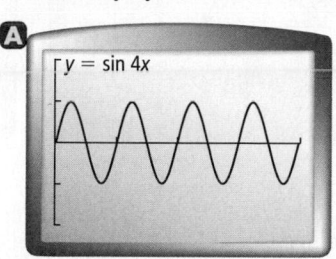

Xmin = 0
Xmax = 2π
Xscl = $\pi/2$
Ymin = -2
Ymax = 2
Yscl = 1

Plan

How do you find the number of cycles?
Identify the smallest repeating section of the graph and count the number of times it occurs.

There are four complete patterns in the graph, so the graph shows 4 cycles. To find the period of the function, divide the length of the horizontal interval of the graph by the number of cycles shown on the graph.

The length of the horizontal interval shown is 2π.

$$2\pi \div 4 = \frac{\pi}{2}$$

The period of $y = \sin 4x$ is $\frac{\pi}{2}$.

B

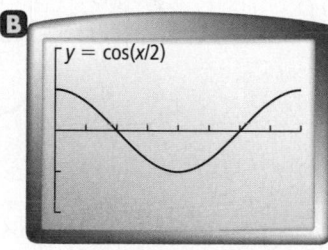

Xmin = 0
Xmax = 4π
Xscl $-$ $\pi/2$
Ymin = -2
Ymax = 2
Yscl = 1

There is only one complete pattern, so the graph shows only 1 cycle. Therefore, the length of the horizontal interval shown in the graph is equal to the period of the function.

The period of $y = \cos \frac{x}{2}$ is 4π.

 Got It? 1. How many cycles occur in the graph? What is the period of the function?

a.

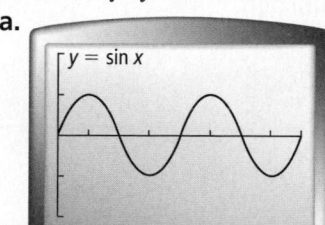

Xmin = 0
Xmax = 4π
Xscl = $\pi/2$
Ymin = -2
Ymax = 2
Yscl = 1

b.

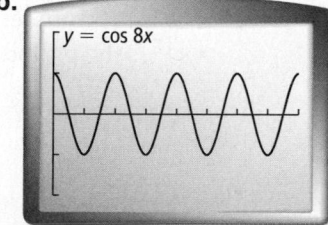

Xmin = 0
Xmax = π
Xscl = $\pi/8$
Ymin = -2
Ymax = 2
Yscl = 1

You can also vary the *amplitude* of a sine or cosine curve. The **amplitude** of a periodic function is half the difference between the maximum and minimum values of the function. It is a way to describe the amount of variation in the function values.

$$\text{amplitude} = \tfrac{1}{2}(\text{maximum value} - \text{minimum value})$$

Problem 2 Finding Amplitudes of Sine and Cosine Curves

The graphing calculator screens at the right show several graphs of $y = a \sin x$ and $y = a \cos x$. Each x-axis shows values from 0 to 2π.

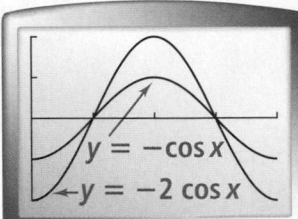

Think

What is the amplitude?
The amplitude is half the difference of the maximum and minimum values of the periodic function.

A What is the amplitude of each sine curve?

The amplitude of $y = \sin x$ is 1, and the amplitude of $y = 2 \sin x$ is 2.

B What is the amplitude of each cosine curve?

The amplitude of $y = -\cos x$ is 1, and the amplitude of $y = -2 \cos x$ is 2.

C How does the value of a affect the amplitude?

In each case, the amplitude of the curve is $|a|$.

Got It? **2.** What is the amplitude of each sine or cosine curve? What is the value of a?

a.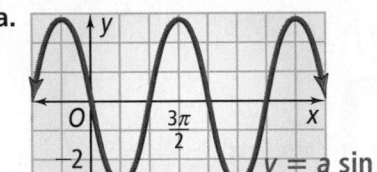

b.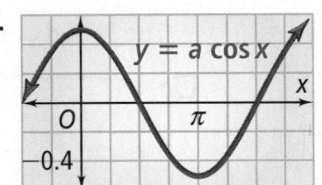

The summary box below lists the properties of sine and cosine functions.

take note

Concept Summary **Properties of Sine and Cosine Functions**

For $a \neq 0$, $b > 0$, and θ in radians, functions of the form $y = a \sin b\theta$ and $y = a \cos b\theta$ have the following properties.

- $|a|$ is the amplitude of the function.
- b is the number of cycles in the interval from 0 to 2π.
- $\frac{2\pi}{b}$ is the period of the function.

You can use five points equally spaced through one cycle to sketch a sine or cosine curve. For $a > 0$ and $b > 0$, the five-point patterns for $y = a \sin b\theta$ and $y = a \cos b\theta$ are shown.

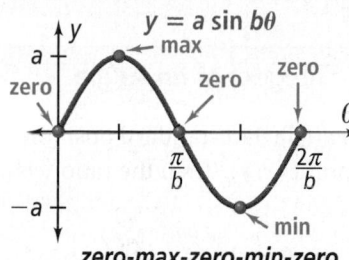

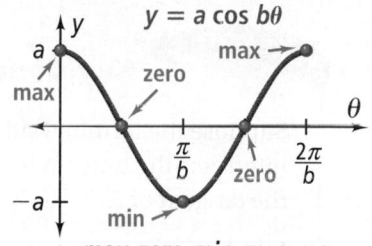

zero-max-zero-min-zero

max-zero-min-zero-max

Problem 3   Graphing From Function Rules

A What is the graph of one cycle of $y = \frac{1}{2} \sin 2\theta$?

Know	Need	Plan
An equation of the form $y = a \sin b\theta$	The graph of one cycle of the equation	• Identify the amplitude and period. • Find the critical values. • Plot the *zero-max-zero-min-zero* pattern.

Step 1 Find the amplitude and period.

$$\text{amplitude} = |a| = \left|\frac{1}{2}\right| = \frac{1}{2}$$

$$\text{period} = \frac{2\pi}{b} = \frac{2\pi}{2} = \pi$$

Step 2 Divide the period into fourths and identify the critical values.

$$\pi \div 4 = \frac{\pi}{4}$$

The critical values on the θ-axis are $0, \frac{\pi}{4}, \frac{\pi}{2}, \frac{3\pi}{4},$ and π.

Step 3 Sketch the graph.
Use $\frac{1}{2}$ for the maximum and $-\frac{1}{2}$ for the minimum.

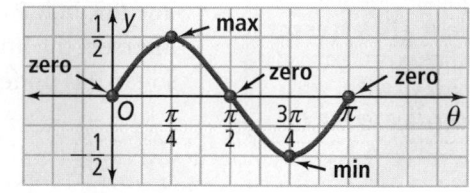

B What is the graph of one cycle of $y = 3 \cos 4\theta$?

$$\text{amplitude} = |a| = |3| = 3$$

$$\text{period} = \frac{2\pi}{b} = \frac{2\pi}{4} = \frac{\pi}{2}$$

Divide the period into fourths.
$\frac{\pi}{2} \div 4 = \frac{\pi}{8}$, so the critical values are $0, \frac{\pi}{8}, \frac{\pi}{4}, \frac{3\pi}{8}, \frac{\pi}{2}$.

Use the critical values to plot the five-point pattern.
Use 3 for the maximum and -3 for the minimum.

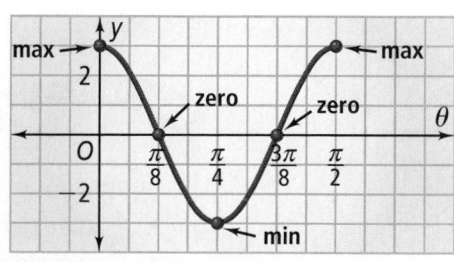

 Got It?   **3.** What is the graph of one cycle of each function?

a. $y = 3 \sin \frac{\pi}{2}\theta$ **b.** $y = 2 \cos \frac{\theta}{3}$

Focus Question How is the graph of the tangent function related to the graphs of sine and cosine functions?

Key Concept   Tangent of an Angle

Suppose the terminal side of an angle θ in standard position intersects the unit circle at the point (x, y). Then the ratio $\frac{y}{x}$ is the tangent of θ.

In this diagram, $x = \cos\theta$, $y = \sin\theta$, and $\frac{y}{x} = \tan\theta$.

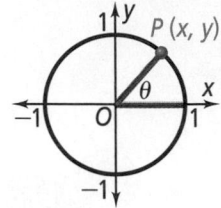

Hint

There is another way to geometrically define tan θ.

The diagram shows the unit circle and the vertical line $x = 1$. The angle θ in standard position determines a point $P(x, y)$.

By similar triangles, the length of the vertical red segment divided by the length of the horizontal red segment is equal to $\frac{y}{x}$. The horizontal red segment has length 1 since it is a radius of the unit circle, so the length of the vertical red segment is $\frac{y}{x}$ or tan θ, which is also the y-coordinate of Q.

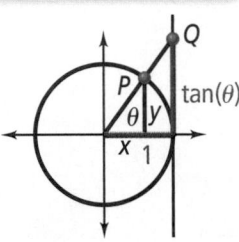

Hint

For any angle θ in standard position (except for θ = odd multiples of $\frac{\pi}{2}$), the line containing the terminal side of angle θ will intersect the line x = 1 at a point Q with y-coordinate tan θ.

The graph at the right shows one cycle of the **tangent function**, $y = \tan\theta$, for $-\frac{\pi}{2} < \theta < \frac{\pi}{2}$. The pattern repeats periodically with period π. At $\theta = \pm\frac{\pi}{2}$, the line through P fails to intersect the line $x = 1$, so tan θ is undefined.

$y = \tan\theta$

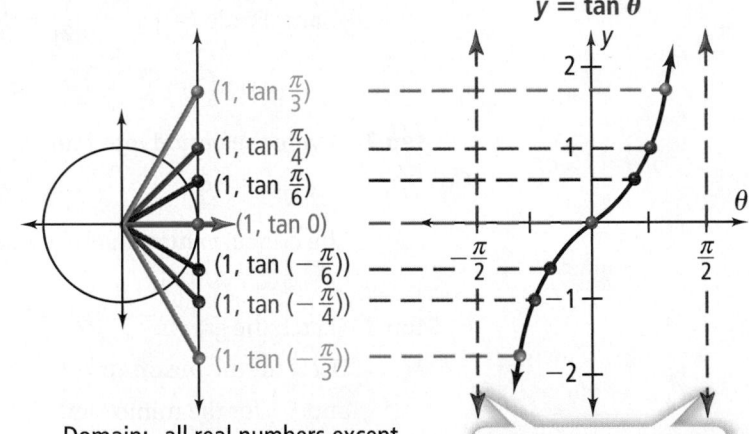

Domain: all real numbers except
odd multiples of $\frac{\pi}{2}$

Range: all real numbers

The graph approaches vertical asymptotes.

Concept Summary   Properties of Tangent Functions

Suppose $y = a \tan b\theta$, with $a \neq 0$, $b > 0$, and θ in radians.

- $\frac{\pi}{b}$ is the period of the function.
- One cycle occurs in the interval from $-\frac{\pi}{2b}$ to $\frac{\pi}{2b}$.
- There are vertical asymptotes at each end of the cycle.

Just as you did with sine and cosine, you can use five values equally spaced through one cycle to sketch a tangent curve. Two of the values are the vertical asymptotes. For $a > 0$ and $b > 0$, graph $y = a \tan b\theta$ by using the pattern *asymptote-(−a)-zero-(a)-asymptote*, as shown.

You can use the period, asymptotes, and points to graph a tangent function.

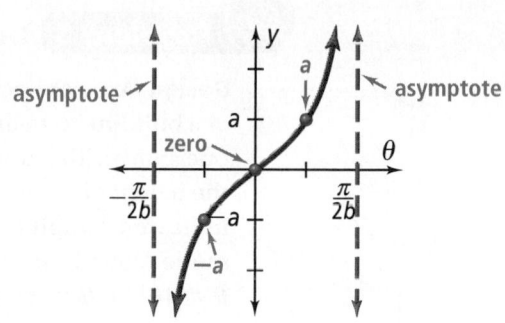

 Problem 4 Graphing a Tangent Function

Sketch two cycles of the graph of $y = \tan \pi\theta$.

Think	Write
Use the formula for the period. Substitute π for b and simplify.	$\text{period} = \frac{\pi}{b} = \frac{\pi}{\pi} = 1$
One cycle occurs in the interval from $-\frac{\pi}{2b}$ to $\frac{\pi}{2b}$.	$\frac{-\pi}{2b} = \frac{-\pi}{2\pi} \qquad \frac{\pi}{2b} = \frac{\pi}{2\pi}$ One cycle is from $-\frac{1}{2}$ to $\frac{1}{2}$. $= -\frac{1}{2} \qquad\qquad = \frac{1}{2}$
Divide the period into fourths and identify the key θ-values for the first cycle.	$1 \div 4 = \frac{1}{4}$
Pair each θ-value with the corresponding y-feature.	$-\frac{1}{2} \quad -\frac{1}{4} \quad 0 \quad \frac{1}{4} \quad \frac{1}{2}$ $\downarrow \qquad \downarrow \qquad \downarrow \quad \downarrow \qquad \downarrow$ asymptote $\quad -a \quad$ zero $\quad a \quad$ asymptote
Asymptotes occur at each end of the cycle.	Asymptotes are at $\theta = -\frac{1}{2}$ and $\frac{1}{2}$.
Locate the 3 points between the asymptotes. Use 1 for a.	$\left(-\frac{1}{4}, -1\right), (0, 0), \left(\frac{1}{4}, 1\right)$
Draw the asymptotes, plot the points, and sketch the curve. Add another cycle on the right, with $\frac{3}{2}$ as an asymptote.	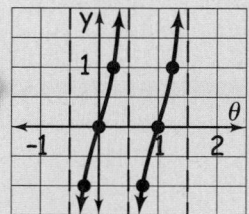

Got It? **4.** Sketch the graph of each tangent curve.
     a. $y = \tan 3\theta, 0 \le \theta \le \pi$ **b.** $y = \tan \frac{\pi}{2}\theta, 0 \le \theta < 3$

Problem 5 Using the Tangent Function to Solve Problems

Design An architect is designing the front facade of a building to include a triangle, similar to the one shown. The function $y = 100 \tan \theta$ models the height of the triangle, where θ is the angle indicated. Graph the function using the degree mode. What is the height of the triangle if $\theta = 16°$? If $\theta = 22°$?

200 ft

Think

How should you graph the function?
"Degree mode" suggests that you use a graphing calculator. Then use TABLE to show y values for different θ values.

Step 1 Graph the function $y = 100 \tan \theta$.

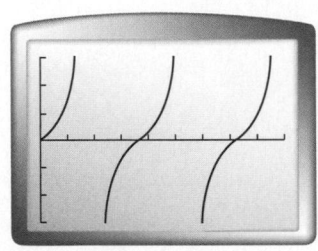

Xmin = 0
Xmax = 470
Xscl = 50
Ymin = −300
Ymax = 300
Yscl = 90

Step 2 Use the **TABLE** feature.

X	Y₁	
16	28.675	
17	30.573	
18	32.492	
19	34.433	
20	36.397	
21	38.386	
22	40.403	
X=16		

When $\theta = 16°$, the height of the triangle is about 28.7 ft. When $\theta = 22°$, the height of the triangle is about 40.4 ft.

 Got It? 5. What is the height of the triangle when $\theta = 25°$?

Focus Question What are the graphs of sine and cosine functions?

Answer The graphs of sine and cosine functions are periodic curves of the form $y = a \sin b\theta$ or $y = a \cos b\theta$. The value of a determines amplitude and reflection of the graph. The value of b determines the period.

Focus Question How is the graph of the tangent function related to the graphs of sine and cosine functions?

Answer The graph of the tangent function is related to the graphs of sine and cosine functions because, in the unit circle, $x = \cos \theta$, $y = \sin \theta$, and $\tan \theta = \frac{y}{x}$. The graph of the tangent curve is not a simple curve like sine or cosine. It has a vertical asymptote every period, the standard period is π instead of 2π, and it has no amplitude.

 Lesson Check

Do you know HOW?

Sketch one cycle of the graph of each function.

1. $y = 2 \sin 6\theta$

2. $y = 2 \cos \frac{\pi}{3}\theta$

Do you UNDERSTAND?

3. Vocabulary Successive asymptotes of a tangent curve are $x = \frac{\pi}{3}$ and $x = -\frac{\pi}{3}$. What is the period?

4. Open-Ended Write a cosine function that has a period greater than the period for $y = 5 \cos \frac{\theta}{2}$.

Practice and Problem-Solving Exercises

 **Practice**

Find the period of each sine curve.

◀ **See Problem 1.**

5. 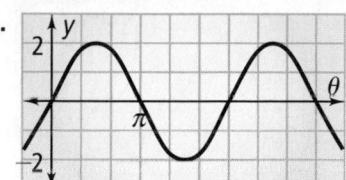   **6.**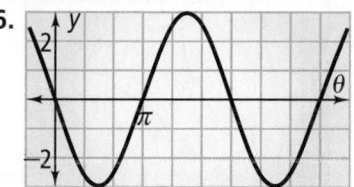

Find the period of each cosine curve.

7.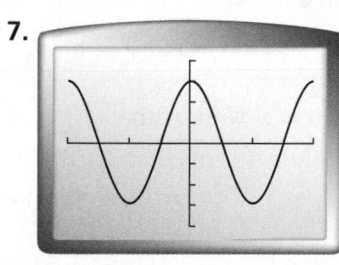

Xmin $= -2\pi$
Xmax $= 2\pi$
Xscl $= \pi$
Ymin $= -4$
Ymax $= 4$
Yscl $= 1$

8.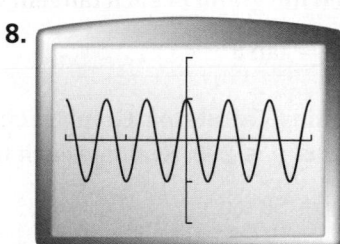

Xmin $= -2\pi$
Xmax $= 2\pi$
Xscl $= \pi$
Ymin $= -2$
Ymax $= 2$
Yscl $= 1$

Find the amplitude and value of *a* for each sine function.

◀ **See Problem 2.**

9. 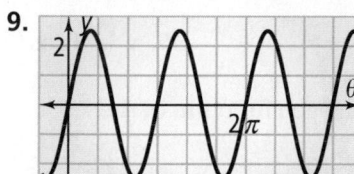   **10.**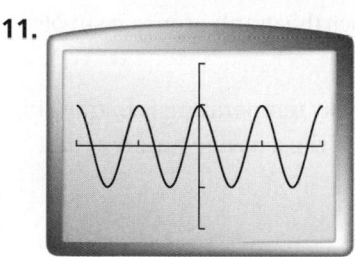

Find the amplitude and value of *a* for each cosine function.

11.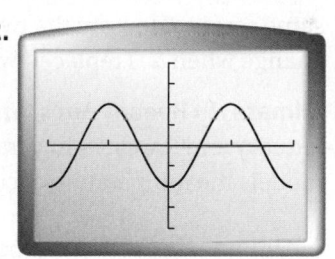

Xmin $= -2\pi$
Xmax $= 2\pi$
Xscl $= \pi$
Ymin $= -2$
Ymax $= 2$
Yscl $= 1$

12.

Xmin $= -2\pi$
Xmax $- 2\pi$
Xscl $= \pi$
Ymin $= -4$
Ymax $= 4$
Yscl $= 1$

Sketch one cycle of the graph of each function.

◀ **See Problem 3.**

13. $y = \sin \pi\theta$ **14.** $y = \sin 3\theta$ **15.** $y = \cos 2\theta$

16. $y = -3\cos\theta$ **17.** $y = -\sin\frac{\pi}{2}\theta$ **18.** $y = -\cos \pi\theta$

19. $y = 2\sin \pi\theta$ **20.** $y = \cos\frac{\pi}{2}\theta$ **21.** $y = 4\sin\frac{1}{2}\theta$

Each graphing calculator screen shows the interval 0 to 2π. What is the period of each graph?

22.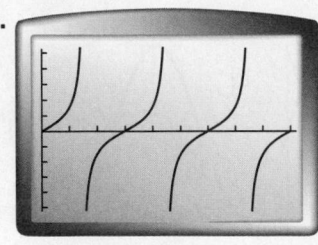

23.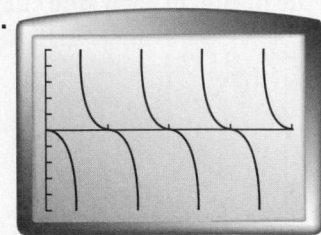

Sketch the graph of each tangent curve in the interval from 0 to 2π.   ◀ **See Problem 4.**

24. $y = \tan \theta$ **25.** $y = \tan 2\theta$ **26.** $y = \tan \frac{2\pi}{3}\theta$

 **Graphing Calculator** Graph each function on the interval $0 \le x \le 2\pi$ with   ◀ **See Problem 5.**
$-200 \le y \le 200$. Evaluate each function at $x = \frac{\pi}{4}, \frac{\pi}{2}$, and $\frac{3\pi}{4}$.

27. $y = 50 \tan x$ **28.** $y = -100 \tan x$ **29.** $y = 125 \tan\left(\frac{1}{2}x\right)$

B Apply

Find the amplitude and period of each function.

30. $y = \sin \pi\theta$ **31.** $y = -5 \sin \theta$ **32.** $y = 3 \sin \theta$

33. $y = -\cos 2t$ **34.** $y = 2 \cos \frac{1}{2}t$ **35.** $y = 3 \cos\left(-\frac{\theta}{3}\right)$

Identify the period for each tangent function. Then graph each function in the interval from -2π to 2π.

36. $y = \tan \frac{\pi}{6}\theta$ **37.** $y = \tan 2.5\theta$ **38.** $y = \tan\left(-\frac{3}{2\pi}\theta\right)$

39. Graphing Calculator Graph the functions $y = 3 \sin \theta$ and $y = -3 \sin \theta$ on the same screen. How are the two graphs related? How does the graph of $y = a \sin b\theta$ change when a is replaced with its opposite?

40. Climate In Buenos Aires, Argentina, the average monthly temperature is highest in January and lowest in July, ranging from 83°F to 57°F. Write a cosine function that models the temperature according to the month of the year.

41. a. Open-Ended Write a tangent function.
   b. Graph the function on the interval -2π to 2π.
   c. Identify the period and the asymptotes of the function.

42. Sound Waves The sound wave for the note A above middle C can be modeled by the function $y = 0.001 \sin 880\pi\theta$. Sketch a graph of the sine curve.

Find the period and amplitude of each sine function. Then sketch each function from 0 to 2π.

43. $y = -3.5 \sin 5\theta$ **44.** $y = \frac{5}{2} \sin 2\theta$ **45.** $y = -2 \sin 2\pi\theta$

Write an equation of a tangent function for each graph.

46.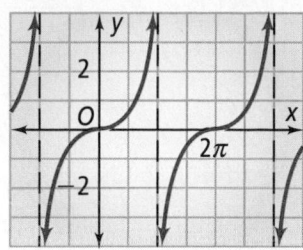

47.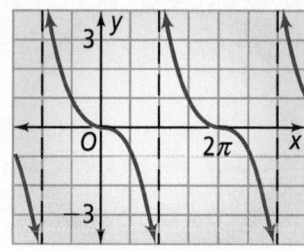

48. Open-Ended Write the equations of three sine functions with the same amplitude that have periods of 2, 3, and 4. Then sketch all three graphs.

49. Music The sound wave for a certain pitch fork can be modeled by the function $y = 0.001 \sin 1320\pi\theta$. Sketch a graph of the sine curve.

Standardized Test Prep

SAT/ACT

50. What is the amplitude of $y = 3 \sin 4\theta$?

Ⓐ $\frac{4}{3}$　　　Ⓑ 3　　　Ⓒ 4　　　Ⓓ 2π

51. Which equation has the same graph as $y = -\cos t$?

Ⓕ $y = \cos(-t)$　　　Ⓗ $y = \cos(t - \pi)$

Ⓖ $y = \sin(t - \pi)$　　　Ⓘ $y = -\sin t$

52. Which value is NOT defined?

Ⓐ $\tan 0$　　　Ⓑ $\tan \pi$　　　Ⓒ $\tan \frac{3\pi}{2}$　　　Ⓓ $\frac{1}{\tan \frac{\pi}{4}}$

53. Which function has a period of 4π and an amplitude of 8?

Ⓕ $y = -8 \sin 8\theta$　　Ⓖ $y = -8 \sin \frac{1}{2}\theta$　　Ⓗ $y = 8 \sin 2\theta$　　Ⓘ $y = 4 \sin 8\theta$

Short Response

54. Does a tangent function have amplitude? Explain.

Mixed Review

Write each measure in radians. Express the answer in terms of π and as a decimal rounded to the nearest hundredth.　　◀ **See Lesson T-4.**

55. $-80°$　　　**56.** $150°$　　　**57.** $-240°$　　　**58.** $320°$

Find the 27th term of each sequence.　　◀ **See Lesson 9-2.**

59. $5, 8, 11, \ldots$　　**60.** $59, 48, 37, \ldots$　　**61.** $-11, -5, 1, \ldots$　　**62.** $6, -7, -20, \ldots$

Get Ready!　**To prepare for Lesson T-6, do Exercises 63–65.**

Determine whether each equation is true for all real numbers x. Explain your reasoning.　　◀ **See Lesson 1-4.**

63. $2x + 3x = 5x$　　　**64.** $-(4x - 10) = 10 - 4x$　　　**65.** $3x + 15 = 5(x - 3) - 2x$

T-6 Basic Identities

Objective To verify trigonometric identities

Dynamic Activity
Trigonometric
Identities

Lesson Vocabulary
• trigonometric identity

Focus Question Why are the interrelationships among the six basic trigonometric functions useful?

A **trigonometric identity** in one variable is a trigonometric equation that is true for all values of the variable for which all expressions in the equation are defined. Some trigonometric identities are definitions or follow immediately from definitions.

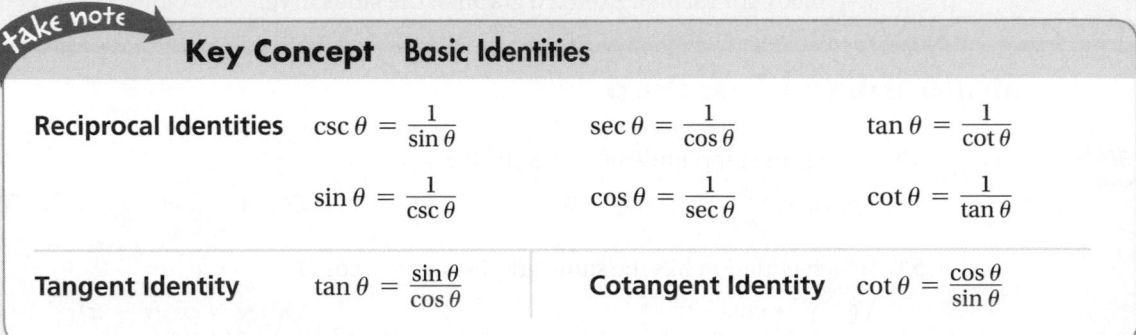

take note

Key Concept   Basic Identities

Reciprocal Identities

$$\csc \theta = \frac{1}{\sin \theta} \qquad \sec \theta = \frac{1}{\cos \theta} \qquad \tan \theta = \frac{1}{\cot \theta}$$

$$\sin \theta = \frac{1}{\csc \theta} \qquad \cos \theta = \frac{1}{\sec \theta} \qquad \cot \theta = \frac{1}{\tan \theta}$$

Tangent Identity $\tan \theta = \dfrac{\sin \theta}{\cos \theta}$ **Cotangent Identity** $\cot \theta = \dfrac{\cos \theta}{\sin \theta}$

You can use trigonometric identities to simplify trigonometric expressions.

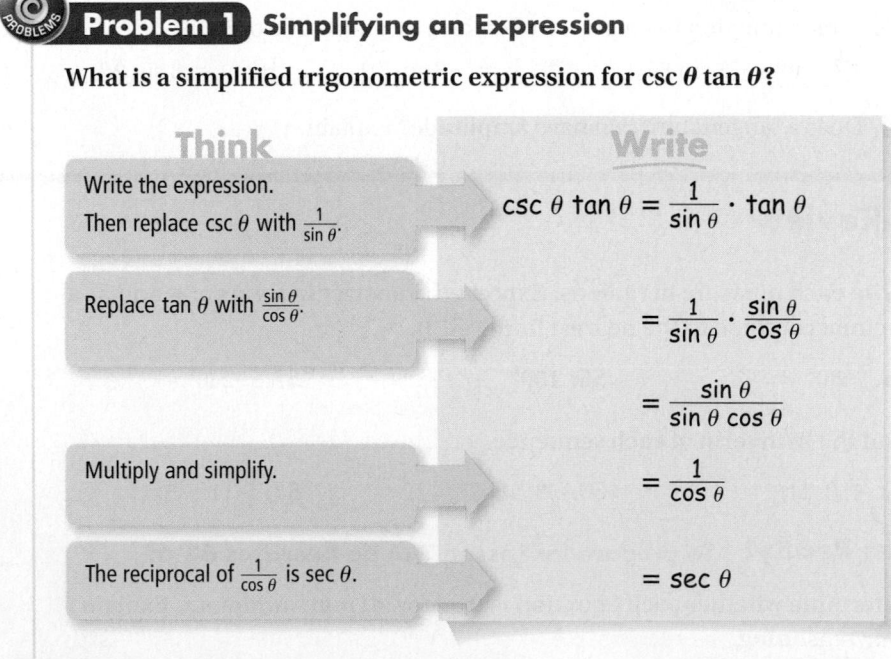

Problem 1   Simplifying an Expression

What is a simplified trigonometric expression for csc θ tan θ?

Think

Write the expression. Then replace $\csc \theta$ with $\frac{1}{\sin \theta}$.

Replace $\tan \theta$ with $\frac{\sin \theta}{\cos \theta}$.

Multiply and simplify.

The reciprocal of $\frac{1}{\cos \theta}$ is $\sec \theta$.

Write

$$\csc \theta \tan \theta = \frac{1}{\sin \theta} \cdot \tan \theta$$

$$= \frac{1}{\sin \theta} \cdot \frac{\sin \theta}{\cos \theta}$$

$$= \frac{\sin \theta}{\sin \theta \cos \theta}$$

$$= \frac{1}{\cos \theta}$$

$$= \sec \theta$$

Got It?   1. What is a simplified trigonometric expression for sec θ cot θ?

You can use known identities to verify other identities. Use previously known identities to transform one side of the equation to look like the other side.

 Problem 2 Verifying an Identity Using Basic Identities

Verify each identity.

A $(\sin \theta)(\sec \theta) = \tan \theta$

Think

What identity do you know that you can use?
Look for a way to write the expression on the left in terms of $\sin \theta$ and $\cos \theta$. Use the identity $\sec \theta = \frac{1}{\cos \theta}$.

To verify this identity, begin with the more complicated side of the equation. Transform the left side of the equation to look like the expression on the right side of the equation.

Use a reciprocal identity.	$(\sin \theta)(\sec \theta) = \sin \theta \cdot \frac{1}{\cos \theta}$
Simplify.	$= \frac{\sin \theta}{\cos \theta}$
Use the tangent identity.	$= \tan \theta$

B $\frac{1}{\cot \theta} = \tan \theta$

Begin with the expression on left side of the equation. Transform it to look like the expression on the right side of the equation.

Use the definition of cotangent.	$\frac{1}{\cot \theta} = \frac{1}{\frac{1}{\tan \theta}}$
Simplify.	$= \tan \theta$

Hint

When verifying an identity, begin with the more complicated side.

 Got It? **2.** Verify the identity $\frac{\csc \theta}{\sec \theta} = \cot \theta$.

Every angle θ determines a point $(x, y) = (\cos \theta, \sin \theta)$ on the unit circle. Also, every point (x, y) on the unit circle satisfies the equation $x^2 + y^2 = 1$. Therefore, for every angle θ, there are three identities related to the Pythagorean Theorem.

Hint

The expression $\cos^2 \theta$ is equivalent to $(\cos \theta)^2$. This simplified notation allows you to write the expression without using parentheses.

take note

Key Concept   Pythagorean Identities

$$\cos^2 \theta + \sin^2 \theta = 1 \qquad\qquad 1 + \tan^2 \theta = \sec^2 \theta \qquad\qquad 1 + \cot^2 \theta = \csc^2 \theta$$

You can use the basic and Pythagorean identities to verify other identities. The method of proof is always the same: transform the expression on one side of the equation to become the expression on the other side.

Problem 3 Verifying a Pythagorean Identity

Verify the Pythagorean identity $1 + \tan^2 \theta = \sec^2 \theta$.

Begin with the expression on left side of the equation. Transform it to look like the expression on the right side.

Plan

With which side should you work? It usually is easier to begin with the more complicated-looking side.

Use the tangent identity. $1 + \tan^2 \theta = 1 + \left(\dfrac{\sin \theta}{\cos \theta}\right)^2$

Simplify. $= 1 + \dfrac{\sin^2 \theta}{\cos^2 \theta}$

Find a common denominator. $= \dfrac{\cos^2 \theta}{\cos^2 \theta} + \dfrac{\sin^2 \theta}{\cos^2 \theta}$

Add. $= \dfrac{\cos^2 \theta + \sin^2 \theta}{\cos^2 \theta}$

Use a Pythagorean identity. $= \dfrac{1}{\cos^2 \theta}$

Use a reciprocal identity. $= \sec^2 \theta$

You have transformed the expression on the left side of the equation to become the expression on the right side. The equation is an identity.

Hint

It often helps to write everything in terms of sines and cosines.

 Got It? **3.** Verify the third Pythagorean identity, $1 + \cot^2 \theta = \csc^2 \theta$.

Focus Question Why are the interrelationships among the six basic trigonometric functions useful?

Answer The basic identities make it possible to write trigonometric expressions in various equivalent forms, some of which can be significantly easier to work with than others in mathematical applications.

 Lesson Check

Do you know HOW?

Verify each identity.

1. $\tan \theta \csc \theta = \sec \theta$

2. $\csc^2 \theta - \cot^2 \theta = 1$

3. $\sin \theta \tan \theta = \sec \theta - \cos \theta$

4. Simplify $\tan \theta \cot \theta - \sin^2 \theta$.

Do you UNDERSTAND?

5. **Vocabulary** How does the identity $\cos^2 \theta + \sin^2 \theta = 1$ relate to the Pythagorean Theorem?

6. **Error Analysis** A student simplified the expression $2 - \cos^2 \theta$ to $1 - \sin^2 \theta$. What error did the student make? What is the correct simplified expression?

Practice and Problem-Solving Exercises

A Practice

Guided Practice

Simplify each trigonometric expression.

◀ See Problem 1.

To start, write the expression and use the reciprocal identity $\sec \theta = \frac{1}{\cos \theta}$.

7. $\sin \theta \sec \theta \cot \theta$

$\sin \theta \sec \theta \cot \theta = \sin \theta \cdot \frac{1}{\cos \theta} \cdot \cot \theta$

8. $\tan \theta \cot \theta$

9. $1 - \cos^2 \theta$

10. $\sec^2 \theta - 1$

11. $1 - \csc^2 \theta$

12. $\sin \theta \csc \theta$

13. $\sec \theta \cos \theta \sin \theta$

Verify each identity.

◀ See Problems 2 and 3.

14. $\cos \theta \cot \theta = \frac{1}{\sin \theta} - \sin \theta$

15. $\sin \theta \cot \theta = \cos \theta$

16. $\cos \theta \tan \theta = \sin \theta$

17. $\sin \theta \sec \theta = \tan \theta$

18. $\cos \theta \sec \theta = 1$

19. $\csc \theta - \sin \theta = \cot \theta \cos \theta$

20. $\sec^2 \theta \cot^2 \theta = \csc^2 \theta$

21. $\cot \theta = \csc \theta \cos \theta$

22. $\sin \theta \tan \theta = \sec \theta - \cos \theta$

B Apply

Simplify each trigonometric expression.

23. $\cos \theta + \sin \theta \tan \theta$

24. $\csc \theta \cos \theta \tan \theta$

25. $\tan \theta (\cot \theta + \tan \theta)$

26. $\sin \theta (1 + \cot^2 \theta)$

27. $\sin^2 \theta \csc \theta \sec \theta$

28. $\sec \theta \cos \theta - \cos^2 \theta$

29. $\csc \theta - \cos \theta \cot \theta$

30. $\dfrac{\csc \theta}{\sin \theta + \cos \theta \cot \theta}$

31. $\dfrac{\cos \theta \csc \theta}{\cot \theta}$

32. $\dfrac{\sin^2 \theta \csc \theta \sec \theta}{\tan \theta}$

Hint

You can also use Pythagorean Identities to simplify an expression.

Express the first trigonometric function in terms of the second.

33. $\sin \theta$; $\cos \theta$

34. $\tan \theta$; $\cos \theta$

35. $\cot \theta$; $\sin \theta$

36. $\csc \theta$; $\cot \theta$

37. $\cot \theta$; $\csc \theta$

38. $\sec \theta$; $\tan \theta$

39. Error Analysis Find the two errors in the verification of the identity $\frac{\sec^2 \theta - \tan^2 \theta}{\tan^2 \theta} = \cot^2 \theta$ shown at the right. Then verify the identity correctly.

40. Open-Ended Develop your own trigonometric identity. (*Hint:* Start with a simple trigonometric expression and work backward.)

41. Writing Only one of the following equations is an identity. Identify the identity and explain your answer.

$$(x - 1)^2 - 1 = x(x - 2) \qquad (x - 1)^2 = x(x - 1)$$

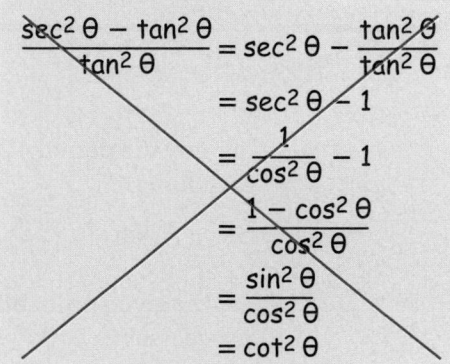

$$\frac{\sec^2 \theta - \tan^2 \theta}{\tan^2 \theta} = \sec^2 \theta - \frac{\tan^2 \theta}{\tan^2 \theta}$$
$$= \sec^2 \theta - 1$$
$$= \frac{1}{\cos^2 \theta} - 1$$
$$= \frac{1 - \cos^2 \theta}{\cos^2 \theta}$$
$$= \frac{\sin^2 \theta}{\cos^2 \theta}$$
$$= \cot^2 \theta$$

Verify each identity.

42. $\sin^2 \theta \tan^2 \theta = \tan^2 \theta - \sin^2 \theta$

43. $\sec \theta - \sin \theta \tan \theta = \cos \theta$

44. $\sin \theta \cos \theta (\tan \theta + \cot \theta) = 1$

45. $\dfrac{1 - \sin \theta}{\cos \theta} = \dfrac{\cos \theta}{1 + \sin \theta}$

46. $\dfrac{\sec \theta}{\cot \theta + \tan \theta} = \sin \theta$

47. $(\cot \theta + 1)^2 = \csc^2 \theta + 2 \cot \theta$

Write each expression in terms of sin θ.

48. $\cos \theta \csc \theta \cot \theta$

49. $\dfrac{\cos \theta}{\sec \theta + \tan \theta}$

Standardized Test Prep

SAT/ACT

50. Which expression is equivalent to $2 \cot \theta$?

Ⓐ $\dfrac{1}{2 \tan \theta}$ 　　　Ⓑ $\dfrac{2}{\cot \theta}$ 　　　Ⓒ $\dfrac{2 \cos \theta}{\sin \theta}$ 　　　Ⓓ $\dfrac{\sin \theta}{\frac{1}{2} \cos \theta}$

51. Which equation is NOT an identity?

Ⓕ $\cos^2 \theta = 1 - \sin^2 \theta$ 　　　Ⓗ $\sin^2 \theta = \cos^2 \theta - 1$

Ⓖ $\cot^2 \theta = \csc^2 \theta - 1$ 　　　Ⓘ $\tan^2 \theta = \sec^2 \theta - 1$

52. Which expressions are equivalent?

I. $(\sin \theta)(\csc \theta - \sin \theta)$ 　　　II. $\sin^2 \theta - 1$ 　　　III. $\cos^2 \theta$

Ⓐ I and II only 　　Ⓑ II and III only 　　Ⓒ I and III only 　　Ⓓ I, II, and III

53. How can you express $\csc^2 \theta - 2 \cot^2 \theta$ in terms of $\sin \theta$ and $\cos \theta$?

Ⓕ $\dfrac{1 - 2 \cos^2 \theta}{\sin^2 \theta}$ 　　Ⓖ $\dfrac{1 - 2 \sin^2 \theta}{\sin^2 \theta}$ 　　Ⓗ $\sin^2 \theta - 2 \cos^2 \theta$ 　　Ⓘ $\dfrac{1}{\sin^2 \theta} - \dfrac{2}{\tan^2 \theta}$

54. Which expression is equivalent to $\dfrac{\tan \theta}{\cos \theta - \sec \theta}$?

Ⓐ $\csc \theta$ 　　　Ⓑ $\sec \theta$ 　　　Ⓒ $-\csc \theta$ 　　　Ⓓ $\tan^2 \theta$

Short Response

55. Show that $(\sec \theta + 1)(\sec \theta - 1) = \tan^2 \theta$ is an identity.

Mixed Review

Identify the period of each function. Then tell where two asymptotes occur for each function.

● **See Lesson T-5.**

56. $y = \tan 6\theta$ 　　**57.** $y = \tan \dfrac{\theta}{4}$ 　　**58.** $y = \tan 1.5\theta$ 　　**59.** $y = \tan \dfrac{\theta}{6}$

For the given probability of success P on each trial, find the probability of x successes in n trials.

● **See Lesson 11-8.**

60. $x = 4, n = 5, p = 0.2$ 　　　　　　**61.** $x = 3, n = 5, p = 0.6$

62. $x = 4, n = 8, p = 0.7$ 　　　　　　**63.** $x = 7, n = 8, p = 0.7$

 **Trigonometry Review**

Connecting **BIG** ideas and Answering the Essential Questions

1 Function
If you know the value of sin θ, use right triangle trigonometry to find values of the other trigonometric functions.

Right Triangles and Trigonometric Ratios (Lesson T-1)

$\sin A = \dfrac{\text{opposite}}{\text{hypotenuse}}$

$\cos A = \dfrac{\text{adjacent}}{\text{hypotenuse}}$

$\tan A = \dfrac{\text{opposite}}{\text{adjacent}}$

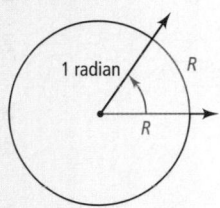

Special Angles (Lesson T-2)

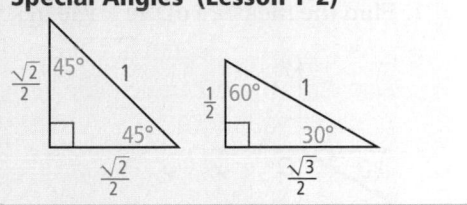

2 Modeling
You can use the sine and cosine functions to model most periodic behavior.

Degrees and Radian Measure (Lesson T-4)

One radian is the measure of a central angle that intercepts an arc of length equal to the radius.

The Unit Circle (Lesson T-3)

$x = \cos \theta$

$\quad = \cos 60° = \dfrac{1}{2}$

$y = \sin \theta$

$\quad = \sin 60° = \dfrac{\sqrt{3}}{2}$

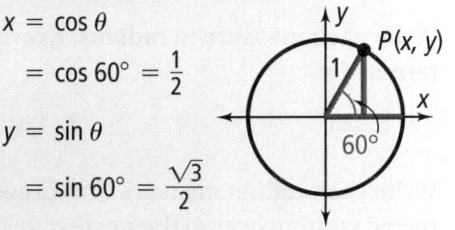

3 Equivalence
To verify that an equation in θ is an identity, show that both of its sides have equal values for each possible replacement for θ.

Basic Identities (Lesson T-6)

$2 \tan \theta \cos^2 \theta = \dfrac{2 \sin \theta \cos^2 \theta}{\cos \theta}$

$\quad = 2 \sin \theta \cos \theta$

Graphs of Sine, Cosine, and Tangent Functions (Lesson T-5)

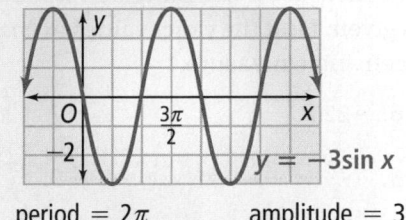

$y = -3\sin x$

period = 2π \qquad amplitude = 3

Vocabulary

- amplitude (p. 850)
- central angle (p. 841)
- cosine function (p. 848)
- cosine of θ (p. 823)
- cycle (p. 849)
- initial side (p. 834)
- intercepted arc (p. 841)
- period (p. 849)
- periodic function (p. 849)
- radian (p. 841)
- reference angle (p. 835)
- sine function (p. 848)
- sine of θ (p. 823)
- standard position (p. 834)
- tangent function (p. 853)
- tangent of θ (p. 823)
- terminal side (p. 834)
- trigonometric identity (p. 858)
- trigonometric ratios (p. 823)
- unit circle (p. 836)

Choose the correct term to complete each sentence.

1. The __?__ of a periodic function is the length of one cycle.

2. Centered at the origin of the coordinate plane, the __?__ has a radius of 1 unit.

3. An asymptote of the __?__ occurs at $\theta = \dfrac{\pi}{2}$ and repeats every π units.

4. The six ratios of the lengths of the sides of a right triangle are known as the __?__ .

5. A trigonometric equation that is true for all values except those for which the expressions on either side of the equal sign are undefined is a __?__ .

MathXL® for School
Go to PowerAlgebra.com

Do you know HOW?

1. Find the measure of the angle in standard position.

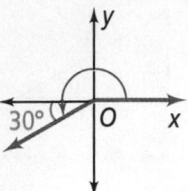

Write each measure in radians. Express your answer in terms of π.

2. $-225°$ **3.** $120°$

Write each radian measure in degrees. If necessary, round your answer to the nearest degree.

4. $\frac{5\pi}{6}$ **5.** -2.5π

The measure θ of an angle in standard position is given. Find the exact values of $\cos\theta$ and $\sin\theta$ for each angle measure.

6. $-225°$ **7.** $120°$

8. $-\frac{4\pi}{3}$ **9.** $\frac{5\pi}{4}$

10. Find the length of the intercepted arc to the nearest tenth for an arc with a central angle of measure $\theta = \frac{\pi}{3}$ on a circle of radius $r = 10$.

Find the amplitude and period of each function. Then sketch one cycle of the graph of each function.

11. $y = 4\sin(2x)$ **12.** $y = 2\sin(4x)$

Graph each function in the interval from 0 to 2π.

13. $y = 2\cos x$ **14.** $y = -\cos x$

15. $y = \sin 2\theta$ **16.** $y = \tan\frac{\pi}{3}\theta$

Simplify each trigonometric expression.

17. $\sin\theta + \cos\theta\cot\theta$ **18.** $\csc\theta\cos\theta\tan\theta$

19. $\cot\theta(\tan\theta + \cot\theta)$ **20.** $\sin\theta\cot\theta$

Verify each identity.

21. $\sec\theta\sin\theta\cot\theta = 1$ **22.** $\csc^2\theta - \cot^2\theta = 1$

23. $\sec\theta\cot\theta = \csc\theta$ **24.** $\sec^2\theta - 1 = \tan^2\theta$

$\triangle ABC$ has right angle C and $AC = 3$. For the given information, find the missing length.

25. $m\angle A = 60°$, $AB = \blacksquare$ **26.** $m\angle B = 60°$, $BC = \blacksquare$

27. $m\angle A = 45°$, $AB = \blacksquare$ **28.** $m\angle A = 30°$, $AB = \blacksquare$

In $\triangle ABC$, find each value as a fraction and as a decimal. Round to the nearest hundredth.

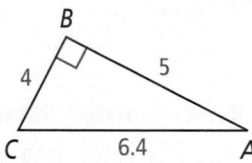

29. $\sin A$ **30.** $\sec A$

31. $\cot A$ **32.** $\csc C$

33. $\sec C$ **34.** $\tan C$

Do you UNDERSTAND?

35. Writing Explain how to convert an angle measure in radians to an angle measure in degrees. Include an example.

36. Physics On each swing, a pendulum 18 inches long travels through an angle of $\frac{3\pi}{4}$ radians. How far does the tip of the pendulum travel in one swing? Round your answer to the nearest inch.

37. Reasoning What are the steps you take to find the asymptotes of the function $y = a\tan bx + c$, $a \neq 0$?

Skills **Handbook**

Percents and Percent Applications

Percent means "per hundred." Find fraction, decimal, and percent equivalents by replacing one symbol for *hundredths* with another.

Example 1

Write each number as a percent.

a. $0.082 = 8.2\%$

Move the decimal point two places to the right and write a percent sign.

b. $\frac{3}{5} = \frac{60}{100} = 60\%$

Write the fraction as hundredths. Then replace the hundredths with a percent sign.

c. $1\frac{1}{6} = \frac{7}{6} = 1.166\overline{6} = 116.\overline{6}\%$

Divide 7 by 6 to write $1\frac{1}{6}$ as a decimal.

Example 2

Write each percent as a decimal.

a. $50\% = 0.50 = 0.5$

Move the decimal point two places to the left and drop the percent sign.

b. $\frac{1}{2}\% = 0.5\% = 00.5\% = 0.005$

Example 3

Use an equation to solve each percent problem.

a. What is 30% of 12?

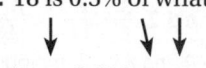

$n = 0.3 \times 12$

$n = 3.6$

b. 18 is 0.3% of what?

$18 = 0.003 \times n$

$\frac{18}{0.003} = \frac{0.003n}{0.003}$

$6000 = n$

c. What percent of 60 is 9?

$n \times 60 = 9$

$60n = 9$

$n = \frac{9}{60} = 0.15 = 15\%$

Exercises

Write each decimal as a percent and each percent as a decimal.

1. 0.46   **2.** 1.506   **3.** 0.007   **4.** 8%   **5.** 103.5%   **6.** 3.3%

Write each fraction or mixed number as a percent.

7. $\frac{1}{4}$ **8.** $\frac{3}{8}$ **9.** $\frac{2}{3}$ **10.** $\frac{4}{9}$ **11.** $1\frac{3}{20}$ **12.** $\frac{1}{200}$

Use an equation to solve each percent problem. Round your answer to the nearest tenth, if necessary.

13. What is 25% of 50?   **14.** What percent of 58 is 37?   **15.** 120% of what is 90?

16. 8 is what percent of 40?   **17.** 15 is 75% of what?   **18.** 80% of 58 is what?

Operations With Fractions

To add or subtract fractions, use a common denominator. The common denominator is the least common multiple of the denominators.

Example 1

Simplify $\frac{2}{3} + \frac{3}{5}$.

For 3 and 5, the least common multiple is 15.

Write $\frac{2}{3}$ and $\frac{3}{5}$ as equivalent fractions with denominators of 15.

Add the numerators.

$$\frac{2}{3} + \frac{3}{5} = \frac{2}{3} \cdot \frac{5}{5} + \frac{3}{5} \cdot \frac{3}{3}$$
$$= \frac{10}{15} + \frac{9}{15}$$
$$= \frac{19}{15} \text{ or } 1\frac{4}{15}$$

Example 2

Simplify $5\frac{1}{4} - 3\frac{2}{3}$.

Write equivalent fractions.

Write $5\frac{3}{12}$ as $4\frac{15}{12}$ so you can subtract the fractions.

Subtract the fractions. Then subtract the whole numbers.

$$5\frac{1}{4} - 3\frac{2}{3} = 5\frac{3}{12} - 3\frac{8}{12}$$
$$= 4\frac{15}{12} - 3\frac{8}{12}$$
$$= 1\frac{7}{12}$$

To multiply fractions, multiply the numerators and multiply the denominators. You can simplify by using a greatest common factor.

Example 3

Simplify $\frac{3}{4} \cdot \frac{8}{11}$

Method 1 $\frac{3}{4} \cdot \frac{8}{11} = \frac{24}{44} = \frac{24 \div 4}{44 \div 4} = \frac{6}{11}$

Divide 24 and 44 by 4, their greatest common factor.

Method 2 $\frac{3}{\cancel{4}} \cdot \frac{\cancel{8}^{2}}{11} = \frac{6}{11}$

Divide 4 and 8 by 4, their greatest common factor.

To divide fractions, use a reciprocal to change the problem to multiplication.

Example 4

Simplify $3\frac{1}{5} \div 1\frac{1}{2}$

Write mixed numbers as improper fractions.

Multiply by the reciprocal of the divisor.

Simplify.

$$3\frac{1}{5} \div 1\frac{1}{2} = \frac{16}{5} \div \frac{3}{2}$$
$$= \frac{16}{5} \cdot \frac{2}{3}$$
$$= \frac{32}{15} \text{ or } 2\frac{2}{15}$$

Exercises

Perform the indicated operation.

1. $\frac{3}{5} + \frac{4}{5}$ 2. $\frac{1}{2} + \frac{2}{3}$ 3. $4\frac{1}{2} + 2\frac{1}{3}$ 4. $5\frac{3}{4} + 4\frac{2}{5}$ 5. $\frac{2}{3} - \frac{3}{7}$

6. $5\frac{1}{2} - 3\frac{2}{5}$ 7. $7\frac{3}{4} - 4\frac{4}{5}$ 8. $3\frac{4}{5} \cdot 10$ 9. $2\frac{1}{2} \cdot 3\frac{1}{5}$ 10. $6\frac{3}{4} \cdot 5\frac{2}{3}$

11. $\frac{1}{2} \div \frac{1}{3}$ 12. $\frac{6}{5} \div \frac{3}{5}$ 13. $8\frac{1}{2} \div 4\frac{1}{4}$ 14. $\frac{8}{9} - \frac{2}{3}$ 15. $5\frac{1}{4} \cdot 8$

Ratios and Proportions

A *ratio* is a comparison of two quantities by division. You can write *equal ratios* by multiplying or dividing each quantity by the same nonzero number.

Ways to Write a Ratio
$a : b \quad a \text{ to } b \quad \frac{a}{b} \ (b \neq 0)$

Example 1

Write $3\frac{1}{3} : \frac{1}{2}$ as a ratio in simplest form.

In simplest form, both terms should be integers. Multiply by the common denominator, 6.

$$3\frac{1}{3} : \frac{1}{2} \rightarrow \frac{3\frac{1}{3}}{\frac{1}{2}} = \frac{20}{3} \text{ or } 20 : 3$$

A rate is a ratio that compares different types of quantities. In simplest form for a rate, the second quantity is one unit.

Example 2

Write **247 mi in 5.2 h** as a rate in simplest form.

Divide by 5.2 to make the second quantity one unit.

$$\frac{247 \text{ mi}}{5.2 \text{ h}} = \frac{47.5 \text{ mi}}{1 \text{ h}} \text{ or } 47.5 \text{ mi/h}$$

A proportion is a statement that two ratios are equal. You can find a missing term in a proportion by using the cross products.

Cross Products of a Proportion
$$\frac{a}{b} = \frac{c}{d} \quad \rightarrow \quad ad = bc$$

Example 3

The Copy Center charges $2.52 for 63 copies. At that rate, how much will the Copy Center charge for 140 copies?

Set up a proportion. $\begin{array}{l} \text{cost} \rightarrow \\ \text{copies} \rightarrow \end{array} \quad \dfrac{2.52}{63} = \dfrac{c}{140}$

Use cross products. $2.52 \cdot 140 = 63c$

Solve for c. $c = \dfrac{2.52 \cdot 140}{63}$

Simplify. $= 5.6 \text{ or } \$5.60$

Exercises

Write each ratio or rate in simplest form.

1. 15 to 20

2. $85 : 34$

3. 38 g in 4 oz

4. 375 mi in 4.3 h

5. $\frac{84}{30}$

Solve each proportion. Round your answer to the nearest tenth, if necessary.

6. $\frac{a}{5} = \frac{12}{15}$

7. $\frac{21}{12} = \frac{14}{x}$

8. $8 : 15 = n : 25$

9. $2.4 : c = 4 : 3$

10. $\frac{17}{8} = \frac{n}{20}$

11. $\frac{13}{n} = \frac{20}{3}$

12. $5 : 7 = y : 5$

13. $\frac{0.4}{3.5} = \frac{5.2}{x}$

14. $\frac{4}{x} = \frac{7}{6}$

15. $4 : n = n : 9$

16. A canary's heart beats 130 times in 12 s. Use a proportion to find about how many times its heart beats in 50 s.

Skills Handbook

Simplifying Expressions With Integers

To add two numbers with the same sign, *add* their absolute values. The sum has the same sign as the numbers. To add two numbers with different signs, find the *difference* between their absolute values. The sum has the same sign as the number with the greater absolute value.

Example 1

Add.

a. $-8 + (-5) = -13$ **b.** $-8 + 5 = -3$ **c.** $8 + (-5) = 3$

To subtract a number, add its opposite.

Example 2

Subtract.

a. $4 - 7 = 4 + (-7)$
$= -3$

b. $-4 - (-7) = -4 + 7$
$= 3$

c. $-4 - 7 = -4 + (-7)$
$= -11$

The product or quotient of two numbers with the same sign is positive. The product or quotient of two numbers with different signs is negative.

Example 3

Multiply or divide.

a. $(-3)(-5) = 15$ **b.** $-35 \div 7 = -5$ **c.** $24 \div (-6) = -4$

Example 4

Simplify $2^2 - 3(4 - 6) - 12$.

$2^2 - 3(4 - 6) - 12 = 2^2 - 3(-2) - 12$

$= 4 - 3(-2) - 12$

$= 4 - (-6) - 12$

$= 4 + 6 - 12 = -2$

Order of Operations

1. Perform any operation(s) inside grouping symbols.

2. Simplify any terms with exponents.

3. Multiply and divide in order from left to right.

4. Add and subtract in order from left to right.

Exercises

Simplify each expression.

1. $-4 + 5$ **2.** $12 - 12$ **3.** $-15 + (-23)$ **4.** $4 - 17$ **5.** $-5 - 12$

6. $3 - (-5)$ **7.** $-8 - (-12)$ **8.** $-19 + 5$ **9.** $(-7)(-4)$ **10.** $-120 \div 30$

11. $(-3)(4)$ **12.** $75 \div (-3)$ **13.** $(-6)(15)$ **14.** $(18)(-4)$ **15.** $-84 \div (-7)$

16. $-2(1 + 5) + (-3)(2)$ **17.** $-4(-2 - 5) + 3(1 - 4)$ **18.** $20 - (3)(12) + 4^2$

19. $\frac{-15}{-5} - \frac{36}{-12} + \frac{-12}{-4}$ **20.** $5^2 - 6(5 - 9)$ **21.** $(-3 + 2^3)(4 + \frac{-42}{7})$

Area and Volume

The *area* of a plane figure is the number of square units contained in the figure.
The *volume* of a space figure is the number of cubic units contained in the figure.
Formulas for area and volume are listed on page 886.

Example 1

Find the area of each figure.

a.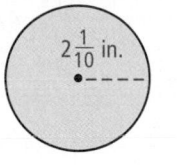
$2\frac{1}{10}$ in.

$$A = \pi r^2$$
$$\approx \frac{22}{7} \cdot \left(\frac{21}{10}\right)^2$$
$$= \frac{693}{50} = 13\frac{43}{50} \text{ in.}^2$$

b.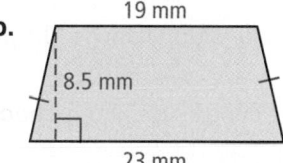
19 mm
8.5 mm
23 mm

$$A = \frac{1}{2}(b_1 + b_2)h$$
$$= \frac{1}{2}(19 + 23) \cdot 8.5$$
$$= 178.5 \text{ mm}^2$$

Example 2

Find the volume of each figure.

a.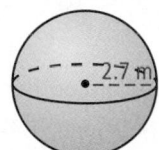
2.7 m

$$V = \frac{4}{3}\pi r^3$$
$$\approx \frac{4}{3} \cdot 3.14 \cdot 2.7^3$$
$$= 82.40616 \approx 82.4 \text{ m}^3$$

b.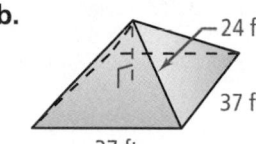
24 ft
37 ft
37 ft

$$V = \frac{1}{3}Bh$$
$$= \frac{1}{3}(37^2) \cdot 24$$
$$= 10,952 \text{ ft}^3$$

Exercises

Find the exact area of each figure.

1.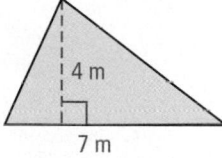
4 m
7 m

2.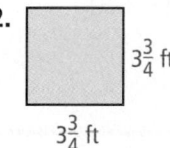
$3\frac{3}{4}$ ft
$3\frac{3}{4}$ ft

3.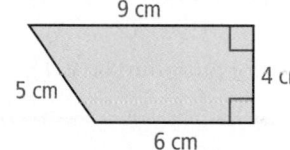
9 cm
5 cm
4 cm
6 cm

4.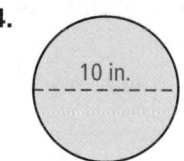
10 in.

Find the exact volume of each figure.

5.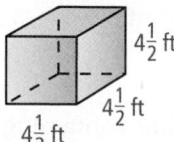
$4\frac{1}{2}$ ft
$4\frac{1}{2}$ ft
$4\frac{1}{2}$ ft

6.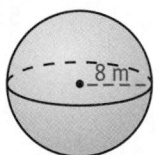
8 m

7.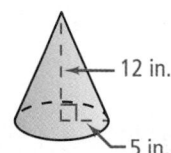
12 in.
5 in.

8.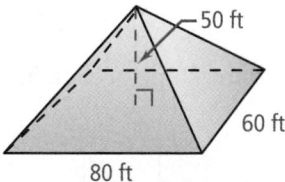
50 ft
60 ft
80 ft

9. Find the area of a triangle with a base of 17 in. and a height of 13 in.

10. Find the volume of a rectangular box 64 cm long, 48 cm wide, and 58 cm high.

11. Find the surface area of the cube in Exercise 5.

The Coordinate Plane, Slope, and Midpoint

The *coordinate plane* is formed when two perpendicular number lines intersect at a point called the origin, forming four quadrants.

Example 1

In which quadrant would you find each point?

a. $(3, -4)$ Move 3 units right and 4 units down. The point is in Quadrant IV.

b. $(-2, -5)$ Move 2 units left and 5 units down. The point is in Quadrant III.

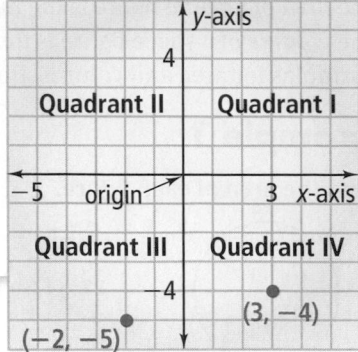

To find the slope of a line on the coordinate plane, choose two points on the line and use the slope formula.

Example 2

Find the slope of each line.

a.

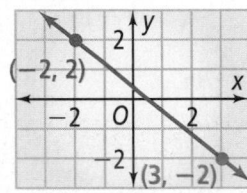

$$m = \frac{y_2 - y_1}{x_2 - x_1}$$
$$= \frac{2 - (-2)}{-2 - 3}$$
$$= \frac{4}{-5} \text{ or } -\frac{4}{5}$$

b.

$$m = \frac{y_2 - y_1}{x_2 - x_1}$$
$$= \frac{2 - 0}{-1 - (-1)} = \frac{2}{0}$$

Since you cannot divide by zero, this line has an undefined slope.

If (x_m, y_m) is the midpoint of the segment joining (x_1, y_1) and (x_2, y_2), then $x_m = \frac{x_1 + x_2}{2}$ and $y_m = \frac{y_1 + y_2}{2}$.

Example 3

Find the coordinates of the midpoint of the segment with endpoints $(-2, 5)$ and $(6, -3)$.

$\frac{-2 + 6}{2} = 2$ and $\frac{5 + (-3)}{2} = 1$ so the midpoint is $(2, 1)$.

Exercises

In which quadrant would you find each point? Graph each point on a coordinate plane.

1. $(3, 2)$ **2.** $(-4, 3)$ **3.** $(2, -3)$ **4.** $(4, -2)$ **5.** $(-4, -5)$ **6.** $(-1, -3)$

Find the slope of each line.

7.

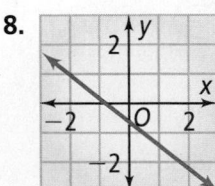

8.

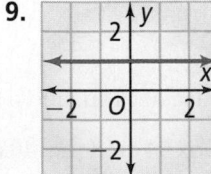

9.

10. the line containing $(-3, 4)$ and $(2, -6)$

11. the line containing $(25, 40)$ and $(100, 55)$

Find the midpoint of the segment with the given endpoints.

12. $(-4, 4), (2, -5)$ **13.** $(3, 3), (7, -6)$ **14.** $(-1, -8), (0, -3)$ **15.** $(3, 4), (2, -6)$

Operations With Exponents

An exponent indicates how many times a number is used as a factor.

Example 1

Write using exponents.

a. $3 \cdot 3 \cdot 3 \cdot 3 \cdot 3 = 3^5$

b. $a \cdot a \cdot b \cdot b \cdot b \cdot b = a^2 b^4$

$2^n = \blacksquare$	$10^n = \blacksquare$
$2^2 = 4$	$10^2 = 100$
$2^1 = 2$	$10^1 = 10$
$2^0 = 1$	$10^0 = 1$
$2^{-1} = \frac{1}{2}$	$10^{-1} = \frac{1}{10}$
$2^{-2} = \frac{1}{4}$	$10^{-2} = \frac{1}{100}$

The patterns shown at the right indicate that $a^0 = 1$ and that $a^{-n} = \frac{1}{a^n}$.

Example 2

Write each expression so that all exponents are positive.

a. $a^{-2}b^3 = \frac{1}{a^2} \cdot b^3 = \frac{b^3}{a^2}$

b. $x^3 y^0 z^{-1} = x^3 \cdot 1 \cdot \frac{1}{z} = \frac{x^3}{z}$

You can simplify expressions that contain powers with the same base.

Example 3

Simplify each expression.

a. $b^5 \cdot b^3 = b^{5+3}$ Add exponents to multiply
     $= b^8$ powers with the same base.

b. $\frac{x^5}{x^7} = x^{5-7}$ Subtract exponents to divide
     $= x^{-2} = \frac{1}{x^2}$ powers with the same base.

You can simplify expressions that contain parentheses and exponents.

Example 4

Simplify each expression.

a. $\left(\frac{ab}{n}\right)^3 = \frac{a^3 b^3}{n^3}$ Raise each factor in the
     parentheses to the third power.

b. $(c^2)^4 = c^{2 \cdot 4} = c^8$ Multiply exponents to raise a
     power to a power.

Exercises

Write each expression using exponents.

1. $x \cdot x \cdot x$

2. $x \cdot x \cdot x \cdot y \cdot y$

3. $a \cdot a \cdot a \cdot a \cdot b$

4. $\frac{a \cdot a \cdot a \cdot a}{b \cdot b}$

Write each expression so that all exponents are positive.

5. c^{-4}

6. $m^{-2} n^0$

7. $x^5 y^{-7} z^{-3}$

8. $ab^{-1} c^2$

Simplify each expression. Use positive exponents.

9. $d^2 d^6$

10. $\frac{a^5}{a^2}$

11. $\frac{c^7}{c}$

12. $\frac{n^3}{n^6}$

13. $\frac{a^5 b^3}{ab^8}$

14. $(3x)^2$

15. $\left(\frac{a}{b}\right)^4$

16. $\left(\frac{xz}{y}\right)^6$

17. $(c^3)^4$

18. $\left(\frac{x^2}{y^5}\right)^3$

19. $(u^4 v^2)^3$

20. $(p^5)^{-2}$

21. $\frac{(2a^4)(3a^2)}{6a^3}$

22. $(x^{-2})^3$

23. $(mg^3)^{-1}$

24. $g^{-3} g^{-1}$

25. $\frac{(3a^3)^2}{18a}$

26. $\frac{c^3 d^7}{c^{-3} d^{-1}}$

Factoring and Operations With Polynomials

Example 1

Perform each operation.

a. $(3y^2 - 4y + 5) + (y^2 + 9y)$

To add, group like terms. $= (3y^2 + y^2) + (-4y + 9y) + 5$

Combine like terms. $= 4y^2 + 5y + 5$

b. $(n + 4)(n - 3)$

Distribute n and 4. $= n(n) + n(-3) + 4(n) + 4(-3)$

Multiply. $= n^2 - 3n + 4n - 12$

Combine like terms. $= n^2 + n - 12$

To factor a polynomial, first find the greatest common factor (GCF) of the terms. Then use the distributive property to factor out the GCF.

Example 2

Factor $6x^3 - 12x^2 + 18x$.

List the factors of each term. The GCF is $6x$. $\quad 6x^3 = 6 \cdot x \cdot x \cdot x; \ -12x^2 = 6 \cdot (-2) \cdot x \cdot x; \ 18x = 6 \cdot 3 \cdot x$

Use the distributive property to factor out $6x$. $\quad 6x^3 - 12x^2 + 18x = 6x(x^2) + 6x(-2x) + 6x(3)$

$$= 6x(x^2 - 2x + 3)$$

When a polynomial is the product of two binomials, you can work backward to find the factors.

$$x^2 + bx + c = (x + \blacksquare)(x + \blacksquare)$$

The *sum* of these numbers must equal *b*.
The *product* of these numbers must equal *c*.

Example 3

Factor $x^2 - 13x + 36$.

Choose numbers that are factors of 36. Look for a pair with the sum -13.

The numbers -4 and -9 have a product of 36 and a sum of -13. The factors are $(x - 4)$ and $(x - 9)$. So, $x^2 - 13x + 36 = (x - 4)(x - 9)$.

Factors	Sum
$-6 \cdot (-6)$	-12
$-4 \cdot (-9)$	-13

Exercises

Perform the indicated operations.

1. $(x^2 + 3x - 1) + (7x - 4)$ **2.** $(5y^2 + 7y) - (3y^2 + 9y - 8)$ **3.** $4x^2(3x^2 - 5x + 9)$

4. $-5d(13d^2 + 7d + 8)$ **5.** $(x - 5)(x + 3)$ **6.** $(n - 7)(n - 2)$

Factor each polynomial.

7. $a^2 - 8a + 12$ **8.** $n^2 - 2n - 8$ **9.** $x^2 + 5x + 4$ **10.** $3m^2 - 9$

11. $y^2 + 5y - 24$ **12.** $s^3 + 6s^2 + 11s$ **13.** $2x^3 + 4x^2 - 8x$ **14.** $y^2 - 10y + 25$

Scientific Notation and Significant Digits

In *scientific notation*, a number has the form $a \times 10^n$, where n is an integer and $1 \le a < 10$.

Example 1

Write 5.59×10^6 in standard form.

A positive exponent indicates a value greater than 1.
Move the decimal point six places to the right.

$$5.59 \times 10^6 = 5\,590\,000 = 5,590,000$$

Example 2

Write 0.0000318 in scientific notation.

Move the decimal point to create a number between 1 and 10.
Since the original number is less than 1, use a negative exponent.

$$0.0000318 = 3.18 \times 10^{-5}$$

When a measurement is in scientific notation, all the digits of the number between 1 and 10 are *significant digits*. When you multiply or divide measurements, your answer should have as many significant digits as the least number of significant digits in any of the numbers involved.

Example 3

Multiply $(6.71 \times 10^8 \text{ mi/h})$ and $(3.8 \times 10^4 \text{ h})$.

Rearrange factors.

$$(6.71 \times 10^8 \text{ mi/h})(3.8 \times 10^4 \text{ h}) = (6.71 \cdot 3.8)(10^8 \cdot 10^4)$$

Add exponents when multiplying powers of 10.

three significant digits, two significant digits

$$= 25.498 \times 10^{12}$$

Write in scientific notation.

$$= 2.5498 \times 10^{13}$$

Round to two significant digits.

$$\approx 2.5 \times 10^{13} \text{mi}$$

Exercises

Change each number to scientific notation or to standard form.

1. 1,340,000 **2.** 6.88×10^{-2} **3.** 0.000775 **4.** 0.0072 **5.** 1.113×10^5

6. 8.0×10^{-4} **7.** 1895 **8.** 2.3×10^3 **9.** 123,400 **10.** 7.985×10^4

Write each product or quotient in scientific notation. Round to the appropriate number of significant digits.

11. $(1.6 \times 10^2)(4.0 \times 10^3)$ **12.** $(2.5 \times 10^{-3})(1.2 \times 10^4)$ **13.** $(4.237 \times 10^4)(2.01 \times 10^{-2})$

14. $\dfrac{7.0 \times 10^5}{2.89 \times 10^3}$ **15.** $\dfrac{1.4 \times 10^4}{8.0 \times 10^2}$ **16.** $\dfrac{6.48 \times 10^6}{3.2 \times 10^5}$

17. $(1.78 \times 10^{-7})(5.03 \times 10^{-5})$ **18.** $(7.2 \times 10^{11})(5 \times 10^6)$ **19.** $(8.90 \times 10^8) \div (2.36 \times 10^{-2})$

20. $(3.95 \times 10^4) \div (6.8 \times 10^8)$ **21.** $(4.9 \times 10^{-8}) \div (2.7 \times 10^{-2})$ **22.** $(3.972 \times 10^{-5})(4.7 \times 10^{-4})$

The Pythagorean Theorem and the Distance Formula

In a right triangle, the sum of the squares of the lengths of the legs is equal to the square of the length of the hypotenuse. Use this relationship, known as the Pythagorean Theorem, to find the length of a side of a right triangle.

The Pythagorean Theorem

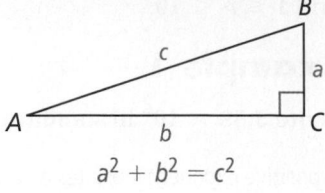

$$a^2 + b^2 = c^2$$

Example 1

Find m in the triangle below, to the nearest tenth.

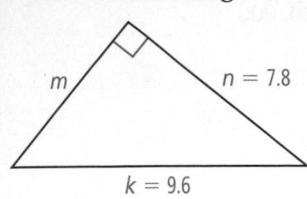

$$m^2 + n^2 = k^2$$
$$m^2 + 7.8^2 = 9.6^2$$
$$m^2 = 9.6^2 - 7.8^2 = 31.32$$
$$m = \sqrt{31.32} \approx 5.6$$

To find the distance between two points on the coordinate plane, use the distance formula.

The distance d between any two points (x_1, y_1) and (x_2, y_2) is

$$d = \sqrt{(x_2 - x_1)^2 + (y_2 - y_1)^2}$$

Example 2

Find the distance between $(-3, 2)$ and $(6, -4)$.

$$d = \sqrt{(6 - (-3))^2 + (-4 - 2)^2}$$
$$= \sqrt{9^2 + (-6)^2}$$
$$= \sqrt{81 + 36}$$
$$= \sqrt{117}$$
$$\approx 10.8$$

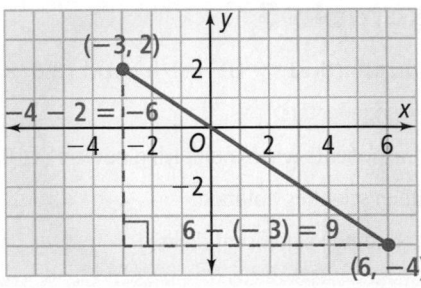

Thus, d is about 10.8 units.

Exercises

In each problem, a and b are the lengths of the legs of a right triangle and c is the length of the hypotenuse. Find each missing length. Round your answer to the nearest tenth.

1. c if $a = 6$ and $b = 8$

2. a if $b = 12$ and $c = 13$

3. b if $a = 8$ and $c = 17$

4. c if $a = 10$ and $b = 3$

5. a if $b = 100$ and $c = 114$

6. b if $a = 12.0$ and $c = 30.1$

Find the distance between each pair of points, to the nearest tenth.

7. $(0, 0), (4, -3)$

8. $(-5, -5), (1, 3)$

9. $(-1, 0), (4, 12)$

10. $(-4, 2), (4, -2)$

11. $(0, 15), (17, 0)$

12. $(-8, 8), (8, 8)$

13. $(-1, 1), (1, -1)$

14. $(-2, 9), (0, 0)$

15. $(-5, 3), (4, 3)$

16. $(2, 1), (3, 4)$

17. $(3, -2), (3, 5)$

18. $(5, 4), (-3, 1)$

Bar and Circle Graphs

Sometimes you can draw different graphs to represent the same data, depending on the information you want to share. A *bar graph* is useful for comparing amounts; a *circle graph* is useful for comparing percents.

Example

Display the 2007 data on immigration to the United States in a bar graph and a circle graph.

To make a circle graph, first find the *percent* of the data in each category. Then express each percent as a decimal and multiply by 360° to find the size of each *central angle*.

$$\text{Africa} \rightarrow \frac{89.3}{1003.7} \approx 0.09 \text{ or } 9\%$$
$$\text{Total} \rightarrow$$

$$0.09 \times 360° \approx 32°$$

Draw a circle and use a protractor to draw each central angle.

Immigration to the United States, 2007

Place of Origin	Immigrants (1000's)
Africa	89.2
Asia	359.4
Europe	120.8
North America	331.7
South America	102.6

Source: Department of Homeland Security

To make a bar graph, place the categories along the bottom axis. Decide on a scale for the side axis. An appropriate scale would be 0–400, marked in intervals of 100. For each data item, draw a bar whose height is equal to the data value.

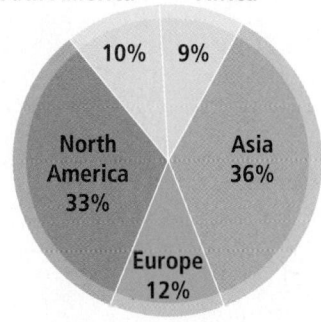
Immigration to the United States, 2007

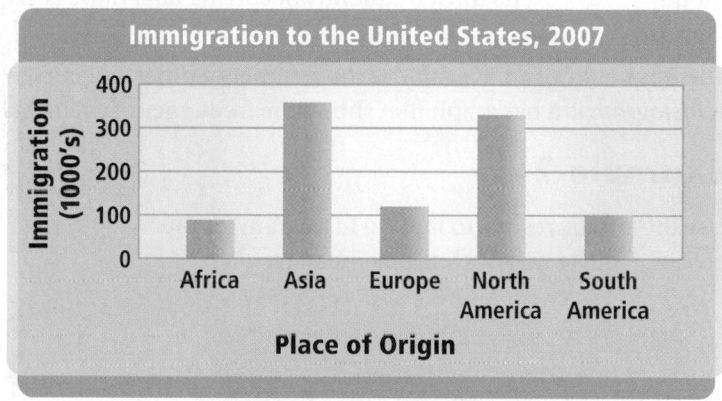

Exercises

Display the data from each table in a bar graph and a circle graph.

1. **NASA Space Shuttle Expenses, 2000**

Operation	Millions of Dollars
Orbiter, integration	698.8
Propulsion	1,053.1
Mission, launch operations	738.8
Flight operations	244.6
Ground operations	510.3

Source: U.S. National Aeronautics and Space Administration

2. **Cable TV Revenue, 2006**

	Millions of Dollars
Airtime	4,566
Basic service	42,918
Pay-per-view, premium services	13,322
Installation	729
Other	27,188

Source: U.S. Census Bureau

Descriptive Statistics and Histograms

For numerical data, you can find the *mean,* the *median,* and the *mode.*

Mean	The sum of the data values in a data set divided by the number of data values
Median	The middle value of a data set that has been arranged in increasing or decreasing order. If the data set has an even number of values, the median is the mean of the middle two values.
Mode	The most frequently occurring value in a data set

Example 1

Find the mean, median, and mode for the following data set.   5 7 6 3 1 7 9 5 10 7

Mean	$\dfrac{5 + 7 + 6 + 3 + 1 + 7 + 9 + 5 + 10 + 7}{10} = 6$
Median	5, 7, 6, 3, 1, 7, 9, 5, 10, 7 Rearrange the numbers from least to greatest.
	1, 3, 5, 5, 6, 7, 7, 7, 9, 10 The median is the mean of the two middle numbers, 6 and 7.
	The median is $\dfrac{6 + 7}{2} = 6.5$.
Mode	The most frequently occurring data value is 7.

The frequency of a data value is the number of times it occurs in a data set.
A *histogram* is a bar graph that shows the frequency of each data value.

Example 2

Use the survey results to make a histogram for the cost of a movie ticket at various theaters.

Survey of Movie Ticket Prices

$7 $8 $7 $9 $8 $9 $8 $10 $8

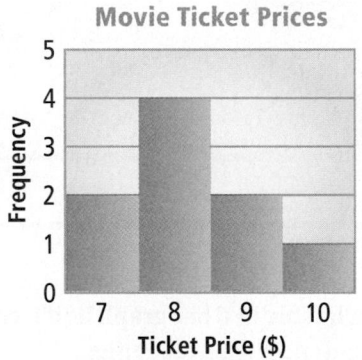

Movie Ticket Prices

Exercises

Find the mean, the median, and the mode of each data set.

1. −3 4 5 5 −2 7 1 8 9

2. 0 0 1 1 2 3 3 5 3 8 7

3. 2.4 2.4 2.3 2.3 2.4 12.0

4. 1 1 1 1 2 2 2 3 3 4

5. 1.2 1.3 1.4 1.5 1.6 1.7 1.8

6. −4 −3 −2 −1 0 1 2 3 4

Make a histogram for each data set.

7. 7 4 8 6 6 8 7 7 5 7

8. 73 75 76 75 74 75 76 74 76 75

Operations With Rational Expressions

A *rational expression* is an expression that can be written in the form $\frac{\text{polynominal}}{\text{polynominal}}$, where the denominator is not zero. A rational expression is in simplest form if the numerator and denominator have no common factors except 1.

Example 1

Write the expression $\frac{4x + 8}{x + 2}$ in simplest form.

Factor the numerator.

$$\frac{4x + 8}{x + 2} = \frac{4(x + 2)}{x + 2}$$

Divide out the common factor $x + 2$.

$$= 4$$

To add or subtract two rational expressions, use a common denominator.

Example 2

Simplify $\frac{x}{2y} + \frac{x}{3y}$.

The common denominator of $3y$ and $2y$ is $6y$.

$$\frac{x}{2y} + \frac{x}{3y} = \frac{x}{2y} \cdot \frac{3}{3} + \frac{x}{3y} \cdot \frac{2}{2}$$

Multiply.

$$= \frac{3x}{6y} + \frac{2x}{6y}$$

Add the numerators.

$$= \frac{5x}{6y}$$

To multiply rational expressions, first find and divide out any common factors in the numerators and the denominators. Then multiply the remaining numerators and denominators. To divide rational expressions, first use a reciprocal to change the problem to multiplication.

Example 3

Simplify $\frac{40x^2}{21} \div \frac{5x}{14}$.

Change dividing by $\frac{5x}{14}$ to multiplying by the reciprocal, $\frac{14}{5x}$.

$$\frac{40x^2}{21} \div \frac{5x}{14} = \frac{40x^2}{21} \cdot \frac{14}{5x}$$

Divide out the common factors 5, x, and 7.

$$= \frac{8}{3}\frac{\cancel{40x^2}^{1}}{\cancel{21}} \times \frac{\cancel{14}^{2}}{\cancel{5x}_{1}}$$

Multiply the numerators ($8x \cdot 2$). Multiply the denominators ($3 \cdot 1$).

$$= \frac{16x}{3}$$

Exercises

Write each expression in simplest form.

1. $\frac{4a^2b}{12ab^3}$

2. $\frac{5n + 15}{n + 3}$

3. $\frac{x - 7}{2x - 14}$

4. $\frac{28c^2(d - 3)}{35c(d - 3)}$

Perform the indicated operation.

5. $\frac{3x}{2} + \frac{5x}{2}$

6. $\frac{3x}{8} + \frac{5x}{8}$

7. $\frac{5}{h} - \frac{3}{h}$

8. $\frac{6}{11p} - \frac{9}{11p}$

9. $\frac{3x}{5} - \frac{x}{2}$

10. $\frac{13}{2x} - \frac{13}{3x}$

11. $\frac{7x}{5} + \frac{5x}{7}$

12. $\frac{5a}{b} + \frac{3a}{5b}$

13. $\frac{7x}{8} \cdot \frac{32x}{35}$

14. $\frac{3x^2}{2} \cdot \frac{6}{x}$

15. $\frac{8x^2}{5} \cdot \frac{10}{x^3}$

16. $\frac{7x}{8} \cdot \frac{64}{14x}$

17. $\frac{16}{3x} \div \frac{5}{3x}$

18. $\frac{4x}{5} \div \frac{16}{15x}$

19. $\frac{x^3}{8} \div \frac{x^2}{16}$

Reference

Table 1 Measures

	United States Customary	Metric
Length	12 inches (in.) = 1 foot (ft) 36 in. = 1 yard (yd) 3 ft = 1 yard 5280 ft = 1 mile (mi) 1760 yd = 1 mile	10 millimeters (mm) = 1 centimeter (cm) 100 cm = 1 meter (m) 1000 mm = 1 meter 1000 m = 1 kilometer (km)
Area	144 square inches (in.^{2}) = 1 square foot (ft^2) 9 ft^2 = 1 square yard (yd^2) 43,560 ft^2 = 1 acre (a) 4840 yd^2 = 1 acre	100 square millimeters (mm^2) = 1 square centimeter (cm^2) 10,000 cm^2 = 1 square meter (m^2) 10,000 m^2 = 1 hectare (ha)
Volume	1728 cubic inches (in.^{3}) = 1 cubic foot (ft^3) 27 ft^3 = 1 cubic yard (yd^3)	1000 cubic millimeters (mm^3) = 1 cubic centimeter (cm^3) 1,000,000 cm^3 = 1 cubic meter (m^3)
Liquid Capacity	8 fluid ounces (fl oz) = 1 cup (c) 2 c = 1 pint (pt) 2 pt = 1 quart (qt) 4 qt = 1 gallon (gal)	1000 milliliters (mL) = 1 liter (L) 1000 L = 1 kiloliter (kL)
Weight or Mass	16 ounces (oz) = 1 pound (lb) 2000 pounds = 1 ton (t)	1000 milligrams (mg) = 1 gram (g) 1000 g = 1 kilogram (kg) 1000 kg = 1 metric ton
Temperature	32°F = freezing point of water 98.6°F = normal human body temperature 212°F = boiling point of water	0°C = freezing point of water 37°C = normal human body temperature 100°C = boiling point of water

Customary Units and Metric Units

Length	1 in. = 2.54 cm 1 ft ≈ 0.305 m 1 mi ≈ 1.61 km	1 cm ≈ 0.39 in. 1 m ≈ 3.28 ft 1 km ≈ 0.62 mi
Area	1 acre = 0.40 ha	1 ha = 2.47 acres
Capacity	1 qt ≈ 0.95 L	1 L ≈ 1.06 qt
Weight and Mass	1 oz ≈ 28.4 g 1 lb ≈ 0.45 kg	1 g ≈ 0.035 oz 1 kg ≈ 2.205 lb

Time

60 seconds (s) = 1 minute (min)	4 weeks (approx.) = 1 month (mo)	12 months = 1 year
60 minutes = 1 hour (h)	365 days = 1 year (yr)	10 years = 1 decade
24 hours = 1 day (d)	52 weeks (approx.) = 1 year	100 years = 1 century
7 days = 1 week (wk)		

Table 2 **Reading Math Symbols**

Symbols	Words
$\cdot$, $\times$	multiplication sign, times
$\pm$	plus or minus positive or negative
$=$	equals
$\overset{?}{=}$	equals?
$\approx$	is approximately equal to
$\neq$	is not equal to
$<$	is less than
$>$	is greater than
$\leq$	is less than or equal to
$\geq$	is greater than or equal to
$\cong$	is congruent to
$\sim$	is similar to
( )	parentheses for grouping
[ ]	brackets for grouping
{ }	braces for a set
%	percent
$\lvert a \rvert$	absolute value of a
$-a$	opposite of a
$a : b$; $\frac{a}{b}$	ratio of a to b
$\frac{1}{a}$, a^{-1}, $a \neq 0$	reciprocal of a
a^n	nth power of a
a^{-n}	$\frac{1}{a^n}$, $a \neq 0$
$\sqrt{a}$	nonnegative square root of a
$\sqrt[n]{a}$	nth root of a (nonnegative if n even)
$\circ$ as in a°	degree(s)
$\circ$ as in $f \circ g$	composition of functions
π	pi, an irrational number, approximately equal to 3.14
e	an irrational number approximately equal to 2.72
i	the imaginary number $\sqrt{-1}$
$a + bi$, $b \neq 0$	a complex number
∞	infinity
$\sum$	sigma, summation
σ	sigma, standard deviation
σ^2	variance
$\overleftrightarrow{AB}$	line through points A and B

Symbols	Words
$\overline{AB}$	segment with endpoints A and B
AB	length of $\overline{AB}$; distance between points A and B
$\angle A$	angle A
$m\angle A$	measure of angle A
$\triangle ABC$	triangle ABC
(x, y)	ordered pair
$x_1, x_2, \ldots$	specific values of the variable x
$y_1, y_2, \ldots$	specific values of the variable y
$\overline{x}$	mean of data values x_i
$f(x)$	f of x; the function value at x
f^{-1}	function inverse
log	logarithm
$\begin{bmatrix} a & b \\ c & d \end{bmatrix}$	matrix
a_{mn}	element in mth row, nth column of matrix A
A^{-1}	inverse of matrix A
$\begin{vmatrix} a & b \\ c & d \end{vmatrix}$	determinant of a matrix
det A	determinant of matrix A
$n!$	n factorial
$_nC_r$	combinations of n things chosen r at a time
$_nP_r$	permutations of n things arranged r at a time
$P(\text{event})$	probability of an event
$P(A|B)$	probability of event A, given event B
sin A	sine of $\angle A$
cos A	cosine of $\angle A$
tan A	tangent of $\angle A$
csc A	cosecant of $\angle A$
sec A	secant of $\angle A$
cot A	cotangent of $\angle A$
$\wedge$	raised to a power (in a spreadsheet formula)
$*$	multiply (in a spreadsheet formula)
$/$	divide (in a spreadsheet formula)
$\ldots$	and so on

Properties and Formulas

Order of Operations
1. Perform any operation(s) inside grouping symbols.
2. Simplify any terms with exponents.
3. Multiply and divide in order from left to right.
4. Add and subtract in order from left to right.

The Pythagorean Theorem
In a right triangle, the sum of the squares of the lengths of the legs is equal to the square of the length of the hypotenuse.

$$a^2 + b^2 = c^2$$

The Distance Formula
The distance d between any two points (x_1, y_1) and (x_2, y_2) is $d = \sqrt{(x_2 - x_1)^2 + (y_2 - y_1)^2}$.

The Midpoint Formula
The midpoint M of a line segment with endpoints $A(x_1, y_1)$ and $B(x_2, y_2)$ is $\left(\dfrac{x_1 + x_2}{2}, \dfrac{y_1 + y_2}{2}\right)$.

Chapter 1 Expressions, Equations, and Inequalities

Closure
For all real numbers a and b, $a + b$ and $a \cdot b$ are real numbers.

The Associative Properties
For all real numbers a, b, and c:

$(a + b) + c = a + (b + c)$
$(a \cdot b) \cdot c = a \cdot (b \cdot c)$

The Commutative Properties
For all real numbers a and b:

$a + b = b + a$ and $a \cdot b = b \cdot a$

The Identity Properties
For every real number a:

$a + 0 = a$ and $0 + a = a$ $a \cdot 1 = a$ and $1 \cdot a = a$
0 is the additive identity.   1 is the multiplicative identity.

The Inverse Properties
For every real number a:

$a + (-a) = 0$ and $a \cdot \dfrac{1}{a} = 1$ $(a \neq 0)$

The Distributive Properties
For all real numbers a, b, and c:

$a(b + c) = ab + ac$ $(b + c)a = ba + ca$
$a(b - c) = ab - ac$ $(b - c)a = ba - ca$

Multiplication
Let a represent a real number.
Multiplication by 0: $0 \cdot a = 0$
Multiplication by -1: $-1 \cdot a = -a$

Opposites
Let a and b represent real numbers.
Opposite of a Sum: $-(a + b) = -a + (-b) = -a - b$
Opposite of a Difference: $-(a - b) = -a + b = b - a$
Opposite of a Product: $-(ab) = -a \cdot b = a \cdot (-b)$
Opposite of an Opposite: $-(-a) = a$

Properties of Equality
Assume a, b, and c represent real numbers.

Reflexive:	$a = a$
Symmetric:	If $a = b$, then $b = a$.
Transitive:	If $a = b$ and $b = c$, then $a = c$.
Substitution:	If $a = b$, then you can replace a with b and vice versa.
Addition:	If $a = b$, then $a + c = b + c$.
Subtraction:	If $a = b$, then $a - c = b - c$.
Multiplication:	If $a = b$, then $ac = bc$.
Division:	If $a = b$ and $c \neq 0$, then $\dfrac{a}{c} = \dfrac{b}{c}$.

Properties of Inequality
Let a, b, and c represent real numbers.

Transitive:	If $a > b$ and $b > c$, then $a > c$.
Addition:	If $a > b$, then $a + c > b + c$.
Subtraction:	If $a > b$, then $a - c > b - c$.
Multiplication:	If $a > b$ and $c > 0$, then $ac > bc$.
	If $a > b$ and $c < 0$, then $ac < bc$.
Division:	If $a > b$ and $c > 0$, then $\dfrac{a}{c} > \dfrac{b}{c}$.
	If $a > b$ and $c < 0$, then $\dfrac{a}{c} < \dfrac{b}{c}$.

Chapter 2 Functions, Equations, and Graphs

Direct Variation
$y = kx$ or $\dfrac{y}{x} = k$, where $k \neq 0$.

Slope of a Line Containing (x_1, y_1) and (x_2, y_2)
$\text{slope} = \dfrac{\text{vertical change (rise)}}{\text{horizontal change (run)}} = \dfrac{y_2 - y_1}{x_2 - x_1}$,
where $x_2 - x_1 \neq 0$

Point-Slope Equation of a Line
The equation of the line through point (x_1, y_1) with slope m is $y - y_1 = m(x - x_1)$.

Function Families

Assume a, k, and h are positive numbers.

Parent	$y = f(x)$
Reflection in x-axis	$y = -f(x)$

Vertical stretch ($a > 1$) Vertical shrink ($0 < a < 1$)	$y = af(x)$

Translation

horizontal to left by h	$y = f(x + h)$
horizontal to right by h	$y = f(x - h)$
vertical up by k	$y = f(x) + k$
vertical down by k	$y = f(x) - k$

Chapter 4 Quadratic Functions and Equations

Quadratic Functions

Parent	$y = x^2$
Reflection across x-axis	$y = -x^2$

Stretch ($a > 1$) Shrink ($0 < a < 1$)	$y = ax^2$

Translation

horizontal by h vertical by k	$y = (x - h)^2 + k$

Vertex Form	$y = a(x - h)^2 + k$
Standard Form	$y = f(x) = ax^2 + bx + c$

The graph is a parabola that opens up
if $a > 0$ and down if $a < 0$.
The vertex is (h, k) (Vertex Form) and
$\left(-\frac{b}{2a}, f\left(-\frac{b}{2a}\right)\right)$ (Standard Form).
The axis of symmetry is $x = h$ (Vertex Form)
and $x = -\frac{b}{2a}$ (Standard Form).

Factoring Perfect-Square Trinomials

$a^2 + 2ab + b^2 = (a + b)^2$
$a^2 - 2ab + b^2 = (a - b)^2$

Factoring a Difference of Two Squares

$a^2 - b^2 = (a + b)(a - b)$

Multiplication Property of Square Roots

For any numbers $a \geq 0$ and $b \geq 0$, $\sqrt{ab} = \sqrt{a} \cdot \sqrt{b}$.

Division Property of Square Roots

For any numbers $a \geq 0$ and $b > 0$, $\sqrt{\frac{a}{b}} = \frac{\sqrt{a}}{\sqrt{b}}$.

Zero-Product Property

If $ab = 0$, then $a = 0$ or $b = 0$.

The Quadratic Formula

If $ax^2 + bx + c = 0$, then $x = \frac{-b \pm \sqrt{b^2 - 4ac}}{2a}$.

Discriminant

The discriminant of a quadratic equation in the form
$ax^2 + bx + c = 0$ is $b^2 - 4ac$.

$b^2 - 4ac > 0 \Rightarrow$ two real solutions
$b^2 - 4ac = 0 \Rightarrow$ one real solution
$b^2 - 4ac < 0 \Rightarrow$ two complex solutions

Square Root of a Negative Real Number

For any positive number a,
$\sqrt{-a} = \sqrt{-1 \cdot a} = \sqrt{-1} \cdot \sqrt{a} = i\sqrt{a}$.
Example: $\sqrt{-5} = i\sqrt{5}$
Note that
$(\sqrt{-5})^2 = (i\sqrt{5})^2 = i^2(\sqrt{5})^2 = -1 \cdot 5 = -5$ (not 5).

Chapter 5 Polynomials and Polynomial Functions

End Behavior of a Polynomial Function

The end behavior of a polynomial function of degree n
with leading term ax^n:

a	n	end behavior
positive	even	up and up
positive	odd	down and up
negative	even	down and down
negative	odd	up and down

Factor Theorem

The expression $x - a$ is a linear factor of a polynomial
if and only if the value a is a zero of the related
polynomial function.

Remainder Theorem

If you divide a polynomial $P(x)$ of degree $n \geq 1$ by $x - a$,
then the remainder is $P(a)$.

Factoring a Sum or Difference of Cubes

$a^3 + b^3 = (a + b)(a^2 - ab + b^2)$
$a^3 - b^3 = (a - b)(a^2 + ab + b^2)$

Rational Root Theorem

Let $P(x) = a_nx^n + a_{n-1}x^{n-1} + \cdots + a_1x + a_0$ be a
polynomial with integer coefficients.
Integer roots of $P(x) = 0$ must be factors of a_0.
Rational roots have reduced form $\frac{p}{q}$ where p is an
integer factor of a_0 and q is an integer factor of a_n.

Conjugate Root Theorems

Suppose $P(x)$ is a polynomial with *rational* coefficients.
If $a + \sqrt{b}$ is an irrational root with a and b rational, then
$a - \sqrt{b}$ is also a root.

Suppose $P(x)$ is a polynomial with *real* coefficients.
If $a + bi$ is a complex root with a and b real, then $a - bi$ is
also a root.

Fundamental Theorem of Algebra

If $P(x)$ is a polynomial of degree $n \geq 1$, then $P(x) = 0$ has exactly n roots, including multiple and complex roots.

Binomial Theorem (Using Pascal's Triangle)

For every positive integer n, $(a + b)^n =$
$P_0 a^n + P_1 a^{n-1} b + P_2 a^{n-2} b^2 + \cdots + P_{n-1} a b^{n-1} + P_n b^n$
where $P_0, P_1, \ldots, P_n$ are the numbers in the nth row of Pascal's Triangle.

Chapter 6 Radical Functions and Rational Exponents

Properties of Exponents

For any nonzero number a and any integers m and n,

$a^0 = 1$ $\qquad (ab)^n = a^n b^n$

$\dfrac{a^m}{a^n} = a^{m-n}$ $\qquad a^m \cdot a^n = a^{m+n}$

$a^{-n} = \dfrac{1}{a^n}$ $\qquad (a^m)^n = a^{mn}$

$\qquad\qquad \left(\dfrac{a}{b}\right)^n = \dfrac{a^n}{b^n}$

nth Roots of nth Powers

For any real number a,

$\sqrt[n]{a^n} = \begin{cases} a & \text{if } n \text{ is odd} \\ |a| & \text{if } n \text{ is even} \end{cases}$

Combining Radical Expressions: Products

If $\sqrt[n]{a}$ and $\sqrt[n]{b}$ are real numbers, then $\sqrt[n]{a} \cdot \sqrt[n]{b} = \sqrt[n]{ab}$.

Combining Radical Expressions: Quotients

If $\sqrt[n]{a}$ and $\sqrt[n]{b}$ are real numbers and $b \neq 0$,

then $\dfrac{\sqrt[n]{a}}{\sqrt[n]{b}} = \sqrt[n]{\dfrac{a}{b}}$.

Properties of Rational Exponents

If the nth root of a is a real number and m is an integer, then $a^{\frac{1}{n}} = \sqrt[n]{a}$ and $a^{\frac{m}{n}} = \sqrt[n]{a^m} = \left(\sqrt[n]{a}\right)^m$. If m is negative, $a \neq 0$.

Composition of Inverse Functions

If f and f^{-1} are inverse functions, then $(f^{-1} \circ f)(x) = x$ and $(f \circ f^{-1})(x) = x$ for x in the domains of f and f^{-1}, respectively.

Radical Functions

	Square Root	nth Root
Parent	$y = \sqrt{x}$	$y = \sqrt[n]{x}$
Reflection in x-axis	$y = -\sqrt{x}$	$y = -\sqrt[n]{x}$
Stretch ($a > 1$) Shrink ($0 < a < 1$)	$y = a\sqrt{x}$	$y = a\sqrt[n]{x}$
Translation horizontal by h vertical by k	$y = \sqrt{x-h} + k$	$y = \sqrt[n]{x-h} + k$

Chapter 7 Exponential and Logarithmic Functions

Exponential Functions

Parent, $b > 0$, $b \neq 1$	$y = b^x$
Reflection in x-axis	$y = -b^x$
Stretch ($a > 1$) Shrink ($0 < a < 1$)	$y = ab^x$
Translation horizontal by h vertical by k	$y = b^{x-h} + k$

Continuously Compounded Interest

$A(t) = P \cdot e^{rt}$, where $A(t)$ represents the total, P represents the principal, r represents the interest rate, and t represents time in years.

Logarithmic Functions

	Base b
Parents, $b > 0$, $b \neq 1$	$y = \log_b x$
Reflection in x-axis	$y = -\log_b x$
Stretch ($a > 1$) Shrink ($0 < a < 1$)	$y = a \log_b x$
Translation horizontal by h vertical by k	$y = \log_b (x - h) + k$

Properties of Logarithms

For any positive numbers m, n, and b where $b \neq 1$

Product Property: $\log_b mn = \log_b m + \log_b n$

Quotient Property: $\log_b \dfrac{m}{n} = \log_b m - \log_b n$

Power Property: $\log_b m^n = n \log_b m$

Change of Base Formula

For any positive numbers, m, b, and c, with

$b \neq 1$ and $c \neq 1$, $\log_b m = \dfrac{\log_c m}{\log_c b}$.

Chapter 8 Rational Functions

Inverse Variation

$xy = k$, $y = \dfrac{k}{x}$, or $x = \dfrac{k}{y}$, where $k \neq 0$.

Combined Variation

z varies jointly with x and y: $z = kxy$

z varies jointly with x and y and inversely with w: $z = \dfrac{kxy}{w}$

z varies directly with x and inversely with the product wy: $z = \dfrac{kx}{wy}$

Reciprocal Functions

Parent	$y = \dfrac{1}{x}$, $x \neq 0$
Reflection in x-axis	$y = -\dfrac{1}{x}$, $x \neq 0$
Stretch ($a > 1$) Shrink ($0 < a < 1$)	$y = \dfrac{a}{x}$, $x \neq 0$
Translation horizontal by h vertical by k	$y = \dfrac{a}{x-h} + k$, $x \neq h$
Asymptotes	$y = k$ (horiz.), $x = h$ (vert.)

Chapter 9 Sequences and Series

Arithmetic Mean of Two Numbers

$$\frac{x + y}{2}$$

Arithmetic Sequence

A recursive definition for an arithmetic sequence with a starting value a and a common difference d has two parts:

$a_1 = a$: initial condition

$a_{n+1} = a_n + d$, for $n \geq 1$: recursive formula

An explicit definition for this sequence is the formula:

$a_n = a + (n - 1)d$ for $n \geq 1$.

Geometric Sequence

A recursive definition for a geometric sequence with a starting value a and a common ratio r has two parts:

$a_1 = a$: initial condition

$a_{n+1} = a_n \cdot r$, for $n \geq 1$: recursive formula

An explicit definition for this sequence is the formula:

$a_n = ar^{n-1}$, for $n \geq 1$.

Sum of a Finite Arithmetic Series

The sum S_n of a finite arithmetic series

$a_1 + a_2 + a_3 + \cdots + a_n$ is $S_n = \frac{n}{2}(a_1 + a_n)$

where a_1 is the first term, a_n is the nth term, and n is the number of terms.

Sum of a Finite Geometric Series

The sum S_n of a finite geometric series

$a_1 + a_1r + a_1r^2 + \cdots + a_1r^{n-1}$ is $S_n = \frac{a_1(1 - r^n)}{1 - r}$

where a_1 is the first term, r is the common ratio, and n is the number of terms.

Sum of an Infinite Geometric Series

An infinite geometric series with $|r| < 1$ converges to the sum S given by the following formula:

$$S = \frac{a_1}{1 - r}.$$

Chapter 10 Quadratic Relations and Conic Sections

Parabolas

	Vertical		
		Vertex $(0, 0)$	Vertex (h, k)
	Equation	$y = \frac{1}{4c}x^2$	$y = \frac{1}{4c}(x - h)^2 + k$
	Focus	$(0, c)$	$(h, c + k)$
	Directrix	$y = -c$	$y = -c + k$

	Horizontal		
		Vertex $(0, 0)$	Vertex (h, k)
	Equation	$x = \frac{1}{4c}y^2$	$x = \frac{1}{4c}(y - k)^2 + h$
	Focus	$(c, 0)$	$(c + h, k)$
	Directrix	$x = -c$	$x = -c + h$

Circles, radius $= r$

	Center $(0, 0)$	Center (h, k)
Equation	$x^2 + y^2 = r^2$	$(x - h)^2 + (y - k)^2 = r^2$

Ellipses

Horizontal, $a > b$ Center $(0, 0)$

Equation	$\frac{x^2}{a^2} + \frac{y^2}{b^2} = 1$
Vertices	$(\pm a, 0)$
Co-Vertices	$(0, \pm b)$
Foci, $c^2 = a^2 - b^2$	$(\pm c, 0)$
Major axis	$y = 0$
Minor axis	$x = 0$

Vertical, $a > b$ Center $(0, 0)$

Equation	$\frac{x^2}{b^2} + \frac{y^2}{a^2} = 1$
Vertices	$(0, \pm a)$
Co-Vertices	$(\pm b, 0)$
Foci, $c^2 = a^2 - b^2$	$(0, \pm c)$
Major axis	$x = 0$
Minor axis	$y = 0$

Hyperbolas

Horizontal, $a > b$ Center $(0, 0)$

Equation	$\frac{x^2}{a^2} - \frac{y^2}{b^2} = 1$
Vertices	$(\pm a, 0)$
Foci, $c^2 = a^2 + b^2$	$(\pm c, 0)$
Transverse axis	$y = 0$
Asymptotes	$y = \pm\frac{b}{a}x$

Vertical, $a > b$ Center $(0, 0)$

Equation	$\frac{y^2}{a^2} - \frac{x^2}{b^2} = 1$
Vertices	$(0, \pm a)$
Foci, $c^2 = a^2 + b^2$	$(0, \pm c)$
Transverse axis	$x = 0$
Asymptotes	$y = \pm\frac{a}{b}x$

Chapter 11 Probability and Statistics

Fundamental Counting Principle
If event M can occur in m ways and is followed by event N that can occur in n ways, then event M followed by event N can occur in $m \cdot n$ ways.

Number of Permutations
The number of permutations of n items of a set arranged r items at a time is

$$_nP_r = \frac{n!}{(n-r)!} \text{ for } 0 \le r \le n.$$

Number of Combinations
The number of combinations of n items of a set chosen r items at a time is

$$_nC_r = \frac{n!}{r!(n-r)!} \text{ for } 0 \le r \le n.$$

Probability of A and B
If A and B are independent events, then
$P(A \text{ and } B) = P(A) \cdot P(B)$.

Probability of A or B
$P(A \text{ or } B) = P(A) + P(B) - P(A \text{ and } B)$
If A and B are mutually exclusive events, then
$P(A \text{ or } B) = P(A) + P(B)$.

Conditional Probability
For any two events A and B with $P(A) \ne 0$, the probability of event B, given event A, is:

$$P(B|A) = \frac{P(A \text{ and } B)}{P(A)}$$

Mean, Variance, and Standard Deviation
Mean: $\bar{x} = \dfrac{x_1 + x_2 + x_3 + \cdots + x_n}{n}$

Variance: $\sigma^2 = \dfrac{\Sigma(x - \bar{x})^2}{n}$

Standard deviation: $\sigma = \sqrt{\dfrac{\Sigma(x - \bar{x})^2}{n}}$

Binomial Probability
For repeated independent trials, each with a probability of success p and a probability of failure q (with $p + q = 1$), the probability of x successes in n trials is
$P(x) = {_nC_x}p^x q^{n-x}$.

Binomial Theorem (Using Combinations)
For every positive integer n, use the combinations formula $_nC_r$ to expand $(a + b)^n$:

$(a + b)^n = {_nC_0}a^n + {_nC_1}a^{n-1}b + {_nC_2}a^{n-2}b^2 +$
$\cdots + {_nC_{n-1}}ab^{n-1} + {_nC_n}b^n$

Chapter 12 Matrices

Properties of Matrix Addition
If A, B, and C are $m \times n$ matrices, then

Closure Property:	$A + B$ is an $m \times n$ matrix
Commutative Property:	$A + B = B + A$
Associative Property:	$(A + B) + C = A + (B + C)$
Identity Property:	There is a unique $m \times n$ matrix O such that $O + A = A + O = A$
Inverse Property:	For each A, there is a unique opposite, $-A$, such that $A + (-A) = O$

Properties of Scalar Multiplication
If A and B are $m \times n$ matrices, c and d are scalars, and O is the $m \times n$ zero matrix, then

Closure Property:	cA is an $m \times n$ matrix
Associative Property:	$(cd)A = c(dA)$
Distributive Property:	$c(A + B) = cA + cB$ $(c + d)A = cA + dA$
Identity Property:	$1 \cdot A = A$
Property of Zero:	$0 \cdot A = O$ and $cO = O$

Properties of Matrix Multiplication
If A, B, and C are $n \times n$ matrices and O is the $n \times n$ zero matrix, then

Closure Property:	AB is an $n \times n$ matrix
Associative Property:	$(AB)C = A(BC)$
Distributive Property:	$A(B + C) = AB + AC$ $(B + C)A = BA + CA$
Property of Zero:	$OA = AO = O$

Determinants of 2 × 2 and 3 × 3 Matrices
The determinant of a 2×2 matrix $\begin{bmatrix} a & b \\ c & d \end{bmatrix}$ is $ad - bc$.

The determinant of a 3×3 matrix $\begin{bmatrix} a_1 & b_1 & c_1 \\ a_2 & b_2 & c_2 \\ a_3 & b_3 & c_3 \end{bmatrix}$ is

$(a_1b_2c_3 + b_1c_2a_3 + c_1a_2b_3) - (a_3b_2c_1 + b_3c_2a_1 + c_3a_2b_1)$.

Inverse of a 2 × 2 Matrix
If $A = \begin{bmatrix} a & b \\ c & d \end{bmatrix}$ and $\det A \ne 0$,

then the inverse of A is

$$A^{-1} = \frac{1}{\det A}\begin{bmatrix} d & -b \\ -c & a \end{bmatrix} = \frac{1}{ad - bc}\begin{bmatrix} d & -b \\ -c & a \end{bmatrix}.$$

Chapter T Trigonometry Concepts

Convert Between Radians and Degrees

Use the proportion $\frac{d°}{180°} = \frac{r\text{ radians}}{\pi\text{ radians}}$ to convert between radians and degrees.

To convert degrees to radians, multiply by $\frac{\pi\text{ radians}}{180°}$.

To convert radians to degrees, multiply by $\frac{180°}{\pi\text{ radians}}$.

Length of an Intercepted Arc

For a circle of radius r and a central angle of measure θ (in radians), the length s of the intercepted arc is $s = r\theta$.

Sine and Cosine Functions

	Sine	Cosine
Parents	$y = \sin x$	$y = \cos x$
Reflection in x-axis	$y = -\sin x$	$y = -\cos x$
Amplitude $|a|$	$y = a \sin x$	$y = a \cos x$
Period $\frac{2\pi}{b}$, $b > 0$	$y = \sin bx$	$y = \cos bx$

Tangent Function

Parent	$y = \tan x$
Reflection across x-axis	$y = -\tan x$
Period $\frac{\pi}{b}$	$y = \tan bx$
Asymptotes ($\tan bx$)	$x = n\frac{\pi}{2b}$, n odd

Basic Identities

Reciprocal Identities:

$\csc \theta = \frac{1}{\sin \theta}$ $\sec \theta = \frac{1}{\cos \theta}$ $\tan \theta = \frac{1}{\cot \theta}$

$\sin \theta = \frac{1}{\csc \theta}$ $\cos \theta = \frac{1}{\sin \theta}$ $\cot \theta = \frac{1}{\tan \theta}$

Tangent Identity: Cotangent Identity:

$\tan \theta = \frac{\sin \theta}{\cos \theta}$ $\cot \theta = \frac{\cos \theta}{\sin \theta}$

Pythagorean Identities

$\cos^2\theta + \sin^2\theta = 1$ $1 + \tan^2\theta = \sec^2\theta$ $\cot^2\theta + 1 = \csc^2\theta$

Reference

Formulas of **Geometry**

You will use a number of geometric formulas as you work through your algebra book. Here are some perimeter, area, and volume formulas.

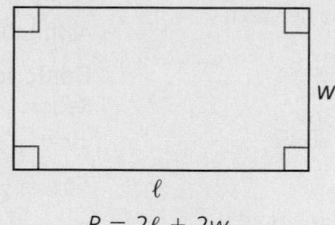

$P = 2\ell + 2w$
$A = \ell w$

Rectangle

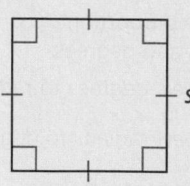

$P = 4s$
$A = s^2$

Square

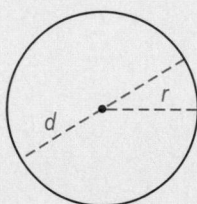

$C = 2\pi r$ or $C = \pi d$
$A = \pi r^2$

Circle

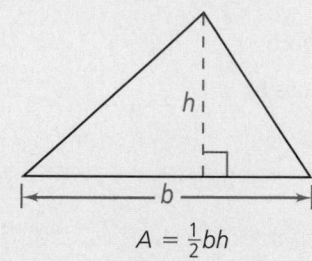

$A = \frac{1}{2}bh$

Triangle

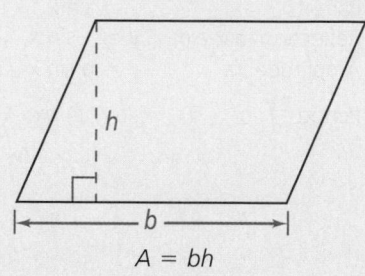

$A = bh$

Parallelogram

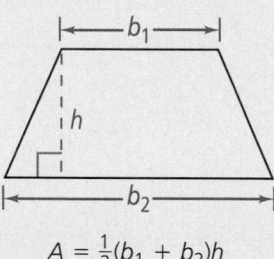

$A = \frac{1}{2}(b_1 + b_2)h$

Trapezoid

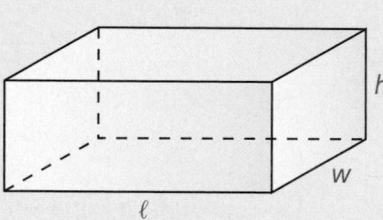

$SA = 2(\ell w + wh + h\ell)$
$V = Bh$
$V = \ell wh$

Right Prism

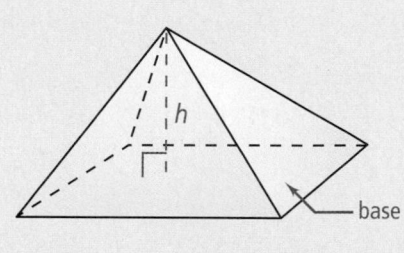

$V = \frac{1}{3}Bh$

Pyramid

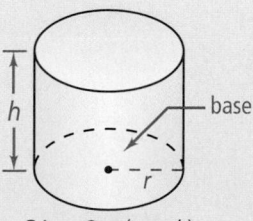

$SA = 2\pi r(r + h)$
$V = Bh$
$V = \pi r^2 h$

Right Cylinder

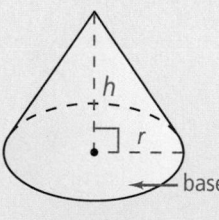

$V = \frac{1}{3}Bh$
$V = \frac{1}{3}\pi r^2 h$

Right Cone

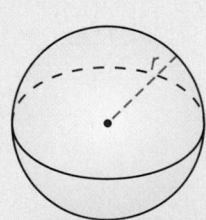

$SA = 4\pi r^2$
$V = \frac{4}{3}\pi r^3$

Sphere

English/Spanish Illustrated **Glossary**

English

A

Spanish

Absolute value (p. 43) The absolute value of a real number, x, written $|x|$, is its distance from zero on the number line.

Valor absoluto de un número real (p. 43) El valor absoluto de un número real, x, escrito como $|x|$, es su distancia desde cero en la recta numérica.

Example $|3| = 3$
$|-4| = 4$

Absolute value function (p. 121) A function of the form $f(x) = |mx + b| + c$, where $m \neq 0$, is an absolute value function.

Función de valor absolute (p. 121) Una función de la forma $f(x) - |mx + b| + c$, donde $m \neq 0$, es una función de valor absoluto.

Example $f(x) = |3x - 2| + 3$
$f(x) = |2x|$

Absolute value of a complex number (p. 269) The absolute value of a complex number is its distance from the origin on the complex number plane. In general, $|a + bi| - \sqrt{a^2 + b^2}$.

Valor absoluto de un número complejo (p. 269) El valor absoluto de un número complejo es la distancia a la que está del origen en el plano de números complejo. Generalmente, $|a + bi| = \sqrt{a^2 + b^2}$.

Example $|3 - 4i| = \sqrt{3^2 + (-4)^2} = 5$

Additive identity (p. 14) The additive identity is 0. The sum of 0 and any number is that number. The sum of opposites is 0.

Identidad aditiva (p. 14) La identidad aditiva es 0. La suma de 0 y cualquier número es ese mismo número. La suma de opuestos es 0.

Additive inverse (p. 14) The opposite or additive inverse of any number a is $-a$. The sum of opposites is 0, the additive identity.

Inverso aditivo (p. 14) El opuesto o inverso aditivo de un número a es $-a$. La suma de opuestos es 0, la identidad aditiva.

Example $3 + (-3) = 0$
$5.2 + (-5.2) = 0$

Algebraic expression (p. 5) An algebraic expression is a mathematical phrase that contains one or more variables.

Expresión algebraica (p. 5) Una expresión algebraica es una frase matemática que contiene una o más variables.

Example $2x + 3$
$z - y$

Amplitude (p. 850) The amplitude of a periodic function is half the difference between the maximum and minimum values of the function.

Amplitud (p. 850) La amplitud de una función periódica es la mitad de la diferencia entre los valores máximo y mínimo de la función.

Example The maximum and minimum values of $y = 4 \sin x$ are 4 and -4, respectively.
amplitude $= \dfrac{4 - (-4)}{2} = 4$

Visual **Glossary**

English

Spanish

Arithmetic mean (p. 594) The arithmetic mean, or average, of two numbers is their sum divided by two.

Media aritmética (p. 594) La media aritmética, o promedio, de dos números es su suma dividida por dos.

Example The arithmetic mean of 12 and 15 is $\frac{12 + 15}{2} = 13.5$.

Arithmetic sequence (p. 592) An arithmetic sequence is a sequence with a constant difference between consecutive terms.

Secuencia aritmética (p. 592) Una secuencia aritmética es una secuencia de números en la que la diferencia entre dos números consecutivos es constante.

Example The arithmetic sequence 1, 5, 9, 13, . . . has a common difference of 4.

Arithmetic series (p. 607) An arithmetic series is a series whose terms form an arithmetic sequence.

Serie aritmética (p. 607) Una serie aritmética es una serie cuyos términos forman una progresión aritmética.

Example $1 + 5 + 9 + 13 + 17 + 21$ is an arithmetic series with six terms.

Asymptote (p. 463) An asymptote is a line that a graph approaches as x or y increases in absolute value.

Asíntota (p. 463) Una asíntota es una recta a la cual se acerca una gráfica a medida que x o y aumentan de valor absoluto.

Example The function $y = \frac{x + 2}{x - 2}$ has $x = 2$ as a vertical asymptote and $y = 1$ as a horizontal asymptote.

Axis of symmetry (pp. 121, 204) The axis of symmetry is the line that divides a figure into two parts that are mirror images.

Eje de simetría (pp. 121, 204) El eje de simetría es la recta que divide una figura en dos partes que son imágenes una de la otra.

Example

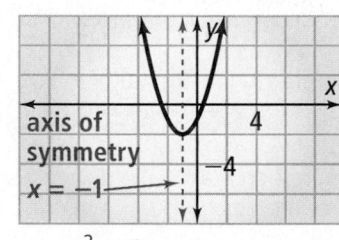

$y = x^2 + 2x - 1$

B

Bias (p. 739) A bias is a systematic error introduced by the sampling method.

Sesgo (p. 739) El sesgo es un error sistemático introducido por medio del método de muestreo.

Bimodal (p. 724) A bimodal data set has two modes.

Bimodal (p. 724) Un conjunto bimodal de datos tiene dos modas.

Example {1, 2, 3, 3, 4, 5, 6, 6} mode = 3 and 6

English	Spanish

Binomial experiment (p. 745) A binomial experiment is one in which the situation involves repeated trials. Each trial has two possible outcomes (success or failure), and the probability of success is constant throughout the trials.

Experimento binomial (p. 745) Un experimento binomial es un experimento que requiere varios ensayos. Cada ensayo tiene dos resultados posibles (éxito o fracaso), y la probabilidad de éxito es constante durante todos los ensayos.

Binomial probability (p. 746) In a binomial experiment with probability of success p and probability of failure q, the probability of x successes in n trials is given by ${}_nC_xp^xq^{n-x}$.

Probabilidad binomial (p. 746) En un experimento binomial con una probabilidad de éxito p y una probabilidad de fracaso q, la probabilidad de x éxitos en n ensayos se expresa con ${}_nC_xp^xq^{n-x}$.

Example Suppose you roll a standard number cube and that you call rolling a 1 a success. Then $p = \frac{1}{6}$ and $q = \frac{5}{6}$. The probability of rolling nine 1's in twenty rolls is ${}_{20}C_9\left(\frac{1}{6}\right)^9\left(\frac{5}{6}\right)^{11} \approx 0.0022$.

Binomial Theorem (pp. 348, 747) For every positive integer n, $(a + b)^n = P_0a^n + P_1a^{n-1}b + P_2a^{n-2}b^2 + \cdots + P_{n-1}ab^{n-1} + P_nb^n$ where $P_0, P_1, \ldots, P_n$ are the numbers in the row of Pascal's Triangle that has n as its second number.

Teorema binomial (pp. 348, 747) Para cada número entero positivo n, $(a + b)^n = P_0a^n + P_1a^{n-1}b + P_2a^{n-2}b^2 + \cdots + P_{n-1}ab^{n-1} + P_nb^n$, donde $P_0, P_1, \ldots, P_n$ son los números de la fila del Triángulo de Pascal cuyo segundo número es n.

Example $(x + 1)^3 = {}_3C_0(x)^3 + {}_3C_1(x)^2(1)^1 + {}_3C_2(x)^1(1)^2 + {}_3C_3(1)^3$
$= x^3 + 3x^2 + 3x + 1$

Boundary (p. 128) A boundary of the graph of a linear inequality is a line in the coordinate plane. It separates the solutions of the inequality from the nonsolutions. Points of the line itself may or may not be solutions.

Límite (p. 128) Un límite de la gráfica de una desigualdad lineal es una línea en el plano de coordenadas. Ésta separa las soluciones de la desigualdad de las no soluciones. Las soluciones pueden ser o no puntos de la línea.

Box-and-whisker plot (p. 725) A box-and-whisker plot is a method of displaying data that uses quartiles to form the center box and the maximum and minimum values to form the whiskers.

Gráfica de cajas (p. 725) Una gráfica de cajas es un método para mostrar datos que utiliza cuartiles para formar una casilla central y los valores máximos y mínimos para formar los conectores.

Example

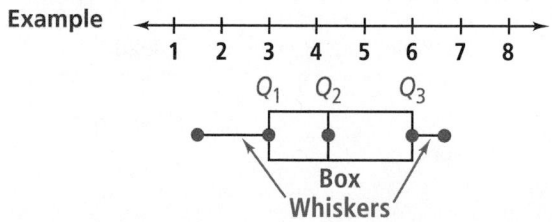

English	Spanish

Branch (p. 531)   Each piece of a discontinuous graph is called a branch.

Rama (p. 531)   Cada segmento de una gráfica discontinua se llama rama.

Example

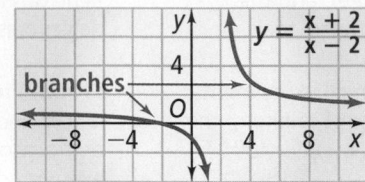

C

Center of a circle (p. 649)   The center of a circle is the point that is the same distance from every point on the circle.

Centro de un círculo (p. 649)   El centro de un círculo es el punto que está situado a la misma distancia de cada punto del círculo.

Example

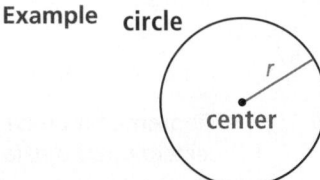

Center of an ellipse (p. 659)   The center of an ellipse is the midpoint of the major axis.

Centro de una elipse (p. 659)   El centro de una elipse es el punto medio entre los dos ejes mayores.

Central angle (p. 841)   A central angle of a circle is an angle whose vertex is at the center of a circle.

Ángulo central (p. 841)   El ángulo central de un círculo es un ángulo cuyo vértice está situado en el centro del círculo.

Example

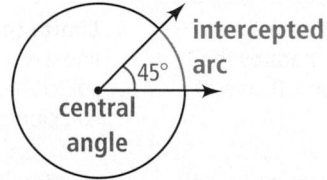

Change of Base Formula (p. 493) $\log_b M = \frac{\log_c M}{\log_c b}$, where M, b, and c are positive numbers, and $b \neq 1$ and $c \neq 1$.

Fórmula de cambio de base (p. 493) $\log_b M = \frac{\log_c M}{\log_c b}$, donde M, b y c son números positivos y $b \neq 1$ y $c \neq 1$.

Example $\log_3 8 = \frac{\log 8}{\log 3} \approx 1.8928$

English

Circle (p. 649)   A circle is the set of all points in a plane at a distance r from a given point. The standard form of the equation of a circle with center (h, k) and radius r is $(x - h)^2 + (y - k)^2 = r^2$.

Spanish

Círculo (p. 649)   Un círculo es el cojunto de todos los puntos situados en un plano a una distancia r de un punto dado. La forma normal de la ecuación cuyo centro es (h, k) y cuyo radio es r es $(x - h)^2 + (y - k)^2 = r^2$.

Example

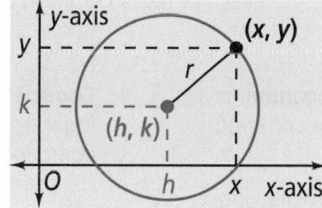

Coefficient (p. 20)   The numerical factor in a term.

Coeficiente (p. 20)   El factor numérico de un término.

Example   The coefficient of $-3k$ is -3.

Coefficient matrix (p. 801)   When representing a system of equations with a matrix equation, the matrix containing the coefficients of the system is the coefficient matrix.

Matriz de coeficientes (p. 801)   Al representar un sistema de ecuaciones con una ecuación de matriz, la matriz que contiene los coeficientes del sistema es la matriz de coeficientes.

Example $\begin{cases} x + 2y = 5 \\ 3x + 5y = 14 \end{cases}$

coefficient matrix $\begin{bmatrix} 1 & 2 \\ 3 & 5 \end{bmatrix}$

Combination (p. 690)   Any unordered selection of r objects from a set of n objects is a combination. The number of combinations of n objects taken r at a time is $_nC_r = \dfrac{n!}{r!(n - r)!}$ for $0 \leq r \leq n$.

Combinación (p. 690)   Cualquier selección no ordenada de r objetos tomados de un conjunto de n objetos es una combinación. El número de combinaciones de n objetos, cuando se toman r objetos cada vez, es $_nC_r = \dfrac{n!}{r!(n - r)!}$ para $0 \leq r \leq n$.

Example   The number of combinations of seven items taken four at a time is $_7C_4 = \dfrac{7!}{4!(7 - 4)!} = 35$. There are 35 ways to choose four items from seven items without regard to order.

Combined variation (p. 523)   A combined variation is a relation in which one variable varies with respect to each of two or more variables.

Variación combinada (p. 523)   Una variación combinada es una relación en la que una variable varía con respecto a cada una de dos o más variables.

Example $y = kx^2\sqrt{z}$
$z = \dfrac{kx}{y}$

English

Spanish

Common difference (p. 592)   A common difference is the difference between consecutive terms of an arithmetic sequence.

Diferencia común (p. 592)   La diferencia común es la diferencia entre los términos consecutivos de una progresión aritmética.

Example   The arithmetic sequence 1, 5, 9, 13, . . . has a common difference of 4.

Common logarithm (p. 482)   A common logarithm is a logarithm that uses base 10. You can write the common logarithm $\log_{10} y$ as $\log y$.

Logaritmo común (p. 482)   El logaritmo común es un logaritmo de base 10. El logaritmo común $\log_{10} y$ se expresa como $\log y$.

Example $\log 1 = 0$
$\log 10 = 1$
$\log 50 = 1.698970004 \ldots$

Common ratio (p. 600)   A common ratio is the ratio of consecutive terms of a geometric sequence.

Razón común (p. 600)   Una razón común es la razón de términos consecutivos en una secuencia geométrica.

Example   The geometric sequence 2.5, 5, 10, 20, . . . has a common ratio of 2.

Completing the square (p. 255)   Completing the square is the process of finding a constant c to add to $x^2 + bx$ so that $x^2 + bx + c$ is the square of a binomial.

Completar el cuadrado (p. 255)   Completar un cuadrado es el proceso mediante el cual se halla una constante c que se le pueda sumar a $x^2 + bx$, de manera que $x^2 + bx + c$ sea el cuadrado de un binomio.

Example $x^2 - 12x + \blacksquare$
$x^2 - 12x + \left(\frac{-12}{2}\right)^2$
$x^2 - 12x + 36$

Complex conjugates (p. 272)   Number pairs of the form $a + bi$ and $a - bi$ are complex conjugates.

Conjugados complejos (p. 272)   Los pares de números de la forma $a + bi$ y $a - bi$ son conjugados complejos.

Example   The complex numbers $2 - 3i$ and $2 + 3i$ are complex conjugates.

Complex fraction (p. 559)   A complex fraction is a rational expression that has a fraction in its numerator or denominator, or in both its numerator and denominator.

Fracción compleja (p. 559)   Una fracción compleja es una expresión racional en la que el numerador, el denominador o ambos son una fracción.

Example $\dfrac{2}{\frac{1}{5}}$, $\dfrac{\frac{2}{7}}{\frac{3}{2}}$

Complex number (p. 269)   Complex numbers are the real numbers and the imaginary numbers.

Número complejo (p. 269)   Los números complejos son los números reales y los números imaginarios.

Example $6 + i$
$7, 2i$

English

Complex number plane (p. 269) The complex number plane is identical to the coordinate plane except each ordered pair (a, b) represents the complex number $a + bi$. The horizontal axis is the Real axis. The vertical axis is the Imaginary axis.

Spanish

Plano de números complejos (p. 269) El plano de los números complejos es idéntico al plano de coordenadas, a excepción de que cada par ordenado (a, b) representa el número complejo $a + bi$. El eje horizontal es el eje real. El eje vertical es el eje imaginario.

Example

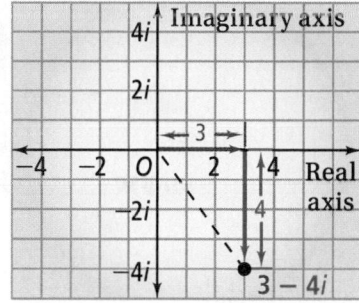

Composite function (p. 428) A composite function is a combination of two functions such that the output from the first function becomes the input for the second function.

Función compuesta (p. 428) Una función compuesta es la combinación de dos funciones. La cantidad de salida de la primera función es la cantidad de entrada de la segunda función.

Example $f(x) = 2x + 1 \quad g(x) = x^2 - 1$

$$(g \circ f)(5) = g(f(5)) = g(2(5) + 1)$$
$$= g(11)$$
$$= 11^2 - 1 = 120$$
$$(f \circ g)(5) = f(g(5)) = f((5)^2 - 1)$$
$$= f(24)$$
$$= 2(24) + 1 = 49$$

Compound inequality (p. 39) You can join two inequalities with the word *and* or the word *or* to form a compound inequality.

Desigualdad compuesta (p. 39) Puedes unir dos desigualdades por medio de la palabra *y* o la palabra *o* para formar una desigualdad compuesta.

Example $-1 < x$ and $x \le 3$
$\qquad\qquad x < -1$ or $x \ge 3$

Conditional probability (p. 711) A conditional probability contains a condition that may limit the sample space for an event. The notation $P(B|A)$ is read "the probability of event B, given event A." For any two events A and B in the sample space, $P(B|A) = \dfrac{P(A \text{ and } B)}{P(A)}$.

Probabilidad condicional (p. 711) Una probabilidad condicional contiene una condición que puede limitar el espacio muestral de un suceso. La notación $P(B|A)$ se lee "la probabilidad del suceso B, dado el suceso A". Para dos sucesos cualesquiera A y B en el espacio muestral,
$$P(B|A) = \frac{P(A \text{ y } B)}{P(A)}.$$

Example $= \dfrac{P(\text{departs and arrives on time})}{P(\text{departs on time})}$

$\qquad\qquad = \dfrac{0.75}{0.83}$

$\qquad\qquad \approx 0.9$

English	Spanish

Conic section (p. 634) A conic section is a curve formed by the intersection of a plane and a double cone.

Sección cónica (p. 634) Una sección cónica es una curva que se forma por la intersección de un plano con un cono doble.

Example

 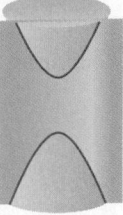

ellipse   **hyperbola**

Conjugate axis (p. 667) The conjugate axis for the hyperbola $\frac{x^2}{a^2} - \frac{y^2}{b^2} = 1$, $a > b > 0$, is the segment from $(0, -b)$ to $(0, b)$. For $\frac{y^2}{a^2} - \frac{x^2}{b^2} = 1$, the conjugate axis is the segment from $(-b, 0)$ to $(b, 0)$.

Eje conjugado (p. 667) El eje conjugado de la hipérbola $\frac{x^2}{a^2} - \frac{y^2}{b^2} = 1$, $a > b > 0$, es el segmento desde el punto $(0, -b)$ hasta el punto $(0, b)$. Para $\frac{y^2}{a^2} - \frac{x^2}{b^2} = 1$, el eje conjugado es el segmento desde el punto $(-b, 0)$ hasta el punto $(b, 0)$.

Conjugate Root Theorem (p. 335) If $P(x)$ is a polynomial with rational coefficients, then the irrational roots of $P(x) = 0$ occur in conjugate pairs. That is, if $a + \sqrt{b}$ is an irrational root with a and b rational, then $a - \sqrt{b}$ is also a root. If $P(x)$ is a polynomial with real coefficients, then the complex roots of $P(x) = 0$ occur in conjugate pairs. That is, if $a + bi$ is a complex root with a and b real, then $a - bi$ is also a root.

Teorema de raíces conjugadas (p. 335) Si $P(x)$ es un polinomio con coeficientes racionales, entonces las raíces irracionales de $P(x) = 0$ ocurren en pares conjugados. Es decir, si $a + \sqrt{b}$ es una raíz irracional donde a y b son racionales, entonces $a - \sqrt{b}$ también es una raíz. Si $P(x)$ es un polinomio con coeficientes reales, entonces las raíces complejas de $P(x) = 0$ ocurren en los pares conjugados. Es decir, si $a + bi$ es una raíz compleja donde a y b son reales, entonces $a - bi$ también es una raíz.

Conjugates (p. 335) Number pairs of the form $a + \sqrt{b}$ and $a - \sqrt{b}$ are conjugates.

Conjugados (p. 335) Los pares de números con la forma $a + \sqrt{b}$ y $a - \sqrt{b}$ son conjugados.

Example $5 + \sqrt{3}$ and $5 - \sqrt{3}$ are conjugates.

Constant (p. 5) A constant is a quantity whose value does not change.

Constante (p. 5) Una constante es una cantidad cuyo valor no cambia.

Constant matrix (p. 801) When representing a system of equations with a matrix equation, the matrix containing the constants of the system is the constant matrix.

Matriz de constantes (p. 801) Al representar un sistema de ecuaciones con una ecuación matricial, la matriz que contiene las constantes del sistema es la matriz de constantes.

Example $\begin{cases} x + 2y = 5 \\ 3x + 5y = 14 \end{cases}$

constant matrix $\begin{bmatrix} 5 \\ 14 \end{bmatrix}$

English

Constant of proportionality (p. 363) If $y = ax^b$ describes y as a power function of x, then y varies directly with, or is proportional to, the bth power of x. The constant a is the constant of proportionality.

Constant of variation (p. 74) The constant of variation is the ratio of the two variables in a direct variation and the product of the two variables in an inverse variation.

Example In $y = 3.5x$, the constant of variation k is 3.5. In $xy = 5$, the constant of variation k is 5.

Constant term (p. 20) A constant term is a term with no variables.

Constraint (p. 169) Constraints are restrictions on the variables of the objective function in a linear programming problem. *See* **Linear programming.**

Continuous graph (p. 539) A graph is continuous if it has no jumps, breaks, or holes.

Continuous probability distribution (p. 752) A continuous probability distribution has as its events any of the infinitely many values in an interval of real numbers.

Continuously compounded interest (p. 477) When interest is compounded continuously on principal P, the value A of an account is $A = Pe^{rt}$.

Example Suppose that $P = \$1200$, $r = 0.05$, and $t = 3$. Then
$$A = 1200e^{0.05 \cdot 3}$$
$$= 1200(2.718 \ldots)^{0.15}$$
$$\approx 1394.20$$

Controlled experiment (p. 739) In a controlled experiment, you divide the sample into two groups. You impose a treatment on one group but not the other "control" group. Then you compare the effect on the treated group to the control group.

Convenience sample (p. 738) In a convenience sample you select any members of the population who are conveniently and readily available.

Spanish

Constante de proporcionalidad (p. 363) Si $y = ax^b$ describe a y como una potencia de la función de x, entonces y varía directamente con, o es proporcional a, la b^{ma} potencia de x. La constante a es la constante de proporcionalidad.

Constante de variación (p. 74) La constante de variación es la razón de dos variables en una variación directa y el producto de las dos variables en una variación inversa.

Término constante (p. 20) Un término constante es un término que no tiene variables.

Restriccion (p. 169) Las restricciones son limitaciones a las variables de una función objetiva en un problema de programación lineal. *Ver* **Linear programming.**

Gráfica continua (p. 539) Una gráfica es continua si no tiene saltos, interrupciones o huecos.

Distribución de probabilidad continua (p. 752) Una distribución de probabilidad continua tiene como sucesos a cualquiera del número infinito de valores en un intervalo de números reales.

Interés compuesto continuo (p. 477) En un sistema donde el interés es compuesto continuamente sobre el capital P, el valor de A de una cuenta es $A = Pe^{rt}$.

Experimento controlado (p. 739) En un experimento controlado, se divide la muestra en dos grupos. Uno de los grupos se manipula y el otro grupo "controlado" se mantiene en su estado original. Luego se comparan el estado del grupo manipulado y el estado del grupo controlado.

Muestra de conveniencia (p. 738) En una muestra de conveniencia se selecciona a cualquier miembro de la población que está convenientemente disponible.

English	Spanish

Converge (p. 617)   An infinite series $a_1 + a_2 + \cdots + a_n + \cdots$ converges if the sum $a_1 + a_2 + \cdots + a_n$ get closer and closer to a real number as n increases.

Convergir (p. 617)   Una serie infinita $a_1 + a_2 + \cdots + a_n + \cdots$ es convergente si la suma $a_1 + a_2 + \cdots + a_n$ se aproxima cada vez más a un número real a medida que el valor de n incrementa.

Example $1 + \frac{1}{2} + \frac{1}{4} + \frac{1}{8} + \cdots$ converges.

Correlation (p. 103)   A correlation indicates the strength of a relationship between two data sets.

Correlación (p. 103)   Una correlación indica la fuerza de una relación entre dos conjuntos de datos.

Correlation coefficient (p. 106)   The correlation coefficient, r, indicates the strength of the correlation. The closer r is to 1 or -1, the more closely the data resembles a line and the more accurate your model is likely to be.

Coeficiente de correlación (p. 106)   El coeficiente de correlación, r, indica la fuerza de la correlación. Mientras más cerca está r de 1 ó -1, más se parecen los datos a una línea y será más probable que tu modelo sea preciso.

Corresponding elements (p. 772)   Corresponding elements are elements in the same position in each matrix.

Elementos correspondientes (p. 772)   Los elementos correspondientes son elementos que se encuentran en la misma posición de cada matriz.

Cosine function, Cosine of θ (pp. 823, 848)   The cosine function, $y = \cos\theta$, matches the measure θ of an angle in standard position with the x-coordinate of a point on the unit circle. This point is where the terminal side of the angle intersects the unit circle. The x-coordinate is the cosine of θ.

Función coseno, Coseno de θ (pp. 823, 848)   La función coseno, $y = \cos\theta$, empareja la medida θ de un ángulo en posición estándar con la coordenada x de un punto en el círculo unitario. Este es el punto en el que el lado terminal del ángulo interseca al círculo unitario. La coordenada x es el coseno de θ.

Example

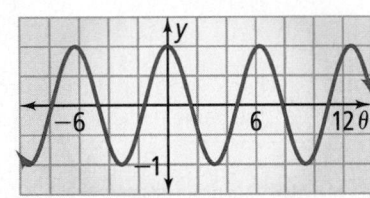

Co-vertices (p. 659)   The endpoints of the minor axis of an ellipse are the co-vertices of the ellipse.

Covértices (p. 659)   Los puntos de intersección entre una elipse y los ejes menores son los covértices de la elipse.

Example

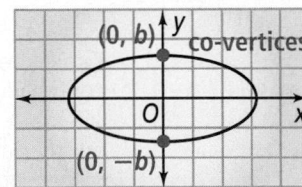

English

Spanish

Cycle (p. 849)   A cycle of a periodic function is an interval of x-values over which the function provides one complete pattern of y-values.

Ciclo (p. 849)   El ciclo de una función periódica es un intervalo de valores de x de los cuales la función produce un patrón completo de valores de y.

Example

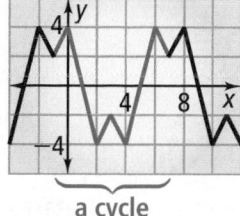

a cycle

D

Decay factor (p. 464)   In an exponential function of the form $y = ab^x$, b is the decay factor if $0 < b < 1$.

Factor de decremento (p. 464)   En una función exponencial de la forma $y = ab^x$, b es el factor de decremento si, $0 < b < 1$.

Example   In the equation $y = 0.3^x$, 0.7 is the decay factor.

Degree of a monomial (p. 292)   The degree of a monomial in one variable is the exponent of the variable.

Grado de un monomio (p. 292)   El grado de un monomio en una variable es el exponente de la variable.

Degree of a polynomial (p. 292)   The degree of a polynomial is the greatest degree among its monomial terms.

Grado de un polinomio (p. 292)   El grado de un polinomio es el grado mayor entre los términos de monomios.

Example $P(x) = x^6 + 2x^3 - 3$ degree 6

Dependent events (p. 704)   Two events are dependent if the occurrence of one event affects the probability of the second event.

Sucesos dependientes (p. 704)   Cuando el resultado de un suceso influye en la probabilidad de que ocurra el segundo suceso, los dos sucesos son dependientes.

Example   You have a bag with red and blue marbles. You draw one marble at random and then another without replacing the first. The colors drawn are dependent events. A red marble on the first draw changes the probability for each color on the second draw.

Dependent variable (p. 70)   If a function is defined by an equation using the variables x and y, where y represents output values, then y is the dependent variable.

Variable dependiente (p. 70)   Si una función es definida por una ecuación que usa las variables x e y, donde y representa valores de salida, entonces y es la variable dependiente.

Example $y = 2x + 1$
y is the dependent variable.

Visual **Glossary**

English

Spanish

Descartes' Rule of Signs (p. 336) Let $P(x)$ be a polynomial with real coefficients written in standard form.
– The number of positive real roots of $P(x) = 0$ is either equal to the number of sign changes between consecutive coefficients of $P(x)$ or is less than that by an even number;
– The number of negative real roots of $P(x) = 0$ is either equal to the number of sign changes between consecutive coefficients of $P(-x)$ or is less than that by an even number. (Count multiple roots according to their multiplicity.)

Regla de los signos de Descartes (p. 336) Sea $P(x)$ un polinomio con coeficientes reales escritos en forma normal.
– El número de raíces positivas reales de $P(x) = 0$ es igual al número de cambios de signos entre coeficientes consecutivos de $P(-x)$ o es menor que eso en un número par;
– El número de raíces negativas reales de $P(x) = 0$ es igual al número de cambios de signos entre coeficientes consecutivos de $P(-x)$ o es menor que eso en un número par. (Cuenta las raíces múltiples según su multiplicidad).

Determinant (p. 790) The determinant of a square matrix is a real number that can be computed from its elements according to a specific formula.

Determinante (p. 790) El determinante de una matriz cuadrada es un número real que se puede calcular a partir de sus elementos por medio de una fórmula específica.

Example The determinant of $\begin{bmatrix} 3 & -2 \\ 5 & 6 \end{bmatrix}$ is

$3(6) - 5(-2) = 28.$

Difference of cubes (p. 311) A difference of cubes is an expression of the form $a^3 - b^3$. It can be factored as $(a - b)(a^2 + ab + b^2)$.

Diferencia de dos cubos (p. 311) La diferencia de dos cubos es una expresión de la forma $a^3 - b^3$. Se puede factorizar como $(a - b)(a^2 + ab + b^2)$.

Example $x^3 - 27 = (x - 3)(x^2 + 3x + 9)$

Difference of two squares (p. 233) A difference of two squares is an expression of the form $a^2 - b^2$. It can be factored as $(a + b)(a - b)$.

Diferencia de dos cuadrados (p. 233) La diferencia de dos cuadrados es una expresión de la forma $a^2 - b^2$. Se puede factorizar como $(a + b)(a - b)$.

Example $25a^2 - 4 = (5a + 2)(5a - 2)$
$m^6 - 1 = (m^3 + 1)(m^3 - 1)$

Direct variation (p. 74) A linear function defined by an equation of the form $y = kx$, where $k \neq 0$, represents direct variation.

Variación directa (p. 74) Una función lineal definida por una ecuación de la forma $y = kx$, donde $k \neq 0$, representa una variación directa.

Example $y = 3.5x, y = 7x, y = -\frac{1}{2}x$

Directrix (p. 641) The directrix of a parabola is the fixed line used to define a parabola. Each point of the parabola is the same distance from the focus and the directrix.

Directriz (p. 641) La directriz de una parábola es la recta fija con que se define una parábola. Cada punto de la parábola está a la misma distancia del foco y de la directriz.

Example

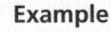

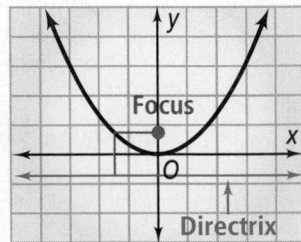

English

Discontinuous graph (p. 539)   A graph is discontinuous if it has a jump, break, or hole.

Discrete probability distribution (p. 752)   A discrete probability distribution has a finite number of Possible events.

Discriminant (p. 262)   The discriminant of a quadratic equation in the form $ax^2 + bx + c = 0$ is the value of the expression $b^2 - 4ac$.

Example $3x^2 - 6x + 1$
$$\text{discriminant} = (-6)^2 - 4(3)(1)$$
$$= 36 - 12 = 24$$

Diverge (p. 617)   An infinite series diverges if it does not converge.

Example $1 + 2 + 4 + 8 + \cdots$ diverges.

Domain (p. 65)   The domain of a relation is the set of all inputs, or *x*-coordinates, of the ordered pairs.

Examples   In the relation $\{(0, 1), (0, 2), (0, 3),$
$(0, 4), (1, 3), (1, 4), (2, 1)\}$, the
domain is $\{0, 1, 2\}$. In the function
$f(x) = x^2 - 10$, the domain is all
real numbers.

Spanish

Gráfica discontinua (p. 539)   Una gráfica es discontinua si tiene un salto, interrupción o hueco.

Distribución de probabilidad discreta (p. 752)   Una distribución de probabilidad discreta tiene un número finito de sucesos posibles.

Discriminante (p. 262)   El discriminante de una ecuación cuadrática en la forma $ax^2 + bx + c = 0$ es el valor de la expresión $b^2 - 4ac$.

Divergir (p. 617)   Una serie infinita es divergente si no es convergente.

Dominio (p. 65)   El dominio de una relación es el conjunto de todos los valores de entrada, o coordenadas *x*, de los pares ordenados.

E

Ellipse (p. 658)   An ellipse is the set of points *P* in a plane such that the sum of the distances from *P* to two fixed points *F*1 and *F*2 is a given constant *k*. The standard form of the equation of an ellipse with its center at the origin is $\frac{x^2}{a^2} + \frac{y^2}{b^2} = 1$ if the major axis is horizontal and $\frac{x^2}{b^2} + \frac{y^2}{a^2} = 1$ if the major axis is vertical, where $a > b$.

Elipse (p. 658)   Una elipse es el conjunto de puntos *P* situados en un plano tal que la suma de las distancias entre *P* y dos puntos fijos F_1 y F_2 es una constante dada *k*. La forma normal de la ecuación de una elipse con su centro en el origen es $\frac{x^2}{a^2} + \frac{y^2}{b^2} = 1$ si el eje mayor es horizontal y $\frac{x^2}{b^2} + \frac{y^2}{a^2} = 1$ si el eje mayor es vertical, donde $a > b$.

Example

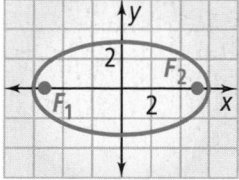

$$\frac{x^2}{36} + \frac{y^2}{9} = 1$$
$$F_1 = (-3\sqrt{3}, 0), F_2 = (3\sqrt{3}, 0)$$

English

End behavior (p. 294) End behavior of the graph of a function describes the directions of the graph as you move to the left and to the right, away from the origin.

Equal matrices (p. 775) Equal matrices are matrices with the same dimensions and equal corresponding elements.

Example Matrices A and B are equal.

$$A = \begin{bmatrix} 2 & 6 \\ \frac{9}{3} & 1 \end{bmatrix} \quad B = \begin{bmatrix} \frac{6}{3} & 6 \\ 3 & \frac{-13}{-13} \end{bmatrix}$$

Equally likely outcomes (p. 698) Equally likely outcomes are events in a sample space that have the same chance of occurring.

Equation (p. 26) An equation is a statement that two algebraic expressions are equal.

Equivalent systems (p. 157) Equivalent systems are systems that have the same solution(s).

Evaluate (p. 19) To evaluate an algebraic expression, substitute a number for each variable in the expression. Then simplify using the order of operations.

Example When $x = 2$ and $y = -1$,
$2x + 3y$ evaluates to 1.

Expand (p. 347) To expand the power of a binomial, multiply as needed, then write the polynomial in standard form.

Example
$$(x + 4)^3 = (x + 4)(x + 4)^2$$
$$= (x + 4)(x^2 + 8x + 16)$$
$$= x^3 + 8x^2 + 16x + 4x^2 + 32x + 64$$
$$= x^3 + 12x^2 + 48x + 64$$

Experimental probability (p. 695) The experimental probability of an event is the ratio
$$\frac{\text{number of times the event occurs}}{\text{number of trials}}.$$

Example Suppose a basketball player has scored 19 times in 28 attempts at a basket. The experimental probability of the player's scoring is
$P(\text{score}) = \frac{19}{28} \approx 0.68$, or 68%.

Spanish

Comportamiento extremo (p. 294) El comportamiento extremo de la gráfica de una función describe las direcciones de la gráfica al moverse a la izquierda y a la derecha, apartándose del origen.

Matrices equivalentes (p. 775) Dos matrices son equivalentes si y sólo si tienen las mismas dimensiones y sus elementos correspondientes son iguales.

Resultados igualmente probables (p. 698) Resultados igualmente probables son sucesos en un espacio muestral con la misma probabilidad de ocurrir.

Ecuación (p. 26) Una ecuación es un enunciado que describe dos expresiones algebraicas iguales.

Sistemas equivalentes (p. 157) Sistemas equivalentes son sistemas que tienen la misma solución o las mismas soluciones.

Evaluar (p. 19) Para evaluar una expresión algebraica, sustituye cada variable de la expresión con un número. Luego, simplifica usando el orden de operaciones.

Expandir (p. 347) Para expandir la potencia de un binomio, multiplica como sea necesario. Luego, escribe el polinomio en forma normal.

Probabilidad experimental (p. 695) La probabilidad experimental de un suceso es la razón
$$\frac{\text{number of times the event occurs}}{\text{number of trials}}.$$

English

Spanish

Explicit formula (p. 585)   An explicit formula expresses the nth term of a sequence in terms of n.

Fórmula explícita (p. 585)   Una fórmula explícita expresa el n-ésimo término de una progresión en función de n.

Example   Let $a_n = 2n + 5$ for positive integers n. If $n = 7$, then $a_7 = 2(7) + 5 = 19$.

Exponential decay (p. 463)   Exponential decay is modeled by a function of the form $y = ab^x$ with $0 < b < 1$.

Decaimiento exponencial (p. 463)   El decaimiento exponencial se expresa con una función $y = ab^x$ donde $0 < b < 1$.

Exponential equation (p. 498)   An exponential equation contains the form b^{cx}, with the exponent including a variable.

Ecuación exponencial (p. 498)   Una ecuación exponencial tiene la forma b^{cx}, y su exponente incluye una variable.

Example
$$5^{2x} = 270$$
$$\log 5^{2x} = \log 270$$
$$2x \log 5 = \log 270$$
$$2x = \frac{\log 270}{\log 5}$$
$$2x \approx 3.4785$$
$$x \approx 1.7392$$

Exponential function (p. 462)   The general form of an exponential function is $y = ab^x$, where x is a real number, $a \neq 0$, $b > 0$, and $b \neq 1$. When $b > 1$, the function models exponential growth with growth factor b. When $0 < b < 1$, the function models exponential decay with decay factor b.

Función exponencial (p. 462)   La forma general de una función exponencial es $y = ab^x$, donde x es un número real, $a \neq 0$, $b > 0$ y $b \neq 1$. Cuando $b > 1$, la función representa un incremento exponencial con factor de incremento b. Cuando $0 < b < 1$, la función representa el decremento exponencial con factor de decremento b.

Example

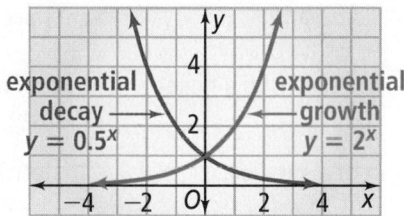

Exponential growth (p. 463)   Exponential growth is modeled by a function of the form $y = ab^x$ with $b > 1$.

Crecimiento exponencial (p. 463)   El crecimiento exponencial se expresa con una función de la forma $y = ab^x$ donde $b > 1$.

Visual **Glossary**

English

Spanish

Extraneous solution (p. 45) An extraneous solution is a solution of an equation derived from an original equation but it is not a solution of the original equation.

Solución extraña (p. 45) Una solución extraña es una solución de una ecuación derivada de una ecuación dada, pero que no satisface la ecuación dada.

Example
$$\sqrt{x - 3} = x - 5$$
$$x - 3 = x^2 - 10x + 25$$
$$0 = x^2 - 11x + 28$$
$$0 = (x - 4)(x - 7)$$
$$x = 4 \text{ or } 7$$
The number 7 is a solution, but 4 is not, since $\sqrt{4 - 3} \neq 4 - 5$.

F

Factor Theorem (p. 302) The expression $x - a$ is a linear factor of a polynomial if and only if the value of a is a root of the related polynomial function.

Teorema de factores (p. 302) La expresión $x - a$ es un factor lineal de un polinomio si y sólo si el valor de a es una raíz de la función polinomial con la que se relaciona.

Example The value 2 makes the polynomial $x^2 + 2x - 8$ equal to zero. So, $x - 2$ is a factor of $x^2 + 2x - 8$.

Factoring (p. 227) Factoring is rewriting an expression as the product of its factors.

Descomposición factorial (p. 227) Descomponer en factores es el proceso de escribir de nuevo una expresión como el producto de sus factores.

Example   expanded form   factored form
$$x^2 + x - 56 \qquad (x + 8)(x - 7)$$

Feasible region (p. 169) In a linear programming problem, the feasible region contains all the values that satisfy the constraints on the objective function.

Región factible (p. 169) En un problema de programación lineal, la región factible contiene todos los valores que satisfacen las restricciones de la función objetiva.

Finite series (p. 607) A finite series is a series with a finite number of terms.

Serie finite (p. 607) Una serie finita es una serie con un número finito de términos.

Focal length (p. 641) The focal length of a parabola is the distance between the vertex and the focus.

Distancia focal (p. 641) La distancia focal de una parábola es la distancia entre el vértice y el foco.

Focus (plural: foci) of a hyperbola (p. 666) A hyperbola is the set of all points P in a plane such that the difference of the distances from P to two fixed points is constant. Each of the fixed points is a focus of the hyperbola.

Foco de una hipérbola (p. 666) Una hipérbola es el conjunto de puntos P en un plano tal que la diferencia de las distancias desde P hasta dos puntos fijos es constante. Cada uno de los puntos fijos es el foco de la hipérbola.

Focus of a parabola (p. 641) A parabola is the set of all points in a plane that are the same distance from a fixed line and a fixed point not on the line. The fixed point is the focus of the parabola.

Foco de una parabola (p. 641) Una parábola es el conjunto de todos los puntos en un plano con la misma distancia desde una línea fija y un punto fijo que no permanece en la línea. El punto fijo es el foco de la parábola.

English

Spanish

Focus (plural: foci) of an ellipse (p. 658)   An ellipse is the set of all points P in a plane such that the sum of the distances from P to two fixed points is constant. Each of the fixed points is a focus of the ellipse.

Foco de una elipse (p. 658)   Una elipse es el conjunto de todos los puntos P en un plano en el cual la suma de las distancias desde P hasta dos puntos fijos es constante. Cada uno de estos puntos fijos es un foco de la elipsis.

Frequency table (p. 724)   A frequency table is a list of the outcomes in a sample space and the number of times each outcome occurs.

Tabla de frecuencias (p. 724)   Una tabla de frecuencias es una lista de los resultados de un espacio muestral y el número de veces que cada resultado ocurre.

Function (p. 66)   A function is a relation in which each element of the domain corresponds with exactly one element in the range.

Función (p. 66)   Una función es una relación en la que cada elemento del dominio corresponde exactamente con un elemento del rango.

Example   The relation $y = 3x^3 - 2x + 3$ is a function. $f(x) = 3x^3 - 2x + 3$ is the same relation written in function notation.

Function notation (p. 70)   If f is the name of a function, the function notation $f(x)$ shows the function name f and also represents the range value $f(x)$ for the domain value x. You read the function notation $f(x)$ as "f of x" or "a function of x." Note that $f(x)$ does *not* mean "f times x."

Notación de una función (p. 70)   Si f es el nombre de una función, la notación de la función $f(x)$ indica el nombre de la función y también representa el valor del rango $f(x)$ para el valor del dominio x. La función de la notación $f(x)$ se lee "f de x" o "una función de x." Observa que $f(x)$ *no* significa "f por x".

Example   When the value of x is 3, $f(3)$, read "f of 3," represents the value of the function at 3.

Function rule (p. 70)   A function rule represents an output value in terms of an input value.

Regla de función (p. 70)   Una regla de función representa un valor de salida en función a un valor de entrada.

Fundamental Counting Principle (p. 686)   The Fundamental Counting Principle is a tool that you can use to quickly count the number of ways certain things can happen.

Principio básico de conteo (p. 686)   El principio básico de conteo es una herramienta que se puede utilizar para hacer un conteo rápido del número de formas en que pueden ocurrir ciertas cosas.

Fundamental Theorem of Algebra (p. 341)   If $P(x)$ is a polynomial of degree $n \geq 1$ with complex coefficients, then $P(x) = 0$ has at least one complex root.

Teorema fundamental de álgebra (p. 341)   Si $P(x)$ es un polinomio de grado $n \geq 1$ con coeficientes complejos, entonces $P(x) = 0$ tiene por lo menos una raíz compleja.

Example $P(x) = 3x^3 - 2x + 3$ is of degree 3, so $P(x) = 0$ has at least one complex root.

G

Geometric mean (p. 603)   The geometric mean of any two positive numbers is the positive square root of the product of the two numbers.

Media geométrica (p. 603)   La media geométrica de dos números positivos es la raíz cuadrada positiva del producto de los dos números.

Example   The geometric mean of 12 and 18 is $\sqrt{12 \cdot 18} \approx 14.6969$.

English

Spanish

Geometric sequence (p. 600) A geometric sequence is a sequence with a constant ratio between consecutive terms.

Secuencia geométrica (p. 600) Una secuencia geométrica es una secuencia con una razón constante entre términos consecutivos.

Example The geometric sequence 2.5, 5, 10, 20, 40 . . . , has a common ratio of 2.

Geometric series (p. 614) A geometric series is the sum of the terms in a geometric sequence.

Serie geométrica (p. 614) Una serie geométrica es la suma de términos en una progresión geométrica.

Example One geometric series with five terms is $2.5 + 5 + 10 + 20 + 40$.

Greatest common factor (p. 229) The greatest common factor (GCF) of an expression is the common factor of each term of the expression that has the greatest coefficient and the greatest exponent.

Máximo factor común (p. 229) El máximo factor común de una expresión es el factor común de cada término de la expresión que tiene el mayor coeficiente y el mayor exponente.

Example The GCF of $4x^2 + 20x - 12$ is 4.

Growth factor (p. 464) In an exponential function of the form $y = ab^x$, b is the growth factor if $b > 1$.

Factor de incremento (p. 464) En una función exponencial de la forma $y = ab^x$, b es el factor de incremento si $b > 1$.

Example In the exponential equation $y = 2^x$, 2 is the growth factor.

Half-plane (p. 128) A half-plane is the set of points in a coordinate plane that are on one side of the boundary of the graph of a linear inequality.

Semiplano (p. 128) Un semiplano es el conjunto de puntos de un plano de coordenadas que están a un lado del límite de la gráfica de desigualdad lineal.

Hyperbola (p. 666) A hyperbola is a set of points P in a plane such that the difference between the distances from P to the foci F_1 and F_2 is a given constant k. $|PF_1 - PF_2| = k$ The standard form of an equation of a hyperbola centered at $(0, 0)$ is $\frac{x^2}{a^2} - \frac{y^2}{b^2} = 1$ if the transverse axis is horizontal and $\frac{y^2}{a^2} - \frac{x^2}{b^2} = 1$ if the transverse axis is vertical.

Hipérbola (p. 666) Una hipérbola es un conjunto de puntos P en un plano tal que la diferencia entre las distancias de P a los focos F_1 y F_2 es una constante k dada. $|PF_1 - PF_2| = k$ La forma normal de la ecuación de una hipérbola centrada en $(0, 0)$ es $\frac{x^2}{a^2} - \frac{y^2}{b^2} = 1$, si el eje transversal es horizontal, y $\frac{y^2}{a^2} - \frac{x^2}{b^2} = 1$, si el eje transversal es vertical.

Example

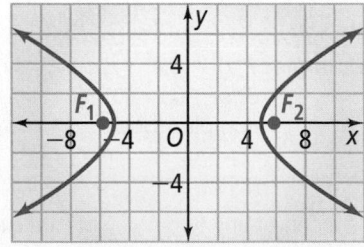

English

i (p. 268) The imaginary number *i* is the principal square root of −1.

Example $i = \sqrt{-1}$ and $i^2 = -1$.

Identity (p. 29) An equation that is true for every value of the variable is an identity.

Imaginary number (p. 269) An imaginary number is any number of the form $a + bi$, where *a* and *b* are real numbers and $b \neq 0$.

Example $2 + 3i$
$7i$
i

Imaginary unit (p. 268) The imaginary unit *i* is the complex number whose square is −1.

Independent events (p. 704) When the outcome of one event does not affect the probability of a second event, the two events are independent.

Example The results of two rolls of a number cube are independent. Getting a 5 on the first roll does not change the probability of getting a 5 on the second roll.

Independent variable (p. 70) If a function is defined by an equation using the variables *x* and *y*, where *x* represents input values, then *x* is the independent variable.

Example $y = 2x + 1$
x is the independent variable.

Index (p. 382) With a radical sign, the index indicates the degree of the root.

Example index 2   index 3   index 4
$\sqrt{16}$ $\sqrt[3]{16}$ $\sqrt[4]{16}$

Infinite series (p. 607) An infinite series is a series with infinitely many terms.

Spanish

i (p. 268) El número imaginario *i* es la raíz cuadrada principal de −1.

Identidad (p. 29) Una ecuación que es verdadera para cada valor de la variable es una identidad.

Número imaginario (p. 269) Un número imaginario es cualquier número de la forma $a + bi$, donde *a* y *b* son números reales y $b \neq 0$.

Unidad imaginaria (p. 268) La unidad imaginaria *i* es el número complejo cuyo cuadrado es −1.

Sucesos independientes (p. 704) Cuando el resultado de un suceso no altera la probabilidad de otro, los dos sucesos son independientes.

Variable independiente (p. 70) Si una función es definida por una ecuación con las variables *x* e *y*, donde *x* representa los valores de entrada, entonces *x* es la variable independiente.

Índice (p. 382) Con un signo de radical, el índice indica el grado de la raíz.

Serie infinita (p. 607) Una serie infinita es una serie con un número infinito de términos.

Visual Glossary

English	Spanish

Initial side (p. 834)   When an angle is in standard position, the initial side of the angle is given to be on the positive *x*-axis. The other ray is the terminal side of the angle.

Lado inicial (p. 834)   Cuando un ángulo está en posición normal, el lado inicial del ángulo se ubica en el eje positivo de las *x*. El otro rayo, o semirrecta, forma el lado terminal del ángulo.

Example

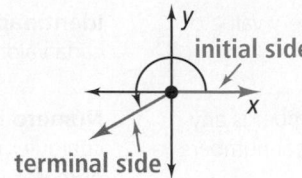

Intercepted arc (p. 841)   An intercepted arc is the portion of a circle whose endpoints are on the sides of a central angle of the circle and whose remaining points lie in the interior of the angle.

Arco interceptado (p. 841)   Un arco interceptado es la porción de un círculo cuyos extremos quedan sobre los lados de un ángulo central del círculo y cuyos puntos restantes quedan en el interior del ángulo.

Example

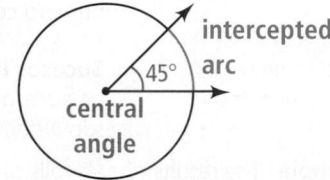

Interquartile range (p. 725)   The interquartile range of a set of data is the difference between the third and first quartiles.

Intervalo intercuartil (p. 725)   El rango intercuartil de un conjunto de datos es la diferencia entre el tercero y el primer cuartiles.

Example   The first and third quartiles of the data set {2, 3, 4, 5, 5, 6, 7, 7} are 3.5 and 6.5. The interquartile range is $6.5 - 3.5 = 3$.

Inverse function (p. 433)   If function *f* pairs a value *b* with *a* then its inverse, denoted f^{-1}, pairs the value *a* with *b*. If f^{-1} is also a function, then *f* and f^{-1} are inverse functions.

Funcion inversa (p. 433)   Si la función *f* empareja un valor *b* con *a*, entonces su inversa, cuya notación es f^{-1}, empareja el valor *a* con *b*. Si f^{-1} también es una función, entonces *f* y f^{-1} son funciones inversas.

Example   If $f(x) = x + 3$, then $f^{-1}(x) = x - 3$.

Inverse operations (p. 27)   Inverse operations are operations that undo each other.

Operaciones inversas (p. 27)   Operaciones inversas son operaciones que se cancelan mutuamente.

Inverse relation (p. 433)   If a relation pairs element *a* of its domain with element *b* of its range, the inverse relation "undoes" the relation and pairs *b* with *a*. If (*a*, *b*) is an ordered pair of a relation, then (*b*, *a*) is an ordered pair of its inverse.

Relación inversa (p. 433)   Si una relación empareja el elemento *a* de su dominio con el elemento *b* de su rango, la relación inversa "deshace" la relación y empareja *b* con *a*. Si (*a*, *b*) es un par ordenado de una relación, entonces (*b*, *a*) es un par ordenado de su inversa.

English	Spanish

Inverse variation (p. 520)   An inverse variation is a relation represented by an equation of the form $xy = k$, $y = \frac{k}{x}$, or $x = \frac{k}{y}$, where $k \neq 0$.

Variación inversa (p. 520)   Una variación inversa es una relación representada por la ecuación $xy = k$, $y = \frac{k}{x}$, ó $x = \frac{k}{y}$, donde $k \neq 0$.

Example

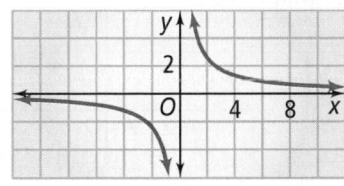

$$xy = 5, \text{ or } y = \frac{5}{x}$$

Joint variation (p. 523)   A joint variation is a relation in which one variable varies directly with respect to each of two or more variables.

Variación conjunta (p. 523)   Una variación conjunta es una relación en la cual el valor de una variable varía directamente con respecto a cada una de dos o más variables.

Example $z = 8xy$
$T = kPV$

L

Like radicals (p. 395)   Like radicals are radical expressions that have the same index and the same radicand.

Radicales semejantes (p. 395)   Los radicales semejantes son expresiones radicales que tienen el mismo índice y el mismo radicando.

Example $4\sqrt[3]{7}$ and $\sqrt[3]{7}$ are like radicals.

Like terms (p. 21)   Like terms have the same variables raised to the same powers.

Términos semejantes (p. 21)   Los términos semejantes tienen las mismas variables elevadas a las mismas potencias.

Limits (p. 610)   Limits in summation notation are the least and greatest integer values of the index n.

Límites (p. 610)   Los límites en notación de sumatoria son el menor y el mayor valor del índice n en números enteros.

Example

$$\text{limits} \nearrow \begin{array}{c} 3 \\ \Sigma \\ n = 1 \end{array} (3n + 5)$$

Line of best fit (p. 106)   The trend line that gives the most accurate model of related data is the line of best fit.

Recta de mayor aproximación (p. 106)   La línea de tendencia que representa con mayor precisión los datos relacionado es la recta de mayor aproximación.

Linear equation (p. 82)   A linear equation in two variables is an equation that can be written in the form $ax + by = c$. *See also* **Standard form of a linear equation.**

Ecuación lineal (p. 82)   Una ecuación lineal de dos variables es una ecuación que se puede escribir de la forma $ax + by = c$. *Ver también* **Standard form of a linear equation.**

Example $y = 2x + 1$ can be written as $-2x + y = 1$.

English

Linear function (p. 82)   A function whose graph is a line is a linear function. You can represent a linear function with a linear equation.

Example

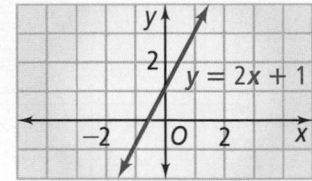

Spanish

Función lineal (p. 82)   Una función cuya gráfica es una recta es una función lineal. La función lineal se representa con una ecuación lineal.

Linear inequality (p. 128)   A linear inequality is an inequality in two variables whose graph is a region of the coordinate plane that is bounded by a line.

Example

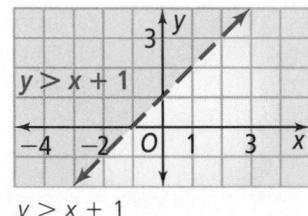

$y > x + 1$

Desigualdad lineal (p. 128)   Una desigualdad lineal es una desigualdad de dos variables cuya gráfica es una región del plano de coordenadas delimitado por una recta.

Linear programming (p. 169)   Linear programming is a method for finding a minimum or maximum value of some quantity, given a set of constraints.

Programación lineal (p. 169)   Programación lineal es un método para hallar el valor mínimo y máximo de una cantidad que se expresa como un conjunto de limitaciones.

Example   Restrictions $x \geq 0$, $y \geq 0$, $x + y \leq 7$, and $y \leq -2x + 8$
Objective function: $B = 2x + 4y$
Evaluate $B = 2x + 4y$ at each vertex.
The minimum value of B occurs when $x = 0$ and $y = 0$. The m aximum value of B occurs when $x = 0$ and $y = 7$.

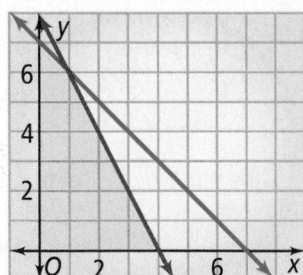

English

Linear system (p. 146)   A linear system is a set of two or more linear equations that use the same variables.

Example

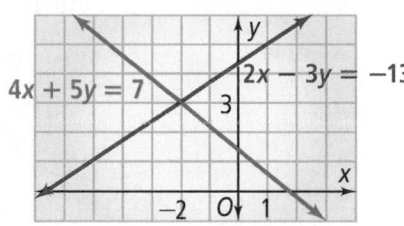

Literal equation (p. 29)   A literal equation is an equation that uses more than one letter as a variable.

Logarithm (p. 480)   The logarithm base b of a positive number x is defined as follows: $\log_b x = y$, if and only if $x = b^y$.

Example $\log_2 8 = 3$
$\log_{10} 100 = \log 100 = 2$
$\log_5 5^7 = 7$

Logarithmic equation (p. 503)   A logarithmic equation is an equation that includes a logarithm involving a variable.

Example $\log_3 x = 4$

Logarithmic function (p. 483)   A logarithmic function is the inverse of an exponential function.

Example

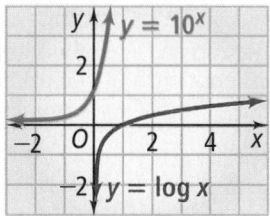

Logarithmic scale (p. 482)   A logarithmic scale is a scale that uses the logarithm of a quantity instead of the quantity itself.

Spanish

Sistema lineal (p. 146)   Un sistema lineal es un conjunto de dos o más ecuaciones lineales con las mismas variables.

Ecuación literal (p. 29)   Una ecuación literal es una ecuación en la cual más de una letra expresa una variable.

Logaritmo (p. 480)   La base del logaritmo b de un número positivo x se define como $\log_b x = y$, si y sólo si $x = b^y$.

Ecuación logarítmica (p. 503)   Una ecuación logarítmica es una ecuación que incluye un logaritmo con una variable.

Función logarítmica (p. 483)   Una función logarítmica es la inversa de una función exponencial.

Escala logarítmica (p. 482)   Una escala logarítmica es una escala que usa el logaritmo de una cantidaden vez de la cantidad misma.

Major axis (p. 659) The major axis of an ellipse is the segment that contains the foci of the ellipse and has endpoints on the ellipse.

Eje mayor (p. 659) En una elipsis, el eje mayor es el segmento que contiene los focos de la elipsis y tiene puntos extremos sobre la elipsis.

Example

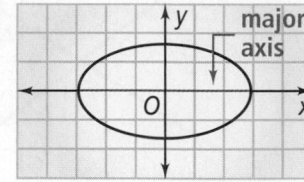

Mapping diagram (p. 64) A mapping diagram describes a relation by linking elements of the domain with elements of the range.

Mapa (p. 64) Un mapa describe una relación al unir los elementos del dominio con los elementos del rango.

Example Domain Range

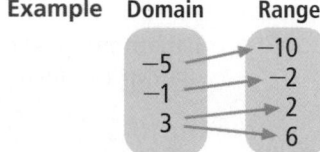

Matrix (p. 184) A matrix is a rectangular array of numbers written within brackets.

Matriz (p. 184) Una matriz es un conjunto de números encerrados en corchetes y dispuestos en forma de rectángulo.

Example $A = \begin{bmatrix} 1 & -2 & 0 & 10 \\ 9 & 7 & -3 & 8 \\ 2 & -10 & 1 & -6 \end{bmatrix}$

The number 2 is the element in the third row and first column. A is a 3×4 matrix.

Matrix element (p. 184) Every item listed in a matrix is an element of the matrix. An element is identified by its position in the matrix.

Elemento matricial (p. 184) Cada cifra de una matriz es un elemento de la matriz. El elemento se identifica según la posición que ocupa en la matriz.

Example $A = \begin{bmatrix} 1 & -2 & 0 & 10 \\ 9 & 7 & -3 & 8 \\ 2 & -10 & 1 & -6 \end{bmatrix}$

Element a_{21} is 9, the element in the second row and first column.

Matrix equation (p. 773) A matrix equation is an equation in which the variable is a matrix.

Ecuación matricial (p. 773) Una ecuación matricial es una ecuación en que la variable es una matriz.

Example

$$\text{Solve } X + \begin{bmatrix} 3 & -2 \\ 5 & 1 \end{bmatrix} = \begin{bmatrix} 4 & 0 \\ 0 & 3 \end{bmatrix}$$

$$X + \begin{bmatrix} 3 & -2 \\ 5 & 1 \end{bmatrix} = \begin{bmatrix} 4 & 0 \\ 0 & 3 \end{bmatrix}$$

$$X = \begin{bmatrix} 4 & 0 \\ 0 & 3 \end{bmatrix} - \begin{bmatrix} 3 & -2 \\ 5 & 1 \end{bmatrix} = \begin{bmatrix} 1 & 2 \\ -5 & 2 \end{bmatrix}$$

English

Maximum value (p. 205) The maximum value of a function $y = f(x)$ is the greatest y-value of the function. It is the y-coordinate of the highest point on the graph of f.

Mean (p. 723) The sum of the data values divided by the number of data values is the mean. *See also* **Arithmetic mean.**

Example $\{1, 2, 3, 3, 6, 6\}$
$$\text{mean} = \frac{1 + 2 + 3 + 3 + 6 + 6}{6}$$
$$= \frac{21}{6} = 3.5$$

Measures of central tendency (p. 723) The mean, the median, and the mode are each central values that help describe a set of data. They are called measures of central tendency.

Example $\{1, 2, 3, 3, 4, 5, 6, 6\}$
mean = 3.75
median = 3.5
modes = 3 and 6

Measure of variation (p. 732) Measures of variation, such as the range, the interquartile range, and the standard deviation, describe how the data in a data set are spread out.

Median (p. 723) The median is the middle value in a data set. If the data set contains an even number of values, the median is the mean of the two middle values.

Example $\{1, 2, 3, 3, 4, 5, 6, 6\}$
$$\text{median} = \frac{3 + 4}{2} = \frac{7}{2} = 3.5$$

Minimum value (p. 205) The minimum value of a function $y = f(x)$ is the least y-value of the function. It is the y-coordinate of the lowest point on the graph of f.

Minor axis (p. 659) The minor axis of an ellipse is the segment that is perpendicular to the major axis at its midpoint and has endpoints on the ellipse.

Example

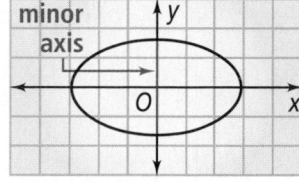

Spanish

Valor máximo (p. 205) El valor máximo de una función $y = f(x)$ es el valor más alto de y de la función. Es la coordenada y del punto más alto de la gráfica de f.

Media (p. 723) La suma de los valores de datos dividida por el número de valores de datos sumados es la media. *Ver también* **Arithmetic mean.**

Medidas de tendencia central (p. 723) La media, la mediana y la moda son los valores centrales que facilitan la descripción de un conjunto de datos. A estos valores se les llama medidas de tendencia central.

Medida de dispersión (p. 732) Las medidas de dispersión, tal como el rango, el intervalo intercuartil y la desviación típica, describen cómo se dispersan los datos en un conjunto de datos.

Mediana (p. 723) La mediana es el valor situado en el medio en un conjunto de datos. Si el conjunto de datos contiene un número par de valores, la mediana es la media de los dos valores del medio.

Valor mínimo (p. 205) El valor mínimo de una función $y = f(x)$ es el valor más bajo de y de la función. Es la coordenada y del punto más bajo de la gráfica de f.

Eje menor (p. 659) En una elipsis, el eje menor es el segmento perpendicular al eje mayor en su punto medio y que tiene puntos extremos sobre la elipsis.

English

Spanish

Mode (p. 723) The mode is the most frequently occurring value (or values) in a set of data.

Moda (p. 723) La moda es el valor o valores que ocurren con mayor frecuencia en un conjunto de datos.

Example $\{1, 2, 3, 3, 4, 5, 6, 6\}$
The modes are 3 and 6.

Monomial (p. 292) A monomial is either a real number, a variable, or a product of real numbers and variables with whole number exponents.

Monomio (p. 292) Un monomio es un número real, una variable o un producto de números reales y variables cuyos exponentes son números enteros.

Example $1, x, 2z, 4ab^2$

Multiple zero (p. 304) If a linear factor is repeated in the complete factored form of a polynomial, the zero related to that factor is a multiple zero.

Cero múltiplo (p. 304) Si un factor lineal se repite en la forma factorizada completa de un polinomio, el cero relacionado con ese factor es un cero múltiplo.

Example The zeros of the function
$P(x) = 2x(x - 3)^2(x + 1)$ are 0, 3,
and -1. Since $(x - 3)$ occurs twice
as a factor, 3 is a multiple zero.

Multiplicative identity (p. 14) The multiplicative identity is 1. The product of 1 and any number is that number. The product of reciprocals is 1.

Identidad multiplicativa (p. 14) La identidad multiplicativa es 1. El producto de 1 y cualquier otro número es ese número. El producto del recíproco es 1.

Multiplicative identity matrix (p. 789) For an $n \times n$ square matrix, the multiplicative identity matrix is an $n \times n$ square matrix I, or $I_{n \times n}$, with 1's along the main diagonal and 0's elsewhere.

Matriz de identidad multiplicativa (p. 789) Para una matriz cuadrada $n \times n$, la matriz de identidad multiplicativa es la matriz cuadrada I de $n \times n$, o $I_{n \times n}$, con unos por la diagonal principal y ceros en los demás lugares.

Example $I_{2 \times 2} = \begin{bmatrix} 1 & 0 \\ 0 & 1 \end{bmatrix}$

$I_{3 \times 3} = \begin{bmatrix} 1 & 0 & 0 \\ 0 & 1 & 0 \\ 0 & 0 & 1 \end{bmatrix}$

Multiplicative inverse (p. 14) The reciprocal or multiplicative inverse of any nonzero number a is $\frac{1}{a}$. The product of reciprocals is 1, the multiplicative identity.

Inverso multiplicativo (p. 14) El recíproco o inverso multiplicativo de cualquier número a, que no sea cero, es $\frac{1}{a}$. El producto de recíprocos es 1, la identidad multiplicativa.

Example $5 \times \frac{1}{5} = 1$

Multiplicative inverse of a matrix (p. 789) If A and X are $n \times n$ matrices, and $AX = XA = I$, then X is the multiplicative inverse of A, written A^{-1}.

Inverso multiplicativo de una matriz (p. 789) Si A y X son matrices $n \times n$, y $AX = XA = I$, entonces X es el inverso multiplicativo de A, expresado como A^{-1}.

Example $A = \begin{bmatrix} 2 & 1 \\ 4 & 0 \end{bmatrix}$

$X = \begin{bmatrix} 0 & \frac{1}{4} \\ 1 & \frac{1}{2} \end{bmatrix}$

$AX = \begin{bmatrix} 1 & 0 \\ 0 & 1 \end{bmatrix} = I$, so $X = A^{-1}$

English

Spanish

Multiplicity (p. 304) The multiplicity of a zero of a polynomial function is the number of times the related linear factor is repeated in the factored form of the polynomial.

Multiplicidad (p. 304) La multiplicidad de un cero de una función polinomial es el número de veces que el factor lineal relacionado se repite en la forma factorizada del polinomio.

Example The zeros of the function
$P(x) = 2x(x - 3)^2(x + 1)$ are 0, 3,
and -1. Since $(x - 3)$ occurs twice as
a factor, the zero 3 has multiplicity 2.

Mutually exclusive events (p. 705) When two events cannot happen at the same time, the events are mutually exclusive. If A and B are mutually exclusive events, then $P(A \text{ or } B) = P(A) + P(B)$.

Sucesos mutuamente excluyentes (p. 705) Cuando dos sucesos no pueden ocurrir al mismo tiempo, son mutuamente excluyentes. Si A y B son sucesos mutuamente excluyentes, entonces $P(A \text{ or } B) - P(A) + P(B)$.

Example Rolling an even number E and
rolling a multiple of five M on a
standard number cube are
mutually exclusive events.

$$P(E \text{ or } M) = P(E) + P(M)$$
$$= \frac{3}{6} + \frac{1}{6}$$
$$= \frac{4}{6}, \text{ or } \frac{2}{3}$$

N

n factorial ($n!$) (p. 687) For any positive integer n, n factorial is $n(n - 1) \cdots 3 \cdot 2 \cdot 1$. Zero factorial $(0!) = 1$.

n factorial ($n!$) (p. 687) Para cualquier entero n, n factorial es $n(n - 1) \cdots 3 \cdot 2 \cdot 1$. El cero factorial $(0!) = 1$.

Example $4! = 4 \times 3 \times 2 \times 1 = 24$

nth root (p. 381) For any real numbers a and b, and any positive integer n, if $a^n = b$, then a is an nth root of b.

raíz n-ésima (p. 381) Para todos los números reales a y b, y todo número entero positivo n, si $a^n = b$, entonces a es la n-ésima raíz de b.

Example $\sqrt[5]{32} = 2$ because $2^5 = 32$.

$\sqrt[4]{81} = 3$ because $3^4 = 81$.

Natural base exponential function (p. 476) A natural base exponential function is an exponential function with base e.

Función exponencial con base natural (p. 476) Una función exponencial con base natural es una función exponencial con base e.

Non-removable discontinuity (p. 539) A non-removable discontinuity is a point of discontinuity that is not removable. It represents a break in the graph of f where you cannot redefine f to make the graph continuous.

Discontinuidad irremovible (p. 539) Una discontinuidad irremovible es un punto de discontinuidad que no se puede remover. Representa una interrupción en la gráfica f donde no se puede redefinir f para volverla una gráfica continua.

English

Spanish

Normal distribution (p. 752)   A normal distribution shows data that vary randomly from the mean in the pattern of a bell-shaped curve.

Distribución normal (p. 752)   Una distribución normal muestra, con una curva en forma de campana, datos que varían alcatoriamente respecto de la media.

Example

Distribution of Test Scores

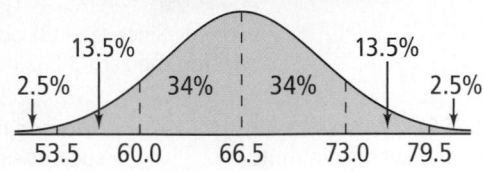

13.5%   13.5%

2.5%   34%   34%   2.5%

53.5   60.0   66.5   73.0   79.5

In a class of 200 students, the scores on a test were normally distributed. The mean score was 66.5 and the standard deviation was 6.5. The number of students who scored greater than 73 percent was about 13.5% + 2,5% of those who took the test.
16% of 200 = 32
About 32 students scored 73 or higher on the test.

Numerical expression (p. 5)   A numerical expression is a mathematical phrase that contains numbers and operation symbols.

Expresión numérica (p. 5)   Una expresión numérica es una expresión matemática compuesta de números y símbolos de operación.

Objective function (p. 169)   In a linear programming model, the objective function is a model of the quantity that you want to make as large or as small as possible. *See* **Linear programming.**

Función objetiva (p. 169)   En un modelo de programación lineal, la función objetiva es un modelo de la cantidad que se quiere aumentar o disminuir cuanto sea posible. *Ver* **Linear programming.**

Observational study (p. 739)   In an observational study, you measure or observe members of a sample in such a way that they are not affected by the study.

Estudio de observación (p. 739)   En un estudio de observación, se miden u observan a los miembros de una muestra de tal manera que no les afecte el estudio.

One-to-one function (p. 439)   A one-to-one function is a function for which each *y*-value in the range corresponds to exactly one *x*-value in the domain. A one-to-one function f has an inverse f^{-1} that is also a function.

Función uno a uno (p. 439)   Una función uno a uno es una función donde cada valor *y* que se encuentra en el rango corresponde exactamente a un valor *x* en el dominio. Una función uno a uno f tiene un inverso f^{-1} que también es una función.

Opposite (p. 14)   The opposite or additive inverse of any number a is $-a$. The sum of opposites is zero, the additive identity.

Opuesto (p. 14)   El opuesto o inverso aditivo de cualquier número a es $-a$. La suma de opuestos es cero, la identidad aditiva.

Example $3 + (-3) = 0$
$5.2 + (-5.2) = 0$

English

Spanish

Outlier (p. 724) An outlier is a value substantially different from the rest of the data in a set.

Valor extremo (p. 724) Un valor extremo es un valor considerablemente diferente al resto de los datos de un conjunto.

Example The outlier in the data set {56, 64, 73, 59, 98, 65, 59} is 98.

Parabola (p. 204) A parabola is the graph of a quadratic function. It is the set of all points *P* in a plane that are the same distance from a fixed point *F*, the focus, as they are from a line *d*, the directrix.

Parábola (p. 204) La parábola es la gráfica de una función cuadrática. Es el conjunto de todos los puntos *P* situados en un plano a la misma distancia de un punto fijo *F*, o foco, y de la recta *d*, o directriz.

Example

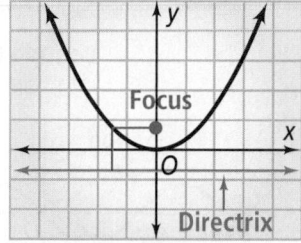

Parallel lines (p. 94) Parallel lines are coplanar lines that do not intersect. In the coordinate plane, parallel lines have the same slope.

Rectas paralelas (p. 94) Rectas paralelas son líneas coplanares que no se intersecan. En un plano de coordenadas, las rectas paralelas tienen la misma pendiente.

Parent function (p. 110) A parent function is the simplest form of a set of functions that form a family.

Función elemental (p. 110) Una función madre es la mínima expresión de un conjunto de funciones que forma una familia.

Example $y = x$ is the parent function for the functions of the form $y = x + k$.

Pascal's Triangle (p. 348) Pascal's Triangle is a triangular array of numbers in which the first and last number is 1. Each of the other numbers in the row is the sum of the two numbers above it.

Triángulo de Pascal (p. 348) El Triángulo de Pascal es una distribución triangular de números en la cual el primer número y el último número son 1. Cada uno de los otros números en la fila es la suma de los dos números de encima.

Example **Pascal's Triangle**

```
            1
          1   1
        1   2   1
      1   3   3   1
    1   4   6   4   1
  1   5  10  10   5   1
```

English

Spanish

Percentiles (p. 728) A percentile is a number from 0 to 100 that you can associate with a value x from a data set. It shows the percent of the data that are less than or equal to x.

Percentiles (p. 728) Un percentil es un número de 0 a 100 que se puede asociar con un valor x de un conjunto de datos. Éste muestra el porcentaje de los datos que son menores o iguales a x.

Perfect square trinomial (p. 232) A perfect square trinomial is a trinomial that is the square of a binomial.

Trinomio cuadrado perfecto (p. 232) Un trinomio cuadrado perfecto es un trinomio que es el cuadrado de un binomio.

Example   perfect square trinominal   binominal square
$$16x^2 - 24x + 9 = (4x - 3)^2$$

Period (p. 849) The period of a periodic function is the horizontal length of one cycle.

Período (p. 849) El período de una función periódica es el intervalo horizontal de un ciclo.

Example

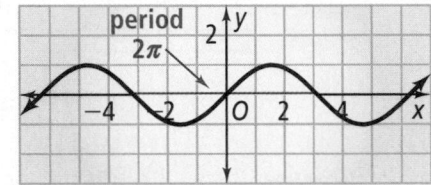

The periodic function $y = \sin x$ has period 2π.

Periodic function (p. 849) A periodic function repeats a pattern of y-values at regular intervals.

Función periódica (p. 849) Una función periódica repite un patrón de valores y a intervalos regulares.

Example

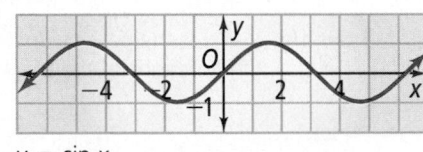

$y = \sin x$

Permutation (p. 687) A permutation is an arrangement of items in a particular order. The number of permutations of n objects taken r at a time is $_nP_r = \frac{n!}{(n-r)!}$ for $1 \le r \le n$.

Permutación (p. 687) Una permutación es la disposición de objetos en un orden determinado. El número de permutaciones de n objetos seleccionados r veces es $_nP_r = \frac{n!}{(n-r)!}$ para $1 \le r \le n$.

Example
$$_8P_5 = \frac{8!}{(8-5)!}$$
$$= \frac{8 \cdot 7 \cdot 6 \cdot 5 \cdot 4 \cdot 3!}{3!}$$
$$= 8 \times 7 \times 6 \times 5 \times 4$$
$$= 6720$$

Perpendicular lines (p. 94) Perpendicular lines are lines that intersect to form right angles. In the coordinate plane, perpendicular lines have slopes with product -1.

Rectas perpendiculares (p. 94) Rectas perpendiculares son rectas que se intersecan y forman ángulos rectos. En un plano de coordenadas, las rectas perpendiculares tienen pendientes cuyo producto es -1.

English

Point of discontinuity (p. 539)   A point of discontinuity is the x-coordinate of a point where the graph of $f(x)$ is not continuous.

Example $f(x) = \dfrac{2}{x-2}$ has a point of discontinuity at $x = 2$.

Point-slope form (p. 88)   The point-slope form of an equation of a line is $y - y_1 = m(x - x_1)$, where m is the slope of the line and (x_1, y_1) is a point on the line.

Example $y - 3 = 2(x - 1)$
$y + 4 = 5(x - 2)$
$y - 2 = 3(x + 2)$

Polynomial (p. 292)   A polynomial is a monomial or the sum of monomials.

Example $3x^3 + 4x^2 - 2x + 5$
$8x$
$x^2 + 4x + 2$

Polynomial function (p. 293)   A polynomial in the variable x defines a polynomial function of x.

Example $P(x) = a_n x^n + a_n - 1x^{n-1} - 1 + \cdots + a_1 x + a_0$ is a polynomial function, where n is a nonnegative integer and the coefficients $a_n, \ldots, a_0$ are real numbers.

Population (p. 738)   A population is the members of a set.

Power function (p. 363)   A power function is a function of the form $y = a \cdot x^b$, where a and b are nonzero real numbers.

Principal root (p. 381)   When a number has two real roots, the positive root is called the principal root. A radical sign indicates the principal root. The principal root of a negative number a is $i\sqrt{|a|}$.

Example   The number 25 has two square roots, 5 and -5. The principal square root, 5, is indicated by $\sqrt{25}$ or $25^{\frac{1}{2}}$.

Spanish

Punto de discontinuidad (p. 539)   Un punto de discontinuidad es la coordenada x de un punto donde la gráfica de $f(x)$ no es continua.

Forma punto-pendiente (p. 88)   La forma punto-pendiente de una ecuación lineal es $y - y_1 = m(x - x_1)$, donde m es la pendiente de la recta y (x_1, y_1) es un punto de la recta.

Polinomio (p. 292)   Un polinomio es un monomio o la suma de dos o más monomios.

Función polinomial (p. 293)   Un polinomio en la variable x define una función polinomial de x.

Población (p. 738)   Una población está compuesta por los miembros de un conjunto.

Función de potencia (p. 363)   Una función de potencia es una función de la forma $y = a \cdot x^b$, donde a y b son números reales diferentes de cero.

Raíz principal (p. 381)   Cuando un número tiene dos raíces reales, la raíz positiva es la raíz principal. El signo del radical indica la raíz principal. La raíz principal de un número negativo a es $i\sqrt{|a|}$.

Probability distribution (p. 748)   A probability distribution is a function that tells the probability of each outcome in a sample space.

Distribución de probabilidades (p. 748)   Una distribución de probabilidades es una función que señala la probabilidad de que cada resultado ocurra en un espacio muestral.

Example

Roll	Fr.	Prob.
1	5	0.125
2	9	0.225
3	7	0.175
4	8	0.2
5	8	0.2
6	3	0.075

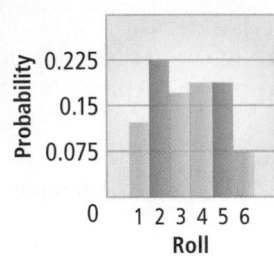

The table and graph both show the experimental probability distribution for the outcomes of 40 rolls of a standard number cube.

Pure imaginary number (p. 269)   If $a = 0$ and $b \neq 0$, the number $a + bi$ is a pure imaginary number.

Número imaginario puro (p. 269)   Si $a = 0$ y $b \neq 0$, el número $a + bi$ es un número imaginario puro.

Quadratic equation (p. 243)   A quadratic equation is one that can be written in the standard form $ax^2 + bx + c = 0$, where $a \neq 0$.

Ecuación cuadrática (p. 243)   Una ecuación cuadrática es una ecuación que se puede expresar en forma normal como $ax^2 + bx + c = 0$, donde $a \neq 0$.

Example $2x^2 + 3x + 1 = 0$

Quadratic Formula (p. 261)   The Quadratic Formula is $x = \frac{-b \pm \sqrt{b^2 - 4ac}}{2a}$. It gives the solutions to the quadratic equation $ax^2 + bx + c = 0$.

Fórmula cuadrática (p. 261)   La fórmula cuadrática es $x = \frac{-b \pm \sqrt{b^2 - 4ac}}{2a}$. Ésta da las soluciones a la ecuación cuadrática $ax^2 + bx + c = 0$.

Example If $-x^2 + 3x + 2 = 0$, then

$$x = \frac{-3 \pm \sqrt{(3)^2 - 4(-1)(2)}}{2(-1)}$$

$$= \frac{-3 \pm \sqrt{17}}{-2}$$

Quadratic function (p. 204)   A quadratic function is a function that you can write in the form $f(x) = ax^2 + bx + c$ with $a \neq 0$.

Función cuadrática (p. 204)   Una función cuadrática es una función que puedes escribir como $f(x) = ax^2 + bx + c$ con $a \neq 0$.

Example

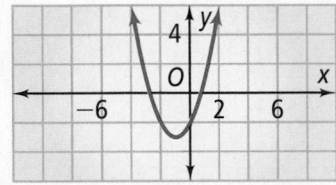

$y = x^2 + 2x - 2$

English

Quantity (p. 5) A mathematical quantity is anything that can be measured or counted.

Quartile (p. 725) Quartiles are values that separate a finite data set into four equal parts. The second quartile (Q_2) is the median of the data. The first and third quartiles (Q_1 and Q_3) are the medians of the lower half and upper half of the data, respectively.

Spanish

Cantidad (p. 5) Una cantidad matemática es cualquier cosa que se puede medir o contar.

Cuartil (p. 725) Los cuartiles son valores que separan un conjunto finito de datos en cuatro partes iguales. El segundo cuartil (Q_2) es la mediana de los datos. Los cuartiles primero y tercero (Q_1 y Q_3) son las medianas de la mitad superior e inferior de los datos, respectivamente.

Example $\{2, 3, 4, 5, 5, 6, 7, 7\}$

$$Q_1 = 3.5$$
$$Q_2 \text{ (median)} = 5$$
$$Q_3 = 6.5$$

R

Radian (p. 841) $\dfrac{a°}{180°} = \dfrac{r \text{ radians}}{\pi \text{ radians}}$

Radián (p. 841) $\dfrac{a°}{180°} = \dfrac{r \text{ radianes}}{\pi \text{ radianes}}$

Example $60° \rightarrow \dfrac{60}{180} = \dfrac{x}{\pi}$

$$x = \dfrac{60\pi}{180}$$
$$= \dfrac{\pi}{3}$$

Thus, $60° = \dfrac{\pi}{3}$ radians.

Radical equation (p. 417) A radical equation is an equation that has a variable in a radicand or has a variable with a rational exponent.

Ecuación radical (p. 417) La ecuación radical es una ecuación que contiene una variable en el radicando o una variable con un exponente racional.

Example $(\sqrt{x})^3 + 1 = 65$

$$x^{\frac{3}{2}} + 1 = 65$$

Radical function (p. 445) A radical function is a function that can be written in the form $f(x) = a\sqrt[n]{x - h} + k$, where $a \neq 0$. For even values of n, the domain of a radical function is the real numbers $x \geq h$. *See also* **Square root function.**

Función radical (p. 445) Una función radical es una función quepuede expresarse como $f(x) = a\sqrt[n]{x - h} + k$, donde $a \neq 0$. Para n par, el dominio de la función radical son los números reales tales que $x \geq h$. *Ver también* **Square root function.**

Example $f(x) = \sqrt{x - 2}$

Radicand (p. 382) The number under a radical sign is the radicand.

Radicando (p. 382) La expresión que aparece debajo del signo radical es el radicando.

Example The radicand in $3\sqrt[4]{7}$ is 7.

English

Spanish

Radius (p. 649)   The radius r of a circle is the distance between the center of the circle and any point on the circumference.

Radio (p. 649)   El radio r de un círculo es la distancia entre el centro del círculo y cualquier punto de la circunferencia.

Example

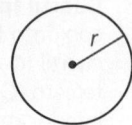

Random sample (p. 738)   In a random sample, all members of the population are equally likely to be chosen as every other member.

Muestra aleatoria (p. 738)   En una muestra aleatoria, la probabilidad de ser seleccionado es igual para todos los miembros.

Example   Let the set of all females between the ages of 19 and 34 be the population. A random selection of 900 females between those ages would be a sample of the population

Range (p. 65)   The range of a relation is the set of all outputs or y-coordinates of the ordered pairs.

Rango (p. 65)   El rango de una relación es el conjunto de todas las salidas posibles, o coordenadas y, de los pares ordenados.

Example   In the relation {(0, 1), (0, 2), (0, 3), (0, 4), (1, 3), (1, 4), (2, 1)}, the range is {1, 2, 3, 4}. In the function $f(x) = |x - 3|$, the range is the set of real numbers greater than or equal to 0.

Range of a set of data (p. 725)   The range of a set of data is the difference between the greatest and least values.

Rango de un conjunto de datos (p. 725)   El rango de un conjunto de datos es la diferencia entre el valor máximo y el valor mínimo de los datos.

Example   The range of the set {3.2, 4.1, 2.2, 3.4, 3.8, 4.0, 4.2, 2.8} is $4.2 - 2.2 = 2$.

Rational equation (p. 565)   A rational equation is an equation that contains a rational expression.

Ecuación racional (p. 565)   Una ecuación racional es una ecuación que contiene una expresión racional.

Rational exponent (p. 403)   If the nth root of a is a real number and m is an integer, then $a^{\frac{1}{n}} = \sqrt[n]{a}$ and $a^{\frac{m}{n}} = \sqrt[n]{a^m} = (\sqrt[n]{a})^m$. If m is negative, $a \neq 0$.

Exponente racional (p. 403)   Si la raíz n-ésima de a es un número real y m es un número entero, entonces $a^{\frac{1}{n}} = \sqrt[n]{a}$ y $a^{\frac{m}{n}} = \sqrt[n]{a^m} = (\sqrt[n]{a})^m$. Si m es negativo, $a \neq 0$.

Example $4^{\frac{1}{3}} = \sqrt[3]{4}$

$5^{\frac{3}{2}} = \sqrt{5^3} = (\sqrt{5})^3$

Rational expression (p. 548)   A rational expression is the quotient of two polynomials.

Expresión racional (p. 548)   Una expresión racional es el cociente de dos polinomios.

English

Rational function (p. 538)   A rational function $f(x)$ can be written as $f(x) = \frac{P(x)}{Q(x)}$, where $P(x)$ and $Q(x)$ are polynomial functions. The domain of a rational function is all real numbers except those for which $Q(x) = 0$.

Spanish

Función racional (p. 538)   Una función racional $f(x)$ se puede expresar como $f(x) = \frac{P(x)}{Q(x)}$, donde $P(x)$ y $Q(x)$ son funciones de polinomios. El dominio de una función racional son todos los números reales excepto aquéllos para los cuales $Q(x) = 0$.

Example

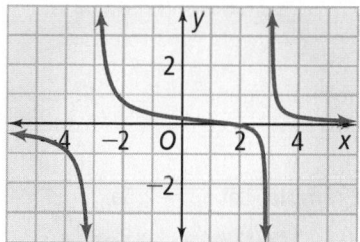

The function $y = \frac{x-2}{x^2-9}$ is a rational function with three branches separated by asymptotes $x = -3$ and $x = 3$.

Rational Root Theorem (p. 332)   Let $P(x) = a_n x^n + a_{n-1} x^{n-1} + \cdots + a_1 x + a_0$ be a polynomial with integer coefficients.
Then there are a limited number of possible roots of $P(x) = 0$:
–Integer roots must be factors of a_0;
–Rational roots must have reduced form p/q where p is an integer factor of a_0 and q is an integer factor of a_n.

Teorema de la Raíz Racional (p. 332)   Sea $P(x) = a_n x^n + a_{n-1} x^{n-1} + \cdots + a_1 x + a_0$ un polinomio con enteros como coeficientes.
Entonces hay un número limitado de raíces posibles para $P(x) = 0$:
–Las raíces enteras deben ser factores de a_0;
–Las raíces racionales deben ser de forma simplificada p/q, donde p es un factor entero de a_0 y q es un factor entero de a_n.

Example   The polynomial equation
$10x^3 + 6x^2 - 11x - 2 = 0$ has
leading coefficient 10 (with factors
$(\pm 1, \pm 2, \pm 5, \pm 10)$ and constant
term -2 (with factors ± 1 and ± 2).
Its only possible rational roots are
$\pm 1, \pm 2, \pm \frac{1}{2}, \pm \frac{1}{5},$
$\pm \frac{2}{5}, \pm \frac{1}{10}.$

Rationalize the denominator (p. 391)   To rationalize the denominator of an expression, rewrite it so there are no radicals in any denominator and no denominators in any radical.

Racionalizar el denominador (p. 391)   Para racionalizar el denominador de una expresión, ésta se escribe de modo que no haya radicales en ningún denominador y no haya denominadores en ningún radical.

Example $\frac{1}{\sqrt{2}} = \frac{1}{\sqrt{2}} \times \frac{\sqrt{2}}{\sqrt{2}} = \frac{\sqrt{2}}{2}$

Reciprocal (p. 14)   The reciprocal or multiplicative inverse of any nonzero number a is $\frac{1}{a}$. The product of reciprocals is 1, the multiplicative identity.

Recíproco (p. 14)   El recíproco o inverso multiplicativo de un número distinto de cero a es $\frac{1}{a}$. El producto de recíprocos es 1, la identidad multiplicativa.

Example $5 \times \frac{1}{5} = 1$

English

Spanish

Reciprocal function (p. 530)   A reciprocal function belongs to the family whose parent function is $f(x) = \frac{1}{x}$ where $x \neq 0$. You can write a reciprocal function in the form $f(x) = \left(\frac{a}{x} - h\right) + k$, where $a \neq 0$ and $x \neq h$.

Función recíproca (p. 530)   Una función recíproca pertenece a la familia cuya función madre es $f(x) = \frac{1}{x}$ donde $x \neq 0$. Se puede escribir una función recíproca como $f(x) = \left(\frac{a}{x} - h\right) + k$, donde $a \neq 0$ y $x \neq h$.

Example $f(x) = \frac{1}{2x + 5}$

$p(v) = \frac{3}{v} + 5$

Recursive formula (p. 586)   A recursive formula defines the terms in a sequence by relating each term to the ones before it.

Fórmula recursiva (p. 586)   Una fórmula recursiva define los términos de una secuencia al relacionar cada término con los términos que lo anteceden.

Example   Let $a_n = 2.5a_{n-1} + 3a_{n-2}$.

If $a_5 = 3$ and $a_4 = 7.5$, then

$a_6 = 2.5(3) + 3(7.5) = 30$.

Reduced row echelon form (p. 188)   A matrix that represents the solution of a system is in reduced row echelon form. The leading 1 in each row has 0's elsewhere in its column.

Forma reducida fila-escalón (p. 188)   Una matriz que representa la solución de un sistema está en forma reducida fila-escalón. El 1 principal en cada fila tiene ceros en otras partes de la columna.

Reference angle (p. 835)   The reference angle is the acute angle formed by the terminal side of an angle in standard position and the x-axis.

Ángulo de referencia (p. 835)   El ángulo de referencia es el ángulo agudo formado por el lado terminal de un ángulo en posición estándar y el eje x.

Example

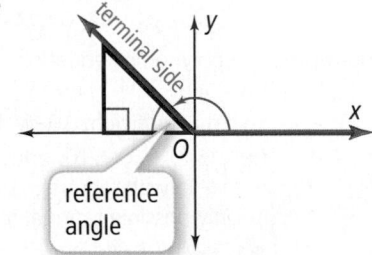

reference angle

Reflection (p. 114)   A reflection flips the graph of a function across a line, such as the x- or y-axis. Each point on the graph of the reflected function is the same distance from the line of reflection as is the corresponding point on the graph of the original function.

Reflexión (p. 114)   Una reflexión voltea la gráfica de una función sobre una línea, como el eje de las x o el eje de las y. Cada punto de la gráfica de la función reflejada está a la misma distancia del eje de reflexión que el punto correspondiente en la gráfica de la función original.

Example

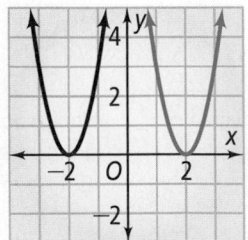

English

Relation (p. 64) A relation is a set of ordered pairs.

Relative maximum (minimum) (p. 305) A relative maximum (minimum) is the value of the function at an up-to-down (down-to-up) turning point.

Example

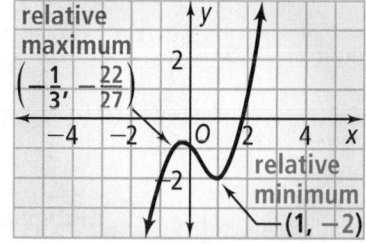

Remainder Theorem (p. 324) If you divide a polynomial $P(x)$ of degree $n > 1$ by $x - a$, then the remainder is $P(a)$.

Example If $P(x) = x^3 - 4x^2 + x + 6$ is divided by $x - 3$, then the remainder is $P(3) = 3^3 - 4(3)^2 + 3 + 6 = 0$ (which means that $x - 3$ is a factor of $P(x)$).

Removable discontinuity (p. 539) A removable discontinuity is a point of discontinuity, a, of function f that you can remove by redefining f at $x = a$. Doing so fills in a hole in the graph of f with the point $(a, f(a))$.

Root (p. 251) A root of a function is the input value for which the value of the function is zero. A root of an equation is a value that makes the equation true. *See also* **Zero of a function.**

Example −2 and 3 are roots of the function $f(x) = (x + 2)(x - 3)$ and the equation $(x + 2)(x - 3) = 0$.

Row operation (p. 186) A row operation on an augmented matrix is any of the following: switch two rows, multiply a row by a constant, add one row to another.

S

Sample (p. 738) A sample from a population is some of the population.

Example Let the set of all males between the ages of 19 and 34 be the population. A random selection of 900 males between those ages would be a sample of the population.

Spanish

Relación (p. 64) Una relación es un conjunto de pares ordenados.

Example {(0, 1), (0, 2), (0, 3), (0, 4), (1, 3)}

Máximo (minimo) relativo (p. 305) El máximo (mínimo) relativo es el valor de la función en un punto de giro de arriba hacia abajo (de abajo hacia arriba).

Teorema del residuo (p. 324) Si divides un polinomio $P(x)$ con un grado $n > 1$ por $x - a$, el residuo es $P(a)$.

Discontinuidad removible (p. 539) Una discontinuidad removible es un punto de discontinuidad a en una función f que se puede remover al redefinir f en $x = a$. Al hacer esto, se llena un hueco en la gráfica f con el punto $(a, f(a))$.

Raíz (p. 251) La raíz de una función es el valor de entrada para el cual el valor de la función es cero. La raíz de una ecuación es un valor que hace verdadera la ecuación. *Ver también* **Zero of a function.**

Operación de fila (p. 186) Una operación de fila en una matriz ampliada es cualquiera de las siguientes opciones: el intercambio de dos filas, la multiplicación de una fila por una constante o la suma de dos filas.

Muestra (p. 738) Una muestra de una población es una parte de la población.

English

Spanish

Sample space (p. 698) The set of all possible outcomes of an experiment is called the sample space.

Espacio muestral (p. 698) El espacio muestral es el conjunto de todos los resultados posibles de un suceso.

Example When you roll a number cube, the sample space is {1, 2, 3, 4, 5, 6}.

Scalar (p. 781) A scalar is a real number factor in a special product.

Escalar (p. 781) Un escalar es un factor que es un número real en un producto especial.

Example $2.5\begin{bmatrix} 1 & 0 \\ -2 & 3 \end{bmatrix} = \begin{bmatrix} 2.5(1) & 2.5(0) \\ 2.5(-2) & 2.5(3) \end{bmatrix}$

$= \begin{bmatrix} 2.5 & 0 \\ -5 & 7.5 \end{bmatrix}$

Scalar multiplication (p. 781) Scalar multiplication is an operation that multiplies a matrix A by a scalar c. To find the resulting matrix cA, multiply each element of A by c.

Multiplicación escalar (p. 781) La multiplicación escalar es la que multiplica una matriz A por un número escalar c. Para hallar la matriz cA resultante, multiplica cada elemento de A por c.

Example $2.5\begin{bmatrix} 1 & 0 \\ -2 & 3 \end{bmatrix} = \begin{bmatrix} 2.5(1) & 2.5(0) \\ 2.5(-2) & 2.5(3) \end{bmatrix}$

$= \begin{bmatrix} 2.5 & 0 \\ -5 & 7.5 \end{bmatrix}$

Scatter plot (p. 103) A scatter plot is a graph that relates two different sets of data by plotting the data as ordered pairs. You can use a scatter plot to determine a relationship between the data sets.

Diagrama de puntos (p. 103) Un diagrama de puntos es una gráfica que relaciona dos conjuntos de datos presentando los datos como pares ordenados. El diagrama de puntos sirve para definir la relación entre conjuntos de datos.

Example

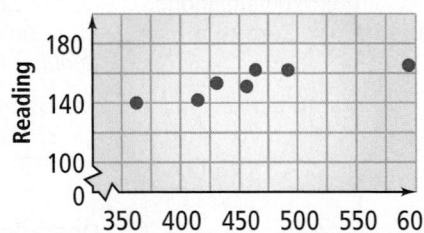

Dollars Spent Per Capita on Entertainment

SOURCE: U.S. Bureau of Labor Statistics

Self-selected sample (p. 738) In a self-selected sample you select only members of the population who volunteered for the sample.

Muestra de voluntarios (p. 738) En una muestra de voluntarios se seleccionan sólo a los miembros de la población que se ofrecen voluntariamente para ser parte de la muestra.

Sequence (p. 584) A sequence is an ordered list of numbers.

Progresión (p. 584) Una progresión es una sucesión de números.

Example 1, 4, 7, 10, . . .

English

Spanish

Series (p. 607) A series is the sum of the terms of a sequence.

Serie (p. 607) Una serie es la suma de los términos de una secuencia.

Example The series $3 + 6 + 9 + 12 + 15$ corresponds to the sequence 3, 6, 9, 12, 15. The sum of the series is 45.

Simplest form of a radical expression (p. 388) A radical expression with index n is in simplest form if there are no radicals in any denominator, no denominators in any radical, and any radicand has no nth power factors.

Mínima expresión de una expresión radical (p. 388) Una expresión radical con índice n está en su mínima expresión si no tiene radicales en ningún denominador ni denominadores en ningún radical y los radicandos no tienen factores de potencia.

Simplest form of a rational expression (p. 548) A rational expression is in simplest form if its numerator and denominator are polynomials that have no common divisor other than 1.

Forma simplificada de una expresión racional (p. 548) Una expresión racional se encuentra en su mínima expresión si su numerador y su denominador son polinomios que no tienen otro divisor aparte de 1.

Example $\dfrac{x^2 - 7x + 12}{x^2 - 9} = \dfrac{(x - 4)(x - 3)}{(x + 3)(x - 3)} = \dfrac{x - 4}{x + 3}$, where $x \neq -3$

Simulation (p. 696) A simulation is a model that imitates one or more events.

Simulación (p. 696) Una simulación es un modelo que imita uno o más sucesos.

Example Suppose a weather forecaster predicts a 50% chance of rain for the next three days. You can use three coins landing heads up to simulate three days in a row of rain.

Sine function, Sine of θ (pp. 823, 848) The sine function, $y = \sin\theta$, matches the measure θ of an angle in standard position with the y-coordinate of a point on the unit circle. This point is where the terminal side of the angle intersects the unit circle. The y-coordinate is the sine of θ.

Función seno, Seno de θ (pp. 823, 848) La función seno, $y = \sin\theta$, empareja la medida θ de un ángulo en posición estándar con la coordenada y de un punto en el círculo unitario. Este es el punto en el que el lado terminal del ángulo interseca al círculo unitario. La coordenada y es el seno de θ.

Example

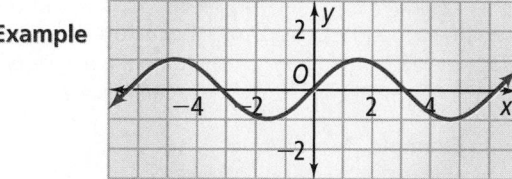
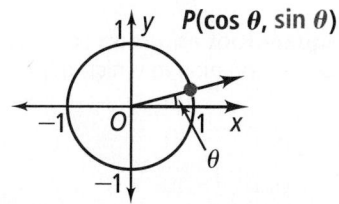

Singular matrix (p. 795) A singular matrix is a square matrix with no inverse. Its determinant is 0.

Matriz singular (p. 795) Una matriz singular es una matriz al cuadrado que no tiene inverso. El determinante de la matriz es 0.

Slope (p. 81) The slope of a non-vertical line is the ratio of the vertical change to the horizontal change between points. You can calculate slope by finding the ratio of the difference in the y-coordinates to the difference in the x-coordinates for any two points on the line. The slope of a vertical line is undefined.

Pendiente (p. 81) La pendiente de una línea no vertical es la razón del cambio vertical al cambio horizontal entre puntos. Puedes calcular la pendiente al hallar la razón de la diferencia de la coordenada y y la diferencia de la coordenada x para dos puntos cualesquiera de la línea. La pendiente de una línea vertical es indefinida.

Example The slope of the line through points $(-1, -1)$ and $(1, -2)$ is

$$\frac{-2 - (-1)}{1 - (-1)} = \frac{-1}{2} = -\frac{1}{2}.$$

Slope-intercept form (p. 83) The slope-intercept form of an equation of a line is $y = mx + b$, where m is the slope and b is the y-intercept.

Forma pendiente-intercepto (p. 83) La forma pendiente-intercepto de una ecuación lineal es $y = mx + b$, donde m es la pendiente y b es el intercepto en y.

Example $y = 8x + 2$

$$y = -x + 1$$

$$y = -\frac{1}{2}x - 14$$

Solution of a system (p. 146) A solution of a system is a set of values for the variables that makes all the equations true.

Solución de un sistema (p. 146) Una solución de un sistema es un conjunto de valores para las variables que hace que todas las ecuaciones sean verdaderas.

Solution of an equation (p. 27) A solution of an equation is a number that makes the equation true.

Solución de una ecuación (p. 27) Una solución de una ecuación es cualquier número que haga verdadera la ecuación.

Example The solution of $2x - 7 = -12$ is $x = -2.5$.

Square matrix (p. 789) A square matrix is a matrix with the same number of columns as rows.

Matriz cuadrada (p. 789) Una matriz cuadrada es la que tiene la misma cantidad de columnas y filas.

Example Matrix A is a square matrix.

$$A = \begin{bmatrix} 1 & 2 & 0 \\ -1 & 0 & -2 \\ 1 & 2 & 3 \end{bmatrix}$$

Square root equation (p. 417) A square root equation is a radical equation in which the radical has index 2.

Ecuación de raíz cuadrada (p. 417) Una ecuación de raíz cuadrada es una ecuación radical en la cual el radical tiene índice 2.

Example $\sqrt{x} = 4$

Square root function (p. 445) A square root function is a function that can be written in the form $f(x) = a\sqrt{x - h} + k$, where $a \neq 0$. The domain of a square root function is all real numbers $x \geq h$.

Función de raíz cuadrada (p. 445) Una función de raíz cuadrada es una función que puede ser expresada como $f(x) = a\sqrt{x - h} + k$, donde $a \neq 0$. El dominio de una función de raíz cuadrada son todos los números reales tales que $x \geq h$.

Example $f(x) = 2\sqrt{x - 3} + 4$

English

Spanish

Standard deviation (p. 732) Standard deviation is a measure of how much the values in a data set vary, or deviate, from the mean, $\bar{x}$. To find the standard deviation, follow five steps:

- Find the mean of the data set.
- Find the difference between each data value and the mean.
- Square each difference.
- Find the mean of the squares.
- Take the square root of the mean of the squares. This is the standard deviation.

Desviación típica (p. 732) La desviación típica denota cuánto los valores de un conjunto de datos varían, o se desvían, de la media, $\bar{x}$. Para hallar la desviación típica, se siguen cinco pasos:

- Se halla la media del conjunto de datos.
- Se calcula la diferencia entre cada valor de datos y la media.
- Se eleva al cuadrado cada diferencia.
- Se halla la media de los cuadrados.
- Se calcula la raíz cuadrada de la media de los cuadrados. Ésa es la desviación típica.

Example $\{0, 2, 3, 4, 6, 7, 8, 9, 10, 11\}$

$\bar{x} = 6$

standard deviation $= \sqrt{12} \approx 3.46$

Standard form of a circle (p. 650) *See* **Circle**.

Forma normal de un círculo (p. 650) *Ver* **Circle**.

Example $(x - 3)^2 + (y - 4)^2 = 4$

Standard form of a linear equation (p. 89) The standard form of a linear equation is $Ax + By = C$, where A, B, and C are real numbers, and A and B are not *both* zero.

Forma normal de una ecuación lineal (p. 89) La forma normal de una ecuación lineal es $Ax + By = C$, donde A, B y C son números reales, y A y B no son cero *ambos*.

Example In standard form, the equation

$y = \frac{4}{3}x - 1$ is

$4x + (-3)y = 3$.

Standard form of a polynomial function (p. 293) The standard form of a polynomial function arranges the terms by degree in descending numerical order. A polynomial function, $P(x)$, in standard form is $P(x) = a_n x^n + a_{n-1} x^{n-1} + \cdots + a_1 x + a_0$, where n is a nonnegative integer and $a_n, \ldots, a_0$ are real numbers.

Forma normal de una función polinomial (p. 293) La forma normal de una función polinomial organiza los términos por grado en orden numérico descendiente. Una función polinomial, $P(x)$, en forma normal es $P(x) = a_n x^n + a_{n-1} x^{n-1} + \cdots + a_1 x + a_0$, donde n es un número entero no negativo y $a_n, \ldots, a_0$ son números reales.

Example $2x^3 - 5x^2 - 2x + 5$

Standard form of a quadratic function (p. 212) The standard form of a quadratic function is $f(x) = ax^2 + bx + c$ with $a \neq 0$.

Forma normal de una función cuadrática (p. 212) La forma normal de una función cuadrática es $f(x) = ax^2 + bx + c$ con $a \neq 0$.

Example $f(x) = 2x^2 + 5x + 2$

Visual **Glossary**

English	Spanish

Standard normal curve (p. 752)   The standard normal curve is a normal distribution centered on the y-axis. The mean of the standard normal curve is 0. The standard deviation is 1.

Curva normal en posición normal (p. 752)   La curva normal es la distribución normal centrada en el eje y. La media de la curva normal es 0. La desviación normal es 1.

Example

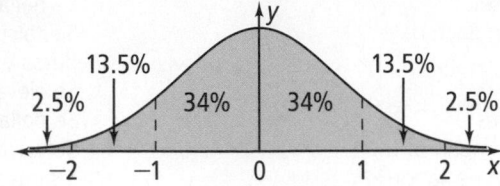

Standard position (p. 834)   An angle in the coordinate plane is in **standard position** when the vertex is at the origin and one ray is on the positive x-axis.

Posición estándar (p. 834)   Un ángulo en el plano de coordenadas se encuentra en **posición estándar** si el vértice se encuentra en el origen y una semirrecta se encuentra en el eje x positivo.

Example

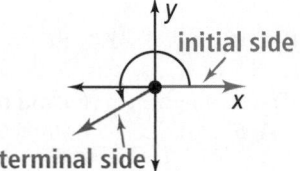

Sum of cubes (p. 311)   The sum of cubes is an expression of the form $a^3 + b^3$. It can be factored as $(a + b)(a^2 - ab + b^2)$.

Suma de dos cubos (p. 311)   La suma de dos cubos es una expresión de la forma $a^3 + b^3$. Se puede factorizar como $(a + b)(a^2 - ab + b^2)$.

Example $x^3 + 27 = (x + 3)(x^2 - 3x + 9)$

Survey (p. 739)   In a survey, you ask every member of a sample the same set of questions.

Encuesta (p. 739)   En una encuesta, se le hace a cada miembro de una muestra la misma serie de preguntas.

Synthetic division (p. 322)   Synthetic division is a process for dividing a polynomial by a linear expression $x - a$. You list the standard-form coefficients (including zeros) of the polynomial, omitting all variables and exponents. You use a for the "divisor" and add instead of subtract throughout the process.

División sintética (p. 322)   La división sintética es un proceso para dividir un polinomio por una expresión lineal $x - a$. En este proceso, escribes los coeficientes de forma normal (incluyendo los ceros) del polinomio, omitiendo todas las variables y todos los exponentes. Usas a como "divisor" y sumas, en vez de restar, a lo largo del proceso.

Example

$$
\begin{array}{r|rrrrr}
-3 & 2 & 5 & 0 & -2 & -8 \\
   &   & -6 & 3 & -9 & 33 \\
\hline
   & 2 & -1 & 3 & -11 & 25
\end{array}
$$

Divide $2x^4 + 5x^3 - 2x - 8$ by $x + 3$. $2x^4 + 5x^3 - 2x - 8$ divided by $x + 3$ gives $2x^3 - x^2 + 3x - 11$ as quotient and 25 as remainder.

English

Spanish

System of equations (p. 146) A system of equations is a set of two or more equations using the same variables.

Sistema de ecuaciones (p. 146) Un sistema de ecuaciones es un conjunto de dos o más ecuaciones que contienen las mismas variables.

$$\textbf{Example}\quad \begin{cases} 2x - 3y = -13 \\ 4x + 5y = 7 \end{cases}$$

Systematic sample (p. 738) In a systematic sample you order the population in some way, and then select from it at regular intervals.

Muestra sistemática (p. 738) En una muestra sistemática se ordena la población de cierta manera y luego se selecciona una muestra de esa población a intervalos regulares.

 T

Tangent function, Tangent of θ (pp. 823, 853) The tangent function, $y = \tan\theta$, matches the measure θ, of an angle in standard position with the y/x ratio of the (x, y) coordinates of a point on the unit circle. This point is where the terminal side of the angle intersects the unit circle. y/x is the tangent of θ.

Función tangente, Tangente de θ (pp. 823, 853) La función tangente, $y = \tan\theta$, empareja la medida θ, de un ángulo en posición estándar con la razón y/x de las coordenadas (x, y) de un punto en el círculo unitario. Este es el punto en el que el lado terminal del ángulo interseca al círculo unitario. y/x es la tangente de θ.

Example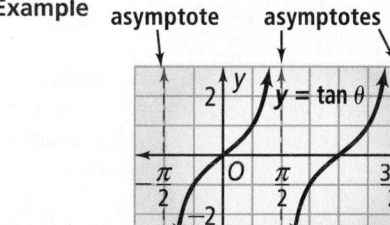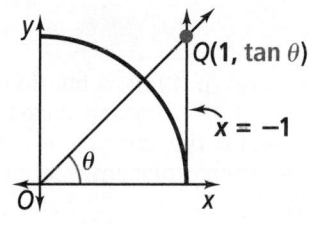

Term of a sequence (p. 584) Each number in a sequence is a term.

Término de una progresión (p. 584) Cada número de una progresión es un término.

Example 1, 4, 7, 10, . . .
The second term is 4.

Term of an expression (p. 20) A term is a number, a variable, or the product of a number and one or more variables.

Término de una expresión (p. 20) Un término es un número, una variable o el producto de un número y una o más variables.

Example The expression $4x^2 - 3y + 7.3$ has 3 terms.

Terminal side (p. 834) *See* **Initial side.**

Lado terminal (p. 834) *Ver* **Initial side.**

Test point (p. 129) A test point is a point that you pick on one side of the boundary of the graph of a linear inequality. If the test point makes the inequality true, then all points on that side of the boundary are solutions of the inequality. If the test point makes the inequality false, then all points on the other side are solutions.

Punto de prueba (p. 129) Un punto de prueba es un punto que escoges a un lado del límite de la gráfica de una desigualdad lineal. Si el punto de prueba hace que la desigualdad sea verdadera, entonces todos los puntos en ese límite son soluciones de la desigualdad. Si el punto de prueba hace que la desigualdad sea falsa, entonces todos los puntos del otro lado del límite son soluciones.

English

Spanish

Theoretical probability (p. 698)   If a sample space has n equally likely outcomes, and an event A occurs in m of these outcomes, then the theoretical probability of event A is $P(A) = \frac{m}{n}$.

Probabilidad teórica (p. 698)   Si un espacio muestral tiene n resultados con la misma probabilidad de ocurrir, y ocurre un suceso A en m de estos resultados, entonces la probabilidad teórica del suceso A es $P(A) = \frac{m}{n}$.

Example   Use the set {1, 4, 9, 16, 25, 36, 49, 64, 81, 100}. The probability that a number selected at random is greater than 50 is $P(A) = \frac{3}{10} = 0.3$.

Tolerance (p. 48)   The difference between a desired measurement and its maximum and minimum allowable values is the tolerance. The tolerance equals one half of the difference between the maximum and minimum values.

Tolerancia (p. 48)   La diferencia entre una medida deseada y sus valores máximo y mínimo permitidos es la tolerancia. La tolerancia equivale a la mitad de la diferencia entre los valores máximo y mínimo.

Example   A manufacturing specification calls for a dimension d of 10 cm with a tolerance of 0.1 cm. The allowable difference between d and 10 is less than or equal to 0.1.

Transformation (p. 110)   A transformation of a function $y = af(x - h) + k$ is a change made to at least one of the values a, h, and k. The four types of transformations are dilations, reflections, rotations, and translations.

Transformación (p. 110)   Una transformación de una función $y = af(x - h) + k$ es un cambio que se le hace a por lo menos uno de los valores a, h y k. Hay cuatro tipos de transformaciones: dilataciones, reflexiones, rotaciones y traslaciones.

Example $g(x) = 2(x - 3)^2$ is a transformation of $f(x) = x^2$.

Translation (p. 110)   A translation shifts the graph of the parent function horizontally, vertically, or both without changing its shape or orientation.

Traslación (p. 110)   Una traslación desplaza la gráfica de la función madre horizontalmente, verticalmente o en ambas direcciones, sin cambiar su forma u orientación.

Example

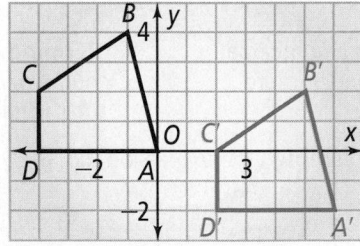

Transverse axis (p. 667)   The transverse axis of a hyperbola is the segment that is on the line containing the foci and has endpoints on the hyperbola.

Eje transversal (p. 667)   El eje transversal de una hipérbola es el segmento que se encuentra sobre la línea que contiene los focos y tiene sus puntos extremos sobre la hipérbola.

Example

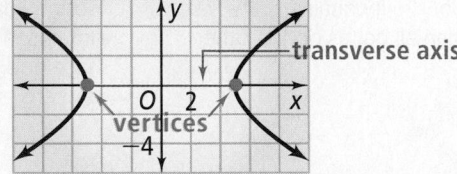

English

Spanish

Trend line (p. 104) A trend line is a line that approximates the relationship between two variables, or data sets, of a scatter plot.

Línea de tendencia (p. 104) Una línea de tendencia es una línea que aproxima la relación entre dos variables o conjuntos de datos de un diagrama de dispersión.

Example

Used Car Prices

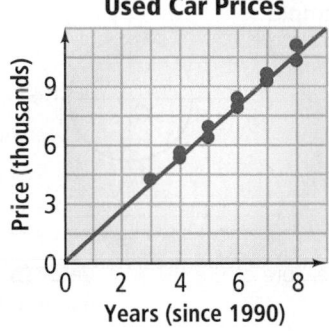

Trigonometric identity (p. 858) A trigonometric identity in one variable is a trigonometric equation that is true for all values of the variable for which both sides of the equation are defined.

Identidad trigonométrica (p. 858) Una identidad trigonométrica en una variable es una ecuación trigonométrica que es verdadera para todos los valores de la variable para los cuales se definen los dos lados de la ecuación.

Example $\tan \theta = \dfrac{\sin \theta}{\cos \theta}$

Trigonometric ratios (p. 823) If θ is an acute angle of a right triangle, x is the length of the adjacent leg (ADJ), y is the length of the opposite leg (OPP), and r is the length of the hypotenuse (HYP), then the trigonometric ratios of θ are

$\sin \theta = \dfrac{y}{r} = \dfrac{\text{OPP}}{\text{HYP}} \qquad \csc \theta = \dfrac{r}{y} = \dfrac{\text{HYP}}{\text{OPP}}$

$\cos \theta = \dfrac{x}{r} = \dfrac{\text{ADJ}}{\text{HYP}} \qquad \sec \theta = \dfrac{r}{x} = \dfrac{\text{HYP}}{\text{ADJ}}$

$\tan \theta = \dfrac{y}{x} = \dfrac{\text{OPP}}{\text{ADJ}} \qquad \cot \theta = \dfrac{x}{y} = \dfrac{\text{ADJ}}{\text{HYP}}$

Razones trigonométricas (p. 823) Si θ es un ángulo agudo de un triángulo, x es la longitud del cateto adyacente (ADJ), y es la longitud del cateto opuesto (OPP) y r es la longitud de la hipotenusa (HYP), entonces las razones trigonométricas son:

$\sin \theta = \dfrac{y}{r} = \dfrac{\text{OPP}}{\text{HYP}} \qquad \csc \theta = \dfrac{r}{y} = \dfrac{\text{HYP}}{\text{OPP}}$

$\cos \theta = \dfrac{x}{r} = \dfrac{\text{ADJ}}{\text{HYP}} \qquad \sec \theta = \dfrac{r}{x} = \dfrac{\text{HYP}}{\text{ADJ}}$

$\tan \theta = \dfrac{y}{x} = \dfrac{\text{OPP}}{\text{ADJ}} \qquad \cot \theta = \dfrac{x}{y} = \dfrac{\text{ADJ}}{\text{HYP}}$

Example

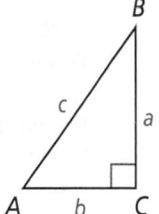

Turning point (p. 294) A turning point of the graph of a function is a point where the graph changes direction from upwards to downwards or from downwards to upwards.

Punto de giro (p. 294) Un punto de giro de la gráfica de una función es un punto donde la gráfica cambia de dirección de arriba hacia abajo o vice versa.

English

U

Unit circle (p. 836)   The unit circle has a radius of 1 unit and its center is at the origin of the coordinate plane.

Example

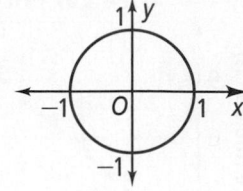

V

Value (p. 5)   The value of a quantity is its measure or the number of items that you count.

Variable (p. 5)   A variable is a symbol, usually a letter, that represents one or more numbers.

Example x, a, k

Variable matrix (p. 801)   When representing a system of equations with a matrix equation, the matrix containing the variables of the system is the variable matrix.

Example $\begin{cases} x + 2y = 5 \\ 3x + 5y = 14 \end{cases}$

variable matrix $\begin{bmatrix} X \\ Y \end{bmatrix}$

Variable quantity (p. 5)   A variable quantity can have values that vary.

Variance (p. 732)   Variance is the square of the standard deviation. $\sigma^2 = \frac{(\sum(x - \bar{x})^2)}{n}$.

Vertex (p. 121)   A vertex of a function is a point where the function reaches a maximum or a minimum value.

Vertex form of a quadratic function (p. 204)   The vertex form of a quadratic function is $f(x) = a(x - h)^2 + k$, where $a \neq 0$ and (h, k) is the coordinate of the vertex of the function.

Example $f(x) = x^2 + 2x - 1 = (x + 1)^2 - 2$
The vertex is $(-1, -2)$.

Spanish

Círculo unitario (p. 836)   El círculo unitario tiene un radio de 1 unidad y el centro está situado en el origen del plano de coordenadas.

Valor (p. 5)   El valor de una cantidad es su medida o el número de datos que cuentas.

Variable (p. 5)   Una variable es un símbolo, generalmente una letra, que representa uno o más valores.

Matriz variable (p. 801)   Al representar un sistema de ecuaciones con una ecuación de matricial, la matriz que contenga las variables del sistema es la matriz variable.

Cantidad variable (p. 5)   Una cantidad variable puede tener valores que varían.

Varianza (p. 732)   La varianza es el cuadrado de la desviación estándar. $\sigma^2 = \frac{(\sum(x - \bar{x})^2)}{n}$.

Vértice (p. 121)   El vértice de una función es el punto donde la función alcanza un valor máximo o mínimo.

Forma del vértice de una función cuadrática (p. 204)   La forma vértice de una función cuadrática es $f(x) = a(x - h)^2 + k$, donde $a \neq 0$ y (h, k) es la coordenada del vértice de la función.

English

Spanish

Vertex of a parabola (p. 204) The vertex of a parabola is the point where the function for the parabola reaches a maximum or a minimum value. The parabola intersects its axis of symmetry at the vertex.

Vértice de una parábola (p. 204) El vértice de una parábola es el punto donde la función de la parábola alcanza un valor máximo o mínimo. La parábola y su eje de simetría se intersecan en el vértice.

Example

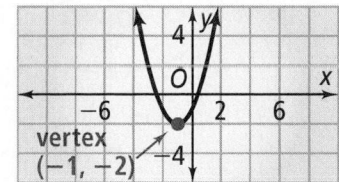

The vertex of the quadratic function
$y = x^2 + 2x - 1$ is $(-1, -2)$.

Vertical compression (p. 115) A vertical compression reduces all *y*-values of a function by the same factor between 0 and 1.

Compresión vertical (p. 115) Una compresión vertical reduce todos los valores de *y* de una función por el mismo factor entre 0 y 1.

Vertical stretch (p. 115) A vertical stretch multiplies all *y*-values of a function by the same factor greater than 1.

Estiramiento vertical (p. 115) Un estiramiento vertical multiplica todos los valores de *y* por el mismo factor mayor que 1.

Vertical-line test (p. 67) You can use the vertical-line test on the graph of a relation to tell whether the relation is a function. If a vertical line passes through more than one point on the graph of a relation, then the relation is *not* a function.

Prueba de la recta vertical (p. 67) Puedes usar la prueba de la línea vertical en la gráfica de una relación para saber si la relación es una función. Si una línea vertical pasa por más de un punto de la gráfica de la relación, entonces la relación *no* es una función.

Example

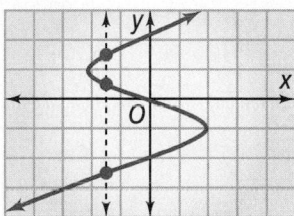

This relation is not a function.

Vertices of a hyperbola (p. 667) The endpoints of the transverse axis of a hyperbola are the vertices of the hyperbola.

Vértices de una hipérbola (p. 667) Los dos puntos de intersección de la hipérbola y su eje mayor son los vértices de la hipérbola.

Example

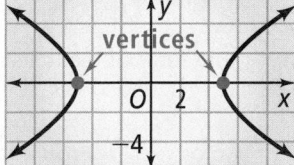

English

Vertices of an ellipse (p. 659)   The endpoints of the major axis of an ellipse are the vertices of the ellipse.

Spanish

Vértices de una elipse (p. 659)   Los dos puntos de intersección de la elipse y su eje mayor son los vértices de la elipse.

Example

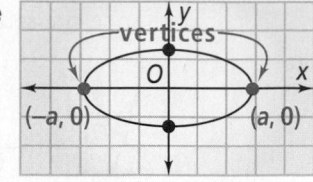

X

x-intercept, y-intercept (p. 83)   The point at which a line crosses the x-axis (or the x-coordinate of that point) is an x-intercept. The point at which a line crosses the y-axis (or the y-coordinate of that point) is a y-intercept.

Intercepto en x, intercepto en y (p. 83)   El punto donde una recta corta el eje x (o la coordenada x de ese punto) es el intercepto en x. El punto donde una recta cruza el eje y (o la coordenada y de ese punto) es el intercepto en y.

Example

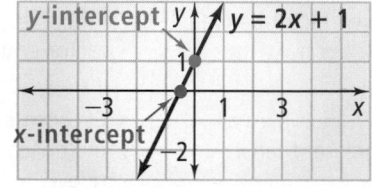

The x-intercept of $y = 2x + 1$ is $\left(-\frac{1}{2}, 0\right)$ or $-\frac{1}{2}$.

The y-intercept of $y = 2x + 1$ is $(0, 1)$ or 1.

Z

Zero matrix (p. 775)   The zero matrix O, or $O_{m \times n}$, is the $m \times n$ matrix whose elements are all zeros. It is the additive identity matrix for the set of all $m \times n$ matrices.

Matriz cero (p. 775)   La matriz cero, O, o $O_{m \times n}$, es la matriz $m \times n$ cuyos elementos son todos ceros. Es la matriz de identidad aditiva para el conjunto de todas las matrices $m \times n$.

Example $\begin{bmatrix} 1 & 4 \\ 2 & -3 \end{bmatrix} + O = \begin{bmatrix} 1 & 4 \\ 2 & -3 \end{bmatrix}$

Zero of a function (p. 243)   A zero of a function $f(x)$ is any value of x for which $f(x) = 0$.

Cero de una función (p. 243)   Un cero de una función $f(x)$ es cualquier valor de x para el cual $f(x) = 0$.

Example

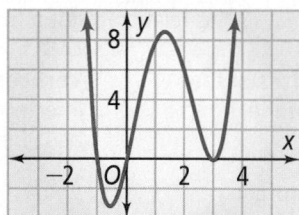

The zeros of the function are $x = -1$, $x = 0$, and $x = 3$.

Zero-Product Property (p. 243)   If the product of two or more factors is zero, then one of the factors must be zero.

Propiedad del cero del producto (p. 243)   Si el producto de dos o más factores es cero, entonces uno de los factores debe ser cero.

Example $(x - 3)(2x - 5) = 0$
$x - 3 = 0$ or $2x - 5 = 0$

Selected Answers

Chapter 1

Get Ready!   p. 1

1. 0   **2.** −2   **3.** −2.09   **4.** 8.05   **5.** $-\frac{3}{4}$ **6.** $\frac{11}{12}$
7. $10\frac{7}{10}$ **8.** $3\frac{1}{2}$ **9.** −42   **10.** 72   **11.** 9   **12.** −9.8
13. $-3\frac{1}{3}$ **14.** $-5\frac{1}{2}$ **15.** $-4\frac{2}{3}$ **16.** $-\frac{3}{4}$ **17.** −21
18. 7.35   **19.** $-\frac{1}{6}$ **20.** $-\frac{3}{5}$ **21.** −20   **22.** 8   **23.** 0.97
24. −5   **25.** 55   **26.** 3   **27.** because the placement of the parentheses changes the order of operations   **28.** 3
29. 3 terms   **30.** Calculate the answer numerically.
31. $\frac{3}{n-3}$

Lesson 1-1   pp. 4–10

Got It? 1. The pattern shows a center square and a yellow square added to each side with the number of squares per side increasing by one.

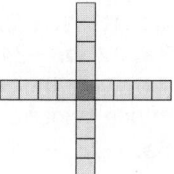

2a. 52;

Input	Process Column	Output
1	2 + 2(1)	4
2	2 + 2(2)	6
3	2 + 2(3)	8
4	2 + 2(4)	10
⋮	⋮	⋮
n	2 + 2(n)	2 + 2n

b. 2 + 2n   **3a.** $12   **b.** $20   **c.** The number of platys must be a whole number whereas the lengths of fish can be a fraction or decimal.
Lesson Check 1. add 35   **2.** rotate 90° clockwise
3.

Input	Process Column	Output
1	2(1)	2
2	2(2)	4
3	2(3)	6
4	2(4)	8
⋮	⋮	⋮
n	2(n)	2n

4.

Input	Process Column	Output
1	3(1)	3
2	3(2)	6
3	3(3)	9
4	3(4)	12
⋮	⋮	⋮
n	3(n)	3n

6. answers may vary. Sample: Tables of values and pictorial representations are both convenient ways to organize data and discover patterns. Tables give more detail. Pictorial representations are easier to visualize.
7. No; the output is $\frac{1}{2}$ the input for all values except the first (Input: 3; Output: 2).
Exercises 9. Base of 3 squares with the number of squares increasing by one. One square is added vertically on each of the outer squares of the base.

11. One square, then 4 squares, then 9 squares, and so on. In general, the number of squares is $n \times n$ or n^2.

13. $4n - 1$

Input	Process Column	Output
1	4(1) − 1	3
2	4(2) − 1	7
3	4(3) − 1	11
4	4(4) − 1	15
⋮	⋮	⋮
n	4(n) − 1	4n − 1

15. Output $= \frac{1}{2}$ Input

Input	Process Column	Output
1	$(1) \cdot \frac{1}{2}$	$\frac{1}{2}$
2	$(2) \cdot \frac{1}{2}$	1
3	$(3) \cdot \frac{1}{2}$	$1\frac{1}{2}$
4	$(4) \cdot \frac{1}{2}$	2
5	$(5) \cdot \frac{1}{2}$	$2\frac{1}{2}$
⋮	⋮	⋮
n	$(n) \cdot \frac{1}{2}$	$\frac{1}{2}n$

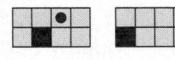
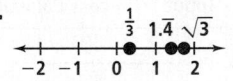

17. 10 **19.** $2n$ **21.** add 3 and then subtract 1; 8, 7, 10 **23.** add 4; 18, 22, 26 **25.** multiply by 5; 2500, 12,500, 62,500

27a.

Input	Output
1	3
2	6
3	9
4	12
5	15
⋮	⋮
n	$3n$

b. 18; 21; 24

29a.

b. Process Column: (1), 2(2), 3(3), 4(4), 5(5); Number of squares: 1, 4, 9, 16, 25 **c.** n^2; each figure contains $n \times n$, or n^2, squares. **31.** -18; $7 - 5n$
33. The shaded square and dot each move clockwise one square.
38. 1.9 **39.** -3.8 **40.** 27 **41.** 0 **42.** -0.4 **43.** 7
44. 50% **45.** 25% **46.** $33.\overline{3}$%, or $33\frac{1}{3}$% **47.** 140%
48. 172% **49.** 123%

Lesson 1-2   pp. 11–17

Got It? 1. rational numbers **2.**

$\frac{1}{3}$ $1.\overline{4}$ $\sqrt{3}$

3a. $\sqrt{26} < 6.25$ **b.** $a < c$; a will be to the left of c on the number line.

Lesson Check 1. Answers may vary. Sample: the number of times a cricket chirps **2.** Answers may vary. Sample: the number of items sold on a given day at a store, where returns are represented by a negative integer **3.** Answers may vary. Sample: the outdoor temperature in tenths of a degree **4.** Inv. Prop. of Add.
5. Assoc. Prop. of Mult. **6.** multiplicative inverse
7. Both properties result in the original term; 0 is the additive identity, whereas 1 is the multiplicative identity.
8. The equation illustrates the Comm. Prop. of Add.
9. answers may vary. Sample: $\sqrt{2}$ is not a rational number because it cannot be written as a quotient of integers.

Exercises 11. y, natural numbers; p, rational numbers

13.

15.

17.

19.

21. > **23.** > **25.** < **27.** Comm. Prop. of Add.
29. Comm. Prop. of Mult. **31.** Inv. Prop. of Mult.
33–39. Answers may vary. Samples are given. **33.** $-3\frac{1}{2}$
35. $\frac{1}{2}$ **37.** $3\frac{1}{3}$ **39.** 4.8 **41.** The point for $\sqrt{5}$ is not at the correct position on the number line; $\sqrt{5} \approx 2.24$.
43. irrational numbers **45.** 8, 1, $\frac{1}{3}$, $-\sqrt{2}$, -3
47. 5.73, $\frac{1}{4}$, -0.06, $-3\sqrt{3}$, -17 **49.** Answers may vary. Sample: $\sqrt{2}$ and $\sqrt{2}$ **51.** Multiply the cost of a drink by 5 and multiply the cost of a sandwich by 5, then add, or add the cost for one drink and one sandwich, then multiply by 5; Distr. Prop. **56.** add 4; 20, 24, 28
57. add 1; 12, 13, 14 **58.** add 1; 0, 1, 2 **59.** $2\frac{1}{4}$
60. $11\frac{2}{3}$ **61.** $1\frac{1}{2}$ **62.** 5 **63.** 38 **64.** 15

Lesson 1-3   pp. 18–24

Got It? 1. H **2.** Let d = the number of days; $150 - 2d$.
3a. 12 **b.** -24 **4.** Let w = the number of two-point shots, r = the number of three-point shots, f = the number of one-point free throws, $2w + 3r + 1f$; 42 points
5a. $-3j^2 - 7k + 5j$ **b.** $12a - 53b$

Lesson Check 1. $\frac{2 + b}{3}$ **2.** $4k + m$ **3.** 12 **4.** 13
5. -5 **6.** -5 **7.** The student did not distribute the -1.
$3p^2q + 2p - (5q + p - 2p^2q) = 3p^2q + 2p - 5q - p + 2p^2q = 5p^2q + p - 5q$ **8.** A constant is a term with no variables whereas a coefficient is the numerical factor in a term. **9.** Answers may vary. Sample: Both algebraic expressions and numerical expressions represent a quantity using numbers, operations and grouping symbols. An algebraic expression includes variables when representing a quantity. Examples: numerical expression: $3 + 6(5 - 2)$; algebraic expression: $2z + 3z(6 + 5z)$.

Exercises 11. $8(x + 3)$ **13.** Let d = the number of days; $25 + 1.5d$ **15.** -30 **17.** -70 **19.** 4 ft
21. Let s = number of shots, $1s$; 8 **23.** $4a$
25. $6a + 3b$ **27.** $-0.5x$ **29.** 3 **31.** -765
33. It is the correct answer's opposite; $a - b = -b + a = -(b - a)$. **35.** $2x - 200$ **37.** $\frac{5x^2}{2}$
39. y **41.** $-2x^2 + 2y^2$. **43.** Answers may vary. Sample: x^2. **45.** Opposite of an Opposite **47.** Mult. by -1
52. -1.5, $-\sqrt{2}$, -1.4, -0.5 **53.** $-\frac{5}{6}$, $-\frac{3}{4}$, $-\frac{3}{8}$, $\frac{1}{2}$
54. -20, 0.2, $\frac{1}{2}$, $\sqrt{2}$ **55.** -3, -0.5, $-\frac{1}{4}$, $\frac{3}{4}$ **56.** $7x - 4$
57. $-p - \frac{2q}{3}$ **58.** $2b - 28$ **59.** $2k - 2m$

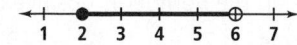

Lesson 1-4   pp. 26–32

Got It? 1. $\frac{3}{2}$ **2.** -1 **3.** 40 m $\times$ 120 m **4a.** never
b. always **5a.** $C = K - 273$ **b.** always
Lesson Check 1. 23.2 **2.** -90 **3.** 12
4. $K = \frac{1}{2}(r - 15)$ **5.** $K = \frac{1}{3}(z + 6)$
6. $K = -\left(\frac{1}{6}\right)(h + 14)$ **7.** To find a solution of an
equation means to find a value of the variable that makes
the equation true. **8.** Four buses are not enough. The
number of buses must be a whole number, so round the
number of buses to 5. **9.** 2nd line incorrect; subtract 10
from both sides: $12x = -12$, $x = -1$
Exercises 11. -81 **13.** 23 **15.** -5 **17.** $\frac{3}{2}$ **19.** 2
21. 300 mi/h; 600 mi/h **23.** sometimes **25.** sometimes
27. $h = \frac{2A}{b}$ **29.** $w = \frac{V}{\ell h}$ **31.** $x = a(b + 5)$, $a \neq 0$
33. $\frac{23}{3}$, or $7\frac{2}{3}$ **35.** 34° and 56° **37.** $b_2 = \frac{2A}{h} - b_1$
39. $h = \frac{S - 2\pi r^2}{2\pi r}$ **41.** 43, 45, 47, and 49 **43.** first stage,
90 s; second stage, 62 s **48.** -7 **49.** $-\frac{16}{3}$ **50.** -20
51. $-\frac{11}{2}$ **52.** $x + 5$ **53.** $16x$ **54.** $3(12 - x)$ **55.** true
56. false **57.** true

Lesson 1-5 Part 1   pp. 33–38

Got It? 1. $\frac{x}{3} \le 15$

2a. $x \le -4$;

b. $x > -1$;

3. at least 33 songs **4a.** always **b.** sometimes **c.** never
Lesson Check 1. $R \ge J$ **2.** $x + 5 < -7$
3. $x \le -\frac{1}{2}$

4. $x \le -2$

5. Answers may vary. Sample: $5 < 6$, but $-5 > -6$.
6. The transitive, addition, and subtraction properties of
inequalities are similar to the properties of equality. The
multiplication and division properties differ. Multiplying or
dividing each side of an inequality by a negative quantity
reverses the direction of the inequality symbol.
Exercises 7. $8x \ge 25$ **9.** $\frac{x}{12} \le 6$

11. $t \le 11$

13. $y \le -6$

15. $n > 8$

17. The width is less than 11.5 in., and the length is 3 in.
greater than the width. **19.** The smaller number is an
integer greater than or equal to 8. **21.** always **23.** never

25. never **27.** $z \ge 6$

29. $x \ge -48$

31. The classmate reversed the direction of the $\ge$ symbol
to $\le$ incorrectly. The correct answer is $y \le -20$.
33. Distr. Prop.; simplify; Subtr. Prop. of Inequality; Mult.
Prop. of Inequality

Lesson 1-5 Part 2   pp. 39–42

Got It? 5a. $2 \le x < 6$

b. sometimes; Sample: The compound inequality is true
when $x = 5$ and not true when $x = 7$.

6a. $w < -3$ or $w > \frac{8}{7}$

b. $x < -1$ or $x > 3$

Lesson Check 1. $40 \le w < 74$ **2.** $a < 12$ or $a > 60$

3. $1 < x < \frac{9}{5}$

4. $x \le 0$ or $x > 3$

5. $x < 8$ or $x > 8$; All real numbers are solutions except
$x = 8$.

6. No; Answers may vary. Sample: $2x < x + 1$ and
$x + 1 > 3$
Exercises 7. $-5 < x < 2$

9. $-4 \le x < 6$

11. $2 \le x < 6$

13. all real numbers

15. $x \le -3$ or $x \ge 9$

17. 98 **19.** $2 < AB < 6$
21. $-1 < x < 8$

23. $x < -2$ or $x > 2$

25. All real numbers

31. $7a + 5$ **32.** $-2x + 14y$ **33.** $\frac{b}{12} + 1$
34. $1.61 - 0.1k$ **35.** 4 **36.** no solution **37.** $\frac{9}{10}$
38. -20

Lesson 1-6 Part 1   pp. 43–46

Got It? 1. $\frac{2}{3}$, -2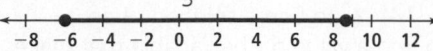

2. -7, -11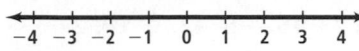

3. -1

Lesson Check 1. -4, 4 **2.** -12, 4 **3.** $-\frac{6}{5}$

4. A solution of an eq. is extraneous if it is a solution to a derived eq., but is not a solution to the original eq.

5. when the number is positive or 0

Exercises 7. -6, 6 **9.** $-\frac{5}{3}$, 3 **11.** no solution

13. -7, 17 **15.** $-\frac{3}{2}$ **17.** $\frac{3}{2}$ **19.** -1, $\frac{3}{2}$ **21.** 1

23. $-\frac{3}{2}$, -1 **25.** $-\frac{1}{3}$ **27.** $\frac{5}{2}$ **29.** $-\frac{71}{36}$ **31.** $|x - 1| = 1$

33. sometimes; when $x \ge 0$

Lesson 1-6 Part 2   pp. 47–52

Got It? 4. $-\frac{4}{3} \le x \le 4$

5a. $x < -5$ or $x > 1$

b. The graph will have two closed circles with an arrow extending to the left of one and to the right of the other.

6. $|h - 52.5| \le .5$

Lesson Check 1. $-11 < x < 9$

2. $x \le -1$ or $x \ge 4$

3. $z < -4$ or $z > 4$

4. Answers may vary. Sample: $d < -5$ and $5d > 25$

5. Answers may vary. Sample: An absolute value equation or inequality represents two equations or inequalities; each equation or inequality is solved in the same manner as a linear equation or inequality.

Exercises 7. $-2\frac{2}{3} < y < 3\frac{1}{3}$

9. $x < -12$ or $x > 6$

11. $x \le -3$ or $x \ge 13$

13. $-3\frac{1}{2} \le w \le \frac{1}{2}$

15. $x \le -3$ or $x \ge 4$

17. $|h - 1.4| \le 0.1$ **19.** $|b - 52.5| \le 2.5$

21. $|d - 0.11885| \le 0.00015$ **23.** $|x| < 4$ **25.** The graph of $|x| < a$ is the set of all points on the number line that lie between a and $-a$. The graph of $|x| > a$ has two parts; the left part consists of the points to the left of $-a$, and the right part consists of the points to the right of a.

27. $-6 \le x \le 8\frac{2}{3}$

29. all real numbers

31. all real numbers

33. $x \le -8.4$ or $x \ge 9.6$

35. $|t - 350| \le 5$ **37.** $|t - 15| \le 30$ **39.** always; if $x > 0$, then $|x| + |x| = 2x$; if $x < 0$, then $|x| + |x| > 2x$.

41. The "3" in the second set of inequalities should be "-3."
$$-4x + 1 < -3$$
$$-4x < -4$$
$$x > 1, \text{ not } x > -\frac{1}{2}$$

43. $|x - 9.55| \le 0.02$; $9.53 \le x \le 9.57$

49. $y < 6$

50. $s < \frac{2}{15}$

51. $a > 4$

52. Each figure has 4 more squares than the previous figure, with one square added at both ends of each row.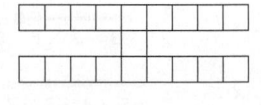

53. Each figure has n more circles than the previous figure, with the new row of circles at the top.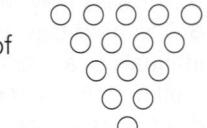

54. 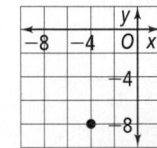 **55.**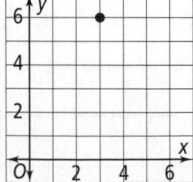

56. **57.**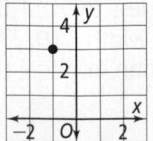

Chapter Review   pp. 54–56

1. solution of an equation **2.** absolute value
3. Reciprocal **4.** compound inequality **5.** add 5; 25, 30, 35
6. add 1; 7, 8, 9 **7.** 12; $n + 8$ **8.** 76; 19n **9.** 20n$
10. irrational numbers **11.** rational numbers, integers
12. rational numbers, integers, whole numbers, natural
numbers **13.** rational numbers **14.** $-\sqrt{60} > -8$
15. $5 < \sqrt{32}$ **16.** Inv. Prop. of Mult. **17.** Assoc. Prop. of
Mult. **18.** 114 **19.** 5b **20.** 11 **21.** 6
22. $z \le \dfrac{2}{5}$

23. $x > 2$

24. no solution
25. $x \le \dfrac{3}{2}$ or $x > 6$

26. 10 cm, 6 cm **27.** 1 **28.** no solution **29.** $x = -8$ or
$x = -12$ **30.** no solution
31. $-\dfrac{1}{3} \le x \le \dfrac{5}{3}$

32. $y < 0$ or $y > 18$

33. $-\dfrac{18}{7} \le x \le \dfrac{18}{7}$

34. $x < -14$ or $x > 10$

35. $|x - 43.6| \le 0.1$

Chapter 2

Get Ready!   p. 61

1. 6s **2.** $4a + b$ **3.** $xy - y + x$ **4.** 1.5g **5.** 0
6. $3b - 2c - 2$ **7.** $6f - 5d$ **8.** $3h + 3g$ **9.** $-2z + 5$
10. $2g - 4dg - 12d$ **11.** $8v - 6$ **12.** $7t - 3st - 5s$
13. -56 **14.** 80 **15.** -10 **16.** -24 **17.** 1075 **18.** 5
19. -1.75 **20.** 1.5 **21.** 20 **22.** 2 **23.** 5 **24.** 4
25. $-2 < x < 8$

26. $a \le 0$

27. $x > -1$

28. $x < -4$ or $x > \dfrac{10}{3}$

29. $-\dfrac{1}{2} \le d \le \dfrac{25}{4}$

30. $-24 \le f \le 18$

31. Answers may vary. Sample: the Civil War, the Great
Depression, the Louisiana Purchase **32.** Answers may
vary. Sample: From 1 to 2 years of age; a person has
usually stopped growing by age 30, but a baby is still
growing at age 1. **33.** Answers may vary. Sample:

The image is a reflection, left to right, of what other people
see; the size is the same. **34.** Answers may vary. Sample:
An inequality determines the limit of a value, or a
boundary, for the solutions on the number line.

Lesson 2-1 Part 1   pp. 64–69

Got It? 1. Let Jan = 1, Feb = 2, Mar = 3, and Apr = 4.

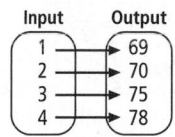

Input	Output
1	69
2	70
3	75
4	78

$\{(1, 69), (2, 70), (3, 75), (4, 78)\}$

x Month	y Temperature (°F)
1	69
2	70
3	75
4	78

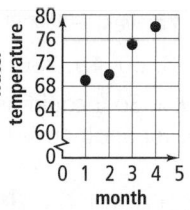

2a. domain: $\{-3, -2, 4, 5\}$; range: $\{-3, 2, 4, 8\}$
b. domain: $\{-3, 0, 2, 4, 9\}$; range: $\{-2, 3, 7, 9, 12\}$
3a. no **b.** yes **c.** In a mapping diagram for a relation that
is not a function, there is at least one element in the
domain that has more than one arrow originating from it.
In a mapping diagram for a function, each element in the
domain has one arrow originating from it. **4.** b and c
Lesson Check 1. domain: $\{0, 3, 4\}$,
range: $\{-2, 1, 2, 4\}$ **2.** domain: $\{-4, -3, 0, 4\}$,
range: $\{-4, -3, 0, 4\}$ **3.** no **4.** yes **5.** Yes; a relation is
any set of pairs of input and output values. No; a function
is a relation in which each element of the domain is paired
with exactly one element of the range. **6.** *Every* vertical
line does not need to intersect a function. Rewrite as: "In
a function, every vertical line must intersect the graph in
at most one point." **7.** A horizontal-line test checks the
pairing of one element of the range with one or more
elements of the domain. A function can have a pairing of
one element of the range with *one or more* elements of
the domain. A horizontal-line test cannot determine
whether a relation is a function.
Exercises 9. domain: $\{1, 2, 3, 4, 5, 6\}$, range:
$\{6, 7, 8, 9, 11\}$ **11.** yes **13.** yes **15.** yes **17.** yes
19. no **21.** domain: $-3 \le x \le 3$, range: $-1 \le y \le 1$;
no **23.** domain: $\{-3, -1, 1, 2, 4\}$, range: $\{0, 1, 2, 3\}$; no

Lesson 2-1 Part 2   pp. 70–73

Got It? 5a. 1 **b.** 0.25 **c.** -8 **6.** Let $x =$ number of
bottles purchased and $C =$ total cost; $C(x) = 1.19x$;
17.85

Lesson Check 1. 14 **2.** −4 **3.** 55 **4.** 19 **5.** range
6. The friend who said the output is 49 is correct.
Substitute 9 for x: $5(9) + 4 = 45 + 4 = 49$.
Exercises 7. 3; $(−5, 3)$ **9.** −15; $(9, −15)$ **11.** −2;
$(3, −2)$ **13.** $−\frac{5}{2}$; $\left(9, −\frac{5}{2}\right)$ **15.** $C(m) = 3.12 + 0.18m$;
$34.62 **17.** 13.5 cm^2 **19.** 11 **21.** 7 **23.** 4
25. $\approx 4849 \text{ cm}^3$ **27a.** into **b.** into **c.** onto **d.** into
32. $\frac{2}{3}$, $−\frac{20}{3}$ **33.** −13, 15 **34.** $x > −3$ **35.** $x \le \frac{3}{2}$
36. $−\frac{3}{2} < x < \frac{3}{2}$ **37.** $x \ge −3$ **38.** $\frac{1}{4}x$ **39.** $−\frac{1}{2}x$
40. $20x$

Lesson 2-2   pp. 74–80

Got It? 1a. yes; $−7, y = −7x$ **b.** no **2a.** yes; $−\frac{5}{3}$
b. yes; $\frac{1}{9}$ **3.** 60 **4a.** 280 **b.** No; if $y^2 = kx^2$ then
$y = \pm\sqrt{k}\,x$. So $\frac{y}{x}$ could be $+\sqrt{k}$ for one pair of values
and $−\sqrt{k}$ for another pair. Then y would not vary directly
with x.
5a. 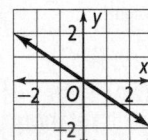 **b.**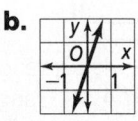

Lesson Check 1. $y = −\frac{1}{2}x$ **2.** $\frac{3}{2}$ **3.** $\frac{5}{4}$ **4.** Answers may
vary. Sample: Two variables are directly related when the
ratio of the output to the input is a constant value. **5.** For
a direct variation, $y = kx$ where k is the constant of
variation. If $x = 0$, then $y = 0$ and the graph of $y = kx$
passes through the origin.
Exercises 7. no **9.** yes; $\frac{1}{3}$, $y = \frac{1}{3}x$ **11.** yes; 12 **13.** no
15. yes; 6 **17.** −3 **19.** $\frac{6}{7}$ **21.** 21 **23.** 13.5 min
25.

x	y
−1	9
1	−9
2	−18

27. no **29.** no
31. $y = 2x$ **33.** $y = −4.5x$ **35.** $y = \frac{3}{5}x$
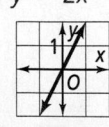 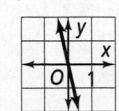

37. 0.625 **39.** 0.225 **41.** Every direct variation
includes the point $(0, 0)$, so x cannot be determined
because k could be any value.

43. Answers may vary.
Sample: $y = 3.2x$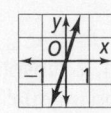

45. Answers may vary. Sample: If y varies directly with x^2,
and $y = 2$ when $x = 4$, then $y = \frac{81}{8}$ when $x = 9$.
47. Answers may vary. Sample: No; the line $y = 0$ passes
through the origin, but is not a direct variation.
53. 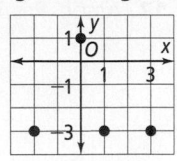 **54.**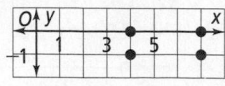

domain: $\{4, 7\}$;
range: $\{0, −1\}$

domain: $\{−2, 0, 1, 3\}$;
range: $\{−3, 1\}$

55. 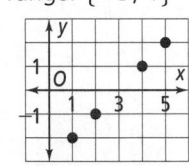 **56.**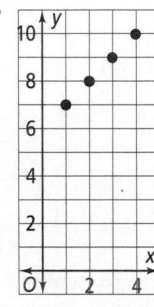

domain: $\{1, 2, 4, 5\}$;
range: $\{−2, −1, 1, 2\}$

domain: $\{1, 2, 3, 4\}$;
range: $\{7, 8, 9, 10\}$
57. $8n$; 40, 48, 56 **58.** $7 − 2n$; −3, −5, −7
59. $12(13 − n)$; 96, 84, 72 **60.** $15(n + 1)$; 90, 105, 120
61. $\frac{17}{3}$; 7; $\frac{23}{3}$, $\frac{29}{3}$ **62.** −5; 1; 4; 13 **63.** −9; −8; −7.5; −6

Lesson 2-3   pp. 81–87

Got It? 1a. −1 **b.** 1 **c.** $\frac{1 − 4}{8 − 5} = \frac{−3}{3} = −1$;
$\frac{4 − 1}{5 − 8} = \frac{3}{−3} = −1$ **2a.** $y = 6x + 5$ **b.** $y = −\frac{1}{2}x − 3$
c. No; any two points on a line can be used to calculate
the slope. **3a.** $y = −\frac{3}{2}x + 9$; $−\frac{3}{2}$; $(0, 9)$
b. $y = −\frac{1}{4}x + 18$; $−\frac{1}{4}$; $(0, 18)$
4a. $y = \frac{4}{7}x − 2$ 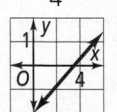 **b.** $y = \frac{1}{2}x$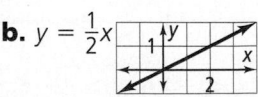

Lesson Check 1. $y = \frac{1}{2}x + 1$ **2.** $y = \frac{4}{3}x + \frac{1}{3}$ **3.** −1
4. 1 **5.** The y-intercept of a line is the point at which the
line crosses the y-axis. The x-intercept is the point at which
the line crosses the x-axis. **6.** She subtracted the
x-coordinates in the wrong order. The x- and y-coordinates
of each point must be subtracted consistently.

Exercises 7. -1 **9.** 3 **11.** 1 **13.** 0 **15.** $y = -5x - 7$
17. $y = 2x + 1$ **19.** $y = -\frac{1}{2}x - \frac{3}{4}$; $-\frac{1}{2}$, $\left(0, -\frac{3}{4}\right)$
21. $y = 7$; 0, $(0, 7)$

23.
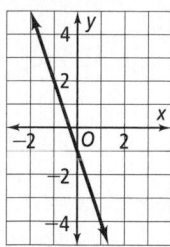

25.
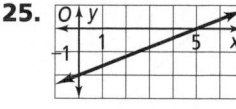

27.
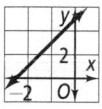

29.
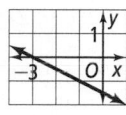

31.
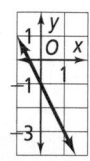

33.
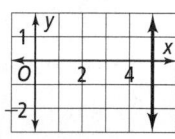

35. 0; $(0, 3)$ **37a.** the rate at which you walk; the slope is the same as the change in distance divided by the change in time, which is the rate at which you walk. **b.** towards your home; the slope is negative and the distance (y-value) decreases as the time (x-value) increases. **39.** He did not isolate y first and then find the coefficient of x. The slope is $\frac{2}{3}$. **41.** $\frac{7}{5}$ **43.** -0.8; $(0, 0.4)$ **45.** 0; $(0, 0)$ **47.** $\frac{A}{B}$; $\left(0, -\frac{C}{B}\right)$, $B \neq 0$ **53.** domain: $\{-2, 1, 2, 3, 4\}$, range: $\{-2, -1, 2, 3\}$; no **54.** domain: all real numbers, range: $y \geq -2$; no **55.** domain: $\{-5, 0, 2, 9\}$, range: $\{-3, -1, 5, 15\}$; no **56.** 2 **57.** 8 **58.** 13

Lesson 2-4 Part 1   pp. 88–91

Got It? 1. $y + 1 = -3(x - 7)$ **2a.** $y - 7 = \frac{7}{5}x$
b. $y = \frac{7}{5}(x + 5)$; Either point can be used to put the equation of the line in point-slope form. **3a.** $-4x + 6y = 1$ **b.** $-91x + 10y = 36$
Lesson Check 1. $y = -3x - 1$ **2.** $y = \frac{1}{2}x + 2$
3. $x + 4y = 20$ **4.** $-2x + 10y = -17$ **5a.** point-slope **b.** slope-intercept **c.** standard **d.** point-slope **6.** Point-slope form; since the x-intercept is the point where y is zero, you know the point on the line, $(x, 0)$, and you know the slope.
Exercises 7. $y - 5 = 3(x - 1)$ **9.** $y + 2 = 0$
11. $y - 3 = -(x + 10)$ or $y + 5 = -(x + 2)$
13. $y - 10 = -\frac{5}{2}(x + 4)$ or $y - 15 = -\frac{5}{2}(x + 6)$
15. $-x + 2y = -4$ **17.** $3x + 5y = 15$
19. $y - \frac{1}{3} = -\frac{5}{13}\left(x + \frac{2}{3}\right)$ or $y + \frac{1}{2} = -\frac{5}{13}\left(x - \frac{3}{2}\right)$

21. $y - \frac{1}{2} = -\frac{7}{10}x$ or $y = -\frac{7}{10}\left(x - \frac{5}{7}\right)$
23. The equation should have $-3x$ instead of $3x$.

Lesson 2-4 Part 2   pp. 92–97

Got It? 4. $(0, -2)$, $(4, 0)$
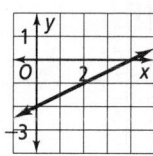

5a.
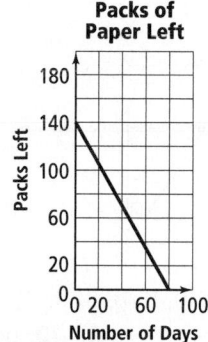

Packs of Paper Left

b. $7x + 4y = 560$ **c.** 87.5 **6a.** $y = -2x + 6$
b. $y = -\frac{3}{2}x + 6$

Lesson Check 1. $(0, 6)$, $(2, 0)$
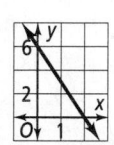

2. $3x + y = -1$ **3.** $3x + 2y = -9$ **4.** Set $y = 0$ to find the x-intercept and set $x = 0$ to find the y-intercept. Plot the intercepts and draw a line through them. **5.** No; one line has a slope of -2 and the other line has a slope of $-\frac{1}{2}$. $-\frac{1}{2}$ is the reciprocal of -2, not the *negative* reciprocal.
Exercises
7. $(0, -2)$, $(-5, 0)$ **9.** $(0, 2)$, $\left(\frac{14}{5}, 0\right)$
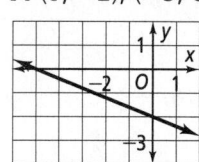   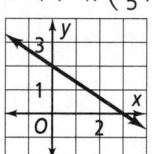

11. Answers may vary. Sample: $y = -2.5x + 20$
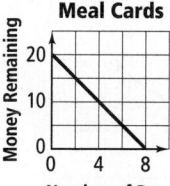

Meal Cards

13. $y = \frac{5}{2}x + \frac{17}{2}$ **15.** $y = \frac{2}{3}x + \frac{44}{3}$

17.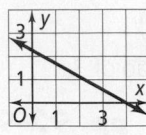

19.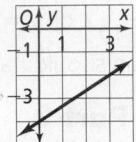

21.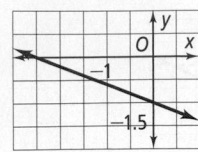

23. $y = \frac{3}{4}x + 3$ **25.** $y = 3x + 2$

27. $y = -1$ **29.** $y = -\frac{3}{2}x - 1$

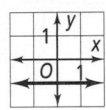 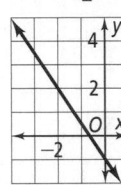

31. $\frac{2}{3}$; $(0, 4)$, $(-6, 0)$ **33.** -0.8; $(0, 0.4)$, $(0.5, 0)$

35. undefined slope; no y-intercept, $(-3, 0)$ **40.** domain: $\{-3, -1, 0, 1, 2\}$, range: $\{-2, 0, 2, 4\}$; yes **41.** domain: all real numbers, range: $\{-2\}$; yes **42.** domain: $\{-18, -2, 0, 3, 39\}$, range: $\{-1, 3, 17, 28, 32\}$; yes **43.** Multiplicative Inv. **44.** Distr. Prop. **45.** Add. Inv., Add. Ident. **46.** $y = 3x - 5$ **47.** $y = \frac{1}{2}x$ **48.** $y = \frac{4}{5}x + 7$ **49.** $y = -\frac{3}{8}x + 12$

Chapter Review for Part A   pp. 98–100

1. relations **2.** sometimes **3.** point-slope **4.** yes; domain: $\{-10, -6, 5, 6, 10\}$, range: $\{2, 3, 4, 7\}$ **5.** no; domain: $\{1, 3, 4, 10\}$, range: $\{5, 6, 8, 12\}$ **6.** no; domain: $\left\{-2, -\frac{3}{2}, -1, \frac{1}{2}, 1, 2, 3\right\}$, range: $\left\{-\frac{7}{2}, -\frac{1}{2}, 0, \frac{1}{2}, \frac{3}{2}, 2, \frac{5}{2}\right\}$

7. yes; domain: $\left\{-2, -1, \frac{1}{2}, 3\right\}$, range: $\{2\}$ **8.** 6, 4.5, 1

9. $-3\frac{3}{4}$, $-3\frac{3}{16}$, $-1\frac{7}{8}$ **10.** no **11.** no **12.** yes; 1; $y = x$

13. -4; 1.2 **14.** $\frac{10}{3}$; -1 **15.** $\frac{7}{2}$; $-1\frac{1}{20}$ **16.** $-\frac{4}{3}$; 0.4

17. $-\frac{2}{5}$ **18.** $\frac{7}{6}$ **19.** $\frac{2}{3}$ **20.** $-\frac{4}{9}$ **21.** $y = -3x + 4$

22. $y = \frac{1}{2}x + 6$

23. $y = 2x - \frac{3}{2}$

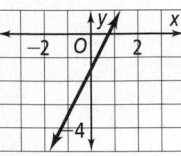

24. $y = \frac{2}{3}x + 3$

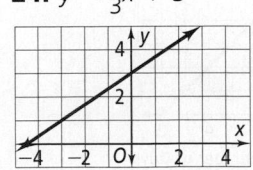

25. $y = -x + 5$

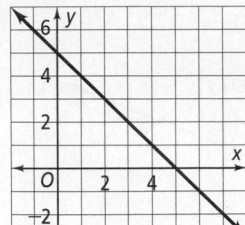

26. $y = -\frac{1}{3}x + \frac{5}{3}$

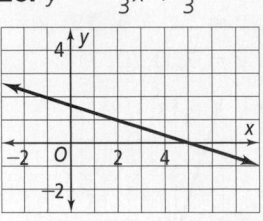

27. $3x + y = 12$ **28.** $5x - y = 6$ **29.** $x + 2y = 12$
30. $2x - 3y = 2$ **31.** $y = -\frac{7}{3}x$ or $y + 7 = -\frac{7}{3}(x - 3)$
32. $y - 3 = 2(x - 2)$ or $y - 5 = 2(x - 3)$
33. $y + 3 = x + 4$ or $y - 2 = x - 1$
34. $y + 5 = -\frac{9}{4}(x - 2)$ or $y - 4 = -\frac{9}{4}(x + 2)$
35. $y = \frac{1}{3}x + \frac{5}{3}$ **36.** $y = -\frac{5}{4}x + \frac{1}{4}$ **37.** $y = -\frac{3}{4}x - \frac{7}{2}$
38. $y = -2x + 9$ **39a.** $y = -\frac{1}{2}x + 7$ **b.** $y = 2x - 13$
c.

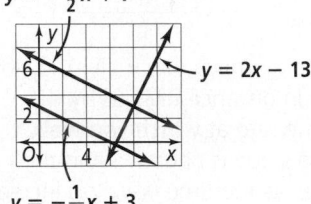

$y = -\frac{1}{2}x + 7$

$y = 2x - 13$

$y = -\frac{1}{2}x + 3$

Lesson 2-5   pp. 103–109

Got It? 1a. strong negative correlation

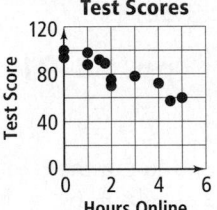

b. about $170

2. Answers may vary. Sample: $y = 3575x + 19{,}354$; $341{,}104 **3.** Answers may vary. Sample: $y = 0.09x + 2.44$, where 1997 is year 0; $4.96
Lesson Check 1. strong positive correlation

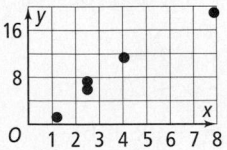

2. no correlation

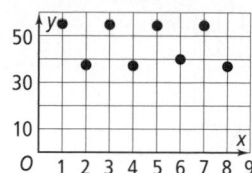

3. strong positive correlation

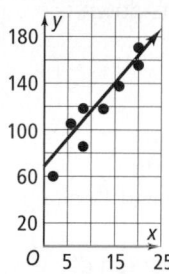

4. Plot the data points in a scatter plot to determine the correlation. The closer the data points fall along a line with a positive or negative slope, the stronger the correlation. **5.** No; answers may vary. Sample: A trend line is determined by using two pts. close to the line drawn through the data sets of the scatter plot. The line of best fit is the most accurate of the trend lines because it uses all the data pts. **6.** The slope of the trend line or line of best fit is positive for data pts. with positive correlation and negative for data pts. with negative correlation. The constant of variation for a direct variation is positive for data pts. with positive correlation.

Exercises 7. strong negative correlation

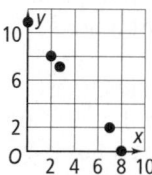

9. Answers may vary. Sample: $y = 4.47x + 33.31$
11. Answers may vary. Sample: $y = -0.7x - 4$
13. 6,055,399 tonnes **15.** positive correlation; no
17. positive correlation; yes

22. 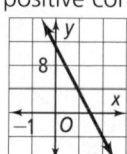 **23.**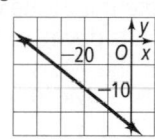

24.

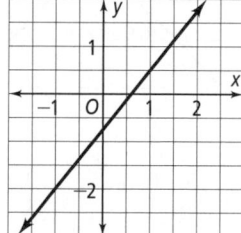

25. $-2x + y = 2$ **26.** $x + y = 0$ **27.** $y = 2$

28.

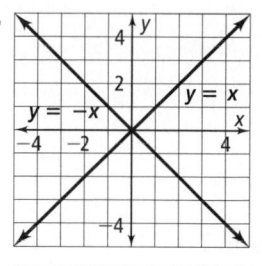

29.

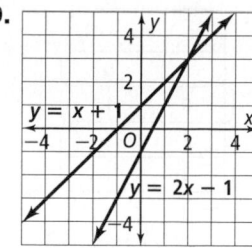

30.

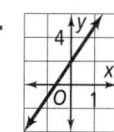

Lesson 2-6 Part 1   pp. 110–113

Got It? 1a. Each output for $y = 2x - 3$ is three less than the corresponding output for $y = 2x$. The graph of $y = 2x - 3$ is the graph of $y = 2x$ translated down three units.

b.

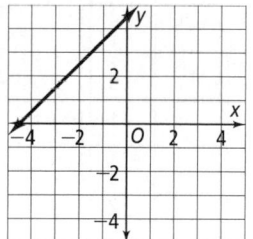

c. $y = x^2 + 2$ **2.** $f\left(x + \frac{1}{2}\right)$

Lesson Check 1. translated 6 units up **2.** translated 4 units to the rt. **3.** Answers may vary. Sample: $f(x) = x$, $f(x - 2) = f(x) - 2$

Exercises 5. The function is $y = x$ translated 4.5 units up.

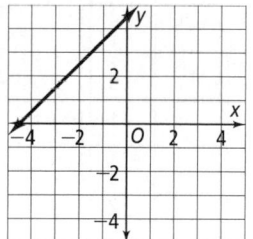

7. The function is $y = x^2$ translated down 5 units.

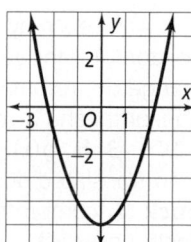

9.

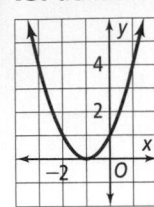

x	$f(x) - 1$
−1	0
0	−1
2	−5
3	1

11. $y = f(x) - \frac{2}{3}$ **13.** $y = f(x) + 2$

15. translated left 1 unit

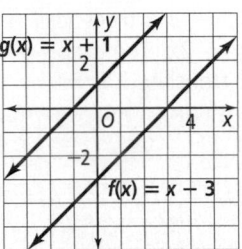

17. translated horizontally right 6 units

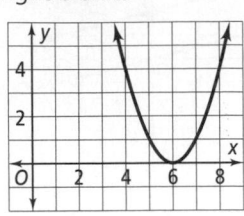

21. translated 4 units up

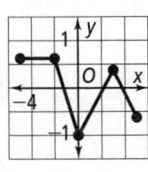

Lesson 2-6 Part 2   pp. 114–120

Got It? 3. $h(x) = -3x - 2$

4a.

x	y
−5	$\frac{2}{3}$
−2	$\frac{2}{3}$
0	−1
3	$\frac{1}{3}$
5	$-\frac{2}{3}$

b. Sometimes; Answers may vary. Sample: switching the order of a horizontal translation and a reflection in the y-axis will change the resulting graph, but switching the order of a horizontal and a vertical translation will not.
5a. $g(x) = 2x - 3$ **b.** $g(x) = f(x + 4) - 2$; translated left 4 units and translated down 2 units
Lesson Check 1. compressed vertically by a factor of 0.25 **2.** reflected over y-axis

3. translated 1 unit to the left and 2 units down

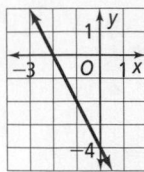

4. stretched vertically by a factor of 2 and translated 1 unit up

5. $g(x)$ is the graph of $h(x)$ translated 2 units up

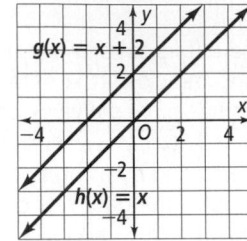

6. $f(x) = -x - 2$; $g(x) = f(-x) = x - 2$
Exercises 7. $g(x) = -x - 1$ **9.** $g(x) = -2x + 4$
11. $y = 2x$ **13.** $y = \frac{1}{4}x$ **15.** $g(x) = 12x - 1$
17. vertically stretched by a factor of 4, reflected over the x-axis, and translated up 4 units **19.** The first two steps are incorrect; the transformations should be: shift 1 unit left, vertically stretch by a factor of 2, and shift 3 units down. **21.** translate to the right 10 s **23.** $f(x) = -2x + 2$; $g(x) = 2x + 2$; reflection in y-axis **25a.** The functions $g(x)$, $h(x)$, and $k(x)$ have the same domain as the function $f(x)$, but different ranges, and the function $m(x)$ has the same range as $f(x)$ but a different domain. **b.** Yes; the transformations in (i), (ii), and (iii) affect only the vert. position of a function, which determines the range. The transformation in (iv) affects only the horizontal position, which determines the domain.
27. translated 7 units down, then reflected over the y-axis, or reflected over the x-axis, then translated 1 unit down

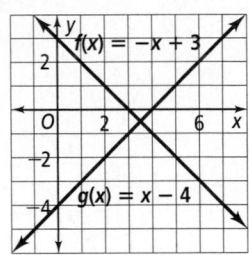

29. translated 3 units up

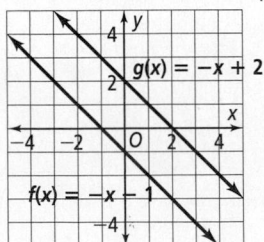

34. $y = -15.82x + 914.59$

35. $x \le -10$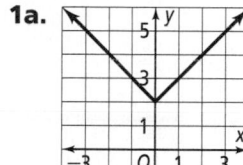

36. $a > 4.5$

37. $b > -1.5$

38. $-2, 8$ **39.** $-12, 11$ **40.** $-3, \frac{21}{5}$

Lesson 2-7   pp. 121–127

Got It?

1a. 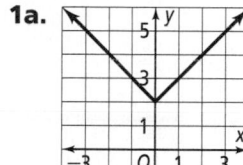 vertex at (0, 2); translated up 2 units from the parent function

b. No; transformations of this form move the vertex up or down along the axis of symmetry, so the axis stays the same.

2.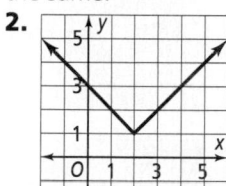

3a. 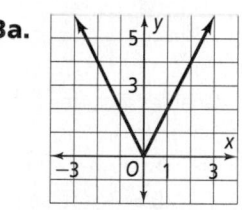   **b.**

4. $(1, -3)$; $x = 1$; translated 1 unit to the rt., vertically stretched by a factor of 2, then reflected over the x-axis and translated down 3 units **5.** $y = \frac{1}{4}|x - 2| - 1$

Lesson Check 1. $(-4, -3)$; $x = -4$ **2.** $(-3, 9)$; $x = -3$ **3.** vertical stretch **4.** vertical stretch
5. Yes; you can determine the position of a graph of an absolute value function by identifying the vertex, axis of symmetry, and the transformation of the absolute value parent function. Answers may vary. Sample: $y = -\frac{1}{2}|x + 3| - 5$; vertex $(-3, -5)$; axis of symmetry, $x = -3$; translated 3 units to the left, vertically compressed by a factor of $\frac{1}{2}$, then reflected over the x-axis and translated down 5 units.
6. Answers may vary. Sample: $y = |x + 1| - 2$ and $y = -|x + 1| - 2$ **7.** $y = |x|$ is the same as $y = x$ when $x \ge 0$ and is the reflection of $y = x$ across the x-axis when $x < 0$.

Exercises 9.

x	y
-2	1
-1	0
0	-1
1	0
2	1

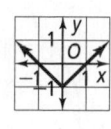

11.

x	y
-4	2
-3	1
-2	0
-1	1
0	2

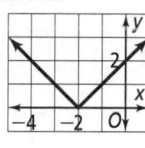

13.

x	y
-8	1
-7	0
-6	-1
-5	0
-4	1

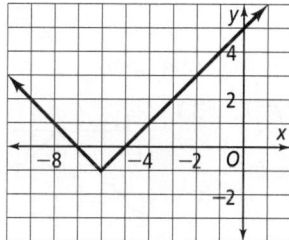

15. 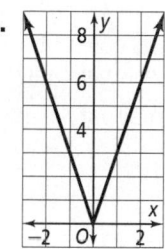   **17.**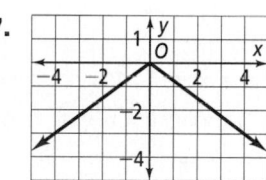

vertically compressed by a factor of $\frac{3}{4}$, reflected across the x-axis

vertically stretched by a factor of 3

19. $(6, 0)$; $x = 6$; vertically stretched by a factor of $\frac{3}{2}$ and translated 6 units to the rt.

21. $(2, -6)$; $x = 2$; translate 2 units to the rt. and 6 units down **23.** $y = 0.5|x + 2| - 6$

25. 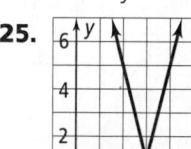 $(3, 1)$; no x-intercept; $(0, 13)$

27a. 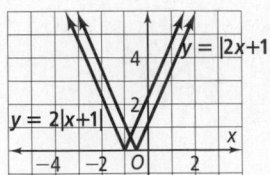 **b.**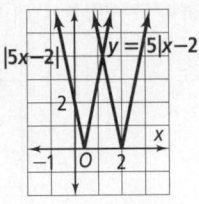

c. The absolute value bars act as grouping symbols, like parentheses.

29a.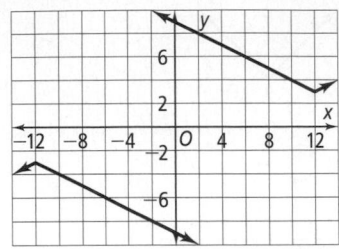

b. Answers may vary. Sample: same shape and size, different vertices, one opens down and one opens up.

31. 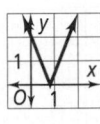 **33.** 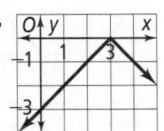 **35.**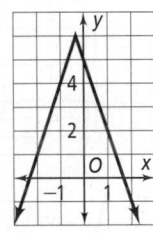

40. $y = x + 1$ **41.** $y = -\frac{1}{2}x + 2$ **42.** Answers may vary. Sample: $y = \frac{4}{5}x + 1$ **43.** Answers may vary. Sample: $y = -\frac{4}{5}x + 8$

44. $p \le 1.25$ ⟵●⟶ 1.25

45. $t > 13$ ⟵○⟶ 13

46. $t \le -3$ ⟵●⟶ −3

Lesson 2-8   pp. 128–134

Got It?

1a. 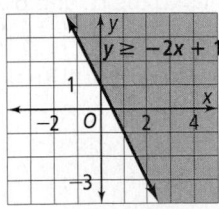 **b.**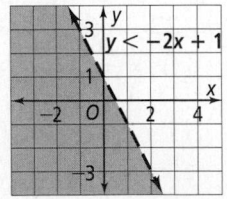

2a.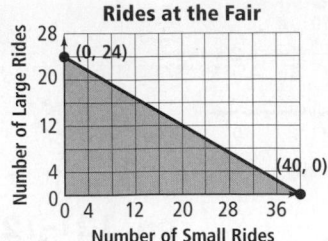

Rides at the Fair

b. The number of rides cannot be negative.

3.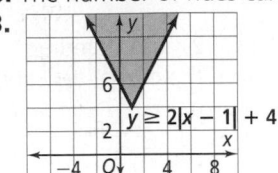

4. $y \le -3x - 1$

Lesson Check

1. 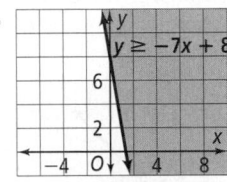 **2.**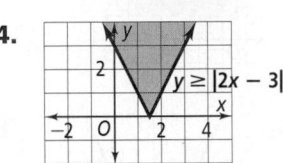

3. 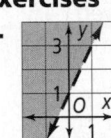 **4.**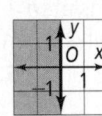

5. Graphing a linear inequality in two variables includes first graphing the boundary line, which is a linear eq. in two variables, and then shading the half-plane. **6.** No; $\left(\frac{3}{4}, 0\right)$ does not satisfy the inequality because $2.25 > 3$ is false.

Exercises

7. 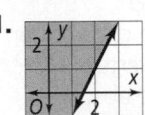 **9.**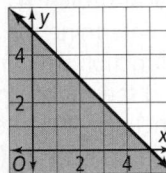

11. 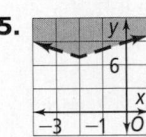 **13.**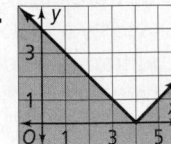

15. **17.**

19. $y < -x - 2$

Selected Answers

21. 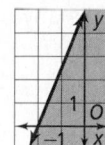 **23.** 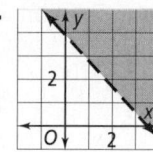 **25.**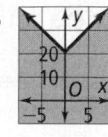

27. domain: $0 \le x \le 28$; $y \le -x + 28$

29a. domain: $0 \le x \le 16$ **b.** There is a limit to the number of gallons in your car's gas tank. **c.** You can't have a negative number of gallons of gas in your tank, nor can you drive a negative number of miles. **d.** $y \le 25x$ **e.** the number of miles you can drive per gallon **f.** Yes; you can use a fraction of a gallon, and you can drive a fraction of a mile. **31.** $x > -3$ **33.** $y \ge -2x + 4$

38. 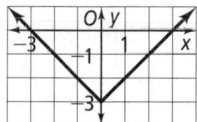 **39.** 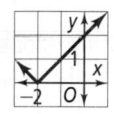 **40.**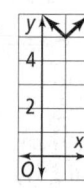

41. yes; 100 **42.** yes; -5 **43.** no
44. strong neg. correlation **45.** no correlation

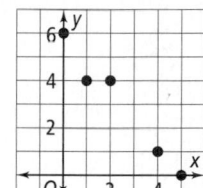 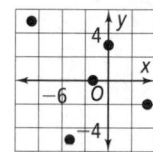

46–48.

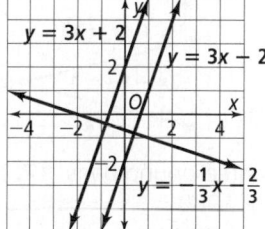

Chapter Review for Part B   pp. 136–138

1. sometimes **2.** half-plane **3.** axis of symmetry

4.

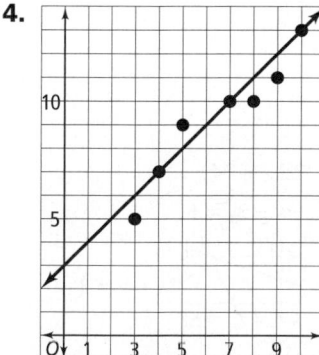

Strong pos. correlation; answers may vary. Sample: $y = x + 3$; 18

5.

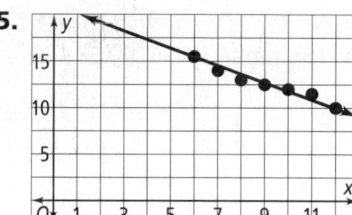

Strong neg. correlation; answers may vary. Sample: $y = -0.9x + 21$; 7.5

6.

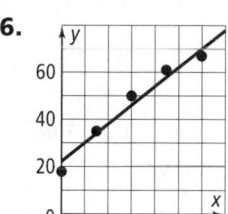

Strong pos. correlation; answers may vary. Sample: $y = 4x + 22$; 82

7. $y = f(x + 2) - 7$ **8.** $y = -f(x - 5)$
9. $y = f(-x) + 3$ **10.** translated 4 units down
11. vertically stretched by a factor of 12, translated 2 units up **12.** vertically stretched by a factor of 2, reflected across the y-axis, reflected across the x-axis
13. $y = |x - 2| + 4$ **14.** $y = |x + 3|$
15. $y = |x - 5| + 2$ **16.** $y = |x - 4| + 1$

17. **18.**

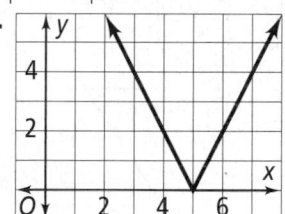

19. **20.**

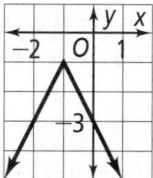

21. $(4, 0)$; $x = 4$ **22.** $(0, 2)$; $x = 0$

23. **24.**

25. **26.**

27a. Answers may vary. Sample: $x + 3y \le 15$

b. Answers may vary. Sample: domain: {0, 1, 2, 3, 4, 5, 6, 7, 8, 9, 10, 11, 12, 13, 14, 15}, range: {0, 1, 2, 3, 4, 5}

c.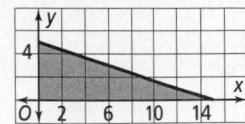

28. Answers may vary. Sample: $y \le -|x| - 1$

Chapter 3

Get Ready!   p. 143

1. 28 **2.** 33 **3.** $-\frac{15}{2}$ **4.** 15 **5.** $y = \frac{1}{2}x - \frac{5}{2}$
6. $y = -2x - 3$ **7.** $y = 5x + 16$ **8.** $y = 3x - 7$
9. $y = \frac{2}{5}x - \frac{3}{2}$ **10.** $y = 4x + 11$ **11.** $y = -6x - 8$
12. $y = -3x + 18$

13. 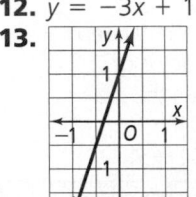 **14.**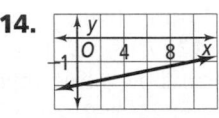

15. 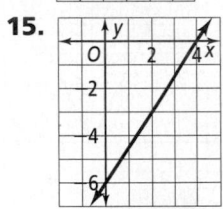 **16.**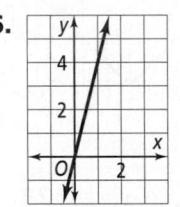

17. 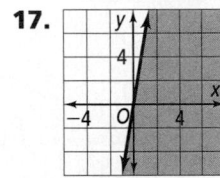 **18.**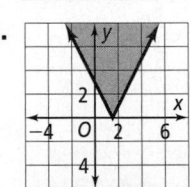

19. 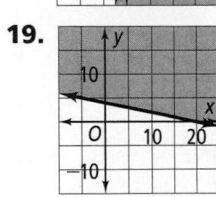 **20.**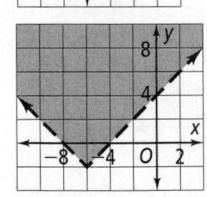

21. Answers may vary. Samples: Rocky Mountains, Appalachian Mountains **22.** 15 books or more; 15 books or more but less than 19, i.e., 15, 16, 17, or 18 books

Lesson 3-1   pp. 146–153

Got It? 1. (2, −1) **2a.** Spiny Dogfish: 59.5 cm; Greenland: 55.75 cm **b.** Each species of shark has a maximum total length; growth rates decrease with increase in age. **3.** in the yr 1990; about 1,100,000

4a. zero solutions **b.** one solution **c.** infinitely many solutions

Lesson Check

1. (2, 1) **2.** (2, 0)

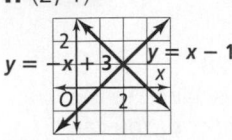 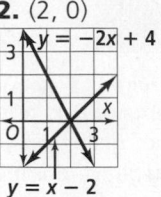

3. 2 pens; 4 pencils **4.** No; straight lines cannot meet in exactly two points.

5. Answers may vary. Sample: $\begin{cases} y = 2x + 1 \\ y = 2x - 3 \end{cases}$

6. One solution; if the slope of one equation is the negative reciprocal of the slope of the other equation, the lines are perpendicular and intersect at exactly one point.

Exercises 7–13. How solutions are determined may vary (graphing or using a table).

7. (3, 1) **9.** (−2, 4)

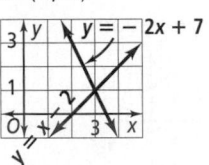 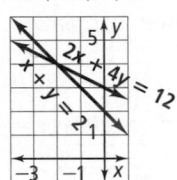

11. no solution **13.** $\left(7, \frac{5}{4}\right)$

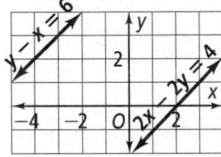 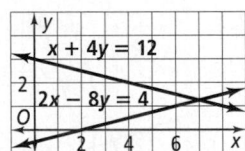

15. 3 one-pound bags; 2 three-pound bags **17.** Models may vary. Sample: Use 0 for 1980.
$\begin{cases} y = 0.232x + 1.328 \\ y = 0.145x + 3.673 \end{cases}$
Around 2007, the quantities were equal. **19.** infinitely many solutions **21.** one solution **23.** zero solutions **25.** infinitely many solutions

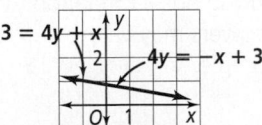

27. no solution **29.** (6, 4)

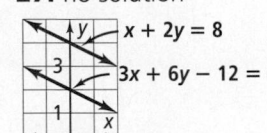 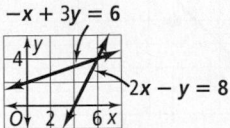

31. zero solutions **33.** zero solutions

35a. $\begin{cases} c = 25h \\ c = 20h + 10 \end{cases}$

b. 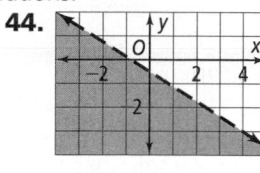 The cost would be the same for 2 hours of instruction.

c. The campus that charges $20 per hour plus a one-time registration of $10 would be cheaper for 10 hours of practice ($210 versus $250).

37. No; they would be the same line, and the system would have infinitely many solutions.

43. **44.**

45.

46. $n < -\frac{8}{7}$ **47.** $x \geq -\frac{29}{2}$ or -14.5 **48.** $x > \frac{5}{8}$

49. 2 **50.** $-\frac{3}{5}$ **51.** 2 **52.** 10 **53a.** -3 **b.** 8 **c.** -10

Lesson 3-2 Part 1   pp. 154–156

Got It? 1. $(-2.5, 2.5)$ **2.** $\$.95$ per download; $\$5.50$ one-time registration fee

Lesson Check 1. $(1, 2)$ **2.** $(-6, -6)$ **3.** Let $r =$ number of regular cups of coffee and $c =$ number of large cups of coffee. First, $r + c = 5$: because a total of 5 cups of coffee were purchased. Second, $r + 1.5c = 6$ because each regular cup of coffee is $1, each large cup is $1.50, and the total spent is $6. Then, solve the system of equations using elimination by subtracting the first equation from the second to eliminate r and solve for c. $c = 2$; 2 large cups

Exercises 5. $(-2, 4)$ **7.** $(10, -1)$ **9.** $(-2, -5)$ **11.** seven $1-bills; eight $5-bills **13.** Error in 5th line: $-4(-7 - x) = 28 + 4x$ *not* $-28 - 4x$; Lines 5–9 should be: $3x + 28 + 4x = 14$; $7x = -14$; $x = -2$; $y = -7 - (-2)$; $y = -5$ **15.** $\left(\frac{2}{3}, \frac{1}{3}\right)$

Lesson 3-2 Part 2   pp. 157–161

Got It? 3. $(4, 0)$ **4a.** $(-2, 3)$ **b.** Answers may vary. Sample: No; the answer will be the same regardless of which variable you solve for first. **5a.** no solution; The eq. is always false. **b.** infinite number of solutions; The eq. is always true.

6. In the substitution method of solving a system of equations, you first solve one equation for one of the variables. Then substitute for this variable in the other equation and solve for the other variable. In the elimination method, you create an equivalent system of equations that contain a pair of additive inverses so that you can eliminate one variable and solve for the remaining variable.

Exercises 7. $(7, 5)$ **9.** $(-1, 3)$ **11.** $(4, 1)$ **13.** $(1, 1)$
15. infinite number of solutions; $\{(a, d) \mid -3a + d = -1\}$
17. no solution **19.** no solution **21.** 10 deliveries
23. $(1, 3)$ **25.** $(-6, 30)$ **27.** $\left(-1, -\frac{1}{2}\right)$ **29.** $(300, 150)$
31. 4 mL of 20% sulfuric acid solution and 2 mL of 50% sulfuric acid solution **33.** In determining whether to use substitution or elimination to solve an equation, look at the equations to determine if one is solved or can be easily solved for a particular variable. If that is the case, substitution can easily be used. Otherwise, elimination might be easier. **35.** Substitution; the second equation is solved for y; $(-7, -26)$ **37.** Elimination; substitution would be difficult since no coefficient is 1 in the original system. Dividing the first equation by 3 and dividing the second equation by 5 results in an equivalent system where y would be eliminated from the system if the equations were subtracted; $(-1, -3)$
43. no solution

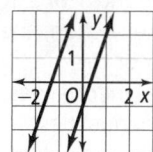

44. infinite number of solutions, $\{(x, y) \mid -9x - 3y = 1\}$

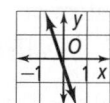

45. no solution

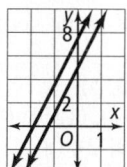

46. function **47.** function **48.** not a function

49. $x < -1$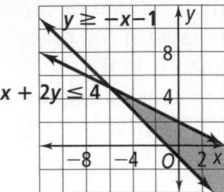

50. $x > -\frac{1}{2}$

51. $y < 1$

Lesson 3-3   pp. 162–167

Got It? 1. (4, 1), (5, 0), (6, 0), (7, 0)

2.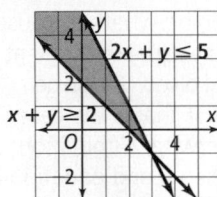

3. 5 meats and no vegetables; 4 meats and 1 or 2 vegetables; 3 meats and 2, 3, or 4 vegetables; 2 meats and 3, 4, 5, or 6 vegetables; 1 meat and 4 − 8 vegetables; no meat 5 − 10 vegetables

Lesson Check

1.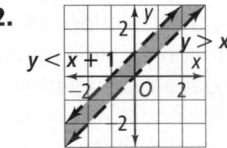

2.

3.

4. 0 h TV and 1, 2, or 3 h football; 1 h TV and 1 or 2 h football; or 2 h TV and 1 h football **5.** Intersection; the solution of two inequalities is the over-lap or the intersection of the graphs of the individual inequalities. **6.** The graphical solution of a system of inequalities consists of the overlap or intersection of the individual half-planes and corresponding boundary lines (either dotted or solid). The graphical solution of a system of equations includes only the intersection of the lines, not the half-planes.
7. For the first inequality, the wrong half-plane has been shaded. The half-plane below $y = \frac{1}{2}x - 1$ should be shaded. Also the boundary line for this half-plane should be dashed.
Exercises 9. (0, 0), (0, 1), (0, 2), (0, 3), (0, 4), (0, 5), (0, 6), (0, 7), (1, 0), (1, 1), (1, 2), (1, 3), (1, 4), (1, 5), (1, 6), (2, 0), (2, 1), (2, 2), (2, 3), (2, 4), (2, 5), (3, 3), (3, 4)
11. (0, 1), (0, 2), (0, 3), (0, 4), (0, 5), (0, 6), (0, 7), (1, 1), (1, 2), (1, 3), (1, 4), (1, 5), (1, 6), (2, 1), (2, 2), (2, 3),

(2, 4), (2, 5), (3, 1), (3, 2), (3, 3), (3, 4), (3, 5), (4, 1), (4, 2), (4, 3), (5, 1), (5, 2), (5, 3), (6, 1), (6, 2), (6, 3), (7, 1), (7, 2), (8, 1), (9, 1)

13.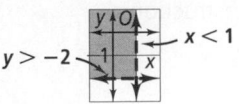

15.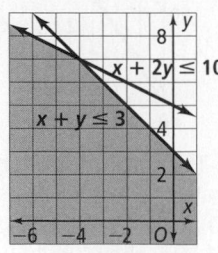

17. Let r = number of rose plants and t = number of tulip plants.
$t + r \geq 50$
$\quad r \leq 20$
Because the number of plants must be a whole number, only the points in the overlap that represent whole numbers are solutions of the system.

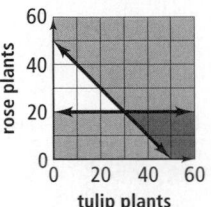

19. $\begin{cases} x + y \leq 1600 \\ y \geq 600 \end{cases}$

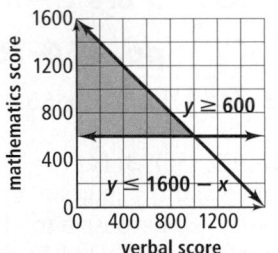

21. Use test pts. that are not on either of the boundary lines and that make the calculations as easy as possible.

23.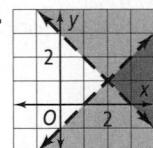

25.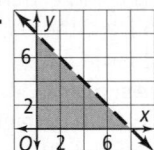

27.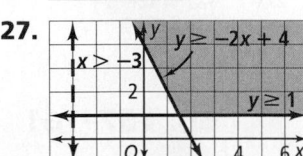

32. (−9, −26) **33.** $\left(\frac{23}{14}, -\frac{13}{14}\right)$ **34.** no solution

35. (−2, −1) **36.** (−1, 2) **37.** $\left(-\frac{4}{7}, \frac{1}{14}\right)$
38–41. Answers may vary. Samples are given for each exercise. **38.** (0, 3) **39.** (0, 3) **40.** (2, −1) **41.** (1, −1)

Lesson 3-4   pp. 169–174

Got It? 1a. *P* has a maximum value of 7.5 at (0, 2.5).
b. Answers may vary. Sample: *P* = 5 has same (maximum) value at all four vertex points. *P* = *x* + 2*y* has maximum value 5 at *R* and *S*. **2.** 108 T-shirts and 5 sweatshirts

Lesson Check

1.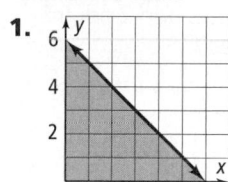

2.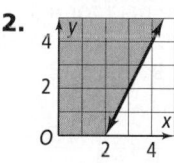

3.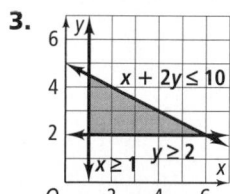

4.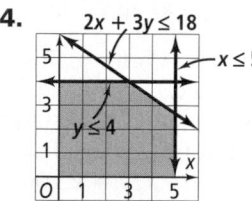

5. 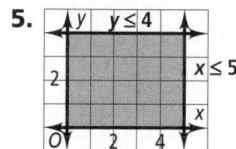 (0, 0), (0, 4), (5, 0), (5, 4)

6. 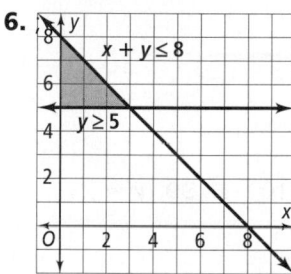 (0, 8), (3, 5), (0, 5)

7. Constraints are limits or restrictions on the variables in the objective function in a linear programming problem. These constraints are written as linear inequalities.
8. Linear programming is an extension of solving linear inequalities. For each, you are given constraints represented by linear inequalities that are graphed. All the points in the overlapping region are solutions, but linear programming problems are usually looking for maximum or minimum values of some quantity modeled with an objective function.

9. Answers may vary. Sample: $\begin{cases} y \le x \\ y \le -x + 4 \\ 0 \le y \le 1 \end{cases}$

$P = 2x + 3y$, $P(0, 0) = 0$, $P(1, 1) = 5$, $P(3, 1) = 9$, $P(4, 0) = 8$; maximum value of *P* is 9 at (3, 1)

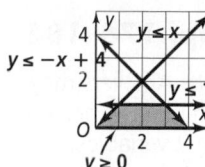

Exercises 11.

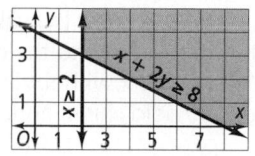 vertices: (8, 0), (2, 3); minimized at (8, 0)

13. 70 spruce trees and 0 maple trees
15. He is not considering the constraint $y \le x + 3$; *P* has a maximum value of 11 at (1, 4)

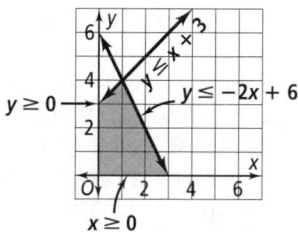

17. 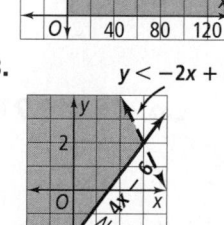 vertices: $\left(75, 20\right)$, $(75, 110)$, $\left(25, 86\frac{2}{3}\right)$, $(25, 110)$; minimized when $C = 633\frac{1}{3}$ at $\left(25, 86\frac{2}{3}\right)$.

19. 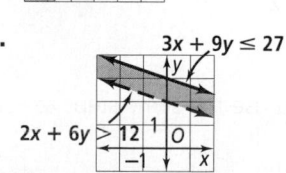 vertices: (0, 0), (150, 0), (100, 100), (0, 200); maximized when $P = 400$ at (0, 200).

23.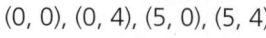

24.

25.

26. 1 **27.** 24 **28.** 65 **29.** (0, 6), (−3, 0) **30.** (0, 4), (18, 0) **31.** (0, −1), (1, 0)

Lesson 3-5   pp. 176–183

Got It? 1. (4, 2, −3) **2a.** (4, −1, 2) **b.** Answers may vary. Sample: Yes; you can choose to eliminate either x, y, or z resulting in a system of equations in 2 variables. **3a.** (2, 1, −4) **b.** No; in Step 1 we solved for x in terms of y only. Therefore, once we found the value of y we could have substituted that value into the equation we wrote in Step 1 and solved for x without ever finding the z-value. **4.** 50 T-shirts, 50 polo shirts, and 100 rugby shirts

Lesson Check 1. (5, −3, −2) **2.** (6, 0, −2) **3.** (0, 3, 4) **4.** Answers may vary. Sample: Substitution is the best method to use when one of the equations can be solved easily for one variable. **5.** Answers may vary. Sample: (0, 0, 0) is a unique solution to a system of three variables. The planes intersect at one common point. When a system has no solution, no point lies in all three planes. **6.** infinitely many solutions

Exercises 7. (4, 2, −3) **9.** (2, 1, −5) **11.** (0, 3, −2) **13.** (2, −1, 1) **15.** (8, −4, 2) **17.** (0, 1, 7) **19.** (1, −1, 2) **21.** Machine A: 112 bolts per hour; Machine B: 90 bolts per hour; Machine C: 85 bolts per hour **23.** Section A has 24,500 seats, Section B has 14,400 seats, and Section C has 10,100 seats.

25. (8, 1, 3) **27.** $\left(\frac{1}{2}, 2, -3\right)$ **29.** (−2, −1, 12)

35. P has a maximum value of 12 at (0, 4).

36. $x \geq -\frac{3}{2};$

37. $x \leq -18;$

38. $x < -1;$

39. $\left(7, \frac{5}{4}\right)$

40. infinite number of solutions,
$$\left\{(x, y) \mid y = -\frac{1}{2}x - \frac{3}{4}\right\}$$

41. no solution

Lesson 3-6   pp. 184–191

Got It? 1a. 17 **b.** −3

2a. $\begin{bmatrix} -4 & -2 & | & 7 \\ 3 & 1 & | & -5 \end{bmatrix}$ **b.** $\begin{bmatrix} 4 & -1 & 2 & | & 1 \\ 0 & 1 & 5 & | & 20 \\ 2 & 1 & 0 & | & 7 \end{bmatrix}$

3. $\begin{cases} 2x = 6 \\ 5x - 2y = 1 \end{cases}$

4a. (1, 2) **b.** elimination; you use the same steps to solve

5. $\left(1, \frac{1}{2}, 3\right)$

Lesson Check 1. 2×1 **2.** 2×4

3. $\begin{bmatrix} 3 & 5 & | & 0 \\ 1 & 1 & | & 2 \end{bmatrix}$ **4.** $\begin{bmatrix} 1 & 3 & -1 & | & 2 \\ 1 & 0 & 2 & | & 8 \\ 0 & 2 & -1 & | & 1 \end{bmatrix}$

5. 16 **6.** a_{21} is 0, the element in row 2, column 1. a_{12} is −9, the element in row 1 and column 2. **7.** Answers may vary. Sample: The entry fee to a school play is $2 for adults. Jamie paid for 4 student entry fees and 2 adult entry fees. What is the student entry fee?
Exercises 9. 1 **11.** 8

13. $\begin{bmatrix} 1 & 2 & | & 11 \\ 2 & 3 & | & 18 \end{bmatrix}$ **15.** $\begin{bmatrix} -3 & 1 & | & -7 \\ 1 & 0 & | & 2 \end{bmatrix}$

17. $\begin{cases} 5x + y = -3 \\ -2x + 2y = 4 \end{cases}$

19. (2, 1) **21.** (4, 6) **23.** (2, 3)
25. $10,000 at 4% and $15,000 at 6%
Let x = amount invested at 4% and
y = amount invested at 6%.
$$\begin{cases} x + y = 25,000 \\ 0.04x + 0.06y = 1300 \end{cases}$$
$$\begin{bmatrix} 1 & 1 & | & 25000 \\ 0.04 & 0.06 & | & 1300 \end{bmatrix} = \begin{bmatrix} 1 & 0 & | & 10000 \\ 0 & 1 & | & 15000 \end{bmatrix}$$

27. (2, 3) **29.** 1 qt. of red paint: $7.75; 1 qt. of yellow paint: $5.75

33. $x \leq -\frac{3}{2};$

34. $x \geq -35;$

35. $x \geq 4;$

36. $\frac{15}{2}, -\frac{9}{2}$ **37.** 10, −10 **38.** 10, −6 **39.** $y = 2x$

40. $y = \frac{1}{3}x$

Chapter Review   pp. 193–196

1. solution of a system **2.** Linear programming; constraints
3. row operations; matrix
4. one solution; (−1, −4)

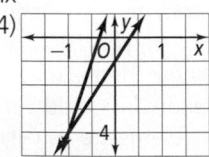

5. infinitely many solutions **6.** zero solutions
7. infinitely many solutions

8. one solution; $(-4, 6)$ **9.** one solution; $(1, 0)$

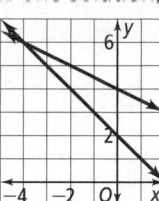 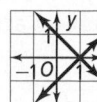

10. 3 pens **11.** $(-1, -2)$ **12.** $(0, -5)$ **13.** $(-2, 3)$
14. no solution **15.** 1 serving of roast beef and 2 servings of mashed potatoes

16. 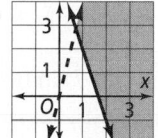 **17.**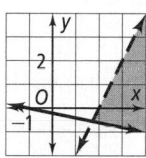

18. 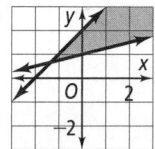 **19.**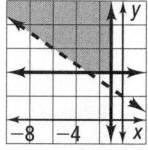

20. Let r = amount of regular coffee and d = amount of decaffeinated coffee
$$\begin{cases} r + d \le 10 \\ r \ge 3d, r \ge 0, d \ge 0 \end{cases}$$

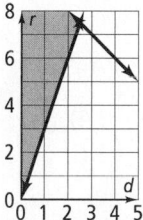

21. vertices: $(4, 0)$ and $(2, 3)$; C has a minimum value of 4 at $(4, 0)$.

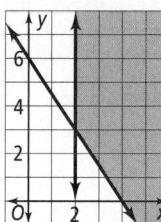

22. 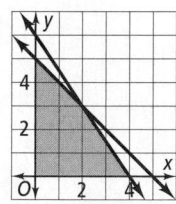 vertices: $(0, 0)$, $(4, 0)$, $(2, 3)$, $(0, 5)$; P has a maximum value of 25 at $(0, 5)$.

23. 50 chef's salads and 50 Caesar salads **24.** $(1, 3, -2)$

25. $(-4, 1, -5)$ **26.** $(6, 0, -2)$ **27.** no solution
28. $\left(\frac{1}{2}, \frac{1}{4}\right)$ **29.** $(1, -1)$ **30.** $(2, -4, 6)$ **31.** $(5, 2, -3)$

Chapter 4

Get Ready! p. 201

1. 6 **2.** 4 **3.** $-2 < x < 6$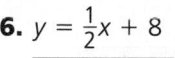
4. $y \le -\frac{5}{4}$ or $y \ge \frac{9}{4}$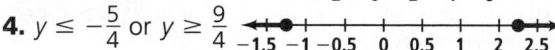
5. $y = 9x - 10$ **6.** $y = \frac{1}{2}x + 8$

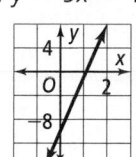 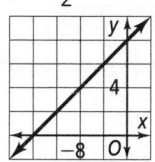

7. translated 4 units to the rt. and 2 units up
8. translated 10 units to the left and 3 units down
9. $(10, -1)$ **10.** $(-6, -6)$ **11.** Answers may vary.
Sample: application forms, registration forms, tests
12. Answers may vary. Sample: monsters, ghosts, tooth fairy **13.** writing

Lesson 4-1 pp. 204–211

Got It?

1a.   **b.** 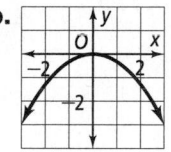 **c.**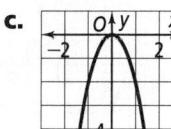

d. If a is a neg. no., the parabola will open downward. There will be a maximum value for y at the vertex of the parabola.
2a. translated 3 units up

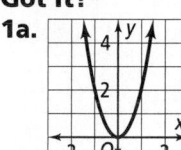

b. translated 1 unit to the left

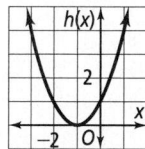

3. vertex: $(-1, 4)$; axis of sym.: $x = -1$; maximum: 4; domain: all real numbers, range: $y \le 4$ **4.** stretch by the factor 2, translate 2 units to the left and 5 units down **5.** $f(x) = -\frac{2}{9}(x - 2)^2 + 7$

Lesson Check

1.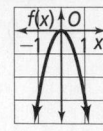

2. minimum **3.** $y = -2(x - 0)^2 + 35$ **4.** when $a > 0$
5. No; a must be > 0 or < 0. **6.** Each graph is a translation of $y = x^2$; $y = (x + 6)^2$ is the graph of $y = x^2$ translated 6 units to the left and has a minimum at $(-6, 0)$; $y = (x - 6)^2$ is the graph of $y = x^2$ translated 6 units to the rt., with a minimum at $(6, 0)$.

Exercises

7.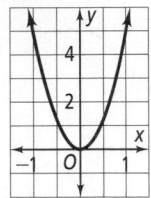

9.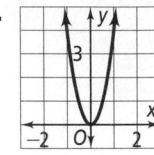

11. translated 3 units up **13.** translated 6 units down

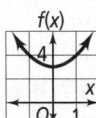

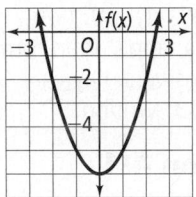

15. translated 9 units down

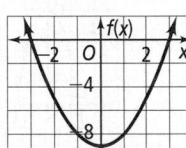

17. vertex: $(-20, 0)$; axis of sym.: $x = -20$; maximum: 0; domain: all real numbers, range: $y \le 0$
19. vertex: $(-5.5, 0)$; axis of sym.: $x = -5.5$; minimum: 0; domain: all real numbers, range: $y \ge 0$
21. $x = 2$ **23.** $x = 7$

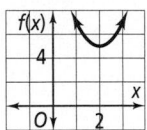

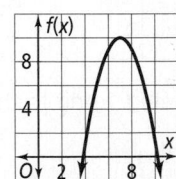

25. $y = 2(x + 1)^2 - 3$ **27.** 25 m² **29.** stretch vertically by a factor of 2, reflect across the x-axis, and translate 1 unit to the rt.

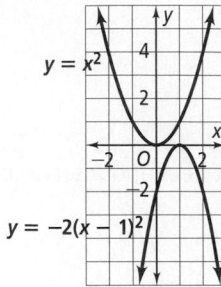

31. stretch vertically by a factor of 3, translate 2 units to the rt. and 3 units up

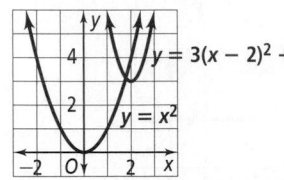

33. compress vertically by a factor of $\frac{1}{4}$, reflect across the x-axis, and translate 3 units up

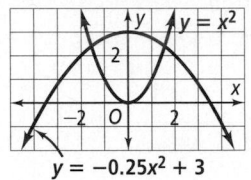

35. parabola $y = a(x - 3)^2 + 4$ with vertex $(3, 4)$ and $a > 0$ or $a < 0$ **37.** $y = -7(x - 1)^2 + 2$
39. $y = -7x^2 + 5$ **41.** $y = 18x - x^2$ or $y = -(x - 9)^2 + 81$.

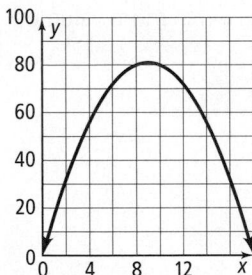

46. $(3, 2)$ **47.** $(-10, 6)$ **48.** $(1, 0, 3)$
49. 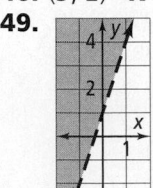   **50.**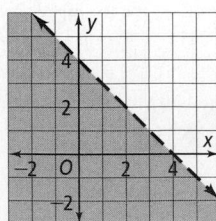

51.

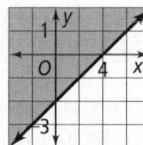

52. yes **53.** no **54.** no **55.** (0, 0) **56.** (−1, 0)
57. (5, 0)

Lesson 4-2 Part 1   pp. 212–215

Got It? 1. vertex: $\left(-\frac{2}{3}, 7\frac{1}{3}\right)$; axis of symmetry: $x = -\frac{2}{3}$;
maximum: $7\frac{1}{3}$; range: $y \le 7\frac{1}{3}$

2.

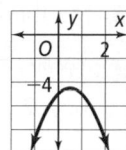

Lesson Check 1. vertex: (0, −4); axis of sym.: $x = 0$;
minimum: −4

2.

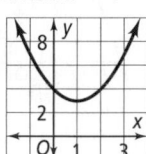

3.

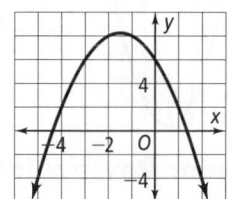

4. Error in calculation of x. The correct calculation is:

$x = \frac{-(-4)}{2(2)} = 1$

$y = 2(1) - 4(1) - 3$
$ = 2 - 4 - 3$
$ = -5$

Vertex: (1, −5)

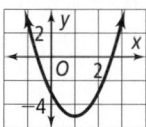

Exercises 5. vertex: (−2, −3); axis of sym.: $x = -2$;
minimum: 3; range: $y \ge -3$ **7.** vertex: (1, 2); axis of
sym.: $x = 1$; maximum: 2; range: $y \le 2$

9. vertex: $\left(-\frac{3}{4}, 5\frac{1}{8}\right)$; axis of sym.: $x = -\frac{3}{4}$; maximum: $5\frac{1}{8}$;

range: $y \le 5\frac{1}{8}$ **11.** vertex: (0, 5); axis of sym.: $x = 0$;
minimum: 5; range: $y \ge 5$

13.

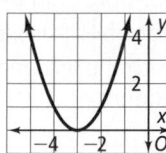

15.

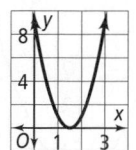

17.

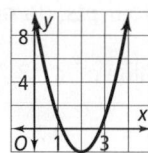

19.

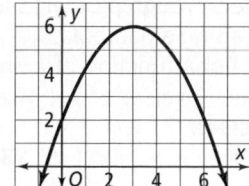

21.

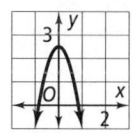

23. $y = \left(-\frac{1}{10}\right)x^2 + 10$

Lesson 4-2 Part 2   pp. 216–219

Got It? 3. $y = -(x - 2)^2 - 1$ **4a.** about 3.84 feet
b. because the y-intercept is (0, 0)
Lesson Check 1. $y = (x - 1)^2 + 8$

2. $y = -\left(x - \frac{3}{2}\right)^2 + \frac{5}{4}$ **3.** The vertex of a function
written in vertex form can easily be determined. It is
(h, k) where $f(x) = a(x - h)^2 + k$. The vertex of a
function in standard form is $\left(\frac{-b}{2a}, f\left(\frac{-b}{2a}\right)\right)$ where
$f(x) = ax^2 + bx + c$.
Exercises 5. $y = (x + 1)^2 + 4$

7. $y = 2\left(x - \frac{5}{4}\right)^2 + \frac{71}{8}$ **9.** \$100; \$25,000 **11.** $b = -6$;
$c = 5$ **13.** $a = 1$; $c = -2$ **15.** 2 s; 64 ft **19.** (0, −16)

24. $\frac{1}{4}$ **25.** −2.5 **26.** (7, −1); elimination **27.** Explanations
may vary. Sample: Substitution because the first equation
is already solved for y; (27, 15) **28.** (3, 2); elimination
29. vertex: (1, 3); axis of sym.: $x = 1$; maximum at
(1, 3); domain: all real numbers, range: $y \le 3$ **30.** vertex:
(−4, 0); axis of sym.: $x = -4$; minimum at (−4, 0);
domain: all real numbers, range: $y \ge 0$ **31.** vertex: (4, 6);
axis of sym.: $x = 4$; maximum at (4, 6); domain: all real
numbers, range: $y \le 6$

Lesson 4-3   pp. 220–225

Got It? 1. $y = -3x^2 + x$ **2a.** No; the ball will only
reach a height of 5 when $x = 5$, which is lower than the
top of the wall at (5, 6). The ball will hit the wall on its
way down. **b.** domain: $0 \le x \le 7$, range: $0 \le y \le 6\frac{1}{8}$
3. $y = -0.329x^2 + 9.798x + 15.571$; 88.5°F at 2:53 P.M.
(although the meteorologist's prediction is 89° at 3 P.M.)
Lesson Check 1. $y = -2x^2 + 3x - 1$
2. $y = 2x^2 + 6x + 7.5$ **3.** $y = -2x^2 + 10x - 13.5$
4. Answers may vary. Sample: A rough plot of the data
will indicate whether the data are collinear (linear
regression) or non-collinear where the data follow a
curve (quadratic regression). **5.** Answers may vary.

Sample: A rough plot will show that the four pts. do **not** lie on a single parabola.
6. y is not a function of x since for one value of x, "3," there are 2 values of y, "4" and "0."
Exercises 7. $y = -x^2 + 3x - 4$ **9.** $y = x^2 + 2x - 2$
11. $y = -x^2 - 4x + 5$ **13a.** $y = -16x^2 + 33x + 46$, where x is the number of seconds after release and y is the height in ft **b.** 28.5 ft **c.** about 63 ft **15.** yes; $y = -2x^2 + 3x + 5$ **17.** yes; $y = 0.625x^2 - 1.75x + 1$
19. B **21.** Answers may vary. Sample: $y = -\frac{1}{25}x^2$, $y = \frac{1}{25}x^2 - \frac{2}{5}x$, $y = \frac{1}{5}x^2 - \frac{6}{5}x$

27. 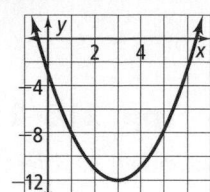 **28.**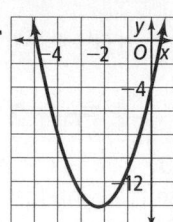

29.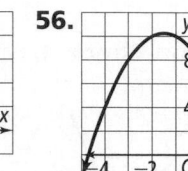

30. (2, 5) **31.** (5, 8) **32.** (−1, −1) **33.** $\frac{4}{5}$ **34.** $-\frac{7}{2}$
35. $x^2 + 5x - 1$ **36.** $6x^2 - 10x - 3$ **37.** $4x^2 - x - 10$

Lesson 4-4 Part 1   pp. 227–230

Got It? 1a. $(x + 10)(x + 4)$ **b.** $(x - 5)(x - 6)$
c. $-(x + 2)(x - 16)$ **2a.** $7(n^2 - 3)$ **b.** $9(x + 2)(x - 1)$
c. $4(x^2 + 2x + 3)$
Lesson Check 1. $(x + 4)(x + 2)$ **2.** $(x - 12)(x - 1)$
3. $5x$ **4.** $4a^2$ **5.** 6 **6.** $7h$ **7.** x is also a factor common to both terms. $27x^2 + 21x = 3x(9x + 7)$, so the GCF is $3x$.
8. 61, 32, 23, 19, 17, 16
Exercises 9. $(x + 2)(x + 3)$ **11.** $(x + 2)(x + 5)$
13. $(y + 3)(y + 12)$ **15.** $(x - 1)(x - 2)$
17. $(x - 4)(x - 6)$ **19.** 3; $3(a^2 + 3)$ **21.** $5b$; $5b(5b - 4)$ **23.** 5; $5(t + 1)(t - 2)$ **25.** 9; $9(3p^2 - p + 2)$ **27.** $(x - 7)(x + 2)$
29. $-(x - 8)(x + 5)$ **31.** $-(t - 11)(t + 4)$
33. b; $b(ab - 1)$ **35.** $3t$; $3t(t - 8)$ **37.** xy; $xy(xy + 1)$
39. To factor $5x^2 + 5x - 60$ completely, first factor the GCF, 5, from the terms to get $5(x^2 + x - 12)$. Then look for numbers whose product is -12 and whose sum is 1. The numbers -3 and 4 work. The complete factorization is $5(x - 3)(x + 4)$; To factor $-5x - 5x + 60$ completely, factor out -5 to get $-5(x^2 + x - 12)$ and proceed as above.

Lesson 4-4 Part 2   pp. 231–236

Got It? 3a. $(x + 1)(4x + 3)$ **b.** $(x - 2)(2x - 3)$
c. No; $2x^2 + 2x + 2 = 2(x^2 + x + 1)$, there are no real factors of a and c whose product is 1 and whose sum is 1.
4. $(8x - 1)^2$ **5.** $(4x - 9)(4x + 9)$

Lesson Check 1. $(x - 9)(x + 9)$ **2.** $(5y - 6)(5y + 6)$
3. $(y - 3)^2$ **4.** $(2x - 1)^2$ **5.** No; the middle term is not twice the product of the square root of the end terms.
6. For $a \neq 1$, look for two factors whose sum is b and whose product is ac. For $a = 1$, look for two factors whose sum is b and whose product is c.
Exercises 7. $(3x + 2)(x + 3)$ **9.** $(x - 8)(2x - 3)$
11. $(m - 3)(2m - 5)$ **13.** $(x - 2)(7x + 6)$
15. $(x + 4)(3x - 4)$ **17.** $(t - 7)^2$ **19.** $(k - 9)^2$
21. $(3x + 8)^2$ **23.** $(c - 8)(c + 8)$ **25.** $(5x - 1)$ cm by $(5x - 1)$ cm **27.** $2(3z + 2)(3z - 2)$ **29.** $2(a - 4)^2$
31. $3(2x + 3)^2$ **33.** $3(x + 1)(x - 9)$
35. $-(x - 1)(x - 4)$ **37.** $(x - y)(x + y)$
39. $-6(z^2 + 100)$ **41.** $(3x - 1)(3x + 1)$ **43.** The third line should be $x(2x - 5) - (2x - 5)$, and the final line should be $(x - 1)(2x - 5)$. **45.** $\pi h(R + r)(R - r)$
52. $y = -0.149x^2 + 5.171x + 16.971$ **53.** penny: 2.5 g, nickel: 5 g, dime: 2.3 g
54. 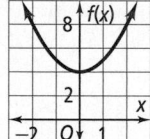 **55.** 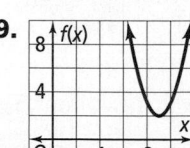 **56.**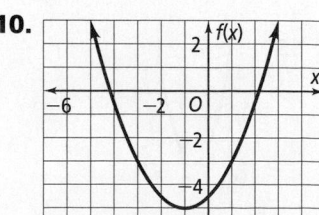

Chapter Review for Part A pp. 237–239

1. standard **2.** axis of symmetry **3.** maximum value
4. vertex: (−2, −6); axis of sym.: $x = -2$; minimum: −6; domain: all real numbers, range: $y \geq -6$ **5.** vertex: (3, 2); axis of sym.: $x = 3$; maximum: 2; domain: all real numbers, range: $y \leq 2$ **6.** vertex: (1, 5); axis of sym.: $x = 1$; minimum: 5; domain: all real numbers, range: $y \geq 5$ **7.** vertex: (−9, −4); axis of sym.: $x = -9$; minimum: −4; domain: all real numbers, range: $y \geq -4$
8. translation 4 units up
9. translation 9 units to the rt. and 2 units up
10. vert. compression by a factor of $\frac{1}{2}$, translation 1 unit to the left and 5 units down

11.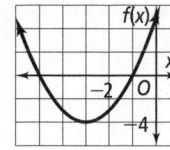

12.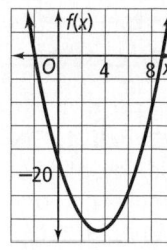

13.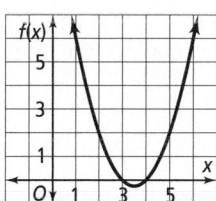

14.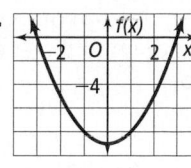

15. $f(x) = 4(x - 1)^2 - 2$ **16.** $f(x) = (x - 4)^2 - 4$
17. $f(x) = 8\left(x + \frac{1}{2}\right)^2 - 14$ **18.** $f(x) = -2\left(x + \frac{3}{2}\right)^2 + \frac{29}{2}$
19. 1 s; 25 ft **20.** $y = x^2 - 6x + 5$
21. $y = -2x^2 + 8x - 8$ **22.** $y = x^2 + 3x - 18$
23. $y = -0.5x^2 + 2.5x - 7$
24. $y = -0.0043x^2 + 0.3521x + 0.3691$
25. $(x - 6)(x - 2)$ **26.** $(3x - 4)(x + 5)$
27. $-2(2x - 1)(x - 3)$ **28.** $(x + 10)(x + 4)$
29. $(x - 7)^2$ **30.** $(3x + 5)^2$ **31.** $4(3x - 2)(3x + 2)$
32. $(5x - 2)(5x + 2)$ **33.** $6x; 6x(x - 4)$
34. $-7; -7(2x^2 + 7)$

Review   p. 242

1. $3\sqrt{2}$ **3.** $-4\sqrt{2}$ **5.** $\frac{-\sqrt{91}}{13}$ **7.** $-10\sqrt{2}$ **9.** 108
11. $|xy|$ **13.** $\frac{-|x|\sqrt{35}}{5}$ **15.** $\frac{5\sqrt{14}}{7}$

Lesson 4-5 Part 1   pp. 243–245

Got It? 1a. 3, 4 **b.** -3, 6 **2.** 3, $\frac{1}{4}$

Lesson Check 1. 3, -3 **2.** -4, -9 **3.** $-\frac{2}{3}$, 1 **4.** -1;
since $y = 0$ when $x = 5$, substitute these values into the
eq. to find b. **5.** One solution: when the table's range
consists of zero and all pos. numbers or zero and all neg.
numbers No solution: when the table does not include
zero and the y-values are either all pos. or all neg.
numbers
Exercises 7. 3, 6 **9.** 5 **11.** 0, 4 **13.** 3, 8 **15.** -1.32, 8.32
17. 1, -0.75 **19.** 0.5, 0.6 **21.** Answers may vary. Samples
are given: **a.** $x^2 - 8x + 15 = 0$ **b.** $x^2 + x - 6 = 0$
c. $x^2 + 7x + 6 = 0$ **23.** (0, -2), (2, 2)

Lesson 4-5 Part 2   pp. 246–250

Got It? 3. -6, 4 **4a.** $53\frac{1}{3}$ m; $21\frac{1}{3}$ m; answers may vary.
Sample: domain: $0 \le x \le 60$, range: $0 \le y \le 30$
b. No; domains and ranges are constrained by real-world
limits.

Lesson Check 1. 4.372, -1.372 **2.** 2.608, -2.108
3. when the coefficients are not integers or no
recognizable factoring pattern is evident
Exercises 5. -0.59, 2.26 **7.** -5.53, 0.36 **9.** -5.16,
1.16 **11a.** about 6.61 s **b.** about 6.89 s **c.** domain:
$0 \le t \le 10.4$, range: $0 \le h \le 1700$ **13.** 3 in.
15. about 3.6 ft **17.** $-\frac{3}{2}$, $-\frac{2}{3}$ **19.** -4, $\frac{5}{2}$ **21.** -1, 4
23. -4, 0 **25.** 4.37, -1.37 **27.** -1, $\frac{10}{3}$ **29.** The
solutions of $x^2 - 10x + 24 = (x - 4)(x - 6) = 0$ are
4 and 6. Average 4 and 6 to get 5. This is the x-coordinate
of the vertex. Substitute 5 in for x in $x^2 - 10x + 24$ to
find that -1 is the y-coordinate of the vertex. So, the
vertex is (5, -1). **34.** $(4x - 1)(4x + 1)$
35. $(5x - 1)(x - 5)$ **36.** $(2x - 1)(x + 7)$ **37.** (2, 0, -2)
38. (-2, 1, 5) **39.** (7, 1, -1) **40.** vertex: (-9, 4); axis
of sym.: $x = -9$; translation 9 units to the left and
4 units up **41.** vertex: $\left(\frac{7}{2}, 0\right)$; axis of sym.: $x = \frac{7}{2}$; stretch
by a factor of 2, translation $3\frac{1}{2}$ units to the rt. **42.** vertex:
(0, -1); axis of sym.: $x = 0$; compression by a factor of $\frac{3}{4}$,
translation 1 unit down **43.** $x^2 + 8x + 13$
44. $4x^2 - 4x + 1$ **45.** $x^2 - 6x + 9$

Lesson 4-6 Part 1   pp. 252–254

Got It? 1a. $\sqrt{5}$, $-\sqrt{5}$ **b.** $\sqrt{2}$, $-\sqrt{2}$
2. 42 in. $\times$ 67.2 in. **3.** 2, 12
Lesson Check 1. 6, -6 **2.** 3, -3 **3.** First, factor the
perfect square trinomial: $(x + 4)^2 = 36$. Then find the
square root of each side of the equation: $x + 4 = \pm 6$.
Rewrite as two equations and solve: $x + 4 = -6$ or
$x + 4 = 6$. The solutions are -10 and 2.
Exercises 5. 2, -2 **7.** $2\sqrt{2}$, $-2\sqrt{2}$ **9.** -4, -2
11. -1, 3 **13.** 1, 11 **15.** $-\frac{10}{3}$, $\frac{2}{3}$ **17.** 20, -20
19. 16, -16 **21.** 10, -10 **23.** 12, -12

Lesson 4-6 Part 2   pp. 255–259

Got It? 4. 9 **5.** $\frac{1}{2} \pm \frac{\sqrt{13}}{2}$
6. $y = \left(x + \frac{3}{2}\right)^2 - \frac{33}{4}$;
vertex: $\left(-\frac{3}{2}, -\frac{33}{4}\right)$;
y-intercept: (0, -6)
Lesson Check 1. 1 **2.** 25 **3.** 4 **4.** 36 **5.** 2500 **6.** 256
7. $x^2 + 12x + 5 = 3$

$x^2 + 12x = -2$	Rewrite to get all terms with x on one side of the eq.
$\left(\frac{12}{2}\right)^2 = 6^2 = 36$	Find $\left(\frac{b}{2}\right)^2 = 36$.
$x^2 + 12x + 36 = -2 + 36$	Add 36 to each side.
$(x + 6)^2 = 34$	Factor the trinomial.

8. Your friend should also have subtracted 49;
$(x^2 - 14x + 49) + 36 - 49 = (x - 7)^2 - 13$

Exercises 9. 81 **11.** 144 **13.** $\frac{9}{4}$ **15.** $-3 \pm 2\sqrt{3}$
17. $-2 \pm \sqrt{2}$ **19.** $5 \pm \sqrt{13}$ **21.** $3 \pm \sqrt{11}$
23. $-\frac{5}{4} \pm \frac{1}{4}\sqrt{37}$ **25.** $y = (x + 2)^2 - 3$
27. $y = -(x + 1)^2 + 4$ **29.** 8 in. **31.** $\frac{-5 \pm \sqrt{37}}{2}$
33. $\frac{2 \pm \sqrt{10}}{3}$ **35.** $\frac{-3 + \sqrt{41}}{8}$ **37.** $\frac{1}{3}, -\frac{2}{3}$
39. $-3 \pm \sqrt{7}$ **44.** $\frac{1}{2}$, 1 **45.** -4, 1 **46.** 8, $-\frac{2}{3}$ **47.** yes;
$y = \frac{1}{2}x^2 + \frac{7}{2}x + 9$ **48.** yes; $y = -\frac{1}{2}x^2 + x + 2$
49. yes; $y = 3x^2 - 5x + 2$ **50.** (2, 0) **51.** (3, 1)
52. (3, 1) **53.** 24 **54.** 84

Lesson 4-7   pp. 260–267

Got It? 1a. -2 **b.** $-2 \pm \sqrt{7}$ **2a.** $10.74 **b.** Yes; a
neg. profit means more money was spent than earned.
3a. no real solutions **b.** two real solutions **4.** Yes;
$b^2 - 4ac = (85)^2 - 4(-16)\left(-109\frac{11}{12}\right) = -190\frac{1}{3}$. The
discriminant is positive. So the eq. has two real solutions.
Lesson Check 1. $\frac{5 \pm \sqrt{53}}{2}$ **2.** $\frac{-3 \pm \sqrt{61}}{2}$ **3.** 3, $-\frac{1}{2}$
4. no real solutions **5.** -32; no real solutions **6.** 273;
two real solutions **7.** 0; one real solution **8.** $k = \pm 6$ for
one real solution; $k > 6$ or $k < -6$ for two real solutions
9. Answers may vary. Sample: The discriminants of eqs.
with one real solution are all zero and thus equal, but
the solutions may or may not be equal. An example is
$x^2 - 8x + 16$ and $x^2 - 4x + 4$. Each has a discriminant
of zero, but the solutions are 4 and 2. **10.** Yes; the eqs.
can share common factors such as for $x^2 + 2x - 8$
where the discriminant is 36 and the solutions are 2 and
-4, and $x^2 - 4x + 4$ where the discriminant is zero and
the solution is 2.
Exercises 11. 1, 3 **13.** $-\frac{7}{2}$, 1 **15.** $\frac{3 \pm \sqrt{5}}{2}$ **17.** 1, 4
19. $.86 **21.** 36; two **23.** -223; no real solutions
25. 0; one **27.** -35; no real solutions **29.** no **31.** 2.29
in. $\times$ 15.71 in. **33.** $-\frac{1}{6}$, 1 **35.** -2.90, 1.90 **37.** 1, 10
39. -3.45, 1.45 **41.** 1.47, -7.47 **43.** two **45.** two
47. two **49.** about 1.89 s **51a.** II **b.** III **c.** I **56.** -2, 10
57. $\frac{2 \pm \sqrt{2}}{2}$ **58.** $\frac{3 \pm \sqrt{41}}{2}$ **59.** $9z^2 + 3z$ **60.** $4x + k$
61. $2y - 8x$ **62.** $2\sqrt{17}$ **63.** 5 **64.** 13

Lesson 4-8 Part 1   pp. 268–273

Got It? 1a. $2i\sqrt{3}$ **b.** $5i$ **c.** $i\sqrt{7}$ **d.** $8i \neq -8$
2a. 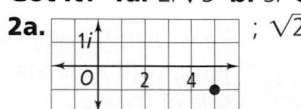 ; $\sqrt{26}$ **b.** 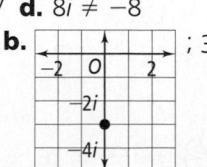 ; 3

c. 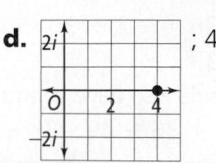 ; $\sqrt{17}$ **d.** 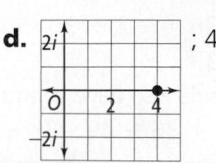 ; 4

3a. $4 - i$ **b.** $-2 + 7i$ **c.** $12i$ **d.** $18i$ **4a.** -21
b. $23 - 2i$ **c.** 41 **5a.** $\frac{7}{25} - \frac{26}{25}i$ **b.** $-\frac{1}{6} - \frac{2}{3}i$
c. $\frac{15}{113} - \frac{112}{113}i$
Lesson Check 1. $5i\sqrt{3}$ **2.** 5 **3.** $7 - 3i$ **4.** $13 - 6i$
5. The add. inv. of a complex no., $a + bi$, is the opposite
of the complex no., or $-a - bi$. The complex conjugate of
a complex no., $a + bi$, is the real part plus the opposite of
the imaginary part of the complex no., or $a - bi$.
6. error in the sign of the last term of the first line, which
carries through to the end of the calculation; the line
should be: "$\ldots = 16 + 28i - 28i - 49i^2$
                        $= 16 + 49$
                        $= 65.$"
Exercises 7. $2i$ **9.** $i\sqrt{15}$
11. 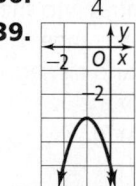 ; 2 **13.** 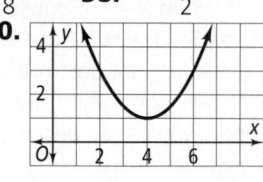 ; $2\sqrt{2}$

15. $6 + 3i$ **17.** $10 + 6i$ **19.** $9 + 58i$ **21.** $65 + 72i$
23. $\frac{8}{17} + \frac{19}{17}i$ **25.** $\frac{8}{13} + \frac{12}{13}i$ **27.** $-1 + 5i$ **29.** $8 - 2i$
31. $10 + 11i$

Lesson 4-8 Part 2   pp. 274–277

Got It? 6a. $\pm 2i$ **b.** $\pm i\sqrt{15}$ **7a.** $\frac{1 \pm i\sqrt{23}}{6}$ **b.** $2 \pm i$
Lesson Check 1. $\pm 4i$ **2.** $\pm i\sqrt{7}$ **3.** $\pm 6i$ **4.** The graph
does not intersect the x-axis, which means that there are
no real solutions to the related equation. The complex
solutions are $3 \pm i$.
Exercises 5. $\pm 5i$ **7.** $\pm 8i\frac{\sqrt{3}}{3}$ **9.** $-1 \pm i\sqrt{2}$
11. $1 \pm i\frac{\sqrt{10}}{2}$ **13.** $2 \pm i$ **15.** $-\frac{5}{2} \pm \frac{\sqrt{15}}{2}i$ **17.** -5, 5
19. trapezoid **21.** $\frac{1}{26} + \frac{3}{52}i$ **23.** $x = -7$, $y = 3$
25. $x = -7$, $y = -3$ **27.** sum: $-\frac{2}{5}$, product: $\frac{1}{5}$
29. Answers may vary. Sample: $x^2 + 36 = 0$
31. Answers may vary. Sample: $x^2 - 8x + 25 = 0$
36. $\frac{-3 \pm \sqrt{41}}{4}$ **37.** $\frac{-1 \pm \sqrt{17}}{8}$ **38.** $\frac{-7 \pm \sqrt{17}}{2}$
39. 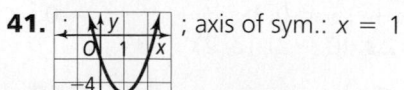 **40.**

    axis of sym.: $x = -1$ axis of sym.: $x = 4$
41. ; ; axis of sym.: $x = 1$

42. $y = 3x - 4$ **43.** $y = -0.5x - 2$
44. $y = -7x + 10$ **45.** $y = 2x + 8$
46. $11q$ **47.** $ab^2 + 2a^2b$ **48.** $-y^2 + 2y$

Chapter Review for Part B pp. 282–284

1. Formula **2.** discriminant **3.** complex **4.** −2, 6
5. −2, $\frac{7}{2}$ **6.** −4, 2 **7.** −9, 2
8. 1, −2.6;

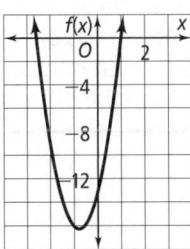

9. 1.345, −3.345;

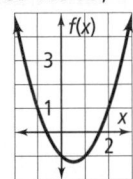

10. 1.618, −0.618; **11.** 3.236, −1.236;

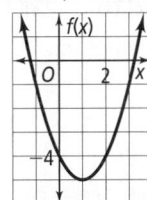

12. 2, 4 **13.** no real solution **14.** 4.56, 0.44 **15.** 2, 4
16. ±2 **17.** ±$\sqrt{5}$ **18.** ±3 **19.** ±2$\sqrt{3}$ **20.** 9 **21.** $\frac{9}{4}$
22. −4 ± $\sqrt{10}$ **23.** 5 ± $\sqrt{38}$ **24.** −1, $\frac{1}{3}$ **25.** 1 ± $i\sqrt{3}$
26. $\frac{-3 \pm i\sqrt{91}}{2}$ **27.** 1, −$\frac{3}{4}$ **28.** 1, −$\frac{8}{3}$ **29.** 3 **30.** 4, −1
31. 1.744, −0.344 **32.** 164; two **33.** −3; none
34. 0; one **35.** 233; two **36.** 10.27 ft × 16.55 ft
37. 2$i\sqrt{6}$ **38.** −3 + $i\sqrt{2}$ **39.** −50 + 40i
40. 6 + 4$i\sqrt{6}$ **41.** 3 + 9i **42.** 13 + 20i **43.** 21 − 25i
44. −12 − 15i **45.** −3 − 2i **46.** −$\frac{1}{2}$ − $\frac{1}{2}i$ **47.** ±3i

48. $\frac{1}{5}$ ± $\frac{2}{5}i$ **49.** 2 ± $i\sqrt{6}$ **50.** $\frac{-4 \pm i\sqrt{26}}{7}$

Chapter 5

Get Ready!   p. 289

1.

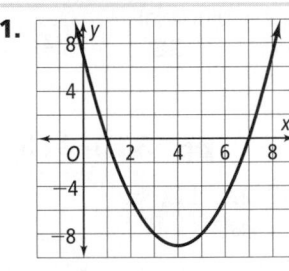

2.

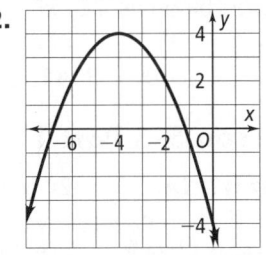

3.

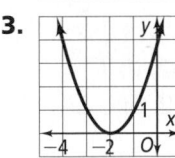

4. $y = x^2 + 3x − 4$ **5.** $y = x^2 − 2x + 1$
6. $y = −x^2 − x + 12$ **7.** 0.25, −1 **8.** −6.39, 4.39
9. −6.38, 0.38 **10.** −4, 5 **11.** −9, 3 **12.** 1, 2 **13.** 24;
two real solutions **14.** 0; one real solution **15.** 0; one real
solution **16.** south **17.** The highest pt. in Maine may be
lower than the highest pt. in the United States. The
relative maximum of a graph for a given region is the
maximum for that region only, whereas the maximum of
the graph may be greater than or equal to the relative
maximum for the region. **18.** $4x^2 + 4x + 1$

Lesson 5-1   pp. 292–299

Got It? 1a. $5x^4 + 3x^3 − x$; quartic trinomial
b. $−4x^5 + 2x^2 + 13$; quintic trinomial **2.** up and down
3a. end behavior: up and down;
two turning pts.

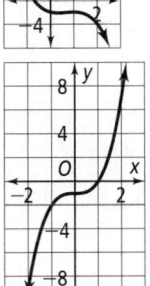

b. end behavior: down and up;
no turning pts.

4a. degree: 4 **b.** Answers may vary. Sample: $y = x^5$
Lesson Check 1. cubic monomial **2.** quadratic
trinomial **3.** $5x^2 + 7x + 3$ **4.** $9x − 3$ **5.** up and down
6. Yes; the graph of a linear binomial or linear monomial
is a straight line. Sample: $y = 2x + 1$. **7.** The graph of
$y = 4x^3 + 4$ has no turning pts., *not* one turning point.
Exercises 9. $10x + 5$; linear binomial **11.** $x^4 − x^3 + x$;
quartic trinomial **13.** $3a^3 + 5a^2 + 1$; cubic trinomial
15. $12x^4 + 3$; quartic binomial **17.** $5x^2 + 4x + 8$;
quadratic trinomial **19.** up and up **21.** down and up
23. up and up **25.** end behavior: up and down; two
turning pts. **27.** end behavior: down and up; no turning pts.
29. 3 **31.** $−4a^4 + a^3 + a^2$; quartic trinomial
33. $2a^3 − 5a^2 − 2a + 5$; cubic polynomial of 4 terms
35a. $\pi r^2 h$ **b.** $\frac{2}{3}\pi r^3$ **c.** $\pi r^2\left(h + \frac{2}{3}r\right)$, or $\frac{2}{3}\pi r^3 + \pi r^2 h$
37. neg.; 3 **39.** pos.; 4 **45.** $−4 + 3i$ **46.** $7 + 7i$
47. $3 + 3i$ **48.** $35x − 5y = −2$ **49.** $6x + 2y = −5$
50. $2x + 7y = 28$ **51.** $(x + 4)(x + 3)$
52. $(x + 10)(x − 2)$ **53.** $(x − 12)(x − 2)$

Lesson 5-2 Part 1   pp. 300–303

Got It? 1. $x(x - 4)(x + 3)$
2. 0, 3, −5;

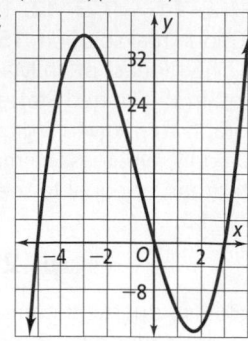

3. a. $f(x) = x^2 - 9$ **b.** $P(x) = x^3 - 3x^2 - 9x + 27$
c.

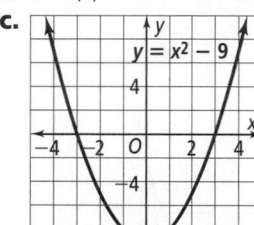 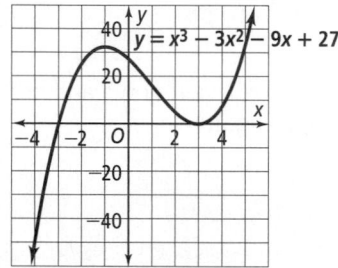

Both graphs have x-intercepts of 3 and −3. The quadratic has up and up end behavior and one turning pt., and the cubic has down and up end behavior and two turning pts.

Lesson Check 1. 0, 6 **2.** −4, 5 **3.** −12, 7, 9
4. $f(x) = x^3 - x$ **5.** Error in writing the factors: a function that has zeros at 3 and −1 has factors of $x - 3$ and $x + 1$, *not* $x + 3$ and $x - 1$, so $f(x) = x^2 - 2x - 3$, *not* $x^2 + 2x - 3$.

Exercises 7. $x(x - 3)(x + 2)$ **9.** $x(x - 7)(x + 3)$
11. $x(x + 4)^2$
13. 1, −2;   **15.** 0, −5, 8;

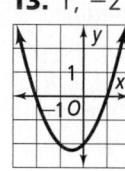   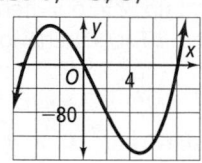

17. −1, 1, 2;

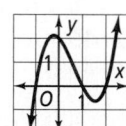

19. $y = x^3 + x^2 - 2x$ **21.** $y = x^3 + 9x^2 + 15x - 25$
23. $y = x^3 + 2x^2 - x - 2$ **25.** $y = x^4 - 5x^3 + 6x^2$
27. $y = -2x(x + 5)(x - 4)$ **29.** B

Lesson 5-2 Part 2   pp. 304–309

Got It? 4. 0 is a zero of multiplicity 1, and the graph looks close to linear at $x = 0$; 2 is a zero of multiplicity 2,

and the graph looks close to quadratic at $x = 2$.
5. relative maximum: (−0.86, 3.13), relative minimum: (0.64, −2) **6.** 2.28 in.³
Lesson Check 1. 2 **2.** 1 **3.** 3 **4.** relative maximum (−2.737, 48.517), relative minimum (2.070, −7.035)
5. $h(x) = x^4 + 4x^3 - 26x^2 - 60x + 225$ **6.** No; Explanations may vary. Sample: A cubic function has either 0 or 2 turning points. Of the two possible turning points, one must be an up-to-down turning point and the other a down-to-up turning point. Relative maximums occur only at up-to-down turning points.
Exercises 7. 0, 1 (multiplicity 3) **9.** −1, 0, 1 **11.** 1, 2 (multiplicity 2) **13.** −1 (multiplicity 2), 1, 2 **15.** relative maximum: (2.15, 12.32), relative minimum: (−0.15, −12.32) **17a.** $\ell = 16 - 2x$; $w = 12 - 2x$; $h = x$ **b.** $V = x(16 - 2x)(12 - 2x)$
c.   194 in.³, 2.26 in.

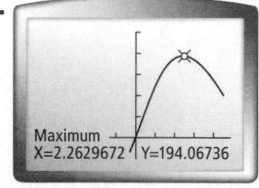

19a. $V_B = (2x + 1)(x + 3)(x + 4)$
$\quad\ V_W = (2x + 1)(x + 1)(x + 2)$
b. $V = 8x^2 + 24x + 10$
21a. $x(x + 3)(2 - x)$; $h = x + 3$; $w = x$
b.   0, −3, 2; where the volume is zero

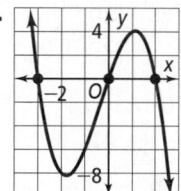

c. $0 < x < 2$ **d.** about 4.06 ft³ **23.** relative maximum: (−0.05, −2.98), relative minimum: (0.88,−6.17); 1.5
25. Answers may vary. Sample: $y = x^4 - x^2$ **27.** −1, 4, $\frac{3}{2}$
33. $-3x^5 + 3x^2 - 1$; quintic trinomial **34.** $-7x^4 - x^3$; quartic binomial **35.** $x^3 - 2$; cubic binomial
36. $(x + 4)(x + 1)$ **37.** $(x - 5)(x + 3)$ **38.** $(x - 6)^2$
39. −3, 2 **40.** $\frac{1}{2}$, 3 **41.** $\pm\frac{5}{2}$

Lesson 5-3 Part 1   pp. 310–313

Got It? 1a. ± 1, $\pm 2i$ **b.** 0, 2, 3 **2a.** ± 2, $\pm 2i$
b. −2, 0, 4 **c.** $\sqrt{5}$, $-\sqrt{5}$, $i\sqrt{2}$, $-i\sqrt{2}$
Lesson Check 1. $(x - 6)(x + 3)$
2. $(x - 3)(x^2 + 3x + 9)$ **3.** $(x^2 + 4)(x + 3)$
4. $(x - 2)(x + 2)(x^2 + 2)$ **5.** −4, $\frac{1}{2}$ **6.** −2, 0, 1
7a. diff. of squares **b.** sum of cubes **c.** diff. of cubes
d. diff. of squares

8. Method 1: Graph $y = x^6 - x^2$. Find the zeros for the real solutions.

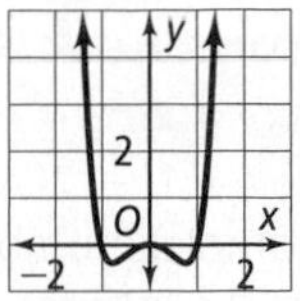

Method 2: Factor and solve $x^6 - x^2 = 0$ for x.

$$x^2(x^4 - 1) = x^2(x^2 - 1)(x^2 + 1)$$
$$= x^2(x - 1)(x + 1)(x^2 + 1)$$
$$x = 0, \pm 1$$

Exercises **9.** $-4, 2 \pm 2i\sqrt{3}$ **11.** $\frac{3}{5}, \frac{-3 \pm 3i\sqrt{3}}{10}$ **13.** $-2, \pm i\sqrt{5}$ **15.** $3, \frac{-3 \pm 3i\sqrt{3}}{2}$ **17.** $\frac{1}{2}, \frac{-1 \pm i\sqrt{3}}{4}$ $\frac{1 \pm i\sqrt{3}}{4}$ **19.** $-4, 0, 2$ **21.** ± 2 **23.** $\pm\sqrt{2}, \pm 3i$ **25.** $-\frac{6}{5}, \frac{3 \pm 3i\sqrt{3}}{5}$ **27.** $\pm 2\sqrt{2}, \pm 2i\sqrt{2}$ **29.** $0, \pm 1, \pm 2$ **31.** C

Lesson 5-3 Part 2 pp. 314–317

Got It? **3.** -1.84 **4.** 7, 8, 9
Lesson Check **1.** 0, 1.536, 8.464 **2.** 0, 1.268, 4.732 **3.** -1.036, 0, 6.036 **4.** Graphing; imaginary numbers don't exist on the x-axis. **5.** 3.13 is the y-value of the intersection point. The solution is the x-value, -1.13.
Exercises **7.** $-1, 0, 3$ **9.** 0, 8 **11.** $0, -3.5, 1$ **13.** $-0.5, 0, 3$ **15.** $-2, 5$
17. 5, 6, 7; $x(x + 1)(x + 2) = 210$;

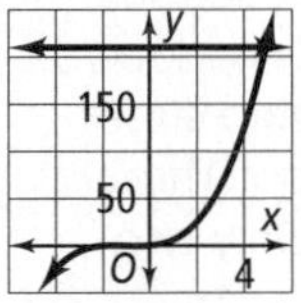

19. $\sqrt{10}, -\sqrt{10}, i\sqrt{10}, -i\sqrt{10}$ **21.** $1, \pm i$ **23.** $-1, 1$
25. 6 ft × 3 ft × 2 ft
27. $-\frac{5}{2}, 1$; $y = (2x + 5)(x - 1)$;

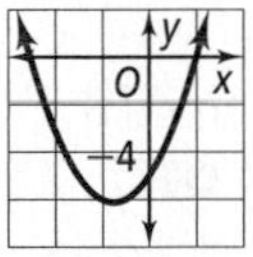

29. $-1, 2$; $y = (x + 1)(x - 2)^2$;

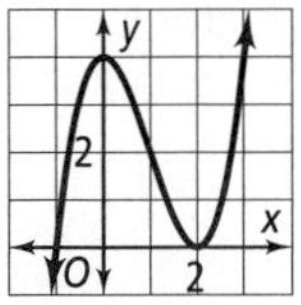

35. $3(x - 4)(x - 2)$ **36.** $2x(x + 3)^2(x - 3)$ **37.** $x^2(x - 5)(x + 1)$ **38.** $-2, 6$ **39.** ± 6 **40.** $-\frac{1}{2}, 3$ **41.** 12 **42.** $-\frac{1}{5}$

Lesson 5-4 Part 1 pp. 318–321

Got It? **1.** $3x - 8$, R 0 **2a.** yes; $P(x) = (x + 5)(x^4 - 1)$ **b.** $(x + 2)(3x + 1)$
Lesson Check **1.** $2x + 3$, R 5 **2.** $9x^2 + 12x + 40$, R120 **3.** $x - a$ is a factor of $P(x)$ by the Factor Theorem.
Exercises **5.** $3x - 5$ **7.** $2x^2 + 5x + 2$ **9.** $9x - 12$, R -32 **11.** no **13.** yes **15.** $5x^3 - 22x^2 - 3x - 53$ **17.** $x + 4$ **19.** no **21.** yes

Lesson 5-4 Part 2 pp. 322–326

Got It? **3.** $x^2 + 7x - 8$, R 0 **4.** width: $(x + 1)$ in.; height: $(x + 2)$ in.; length: $(x + 3)$ in. **5.** 0
Lesson Check **1.** $x^2 + 2x + 5$ **2.** $x^2 + x - 2$ **3.** $4x^2 + x - 6$, R 6 **4.** The polynomials need to be written in standard form since the leading coefficient of both polynomials determines the leading term of the quotient.
Exercises **7.** $x^2 - 2x + 2$ **9.** $x^2 + 2x + 5$ **11.** $3x^2 + 8x - 3$ **13.** $y = (x + 1)(x + 3)(x - 2)$ **15.** length $= x + 3$; height $= x - 2$ **17.** 0 **19.** 168 **21.** yes **23.** no **25.** $x^3 - x^2 + 1$ **27.** $x^3 - 3x^2 + 12x - 35$, R 109 **29.** There are two errors. The constant term of the dividend is missing and the divisor is -1 *not* 1: $x^3 - x^2 - 2x = (x + 1)(x^2 - 2x) = x(x + 1)(x - 2)$. **35.** $0, -1$ **36.** 0, 1 **37.** $-5, 0, 5$ **38.** $\frac{-3 \pm \sqrt{17}}{2}$ **39.** $-1 \pm \sqrt{3}$ **40.** $1, -\frac{5}{7}$ **41.** $\frac{5 \pm \sqrt{5}}{2}$ **42.** $3 \pm \sqrt{2}$ **43.** $\frac{-7 \pm \sqrt{5}}{2}$

44.

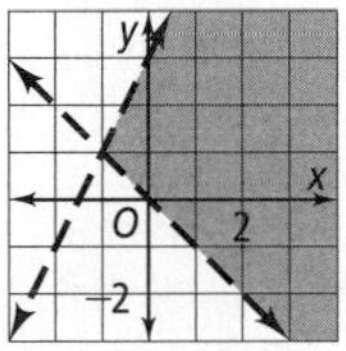

45.

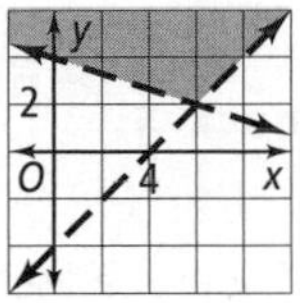

46.

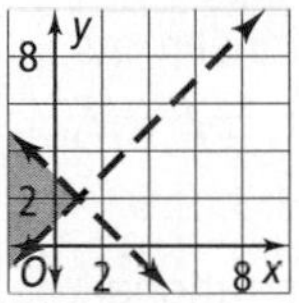

47. 24 **48.** 5 **49.** $23 - 11i$

Chapter Review for Part A pp. 327–329

1. relative minimum **2.** degree **3.** standard form of a polynomial function **4.** synthetic division **5.** multiplicity **6.** $y = -x^4 + 12$; quartic binomial; down and down **7.** $y = x^2 - x + 7$; quadratic trinomial; up and up **8.** $y = -x^4 + 2x^3 + 3x^2 - 6x + 12$; quartic polynomial of five terms; down and down **9.** $y = x^3 + 2x^2 - 4x + 8$; cubic polynomial of four terms; down and up **10.** $y = x^4 - 3x^3 + 3x^2 + 10$; quartic polynomial of four terms; up and up **11.** 3 **12.** If n is even, there are an odd no. of turning pts.; if n is odd, there are an even no. of turning pts. **13.** $f(x) = x^3 - 4x^2 - 11x - 6$ **14.** $f(x) = x^3 - x^2 - 2x$ **15.** $f(x) = x^3 - 6x^2 + 11x - 6$

16. $f(x) = x^3 - 3x^2 - 6x + 8$ **17.** 0, −2 (multiplicity 3)
18. 2 (multiplicity 2), −2 (multiplicity 2) **19.** 0, $-\frac{1}{2}$, 1
20. 5, −2 (multiplicity 2) **21.** relative maximum:
(0.8672, −1.9351), relative minimums: (0, −3),
(2.8828, −12.1704); zeros: $x \approx -0.5992$, $x \approx 3.7115$
22. relative maximum: (−0.8441, 9.3023), relative
minimum: (0.7108, −0.0964); zeros: $x = -1.6180$,
$x \approx 0.6180$, $x \approx 0.8$ **23.** relative minimum: (1, −4);
zeros: $x \approx -0.2490$, $x \approx 1.6633$ **24.** relative
maximum: (−0.4142, −3.3431), relative minimum:
(2.4142, −14.6569); zero: $x = 4$ **25.** 3, 8 **26.** $-\frac{1}{2}$
27. 0, $\frac{-1 \pm \sqrt{37}}{2}$ **28.** $\frac{2 \pm i\sqrt{2}}{2}$
29. no real roots; **30.** 2.3949;

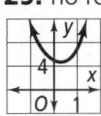 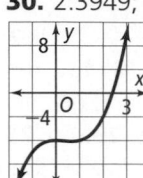

31. 4.87 in. × 2.87 in. × 2.87 in. **32.** $x^2 + 6x + 9$
33. $2x^2 + x - 3$, R 1 **34.** yes **35.** no **36.** $x^2 - 1$
37. $2x^2 - 6x + 2$, R −20 **38.** $5x^2 + 18x + 36$, R 12
39. −14 **40.** 2

Lesson 5-5 Part 1   pp. 332–334

Got It? 1. $\frac{2}{3}$ **2.** 2, −1, $-\frac{3}{2}$
Lesson Check 1. ±1, ±2 **2.** ±1, ±2, ±3, ±6, $\pm\frac{1}{2}$,
$\pm\frac{3}{2}$ **3.** ±1, ±2, ±3, ±4, ±6, ±12, $\pm\frac{1}{3}$, $\pm\frac{2}{3}$, $\pm\frac{4}{3}$
4a. never; 5 is not a factor of 8. **b.** always; −2 is a
factor of 8.
Exercises 5. ±1, ±2, ±4, $\pm\frac{1}{2}$; no rational roots
7. ±1, ±3, ±9; no rational roots **9.** ±1, ±2, ±3, ±6,
$\pm\frac{1}{3}$, $\pm\frac{2}{3}$; no rational roots **11.** ±1, ±2, ±3, ±6,
±9, ±18, $\pm\frac{1}{6}$, $\pm\frac{1}{3}$, $\pm\frac{1}{2}$, $\pm\frac{3}{2}$, $\pm\frac{2}{3}$, $\pm\frac{9}{2}$; no rational roots
13. ±1, $\pm\frac{1}{8}$, $\pm\frac{1}{4}$, $\pm\frac{1}{2}$; −1, $\frac{1}{4}$, $\frac{1}{2}$ **15.** no rational roots
17. no rational roots **19.** no rational roots **21.** The roots
were written as the factors of the leading coefficients over
the factors of the constant term. The possible roots should
list the factors of the constant term over the factors of the
leading coefficient.

Lesson 5-5 Part 2   pp. 335–339

Got It? 3. 3 + 2i **4.** $P(x) = x^4 - 14x^3 + 69x^2 - 194x + 208$ **5a.** There are three or one pos. real roots
and one neg. real root. The graph confirms one neg. and
one pos. real root. **b.** Real roots can be confirmed
graphically because they are x-intercepts. Complex roots
cannot be confirmed graphically because they have an
imaginary component.

Lesson Check 1. $P(x) = x^2 - 14x + 45$
2. $P(x) = x^3 + 4x^2 + 4x + 16$ **3.** Answers may vary.
Samples: 1 + 2i and 1 − 2i; 1 + $\sqrt{2}$ and 1 − $\sqrt{2}$
4. Complex number roots come in pairs if the equation
has real coefficients; if −4i is a root, so is 4i.
Exercises 5. 2i, −$\sqrt{10}$ **7.** −i, 7 − 8i
9. $P(x) = x^2 + 100$ **11.** $P(x) = x^2 + 24x + 135$
13. $P(x) = x^4 - 22x^3 + 466x^2 - 7368x + 23{,}168$
15. $P(x) = x^4 - 38x^3 + 710x^2 - 7126x + 29{,}125$
17. two or no pos. real roots; one neg. real root
19. ≈5.67 cm **21.** $P(x) = x^4 - 8x^3 + 75x^2 - 512x + 704$ **23.** Error in second line, sign of second
term; the line should be: $P(-x) = -x^3 + x^2 - x + 1$.
Since there are three sign changes in $P(-x)$, there are
three or one neg. real roots. **25.** height: 5 ft; bases: 10 ft,
14 ft **32.** $x^2 + 6x + 6$, R 3 **33.** $7x - 3$, R 2
34. $8x^2 - 36x + 216$, R −1289 **35.** ±3i **36.** ±9i
37. ±12i **38.** $-5x^4 + 6x^2 + 9x + 11$; quartic
polynomial of four terms **39.** $-4x^5 + 7x^3 + 13x + 2$;
quintic polynomial of four terms

Lesson 5-6   pp. 340–345

Got It? 1. 0, 1, −5, 2 **2a.** −1, 2, $\frac{1 \pm i\sqrt{23}}{4}$
b. i. A 5th degree polynomial function has four, two, or
zero turning pts. Three turning pts. are visible, so there
must be a fourth one. This will turn the graph back across
the x-axis. **ii.** The Fundamental Thm. of Algebra states
there will be five roots, and the Conjugate Root Thm.
requires pairs of irrational or complex roots. Only two
zeros appear in the graph, so there are three zeros
remaining. Of the remaining roots, either there are
three real roots, or one real and two complex roots.
Either way, there is at least one real root that does not
appear as a real zero in the graph.
Lesson Check 1. four roots **2.** fourteen roots
3. 5, ±4i **4.** 0, 2, ±i **5.** By the Fundamental Thm. of
Algebra, a polynomial equation of degree n has exactly
n complex roots. **6.** Answers may vary. Sample:
$y = x^4 + 8x^2 + 16$ **7.** Use synthetic division to test for
and factor out linear factors until a quadratic factor is
obtained. Then use the Quadratic Formula if the quadratic
factor cannot be factored further.
Exercises 9. −3, −2, 1 **11.** −3, −1, ±2i
13. −1, $\frac{1 \pm i\sqrt{7}}{4}$ **15.** 2, ±$\sqrt{3}$ **17.** ±2, ±i
19. −6, ±i **21.** five complex roots; one, three,
or five real roots; possible rational roots:
±1, ±2, ±3, ±6, ±9, ±18 **23.** six complex roots; zero,
two, four, or six real roots; possible rational roots: $\pm\frac{1}{4}$, $\pm\frac{1}{2}$,
$\pm\frac{3}{4}$, ±1, $\pm\frac{3}{2}$, ±2, ±3, ±4, ±6, ±8, ±12, ±24
25. −2, $-\frac{1}{2}$, 4 **27.** 3, −1 ± $i\sqrt{2}$ **29.** 3 bridges **31.** No;
a 4th degree polynomial has four complex roots. If 5 − i

is a root, then by the Conjugate Root Thm. $5 + i$ must also be a root. Likewise, if $4 + i$ is a root, then $4 - i$ must also be a root. This would result in five roots, which is impossible. **33.** always **35.** Maurice is incorrect. Although every function of degree 1 has exactly one zero, $y = 2$ is a function of degree 0 but is still a linear function. So linear functions with degree zero may have no zero or x-intercept. Therefore, $y = 2$ has no zero or x-intercept. **40.** $x^4 + 6x^3 + 14x^2 + 24x + 40 = 0$

41. $3 \pm 2\sqrt{2}$ **42.** $\frac{-5 \pm i\sqrt{47}}{4}$ **43.** $\frac{3 \pm i\sqrt{23}}{4}$

44. $f(x) = -x^2 + 2x + 3$ **45.** $f(x) = 2x^2 + 24x + 75$
46. $x^3 + 3x^2 + 3x + 1$ **47.** $x^3 - 9x^2 + 27x - 27$
48. $x^3 + 15x^2 + 75x + 125$

Lesson 5-7   pp. 347–352

Got It? 1. $a^8 + 8a^7b + 28a^6b^2 + 56a^5b^3 + 70a^4b^4 + 56a^3b^5 + 28a^2b^6 + 8ab^7 + b^8$ **2a.** $16x^4 - 96x^3 + 216x^2 - 216x + 81$ **b.** If you express 11 as $(10 + 1)$ and calculate the powers of $(10 + 1)$ using Pascal's Triangle, the result is the indicated pattern.
Lesson Check 1. $x^3 + 3x^2a + 3xa^2 + a^3$
2. $x^5 - 10x^4 + 40x^3 - 80x^2 + 80x - 32$
3. $4x^2 + 16x + 16$ **4.** $27a^3 - 54a^2 + 36a - 8$
5a. yes **b.** yes **c.** no **6.** The coefficients for the expansion of $(a + b)^n$ are equal to the numbers in the nth row of Pascal's Triangle, respectively.
Exercises 7. $a^4 + 8a^3 + 24a^2 + 32a + 16$
9. $46,656 + 46,656a + 19,440a^2 + 4320a^3 + 540a^4 + 36a^5 + a^6$ **11.** $y^8 + 8y^7 + 28y^6 + 56y^5 + 70y^4 + 56y^3 + 28y^2 + 8y + 1$ **13.** $128x^7 - 448x^6y + 672x^5y^2 - 560x^4y^3 + 280x^3y^4 - 84x^2y^5 + 14xy^6 - y^7$
15. $4096x^6 + 12,288x^5 + 15,360x^4 + 10,240x^3 + 3840x^2 + 768x + 64$ **17.** $16x^2 + 40x + 25$
19. $81y^4 - 1188y^3 + 6534y^2 - 15,972y + 14,641$
21a. 6 **b.** 489,888 **23.** $135x^4$ **25.** $625b^8$ **27.** The challenge of the Binomial Thm. occurs when there is a coefficient with the x. However, it is much more efficient to use the Binomial Thm. than FOIL when expanding a binomial that is raised to a high power. **29.** $x^{12} + 24x^{10} + 240x^8 + 1280x^6 + 3840x^4 + 6144x^2 + 4096$
31. $a^5 - 5a^4b^2 + 10a^3b^4 - 10a^2b^6 + 5ab^8 - b^{10}$
33. $256x^4 - 1792x^3y + 4704x^2y^2 - 5488xy^3 + 2401y^4$
35. $4096x^{18} + 12,288x^{15}y^2 + 15,360x^{12}y^4 + 10,240x^9y^6 + 3840x^6y^8 + 768x^3y^{10} + 64y^{12}$
37. $125a^3 + 150a^2b + 60ab^2 + 8b^3$ **39.** $-32y^{10} + 80y^8x - 80y^6x^2 + 40y^4x^3 - 10y^2x^4 + x^5$ **41.** Answers may vary. Sample: One of the terms is neg. $(-y)$ and it is alternately raised to odd and even powers; the term is neg. when raised to an odd power and pos. when raised to an even power. **48.** $-3, -1, \frac{-3 \pm i\sqrt{11}}{2}$
49. $1, \pm i, \pm 3i$ **50.** $-4, \frac{-3 \pm i\sqrt{7}}{4}$

51. $1, \frac{-1 \pm 3i\sqrt{3}}{2}$ **52.** $-18 + 43i$ **53.** -2
54. $2x^3 + 5x^2 - x + 9$; cubic polynomial of 4 terms
55. $-7x^2 + 4x + 1$; quadratic trinomial

Lesson 5-8   pp. 353–360

Got It? 1. $y = 1.667x^3 - 4.667x + 5$ **2.** about 22.7 billion lb **3.** Answers may vary. Sample: The cubic model would fit the data better than the linear model because of the $(n + 1)$ Pt. Principle. Both models have down and up end behavior and increasing growth. The cubic shows slowing growth followed by rapidly increasing growth.
4a. $y = 0.269867411x - 3.919692952$

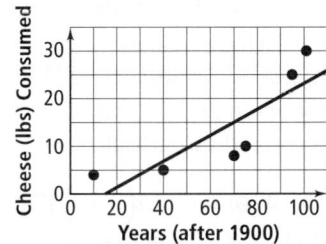

b. 1980: 17.67 lb; 2000: 23.07 lb; 2012: 26.31 lb; most confident for the year 1980, since it is within the domain of the data set; least confident for the year 2012, since it is outside of the domain of the data set
Lesson Check 1. linear **2.** quadratic **3.** cubic
4. quartic **5.** interpolation since the data pt. is within the domain of the data set **6.** yes; $y = -x^3 - 3x^2 - 3x$
7. cubic model; the closer R^2 is to 1, the better the fit.
Exercises 9. $y = -9x + 5$ **11.** $y = x^2 - 6x + 1$
13. (where $x =$ yrs after 1900) linear: $y = 49.238x - 2614.286$, cubic: $y = 0.028x^3 - 6.711x^2 + 578.194x - 16,226.666$; cubic; linear **15.** (where $x =$ yrs after 1900) linear: $y = 5.8x - 379.667$, quadratic: $y = 0.8x^2 - 146.2x + 6827$; quadratic; linear
17. 1990: $1700 billion; 2010: $3141 billion **19.** 1985: $180,000; 1999: $194,000; 2020: $803,000 **21.** cubic: $y = 0.922x^3 - 1.462x^2 + 7.978x + 4.681$; quartic: $y = -\frac{1}{3}x^4 + \frac{5}{3}x^3 + \frac{1}{3}x^2 + \frac{16}{3}x + 3$; quartic, $(R^2 = 1)$
23. $y = 0.000508x^4 - 0.00234x^3 - 0.0349x^2 + 0.293x - 1$ **25.** Sample: 405.7 ppm; not very confident because 2022 is outside the domain of the data
27. $y = -0.0288800705x^3 - 0.469356261x^2 - 7.401675485x + 3.038800705$; $R^2 = 1$; good fit
29. Sample: A quadratic model would be more appropriate, given the real–world context. According to the cubic model, there would be a neg. no. of Americans in the year 2024.
36. $32x^5 + 240x^4 + 720x^3 + 1080x^2 + 810x + 243$ **37.** $1331x^3 - 363x^2 + 33x - 1$
38. $4096 - 6144x + 3456x^2 - 864x^3 + 81x^4$
39. $|x - 8| < 1$ **40.** $|y - 2.8| < 1.1$
41. $|t - 750| < 250$ **42.** $s = \sqrt{A}$ **43.** $\ell = \frac{P}{2} - w$

44. $r = \frac{C}{2\pi}$

45. 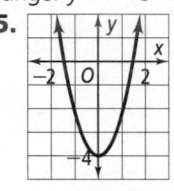 **46.** 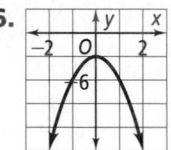 **47.**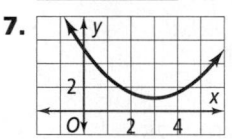

Lesson 5-9   pp. 361–367

Got It? 1. $y = 2(x + 3)^3 - 4$ **2.** $1 - \sqrt[3]{2}$ **3a.** Answers may vary. Sample: $y = x^4 - 6x^3 + x^2 - 6x$ **b.** Yes; $-f(x)$ is the function reflected across the x-axis, so the zeros will stay the same. **4.** 972.2 kW

Lesson Check 1. -2 **2.** 3 **3.** $\frac{1}{3}$ **4.** No; a power function is of the form $y = ax^b$, where y varies directly with the bth power of x. **5.** Both $y = x^3$ and $y = 4x^3$ have the same end behavior of down and up and no turning pts. $y = 4x^3$ is $y = x^3$ stretched vertically by a factor of 4.

Exercises 7. $y = 2(x + 3)^3 + 4$ **9.** $y = -3\left(x + \frac{1}{2}\right)^3 + \frac{3}{4}$ **11.** $\frac{8}{3}$ **13.** $-\frac{2}{15}$ **15.** $1 - \frac{1}{2}\sqrt[3]{20}$ **17.** Answers may vary. Sample: $x^4 - x^3 - x^2 - x - 2$ **19.** Answers may vary. Sample: $x^4 - 2x^3 - 2x^2 - 2x - 3$ **21.** Answers may vary. Sample: $x^4 + x^3 - 5x^2 + x - 6$

23. 17,155.9 ft³ **25.** Yes; using parent function $y = x^3$, stretch vertically by a factor of 3. **27.** no **29.** Yes; using parent function $y = x^4$, translate 2 units to the left. **31.** translation 4 units up and 1 unit to the left **33.** vert. stretch by a factor of 5, translation 1 unit up and 1 unit to the rt. **35.** 40 lb-ft²/s² **37.** Error in (2) "a transformation of $y = x^2$." Some polynomials do not contain an x^2 term. **42.** $y = -2x^3 + 3x^2 - x - 2$ **43.** $y = 3x^3 - 5x - 3$ **44.** $y = -\frac{4}{5}x + \frac{16}{5}$ **45.** $y = -3x + 5$ **46.** yes **47.** no **48.** $x^2(x^8 + 1)$ **49.** $(x - y)(x + y)(x^2 + y^2)$ **50.** $9x^3y^6(9x^3y^6 - 1)$

Chapter Review for Part B pp. 369–372

1. D **2.** B **3.** C **4.** A **5.** $\pm1, \pm2, \pm3, \pm6$ **6.** $\pm1, \pm2, \pm\frac{1}{3}, \pm\frac{2}{3}$ **7.** $\pm1, \pm2, \pm3, \pm4, \pm6, \pm12, \pm\frac{1}{4}, \pm\frac{1}{2}, \pm\frac{3}{4}, \pm\frac{3}{2}$ **8.** $\pm1, \pm7, \pm\frac{1}{3}, \pm\frac{7}{3}$ **9.** -3 **10.** -5

11. $1, -4, -\frac{1}{2}$ **12.** $1, -2, -\frac{2}{3}$ **13.** $1 + i$ **14.** $5 - \sqrt{3}, \sqrt{2}$ **15.** $3i, -7i$ **16.** $-2 - \sqrt{11}, -4 + 6i$
17. $y = x^2 - 17x + 70$ **18.** $y = x^3 + 3x^2 + 25x + 75$ **19.** $y = x^2 - 12x + 37$ **20.** $y = x^4 - 4x^3 - 10x^2 + 68x - 80$ **21.** one pos. real zero; two or no neg. real zeros **22.** two or no pos. real zeros; one neg. real zero **23.** four, two, or no pos. real zeros; no neg. real zeros **24.** two or no pos. real zeros; two or no neg. real zeros **25.** 3 **26.** 5 **27.** 6 **28.** $1, -3 \pm \sqrt{7}$ **29.** $2, \pm\sqrt{5}$
30. $-3, 6, \frac{1 \pm \sqrt{5}}{2}$ **31.** 9 **32.** 1, 8, 28, 56, 70, 56, 28, 8, 1

33. $x^3 + 27x^2 + 243x + 729$ **34.** $b^4 + 8b^3 + 24b^2 + 32b + 16$ **35.** $27a^3 + 27a^2 + 9a + 1$ **36.** $x^3 - 15x^2 + 75x - 125$ **37.** $x^3 - 6x^2y + 12xy^2 - 8y^3$ **38.** $243a^5 + 1620a^4b + 4320a^3b^2 + 5760a^2b^3 + 3840ab^4 + 1024b^5$ **39.** $x^6 + 6x^5 + 15x^4 + 20x^3 + 15x^2 + 6x + 1$ **40.** $64x^6 - 192x^5 + 240x^4 - 160x^3 + 60x^2 - 12x + 1$ **41.** 108 **42.** $6a^2c^2$ **43.** $y = 3.5x^2 - 4.5x + 5$ **44.** $y = 2.082999x - 2.475234$; $y = 0.086232x^2 + 0.008929x + 5.963724$; $y = -0.002554x^3 + 0.178307x^2 - 0.913645x + 8.205128$; cubic is best fit since $R^2 = 1$.
45. $y = -5.8667x^3 + 120.5333x^2 - 629.2667x + 1421$; $1097.3 \approx 1097$ **46.** $y = -(x - 2)^3 + 1$
47. $y = 6(x + 3)^3$ **48.** Answers may vary. Sample: $y = x^4 - 10x^3 + 25x^2 - 10x + 24$ **49.** $y = 0.3x^5 + 3$

Chapter 6

Get Ready!   p. 377

1. domain: {1, 2, 3, 4}, range: {2, 3, 4, 5} **2.** domain: {1, 2, 3, 4}, range: {2} **3.** domain: all real numbers, range: $y \geq -8$ **4.** domain: all real numbers, range: $y \geq 3$
5. **6.**

7.

8. $3y^2 - 14y + 8$ **9.** $49a^2 - 100$ **10.** $x^3 + 4x^2 - 15x - 18$ **11.** $-2, 7$ **12.** $\frac{5}{2}, 3$ **13.** $-4, \frac{2}{3}$ **14.** $\frac{1}{2}$
15. $\pm\frac{7}{2}$ **16.** $\pm\sqrt{7}$ **17.** Yes; it is a better deal to first take 50% off the shirt and then use the $10 coupon. **18.** A "one-to-one function" is a function where there is exact correspondence of every element of the domain with exactly one element of the range. **19.** the nonnegative root

Lesson 6-1   pp. 381–386

Got It? 1a. $0; -1; 2$ **b.** ±0.1; no real square root; $\pm\frac{6}{11}$ **c.** Any negative number multiplied by itself an even number of times will always be positive. Therefore, there can be no real nth roots (where n is even) for a negative number b. **2a.** -3 **b.** no real root **c.** 7 **d.** no real root **3a.** $9x^2$ **b.** a^4b^5 **c.** $|x^3|y^4$ **4.** 0; 100

Lesson Check 1. ±5 **2.** ±0.4 **3.** no real square roots **4.** $3|b|$ **5.** $a^4|b^9|$ **6.** $-5a$ **7.** 16 has two real fourth roots, 2 and −2. **8.** The real roots of a number are the positive and negative (but not imaginary) roots of the number; the principal root of a number is the nonnegative root of the number. **9.** n is odd.

Exercises 11. ± 0.07 **13.** -4 **15.** $-\frac{1}{2}$ **17.** 6 **19.** -3
21. $3y^2$ **23.** $2y^2$ **25.** ± 10 **27.** ± 0.5 **29.** about 0.8 in.
31. 0.5 **33.** 0.2 **35.** Answers may vary. Sample:
$\sqrt[3]{-8x^6}$, $-\sqrt[4]{16x^8}$, $\sqrt[5]{-32x^{10}}$ **37.** sometimes; they are
equal for $x \geq 0$ **43.** $y = (x + 2)^3 + 3$ **44.** $y = \frac{1}{2}x^3 - 2$

45. $1, \frac{3}{4}$ **46.** $\frac{5 \pm i\sqrt{11}}{6}$ **47.** $\frac{11}{6}$ **48.** $2x^3y^3$ **49.** $\frac{ac}{3}$

50. $\frac{4}{x^2}$

Lesson 6-2 Part 1   pp. 387–389

Got It? 1a. Yes; $\sqrt[4]{60}$ **b.** No; the indexes are different.
c. Yes; $\sqrt[5]{10}$ **2.** $4x^2\sqrt[3]{2x}$ **3.** $10x^3y^3\sqrt{3y}$
Lesson Check 1. $\sqrt{10}$ **2.** $-3\sqrt[3]{4}$ **3.** Cannot be
simplified; the indexes are different. **4.** No real solutions;
$\sqrt{-4}$ is not a real number. **5.** $x \leq 0$; for $x \leq 0$, $-4x^3 \geq 0$
and $\sqrt{-4x^3}$ is real. **6.** A product of two square roots can
be simplified in this way only if the square roots are real
numbers. $\sqrt{-2}$ and $\sqrt{-8}$ are not real numbers.
Exercises 7. 16 **9.** -9 **11.** $2x\sqrt{5x}$ **13.** $10|a^3|b^3\sqrt{2b}$
15. $2\sqrt[3]{12}$ **17.** $40x|y|\sqrt{3}$ **19.** $-2x^2y\sqrt[3]{30x}$ **21.** $5\sqrt{10}$
23. $10 + 7\sqrt{2}$ **25.** sometimes **27.** $20\sqrt{22}$ cm²

Lesson 6-2 Part 2   pp. 390–394

Got It? 4a. $5|x|$ **b.** yes; $\frac{3x^2\sqrt{2x}}{x\sqrt{2x}} = 3x$ **5a.** $\frac{\sqrt[3]{175xy}}{5y}$
b. D; there is no y in the expression.
Lesson Check 1. $\sqrt[3]{3x}$ **2.** $x^2\sqrt{3x}$ **3.** Write the
root of the quotient as the quotient of roots:

$\sqrt[3]{\frac{3y}{20xy^2}} = \frac{\sqrt[3]{3y}}{\sqrt[3]{20xy^2}} = \frac{\sqrt[3]{3y}}{\sqrt[3]{2^2 \cdot 5xy^2}}$. Then rationalize the

denominator by multiplying by $\frac{\sqrt[3]{2 \cdot 5^2x^2y}}{\sqrt[3]{2 \cdot 5^2x^2y}}$ to get

$\frac{\sqrt[3]{2 \cdot 3 \cdot 5^2x^2y^2}}{\sqrt[3]{(2 \cdot 5xy)^3}} = \frac{\sqrt[3]{150x^2y^2}}{2 \cdot 5xy}$

Exercises 5. $\frac{4x}{y}$ **7.** $5x\sqrt[3]{x^2y^2}$ **9.** $\frac{2\sqrt{a}}{3ab}$ **11.** $\frac{\sqrt{2x}}{2}$

13. $\frac{\sqrt[3]{45x^2}}{3x}$ **15.** $5x^2\sqrt{5}$ **17.** $\frac{\sqrt[3]{150ab^2c}}{5a}$ **19.** 6 cm²

21. about 212 mi/h **23.** $\frac{5\sqrt{14x}}{21x}$ **25.** error in line 1:

$\frac{\sqrt[7]{x^5}}{\sqrt[4]{x^2}} \neq \sqrt[7-4]{\frac{x^5}{x^2}}$ **33.** $11|a^{45}|$ **34.** $9c^{24}d^{32}$ **35.** $4a^{27}$
36. $y^2 - 4y + 16$, R -128 **37.** $6a^2 - 5a + 4$

38. 25 **39.** 25 **40.** $\frac{121}{4}$ **41.** $\frac{3}{5} + \frac{1}{5}i$ **42.** $\frac{10}{13} - \frac{15}{13}i$
43. $\frac{16}{17} - \frac{4}{17}i$ **44.** $\frac{-7}{74} - \frac{5}{74}i$

Lesson 6-3   pp. 395–401

Got It? 1a. The indexes are different. You cannot
combine the expressions. **b.** $7x\sqrt{xy}$ **c.** $2\sqrt[5]{3x^2}$
2a. about 84.9 in. **b.** The length of the diagonal of a
square of side 6 can be found using the Pythagorean
Thm. to be $\sqrt{6^2 + 6^2} = \sqrt{72}$. Using this information
you can calculate the perimeter of the window and
simplify the expression at the end. **3.** $6\sqrt[3]{2}$
4. $46 + 16\sqrt{5}$ **5a.** 24 **b.** 1 **6a.** $-\sqrt{21} - \sqrt{35}$
b. $\frac{1}{3}(12x + 4x\sqrt{6})$ **c.** after rationalizing; When the
numerator is multiplied by the conjugate of the
denominator, it is more convenient if $\sqrt{8}$ is not yet
simplified.
Lesson Check 1. $12\sqrt{6}$ **2.** cannot combine **3.** $3\sqrt{3x}$
4. $7\sqrt{3}$ **5.** 13 **6.** $75 + 34\sqrt{5}$ **7.** $-16 - 3\sqrt{2}$ **8.** -166
9a. not like radicals **b.** like radicals; $9\sqrt{3xy}$ **c.** not like
radicals **10.** They are alike in that you can also use the
Distr. Prop. to multiply binomial radical expressions; they are
different in that you cannot multiply radicands together if
they do not have the same index.
Exercises 11. $6\sqrt{6}$ **13.** cannot combine **15.** $90\sqrt{2}$ in.,
or about 127.3 in. **17.** $13\sqrt{5}$ **19.** $2\sqrt[4]{2} + 2\sqrt[4]{3}$
21. $23 + 7\sqrt{7}$ **23.** $8 + 2\sqrt{15}$ **25.** $38 + 12\sqrt{10}$
27. 4 **29.** -2 **31.** $13 + 7\sqrt{3}$ **33.** 140.3 in.² **35.** $8\sqrt{3}$
37. $5\sqrt{3} - 4\sqrt{2}$ **39.** $-2\sqrt[3]{2}$ **41.** $-11 + \sqrt{21}$
43. $4x\sqrt{3}$ s **45.** $\frac{\sqrt{2} - 1}{\sqrt{2} + 1} = \frac{6 - \sqrt{32}}{2} = 3 - 2\sqrt{2}$
47. $\frac{89 + 42\sqrt{3}}{-239}$ **49.** $\frac{1}{2}(\sqrt{3} - \sqrt{7})$ **51.** $1 + 2\sqrt[3]{4}$
58. $3\sqrt[3]{2}$ **59.** $\frac{2\sqrt[3]{x^2}}{x}$ **60.** 4 **61.** $2x$ **62.** $7x^2\sqrt{2}$
63. $x\sqrt{15}$ **64.** $2, -1 \pm i\sqrt{3}$ **65.** $-10, 5 \pm 5i\sqrt{3}$
66. $\frac{1}{5}, \frac{-1 \pm i\sqrt{3}}{10}$ **67.** $\sqrt{7}$ (multiplicity 2), $-\sqrt{7}$
(multiplicity 2) **68.** $\frac{2\sqrt{5}}{5}$ (multiplicity 2), $-\frac{2\sqrt{5}}{5}$
(multiplicity 2) **69.** $\pm\frac{1}{3}, \pm\frac{1}{3}i$ **70.** x^6 **71.** p^5q^5
72. 2^9, or 512

Lesson 6-4 Part 1   pp. 402–405

Got It? 1a. 8 **b.** 11 **c.** 6 **2a.** $\frac{\sqrt[8]{w^3}}{w}$, $\sqrt[5]{x}$ **b.** $x^{\frac{3}{4}}$, $z^{\frac{4}{5}}$
c. If m is negative, a is in the denominator and $\frac{1}{a}$ is
undefined when $a = 0$. **3a.** about 0.61 Earth years
b. about 12.76 Earth years

Lesson Check 1. 5 **2.** 5 **3.** $\frac{1}{128}$ **4.** $(-64)^{\frac{1}{3}} =$
$\sqrt[3]{-64} = -4$ and $-64^{\frac{1}{3}} = -\sqrt[3]{64} = -4$;

$(-64)^{\frac{1}{2}} = \sqrt{-64}$, which is not a real number, but $-64^{\frac{1}{2}} = -\sqrt{64} = -8$, which is a real number.

Exercises 5. 6 **7.** 7 **9.** $7\sqrt{3}$ **11.** $\frac{1}{\sqrt[8]{y^9}}$ or $\frac{1}{(\sqrt[8]{y})^9}$

13. $\sqrt[7]{x^2}$ or $(\sqrt[7]{x})^2$ **15.** $\frac{1}{\sqrt[4]{t^3}}$ or $\frac{1}{(\sqrt[4]{t})^3}$ **17.** $\sqrt[5]{y^6}$ or

$(\sqrt[5]{y})^6$ **19.** $(7x)^{\frac{3}{2}}$ **21.** $a^{\frac{2}{3}}$ **23.** $c^{\frac{1}{2}}$ **25.** ≈ 7.9 m **27.** -7

29. 64 **31.** 1,000,000,000 or 10^9

33a. $4^{\frac{1}{2}} \times 4^{\frac{1}{2}} = 4^1 = 4$ **b.** $4^{\frac{1}{2}} \times 4^{\frac{1}{2}} = 2 \times 2 = 4$

c. $\sqrt{4} \times \sqrt{4} = \sqrt{16} = 4$

Lesson 6-4 Part 2   pp. 406–411

Got It? 4a. $\sqrt[6]{x^5}$ **b.** $\sqrt[4]{27}$ **5a.** $\frac{1}{8}$ **b.** 8 **c.** $\frac{1}{2187}$

6a. $\frac{1}{2x^5}$ **b.** $27x\sqrt[8]{x^4y^3}$

Lesson Check 1. $\sqrt[4]{11^3}$ **2.** $\frac{\sqrt{x}}{x}$ **3.** error in third line,

second term; $5(5^{\frac{1}{2}}) = 5^{\frac{3}{2}}$. The third and fourth lines should be:

$20 - 5^{\frac{3}{2}}$

$20 - 5\sqrt{5}$

4. $(1 + \sqrt{2})$ or any nonzero rational number times $(1 + \sqrt{2})$

Exercises 5. $\sqrt[12]{6^7}$ **7.** $\sqrt[10]{5^7}$ **9.** $\frac{\sqrt[6]{16}}{2}$ **11.** $\frac{\sqrt[6]{7776}}{6}$ **13.** 16

15. 64 **17.** 8 **19.** $\frac{1}{x^2}$ **21.** $\frac{\sqrt[3]{x}}{3x}$ **23.** $-\frac{3}{x^3}$ **25.** $\frac{y^4}{x^3}$ **27.** $\frac{1}{x}$

29. about 251,000,000 in., or 3961 mi **31.** $y^{\frac{4}{5}}$

33. $x^{\frac{1}{6}}y^{\frac{1}{4}}$ **35.** $\frac{2x^2}{3y^3}$ **37a.** $\sqrt{x} \cdot \sqrt{x} \cdot \sqrt{x} \cdot \sqrt{x} = x \cdot x = x^2$

so $\sqrt[4]{x^2} = \sqrt{x}$ **b.** $\sqrt[4]{x^2} = (x^2)^{\frac{1}{4}} = x^{\frac{2}{4}} = x^{\frac{1}{2}} = \sqrt{x}$

43. $4\sqrt[3]{3}$ **44.** $21\sqrt{2}$ **45.** $1 + 3\sqrt{5}$ **46.** -7

47. $-8\sqrt{3}$ **48.** $9\sqrt[4]{2}$ **49.** $4x(x^2 - 2x + 4)$

50. $(x + 2)^2$ **51.** $(x - 9)^2$ **52.** $(4a - 3b)(4a + 3b)$

53. $(5x - 4y)^2$ **54.** $(3x + 8)^2$ **55.** $-3, 2$ **56.** $7, -2$

57. $-\frac{3}{2}, 1$ **58.** $-\frac{1}{3}, 2$ **59.** $-\frac{5}{2}, \frac{1}{2}$ **60.** $-\frac{2}{3}, \frac{3}{2}$

Chapter Review for Part A   pp. 412–414

1. radicand **2.** rational exponent **3.** are not **4.** 5
5. 0.7 **6.** -2 **7.** -2 **8.** $9|x|$ **9.** $4x^2$ **10.** $2|x^3|$
11. $0.2x$ **12.** $\frac{x^2}{2}$ **13.** $5x^2y^3$ **14.** 3 **15.** -7 **16.** 4
17. $4x^2$ **18.** $30y$ **19.** 4 **20.** $3xy$ **21.** $\frac{3|x|}{y^2}$ **22.** $\frac{2\sqrt{3}}{3}$
23. $\frac{\sqrt{3x}}{8}$ **24.** $\frac{y\sqrt[3]{150x}}{10x^2}$ **25.** $22\sqrt{3}$ **26.** $26\sqrt{5x}$
27. $x\sqrt[3]{2}$ **28.** $14 + 7\sqrt{2}$ **29.** -6 **30.** $100 + 10\sqrt{6} - 10\sqrt{3} - 3\sqrt{2}$ **31.** $\frac{5 + 2\sqrt{5}}{5}$ **32.** $\frac{9 + 3\sqrt{2}}{7}$ **33.** 5

34. 3 **35.** 4 **36.** 25 **37.** x **38.** $-2y^3$ **39.** $81x^2y^4$
40. $\frac{1}{x^3y^6}$ **41.** $\frac{1}{x}$ **42.** x^3y^6

Lesson 6-5 Part 1   pp. 417–420

Got It? 1. 6 **2a.** 5, -11 **b.** 93 **3.** 37,500,000 m^3
Lesson Check 1. 12 **2.** 27 **3.** Solving square root equations is different from solving absolute value equations in that you use a different technique to isolate the variable. In square root equations, you square each side. In absolute value equations, you write two new equations and solve both. Solving square root equations is similar to solving absolute value equations in that both can introduce extraneous solutions.
Exercises 5. 1 **7.** 15 **9.** 4 **11.** 3, -13 **13.** 18 **15.** 8
17. about 25.8 ft **19.** 5 **21.** 8 **23.** 5

Lesson 6-5 Part 2   pp. 421–425

Got It? 4a. 10 **b.** when you raise each side of an equation to a power **5.** 9
Lesson Check 1. $\frac{1}{25}$ **2.** 4 **3.** 1 **4.** 512 **5.** 3; The solution of 3 yields a negative value for the left side of the equation, but the right side of the equation $(\sqrt{3(3)})$ cannot be negative.
Exercises 7. 1 **9.** 1, 4 **11.** 1 **13.** 3 **15.** 1 **17.** 6 **19.** 8
21. $-1, 2$ **23.** $36\sqrt{2} - 36$ **25.** $x = 4$ is a solution, but $x = 1$ is an extraneous solution. **27.** Answers may vary. Sample: $\sqrt{x - 3} = \sqrt{3x + 5}$ **29.** 1 **31.** 9, -7 **33.** 9
39. 3 **40.** 16 **41.** 625 **42.** 512 **43.** $\frac{1}{1000}$ **44.** $6\sqrt{2}$
45. 3, 4 **46.** 3, 5 **47.** $-5, -4$ **48.** $-2, -\frac{2}{3}$ **49.** $-\frac{1}{3}, -\frac{4}{3}$
50. $-2, -\frac{3}{4}$ **51.** domain: {0, 2, 4}, range: {$-5, -3, -1$}; yes **52.** domain: {$-1, 0, 1$}, range: {2, 0, 1}; yes
53. domain: {$-2, 0, 1$}, range: {$-2, 0, 1$}; yes
54. domain: {3, 4, 5}, range: {-1}; yes **55.** domain: {0, 1, 2}, range: {0, 1, 2}; no **56.** domain: {0}, range: {$-2, 0, 2$}; no

Lesson 6-6   pp. 426–432

Got It? 1. $(f + g)(x) = 2x^2 + x + 5$, domain: all real numbers $(f - g)(x) = 2x^2 - x + 11$, domain: all real numbers **2.** $(f \cdot g)(x) = 9x^3 - 30x^2 - 23x - 4$, domain: all real numbers; $(\frac{f}{g})(x) = x - 4$, domain: all real numbers except $x = -\frac{1}{3}$ **3.** 4 **4.** Let $D(x) = $ cost after applying the 15% store discount, $E(x) = $ cost after applying the 20% employee discount, and $x = $ cost of items. Then $D(x) = 0.85x$ and $E(x) = 0.80x$. **a.** $(E \circ D)(x) = 0.68x$ **b.** $(D \circ E)(x) = 0.68x$ **c.** The total discounts are the same.
Lesson Check 1. $3x^3 - 2x^2 + 3x - 2$
2. $-x^2 + 3x - 3$ **3.** $3x^2 + 1$ **4.** $x^2 + 3x - 1$
5. $x^2 - 3x + 3$ **6.** $-x^2 + 3x - 3$ **7.** Answers may vary. Sample: $f(x) = 3x^2 + 1, g(x) = 2x + 1; (f \circ g) = 12x^2 + 12x + 4; (g \circ f) = 6x^2 + 3$ **8.** Answers may vary.

Sample: $f(x) - 2x$, $g(x) = 0.5x$; $f(g(x)) = x$

Exercises 9. $x^2 + 7x + 5$; domain: all real numbers

11. $7x^3 + 5x^2$; domain: all real numbers

13. $\frac{x^2}{7x + 5}$; domain: all real numbers except $x = -\frac{5}{7}$

15. $\frac{1}{x} + x - 2$; domain: all real numbers except $x = 0$

17. $2x - x^2$; domain: all real numbers except $x = 0$

19. 20 **21.** 8 **23.** 25 **25.** 9 **27.** 0.25

29a. $(g \circ f)(x) = 2.1105x$ **b.** 31.6575 pesos

31. $x^2 - x + 7$; domain: all real numbers

33. $-2x^2 + 8x + 1$; domain: all real numbers

35. $2x^2 + 2x + 24$; domain: all real numbers

37. $-6x^3 + 3x^2 + 33x - 30$; domain: all real numbers

39. $\frac{10x + 25}{x^2 - 3x + 2}$; domain: all real numbers except $x = 1$ and 2 **41a.** $g(x)$ is the bonus earned when x is the amount of sales over \$5000. $h(x)$ is the excess sales over \$5000. **b.** $(g \circ h)(x)$; you first need to find the excess sales over \$5000 to calculate the bonus. **43.** -4 **45.** 17

47. $-\frac{8}{9}$ **49.** $12x^2 + 2$; $6x^2 + 4$ **55.** 1 **56.** -3 **57.** 4

58. 3 **59.** 2 **60.** 3 **61.** $x^6 + 6x^5y + 15x^4y^2 + 20x^3y^3 + 15x^2y^4 + 6xy^5 + y^6$ **62.** $16x^4 - 32x^3y + 24x^2y^2 - 8xy^3 + y^4$ **63.** $59{,}049 - 65{,}610x + 29{,}160x^2 - 6480x^3 + 720x^4 - 32x^5$ **64.** $1024x^5 - 1280x^4y + 640x^3y^2 - 160x^2y^3 + 20xy^4 - y^5$

65. $x^8 + 4x^7 + 6x^6 + 4x^5 + x^4$ **66.** $x^{12} + 12x^{10}y^3 + 60x^8y^6 + 160x^6y^9 + 240x^4y^{12} + 192x^2y^{15} + 64y^{18}$

67. no solution

68. (2, 2)

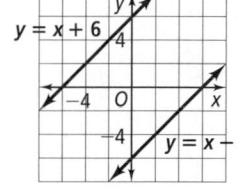

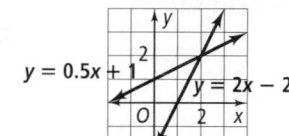

69. (1, 1)

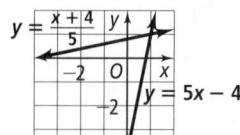

Lesson 6-7 Part 1   pp. 433–436

Got It?

1a.

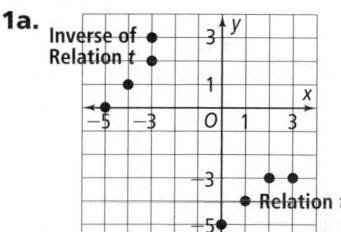

b. t is a function; the inverse of t is not a function; there are 2 y-values for one x-value

2a. $y = \frac{x}{2} - 4$ **b.** $y = \pm\sqrt{x - 2}$

3.

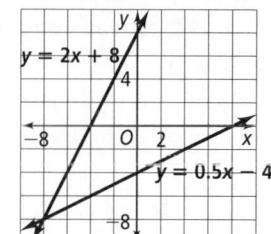

Lesson Check 1. $f^{-1}(x) = \frac{x - 3}{4}$; yes

2. $f^{-1}(x) = \pm\sqrt{x + 1}$; no **3.** $f^{-1}(x) = -1 \pm \sqrt{x}$; no

4. no; yes **5.** 2, 5

Exercises

7.

x	0	1	2	3
y	1	2	3	4

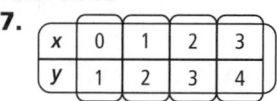

9. $y = \frac{1}{3}x - \frac{1}{3}$; yes **11.** $y = -\frac{1}{3}x + \frac{4}{3}$; yes

13. $y = \pm\sqrt{\frac{x + 5}{3}}$; no **15.** $y = \frac{1 \pm \sqrt{x - 5}}{2}$; no

17.

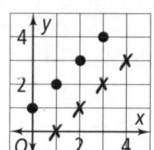

19.

21.

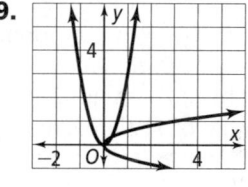

23. $f^{-1}(x) = \sqrt[3]{x}$; yes **25.** $f^{-1}(x) = \pm\sqrt{\frac{5x - 5}{2}}$; no

27. $f^{-1}(x) = \pm 2\sqrt{\frac{x}{3}}$; no

29a.

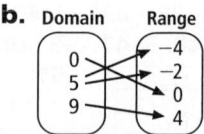

Domain   Range

b. Domain   Range

Lesson 6-7 Part 2   pp. 437–442

Got It? 4a. domain: all real numbers; range: all real numbers **b.** $g^{-1}(x) = -\frac{1}{4}x + \frac{3}{2}$ **c.** domain: all real numbers; range: all real numbers **d.** Yes; for each x in the domain of g^{-1}, there is only one value of y in the range.

5. $v = \sqrt{19.6d}$; about 21.7 m/s **6a.** $g^{-1}(x) = \frac{4 - 2x}{x}$ **b.** 0 is not in the domain of g^{-1} so $(g \circ g^{-1})(0)$ does not exist. **c.** 0

Lesson Check 1a. $h^{-1}(x) = -\frac{1}{x} - 2$ **b.** −2.25 **c.** 0

2. Answers may vary. Samples: $f(x) = 2x + 1$ and $g(x) = x - 2$; $f(x) = x^2$ and $g(x) = x + 1$

Exercises 3. $f^{-1}(x) = \frac{x - 4}{3}$, domain of f: all real numbers, range of f: all real numbers, domain of f^{-1}: all real numbers, range of f^{-1}: all real numbers; f^{-1} is a function. **5.** $f^{-1}(x) = x^2 + 5$, domain of f: $x \geq 5$, range of f: $y \geq 0$, domain of f^{-1}: $x \geq 0$, range of f^{-1}: $y \geq 5$; f^{-1} is a function **7.** $f^{-1}(x) = \frac{3 - x^2}{2}$, domain of f: $x \leq \frac{3}{2}$, range of f: $y \geq 0$, domain of f^{-1}: $x \geq 0$, range of f^{-1}: $y \leq \frac{3}{2}$; f^{-1} is a function. **9.** $f^{-1}(x) = \pm\sqrt{1 - x}$, domain of f: all real numbers, range of f: $y \leq 1$, domain of f^{-1}: $x \leq 1$, range of f^{-1}: all real numbers; f^{-1} is not a function. **11a.** $r = \sqrt[3]{\frac{3V}{4\pi}}$; yes **b.** about 20.29 ft

13. −10 **15.** d **17.** −1 **19.** $f^{-1}(x) = x^2$, domain of f: $x \geq 0$, range of f: $y \leq 0$, domain of f^{-1}: $x \leq 0$, range of f^{-1}: $y \geq 0$; f^{-1} is a function. **21.** $f^{-1}(x) = 3 - x^2$, domain of f: $x \leq 3$, range of f: $y \geq 0$, domain of f^{-1}: $x \geq 0$, range of f^{-1}: $y \leq 3$; f^{-1} is a function.

23. $f^{-1}(x) = \pm\sqrt{2x}$, domain of f: all real numbers, range of f: $y \geq 0$, domain of f^{-1}: $x \geq 0$, range of f^{-1}: all real numbers; f^{-1} is not a function. **25.** $f^{-1}(x) = \pm\sqrt{x} + 4$, domain of f: all real numbers, range of f: $y \geq 0$, domain of f^{-1}: $x \geq 0$, range of f^{-1}: all real numbers; f^{-1} is not a function. **27.** $f^{-1}(x) = \pm\frac{1}{\sqrt{x}} - 1$, domain of f: $x \neq -1$, range of f: $y > 0$, domain of f^{-1}: $x > 0$, range of f^{-1}: $y \neq -1$; f^{-1} is not a function. **29.** $f^{-1}(x) = \left(\frac{3}{x}\right)^2$, domain of f: $x > 0$, range of f: $y > 0$, domain of f^{-1}: $x > 0$, range of f^{-1}: $y > 0$; f^{-1} is a function.

31. r is not a function because there are two y-values for one x-value. r^{-1} is a function because each of its x-values has one y-value. **33.** Answers may vary. Sample: $f(x) = \sqrt{-(x + 1)} - 2$

38. $2x + 7$ **39.** $-x - 10$ **40.** $-\frac{3}{2}x + 11$

41. $2x^2 + 28x$ **42.** 32 **43.** $2x + 28$ **44.** −2 **45.** no real root **46.** 3 **47.** −3 **48.** −3 **49.** 0.4

50. 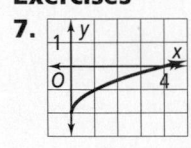 **51.** 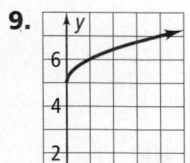 **52.**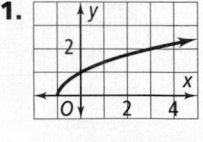

Lesson 6-8   pp. 444–450

Got It?

1.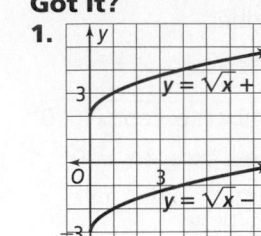

2. 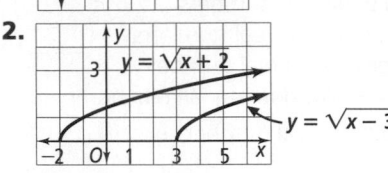 **3.**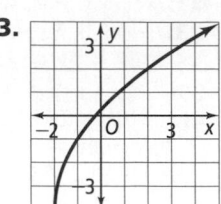

4. 1999

5.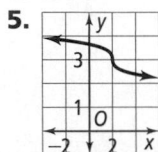

6a. $y = \sqrt[3]{8x + 32} - 2$ is the graph of $y = 2\sqrt[3]{x}$ translated 4 units to the left and 2 units down. **b.** $y = 9|x + 2|$; the graph of $y = 9|x + 2|$ is the graph of $y = 9|x|$ translated 2 units to the left; You are rewriting the function so that x has a coefficient of 1.

Lesson Check

1. 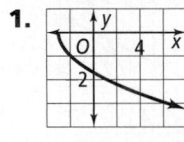 **2.**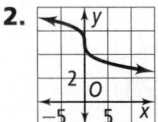

3. 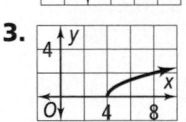 **4.**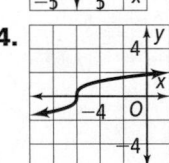

5. When $|a| < 1$, a will vertically compress $y = \sqrt{x}$ and when $|a| > 1$, a will vertically stretch $y = \sqrt{x}$; this is similar to its effect on other functions. When $a < 0$, the graph will also be reflected in the x-axis. **6.** $g(x)$ is the reflection of $f(x)$ across the x-axis and again across $x = -1$.

Exercises

7. **9.** **11.**

13. 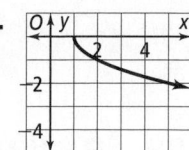 **15.**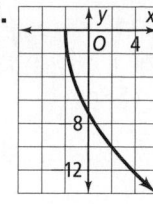

17. 147 **19.** −1

21. 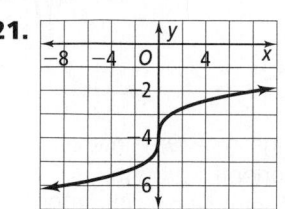 **23.**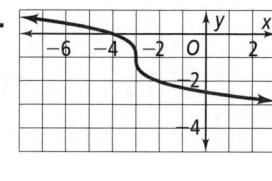

25. ≈16.44 ft; ≈29.22 ft

27. 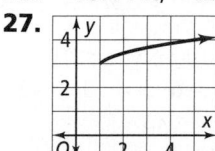 domain: $x \geq 1$, range: $y \geq 3$

29a. $y = \sqrt{x - 2} - 2$ **b.** domain: $x \geq 2$, range: $y \geq -2$ **c.** No; the function pairs the number 3 with the number −1, which is not a nonnegative real number.

31. $\frac{1}{3}$ **33.** 0, 1, 9

35a. 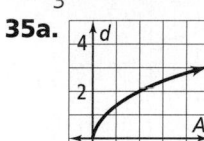 **b.** about 21.2 in.

41. $f^{-1}(x) = \frac{3(x + 3)}{2}$; yes **42.** $f^{-1}(x) = (x + 4)^2 - 3$, $x \geq -4$; yes **43.** $f^{-1}(x) = \frac{-1 \pm \sqrt{x}}{2}$; no **44.** $\frac{x\sqrt{3xy}}{y}$

45. $\frac{\sqrt[3]{9xy^2}}{3y}$ **46.** $\frac{\sqrt[5]{48x^3y^4}}{2y}$ **47.** $\frac{9 \pm \sqrt{21}}{2}$ **48.** $\frac{-3 + 3\sqrt{5}}{2}$

49. $\frac{-1 \pm \sqrt{61}}{10}$ **50.** 8 **51.** 16 **52.** 2

Chapter Review for Part B pp. 452–454

1. radical functions **2.** composite function **3.** inverse function **4.** −1 **5.** 15 **6.** 5 **7.** −8, 10 **8.** 2, −1 **9.** −2 **10.** 0, 16 **11.** 0, 36 **12.** 9.05 W **13.** $x^2 + x - 20$; domain: all real numbers **14.** $x^2 - x - 12$; domain: all real numbers **15.** $x^3 - 4x^2 - 16x + 64$; domain: all real numbers **16.** $x + 4$; domain: all real numbers except $x = 4$ **17.** 50 **18.** 5 **19.** 23 **20.** $5a^2 + 3$
21. $D(C(x)) = 0.5x - 0.5$, $C(D(x)) = 0.5x - 1$; use the coupon after the store discount. **22.** $f^{-1}(x) = \pm\sqrt{\frac{x + 8}{2}}$; no **23.** $f^{-1}(x) = 5 - \frac{1}{3}x$; yes **24.** $f^{-1}(x) = x^2 - 6$; yes
25. $f^{-1}(x) = \frac{3 \pm \sqrt{x}}{2}$; no

26. 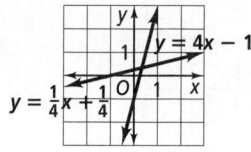 domain of f: all real numbers, range of f: all real numbers, domain of f^{-1}: all real numbers, range of f^{-1}: all real numbers

27. domain of f: all real numbers, range of f: $y \geq 0$; domain of f^{-1}: $x \geq 0$, range of f^{-1}: all real numbers

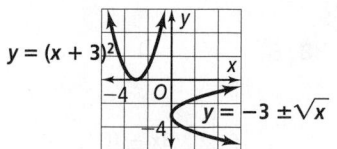

28. domain of f: $x \geq 3$, range of f: $y \geq 0$, domain of f^{-1}: $x \geq 0$, range of f^{-1}: $y \geq 3$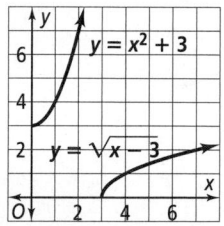

29. domain of f: all real numbers, range of f: $y \leq 6$, domain of f^{-1}: $x \leq 6$, range of f^{-1}: all real numbers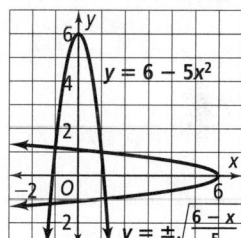

30. $s = \sqrt[3]{V}$; 4 ft

31. domain: $x \geq 0$, range: $y \geq -5$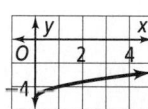

32. domain: $x \geq -8$, range: $y \geq 0$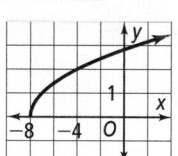

33. domain: $x \geq 0$, range: $y \geq 9$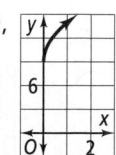

34. domain: $x \geq 4$, range: $y \leq 0$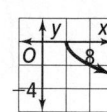

35. domain: all real numbers, range: all real numbers

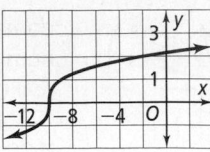

36. domain: all real numbers, range: all real numbers

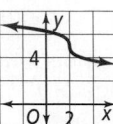

37. no solution

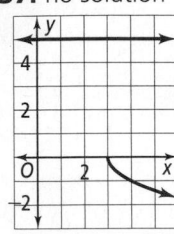

38. 6

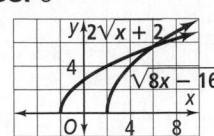

Chapter 7

Get Ready!

p. 459

1. 0.1; 10; 1000 **2.** $\frac{4}{9}$; 1; $\frac{9}{4}$ **3.** $-\frac{1}{625}$; $-\frac{1}{25}$; -1

4. $-\frac{1}{3}$; -1; -3

5.

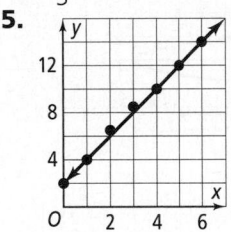

; $y = 2x + 2$

6.

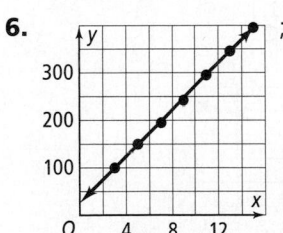

; $y = 25x + 25$

7. $y = x^2$

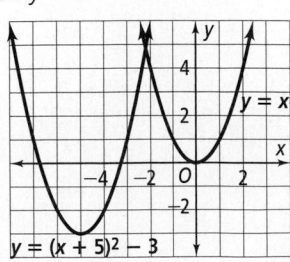

8. $y = x^3$

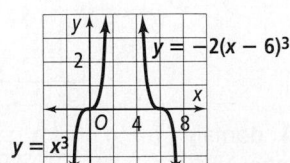

9. x^2 **10.** $16x^4$ **11.** $y = \pm\sqrt{\frac{10-x}{2}}$; no

12. $y = -4 + \sqrt[3]{x+1}$; yes **13.** decrease

14. exponential **15.** no

Lesson 7-1

pp. 462–469

Got It?

1a.

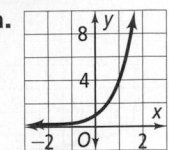

b.

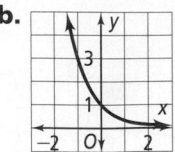

c.

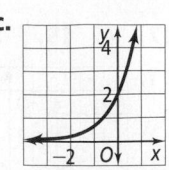

d. domain: all real numbers, range: $y > 0$; y-intercept: $(0, a)$ where $y = ab^x$ **2a.** exponential growth; 3
b. exponential decay; 11 **c.** exponential growth; 2000
3a. $593.84 **b.** Because interest is paid annually, the function is not continuous. The account contains $1276.28 after 5 years, and $1340.10 after 6 years. The account will never contain any value in between. **4a.** ≈3
b. No; the function is asymptotic to the x-axis.

Lesson Check 1. decay; 10 **2.** growth; 0.75
3. growth; 1 **4.** decay; 1

5.

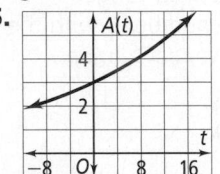

6.

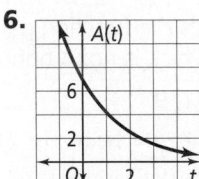

7. If $a > 0$ and $b > 1$, then the function represents exponential growth; if $a > 0$ and $0 < b < 1$, then the function represents exponential decay. **8a.** quadratic; degree 2 with $3x^2$ as the leading term **b.** exponential; the equation is of the form $y = ab^x$ **c.** linear; degree 1 with x as the leading term **d.** exponential; the equation is of the form $y = ab^x$ **9.** $0.3 < 1$, so 0.3 is the decay factor

Exercises

11.

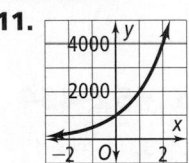

13.

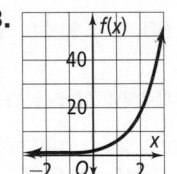

15.

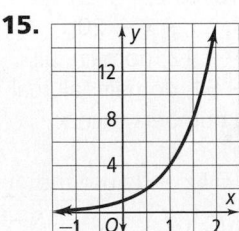

17. exponential decay; 2 **19.** exponential decay; 0.8
21. exponential growth; $\frac{1}{100}$ **23a.** $2249.73
b. $4051.63 **c.** 6 yrs **d.** 11 yrs
25. $y = 1,860,000(0.985)^x$; 1,551,485 **27.** $262.48
29. 0.25 **31.** 0.999 **33.** 2
35a. $y = 80(0.965)^x$

b.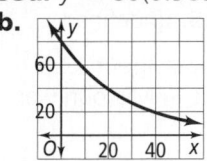
about 47 yrs

42. 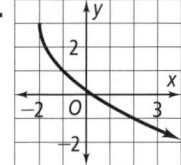 **43.**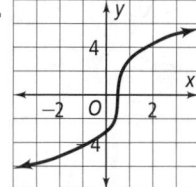

44.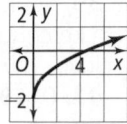

45. $(2 + 3x)(4 - 6x + 9x^2)$ **46.** $(3x - 1)(x + 4)$
47. $(4x - 5)(4x - 5)$ **48.** $(1, -1)$ **49.** $(0, 0)$
50. $(1.2, 0.6)$

51. 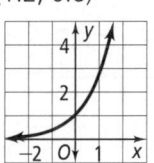 **52.**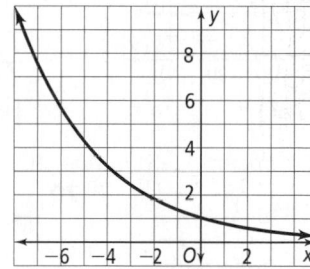

53.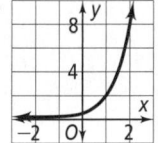

Lesson 7-2 Part 1   pp. 470–475

Got It? 1a. Stretches by a factor of 2

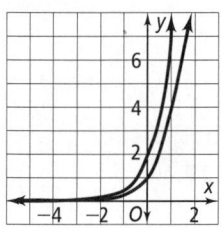

b. Reflects in the x-axis, compresses by a factor of 0.5;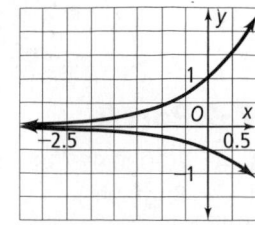

2a. translate 2 units to the left; the y-intercept becomes 16
b. Stretch the graph of $y = (0.25)^x$ by a factor of 5 and translate the graph of $y = 5 \cdot 0.25^x$ up 5 units
3a. about 31.9 min **b.** No; a cup of hot coffee cannot cool below room temperature. So, to use exponential data, it is important to translate the data by 68 units.
Lesson Check 1. stretch by a factor of 2 and reflection across the x-axis **2.** compress by a factor of $\frac{1}{2}$ **3.** translate 5 units to the right **4.** translate 3 units up **5.** The graph is a shift of the parent function 2 units to the left and 1 unit up.

Exercises
7. 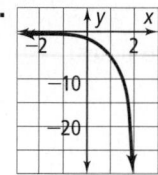 **9.**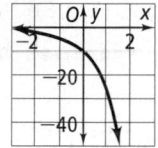

11. 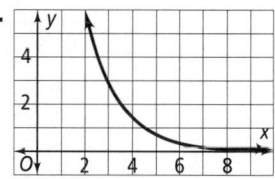 **13.**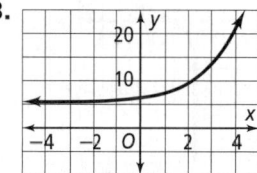

15. 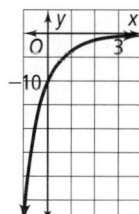 **17.**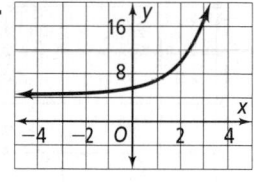

19a. $y = 127.27(0.837)^x + 70$ **b.** about 5.2 min

21. As the value of b approaches 1, the graph comes closer to being a straight line.

23. $y = -3^x$; $y = -3^{x-8} + 2$ **25.** $y = -3\left(\frac{1}{3}\right)^x$; $y = -3\left(\frac{1}{3}\right)^{x+15} - 1$

Lesson 7-2 Part 2   pp. 476–479

Got It? 4. $e^8 \approx 2980.957987$; two methods: use the e^x key and let $x = 8$; graph $y = e^x$ and trace to $x = 8$.
5. about $4475
Lesson Check 1. 403.4288 **2.** 0.3679 **3.** 22,026.4658
4. no; $2000e^{0.05t} \neq 1000(e^{0.04t} + e^{0.06t})$
Exercises 5. 0.1353 **7.** 15.1543 **9.** $448.30
11. $6168.41 **13.** $y = 50\left(\frac{1}{2}\right)^{\frac{1}{14.3}x}$; 0.85 mg
15. $\approx$61.4 pascals **22.** exponential growth; 23
23. exponential growth; 3 **24.** exponential decay; 2
25. $6\sqrt{5}$ **26.** $-\sqrt[3]{4}$ **27.** $5(\sqrt{3} + \sqrt{5})$ **28.** $2(\sqrt[4]{2} + \sqrt[4]{8})$
29. $\sqrt{3}$ **30.** $11\sqrt{7}$ **31.** $f^{-1}(x) = \frac{x+1}{4}$; yes
32. $f^{-1}(x) = x^{\frac{1}{7}}$; yes **33.** $f^{-1}(x) = \left(\frac{x-1}{5}\right)^{\frac{1}{3}}$; yes

Lesson 7-3   pp. 480–487

Got It? 1a. $\log_6 36 = 2$ **b.** $\log_3 1 = 0$
c. $\log_{\frac{2}{3}} \frac{8}{27} = 3$ **2a.** 3 **b.** $\frac{5}{2}$ **c.** $-\frac{5}{6}$ **3.** $\approx$16 times
4a. domain: $x > 0$; range: all real numbers; no y-intercept; vertical asymptote: $x = 0$

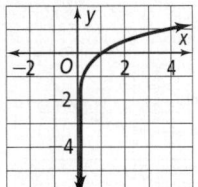

b.

x	$2^y = x$	y
-1	$2^y = -1$	undefined
0	$2^y = 0$	undefined
1	$2^y = 1$	0
2	$2^y = 2$	1

5a. translates the graph of the parent function 3 units to the right and 4 units up; The asymptote changes from $x = 0$ to $x = 3$. The domain changes from $x > 0$ to $x > 3$. The range remains all real numbers. **b.** stretches the graph of the parent function by a factor of 5; The asymptote, domain, and the range remain the same.
Lesson Check 1. $\log_5 25 = 2$ **2.** $\log_4 64 = 3$
3. $\log_3 243 = 5$ **4.** $\log_5 25 = 2$ **5.** 3 **6.** 1 **7.** 2 **8.** -2
9a. no **b.** yes **c.** yes **d.** no **10.** Choose a few points on

the graph of $y = 6^x$, reverse their coordinates, and plot them. **11.** $y = \log_2 (x + 4)$ translates the graph of $y = \log_2 x$ 4 units to the left. Asymptote changes from $x = 0$ to $x = -4$. Domain changes from $x > 0$ to $x > -4$. Range remains the same.
Exercises 13. $\log 1000 = 3$ **15.** $\log \frac{1}{10} = -1$
17. $\log_{\frac{1}{3}} \frac{1}{27} = 3$ **19.** 4 **21.** 1 **23.** 3 **25.** undefined
27. 4 **29.** The earthquake in Missouri was about 1.58 times more intense. **31.** The earthquake in Missouri was about 50,119 times more intense.
33–35.

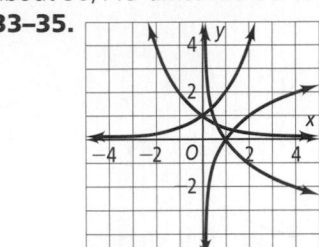

37. translate the graph 2 units to the right **39.** apple juice: acidic; buttermilk: acidic; cream: acidic; ketchup: acidic; shrimp sauce: basic; strained peas: acidic
41. $2^7 = 128$ **43.** $6^1 = 6$ **45.** $2^{-1} = \frac{1}{2}$ **47.** 0 **49.** 1
51. First rewrite $y = \log_1 x$ as $1^y = x$. For any real number y, $x = 1$. **53.** $y = 4^x$ **55.** $y = 2^{x-1}$
57. $y = 10^{x-1}$
59.

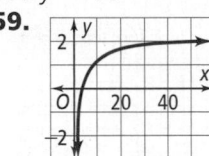

61.

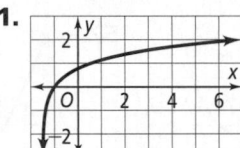

63. domain: $x > 0$, range: all real numbers
69.

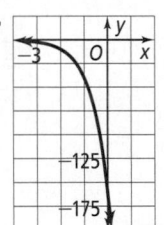

70.

71.

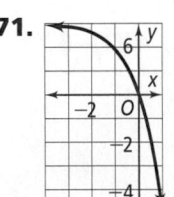

72. $(2x - 3)(2x - 1)$ **73.** $4(b - 5)(b + 5)$
74. $(5x - 2)(x + 3)$ **75.** 2 **76.** 256 **77.** $\frac{1}{4}$

Lesson 7-4   pp. 491–497

Got It? 1a. $\log_4 15x^2$ **b.** 1
2a. $\log_3 2 + 3\log_3 5 - \log_3 37$ **b.** $2 + 5\log_3 x$
3a. $\frac{5}{3}$ **b.** ≈ 2.085 **4.** Substance B; log 2; $-\log[H^+_B] + \log[H^+_B] = \log 2$

Lesson Check 1. $\log_4 16$ **2.** $\log_6 6$ **3.** $\log_3 x - \log_3 y$
4. $2\log m + 5\log n$ **5.** $\frac{1}{2}\log_2 x$ **6a.** Product Prop. and Power Prop. **b.** Quotient Prop. **7.** 0.00001 **8.** Answers may vary. Sample: log 150 = log 25 + log 6

Exercises 9. $\log_2 3$ **11.** log 972 **13.** $3\log x + 5\log y$
15. $\log_3 7 + 2\log_3 (2x - 3)$ **17.** ≈ 3.17 **19.** ≈ 1.75
21. ≈ 3.63 **23.** 12 **25.** about 3 dB **27.** 1 **29.** 2

31. false; $\frac{1}{2}\log_3 3 = \log_3 3^{\frac{1}{2}}$, not $\log_3 \frac{3}{2}$ **33.** false;

$(\log x)^2 = (\log x) \cdot (\log x) \neq \log x^2$ **35.** $\log_4 \frac{m^x n^{\frac{1}{y}}}{p}$

37. No; the expression $(2x + 1)$ is a sum, so it is not covered by the Product, Quotient, or Power Props. **39.** $\frac{1}{2}\log 2 + \frac{1}{2}\log x - \frac{1}{2}\log y$ **41.** $3\log 2 + \frac{3}{2}\log x - 3\log 5$
43. $3\log 2 + \frac{1}{2}\log r - \log s$ **45.** $\frac{\log 2}{\log 7}$ **47.** $\frac{\log 3x}{\log 4}$
49. Capella is about 1.02 times brighter than Rigel.
54. $\log_7 49 = 2$ **55.** $\log_8 \frac{1}{4} = -\frac{2}{3}$ **56.** $-3 = \log_5 \frac{1}{125}$
57. ± 8 **58.** $\frac{64}{7}$ **59.** 2 **60.** $f(x) = x^3 + 5x^2 - 3x - 15$
61. $f(x) = x^4 + 17x^2 + 16$
62. $f(x) = x^4 - 2x^3 - 2x^2 + 14x - 35$
63. 2 **64.** 3 **65.** $\frac{1}{3}$

Lesson 7-5 Part 1   pp. 498–502

Got It? 1. $\frac{4}{9}$ **2a.** ≈ 1.5122 **b.** because the terms cannot be written with a common base **3a.** ≈ 0.8588
b. ≈ 1.2114 **4.** ≈ 13.51 yrs
Lesson Check 1. 2 **2.** 3 **3.** ≈ 3.6439 **4.** Yes; $5^x = 0$ has no solution.
Exercises 5. $\frac{3}{2}$ **7.** -1 **9.** -1 **11.** $\frac{2}{5}$ **13.** 2.1240
15. 3.4650 **17.** 0.2720 **19.** 0.5690 **21.** 4.7027
23. 4.89 **25.** about the yr 2012 **27.** ≈ 7.6 yrs **29.** 3
31. $-\frac{1}{2}$ **33a.** 13 yrs after July 2007 **b.** 35 yrs after July 2007 **c.** 25 yrs after July 2007 **35.** 0.8505 **37.** 1
39. 3.0389

Lesson 7-5 Part 2   pp. 503–506

Got It? 5. 1.45 **6.** 200

Lesson Check 1. 25 **2.** 2000 **3.** $\frac{\sqrt{10}}{10}$ or about ≈ 0.3162

4. The log bases are not equal.
$\log_2 x = 2\log_3 9$
$\log_2 x = \log_3 9^2$
$\log_2 x = 4$
    $x = 2^4$
    $x = 16$

Exercises 5. 0.05 **7.** 10,000 **9.** $\sqrt{10}$ or ≈ 3.1623
11. 2 **13.** 20 **15.** 5 **17.** ≈ 1357.2 **19.** 5.8 **21a.** 1 W/m²; 10^4 W/m² **b.** 10,000 times as intense **23.** 625 **25.** 1.5
27. 500 **29.** $\frac{1}{2}$ **31.** $\frac{1}{3}$ **33.** Answers may vary. Sample: log x = 1.6; $x \approx 39.81$ **40.** $\log 2 + 3\log x - 2\log y$
41. $\log_3 x - \log_3 y$ **42.** $1 + \frac{1}{2}\log_3 x$ **43.** $x^2 - 3x - 1$
44. $3x^2 - 3$ **45.** $9x^2 - 1$ **46.** 1, $\pm i$ **47.** ± 2, $\pm 2i$
48. $\pm\sqrt{3}$, $\pm\sqrt{2}$ **49.** 10 **50.** 15

Chapter Review   pp. 509–512

1. exponential decay; exponential growth **2.** asymptote
3. exponential function; natural base exponential function
4. continuously compounded interest **5.** common logarithm **6.** exponential growth; (0, 1) **7.** exponential growth; (0, 2) **8.** exponential growth; (0, 0.2)
9. exponential decay; (0, 3) **10.** exponential growth; $\left(0, \frac{25}{7}\right)$ **11.** exponential growth; (0, 0.0015)
12. exponential decay; (0, 2.25) **13.** exponential decay; (0, 0.5) **14.** $y = 12,500(0.91)^x$; $7800
15. $y = 50(1.03)^x$; $58 **16.** The parent graph $y = 2^x$ is stretched by a factor of 5, translated 1 unit to the left, and 3 units up. **17.** The parent graph $y = \left(\frac{1}{3}\right)^x$ is reflected across the x-axis, stretched by a factor of 2, and translated 2 units to the right. **18.** $1100.76
19. $291.91 **20.** 0.0498 **21.** 0.3679 **22.** 148.4132
23. 0.6065 **24.** $2 = \log_6 36$ **25.** $-3 = \log_2 0.125$
26. $3 = \log_3 27$ **27.** $-3 = \log 0.001$ **28.** 6 **29.** -2
30. -5 **31.** 0

32.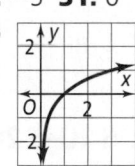

33.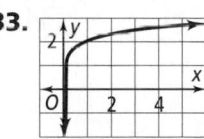

34.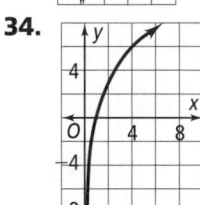

35.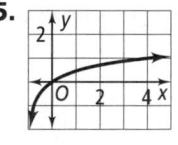

36. The parent graph $y = \log_4 x$ is stretched by a factor of 3 and translated 1 unit to the left. **37.** The parent graph $y = \log_3 x$ is translated 5 units right and 3 units up. **38.** log 24; Product Prop. **39.** $\log_2 \frac{5}{3}$; Quotient Prop. **40.** 0 Power and Product Prop. **41.** $\log \frac{x}{y}$; Quotient Prop. **42.** $\log \frac{5}{x^2}$; Power and Quotient Prop. **43.** $\log_4 x^5$; Power and Product Prop. **44.** $2 \log_4 x + 3 \log_4 y$; Product and Power Prop. **45.** $\log 4 + 4 \log s + \log t$; Product and Power Prop. **46.** $\log_3 2 - \log_3 x$; Quotient Prop. **47.** $2 \log(x + 3)$; Power Prop. **48.** $3 \log_2 2 + 3 \log_2 (y - 2)$; Power and Product Prop. **49.** $2 \log z - \log 5$; Power and Quotient Prop. **50.** ≈ 2.8 **51.** ≈ 2.1 **52.** 0.75 **53.** 3.2619 **54.** 4.6542 **55.** 1.3652 **56.** 3.3333 **57.** 8 **58.** 50 **59.** 15.5885 **60.** 0.9307 **61.** 0.6599 **62.** 0.6658 **63.** 3.0589 **64.** ≈ 18.2 h

Chapter 8

Get Ready!   p. 517

1. $\frac{4}{3}$; -4 **2.** $-\frac{2}{3}$; 2 **3.** $-\frac{10}{3}$; 10 **4.** $-\frac{16}{7}, \frac{48}{7}$ **5.** $(x + 3)$ $(x - 2)$ **6.** $(4x + 5)(x + 3)$ **7.** $(3x - 5)(3x + 5)$ **8.** $(x - 6)^2$ **9.** $(3x + 4)(x + 2)$ **10.** $(x - 3)(x - 2)$ **11.** 1, -8 **12.** -6, -8 **13.** 4, 2 **14.** 0, $-\frac{2}{3}$ **15.** 8, $\frac{1}{2}$ **16.** 15, -2 **17.** Answers may vary. Sample: Inverse is used when one quantity increases as the other quantity decreases.

18. Answers may vary.
Sample:

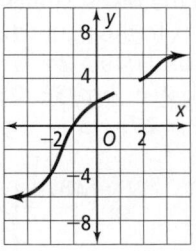

Lesson 8-1   pp. 520–528

Got It? 1a. direct; $y = 40x$ **b.** inverse; $y = \frac{8}{x}$
c. neither
2.

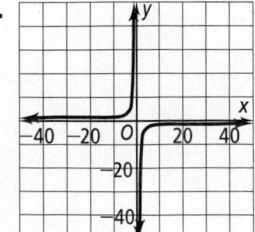

$y = -28$ when $x = 2$.

3a. $t = \frac{225}{n}$ **b.** 9 students **4.** 23 bags **5a.** 4018 joules **b.** 12 m; No, you need not calculate P to find the height. Substitute the mass and height of the first diver, and the mass of the second diver in $P = mgh$ and set the two quantities equal to calculate the height of the second diver. Solve the equation for h.

Lesson Check 1. inverse; $y = \frac{6}{x}$ **2.** direct; $y = 5x$ **3.** In direct variation, two positive quantities either increase together or decrease together. In an inverse variation, as one quantity increases, the other quantity decreases and vice versa. **4.** p varies directly with q, r, and t and inversely with s. **5.** d varies directly with the cube root of r and inversely with the square of t.

Exercises 7. neither

9. $y = \frac{11}{x}$; 1.1; 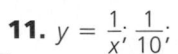 **11.** $y = \frac{1}{x}, \frac{1}{10}$;

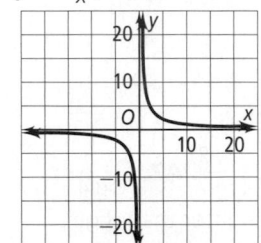 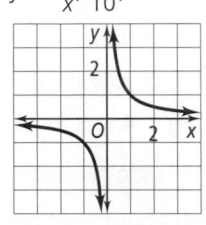

13. $y = \frac{3.6}{x}$; 0.36; 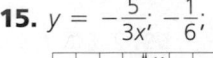 **15.** $y = -\frac{5}{3x}, -\frac{1}{6}$;

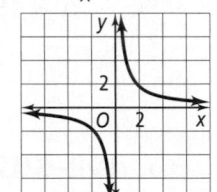 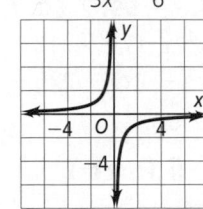

17. ≈ 4 buckets **19.** $PE = 2gh$ **21.** $F = \frac{km}{d^2}$ **23a.** ≈ 76.58 L **b.** ≈ 20 moles **25.** $z = 10xy$; 360 **27.** 10 **29.** $18\frac{2}{3}$ **31.** 3.6 **33.** 2.5 **35.** 2.625 **41.** 4 **42.** 2.846 **43.** $3333.\overline{3}$ **44.** $-90x^2$ **45.** $84x^2$ **46.** $10x^2y^3\sqrt{2y}$ **47.** $|x^5|y^{50}$ **48.** $-4ab^2$ **49.** $2m^2|n|\sqrt[4]{4}$ **50.** $y = |x|$ translated 2 units up;

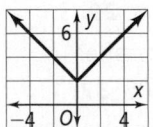

51. $y = |x|$ translated 2 units to the left;

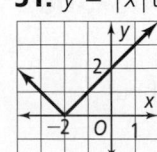

52. $y = |x|$ translated 3 units down;

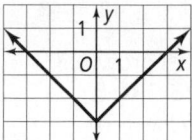

53. $y = |x|$ translated 3 units to the rt.;

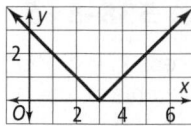

54. $y = |x|$ translated 4 units to the left and 5 units down;

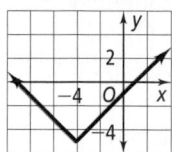

55. $y = |x|$ translated 10 units to the rt. and 7 units up;

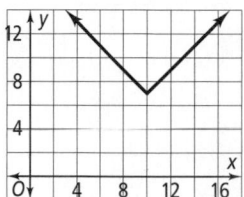

Lesson 8-2   pp. 530–537

Got It?

1a.

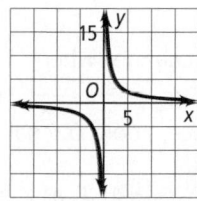

no x- or y-intercept; horizontal asymptote: $y = 0$; vertical asymptote: $x = 0$; domain: all real numbers except $x = 0$, range: all real numbers except $y = 0$

b. Yes; they have similar graphs.

2a. $y = \frac{1}{2x}$ is a shrink of the graph of $y = \frac{1}{x}$ by a factor of $\frac{1}{2}$. **b.** $y = \frac{2}{x}$ is a stretch of the graph of $y = \frac{1}{x}$ by a factor of 2. **c.** $y = -\frac{1}{2x}$ is a reflection across the x-axis and a shrink of the graph of $y = \frac{1}{x}$ by a factor of $\frac{1}{2}$.

3.

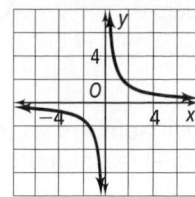

domain: all real numbers except $x = 2$, range: all real numbers except $y = 4$

4. $y = \frac{2}{x - 1} - 4$ **5a.** $C = \frac{1200}{n}$; **b.** domain: whole numbers from 1 to 312; **c.** 160 students

Lesson Check

1.

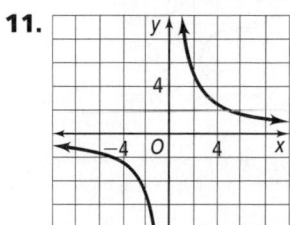

2. $y = \frac{1}{x}$ translated 5 units up **3.** $y = \frac{1}{x}$ reflected across the x-axis and stretched by a factor of 4 **4.** horizontal asymptote: $y = -7$, vertical asymptote: $x = -2$
5. shrink of the graph of $y = \frac{1}{x}$ by a factor of $\frac{1}{2}$

6. Answers may vary. Sample: $y = -\frac{2}{x}$ **7.** for $y = \frac{a}{x}$: stretch if $|a| > 1$ and compression if $0 < |a| < 1$

Exercises

9.

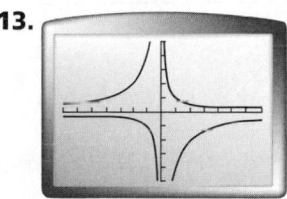

no x- or y-intercept; horizontal asymptote: $y = 0$, vertical asymptote: $x = 0$; domain: all real numbers except $x = 0$, range: all real numbers except $y = 0$

11.

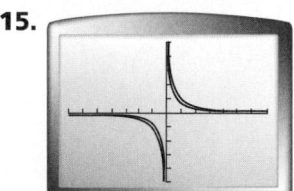

no x- or y-intercept; horizontal asymptote: $y = 0$, vertical asymptote: $x = 0$; domain: all real numbers except $x = 0$, range: all real numbers except $y = 0$

13.

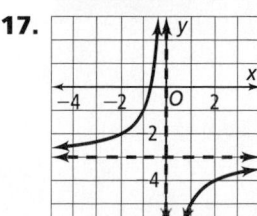

reflection across the x-axis and a stretch by a factor of 4

15.

compression by a factor of 0.75

17.

domain: all real numbers except $x = 0$, range: all real numbers except $y = -3$

19. 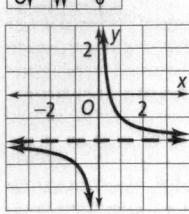 domain: all real numbers except $x = 3$, range: all real numbers except $y = 4$

21. 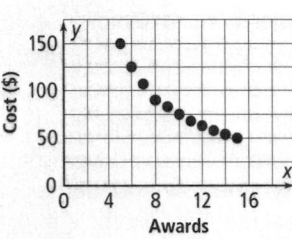 domain: all real numbers except $x = 0$, range: all real numbers except $y = -2$

23. $y = \frac{2}{x} + 4$ **25.** $y = \frac{2}{x - 4} - 8$

27.
$c = \frac{750}{a}$; domain: whole numbers from 5 to 15, range: $50 \leq c \leq 750$

29. 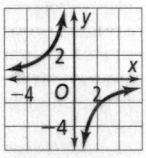 **31.**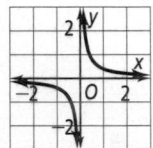

33. B
35. 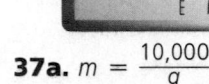 ; (2.92, 6.2)

37a. $m = \frac{10,000}{g}$

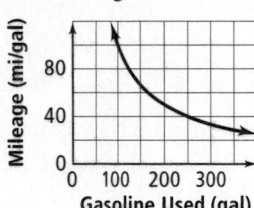

b. $m = \frac{10,000}{g - 50}$

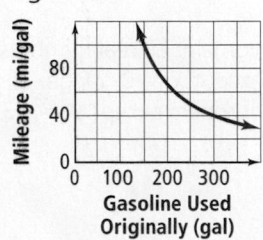

c. 25 mi/gal; 28.57 mi/gal
43. $y = \frac{24}{x}$; $-\frac{24}{5}$ **44.** $y = \frac{50}{x}$; -10 **45.** $y = \frac{48}{x}$; $-\frac{48}{5}$
46. exponential growth; 3 **47.** exponential growth; 0.1
48. exponential decay; 5 **49.** $79 - 20\sqrt{3}$ **50.** 6
51. -2 **52.** $(x + 9)(x - 3)$ **53.** $(2x - 7)(x + 4)$
54. $(2x - 3)(x - 8)$

Lesson 8-3   pp. 538–546

Got It? 1a. domain: all real numbers except $x = 4$ and $x = -4$; points of discontinuity: non-removable at $x = 4$ and $x = -4$; no x-intercept, y-intercept: $\left(0, -\frac{1}{16}\right)$
b. domain: all real numbers; no pts. of discontinuity; x-intercepts: $(1, 0)$ and $(-1, 0)$, y-intercept: $\left(0, -\frac{1}{3}\right)$
c. domain: all real numbers except $x = -2$ and $x = -1$; points of discontinuity: non-removable at $x = -2$, removable at $x = -1$; no x-intercept, y-intercept: $\left(0, \frac{1}{2}\right)$
2a. $x = 1$ and $x = -3$ **b.** $x = -3$ **c.** no vertical asymptotes **3a.** $y = -2$ **b.** $y = 0$ **c.** no horizontal asymptote
4.

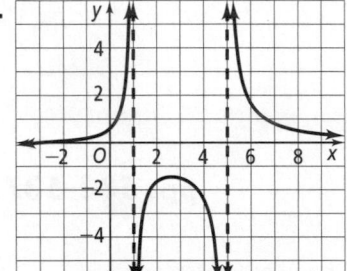

5a. 4 gal **b.** No, because the graph changes when $y_1 = 0.8$ and intersects the graph of $y_2 = \frac{2 + (0.1)x}{2 + x}$ at $x \approx 0.6$. So, to have 80% orange juice, about 0.6 gal should be added.
Lesson Check 1. at $x = -5$ and $x = -4$ **2.** at $x = 9$ and $x = -2$ **3.** at $x = -1$ **4.** at $x = \frac{1}{3}$ and $x = 2$
5. $x = -5$ **6.** $x = -2$ and $x = -3$ **7.** $x = 1$ **8.** $x = 1$ and $x = -3$
9.

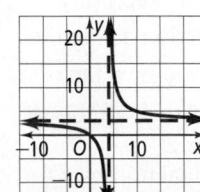

10.

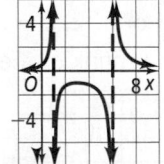

11. at $x = 1$ and $x = -3$; The function is undefined.
12. degree 2; function is discontinuous at 2 values of x
Exercises 13. domain: all real numbers except $x = 0$ and $x = 2$; points of discontinuity: non-removable at $x = 0$ and $x = 2$; no x- or y-intercept **15.** domain: all real numbers except $x = \pm 1$; pts. of discontinuity: non-removable at $x = -1$, removable at $x = 1$; no x-intercept;

y-intercept: (0, 3) **17.** hole at $x = -5$ **19.** vertical asymptote at $x = -1$, hole at $x = 2$ **21.** $y = 1$ **23.** $y = 0$

25.
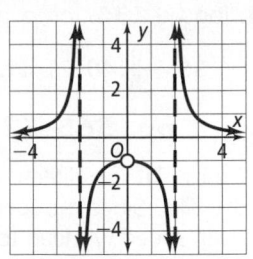

27.
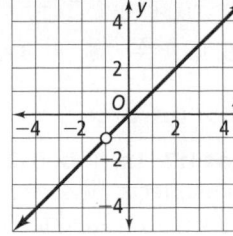

29.
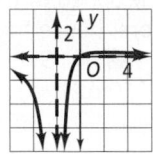

31. vertical asymptotes at $x = -3$ and $x = 3$, horizontal asymptote at $y = 0$ **33.** horizontal asymptote at $y = 0$ **35.** 3 test scores **37.** Answers may vary. Sample: There is no value of x for which the denominator equals 0.

39.
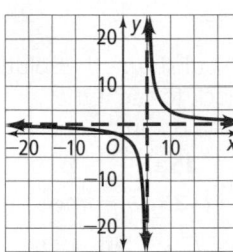

41.
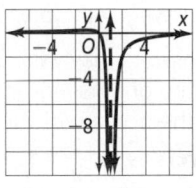

47.
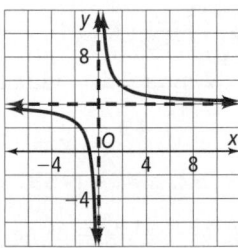
domain: all real numbers except $x = 0$, range: all real numbers except $y = 4$

48.
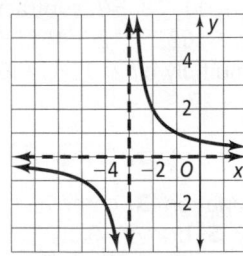
domain: all real numbers except $x = -3$, range: all real numbers except $y = 0$

49.
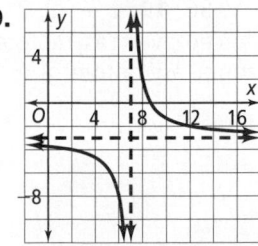
domain: all real numbers except $x = 7$, range: all real numbers except $y = -3$

50. $y = \frac{x + 3}{2}$; yes **51.** $y = \pm\sqrt{\frac{x}{2}}$; no **52.** $y = \frac{1}{x} - 2$; yes

53. $a < 10\frac{2}{3}$

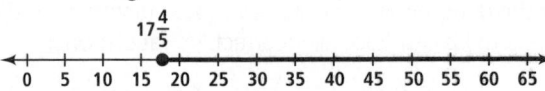

54. $x \geq 17\frac{4}{5}$

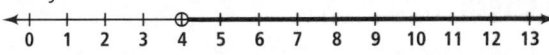

55. $y > 4$

56. $(2x - 1)(x - 1)$ **57.** $(2x - 3)(2x + 3)$
58. $(5x + 1)(x + 1)$

Lesson 8-4   pp. 548–554

Got It? 1a. $-\frac{4x}{y}$; $x \neq 0$, $y \neq 0$ **b.** $\frac{x + 4}{x - 3}$; $x \neq 2$ or 3
c. $-\frac{4}{x + 3}$; $x \neq \pm 3$ **2.** $\frac{2(x + 1)}{(x + 4)^2}$; $x \neq \pm 4$ **3a.** $\frac{2x}{x - 1}$; $x \neq 1$,
-1, -4, or 3 **b.** Six restrictions; two in each of the original denominators, and two in the reciprocal of the second rational expression. **4.** a square

Lesson Check 1. $\frac{z - 3}{2(z + 3)}$; $z \neq -3$ **2.** $\frac{3}{x}$; $x \neq 0$ or 1
3. $\frac{3(x + 5)}{x + 3}$; $x \neq -3$, -6, or 2 **4.** $-\frac{x + 6}{x + 2}$; $x \neq$
-6, -2, 2, 3, or 5 **5.** Yes; the numerator and denominator are polynomials with no common factor. **6.** No; $x = 2$ will make the denominator of $\frac{x}{x - 2}$ equal to 0, so $x = 2$ is not a solution. There is no solution to the eq.
7. Length $= \frac{2(a + 8)}{a + 5}$; $-10 < a < -5$, $a \neq -8$

Exercises 9. $\frac{1}{2x - 1}$; $x \neq 0$ or $\frac{1}{2}$ **11.** $7 - z$; $z \neq -7$
13. $-\frac{x + 4}{x - 5}$; $x \neq 5$ or 3 **15.** $\frac{xy^5}{4}$; $x \neq 0$, $y \neq 0$
17. $-\frac{4(x + 6)}{3(3x + 8)}$; $x \neq 3$ or $-\frac{8}{3}$ **19.** $\frac{2}{3x^2y^2}$; $x \neq 0$, $y \neq 0$
21. $\frac{-5(x + y)}{3}$; $x \neq y$ **23.** $\frac{4(y - 3)}{y(y + 5)}$; $y \neq 2$, -5, or 0
25a. $\frac{\pi r^2(2r)}{2\pi r^2 + 2\pi r(2r)} = \frac{r}{3}$ **b.** $\frac{\pi(2r)^2(r)}{2\pi(2r)^2 + 2\pi(2r)(r)} = \frac{r}{3}$
c. The ratios are equal. The buildings are equally efficient.
27. $\frac{y + 6}{y - 2}$; $y \neq 2$ **29.** $\frac{x(x - 1)^3}{x + 4}$; $x \neq -4$, 0, or 1
31. $\frac{18x^5}{y^2}$; $x \neq 0$, $y \neq 0$ **33.** $\frac{4}{x}$; $x \neq 0$, -5, 4, or 1
35. $\frac{x + 1}{x - 4}$; $x \neq -3$, $\frac{1}{2}$, 2, or 4 **37.** $\frac{6(a + 1)}{a - 3}$; $|a| > 3$
41. never **46.** hole at $x = 3$ **47.** vertical asymptotes at $x = -\frac{2}{3}$ and $x = -1$ **48.** hole at $x = 4$, vertical

asymptote at $x = -3$ **49.** 3 **50.** -5 **51.** $\frac{3}{4}$ **52.** 49
53. 168 **54.** 2 **55.** $\frac{17}{38}$ **56.** $\frac{11}{72}$ **57.** $\frac{137}{180}$

Lesson 8-5 Part 1   pp. 555–558

Got It? 1a. $2(x + 2)(x - 3)$ **b.** $(x - 1)(x - 2)^2(x + 4)$

2a. $\frac{x + 2}{x}$, $x \neq 1$ or 0 **b.** $\frac{2(x - 1)}{x^2 - 4}$; $x \neq \pm 2$ **c.** Yes, however the denominator would have to be factored more and there could be additional, incorrect limitations on x.

3a. $\frac{x - 2}{x - 1}$, $x \neq 1$ or 2 **b.** $\frac{x^2 - x - 4}{x^2 + 6x + 5}$; $x \neq -5$ or -1

Lesson Check 1. $\frac{2a - 10}{3a - 5}$; $a \neq \frac{5}{3}$ **2.** $\frac{6x - 11}{x^2 - 4}$; $x \neq \pm 2$

3. $\frac{-11m}{3m + 6}$; $m \neq -2$ **4.** $\frac{-4(2b - 5)}{(b - 4)(b + 4)(b - 2)}$; $b \neq 2$ or ± 4

5. Answers may vary. Sample: $\frac{x^2 - 1}{x^2 - 6x + 5}$, $\frac{x^2 + 6x + 5}{x^2 - 25}$

6. Factor the polynomials completely. Then identify the greatest power of each factor that occurs in either expression. The least common multiple is the product of those factors.

Exercises 7. $9(x + 2)(2x - 1)$ **9.** $2(x + 5)(x^2 -$
$32x - 10)$ **11.** $\frac{2(d - 2)}{2d + 1}$; $d \neq -\frac{1}{2}$ **13.** $\frac{-3(2y + 1)}{2y - 1}$;
$y \neq \frac{1}{2}$ **15.** $\frac{y - 6}{2(y + 2)}$; $y \neq -2$ **17.** $\frac{3x - 8}{4x^2}$; $x \neq 0$

19. $\frac{7x - 17}{(x - 3)(x + 3)}$; $x \neq \pm 3$ **21.** $\frac{x(3x^2 + x - 1)}{x^2 - 2}$; $x \neq \pm\sqrt{2}$

Lesson 8-5 Part 2   pp. 559–564

Got It? 4a. $\frac{x^2 y}{x + y}$ **b.** $\frac{(x - 1)^2}{2x}$ **c.** Answers may vary. Samples: Method 1; it requires fewer steps. Method 2; it is easier to simplify the numerator and denominator separately. **5.** Option 1 still gives the better combined mpg since Option 3 gives 18.46 mpg.

Lesson Check 1. $\frac{y}{2x}$ **2.** $\frac{b}{9}$

3. error in dividing by the denominator:

$$\frac{1 + \frac{1}{x}}{\frac{3}{x}} = \frac{\frac{x + 1}{x}}{\frac{3}{x}}$$
$$= \frac{x + 1}{x} \cdot \frac{x}{3}$$
$$= \frac{x + 1}{3}$$

Exercises 5. $\frac{2}{3(x + y)}$ **7.** $\frac{y}{x + y}$ **9.** $\frac{2}{5}$ **11.** $\frac{-3x}{5 + xy}$

13. $\frac{2(x + 5)}{x + 7}$ **15.** 3.84 in. **17.** $\frac{-x + 6}{(x - 3)(x + 3)}$; $x \neq \pm 3$

19. $\frac{-2x(x + 3)}{(x - 2)(x - 1)(x + 1)}$; $x \neq \pm 1$ or 2 **21.** $\frac{3x + 2y}{7x - 5y}$

23. x **30.** $\frac{12x}{x + 3}$; $x \neq 2$ or ± 3 **31.** $\frac{3(x + 2)}{4(x - 3)}$; $x \neq \pm 2$ or 3

32. $\frac{3(x + 1)}{2(x + 3)}$; $x \neq \pm 1$ or -3 **33.** $\log_3 yt^4$ **34.** $\log p^7 q^2$

35. $\log_5 \frac{x}{\sqrt[5]{y}}$ **36.** 30 **37.** 82 **38.** $\frac{15}{4}$ **39.** $-\frac{4}{5}$ **40.** 21 **41.** 18

Lesson 8-6   pp. 565–571

Got It? 1a. 1 **b.** 0 **2a.** ≈ 4.47 mi/h **b.** The direction of wind affects the speed (rate) of the bike. Since the speed is inversely related to time, change in speed will lead to change in time. Since there is no wind, the speed of the bike will remain same to and from the store, hence the time to and from the store will remain the same. **3.** $0.\overline{27}$

Lesson Check 1. 5 **2.** -1 **3.** -2 **4.** 310 mi/h
5. LCD was not found; the correct answer is

$$\frac{35 + 9x}{7x} = \frac{28(7)}{7x}, \; x \neq 0$$
$$9x = 161$$
$$x = \frac{161}{9} = 17.\overline{8}.$$

6. Answers may vary. Sample: $\frac{2}{x - 3} + \frac{1}{x + 3} = \frac{5x}{x^2 - 9}$

7. Answers may vary. Sample: (1) Substitute the solution into the original equation. (2) Check to see if the solution is in the domain of the graph of the original equation.

Exercises 9. $\frac{2}{9}$ **11.** $-1, 2$ **13.** 1 **15a.** $\frac{35}{18}$ h **b.** 90 mi/h

17. 1.5 **19.** ± 2 **21.** 1.69, -0.44 **23.** $E = mc^2$

25. $c = \pm\sqrt{a^2 - b^2}$ **27.** $B = \pm\sqrt{\frac{2Vm}{r^2 q}}$ **29.** $1\frac{5}{7}$ h

31. 4 test scores **33a.** $2250 **b.** $\frac{15,000}{24 + x}$ (3.60)

c. $2250 - \frac{15,000}{24 + x}$ (3.60) **d.** ≈ 32.7 mpg **35.** no solution

37. 30 **39.** -4 **41.** -1 **48.** $\frac{-y - 13}{4(y + 1)}$ **49.** $\frac{5xy - 12}{2y(y + 2)}$

50. $\frac{x^2 + 3}{2(x - 1)(x + 3)}$ **51.** $x = -3$ **52.** $x = -1$ **53.** $x =$

-0.875 **54.** $y = \frac{5 - x}{2}$; yes **55.** $y = \pm\sqrt{x - 1}$; no

56. $y = \sqrt[3]{x + 4}$; yes **57.** add 2; 9, 11, 13 **58.** subtract 2; $-10, -12, -14$ **59.** multiply by 5; 625, 3125, 15625
60. subtract 5; 30, 25, 20 **61.** multiply by 2; 128, 256, 512 **62.** subtract 4; $-19, -23, -27$

Chapter Review   pp. 573–576

1. simplest form **2.** combined variation **3.** complex fraction **4.** point of discontinuity **5.** branch **6.** 12

7. $y = \frac{72}{x}$ **8.** $y = 6x$ **9.** $z = \frac{7}{4}xy$; 56 **10.** $z = \frac{4x}{y}$; 2

11.

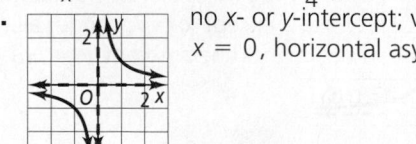

no x- or y-intercept; vert. asymptote: $x = 0$, horizontal asymptote: $y = 0$

12.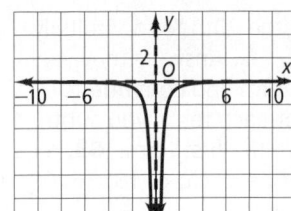
no x- or y-intercept; vert. asymptote: $x = 0$, horizontal asymptote: $y = 0$

13.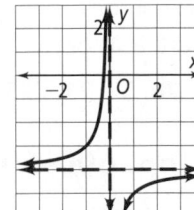
x-intercept: $(-0.25, 0)$, no y-intercept; vert. asymptote: $x = 0$, horizontal asymptote: $y = -4$

14.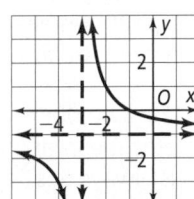
x-intercept: $(-1, 0)$, y-intercept: $(0, -\frac{1}{3})$; vert. asymptote: $x = -3$, horizontal asymptote: $y = -1$

15. $y = \dfrac{4}{x} + 3$ **16.** $y = \dfrac{4}{x - 2} + 2$

17. $y = \dfrac{4}{x + 3} - 4$ **18.** $y = \dfrac{4}{x - 4} - 3$

19. pts. of discontinuity: $x = -2, 1$;
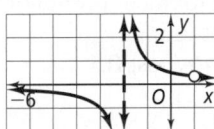
vert. asymptote: $x = -2$, horizontal asymptote: $y = 0$; hole at $x = 1$

20. pts. of discontinuity: $x = 1, -1$
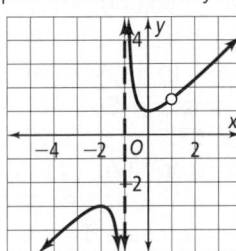
vert. asymptote: $x = -1$; hole at $x = 1$

21. no pts. of discontinuity
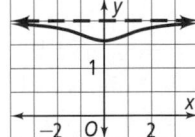
horizontal asymptote: $y = 2$

22.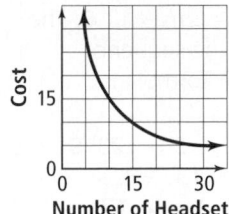
$\approx 31{,}056$ headsets

23. $\dfrac{x + 5}{x + 4}$; $x \neq -4$ or -5 **24.** $\dfrac{(x - 1)(x + 1)}{x + 3}$; $x \neq -4, -3,$ or 6 **25.** $\dfrac{(2x - 1)(x + 1)}{x + 4}$; $x \neq -4, -1,$ or 0 **26.** $\dfrac{r}{3}$, where r is the radius **27.** $\dfrac{3(3x - 4)}{(x - 2)(x + 2)}$; $x \neq \pm 2$

28. $\dfrac{-x^2 + 3x + 2}{x(x + 1)(x - 1)(x + 3)}$; $x \neq \pm 1, 0,$ or -3 **29.** $\dfrac{2(x - 1)}{3x - 1}$

30. $\dfrac{1}{4(x + y)}$ **31.** -1 **32.** no solution **33.** $-12, 9$

34. you: 10 mi/h friend: 8 mi/h

Chapter 9

Get Ready! p. 581

1. 9, 11, 13, 15 **2.** 1, 6, 11, 16 **3.** 0.9, 1.1, 1.3, 1.5
4. $-2, -7, -12, -17$ **5.** $3\frac{1}{3}, 7\frac{1}{3}, 11\frac{1}{3}, 15\frac{1}{3}$ **6.** $-12, -15,$
$-18, -21$ **7.** subtract 5; $-11, -16, -21$ **8.** mult. by 2;
16, 32, 64 **9.** alternate subtract 9 and add 1; $-7, -6,$
-15 **10.** add 3; 19, 22, 25 **11.** $\frac{4}{3}$ **12.** $\frac{3}{4}$ **13.** $\frac{5}{3}$
14. $\frac{5}{18}$ **15.** Answers may vary. Sample: $f(x) = 2x - 1$;
1, 3, 5, 7, 9 **16.** Answers may vary. Sample:
$g(x) = 1 - 2x$; $-1, -3, -5, -7, -9$; yes; common
difference: -2 **17.** Answers may vary. Sample:
$h(x) = 5(2)^x$; 10, 20, 40, 80, 160; yes; common ratio: 2

Lesson 9-1 pp. 584–591

Got It? 1. 147 **2a.** $a_1 = 1$ and $a_n = na_{n-1}$ **b.** $a_1 = 1$
and $a_n = a_{n-1} + n^2$ **3a.** $a_n = n^2 - 1$; 399 **b.** To find
the nth term using an explicit formula, you simply
substitute for n in the formula. To find the nth term using
a recursive definition may require many iterations.
4. 18 months
Lesson Check 1. 2, 7, 12, 17, 22 **2.** $-1, 0, 3, 8, 15$
3. $a_1 = 3$ and $a_n = 2a_{n-1}$ **4.** $a_n = 2 + 3n$ **5.** A
recursive formula defines the terms in a sequence by
relating each term after the first term to the one before it
and requires that the previous term be known to find a
given term. An example of a recursive formula for the
sequence 8, 4, 2, 1, . . . is $a_1 = 8$ and $a_n = \frac{1}{2}a_{n-1}$. An
explicit formula describes the nth term of a sequence
using the variable n and only requires the number of the
term to be known. An example of an explicit formula for

the sequence 1, 3, 5, 7, . . . is $a_n = 2n - 1$. **6.** The " $+1$ " in $a_n = 3n + 1$ is incorrect for the sequence 1, 4, 7, 10, . . . The correct explicit formula is $a_n = -2 + 3n$.

Exercises 7. $-4, -9, -14, -19, -24, -29$ **9.** 2, 5, 10, 17, 26, 37 **11.** 1, 3, 7, 15, 31, 63 **13.** $-3, 9, -27, 81,$ $-243, 729$ **15.** $a_1 = 4$ and $a_n = 2a_{n-1}$ **17.** $a_1 = 1$ and $a_n = a_{n-1} + 3$ **19.** $a_1 = \frac{1}{2}$ and $a_n = \frac{1}{2}a_{n-1}$
21. $a_n = n + 3$; 13 **23.** $a_n = \frac{n-6}{2}$; 2 **25.** $a_n = \frac{1}{n+1}$; $\frac{1}{11}$ **27.** 5 **29.** $\frac{5}{16}$ **31.** $\frac{1}{256}$ **33.** 13.8 mi **35.** explicit; $-24, -21, -16, -9, 0$ **37.** explicit; $-6, -18, -38,$ $-66, -102$ **39.** 15; 26; 40 **41.** 96, 192; $a_n = 3 \cdot 2^{n-1}$, explicit OR $a_n = 2a_{n-1}$, $a_1 = 3$, recursive **43.** 4096, 16,384; $a_n = 4^n$, explicit OR $a_n = 4a_{n-1}$, $a_1 = 4$, recursive **45.** $-1, 1$; $a_n = (-1)^n$, explicit OR $a_n = -1(a_{n-1})$, $a_1 = -1$, recursive **47.** $-47, -40$; $a_n = -82 + 7n$, explicit OR $a_n = a_{n-1} + 7$, $a_1 = -75$, recursive **49a.** 25 boxes **b.** 110 boxes **c.** 9 levels
51. $\frac{16}{5}, \frac{25}{6}, \frac{36}{7}, \frac{49}{8}$ **53.** Answers may vary. Sample:
a. 1, $-2, 4, -8, . . .$ **b.** $a_n = -2(a_{n-1})$, and $a_1 = 1$; $a_n = (-2)^{n-1}$ **c.** $-524,288$ **59.** 2 **60.** 4 **61.** -5
62. -1 **63.** 1 **64.** 2 **65.** subtract 2; $-2, -4, -6$
66. add 17; 185, 202, 219 **67.** add $\frac{3}{7}$; $\frac{17}{7}, \frac{20}{7}, \frac{23}{7}$

Lesson 9-2   pp. 592–598

Got It? 1a. no **b.** yes **2a.** 93 **b.** 95, 110 **3a.** 115 **b.** yes, use the formula for arithmetic mean and solve for a_7, $a_7 = 2a_6 - a_5$ **4.** 65 seats
Lesson Check 1. 56 **2.** 87 **3.** 13 **4.** 39 **5.** In an arithmetic sequence, the diff. between any two consecutive terms is always the same number. **6.** Answers may vary. Sample: 2, 4, 8, 16, 32, . . .
Exercises 7. yes; 10 **9.** yes; 3 **11.** yes; 4 **13.** 127
15. -59 **17.** -146 **19.** 12.5 **21.** 21 **23.** -8
25. 7.5 **27.** \$135 **29.** 18 **31.** 36 **33.** 2 **35.** 4
37. -20 **39.** 1.1 **41.** The student multiplied the third term by 2 instead of adding 2. The correct answer is 6.
43. $a_n = -5 + 1(n - 1)$; $a_n = a_{n-1} + 1$, $a_1 = -5$
45. $a_n = -5 + 1.5(n - 1)$; $a_n = a_{n-1} + 1.5$, $a_1 = -5$
47. $a_n = 27 - 12(n - 1)$; $a_n = a_{n-1} - 12$, $a_1 = 27$
49. Answers may vary. Sample: An advantage of a recursive formula is that only the preceding term must be known to find the next term; a disadvantage is that many calculations may be required to find a term. An advantage of an explicit formula is that it is easy to find any term. Use the recursive formula when the previous term and common diff. are known. Use the explicit formula when the term number and common diff. are known.
51. $-4, -10, -16$ **53.** $-8, -17, -26$ **55.** 17, 17, 17
57. \$5055 **59a.** Answers may vary. Sample: 25, 18, 11, 4, $-3, -10, . . .$; to find the 6th term, multiply 5 times (-7) and add to a_1; to find the 8th term, multiply 7 times

(-7) and add to a_1; to find the 20th term, multiply 19 times (-7) and add to a_1. **b.** Answers may vary. Sample: Start with the first term and continue to subtract 7 for each term. For each term, you subtract $7 \cdot$ (term number $- 1$) from the first term. **63.** recursive; $-2, -7, -12, -17, -22$ **64.** explicit; 6, 18, 36, 60, 90
65. explicit; 0, 3, 8, 15, 24 **66.** $y - 3 = \frac{8}{3}x$ or $y - 11 = \frac{8}{3}(x - 3)$ **67.** $y - 6 = 4(x - 4)$ or $y - 30 = 4(x - 10)$ **68.** $y - 10 = 8(x - 1)$ or $y - 42 = 8(x - 5)$ **69.** $r = \frac{\sqrt[3]{6\pi^2 V}}{2\pi}$ **70.** 32 **71.** 625
72. -81

Lesson 9-3   pp. 600–606

Got It? 1a. yes; $a_1 = 2$, $r = 2$ **b.** no **c.** yes; $a_1 = 2^3$, $r = 2^4$ **2a.** 156,250 **b.** 60; 30 **3a.** explicit; it is easier to use because only one calculation is needed. **b.** about 16.8 cm, about 4 cm **4.** ± 60
Lesson Check 1. no **2.** yes; 2 **3.** 729 **4.** 0.0064
5. The third term would be the geometric mean of 5 and 80 which is 20. Since a is pos. and r^2 is always pos., the third term, ar^2, cannot be neg. **6.** For both the arithmetic mean and the geometric mean, the middle term of any three consecutive terms can be determined using the first and last of the three terms. The arithmetic mean is the sum of the first and last terms divided by 2, whereas the geometric mean is the square root (or its opposite) of the product of the first and the last terms.
Exercises 7. yes; 2 **9.** yes; -2 **11.** yes; 0.1
13. 6561 **15.** $\frac{-3}{2048}$ **17.** about 656.1 g; about 182.5 g; about 96.2 g **19.** $\pm \frac{4}{15}$ **21.** ± 3.75
23. $a_n = 100(-20)^{n-1}$; 100, $-2000, 40,000, -800,000,$ 16,000,000 **25.** $a_n = 1024(0.5)^{n-1}$; 1024, 512, 256, 128, 64 **27.** $a_n = 10(-1)^{n-1}$; 10, $-10, 10, -10, 10$
29. arithmetic; 125, 150 **31.** geometric; $-80, 160$
33. neither; 25, 36 **35.** 7.5, 22.5, 67.5 or $-7.5, 22.5,$ -67.5 **37.** $-6.64, -11.02, -18.30$ or 6.64, $-11.02,$ 18.30 **39.** about 74.3 mi **41.** 3×4^{16}, or 12,884,901,888
43. $3(4^{n-1})$ **45.** 2.5 **47.** Both the common diff. and the common ratio are used to find the next term in a sequence, but a common diff. is added and a common ratio is multiplied. **52.** $a_n = -3 + 3(n - 1)$; $a_n = a_{n-1} + 3$, $a_1 = -3$ **53.** $a_n = 17 - 9(n - 1)$; $a_n = a_{n-1} - 9$, $a_1 = 17$ **54.** $a_n = -2 - 11(n - 1)$; $a_n = a_{n-1} - 11$, $a_1 = -2$ **55.** $a^4 + 20a^3 + 150a^2 + 500a + 625$
56. $x^3 - 27x^2 + 243x - 729$ **57.** $32x^5 + 80x^4y + 80x^3y^2 + 40x^2y^3 + 10xy^4 + y^5$ **58.** $b^{12} - 18b^{10} + 135b^8 - 540b^6 + 1215b^4 - 1458b^2 + 729$ **59.** vert. asymptote: $x = -3$ **60.** vert. asymptote: $x = -1$
61. vert. asymptotes: $x = 0$, 1 **62.** vert. asymptote: $x = 3$; hole at $x = -3$ **63.** $a_n = a_{n-1} + n$, $a_1 = 1$
64. $a_n = a_{n-1} + (2n - 1)$, $a_1 = 1$
65. $a_n = a_{n-1} + n^2$, $a_1 = 1$

Lesson 9-4   pp. 607–613

Got It? 1a. 2500 **b.** 1863 **c.** Yes; no; the sum of any number of even numbers is always even. The sum of an odd number of odd numbers is odd, but the sum of an even number of odd numbers is even. **2.** 59 sales; 1725 sales **3a.** $\sum_{n=1}^{40}(7n - 12)$ **b.** $\sum_{n=1}^{50}(510 - 10n)$

Lesson Check 1. 91 **2.** 780 **3.** $\sum_{n=1}^{7} 3n$ **4.** $\sum_{n=1}^{12}(4n - 3)$
5. An arithmetic sequence is a list of numbers for which successive numbers have a common difference. An arithmetic series is an expression for the sum of the terms of an arithmetic sequence. **6.** The lower limit should not be 3, it should be zero. The correct summation notation is $\sum_{n=0}^{8}(3 + 5n)$. **7.** Yes; $44 = 2(a_1 + a_4)$, so any combination of a_1 and a_4 with a sum of 22 is a possible series.

Exercises 9. 56 **11.** 840 **13.** −165 **15a.** 95 **b.** 510
17. $\sum_{n=1}^{8}(2n + 5)$ **19.** $\sum_{n=1}^{10}(110 - 10n)$ **21.** sequence; infinite **23.** series; infinite **25.** 32 **27.** 264 **29.** 4292
31a. $\sum_{n=1}^{20}(3n + 15)$, or $18 + 21 + 24 + \cdots + 75$ **b.** 930 seats **c.** \$46,950 **33.** 110 **41.** $a_n = 2^{n-1}$; 1, 2, 4
42. $a_n = -1(-1)^{n-1}$; −1, 1, −1 **43.** $a_n = 3\left(\frac{3}{2}\right)^{n-1}$;
$3, \frac{9}{2}, \frac{27}{4}$ **44.** $\frac{x + 3}{x - 4}$; $x \neq 4, x \neq -1$ **45.** $\frac{c - 2}{c - 5}$; $c \neq 5$,
$c \neq 6$ **46.** $\frac{z^2 + 12z + 20}{z - 1}$; $z \neq 1, z \neq 0$ **47.** $-\frac{1}{3}$
48. $\frac{3}{4}$ **49.** $-\frac{1}{2}$

Lesson 9-5   pp. 614–621

Got It? 1a. 315 **b.** −1705 **2.** about \$2138.43
3a. diverges **b.** converges; $\frac{1}{4}$ **c.** Yes; if $|r| < 1$, the series converges. If $|r| \geq 1$, the series diverges.
Lesson Check 1. $\frac{31}{80}$ **2.** $\frac{55}{9}$ **3.** converges **4.** diverges
5. Since $r = 1.1 > 1$, the series diverges and does not have a sum. **6.** An infinite geometric series has a sum only when $|r| < 1$. **7.** The sum of a finite arithmetic series is $S_n = \frac{n}{2}(a_1 + a_n)$. The sum of finite geometric series is $S_n = \frac{a_1(1 - r^n)}{1 - r}$. The formulas are similar in that each sum requires the first term and the number of terms in the series. The formulas are different in that the sum of a finite arithmetic series needs the last term, while the sum of a finite geometric series needs the common ratio.
Exercises 9. 1456 **11.** −5115 **13.** no; \$133.76
15. converges; $\frac{2}{3}$ **17.** diverges **19.** converges; −81
21. $1.\overline{2}$ **23.** $\frac{9}{5}$ **25.** geometric; 2046 **27.** geometric; −1,627,605 **29.** arithmetic; 500,500

31a.

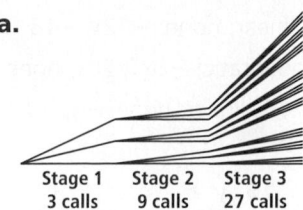

Stage 1   Stage 2   Stage 3
3 calls   9 calls   27 calls

b. 3 + 9 + 27 + 81 + 243 + 729 **c.** 1092
35. choice (b); (a) yields \$26,000; using the formula for finding the sum of a finite geometric series, (b) yields \$1,342,177.26. **42.** 140 **43.** −825 **44.** $\frac{7c - 4}{2c^2}$
45. $\frac{10(2y + 3)}{(y + 3)(y - 3)}$ **46.** $\frac{x^2 + 6x + 4}{(x + 6)(x - 6)}$ **47.** 0 **48.** 2 **49.** 1

Chapter Review   pp. 623–626

1. limits **2.** sequence **3.** converges **4.** common ratio
5. explicit formula **6.** 1, −1, −3, −5, −7 **7.** 1, 0, −3, −8, −15 **8.** 2, 3, 5, 9, 17 **9.** 20, 10, 5, 2.5, 1.25
10. $a_n = a_{n-1} + 17, a_1 = 5$ **11.** $a_n = a_{n-1} + 9$, $a_1 = -2$ **12.** $a_n = 3n - 2$ **13.** $a_n = 6.5 - 2.5n$
14. no **15.** yes; $d = 15, a_{32} = 468$ **16.** yes; $d = 3$, $a_{32} = 100$ **17.** no **18.** 5 **19.** 101.5 **20.** 5 **21.** −4.9
22. −10.5, −8, −5.5 **23.** 1.4, 0.8, 0.2 **24.** $a_n = -2 + 9(n - 1)$ **25.** $a_n = 62 - 3(n - 1)$ **26.** yes;
$r = \frac{1}{2}; \frac{1}{16}, \frac{1}{32}$ **27.** no **28.** yes; $r = 1.2$; 6.2208, 7.46496
29. ±6 **30.** ±0.04 **31.** +10, −5, ±2.5 **32.** $a_n = 2^{n-1}$
33. $a_n = 25\left(\frac{1}{5}\right)^{n-1}$ **34.** 2560 **35.** 1536 **36.** $\sum_{n=1}^{5}(13 - 3n)$;
20 **37.** $\sum_{n=1}^{7}(45 + 5n)$; 455 **38.** $\sum_{n=1}^{11}(4.6 + 1.4n)$; 143
39. $\sum_{n=1}^{8}(23 - 2n)$; 112 **40.** 31 **41.** $53\frac{1}{8}$ **42.** $14\frac{7}{18}$
43. converges; $S = 187.5$ **44.** diverges **45.** diverges
46. converges; $S = 2$

Chapter 10

Get Ready!   p. 631

1.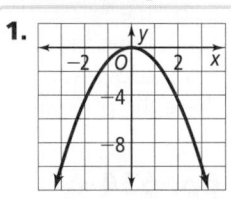

2.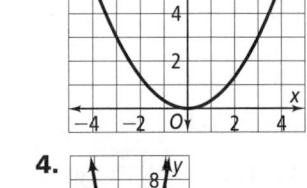

3.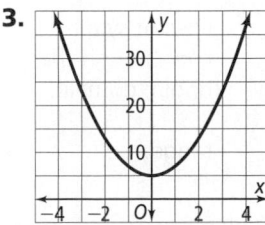

4.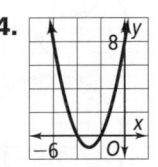

5. quadratic; $-x^2$, $6x$, 1 **6.** linear; none, $-12x$, -18

7. linear; none, x, $-\frac{13}{2}$ **8.** quadratic; $-8x^2$, $28x$, none

9. quadratic; $-2x^2$, $-3x$, 6 **10.** linear; none, $-x$, -10

11. 16 **12.** $\frac{25}{4}$ **13.** 49

14. $y = (x + 3)^2 - 2$ **15.** $y = 2(x - 1)^2 + 8$

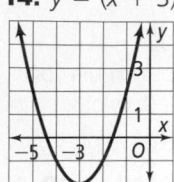 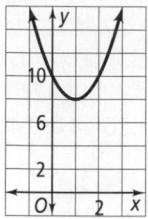

16. $y = -3\left(x - \frac{1}{6}\right)^2 + \frac{1}{12}$ **17.**

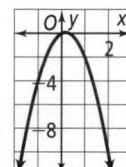 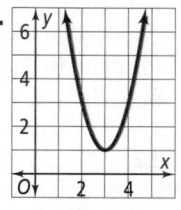

18. **19.**

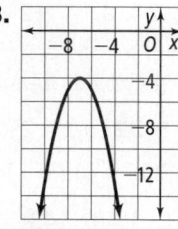 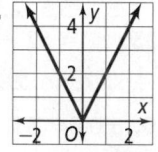

20.

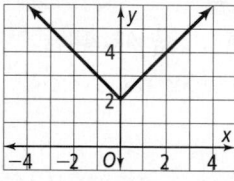

21. The radius of a circle is the distance from the center of the circle to any pt. on the circle. The radius extends in every direction from the center and ends on the circumference of the circle. All radii of the same circle are equal. **22.** The vertex of a parabola is the lowest or highest pt. of a parabola; it is the pt. where the parabola changes direction.

Lesson 10-1   pp. 634–640

Got It? 1a.

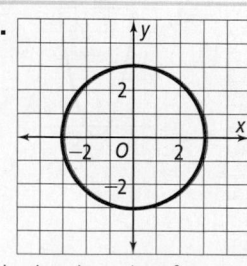

lines of sym.: every line through the origin; domain: $-3 \le x \le 3$, range: $-3 \le y \le 3$

b. 6 is outside the domain of x.

2.

lines of sym.: x-axis and y-axis; domain: $-3 \le x \le 3$, range: $-3\sqrt{2} \le y \le 3\sqrt{2}$

3.

lines of sym.: x-axis and y-axis; domain: $x \le -4$ or $x \ge 4$, range: all real numbers

Lesson Check

1.

lines of sym.: x-axis and y-axis; domain: $-6 \le x \le 6$, range: $-3 \le y \le 3$

2.

lines of sym.: x-axis and y-axis; domain: $x \le -3$ or $x \ge 3$, range: all real numbers

3. domain: $x \le -2.5$ or $x \ge 2.5$, range: all real numbers
4. domain: $-6 \le x \le 6$, range: $-1.5 \le y \le 1.5$
5a. hyperbola **b.** circle **6.** Answers may vary. Sample: The domain of an ellipse is an interval of two real numbers, such as $-a \le x \le a$. The domain of a hyperbola is two intervals, such as $x \le -a$ or $x \ge a$, if there are x-intercepts, or all real numbers if there are no x-intercepts.

Exercises

7.

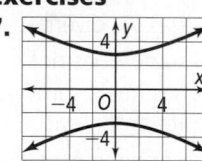

hyperbola; center: (0, 0); no x-intercepts, y-intercepts: $\left(0, \pm\frac{5\sqrt{3}}{3}\right)$; lines of sym.: x-axis and y-axis; domain: all real numbers, range: $y \le -\frac{5\sqrt{3}}{3}$ or $y \ge \frac{5\sqrt{3}}{3}$

9.

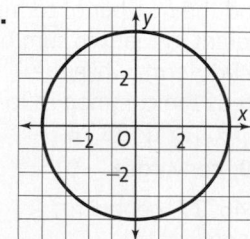

circle; center: (0, 0); radius: 4; x-intercepts: $(\pm 4, 0)$, y-intercepts: $(0, \pm 4)$; infinitely many lines of sym.; domain: $-4 \le x \le 4$, range: $-4 \le y \le 4$

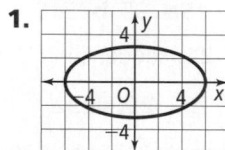
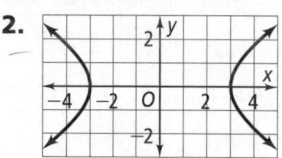

11. 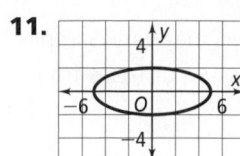 ellipse; center: (0, 0); x-intercepts: (±5, 0), y-intercepts: (0, ±2); lines of sym.: x-axis and y-axis; domain: −5 ≤ x ≤ 5, range: −2 ≤ y ≤ 2

13. 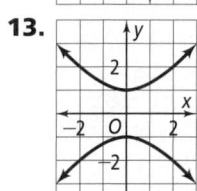 hyperbola; center: (0, 0); no x-intercepts, y-intercepts: (0, ±1); lines of sym.: x-axis and y-axis; domain: all real numbers, range: $y \leq -1$ or $y \geq 1$

15. 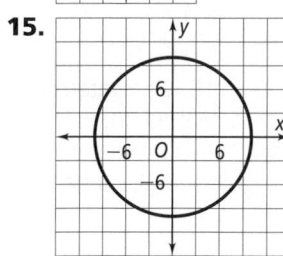 circle; center: (0, 0); radius: 10; x-intercepts: (±10, 0), y-intercepts: (0, ±10); infinitely many lines of sym.; domain: −10 ≤ x ≤ 10, range: −10 ≤ y ≤ 10

17. 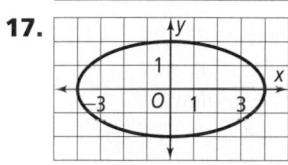 ellipse; center: (0, 0); x-intercepts: (±4, 0), y-intercepts: (0, ±2); lines of sym.: x-axis and y-axis; domain: −4 ≤ x ≤ 4, range: −2 ≤ y ≤ 2

19. 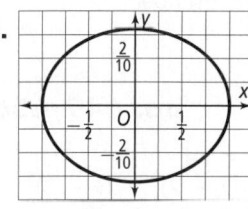 ellipse; center: (0, 0); x-intercepts: (±1, 0), y-intercepts: $\left(0, \pm\frac{1}{3}\right)$; lines of sym.: x-axis and y-axis; domain: −1 ≤ x ≤ 1, range: $-\frac{1}{3} \leq y \leq \frac{1}{3}$

21. 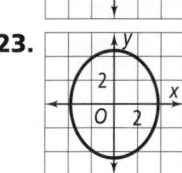 circle; center: (0, 0); radius: 2; x-intercepts: (±2, 0), y-intercepts: (0, ±2); infinitely many lines of sym.; domain: −2 ≤ x ≤ 2, range: −2 ≤ y ≤ 2

23. ellipse; center: (0, 0); x-intercepts: $\left(\pm\frac{8\sqrt{5}}{5}, 0\right)$, y-intercepts: (0, ±2√5); lines of sym.: x-axis and y-axis; domain: $-\frac{8\sqrt{5}}{5} \leq x \leq \frac{8\sqrt{5}}{5}$, range: −2√5 ≤ y ≤ 2√5

25a. All lines in the plane that pass through the center of a circle are axes of sym. of the circle. **b.** The axes of sym. of an ellipse intersect at the center of the ellipse. The same is true for a hyperbola. This can be confirmed using, for example, $4x^2 + 9y^2 = 36$ and $4x^2 - 9y^2 = 36$.

27. 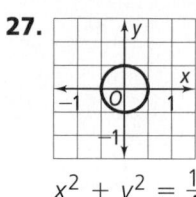   **29.**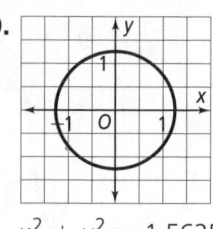

$x^2 + y^2 = \frac{1}{4}$

$x^2 + y^2 = 1.5625$

31. (√2, 1) **33.** (2, 0) **35.** (0, −√7) **42.** diverges
43. diverges **44.** converges **45.** $x^3 - 3x^2y + 3xy^2 - y^3$
46. $p^6 + 6p^5q + 15p^4q^2 + 20p^3q^3 + 15p^2q^4 + 6pq^5 + q^6$ **47.** $x^4 - 8x^3 + 24x^2 - 32x + 16$

48.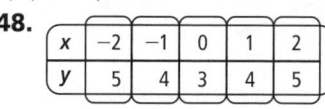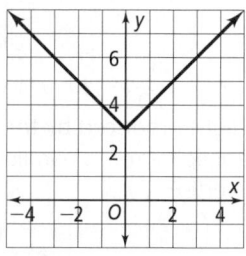

x	−2	−1	0	1	2
y	5	4	3	4	5

49.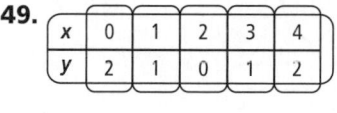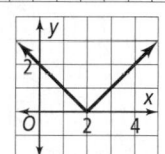

x	0	1	2	3	4
y	2	1	0	1	2

50.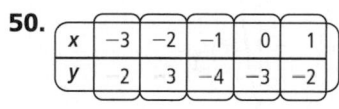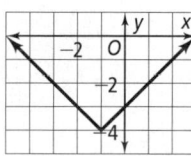

x	−3	−2	−1	0	1
y	2	−3	−4	−3	−2

Lesson 10-2   pp. 641–648

Got It? 1a. $y = -\frac{1}{6}x^2$ **b.** vertex: (0, 0); focus: (0, 1); directrix: $y = -1$ **c.** As the distance between the vertex and focus increases, the width of the parabola increases.
2a. $x = \frac{1}{10}y^2$ **b.** vertex: (0, 0); focus: $\left(-\frac{1}{16}, 0\right)$; directrix: $x = \frac{1}{16}$ **3.** 1 cm **4.** vertex: (−4, 2); focus: $\left(-4, 2\frac{1}{4}\right)$; directrix: $y = 1\frac{3}{4}$ **5.** $y = \frac{1}{8}(x - 1)^2 + 4$

Lesson Check 1. $y = \frac{1}{2}x^2$ **2.** $x = \frac{1}{4}(y - 2)^2 + 3$
3. vertex: (0, 0); focus: (4, 0); directrix: $x = -4$
4. vertex: (−3, −4); focus: (−3, −3.75); directrix: $y = -4.25$ **5.** 6 units **6.** With the focus one unit away from the vertex of a parabola at the origin, $c = \pm1$. Given this information, the student cannot tell whether the parabola opens in the vert. direction, with one of the eqs. $y = \frac{1}{4}x^2$ or $y = -\frac{1}{4}x^2$, or whether the parabola opens in the horizontal direction, with one of the eqs. of $x = \frac{1}{4}y^2$ or $x = -\frac{1}{4}y^2$.

Exercises 7. $x = \frac{1}{24}y^2$ **9.** $x = -\frac{1}{4}y^2$

11. vertex: (0, 0);

focus: $\left(0, \frac{1}{16}\right)$;

directrix: $y = -\frac{1}{16}$

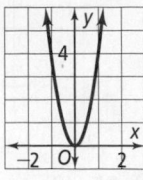

13. vertex: (0, 0);

focus: $\left(\frac{1}{2}, 0\right)$;

directrix: $x = -\frac{1}{2}$

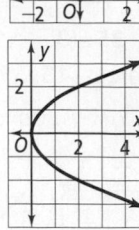

15. $y = -\frac{1}{20}x^2$ **17.** Answers may vary. Sample: $y = x^2$.
The light produced by the bulb will reflect off the
parabolic mirror in parallel rays.

19. vertex: (3, 2);

focus: $\left(3, \frac{9}{4}\right)$;

directrix: $y = \frac{7}{4}$

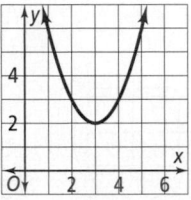

21. vertex: (−1, −4);

focus: $\left(-1, -3\frac{7}{8}\right)$;

directrix: $y = -4\frac{1}{8}$

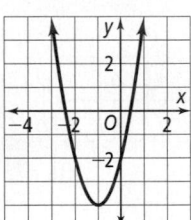

23. $x = -\frac{1}{32}(y - 3)^2$ **25.** $y = -\frac{1}{16}(x - 7)^2 + 2$

27. 3.5 in.

29. vertex: (0, 0);
focus: (0, −1);
directrix: $y = 1$

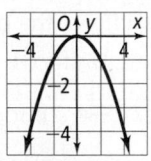

31. vertex: (0, 0);
focus: (−2, 0);
directrix: $x = 2$

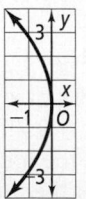

33. vertex: (4, 0);
focus: (4, −6);
directrix: $y = 6$

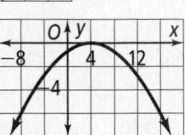

35. $x = -\frac{1}{2}(y - 1)^2 + 1$ **37.** Answers may vary. Sample:
Write the eq. in the form $x = \dfrac{1}{4\left(\frac{1}{8}\right)}y^2$. The distance from

the focus to the directrix is $2\left(\frac{1}{8}\right)$, or $\frac{1}{4}$.

42.

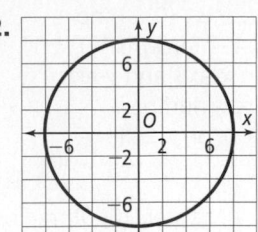

circle: center (0, 0), radius 8;
x-intercepts: (±8, 0),
y-intercepts: (0, ±8);
infinitely many lines of sym.;
domain: $-8 \le x \le 8$,
range: $-8 \le y \le 8$

43.

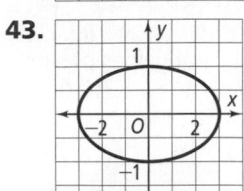

ellipse: center (0, 0); x-intercepts:
(±3, 0), y-intercepts: (0, ±1);
lines of sym.: x-axis and y-axis;
domain: $-3 \le x \le 3$, range:
$-1 \le y \le 1$

44.

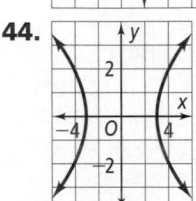

hyperbola: center (0, 0);
x-intercepts (±3, 0), no
y-intercept; lines of sym.:
x-axis and y-axis;
domain: $x \le -3$ or $x \ge 3$,
range: all real numbers

45. 1 **46.** 25 **47.** 9

Lesson 10-3   pp. 649–656

Got It? 1. $(x - 5)^2 + (y + 2)^2 = 64$
2a. $(x + 5)^2 + (y + 3)^2 = 1$ **b.** $(x - 2)^2 + (y - 3)^2 = 9$
3a. $(x - 7)^2 + (y + 10)^2 = 144$ **b.** Yes; the values of h
and k determine the position of the circle, and r
determines the size of the circle.
4a. center (−8, −3), radius 11 **b.** center (3, −7),
radius $\sqrt{66}$

5.

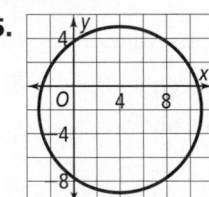

Lesson Check 1. $(x + 1)^2 + (y + 5)^2 = 4$
2. $x^2 + y^2 = 36$ **3.** $x^2 + (y - 3)^2 = 121$
4. $(x + 5)^2 + (y + 3)^2 = 16$ **5.** The circle with equation
$(x + 7)^2 + (y - 7)^2 = 8$ is a translation of the circle with
equation $x^2 + y^2 = 8$ as 7 units left and 7 units down,
not right and down. **6.** If $P(x, y)$ is one of the pts.
$(r, 0)$, $(−r, 0)$, $(0, r)$, or $(0, −r)$, subst. shows that

$x^2 + y^2 = r^2$. If $P(x, y)$ is any other pt. on the circle, drop a perpendicular $\overline{PK}$ from P to K on the x-axis. $\triangle OPK$ is a rt. triangle with legs of lengths $|x|$ and $|y|$ and with hypotenuse of length r. By the Pythagorean Thm., $|x|^2 + |y|^2 = r^2$, so $x^2 + y^2 = r^2$.

Exercises 7. $x^2 + y^2 = 100$ **9.** $(x - 2)^2 +$ $(y - 3)^2 = 20.25$ **11.** $(x - 1)^2 + (y + 3)^2 = 100$ **13.** $(x + 1)^2 + (y - 3)^2 = 81$ **15.** $(x - 2)^2 +$ $(y + 4)^2 = 25$ **17.** $(x - 3)^2 + (y - 2)^2 = 49$ **19.** $(x - 2)^2 + (y + 6)^2 = 16$ **21.** center $(1, 1)$, radius 1 **23.** center $(0, -3)$, radius 5

25. 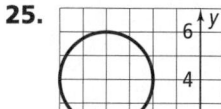 **27.**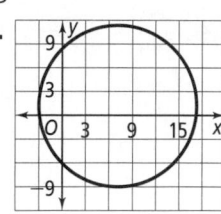

29. $x^2 + y^2 = 36$, $(x - 8)^2 + (y - 6)^2 = 16$, $(x - 8)^2 + (y)^2 = 4$ **31.** $x^2 + y^2 = 16$

33. $x^2 + y^2 = 25$ **35.** $x^2 + y^2 = 26$ **37.** Gear A: $(x + 7)^2 + y^2 = 16$, Gear B: $x^2 + y^2 = 9$, Gear C: $(x - 4)^2 + y^2 = 1$ **39.** $(x - 1)^2 + (y + 2)^2 = 10$ **41.** $(x - 6)^2 + (y - 4)^2 = 25$ **43.** center $(0, 0)$, radius $\sqrt{2}$ **45.** center $(-5, 0)$, radius $3\sqrt{2}$ **47.** center $(-3, 5)$, radius $\sqrt{38}$ **49.** center $(3, 1)$, radius $\sqrt{6}$

56. $x = -\frac{1}{12}y^2$ **57.** at $x = -1$ **58.** $x = 2, x = 3$

59. no points of discontinuity **60.** 4 **61.** 2 **62.** -3

63. 4 **64.** $\frac{1}{2}$ **65.** 1 **66.** $-2, -9$ **67.** $0, \pm4, \pm4i$

68. $\pm2, \pm2\sqrt{2}$

Lesson 10-4   pp. 658–665

Got It? 1. $\frac{x^2}{4} + \frac{y^2}{25} = 1$

2a. $(\pm8, 0)$.

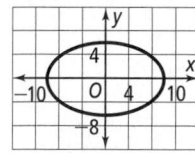

b. The vertex and co-vertex approach the same distance from the center of the ellipse; a circle

3. 24 ft **4.** $\frac{x^2}{36} + \frac{y^2}{53} = 1$

Lesson Check 1. $\frac{x^2}{64} + \frac{y^2}{36} = 1$ **2.** $(\pm\sqrt{21}, 0)$

3. $\frac{x^2}{169} + \frac{y^2}{25} = 1$ **4.** $6\sqrt{23}$ ft ≈ 28.77 ft

5. The student used a and b instead of a^2 and b^2; $\frac{x^2}{1681} + \frac{y^2}{841} = 1$ **6.** The eq. of an ellipse with center at

the origin is $\frac{x^2}{a^2} + \frac{y^2}{b^2} = 1$. For a circle, the major axis and the minor axis are of equal length such that $a = b = r$. Thus, by subst., $\frac{x^2}{r^2} + \frac{y^2}{r^2} = 1$ or $x^2 + y^2 = r^2$.

Exercises 7. $\frac{x^2}{16} + \frac{y^2}{9} = 1$ **9.** $\frac{x^2}{9} + y^2 = 1$

11. $\frac{x^2}{16} + \frac{y^2}{49} = 1$ **13.** $\frac{x^2}{9} + \frac{y^2}{25} = 1$

15. $(0, \pm\sqrt{5})$ **17.** $(\pm4\sqrt{2}, 0)$

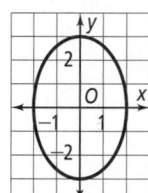   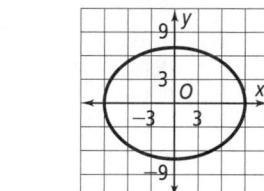

19. $(0, \pm6)$

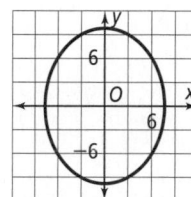

21. 32 **23.** $2\sqrt{39}$ **25.** $8\sqrt{2}$ **27.** $\frac{x^2}{89} + \frac{y^2}{64} = 1$

29a. about 22.25 ft **b.** Due to the reflective prop. of an ellipse, you can aim your putt at any part of the border. The ball will reflect off the border and go directly into the hole. **31.** $(0, \pm2\sqrt{3})$ **33.** $(0, \pm1)$ **35a.** 0.9 **b.** 0.1 **c.** The shape is close to a circle. **d.** The shape is close to a line segment. **37.** $\frac{x^2}{16} + y^2 = 1$ **39.** $\frac{x^2}{1681} + \frac{y^2}{841} = 1$

41. $\frac{x^2}{25} + \frac{y^2}{4} = 1$ **43.** $\frac{x^2}{169} + \frac{y^2}{144} = 1$ **45.** $\frac{x^2}{16} + \frac{y^2}{12} = 1$

47. $\frac{x^2}{36} + \frac{y^2}{27} = 1$ **52.** $(x - 1)^2 + (y + 5)^2 = 9$

53. $(x + 2)^2 + (y - 4)^2 = 81$ **54.** $\frac{1}{2x - 3x^4}$; $x \neq 0$ or $\sqrt[3]{\frac{2}{3}}$ **55.** $\frac{x - 6}{x - 1}$; $x \neq 1$ or -6

56. $\frac{x - 5}{x^2 - 2x + 4}$; $x \neq -2$ **57.** $\log 15$ **58.** $\log_3 6$

59. $\log 2$ **60.** $y = 2x + 4$ **61.** $y = \frac{1}{3}x$

Lesson 10-5   pp. 666–673

Got It? 1a. $\frac{y^2}{16} - \frac{x^2}{9} = 1$

b.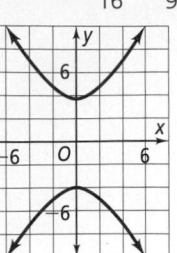

c. when $a = b$

2. vertices: $(\pm 2, 0)$;
foci: $(\pm \sqrt{13}, 0)$;
asymptotes: $y = \pm \frac{3}{2}x$

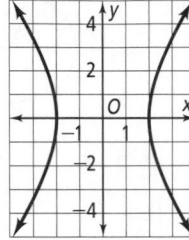

3. $\frac{x^2}{49} - \frac{y^2}{72} = 1$

Lesson Check

1. vertices: $(\pm 6, 0)$;
foci: $(\pm \sqrt{61}, 0)$;
slopes of asymptotes: $\pm \frac{5}{6}$

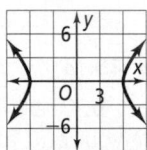

2. vertices: $(0, \pm 4)$;
foci: $(0, \pm \sqrt{41})$;
slopes of asymptotes: $\pm \frac{4}{5}$

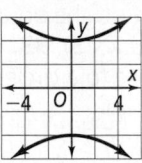

3. vertices: $(0, \pm 2)$;
foci: $(0, \pm 2\sqrt{5})$;
slopes of asymptotes: $\pm \frac{1}{2}$

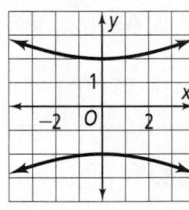

4. vertices: $(\pm 5, 0)$;
foci: $(\pm \sqrt{41}, 0)$;
slopes of asymptotes: $\pm \frac{4}{5}$

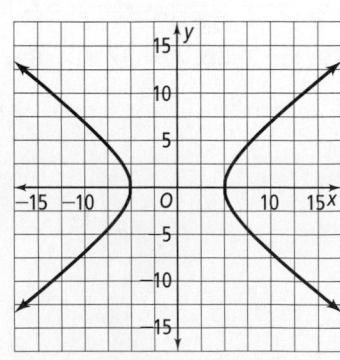

5. $\frac{x^2}{25} - \frac{y^2}{24} = 1$ **6.** Answers may vary. Sample:
Similarities—Both have two axes of sym. that intersect at the center of the figure and two foci that lie on the same line as the two "principal" vertices. Differences—An ellipse consists of pts. whose distances from the foci have a constant sum, whereas a hyperbola consists of pts. whose distances from the foci have a constant diff.
7. Answers may vary. Sample: A hyperbola is vert. or horizontal depending on whether it has a positive coefficient, not because the larger denominator is under the y^2 term.

Exercises 9. $\frac{x^2}{144} - \frac{y^2}{25} = 1$ **11.** $\frac{x^2}{144} - \frac{y^2}{25} = 1$

13. vertices: $(0, \pm 9)$;
foci: $(0, \pm \sqrt{97})$;
asymptotes: $y = \pm \frac{9}{4}x$

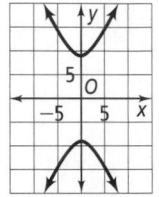

15. vertices: $(0, \pm 5)$;
foci: $(0, \pm 5\sqrt{5})$;
asymptotes: $y = \pm \frac{1}{2}x$

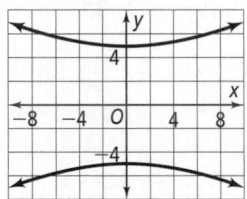

17. vertices: $(0, \pm 5)$;
foci: $(0, \pm \sqrt{29})$;
asymptotes: $y = \pm \frac{5}{2}x$

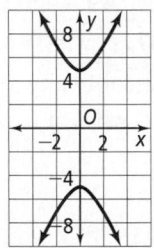

19. vertices: $(0, \pm 4\sqrt{2})$;
foci: $(0, \pm 4\sqrt{3})$;
asymptotes: $y = \pm \sqrt{2}x$

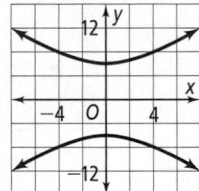

21. $\frac{x^2}{4.770 \times 10^{12}} - \frac{y^2}{3.668 \times 10^{12}} = 1$ **23.** $\frac{y^2}{25} - \frac{x^2}{144} = 1$

25. $\frac{x^2}{4} - y^2 = 1$ **27.** $\frac{y^2}{9} - x^2 = 1$

29. $y = \pm\sqrt{3x^2 - 2}$; $(\pm 0.816, 0)$

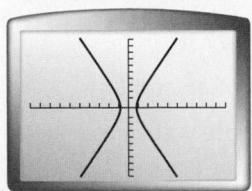

33.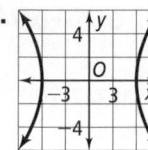

39. foci: $(\pm 3, 0)$
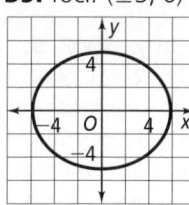

40. foci: $(0, \pm 1)$
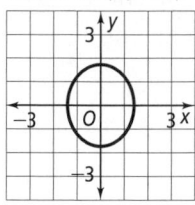

41. foci: $(0, \pm 6)$
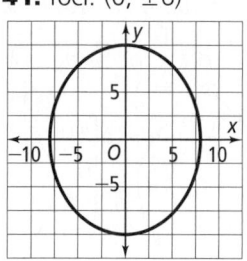

42. $\frac{1}{3}$ **43.** 125 **44.** 6 **45.** −19 **46.** 6

Chapter Review
pp. 675–678

1. directrix **2.** major axis **3.** standard form of an eq. of a circle **4.** radius **5.** transverse axis

6.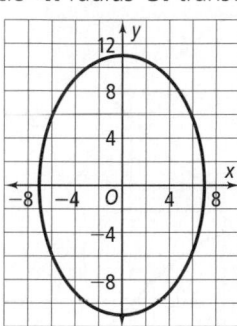
ellipse; lines of sym.: x-axis and y-axis; domain: $-7 \le x \le 7$, range: $-11 \le y \le 11$

7.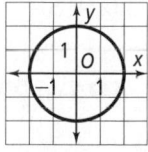
circle; lines of sym.: every line through the center; domain: $-2 \le x \le 2$, range: $-2 \le y < 2$

8.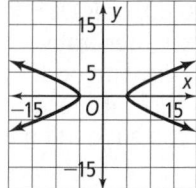
hyperbola; lines of sym.: x-axis and y-axis; domain: $x \le -5$ or $x \ge 5$, range: all real numbers

9.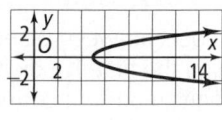
parabola; line of sym.: x-axis; domain: $x \ge 5$, range: all real numbers

10. center $(0, 0)$; domain: $x \le -4$ or $x \ge 4$, range: all real numbers **11.** center $(0, 0)$; domain: $-3 \le x \le 3$, range: $-2 \le y \le 2$ **12.** $x = \frac{1}{20}y^2$ **13.** $y = -\frac{1}{20}x^2$

14. $y = \frac{1}{24}x^2$ **15.** $y = \frac{1}{10}x^2$ **16.** $y = 3x^2$

17. $y = \frac{1}{8}x^2 + 1$ **18.** $x = -\frac{1}{12}y^2 + 1$

19. focus: $\left(0, \frac{1}{20}\right)$, directrix: $y = -\frac{1}{20}$
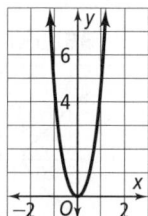

20. focus: $\left(\frac{1}{8}, 0\right)$, directrix: $x = -\frac{1}{8}$
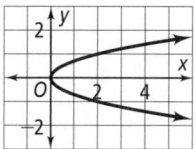

21. focus: $(-2, 0)$, directrix: $x = 2$
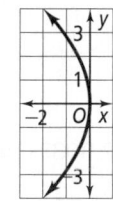

22. $x^2 + y^2 = 16$ **23.** $(x - 8)^2 + (y - 1)^2 = 25$
24. $(x + 3)^2 + (y - 2)^2 = 100$
25. $(x - 5)^2 + (y + 3)^2 = 64$
26. center $(1, 0)$, radius 8 **27.** center $(-7, -3)$, radius 7

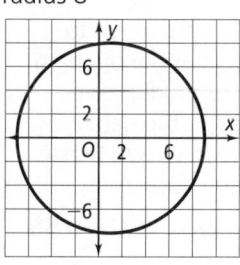 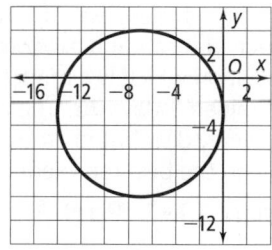

circle with radius 8 translated 1 unit to the rt.

circle with radius 7 translated 7 units to the left and 3 units down

28. $\frac{x^2}{17} + \frac{y^2}{16} = 1$ **29.** $\frac{x^2}{25} + \frac{y^2}{29} = 1$ **30.** $\frac{x^2}{9} + \frac{y^2}{10} = 1$

31. $\frac{x^2}{40} + \frac{y^2}{36} = 1$ **32.** $\frac{x^2}{64} + \frac{y^2}{16} = 1$

33. foci: $(0, \pm\sqrt{5})$

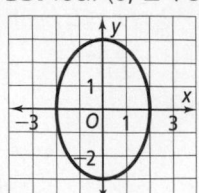

34. foci: $(\pm 3\sqrt{29}, 0)$

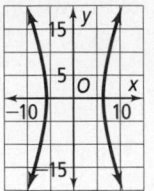

35. foci: $(0, \pm\sqrt{569})$

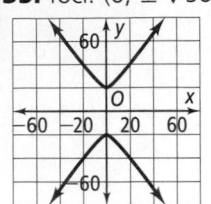

36. foci: $(\pm\sqrt{202}, 0)$

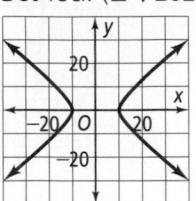

37. $\dfrac{x^2}{64} - \dfrac{y^2}{225} = 1$ **38.** $\dfrac{y^2}{49} - \dfrac{x^2}{576} = 1$

39. $\dfrac{x^2}{1.148 \times 10^{10}} - \dfrac{y^2}{3.395 \times 10^{10}} = 1$

Chapter 11

Get Ready!   p. 683

1. $83.\overline{3}\%$ **2.** $19.\overline{4}\%$ **3.** $\approx 92.308\%$ **4.** 30.56%
5. 6720 **6.** 22,100 **7.** 10
8. $a^5 + 5a^4b + 10a^3b^2 + 10a^2b^3 + 5ab^4 + b^5$
9. $j^3 + 9j^2k + 27jk^2 + 27k^3$ **10.** $m^2 + 1.4m + 0.49$
11. $16 + 32t + 24t^2 + 8t^3 + t^4$ **12.** $m^2 + 2mn + n^2$
13. $x^4 + 12x^3y + 54x^2y^2 + 108xy^3 + 81y^4$ **14.** $\pm\dfrac{1}{10}$
15. $\pm\dfrac{1}{20}$ **16.** $\pm\dfrac{1}{14}$ **17.** $\pm\dfrac{1}{2}$ **18.** $\pm\dfrac{1}{3}$ **19.** $\pm\dfrac{1}{24}$
20. In a math class, when actual trials are difficult to conduct, you can find experimental probability by using a simulation which is a model of one or more events.
21. It rained today. **22.** The mean, $12.\overline{6}$; the data are fairly evenly distributed around the mean which, makes the mean the best representation of the data given.

Lesson 11-1 Part 1   pp. 686–689

Got It? 1. 6,760,000 **2.** 40,320
3a. 2730 **b.** Yes; because $n = 10$ and $r = 3$ in the formula $_nP_r$ for both cases.
Lesson Check 1. 120 **2.** 3024 **3.** 20
Exercises 5. 26,000 **7.** 120 **9.** 720
11. 120 **13a.** 24 **b.** 120 **15.** 56 **17.** 1680
19. 840 **21.** 10,897,286,400 **23.** True; Assoc. Prop. of Mult. **25.** false; answers may vary. Sample: $(3 \cdot 2)! = 6! = 720$ and $3! \cdot 2! = 6 \cdot 2 = 12$ **27.** false; answers may vary. Sample: $(3!)^2 = 6^2 = 36$ and $3^{(2!)} = 3^2 = 9$

Lesson 11-1 Part 2   pp. 690–694

Got It? 4a. 56 **b.** 36 **c.** 3003 **5.** 1680
Lesson Check 1. 20 **2.** 21 **3.** 4 **4.** 4,151,347,200
5. A permutation is an arrangement of items in a particular order; order is important. A grouping in which order does not matter is a combination.
Exercises 7. 15 **9.** 1 **11.** 15 **13.** $\dfrac{5}{18}$ **15.** combination; 4368 **17.** combination; 70 **19.** C **21.** Sometimes; $_nC_r = {}_nP_r$ when $\dfrac{n!}{r!(n-r)!} = \dfrac{n!}{(n-r)!}$; that is, when $r! = 1$, or $r = 0$ or $r = 1$.
27. foci: $(\pm\sqrt{85}, 0)$;

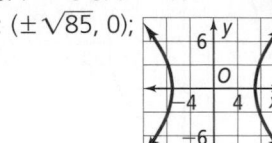

28. foci: $(0, \pm\sqrt{21})$;

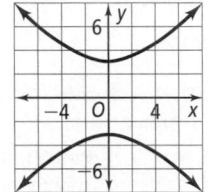

29. foci: $(0, \pm 2\sqrt{26})$;

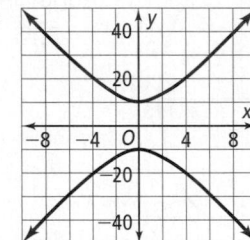

30. $4(x - 1)^2$ **31.** $-(x + 3)^2$ **32.** $3(x - 5)(x + 5)$
33. 30,240 **34.** $\dfrac{4}{5}$ **35.** 210

Lesson 11-2 Part 1   pp. 695–697

Got It? 1. 0.40, or 40% **2.** 0.20, or 20%
Lesson Check 1. 0.75, or 75% **2.** 0.80, or 80%
3. Answers may vary. Samples: Flip a coin; generate random numbers on a calculator; roll a die with odd numbers as true and even numbers as false. **4.** Because you are averaging over more samples, you are getting a more accurate average.
Exercises 5. $\dfrac{161}{340} \approx 47\%$; $\dfrac{179}{340} \approx 53\%$ **7.** Answers may vary. Sample: Generate random numbers between 0 and 1 using a graphing calculator. Examine the first five digits of each random number. Let even digits represent correct answers and odd digits incorrect answers. If there are two or more even digits, make a tally mark for that number. The total number of tally marks for 100 numbers, as a percent, gives the experimental probability. The simulated probability should be about 0.8.

9. Answers may vary. Sample: Randomly generate a 1, 2, 3, 4, or 5 five times. Let 1 represent a correct guess and 2–5 represent incorrect guesses. Tally the recorded numbers with exactly one digit that represents a correct answer. Tally the recorded numbers with exactly two digits that represent correct answers. Tally the recorded numbers with exactly three digits that represent correct answers. The tally totals, as percents, give the experimental probabilities. They should be in the neighborhood of 40%, 20%, and 5%, respectively.

Lesson 11-2 Part 2   pp. 698–703

Got It? 3a. $\frac{1}{2}$ **b.** The likelihoods of getting an even or odd are the same, i.e. $\frac{1}{2}$. **4.** $\frac{48}{2,598,960}$ or 0.0000184689 or $\approx 0.00185\%$ **5.** 0.05 or 5%

Lesson Check 1. $\frac{1}{6}$ **2.** $\frac{1}{3}$ **3.** Experimental probabilities are calculated on the basis of data from an experiment, actual or simulated. Given equally likely outcomes, the basis for calculating theoretical probability is being able to determine the no. of ways that an event can occur within these outcomes. Comparisons of measures such as length and area are the basis of geometric probability. **4.** $\frac{3}{10}$, or 30% **5.** $\frac{1}{2}$, or 50% **6.** $\frac{1}{2}$, or 50%

Exercises 7. $\frac{4}{5}$, or 80% **9.** $\frac{48}{125}$, or 38.4%
11. $\frac{103}{125}$, or 82.4% **13.** $\frac{77}{125}$, or 61.6%

15. $\frac{_{30}C_3 \cdot _{120}C_6}{_{150}C_9} \approx 0.17879 \approx 17.9\%$ **17.** $\frac{5}{8}$, or 62.5%

19. $\frac{3}{4}$, or 75% **21.** $\frac{116}{147} \approx 78.9\%$ **23.** $\frac{43}{147} \approx 29.3\%$

25. 1 chance in 2,869,685 or $\approx 0.00003485\%$ **32.** 20
33. 840 **34.** 10 **35.** 45 **36.** $\frac{25b - 7a^3}{5a^2b^2}$ **37.** $\frac{3q + 7p}{pq}$
38. 0 **39.** $\frac{7}{36} = 19.\overline{4}\%$ **40.** $\frac{25}{36} \approx 69.\overline{4}\%$ **41.** $\frac{1}{2}$, or 50%

Lesson 11-3   pp. 704–710

Got It? 1. Independent; the number of coins is the same after the coin is replaced. **2.** 0.20, or 20%
3a. Not mutually exclusive; 2 is a prime number and an even number. **b.** Mutually exclusive; there is no even number less than 2 in the roll of a number cube.
4a. 0.61, or 61% **b.** Yes; the percentage of students tells which language is chosen by more students. **5a.** $\frac{5}{9}$ **b.** $\frac{5}{9}$

Lesson Check 1. $\frac{1}{15}$ or 6.$\overline{6}$% **2.** $\frac{27}{80}$ or 33.75% **3.** 1
4. $\frac{7}{8}$ or 87.5% **5.** $\frac{5}{8}$ or 62.5% **6.** Events A and B are independent if the outcomes of A do not affect the outcomes of B. The events are mutually exclusive if A and B cannot occur at the same time. For independent events, $P(A \text{ and } B) = P(A) \cdot P(B)$. For mutually exclusive events, $P(A \text{ and } B) = 0$. For any events, $P(A \text{ or } B) =$

$P(A) + P(B) - P(A \text{ and } B)$. **7.** Since these are not mutually exclusive events, $P(A \text{ and } B) \neq 0$. The student should have calculated $P(A \text{ or } B) = P(A) + P(B) - P(A \text{ and } B)$, which is 0.79, or 79%.
Exercises 9. independent **11.** dependent **13.** $\frac{9}{34}$
15. $\frac{9}{25}$ **17.** mutually exclusive; if the numbers are equal, then the sum is even **19.** $\frac{14}{15}$ **21.** 47% **23.** $\frac{5}{6}$ **25.** $\frac{2}{3}$
27. $\frac{2}{5}$ **29.** 38% **31.** $\frac{4}{15}$ **33.** $\frac{8}{15}$ **35.** not mutually exclusive **43.** $\frac{1}{6}$ **44.** $\frac{1}{2}$ **45.** $\frac{1}{2}$ **46.** $\frac{3}{7}$ **47.** $-\frac{3}{2}$, 2 **48.** $\frac{1}{6}$
49. 500 **50.** 500,000 **51.** ± 100 **52.** $\frac{1}{16}$ **53.** $\frac{1}{16}$ **54.** $\frac{3}{16}$

Lesson 11-4   pp. 711–717

Got It? 1a. ≈ 0.57355 or $\approx 57.355\%$ **b.** Female; there are more females enrolled. **2a.** ≈ 0.026448 or $\approx 2.64\%$ **b.** ≈ 0.040302 or $\approx 4.03\%$ **3.** 0.2 **4.** 9%

Lesson Check 1. $\frac{1}{2}$ **2.** $\frac{1}{13}$, or 7.7% **3.** 0% **4.** 50%
5. The sum of the probability of an event happening and the probability of an event not happening is 1. Each branch represents either the event happening or the event not happening. **7.** Answers may vary. Sample: Tree diagrams apply to cases in which more than one event occurs in a sequence. The Fundamental Counting Principle applies to situations in which there are multiple outcomes of a single event. With a tree diagram, but not with the Fundamental Counting Principle, you can determine probabilities of dependent events, or conditional probabilities.
Exercises 9. 0.6 **11.** ≈ 0.682 **13.** ≈ 0.709 **15.** $\approx 23\%$
17.

M = male
F = female
R = right-handed
L = left-handed

$P(L|F) = 10\%$; $P(M \text{ and } R) \approx 8.3\%$
19. 75% **21.** $P(R|W)$ **23.** 0.08, or 8% **25.** 0.84

30. $\frac{1}{3} = 33.\overline{3}\%$ **31.** $\frac{17}{76} \approx 0.22368 \approx 22.37\%$

32. $x = \frac{1}{4}(y - 2)^2 + 5$ **33.** $y = \frac{1}{12}(x + 2)^2 + 3$

44. 0.2, 0.3, 0.6, 0.7, 0.8, 0.9, 1.2; 0.7
45. 11, 15, 17, 18, 21, 21, 23; 18

Chapter Review for Part A pp. 718–720

1. permutation **2.** Conditional **3.** simulation **4.** mutually exclusive **5.** 6 **6.** 362,880 **7.** 12 **8.** 30 **9.** 21 **10.** 10
11. 30 **12.** 744 **13.** 220; 84; 20; 1 **14.** 3.315312×10^9
15. 216 **16.** $\frac{47}{70}$ **17.** 0 **18.** $\frac{2}{5}$ **19.** Not necessarily; you may pick a 5 zero times, one time, or more than once. Each time you pick, the prob. that it will be a 5 is $\frac{1}{20}$.
20. dependent **21.** independent **22.** 0.21 **23.** 0.79
24. 0.3 **25.** 0.7 **26.** $\frac{1}{4}$ **27.** $\frac{1}{5}$ **28.** $\frac{1}{8}$

Lesson 11-5   pp. 723–731

Got It? 1. mean: 5.25, median: 5, mode: 5 **2a.** Yes; it is unlikely that the water temperature of a lake would change by 25 degrees. **b.** No; 98 would represent the busiest night of the week, and it may relate to a weekly event. **3.** Dauphin Island: mean: 69.08$\overline{3}$, mode: 84, range: 33, Q_1 = 58, median: 71, Q_3 = 81, interquartile range: 23; Grand Isle: mean: 73.41$\overline{6}$, modes: 61, 70, 77, 83, 85, range: 24, Q_1 = 64.5, median: 73.5, Q_3 = 83, interquartile range: 18.5; The range and the interquartile range show the temperatures varying less at Grand Isle than at Dauphin Island. Also, the temperatures at Grand Isle are generally higher. **4a.** Use STAT PLOT, select a box-and-whisker plot. Enter data for the three remaining Gulf Coast sites. Enter the window values. Draw the box-and-whisker plots. Use TRACE on the plot to find quartiles Q_1, Q_2, and Q_3.

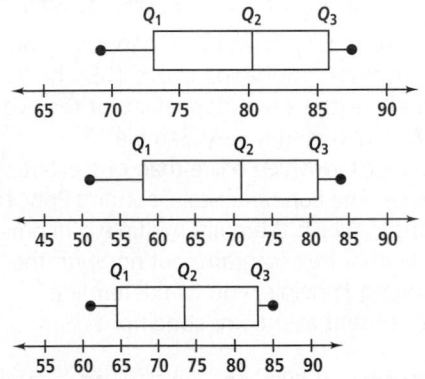

b. Yes, a box-and-whisker plot uses minimum and maximum values, the median, and the first and third quartiles to display the variability in a data set.
5a. 79 **b.** 98
Lesson Check 1. outlier: 54; outlier included: mean: 22.8, median: 19.5, mode: 18; outlier not included: mean: 19.$\overline{3}$, median: 19, mode: 18 **2.** outlier: 40; outlier included: mean: 92.$\overline{6}$, median: 98, mode: 90; outlier not included: mean: 99.25, median: 99, mode: 90 **3.** 40%: 49 and below; 80%: 58 and below **4.** The error is in how to calculate the median. The median is the middle value, or the 11th value, which is 90.
Exercises 5. mean: 112.$\overline{3}$, median: 95, mode: none
7. 9.8 **9.** Jacksonville: mean: 67.991$\overline{6}$, mode: none, range: 29.2, Q_1 = 58.15, median: 68.4, Q_3 = 78.6, interquartile range: 20.45; Austin: mean: 68.58$\overline{3}$, mode: none, range: 36, Q_1 = 56.85, median: 70.5, Q_3 = 80.75, interquartile range: 23.9; the range and the interquartile range show the temperatures varying less at Jacksonville than at Austin.

11.

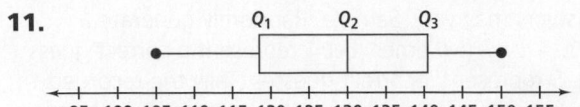

13. 5; 17 **15.** outliers: 22.2 and 99.9; outliers included: mean: ≈60.74, median: 58, mode: none; both outliers not included: mean: 60.6$\overline{81}$, median: 58, mode: none
17a.

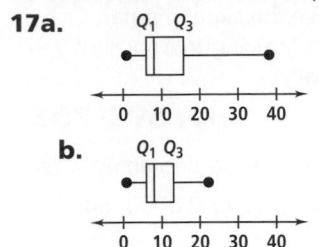

c. The main effect of removing the outlier is a shortening of the long whisker. The median decreases from 8.5 to 8.
19. 65th **21a.** mean: $1047.88, median: $1049.50, mode: $695 **b.** mode; it gives the lowest price **c.** median; when extreme values (outliers) are involved ($695 and $1499), the median gives a more accurate measure of central tendency **27.** ≈0.20 **28.** ≈0.56 **29.** yes; −9 **30.** yes; 17 **31.** no **32.** ±16 **33.** ±0.09 **34.** ±$\frac{11}{4}$

Lesson 11-6   pp. 732–737

Got It? 1. $\bar{x}$ = 69.8$\overline{3}$, σ^2 ≈ 115.1389, σ ≈ 10.7303
2. $\bar{x}$ = 7.2$\overline{6}$, σ ≈ 3.214 **3a.** within 3 standard deviations of the mean **b.** FEMA can expect that the no. of hurricanes for a 15-year period will fall within 3 standard deviations of the mean.
Lesson Check 1. $\bar{x}$ = 10, σ^2 = 19.8, σ ≈ 4.45
2. within 2 standard deviations of the mean **3.** Measures of central tendency are specific data pts. which give a summary of the middle of the data set, whereas the measures of variation give a summary of the variation of the data set within the range of distribution. **4.** Standard deviation measures how widely spread the data values are. If the data pts. are close to the mean, the standard deviation is small; if the data pts. are far from the mean, the standard deviation is large. The data pts. of Set B are closer to the mean of 70 than the data pts. of Sets A and C; likewise, the data pts. of Set A are closer to 70 than the data pts. of Set C.
Exercises 5. $\bar{x}$ ≈ 258.6, σ^2 ≈ 52,136.8, σ ≈ 228.3
7. $\bar{x}$ = 5.5, σ^2 ≈ 10.9, σ ≈ 3.3
9. $\bar{x}$ = 1992.$\overline{3}$, σ ≈ 61.85 **11.** 2 standard deviations
13. $\bar{x}$ = 53.8, σ ≈ 3.4; 1σ: 7; 2σ: 9; 3σ: 10 **15.** Overall farm income increased slightly, but there was less variability among the states in 2002. The income in 2001 clustered more tightly around the mean.
(2001: σ ≈ 2679, 2002: σ ≈ 2758)
17a. $\bar{x}$ = 82.3, σ ≈ 4.3 **b.** 1σ: 7; 2σ: 9; 3σ: 10

23.

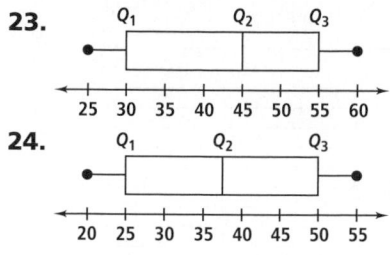

24.

25. center $(2, -1)$; radius 6 **26.** center $(1, 1)$; radius 2
27. $\frac{1}{2}$ **28.** $-\frac{1}{3}$ **29.** $\frac{1}{6}$

Lesson 11-7   pp. 738–743

Got It? 1a. convenience sample; yes; since the location is at the food court in the mall, the sample may over represent food court or fast food supporters. **b.** Answers may vary. Sample: population data for the US census **2a.** Yes; the question asks about two issues, nutrition and taste. **b.** Yes; the question is "loaded," suggesting the student council is "highly effective" and that you want a particular answer. **3a.** Answers may vary. Sample: Have pictures of five well known figures, the swimmer and four others who are not sports figures, such as an actor, the president, etc. Ask a member in every fifth house in your neighborhood to identify the five figures. **b.** Explanations may vary. Sample: The sampling method is not appropriate because the members of a swim team are more likely than a person not on a swim team to know the name of a famous swimmer. Also, the question is not appropriate as it identifies that the person in the photograph is a swimmer.
Lesson Check 1a. convenience sample **b.** Yes; since the location is near the exit of a history museum, the sample may overrepresent people who enjoy learning history and the results will have a bias. **2.** Yes; the question is leading and loaded. It suggests the person wants a particular answer. **3.** All members of the set are the population. A sample is a subset of the population. Answers may vary. Sample: population: students in a high school; sample: students who like to snowboard. **4.** It is important to have as little error as poss. in a sample, thus giving an unbiased sample. An unbiased sample is more representative of an entire population. **5.** A large sample size would give a better estimate. The size of the sample is important to the reliability of the sample.
Exercises 7. systematic sampling; no **9.** The question asks about two issues, academic homework and household chores. **11.** The question is leading. It suggests you want a certain answer, that the wrestling team doesn't get enough coverage in the school newspaper. **13.** Answers may vary. Sample: Convenience sampling; interview students at a local high school. **15.** Answers may vary. Sample: Self-selected sampling; a newspaper article invites females over the age of 21 to call the paper

and express their opinions. **17.** self-selected sampling; biased because only those who spend time online will respond. **19.** Answers may vary. Sample: Do you think career opportunitites will decrease if Congress considers additional unemployment control laws? **21.** Answers may vary. Sampling: Do you think opening more colleges and encouraging students to complete their education will help provide careers to financially challenged people?
23. systematic sampling; This sample may have a bias since people with no strong interest in any leisure-time activity may choose not to respond.
25. $\approx \pm 0.019988$, or $\pm 1.9988\%$ **30.** $\bar{x} \approx 2.83$, $\sigma \approx 2.54$
31. $\bar{x} \approx 5.62$, $\sigma \approx 3.67$ **32.** $y = \frac{1}{2}(x - 5)$; yes
33. $y = \pm\sqrt{x}$; no **34.** $y = \frac{x^2}{9}$, $x \geq 0$; yes **35.** 6 **36.** 1
37. 10

Lesson 11-8   pp. 745–751

Got It? 1. $P(0) = 0.07776$; $P(1) = 0.2592$; $P(2) = 0.3456$; $P(3) = 0.2304$; $P(5) = 0.01024$
2. $81x^4 + 108x^3y + 54x^2y^2 + 12xy^3 + y^4$ **3.** ≈ 0.1035, or about 10.4%
Lesson Check 1. ≈ 0.3110, or $\approx 31.10\%$ **2.** ≈ 0.1641, or $\approx 16.41\%$ **3.** $20c^3d^3$ **4.** $-10x^4y$ **5.** 0.2646, or 26.46%
6. Answers may vary. Sample: A binomial experiment has three important features: a. The situation involves repeated trials; flipping a coin 10 times has 10 trials. b. Each trial has two possible outcomes; in this case, heads or tails. c. The probability of success is constant throughout the trials; the trials of flipping a coin, are independent. **7.** The student wrote "5" instead of "4". It should be: $_nC_{(5-1)}a^{n-4}b^4 = {_7}C_4 j^3(-k)^4 = 35j^3k^4$
Exercises 9. ≈ 0.2461, or $\approx 24.61\%$ **11.** 0.6561, or 65.61% **13.** $256c^4 - 256c^3d + 96c^2d^2 - 16cd^3 + d^4$
15. $5xy^4$ **17.** $P(0) \approx 0.1176$, $P(1) \approx 0.3025$, $P(2) \approx 0.3241$, $P(3) \approx 0.1852$, $P(4) \approx 0.0595$, $P(5) \approx 0.0102$, $P(6) \approx 0.0007$ **19.** 0.99328
21. ≈ 0.2824 **23.** ≈ 0.2461 **25.** ≈ 0.6230 **27a.** 0.0914
b. The probability that three boxes would be underweight is 0.0001. You can conclude that there might be a malfunction in the machinery or that the company's claim may be false. **29.** Answers may vary. Sample: 60% of the summer days in Eastport are sunny. What is the probability of a week containing exactly two sunny days? **36.** loaded and leading question by the use of the words "beautiful" and "Do you agree" **37.** not enough information about the amendments to make a decision **38.** vertices: $(0, \pm 7)$; foci: $(0, \pm\sqrt{74})$; asymptotes: $y = \pm\frac{7}{5}x$
39. vertices: $(0, \pm 3)$; foci: $(0, \pm\sqrt{13})$; asymptotes: $y = \pm\frac{3}{2}x$ **40.** vertices: $(0, \pm 3)$; foci: $(0, \pm 5)$; asymptotes: $y = \pm\frac{3}{4}x$ **41.** $\frac{2}{3}$ **42.** $\frac{1}{2}$ **43.** $\frac{2}{3}$ **44.** $\bar{x} = 24.4$, $\sigma \approx 5.04$
45. $\bar{x} = 81.8$, $\sigma \approx 4.77$ **46.** $\bar{x} = 8.6$, $\sigma \approx 0.47$
47. $\bar{x} \approx 24.74$, $\sigma \approx 2.046$

Lesson 11-9   pp. 752–759

Got It? 1a. 71% **b.** 88%

2.

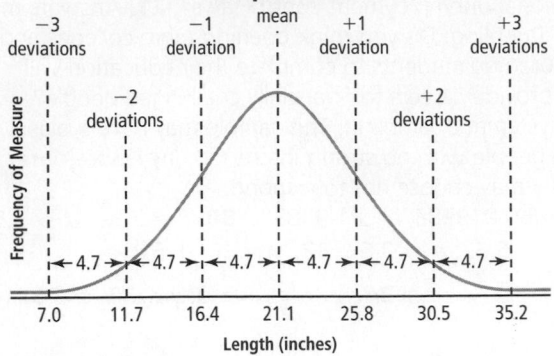

Distribution of Female European Eels

3a. 2.5% **b.** 210 students **c.** The students that received a B had scores between 165 and 180.

Lesson Check 1. 94%

2.

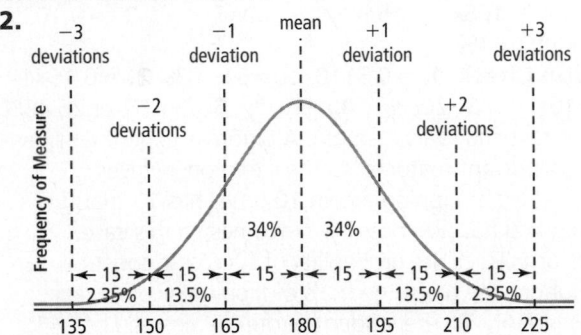

3. 47.5% **4.** Normal distribution means that most of the examples in a data set are close to the mean; the distribution of the data is within 1, 2, or 3 standard deviations of the mean. **5.** The mean and median are equivalent in a normal distribution. **6.** mean increases by 10: the bell curve is translated 10 units to the rt.

Exercises 7. ≈43% **9.** ≈43 men

11.

30 35 40 45 50 55 60

13.

34.5 38 41.5 45 48.5 52 55.5

15. 97.5%

17a. Set 2

b-c.

4 5 6 7 8 9 10 11

19. Yes; 99% of all grades are expected to be within 3 standard deviations of the mean, and this score is 4.4 standard deviations above the mean. **21.** 47.5%

23. 84%

25a.

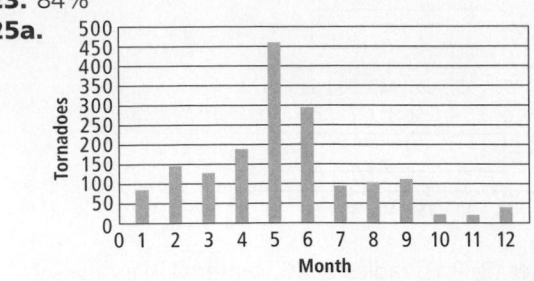

b. Yes; the curve is skewed to the left. **27.** Yes; Elena scored within the top 10% of her group. Her score is 2.75 standard deviations above the mean, which places her in the top 1%. Jake did not score in the top 10%. His score is 1.16 standard deviations above the mean, or at the 88th percentile. **32.** 0.02867 **33.** 0.1612 **34.** 0.03676

35.

circle; center: (0, 0), radius: 8; lines of sym.: all lines through the center; domain: $-8 \le x \le 8$, range: $-8 \le y \le 8$

36.

hyperbola; center: (0, 0), foci: $(\pm 3\sqrt{2}, 0)$; lines of sym.: $x = 0$, $y = 0$; domain: $x \le -3$ or $x \ge 3$; range: all real numbers

37.

ellipse; center: (0, 0), foci: $(\pm 4, 0)$; lines of sym.: $x = 0$, $y = 0$; domain: $-5 \le x \le 5$, range: $-3 \le y \le 3$

38. $y = x - 3$;

39. $y = x$;

40. $y = x - \frac{5}{4}$;

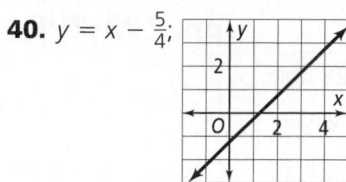

Chapter Review for Part B pp. 761–764

1. sample **2.** outlier **3.** probability distribution **4.** range of a set of data **5.** 9 **6.** mean: 6, median: 6, mode: 9 **7.** mean: $10.\overline{6}$, median: 7, modes: 3 and 7 **8.** mean: 15, median: 15, mode: 18 **9.** mean: 9.5, median: 9.5, mode: none **10.** range: 35; $Q_1 = 30$; $Q_3 = 55$ **11.** range: 35; $Q_1 = 25$; $Q_3 = 50$ **12.** range: 65; $Q_1 = 42$; $Q_3 = 87$ **13.** heights of 3 ppl. **14.** ages of thirty college students **15.** gas mileage of 18 automobiles of various types **16.** $\bar{x} \approx 6.64$, $\sigma \approx 5.12$ **17.** $\bar{x} \approx 17.14$, $\sigma \approx 3.52$ **18.** $\bar{x} = 7.5$, $\sigma \approx 2.67$ **19.** not a random sample; they will all begin with the letter "a" **20.** not a random sample; the lawyers will choose jurors that are likely to support their side **21.** random sample; all students have an equal chance to be chosen **22.** not a random sample; the five with the largest (or smallest) circulation size will be picked **23.** not a random sample; people at the bus station may be less likely to own a car and therefore less likely to be in favor of a new garage. **24.** $\frac{1}{2}$ **25.** $\frac{1}{3}$ **26.** ≈ 0.14 **27.** ≈ 0.0710 **28.** ≈ 0.2066 **29.** ≈ 0.1766 **30.** $21a^5b^2$ **31.** $56a^3b^5$ **32.** continuous **33.** discrete **34.** discrete **35.** continuous **36.** 16%; 2.5%

Chapter 12

Get Ready! p. 769

1. 6 **2.** $\frac{1}{3}$ **3.** $-\frac{3}{8}$ **4.** $\frac{7}{72}$ **5.** -9 **6.** 11 **7.** 3 **8.** $\left(\frac{1}{2}, -4\right)$ **9.** $\left(-\frac{2}{3}, -\frac{2}{3}\right)$ **10.** $\left(\frac{3}{4}, \frac{11}{4}\right)$ **11.** $(7, 9, -6)$ **12.** $(0, 0, 8)$ **13.** $(7, 5, 0)$

Lesson 12-1 pp. 772–779

Got It? 1a. $\begin{bmatrix} -15 & 25 \\ -1 & 1 \\ -2 & 15 \end{bmatrix}$ **b.** $\begin{bmatrix} -9 & 23 \\ -5 & 9 \\ 0 & 5 \end{bmatrix}$

c. Yes; it does not matter in which order you add matrices.

2. $A = \begin{bmatrix} 3 & 6 & -1 \\ 1 & 3 & 7 \\ 1 & 1 & 3 \end{bmatrix}$ **3a.** $\begin{bmatrix} 0 & 0 \\ 0 & 0 \end{bmatrix}$ **b.** $\begin{bmatrix} -1 & 10 & -5 \\ 0 & 2 & -3 \end{bmatrix}$

4a. $x = 6$, $y = -6$ **b.** $x = 4$, $y = -3$

Lesson Check 1. $\begin{bmatrix} 1 & 1 \\ -2 & 8 \end{bmatrix}$ **2.** $\begin{bmatrix} 1 & -9 & 8 \\ -3 & -1 & 8 \end{bmatrix}$

3. $\begin{bmatrix} -3 & 4 \\ -5 & 11 \end{bmatrix}$ **4.** Yes; the elements in each of the corresponding positions are equal. **5.** The elements were not subtracted. The correct answer is $\begin{bmatrix} 6 \\ 5 \end{bmatrix} - \begin{bmatrix} 3 \\ 7 \end{bmatrix} = \begin{bmatrix} 3 \\ -2 \end{bmatrix}$

Exercises 7. $\begin{bmatrix} 3.9 & -2.3 \\ -0.6 & 9.1 \end{bmatrix}$ **9.** $\begin{bmatrix} 6 & 2 \\ -1 & 3 \end{bmatrix}$

11. $\begin{bmatrix} -9 & -2 & 12 \\ -15 & 11 & -7 \end{bmatrix}$ **13.** $\begin{bmatrix} 0 & 0 \\ 0 & 0 \end{bmatrix}$ **15.** $x = 2$, $t = \frac{1}{10}$

17. B and D cannot be added because they do not have the same dimensions.

19.

	Plant 1			Plant 2	
	Plastic	Rubber		Plastic	Rubber
1-color	1000	1400	1-color	1200	3600
3-color	2600	3800	3-color	1800	4800

Plant 1 − Plant 2 = $\begin{bmatrix} -200 & -2200 \\ 800 & -1000 \end{bmatrix}$, where the top row represents 1-color balls and the bottom represents 3-color balls. **21.** $c = \frac{5}{2}$, $d = \frac{2}{5}$, $f = 7$, $g = 5$, $h = -1$

23a. $\begin{bmatrix} 124.6 \\ 113.3 \\ 71.6 \\ 87.2 \end{bmatrix}$ **b.** $\begin{bmatrix} -6.2 \\ -4.7 \\ 9.4 \\ 3.6 \end{bmatrix}$

c. Yes; order matters because subtraction is not comm. **29.** 68% **30.** 97.5% **31.** 47.5% **32.** 2, −6

33. $\frac{2}{3}$, 2 **34.** 5, 0 **35.** $\begin{bmatrix} 9 & 15 \\ 6 & 24 \end{bmatrix}$ **36.** $\begin{bmatrix} -20 \\ 35 \end{bmatrix}$

Lesson 12-2 pp. 781–788

GotIt? 1. $\begin{bmatrix} 8 & 24 & -19 \\ -3 & 9 & 10 \end{bmatrix}$ **2.** $\begin{bmatrix} 5 & -1 \\ \frac{7}{3} & 0 \end{bmatrix}$ **3a.** $\begin{bmatrix} -6 & 0 \\ -9 & 11 \end{bmatrix}$

b. $\begin{bmatrix} -3 & 7 \\ 6 & 8 \end{bmatrix}$ **c.** No; explanations may vary. Sample: For the matrices in parts (a) and (b), $AB = \begin{bmatrix} -6 & 0 \\ -9 & 11 \end{bmatrix}$ and $BA = \begin{bmatrix} -3 & 7 \\ 6 & 8 \end{bmatrix}$, so $AB \neq BA$.

4. player from 1994: 100 pts., player from 2006: 81 pts. **5a.** no **b.** yes **c.** yes **d.** no **e.** yes

Lesson Check 1. $\begin{bmatrix} 6 & -2 \\ 4 & 0 \end{bmatrix}$ **2.** $\begin{bmatrix} -3 & 11 \\ -10 & 6 \end{bmatrix}$

3. $\begin{bmatrix} 5 & 7 \\ 2 & 6 \end{bmatrix}$ **4.** $\begin{bmatrix} 9 & -1 \\ -2 & 2 \end{bmatrix}$

5. Scalar; repeated matrix addition is repeated addition of each element of the matrix, which is the same as scalar multiplication of the matrix. **6.** The product of two matrices A and B exists only if the number of columns of A is equal to the number of rows of B. Since A is a 2×4

matrix with 4 columns and B is a 3×6 matrix with 3 rows and $4 \neq 3$, the product AB does not exist. Likewise, since $6 \neq 2$, the product BA does not exist.

Exercises 7. $\begin{bmatrix} 9 & 12 \\ 18 & -6 \\ 3 & 0 \end{bmatrix}$ **9.** $\begin{bmatrix} -5 & -1 \\ 0 & -2 \end{bmatrix}$ **11.** $\begin{bmatrix} 19 & 11 \\ -12 & 10 \end{bmatrix}$

13. $\begin{bmatrix} -1 & 2 \\ 3 & -4 \end{bmatrix}$ **15.** $\begin{bmatrix} -4 & 8 \\ -22 & 2 \end{bmatrix}$ **17.** $\begin{bmatrix} -3 & 4 \\ -21 & 2 \end{bmatrix}$ **19.** $[34]$

21. $[0 \quad 34]$

23a.

	Lilies	Carnations	Daisies
Arrangement 1	3	0	0
Arrangement 2	3	4	0
Arrangement 3	0	3	4

b.

	Cost
Lilies	\$2.15
Carnations	\$0.90
Daisies	\$1.30

c.

	Cost
Arrangement 1	\$6.45
Arrangement 2	\$10.05
Arrangement 3	\$7.90

25. yes **27.** yes **29a.** River's Edge: 99 pts.; West River: 97 pts. **b.** West River

31. $\begin{bmatrix} 1 & -6 & -5 \\ 6 & 1 & -5 \\ -3 & -12 & 0 \end{bmatrix}$ **33.** $\begin{bmatrix} 17 & -24 \\ -33 & -7 \\ 69 & -18 \end{bmatrix}$

35. $\begin{bmatrix} 34 & -1 \\ 6 & -13 \\ -7 & 16 \end{bmatrix}$ **42.** $\begin{bmatrix} -33 & -12 \\ -6 & 27 \end{bmatrix}$

43. $\begin{bmatrix} 9 & -6 & 12 \\ 2 & 20 & 12 \end{bmatrix}$ **44a.** 12 **b.** 12 **c.** 0

45a. −12 **b.** −12 **c.** 0

Lesson 12-3 Part 1   pp. 789–792

Got It? 1a. yes **b.** yes **c.** No; no matrix that is multiplied by the zero matrix will give an identity matrix. **2a.** 3 **b.** −48

Lesson Check 1. 16 **2.** 7
3. The student added $ad + bc$ instead of subtracting $ad - bc$.
$\det\begin{bmatrix} 2 & 5 \\ -3 & 1 \end{bmatrix} = (2)(1) - (-3)(5) = 2 - (-15)$
$= 2 + 15 = 17$

Exercises 5. yes **7.** no **9.** 0 **11.** 11 **13.** −5 **15.** 36 **17.** 25 **19a.** 0 **b.** 0 **c.** 0 **d.** 0 Answers may vary. Sample: When the top row and bottom row are identical and the middle row has the same numbers as both rows, then the determinant is zero.

Lesson 12-3 Part 2   pp. 793–798

Got It? 3a. 12 units^2 **b.** 28 units^2
4a. yes; $\begin{bmatrix} 1 & -1 \\ -\frac{3}{2} & 2 \end{bmatrix}$ **b.** no **c.** yes; $\begin{bmatrix} 3 & -4 \\ -5 & 7 \end{bmatrix}$
5a. 88, 68, 84, 60, 12, 32, 52, 72, 28, 30, 14, 18, 2, 8, 14, 20 **b.** Multiply the coded information by the inverse of the coding matrix and get the following:
$\begin{bmatrix} 4 & 1 & 7 & 3 & 1 & 2 & 3 & 4 \\ 9 & 8 & 7 & 6 & 1 & 3 & 5 & 7 \end{bmatrix}$

Lesson Check 1. does not exist **2.** $\begin{bmatrix} 3 & -2 \\ -7 & 5 \end{bmatrix}$

3. Multiplicative inverses are only defined for square matrices because a pair of square matrices can be multiplied in either order, and can therefore be defined as multiplicative inverses of each other.

Exercises 5. yes; $\begin{bmatrix} 0 & 1 \\ -1 & 2 \end{bmatrix}$ **7.** yes; $\begin{bmatrix} 2 & -1.5 \\ -1 & 1 \end{bmatrix}$ **9.** no

11. 44 units^2 **13.** 34 units^2 **15.** 0 **17.** −30

19. yes; $\begin{bmatrix} -3 & 4 \\ 1 & -1 \end{bmatrix}$ **21.** yes; $\begin{bmatrix} 0.5 & 0 \\ 0 & 0.5 \end{bmatrix}$

23. yes; $\begin{bmatrix} 0.4 & 0.4 & 0.2 \\ -0.6 & -0.6 & 0.2 \\ -0.2 & 0.8 & 0.4 \end{bmatrix}$ **25.** 6 **31.** $\begin{bmatrix} 2 & 5 \\ 1 & 1 \end{bmatrix}$

32. $\begin{bmatrix} -10 & 19 \\ -20 & 7 \end{bmatrix}$ **33.** 720 **34.** 362,880
35. $1.08972864 \times 10^{10}$ **36.** 110,880
37. no solution **38.** (6, 0, −3)

Lesson 12-4 Part 1   pp. 799–802

Got It? 1a. $\begin{bmatrix} -8 \\ 9 \end{bmatrix}$ **b.** $\begin{bmatrix} -14 & -20 \\ 19 & 28 \end{bmatrix}$
c. Since matrix A has no inverse, the eq. has no solution.
2a. $\begin{bmatrix} 3 & -7 \\ 5 & 1 \end{bmatrix}\begin{bmatrix} x \\ y \end{bmatrix} = \begin{bmatrix} 8 \\ -2 \end{bmatrix}$

b. $\begin{bmatrix} 1 & 3 & 5 \\ -2 & 1 & -4 \\ 7 & -2 & 0 \end{bmatrix}\begin{bmatrix} x \\ y \\ z \end{bmatrix} = \begin{bmatrix} 12 \\ -2 \\ 7 \end{bmatrix}$

c. $\begin{bmatrix} 2 & -8 \\ -1 & 1 \end{bmatrix}\begin{bmatrix} x \\ y \end{bmatrix} = \begin{bmatrix} -3 \\ -4 \end{bmatrix}$

Lesson Check 1. $\begin{bmatrix} -6 & 3 \\ 4 & -2 \end{bmatrix}\begin{bmatrix} x \\ y \end{bmatrix} = \begin{bmatrix} 8 \\ 10 \end{bmatrix}$

2. $\begin{bmatrix} 2 & 3 & 0 \\ 1 & -2 & 1 \\ 0 & 6 & -4 \end{bmatrix}\begin{bmatrix} x \\ y \\ z \end{bmatrix} = \begin{bmatrix} 12 \\ 9 \\ 8 \end{bmatrix}$

3. Use matrix multiplication to combine the coefficient matrix and the variable matrix into a product matrix. Then set the first element in the product matrix equal to the first element in the constant matrix and set the second element in the product matrix equal to the second

element in the constant matrix. The result will be a system of equations:
$$-2p + 3q = 2$$
$$4p + q = -5$$

Exercises

5. $\begin{bmatrix} \frac{29}{31} \\ -\frac{66}{217} \\ \frac{34}{217} \end{bmatrix}$ **7.** $\begin{bmatrix} \frac{2487}{253} \\ \frac{1192}{253} \\ -\frac{430}{253} \end{bmatrix}$

9. $\begin{bmatrix} -3 & 1 \\ 1 & 0 \end{bmatrix}\begin{bmatrix} x \\ y \end{bmatrix} = \begin{bmatrix} -7 \\ 2 \end{bmatrix}$; coefficient matrix: $\begin{bmatrix} -3 & 1 \\ 1 & 0 \end{bmatrix}$,

variable matrix: $\begin{bmatrix} x \\ y \end{bmatrix}$, constant matrix: $\begin{bmatrix} -7 \\ 2 \end{bmatrix}$

11. (6, 2) **13.** (16, −22)

Lesson 12-4   Part 2 pp. 804–808

Got It? 3a. (5, −21) **b.** no solution **4.** run: 32 min; jog: 8 min
Lesson Check 1. (5, 3) **2.** (−6, −6) **3.** The student did not separate the coefficient matrix and the variable matrix. The matrix eq. should be written
as $\begin{bmatrix} 2 & 3 \\ -4 & 5 \end{bmatrix}\begin{bmatrix} x \\ y \end{bmatrix} = \begin{bmatrix} 5 \\ 1 \end{bmatrix}$.

Exercises 5. $\left(\frac{1}{2}, 20\right)$ **7.** (3, 2) **9.** (2, −1, 3) **11.** about 22 min at 11 mph and about 38 min at 15 mph **13.** 1 lb of almonds, 1 lb of peanuts, and 1 lb of raisins **15.** (2, 4) **17.** (5, 0, 1) **19.** (2, −1, 3) **21.** length = 280 ft, width = 140 ft **23.** (2, 40) **25.** (12.5, 1187.5) **27.** no unique solution **33.** −44 **34.** 4913 **35.** −218 **36.** 34.$\overline{4}$; 30.9; 5.56 **37.** 4.17; 1.32; 1.15 **38.** 19.$\overline{6}$ m; 22.$\overline{2}$ m; 4.7 m **39.** 57.4 mi; 345.44 mi²; 18.6 mi **40.** 4 **41.** 21 **42.** 52.5

Chapter Review   pp. 810–812

1. equal matrices **2.** zero matrix **3.** matrix equation **4.** square matrix

5. $\begin{bmatrix} -1 & 9 & -8 \\ 4 & 0 & 6 \end{bmatrix}$ **6.** $\begin{bmatrix} 5 & -4 \\ 5 & 0 \end{bmatrix}$ **7.** $[1 \quad -8 \quad 12]$

8. $\begin{bmatrix} -3 & 10 \\ -3 & 3 \end{bmatrix}$ **9.** $x = -2, w = 8, r = 4, t = -1$
10. $t = -4, y = \frac{11}{2}, r = 4, w = 4$

11. $\begin{bmatrix} 18 & 3 & 0 & 24 \\ -12 & 9 & 21 & 33 \end{bmatrix}$ **12.** undefined **13.** undefined

14. $\begin{bmatrix} -6 & 10 & 21 & 41 \\ -28 & 10 & 28 & 28 \end{bmatrix}$ **15.** $\begin{bmatrix} -14 & -2 \\ 43 & -7 \end{bmatrix}$

16. $\begin{bmatrix} -11 & 18 \\ -17 & -2 \end{bmatrix}$ **17.** 24; $\begin{bmatrix} \frac{1}{6} & -\frac{1}{24} \\ 0 & \frac{1}{4} \end{bmatrix}$

18. 0; does not exist **19.** 42; $\begin{bmatrix} \frac{5}{42} & -\frac{1}{42} \\ -\frac{4}{21} & \frac{5}{21} \end{bmatrix}$

20. 6; $\begin{bmatrix} \frac{1}{3} & -\frac{2}{3} & 0 \\ -\frac{1}{6} & \frac{1}{3} & -\frac{1}{2} \\ \frac{1}{3} & \frac{1}{3} & 0 \end{bmatrix}$ **21.** $\begin{bmatrix} 1 & 2 \\ -1 & 0 \end{bmatrix}$ **22.** (−4, −7)

23. $\begin{bmatrix} 2 \\ 2 \end{bmatrix}$ **24.** $\begin{bmatrix} 2 & 1 \\ 3 & 2 \end{bmatrix}$ **25.** no unique solution

26. no unique solution

Chapter T

T-1   pp. 823–827

Got It? 1. a. $\frac{4}{5}$ **b.** $\frac{5}{3}$ **c.** $\frac{4}{3}$ **2.** $\sin E = \frac{3}{5}$, $\sec F = \frac{5}{3}$
3a. 27.1 m **b.** 32.2 m
Lesson Check 1. $\sin 57° = \frac{b}{c}$, $\cos 57° = \frac{a}{c}$, $\tan 57° = \frac{b}{a}$ **2.** 15.4 **3.** $\sin 33° = \frac{a}{c} = 0.5$, $\cos 33° = \frac{b}{c} = 0.8$, $\tan 33° = \frac{a}{b} = 0.6$ **4.** The cotangent is $\frac{\text{adjacent}}{\text{opposite}}$ and he used $\frac{\text{opposite}}{\text{adjacent}}$. So $\cot Q = \frac{p}{q}$. **5.** Answers may vary. Sample: Use the inverse of sine to find the measure of the angle opposite the shortest side, $\theta = \sin^{-1}\frac{3}{5} \approx 36.9°$. Then find the tangent of the angle opposite the shortest side, $\tan 36.9° \approx 0.75$.
Exercises 7. $\frac{17}{8} \approx 2.13$ **9.** $\frac{17}{8} \approx 2.13$ **11.** $\frac{8}{15} \approx 0.53$

(Right triangle with vertices I (top left), H (bottom left), G (bottom right); legs: $IH = 9$, $HG = 40$, hypotenuse $IG = 41$)

13. $\frac{40}{41} \approx 0.98$ **15.** $\frac{41}{9} \approx 4.56$ **17.** not defined
19a. 300 ft **b.** 445 ft
21.

(Right triangle with hypotenuse 20, legs $3\sqrt{39}$ and 7, angle θ)

$\sin \theta = \frac{3\sqrt{39}}{20}$, $\tan \theta = \frac{3\sqrt{39}}{7}$, $\csc \theta = \frac{20\sqrt{39}}{117}$, $\sec \theta = \frac{20}{7}$, $\cot \theta = \frac{7\sqrt{39}}{117}$

23.

(Right triangle with hypotenuse 25, legs 24 and 7, angle θ)

$\sin \theta = \frac{24}{25}$, $\cos \theta = \frac{7}{25}$, $\csc \theta = \frac{25}{24}$, $\sec \theta = \frac{25}{7}$, $\cot \theta = \frac{7}{24}$

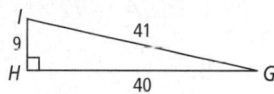

25.

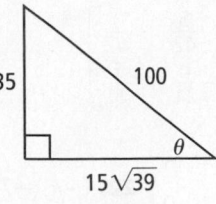

$$\cos \theta = \frac{3\sqrt{39}}{20}, \tan \theta = \frac{7\sqrt{39}}{117}, \csc \theta = \frac{20}{7},$$
$$\sec \theta = \frac{20\sqrt{39}}{117}, \cot \theta = \frac{3\sqrt{39}}{7}$$

27. 20.3 m² **29.** $c \approx 12.2, m\angle A \approx 35.0°, m\angle B \approx 55.0°$
34. $(3, -2)$ **35.** $(1, -1, 2)$ **36.** $(0, 1, -2)$
37. $2\sqrt{3} \approx 3.464$ **38.** $4\sqrt{2} \approx 5.657$ **39.** $\frac{9\sqrt{3}}{2} \approx 7.794$

T-2   **pp. 828–833**

Got It? 1. a. $y = 8\sqrt{2}$ **b.** $x = 5\sqrt{2}$ **2.** shorter leg:
$\frac{10\sqrt{3}}{3}$ units; hypotenuse: $\frac{20\sqrt{3}}{3}$ units **3.** $a = 20\sqrt{3}$;
$b = 20$

Lesson Check 1. $x = 7\sqrt{2}$ **2.** $x = 3$ **3.** No; in a
30°-60°-90° triangle, the length of the shorter leg is half
the length of the hypotenuse, so the length is half of 5,
or 2.5.

Exercises 5. $x = 8$; $y = 8\sqrt{2}$ **7.** $p = 12\sqrt{3}$;
$q = 24$ **9.** $w = 2$; $z = 4$ **11.** 0.24 min, or 14.4 s
13. $p = 14$; $q = 7$; $r = 7\sqrt{3}$; $s = 7$ **15.** about 424 ft
17. leg: $\frac{\sqrt{6}}{2}$ ft **19.** hypotenuse: 6 in.; longer leg:
$3\sqrt{3}$ in. **21.** shorter leg: $\sqrt{2}$ ft; longer leg: $\sqrt{6}$ ft
23. shorter leg: $\frac{3\sqrt{2}}{2}$ m; longer leg: $\frac{3\sqrt{6}}{2}$ m **25a.** about
4.2 m **b.** about 1.6 m **30.** $a \approx 3.9, c \approx 6.9$,
$m\angle B = 55.8°$ **31.** $a \approx 26.8, c \approx 28.1, m\angle A = 72.8°$
32. $a \approx 19.8, c \approx 2.9, m\angle A = 81.7°$
33. $x^2 + y^2 = 1$ **34.** $x^2 + y^2 = 1$ **35.** $x^2 + y^2 = 1$

T-3   **pp. 834–840**

Got It?

1. 225°

2a.

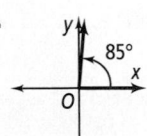

b. 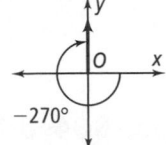 ; reference angle: 40°

c. ; reference angle: 40°

3a. $\frac{\sqrt{3}}{2}, \frac{1}{2}$ **b.** 1, 0 **c.** −1, 0 **4a.** $\frac{\sqrt{3}}{2}, -\frac{1}{2}$ **b.** $\frac{\sqrt{3}}{2}, -\frac{1}{2}$
c. Yes; for example, when $\theta = 45°$, $\cos \theta = \sin \theta$.
Lesson Check 1. 135° **2.** 240° **3.** 45° **4.** A 310°
angle in standard position does not have the same
terminal side as a 50° angle in standard position; it has
the same terminal side as a −50° angle.
Exercises 5. −315° **7.** −90°
9. 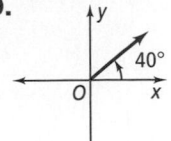 ; reference angle: 40°

11. ; reference angle: 90°

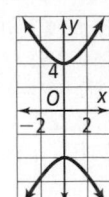

13. $\frac{\sqrt{2}}{2}, \frac{\sqrt{2}}{2}$ **15.** −1, 0 **17.** $-\frac{\sqrt{3}}{2}, \frac{1}{2}$ **19.** $-\frac{1}{2}, \frac{\sqrt{3}}{2}$
21. $\frac{\sqrt{3}}{2}, -\frac{1}{2}$ **23.** 0.98, −0.17 **25.** −0.87, −0.5 **27.** II
29. negative x-axis **31.** −276° **33a.** 0.77, 0.77, 0.77
b. The cosines of the three angles are equal because the
angles are coterminal. **38.** $x = 7\sqrt{2}$; $y = 7\sqrt{2}$
39. $a = 6\sqrt{3}$; $b = 3\sqrt{3}$ **40.** $m = 23$; $n = 23\sqrt{3}$
41. $(0, 2\sqrt{5}), (0, -2\sqrt{5})$;

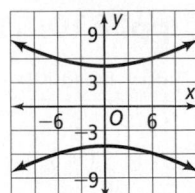

42. $(0, 5\sqrt{5}), (0, -5\sqrt{5})$;

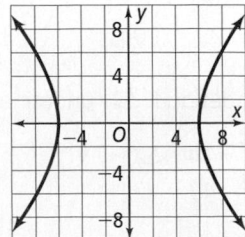

43. $(\sqrt{85}, 0), (-\sqrt{85}, 0)$;

44. $y - 1 = -3x$ or $y + 5 = -3(x - 2)$

45. $y + 4 = -\frac{7}{5}(x + 4)$ or $y - 3 = -\frac{7}{5}(x + 9)$
46. $y - 2 = -(x - 7)$ or $y - 8 = -(x - 1)$
47. 50.24 in.^{2} **48.** 200.96 mi^2 **49.** 9.0746 ft^2

46. mean = 12.9, s.d. = 3.53 **47.** mean = 30, s.d. = 8.09 **48.** $\frac{8}{17}$ **49.** $\frac{8}{15}$ **50.** $\frac{15}{8}$ **51.** $\frac{8}{17}$

T-4 pp. 841–847

Got It? 1a. 90° **b.** $\frac{5\pi}{4}$ radians **c.** $\frac{360°}{\pi} \approx 114.59°$

d. $\frac{5\pi}{6}$ radians **2.** $-\frac{\sqrt{3}}{2}$, $-\frac{1}{2}$ **3a.** 6.3 in. **b.** arc length would also double. **4.** $\approx 15{,}708$ km

Lesson Check 1. $\frac{5\pi}{3}$ radians ≈ 5.24 radians

2. 135° **3.** $\frac{20\pi}{3} \approx 20.94$ in. **4.** 1 radian **5.** 6 "perfect" slices

Exercises 7. $\frac{5\pi}{6}$, 2.62 **9.** $\frac{\pi}{9}$, 0.35 **11.** 198°

13. −172° **15.** $\frac{1}{2}$, $\frac{\sqrt{3}}{2}$ **17.** $-\frac{1}{2}$, $\frac{\sqrt{3}}{2}$ **19.** $-\frac{\sqrt{3}}{2}$, $-\frac{1}{2}$

21. 51.8 ft **23.** ≈ 746 ft **25a.** $\approx 11{,}048$ km, $\approx 33{,}144$ km, $\approx 27{,}620$ km, $\approx 276{,}198$ km **b.** 18.1 h
27a. 15°, $\frac{\pi}{12}$ **b.** ≈ 1036.7 mi **c.** ≈ 413.6 mi **29.** II

31.

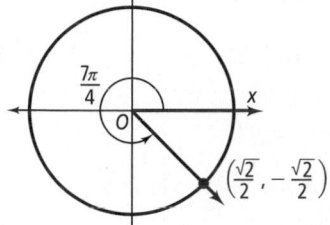

0.71, −0.71

33.

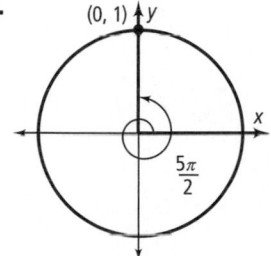

0.00, 1.00

35. ≈ 11 radians **37.** ≈ 6.3 cm

42.

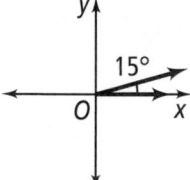

43.

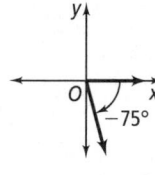

44.

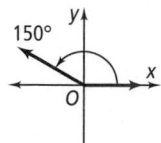

45.

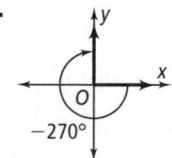

T-5 pp. 848–857

Got It? 1a. 2; 2π **b.** 4; $\frac{\pi}{4}$ **2a.** 3; −3 **b.** 0.5; 0.5

3a.

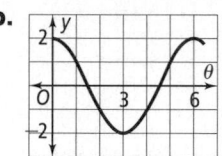

b.

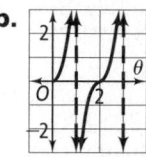

4a.

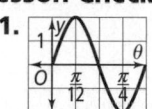

b.

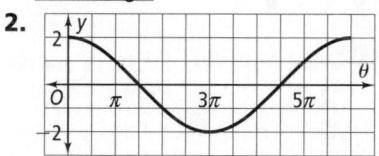

5. ≈ 46.6 ft

Lesson Check

1.

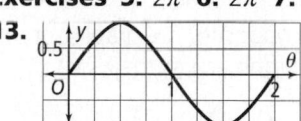

2.

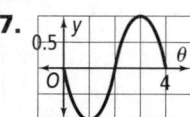

3. $\frac{2\pi}{3}$ **4.** Answers may vary. Sample: $y = 5 \cos \frac{\theta}{3}$

Exercises 5. 2π **6.** 2π **7.** 2π **9.** $\frac{5}{2}$; $\frac{5}{2}$ **11.** 1; 1

13.

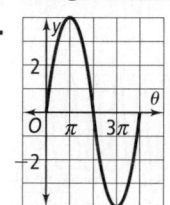

15.

17.

19.

21.

23. $\frac{\pi}{2}$

25.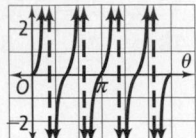

27.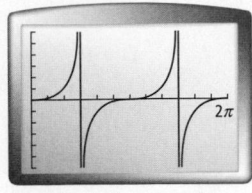

50, undefined, −50

29.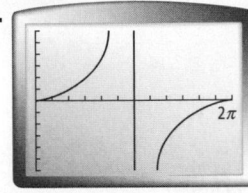

≈51.8, 125, ≈301.8

31. 5; 2π **33.** 1; π **35.** 3; 6π

37. $\frac{2\pi}{5}$;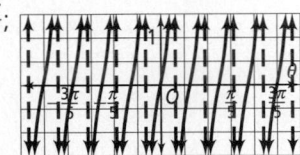

39.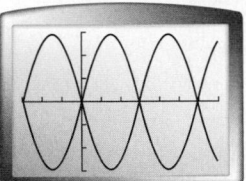

They are reflections of each other across the *x*-axis.

When *a* is replaced by its opposite, the graph is a reflection of the original graph across the *x*-axis.

43. $\frac{2\pi}{5}$, 3.5;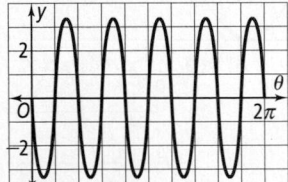

45. 1, 2;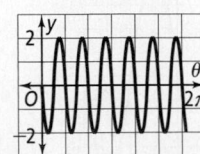

47. $y = -\tan\left(\frac{1}{2}x\right)$

49.
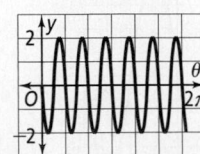

55. $-\frac{4\pi}{9}$, −1.40 **56.** about 83 **57.** $\frac{-4\pi}{3}$, −4.19

58. $\frac{16\pi}{9}$, 5.59 **59.** 83 **60.** −227 **61.** 145 **62.** −332

63. true; Distr. Prop. **64.** true; Distr. Prop. and Comm. Prop. of Add. **65.** not true

T-6 pp. 858–862

Got It? 1. $\csc \theta$ **2.** $\dfrac{\csc \theta}{\sec \theta} = \dfrac{\left(\frac{1}{\sin \theta}\right)}{\left(\frac{1}{\cos \theta}\right)} = \dfrac{\cos \theta}{\sin \theta} = \cot \theta$

3.
$$\begin{aligned} 1 + \cot^2 \theta &= 1 + \left(\frac{\cos \theta}{\sin \theta}\right)^2 \\ &= 1 + \frac{\cos^2 \theta}{\sin^2 \theta} \\ &= 1 + \frac{1 - \sin^2 \theta}{\sin^2 \theta} \\ &= 1 + \frac{1}{\sin^2 \theta} - \frac{\sin^2 \theta}{\sin^2 \theta} \\ &= 1 + \csc^2 \theta - 1 \\ &= \csc^2 \theta \end{aligned}$$

Lesson Check

1. $\tan \theta \csc \theta$

$$\begin{aligned} &= \frac{\sin \theta}{\cos \theta} \cdot \frac{1}{\sin \theta} \\ &= \frac{1}{\cos \theta} \\ &= \sec \theta \end{aligned}$$

2. $\csc^2 \theta - \cot^2 \theta$

$$\begin{aligned} &= \left(\frac{1}{\sin \theta}\right)^2 - \left(\frac{\cos \theta}{\sin \theta}\right)^2 \\ &= \frac{1}{\sin^2 \theta} - \frac{\cos^2 \theta}{\sin^2 \theta} \\ &= \frac{1 - \cos^2 \theta}{\sin^2 \theta} \\ &= \frac{\sin^2 \theta}{\sin^2 \theta} \\ &= 1 \end{aligned}$$

3. $\sin \theta \tan \theta$

$$\begin{aligned} &= \sin \theta \cdot \frac{\sin \theta}{\cos \theta} \\ &= \frac{\sin^2 \theta}{\cos \theta} \\ &= \frac{1 - \cos^2 \theta}{\cos \theta} \\ &= \frac{1}{\cos \theta} - \frac{\cos^2 \theta}{\cos \theta} \\ &= \sec \theta - \cos \theta \end{aligned}$$

4. $\tan \theta \cot \theta - \sin^2 \theta$

$$\begin{aligned} &= \tan \theta \frac{1}{\tan \theta} - \sin^2 \theta \\ &= \frac{\tan \theta}{\tan \theta} - \sin^2 \theta \\ &= 1 - \sin^2 \theta \\ &= \cos^2 \theta \end{aligned}$$

5. Answers may vary. Sample: Letting a and b be the legs, and c the hypotenuse o f a right triangle, the Pythagorean Theorem states that $a^2 + b^2 = c^2$. Dividing both sides by c^2, then $\frac{a^2}{c^2} + \frac{b^2}{c^2} = \left(\frac{a}{c}\right)^2 + \left(\frac{b}{c}\right)^2 = 1$. Calling the angle between a and c θ, then $\sin\theta = \frac{b}{c}$ and $\cos\theta = \frac{a}{c}$. By substitution, $\cos^2\theta + \sin^2\theta = 1$. **6.** wrong calculation: $2 - \cos^2\theta = 2 - (1 - \sin^2\theta) = 2 - 1 + \sin^2\theta = 1 + \sin^2\theta$

Exercises 7. 1 **9.** $\sin^2\theta$ **11.** $-\cot^2\theta$ **13.** $\sin\theta$

15. $\sin\theta\cot\theta$
$= \sin\theta\left(\frac{\cos\theta}{\sin\theta}\right) = \cos\theta$

17. $\sin\theta\sec\theta$
$= \sin\theta\left(\frac{1}{\cos\theta}\right) = \frac{\sin\theta}{\cos\theta} = \tan\theta$

19. $\csc\theta - \sin\theta$
$= \frac{1}{\sin\theta} - \sin\theta$
$= \frac{1 - \sin^2\theta}{\sin\theta} = \frac{\cos^2\theta}{\sin\theta}$
$= \frac{\cos\theta}{\sin\theta} \cdot \cos\theta = \cot\theta\cos\theta$

21. $\cot\theta = \frac{\cos\theta}{\sin\theta}$
$= \left(\frac{1}{\sin\theta}\right)\cos\theta = \csc\theta\cos\theta$

23. $\sec\theta$ **25.** $\sec^2\theta$ **27.** $\tan\theta$ **29.** $\sin\theta$ **31.** 1

33. $\pm\sqrt{1 - \cos^2\theta}$ **35.** $\pm\frac{\sqrt{1 - \sin^2\theta}}{\sin\theta}$
37. $\pm\sqrt{\csc^2\theta - 1}$ **39.** Errors are in the first line and the last 2 lines: first line, incorrect cancellation of $\tan^2\theta$; last 2 lines, $\frac{\sin^2\theta}{\cos^2\theta} = \tan^2\theta$, not $\cot^2\theta$. A correct identity verification is:

$$\frac{\sec^2\theta - \tan^2\theta}{\tan^2\theta} = \frac{\frac{1}{\cos^2\theta} - \frac{\sin^2\theta}{\cos^2\theta}}{\frac{\sin^2\theta}{\cos^2\theta}}$$

$$= \frac{1 - \sin^2\theta}{\cos^2\theta} \cdot \frac{\cos^2\theta}{\sin^2\theta} = \frac{1 - \sin^2\theta}{\sin^2\theta} = \frac{\cos^2\theta}{\sin^2\theta} = \cot^2\theta$$

41. $(x - 1)^2 - 1 = x(x - 2)$ is an identity since: $(x - 1)^2 - 1 = x^2 - 2x + 1 - 1 = x^2 - 2x = x(x - 2)$. $(x - 1)^2 = x(x - 1)$ is an eq. since it has a unique solution:
$$(x - 1)^2 = x(x - 1)$$
$$x^2 - 2x + 1 = x^2 - x$$
$$-x = -1$$
$$x = 1$$

43. $\sec\theta - \sin\theta\tan\theta$
$= \frac{1}{\cos\theta} - \sin\theta\left(\frac{\sin\theta}{\cos\theta}\right)$
$= \frac{1}{\cos\theta} - \frac{\sin^2\theta}{\cos\theta} = \frac{1 - \sin^2\theta}{\cos\theta} = \frac{\cos^2\theta}{\cos\theta} = \cos\theta$

45. $\frac{1 - \sin\theta}{\cos\theta} = \frac{1 - \sin\theta}{\cos\theta} \cdot \frac{\cos\theta}{\cos\theta}$
$= \frac{(1 - \sin\theta)\cos\theta}{\cos^2\theta}$
$= \frac{(1 - \sin\theta)\cos\theta}{1 - \sin^2\theta}$
$= \frac{(1 - \sin\theta)\cos\theta}{(1 - \sin\theta)(1 + \sin\theta)}$
$= \frac{\cos\theta}{1 + \sin\theta}$

47. $(\cot\theta + 1)^2 = \cot^2\theta + 2\cot\theta + 1$
$= \cot^2\theta + 1 + 2\cot\theta = \csc^2\theta + 2\cot\theta$

49. $1 - \sin\theta$ **56.** $\frac{\pi}{6}$; $\theta = -\frac{\pi}{12}, \frac{\pi}{12}$

57. 4π; $\theta = -2\pi, 2\pi$ **58.** $\frac{2\pi}{3}$; $\theta = -\frac{\pi}{3}, \frac{\pi}{3}$
59. 6π; $\theta = -3\pi, 3\pi$ **60.** 0.0064 **61.** 0.3456
62. ≈ 0.136 **63.** ≈ 0.198

Trigonometry Review   p. 863

1. period **2.** unit circle **3.** tangent function
4. trigonometric ratios **5.** trigonometric identity

Skills Handbook

p. 865 1. 46% **3.** 0.7% **5.** 1.035 **7.** 25% **9.** $66.\overline{6}$%
11. 115% **13.** 12.5 **15.** 75 **17.** 20%
p. 866 1. $1\frac{2}{5}$ **3.** $6\frac{5}{6}$ **5.** $\frac{5}{21}$ **7.** $2\frac{19}{20}$ **9.** 8. **11.** $1\frac{1}{2}$
13. 2 **15.** 42
p. 867 1. 3 to 4 **3.** 19 g in 2 oz **5.** $\frac{14}{5}$ **7.** 8 **9.** 1.8
11. 1.95 **13.** 45.5 **15.** ± 6
p. 868 1. 1 **3.** -38 **5.** -17 **7.** 4 **9.** 28 **11.** -12
13. -90 **15.** 12 **17.** 19 **19.** 9 **21.** -10
p. 869 1. 14 m^2 **3.** 30 cm^2 **5.** $91\frac{1}{8}$ ft^3 **7.** 100π in.^{3}
9. 110.5 in.^{2} **11.** $121\frac{1}{2}$ ft^2
p. 870 1. I **3.** IV **5.** III **7.** $\frac{4}{5}$ **9.** 0 **11.** $\frac{1}{5}$ **13.** $\left(5, -\frac{3}{2}\right)$
p. 871 1. x^3 **3.** a^4b **5.** $\frac{1}{c^4}$ **7.** $\frac{x^5}{y^7z^3}$ **9.** d^8 **11.** c^6
13. $\frac{a^4}{b^5}$ **15.** $\frac{a^4}{b^4}$ **17.** c^{12} **19.** $u^{12}v^6$ **21.** a^3 **23.** $\frac{1}{mg^3}$
25. $\frac{a^5}{2}$
p. 872 1. $x^2 + 10x - 5$ **3.** $12x^4 - 20x^3 + 36x^2$
5. $x^2 - 2x - 15$ **7.** $(a - 6)(a - 2)$ **9.** $(x + 4)(x + 1)$
11. $(y + 8)(y - 3)$ **13.** $2x(x^2 + 2x - 4)$
p. 873 1. 1.34×10^6 **3.** 7.75×10^{-4} **5.** 111,300
7. 1.895×10^3 **9.** 1.234×10^5 **11.** 6.4×10^5
13. 8.52×10^2 **15.** 17.5 **17.** 8.95×10^{-12}
19. 3.77×10^{10} **21.** 1.8×10^{-6}
p. 874 1. 10 **3.** 15 **5.** 54.7 **7.** 5 **9.** 13 **11.** 22.7
13. 2.8 **15.** 9 **17.** 7

p. 875

1.

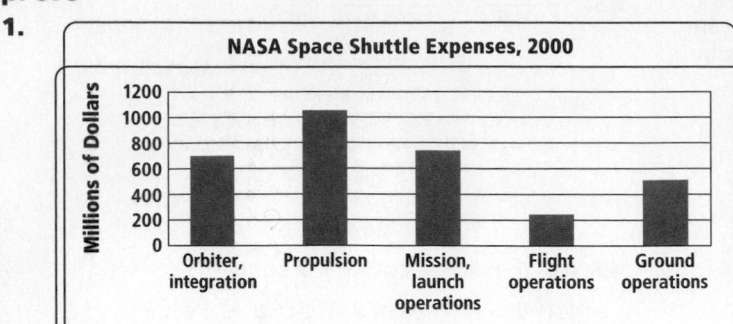

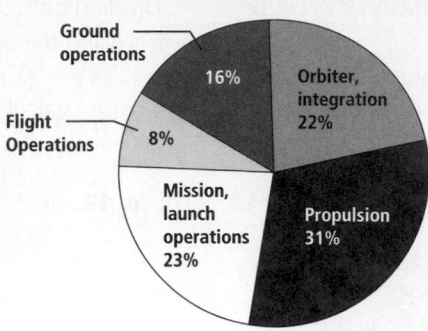

p. 876 **1.** $3.\overline{7}$; 5; 5 **3.** $3.9\overline{6}$; 2.4; 2.4 **5.** 1.5; 1.5;
no mode

7.

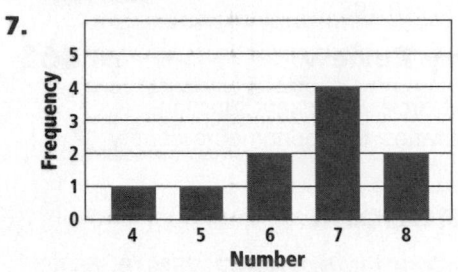

p. 877 **1.** $\frac{a}{3b^2}$ **3.** $\frac{1}{2}$ **5.** $4x$ **7.** $\frac{2}{h}$ **9.** $\frac{x}{10}$ **11.** $\frac{74x}{35}$
13. $\frac{4x^2}{5}$ **15.** $\frac{16}{x}$ **17.** $\frac{16}{5}$ **19.** $2x$

Index

Index

Index

86, 91, 95, 118, 126, 152, 156,
165, 173, 181, 191, 214, 219, 223,
229, 235, 245, 257, 265, 273, 297,
303, 316, 326, 338, 339, 345, 351,
359, 367, 384, 389, 393, 400, 415,
424, 430, 440, 447, 467, 474, 486,
490, 496, 504, 525, 546, 551, 562,
569, 570, 588, 597, 604, 611, 618,
620, 646, 654, 662, 671, 672, 707,
721, 728, 730, 737, 749, 758, 776,
786, 792, 797, 806, 825, 831, 838,
847, 860, 861

evaluating
algebraic expressions, 19, 20, 56
e^x, 476
functions, 70–73
logarithmic expressions, 480–487
sequences, 593, 601
series, 617

expanding
binomial(s), 347–351
logarithms, 492

experimental probability, 695

explicit formulas, 585, 587, 624

exponential
growth and decay, 462–468, 510
models, 462–468, 473, 507, 510

exponential equations
base e, 476
common base, 498
defined, 498, 512
different base, 499
modeling, 500
solving by graphing, 499
solving using tables, 499
writing, 481

exponential functions
base e, 476
defined, 463
families of, 473, 484
general form of, 462, 510
graphing, 462–463, 471
inverses of, 483
natural base, 476
properties of, 470–478, 510
writing, 466

exponents
properties of, 380, 491
rational, 402–410

expressions
algebraic. *See* algebraic expressions
equivalent, 402
greatest common factor (GCF), 229
logarithmic, 480
numerical, 5
quadratic. *See* quadratic expressions
radical. *See* radical expressions
rational. *See* rational expressions
representing patterns using, 6
writing, 20

F

Factor Theorem, 302

factor(s)
binomial, 231–233
checking, 320
greatest common (GCF), 229, 239
integer, 332

factorial, *n*, 687

factoring
by grouping, 311
defined, 227
perfect square trinomials, 232
quadratic expressions, 227–235, 239
rational expressions, 548
solving polynomial equations by,
310–313, 328
solving quadratic equations by,
243–247
the GCF out, 311
to find discontinuities, 539–540

family(ies)
of absolute value functions, 122, 137
of reciprocal functions, 530–535, 574

feasible region, 169, 195

finite geometric series, 614, 615

finite sequences, 607

finite series, 607, 614, 615

flips. *See* reflections

FLOAT feature, 588

focal length, of parabola, 641

focus
of ellipse, 658, 660
of hyperbola, 666
of parabola, 641

formulas
arithmetic sequences, 592, 624
Change of Base, 493
earthquake intensity, 482
electric current, 16
error of margin for drilling a hole, 52
explicit, 585, 587, 624
for distance, 438
for geometric series, 616
generating mathematical patterns, 585
interest, 477, 510
inverses of, 438
perimeter of a rectangle, 28
point-slope form, 88
quadratic, 260–267, 284
recursive, 586, 624
slope, 81
sum of arithmetic series, 607
sum of geometric series, 614
surface area, 72
temperature conversions, 29
volume of sphere, 72

fractions, complex, 559, 576

function notation, 70

function rule, 70

function(s). *See also* equation(s)
absolute value, 121–127
adding, 426, 427
as Big Idea, 63, 102, 136, 145, 192,
203, 241, 281, 291, 331, 379, 416,
451, 452, 461, 508, 519, 572, 822,
863
composite, 428, 429
composition of, 428, 438
continuous, 539
cosine, 848, 850
cubic, 295
defined, 66, 98
discontinuous, 539
dividing, 426, 427
domain of, 66, 426, 438, 538, 539

Index

Index

Acknowledgments

Staff Credits

The people who made up the High School Mathematics team—representing composition services, core design digital and multimedia production services, digital product development, editorial, editorial services, manufacturing, marketing, and production management—are listed below.

Dan Anderson, Scott Andrews, Christopher Anton, Carolyn Artin, Michael Avidon, Margaret Banker, Charlie Bink, Niki Birbilis, Suzanne Biron, Beth Blumberg, Kyla Brown, Rebekah Brown, Judith Buice, Sylvia Bullock, Stacie Cartwright, Carolyn Chappo, Christia Clarke, Tom Columbus, Andrew Coppola, AnnMarie Coyne, Bob Craton, Nicholas Cronin, Patrick Culleton, Damaris Curran, Steven Cushing, Sheila DeFazio, Cathie Dillender, Emily Dumas, Patty Fagan, Frederick Fellows, Jorgensen Fernandez, Mandy Figueroa, Suzanne Finn, Sara Freund, Matt Frueh, Jon Fuhrer, Andy Gaus, Mark Geyer, Mircea Goia, Andrew Gorlin, Shelby Gragg, Ellen Granter, Jay Grasso, Lisa Gustafson, Toni Haluga, Greg Ham, Marc Hamilton, Chris Handorf, Angie Hanks, Scott Harris, Cynthia Harvey, Phil Hazur, Thane Heninger, Aun Holland, Amanda House, Chuck Jann, Linda Johnson, Blair Jones, Marian Jones, Tim Jones, Gillian Kahn, Brian Keegan, Jonathan Kier, Jennifer King, Tamara King, Elizabeth Krieble, Meytal Kotik, Brian Kubota, Roshni Kutty, Mary Landry, Christopher Langley, Christine Lee, Sara Levendusky, Lisa Lin, Wendy Marberry, Dominique Mariano, Clay Martin, Rich McMahon, Eve Melnechuk, Cynthia Metallides, Hope Morley, Christine Nevola, Michael O'Donnell, Michael Oster, Ameer Padshah, Jeffrey Paulhus, Jonathan Penyack, Valerie Perkins, Brian Reardon, Wendy Rock, Marcy Rose, Carol Roy, Irene Rubin, Hugh Rutledge, Vicky Shen, Jewel Simmons, Ted Smykal, Emily Soltanoff, William Speiser, Jayne Stevenson, Richard Sullivan, Dan Tanguay, Dennis Tarwood, Susan Tauer, Tiffany Taylor-Sullivan, Catherine Terwilliger, Mark Tricca, Maria Torti, Leonid Tunik, Ilana Van Veen, Lauren Van Wart, John Vaughan, Laura Vivenzio, Samuel Voigt, Kathy Warfel, Don Weide, Laura Wheel, Eric Whitfield, Sequoia Wild, Joseph Will, Kristin Winters, Allison Wyss, Dina Zolotusky

Additional Credits: Michele Cardin, Robert Carlson, Kate Dalton-Hoffman, Dana Guterman, Narae Maybeth, Carolyn McGuire, Manjula Nair, Rachel Terino, Steve Thomas

Illustration

Stephen Durke: 574; **Phil Guzy:** 596, 597; **Rob Schuster:** 4, 5, 11, 18, 26, 33, 39, 41, 48, 60, 68, 74, 81, 84, 99, 107, 114, 116, 134, 142, 143, 149, 157, 165, 166, 168, 171, 174, 194, 202, 207, 216, 226, 233, 240, 258, 280, 288, 294, 296, 303, 308, 312, 325, 326, 331, 367, 374, 375, 381, 390, 395, 398, 405, 414, 429, 434, 449, 451, 469, 498, 515, 522, 527, 534, 542, 547, 564, 566, 567, 570, 571, 572, 580, 587, 595, 609, 614, 617, 619, 630, 639, 641, 649, 687; **Pronk&Associates:** 12, 362, 399, 462, 589; **XNR Productions:** 797

Technical Illustration

GGS Book Services

Photography

All photographs not listed are the property of Pearson Education

Back Cover: Klein J.-L & Hube/Biosphoto

Page 3, ©Franck Seguin/Corbis; **28,** ©BL Images Ltd/Alamy; **41,** ©Richard Wahlstrom/JupiterImages; **49,** ©UPI Photo/Roger Williams/Newscom; **63,** ©Joe McBride/Getty Images; **65,** ©JUPITERIMAGES/Brand X/Alamy; **65,** ©JUPITERIMAGES/Brand X/Alamy; **65,** ©JUPITERIMAGES/Brand X/Alamy; **65,** ©JUPITERIMAGES/Brand X/Alamy; **65,** ©Roberto Mettifogo/Getty Images; **93,** ©www.indepthexposure.com; **93,** ©Zen Shui/SuperStock; **145,** ©Hisham Ibrahim/Getty Images; **147,** ©Doug Perrine/Peter Arnold Inc.; **147,** ©PAUL NICKLEN/National Geographic Stock; **171,** ©Andy Crawford/Dorling Kindersley; **171,** ©Thomas Northcut/Photodisc/Getty Images; **171,** ©Steve Gorton/Dorling Kindersley; **203,** ©Atlantide Phototravel/Corbis; **208,** ©Stuart Westmorland/Getty Images; **217,** Jeff Greenberg/PhotoEdit Inc.; **221,** ©Thomas Barwick/Getty Images; **247,** ©Andy Harmer/Photo Researchers, Inc.; **247,** ©Harvey Lloyd/Getty Images; **253,** ©Rolf Hicker Photography/Alamy; **291,** ©Claudius/zefa/Corbis; **323,** ©James Baigrie/Botanica/Jupiterimages; **355,** ©D. Hurst/Alamy; **355,** ©Peter Cade/Getty Images; **355,** ©D. Hurst/Alamy; **355,** ©FOOD DRINK AND DIET/MARK SYKES/Alamy; **355,** ©Andre Gallant/Getty Images; **364,** ©Ed Darack/Getty Images; **379,** ©Jake Norton/Getty Images; **396,** ©Panoramic Images/Getty Images; **404,** ©Detlev van Ravenswaay/Photo Researchers, Inc.; **419,** ©Bob Llewellyn/Jupiterimages; **438,** ©Bob Krist/CORBIS; **461,** ©Peter Mason/Getty Images; **466,** ©Jose B. Ruiz/npl/Minden Pictures; **482,** ©Earth Imaging/Getty Images; **496,** ©Jerry Lodriguss/Photo Researchers, Inc; **519,** ©Stephen Dalton/Minden Pictures; **524,** ©Corbis Super RF/Alamy; **524,** ©Chase Jarvis/Photolibrary; **536,** ©NASA-HQ-GRIN; **567,** ©NASA - JPL; **583,** ©Yu Xiangquan/Xinhua Press/Corbis; **638,** ©B.A.E. Inc./Alamy; **661,** ©Museum of Science and Industry; **673,** Photolibrary; **675,** Ron Chapple Stock/Corbis; **684,** Koji Aoki/Aflo/Getty Images; **755,** Jim Sanborn; **767 both,** Jason Lugo/iStockphoto; **795,** Wolfgang Spunbarg/PhotoEdit; **819,** Ron Watts/Getty Images; **839 t,** Steve Gorton/Dorling Kindersley; **839 b,** European Space/Photo Researchers; **881,** Demetrio Carrasco/Dorling Kindersley; **895,** AFP PHOTO/Fabrice/Newscom; **913,** age footstock/SuperStock, **923,** mediacolor's/Alamy.